THE WESTERN HERITAGE
SINCE 1648

Donald Kagan

YALE UNIVERSITY

Steven Ozment

HARVARD UNIVERSITY

Frank M. Turner

YALE UNIVERSITY

THE

WESTERN

Volume II: Since 1648

HERITAGE

Fourth Edition

Macmillan Publishing Company
New York

Collier Macmillan Canada
Toronto

Acquisitions Editor: Bruce Nichols
Developmental Editor: Johnna Barto
Production Supervisor: J. Edward Neve
Production Manager: Richard C. Fischer
Text Designer: Sheree L. Goodman
Cover Designer: Sheree L. Goodman
Photo Researcher: Elsa Peterson
Maps: Maryland CartoGraphics

This book was set in Trump Mediaeval by York Graphic Services, Inc.,
printed and bound by Rand McNally & Co.
The cover was printed by Lehigh Press, Inc.

Printed in the United States of America

Note: The dates cited for monarchs and popes are generally the years of
their reign rather than of their births and deaths.

This book is a portion of *The Western Heritage,*
copyright © 1979, 1983, and 1987 by Macmillan Publishing Company.

Macmillan Publishing Company
866 Third Avenue, New York, New York 10022

Collier Macmillan Canada, Inc.
1200 Eglinton Avenue East
Suite 200
Don Mills, Ontario, M3C 3N1

Library of Congress Cataloging-in-Publication Data

Kagan, Donald.
    The Western heritage / Donald Kagan, Steven Ozment, Frank M.
Turner. — 4th ed.
        p.   cm.
    Includes bibliographical references and indexes.
    Contents: v. 1. To 1715 — v. 2. Since 1648.
    ISBN 0-02-361911-2 (v. 1). — ISBN 0-02-361912-0 (v. 2)
    1. Civilization, Occidental.   I. Ozment, Steven E.   II. Turner,
Frank M. (Frank Miller).   III. Title.
CB245.K28   1991d
909'.09821—dc20
                                                                    90-46893
                                                                    CIP

Printing: 2 3 4 5 6 7 8   Year: 1 2 3 4 5 6 7 8 9 0

Preface

As *The Western Heritage* enters its second decade, Europe is experiencing the most rapid and extensive changes since the end of World War II. The implications for both Europeans and Americans of the revolutionary events in the Soviet Union and Eastern Europe, the emergence of a reunited Germany, and the movement toward West European economic integration are yet to be understood. These current events make more crucial than ever the need for students to be aware of the social, political, and intellectual forces that have established Western civilization and that have determined its destinies.

Goals of the Text

From the beginning, in 1979, it has been our intention to provide our readers with a volume that does justice to the richness and variety of Western civilization. We believe there is a new urgency in that purpose. To that end, we have attempted to present

- a strong central narrative of the emergence of Western society
- the development of constitutionalism
- the shifting relationships of religion to political order
- the expansion of science
- and development of the major social, religious, and intellectual currents that have characterized the Western cultural experience.

We believe all of these factors have been fundamental to the history of Western civilization and that none of them can be omitted. Each belongs to the present as well as the past and each has made itself felt in recent years.

BALANCED PRESENTATION Our goal has been and remains that of a fair and balanced presentation of Western history. We believe that history has many sides and that no one of these can explain the others. The attempt to tell the story of Western civilization from a single overarching perspective, no matter how timely it may seem at any particular moment, will end up suppressing major parts of the story. One of our chief goals has been to avoid any such impoverishment of the study of Western civilization by presenting political, social, economic, intellectual, cultural, and religious aspects of history.

RECENT SCHOLARSHIP While seeking to provide balanced coverage, we have also been determined that our narrative present the most recent developments in historical scholarship and reflect the expanding concerns of professional historians. For that reason we have in this edition, as in previous revisions, expanded our coverage of social history. We have added new sections to the text, new documents, and new photographs to reflect this ever growing area of research and teaching. In particular we have attempted to provide major coverage of the role of women, the family, and minorities in Western culture. We believe the particular strength of our volume is to show the clear relationship of the concerns of social history to political, economic, religious, and intellectual issues and developments.

Changes in Fourth Edition

Over the years we have been fortunate in both the positive responses and constructive criticisms we have received from readers and teachers. The major revisions in this edition reflect what we genuinely regard as the ongoing partnership between our readers and ourselves. Responding to such suggestions, we have in this edition made a number of extensive changes in our coverage and organization. These include

- expanded attention to social history and to the role of minorities throughout the book

- reorganization and addition of new subheads to the chapters on ancient history
- expansion of the chapter (6) on the early Middle Ages to provide increased coverage of the Byzantine Empire and Islam
- revision and restructuring the two chapters (7 and 8) on the high Middle Ages, with the first focusing on church and state and the latter including extended coverage of towns, townspeople, schools, and universities
- division of the previous single chapter on the later Middle Ages into two separate chapters (9 and 10) with one dealing with the plagues, wars, and schisms of the fourteenth and fifteenth centuries, and the other with rebirth and renewal during the Renaissance
- inclusion of new sections on printing and the social history of the Reformation (Chapter 11)
- addition of a new section of black African slavery in the eighteenth-century colonial economy (Chapter 17)
- expanded coverage of the unrest of nationalities in the late nineteenth century (Chapter 23)
- new sections on eighteenth and nineteenth-century Jewish history (Chapters 16 and 24)
- a new discussion of women in Nazi Germany (Chapter 28)
- reorganization of the treatment of World War II and the inclusion of material of the domestic fronts (Chapter 29)
- complete reorganization and revision of the chapters (30 and 31) dealing with Europe since World War II
- a separate chapter (30) dealing with the Cold War confrontations, domestic politics in the United States, the Vietnam conflict, and the Arab-Israeli conflict
- a completely reorganized and largely rewritten concluding chapter (31) dealing with European domestic politics and cultural forces since World War II
- an extensive discussion and analysis of the recent changes in the Soviet Union and Eastern Europe (Chapter 31).

All of these revisions are designed to provide clearer coverage and to include consideration of important new issues.

Pedagogical Features

In this edition we have also made major changes in the presentation of the book in order to aid student study and understanding.

LEARNING AIDS We have revised the *part opening essays* that survey the six major sections of the book. Each chapter includes an *outline*, and *introductory* and *concluding sections*. There are many new section introductions and subheads to guide students. We have added many more *chronologies* and *timelines*. Over a third of the *primary source documents* are new; each chapter contains an average of seven documents. New titles reflecting recent scholarship have been added to the lists of *suggested readings*.

NEW MAP PROGRAM We have introduced an entirely new map program in this edition. There are now 89 maps executed in two colors. Compiled by a skilled and professional cartographer, these maps reflect a consistency in style and creative use of color for ease of reading.

FULL-COLOR PORTFOLIOS This volume also includes six full-color portfolios. Each of these picture inserts is organized around a particular theme and includes an introductory essay. The themes are Ancient Empires, Medieval Towns, Family Life in Early Modern Europe, the Old Regime and Revolution, Workplaces in the Nineteenth Century, and the New Europe. Instructors and students should find that these photo essays will provide the materials for interesting and lively discussions.

Ancillary Instructional Materials

Finally there is available an extensive program of ancillary materials to be used with *The Western Heritage*. The supplements package has been expanded for the Fourth Edition with the addition of Computerized Study Guide, Slide Set, and Telecourse. The following components are available to adopters of the text:

- **Instructor's Manual** prepared by Perry M. Rogers of Ohio State University is a 228 page manual which includes chapter summary, key points and vital concepts, identification questions, multiple-choice questions, discussion questions, and suggested films.
- **Map Transparencies** consisting of 50 full-color maps from the text.
- **Slide Package** consisting of 150 slides of important art and architecture.
- **Telecourse,** *The Western Tradition,* an Annenberg/CPB project, with Study Guides, volumes I and II, and Administrative Handbook by Jay Boggis.
- **Study Guide** prepared by Anthony M. Brescia of Nassau Community College which includes commentary, definitions, identifications, map exercises, short-answer exercises, and essay questions.
- **Computerized Study Guide** consisting of 15 multiple-choice questions from each chapter with reinforcing feedback on right answers and clarifying feedback on wrong answers. All answers are page referenced to the text material.
- **Computerized Test Bank** consisting of 1,000 multiple-choice questions from the Instructor's Manual, for IBM and compatibles.

Acknowledgments

We are especially grateful to the following readers who were good enough to criticize and evaluate the previous editions and early drafts of our revision:

Brandon H. Beck, *Shenandoah College and Conservatory*
John Beer, *University of Delaware*
Jay Bregman, *University of Maine*
Ted Carageorge, *Pensacola Junior College*
Carlos A. Contreras, *California State University, Fresno*
John J. Cronin, *Delaware County Community College*
Paige Cubbison, *Miami Dade Community College*
Donald E. Davis, *Illinois State University*
Thomas A. Devasia, *Bellarmine College*
Paul J. Devendittis, *Nassau Community College*
Paul J. Enea, *Delaware County Community College*
Steven Fanning, *University of Illinois at Chicago*
Marsha Frey, *Kansas State University*
Frank Frost, *University of California, Santa Barbara*
Frank Garosi, *California State University, Sacramento*
Joseph Gonzalez, *Moorpark College*

Brison D. Gooch, *Texas A & M University*
Paul B. Harvey, Jr., *Pennsylvania State University*
John Hatch, *Texas A & M University*
Peter Hayes, *Northwestern University*
C. James Haug, *Mississippi State University*
Gordon L. Iseminger, *University of North Dakota*
Sharon Johnson, *Miami Dade Community College*
David Jordan, *University of Illinois at Chicago*
Alexandra Korros, *Xavier University*
Patricia Lowman, *Bellarmine College*
David MacDonald, *Illinois State University*
Joan H. MacMaster, *L. A. Pierce College*
Margaret H. Mahoney, *Bellarmine College*
Donna J. E. Maier, *University of Northern Iowa*
John F. McCormack, *Delaware County Community College*
William K. Miller, *University of Minnesota*
Michael Mini, *Montgomery County Community College*
Gordon R. Mork, *Purdue University*
LeRoy H. Musselman, *Louisiana State University, Shreveport*
Thomas F. X. Noble, *University of Virginia*
George B. Oliver, *Randolph-Macon College*
Theodore M. Porter, *University of Virginia*
Paul G. Randolph, *Pepperdine University*
William Richardson, *Wichita State University*
Eric C. Rust, *Baylor University*
Joseph Scalzo, *Lemoyne College*
Carolyn P. Schriber, *Colorado State University*
Gerald M. Straka, *University of Delaware*
William H. TeBrake, *University of Maine*
Jeffrey von Arx, *Georgetown University*
James J. Ward, *Cedar Crest College*
John C. White, *University of Alabama at Huntsville*
L. Pearce Williams, *Cornell University*
Larry Yarak, *Texas A & M University*

We greatly benefitted from their work, and we hope that this edition reflects their contributions.

As in the past, we hope that our readers will find this volume both informative and enjoyable. We also hope that it will mark just the beginning of their interest in history and their exploration of the past.

D.K.
S.O.
F.M.T.

New Haven and Cambridge

CONTENTS

Documents

MAPS

Louis XIV (1643–1715) was the dominant European monarch in the second half of the seventeenth century. His rule became the prototype of the modern centralized state. [Giraudon]

13

ENGLAND AND FRANCE IN THE SEVENTEENTH CENTURY

The religious wars made a deep impression on people. By the seventeenth century many had concluded that only a strong, centralized government, free of competition from noblemen and commanding the loyalty of all its people, could provide the order and security required for a tranquil and productive life. The successful ruler must be absolute. In such a state, the ruler had a standing army capable of crushing his opponents and forcing local customs and laws to conform to "national" policy. He also had at his command a bureaucracy spread across the land capable of collecting all the taxes needed to attain the government's goals and of creating a transregional culture. In such a state there could be only one king, one law, and one faith.

By the seventeenth century absolute states were coming into existence in some places and life was in the process of being conformed to the will of a powerful monarch. Nowhere was this more impressively and oppressively underway than in the France of Louis XIV. The Stuart kings of England also aspired to such autocracy, and some English philosophers eloquently defended the divine right of kings and absolute rule. But during the course of the seventeenth century a very different kind of state came into being in England than in France. The English found a way to have both a strong monarchy and a representative government and even to attain a degree of religious diversity and toleration.

Constitutional Crisis and Settlement in Stuart England

Between 1603 and 1715 England experienced the most tumultuous years of its long history. In this period Puritan resistance to the Elizabethan religious settlement merged with fierce parliamentary opposition to the aspirations to absolute monarchy of the Stuart kings. During these years no fewer than three foreigners occupied the English throne, and between 1649 and 1660 England was without a king altogether. Yet by the end of this century of crisis, England provided a model to Europe of limited monarchy, parliamentary government, and measured religious toleration.

James I

The first of England's foreign monarchs was James VI of Scotland (the son of Mary Stuart, Queen of Scots), who in 1603 succeeded the childless Elizabeth as James I of England. This first Stuart king inherited not only the crown but also a royal debt of almost one-half million pounds, a fiercely divided church, and a Parliament already restive over the extent of his predecessor's claims to royal authority. Under James each of these problems worsened. The new king utterly lacked tact and was ignorant of English institutions. He strongly advocated the divine right of kings, a subject on which he had written a book in 1598 entitled *A Trew Law of Free Monarchies*. He rapidly alienated both Parliament and the politically powerful Puritans.

The breach with Parliament was opened by James' seeming usurpation of the power of the purse. Royal debts, his own extravagance, and an inflation he could not control made it necessary for the king to be constantly in quest of additional revenues. These he sought largely by levying—solely on the authority of ill-defined privilege claimed to be attached to the office of king—new custom duties known as *impositions*. These were a version of the older such duties known as *tonnage* and *poundage*. Parliament resented such independent efforts to raise revenues as an affront to its power, and the result was a long and divisive court struggle between the king and Parliament.

As the distance between king and Parliament widened, the religious problems also worsened. Prominent among the lesser landed gentry and within Parliament were the Puritans. They had hoped that James' experience with the Scottish Presbyterian church and his own Protestant upbringing would incline him to favor their efforts to "purify" the Anglican church. Since the days of Elizabeth, the Puritans had sought to eliminate elaborate religious ceremonies and to replace the hierarchical episcopal system of church governance with a more representative Presbyterian form like that of the Calvinist churches on the Continent.

In January 1604 they had their first direct dealing with the new king. James responded in that month to a statement of Puritan grievances, the so-called Millenary Petition, at a special religious conference at Hampton Court. To the dismay of the Puritans the king firmly declared his intention to maintain and even enhance the Anglican episcopacy. "A Scottish presbytery," he snorted, "agreeth as well with monarchy as God and the devil. No bishops, no king." Nonconformists were clearly forewarned.

Both sides departed the conference with their worst suspicions of one another largely confirmed. As the years passed, the distrust between them only deepened. During James' reign in 1620 Puritan separatists founded Plymouth Colony in Cape Cod Bay in North America, preferring flight from England to Anglican conformity. The Hampton Court conference did, however, sow one fruitful seed. A commission was appointed to render a new translation of the Bible. That mission was fulfilled in 1611 when the eloquent Authorized or King James Version of the Bible was published.

Though he inherited major political and religious difficulties, James also created special problems for himself. His court became a center of scandal and corruption. He governed by favorites, the most influential of whom was the duke of Buckingham, whom rumor made the king's homosexual lover. Buckingham controlled royal patronage and openly sold peerages and titles to the highest bidders—a practice that angered the nobility because it cheapened their rank.

James' pro-Spanish foreign policy also displeased the English. In 1604 he concluded a much-needed peace with Spain, England's chief adversary during the second half of the sixteenth century. His subjects viewed it as a sign of pro-Catholic sentiment. James further increased suspicions when he attempted unsuccessfully to relax the penal laws against Catholics. The English had not forgotten the brutal reign of Mary Tudor and the acts of treason by Catholics during Elizabeth's reign. In 1618 James hesitated, not unwisely, to rush English troops to the aid of Protestants in Germany at the outbreak of the Thirty Years' War. This hesitation caused his loyalty to the Anglican church to be openly questioned by some. In the king's last years, as his health failed and the reins of government were increasingly given over to his son Charles and Buckingham, parliamentary power and Protestant sentiment combined to undo his pro-Spanish foreign policy. Indeed, it was a foreign policy that had also failed to meet the king's own expectations. In 1624 England entered a continental war against Spain.

Charles I

Charles I (1625–1649) flew even more brazenly in the face of Parliament and the Puritans than did his father. Unable to gain adequate funds from Parliament for the Spanish war, Charles, like his father, resorted to extraparliamentary measures. He levied new tariffs and duties and attempted to collect discontinued taxes. He even subjected the English people to a so-called forced loan (a tax theoretically to be repaid), imprisoning those who refused to pay. Troops in transit to war zones were quartered in private English homes.

Charles I (1625–1649) poses with his family. Both children in this painting became king. The future Charles II (1660–1685) is clasping his father's knee; the future James II (1685–1688) is in the arms of his mother, Queen Henrietta Marie, the daughter of Henry IV of France. [Metropolitan Museum of Art]

When Parliament met in 1628, its members were furious. Taxes were being illegally collected for a war that was going badly for England and that now, through royal blundering, involved France as well as Spain. Parliament expressed its displeasure by making the king's request for new funds conditional on his recognition of the Petition of Right. This major document of constitutional freedom declared that henceforth there should be no forced loans or taxation without the consent of Parliament, that no freeman should be imprisoned without due cause, and that troops should not be billeted in private homes. Though Charles agreed to the petition, there was little confidence that he would keep his word.

DISMISSAL OF PARLIAMENT In August 1628 Charles' chief minister, Buckingham, with whom Parliament had been in open dispute since 1626, was assassinated. His death, while sweet to many, did not resolve the hostility between king and Parliament. In January 1629 Parliament further underscored its resolve to limit royal prerogative. It declared that religious innovations leading to "popery"—Charles' high-church policies were meant—and the levying of taxes without parliamentary consent were acts of treason. Perceiving that things were getting out of hand, Charles promptly dissolved Parliament and did not recall it again until 1640, when war with Scotland forced him to do so.

To conserve his limited resources, Charles made peace with France and Spain in 1629 and 1630, respectively. His chief minister, Thomas Wentworth (after 1640, earl of Stafford), instituted a policy known as *thorough*, that is, strict efficiency and administrative centralization in government. This policy aimed at absolute royal control of England and required for its success the king's ability to operate independently of Parliament.

Every legal fundraising device was exploited to the full. Neglected laws suddenly were enforced, and existing taxes were extended into new areas. An example of the latter tactic was the inland collection of "ship money." This tax normally was levied only on coastal areas to pay for naval protection, but after 1634 it was gradually applied to the whole of England, interior and coastal towns alike. A great landowner named John Hampden unsuccessfully challenged its extension in a close legal con-

test. Although the king prevailed, it was a costly victory, for it deepened the animosity toward him among the powerful landowners, who both elected the Parliament and sat in it.

Charles had neither the royal bureaucracy nor the standing army to rule as an absolute monarch. This became abundantly clear when he and his religious minister, William Laud (1573–1645; after 1633, the archbishop of Canterbury), provoked a war with Scotland. They tried to impose the English episcopal system and a prayer book almost identical to the Anglican *Book of Common Prayer* on the Scots as they had done throughout England. From his position within the Court of High Commission, Laud had already radicalized the Puritans by denying them the right to publish and preach.

Facing resistance from the Scots, Charles was forced to seek financial assistance from a Parliament that opposed his policies almost as much as it opposed the foreign invaders. Led by John Pym (1584–1643), Parliament refused even to consider funds for war until the king agreed to redress a long list of political and religious grievances. The result was the king's immediate dissolution of Parliament—hence its name, the Short Parliament (April–May 1640). When the Presbyterian Scots invaded England and defeated an English army at the battle of Newburn in the summer of 1640, Charles found himself forced to reconvene Parliament. This time it was on the latter's terms and for what would be a long and most fateful duration.

THE LONG PARLIAMENT The landowners and the merchant classes represented by Parliament had resented the king's financial measures and paternalistic rule for some time. To this resentment was added fervent Puritan opposition. Hence the Long Parliament (1640–1660) acted with widespread support and general unanimity when it convened in November 1640.

Both the earl of Stafford and Archbishop Laud were impeached by the House of Commons. Disgraced and convicted by a Parliamentary bill of attainder (a judgment of treason entailing loss of civil rights), Stafford was executed in 1641. Laud was imprisoned and later executed (1645). The Court of Star Chamber and the Court of High Commission, royal instruments of political and religious *thor-*

Why Englishmen Emigrated to America

*Conditions in England during the reign of Charles I deteriorated
to the point that a number of English people chose to emigrate to
Holland and New England. Writing in 1629, John Winthrop, a
Suffolk gentleman who would become the governor of the Massachusetts Bay Colony, cited his reasons for going to America. He
makes clear the religious and moral zeal that inspired the first
settlers in New England.*

1. It will be a service to the Church of great consequence to carry the gospel into those parts of the world, . . . and to raise a bulwark against the kingdom of Antichrist which the Jesuits labor to rear up in those parts.

2. All other churches of Europe are brought to desolation, and our sins, for which the Lord begins already to frown upon us and to cut us short, do threaten evil times to be coming upon us; and who knows but that God hath provided this place to be a refuge for many whom he means to save out of the general calamity, and seeing the Church hath no place left to fly into but the wilderness, what better work can there be than to go and provide tabernacles and food for her. . . .

3. This land [England] grows weary of her inhabitants, so as man, who is the most precious of all creatures, is here more vile and base than the earth we tread upon, and of less price among us than an horse or a sheep . . . and thus it is come to pass that children, servants, and neighbors, especially if they be poor, are counted the greatest burdens, which, if things were right, would be the chiefest earthly blessings.

4. The whole earth is the Lord's garden, and he hath given it to the sons of men with a general commission (Gen. i. 28) to increase and multiply, and replenish the earth and subdue it, which was again renewed to Noah; the end is double and natural, that man might enjoy the fruits of the earth and God might have his due glory from the creature. Why then should we stand here striving for places of habitation, etc. (many men spending as much labor and cost to recover or keep sometimes an acre or two of land as would procure them many, and as good or better, in another country), and in the meantime suffer a whole continent as fruitful and convenient for the use of man to lie waste without any improvement? . . .

7. What can be a better work and more honorable and worthy a Christian than to help raise and support a particular church while it is in its infancy, and join his forces with such a company of faithful people as by a timely assistance may grow strong and prosper, and for want of it may be put to great hazard, if not wholly ruined? . . .

James Harvey Robinson (Ed.), Readings in European History, *Vol. 2 (Boston: Athenaeum, 1906), pp. 225–226.*

ough, respectively, were abolished. The levying of new taxes without consent of Parliament and the inland extension of ship money now became illegal. Finally, it was resolved that no more than three years should elapse between meetings of Parliament and that Parliament could not be dissolved without its own consent.

Marxist historians have seen in these measures a major triumph of the "bourgeoisie" over the aristocracy. Yet lesser aristocratic groups (the gentry) were actually divided between the parliamentary and royal camps. Therefore, more was obviously at issue than simple class warfare. The accomplishment of the Long Parliament was to issue a firm and

*modern +
Extreme
Puritans*

lasting declaration of the political and religious rights of the many English people represented in Parliament, both high and low, against autocratic royal government.

There remained division within Parliament over the precise direction of religious reform. Both moderate Puritans (the Presbyterians) and extreme Puritans (the Independents) wanted the complete abolition of the episcopal system and the *Book of Common Prayer*. The majority Presbyterians sought to reshape England religiously along Calvinist lines, with local congregations subject to higher representative governing bodies (presbyteries). Independents wanted every congregation to be its own final authority. There was also a considerable number of conservatives in both houses who were determined to preserve the English church in its current form. However, their numbers fell dramatically after 1642, when those who sympathized with the present Anglican church departed the House of Commons.

The division within Parliament was further intensified in October 1641, when a rebellion erupted in Ireland, requiring an army to suppress it. Pym and his followers, loudly reminding the House of Commons of the king's past misdeeds, argued that Charles could not be trusted with an army and that Parliament should become the commander-in-chief of English armed forces. Parliamentary conservatives, who had winced once at Puritan religious reforms, winced thrice at this bold departure from English practice. On December 1, 1641, Parliament presented Charles with the "Grand Remonstrance," a more-than-200-article summary of popular and parliamentary grievances against the crown.

ERUPTION OF CIVIL WAR Charles saw the division within Parliament as a last chance to regain power. In January 1642 he invaded Parliament with his soldiers. He intended to arrest Pym and the other leaders, but they had been forewarned and managed to escape. Shocked by the king's action, a majority of the House of Commons thereafter passed the Militia Ordinance, a measure that gave Parliament control of the army. The die was now cast. For the next four years (1642–1646) civil war engulfed England.

Charles assembled his forces at Nottingham, and in August the civil war began. The main issues were (1) whether England would be ruled by an absolute monarchy or by a parliamentary government and (2) whether English religion would be conformist high Anglican and controlled by the king's bishops or cast into a more decentralized, Presbyterian system of church governance. Charles' supporters, known as *Cavaliers*, were located in the northwestern half of England. The parliamentary opposition, known as *Roundheads* because of their close-cropped hair, had its stronghold in the southeastern half of the country. The no-

MAP 13-1 THE ENGLISH CIVIL WAR *In the English Civil War, 1645 was a crucial year; here the rapidly deteriorating Royalist position is shown.*

THE ENGLISH CIVIL WAR 1642-1646

Controlled by the Parliamentarians, Beginning of 1645.
Controlled by the Royalists, Beginning of 1645.
Conquered by the Parliamentarians, in 1645.
Battle Site

White Hall

BANCKET HAVS

The bleeding head of Charles I is exhibited to the crowd after his execution on a cold day in January 1649. The contemporary Dutch artist also professed to see the immediate ascension of Charles' soul to heaven. In fact, to many the king was seen as a martyr.

bility, identifying the power of their peerage with the preservation of the current form of the monarchy and the Church, became prominent supporters of the king, whereas the townspeople supported the Parliamentary army.

Oliver Cromwell and the Puritan Republic

Two factors led finally to Parliament's victory. The first was an alliance with Scotland in 1643 consummated when John Pym persuaded Parliament to accept the terms of the Solemn League and Covenant. This agreement com-

Cromwell's New Model Army defeated the royalists in the English Civil War. After the execution of Charles I in 1649, Cromwell dominated the short-lived English republic, conquered Ireland and Scotland, and ruled as Lord Protector from 1653 until his death in 1658. [Bettmann Archive]

mitted Parliament, with the Scots, to a Presbyterian system of church government. The second was the reorganization of the parliamentary army under Oliver Cromwell (1599–1658), a middle-aged country squire of iron discipline and strong Independent religious sentiment. Cromwell and his "godly men" favored neither the episcopal system of the king nor the pure Presbyterian system of the Solemn League and Covenant. They were willing to tolerate an established majority church, but only if it also permitted Protestant dissenters to worship outside it.

The allies won the Battle of Marston Moor in 1644, the largest engagement of the war. In June 1645 Cromwell's New Model Army, which fought with a disciplined fanaticism, decisively defeated the king at Naseby.

Though defeated militarily, Charles again took advantage of the deep divisions within Parliament, this time seeking to win the Presbyterians and the Scots over to the royalist side. But Cromwell's army firmly imposed its will. In December 1648 Colonel Thomas Pride physically barred the Presbyterians, who made up a majority of Parliament, from taking their seats. After "Pride's Purge," only a "rump" of fewer than fifty members remained. Though

---

A Portrait of Oliver Cromwell

Statesman and historian Edward Hyde, the earl of Clarendon (1609–1674), was an enemy of Oliver Cromwell. However, his portrait of Cromwell, which follows, mixes criticism with grudging admiration for the Puritan leader.

He was one of those men whom his enemies cannot condemn without at the same time also praising. For he could never have done half that mischief without great parts of courage and industry and judgment. And he must have had a wonderful understanding of the natures and humours of men and a great dexterity in applying them . . . [to] raise himself to such a height. . . .

When he first appeared in the Parliament, he seemed to have a person in no degree gracious, no ornament of discourse, none of those talents which reconcile the affections of the standers-by; yet as he grew into his place and authority, his parts seemed to be renewed, as if he concealed faculties til he had occasion to use them. . . .

After he was confirmed and invested Protector . . . he consulted with very few . . . nor communicated any enterprise he resolved upon with more than those who were to have principal parts in the execution of it; nor to them sooner than was absolutely necessary. What he once resolved . . . he would not be dissuaded from, nor endure any contradiction. . . .

In all other matters which did not concern . . . his jurisdiction, he seemed to have great reverence for the law. . . . And as he proceeded with . . . indignation and haughtiness with those who were refractory and dared to contend with his greatness, so towards those who complied with his good pleasure, and courted his protection, he used a wonderful civility, generosity, and bounty.

To reduce three nations [England, Ireland, and Scotland], which perfectly hated him, to an entire obedience to all his dictates; to awe and govern those nations by an army that was not devoted to him and wished his ruin; this was an instance of a very prodigious address. But his greatness at home was but a shadow of the glory he had abroad. It was hard to discover which feared him most, France, Spain, or the Netherlands. . . . As they did all sacrifice their honour and their interest to his pleasure, so there is nothing he could have demanded that any of them would have denied him.

James Harvey Robinson (Ed.), Readings in European History, *Vol. 2 (Boston: Atheneum, 1906), pp. 248–250.*

An Account of the Execution of Charles I

Convicted of "high treason and other high crimes," Charles I was beheaded on January 30, 1649. In his last minutes he conversed calmly with the attending bishop and executioner, anxious only that the executioner not strike before he gave the signal.

To the executioner he said, "I shall say but very short prayers, and when I thrust out my hands—"

Then he called to the bishop for his cap, and having put it on, asked the executioner, "Does my hair trouble you?" and the executioner desired him to put it under his cap, which as he was doing by help of the bishop and the executioner, he turned to the bishop and said, "I have a good cause, and a gracious God on my side."

The bishop said, "There is but one stage more, which, though turbulent and troublesome, yet is a very short one. . . . It will carry you from earth to heaven . . . to a crown of glory. . . . "

Then the king asked the executioner, "Is my hair well?"

And taking off his cloak and George [the Order of the Garter, bearing a figure of Saint George], he delivered his George to the bishop. . . .

Then putting off his doublet and being in his waistcoat, he put on his cloak again, and looking upon the block, said to the executioner, "You must set it fast."

The executioner. "It is fast, sir."

King. "It might have been a little higher."

Executioner. "It can be no higher, sir."

King. "When I put out my hands this way, then—"

Then having said a few words to himself, as he stood with hands and eyes lifted up, immediately stooping down he laid his neck upon the block; and the executioner, again putting his hair under his cap, his Majesty, thinking he had been going to strike, bade him, "Stay for the sign."

Executioner. "Yes, I will, as it please your Majesty."

After a very short pause, his Majesty stretching forth his hands, the executioner at one blow severed his head from his body; which being held up and showed to the people, was with his body put into a coffin covered with black velvet and carried into his lodging.

His blood was taken up by divers persons for different ends; by some as trophies of the villainy; by others as relics of a martyr.

James Harvey Robinson (Ed.), Readings in European History, *Vol. 2 (Boston: Atheneum, 1906), pp. 244–245.*

small in numbers, this Independent Rump Parliament had supreme military power within England. It did not hesitate to use this power.

On January 30, 1649, after trial by a special court, it executed Charles as a public criminal and thereafter abolished the monarchy, the House of Lords, and the Anglican church. The revolution was consummated by events hardly contemplated at its outset.

From 1649 to 1660 England became officially a Puritan republic. During this period Cromwell's army conquered Ireland and Scotland, creating the single political entity of Great Britain. Cromwell, however, was a military man and no politician. He was increasingly frustrated by what seemed to him to be pettiness and dawdling on the part of Parliament. When in 1653 the House of Commons entertained a motion to disband the expensive army of fifty thousand, Cromwell responded by marching in and disbanding Parliament. He ruled thereafter as Lord Protector.

But his military dictatorship proved no more effective than Charles' rule had been and became just as harsh and hated. Cromwell's great army and foreign adventures inflated his budget to three times that of Charles. Trade and commerce suffered throughout England, as

The Abolition of Kingship

After the English Civil War, Parliament passed three acts designed to create the Commonwealth of England. Together, the three acts defined English Parliamentary government as it would develop into the modern world. The first of these, passed on March 17, 1649, abolished the office of the king and set in his place government by elected representatives meeting in council.

And whereas it is and hath been found by experience, that the office of a King in this nation and Ireland, and to have the power thereof in any single person, is unnecessary, burdensome, and dangerous to the liberty, safety, and public interest of the people, and that for the most part, use hath been made of the regal power and prerogative to oppress and impoverish and enslave the subject; and that usually and naturally any one person in such power makes it his interest to incroach upon the just freedom and liberty of the people, and to promote the setting up of their own will and power above the laws, that so they might enslave these kingdoms to their own lust; be it therefore enacted and ordained by this present Parliament, and by authority of the same, that the office of a King in this nation shall not henceforth reside in or be exercised by any one single person; and that no one person whatsoever shall or may have, or hold the office, style, dignity, power, or authority of King of the said kingdoms and dominions, or any of them, or of the Prince of Wales, any law, statute, usuage, or custom to the contrary thereof in any wise notwithstanding. . . .

And whereas by the abolition of the kingly office provided for in this Act, a most happy way is made for this nation (if God see it good) to return to its just and ancient right, of being governed by its own representatives or national meetings in council, from time to time chosen and entrusted for that purpose by the people, it is therefore resolved and declared by the Commons assembled in Parliament that they will put a period to the sitting of this present Parliament, and dissolve the same so soon as may possibly stand with the safety of the people that hath betrusted them, and with what is absolutely necessary for the preserving and upholding the Government now settled in the way of a Commonwealth: and that they will carefully provide for the certain choosing, meeting, and sitting of the next and future representatives, with such other circumstances of freedom in choice and equality in distribution of members to be elected thereunto, as shall most conduce to the lasting freedom and good of this Commonwealth.

S. R. Gardiner, Constitutional Documents of the Puritan Revolution *(Oxford: The Clarendon Press, 1906), pp. 384–386.*

near chaos reigned in many places. Puritan prohibitions of such pastimes as theaters, dancing, and drunkenness were widely resented. Cromwell's treatment of Anglicans came to be just as intolerant as Charles' treatment of Puritans had been. In the name of religious liberty, political liberty had been lost. Cromwell was unable to get along even with the new Parliaments that were elected under the auspices of his army. By the time of his death in 1658, a majority of the English were ready to end the Puritan experiment and return to the traditional institutions of government.

Charles II and the Restoration of the Monarchy

The Stuart monarchy was restored in 1660 when Charles II (1660–1685), son of Charles I, returned to England amid great rejoicing. A man of considerable charm and political skill, Charles set a refreshing new tone after eleven years of somber Puritanism. His restoration returned England to the status quo of 1642, as once again a hereditary monarch sat on the throne and the Anglican church was religiously supreme.

Because of his secret Catholic sympathies the king favored a policy of religious toleration. He wanted to allow all persons outside the Church of England, Catholics as well as Puritans, to worship freely so long as they remained loyal to the throne. But the ultraroyalist Anglicans in Parliament decided otherwise. They did not believe patriotism and religion could be so disjointed. Between 1661 and 1665, through a series of laws known as the Clarendon Code, Parliament excluded Roman Catholics, Presbyterians, and Independents from the religious and political life of the nation. Penalties were imposed for attending non-Anglican worship services; strict adherence to the *Book of Common Prayer* and the Thirty-Nine Articles was required; and all who desired to serve in local government were made to swear oaths of allegiance to the Church of England. This trampling of Puritan sentiments did not go unopposed in Parliament, but the opposition was not strong enough to override the majority.

Under Charles II England stepped up its challenge of the Dutch to become Europe's commercial and business center. Navigation Acts were passed that required all imports into England to be carried either in English ships or in ships registered to the same country as the

Charles II (1660–1685) was a man of considerable charm and political skill. Charles was a popular and astute ruler. [Robert Harding Picture Collection]

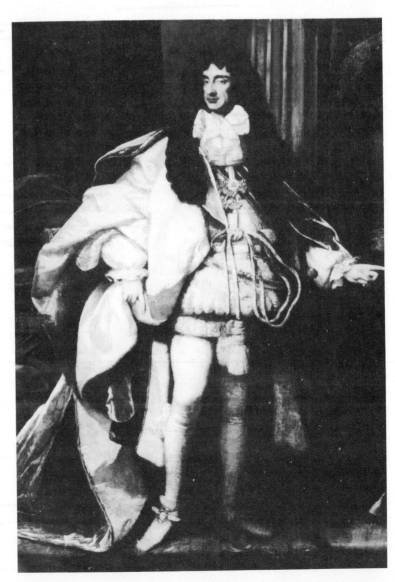

Dutch Dominance

imports they carried. Such laws struck directly at Dutch dominance in the shipping industry. Because the Dutch were the original suppliers of hardly more than tulips and cheese, these laws threatened to end their lucrative role as Europe's commercial middlemen. A series of naval wars between England and Holland ensued. Charles also undertook at this time to tighten his grasp on the rich English colonies in North America and the Caribbean, many of which had been settled and developed by separatists who desired independence from English rule.

Although Parliament strongly supported the monarchy, Charles, following the habit of his predecessors, required greater revenues than Parliament appropriated. These Charles managed to get in part by increased customs. He also received French aid. In 1670 England and France formally allied against the Dutch in the Treaty of Dover. A secret portion of this treaty pledged Charles to announce his conversion to Catholicism as soon as conditions in England permitted; for this declaration Louis XIV of France promised to pay 167,000 pounds. (Such a declaration never came to pass.) Charles also received a French war chest of 250,000 pounds per annum.

In an attempt to unite the English people behind the war with Holland, and as a sign of good faith to Louis XIV, Charles issued a Declaration of Indulgence in 1672. This document suspended all laws against Roman Catholics and Protestant nonconformists. But again, the conservative Tory Parliament proved less generous than the king and refused to grant money for the war until Charles rescinded the measure. After Charles withdrew the declaration, Parliament passed the Test Act. It required all officials of the crown, civil and military, to swear an oath against the doctrine of transubstantiation—a requirement that no loyal Roman Catholic could honestly meet.

The Test Act was aimed in large measure at the king's brother, James, duke of York, heir to the throne and a recent, devout convert to Catholicism. In 1678 a notorious liar named Titus Oates swore before a magistrate that Charles' Catholic wife, through her physician, was plotting with Jesuits and Irishmen to kill the king so that James could assume the throne. The matter was taken before Parliament, where it was believed. In the ensuing hysteria, known as the *Popish Plot*, several people were tried and executed. Riding the crest of anti-Catholic sentiment, opposition Whig members of Parliament, led by the earl of Shaftesbury (1621–1683), made an impressive but unsuccessful effort to enact a bill excluding James from succession to the throne.

More suspicious than ever of Parliament, Charles II turned again to increased customs revenue and the assistance of Louis XIV for extra income. Therefore, he was able to rule from 1681 to 1685 without recalling Parliament. In these years Charles suppressed much of his opposition. He drove the earl of Shaftesbury into exile, executed several Whig leaders for treason, and bullied local corporations into electing members of Parliament submissive to the royal will. When Charles died in 1685 (after a deathbed conversion to Catholicism), he left James the prospect of a Parliament filled with royal friends.

James II and Renewed Fears of a Catholic England

James II (1685–1688) did not know how to make the most of a good thing. He alienated Parliament by insisting upon the repeal of the Test Act. When Parliament balked, he dissolved it and proceeded openly to appoint known Catholics to high positions in both his court and the army. In 1687 James issued a Declaration of Indulgence, which suspended all religious tests and permitted free worship. Local candidates for Parliament who opposed the declaration were removed from their offices by the king's soldiers and were replaced by Catholics. In June 1688 James went so far as to imprison seven Anglican bishops who had refused to publicize his suspension of laws against Catholics.

Under the guise of a policy of enlightened toleration, James was actually seeking to subject all English institutions to the power of the monarchy. His goal was absolutism, and even conservative, loyalist Tories could not abide this. The English had reason to fear that James planned to imitate the policy of Louis XIV. In 1685 Louis had revoked the Edict of Nantes (which had protected French Protestants for almost a century) and had returned France to Catholicism using dragoons when people protested and resisted. A national consensus very quickly formed against the monarchy of James II.

The direct stimulus for parliamentary action came when on June 20, 1688, James' second wife, a Catholic, gave birth to a son, a male Catholic heir to the English throne. The English had hoped that James would die without a male heir and that the throne would revert to his Protestant eldest daughter, Mary. Mary was the wife of William III of Orange, *stadholder* of the Netherlands, great-grandson of William the Silent, and the leader of European opposition to Louis XIV's imperial designs. Within days of the birth of a Catholic male heir, Whig and Tory members of Parliament formed a coalition and invited Orange to invade England to preserve "traditional liberties," that is, the Anglican church and parliamentary government.

The "Glorious Revolution"

William of Orange arrived with his army in November 1688 and was received without opposition by the English people. In the face of sure defeat James fled to France and the protection of Louis XIV. With James gone, Parliament declared the throne vacant and on its own authority proclaimed William and Mary the new monarchs in 1689. Thus they completed a successful bloodless revolution. William and Mary, in turn, recognized a Bill of Rights that limited the powers of the monarchy and guaranteed the civil liberties of the English privileged classes. Henceforth, England's monarchs would rule by the consent of Parliament and would be subject to law. The Bill of Rights also pointedly prohibited Roman Catholics from occupying the English throne. The Toleration Act of 1689 permitted worship by all Protestants and outlawed Roman Catholics and anti-Trinitarians (those who denied the Christian doctrine of the Trinity).

The final measure closing the century of strife was the Act of Settlement in 1701. This bill provided for the English crown to go to the Protestant House of Hanover in Germany if Queen Anne (1702–1714), the second daughter of James II and the last of the Stuart monarchs, was not survived by her children. Consequently in 1714 the Elector of Hanover became King George I of England, the third foreign

ENGLAND IN THE SEVENTEENTH CENTURY	
1603	James VI of Scotland becomes James I of England
1604	Hampton Court Conference
1611	Publication of the Authorized or King James Version of the English Bible
1625	Charles I becomes English Monarch
1628	Petition of Right
1629	Charles I dissolves Parliament and embarks on eleven years of personal rule
1640	April–May Short Parliament / November Long Parliament convenes
1641	Great Remonstrance
1642	Outbreak of the Civil War
1645	Charles I defeated at Naseby
1648	Pride's Purge
1649	Charles I executed
1649–1660	Various attempts at a Puritan Commonwealth
1660	Charles II restored to the English throne
1670	Secret Treaty of Dover between France and England
1672	Parliament passes the Test Act
1678	Popish Plot
1685	James II becomes king of England
1688	Glorious Revolution
1689	William and Mary come to the throne of England
1701	Act of Settlement provides for Hanoverian Succession
1702–1715	Reign of Queen Anne, the last of the Stuarts

monarch to occupy the English throne in just over a century.

The "Glorious Revolution" of 1688 established a framework of government by and for the governed. It received classic philosophical justification in John Locke's *Second Treatise of Government* (1690), in which Locke described the relationship of a king and his people in terms of a bilateral contract. If the king broke that contract, the people, by whom Locke meant the privileged and powerful, had the right to depose him. Although it was neither in fact nor in theory a "popular" revolution such as would occur in France and America a hundred years later, the Glorious Revolution did establish in England a permanent check on monarchical power by the classes represented in Parliament.

Rise of Absolutism in France

Both regional rights and a degree of religious diversity were recognized within the Holy Roman Empire, England, and the Netherlands during the seventeenth century. The assertion of local political autonomy by the numerous member states and cities of the Holy Roman Empire made a strong central government there unthinkable. In England and the Netherlands centuries of parliamentary practice permitted regional freedoms to coexist with a strong central government. Following the Thirty Years' War, the Peace of Westphalia (1648) reaffirmed religious pluralism within the Holy Roman Empire. A degree of religious diversity, long a Netherlands tradition, received final confirmation also in England after decades of dogged Puritan resistance, when the Toleration Act of 1689 granted rights of worship to Protestant nonconformists.

England was arguably the most exemplary of the lands where a form of representative government became law. Seventeenth-century France, in contrast, saw both representative government and religious pluralism crushed by the absolute monarchy and the closed Catholic state of Louis XIV (1643–1715). Louis sought with great success to vest in himself and his government not only all French military power and legal authority, but the norms of religion and culture as well. An aggressive ruler who sought glory (*la gloire*) in foreign wars, Louis subjected his subjects at home to "one king, one law, one faith."

Henry IV and Sully

The foundation was well laid for Louis' grand reign by his predecessors and their exceptional ministers. Henry IV (1589–1610; see Chapter 12) began in earnest the curtailment of the privileges of the French nobility necessary for the creation of a strong centralized state. His targets were the provincial governors and the regional *parlements*, especially the powerful Parlement of Paris, where a divisive spirit lived on. Here were to be found the old privileged groups, tax-exempt magnates whose sole pre-

occupation was to protect their self-interests. During Louis XIV's reign their activities came under the strict supervision of royal civil servants known as *intendants*, who implemented the king's will with remarkable success in the provinces.

Also during Henry IV's reign an economy more amenable to governmental regulation emerged after the long decades of religious and civil war. Henry and his finance minister, the duke of Sully (1560–1641), prepared the way for the mercantilist policies of Louis XIV and his minister Colbert by establishing government monopolies on gunpowder, mines, and salt. A canal system was begun to link the Atlantic and the Mediterranean by joining the Saône, the Loire, the Seine, and the Meuse rivers. An involuntary national labor force emerged with the introduction of a royal *corvée*; this drafting of workers provided the labor to improve roads and the conditions of internal travel. Sully even dreamed of the political and commercial organization of the whole of Europe in a kind of common market.

Louis XIII and Richelieu

Henry IV was assassinated in 1610, and the following year Sully retired. Because Henry's successor, Louis XIII (1610–1643), was only nine years old when his father was assassinated, the task of governing fell to the queen mother, Marie de Médicis (d. 1642). Finding herself in a vulnerable position, she sought security abroad by signing a ten-year mutual defense pact with arch-rival Spain in the Treaty of Fontainebleau (1611). This alliance also arranged for the later marriage of Louis XIII to the Spanish infanta as well as for the marriage of the queen's daughter Elizabeth to the heir to the Spanish throne. The queen sought internal security against the French nobility by promoting the career of Cardinal Richelieu (1585–1642) as the king's chief adviser. However, he never became her pawn. Richelieu, loyal and shrewd, aspired to make France a supreme European power. He, more than any one person, was the secret of French success in the first half of the seventeenth century.

An apparently devout Catholic who also believed that the Church best served both his own ambition and the welfare of France, Richelieu was strongly anti-Habsburg in politics. On the one hand, he supported the Spanish alliance of the queen and Catholic religious unity within France. On the other hand, he was determined to contain Spanish power and influence, even when that meant aiding and abetting Protestant Europe. It is an indication both of Richelieu's awkward political situation and of his diplomatic agility that he could, in 1631, pledge funds to the Protestant army of Gustavus Adolphus, while at the same time insisting that Catholic Bavaria be spared from attack and that Catholics in conquered countries be permitted to practice their religion.

At home Richelieu pursued his policies utterly without sentiment. Supported by the king, whose best decision was to let his chief minister make all the decisions of state, Richelieu stepped up the campaign against the separatist provincial governors and *parlements*. He made it clear to all that there was only one law, that of the king, and that none could stand above it. When disobedient noblemen defied his edicts, they were imprisoned and even executed. Louis XIV had Richelieu to thank for the fact that many of the French nobility became docile beggars at his court. Such treatment of the nobility won Richelieu much enmity, even from the queen mother who, unlike Richelieu, was not always willing to place the larger interests of the state above the pleasure of favorite princes.

The king let no criticism weaken his chief minister, not even that of his mother. The queen mother had largely ignored Louis during his youth—he was educated mostly at the hands of his falconer—and the two remained estranged. This was doubtless a factor in the king's firm support of Richelieu when his mother became Richelieu's accuser.

Richelieu inspired the campaign against the Huguenots that would end in 1685 with Louis XIV's revocation of the Edict of Nantes. Royal armies conquered major Huguenot cities in 1629. The subsequent Peace of Alais (1629) truncated the Edict of Nantes by denying Protestants the right to maintain garrisoned cities, separate political organizations, and independent law courts. Only Richelieu's foreign policy prevented the earlier implementation of the extreme intolerance of Louis XIV. In the same year that the independent political status of the Huguenots was rescinded, Richelieu also entered negotiations to make Gustavus Adolphus his counterweight to the expansion of Habsburg power within the Holy Roman

Cardinal Richelieu was the mastermind behind French royal power in the seventeenth century. This striking triple portrait is by Philippe de Champaigne (1602–1674). [Courtesy of the Trustees, The National Gallery, London]

Empire. By 1635 the Catholic soldiers of France were fighting openly with Swedish Lutherans against the emperor's army in the final phase of the Thirty Years' War.

In the best Machiavellian tradition Richelieu employed the arts and the printing press to defend his actions and to indoctrinate the French people in the meaning of *raison d'état* ("reason of state"). This also set a precedent for Louis XIV's elaborate use of royal propaganda and spectacle to assert and enhance his power. One measure of Richelieu's success is France's substantial gains in land and political influence when the Treaty of Westphalia (1648) ended hostilities in the Holy Roman Empire and the Treaty of the Pyrenees (1659) sealed peace with Spain.

Young Louis XIV and Mazarin

Richelieu's immediate legacy, however, was strong resentment of the monarchy by the French aristocracy and the privileged bourgeoisie. Louis XIV was only five years old when Louis XIII died in 1643. During his minority the queen mother, Anne of Austria (d. 1666), placed the reins of government in the hands of Cardinal Mazarin (1602–1661), who continued Richelieu's determined policy of centralization. During his regency the long-building backlash occurred. Named after the slingshot used by street boys, the Fronde (1649–1652) was a series of widespread rebellions by segments of the French nobility and townspeople aimed at reversing the drift toward absolute monarchy. This was a last-ditch effort to preserve their local autonomy. These privileged groups saw their traditional position in French society thoroughly undermined by the crown's steady multiplication of royal offices, the replacement of local authorities by "state" agents, and the reduction of their accustomed power of patronage.

The Parlement of Paris initiated the revolt in 1649, and the nobility at large soon followed. The latter were urged on by the influential wives of princes who had been imprisoned by Mazarin for treason. The many briefly triumphed over the one when Mazarin released the imprisoned princes in February 1651. He and Louis XIV thereafter entered a short exile (Mazarin leaving France, Louis fleeing Paris). They returned to Paris in October 1652, by which time the inefficiency and near anarchy of government by the nobility made them very welcome. The period of the Fronde convinced a majority of the French that a strong king was

This medallion depicts Louis XIV as a child with his mother, Anne of Austria. [Giraudon/Art Resource]

preferable to the competing and irreconcilable claims of many regional powers. After 1652 the French were ready to experiment in earnest with absolute rule.

The World of Louis XIV

Thanks to the forethought of Mazarin, Louis XIV was well prepared to rule France. The turbulent period of his youth seems also to have made an indelible impression. Louis wrote in his memoirs that the Fronde caused him to loathe "kings of straw" and made him determined never to become one. Indoctrinated with a strong sense of the grandeur of his crown, he never missed an opportunity to impress it on the French people. When the dauphin (the heir to the French throne) was born in 1662, for example, Louis appeared for the celebration dressed as a Roman emperor. Although his rule became the prototype of the modern centralized state, its inspiration remained a very narrow ideal of personal glory.

King by Divine Right

Reverence for the king and the personification of government in his person had been nurtured in France since Capetian times. It was a maxim of French law and popular opinion that "the king of France is emperor in his realm," that the king's wish is the law of the land.

An important theorist for Louis' even grander concept of royal authority was the devout tutor of the dauphin, Bishop Jacques-Bénigne Bossuet (1627–1704). An ardent champion of the Gallican Liberties—the traditional rights of the French king and Church in matters of ecclesiastical appointments and taxation—Bossuet defended what he called the "divine right of kings." He cited the Old Testament example of rulers divinely appointed by and answerable only to God. As medieval popes had insisted that only God could judge a pope, so Bossuet argued that none save God could sit in judgment on the king. Kings may have remained duty-bound to reflect God's will in their rule—in this sense Bossuet considered them always subject to a higher authority. Yet as God's regents on earth they could not be bound to the dictates of mere princes and parliaments. Such were among the assumptions that lay behind Louis XIV's al-

Bishop Bossuet Defends the Divine Right of Kings

The revolutions of the seventeenth century caused many to fear anarchy far more than tyranny, among them the influential French bishop Jacques-Bénigne Bossuet (1627–1704), the leader of French Catholicism in the second half of the seventeenth century. Louis XIV made him court preacher and tutor to his son, for whom Bossuet wrote a celebrated Universal History. *In the following excerpt Bossuet defends the divine right and absolute power of kings. He depicts kings as embracing in their person the whole body of the state and the will of the people they govern and, as such, as being immune from judgment by any mere mortal.*

The royal power is absolute. . . . The prince need render account of his acts to no one. "I counsel thee to keep the king's commandment, and that in regard of the oath of God. Be not hasty to go out of his sight; stand not on an evil thing for he doeth whatsoever pleaseth him. Where the word of a king is, there is power; and who may say unto him, What doest thou? Whoso keepeth the commandment shall feel no evil thing" [Eccles. 8:2–5]. Without this absolute authority the king could neither do good nor repress evil. It is necessary that his power be such that no one can hope to escape him, and finally, the only protection of individuals against the public authority should be their innocence. This confirms the teaching of St. Paul: "Wilt thou then not be afraid of the power? Do that which is good" [Rom. 13:3].

God is infinite, God is all. The prince, as prince, is not regarded as a private person: he is a public personage, all the state is in him; the will of all the people is included in his. As all perfection and all strength are united in God, so all the power of individuals is united in the person of the prince. What grandeur that a single man should embody so much! . . .

Behold an immense people united in a single person; behold this holy power, paternal and absolute; behold the secret cause which governs the whole body of the state, contained in a single head: you see the image of God in the king, and you have the idea of royal majesty. God is holiness itself, goodness itself, and power itself. In these things lies the majesty of God. In the image of these things lies the majesty of the prince.

From Politics Drawn from the Very Words of Holy Scripture, *in James Harvey Robinson (Ed.),* Readings in European History, *Vol. 2 (Boston: Atheneum, 1906), pp. 275–276.*

leged declaration: *"L'état, c'est moi"* ("I am the state").

Versailles

The palace court at Versailles on the outskirts of Paris became Louis' permanent residence after 1682. It was a true temple to royalty, architecturally designed and artistically decorated to proclaim the glory of the Sun King, as

Louis was known. A spectacular estate with magnificent fountains and acres of orange groves, it became home to thousands of aristocrats, royal officials, and servants. Although its physical maintenance and new additions, which continued throughout Louis' lifetime, consumed over half his annual revenues, Versailles paid political dividends well worth the investment.

Life at court was organized around the king's daily routine. During his rising and dressing, nobles whispered their special requests in Louis' ear. After the morning mass, which Louis always observed, there followed long hours in council with the chief ministers, assemblies from which the nobility was carefully excluded.

Louis' ministers and councilors were hand-picked townsmen who owed everything they had to the king's favor and who for that reason served him faithfully and without question. The three main councils were: (1) the Council of State, a small group of four or five who met

MAP 13-2   THE WARS OF LOUIS XIV   *A bit later in France we see the territorial changes resulting from Louis XIV's first three major wars. The War of the Spanish Succession was yet to come.*

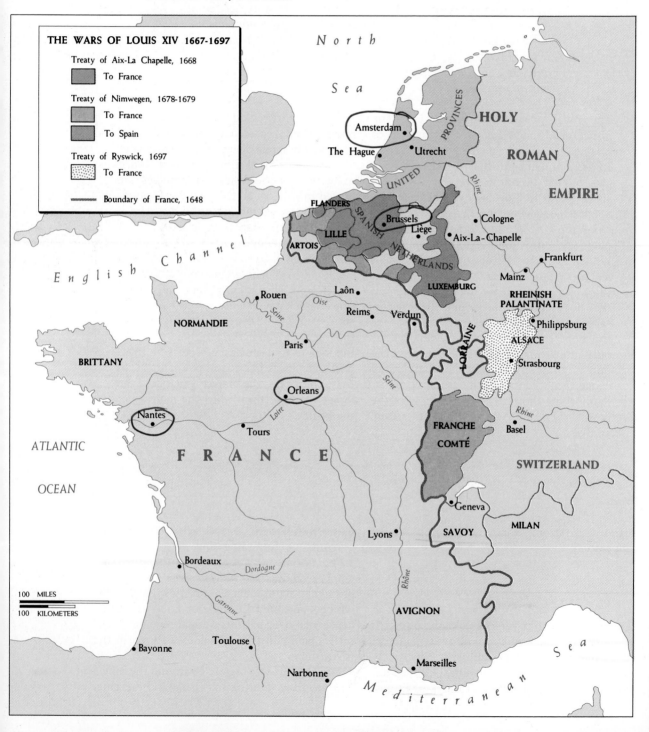

THE WARS OF LOUIS XIV 1667-1697

Treaty of Aix-La Chapelle, 1668
□ To France

Treaty of Nimwegen, 1678-1679
□ To France
□ To Spain

Treaty of Ryswick, 1697
□ To France

⸺ Boundary of France, 1648

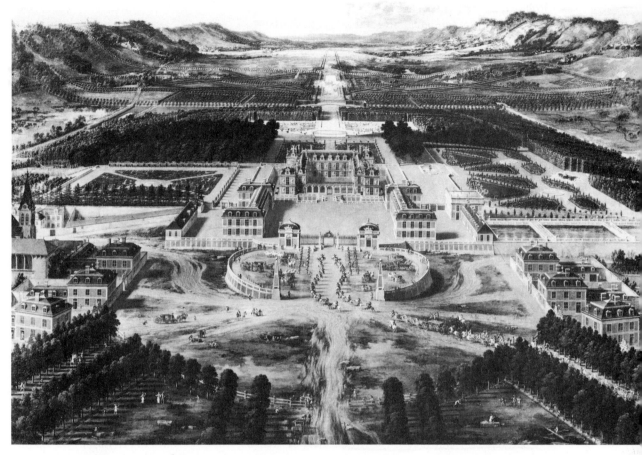

Versailles was painted in 1668 by Pierre Patel the Elder (1605–1676). The central building is the hunting lodge built for Louis XIII earlier in the century; some of the first expansion undertaken by Louis XIV appears as wings. [Cliché des Musées Nationaux, Paris]

During the glory days of Versailles in the seventeenth century, French court life displayed opulent costumes and mannered behavior. [The Granger Collection]

thrice weekly to rule on all matters of state, but especially on foreign affairs and war policy; (2) the Council of Dispatches, which regularly assessed the reports from the *intendants* in the towns and provinces, a boring business that the king often left to his ministers; and finally (3) the Council of Finances, which handled matters of taxation and commerce.

Members of the royal court spent the afternoons hunting, riding, or strolling about the lush gardens. Evenings were given over to planned entertainment in the large salons (plays, concerts, gambling, and the like), followed by supper at 10:00 P.M. Even the king's retirement became a part of the day's spectacle. Fortunate nobles held his night candle as they accompanied him to his bed.

Although only five feet four inches in height, the king had presence and was always engaging in conversation. An unabashed ladies' man, he encouraged the belief at court that it was an honor to lie with the king. Married to the Spanish Infanta (that is, daughter of the Spanish king) Marie Thérèse, for political reasons in 1660, he kept many mistresses. After Marie's death in 1683, he settled down in secret marriage to Madame de Maintenon and apparently became much less the philanderer.

All this ritual and play served the political purpose of keeping an impoverished nobility, barred by law from high government positions, busy and dependent so that they had little time to plot revolt. The dress codes and the high-stakes gaming at court contributed to the indebtedness and dependency of the nobility on the king. Court life was a carefully planned and successfully executed domestication of the nobility.

Suppression of the Jansenists

Like Richelieu before him, Louis believed that political unity also required religious conformity. To that end he suppressed two groups of influential religious dissenters: the Catholic Jansenists, who were opponents of the Jesuits, and the Protestant Huguenots.

The king and the French church jealously guarded their traditional independence from Rome (long proclaimed in the so-called Gallican Liberties, championed since the fourteenth century). Nevertheless, the years following the conversion of Henry IV to

Cornelis Jansen, Bishop of Ypres (1585–1638), wrote that individuals could do nothing to contribute to their salvation unless they were assisted by divine grace. This teaching, which came to be called Jansenism, was condemned as heretical by the Church because it seemed to deny the doctrine of human free will. [Library of Congress]

Catholicism had seen a great influx of Catholic religious orders into France, prominent among them the Jesuits. Because of their leadership at the Council of Trent and their close Spanish connections, the Jesuits had earlier been banned from France by Catherine de Médicis. Henry IV lifted the ban in 1603, with certain conditions: there was to be a limitation on the number of new colleges they could open; special licenses were required for their public activities; and each member of the order was subjected to an oath of allegiance to the king.

The Jesuits were not, however, easily harnessed. They rapidly monopolized the education of the upper classes, and their devout students promoted the religious reforms and doctrine of the Council of Trent throughout France. It is a measure of their success that Jesuits served as confessors to Henry IV, Louis XIII, and Louis XIV.

In the 1630s a group known as *Jansenists* formed an intra-Catholic opposition to both the theology and the political influence of the Jesuits. They were Catholics who adhered to the tradition of Saint Augustine, out of which many Protestant teachings had also come. Serious and uncompromising in their religious doctrine and practice, the Jansenists particularly opposed Jesuit teachings about free will. They believed with Saint Augustine that original sin dominated humankind so completely that individuals could do absolutely nothing good or contribute to their salvation unless they were first specially assisted by the grace of God. The namesake of the Jansenists was Cornelis Jansen (d. 1638), a Flemish theologian and the bishop of Ypres. He was the author of a posthumously published book entitled *Augustinus* (1640), which assailed Jesuit teaching on grace and salvation.

Through one of Jansen's close friends, a prominent Parisian family, the Arnaulds, who also opposed the Jesuits, became Jansenist allies. Like many other French people, the Arnauld family believed that the Jesuits had been behind the assassination of Henry IV in 1610. Arnauld support added a strong political element to the Jansenists' theological opposition to the Jesuits. Jansenist communities at Port-Royal and Paris were dominated by the Arnaulds during the 1640s. In 1643 Antoine Arnauld published a work entitled *On Frequent Communion* in which he criticized the Jesuits for confessional practices that permitted the easy redress of almost any sin. The Jesuits, in turn, condemned the Jansenists as "crypto-Calvinists" in their theology.

On May 31, 1653, Pope Innocent X declared heretical five Jansenist theological propositions on grace and salvation. In 1656 the pope banned Jansen's *Augustinus*, and the Sorbonne censured Antoine Arnauld. In this same year Antoine's friend, Blaise Pascal (d. 1662), the most famous of Jansen's followers, published the first of his *Provincial Letters* in defense of Jansenism. A deeply religious man, Pascal tried to reconcile the "reasons of the heart" with growing seventeenth-century reverence for the clear and distinct ideas of the mind. He found Jesuit moral theology to be not only lax and shallow, but also a rationalized approach to religion that did injustice to religious experience.

In 1660 Louis permitted the papal bull *Ad Sacram Sedem* (1656) to be enforced in France, thus banning Jansenism. He also closed down the Port-Royal community. Thereafter, Jansenists either retracted their views or went underground. At a later date (1710) the French king lent his support to a still more thorough purge of Jansenist sentiment. With the fall of the Jansenists went a Catholicism broad enough to attract the Huguenots. Jansenism had been the French church's last best hope of religious unity.

Revocation of the Edict of Nantes

Since the Edict of Nantes in 1598, a cold war had existed between the great Catholic majority (nine tenths of the French population) and the Protestant minority. Despite their respectable numbers (about 1.75 million by the 1660s), the Huguenots were in decline in the second half of the seventeenth century. Government harassment had forced the more influential members to withdraw their support. Officially the French Catholic church had long denounced Calvinists as heretical and treasonous and had supported their persecution as both a pious and a patriotic act.

Following the Peace of Nijmegen in 1678–1679, which halted for the moment Louis' aggression in Europe, Louis launched a methodical government campaign against the French Huguenots in a determined effort to unify France religiously. He hounded the Huguenots out of public life, banned them from government office, and excluded them from such professions as printing and medicine. Subsidies and selective taxation also became weapons to encourage their conversion to Catholicism. In 1681 Louis further bullied Huguenots by quartering his troops in their towns. The final stage of the persecution came in October 1685, when Louis revoked the Edict of Nantes. In practical terms the revocation meant the closing of Protestant churches and schools, the exile of Protestant ministers, the placement of nonconverting laity in galleys as slaves, and the ceremonial baptism of Protestant children by Catholic priests.

The revocation of the Edict of Nantes became the major blunder of Louis' reign. Thereafter, he was viewed throughout Protestant Europe as a new Philip II, intent on a Catholic reconquest of the whole of Europe, who must be resisted at all costs. Within France the revocation of the Edict of Nantes led to the voluntary emigration of over a quarter million

French. They formed new communities and joined the French resistance movement in England, Germany, Holland, and the New World. Thousands of French Huguenots served in the army of Louis' arch foe, William III of the Netherlands, later King William III of England.

Louis XIV Revokes the Edict of Nantes

Believing that a country could not be under one king and one law unless it was also under one religious system, Louis XIV stunned much of Europe in October 1685 by revoking the Edict of Nantes, which had protected the religious freedoms and civil rights of French Protestants since 1598.

Art. 1. Know that we . . . with our certain knowledge, full power and royal authority, have by this present, perpetual and irrevocable edict, suppressed and revoked the edict of the aforesaid king our grandfather, given at Nantes in the month of April, 1598, in all its extent . . . together with all the concessions made by [this] and other edicts, declarations, and decrees, to the people of the so-called Reformed religion, of whatever nature they be . . . and in consequence we desire . . . that all the temples of the people of the aforesaid so-called Reformed religion situated in our kingdom . . . should be demolished forthwith.

Art. 2. We forbid our subjects of the so-called Reformed religion to assembly any more for public worship of the abovementioned religion. . . .

Art. 3. We likewise forbid all lords, of whatever rank they may be, to carry out heretical services in houses and fiefs . . . the penalty for . . . the said worship being confiscation of their body and possessions.

Art. 4. We order all ministers of the aforesaid so-called Reformed religion who do not wish to be converted and to embrace the Catholic, Apostolic, and Roman religion, to depart from our kingdom and the lands subject to us within fifteen days from the publication of our present edict . . . on pain of the galleys.

Art. 5. We desire that those among the said [Reformed] ministers who shall be converted [to the Catholic religion] shall continue to enjoy during their life, and their wives shall enjoy after their death as long as they remain widows, the same exemptions from taxation and billeting of soldiers, which they enjoyed while they fulfilled the function of ministers. . . .

. . . .

Art. 8. With regard to children who shall be born to those of the aforesaid so-called Reformed religion, we desire that they be baptized by their parish priests. We command the fathers and mothers to send them to the churches for that purpose, on penalty of a fine of 500 livres or more if they fail to do so; and afterwards, the children shall be brought up in the Catholic, Apostolic, and Roman religion. . . .

. . . .

Art. 10. All our subjects of the so-called Reformed religion, with their wives and children, are to be strongly and repeatedly prohibited from leaving our aforesaid kingdom . . . or of taking out . . . their possessions and effects. . . .

. . . .

The members of the so-called Reformed religion, while awaiting God's pleasure to enlighten them like the others, can live in the towns and districts of our kingdom . . . and continue their occupation there, and enjoy their possessions . . . on condition . . . that they do not make public profession of [their religion].

Church and State Through the Centuries: A Collection of Historic Documents, trans. and ed. by S. Z. Ehler and John B. Morrall (New York: Biblo and Tannen, 1967), pp. 209–213.

Those who remained in France became an uncompromising guerilla force. Despite the many domestic and foreign liabilities created for France by the revocation of the Edict of Nantes, Louis, to his death, considered it his most pious act, one that placed God in his debt.

War Abroad

War was the normal state of affairs for seventeenth-century rulers and for none more than for Louis XIV, who had the means to pursue it to his hearts content. He confessed on his deathbed that he had "loved war too much." Periods of peace became opportunities for the discontented in town and countryside to plot against the king; war served national unity as well as "glory." By the 1660s France was superior to any other nation in administrative bureaucracy, armed forces, and national unity. It had a population of nineteen million, prosperous farms, vigorous trade, and much taxable wealth. By every external measure Louis was in a position to dominate Europe.

LOUVOIS, VAUBAN, AND COLBERT

The great French war machine became the work of three ministers: Louvois, Vauban, and Colbert. The army, about a quarter of a million men strong, was the creation of Michel le Tellier and his more famous son, the marquis of Louvois (1641–1691). Louis' war minister from 1677 to 1691, Louvois was a superior military tactician.

Before Louvois the French army had been an amalgam of local recruits and mercenaries, uncoordinated groups whose loyalty could not always be counted on. Louvois disciplined the French army and made it a respectable profession. He placed a limit on military commissions and introduced a system of promotion by merit, policies that brought dedicated fighting men into the ranks. Enlistment was for four years and was restricted to single men. The pay was good. _Intendants_, the king's ubiquitous civil servants, carried out regular inspections, monitoring conduct at all levels and reporting to the king.

What Louvois was to military organization, Sebastien Vauban (1633–1707) was to military engineering. He perfected the arts of fortifying and besieging towns. He also devised the system of trench warfare and developed the con-

The policies of Jean-Baptiste Colbert (1619–1683) transformed France into a major industrial and commercial power. [Giraudon]

cept of defensive frontiers that remained basic military tactics through World War I.

War cannot be successful without financing, and here Louis had the guidance of his most brilliant minister, Jean-Baptiste Colbert (1619–1683). Colbert worked to centralize the French economy with the same rigor that Louis had worked to centralize the French government. He put the nation to work under state supervision and carefully regulated the flow of imports and exports through tariffs. He created new national industries and organized factories around a tight regimen of work and ideology. Administrative bureaucracy was simplified, unnecessary positions were abolished, and the number of tax-exempt nobles was reduced. Colbert also increased the _taille_ on the peasantry, the chief source of royal wealth.

Although the French economy continued to be a puppet controlled by many different strings, more of these strings were now in the hand of the king than had been the case in centuries past. This close government control of the economy came to be known as _mercantilism_. Its aim was to maximize foreign exports and the internal reserves of bullion, the gold and silver necessary for making war. Modern scholars argue that Colbert overcontrolled the French economy and cite his "paternalism" as a major reason for French failures in the New

Colbert Revives French Manufacture and Trade

*Political power goes hand in hand with economic power. In this
letter to the officials of Marseilles (1664), Louis XIV summarized
the new policies proposed by Colbert to improve French business.
Every effort was made to improve the means of manufacture and
trade by freeing merchants from restrictive rules and regulations
and by subsidizing new ventures from the royal treasury.*

Considering how advantageous it would
be to this realm to reëstablish its foreign
and domestic commerce, . . . we have resolved to establish a council particularly
devoted to commerce, to be held every
fortnight in our presence, in which all the
interests of merchants and the means con-
ducive to the revival of commerce shall be
considered and determined upon, as well
as all that which concerns manufactures.

We also inform you that we are setting
apart, in the expenses of our state, a million livres each year for the encouragement of manufactures and the increase of
navigation, to say nothing of the considerable sums which we cause to be raised to
supply the companies of the East and West
Indies;

That we are working constantly to abolish all the tolls which are collected on the
navigable rivers;

That there has already been expended
more than a million livres for the repair of
the public highways, to which we shall
also devote our constant attention;

That we will assist by money from our
royal treasury all those who wish to reëstablish old manufactures or to undertake
new ones;

That we are giving orders to all our ambassadors or residents at the courts of the
princes, our allies, to make, in our name,
all proper efforts to cause justice to be rendered in all cases involving our merchants,
and to assure for them entire commercial
freedom;

That we will comfortably lodge at our
court each and every merchant who has
business there during all the time that he
shall be obliged to remain there, having
given orders to the grand marshal of our
palace to indicate a proper place for that
purpose, which shall be called the House
of Commerce; . . .

That all the merchants and traders by
sea who purchase vessels, or who build
new ones, for traffic or commerce shall
receive from us subsidies for each ton of
merchandise which they export or import
on the said voyages.

James Harvey Robinson (Ed.), Readings in European History, *Vol. 2 (Boston: Athenaeum, 1906), pp. 280–281.*

World. Be that as it may, Colbert's policies
unquestionably transformed France into a
major industrial and commercial power, with
foreign bases in Africa, India, and the Americas
from Canada to the Caribbean.

THE WAR OF DEVOLUTION   Louis' first
great foreign adventure was the War of Devolution (1667–1668). It was fought, as still a later
and greater war would be, over Louis' claim to
a Spanish inheritance through his wife, Marie
Thérèse (1638–1683). According to the terms
of the Treaty of the Pyrenees (1659), Marie had

renounced her claim to the Spanish succession
on condition that a 500,000-crown dowry be
paid to Louis within eighteen months of the
marriage. (The condition was not met.) When
Philip IV of Spain died in September 1665, he
left all his lands to his sickly four-year-old son
by a second marriage, Charles II (1665–1700);
his daughter Marie was explicitly excluded.
Louis had always harbored the hope of turning
the marriage to territorial gain and even before
Philip's death had argued that Marie was entitled to a portion of the inheritance.

Louis had a legal argument on his side,

which gave the war its name. He maintained that in certain regions of Brabant and Flanders, which were part of the Spanish inheritance, property "devolved" to the children of a first marriage rather than to those of a second. Therefore, Marie had a higher claim than Charles II to these regions. The argument was not accepted, for such regional laws could hardly bind the king of Spain. However, Louis was not deterred from sending his armies, under the viscount of Turenne, into Flanders and the Franche-Comté in 1667. In response to this aggression England, Sweden, and the United Provinces of Holland formed the Triple Alliance, a force sufficient to bring Louis to peace terms in the Treaty of Aix-la-Chapelle (1668).

INVASION OF THE NETHERLANDS In 1670 England and France became allies against the Dutch by signing the Treaty of Dover. That move set the Stuart monarchy of Charles II on a new international course. With the departure of the English from its membership, the Triple Alliance crumbled. This left Louis in a stronger position to invade the Netherlands for a second time, which he did in 1672. This second invasion was aimed directly at Holland, the organizer of the Triple Alliance in 1667 and the country held accountable by Louis for foiling French designs in Flanders. Louis had been mightily offended by Dutch boasting after the Treaty of Aix-la-Chapelle. Cartoons like one depicting the sun (Louis was the "Sun King") eclipsed by a great moon of Dutch cheese cut the French king to the quick. It was also clear that there could be no French acquisition of land in the Spanish Netherlands, nor European hegemony beyond that, until Holland was neutralized.

Louis' successful invasion of the United Provinces in 1672 brought the downfall of Dutch statesmen Jan and Cornelius De Witt. In their place came the twenty-seven-year-old Prince of Orange, destined after 1689 to become King William III of England. Orange was the great-grandson of William the Silent, who had repulsed Philip II and dashed Spanish hopes of dominating the Netherlands in the sixteenth century.

Orange proved to be Louis' undoing. This unpretentious Calvinist, who was in almost every way Louis' opposite, galvanized the seven provinces into a fierce fighting unit. In 1673 he united the Holy Roman Emperor, Spain, Lorraine, and Brandenburg in an alliance against Louis—the proclaimed "Christian Turk," a menace to the whole of western Europe, Catholic and Protestant alike. Subsequent battles saw the loss of Louis' ablest generals, Turenne and Condé, in 1675, whereas the defeat of the Dutch fleet by Admiral Duquesne established French control of the Mediterranean in 1676. The Peace of Nimwegen, signed with different parties in successive years (1678, 1679), ended the hostilities of this second war. The settlements were not unfavor-

THE REIGN OF LOUIS XIV (1643–1715)

1648	Peace of Westphalia reaffirms religious pluralism in Holy Roman Empire
1649–1652	The Fronde, a revolt of nobility and townsmen against confiscatory policies of the crown
1653	Jansenism declared a heresy by the pope
1659	Treaty of Pyrenees ends hostilities between France and Spain
1660	Louis XIV enforces papal ban on Jansenists
1667–1668	War of Devolution fought over Louis' claims to lands in Brabant and Flanders by virtue of his Spanish inheritance through his wife
1668	The Triple Alliance (England, Sweden, and the United Provinces) repels Louis' army from Flanders and forces the Treaty of Aix-la-Chapelle
1670	Treaty of Dover brings French and English together against the Netherlands
1672	France invades the United Provinces
1678–1679	Peace of Nimwegen ends French wars in United Provinces
1685	Louis XIV revokes Edict of Nantes
1689–1697	Nine Years' War between France and League of Augsburg, a Europe-wide alliance against Louis XIV
1697	Peace of Ryswick ends French expansion into Holland and Germany
1702–1714	England, Holland, and Holy Roman Emperor resist Louis' claim to the Spanish throne in the War of Spanish Succession
1712	Treaty of Utrecht between England and France
1714	Treaty of Rastadt between Spain and France

able to France. Spain, for example, surrendered the Franche-Comté. However, France still fell far short of the European empire to which Louis aspired.

THE LEAGUE OF AUGSBURG

Between the Treaty of Nimwegen and the renewal of full-scale war in 1689, Louis restlessly probed his perimeters. The army was maintained at full strength. In 1681 it conquered the free city of Strasbourg, setting off the formation of new defensive coalitions against Louis. The League of Augsburg was created in 1686 to resist French expansion into Germany. It grew by 1689 to include the Emperor Leopold; Spain; Sweden; the United Provinces; the electorates of Bavaria, Saxony, and the Palatinate; and the England of William and Mary. That year saw the beginning of the Nine Years' War (1689–1697) between France and the League of Augsburg. For the third time stalemate and exhaustion forced the combatants into an interim settlement.

The Peace of Ryswick in September 1697 became a personal triumph for William of Orange, now William III of England, and the Emperor Leopold. It secured Holland's borders and thwarted Louis' expansion into Germany. During this same period England and France fought for control of North America in what came to be known as King William's War (1689–1697).

WAR OF THE SPANISH SUCCESSION: TREATIES OF UTRECHT–RASTADT

After Ryswick, Louis, who seemed to thrive on partial success, made still a fourth attempt to realize his grand design of French European domination. This time he was assisted by an unforeseen turn of events. On November 1, 1700, Charles II of Spain, known as "the Sufferer" because of his genetic deformities and lingering illnesses, died.

Both Louis and the Austrian Emperor Leopold had claims to the Spanish inheritance through their grandsons: Louis by way of his marriage to Marie Thérèse and Leopold through his marriage to her younger sister, Margaret Thérèse. Although the dauphin had the higher blood claim, it was assumed that the inheritance would go to the grandson of the emperor. The French raised the specter of Habsburg domination of the whole of Europe should Spain come under the imperial crown. Marie Thérèse, however, had renounced her right to the Spanish inheritance in the Treaty of the Pyrenees (1659).

The nations of Europe feared a union of the French and Spanish crowns more than they did a union of the imperial and Spanish crowns.

The siege of Tournai in 1709 occurred during the War of the Spanish Succession. Tournai, a fortress city on the border between France and the Spanish Netherlands, had been captured by the French in 1667. Here it is beseiged by the English and Imperial forces under Marlborough and Prince Eugene. Under the terms of the Treaty of Utrecht (1713), France ceded Tournai to Austria. [Engraving by P. Mortier. BBC Hulton Picture Library]

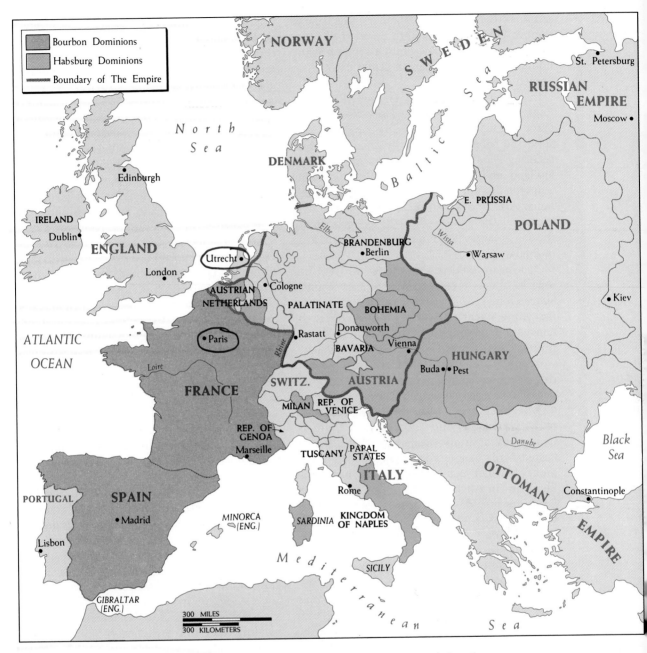

MAP 13-3 EUROPE IN 1714 *The War of the Spanish Succession ended in the year before the death of the aged Louis XIV. By then France and Spain, although not united, were ruled by members of the Bourbon family, and Spain had lost her non-Iberian possessions. Austria had continued to grow.*

They determined that the former alliance should not occur. Hence, before Charles' death, negotiations began to partition the inheritance in such a way that the current balance of power would be maintained.

Charles II upset all such plans by leaving the entire Spanish inheritance to Philip of Anjou, Louis' grandson. At a stroke the Spanish inher-

itance had fallen to France. Although Louis had been party to the partition agreements in advance of Charles' death, he now saw God's hand in Charles' will; he chose to enforce its terms rather than abide by those of the partition treaty. Philip of Anjou moved to Madrid and became Philip V of Spain. Louis, in what was interpreted as naked French aggression, sent his troops again into Flanders, this time to remove Dutch soldiers from Spanish territory in the name of the new French king of Spain. Louis also declared Spanish America open to French ships.

In September 1701 the Grand Alliance of England, Holland, and the Holy Roman Emperor formed against Louis. It sought to preserve the balance of power by once and for all securing Flanders as a neutral barrier between Holland and France and by gaining for the emperor his fair share of the Spanish inheritance. After the formation of the alliance Louis increased the stakes of battle by recognizing the son of James II of England as James III, king of England.

Once again total war enveloped western Europe as the twelve-year War of the Spanish Succession (1702–1714) began. France, for the first time, went to war with inadequate finances, a poorly equipped army, and mediocre military leadership. The English had advanced weaponry (flintlock rifles, paper cartridges, and ring bayonets) and superior tactics (thin, maneuverable troop columns rather than the traditional deep ones). John Churchill, the duke of Marlborough, who succeeded William of Orange as military leader of the alliance, bested Louis' soldiers in every major engagement. Marlborough routed French armies at Blenheim in August 1704 and on the plain of Ramillies in 1706—two decisive battles of the war. In 1708–1709 famine, revolts, and uncollectable taxes tore France apart internally. Despair pervaded the French court. Louis wondered aloud how God could forsake one who had done so much for Him.

Though ready to make peace in 1709, Louis could not bring himself to accept the stiff terms of the alliance. They demanded that he transfer all Spanish possessions to the emperor's grandson Charles and remove Philip V

from Madrid. The result was a clash of forces at Malplaquet (September 1709), which left carnage on the battlefield unsurpassed until modern times.

France finally signed an armistice with England at Utrecht in July 1712 and concluded hostilities with Holland and the emperor in the Treaty of Rastadt in March 1714. This agreement confirmed Philip V as king of Spain. It gave England Gibraltar, which made England thereafter a Mediterranean power. Also it won Louis' recognition of the House of Hanover's right of accession to the English throne.

Politically the eighteenth century would belong to England as the sixteenth had belonged to Spain and the seventeenth to France. Although France remained intact and quite strong, the realization of Louis XIV's ambition had to await the rise of Napoleon Bonaparte. On his deathbed on September 1, 1715, a dying Louis fittingly warned the dauphin not to imitate his love of buildings and his liking for war.

Louis XIV's Legacy

When one looks back on Louis' reign, the grandeur and power of it still remain undimmed by his glory-seeking and military ambitions. One remembers not only a king who loved war too much, but also one who built the palace of Versailles and brought a new majesty to France; a king who orchestrated the fractious French aristocracy and bourgeoisie at court and controlled a French peasantry that had all too many just grievances; a king who raised up skilled and trustworthy ministers, councilors, and *intendants* from the middle classes; and a king who created a new French empire by expanding trade into Asia and colonizing North America. There is a record of building as well as one of war and destruction.

In the seventeenth century, England and France exhibited two divergent models for governing a nation. England became the model for parliamentary government, France for absolute monarchy. In England, the monarch was limited and the parliament was strong. In France, the monarch was strong, and the regional parlements *were rendered silent.*

The English people struggled throughout the century, both with Oliver Cromwell and with the Stuart monarchs, to ensure that their rulers would be answerable to someone other than themselves or God. At the same time, the English fought to guarantee civil liberties, at least for the privileged classes, who represented the interests of Englishmen beyond the king. The acceptance of the Bill of Rights

(1689) by William and Mary achieved this goal. In the very same year, the Toleration Act permitted worship by all English Protestants. These acts represented neither democracy nor religious freedom in a modern sense—the Bill of Rights protected only the privileged, not all English people, and the Toleration Act outlawed Catholics and unitarians. Still, these acts firmly established representative government and legally recognized, at least in principle, a variety of religious belief.

In France, by contrast, the king remained supreme. His standing army was his "dialogue" with his subjects. He ruled by "divine right" and his actions were subject to God's judgment alone; the dictates of mere parliaments could not bind him. There could be but one ruler, one law, and one religion within a country that would be well-governed.

Measured by their accomplishments, both the French and English governments worked exceedingly well. Each contained the traditional fragmenting forces of the age, the French more effectively than the English. In both England and France, the king restrained powerful noblemen and subordinated the Church and religion to secular political goals.

The British model exerted its influence wherever the British went, becoming particularly successful in the North American colonies. The French model persisted in France until the French Revolution. The two models, in developed forms, still contest one another today.

Suggested Readings

MAURICE ASHLEY, *The Greatness of Oliver Cromwell* (1966). Detailed biography.

MAURICE ASHLEY, *England in the Seventeenth Century* (1980). Readable survey.

TREVOR ASTON (Ed.), *Crisis in Europe 1560–1660* (1965). Essays by major scholars focused on social and economic forces.

PETER BURKE, *Popular Culture in Early Modern Europe* (1978). A journalistic romp.

WILLIAM F. CHURCH (Ed.), *The Greatness of Louis XIV: Myth or Reality?* (1959). Excerpts from the scholarly debate over Louis' reign.

R. S. DUNN, *The Age of Religious Wars, 1559–1715* (1979). Lucid survey setting the conflicting political systems of France and England in larger perspective.

J. H. ELLIOTT, *Imperial Spain, 1469–1716* (1977). Authoritative study of an authoritarian government.

ANTONIA FRASER, *Royal Charles: Charles II and the Restoration* (1979). Delightful popular biography.

WILLIAM HALLER, *The Rise of Puritanism* (1957). Interesting study based largely on Puritan sermons.

CHRISTOPHER HILL, *The Century of Revolution 1603–1714* (1961). Bold, imaginative synthesis by a controversial master.

DEREK HIRST, *Authority and Conflict: England 1603–1658* (1986). Scholarly survey integrating history and historiography.

W. H. LEWIS, *The Splendid Century* (1953). Focuses on society, especially in the age of Louis XIV.

MICHAEL MACDONALD, *Mystical Bedlam: Madness, Anxiety and Healing in Seventeenth Century England* (1981). Interesting analysis of a physician's record of illnesses treated.

DAVID OGG, *Europe in the Seventeenth Century* (1925). Among the most authoritative syntheses.

STUART E. PRALL, *The Puritan Revolution: A Documentary History* (1968). Comprehensive document collection.

LAWRENCE STONE, *The Causes of the English Revolution 1529–1642* (1972). Brief survey stressing social history and ruminating over historians and historical method.

G. R. R. TREASURE, *Seventeenth Century France* (1966). Broad, detailed survey of entire century.

DAVID UNDERDOWN, *Revel, Riot, and Rebellion* (1985). On popular culture and the English civil war.

MICHAEL WALZER, *The Revolution of the Saints: A Study in the Origins of Radical Politics* (1965). Effort to relate ideas and politics that depicts Puritans as true revolutionaries.

C. V. WEDGWOOD, *Richelieu and the French Monarch* (1950). Fine biography.

JOHN B. WOLF, *Louis XIV* (1968). Very detailed political biography.

Tycho Brahe made the most important observations of the stars since antiquity. He opposed Copernicus's ideas, but the data that he collected from his observations became important for the work and theories of Kepler. [The Bettmann Archive]

14

New Directions in Science and Thought in the Sixteenth and Seventeenth Centuries

The sixteenth and seventeenth centuries witnessed a sweeping change in the scientific view of the universe. An earth-centered picture of the universe gave way to one in which the earth was only another planet orbiting about the sun. The sun itself became one of millions of stars. This transformation of humankind's perception of its place in the larger scheme of things led to a vast rethinking of moral and religious matters as well as of scientific theory. Faith and reason needed new modes of reconciliation as did faith and science. The new ideas and methods of science challenged modes of thought associated with medieval times and Scholasticism. The literary imagination was touched by the new outlook on physical nature, and religious thinkers had to reconsider many traditional ideas. Philosophers applied rational, scientific thought to the realm of politics. Some of those writers supported absolutism; others, parliamentary systems.

The new scientific concepts and the methods of their construction became so impressive that subsequent knowledge in the Western world has been deemed correct largely to the extent that it has approximated knowledge as defined by science. Perhaps no single intellectual development proved to be more significant for the future of European and Western civilization.

The Scientific Revolution

The process by which the new view of the universe and of scientific knowledge came to be established is normally termed the *Scientific Revolution*. However, care must be taken in the use of this metaphor. The word *revolution* normally denotes fairly rapid changes in the political world, involving large numbers of people. The Scientific Revolution was not rapid, nor did it involve more than a few hundred human beings. It was a complex movement with many false starts and many brilliant people with wrong as well as useful ideas. It took place in the studies and the crude laboratories of thinkers in Poland, Italy, Bohemia, France, and Great Britain.

The Scientific Revolution stemmed from two major tendencies. The first, as illustrated by Nicolaus Copernicus, was the imposition of important small changes on existing models of thought. The second, as embodied by Francis Bacon, was the desire to pose new kinds of questions and to use new methods of investigation. In both cases, scientific thought changed current and traditional opinions in other fields.

Nicolaus Copernicus: Rejection of an Earth-Centered Universe

Nicolaus Copernicus (1473–1543) was a Polish astronomer who enjoyed a very high reputation throughout his life. He had been educated in Italy and corresponded with other astronomers throughout Europe. However, he had not been known for strikingly original or unorthodox thought. In 1543, the year of his death, Copernicus published *On the Revolutions of the Heavenly Spheres*. Because he died near the time of publication, the fortunes of his work are not the story of one person's crusade for progressive science. Copernicus' book was "a revolution-making rather than a revolutionary text."[1] What Copernicus did was to provide an intellectual springboard for a complete criticism of the then-dominant view of the position of the earth in the universe.

THE PTOLEMAIC SYSTEM At the time of Copernicus the standard explanation of the earth and the heavens was that associated with Ptolemy and his work entitled the *Almagest* (A.D. 150). There was not just one Ptolemaic system; rather, several versions had been developed over the centuries by commentators on the original book. Most of these systems assumed that the earth was the center of the universe. Above the earth lay a series of crystalline spheres, one of which contained the moon, another the sun, and still others the planets and the stars. This was the astronomy found in such works as Dante's *Divine Comedy*. At the outer regions of these spheres lay the realm of God and the angels. Aristotelian physics provided the intellectual underpinnings of the Ptolemaic systems. The earth had to be the center because of its heaviness. The stars and the other heavenly bodies had to be enclosed in the crystalline spheres so that they could move. Nothing could move unless something was actually moving it. The state of rest was natural; motion was the condition that required explanation.

Numerous problems were associated with this system, and these had long been recognized. The most important was the observed motions of the planets. Planets could be seen moving in noncircular patterns around the earth. At certain times the planets actually appeared to be going backward. The Ptolemaic systems explained these strange motions primarily through *epicycles*. An epicycle is an orbit upon an orbit, like a spinning jewel on a ring. The planets were said to make a second revolution in an orbit tangent to their primary orbit around the earth. Other intellectual but nonobservational difficulties related to the immense speed at which the spheres had to move around the earth. To say the least, the Ptolemaic systems were cluttered. However, they were effective explanations as long as one assumed Aristotelian physics and the Christian belief that the earth rested at the center of the created universe.

---

[1] *Thomas S. Kuhn,* The Copernican Revolution: Planetary Astronomy in the Development of Western Thought *(New York: Vintage, 1959), p. 135.*

COPERNICUS' UNIVERSE Copernicus' *On the Revolution of the Heavenly Spheres* challenged this picture in the most conserva-

497

NEW DIRECTIONS IN SCIENCE AND THOUGHT IN THE SIXTEENTH AND SEVENTEENTH CENTURIES

tive manner possible. It suggested that if the earth were assumed to move about the sun in a circle, many of the difficulties with the Ptole-

---

Copernicus Ascribes Movement to the Earth

Copernicus published De Revolutionibus Orbium Caelestium (On the Revolutions of the Heavenly Spheres) *in 1543. In his preface, which was addressed to Pope Paul III, he explained what had led him to think that the earth moved around the sun and what he thought were some of the scientific consequences of the new theory. The reader should note how important Copernicus considered the opinions of the ancient writers who had also ascribed motion to the earth. This is a good example of the manner in which familiarity with the ancients gave many Renaissance writers the self-confidence to criticize medieval ideas.*

I may well presume, most Holy Father, that certain people, as soon as they hear that in this book about the Revolutions of the Spheres of the Universe I ascribe movement to the earthly globe, will cry out that, holding such views, I should at once be hissed off the stage. . . .

So I should like your Holiness to know that I was induced to think of a method of computing the motions of the spheres by nothing else than the knowledge that the Mathematicians [who had previously considered the problem] are inconsistent in these investigations.

For, first, the mathematicians are so unsure of the movements of the Sun and Moon that they cannot even explain or observe the constant length of the seasonal year. Secondly, in determining the motions of these and of the other five planets, they use neither the same principles and hypotheses nor the same demonstrations of the apparent motions and revolutions. . . . Nor have they been able thereby to discern or deduce the principal thing—namely the shape of the Universe and the unchangeable symmetry of its parts. . . .

I pondered long upon this uncertainty of mathematical tradition in establishing the motions of the system of the spheres. At last I began to chafe that philosophers could by no means agree on any one certain theory of the mechanism of the Universe, wrought for us by a supremely good and orderly Creator. . . . I therefore took pains to read again the works of all the philosophers on whom I could lay hand to seek out whether any of them had ever supposed that the motions of the spheres were other than those demanded by the [Ptolemaic] mathematical schools. I found first in Cicero that Hicetas [of Syracuse, fifth century B.C.] I had realized that the Earth moved. Afterwards I found in Plutarch that certain others had held the like opinion. . . .

Thus assuming motions, which in my work I ascribe to the Earth, by long and frequent observations I have at last discovered that, if the motions of the rest of the planets be brought into relation with the circulation of the Earth and be reckoned in proportion to the circles of each planet, not only do their phenomena presently ensue, but the orders and magnitudes of all stars and spheres, nay the heavens themselves, become so bound together that nothing in any part thereof could be moved from its place without producing confusion of all the other parts of the Universe as a whole.

As quoted in Thomas S. Kuhn, The Copernican Revolution: Planetary Astronomy in the Development of Western Thought *(New York: Vintage Books, 1959), pp. 137–139, 141–142.*

Two seventeenth-century armillary spheres, astronomical devices composed of rings represent the orbits of important celestial bodies. The left one was built on the Copernican model, the right sphere reflects the much more complicated Ptolemaic universe. [Museum of the History of Science, Oxford, England]

maic systems would disappear or become simpler. Although not wholly eliminated, the number of epicycles would be somewhat fewer. The motive behind this shift away from the earth-centered universe was to find a solution to the problems of planetary motion. By allowing the earth to move around the sun, Copernicus was able to construct a more mathematically elegant basis for astronomy. He had been discontented with the traditional system because it was mathematically clumsy and inconsistent. The primary appeal of his new system was its mathematical aesthetics: with the sun at the center of the universe, mathematical astronomy would make more sense. A change in the conception of the position of the earth meant that the planets were actually moving in circular orbits and only seemed to be doing otherwise because of the position of the observers on earth.

Except for the modification in the position of the earth, most of the other parts of Copernicus' book were Ptolemaic. The path of the planets remained circular. Genuine epicycles still existed in the heavens. His system was no more accurate than the existing ones for predicting the location of the planets. He had used no new evidence. The major impact of his work was to provide another way of confronting some of the difficulties inherent in Ptolemaic astronomy. This work did not immediately replace the old astronomy, but it did allow other people who were also discontented with the Ptolemaic systems to think in new directions.

Copernicus' concern about mathematics provided an example of the single most important factor in the developing new science. The key to the future development of the Copernican revolution lay in the fusion of mathematical astronomy with further empirical data and observation. Mathematics became the model to which the new scientific thought would conform. The new empirical evidence helped to persuade the learned public.

Tycho Brahe and Johannes Kepler: New Scientific Observations

The next major step toward the conception of a sun-centered system was taken by Tycho Brahe (1546–1601). He actually spent most of his life opposing Copernicus and advocating a different kind of earth-centered system. He suggested that the moon and the sun revolved around the earth and that the other planets revolved around the sun. However, in attacking Copernicus, he gave the latter's ideas more publicity. More important, this Danish astronomer's major weapon against Copernican astronomy was a series of new naked-eye astronomical observations. Brahe constructed the most accurate tables of observations that had been drawn up for centuries.

When Brahe died, these tables came into the possession of Johannes Kepler (1571–1630), a German astronomer. Kepler was a convinced Copernican, but his reasons for taking that position were not scientific. Kepler was deeply influenced by Renaissance Neoplatonism and its honoring of the sun. These Neoplatonists were also determined to discover mathematical harmonies in those numbers that would support a sun-centered universe. After much work Kepler discovered that to keep the sun at the center of things, he must abandon the Copernican concept of circular orbits. The mathematical relationships that emerged from a consideration of Brahe's observations suggested that the orbits of the planets were elliptical. Kepler published his findings in 1609 in a book entitled *On the Motion of Mars.* He had solved the problem of planetary orbits by using Copernicus' sun-centered universe and Brahe's empirical data.

Kepler had also defined a new problem. None of the available theories could explain why the planetary orbits were elliptical. That solution awaited the work of Sir Isaac Newton.

Galileo Galilei: A Universe of Mathematical Laws

From Copernicus to Brahe to Kepler there had been little new information about the heavens that might not have been known to Ptolemy. However, in the same year that Kepler published his volume on Mars, an Italian scientist named Galileo Galilei (1564–1642) first turned a telescope on the heavens. Through that re-

Galileo, working at first from others' suggestion, effectively invented the telescope. This is his 1609 instrument. His observations of the physical features on earth's moon and of the cyclical phases of the planet Venus and his discovery of the most prominent moons of the planet Jupiter were the first major astronomical observations since antiquity and had revolutionary intellectual and theological implications. [Istituto e Museo de Storia della Scienza, Florence. Alinari/Art Resource]

cently invented instrument he saw stars where none had been known to exist, mountains on the moon, spots moving across the sun, and moons orbiting Jupiter. The heavens were far more complex than anyone had formerly suspected. None of these discoveries proved that the earth orbited the sun, but they did suggest the complete inadequacy of the Ptolemaic system. It simply could not accommodate itself to all of these new phenomena. Some of Galileo's colleagues at the university of Padua were so unnerved that they refused to look through the telescope.

Galileo publicized his findings and arguments for the Copernican system in numerous works, the most famous of which was his *Dialogues on the Two Chief Systems of the World* (1632). This book brought down on him the condemnation of the Roman Catholic church. He was compelled to recant his opinions. However, he is reputed to have muttered after the recantation, *"E pur si muove"* ("It [the earth] still moves").

Galileo's discoveries and his popularization of the Copernican system were of secondary importance in his life work. His most important achievement was to articulate the concept of a universe totally subject to mathematical laws. More than any other writer of the century he argued that nature in its most minute details displayed mathematical regularity. He once wrote:

> Philosophy is written in that great book which ever lies before our eyes—I mean the universe—but we cannot understand it if we do not first learn the language and grasp the symbols in which it is written. This book is written in the mathematical language, and the symbols are triangles, circles, and other geometrical figures, without whose help it is impossible to comprehend a single word of it; without which one wanders through a dark labyrinth.[2]

The universe was rational; however, its rationality was not that of Scholastic logic but of mathematics. Copernicus had thought that the heavens conformed to mathematical regularity; Galileo saw this regularity throughout all physical nature. He believed that the smallest atom behaved with the same mathematical precision as the largest heavenly sphere.

Galileo's thought meant that a world of quantity was replacing one of qualities. Mathematical quantities and relationships would henceforth increasingly be used to describe nature. Color, beauty, taste, and the like would be reduced to numerical relationships. And eventually social relationships would be envisioned in a mathematical model. Nature was cold, rational, mathematical, and mechanistic. What was real and lasting in the world was what was mathematically measurable. Few intellectual shifts have wrought such momentous changes for Western civilization.

Isaac Newton: The Laws of Gravitation

Englishman Isaac Newton (1642–1727) drew on the work of his predecessors and his own brilliance to solve the major remaining problem of planetary motion and to establish a basis for physics that endured more than two

Sir Isaac Newton, discoverer of the mathematical and physical laws governing the force of gravity, believed that religion and science were compatible and mutually supportive. To study nature was to gain a better understanding of the Creator. [New York Public Library Picture Collection]

[2] Quoted in E. A. Burtt, The Metaphysical Foundations of Modern Physical Science (Garden City, N.Y.: Anchor-Doubleday, 1954), p. 75.

501

NEW
DIRECTIONS IN
SCIENCE AND
THOUGHT IN
THE SIXTEENTH
AND
SEVENTEENTH
CENTURIES

Galileo Discusses the Relationship of Science and the Bible

The religious authorities were often critical of the discoveries and theories of sixteenth- and seventeenth-century science. For many years, religious and scientific writers debated the implications of the Copernican theory in the reading of the Bible. For years before his condemnation by the Roman Catholic church in 1633, Galileo had contended that scientific theory and religious piety were compatible. In his Letter to the Grand Duchess Christiana *(of Tuscany) written in 1615, Galileo argued that God had revealed truth in both the Bible and physical nature and that the truth of physical nature did not contradict the Bible if the latter were properly understood.*

The reason produced for condemning the opinion that the earth moves and the sun stands still is that in many places in the Bible one may read that the sun moves and the earth stands still. . . .

With regard to this argument, I think in the first place that it is very pious to say and prudent to affirm that the holy Bible can never speak untruth—whenever its true meaning is understood. But I believe nobody will deny that it is often very abstruse, and may say things which are quite different from what its bare words signify. . . .

This being granted, I think that in discussions of physical problems we ought to begin not from the authority of scriptural passages, but from sense-experiences and necessary demonstrations; for the holy Bible and the phenomena of nature proceed alike from the divine Word, the former as the dictate of the Holy Ghost and the latter as the observant executrix of God's commands. It is necessary for the Bible, in order to be accommodated to the understanding of every man, to speak many things which appear to differ from the absolute truth so far as the bare meaning of the words is concerned. But Nature, on the other hand, is inexorable and immutable; she never transgresses the laws imposed upon her, or cares a whit whether her abstruce reasons and methods of operation are understandable to men. For that reason it appears that nothing physical which sense-experience sets before our eyes, or which necessary demonstrations prove to us, ought to be called in question (much less condemned) upon the testimony of biblical passages which may have some different meaning beneath their words. For the Bible is not chained in every expression to conditions as strict as those which govern all physical effects; nor is God any less excellently revealed in Nature's actions than in the sacred statements of the Bible. . . .

From this I do not mean to infer that we need not have an extraordinary esteem for the passages of holy Scripture. On the contrary, having arrived at any certainties in physics, we ought to utilize these as the most appropriate aids in the true exposition of the Bible and in the investigation of those meanings which are necessarily contained therein for these must be concordant with demonstrated truths. I should judge the authority of the Bible was designed to persuade men of those articles and propositions which, surpassing all human reasoning, could not be made credible by science, or by any other means than through the very mouth of the Holy Spirit. . . .

But I do not feel obliged to believe that the same God who has endowed us with senses, reason, and intellect has intended to forgo their use and by some other means to give us knowledge which we can attain by them.

Discoveries and Opinions of Galileo, *trans. and ed. by Stillman Drake (Garden City, N.Y.: Doubleday Anchor Books, 1957), pp. 181–183.*

Newton Contemplates the Nature of God

Issac Newton believed there was a close relationship between his scientific theory and the truths of religion. He and many other scientists of his generation were convinced that the investigation of physical nature would lead to proofs for the existence of God. In this passage, which is taken from comments he added to later editions of the Principia Mathematica, *Newton explains how the character of planetary motion leads one to conclude that God exists. He then argues that the nature of God is that of a person rather than that of an impersonal natural force. Through arguments such as these Newton believed science could be defended against those who claimed its discoveries would lead to materialism.*

The six primary planets are revolved about the sun in circles concentric with the sun. . . . Ten moons are revolved about the earth, Jupiter, and Saturn in circles concentric with them . . . ; but it is not to be conceived that mere mechanical causes could give birth to so many regular motions. . . . This most beautiful system of sun, planets, and comets could only proceed from the counsel and dominion of an intelligent and powerful Being. And if the fixed stars are the centers of other like systems, these, being formed by the like wise counsel, must be all subject to the dominion of One, especially since the light of the fixed stars is of the same nature with the light of the sun and from every system light passes into all the other systems; and lest the systems of the fixed stars should, by their gravity, fall on each other, he hath placed those systems at immense distances from one another.

This Being governs all things, not as the soul of the world, but as Lord over all; and on account of his dominion he is wont to be called "Lord God." . . . The word "God" usually signifies "Lord," but every lord is not a God. It is the dominion of a spiritual being which constitutes a God: a true, supreme, or imaginary dominion makes a true, supreme, or imaginary god. And from his true dominion it follows that the true God is a living, intelligent, and powerful Being; and, from his other perfections, that he is supreme or most perfect. He is eternal and infinite, omnipotent, and omniscient; that is, his duration reaches from eternity to eternity; his presence from infinity to infinity; he governs all things and knows all things that are or can be done. He is not eternity and infinity, but eternal and infinite; he is not duration or space, but he endures and is present. He endures forever and is everywhere present; and, by existing always and everywhere, he constitutes duration and space. . . . We have ideas of his attributes, but what the real substance of anything is we know not. . . . We know him only by his most wise and excellent contrivances of things and final causes; we admire him for his perfections, but we reverence and adore him on account of his dominion, for we adore him as his servants; and a god without dominion, providence, and final causes is nothing else but Fate and Nature.

H. S. Thayer (Ed.), Newton's Philosophy of Nature: Selections from His Writings *(New York: Hafner Press, 1974), pp. 42–44.*

centuries. The question that continued to perplex seventeenth-century scientists who accepted the theories of Copernicus, Kepler, and Galileo was how the planets and other heavenly bodies moved in an orderly fashion. The Ptolemaic and Aristotelian answer had been the crystalline spheres and a universe arranged in the order of the heaviness of its parts. Numerous unsatisfactory theories had been set forth to deal with the question.

In 1687 Newton published *The Mathematical Principles of Natural Philosophy*, better known by its Latin title of *Principia Mathematica*. Much of the research and thinking for this great work had taken place more than fifteen years earlier. Newton was heavily indebted to the work of Galileo and particularly to the latter's view that inertia could exist in either a state of motion or a state of rest. Galileo's mathematical bias permeated Newton's thought. Newton reasoned that the planets and all other physical objects in the universe moved through mutual attraction. Every object in the universe affected every other object through gravity. The attraction of gravity explained why the planets moved in an orderly rather than a chaotic manner. He had found that "the force of gravity towards the whole planet did arise from and was compounded of the forces of gravity towards all its parts, and towards every one part was in the inverse proportion of the squares of the distances from the part."[3] Newton demonstrated this relationship mathematically. He made no attempt to explain the nature of gravity itself.

Newton was a great mathematical genius, but he also upheld the importance of empirical data and observation. He believed, in good Baconian fashion, that one must observe phenomena before attempting to explain them. The final test of any theory or hypothesis for him was whether it described what could actually be observed. He was a great opponent of Descartes' rationalism, which he believed included insufficient guards against error. As Newton's own theory of universal gravitation became increasingly accepted, the Baconian bias also became more fully popularized.

Newton's Reconciliation of Science and Faith

With the work of Newton the natural universe became a realm of law and regularity. Beliefs in spirits and divinities were no longer necessary to explain its operation. Thus the Scientific Revolution liberated human beings from the fear of a chaotic or haphazard universe. Most of the scientists were very devout people. They saw the new picture of physical nature as sug-

MAJOR WORKS OF THE SCIENTIFIC REVOLUTION	
1543	*On the Revolutions of the Heavenly Spheres* (Copernicus)
1605	*The Advancement of Learning* (Bacon)
1609	*On the Motion of Mars* (Kepler)
1620	*Novum Organum* (Bacon)
1632	*Dialogues on the Two Chief Systems of the World* (Galileo)
1637	*Discourse on Method* (Descartes)
1687	*Principia Mathematica* (Newton)

gesting a new picture of God. The Creator of this rational, lawful nature must also be rational. To study nature was to come to a better understanding of that Creator. Science and religious faith were not only compatible but mutually supporting. As Newton wrote, "The main Business of Natural Philosophy is to argue from Phaenomena without feigning Hypothesis, and to deduce Causes from Effects, till we come to the very first Cause, which certainly is not mechanical."[4]

This reconciliation of faith and science allowed the new physics and astronomy to spread rapidly. At the very time when Europeans were finally tiring of the wars of religion, the new science provided the basis for a view of God that might lead away from irrational disputes and wars over religious doctrine. Faith in a rational God encouraged faith in the rationality of human beings and in their capacity to improve their lot once liberated from the traditions of the past. The Scientific Revolution provided the great model for the desirability of change and of criticism of inherited views. Yet at the same time the new science caused some people to feel that the mystery had been driven from the universe and that the rational Creator was less loving and less near to humankind than the God of earlier ages.

Literary Imagination in Transition

The world of the new science developed in the midst of a society where medieval outlooks

---

[3] *Quoted in A. Rupert Hall,* From Galileo to Newton, 1630–1720 *(London: Fontana, 1970), p. 300.*

[4] *Quoted in Franklin Baumer,* Main Currents of Western Thought, *4th ed. (New Haven: Yale, 1978) p. 323.*

and religious values remained very much alive. Literary figures of the same period often reflected both the new and the old. In Cervantes one sees a brilliant writer raising questions about the adequacy of medieval values of chivalry and honor and probing the character of human perceptions of reality. Shakespeare's dramas provide an insight into virtually the entire range of late sixteenth- and early seventeenth-century English world views. John Milton could attempt to justify the ways of the Christian God to doubting human beings and in the same work have characters debate the adequacy of the Ptolemaic and Copernican systems. John Bunyan during the same years that Newton reached his deepest insights about nature could write one of the classic works of simple Christian piety. It is the combination of past and future world views that makes the thought of the seventeenth century so remarkable and rich.

Miguel de Cervantes Saavedra: Rejection of Idealism

Spanish literature of the sixteenth and seventeenth centuries reflects the peculiar religious and political history of Spain in this period. Spain was dominated by the Catholic church and this was a major influence on its literature. Since the joint reign of Ferdinand and Isabella (1479–1504) the Church had received the unqualified support of reigning political power. Although there was religious reform in Spain, a Protestant Reformation never occurred, thanks largely to the entrenched power of the Church and the Inquisition.

The second influence was the aggressive piety of Spanish rulers. The intertwining of Catholic piety and Spanish political power underlay the third major influence on Spanish literature: preoccupation with medieval chivalric virtues—in particular, questions of honor and loyalty. The novels and plays of the period almost invariably focus on a special decision involving a character's reputation as his honor or loyalty is tested. In this regard Spanish literature may be said to have remained more Catholic and medieval than that of England and France, where major Protestant movements had occurred. Two of the most important Spanish writers in this period became priests (Lope de Vega and Pedro Calderón de la Barca). The one generally acknowledged to be the greatest Spanish writer of all time, Cervantes, was preoccupied in his work with the strengths and weaknesses of religious idealism.

Cervantes (1547–1616) was born in Alcalá, the son of a nomadic physician. Having received only a smattering of formal education, he educated himself by insatiable reading in vernacular literature and immersion in the "school of life." As a young man he worked in Rome for a Spanish cardinal. In 1570 he became a soldier and was decorated for gallantry in the Battle of Lepanto (1571). While he was returning to Spain in 1575, his ship was captured by pirates, and Cervantes spent five years as a slave in Algiers. On his release and return

The author of Don Quixote *was Miguel de Cervantes Saavedra (1547–1616), generally acknowledged to be the greatest Spanish writer. [Library of Congress]*

to Spain, he held many odd jobs, among them that of a tax collector. He was several times imprisoned for padding his accounts. He began to write his most famous work, _Don Quixote,_ in 1603, while languishing in prison.

The first part of _Don Quixote_ appeared in 1605. If, as many argue, the intent of this work was to satirize the chivalric romances so popular in Spain, Cervantes nonetheless failed to conceal his deep affection for the character he created as an object of ridicule, Don Quixote. The work is satire only on the surface and has remained as much an object of study by philosophers and theologians as by students of Spanish literature. Don Quixote, a none-too-stable middle-aged man, was presented by Cervantes as one driven mad by reading too many chivalric romances. Don Quixote finally comes to believe that he is an aspirant to knighthood and must prove by brave deeds his worthiness of knightly rank. To this end he acquires a rusty suit of armor, mounts an aged steed (named Rozinante), and chooses for his inspiration a quite unworthy peasant girl, Dulcinea, whom he fancies to be a noble lady to whom he can, with honor, dedicate his life.

Don Quixote's foil in the story—Sancho Panza, a clever, worldly-wise peasant who serves as his squire—is an equally fascinating character. Sancho Panza watches with bemused skepticism, but also with genuine sympathy, as his lord does battle with a windmill (which he mistakes for a dragon) and repeatedly makes a fool of himself as he gallops across the countryside. The story ends tragically with Don Quixote's humiliating defeat by a well-meaning friend, who, disguised as a knight, bests Don Quixote in combat and forces him to renounce his quest for knighthood. The humiliated Don Quixote does not, however, come to his senses as a result. He returns sadly to his village to die a shamed and broken-hearted old man.

Throughout _Don Quixote_ Cervantes juxtaposes the down-to-earth realism of Sancho Panza with the old-fashioned religious idealism of Don Quixote. The reader perceives that Cervantes admired the one as much as the other and meant to portray both as representing attitudes necessary for a happy life. If they are to be truly happy, men and women need dreams, even impossible ones, just as much as they need a sense of reality.

William Shakespeare: Dramatist of the Age

Shakespeare (1564–1616), the greatest playwright in the English language, was born in Stratford-on-Avon. He lived there almost all of his life except for the years when he wrote in London. There is much less factual knowledge about him than one would expect of such an important figure. Shakespeare married in 1582 at the early age of eighteen, and he and his wife, Anne Hathaway, had three children (two were twins) by 1585. He apparently worked as a schoolteacher for a time and in this capacity acquired his broad knowledge of Renaissance learning and literature. The argument of some scholars that he was an untutored natural genius is highly questionable. His own learning and his enthusiasm for the education of his day are manifest in the many learned allusions that appear in his plays.

Shakespeare enjoyed the life of a country gentleman. There is none of the Puritan dis-

The dramatist and poet William Shakespeare is considered the greatest playwright in the English language. This engraving by Martin Droeshout appears on the title page of the collected edition of his plays published in 1623 and is probably as close as we shall come to knowing what he looked like. [New York Public Library Picture Collection]

tress over worldliness in his work. He took the new commercialism and the bawdy pleasures of the Elizabethan Age in stride and with amusement. The few allusions to the Puritans that exist in his works appear to be more critical than complementary. In matters of politics, as in those of religion, he was very much a man of his time and inclined to offend his queen.

That Shakespeare was interested in politics is apparent from his history plays and the references to contemporary political events that fill all his plays. He seems to have viewed government simply, however, through the character of the individual ruler, whether Richard III or Elizabeth Tudor, not in terms of ideal systems or social goals. By modern standards he was a political conservative, accepting the social rankings and the power structure of his day and demonstrating unquestioned patriotism.

Shakespeare knew the theater as one who participated in every phase of its life—as a playwright, an actor, and a part owner of a theater. He was a member and principal dramatist of a famous company of actors known as the King's Men. During the tenure of Edmund Tilney, who was Queen Elizabeth's Master of Revels during the greater part of Shakespeare's active period (1590–1610), many of Shakespeare's plays were performed at court. The queen enthusiastically patronized plays and pageants.

Elizabethan drama was already a distinctive form when Shakespeare began writing. Unlike French drama of the seventeenth century, which was dominated by the court and classical models, English drama developed in the sixteenth and seventeenth centuries as a blending of many extant forms. It ranged from classical comedies and tragedies to the medieval morality play and contemporary Italian short stories.

Two contemporaries, Thomas Kyd and Christopher Marlowe, especially influenced Shakespeare's tragedies. Kyd (1558–1594) was the author of the first dramatic version of Hamlet and a master at weaving together motive and plot. The tragedies of Marlowe (1564–1593) set a model for character, poetry, and style that only Shakespeare among the English playwrights of the period surpassed. Shakespeare's work was an original synthesis of the best past and current achievements. He mas-

tered the psychology of human motivation and passion and had a unique talent for psychological penetration.

Shakespeare wrote histories, comedies, and tragedies. Richard III (1593), a very early play, stands out among the examples of the first genre, although some historians have criticized as historically inaccurate his patriotic depiction of Richard, the foe of Henry Tudor, as an unprincipled villain. Shakespeare's comedies, although not attaining the heights of his tragedies, surpass in originality his history plays. Save for The Tempest (1611), his last play, the comedies most familiar to modern readers were written between 1598 and 1602: Much Ado About Nothing (1598–1599), As You Like It (1598–1600), and Twelfth Night (1602).

The tragedies are considered his unique achievement. Four of these were written within a three-year period: Hamlet (1603), Othello (1604), King Lear (1605), and Macbeth (1606). The most original of the tragedies, Romeo and Juliet (1597), transformed an old popular story into a moving drama of "star-cross'd lovers." Both Romeo and Juliet, denied a marriage by their factious families, die tragic deaths. Romeo, finding Juliet and thinking her dead after she has taken a sleeping potion, poisons himself. Juliet, awakening to find Romeo dead, stabs herself to death with his dagger.

Throughout his lifetime and ever since, Shakespeare has been immensely popular with both the playgoer and the play reader. As Ben Jonson, a contemporary classical dramatist who created his own school of poets, aptly put it in a tribute affixed to the First Folio edition of Shakespeare's plays (1623): "He was not of an age, but for all time."

John Milton: Puritan Poet

John Milton (1608–1674) was the son of a devout Puritan father. Educated at Saint Paul's School and then at Christ's College of Cambridge University, he became a careful student of Christian and pagan classics. In 1638 he traveled to Italy, where he found in the lingering Renaissance a very congenial intellectual atmosphere. The Phlegraean Fields near Naples, a volcanic region, later became the model for hell in Paradise Lost, and it is suspected by some scholars that the Villa d'Este provided the model for paradise in Paradise Regained.

The English writer and poet John Milton is shown in an engraving by William Faithorne. It is one of the few authentic contemporary likenesses of him. [Library of Congress]

Milton remained throughout his life a man more at home in the Italian Renaissance, with its high ideals and universal vision, than in the strife-torn England of the seventeenth century.

A man of deep inner conviction and principle, Milton believed that standing a test of character was the most important thing in an individual's life. This belief informed his own personal life and is the subject of much of his literary work. An early poem, *Lycidas*, was a pastoral elegy dealing with one who lived well but not long, Edward King, a close college friend who tragically drowned.

In 1639 Milton joined the Puritan struggle against Charles I and Archbishop Laud. Employing his literary talents as a pamphleteer, he defended the Presbyterian form of church government against the episcopacy and supported other Puritan reforms. After a month-long unsuccessful marriage in 1642 (a marriage later reconciled), he wrote several tracts in defense of the right to divorce. These writings became a factor in Parliament's passage of a censorship law in 1643, against which Milton wrote an eloquent defense of the freedom of the press, *Areopagitica* (1644).

Until the upheavals of the civil war moderated his views, Milton believed that government should have the least possible control over the private lives of individuals. When Parliament divided into Presbyterians and Independents, he took the side of the latter, who wanted to dissolve the national church altogether in favor of the local autonomy of individual congregations. He also defended the execution of Charles I in a tract on the *Tenure of Kings and Magistrates.* After his intense labor on this tract his eyesight failed. Milton was totally blind when he wrote his acclaimed masterpieces.

Paradise Lost, completed in 1665 and published in 1667, is a study of the destructive qualities of pride and the redeeming possibilities of humility. It elaborates in traditional Christian language and concept the revolt of Satan in heaven and the fall of Adam on earth. The motives of Satan and all who rebel against God intrigued Milton. His proud but tragic Satan, one of the great figures in all literature, represents the absolute corruption of potential greatness.

In *Paradise Lost* Milton aspired to give England a lasting epic like that given Greece in Homer's *Iliad* and ancient Rome in Vergil's *Aeneid.* In choosing biblical subject matter, he revealed the influence of contemporary theology. Milton tended to agree with the Arminians, who, unlike the extreme Calvinists, did not believe that all worldly events, including the Fall of Man, were immutably fixed in the eternal decree of God. Milton shared the Arminian belief that human beings must take responsibility for their fate and that human efforts to improve character could, with God's grace, bring salvation.

Perhaps his own blindness, joined with the hope of making the best of a failed religious revolution, inclined Milton to sympathize with those who urged people to make the most of what they had, even in the face of seemingly sure defeat. That is a manifest concern of his last works, *Samson Agonistes,* which recounts the biblical story of Samson, and *Paradise Regained*, the story of Christ's temptation in the wilderness, both published in 1671.

John Bunyan: Visions of Christian Piety

Bunyan (1628–1688) was the English author of two classics of sectarian Puritan spirituality: *Grace Abounding* (1666) and *The Pilgrim's*

John Milton Defends Freedom to Print Books

During the English Civil War the Parliament passed a very strict censorship measure. In Areopagitica *(1644) John Milton attacked this law and contributed one of the major defenses for the freedom of the press in the history of Western culture. In the passage below he compares the life of a book with the life of a human being. He argues that it may be more dangerous and harmful to attack a book than to attack a person. One reason for this view is that books may contain the wisdom of human beings over many ages rather than the wisdom of a single life.*

I deny not, but that it is of greatest concernment in the Church and Commonwealth, to have a vigilant eye how books demean themselves, as well as men; and thereafter to confine, imprison, and do sharpest justice on them as malefactors; for books are not absolutely dead things, but do contain a progeny of life in them to be as active as that soul was whose progeny they are; nay, they do preserve as in a vial the purest efficacy and extraction of that living intellect that bred them. I know they are as lively, and as vigorously productive, as those fabulous dragon's teeth; and being sown up and down, may chance to spring up armed men. And yet on the other hand unless wariness be used, as good almost kill a man as kill a good Book; who kills a man kills a reasonable creature, God's Image; but he who destroys a good book, kills reason itself, kills the Image of God, as it were, in the eye. Many a man lives a burden to the Earth; but a good book is the precious life-blood of a master spirit, embalmed and treasured up on purpose to a life beyond life. It is true, no age can restore a life, whereof, perhaps there is no great loss; and revolutions of ages do not oft recover the loss of a rejected truth, for the want of which whole nations fare the worse. We should be wary, therefore, what persecution we raise against the living labours of public men, how we spill that seasoned life of man preserved and stored up in books; since we see a kind of homicide may be thus committed, sometimes a martyrdom, and if it extends to the whole impression, a kind of massacre, whereof the execution ends not in the slaying of an elemental life, but strikes at that ethereal . . . essence, the breath of reason itself; slays an immortality rather than a life.

J. A. St. John (Ed.), The Prose Works of John Milton *(London: H. G. Bohn, 1843–1853), 2:8–9.*

Progress (1678). A Bedford tinker, his works speak especially for the seventeenth-century working people and popular religious culture. Bunyan received only the most basic education before taking up his father's craft. He was drafted into Oliver Cromwell's revolutionary army in 1644 and served for two years, although without seeing actual combat. The visionary fervor of the New Model Army and the imagery of warfare abound in Bunyan's work.

After the restoration of the monarchy in 1660, Bunyan went to prison for his fiery preaching and remained there for twelve years. Had he been willing to agree to give up preaching, he might have been released much sooner. But Puritans considered the compromise of one's beliefs a tragic flaw, and Bunyan steadfastly refused all such suggestions.

During this period of imprisonment, Bunyan wrote his famous autobiography, *Grace Abounding.* It is both a very personal statement and a model for the faithful. Like *The Pilgrim's Progress,* Bunyan's later masterpiece, *Grace Abounding* expresses Puritan piety at its most fervent. Puritans believed that individuals could do absolutely nothing to save themselves, and this made them extremely restless and introspective. The individual believer could only trust that God had placed her or him among the elect and try each day to live a life that reflected such a favored status. So long as men and women struggled successfully against the flesh and the world, they had presumptive evidence that they were among God's elect. To falter or to become complacent in the face of temptation was to cast doubt on one's faith and salvation and even to raise the specter of eternal damnation.

This anxious questing for salvation was the subject of _The Pilgrim's Progress_, a work unique in its contribution to Western religious symbolism and imagery. It is the story of the journey of Christian and his friends Hopeful and Faithful to the Celestial City. It teaches that one must deny spouse, children, and all earthly security and go in search of "Life, life, eternal life." During the long journey, the travelers must resist the temptations of Worldly-Wiseman and Vanity Fair, pass through the Slough of Despond, and endure a long dark night in Doubting Castle, their faith being tested at every turn. Bunyan later wrote a work tracing the progress of Christian's opposite, _The Life and Death of Mr. Badman_ (1680). It tells the story of a man so addicted to the bad habits of Restoration society, of which Bunyan strongly disapproved, that he journeyed steadfastly not to heaven but to hell.

Philosophy in the Wake of Changing Science

The end of the sixteenth century saw weariness with religious strife and incipient unbelief as many people no longer embraced either old Catholic or new Protestant absolutes. Intellectually as well as politically the seventeenth century was a period of transition. The thinkers of the Renaissance had already prepared the way be reacting strongly against medieval intellectual traditions, especially those informed by Aristotle and Scholasticism.

The thinkers of the Renaissance and the Reformation nonetheless paved the way for the new science and philosophy, both by their attacks on tradition and by their own failure to implement radical reforms. The Humanist revival of ancient skepticism proved an effective foundation for attacks on traditional views of

MAJOR WORKS OF SEVENTEENTH-CENTURY LITERATURE AND PHILOSOPHY	
1605	_King Lear_ (Shakespeare)
1605	_Don Quixote,_ Part I (Cervantes)
1651	_Leviathan_ (Hobbes)
1656–1657	_Provincial Letters_ (Pascal)
1667	_Paradise Lost_ (Milton)
1677	_Ethics_ (Spinoza)
1678	_The Pilgrim's Progress_ (Bunyan)
1690	_Treatises of Government_ (Locke)
1690	_An Essay Concerning Human Understanding_ (Locke)

authority and rationality in both religion and science. Already such thinkers as the Italian Pico Della Mirandola (1463–1494), the German Cornelius Agrippa of Nettisheim (1486–1535), and the Frenchman François Rabelais (1494–1553) had questioned the ability of reason to obtain certitude. Sebastian Castellio (1515–1563), Michel de Montaigne (1533–1592), and Pierre Charron (1541–1603) had been as much repelled by the new Calvinist religion as John Calvin had been by medieval religion. The ground had thus been prepared for philosophers who would look for new ways to certainty beyond the bounds of Scholasticism or of Catholic or Protestant theology.

The revolution in scientific thought contributed to this major reconsideration of Western philosophy. Several of the most important figures in the scientific revolution, such as Descartes and Bacon, were themselves philosophers. They had been discontent with the Scholastic heritage. Bacon insisted on attention to empirical research. Descartes attempted to find certainty through the exploration of his process of thinking. Newton wrote widely on both scientific method and theological issues.

The new methods of science had a broad impact on philosophers. The emphasis that Galileo placed on mathematics spread to other areas of thought. Pascal, who was himself a very gifted mathematician, became concerned about the issue of certain knowledge and religious faith. Spinoza would write his ethical discourses in the form of geometrical theorems. Hobbes produced a great political treatise through a mode of rational reasoning resembling mathematics. Locke would attempt to explore the human mind in a fashion that he believed resembled Newton's approach to the physical universe. Virtually all of these writers found a tension that they hoped to resolve between the new science and religious belief.

Francis Bacon: Empirical Method

Bacon (1561–1626) was an Englishman of almost universal accomplishment. He was a lawyer, a high royal official, and the author of histories, moral essays, and philosophical discourses. Traditionally he has been regarded as the father of empiricism and of experimentation in science. Much of this reputation is unearned. Bacon was not a scientist except in the most amateur fashion. His accomplishment was setting a tone and helping to create a climate in which other scientists worked.

By teaching that knowledge should proceed inductively, Sir Francis Bacon, Viscount St. Albans (1561–1626) became a major champion of the scientific method. [National Portrait Gallery, London]

In books such as *The Advancement of Learning* (1605), the *Novum Organum* (1620), and the *New Atlantis* (1627), Bacon attacked the Scholastic belief that most truth had already been discovered and only required explanation, as well as the Scholastic reverence for intellectual authority in general. He believed that Scholastic thinkers paid too much attention to tradition and to knowledge achieved by the ancients. He urged contemporaries to strike out on their own in search of a new understanding of nature. He wanted seventeenth-century Europeans to have confidence in themselves and their own abilities rather than in the people and methods of the past. Bacon was one of the first major European writers to champion the desirability of innovation and change.

Bacon believed that human knowledge should produce useful results. In particular, knowledge of nature should be brought to the aid of the human condition. Those goals required the modification or abandonment of Scholastic modes of learning and thinking. Bacon contended, "The [Scholastic] logic now in use serves more to fix and give stability to the errors which have their foundation in commonly received notions than to help the search after truth."[5] Scholastic philosophers could not escape from their syllogisms to examine the foundations of their thought and intellectual presuppositions. Bacon urged that philosophers and investigators of nature examine the evidence of their senses before constructing logical speculations. In a famous passage he divided all philosophers into "men of experiment and men of dogmas." He observed:

The men of experiment are like the ant, they only collect and use; the reasoners resemble spiders, who make cobwebs out of their own substance. But the bee takes a middle course: it gathers its material from the flowers of the garden and of the field, but transforms and digests it by a power of its own. Not unlike this is the true business of philosophy.[6]

By directing scientists toward an examination of empirical evidence, Bacon hoped that they would achieve new knowledge and thus new capabilities for humankind.

Bacon compared himself with Columbus

---

[5] *Quoted in Baumer, p. 281.*
[6] *Quoted in Baumer, p. 288.*

511

NEW
DIRECTIONS IN
SCIENCE AND
THOUGHT IN
THE SIXTEENTH
AND
SEVENTEENTH
CENTURIES

Bacon Attacks the Idols That Harm Human Understanding

Francis Bacon wanted the men and women of his era to have the courage to change the way in which they thought about physical nature. In this famous passage from the Novum Organum *(1620) Bacon attempted to explain why people had such difficulty in asking new questions and seeking new answers. His observations may still be relevant to the manner in which people form and hold their opinions in our own day.*

The idols and false notions which are now in possession of the human understanding, and have taken deep root therein, not only so beset men's minds that truth can hardly find entrance, but even after entrance is obtained, they will again in the very instauration of the sciences meet and trouble us, unless men being forewarned of the danger fortify themselves as far as may be against their assaults.

There are four classes of Idols which beset men's minds. To these for distinction's sake I have assigned names,— calling the first class *Idols of the Tribe*; the second, *Idols of the Cave*; the third, *Idols of the Marketplace*; the fourth, *Idols of the Theatre.*

The Idols of the Tribe have their foundation in human nature itself; and in the tribe or race of men. For it is a false assertion that the sense of man is the measure of things. On the contrary, all perceptions as well as the sense as of the mind are according to the measure of the universe. And the human understanding is like a false mirror, which, receiving rays irregularly, distorts and discolours the nature of things by mingling its own nature with it.

The Idols of the Cave are the idols of the individual man. For every one (besides the errors common to human nature in general) has a cave or den of his own, which refracts and discolours the light of nature; owing either to his own proper and peculiar nature; or to his education and conversation with others; or to the reading of books, and the authority of those whom he esteems and admires. . . .

There are also Idols formed by the intercourse and association of men with each other, which I call Idols of the Marketplace, on account of the commerce and consort of men there. For it is by discourse that men associate; and words are imposed according to the apprehension of the vulgar. And therefore the ill and unfit choice of words wonderfully obstructs the understanding. . . .

Lastly, there are Idols which have immigrated into men's minds from the various dogmas of philosophies, and also from wrong laws of demonstration. These I call Idols of the Theatre; because in my judgment all the received systems are but so many stage plays, representing worlds of their own creation after an unreal and scenic fashion.

Francis Bacon, Essays, Advancement of Learning, New Atlantis, and Other Pieces, *ed. by Richard Foster Jones (New York: Odyssey, 1937), pp. 278–280.*

plotting a new route to intellectual discovery. The comparison is significant, because it displays the consciousness of a changing world that appears so often in writers of the late sixteenth and early seventeenth centuries. They were rejecting the past not from simple hatred but rather from a firm understanding that the world was much more complicated than their medieval forebears had thought.

Neither Europe nor European thought could

The microscope was the telescope's companion as a major optical invention of the seventeenth century. Several people, including Galileo, had a hand in its development, but the greatest progress was made by the Dutchman Anton von Leeuwenhoek (1632–1723) and the Englishman Robert Hooke (1635–1703). Hooke designed this microscope in 1670. [IBM Gallery of Science and Art]

remain self-contained. There were not only new worlds on the globe but also new worlds of the mind. Most of the people in Bacon's day, including the intellectuals, thought that the best era of human history lay in antiquity. Bacon dissented vigorously from that point of view. He looked to a future of material improvement achieved through the <u>empirical</u> examination of nature. His own theory of induction from empirical evidence was quite unsystematic, but his insistence on appeal to experience influenced others whose methods were more productive. His great achievement was persuading increasing numbers of thinkers that scientific thought must conform to empirical experience.

Bacon gave science a progressionist bias. Science was to have a practical purpose and its goal was to be human improvement. Some scientific investigation does possess this character. Much pure research does not. However, Bacon linked in the public mind the concepts of science and material progress. This was a powerful idea and has continued to influence Western civilization to the present day. It has made science and those who can appeal to the authority of science major forces for change and innovation. Thus, though not making any major scientific contribution himself, Bacon directed investigators of nature to a new method and a new purpose.

René Descartes: The Method of Rational Deduction

No writer of the seventeenth century more fully adopted the geometric spirit of contemporary mathematics than René Descartes (1596–1650). He was a gifted mathematician who invented analytic geometry. He also was the author of major works on numerous scientific topics. However, his most important con-

René Descartes (1596–1650), believed that because the material world operated according to mathematical laws it could therefore be understood by the exercise of human reasoning. [Giraudon]

tribution was to scientific method. He wanted to proceed by deduction rather than by empirical observation and induction.

In 1637 Descartes published his *Discourse on Method* in which he attempted to provide a basis for all thinking founded on a mathematical model. He published the work in French rather than in Latin because he wanted it to have wide circulation and application. He began by saying that he would doubt everything except those propositions about which he could have clear and distinct ideas. This approach rejected all forms of intellectual authority except the conviction of his own reason. He concluded that he could not doubt his own act of thinking and his own existence. From this base he proceeded to deduce the existence of God. The presence of God was important to Descartes because God was the guarantor of the correctness of clear and distinct ideas. Because God was not a deceiver, the ideas of God-given reason could not be false.

Descartes believed that this powerful human reason could fully comprehend the world. He divided existing things into mind and body. Thinking was the characteristic of the mind and extension of the body. Within the material world, mathematical laws reigned supreme. These could be grasped by the human reason. Because the laws were mathematical, they could be deduced from each other and constituted a complete system. The world of extension was the world of the scientist, whereas the mind was related to theology and philosophy. In the material world there was no room for spirits, divinity, or anything nonmaterial. Descartes had separated mind from body in order to banish the former from the realm of scientific speculation. He wanted to resurrect the speculative use of reason, but in a limited manner. It was to be applied only to the mechanical and mathematical realm of matter.

Descartes' emphasis on deduction and rational speculation exercised broad influence. Well into the eighteenth century European thinkers appealed to Descartes' method, which moved from broad intellectual generalizations to specific phenomena. The method then attempted to see how the phenomena could be interpreted so as to mesh with the generalization.

However, that method was eventually over-

come by the force of scientific induction, whereby the observer or scientist began with observations of empirical data and then attempted to draw generalizations from those observations. The major champion of the inductive method during the early seventeenth century had been Francis Bacon.

Blaise Pascal: Reason and Faith

Pascal (1623–1662), a French mathematician and a physical scientist widely acclaimed by his contemporaries, surrendered all his wealth to pursue an austere, self-disciplined life. Torn between the continuing dogmatism and the skepticism of the seventeenth century, he aspired to write a work that would refute both the Jesuits and the skeptics. He considered the Jesuits' casuistry (i.e., arguments designed to minimize and even excuse sinful acts) a distortion of Christian teaching. The skeptics of his age either denied religion altogether (as atheists) or accepted it only as it conformed to reason (as deists). Such a definitive work was never realized, and his views on these matters exist only in piecemeal form. He wrote against the Jesuits in his *Provincial Letters* (1656–1657). He also left behind a provocative collection of reflections on humankind and religion that was published posthumously under the title *Pensées*.

Pascal allied himself with the Jansenists, seventeenth-century Catholic opponents of the Jesuits. His sister was a member of the Jansenist community of Port-Royal near Paris. The Jansenists shared with the Calvinists Saint Augustine's belief in human beings' total sinfulness, their eternal predestination by God, and their complete dependence on faith and grace for knowledge of God and salvation.

Pascal believed that reason and science, although attesting to human dignity, remained of no avail in matters of religion. Here only the reasons of the heart and a "leap of faith" could prevail. Pascal saw two essential truths in the Christian religion: that a loving God, worthy of human attainment, exists, and that human beings, because they are corrupted in nature, are utterly unworthy of God. Pascal believed that the atheists and the deists of the age had spurned the lesson of reason. For him rational analysis of the human condition attested humankind's utter mortality and corruption; it also exposed the weakness of reason itself in

Pascal Meditates on Human Beings
As Thinking Creatures

Pascal was both a religious and a scientific writer. Unlike other scientific thinkers of the seventeenth century, he was not overly optimistic about the ability of science to improve the human condition. Pascal believed that science and philosophy would instead help human beings to understand their situation better. In these passages from his Pensées (Thoughts), *he discussed the uniqueness of human beings as the creatures who alone in all the universe are capable of thinking.*

339

I can well conceive a man without hands, feet, head (for it is only experience which teaches us that the head is more necessary than feet). But I cannot conceive man without thought; he would be a stone or a brute.

344

Reason commands us far more imperiously than a master; for in disobeying the one we are unfortunate, and in disobeying the other we are fools.

346

Thought constitutes the greatness of man.

347

Man is but a reed, the most feeble thing in nature; but he is a thinking reed. The entire universe need not arm itself to crush him. A vapour, a drop of water suffices to kill him. But, if the universe were to crush him, man would still be more noble than that which killed him, because he knows that he dies and the advantage which the universe has over him; the universe knows nothing of this.

All our dignity consists, then, in thought. By it we must elevate ourselves, and not by space and time which we cannot fill. Let us endeavour, then, to think well; this is the principle of morality.

348

A thinking reed—It is not from space that I must seek my dignity, but from the government of my thought. I shall have no more if I possess worlds. By space the universe encompasses and swallows me up like an atom; by thought I comprehend the world.

Blaise Pascal, Pensées and The Provincial Letters *(New York: Modern Library, 1941), pp. 115–116.*

resolving the problems of human nature and destiny. Reason should rather drive those who truly heed it to faith and dependence on divine grace.

Pascal made a famous wager with the skeptics. It is a better bet, he argued, to believe that God exists and to stake everything on his promised mercy than not to do so. This is because if God does exist, everything will be gained by the believer, whereas, should He prove not to exist, the loss incurred by having believed in Him is by comparison very slight.

Convinced that belief in God improved life psychologically and disciplined it morally (whether or not God proved in the end to exist), Pascal worked to strengthen traditional religious belief. He urged his contemporaries to seek self-understanding by "learned ignorance" and to discover humankind's greatness by recognizing its misery. Thereby he hoped to

515

NEW
DIRECTIONS IN
SCIENCE AND
THOUGHT IN
THE SIXTEENTH
AND
SEVENTEENTH
CENTURIES

Pascal invented this adding machine, the ancestor of all mechanical calculators, about 1644. It has eight wheels with ten cogs each, corresponding to the numbers 0–9. The wheels move forward for addition, backward for subtraction. [Musée des Techniques, Paris]

counter what he believed to be the false optimism of the new rationalism and science.

Baruch Spinoza: The World as Divine Substance

The most controversial thinker of the seventeenth century was Baruch Spinoza (1632–1677), the son of a Jewish merchant of Amsterdam. Spinoza's philosophy caused his excommunication by his own synagogue in 1656. In 1670 he published his *Treatise on Religious and Political Philosophy*, a work that criticized the dogmatism of Dutch Calvinists and championed freedom of thought. During his lifetime both Jews and Protestants attacked him as an atheist.

Spinoza's most influential writing, the *Ethics*, was published after his death in 1677. Religious leaders universally condemned it for its apparent espousal of pantheism (i.e., a doctrine equating God and nature). God and nature

were so closely identified by Spinoza that little room seemed left either for divine revelation in Scripture or for the personal immortality of the soul—denials equally repugnant to Jews and to Christians. The *Ethics* was a very complicated work, written in the spirit of the new science, as a geometrical system of definitions, axioms, and propositions. Spinoza divided the

Even before Pascal's day, of course, there was a tradition of elaborate mechanical devices throughout Europe. For example, by 1500, there were public clocks in practically every town. One of the most famous is the astronomical clock of Strasbourg cathedral in France, which presents a parade of allegorical figures every day at noon. [French Government Tourist Office, New York]

work into five parts, which dealt with God, the mind, emotions, human bondage, and human freedom.

The most controversial part of the *Ethics* deals with the nature of substance and of God. According to Spinoza, there is but one substance, which is self-caused, free, and infinite, and God is that substance. From this definition it follows that everything that exists is in God and cannot even be conceived of apart from Him. Such a doctrine is not literally pantheistic because God is still seen to be more than the created world that He, as primal substance, embraces. It may perhaps best be described as *panentheism*: the teaching that all that exists is within God, yet God remains more than and beyond the natural world. Nonetheless, in Spinoza's view, statements about the natural world are also statements about divine nature. Mind and matter are seen to be extensions of the infinite substance of God; what transpires in the world of humankind and nature is a necessary outpouring of the divine.

Such teaching seemed to portray the world as eternal and human actions as unfree and inevitable. Jews and Christians have traditionally condemned such teachings because they deny the creation of the world by God in time and destroy any voluntary basis for personal reward and punishment.

Spinoza found enthusiastic supporters, however, in the nineteenth-century German philosopher Georg Wilhelm Friedrich Hegel and in Romantic writers of the same century, especially Johann Wolfgang von Goethe and Percy Bysshe Shelley. Modern thinkers who are unable to accept traditional religious language and doctrines have continued to find in the teaching of Spinoza a congenial rational religion.

Thomas Hobbes: Apologist for Absolutism

Thomas Hobbes (1588–1679) was incontestably the most original political philosopher of the seventeenth century. The son of a clergyman, he was educated at Oxford University. Although he never broke with the Church of England, he came to share basic Calvinist beliefs. Their low view of human nature and the ideal of a commonwealth based on a covenant both found eloquent expression in Hobbes' political philosophy.

An urbane and much-traveled man, Hobbes enthusiastically supported the new scientific movement. He worked as tutor and secretary to three earls of Devonshire over a fifty-year period. During the 1630s he visited Paris, where he came to know Descartes. After the outbreak of the Puritan Revolution in 1640, he lived as an exile in Paris until 1651. In 1646 Hobbes became the tutor of the Prince of Wales, the future Charles II, and remained on good terms with him after the restoration of the Stuart monarchy. Hobbes also spent time with Galileo in Italy.

He took a special interest in the works of William Harvey (1578–1657). Harvey was a physiologist famed for the discovery of how blood circulated through the body; his scientific writings influenced Hobbes' own tracts on bodily motions. Hobbes became an expert in geometry and optics. He was also highly trained in classical languages. His first published work was a translation of Thucydides' *History of the Peloponnesian War*, the first English translation of this work, which is still reprinted today.

The English Civil War made Hobbes a political philosopher. In 1651 his *Leviathan* appeared. Written as the concluding part of a broad philosophical system that analyzed physical bodies and human nature, the work established Hobbes as a major European thinker.

Hobbes viewed humankind and society in a thoroughly materialistic and mechanical way. Human beings are defined as a collection of material particles in motion. All their psychological processes begin with and are derived from bare sensation, and all their motivations are egoistical, intended to increase pleasure and minimize pain. The human power of reasoning, which Hobbes defined unspectacularly as a process of adding and subtracting the consequences of agreed-upon general names of things, develops only after years of concentrated industry. Human will Hobbes defined as simply "the last appetite before choice."

Despite this mechanistic view of human beings, Hobbes believed they could accomplish much by the reasoned use of science. All was contingent, however, on the correct use of that greatest of human creations (one compounded of the powers of most people): the commonwealth, in which people are united by their consent in one all-powerful person.

The key to Hobbes' political philosophy is a brilliant myth of the original state of human-

Non est potestas Super Terram quæ Comparetur ei Iob. 41. 24.

Shown here is the famous title-page illustration for Hobbe's Leviathan. *The ruler is pictured as absolute lord of his lands, but note that he incorporates the mass of individuals whose self-interests are best served by their willingness to accept him and cooperate with him.*

kind. According to this myth, human beings in the natural state are generally inclined to a "perpetual and restless desire of power after power that ceases only in death."[7] As all people desire and, in the state of nature, have a natural right to everything, their equality breeds enmity, competition, diffidence, and desire for glory begets perpetual quarreling—"a way of every man against every man."[8] As Hobbes put it in a famous summary:

In such condition there is no place for industry, because the fruit thereof is uncertain; and consequently no culture of the earth; no navigation nor use of the commodities that may be imported by sea; no commodious building; no instruments of moving and removing such things as require much force; no knowledge of the face of the earth; no account of time; no arts; no letters; no society; and, which is worst of all, continual fear and danger of violent death; and the life of man solitary, poor, nasty, brutish, and short.[9]

Whereas earlier and later philosophers saw the original human state as a paradise from which humankind had fallen, Hobbes saw it as a corruption from which only society had de-livered people. Contrary to the views of Aristotle and Christian thinkers like Thomas Aquinas, in the view of Hobbes human beings are not by nature sociable, political animals; they are self-centered beasts, laws unto themselves, utterly without a master unless one is imposed by force.

According to Hobbes, people escape the impossible state of nature only by entering a social contract that creates a commonwealth tightly ruled by law and order. They are driven to this solution by their fear of death and their desire for "commodious living." The social contract obliges every person, for the sake of peace and self-defense, to agree to set aside personal rights to all things and to be content with as much liberty against others as he or she would allow others against himself or herself. All agree to live according to a secularized version of the golden rule: "Do not that to another which you would not have done to yourself."[10]

Because words and promises are insufficient to guarantee this state, the social contract also establishes the coercive force necessary to compel compliance with the covenant. Hobbes believed that the dangers of anarchy were always far greater than those of tyranny; he con-

[7] *Thomas Hobbes,* Leviathan Parts I and II, *ed. by H. W. Schneider (Indianapolis: Bobbs-Merrill, 1958), p. 86.*
[8] *Hobbes, p. 106.*
[9] *Hobbes, p. 107.*

[10] *Hobbes, p. 130.*

ceived of the ruler as absolute and unlimited in power, once established in office. There is no room in Hobbes' political philosophy for political protest in the name of individual conscience, nor for resistance to legitimate authority by private individuals. These features of the *Leviathan* were criticized by contemporary Catholics and Puritans alike. To his critics, who lamented the loss of their individual liberty in such a government, Hobbes pointed out the alternative:

> The greatest that in any form of government can possibly happen to the people in general is scarce sensible in respect of the miseries and horrible calamities that accompany a civil war or that dissolute condition of masterless men, without subjection to laws and a coercive power to tie their hands from rapine and revenge.[11]

It is puzzling why Hobbes believed that absolute rulers would be more benevolent and less egoistic than all other people. He simply placed the highest possible value on a strong, efficient ruler who could save human beings from the chaos attendant on the state of nature. In the end it mattered little to Hobbes whether this ruler was Charles I, Oliver Cromwell, or Charles II, each of whom received Hobbes' enthusiastic support, once he was established in power.

John Locke: Defender of Moderate Liberty

Locke (1632–1704) has proved to be the most influential political thinker of the seventeenth century. Although he was not as original as Hobbes, his political writings became a major source of the later Enlightenment criticism of absolutism. They gave inspiration to both the American and the French revolutions.

Locke's sympathies lay with the Puritans and the Parliamentary forces that challenged the Stuart monarchy. His father fought with the Parliamentary army during the English Civil War. Locke read deeply in the works of Francis Bacon, René Descartes, and Isaac Newton and was a close friend of the English physicist and chemist Robert Boyle (1627–1691). Some view Locke as the first philosopher to synthesize the rationalism of Descartes and

John Locke's philosophy was influential in the areas of politics and the theory of human knowledge. [Bettmann Archive]

the experimental science of Bacon, Newton, and Boyle.

Locke was for a brief period strongly influenced by the political views of Hobbes. This influence changed, however, after his association with Anthony Ashley Cooper, the earl of Shaftesbury. In 1667 Locke moved into Shaftesbury's London home and served him as physician, secretary, and traveling companion. A zealous Protestant, Shaftesbury was considered by his contemporaries a radical in both religion and politics. He organized an unsuccessful rebellion against Charles II in 1682. Although Locke had no part in the plot, both he and Shaftesbury were forced to flee to Holland after its failure.

Locke's two most famous works are the *Essay Concerning Human Understanding* (1690), completed during his exile in Holland, and the *Two Treatises of Government* (1690). In the *Essay Concerning Human Understanding* Locke explored the function of the human mind. He believed that the mind at birth was a blank tablet. There are no innate ideas; all knowledge is derived from actual sensual experience. Human ideas are either simple (that is, passive receptions from daily experience) or complex (that is, products of sustained mental exercise). What people know is not the exter-

---

[11] *Hobbes*, p. 152.

519

NEW
DIRECTIONS IN
SCIENCE AND
THOUGHT IN
THE SIXTEENTH
AND
SEVENTEENTH
CENTURIES

John Locke Explains the Sources of Human Knowledge

An Essay Concerning Human Understanding (1690) may be the most influential philosophical work ever written in English. Locke's most fundamental idea, which is explicated in the passage below, is that human knowledge is grounded in the experiences of the senses and in the reflection of the mind on those experiences. He rejected any belief in innate ideas. His emphasis on experience led to the wider belief that human beings are creatures of their environment. After Locke, numerous writers argued that human beings could be improved if the environment in which they lived were reformed.

Let us then suppose the mind to be, as we say, white paper void of all characters, without any *ideas*. How comes it to be furnished? Whence comes it by that vast store which the busy and boundless fancy of man has painted on it with an almost endless variety? Whence has it all the materials of reason and knowledge? To this I answer, in one word, from *experience;* in that all our knowledge is founded, and from that it ultimately derives itself. Our observation, employed either about *external sensible objects, or about the internal operations of our minds perceived and reflected on by ourselves, is that which supplies our understanding with all the materials of thinking.* These two are the fountains of knowledge, from whence all the ideas we have, or can naturally have, do spring.

First, *our senses,* conversant about particular sensible objects, do *convey into the mind* several distinct *perceptions* of things, according to those various ways wherein those objects do affect them. And thus we come by those *ideas* we have of *yellow, white, heat, cold, soft, hard, bitter, sweet,* and all those which we call sen-

sible qualities. . . . This great source of most of the *ideas* we have, depending wholly upon our senses, and derived by them to the understanding, I call SENSATION.

Secondly, the other fountain from which experience furnisheth the understanding with ideas is the *perception of the operations of our own minds* within us, as it is employed about the *ideas* it has got. . . . And such are *perception, thinking, doubting, believing, reasoning, knowing, willing,* and all the different actings of our own minds. . . . I call this REFLECTION, the *ideas* it affords being such only as the mind gets by reflecting on its own operations within itself. . . . These two, I say, viz. external material things as the objects of SENSATION, and the operations of our own minds within as the objects of REFLECTION, are to me the only originals from whence all our *ideas* take their beginnings. . . .

The understanding seems to me not to have the least glimmering of any *ideas* which it doth not receive from one of these two.

John Locke, An Essay Concerning Human Understanding, *Vol. 1 (London: Everyman's Library, 1961), pp. 77–78.*

nal world in itself but the results of the interaction of the mind with the outside world.

Locke also denied the existence of innate moral norms. Moral ideas are the product of

humankind's subjection of their self-love to their reason—a freely chosen self-disciplining of natural desires so that conflict in conscience may be avoided and happiness attained. Locke also believed that the teachings of Christianity were identical to what uncorrupted reason taught about the good life. A rational person would therefore always live according to simple Christian precepts. Although Locke firmly denied toleration to Catholics and atheists—both were considered subversive in England—he otherwise sanctioned a variety of Protestant religious practice.

Locke wrote *Two Treatises of Government* during the reign of Charles II. They oppose the argument that rulers are absolute in their power. According to the preface of the published edition, which appeared after the Glorious Revolution, the treatises were written "to justify to the world the people of England, whose love of their just and natural rights, with their resolution to preserve them, saved the nation when it was on the brink of slavery and ruin."[12] Locke rejected particularly the views of Sir Robert Filmer and Thomas Hobbes.

Filmer had written a work entitled *Patriarcha, or the Natural Power of Kings* (published in 1680), in which the rights of kings over their subjects were compared with the rights of fathers over their children. Locke devoted his entire first treatise to a refutation of Filmer's argument. He maintained not only that the analogy was inappropriate, but that even the right of a father over his children could not be construed as absolute but was subject to a higher natural law. Both fathers and rulers, Locke argued, remain bound to the law of nature. That is, the voice of reason, which teaches that "all mankind [are] equal and independent, [and] no one ought to harm another in his life, health, liberty, or possessions,"[13] inasmuch as all human beings are the images and property of God. According to Locke, people enter into social contracts, empowering legislatures and monarchs to "umpire" their disputes, precisely in order to preserve their natural rights, not to give rulers an absolute power over them. Rulers are rather "entrusted" with the preservation of the law of nature and transgress it at their peril:

> Whenever that end [namely, the preservation of life, liberty, and property for which power is given to rulers by a commonwealth] is manifestly neglected or opposed, the trust must necessarily be forfeited and the power devolve into the hands of those that gave it, who may place it anew where they think best for their safety and security.[14]

From Locke's point of view, absolute monarchy is "inconsistent" with civil society and can be "no form of civil government at all."

Locke's main differences with Hobbes stemmed from the latter's well-known views on the state of nature. Locke believed that the natural human state was one of perfect freedom and equality. Here all enjoyed, in unregulated fashion, the natural rights of life, liberty, and property. The only thing lacking in the state of nature was a single authority to give judgment when disputes inevitably arose because of the natural freedom and equality possessed by all.

Contrary to the view of Hobbes, human beings in their natural state were creatures not of monomaniacal passion but of extreme goodwill and rationality. And they did not surrender their natural rights unconditionally when they entered the social contract; rather they established a means whereby these rights could be better preserved. The state of warfare (that Hobbes believed characterized the state of nature) emerged for Locke only when rulers failed in their responsibility to preserve the freedoms of the state of nature and attempted to enslave people by absolute rule (that is, to remove them from their "natural" condition). Only then did the peace, goodwill, mutual assistance, and preservation in which human beings naturally live—and socially ought to live—come to an end and a state of war emerge.

The Scientific Revolution and the thought of writers whose work was contemporaneous with it mark one of the major turning points in the history of Western thought and eventually of world thought. The scientific and political ideas of the late sixteenth and seventeenth centuries gradually overturned many of the most fundamental premises of the medieval world view. The sun replaced the earth as the center of the solar system. The solar system itself came to be viewed as one of

[12] *John Locke*, The Second Treatise of Government, *ed. by T. P. Peardon (Indianapolis: Bobbs-Merrill, 1952), Preface.*

[13] *Locke, Ch. 2, sects. 4–6, pp. 4–6.*

[14] *Locke, Ch. 13, sect. 149, p. 84.*

many possible systems in the universe. The new knowledge of the physical universe provided occasions for challenges to the authority of the Church and of Scripture. Mathematics began to replace theology and metaphysics as the mode of understanding nature.

Parallel to these developments and sometimes related to them, political thought became much less concerned with religious issues. Hobbes generated a major theory of political obligation with virtually no reference to God. Locke theorized about politics with a recognition of God but with little attention to Scripture. Both Locke and Spinoza championed greater freedom of religious and political expression. Locke produced a psychology that emphasized the influence of environment on human character and action. All of these new ideas gradually displaced or reshaped theological and religious modes of thought and placed humankind and life on earth at the center of Western thinking. Intellectuals in the West consequently developed greater self-confidence in their own capacity to shape the world and their own lives.

521

NEW
DIRECTIONS IN
SCIENCE AND
THOUGHT IN
THE SIXTEENTH
AND
SEVENTEENTH
CENTURIES

Suggested Readings

R. ASHCRAFT, *Revolutionary Politics and Locke's Two Treatises of Government* (1986). The most important study of Locke to appear in recent years.

V. M. BRITTAIN, *Valiant Pilgrim: The Story of John Bunyan and Puritan England* (1950). Illustrated historical biography.

K. C. BROWN, *Hobbes Studies* (1965). A collection of important essays.

HERBERT BUTTERFIELD, *The Origins of Modern Science 1300–1800* (1949). An authoritative survey.

JOHN CAIRD, *Spinoza* (1971). Intellectual biography by a philosopher.

I. B. COHEN, *Revolution in Science* (1985). A general consideration of the concept and of historical examples of change in scientific thought.

HARDIN CRAIG, *Shakespeare: A Historical and Critical Study with Annotated Texts of Twenty-one Plays* (1958).

MAURICE CRANSTON, *Locke* (1961). Brief biographical sketch.

J. DUNN, *The Political Thought of John Locke; An Historical Account of the "Two Treatises of Government"* (1969). An excellent introduction.

MÀNUEL DURAN, *Cervantes* (1974). Detailed biography.

M. A. FINOCCHIARO, *The Galileo Affair: A Documentary History* (1989). A collection of all the relevant documents and introductory commentary.

GALILEO GALILEI, *Discoveries and Opinions of Galileo*, ed. and trans. by Stillman Drake (1957).

A. R. HALL, *The Scientific Revolution 1500–1800: The Formation of the Modern Scientific Attitude* (1966). Traces undermining of traditional science and rise of new sciences.

C. HILL, *Milton and the English Revolution* (1977). A major biography.

M. HUNTER, *Science and Society in Restoration England* (1981). Examines the social relations of scientists and scientific societies.

MARGARET JACOB, *The Newtonians and the English Revolution* (1976). A controversial book that attempts to relate science and politics.

D. JOHNSTON, *The Rhetoric of Leviathan: Thomas Hobbes and the Politics of Cultural Transformation* (1986). An important study that links Hobbes' thought to the rhetoric of the Renaissance.

ALEXANDER KOYRÉ, *From the Closed World to the Infinite Universe* (1957). Treated from perspective of the historian of ideas.

THOMAS S. KUHN, *The Copernican Revolution* (1957). A scholarly treatment.

PETER LASLETT, *Locke's Two Treatises of Government*, 2nd ed. (1970). Definitive texts with very important introductions.

D. LINDBERG AND R. L. NUMBERS, eds., *God and Nature: Historical Essays on the Encounter between Christianity and Science* (1986). The best collection of essays on the subject.

O. MAYER, *Authority, Liberty, and Automatic Machinery in Early Modern Europe* (1986). A lively study that seeks to relate thought about machinery to thought about politics.

R. POPKIN, *The History of Scepticism from Erasmus to Spinoza* (1979). A classic study of the fear of loss of intellectual certainty.

P. REDONDI, *Galileo: Heretic* (1987). A controversial work that examines the relationship of Galileo's thought to the Church's teaching on the Eucharist rather than to planetary motion.

S. SHAPIN AND S. SCHAFFER, *Leviathan and the Air-Pump: Hobbes, Boyle, and the Experimental Life* (1985). A study of the debate over the validity of scientific experiment during the age of the scientific revolution.

B. SHAPIRO, *Probability and Certainty in Seventeenth-Century England: A Study of the Relationships between Natural Science, Religion, History, Law, and Literature* (1983). As the title indicates, a very broad study and an important one.

RICHARD S. WESTFALL, *Never at Rest: A Biography of Isaac Newton* (1981). A new important major study.

During the late seventeenth and early eighteenth centuries the monarchs remained
the center of public political ceremony and attention. Here Louis XV of France
approaches Sainte-Chapelle in Paris and is surrounded by crowds of spectators
as well as by nobles and soldiers. [The Bettmann Archive]

15

SUCCESSFUL AND UNSUCCESSFUL PATHS TO POWER (1686–1740)

The late seventeenth and early eighteenth centuries witnessed significant shifts of power and influence among the states of Europe. Nations that had been strong lost their status as significant military and economic units. Other countries, which had in some cases figured only marginally in international relations, came to the fore. Great Britain, France, Austria, Russia, and Prussia emerged during this period as the powers that would dominate Europe until at least World War I. The establishment of their political and economnic

dominance occurred at the expense of Spain, the United Netherlands, Poland, Sweden, and the Ottoman Empire. Equally essential to their rise was the weakness of the Holy Roman Empire after the Treaty of Westphalia (1648).

The successful competitors for international power were those states that in differing fashions created strong central political authorities. Farsighted observers in the late seventeenth century already understood that in the future those domains that would become or remain great powers must imitate the political and military organization of Louis XIV. Monarchy alone could impose unity of purpose on the state. The turmoil of seventeenth-century civil wars and aristocratic revolts had impressed people with the value of the monarch as a guarantor of minimum domestic tranquility.

Imitation of French absolutism involved other factors besides belief in a strong monarchy. It usually required building a standing army, organizing an efficient tax structure to support the army, and establishing a bureaucracy to collect the taxes. Moreover, the political classes of the country, especially the nobles, had to be converted to a sense of duty and loyalty to the central government that was more intense than their loyalty to other competing political and social institutions.

The waning powers of Europe were those whose leaders failed to achieve such effective organization. They were unable to employ their political, economic, and human resources to resist external aggression or to overcome the forces of domestic dissolution. The internal and external failures were closely related. If a state failed to maintain or establish a central political authority with sufficient power over the nobility, the cities, the guilds, and the Church, it could not raise a strong army to defend its borders or its economic interests. More often than not, the key element leading to success or failure was the character, personality, and energy of the monarch.

The Maritime Powers

In western Europe, Britain and France emerged as the dominant powers. This development represented a shift of influence away from Spain and the United Netherlands. Both the latter countries had been quite strong and important during the sixteenth and seventeenth centuries, but they became negligible during the course of the eighteenth century. However, neither disappeared from the map. Both retained considerable economic vitality and influence. The difference was that France and Britain attained so much more power and economic strength.

Spain

Spanish power had depended on the influx of wealth from the Americas and on the capacity of the Spanish monarchs to rule the still largely autonomous provinces of the Iberian peninsula. The economic life of the nation was never healthy. Except for wool Spain had virtually no exports with which to pay for its imports. Instead of promoting domestic industries, the Spanish government financed imports by using the gold and silver mined in its New World empire. This external source of wealth was not certain because the treasure fleets from the New World could be and sometimes were captured by pirates or the navies of other nations.

The political life of Spain was also weak. Within Castile, Aragon, Navarre, the Basque provinces, and other districts, the royal government could not operate without the close cooperation of strong local nobles and the Church. From the defeat of the Spanish Armada in 1588 to the Treaty of the Pyrenees in 1659, Spain experienced a series of foreign policy reverses that harmed the domestic prestige of the monarchy. Furthermore, between 1665 and 1700 the physically malformed, dull-witted, and sexually impotent Charles II was monarch. Throughout his reign the local provincial estates and the nobility increased their power. On his death the War of the Spanish Succession saw the other powers of Europe contesting the issue of the next ruler of Spain. The Treaty of Utrecht (1713) gave the Spanish crown to Philip V (1700–1746), who was a Bourbon and the grandson of Louis XIV. The new king should have attempted to consolidate his internal power and to protect Spanish overseas trade. However, his second wife, Elizabeth Farnese, wanted to use Spanish power to carve out interests for her sons on the Italian peninsula. Such machinations diverted government resources and allowed the nobility and the provinces to continue to assert their privileges against the authority of the monarchy. Not until the reign of Charles III (1759–1788) did Spain possess a monarch concerned with efficient administration and internal improvement. By the third quarter of the century the country was better governed, but it could no longer compete effectively in power politics.

The Netherlands

The demise of the United Provinces of the Netherlands occurred wholly within the eighteenth century. After the death of William III of England in 1702, the various local provinces successfully prevented the emergence of another strong _stadtholder._ Unified political leadership therefore vanished. During the earlier long wars of the Netherlands with Louis XIV and England, naval supremacy slowly but steadily had passed to the British. The fishing industry declined, and the Dutch lost their technological superiority in shipbuilding. Countries between which Dutch ships had once carried goods now came to trade directly with each other. For example, the British began to use more and more of their own vessels in the Baltic traffic with Russia.

Similar stagnation overtook the Dutch domestic industries, such as textile finishing, paper making, and glass blowing. The disunity of the provinces and the absence of vigorous leadership hastened this economic decline and prevented action that might have slowed or halted it.

What saved the United Provinces from becoming completely insignificant in European matters was their continued dominance of the financial community. Well past the middle of the century their banks continued to provide loans and financing for European trade.

France After Louis XIV

Despite its military losses in the War of the Spanish Succession, France remained a great power. It was less strong in 1715 than in 1680, but it still possessed a large population, an advanced if troubled economy, and the adminis-

By the mid-seventeenth century, when this picture of the Amsterdam Exchange was painted, Amsterdam had replaced the cities of Italy and south Germany as the leading banking center of Europe. Amsterdam retained this position until the late eighteenth century. [Museum Boymans-van Beuningen, Rotterdam]

The collapse of the bank of John Law (1671–1729) in 1720 damaged both the French economy and the prestige of the government. [Library of Congress]

trative structure bequeathed it by Louis XIV. Moreover, even if France and its resources had been badly drained by the last of Louis' wars, the other major states of Europe emerged from the conflict similarly debilitated. What the country required was a period of economic recovery and consolidation, wiser political leadership, and a less ambitious foreign policy. It did enjoy a period of recovery, but the quality of its leadership was at best indifferent. Louis XIV was succeeded by his five-year-old great-grandson Louis XV (1715–1774). The young boy's uncle, the duke of Orléans, became regent and remained so until 1720. The regency further undermined the already faltering prestige of the monarchy.

JOHN LAW AND THE MISSISSIPPI BUBBLE The duke of Orléans was a gambler, and for a time he turned over the financial management of the kingdom to John Law (1671–1729), a Scottish mathematician and fellow gambler. Law believed that an increase in the paper money supply would stimulate the postwar economic recovery of the country. With the permission of the regent he established a bank in Paris that issued paper money. Law then organized a monopoly on trading privileges with the French colony of Louisiana in North America.

The Mississippi Company also assumed the management of the French national debt. The company issued shares of its own stock in exchange for government bonds, which had fallen sharply in value. In order to redeem large quantities of bonds, Law encouraged speculation in Mississippi Company stock. In 1719 the price of the stock rose handsomely. However, smart investors took their profits by selling their stock in exchange for money from Law's bank. Then they sought to exchange the currency for gold. To make the second transaction, they went to Law's bank, but that institution lacked sufficient gold to redeem all the money brought to it.

In February 1720 all gold payments were

The impending collapse of Law's bank engendered a financial panic throughout France, as desperate investors, such as these shown here in the city of Rennes, sought to exchange their paper currency for gold and silver before the bank's supply of precious metals was exhausted. [Musee de Bretagne, Rennes]

halted in France. Soon thereafter Law himself fled the country. The Mississippi Bubble, as the affair was called, had burst. The fiasco brought disgrace on the government that had made Law its controller general. The Mississippi Company was later reorganized and functioned quite profitably, but fear of paper money and speculation marked French economic life for the rest of the century.

RENEWED AUTHORITY OF THE PARLEMENTS

The duke of Orléans made a second departure that also lessened the power of the monarchy. He attempted to draw the French nobility once again into the decision-making processes of the government. Louis XIV had downgraded the nobility and had filled his ministries and bureaucracies with persons of nonnoble families. The regent was seeking

to restore a balance. He adopted a system of councils on which the nobles were to serve along with the bureaucrats. However, the years of noble domestication at Versailles had worked too well, and the nobility seemed to lack both the talent and the desire to govern. The experiment failed.

The failure of the great French nobles to function as satisfactory councilors did not mean that they had surrendered their ancient ambition to assert their rights, privileges, and local influence over those of the monarchy. The chief feature of French political life from this time until the French Revolution was the attempt of the nobility to impose its power on the monarchy. The most effective instrument in this process was the *parlements*, or courts dominated by the nobility.

The French *parlements* were very different

527

SUCCESSFUL
AND
UNSUCCESSFUL
PATHS TO
POWER (1686–1740)

Saint-Simon Shows the French Nobility's Incapacity to Govern

The regent under the young Louis XV hoped that France's nobility might assume an active role in government in place of the passive role assigned to them by Louis XIV. This plan involved displacing many nonnoble bureaucrats and others who were regarded as noble by virtue of holding office rather than by virtue of noble birth ("nobles of the robe"). As described by the duke of Saint-Simon (1675–1755), the plan failed because the real nobles proved unequal to their new duties.

The design was to begin to put the nobility into the ministry, with the dignity and authority befitting them, at the expense of the high civil servants and nobles of the robe, and by degree and according to events to guide affairs wisely so that little by little those commoners would lose all those administrative duties that are not purely judicial . . . in order to submit to the nobility all modes of administration. The difficulty was the ignorance, the frivolity, and the lack of diligence of the nobility who were accustomed to being good for nothing except getting killed, succeeding at war only by seniority, and romping around for the rest of the time in the most mortal uselessness. As a result they were devoted to idleness and disgusted with all knowledge outside war by their conditioned incapacity for being able to provide themselves with anything useful to do. It was impossible to make the first step in this direction without overturning the monster that had devoured the nobility, the controller general and the secretaries of state.

Duc de Saint-Simon, Memories, *trans. by Frank M. Turner, cited in John Lough,* An Introduction to Eighteenth-Century France *(New York: David MacKay, 1964), pp. 135–136.*

institutions from the English Parliament. These French courts, the most important of which was the Parlement of Paris, did not have the power to legislate. Rather, they had the power to recognize or not to recognize the legality of an act or law promulgated by the monarch. By long tradition their formal approval had been required to make a royal law valid. Louis XIV had often overridden stubborn, uncooperative *parlements*. However, in another of his many major political blunders, the duke of Orléans had formally approved the reinstitution of the *parlements'* power to allow or disallow laws. Thereafter the growing financial and moral weakness of the eighteenth-century monarchy allowed these aristocratic judicial institutions to reassert their authority. This situation meant that for the rest of the century until the revolution the *parlements* became natural centers for aristocratic resistance to royal authority.

ADMINISTRATION OF CARDINAL FLEURY

By 1726 the chief minister of the French court was Cardinal Fleury (1653–1743). He was the last of those great churchmen who had so loyally and effectively served the French monarchy. Like his seventeenth-century predecessors, the cardinals Richelieu and Mazarin, Fleury was a realist. He understood the political ambition and incapacity of the nobility and worked quietly to block their undue influence. Fleury was also aware of the precarious financial situation in which the wars of Louis XIV had left the royal treasury.

The cardinal, who was seventy-three years old when he came to office, was determined to give the country a period of peace. He surrounded himself with generally able assistants who attempted to solve the financial problems. Part of the national debt was repudiated. New industries enjoying special privileges were established, and new roads and bridges were built. On the whole the nation prospered, but Fleury was never able to draw from the nobles or the Church sufficient tax revenues to put the state on a stable financial footing.

Fleury died in 1743, having unsuccessfully attempted to prevent France from intervening in the war then raging between Austria and Prussia. All of his financial pruning and planning had come to naught. Another failure must also be credited to this elderly churchman. Despite his best efforts he had not trained

Cardinal Fleury (1653–1743), was tutor and chief minister from 1726 to 1743 of Louis XV. He gave France a period of peace and prosperity, but was unable to solve the long-term financial problems of the state. [Bulloz]

Louis XV to become an effective monarch. Louis XV possessed most of the vices and almost none of the virtues of his great-grandfather. He wanted to hold on to absolute power but was unwilling to work the long hours required. He did not choose many wise advisers after Fleury. He was tossed about by the gossip and intrigues of the court nobles. His personal life was scandalous. His reign became more famous for his mistress, Madame de Pompadour, than for anything else. Louis XV was not an evil person but a mediocre one. And in a monarch, mediocrity was unfortunately often a greater fault than vice.

Despite this political drift France remained a great power. Its army at mid-century was still the largest and strongest military force on the Continent. Its commerce and production expanded. Its colonies produced wealth and spurred domestic industries. Its cities grew and prospered. The wealth of the nation waxed as the absolutism of the monarchy waned. France did not lack sources of power and strength, but

Madame de Pompadour (1721–1764), was the mistress of Louis XV. A woman of beauty, cultivation, and taste, she was a notable patroness of artists, craftsmen, and writers. This portrait, which captures her grace and elegance, is by Francois Boucher (1703–1770), one of her favorite painters. [National Galleries of Scotland]

it did lack the political leadership that could organize, direct, and inspire its people.

Great Britain: The Age of Walpole

In 1713 Britain had emerged as a victor over Louis XIV, but the nation required a period of recovery. As an institution the British monarchy was not in the degraded state of the French monarchy, yet its stability was not certain.

THE HANOVERIAN DYNASTY In 1714 the Hanoverian dynasty, designated by the Act of Settlement (1701), came to the throne. Almost immediately George I (1714–1727) confronted a challenge to his new title. The Stuart pretender James Edward (1688–1766), the son of James II, landed in Scotland in December 1715. His forces marched southward but met defeat less than two months later. Although militarily successful against the pretender, the new dynasty and its supporters saw the need for consolidation.

WHIGS AND TORIES During the seventeenth century England had been one of the most politically restive countries in Europe. The closing years of Queen Anne's reign

(1702–1714) had seen sharp clashes between the political factions of Whigs and Tories over the coming Treaty of Utrecht. The Tories had urged a rapid peace settlement and after 1710 had opened negotiations with France. During the same period the Whigs were seeking favor from the Elector of Hanover, who would soon be their monarch. His concern for his domains in Hanover made him unsympathetic to the Tory peace policy. In the final months of Anne's reign, some Tories, fearing loss of power under the waiting Hanoverian dynasty, opened channels of communication with the Stuart pretender; and a few even rallied to his losing cause.

Under these circumstances it was little wonder that George I, on his arrival in Britain, clearly favored the Whigs and proceeded with caution. Previously the differences between the Whigs and the Tories had been vaguely related to principle. The Tories emphasized a strong monarchy, low taxes for landowners, and firm support of the Anglican church. The Whigs supported monarchy but wanted Parliament to retain final sovereignty. They tended to favor urban commercial interests as well as the prosperity of the landowners. They encouraged a policy of religious toleration toward the Protestant nonconformists in England. Socially both groups supported the status quo.

Neither group was organized like a modern political party. Organizationally, outside of Parliament, each party consisted of political networks based on local political connections and local economic influence. Each group acknowledged a few spokesmen on the national level who articulated positions and principles. However, after the Hanoverian accession and the eventual Whig success in achieving the firm confidence of George I, the chief difference for almost forty years between the Whigs and the Tories was that one group did have access to public office and patronage and the other did not. This early Hanoverian proscription of Tories from public life was one of the most prominent features of the age.

THE LEADERSHIP OF ROBERT WALPOLE

The political situation after 1715 remained in a state of flux, until Robert Walpole

Sir Robert Walpole (1676–1745) left, is shown talking to the Speaker of the House of Commons. Walpole, who dominated British political life from 1721 to 1742, is considered the first prime minister of Britain. [The Mansell Collection]

(1676–1745) took over the helm of government. This Norfolk squire had been active in the House of Commons since the reign of Queen Anne, and he had served as a cabinet minister. What gave him special prominence under the new dynasty was a British financial scandal similar to the French Mississippi Bubble.

Management of the British national debt had been assigned to the South Sea Company, which exchanged government bonds for company stock. As in the French case, the price of the stock flew high, only to crash in 1720 when prudent investors sold their holdings and took their speculative profits. Parliament intervened and, under Walpole's leadership, adopted measures to honor the national debt. To most comtemporaries Walpole had saved the financial integrity of the country and, in so doing, had proved himself a person of immense administrative capacity and political ability.

George I gave Walpole his full confidence. For this reason Walpole has often been regarded as the first prime minister of Great Britain and the originator of the cabinet system of government. However, unlike a modern prime minister, he was not chosen by the majority of the House of Commons. His power largely depended on the goodwill of George I and later of George II (1727–1760).

Walpole generally demanded that all of the ministers in the cabinet agree on policy, but he could not prevent frequent public differences on policy. The real source of Walpole's power was the combination of the personal support of the king, his ability to handle the House of Commons, and his iron-fisted control of government patronage. To oppose Walpole on either minor or more substantial matters was to risk the almost certain loss of government patronage for oneself, one's family, or one's friends. Through the skillful use of patronage Walpole bought support for himself and his policies from people who wanted to receive jobs, appointments, favors, and government contracts. Such corruption supplied the glue of political loyalty.

Walpole's favorite slogan was *"Quieta non movere"* (roughly, "Let sleeping dogs lie"). To that end he pursued a policy of peace abroad and promotion of the status quo at home. In this regard he and Cardinal Fleury were much alike.

531

SUCCESSFUL
AND
UNSUCCESSFUL
PATHS TO
POWER (1686–
1740)

THE STRUCTURE OF PARLIAMENT

The structure of the eighteenth-century British House of Commons aided Walpole in his pacific policies. It was neither a democratic nor a representative body. Each of the counties elected two members. But if the more powerful landed families in a county agreed on the candidates, there was no contest. Other members were elected from units called *boroughs*, of which there were a considerable variety. There were many more borough seats than county seats. A few were large enough for elections to be relatively democratic.

However, most boroughs had a very small number of electors. For example, a local municipal corporation or council of only a dozen members might have the legal right to elect a member of Parliament. In Old Sarum, one of the most famous corrupt or "rotten" boroughs, the Pitt family for many years simply bought up those pieces of property to which a vote was attached and thus in effect owned a seat in the

---

Lady Mary Wortley Montagu Gives Advice on Election to Parliament

In this letter of 1714 Lady Mary Wortley Montagu discussed with her husband the various paths that he might follow to gain election to the British House of Commons. Note the emphasis she placed on knowing the right people and on having large amounts of money to spend on voters. Eventually her husband was elected to Parliament in a borough that was controlled through government patronage.

You seem not to have received my letters, or not to have understood them: you had been chose undoubtedly at York, if you had declared in time; but there is not any gentleman or tradesman disengaged at this time; they are treating every night. Lord Carlisle and the Thompsons have given their interest to Mr. Jenkins. I agree with you of the necessity of your standing this Parliament, which, perhaps, may be more considerable than any that are to follow it; but, as you proceed, 'tis my opinion, you will spend your money and not be chose. I believe there is hardly a borough unengaged. I expect every letter should tell me you are sure of some place; and, as far as I can perceive you are sure of none. As it has been managed, perhaps it will be the best way to deposit a certain sum in some friend's hands, and buy some little Cornish borough: it would, undoubtedly, look better to be chose for a considerable town; but I take it to be now too late. If you have any thoughts of Newark, it will be absolutely necessary for you to enquire after Lord Lexington's interest; and your best way to apply yourself to Lord Holdernesse, who is both a Whig and an honest man. He is now in town, and you may enquire of him if Brigadier Sutton stands there; and if not, try to engage him for you. Lord Lexington is so ill at the Bath, that it is a doubt if he will live 'till the elections; and if he dies, one of his heiresses, and the whole interest of his estate, will probably fall on Lord Holdernesse.

'Tis a surprize to me, that you cannot make sure of some borough, when a number of your friends bring in so many Parliament-men without trouble or expense. 'Tis too late to mention it now, but you might have applied to Lady Winchester, as Sir Joseph Jekyl did last year, and by her interest the Duke of Bolton brought him in for nothing; I am sure she would be more zealous to serve me, than Lady Jekyl.

Lord Wharncliffe (Ed.), Letters and Works of Lady Mary Wortley Montagu, *3rd ed., Vol. 1 (London, 1861), p. 211.*

A series of four Hogarth etchings satirizing an English parliamentary election. In a savage indictment of the notoriously corrupt English electoral system, Hogarth shows the voters going to the polls after having been bribed and intoxicated with free gin. (Note that voting was public. The secret ballot was not introduced in England until 1872.) The fourth etching, Chairing the Member, shows the triumphal procession of the victorious candidate, which is clearly turning into a brawl. [Metropolitan Museum of Art, Harris Brisbane Dick Fund, 1932. Acc. #32.35.(124)]

533

SUCCESSFUL
AND
UNSUCCESSFUL
PATHS TO
POWER (1686–1740)

House of Commons. Through proper electoral management, which involved favors to the electors, the House of Commons could be controlled.

The structure of Parliament and the manner in which it was elected meant that the government of England was dominated by the owners of property and by especially wealthy nobles. They did not pretend to represent people and districts or to be responsive to what would later be called public opinion. They regarded themselves as representing various economic and social interests, such as the West Indian interest, the merchant interest, or the landed interest. These owners of property were suspicious of an administrative bureaucracy controlled by the crown or its ministers. For this reason they or their agents served as local government administrators, judges, militia commanders, and tax collectors. In this sense the British nobility and other substantial landowners actually did govern the nation. And because they regarded the Parliament as the political sovereign, there was no absence of central political authority and direction. Consequently the supremacy of Parliament provided Britain with the kind of unity that elsewhere in Europe was sought through the institutions of absolutism.

FREEDOM OF POLITICAL LIFE British political life was genuinely more free than that on the Continent. There were real limits on the power of Robert Walpole. Parliament could not be wholly unresponsive to popular political pressure. Even with the extensive use of patronage many members of Parliament maintained independent views. Newspapers and public debate flourished. Free speech could be exercised, as could freedom of association. There was no large standing army. Those Tories barred from political office and the Whig enemies of Walpole could and did voice their opposition to his policies—this would not have been possible on the Continent.

For example, in 1733 Walpole presented to the House of Commons a scheme for an excise tax that would have raised revenue somewhat in the fashion of a modern sales tax. The public outcry in the press, on the public platform, and in the streets was so great that he eventually withdrew the measure. What the English regarded as their traditional political rights raised a real and potent barrier to the power of the government. Again in 1739, the public outcry over the Spanish treatment of British merchants in the Caribbean pushed Britain into a war, which Walpole opposed and deplored.

Walpole's ascendancy, which lasted until 1742, did little to raise the level of British political morality, but it brought the nation a kind of stability that it had not enjoyed for well over a century. Its foreign trade grew steadily and spread from New England to India. Agriculture improved its productivity. All forms of economic enterprise seemed to prosper. The navy became stronger. As a result of this political stability and economic growth, Great Britain became a European power of the first order and stood at the beginning of its era as a world power. Its government and economy during the next generation became a model for all progressive Europeans.

FRANCE AND GREAT BRITAIN IN THE EARLY EIGHTEENTH CENTURY

1713	Treaty of Utrecht ends the War of the Spanish Succession
1714	George I becomes king of Great Britain and thus establishes the Hanoverian dynasty
1715	Louis XV becomes King of France
1715–1720	Regency of the duke of Orléans in France
1720	Mississippi Bubble bursts in France and South Sea Bubble bursts in Great Britain
1720–1742	Robert Walpole dominates British politics
1726–1743	Cardinal Fleury serves as Louis XV's chief minister
1727	George II becomes king of Great Britain
1733	Excise bill crisis in Britain
1739	War of Jenkins' Ear begins between England and Spain

Central and Eastern Europe

The major factors in the shift of political influence among the maritime nations were naval strength, economic progress, foreign trade, and sound domestic administration. The conflicts among them occurred less in Europe than on the high seas and in their overseas empires. These nations already existed in well-defined geographical areas with established borders. Their populations generally accepted the authority of the central government.

The situation in central and eastern Europe was rather different. Except for the cities on the Baltic, the economy was agrarian. There were fewer cities and many more large estates populated by serfs. The states in this region did not possess overseas empires. Changes in the power structure normally involved changes in borders, or at least in the prince who ruled a particular area. Military conflicts took place at home rather than overseas.

The political structure of this region, which lay largely east of the Elbe River, was very "soft." The almost constant warfare of the seventeenth century had led to a habit of temporary and shifting political loyalties. The princes and aristocracies of small states and principalities were unwilling to subordinate themselves voluntarily to a central monarchical authority. Consequently the political life of the region and the kind of state that emerged there were different from those of western Europe.

Beginning in the last half of the seventeenth century, eastern and central Europe began to assume the political and social contours that would characterize it for the next two hundred years. After the Peace of Westphalia the Austrian Habsburgs recognized the basic weakness of the position of Holy Roman Emperor and began a new consolidation of their power. At the same time the state of Prussia began to emerge as a factor in north German politics and as a major challenger to Habsburg domination of Germany. Most important, Russia at the opening of the eighteenth century rose to the status of a military power of the first order. These three states (Austria, Prussia, and Russia) achieved their new status largely as a result of the political decay or military defeat of Sweden, Poland, and the Ottoman Empire.

Sweden: The Ambitions of Charles XII

Under Gustavus Adolphus II (1611–1632), Sweden had played an important role as a Protestant combatant in the Thirty Years' War. During the rest of the seventeenth century Sweden had consolidated its control of the Baltic, thus preventing Russian possession of a Baltic port and permitting Polish and German access to the sea only on Swedish terms. The Swedes also possessed one of the better armies in Europe. However, Sweden's economy, based primarily on the export of iron, was not strong enough to ensure continued political success.

In 1697 Charles XII (1697–1718) came to the throne. He was headstrong, to say the least, and perhaps insane. In 1700 Russia began a drive to the west against Swedish territory. The Russian goal was a foothold on the Baltic. In the resulting Great Northern War (1700–1721), Charles XII led a vigorous and often brilliant campaign, but one that eventually resulted in the defeat of Sweden. In 1700 he defeated the Russians at the battle of Narva, but then he turned south to invade Poland. The conflict dragged on, and the Russians were able to strengthen their forces.

In 1708 the Swedish monarch began a major invasion of Russia but became bogged down in the harsh Russian winter. The next year his army was decisively defeated at the battle of Poltava. Thereafter the Swedes could maintain only a holding action. Charles himself sought refuge with the Ottoman army and then eventually returned to Sweden in 1714. He was shot four years later while fighting the Norwegians.

The Great Northern War came to a close in 1721. Sweden had exhausted its military and economic resources and had lost its monopoly on the Baltic coast. Russia had conquered a large section of the eastern Baltic, and Prussia had gained a portion of Pomerania. Internally, after the death of Charles XII, the Swedish nobles were determined to reassert their power over that of the monarchy. They did so but then fell into quarrels among themselves. Sweden played a very minor role in European affairs thereafter.

The Ottoman Empire

At the southeastern extreme of Europe the Ottoman Empire lay as a barrier to the territorial ambitions of the Austrian Habsburgs and of Poland and Russia. The empire in the late seventeenth century still controlled most of the Balkan peninsula and the entire coastline of the Black Sea. It was an aggressive power that had for two centuries attempted to press its control further westward in Europe. The Ottoman Empire had probably made its great-

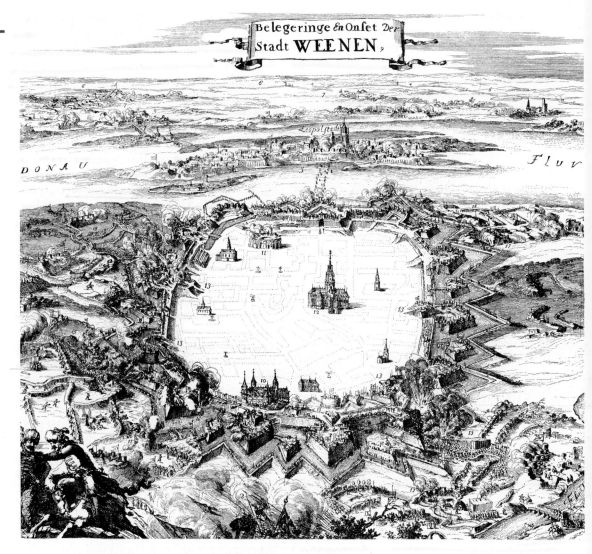

A contemporary Dutch print views the 1683 Turkish siege of Vienna from a remarkably revealing position in the hills west of the city. The scene shows the Turkish forces deciding to give up the summer-long attack; their commanders, the Ottoman Grand Vizier and the Pasha of Adrianople, lower left, were just beginning their flight. Polish and other Christian aid for the beleaguered Habsburg forces had arrived, and the battle was clearly going against the Turks. Never again did the weakened Muslim Ottoman Empire threaten the west. Note the Danube River toward the top, the elaborate zig-zag fortifications outside the walls, and bursts of artillery fire at several points. Most details inside the walled city are omitted, but the central cathedral and the imperial palace, toward the bottom, are shown. One unforeseen lasting social result of the siege was the boost given to coffee drinking by the Viennese discovery of coffee beans in the Turkish camps around the city. [British Museum]

est military impression on Europe in 1683, when it laid siege to the city of Vienna.

However, the Ottomans had overextended themselves politically, economically, and militarily. The major domestic political groups resisted any substantial strengthening of the central government in Constantinople. Rival-

ries for power among army leaders and nobles weakened the effectiveness of the government. In the Outer provinces, such as Transylvania, Wallachia, and Moldavia (all parts of modern Romania), the empire depended on the good-will of local rulers, who never submitted themselves fully to the imperial power. The empire's economy was weak, and its exports were primarily raw materials. Moreover the actual conduct of most of its trade had been turned over to representatives of other nations.

By the early eighteenth century the weakness of the Ottoman Empire meant that on the southeastern perimeter of Europe there existed an immense political vacuum. In 1699 the Turks concluded a treaty with their longtime Habsburg enemy and surrendered all pretensions of control over Hungary, Transylvania, Croatia, and Slavonia. From this time onward Russia also attempted to extend its territory and influence at the expense of the empire. For almost two hundred years the decay of the Ottoman Empire constituted a major factor in European international relations. The area always proved tempting to the major powers. However, their distrust of each other and their conflicting rivalries, as well as a considerable residual strength on the part of the Turks, prevented the dismemberment of the empire.

Poland: Absence of Strong Central Authority

In no other part of Europe was the failure to maintain a competitive political position so complete as in Poland. In 1683 King John III Sobieski (1674–1696) had led a Polish army to rescue Vienna from the Turkish siege. Following that spectacular effort, however, Poland became little more than a byword for the dangers of aristocratic independence. In Poland as nowhere else on the Continent, the nobility became the single most powerful political factor in the country. Unlike the British nobility and landowners, the Polish nobility would not

537

SUCCESSFUL
AND
UNSUCCESSFUL
PATHS TO
POWER (1686–
1740)

John III Sobieski (1624–1696) was elected king of Poland in 1674, Sobieski was a military hero in the wars against the Turks. However, he failed in his attempt to give Poland a strong, national monarchy. [Art Resource]

even submit to a central authority of their own making. There was no effective central authority in the form of either a king or a parliament.

The Polish monarchy was elective, but the deep distrust and divisions among the nobility prevented their electing a king from among their own numbers. Sobieski was a notable exception. Most of the Polish monarchs came from outside the borders of the kingdom and were the tools of foreign powers. The Polish nobles did have a central legislative body called the *Sejm, or Diet*. It included only the nobles and specifically excluded representatives from corporate bodies, such as the towns. In the Diet, however, there existed a practice known as the *liberum veto*, whereby the staunch opposition of any single member could require the body to disband. Such opposition was termed *exploding the Diet*. More often than not, this practice was the work of a group of dissatisfied nobles rather than of one person. Nonetheless, the rule of unanimity posed a major stumbling block to effective government.

Government as it was developing elsewhere in Europe simply was not tolerated in Poland. Localism reminiscent of the Middle Ages continued to hold sway as the nobles used all their energy to maintain their traditional "Polish liberties." There was no way to collect sufficient taxes to build up an army. The price of this noble liberty was eventually the disappearance of Poland from the map of Europe during the last half of the eighteenth century.

The Habsburg Empire and the Pragmatic Sanction

The close of the Thirty Year's War marked a fundamental turning point in the history of the Austrian Habsburgs. Previously, in alliance with the Spanish branch of the family, they had hoped to dominate all of Germany politically and to bring it back to the Catholic fold. They had failed to achieve either goal, and the decline of Spanish power meant that in future diplomatic relations the Austrian Habsburgs were very much on their own. The Treaty of Westphalia permitted Protestantism within the Holy Roman Empire, and the treaty also recognized the political autonomy of more than three hundred corporate German political entities within the empire. These included large units (such as Saxony, Hanover, Bavaria,

and Brandenburg) and also scores of small cities, bishoprics, principalities, and territories of independent knights.

After 1648 the Habsburg family retained firm hold on the title of Holy Roman Emperor, but the effectiveness of the title depended less on force of arms than on the cooperation that the emperor could elicit from the various political bodies in the empire. The Diet of the empire sat at Regensburg from 1663 until its dissolution in 1806. The Diet and the emperor generally regulated the daily economic and political life of Germany. The post-Westphalian Holy Roman Empire in many ways resembled Poland in its lack of central authority. However, unlike its Polish neighbor, the Holy Roman Empire was reorganized from within as the Habsburgs attempted to regain their authority. As will be seen shortly, Prussia set out on its course toward European power at the same time.

CONSOLIDATION OF AUSTRIAN POWER While establishing a new kind of position for their Austrian holdings among the German states, the Habsburgs began to consolidate their power and influence within their other hereditary possessions. These included, first, the Crown of Saint Wenceslas encompassing the kingdom of Bohemia (in modern Czechoslovakia) and the Duchies of Moravia and Silesia and, second, the Crown of Saint Stephen which ruled Hungary, Croatia, and Transylvania. In the middle of the seventeenth century much of Hungary remained occupied by the Turks and was liberated only at the end of the century.

In the early eighteenth century the family further extended its domains, receiving the former Spanish (thereafter Austrian) Netherlands, Lombardy in northern Italy, and the Kingdom of Naples in southern Italy through the Treaty of Utrecht in 1713. The Kingdom of Naples was lost relatively quickly and played no considerable role in the Habsburg fortunes. During the eighteenth and nineteenth centuries the Habsburgs' power and influence in Europe would be based primarily on their territories located outside Germany.

In the second half of the seventeenth century and later the Habsburgs confronted immense problems in these hereditary territories. In each they ruled by virtue of a different title and had to gain the cooperation of the local

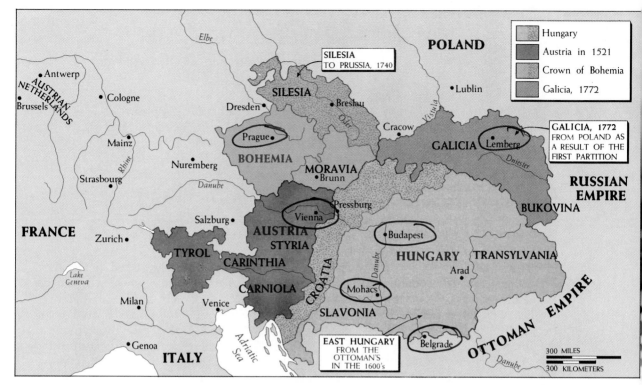

MAP 15-1   THE AUSTRIAN HABSBURG EMPIRE, 1521–1772   *The Empire had three main units—Austria, Bohemia, Hungary. Expansion was mainly eastward: east Hungary from the Ottomans (17th century) and Galicia from Poland (1772). Meantime, Silesia was lost, but Habsburgs retained German influence as Holy Roman Emperors.*

nobility. The most difficult province was Hungary, where the Magyar nobility seemed ever ready to rebel. There was almost no common basis for political unity among peoples of such diverse languages, customs, and geography. Even the Habsburg zeal for Roman Catholicism no longer proved a bond for unity as they continued to confront the equally zealous Calvinism of the Magyar nobles. Over the years the Habsburgs established various central councils to chart common policies for their far-flung domains. Virtually all of these bodies dealt with only a portion of the Habsburgs' holdings. Repeatedly they found themselves compelled to bargain with nobles in one part of Europe in order to maintain their position in another.

Despite all these internal difficulties Leopold I (1657–1705) rallied his domains to resist the advances of the Turks and to resist the aggression of Louis XIV. He achieved Ottoman recognition of his sovereignty over Hungary in 1699 and suppressed the long rebellion of his new Magyar subjects between 1703 and 1711.

He also extended his territorial holdings over much of what is today Yugoslavia and western Romania. These southeastward extensions allowed the Habsburgs to hope to develop Mediterranean trade through the port of Trieste. The expansion at the cost of the Ottoman Empire also helped the Habsburgs to compensate for their loss of domination over the Holy Roman Empire. Strength in the East gave them greater political leverage in Germany. Leopold was succeeded by Joseph I (1705–1711), who continued his policies.

THE DYNASTIC PROBLEM OF CHARLES VI When Charles VI (1711–1740) succeeded Joseph, he added a new problem to the old chronic one of territorial diversity. He had no male heir, and there was only the weakest of precedents for a female ruler of the Habsburg domains. Charles feared that on his death the Austrian Habsburg lands might fall prey to the surrounding powers, as had those of the Spanish Habsburgs in 1700. He was determined to prevent that disaster and to provide his do-

Maria Theresa Discusses One Weakness of Her Throne

Scattered subjects of the multilingual Austrian Empire (Germans, Hungarians, Czechs, Slovaks, Slovenes, Croatians, Poles, and Romanians, for example) made impossible the unifying of the empire into a strong centralized monarchy. Maria Theresa, writing in 1745, explained how previous Habsburg rulers had impoverished themselves by attempting, with little success, to purchase the political and military support of the nobles in different provinces. The more privileges they gave the nobles, the more they were expected to give.

The return once again to my ancestors, these individuals not only gave away most of the crown estates, but absorbed also the debts of those properties confiscated in time of rebellion, and these debts are still in arrears. Emperor Leopold [1658–1705] found little left to give away, but the terrible wars he fought no doubt forced him to mortgage or pawn additional crown estates. His successors did not relieve these burdens, and when I became sovereign, the crown revenues barely reached eighty thousand gulden. Also in the time of my forebears, the ministers received enormous payments from the crown and from the local Estates because they knew not only how to exploit selfishly the good will, grace, and munificence of the Austrian house by convincing each ruler that predecessor had won fame by giving freely but also how to win the ears of the provincial lords and clergy so that these ministers acquired all that they wished. In fact they spread their influence so wide that in the provinces they were more feared and respected than the ruler himself. And when they had finally taken everything from the sovereign, these same ministers turned for additional compensation to their provinces, where their great authority continuously increased. Even though complaints reached the monarch, out of grace and forebearance toward the ministers, he simply allowed the exploitations to continue. . . .

This system gave the ministers such authority that the sovereign himself found it convenient for his own interests to support them because he learned by experience that the more prestige enjoyed by the heads of the provinces, the more of the sovereign's demands these heads could extract from their Estates.

Maria Theresa, Political Testament, *cited in Karl A. Roider (Ed. and Trans.),* Maria Theresa *(Englewood Cliffs, N.J.: Prentice-Hall, 1973), pp. 32–33.*

mains with the semblance of legal unity. To those ends, he devoted most of his reign to seeking the approval of his family, the estates of his realms, and the major foreign powers for a document called the *Pragmatic Sanction.*

This instrument provided the legal basis for a single line of inheritance within the Habsburg dynasty through Charles VI's daughter Maria Theresa (1740–1780). Other members of the Habsburg family recognized her as the rightful heir. The nobles of the various Habsburg domains did likewise after extracting various concessions from Charles. Consequently, when Charles VI died in October 1740, he believed that he had secured legal unity for the Habsburg Empire and a safe succession for his daughter.

He had indeed established a permanent line of succession and the basis for future legal bonds within the Habsburg holdings. However, he failed to protect his daughter from foreign aggression, either through the Pragmatic Sanction or, more important, by leaving her a strong army and a filled treasury. Less than two months after his death the fragility of the foreign agreements became all too apparent. In December 1740 Frederick II of Prussia invaded the Habsburg province of Silesia. Maria Theresa would now have to fight to defend her inheritance.

Prussia and the Hohenzollerns

The Habsburg achievement had been to draw together into an uncertain legal unity a collection of domains possessed by <u>dint</u> of separate feudal titles. The achievement of the Hohenzollerns of Brandenburg-Prussia was to acquire a similar collection of <u>titular</u> holdings and then to forge them into a centrally administered unit. In spite of the geographical separation of their territories and the paucity of their natural economic resources, they transformed feudal ties and structures into bureaucratic ones. They subordinated every social class and most economic pursuits to the strengthening of the institution that united their far-flung realms: the army. In so doing they made the term *Prussian* <u>synonymous</u> with administrative rigor and military discipline.

A STATE OF DISCONNECTED TERRITORIES The rise of Prussia occurred within the German power vacuum created by the Peace of Westphalia. It is the story of the extraordinary Hohenzollern family, which had ruled the German territory of Brandenburg since 1417. Through inheritance the family had acquired the duchy of Cleves and the counties of Mark and Ravensburg in 1609, the duchy of East Prussia in 1618, and the duchy of Pomerania in 1637. Except for Pomerania, none of these lands was <u>contiguous</u> with Brandenburg. East Prussia lay inside Poland and outside the authority of the Holy Roman Emperor. All of the territories lacked good natural

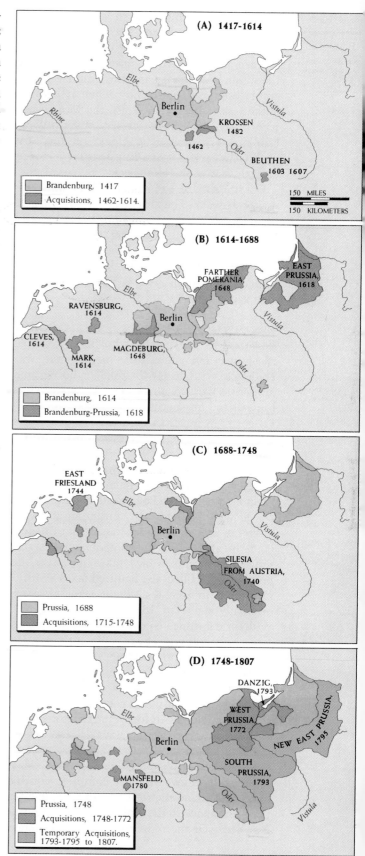

MAP 14-2 EMPANSION OF BRANDENBURG-PRUSSIA *Seventeenth-century Brandenburg-Prussia expanded mainly by acquiring dynastic titles in geographically separated lands. Eighteenth-century expansion occurred through aggression to the east: Silesia seized in 1740 and various parts of Poland in 1772, 1793, and 1795.*

resources, and many of them were devastated during the Thirty Years' War. At Westphalia the Hohenzollerns lost part of Pomerania to Sweden but were compensated by receiving three more bishoprics and the promise of the archbishopric of Magdeburg when it became vacant, as it did in 1680. By the late seventeenth century the scattered Hohenzollern holdings represented a block of territory within the Holy Roman Empire second in size only to that of the Habsburgs.

Despite its size, the Hohenzollern conglomerate was weak. The areas were geographically separate, and there was no mutual sympathy or common concern among them. In each there existed some form of local noble estates that limited the power of the Hohenzollern prince. The various areas were exposed to foreign aggression.

FREDERICK WILLIAM, THE GREAT ELECTOR

The person who began to forge these areas and nobles into a modern state was Frederick William (1640–1688), who became known as the Great Elector. He established himself and his successors as the central uniting power by breaking the estates, organizing a royal bureaucracy, and establishing a strong army.

Between 1655 and 1660 Sweden and Poland engaged in a war that endangered the Great Elector's holdings in Pomerania and East Prussia. Frederic William had neither an adequate army nor the tax revenues to confront this foreign threat. In 1655 the Brandenburg estates refused to grant his new taxes; however, he proceeded to collect the required taxes by military force. In 1659 a different grant of taxes, originally made in 1653, elapsed; Frederick William continued to collect them as well as those he had imposed by his own authority. He used the money to build up an army, which allowed him to continue to enforce his will without the approval of the nobility. Similar processes of threats and coercion took place against the nobles in his other territories.

However, there was a political and social trade-off between the elector and his various nobles. These *Junkers*, or German noble landlords, were allowed almost complete control over the serfs on their estates. In exchange for their obedience to the Hohenzollerns, the *Junkers* received the right to demand obedience

from their serfs. Frederick William also tended to choose as the local administrators of the tax structure men who would normally have been members of the nobles estates. In this fashion he co-opted potential opponents into his service. The taxes fell most heavily on the backs of the peasants and the urban classes.

As the years passed, sons of *Junkers* increasingly dominated the army officer corps, and this practice became even more pronounced during the eighteenth century. All officials and army officers took an oath of loyalty directly to the elector. The army and the elector thus came to embody the otherwise absent unity of the state. The existence of the army made Prussia a valuable potential ally and a state with which other powers needed to curry favor.

FREDERICK WILLIAM I, KING OF PRUSSIA

Yet, even with the considerable accomplishments of the Great Elector, the house of Hohenzollern did not possess a crown. The achievement of a royal title was one of the few state-building accomplishments of Frederick I (1688–1713). This son of the Great Elector was the least "Prussian" of his family during these crucial years. He built palaces, founded Halle University (1694), patronized the arts, and lived luxuriously. However, in 1700, at the outbreak of the War of the Spanish Succession, he put his army at the disposal of the Habsburg Holy Roman Emperor. In exchange for this loyal service the emperor permitted Frederick to assume the title of "King of Prussia." Thereafter Frederick became Frederick I, and he passed the much-desired royal title to his son Frederick William I in 1713.

Frederick William I (1713–1740) was both the most eccentric personality to rule the Hohenzollern domains and one of its most effective monarchs. After giving his father a funeral that matched the luxury of his life, Frederick William I immediately imposed policies of strict austerity. In some cases jobs were abolished, and in others salaries were lowered. His political aims seem to have been nothing else than the consolidation of an obedient, compliant bureaucracy and the expansion of the army. He initiated a policy of *Kabinett* government, which meant that lower officials submitted all relevant documents to him in his office, or *Kabinett*. Then he alone examined

543

SUCCESSFUL
AND
UNSUCCESSFUL
PATHS TO
POWER (1686–
1740)

The Great Elector Welcomes Protestant Refugees from France

The Hohenzollern dynasty of Brandenburg-Prussia pursued a policy of religious toleration. The family itself was Calvinist, whereas most of its subjects were Lutherans. When Louis XIV of France revoked the Edict of Nantes in 1685, Frederick William, the Great Elector, seized on the opportunity to invite into his realms French Protestants. As his proclamation indicates, he was quite interested in attracting persons with productive skills who could aid the economic development of his domains.

We, Friedrich Wilhelm, by Grace of God Margrave of Brandenburg. . . .

Do hereby proclaim and make known to all and sundry that since the cruel persecutions and rigorous ill-treatment in which Our co-religionists of the Evangelical-Reformed faith have for some time past been subjected in the Kingdom of France, have caused many families to remove themselves and to betake themselves out of the said Kingdom into other lands, We now . . . have been moved graciously to offer them through this Edict . . . a secure and free refuge in all Our Lands and Provinces. . . .

Since Our Lands are not only well and amply endowed with all things necessary to support life, but also very well-suited to the reestablishment of all kinds of manufactures and trade and traffic by land and water, We permit, indeed, to those settling therein free choice to establish themselves where it is most convenient for their profession and way of living. . . .

The personal property which they bring with them, including merchandise and other wares, is to be totally exempt from any taxes, customs dues, licenses, or other imposts of any description, and not detained in any way. . . .

As soon as these Our French co-religionists of the Evangelical-Reformed faith have settled in any town or village, they shall be admitted to the domiciliary rights and craft freedoms customary there, gratis and without payments of any fee; and shall be entitled to the benefits, rights, and privileges enjoyed by Our other, native, subjects, residing there. . . .

Not only are those who wish to establish manufacture of cloth, stuffs, hats, or other objects in which they are skilled to enjoy all necessary freedoms, privileges and facilities, but also provision is to be made for them to be assisted and helped as far as possible with money and anything else which they need to realize their intention. . . .

Those who settle in the country and wish to maintain themselves by agriculture are to be given a certain plot of land to bring under cultivation and provided with whatever they need to establish themselves initially. . . .

C. A. Macartney (Ed.), The Habsburg and Hohenzollern Dynasties in the Seventeenth and Eighteenth Centuries *(New York: Walker, 1970), pp. 270–273.*

the papers, made his decision, and issued his orders. Frederick William I thus skirted the influence of ministers and ruled alone.

Frederick William organized the bureaucracy along the lines of military discipline. He united all departments under the *General-Ober-Finanz - Kriegs - und - Domänen - Direktorium*, which is more happily known to us as the *General Directory*. He imposed taxes on the nobility and changed most remaining feudal

Economically weak, with a small population, Prussia became an important state because it developed a large, well-trained army. The discipline for which Prussian troops were noted was the result of constant drill and harsh punishment. The parade-ground formation shown here was actually meant to be performed on the battlefield. The wooden horse (left) was used for punishment, not exercise. [Bildarchiv Preussischer Kulturbesitz]

dues into money payments. He sought to transform feudal and administrative loyalties into a sense of duty to the monarch as a political institution rather than as a person. He once described the perfect royal servant as

> *an intelligent, <u>assiduous</u>, and alert person who after God values nothing higher than his king's pleasure and serves him out of love and for the sake of honor rather than money and who in his conduct solely seeks and constantly bears in mind his king's service and interests, who, moreover, abhors all intrigues and emotional deterrents.*[1]

---

[1] *Quoted in Hans Rosenberg,* Bureaucracy, Aristocracy, and Autocracy *(Boston: Beacon Press, 1958), p. 93.*

Service to the state and the monarch was to become impersonal, mechanical, and, in effect, unquestioning.

THE PRUSSIAN ARMY The discipline that Frederick William applied to the army was little less than fanatical. During his reign the size of the military force grew from about thirty-nine thousand in 1713 to over eighty thousand in 1740. It was the third or fourth largest army in Europe, whereas Prussia ranked thirteenth in size of population. Rather than using recruiters, the king made each canton or local district responsible for supplying a certain number of soldiers.

After 1725 Frederick William always wore

an officer's uniform. He built one regiment from the tallest soldiers he could find in Europe. Separate laws applied to the army and to civilians. Laws, customs, and royal attention made the officer corps the highest social class of the state. Military service attracted the sons of *Junkers*. In this fashion the army, the *Junker* nobility, and the monarchy became forged into a single political entity. Military priorities and values dominated Prussian government, society, and daily life as in no other state of Europe. It has often been said that whereas other nations possessed armies, the Prussian army possessed its nation.

Although Frederick William I built the best army in Europe, he followed a policy of avoiding conflict. He wanted to drill his soldiers but not to order them into battle. Although Frederick William terrorized his family and associates and on occasion knocked out teeth with his walking stick, he was not a militarily aggressive monarch. The army was for him a symbol of Prussian power and unity, not an instrument to be used for foreign adventures or aggression.

At his death in 1740 he passed to his son Frederick II (1740–1786; Frederick the Great) this superb military machine, but he could not pass to his son the wisdom to refrain from using it. Almost immediately on coming to the throne, Frederick II upset the Pragmatic Sanction and invaded Silesia. He thus crystallized the Austrian-Prussian rivalry for control of Germany that would dominate central European affairs for over a century.

The Entry of Russia into the European Political Arena

Though ripe with consequences for the future, the rise of Prussia and the new consolidation of Austrian Habsburg domains seemed to many at the time only one more shift in the long-troubled German scene. However, the emergence of Russia as an active European power constituted a wholly new factor in European politics. Previously Russia had been considered a part of Europe only by courtesy. Geographically and politically it lay on the periphery of Europe. Hemmed in by Sweden on the Baltic and by the Ottoman Empire on the

AUSTRIA AND PRUSSIA IN THE LATE SEVENTEENTH AND EARLY EIGHTEENTH CENTURIES

1640–1688	Reign of Frederick William, the Great Elector
1657–1705	Leopold I rules Austria and resists the Turkish invasions
1683	Turkish siege of Vienna
1688–1713	Reign of Frederick I of Prussia
1699	Peace treaty between Turks and Habsburgs
1711–1740	Charles VI rules Austria and secures agreement to the Pragmatic Sanction
1713–1740	Frederick William I builds up the military power of Prussia
1740	Maria Theresa succeeds to the Habsburg throne
1740	Frederick II violates the Pragmatic Sanction by invading Silesia

Black Sea, the country had no warm-water ports. Its chief outlet to the west was Archangel on the White Sea, which was open to ships during only part of the year. There was little trade. What Russia did possess was a vast reserve of largely undeveloped natural and human resources.

Birth of the Romanov Dynasty

The reign of Ivan the Terrible, which had begun so well and closed so frighteningly, was followed by a period of anarchy and civil war known as the "Time of Troubles," In 1613, hoping to resolve the tension and end the uncertainty, an assembly of nobles elected as tsar a seventeen-year-old boy named Michael Romanov (1613–1654). Thus began the dynasty that in spite of palace revolutions, military conspiracies, assassinations, and family strife ruled Russia until 1917.

Michael Romanov and his two successors, Alexis I (1654–1676) and Theodore III (1676–1682), brought stability and bureaucratic centralization to Russia. However, Russia remained militarily weak and financially impoverished. The bureaucracy after these years of turmoil still remained largely controlled by the boyars, the old nobility. This administrative apparatus was only barely capable of putting down a revolt of peasants and cossacks (adventurous horsemen) under Stepan Razin in

1670–1671. Furthermore, the government and the tsars faced the danger of mutiny from the *streltsy,* or guards of the Moscow garrison.

Peter the Great

In 1682 another boy—ten years old at the time—ascended the fragile Russian throne as co-ruler with his half brother. His name was Peter (1682–1725), and Russia would never be the same after him. He and his ill half-brother, Ivan V, had come to power on the shoulders of the *streltsy,* who expected rewards from the persons they favored. Much violence and bloodshed had surrounded the disputed succession. Matters became even more confused when the boys' sister, Sophia, was named regent. Peter's followers overthrew her in 1689. From that date onward Peter ruled personally, although in theory he shared the crown with Ivan, until Ivan died in 1696. The dangers and turmoil of his youth convinced Peter of two

things. First, the power of the tsar must be made secure from the jealousy of the boyars and the greed of the *streltsy.* Second, the military power of Russia must be increased.

Peter I, who became Peter the Great, was fascinated by western Europe, particularly its military resources. He was an imitator of the first order. The products and workers from the West who had filtered into Russia impressed and intrigued him. In 1697 he made a famous visit in rather weak disguises throughout western Europe. There he dined and talked with the great and the powerful, who considered this almost seven-foot-tall ruler both crude and rude. His happiest moments on the trip were spent inspecting shipyards, docks, and the manufacture of military hardware.

He returned to Moscow determined by whatever means necessary to copy what he had seen abroad, for he knew that warfare would be necessary to make Russia a great power. The tsar's drive toward westernization,

Peter the Great (1682–1725) studied ship building in Holland. In 1697, the Tsar visited western Europe incognito to study the skills that he considered necessary for Russia to build a strong, modern state. [The Bettmann Archive]

though unsystematic, had four general areas of concern: taming the boyars and the *streltsy*, achieving secular control of the Church, reorganizing the internal administration, and developing the economy. Peter pursued each of these goals with violence and ruthlessness.

TAMING THE BOYARS AND STRELTSY

Peter made a sustained attack on the Russian boyars. In 1698, immediately on his return from abroad, he personally shaved the long beards of the court boyars and sheared off the customary long, hand-covering sleeves of their shirts and coats, which had made them the butt of jokes throughout Europe. More important, he demanded that the nobles provide his state with their services.

In 1722 Peter published a Table of Ranks, which henceforth equated a person's social position and privileges with his rank in the bureaucracy or the army rather than with his position in the nobility. However, unlike the

547

SUCCESSFUL
AND
UNSUCCESSFUL
PATHS TO
POWER (1686–
1740)

Peter the Great Issues Decrees on Dress and Shaving

In his determination to transform Russia and to make it resemble a western European nation, Peter the Great issued decrees mandating western European clothing and forbidding beards and moustaches. By "western" clothing, the decree meant clothing designed according to German styles unless otherwise specified. The tax imposed on those persons who refused to shave was graduated according to social rank.

Decree of 1701

Western Dress shall be worn by all the boyars, . . . members of our councils and of our court . . . gentry of Moscow, secretaries . . . provincial gentry, . . . government officials, strel'tsy, members of the guilds purveying for our household, citizens of Moscow of all ranks, and residents of provincial cities . . . excepting the clergy . . . and peasant tillers of the soil. The upper dress shall be of French or Saxon cut, and the lower dress and underwear—[including] waistcoat, trousers, boots, shoes, and hats—shall be of the German type. They shall also ride German saddles. [Likewise] the womenfolk of all ranks, including the priests', deacons', and church attendants' wives, the wives of the dragoons, the soldiers, and the strel'tsy, and their children shall wear Western . . . dresses, hats, jackets, and underwear—undervests and petticoats and shoes. From

now on no one [of the above-mentioned] is to wear Russian dress or Circassian coats, sheepskin coats, or Russian peasant coats, trousers, boots, and shoes. It is also forbidden to ride Russian saddles, and the craftsmen shall not manufacture them or sell them at the marketplaces.

The Decree of 1705

A decree to be published in Moscow and in all the provincial cities: Henceforth, in accordance with this, His Majesty's decree, all court attendants . . . provincial service men, government officials of all ranks, military men, . . . members of the wholesale merchants' guild, and members of guilds purveying for our household must shave their beards and moustaches. But, if it happens that some of them do not wish to shave their beards and moustaches, let a year tax be collected from such persons. . . .

George Vernadsky (Ed.), A Source Book from Russian History from Early Times to 1917 (New Haven: Yale University Press, 1972), 2: 347.

As part of this effort to bring Russia into the modern age, Peter the Great required nobles to change the style of their dress and to trim their beards. In this contemporary woodcut, Peter is portrayed cutting the beard of a Russian noble.

case in Prussia, the Russian nobility never became perfectly loyal to the state. They repeatedly sought to reassert their independence and their control of the Russian imperial court.

The *streltsy* fared less well than the boyars. In 1698 they had rebelled while Peter was on his European tour. When he returned and put down the revolt of these Moscow troops, he directed massive violence and brutality against both leaders and followers. There were private tortures and public executions, in which Peter's own ministers took part. Almost twelve hundred of the rebels were put to death, and their corpses long remained on public display to discourage future disloyalty.

ACHIEVING SECULAR CONTROL OF THE CHURCH
Peter dealt with the potential independence of the Russian Orthodox church with similar ruthlessness. Here again, Peter had to confront a problem that had arisen in the turbulent decades that had preceded his reign. The Russian church had long opposed the scientific as well as the theological thought of the West. In the mid-seventeenth century a reformist movement led by Patriarch Nikon arose in the Church. In 1667 certain changes had been introduced into the texts and the ritual of the Church. These reforms caused great unrest because the Russian church had always claimed to be the protector of the ritual. The Old Believers, a group of Russian Christians who strongly opposed these changes, were condemned by the hierarchy, but they persisted in their opposition. Late in the century thousands of them committed suicide rather than submit to the new rituals. The Old Believers' movement represented a rejection of change and innovation; its presence discouraged the Church hierarchy from making any further substantial moves toward modern thought.

In the future Peter wanted to avoid two kinds of difficulties with the Russian church. First, the clergy must not constitute a group within the state that would oppose change and westernization. Second, the hierarchy of the Church must not be permitted to reform liturgy, ritual, or doctrine in a way that might again give rise to discontent such as that of the Old Believers. Consequently, in 1721, Peter simply abolished the position of patriarch of the Russian church. In its place he established a synod headed by a layman to rule the Church in accordance with secular requirements. So far as transforming a traditional institution was concerned, this action toward the Church was the most radical policy of Peter's reign. It produced still further futile opposition from the Old Believers, who saw the tsar as leading the Church into new heresy.

REORGANIZING DOMESTIC ADMINISTRATION
In his reorganization of domestic administration, Peter looked to institutions then used in Sweden. These were "colleges," or bureaus, composed of several persons rather than departments headed by a single minister. These colleges, which he imposed on Russia, were to look after matters such as the collection of taxes, foreign affairs, war, and economic matters. This new organization was an attempt to breathe life into the generally stagnant and inefficient administration of the country.

In 1711 he created a central senate of nine members who were to direct the Moscow government when the tsar was away with the army. The purpose of these and other local administrative reforms was to establish a bureaucracy that could collect and spend tax revenues to support an efficient army.

DEVELOPING THE ECONOMY AND WAGING WAR The economic development advocated by Peter the Great was closely related to his military needs. He encouraged the establishment of an iron industry in the Ural Mountains, and by mid-century Russia had become the largest iron producer in Europe. He sent prominent young Russians abroad to acquire technical and organizational skills. He attempted to attract west European craftsmen to live and work in Russia. Except for the striking growth of the iron industry, which later languished, all these efforts had only marginal success.

The goal of these internal reforms and political departures was to support a policy of war-fare. Peter was determined to secure warm-water ports that would allow Russia to trade with the West and to have a greater impact of European affairs. This policy led him into wars with the Ottoman Empire and with Sweden. His armies commenced fighting the Turks in 1695 and captured Azov on the Black Sea in 1696. It was a temporary victory, for in 1711 he was compelled to return the port.

Peter had more success against Sweden, where the inconsistency and irrationality of Charles XII was no small aid. In 1700 Russia moved against the Swedish territory on the Baltic. The Swedish king's failure to follow up his victory at Narva in 1700 allowed Peter to regroup his forces and hoard his resources. In 1709, when Charles XII returned to fight Russia again, Peter was ready, and the Battle of Poltava sealed the fate of Sweden. In 1721, at the Peace of Nystad, which ended the Great Northern War, the Russian conquest of

Peter the Great built St. Petersburg (now Leningrad) on the Gulf of Finland to provide Russia with better contact with Western Europe. He moved the capital there from Moscow in 1703. This is an eighteenth-century view of the city. [John R. Freeman]

cies of Peter the Great literally intersected. This was at the spot on the Gulf of Finland where Peter founded his new capital city of Saint Petersburg (now Leningrad). There he built government structures and compelled his boyars to construct town houses. In this fashion he imitated those west European monarchs who had copied Louis XIV by constructing smaller versions of Versailles. However, the founding of Saint Petersburg went beyond the construction of a central court. It symbolized a new western orientation of Russia and Peter's determination to hold his position on the Baltic coast. He had begun the construction of the city and had moved the capital there in 1703, even before his victory over Sweden was assured.

Despite his notable success on the Baltic, Peter's reign ended with a great question mark. He had long quarreled with his only son, Alexis. Peter was jealous of the young man and was fearful that he might undertake sedition. In 1718 Peter had his son imprisoned, and during this imprisonment the presumed successor to the throne died mysteriously. Thereafter Peter claimed for himself the right of naming a successor, but he could never bring himself to designate the person either orally or in writing. Consequently, when he died in 1725, there was no firmer policy on the succession to the throne than when he had acceded to the title. For over thirty years, once again soldiers and nobles would determine who ruled Russia. Peter had laid the foundations of a modern Russia, but he had failed to lay the foundations of a stable state.

Estonia, Livonia, and part of Finland was confirmed. Henceforth Russia possessed warm-water ports and a permanent influence on European affairs.

At one point the domestic and foreign poli-

By the second quarter of the eighteenth century the major European powers were not yet nation-states in which the citizens felt themselves united by a shared sense of community, culture, language, and history. They were still monarchies in which the personality of the ruler and the personal relationships of the great noble families exercised considerable influence over public affairs. The monarchs, except in Great Britain, had generally succeeded in making their power greater than the nobility's. However, the power of the aristocracy and its capacity to resist or obstruct the policies of the monarch were not destroyed. In Britain, of course, the nobility had tamed the monarchy, but even there tension between

nobles and monarchs would continue through the rest of the century.

In foreign affairs the new arrangement of military and diplomatic power established during the early years of the century prepared the way for two long-term conflicts. The first was a commercial rivalry for trade and overseas empire between France and Great Britain. During the reign of Louis XIV these two nations had collided over the French bid for dominance in Europe. During the eighteenth century they dueled for control of commerce on other continents. The second arena of warfare was central Europe, where Austria and Prussia fought for the leadership of the states of Germany.

However, behind these international conflicts and the domestic rivalry of monarchs and nobles, the society of eighteenth-century Europe began to experience momentous change. The character and the structures of the society over which the monarchs ruled were beginning to take on some features associated with the modern age. These economic and social developments would, in the long run, produce transformations in the life of Europe beside which the state building of the early eighteenth-century monarchs paled.

Suggested Readings

M. S. ANDERSON, *Europe in the Eighteenth Century, 1713–1783* (1961). The best one-volume introduction.

T. M. BARKER, *Army, Aristocracy, Monarchy: Essays in War, Society and Government in Austria, 1618–1780* (1982). Examines the intricate power relationships among these major institutions.

R. BROWNING, *Political and Constitutional Ideas of the Court Whigs* (1982). An excellent overview of the ideology of Walpole's supporters.

F. L. CARSTEN, *The Origins of Prussia* (1954), Discusses the groundwork laid by the Great Elector in the seventeenth century.

J. C. D. CLARK, *English Society: 1688–1832: Social Structure and Political Practice during the Ancien Regime* (1985). An important, controversial work that emphasizes the role of religion in English political life.

A. COBBAN, *A History of Modern France*, 2nd ed., Vol. 1 (1961). A lively and opinionated survey.

L. COLLEY, *In Defiance of Oligarchy: The Tory Party, 1714–60.* (1982) An important study that challenges much conventional opinion about eighteenth-century British politics.

P. DUKES, *The Making of Russian Absolutism: 1613–1801* (1982). An overview based on recent scholarship.

R. R. ERGANG, *The Potsdam Führer* (1941). The biography of Frederick William I.

R. J. W. EVANS, *The Making of the Habsburg Monarchy, 1550–1700: An Interpretation* (1979). Places much emphasis on intellectual factors and the role of religion.

F. FORD, *Robe and Sword: The Regrouping of the French Aristocracy After Louis XIV* (1953). An important book for political, social, and intellectual history.

G. P. GOOCH, *Maria Theresa and Other Studies* (1951). A sound introduction to the problems of the Habsburgs.

G. P. GOOCH, *Louis XV, The Monarchy in Decline* (1956). A discussion of the problems of France after the death of Louis XIV.

J. M. HITTLE, *The Service City: State and Townsmen in Russia, 1600–1800* (1979). Examines the relationship of cities in Russia to the growing power of the central government.

H. HOLBORN, *A History of Modern Germany*, 1648–1840 (1966). The best and most comprehensive survey in English.

H. C. JOHNSON, *Frederick the Great and His Officials* (1975). An excellent examination of the Prussian administration.

R. A. KANN AND Z. V. DAVID, *The Peoples of the Eastern Habsburg Lands, 1526–1918* (1984). The best overview of the subject.

R. K. MASSIE, *Peter the Great: His Life and His World* (1980). A good popular biography.

L. B. NAMIER AND J. BROOKE, *The History of Parliament: The House of Commons, 1754–1790*, 3 vols. (1964). A detailed examination of the unreformed British House of Commons and electoral system.

L. J. OLIVA (Ed.), *Russia and the West from Peter the Great to Khrushchev* (1965). An anthology of articles tracing an important and ambiguous subject.

J. B. OWEN, *The Eighteenth Century* (1974). An excellent introduction to England in the period.

J. H. PLUMB, *Sir Robert Walpole*, 2 vols. (1956, 1961). A masterful biography ranging across the sweep of European politics.

J. H. PLUMB, *The Growth of Political Stability in England, 1675–1725* (1969). An important interpretive work.

N. V. RIASANOVSKY, *A History of Russia*, 3rd ed. (1977). The best one-volume introduction.

N. V. RIASANOVSKY, *The Image of Peter the Great in Russian History and Thought* (1985). Examines the ongoing legacy of Peter in Russian history.

H. ROSENBERG, *Bureaucracy, Aristocracy, and Autocracy: The Prussian Experience, 1660–1815* (1960). Emphasizes the organization of Prussian administration.

E. N. WILLIAMS, *The Ancien Régime in Europe* (1972). A state-by-state survey of very high quality.

LE GRAND ABUS.

The Old Regime was a society in which privilege prevailed. In this remarkable French cartoon from the period a woman from the common classes is shown carrying on her back a nun representing the privileges of the Church and a wealthy noble lady representing the privileges of the aristocracy. [The Bettmann Archive]

16

SOCIETY AND ECONOMY UNDER THE OLD REGIME IN THE EIGHTEENTH CENTURY

During the French Revolution and the turmoil spawned by that upheaval, it became customary to refer to the patterns of social, political, and economic relationships that had existed in France before 1789 as the ancien régime, or the "old regime." The term has come to be applied generally to the life and institutions of prerevolutionary Europe. Politically the term indicated the rule of theoretically absolute monarchies with growing bureaucracies and aristocratically led armies. Economically the old regime was characterized by scarcity of food, the predominance of agriculture, slow transport, a low level of iron production, rather unsophisticated financial institutions, and in some cases competitive commercial overseas empires.

Socially, prerevolutionary Europe was based on (1) aristocratic elites possessing a wide variety of inherited legal privileges; (2) established Roman Catholic and Protestant churches intimately related to the state and the aristocracy; (3) an urban labor force usually organized into guilds; and (4) a rural peasantry subject to high taxes and feudal dues. It should be remembered that the men and women living during this period did not know it was the old regime. In most cases they earned their livelihoods and went through the various stages of life as their forebears had done for generations before them and as they expected their children to do after them.

Tradition, hierarchy, corporateness, and privilege were the chief social characteristics of the old regime. Yet it was by no means a static society. Factors of change and innovation were fermenting in its midst. There was a strong demand from the colonies in the Americas for European goods and manufactures. Merchants in seaports and other cities were expanding their businesses. By preparing their states for war, the various governments put new demands on the resources and the economic organizations of their nations. The spirit of rationality that had been so important to the Scientific Revolution of the seventeenth century continued to manifest itself in the economic life of the eighteenth century. Perhaps most important, the population of Europe grew rapidly. The old regime itself fostered the changes that eventually transformed it into a very different kind of society.

Major Features of Life in the Old Regime

World of Contrasts

Probably the most striking feature of the old regime was the marked contrasts in the lives and experiences of people in different social ranks, different countries, and even different regions of the same country. The bonds created by rapid transport and communication that have today led to similar patterns of life throughout the Western world simply did not yet exist.

Within the major monarchies there was usually no single standard of uniform law, money, or weights and measures. Except in Britain, internal tolls hampered the passage of goods. The nobility of Great Britain lived in the most magnificent luxury the order had ever known. On the Continent some groups of nobles were also very wealthy, but other members of the continental nobility were little better off than the wealthier peasants. So far as the peasantry was concerned, it tended to prosper in western Europe while reaching new depths of social and economic degradation east of the Elbe River.

In Britain, Holland, and parts of France there was a healthy and growing middle class, but such an order hardly existed in the German principalities, the Austrian Empire, or Russia. Finally, there was a stark contrast between the refinement of taste, fashion, and manners of the upper levels of society and the simultaneous presence of public whipping, torture, and executions inflicted on the lower classes. Historians often point to the difficulties of life and the differences in wealth in our industrial society, but these were far more extreme in the society of the old regime.

Maintenance of Tradition

Eighteenth-century society was traditional. The past weighed more heavily on people's minds than did the future. Few persons outside the government bureaucracies and the movement for reform called the *Enlightenment* (see Chapter 18) considered change or innovation desirable. This was especially true of social relationships. Both nobles and peasants, for very different reasons, repeatedly called for the restoration of traditional or customary rights. The nobles asserted what they considered their ancient rights against the intrusion of the expanding monarchical bureaucracies. The peasants, in petitions and revolts, called for the revival or the maintenance of the customary manorial rights that provided them access to particular lands, courts, or grievance proce-dures.

With the exception of the early industrial development in Britain, the eighteenth-century economy was also quite traditional. The quality and quantity of the harvest re-mained the single most important fact of life for the overwhelming majority of the popula-tion and the gravest concern of the govern-ments.

Hierarchy and Privilege

Closely related to this traditional social and economic outlook was the hierarchical struc-ture of the society. The medieval sense of rank and degree not only persisted but became more rigid in the course of the century. In several continental cities "sumptuary laws" regulat-ing the dress of the different classes remained on the books. These laws forbade persons in one class or occupation to wear clothes like those worn by people in a socially higher posi-tion. The point of such laws, which were largely ineffective in the eighteenth century, was to make the social hierarchy actually visi-ble. Rather than by such legislation, the hierar-chy was really enforced through the corporate nature of social relationships.

Each state or society was considered a com-munity of numerous smaller communities. People in eighteenth-century Europe did not enjoy what Americans regard as individual rights. A person enjoyed such rights and privi-leges as were guaranteed to the particular com-munities or groups of which she or he was a part. The "community" might include the vil-lage, the municipality, the nobility, the church, the guild, or the parish. In turn, each of these bodies enjoyed certain privileges, some of which were great and some small. The privi-leges might involve exemption from taxation or from some especially humiliating punish-ment, the right to practice a trade or craft, the right of one's children to pursue a particular occupation, or, in the case of the Church, the right to collect the tithe.

Family Structures and the Family Economy

In preindustrial Europe the household was the basic unit of production and consumption.

That is to say, only the most limited number of productive establishments employed more than a handful of people not belonging to the family of the owner. Those very few establish-ments employing significant numbers of wage earners who were not members of the owner's family were located in cities. But the over-whelming majority of Europeans lived in rural areas. There, as well as in small towns and cit-ies, the household mode of organization pre-dominated on farms, in artisans' workshops, and in small merchants' shops. With that mode of economic organization there devel-oped what is known as the *family economy*.

Households

What was a household in preindustrial Europe of the old regime? There were two basic mod-els, one characterizing northwestern Europe and the other eastern Europe.

NORTHWESTERN EUROPE In the north-western part of the continent, the household almost invariably consisted of a married cou-ple, their children through their early teen-age years, and their servants. Except for the rela-tively few very wealthy people, households were quite small, rarely consisting of more than five or six members. Furthermore, in these households, more than two generations of a family rarely lived under the same roof. High mortality and late marriage prevented families of three generations. In other words, grandparents rarely lived in the same house-hold as their grandchildren. In this regard the family structure of northwestern Europe was nuclear rather than extended. That is to say, these families consisted of parents and chil-dren rather than of several generations under the same roof.

This particular characteristic of the north-western European household is one of the most major discoveries of recent research into family history. Previously it had been assumed that before industrialization the European family lived in extended familial settings with several generations inhabiting a household. Recent demographic investigation has sharply reversed this picture. Children lived with their parents only until their early teens. Then they normally left home, usually to enter the work force of young servants who lived and worked in a household other than that of their parents.

A child of a skilled artisan might remain with his or her parents in order to acquire the valuable skill; only rarely would more than one of the children do so because their labor would be more valuable and remunerative elsewhere.

These young men and women who had left home would eventually marry, and they would then begin to form an independent household of their own. This practice of moving away from home is known as *neolocalism*. The age of their marriage would be relatively late. For men it was over twenty-six, and for women over twenty-three. At the time of marriage the couple usually quickly began a family. It was not unusual for the marriage to occur at the end of a long courtship when the woman was already pregnant. Family and community pressures seem more often than not to have compelled the man to marry the woman. In any case premarital sexual relations were common, though illegitimate births were rare. The new couple would soon employ a servant, who with their growing children would undertake

whatever form of livelihood the household used to support itself.

Servant in this context is a word that may seem confusing. It does not refer to someone looking after the needs of wealthy people. Rather in preindustrial Europe, a servant was a person—either male or female—who was hired, often under a clear contract, to work for the head of the household in exchange for room, board, and wages. The servant was usually young and by no means necessarily of a social position lower than that of his or her employer. Normally the servant was an integral part of the household and took meals with the family.

Young men and women became servants when their labor was no longer needed in their parents' household or when they could earn more money for their family outside the parental household. Being a servant for several years—often as many as eight or ten—was a means of acquiring the productive skills and the monetary savings necessary for young peo-

Most eighteenth-century Europeans worked with their families in agriculture as in this French dairy barn c. 1780. [Charles Farrell Collection]

557

SOCIETY AND
ECONOMY
UNDER THE
OLD REGIME
IN THE
EIGHTEENTH
CENTURY

Servant girls make butter and cheese on a family farm. The farmer's wife, at left, is supervising their labor. Being a servant was a way for young people to acquire the skills and savings needed to start a household of their own when they married. [Bildarchiv Preussischer Kulturbesitz]

ple to begin their own household. This period of working as a servant between leaving home and beginning a new household accounts in a large measure for the late age of marriage in northwestern Europe.

EASTERN EUROPE As one moved toward the eastern areas of the continent, the structure of the household and the pattern of marriage changed. There marriage occurred quite early, before the age of twenty for both men and women. Consequently children were born to parents of a much younger age. Quite often, especially among Russian serfs, wives were older than their husbands. Eastern European households tended to be quite large in comparison with those in the West. Often the Russian household in the countryside had more than nine and possibly more than twenty members with three or perhaps even four generations of the same family living together. Early marriage made this situation more likely. In Russia marrying involved not starting a new house-

hold but continuing in and expanding one already established.

The landholding pattern in eastern Europe accounts, at least in part, for these patterns of marriage and the family. The lords of the manor who owned land wanted to ensure that it would be cultivated so that they could receive their rents. To that end, for example, in Poland, landlords might forbid marriage between their own serfs and those from another estate. They might also require widows and widowers to remarry so that there would be adequate labor for a particular plot of land. Polish landlords also frowned on the hiring of free laborers—the equivalent of servants in the West—to aid land cultivation. The landlords preferred other serfs to be used. This practice inhibited the possible formation of independent households. In Russia, landlords ordered the families of young people in their villages to arrange marriages within a short, set period of time. These lords discouraged single-generation family households because the death or

*Depending on their ages and skills, everyone in an eighteenth-century family worked
to help support the household. This engraving depicts a family of chimney sweeps.
[British Museum]*

serious illness of a person in such a household might mean that the land assigned to that household would go out of cultivation.

The Family Economy

In both northwestern and eastern Europe, most Europeans worked within the context of the *family economy*. That is to say, the household was the fundamental unit of production and consumption. People thought and worked in terms of sustaining the economic life of the family, and family members saw themselves as working together in an interdependent rather than an independent or individualistic manner. The goal of the family household was to produce or to secure through wages enough food to support its members. In the counryside that effort virtually always involved farming. In cities and towns artisan production or working for another person was the usual pattern.

Almost everyone lived within a household of some kind because it was virtually impossible for ordinary people to support themselves independently. Indeed, except for members of religious orders, people living outside a household were viewed with great suspicion. It was assumed that they were potentially criminal or disruptive or, at the very minimum, potentially dependent on the charity of others.

Marriage and the family within this economy meant that all members of the household had to work. On a farm much of the effort went directly into raising food or producing other agricultural goods that could be exchanged for food. In the countryside of western Europe, however, very few people had enough land to support their household from farming alone. For this reason one or more family members might work elsewhere and send wages home. For example, the father or older children might work as a harvest picker or might fish or might engage in some other kind of labor, either in the local neighborhood or perhaps many miles from home. If the father was such a migrant worker, the burden of the farm work would fall on his wife and their younger children. This was not an uncommon pattern. Within this family economy all of the goods and income produced went to the benefit of the household rather than to the individual family member. Depending on their ages and skills, everyone in the family worked. The very necessity of survival in the face of poor harvests or economic slumps meant that no one could be idle.

The family economy also dominated the life of skilled urban artisans. The father was usually the chief craftsman. He usually had one or more servants in his employ, but would expect his children to work in the enterprise also. His eldest child was usually trained in the trade. His wife often contributed to his business by selling the wares, or she might open a small shop of her own. Wives of merchants also often ran their husbands' businesses, especially when the husband traveled to purchase new goods. In any case, everyone in the family was involved. If business was poor, family members would look for employment elsewhere, not to support themselves but to support the survival of the family unit.

In western Europe the death of a father often brought disaster to the economy of the household. The ongoing economic life of the family usually depended on his land or his skills. The widow might take on the farm or the business, or his children might do so. The widow usually sought to remarry quickly in order to have the labor and skills of a male once more in the household and to prevent herself from falling into a state of dependence.

The high mortality rate of the time meant that there were many households in which there were stepchildren and reconstituted second family groups. But in some cases, because of the advanced age of the widow or economic hard times, the household simply dissolved. The widow became dependent on charity or relatives. The children became similarly dependent or moved earlier than they would otherwise have done into the work force of servants. In other cases, the situation could be so desperate that they would resort to crime or to begging. The personal, emotional, and economic vulnerability of the family economy cannot be overemphasized.

In eastern Europe the family economy was

Working women in eighteenth-century France crush clay shards as a first step in making glass. It was common for the wives and daughters of artisans to help with the family trade. [New York Public Library]

also in place, but in the context of serfdom and landlord domination. Peasants clearly thought in terms of their families and of expanding the land available for cultivation. In some measure, the village structure may have mitigated the pressures of the family economy, as did the multigenerational family. Dependence on the available land was the chief fact of life, and there were many fewer artisan and merchant households. There was also far less mobility than in western Europe.

Women and the Family Economy

The family economy established many of the chief constraints on the lives and the personal experiences of women in preindustrial society. Most of the historical research that has been undertaken on this subject relates to western Europe. There, a woman's life experience was, in large measure, the function of her capacity to establish and maintain a household. For women, marriage was an institution of economic necessity as well as one that fulfilled sexual and psychological needs. A woman outside a household situation lived in a highly vulnerable and precarious position. Unless she were an aristocrat or a member of a religious order, she probably could not support herself by her own efforts alone. Consequently, much of a woman's life was devoted first to aiding the maintenance of her parents' household and then to devising some means of assuring having her own household to live in as an adult. In most cases the bearing and rearing of children were subordinate to these goals.

As a child, certainly by the age of seven, a girl was expected to begin to make contributions to the household work. On a farm this might mean looking after chickens or watering animals or carrying food to adult men and women working the land. In an urban artisan's household, she would do some form of light work, perhaps involving cleaning or carrying and later sewing or weaving. The girl would remain in her parents' home as long as she made a real contribution to the family enterprise or as long as her labor elsewhere was not more valuable and remunerative to the family.

An artisan's daughter might not leave home until marriage because she could learn increasingly valuable skills associated with the trade. The situation was quite different for the much larger number of girls growing up on farms. There, the girl's parents and brothers could often do all the necessary farm work, and her labor at home quickly became of little value to the family. She would then leave home, usually between the age of twelve and fourteen. She might take up residence on another farm, but more likely, she would migrate to a nearby town or city. She would rarely travel more than thirty miles from her parents' household. She would then normally become a servant, once again living in a household, but this time in the household of an employer.

Having migrated from home, the young woman's chief goal was to accumulate sufficient capital for a dowry. Her savings would make her eligible for marriage because they would allow her to make the necessary contribution to form a household with her husband. The dowry would thus permit her to become an economic partner in the context of the family economy. It must be emphasized that marriage within the family economy was a joint economic undertaking, and that the wife was expected to make an immediate contribution of capital for the establishment of the household. A young woman might well work for ten years or more to accumulate a dowry. This practice meant that marriage was usually postponed until her mid- to late twenties.

Within the marriage the necessity of earning enough money or producing enough farm goods to ensure an adequate food supply was always the dominant concern. Domestic duties, childbearing, and child rearing were subordinate to the economic situation. Consequently, the number of children might very well be limited, usually through the practice of *coitus interruptus* or withdrawal of the male prior to ejaculation. Young children were often placed with wet-nurses so that the mother could continue to make her economic contribution to the household. The wet-nurse, in turn, was making such a contribution to her own household. The child would be fully reintegrated into its family when it was weaned and would be expected to aid the family at a very early age.

The kind of work a married woman did differed markedly between city and country and was in many ways a function of the husband's occupation. If the peasant household possessed enough land to support itself, the wife spent much of her time quite literally carrying things for her husband—water, food, seed, harvested grain, and the like. But there were few such adequate landholdings. If the husband had to do work other than farming, such as fishing or migrant labor, the wife might actually be in charge of the farm and do the ploughing, planting, and harvesting. In the city the wife of an artisan or merchant often acted somewhat in the capacity of a business manager. She might well be in charge of the household finances, and she actively participated in the trade or manufacturing enterprise. When her husband died, she might take over the business and perhaps hire an artisan.

Finally, if economic disaster struck the family, more often than not it was the wife who organized what Olwen Hufton has called the "economy of expedients,"[1] within which family members might be sent off to find work elsewhere or even to beg in the streets.

In all phases of life within the family economy, women led active, often decisive roles. Industriousness rather than idleness was their lot in life. Finding a functional place in the household was essential to their well-being. Once that place had been found, their function was essential to the ongoing well-being of the household.

---

[1] Olwen Hufton, "Women and the Family Economy in Eighteenth-Century France," French Historical Studies, 9 (1976):19.

561

SOCIETY AND
ECONOMY
UNDER THE
OLD REGIME
IN THE
EIGHTEENTH
CENTURY

Women of the poorer classes did the same manual work as men. This woman was a Parisian street sweeper. [British Library]

Children and the World of the Family Economy

Under the social and medical conditions of the day, the birth of a child was a time of grave danger to both mother and the infant. Both mother and child were immediately exposed to the possible contraction of contagious diseases. Puerperal fever was frequent, as were other infections from unsterilized medical instruments. By no means were all midwives skillful practitioners of their profession. Furthermore, the immense poverty and the wretched housing conditions of the vast majority of Europe's population endangered the lives of the newborn child and the mother. For large numbers of women childbirth constituted a time of great fearfulness of personal vulnerability.

Assuming that both mother and child survived, the mother might nurse the infant, but quite often the child would be sent to a wet-nurse. Convenience may have led to this practice among the wealthy, but economic necessity dictated it for the poor. The structures and customs of the family economy did not permit a woman the time away from work to devote herself entirely to rearing a child. The wet-nursing industry was quite well organized, and

children born in cities might be transported to wet-nurses in the country, where they would remain for months or even years.

However, throughout Europe the birth of a child was not always a welcome event. The child might be illegitimate or it might represent still one more economic burden on an already hard-pressed household. Through at least the end of the seventeenth century and to a lesser degree beyond it, various forms of infanticide were practiced, especially among the poor. The infant might be smothered or left exposed to the elements. These practices were one result of both the ignorance and the prejudice surrounding contraception.

Though many married couples seem to have succeeded in limiting their families, young men and women who were unmarried and whose sexual relationships may have been the result of a fleeting acquaintance were less fortunate. Numerous young women, especially among servants, found themselves pregnant and without husbands. This situation and the consequent birth of illegitimate children seem to have become much more frequent over the course of the eighteenth century. The reasons for this development remain uncertain, but it probably arose from the more frequent migration of young people from their homes and the disturbance of traditional village life through enclosures (to be discussed later), the commercialization of agriculture, wars, and the late-century revolutions.

The late seventeenth and the early eighteenth centuries saw a new interest in preserving the lives of abandoned children. Large foundling hospitals were established in all the major nations. Hospitals created to care for abandoned children had existed before, but these years saw an expansion in their size and numbers. These hospitals, two of the most famous of which were the Paris Foundling Hospital (1670) and the London Foundling Hospital (1739), cared for thousands of European children. The demands on their resources vastly increased in the course of the eighteenth century. For example, early in the century, the average number of children admitted to the Paris Foundling Hospital was approximately 1,700 annually. But in the peak year of 1772, that number rose to 7,676 children. Not all of those children came from Paris. Many had been brought to the city from the provinces, where local foundling homes and hospitals

A Lottery Is Provided for Admission of Children to the London Foundling Hospital

The London Foundling Hospital was established in 1739. The institution soon found that the demand for admission was greater than the facilities available. In 1742 its officers adopted the following policy for admitting children. The goal of the lottery was to ensure fairness. This system continued in use until 1756, when new funds allowed for the expansion of the hospital.

That all the Women who bring any Children be let into the Court Room as they come, and there set on Benches to be placed round the Room. . . . That as many White Balls as there shall be Children to be taken in, and with five red Balls for every Twenty Children who are to be taken in and so in Proportion for any greater or lesser number, and as many black Balls as with the white and red shall be Equal to the number of Women present, shall be put into a Bag or Box and drawn out by the Women who bring the Children. That each Woman who draws a white Ball shall be carried with her Child into the Inspecting Room in order to have the Child examined. That each Woman who draws a red Ball be carried with her child into another Room there to remain till the Examination of the Children, whose Nurses drew white Balls is ended. That each Woman who draws a black Ball shall be immediately turned out of the Hospital with her Child. If on such Examination any of those Children are rejected but not so many as there be red Balls drawn, there shall be a second Drawing of Lotts by putting into the Bag or Box as many white Balls as there are Children wanting to make up the number ordered to be taken in, And as many black Balls as with the white will be equal to the whole number of red Balls drawn in the first Drawing. And the children whose Nurses draw those white Balls to be taken in if duly qualified, and so on till the whole number be compleated. . . . The Lotts to be drawn in the Court Room in the presence of all the Women to prevent all Suspicion of Fraud or Partiality.

Minutes of the Foundling Hospital's General Committee, as quoted in Ruth K. McClure, Coram's Children: The London Foundling Hospital in the Eighteenth Century *(New Haven: Yale University Press, 1981), pp. 77–78.*

were also overburdened. The London Foundling Hospital lacked the income to deal with all of the children brought to it. In the middle of the eighteenth century, the hospital found itself compelled to choose children for admission by a lottery system.

Sadness and tragedy surrounded almost every aspect of abandoned children. The overwhelming majority of them were illegitimate infants drawn from across the social spectrum. However, a substantial portion seem to have been left with the foundling hospitals because their parents were encountering difficult economic times. There existed a quite close rela-

tionship between rising Paris food prices and increasing numbers of abandoned children. Parents would sometimes leave personal tokens or saints' medals on the abandoned baby in the vain hope that at some future time they might be able to reclaim the child. The number of children so reclaimed was negligible. Leaving a child at a foundling hospital did not guarantee its survival. Again, to cite the situation in Paris, only about 10 per cent of all abandoned children lived to the age of ten years.

Despite all of these perils of early childhood, children did grow up and come of age across Europe. The world of the child may not have received the kind of attention that it does today, but in the course of the eighteenth century the seeds of that modern sensibility were sown. Particularly among the upper classes new interest arose in the education of children. As economic skills became more demanding, literacy became more valuable, and there was a marked improvement in literacy during the century. However, in most areas education remained firmly in the hands of the churches. The overwhelming majority of the European population remained illiterate. It was not until the late nineteenth century that the world of childhood and the process of education became inextricably linked. Then children would be reared to become members of a national citizenry. In the old regime they were reared to make their contribution to the economy of their parents' family and then to set up their own household.

The Land and Its Tillers 563

SOCIETY AND
ECONOMY
UNDER THE
OLD REGIME
IN THE
EIGHTEENTH
CENTURY

Land constituted the economic basis of eighteenth-century life. Well over three-fourths of all Europeans lived in the country, and few of these people ever traveled more than a few miles from their birthplace. With the exception of the nobility and the wealthier nonaristocratic landowners, the dwellers on the land were poor. By any modern standard their lives were difficult. They lived in various modes of economic and social dependency, exploitation, and vulnerability.

Peasants and Serfs

The major forms of rural social dependency related directly to the land. Those who worked the land were subject to immense influence

Eighteenth-century France had some of the best roads in the world, but they were often built with forced labor. French peasants were required to work for part of each year on such projects. This system, called the corvée, *was not abolished until the French Revolution in 1789. [Giraudon]*

and in some cases direct control by the landowners. This situation prevailed in differing degrees for free peasants, such as English tenants and most French cultivators, and for the serfs of Germany, Austria, and Russia, who were legally bound to a particular plot of land and a particular lord. In all cases the class that owned most of the land also controlled the local government and the courts. For example, in Great Britain all farmers and smaller tenants had the legal rights of English citizens. However, the justices of the peace who presided over the county courts and who could call out the local militia were always substantial landowners, as were the members of Parliament, who made the laws.

A Commission of Inquiry Describes the Burden of Bohemian Serfs

Over the course of her reign the Habsburg Empress Maria Theresa became increasingly concerned about the plight of serfs in her various domains. By the 1760s she would have abolished serfdom except for the strong resistance of the landlords. However, she did order an official Commission of Enquiry into the situation of serfs in Bohemia. The Commission reported in June 1769 and included the following comments in its report. Robot *is the Slavonic term for payments of compulsory labor by serfs to landlords.*

The *robot* give rise to continual vexations. Even those nobles who have the best intentions are unable to protect their peasants, because their agents are rough, evil, violent and grasping. These burdens are terrifyingly heavy, and it is not surprising that the peasants try to evade them by every means. In consequence of the arbitrary allocation of the *robot*, the peasants live in a condition of real slavery; they become savage and brutalized, and cultivate the lands in their charge badly. . . . In their ruinous huts, the parents sleep on straw, the children naked on the wide shelves of earthenware stoves; they never wash, which promotes the spread of epidemics; there are no doctors to look after them. . . . Even their personal effects are not safe from the greed of the great lords. If they own a good horse, the lord forces them to sell it to him. . . . In many places the serfs are forced to buy sick sheep from their lord at an arbitrarily fixed price. Implements of torture are set up in every village market square, or in front of the castle; recalcitrant peasants are thrown into irons, they are forced to sit astride a sharp wooden horse, which cuts deeply into their flesh; stones are hung on their legs; for the most trifling offence they are given fifty strokes of the rod; the serf who arrives late for his *robot*, be it only half an hour, is beaten half-dead. Many flee into Prussia to escape this reign of terror; there are hundreds of huts which their occupants have abandoned because they threatened to collapse and they had not the means to repair them. In other places the thatches have been taken off to feed the horses for lack of fodder, because these wretched creatures are forbidden to gather leaves in the forest for fear of their disturbing the game. Even when the harvest has been good they are obliged to ask for seed from their lord, and he sells it them at an extortionate price. The big landlords drive away the Jews, who make loans on better terms. . . . The Kingdom of Bohemia is like a statue which is collapsing because its pedestal has been taken away, because all the charges of the Kingdom are born by the peasants, who are the sole taxpayers.

C. A. *Macartney,* The Habsburg and Hohenzollern Dynasties in the Seventeenth and Eighteenth Centuries *(New York: Walker and Company, 1970), pp. 173–174.*

565

SOCIETY AND
ECONOMY
UNDER THE
OLD REGIME
IN THE
EIGHTEENTH
CENTURY

OBLIGATIONS OF PEASANTS The intensity of landlord power increased as one moved from west to east. In France the situation differed somewhat from province to province. Most French peasants owned some land, but there were a few serfs. However, nearly all peasants were subject to certain feudal dues, called *banalités*. These included the required use-for-payment of the lord or seigneur's mill to grind grain and his oven to bake bread. The seigneur could also require a certain number of days each year of the peasant's labor. This practice of forced labor was termed the *corvée*. Because even landowning French peasants rarely possessed enough land to support their families, they were also subject to feudal dues attached to the plots of land they rented. In Prussia and Austria, despite attempts by the monarchies late in the century to improve the lot of the serfs, the landlords continued to exercise almost complete control over them. In many of the Habsburg lands law and custom required the serfs to provide service, or *robot*, to the lords.

Moreover, throughout continental Europe, in addition to these feudal services, the burden of state taxation fell on the tillers of the soil. Many peasants, serfs, and other agricultural laborers were forced to undertake supplemental work to raise the cash required to pay the tax collector. Through various legal privileges and the ability to demand further concessions from the monarchs, the landlords escaped the payment of numerous taxes. They also presided over the manorial courts.

The condition of the serfs was the worst in Russia. The Russian custom of reckoning one's wealth by the number of "souls" (that is, male serfs) owned rather than by the acreage possessed reveals the contrast. The serfs were, in effect, regarded merely as economic commodities. Russian landlords could demand as many as six days a week of labor. Like Prussian and Austrian landlords they enjoyed the right to punish their serfs. On their own authority alone they could even exile a serf to Siberia. The serfs had no legal recourse against the orders and whims of their lords. There was actually little difference between Russian serfdom and slavery.

PEASANT REBELLIONS The Russian monarchy itself contributed to the degradation of the serfs. Peter the Great gave whole villages to favored nobles. Later in the century Catherine the Great (1762–1796) confirmed the authority of the nobles over their serfs in exchange for the political cooperation of the landowners. The situation in Russia led to considerable unrest. There were well over fifty peasant revolts between 1762 and 1769. These culminated between 1773 and 1775 in Pugachev's rebellion, during which all of southern Russian experienced intense unrest. Emelyan Pugachev (1726–1775) promised the serfs land of their own and freedom from their lords. The rebellion was brutally suppressed. Thereafter, any thought of liberalizing or improving the condition of the serfs was set aside for a generation.

Pugachev's was the greatest rebellion in Russian history and the largest peasant uprising of the eighteenth century. Smaller peasant revolts or disturbances occurred outside Russia. Rebellions took place in Bohemia in 1775,

Emelyan Pugachev (1726–1775) led the largest peasant revolt in Russian history. Here in a contemporary propaganda picture he is shown in chains. An inscription in Russian and German was printed below the picture discussing the evil of revolution and insurrection. [Bildarchiv Preussischer Kulturbesitz.]

Catherine the Great Issues a Proclamation Against Pugachev

Against a background of long-standing human degradation, and ever-increasing landowner authority, the greatest serf rebellion in Russian history was led from 1773 to 1775 by a Don Cossack named Emelyan Pugachev. Empress Catherine the Great's proclamation of 1773 argues that he was alienating the serfs from their natural and proper allegiance to her and their masters.

By the grace of God, we Catherine II . . . make known to our faithful subjects, that we have learnt, with the utmost indignation and extreme affliction, that a certain Cossack, a deserter and fugitive from the Don, named Emelyan Pugachev, after having traversed Poland, has been collecting, for some time past, in the districts that border on the river Irghis, in the government of Orenburg, a troop of vagabonds like himself; that he continues to commit in those parts all kinds of excesses, by inhumanly depriving the inhabitants of their possessions, and even of their lives. . . .

In a word, there is not a man deserving of the Russian name, who does not hold in abomination the odious and insolent lie by which Pugachev fancies himself able to seduce and to deceive persons of a simple and credulous disposition, by promising to free them from the bonds of submission, and obedience to their sovereign, as if the Creator of the universe had established human societies in such a manner as that they can subsist without an intermediate authority between the sovereign and the people.

Nevertheless, as the insolence of this vile refuse of the human race is attended with consequences pernicious to the provinces adjacent to that district; as the report of the flagrant enormities which he has committed, may affright those persons who are accustomed to imagine the misfortunes of others as ready to fall upon them, and as we watch with indefatigable care over the tranquility of our faithful subjects, we inform them . . . that we have taken . . . such measures as are the best adapted to stifle the sedition. . . .

We trust . . . that every true son of the country will unremittedly fulfill his duty, of the contributing to the maintenance of good order and of public tranquility, by preserving himself from the snares of seduction, and by discharging his obedience to his lawful sovereign.

William Tooke, Life of Catherine II, Empress of Russia, *4th ed., Vol. 2 (London: T. N. Longman and O. Rees, 1800), pp. 460–461 (spelling modernized).*

in Transylvania in 1784, in Moravia in 1786, and in Austria in 1789. Revolts in western Europe were almost nonexistent, but England experienced numerous local enclosure riots. Rural rebellions were violent, but the peasants and serfs normally directed their wrath against property rather than persons. The rebels usually sought to reassert traditional or customary rights against practices that they perceived as innovations. Their targets were carefully chosen and included unfair pricing, onerous new or increased feudal dues, changes in methods of payment or land use, unjust officials, or extraordinarily brutal overseers and landlords. In this respect the peasant revolts were quite conservative in nature.

The main goal of peasant society was a stability that would ensure the local food supply. In western Europe most rural society was organized into villages; on about half of the land, the owners of individual plots or strips would decide communally what crops would be planted. In eastern Europe, with its great estates of hundreds or thousands of acres, the landlords decided how to use the land. In either case the tillers resisted changes that might endanger the sure supply of food, which they generally believed to be promised by traditional cultivation.

However, throughout the eighteenth century landlords across the Continent began to search for higher profits from their holdings. They embraced innovation in order to increase their own prosperity. They commercialized agriculture and thereby challenged the traditional peasant ways of production. Peasant revolts and disturbances often resulted. The governments of Europe, hungry for new taxes and dependent on the goodwill of the nobility, used their armies and militias to smash the peasants who defended the past. In certain areas, such as the Low Countries and parts of Germany, the peasants themselves began to innovate so that they could more easily raise the cash they needed for tax payments.

567

SOCIETY AND
ECONOMY
UNDER THE
OLD REGIME
IN THE
EIGHTEENTH
CENTURY

The Revolution in Agriculture

Even more basic than the social dependency of peasants and small tenant farmers was their dependency on the productiveness of nature. The quantity and quality of the annual grain harvest was the most fundamental fact in their lives. On the Continent bread was the primary

Turgot Describes the Results of Poor Harvests in France

Failure of the grain crop and other plantings could bring both hunger and social disruption during the eighteenth century. Anne Robert Jacques Turgot (1727–1781), who later became finance minister of France, emphasized the role of private charity and government policy in relieving the suffering. His description, written in 1769, also provides a brief survey of the diet of the French peasant.

Everyone has heard of the terrible dearth that has just afflicted this generality [a local administrative district]. The harvest of 1769 in every respect proved to be one of the worst in the memory of man. The dearths of 1709 and 1739 were incomparably less cruel. To the loss of the greatest part of the rye was added the total loss of the chestnuts, of the buckwheat, and of the Spanish wheat—cheap food stuffs with which the peasant sustained himself habitually a great part of the year, reserving as much as he could of his corn [grain] in order to sell it to the inhabitants of the towns. . . . The people could exist only by exhausting their resources, by selling at a miserable price their articles of furniture and even their clothes. Many of the inhabitants have been obliged to disperse themselves through other provinces to seek work or to beg, leaving their wives and children to the charity of the parishes. It has been necessary for the public authority to require the proprietors and inhabitants in better circumstances in each parish to assess themselves for the relief of the poor people; nearly a fourth of the population is dependent upon charitable contributions. After these melancholy sufferings which the province has already undergone, and with the reduced condition in which it was left by the dearth of last year, even had the harvest of the present year been a good one, the poverty of the inhabitants would have necessitated the greatest efforts to be made for their relief. But we have now to add the dismal fact of our harvest being again deficient. . . .

W. W. Stephens (Ed.), The Life and Writings of Turgot (London: Longmans, Green, 1895), p. 50.

component of the diet of the lower classes. The food supply was never certain, and the farther east one traveled, the more uncertain it became. Failure of the harvest meant not only hardship but actual death from either outright starvation or protracted debility. Quite often people living in the countryside encountered more difficulty finding food than did city-dwellers, whose local government usually stored reserve supplies of grain.

Poor harvests also played havoc with prices. Smaller supplies or larger demand raised grain prices. Even small increases in the cost of food could exert heavy pressure on peasant or artisan families. If prices increased sharply, many of those families fell back on poor relief from their local municipality or county or the Church. What made the situation of food supply and prices so difficult was the peasants' sense of helplessness before the whims of nature and the marketplace.

Over the course of the century, historians now believe, there occurred a slow but steady inflation of bread prices, spurred largely by population growth. This inflation put pressure on all of the poor. The prices rose faster than urban wages and brought no appreciable advantage to the very small peasant producer. On

Jethro Tull's wheat drill was one of the major inventions that allowed agricultural production to increase. It was a device to plant wheat more efficiently. [Mary Evans Picture Library]

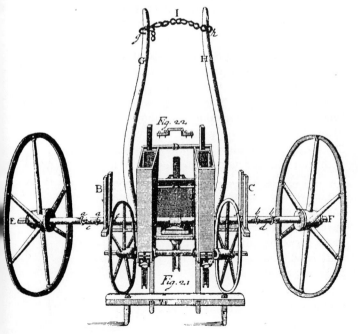

the other hand, the rise in grain prices benefited landowners and those wealthier peasants who had surplus grain to sell.

NEW CROPS AND NEW METHODS

The increasing price of grain presented landlords with an opportunity to improve their incomes and lifestyle. To those ends they began a series of innovations in farm production that became known as the *agricultural revolution*.

This movement began during the sixteenth and seventeenth centuries in the Low Countries, where the pressures of the growing population and the shortage of land required changes in cultivation. Dutch landlords and farmers devised better ways to build dykes and to drain land so that they could farm more extensive areas. They also experimented with new crops, such as clover and turnips, that would increase the supply of animal fodder and restore the soil. These improvements became so famous that early in the seventeenth century Cornelius Vermuyden, a Dutch drainage engineer, was hired in England to drain thousands of acres of land around Cambridge.

The methods that the Dutch farmers had pioneered were extensively adopted in England during the early eighteenth century. The major agricultural innovations undertaken by the English included new methods of farming, new crops, and new modes of landholding, all of which eventually led to greater productivity. This advance in food production was necessary for the development of an industrial society. It ensured adequate food for people living in cities and freed agricultural labor for industrial production. The changing modes of agriculture sponsored by the landlords undermined the assumptions of traditional peasant production. Farming now took place not only for the local food supply but also to assure the landlord a handsome profit. The latter goal meant that the landlords began to exert new pressures on their tenants and serfs.

Landlords in Great Britain during the eighteenth century provided the most striking examples of the agricultural improvement. They originated almost no genuinely new methods of farming, but they provided leadership in popularizing ideas developed in the previous century either in the Low Countries or in England. Some of these landlords and agricultural innovators became very famous. For example, Jethro Tull (1674–1741) contributed a willingness to experiment and to finance the experiments of others. Many of his ideas, such as the refusal to use manure as fertilizer, were wrong. Others, however, such as using iron plows to overturn earth more deeply and planting wheat by a drill rather than by casting, were excellent. His methods permitted land to be cultivated for longer periods without having to be left fallow.

Charles "Turnip" Townsend (1674–1738) encouraged even more important innovations. He learned from the Dutch how to cultivate sandy soil with fertilizers. He also instituted crop rotation, using wheat, turnips, barley, and clover. This new system of rotation abolished the fallow field and replaced it with a field sown in a crop that both replaced soil nutrients and supplied animal fodder. The additional fodder meant that more livestock could be raised. The larger number of animals increased the quantity of manure available as fertilizer for the grain crops. Consequently, in the long run, there was more food for both animals and human beings.

A third British agricultural improver was Robert Bakewell (1725–1795), who pioneered new methods of animal breeding that produced more and better animals and more milk and meat.

These and other innovations received widespread discussion in the works of Arthur Young (1741–1820), who edited the *Annals of Agriculture*. In 1793 he became secretary of the British Board of Agriculture. Young traveled widely across Europe, and his books are among the most important documents of life during the second half of the eighteenth century.

ENCLOSURE REPLACES OPEN-FIELD METHOD Many of the agriculture innovations, which were adopted only very slowly, were incompatible with the existing organization of land in Britain. Small cultivators who lived in village communities still farmed most of the soil. Each farmer tilled an assortment of unconnected strips. The two- or three-field systems of rotation left large portions of land annually fallow and unproductive. Animals grazed on the common land in the summer and on the stubble of the harvest in the winter. Until at least the middle of the eighteenth century the decisions about what crops would be planted were made communally. The entire

system discouraged improvement and favored the poorer farmers, who needed the common land and stubble fields for their animals. The village method provided little possibility of expanding the pasture land to raise more animals that would, in turn, produce more manure, which could be used for fertilizer. Thus, the methods of traditional production aimed at a steady but not a growing supply of food.

In 1700 approximately half the arable land in Britain was farmed by this open-field method. By the second half of the century the rising price of wheat encouraged landlords to consolidate or enclose their lands to increase production. The enclosures were intended to use land more rationally and to achieve greater commercial profits. The process involved the fencing of common lands, the reclamation of previously untilled waste, and the transformation of strips into block fields. These procedures brought turmoil to the economic and social life of the countryside. Riots often ensued.

Because many British farmers either owned their strips or rented them in a manner that amounted to ownership, the larger landlords had usually to resort to parliamentary acts to legalize the enclosure of the land, which they owned but rented to the farmers. Because the large landowners controlled Parliament, there was little difficulty in passing such measures. Between 1761 and 1792 almost 500,000 acres were enclosed through parliamentary act, as compared with 75,000 acres between 1727 and 1760. In 1801 a general enclosure act streamlined the process.

The enclosures were at the time and have remained among historians a very controversial topic. They permitted the extension of both farming and innovation. In that regard they increased food production on larger agricultural units. At the same time they disrupted the small traditional communities. They forced off the land some independent farmers, who had needed the common pasturage, and very poor cottagers, who had lived on the reclaimed waste land. However, the enclosures did not depopulate the countryside. In some counties where the enclosures took place, the population increased. New soil had come into production, and services subsidiary to farming also expanded.

The enclosures did not create the labor force for the British Industrial Revolution. What the enclosures most conspicuously displayed was

or alleviation of rents during depressed periods. However, as the landlords became increasingly concerned about profits, they began to leave the peasants to the mercy of the marketplace.

LIMITED IMPROVEMENTS IN EASTERN EUROPE Improving agriculture tended to characterize farm production west of the Elbe. Dutch farming was quite efficient. In France, despite the efforts of the government to improve agriculture, enclosures were restricted. Yet there was much discussion in France about improving agricultural methods. These new procedures benefited the ruling classes because better agriculture increased their incomes and assured a larger food supply, which tended to discourage social unrest.

In Prussia, Austria, Poland, and Russia only very limited agricultural improvement took place. Nothing in the relationship of the serfs to their lords encouraged innovation. In eastern Europe the chief method of increasing production was to extend farming to previously untilled lands. The management of farms was usually under the direction of the landlords or their agents rather than of the villages. By extending tillage, the great landlords sought to squeeze more labor from their serfs rather than greater productivity from the soil. As in the west, the goal was increased profits for the landlords. But on the whole, east European landlords were much less ambitious and successful. The only significant nutritional gain achieved through their efforts was the introduction of maize and the potato. Livestock production did not increase significantly.

Population Expansion

The assault on human dependence on nature through improved farming was both a cause and a result of an immense expansion in the population of Europe. The population explosion with which the entire world must contend today seems to have had its origins in the eighteenth century. Before this time Europe's population had experienced dramatic increases, but plagues, wars, or harvest failures had in time decimated the increase. Beginning in the second quarter of the eighteenth century, the population began to grow without decimation.

Our best estimates suggest that in 1700

Part of the commercialization of agriculture that occurred in the eighteenth century was the "farming" of forests for saleable timber. This was particularly lucrative in Britain, Scandinavia, and parts of France, where there was a large demand for lumber for ship building. [British Library]

the introduction of the entrepreneurial or capitalistic attitude of the urban merchant into the countryside. This commercialization of agriculture, which spread from Britain very slowly across the Continent during the next century, strained the parental relationship between the governing and governed classes. Previously the landlords had somewhat looked after the welfare of the lower orders through price controls

Europe's population, excluding the European provinces of the Ottoman Empire, stood between 100 million and 120 million people. By 1800 the figures had risen to almost 190 million, and by 1850 to 260 million. The population of England and Wales rose from 6 million in 1750 to over 10 million in 1800. France grew from 18 million in 1715 to approximately 26 million in 1789. Russia's population increased from 19 million in 1722 to 29 million in 1766. Such extraordinary, sustained growth put new demands on all resources and considerable pressure on existing social organization.

The population expansion occurred across the Continent in both the country and the cities. Only a limited consensus exists about the causes of this growth. There was a clear decline in the death rate. There were fewer wars and somewhat fewer epidemics in the eighteenth century. Hygiene and sanitation also improved. Better medical knowledge and techniques were once thought to have contributed to the decline in deaths. This factor is now discounted because the more important medical advances came after the initial population explosion or would not have contributed directly to it.

Rather, changes in the food supply itself may have provided the chief factor that allowed the population growth to be sustained. The improved and expanding grain production made one contribution. Another and even more important modification was the cultivation of the potato. This tuber was a product of the New World and came into widespread European production during the eighteenth century. On a single acre enough potatoes could be raised to feed one peasant's family for an entire year. With this more certain food supply, more children could be reared, and more could survive.

This impact of the population explosion can hardly be overestimated. It created new demands for food, goods, jobs, and services. It provided a new pool of labor. Traditional modes of production and living had to be revised. More people came to live in the countryside than could find employment there. Migration increased. There were also more people who might become socially and politically discontented. And because the population growth fed on itself, all of these pressures and demands continued to increase. The society and the social practices of the old regime literally outgrew their traditional bounds.

The second half of the eighteenth century witnessed the beginning of the industrialization of the European economy. The Industrial Revolution constituted the achievement of sustained economic growth. Previously production had been limited. The economy of a province or a country might grow, but it soon reached a plateau. However, since the late eighteenth century the economy of Europe has managed to expand relatively uninterrupted. Depressions and recessions have been temporary, and even during such economic downturns the Western economy has continued to grow.

At considerable social cost, industrialization has made possible more goods and more services than ever before in human history. Industrialization in Europe eventually overcame the economy of scarcity. The new means of production demanded new kinds of skills, new discipline in work, and a large labor force. The goods produced met immediate consumer demand and also created new demands. In the long run, industrialization clearly raised the standard of living and overcame the poverty that had been experienced by the overwhelming majority of Europeans who lived during the eighteenth century and earlier. Industrialization provided human beings greater control over the forces of nature than they had ever known before. The wealth produced by industrialization upset the political structures of the old regime and led to reforms. The economic elite of the emerging industrial society would eventually challenge the political dominance of the aristocracy.

Industrial Leadership of Great Britain

Great Britain was the home of the Industrial Revolution and, until the middle of the nineteenth century, maintained the industrial leadership of Europe. Several factors contributed to the early start in Britain. The nation constituted the single largest free-trade area in Europe. The British possessed good roads and waterways without internal tolls or other internal trade barriers. The country was endowed with rich deposits of coal and iron ore. The political structure was stable, and prop-

This shows the pithead of an eighteenth-century coal mine in England. The machinery on the left included a steam engine that powered equipment either to bring the mined coal to the surface or to pump water from the mine. Britain's large supply of coal was one of the contributing factors to its early industrialization. [Walker Art Gallery, Liverpool]

erty was absolutely secure. Taxation was not especially heavy. In addition to the existing domestic consumer demand, the British economy also benefited from demand from the colonies in North America.

Finally, British society was relatively mobile by the standards of the time. Persons who had money or could earn money could rise socially. The British aristocracy would receive into its midst people who had amassed very large fortunes. No one of these factors preordained the British advance toward industrialism. However, the combination of them plus the progressive state of British agriculture provided the nation with the marginal advantage in the creation of a new mode of economic production.

While this economic development was occurring, people did not call it a *revolution*. That term came to be applied to the British economic phenomena only after the French Revolution. The continental writers observed that what had taken place in Britain was the economic equivalent of the political events in France; hence the concept of an *industrial revolution*. It was revolutionary less in its speed, which was on the whole rather slow, than in its implications for the future of European society.

New Methods of Textile Production

Although eighteenth-century society was primarily devoted to agriculture, manufacturing permeated the countryside. The same peasants who tilled the land in spring and summer often spun thread or wove textiles in the winter.

573

SOCIETY AND
ECONOMY
UNDER THE
OLD REGIME
IN THE
EIGHTEENTH
CENTURY

Under what is termed the *domestic* or *putting-out system*, agents of urban textile merchants took wool or other unfinished fibers to the homes of peasants, who spun it into thread. The agent then transported the thread to other peasants, who wove it into the finished product. The merchant sold the wares. In literally thousands of peasant cottages from Ireland to Austria, there stood either a spinning wheel or a handloom. Sometimes the spinners or weavers owned their own equipment, but more often than not, by the middle of the century the merchant capitalist owned the machinery as well as the raw material.

What must be kept constantly in mind is the rather surprising fact that eighteenth-century industrial development took place within a rural setting. The peasant family living in a one- or two-room cottage was the basic unit of production rather than the factory. The family economy, rather than the industrial factory economy, characterized the century.

The domestic system of textile production was a basic feature of this family economy. However, by mid-century a series of production bottlenecks had developed within the domestic system. The demand for cotton textiles was growing more rapidly than production. This demand arose particularly in Great Britain, where there existed a large domestic demand for cotton textiles from the growing population. There was a similar foreign demand on British production from its colonies in North America. It was in response to this consumer demand for cotton textiles that the most famous inventions of the Industrial Revolution were devised.

THE SPINNING JENNY   Cotton textile weavers had the technical capacity to produce the quantity of fabric that was in demand. However, the spinners did not possess the equipment to produce as much thread as the weavers needed and could use. This imbalance had been created during the 1730s by James Kay's invention of the flying shuttle, which increased the productivity of the weavers. Thereafter, various groups of manufacturers and merchants offered prizes for the invention of a machine to eliminate this bottleneck.

About 1765 James Hargreaves (d. 1778) invented the spinning jenny. Initially this machine allowed 16 spindles of thread to be spun, but by the close of the century its capacity had been increased to as many as 120 spindles.

THE WATER FRAME   The spinning jenny broke the bottleneck between the productive capacity of the spinners and the weavers, but it was still a piece of machinery that was used in the cottage. The invention that took cotton textile manufacture out of the home and put it

Under the domestic *or putting-out system,* urban textile merchants took unfinished fiber to peasants, who then spun it into thread or wove it into cloth in their homes, as this English family is doing. [Library of Congress]

Josiah Tucker Praises the New Use of Machinery in England

The extensive use of recently invented machines made the Industrial Revolution possible in England. This passage from a 1757 travel guide illustrates how contemporaries regarded the application of machines to various manufacturing processes as new and exciting.

Few countries are equal, perhaps none excel, the English in the number of contrivances of their Machines to abridge labour. Indeed, the Dutch are superior to them in the use and application of Wind Mills for sawing Timber, expressing Oil, making Paper and the like. But in regard to Mines and Metals of all sorts, the English are uncommonly dexterous in their contrivance of the mechanic Powers; some being calculated for landing the Ores out of the Pits, such as Cranes and Horse Engines; others for draining off superfluous Water, such as Water Wheels and Steam Engines; others again for easing the Expense of Carriage such as machines to run on inclined planes or Roads downhill with wooden frames, in order to carry many Tons of Material at a Time. And to these must be added the various sorts of Levers used in various processes; also the Brass Battery works, the Slitting Mills, Plate and Flatting Mills, and those for making Wire of Different Fineness. Yet all these, curious as they may seem, are little more than Preparations or Introductions for further Operations. Therefore, when we still consider that at Birmingham, Wolverhampton, Sheffield and other manufacturing Places, almost every Master Manufacturer hath a new Invention of his own, and is daily improving on those of others; we may aver with some confidence that those parts of England in which these things are seen exhibit a specimen of practical mechanics scarce to be paralleled in any part of the world.

Josiah Tucker, Instructions to Travellers *(London: Privately Printed, 1757), p. 20.*

into the factory was Richard Arkwright's (1732–1792) water frame, patented in 1769. It was a water-powered device designed to permit the production of a purely cotton fabric rather than a cotton fabric containing linen fiber for durability. Eventually Arkwright lost his patent rights, and other manufacturers were able to use his invention freely. As a result, numerous factories sprang up in the countryside near streams that provided the necessary waterpower. From the 1780s onward the cotton industry could meet an ever-expanding demand. In the last two decades of the century cotton output increased by 800 per cent over the production of 1780. By 1815 cotton composed 40 per cent of the value of British domestic exports, and by 1830 just over 50 per cent.

The Industrial Revolution had commenced in earnest by the 1780s, but the full economic and social ramifications of this unleashing of human productive capacity were not really felt until the early nineteenth century. The expansion of industry and the incorporation of new inventions often occurred rather slowly. For example, Edmund Cartwright (1743–1822) invented the power loom for machine weaving in the late 1780s. Yet not until the 1830s were there more power-loom weavers than hand-loom weavers in Britain. Nor did all of the social ramifications of industrialism appear immediately. The first cotton mills used waterpower, were located in the country, and rarely employed more than two dozen workers. Not until the late-century application of the steam engine, perfected by James Watt (1736–1819) in 1769, to the running of textile machinery could factories easily be located in or near existing urban centers. The steam engine not only vastly increased and regularized the available energy but also made possible the combination of urbanization and industrialization.

The Steam Engine

The new technology in textile manufacture vastly increased cotton production and revolutionized a major consumer industry. However, the invention that more than any other permitted industrialization to grow on itself and to expand into one area of production after another was the steam engine. This machine provided for the first time in human history a steady and essentially unlimited source of inanimate power. Unlike engines powered by water or the wind, the steam engine, driven by the burning of coal, was a portable source of industrial power that did not fail or falter as the seasons of the year changed. Unlike human power or animal power the steam engine depended on mineral energy that did not tire over the course of a day. Finally, the steam engine could be applied to a very large number of industrial and, eventually, transportation uses.

Manchester's Calico Printers Protest the Use of New Machinery

The introduction of the new machines associated with the Industrial Revolution stirred much protest. Machine labor was replacing human labor; machines were duplicating the skills of laborers. This situation could mean the loss of jobs. It also brought about the loss of status for workers whose chief means of livelihood lay in their possession of those displaced and now mechanized skills. The following letter was sent anonymously to a Manchester manufacturer by English workers. It indicates the outrage of those workers, the modes of intimidation they were willing to use as threats, and their own economic fears.

Mr. Taylor, If you dont discharge James Hobson from the House of Correction we will burn your House about your Ears for we have sworn to stand by one another and you must immediately give over any more Mashen Work for we are determined there shall be no more of them made use of in the Trade and it will be madness for you to contend with the Trade as we are combined by Oath to fix Prices we can afford to pay him a Guinea Week and not hurt the fund if you was to keep him there till Dumsday therefore mind you comply with the above or by God we will keep our Words with you we will make some rare Bunfires in this Countey and at your Peril to call any more Meetings mind that we will make the Mosney Pepel shake in their Shoes we are determined to destroy all Sorts of Masheens for Printing in the Kingdom for there is more hands then is work for so no more from the ingerd Gurnemen Rember we are a great number sworn nor you must not advertise the Men that you say run away from you when your il Usage was the Cause of their going we will punish you for that our Meetings are legal for we want nothing but what is honest and to work for selvs and familers and you want to starve us but it is better for you and a few more which we have marked to die then such a Number of Pore Men and their famerles to be starved.

London Gazette, 1786, p. 36, as reprinted in Douglas Hay (Ed.), Albion's Fatal Tree (New York: Pantheon Books, 1975), p. 318.

Richard Arkwright's (1732–1792) water frame led to the production of purely cotton fabric. This is his cotton mill in Derbyshire, England, in the 1780s. [Art Resource]

This improved steam engine was built in 1784 by James Watt. Pressure in the cylinder on the left forces the beam upwards, while the descending arm sets the large flywheel in continuous motion. Instead of just pumping, this improved engine could be used to drive every sort of machine. [Science Museum, London]

The first practical engine using steam power had been the invention of Thomas Newcomen in the early eighteenth century. The piston of this device was moved when the steam that had been induced into the cylinder condensed, causing the piston to fall. The Newcomen machine was very large. It was inefficient in its use of energy because both the condenser and the cylinder were heated, and it was practically untransportable. Despite these problems English mine operators employed the Newcomen machines to pump water out of coal and tin mines. By the third quarter of the eighteenth century almost a hundred Newcomen machines were operating in the mining districts of England.

During the 1760s James Watt, a Scottish engineer and machine maker, began to experiment with a model of a Newcomen machine at the University of Glasgow. He gradually understood that if the condenser were separated from the piston and the cylinder, much greater efficiency would result. In 1769 he patented his new invention, but transforming his idea into application presented difficulties. His design required exceedingly precise metalwork. Watt soon found a partner in Matthew Boulton, a toy manufacturer in Birmingham, the city with the most skilled metalworkers in Britain. Watt and Boulton, in turn, consulted with John Wilkinson, a cannon manufacturer, to find ways to drill the precise metal cylinders required by Watt's design. In 1776 the Watt steam engine found its first commercial application pumping water from mines in Cornwall.

The use of the steam engine spread slowly because until 1800 Watt retained the exclusive patent rights. He was also reluctant to make further changes in his invention that would permit the engine to operate more rapidly. Boulton eventually persuaded him to make modifications and improvements. These allowed the engines to be used not only for pumping but also for running cotton mills. By the early nineteenth century the steam engine had become the prime mover for all industry. With its application to ships and then to wagons on iron rails, the steam engine also revolutionized transportation.

Iron Production

The manufacture of high-quality iron has been basic to modern industrial development. It constitutes the chief element of all heavy industry and land or sea transport. Iron has also been the material out of which most productive machinery itself has been manufactured. During the early eighteenth century British ironmakers produced somewhat less than twenty-five thousand tons annually. Three factors held back the production of the metal. Charcoal rather than coke was used to smelt the ore. Charcoal, which is derived from wood, was becoming a scarce commodity, and it did not burn at as high a temperature as coke, which is derived from coal. Second, until the perfection of the steam engine, insufficient blasts could be achieved in the furnaces. Finally, the demand for iron was limited. The elimination of the first two problems eliminated the third.

In the course of the century British ironmakers began to use coke, and the steam engine provided new power for the blast furnaces. Coke was an abundant fuel because of Britain's large coal deposits. The existence of the steam

---

Major Inventions in the Textile-Manufacturing Revolution

1733	James Kay's flying shuttle
1765	James Hargreaves' spinning jenny (patent 1770)
1769	James Watt's steam engine patent
1769	Richard Arkwright's waterframe patent
1787	Edmund Cartwright's power loom

---

engine both improved iron production and increased the demand for iron.

In 1784 Henry Cort (1740–1800) introduced a new puddling process, that is, a new method for melting and stirring the molten ore. Cort's process allowed more slag (the impurities that bubbled to the top of the molten metal) to be removed and a purer iron to be produced. Cort also developed a rolling mill that continuously shaped the still-molten metal into bars, rails, or other forms. Previously the metal had been pounded into these forms.

All of these innovations achieved a better, more versatile product at a lower cost. The demand for iron grew as its price became lower. By the early years of the nineteenth century British iron production amounted to over a million tons annually. The lower cost of iron, in turn, lowered the cost of steam engines and allowed them to be used more widely.

The Aristocracy

Despite the emerging Industrial Revolution, the eighteenth century remained the age of the aristocracy. The nobility of every country was the single wealthiest sector of the population; possessed the widest degree of social, political, and economic power; and set the tone of polite society. Land continued to provide the aristocracy with its largest source of income, but the role of the aristocrat was not limited to the estate. The influence of aristocrats was felt in every area of life.

Varieties of Aristocratic Privilege

To be an aristocrat was a matter of birth and legal privilege. This much they had in common across the Continent. In almost every other respect they differed markedly from country to country.

BRITISH NOBILITY

BRITISH NOBILITY The smallest, wealthiest, best-defined, and most socially responsible aristocracy resided in Great Britain. It consisted of about four hundred families, whose eldest male member sat in the House of Lords. Through the corruptions of the electoral system these families also controlled a large number of seats in the House of Commons. The estates of the British nobility ranged from a few thousand to fifty thousand acres, from which they received their rents. The nobles owned approximately one fourth of all the arable land in the country. Increasingly the money of the aristocracy was being invested in commerce, canals, urban real estate, mines, and sometimes industrial ventures. Because only the eldest son inherited the title and the land, younger sons moved into commerce, the army, the professions, and the Church. The British landowners in the House of Commons levied taxes in Parliament and also paid taxes. They had almost no significant legal privileges, but their direct or indirect control of local government gave them immense political power and social influence. The aristocracy quite simply dominated the society and the politics of the English counties.

FRENCH NOBILITY The situation of the continental nobilities was less clear-cut. In France the nobility was divided between nobles of the sword and those of the robe. The former families enjoyed privileges deriving from military service; the latter had either gained their titles by serving in the bureaucracy or had purchased them. The two groups had frequently quarreled in the past but tended to cooperate during the eighteenth century to defend their common privileges.

The French nobility were also divided between those who held office or favor with the royal court at Versailles and those who did not. The court nobility reaped the immense wealth that could be gained from holding high offices. The noble hold on such offices intensified over the course of the century. By the late 1780s appointments to the Church, the army, and the bureaucracy, as well as other profitable positions, tended to go to the nobles already established in court circles. Whereas these well-connected aristocrats were quite rich, other nobles who lived in the provinces were often rather poor. These *hobereaux*, as the poverty-stricken nobles were called, were sometimes little or no better off than wealthy peasants.

Despite differences in rank, origin, and wealth, all French aristocrats enjoyed certain hereditary privileges that set them apart from the rest of society. They were exempt from many taxes. For example, most French nobles did not pay the *taille*, which was the basic tax of the old regime. The nobles were technically liable for payment of the *vingtième*, or the "twentieth," which resembled an income tax. However, by virtue of protests and legal procedures, the nobility rarely felt the entire weight of this tax. The nobles were not liable for the royal *corvées*, or labor donations, which fell on the peasants. In addition to these exemptions, the approximately 400,000 French nobles could collect feudal dues from their tenants and enjoyed hunting and fishing privileges denied their tenants.

EASTERN EUROPEAN NOBILITIES East of the Elbe River the character of the nobility became even more complicated and repressive. In Poland there were thousands of nobles, or *szlachta*, who after 1741 were entirely exempt from taxes. Until 1768 these Polish aristocrats possessed the right of life and death over their serfs. Most of the Polish nobility were relatively poor. The political power of the fragile Polish state resided in the few very rich nobles.

In Austria and Hungary the nobility continued to possess broad judicial powers over the peasantry through manorial courts.

In Prussia, after the accession of Frederick the Great in 1740, the position of the *Junker* nobles became much stronger. Frederick's various wars required the full support of his nobles. He drew his officers almost wholly from the *Junker* class. The bureaucracy was also increasingly composed of nobles. As in other parts of eastern Europe, the Prussian nobles enjoyed extensive judicial authority over the serfs.

In Russia the eighteenth century saw what amounted to the creation of the nobility. Peter the Great's linking of state service and noble social status through the Table of Ranks (1722) established among Russian nobles a self-conscious class identity that had not previously existed. Thereafter they stood united in

579

SOCIETY AND
ECONOMY
UNDER THE
OLD REGIME
IN THE
EIGHTEENTH
CENTURY

The Earl of Chesterfield Advises His Son about Good Behavior

In the middle of the eighteenth century the English Earl of Chesterfield wrote a long series of letters to his son. They were intended to instruct the young man on the manners that would be required for him to be accepted into aristocratic society. In this letter of October 19, 1748, the father wrote to his son about the art of polite conversation. In other parts of the letter not quoted here the Earl advises his son to avoid swearing and the use of oaths.

Having, in my last [letter], pointed out what sort of company you should keep, I will now give you some rules for your conduct in it. . . .

Talk often, but never long: in that cast, if you do not please, at least you are sure not to tire your hearers. . . .

Tell stories very seldom, and absolutely never but where they are very apt and very short. Omit every circumstance that is not material, and beware of digressions. To have frequent recourse to narrative betrays great want of imagination.

Never hold any body by the button, or the hand, in order to be heard out; for if people are not willing to hear you, you had much better hold your tongue than them. . . .

. . . .

Avoid as much as you can, in mixed companies, argumentative, polemical conversations; which though they should not, yet certainly do, indispose for a time, the contending parties towards each other; and if the controversy grows warm and noisy, endeavor to put an end to it, by some genteel levity or joke. . . .

Above all things, and upon all occasions, avoid speaking of yourself, if it possible. Such is the natural pride and vanity of our hearts, that it perpetually breaks out, even in the people of the best parts, in all the various modes and figures of the egotism. . . .

. . . .

Take care never to seem dark and mysterious; which is not only a very unamiable character, but a very suspicious one too; if you seem mysterious with others, they will be really so with you, and you will know nothing. . . .

Neither retail nor receive scandal willingly. . . .

Mimicry, which is the common and favourite amusement of little, low minds, is in the utmost contempt with great ones. It is the lowest and most illiberal of all buffoonery. . . .

I need not (I believe) advise you to adapt your conversation to the people you are conversing with: for I suppose you would not, without this caution, have talked upon the same subject, and in the same manner, to a minister of state, a bishop, a philosopher, a captain, and a woman. A man of the world must, like the Cameleon, be able to take very different hue; which is by no means a criminal or abject, but a necessary complaisance; for it relates only to manners and not to morals.

Charles Strachey (Ed.), The Letters of the Earl of Chesterfield to His Son *(New York and London, 1925), 1:280–285.*

their determination to resist compulsory state service. In 1736 Empress Ann reduced such service to a period of twenty-five years. In 1762 Peter III removed the liability for compulsory service entirely from the greatest nobles. In 1785, in the Charter of the Nobility, Catherine the Great granted an explicit legal definition of noble rights and privileges in exchange for assurances of voluntary state service from the nobility. The noble privileges included the right of transmitting noble status to one's wife and children, the judicial protection of noble rights and property, considerable power over the serfs, and exemption from personal taxes.

Aristocratic Resurgence

The Russian Charter of the Nobility constituted one aspect of the broader European-wide development termed the *aristocratic resurgence*. Throughout the century the various nobilities felt their social position and privileges threatened by the expanding power of the monarchies and the growing wealth of merchants, bankers, and other commercial groups. First, all nobilities attempted to preserve their exclusiveness by making entry into their ranks and institutions more difficult. Second, they pushed for exclusively noble appointments to the officer corps of the armies, the bureaucracies, the government ministries, and the Church. In that manner the nobles hoped to control the power of the monarchies.

On a third level, the nobles attempted to use the authority of existing aristocratically controlled institutions against the power of the monarchies. These institutions included the British Parliament and on the Continent the French courts, or *parlements;* the local aristocratic estates; and the provincial diets. Economically the aristocratic resurgence took the form of pressing the peasantry for higher rents or collecting long-forgotten feudal dues. There was a general tendency for the nobility to shore up its position by various appeals to traditional and often ancient privileges that had lapsed over the course of time. To contemporaries this aristocratic challenge to the monarchies and to the rising commercial classes constituted one of the most fundamental political facts of the day.

Aristocratic Protection of Self-Interest in the Countryside: The Case of the English Game Laws

Although the various aristocracies put new pressures on the monarchies during the eighteenth century, the chief area in which they sought to maintain themselves was in the countryside itself.

Landlords set traps to catch and injure persons who attempted to poach animals on their estates. The poachers were thus treated as little more than animals. [Mary Evans Picture Library]

One of the clearest examples of aristocratic domination of the countryside and of aristocratic manipulation of the law to its own advantage was English legislation in regard to the hunting of game.

Between 1671 and 1831 English landowners had the exclusive legal right to hunt game animals. These specifically included hares, partridges, pheasants, and moorfowl. Similar legislation covered other animals such as deer, the killing of which became a capital offense in the eighteenth century. By law, only persons owning a particular amount of landed property could hunt these animals. Excluded from the right to hunt were all persons renting land, wealthy city merchants who did not own land, and poor people in cities, villages, and the countryside. The poor were excluded because it was widely believed among the elite classes that allowing them to enjoy the sport of hunting would undermine necessary work habits. The city merchants were excluded in an attempt by the landed gentry in Parliament to give visible and legal demonstration of the superiority of landed wealth over commercial wealth. In other words, the various game laws were intended to uphold the status of the aristocracy and the landed gentry.

The game laws represent a prime example of class legislation: the gentry who benefited from the laws and whose parliamentary representatives had passed them also served as the local justices of the peace who administered the laws and imposed penalties for their violation. The justices of the peace could levy fines and even have poachers impressed into the army. Gentry could also take civil legal action against wealthier poachers, such as rich farmers who did not own land, and thus saddle those persons with immense legal fees. The gentry also took other actions. They employed gamekeepers to protect game from poachers. The gamekeepers were known to kill the dogs belonging to people suspected of poaching. By the middle of the century violent conflicts involving death were not uncommon as gamekeepers confronted poachers. Trapguns were devised to shoot poachers who tripped the hidden levers.

In response to these laws and practices, a small industry arose to circumvent them. Many poor local people living either on the estate or in a nearby village would kill game for food. They believed that the game actually belonged to the community, and this practice increased during economic hard times. In this regard poaching was one way for the poor to find food.

Even more important was the black market in game animals sustained by the demand of

Thomas Gainsborough (1728–1788) painted this portrait of the English gentry on its estates: Robert Andrews and His Wife. *Note the rifle and hunting dog, symbols of Andrews' status as a gentleman and landowner. By law only persons owning a particular amount of land could hunt game animals in England. [The National Gallery, London]*

urban people for this kind of luxury meat. Here there arose the possibility of poaching for profit, and indeed, the technical meaning of *poaching* was the stealing or killing of game for sale. Local people from both the countryside and the villages would steal the game and then sell it to middlemen called *higglers*. Later, coachmen took over this middleman function. The higglers and the coachmen would smuggle the game into the cities, where poulterers would sell it at a premium price. Everyone involved made a bit of money along the way. During the second half of the century English aristocrats began to construct large game preserves, which, in turn, became hunting grounds to organized gangs of poachers. These preserves became the occasion for great resentment among the countryside poor, who had lost their rights to communal land as a result of the enclosures.

Over the course of the eighteenth century the game laws became harsher. Penalties against poaching increased in the years after the outbreak of the French Revolution. During those same years the amount of poaching increased as the economic hardships of the war put a greater burden on poor people and as the demand for food in English cities grew along with their population. By the 1820s there were calls among landowners, as well as from reformers, for a change in the law. In 1831 the game laws were rewritten to make the landowners the possessors of the game but permitting them to allow other people to hunt it. Poaching continued, but the exclusive right of the landed classes to hunt game had ended.

Cities

Remarkable changes occurred in the pattern of city growth between 1500 and 1800. In 1500 within Europe (excluding Hungary and Russia) there were approximately 156 cities with a population greater than 10,000. Only 4 of those cities, Paris, Milan, Venice, and Naples, had populations larger than 100,000. By 1800 there existed approximately 363 cities of 10,000 or more inhabitants, and 17 of those had populations larger than 100,000. The percentage of the European population living in urban areas had risen from just over 5 per cent to just over 9 per cent. There had also occurred a major

shift in urban concentration from southern, Mediterranean Europe to the north.

Patterns of Preindustrial Urbanization

The eighteenth century witnessed a considerable growth of towns. The tumult of the day and the revolutions with which the century closed had a strong relationship to that urban expansion. London grew from about 700,000 inhabitants in 1700 to almost 1 million in 1800. By the time of the French Revolution the population of Paris stood over 500,000. Berlin's population tripled over the course of the century, reaching 170,000 in 1800. Saint Petersburg, founded in 1703, numbered over 250,000 inhabitants a century later. In addition to the growth of these capitals, the number of smaller urban units of 20,000–50,000 people increased considerably. However, this urban growth must be kept in perspective. Even in France and Great Britain probably somewhat less than 20 per cent of the population lived in cities. And the town of 10,000 inhabitants was much more common than the giant urban center.

These raw figures conceal significant changes that took place in how cities grew and how population distributed itself. A major time of urban development was the sixteenth century. This development was followed by a leveling off and even a decline in the seventeenth. New growth began in the early eighteenth century and became much accelerated in the late eighteenth and the early nineteenth centuries. Between 1500 and 1750 the major urban expansion took place within already-established and generally already-large cities. It was not a period of the emergence and growth of new cities. After 1750 the pattern changed with the birth of new cities and the rapid growth of already-existing smaller cities.

GROWTH OF CAPITALS AND PORTS
In particular, between 1600 and 1750, the urban areas that displayed the most growth and vigor were capitals and ports. This situation reflects the success of monarchical state building during those years and the consequent burgeoning of bureaucracies, armies, courts, and other groups who lived in the capitals. The growth of port cities, in turn, reflects the expansion of European overseas trade and most especially that of the Atlantic routes.

Nearly all of these urban conglomerates were nonindustrial cities. They grew and expanded for reasons other than being the location of factories or other large manufacturing establishments. Only Manchester in England and Lyons in France had experienced such industrial growth. Significant growth did not take place in the cases of industrial cities.

Furthermore, between 1600 and 1750, cities with populations of less than 40,000 inhabitants declined. These included older landlocked trading centers, medieval industrial cities, and ecclesiastical centers. They contributed less to the new political regimes, and the expansion of the putting-out system transferred much production that had once occurred in medieval cities into the countryside. Rural labor was cheaper than urban labor, and cities with concentrations of labor declined as the site of production was moved from the urban workshop into the country.

EMERGENCE OF NEW CITIES AND GROWTH OF SMALL TOWNS In the middle of the eighteenth century a new pattern emerged. The rate of growth of existing large cities declined. New cities began to emerge and existing smaller cities began to grow. Several factors were at work in the process, which Jan De Vries has termed "an urban growth from below."[2] First, there was the general overall population increase. Second, the early stages of the Industrial Revolution, particularly in Britain, occurred in the countryside and tended to aid the growth of smaller towns and cities located nearby the factories. Factory organization itself fostered new concentrations of population.

However, cities also grew where there was little industrialization. The reason for this growth would seem to have been the new prosperity of European agriculture. Greater agricultural production aided the growth of nearby market towns and other urban centers that served agriculture or allowed more prosperous farmers to have access to the consumer goods and recreation they wanted. This new pattern of urban growth—new cities and the expansion of smaller existing ones—would continue into the nineteenth century.

[2]J. De Vries, "Patterns of Urbanization in Pre-Industrial Europe, 1500–1800," in H. Schnal, ed., Patterns of Urbanization Since 1500 (London: Croom Helm, 1981), p. 103.

Social divisions were as marked in the cities of the eighteenth century as they were in the industrial centers of the nineteenth.

Visible segregation often existed between the urban rich and the urban poor. The nobles and the upper middle class lived in fashionable town-houses, often constructed around newly laid-out green squares. The poorest town dwellers usually congregated along the rivers. Small merchants and craftsmen lived above their shops. Whole families might live in a single room. Sanitary facilities such as now exist were still unknown. There was little pure water. Cattle, pigs, goats, and other animals walked the streets with the people. All reports on the cities of Europe during this period emphasize both the striking grace and beauty of the dwellings of the wealthy and the dirt, filth, and stench that filled the streets.

Poverty was not just a city problem; it was usually worse in the countryside. But in the city poverty more visibly manifested itself in terms of crime, prostitution, vagrancy, begging, and alcoholism. Many a young man or woman from the countryside migrated to the nearest city to seek a better life, only to discover poor housing, little food, disease, degradation, and finally death. It did not require the Industrial Revolution and the urban factories to make the cities into hellholes for the poor and the dispossessed. The full darkness of London life during the mid-century "gin age," when consumption of that liquor blinded and killed many poor people, is evident in the engravings of William Hogarth (1697–1764).

Also contrasting with the serenity of the aristocratic and upper-commercial-class lifestyle were the public executions that took place all over Europe, the breaking of men and women on the wheel in Paris, and the public floggings in Russia. Brutality condoned and carried out by the ruling classes was quite simply a fact of everyday life.

THE UPPER CLASSES At the top of the urban social structure stood a generally small group of nobles, large merchants, bankers, financiers, clergy, and government officials. These men (and they were always men) controlled the political and economic affairs of the town. Normally they constituted a self-appointed and self-electing oligarchy who gov-

By the eighteenth century the drinking of vast quantities of gin, a very cheap liquor, had become a major social problem for the working class in England. This 1750 etching by Hogarth illustrates the social evils that resulted from gin consumption, including debt, child abuse, death, and general disorder. [Metropolitan Museum of Art, Harris Brisbane Dick Fund, 1932 Acc. #32.35.(124)]

erned the city through its corporation or city council. These rights of self-government had normally been granted by some form of royal charter that gave the city corporation its authority and the power to select its own members. In a few cities on the Continent, artisan guilds controlled the corporations, but more generally the councils were under the influence of the local nobility and the wealthiest commercial people.

THE MIDDLE CLASS Another group in the city were the prosperous but not immensely wealthy merchants, tradesmen, bankers, and professional people. These were the most dynamic element of the urban population and constituted the persons traditionally regarded as the middle class, or *bourgeoisie*.

The concept of the middle class was much less clear-cut than that of the nobility. They had less wealth than most nobles but more

than urban artisans. The middle-class people lived in the cities and towns, and their sources of income had little or nothing to do with the land. The middle class normally stood on the side of reform, change, and economic growth. The middle-class commercial figures—traders, bankers, manufacturers, and lawyers—often found their pursuit of both profit and prestige blocked by the privileges of the nobility and its social exclusiveness. The bourgeoisie also wanted more rational regulations for trade and commerce, as did some of the more progressive aristocrats.

During the eighteenth century the relationship between the middle class and the aristocracy was a complicated one. Wealthy members of the former often attempted to imitate the lifestyle of the latter and might purchase landed estates. The nobles especially in England and France were increasingly embracing the commercial spirit associated with the middle class; they improved their estates and invested in cities. The *bourgeoisie* were not rising to challenge the nobility; rather, both were seeking to add new dimensions to their existing power and prestige. In that regard the tensions between the middle class and the aristocracy in the eighteenth century involved more nearly issues of power sharing than a clash over values or goals associated with class. However, privilege, tradition, and political connection gave many advantages to the nobility.

Consequently, as the century passed, many members of the middle class felt and voiced increasing resentment of the aristocracy and especially of those privileges enjoyed by the aristocracy on the basis of birth. That resentment increased as the wealth and the numbers of the *bourgeoisie* grew and as aristocrats, especially on the Continent, attempted to tighten control of political and ecclesiastical power. The expanding influence of the nobility seemed to mean that the middle class would continue to be excluded from the political decisions of the day.

On the other hand, the middle class in the cities tended to fear the lower urban classes as much as they resented the nobility. The lower orders constituted a potentially violent element in the society, a potential threat to property, and, in their poverty, a drain on national resources. However, the lower classes were much more varied than either the city aristocracy or the middle class cared to admit.

ARTISANS The segment of the urban population that suffered from both the grasping of the middle class and the local nobility was that made up of the shopkeepers, the artisans, and the wage earners. These people constituted the single largest group in any city. The lives and experience of this class were very diverse. They included grocers, butchers, fishmongers, carpenters, cabinetmakers, smiths, printers, handloom weavers, and tailors, to give but a few examples. They had their own culture, values, and institutions. Like the peasants of the countryside, they were in many respects very conservative. Their economic position was highly vulnerable. If a poor harvest raised the price of food, their own businesses suffered.

The entire life of these artisans and shopkeepers centered on their work. They usually lived near or at their place of employment. Most of them worked in shops with fewer than a half dozen other craftsmen. Their primary institution had historically been the guild, but by the eighteenth century the guilds rarely possessed the influence of their predecessors in medieval or early modern Europe.

Nevertheless, the guilds were not to be ignored. They played a conservative role. They did not seek economic growth or innovation. They attempted to preserve the jobs and skills of their members. The guilds still were able in many countries to determine who might and might not pursue a particular craft. They attempted to prevent too many people from learning a particular skill.

The guilds also provided a framework for social and economic advancement. A boy might at an early age become an apprentice to learn a craft or trade. After several years he would be made a journeyman. Still later, if successful and sufficiently competent, he might become a master. The artisan could also receive certain social benefits from the guilds. These might include aid for his family during sickness or the promise of admission for his son. The guilds constituted the chief protection for artisans against the operation of the commercial market. They were particularly strong in central Europe.

The Urban Riot

The artisan class, with its generally conservative outlook, maintained a rather fine sense of social and economic justice. These ideals were based largely on traditional practices. If the collective sense of what was economically "just" was offended, artisans frequently manifested their displeasure through the instrument of the riot. The most sensitive area was the price of bread. If a baker or a grain merchant announced a price that was considered unjustly high, a bread riot might well ensue. Artisan leaders would confiscate the bread or grain and sell it for what the urban crowd considered a "just price." They would then give the money paid for the grain or bread to the baker or merchant.

The possibility of bread riots acted as a restraint on the greed of merchants. Such disturbances represented a collective method of imposing the "just price" in place of the price set by the commercial marketplace. In other

Newgate Prison, London was burned in June 1780 during the anti-Catholic Gordon riots which raged for several days. Some three hundred prisoners were released and the unfortunate warden, Mr. Akerman, lost all his furniture in the fire.

words, bread and food riots, which occurred throughout Europe, were not irrational acts of screaming hungry people but highly ritualized social phenomena of the old regime and its economy of scarcity.

Other kinds of riots were also a basic characteristic of eighteenth-century society and politics. The riot was a way in which people who were excluded in every other way from the political processes could make their will known. Sometimes urban rioters were incited by religious bigotry. For example, in 1753 London Protestant mobs compelled the government ministry to withdraw an act meant to legalize Jewish naturalization. In 1780 the same rabidly Protestant spirit manifested itself in the Gordon riots. Lord George Gordon had raised the specter of an imaginary Catholic plot after the government relieved military recruits from having to take specifically anti-Catholic oaths.

In these riots and in food riots, violence was normally directed against property rather than against people. The rioters themselves were not "riff-raff" but usually small shopkeepers, freeholders, craftsmen, and wage earners. They usually had no other purpose than to restore a traditional right or practice that seemed endangered. Nevertheless, considerable turmoil and destruction could result from their actions.

During the last half of the century urban riots increasingly involved political ends. Though often simultaneous with economic disturbances, the political riot always had non-artisan leadership or instigators. In fact, the "crowd" of the eighteenth century was often the tool of the upper classes. In Paris the aristocratic Parlement often urged crowd action in their disputes with the monarchy. In Geneva middle-class citizens supported artisan riots against the local urban oligarchy. In Great Britain in 1792 the government turned out mobs to attack English sympathizers of the French Revolution. Such outbursts of popular unrest suggest that the crowd or mob first entered the European political and social arena well before the revolution in France.

The Jewish Population: The Age of the Ghetto

Although the small Jewish communities of Amsterdam and other west European cities became famous for their intellectual life and financial institutions, the vast majority of European Jews lived in eastern Europe. In the eighteenth century and thereafter the Jewish population of Europe was concentrated in Poland, Lithuania, and the Ukraine, where no fewer than three million Jews dwelled. There were perhaps as many as 150,000 in the Habsburg lands, primarily Bohemia, around 1760. Fewer than 100,000 lived in Germany. There were approximately 40,000 in France. Much smaller Jewish populations resided in nations such as England and Holland each of which had a Jewish population of less than 10,000. There were even smaller groups of Jews elsewhere.

In 1762 Catherine the Great of Russia specifically excluded Jews from a manifesto that welcomed foreigners to settle in Russia. She relaxed the exclusion somewhat a few years later. After the first partition of Poland of 1772, to be discussed in Chapter 18, Russia included a very large Jewish population. There were also larger Jewish communities in Prussia and under Austrian rule.

Jews dwelled in most nations without enjoying the rights and privileges of other subjects of the monarchs unless such rights were specifically granted to them. They were regarded as a kind of resident alien whose residence might well be temporary or changed at the whim of local rulers or the monarchical government.

No matter where they dwelled, the Jews of Europe under the Old Regime lived apart in separate communities from non-Jewish Europeans. These might be distinct districts of cities known as *ghettos* or in primarily Jewish villages in the countryside. Jews were also treated as a distinct people religiously and legally. In Poland for much of the century they were virtually self-governing. In other areas they lived under the burden of discriminatory legislation. Except in England, Jews could not and did not mix in the mainstream of the societies in which they dwelled. This period, which really may be said to have begun with the expulsion of the Jews from Spain at the end of the fifteenth century, is known as the age of the ghetto or separate community.

During the seventeenth century a very small number of Jews had financed the wars of major rulers. These financiers often became quite close to the rulers and became known as "court Jews." Perhaps the most famous was Samuel Oppenheimer (1630–1703), who helped the Habsburgs finance their struggle against the Turks and the defense of Vienna. But even these privileged Jews, including Oppenheimer, often failed to have their loans repaid. The "court Jews" and their financial abilities became famous. They tended to marry among themselves.

However, the overwhelming majority of the Jewish population of Europe lived in poverty. They occupied the most undesirable sections of cities or poor rural villages. They pursued money lending in some cases, but quite often worked at the lowest occupations. Their religious beliefs, rituals, and community set them apart. Virtually all of the laws and social institutions were directed at keeping them in situations of social inferiority and apart from their Christian neighbors.

Under the Old Regime, it is important to emphasize, all of this discrimination was based on religious separateness. Jews who converted to Christianity were welcomed, even if not always warmly, into the major political and social institutions of gentile European society. But until the last two decades of the eighteenth century in every part of Europe those Jews who remained loyal to their faith were subject to various religious, civil, and social disabilities. They could not pursue the professions freely; often they could not change residence freely; and they stood outside the political structures of the nations in which they lived. Jews could be expelled from the cities where they lived and their property could be confiscated. They were regarded as socially and religiously inferior. They could be required to listen to sermons that insulted them and their religion. Jews might find their children taken away from them and given Christian instruction. They knew that their non-Jewish neighbors might suddenly turn against them and take their lives or the lives of their fellow religious believers.

As will be seen in subsequent chapters, the end of the Old Regime brought major changes in the life of these Jews and in their relationship to the larger culture.

587

SOCIETY AN
ECONOMY
UNDER THE
OLD REGIM
IN THE
EIGHTEENTH
CENTURY

Near the close of the eighteenth century European society was on the brink of a new era. That society had remained traditional and corporate largely because of the economy of scarcity. Beginning in the eighteenth century the commercial spirit and the value of the marketplace, although not new, were permitted fuller play than ever before in European history. The newly unleashed commercial spirit led increasingly to a conception of human beings as individuals rather than as members of communities. In particular that spirit manifested itself in agricultural and industrial revolutions. Together those two vast changes in production overcame most of the scarcity that had haunted Europe and the

West generally. The accompanying changes in landholding and production would bring major changes to the European social structure.

The expansion of population provided a further stimulus for change. More people meant more labor, more energy, and more minds contributing to the creation and solution of social difficulties. Cities had to accommodate themselves to expanding populations. Corporate groups, such as the guilds, had to confront the existence of a larger labor force. New wealth meant that birth would eventually become less and less a determining factor in social relationships, except in regard to the social roles assigned to the two sexes. Class structure and social hierarchy remained, but the boundaries became somewhat blurred.

Finally, the conflicting political ambitions of the monarchs, the nobilities, and the middle class generated innovation. In the pursuit of new revenues the monarchs interfered with the privileges of the nobles. In the name of ancient rights the nobles attempted to secure and expand their existing social privileges. The middle class, in all of its diversity, was growing wealthier from trade, commerce, and the practice of the professions. Its members wanted social prestige and influence equal to their wealth. They resented privileges, frowned on hierarchy, and rejected tradition.

All of these factors meant that the society of the eighteenth century stood at the close of one era in European history and at the opening of another.

Suggested Readings

I. T. BEREND AND G. RANKI, The European Periphery and Industrialization, 1780–1914 (1982). Examines the experience of eastern and Mediterranean Europe.

J. BLUM, Lord and Peasant in Russia from the Ninth to the Nineteenth Century (1961). A thorough and wide-ranging discussion.

J. BLUM, The End of the Old Order in Rural Europe (1978). The most comprehensive treatment of life in rural Europe, especially central and eastern, from the early eighteenth through the mid-nineteenth centuries.

F. BRAUDEL, Capitalism and Material Life, 1400–1800 (1974). An investigation of the physical resources and human organization of preindustrial Europe.

F. BRAUDEL, The Structures of Everyday Life: The Limits of the Possible, trans. by M. Kochan (1982). A magisterial survey by the most important social historian of our time.

J. CANNON, Aristocratic Century: The Peerage of Eighteenth-Century England (1985). A useful treatment based on the most recent research.

P. DEANE, The First Industrial Revolution, 2nd ed. (1979). A well-balanced and systematic treatment.

J. DE VRIES, The Economy of Europe in an Age of Crisis, 1600–1750 (1976). An excellent overview that sets forth the main issues.

J. DE VRIES, European Urbanization 1500–1800 (1984). The most important and far-ranging of recent treatments of the subject.

M. W. FLINN, The European Demographic System, 1500–1820 (1981). A major summary.

R. FORSTER, The Nobility of Toulouse in the Eighteenth Century (1960). A local study that displays the variety of noble economic activity.

R. FORSTER AND O. RANUM, Deviants and Abandoned in French Society (1978). This and the following volume contain important essays from the French Journal Annales.

R. FORSTER AND O. RANUM, Medicine and Society in France (1980).

D. V. GLASS AND D. E. C. EVERSLEY (Eds.), Population in History: Essays in Historical Demography (1965). Fundamental for an understanding of the eighteenth-century increase in population.

A. GOODWIN (Ed.), The European Nobility in the Eighteenth Century (1953). Essays on the nobility in each state.

P. GOUBERT, The Ancien Régime: French Society, 1600–1750, trans. by Steve Cox (1974). A superb account of the peasant social order.

H. J. HABAKKUK AND M. POSTAN (Eds.), The Cambridge Economic History of Europe (1965). Separate chapters by different authors on major topics.

D. HAY ET AL., Albion's Fatal Tree: Crime and Society in Eighteenth-Century England (1976). Separate essays on a previously little explored subject.

O. H. HUFTON, The Poor of Eighteenth-Century France, 1750–1789 (1975). A brilliant study of poverty and the family economy.

R. M. ISHERWOOD, Farce and Fantasy: Popular Entertainment in Eighteenth-Century Paris (1986). A study that concentrates primarily on the theater and related spectacles.

C. JONES, Charity and Bienfaisance: The Treatment of the Poor in the Montpellier Region, 1740–1815 (1982). An important local French study.

E. L. JONES, Agriculture and Economic Growth in England, 1650–1815 (1968). A good introduction to an important subject.

A. KAHAN, The Plow, the Hammer, and the Knout: An Economic History of Eighteenth-Century Russia (1985). An extensive and detailed treatment.

589

SOCIETY AND
ECONOMY
UNDER THE
OLD REGIME
IN THE
EIGHTEENTH
CENTURY

H. KAMEN, *European Society, 1500–1700* (1985). The best one-volume treatment.

P. LASLETT, *The World We Have Lost* (1965). Examination of English life and society before the coming of industrialism.

R. K. McCLURE, *Coram's Children: The London Foundling Hospital in the Eighteenth Century* (1981). A moving work that deals with the plight of all concerned with the problem.

N. McKENDERICK (Ed.), *The Birth of a Consumer Society: The Commercialization of Eighteenth-Century England* (1982). Deals with several aspects of the impact of commercialization.

M. A. MEYER, *The Origins of the Modern Jew: Jewish Identity and European Culture in Germany, 1749–1824* (1967). A general introduction organized around individual case studies.

P. B. MUNSCHE, *Gentlemen and Poachers: The English Game Laws, 1671–1831* (1981). An excellent analysis of these laws.

S. POLLARD, *The Genesis of Modern Management: A Study of the Industrial Revolution in Great Britain* (1965). Treats the issue of industrialization from the standpoint of factory owners.

S. POLLARD, *Peaceful Conquest: The Industrialization of Europe, 1760–1970* (1981). A useful survey.

A. RIBEIRO, *Dress in Eighteenth Century Europe, 1715–1789* (1985). An interesting examination of the social implication of style in clothing.

G. RUDÉ, *The Crowd in History 1730–1848* (1964). This and the following work were pioneering studies.

G. RUDÉ, *Europe in the Eighteenth Century* (1972). A survey with emphasis on social history.

H. SCHMAL (Ed.), *Patterns of European Urbanization Since 1500* (1981). Major revisionist essays.

L. STONE, *The Family, Sex and Marriage in England 1500–1800* (1977). A pioneering study of a subject receiving new interest from historians.

L. STONE, *An Open Elite?* (1985). Raises important questions about the traditional view of open access to social mobility in England.

T. TACKETT, *Priest and Parish in Eighteenth-Century France: A Social and Political Study of the Curés in a Diocese of Dauphiné, 1750–1791* (1977). A very important local study that displays the role of the church in the fabric of social life in the old regime.

L. A. TILLY AND J. W. SCOTT, *Women, Work, and Family* (1978). An excellent survey of the issues in western Europe.

R. WALL (Ed.), *Family Forms in Historic Europe* (1983). Essays that cover the entire continent.

C. WILSON, *England's Apprenticeship, 1603–1763* (1965). A broad survey of English economic life on the eve of industrialism.

E. A. WRIGLEY AND R. S. SCHOFIELD, *The Population History of England, 1541–1871: A Reconstruction* (1982). One of the most ambitious demographic studies ever undertaken.

E. A. WRIGLEY, *Continuity, Chance and Change: The Character of the Industrial Revolution in England* (1988). A major conceptual reassessment.

George III, as painted by Benjamin West, became the English monarch near the close of the Seven Years War and then presided over policies that led to the revolt and loss of the American colonies. [Her Majesty the Queen]

17

EMPIRE, WAR, AND COLONIAL REBELLION

The middle of the eighteenth century witnessed a renewal of European warfare on a worldwide scale. The conflict involved two separate but interrelated rivalries. Austria and Prussia fought for dominance in central Europe while Great Britain and France dueled for commercial and colonial supremacy. The wars were long, extensive, and very costly in both effort and money. They resulted in a new balance of power on the Continent and on the high seas. Great Britain gained a world empire, and Prussia was recognized as a great power.

Moreover, the expense of these wars led every major European government after the Peace of Paris of 1763 to reconstruct its policies of taxation and finance. These revised fiscal programs produced internal conditions for the monarchies of Europe that had most significant results for the rest of the century. These included the American Revolution, enlightened absolutism on the Continent, a continuing financial crisis for the French monarchy, and reform of the Spanish Empire in South America.

Periods of European Overseas Empires

Since the Renaissance, European contacts with the rest of the world have gone through four distinct stages. The *first* was that of the discovery, exploration, and initial conquest and settlement of the New World. This period had closed by the end of the seventeenth century.

The *second* era, which is largely the concern of this chapter, was one of colonial trade rivalry among Spain, France, and Great Britain. The Anglo-French side of the contest has often been compared to a second Hundred Years' War. During this second period, both the British colonies of the North American seaboard and the Spanish colonies of Central and South America emancipated themselves from European control. It may be said to have closed during the 1820s.

The *third* stage of European contact with the non-European world occurred in the nineteenth century. During that period new formal empires involving the European administration of indigenous peoples were carved out in Africa and Asia. Those nineteenth-century empires also included new areas of European settlement, such as Australia, New Zealand, and South Africa. The bases of these empires were trade, national honor, and military strategy.

The *last* period of European empire came in the twentieth century, with the decolonization of peoples who had previously been under European colonial rule.

During the four and a half centuries before decolonization, Europeans exerted political dominance over much of the rest of the world. They frequently treated other peoples as social, intellectual, and economic inferiors. They ravaged existing cultures because of greed, religious zeal, or political ambition. These actions are major facts of European history and significant factors in the contemporary relationship of Europe and its former colonies. What allowed the Europeans to exert such influence and domination for so long over so much of the world was not any innate cultural superiority but a technological supremacy closely related to naval power and gunpowder. Ships and guns allowed the Europeans to exercise their will almost wherever they chose.

Eighteenth-Century Empires

European empires of the eighteenth century existed primarily to enrich trade. They were empires based on commerce. Extensive trade rivalries sprang up around the world. Consequently, the protection of these empires required extensive naval power. Spain dominated the largest of these empires and constructed elaborate naval, commercial, and political structures to exploit and govern it. Finally, these empires depended in large measure upon slave labor. Indeed, the Atlantic slave trade itself represented one of the major ways in which European merchants enriched themselves. That trade in turn forcibly brought the peoples of Africa into the life and culture of the New World.

Mercantile Empires

Navies and merchant shipping were the keystones of the mercantile empires of the eighteenth century. These empires were meant to bring profit to a nation rather than to provide areas for settlement. The Treaty of Utrecht (1713) established the boundaries of empire during the first half of the century.

Except for Brazil, which was governed by Portugal, Spain controlled all of mainland South America. In North America it controlled Florida, Mexico, and California. The Spanish also governed the island of Cuba and half of Hispaniola.

The British Empire consisted of the colonies along the North Atlantic seaboard, Nova Scotia, Newfoundland, Jamaica, and Barbados. Britain also possessed a few trading stations on the Indian subcontinent.

The French domains covered the Saint Lawrence River valley and the Ohio and Mississippi river valleys. They also included the West Indian islands of Saint Domingue, Guadeloupe, and Martinique; and stations in India.

The Dutch controlled Surinam, or Dutch Guiana, in South America; and various trading stations in Ceylon and Bengal. Most important, they controlled the trade with Java in what is now Indonesia.

All of these powers also possessed numerous smaller islands in the Caribbean. So far as eighteenth-century developments were concerned, the major rivalries existed among the Spanish, the French, and the British.

MERCANTILIST GOALS To the extent that any formal economic theory lay behind the conduct of these empires, it was *mercantilism*, that practical creed of hard-headed businessmen. Initially, the fundamental point of this outlook was the necessity of acquiring a favorable trade balance of gold and silver bullion. Such bullion was regarded as the measure of a country's wealth, and a nation was truly wealthy only if it amassed more bullion than its rivals.

From beginning to end, the economic well-being of the home country was the first concern of mercantilist writers. Colonies were to provide markets and natural resources for the industries of the home country. In turn, the home country was to furnish military security and political administration for the colonies. For decades both sides assumed that the colo-

nies were the inferior partner in the relationship. The mercantilist statesmen and traders regarded the world as an arena of scarce resources and economic limitation. They assumed that one national economy could grow only at the expense of others. The home country and its colonies were to trade only with each other. To that end they attempted to forge trade-tight systems of national commerce through navigation laws, tariffs, bounties to encourage production, and prohibitions against trading with the subjects of other monarchs. National monopoly was the ruling principle.

Mercantilist ideas had always been neater on paper than in practice. By the early eighteenth century mercantilist assumptions were held only in the vaguest manner. They stood too far removed from the economic realities of the colonies and perhaps from human nature. The colonial and home markets simply failed to mesh. Spain could not produce sufficient goods

The Mercantilist Position Stated

One of the earliest discussions of the economic theory of mercantilism appeared in England's Treasure by Forraign Trade (1664) *by Thomas Mun. In this passage from that work Mun explained why it was necessary to the prosperity of the nation for more goods to be exported than imported. Although later mercantilist theory became somewhat more sophisticated, all writers in the eighteenth century emphasized the necessity of a favorable balance of trade.*

The ordinary means therefore to increase our wealth and treasure is by *Forraign Trade* wherein wee must ever observe this rule; to sell more to strangers yearly than wee consume of theirs in value. For suppose that when this Kingdom is plentifully served with the Cloth, Lead, Tinn, Iron, Fish and other native commodities, we doe yearly export the overplus to forraign countries to the value of twenty two hundred thousand pounds; by which means we are enabled beyond the Seas to buy and bring in forraign wares for our use and Consumptions, to the value of twenty hundred thousand pounds; By this order duly kept in our trading, we may rest assured that the Kingdom shall be enriched yearly two hundred thousand pounds, which must be brought to us in so much Treasure; because that part of our stock which is not returned to us in wares must necessarily be brought home in treasure [i.e., gold or silver bullion].

Thomas Mun, England's Treasure by Forraign Trade, *as quoted in Charles Wilson,* England's Apprenticeship, 1603–1763 *(London: Longman, 1965), p. 60*

The English factory at Surat in India, was owned and operated by the East India Company. Here Indian goods were purchased and stored until British ships arrived to take them to Britain. [The Mansell Collection]

for South America. Economic production in the British North American colonies challenged English manufacturing and led to British attempts to limit certain colonial industries, such as iron and hat making.

Colonists of different countries wished to trade with each other. English colonists could buy sugar more cheaply from the French West Indies than from English suppliers. The traders and merchants of one nation always hoped to break the monopoly of another. For all these reasons the eighteenth century became the "golden age of smugglers."[1] The governments could not control the activities of all their subjects. Clashes among colonists could and did bring about conflict between governments.

FRENCH-BRITISH RIVALRY Neither the French nor the British colonies of North

America fit particularly well into the mercantile pattern of empire. Trade with these areas during the early part of the century was smaller than with the West Indies. These mainland colonies were settlements rather than arenas for economic exploitation. The French lands of Canada were quite sparsely populated. Relations with the native Americans were troublesome. The economic interests and the development of the colonies were not wholly compatible with those of the home countries. Major flash points existed between France and Britain on the North American continent. Their colonists quarreled endlessly with each other. Both groups of settlers were jealous over rights to the lower Saint Lawrence River valley, upper New England, and later the Ohio River valley. There were other rivalries over fishing rights, fur trade, and relationships with the Indians.

Unlike North America or the West Indies, India was neither the home of migrating Euro-

[1] *Walter Dorn*, Competition for Empire, 1740–1763 *(New York: Harper, 1940), p. 266.*

peans nor an integral part of their imperial schemes. The Indian subcontinent was an area where both France and Britain traded through privileged, chartered companies that enjoyed a legal monopoly. The East India Company was the English institution; the French equivalent was the Compagnie des Indes. The trade of India and Asia figured only marginally in the economics of empire.

Nevertheless, throughout the century trade and involvement on the subcontinent continued. Enterprising Europeans always hoped that in some fashion profitable commerce with India might develop. Others regarded India as a springboard into the even larger potential market of China. The original European footholds in India were trading posts called *factories*. They existed through privileges granted by the various Indian governments.

Two circumstances arose during the middle of the eighteenth century to change this situation. First, in several of the Indian states decay occurred in the indigenous administration and government. Second, Joseph Dupleix (1697–1763) for the French and Robert Clive (1725–1774) for the British saw these developments as opportunities for expanding the control of their respective companies (the Compagnie des Indes and the East India Company). To maintain their own security and to expand their privileges, the companies began to fill the power vacuum and in effect took over the government of some regions. Each group of Europeans hoped to checkmate the other.

The Spanish Colonial System

Spanish control of its American empire involved a system of government and a system of monopolistic trade regulation. Both were more rigid in appearance than in practice. Actual government was often informal, and the trade monopoly was often breached.

COLONIAL GOVERNMENT Because Queen Isabella had commissioned Columbus, the technical legal link between the New World and Spain was the crown of Castile. Its powers both at home and in America were subject to few limitations. Government of America was assigned to the Council of the Indies, which, in conjunction with the monarch, nominated the persons who served as viceroys of New Spain and Peru. These viceroys served as the chief executives in the New World and carried out the laws promulgated by the Council of the Indies.

Within each of the viceroyalties were established a number of subordinate judicial councils known as *audiencias*. There was also a variety of local officers, the most important of which were the *corregidores*, who presided over municipal councils. All of these offices provided the monarchy with a vast array of patronage, usually bestowed on persons born in Spain. Virtually all political power flowed from the top of this political structure downward; in effect, there was little or no substantial local initiative or self-government.

TRADE REGULATION The colonial political structures existed, in large measure, to support the commercial goals of Spain. The Casa de Contratación (House of Trade) in Seville regulated all trade with the New World. Cádiz was the only port to be used for the American trade. The Casa de Contratación was the single most influential institution of the Spanish Empire. Its members worked closely with the Consulado (Merchant Guild)

The fortress of El Morro in the harbor of San Juan, Puerto Rico. This massive citadel protected the Spanish treasure fleets that carried gold and silver each year to Spain from the mines of Mexico and Peru. [Commonwealth of Puerto Rico]

of Seville and other groups involved with the American commerce in Cádiz.

The key device for maintaining the trade monopoly administered in Seville was a complicated system of trade and bullion fleets. The Seville merchants sought to sell goods in

Visitors Describe the Portobello Fair

The Spanish attempted to restrict all trade within their Latin American empire to a few designated ports. The most famous of these was Portobello on the Isthmus of Panama. In the 1730s, two visitors saw the event and described it. Note the wide variety of goods traded and the vast distances over which products had to be transported. This fair was the chief means of facilitating trade between the western coast of South America and Spain.

The town of Portobello, so thinly inhabited, by reason of its noxious air, the scarcity of provisions, and the soil, becomes, at the time of the [Spanish] galleons one of the most populous places in all South America. . . .

The ships are no sooner moored in the harbour, than the first work is, to erect, in the square, a tent made of the ship's sails, for receiving its cargo; at which the proprietors of the goods are present, in order to find their bales, by the marks which distinguish them. These bales are drawn on sledges, to their respective places by the crew of every ship, and the money given them is proportionally divided.

Whilst the seamen and European traders are thus employed, the land is covered with droves of mules from Panama, each drove consisting of above an hundred, loaded with chests of gold and silver, on account of the merchants of Peru. Some unload them at the exchange, others in the middle of the square; yet, amidst the hurry and confusion of such crowds, no theft, loss, or disturbance, is ever known. He who has seen this place during the *tiempo muerto*, or dead time, solitary, poor, and a perpetual silence reigning everywhere; the harbour quite empty, and every place wearing a melancholy aspect; must be filled with astonishment at the sudden change, to see the bustling multitudes,

every house crowded, the square and streets encumbered with bales and chests of gold and silver of all kinds; the harbour full of ships and vessels, some bringing by the way of Rio de Chape the goods of Peru, such as cacao, quinquina, or Jesuit's bark, Vicuña wool, and bezoar stones; others coming from Carthagena, loaded with provisions; and thus a spot, at all times detested for its deleterious qualities, becomes the staple of the riches of the old and new world, and the scene of one of the most considerable branches of commerce in the whole earth.

The ships being unloaded, and the merchants of Peru, together with the president of Panama, arrived, the fair comes under deliberation. And for this purpose the deputies of the several parties repair on board the commodore of the galleons, where, in the presence of the commodore, and the president of Panama, . . . the prices of the several kinds of merchandizes are settled. . . . The purchases and sales, as likewise the exchanges of money, are transacted by brokers, both from Spain and Peru. After this, every one begins to dispose of his goods; the Spanish brokers embarking their chests of money, and those of Peru sending away the goods they have purchased, in vessels called chatas and bongos, up the river Chagres. And thus the fair of Porto Bello ends.

George Juan and Antonio de Ulloa, A Voyage to South America *(London, 1772), Vol. 1, pp. 103–110, quoted in Benjamin Keen (Ed.),* Readings in Latin-American Civilization 1492 to the Present *(New York: Houghton Mifflin, 1955), pp. 107–108.*

America and to draw back to Spain as much precious metal as possible. They and they alone were to be the link between the New World and Europe. Merchants from other nations were to be excluded from the American routes. Even the Spanish colonists from the various parts of the American empire were prohibited from establishing direct trade with each other and from building their own shipping and commercial industry.

Each year, a fleet of commercial vessels (the *flota*), accompanied by protective naval ships, carried merchandise from Spain to a few specified ports in America. These included Portobello, Veracruz, and Cartagena. There were no authorized ports on the Pacific Coast. Areas far to the south, such as Buenos Aires on the Rio de la Plata, received shipments only after the shipments had been received at one of the authorized ports. After selling their wares, the ships were loaded with silver and gold bullion, usually wintered in heavily fortified Caribbean ports, and then sailed back to Spain. The *flota* system always worked imperfectly.

COLONIAL REFORM UNDER THE SPANISH BOURBON MONARCHS A crucial change occurred in the Spanish colonial system during the eighteenth century. The War of the Spanish Succession and the Treaty of Utrecht replaced the Spanish Habsburgs with the Bourbons of France on the Spanish throne. Philip V (1700–1746) and his successors brought with them to Spain the administrative skills and expectations that had been forged by the bureaucrats of Louis XIV. The Bourbon Spanish monarchy was determined to reassert the imperial trade monopoly, which had decayed under the last Spanish Habsburgs, and thus to improve the domestic economy and revive the role of Spain in European affairs.

Under Philip V, attempts were made to suppress smuggling by the use of coastal patrol vessels in American waters. An incident arising from this policy (to be discussed later in this chapter) eventually led to war with England. In 1739, Philip established the viceroyalty of New Granada in the area that is today made up of Venezuela, Colombia, and Ecuador. The purpose of this new administrative unit was to increase direct royal government in the area.

During the reign of Ferdinand VI (1746–1759), the great mid-century wars exposed the vulnerability of the empire to naval attack and economic penetration. As an ally of France, Spain emerged as one of the defeated powers in 1763. Government circles were convinced that some changes in the colonial system had to be undertaken.

Charles III (1759–1788) made the most important strides toward imperial reform. What this reform meant was an attempt to reassert Spanish peninsular control of the empire. Like his two Bourbon predecessors, Charles III put more emphasis on royal ministers than on councils. Consequently the role of both the Council of the Indies and the Casa de Contratación diminished. After 1765, Charles abolished the monopolies of Seville and Cádiz and permitted other Spanish commercial centers to trade with America. He also opened more South American and Caribbean ports to trade and authorized some commerce between ports in America. In 1776, he organized a fourth viceroyalty in the region of Rio de la Plata, which included much of present-day Argentina, Uruguay, Paraguay, and Bolivia.

While in one sense somewhat freeing trade with and in America, Charles III attempted to increase the efficiency of tax collection and to eliminate bureaucratic corruption. To achieve those ends, he introduced the institution of the *intendent* into the Spanish Empire. These loyal, royal bureaucrats were patterned on the French *intendants* made so famous and effective as agents of the absolutism of Louis XIV.

These late-eighteenth-century Bourbon reforms helped to stimulate the imperial economy. Trade expanded and was somewhat more varied. But first and foremost, these reforms were attempts to bring the empire back under direct Spanish control. *Peninsulares* (persons born in Spain) entered the New World in large numbers to fill new posts. Expanding trade brought more Spanish merchants to Latin America. The export orientation of the economy remained, and economic life was still organized to the benefit of Spain. A major result of these policies was to make the creoles (persons of European descent born in the Spanish colonies) feel that they were second-class subjects. In time, their resentment provided a major source of the discontent leading to the wars of independence in the early nineteenth century. Finally, it should be observed that the new imperial policies of Charles III were the Spanish equivalent of the new colonial direc-

DISPUTED BY
ENGLAND,
RUSSIA, AND
SPAIN

VICEROYALTY OF
NEW SPAIN

A T L A N T I C

Mississippi

Rio

Grande

EFFECTIVE FRONTIER OF
SPANISH SETTLEMENT

O C E A N

Mexico
City •

Santo Domingo

Caracas

VICEROYALTY OF
Bogotá NEW GRANADA
• Separated From
Viceroyalty of
Peru,
1717, 1739

GUIANA

Quito •

Amazon

P A C I F I C

VICEROYALTY

OF

BRAZIL

VICEROYALTY

Pernambuco
•

Lima • OF

Bahia
•

PERU

O C E A N

VICEROYALTY
São Paulo
•
Rio de Janeiro
•

OF LA PLATA
Separated From the
Viceroyalty of Peru,
1776

Santiago •

Buenos
Aires
•

AUDIENCIA
OF CHILE
Retained by the
Viceroyalty of Peru,
1776

Claimed but not
settled by Spain

MAP 17-1 VICEROYALTIES IN LATIN AMERICA
IN 1780 *The late-eighteenth century viceroyalties
in Latin America display the effort of the Spanish
Bourbon monarchy to establish more direct control
of the continent. They sought this through the introduction of a larger number of royal officials by establishing more governmental districts.*

599

EMPIRE, WA
AND COLON
REBELLION

tions undertaken by the British government in
1763, which led to the American Revolution.

Black African Slavery and the Atlantic Economy

The heart of the eighteenth-century colonial
rivalry was situated in the West Indies. These
islands, close to the American continents, constituted the jewels of empire. The West Indies
raised tobacco, cotton, indigo, coffee, and
sugar, for which there existed strong markets
in Europe. Sugar in particular had become a
product of standard consumption rather than a
luxury. It was used in coffee, tea, and cocoa; for
making candy and preserving fruits; and in the
brewing industry. There seemed no limit to its
uses.

Basic to the economy of the West Indies as
well as to that of Spanish and Portuguese settlements in South America and the British colonies on the South Atlantic seaboard of North
America was the institution of slavery. The
major source of those slaves were black peoples from West Africa.

Slavery was an institution that had existed
in various parts of Europe since ancient times.
There was no moral or religious stigma attached to slave owning or slave trading. It had
a continuous existence in the Mediterranean
world where only the sources of slaves
changed over the centuries. After the conquest
of Constantinople in the mid-fifteenth century, the Ottoman Empire forbade the importation of white slaves from regions under its
control. At this time the Portuguese had begun
to import black African slaves into the Iberian
peninsula from the Canary Islands and West
Africa. Black slaves from Africa were also not
uncommon in other parts of the Mediterranean, and a few found their way into northern
Europe. There they might be used as personal
servants or displayed because of the novelty of
their blackness at the courts of royalty or
homes of the wealthy.

THE ECONOMICS OF SLAVERY When

the New World was discovered and settled, the
conquering Spanish and Portuguese confronted
a vast shortage of labor. They and most of the
French and English settlers who came later had
no intention of undertaking physical manual
work themselves. At first they attempted to
use native Americans. However, hundreds of
thousands of native Americans died of disease
during the sixteenth and seventeenth centuries, resulting in the persistence of the labor
shortage. The Spanish and Portuguese then
turned to the labor of imported African slaves.
By the late sixteenth century in the islands of
the West Indies and the major cities of South
America black slaves equalled or surpassed the
numbers of white European settlers.

On much of the South American continent
dominated by Spain the numbers of slaves declined during the late seventeenth century,
and the institution became less fundamental
there than elsewhere. Slavery continued to
prosper, however, in Brazil and in the Caribbean where sugar had become the basic staple
commodity of production. Later slavery spread
into the British North American colonies. The
first slaves were bought at Jamestown in 1619.
They soon became a fundamental institution
in North American colonial life. At one time
or another slaves were held in all the colonies.

One of the forces that led to the spread of
slavery in Brazil and the West Indies was the
cultivation of sugar. It could not be cultivated
by small landowners because it required a large
investment in land and equipment. Only slave
labor could provide enough workers for the
extremely profitable sugar plantations. As the
production of sugar expanded so also did the
demand for slaves and their consequent importation. By the close of the seventeenth century
the Caribbean Islands were the world center
for the production of sugar with its ever growing demand. The slave population continued
to expand. It has been estimated that by 1725
almost 90 per cent of the population of Jamaica
were black slaves. The situation was similar
throughout the West Indies. There and elsewhere, in Brazil and the southern British colonies, prosperity and slavery went hand in hand.
The wealthiest and most prized of the colonies
were those that raised staples such as sugar,
rice, tobacco, or cotton by slave labor.

The profits to the home country as well as to
the planters were enormous. Throughout the
eighteenth century more goods were exported
from the British West Indies islands to Britain

On a French West Indian plantation slaves pick cotton on the right while other slaves on the left remove the seeds from the fiber. The particular variety of cotton shown in this engraving grew on shrubs rather than on the bushes grown in the American south. [The Granger Collection]

than from any other area of British trade. The islands also were among the largest importers of British goods. Similar trade patterns existed with the other colonies with slave-based populations. Many of the plantation owners, especially from the West Indies, were absentee owners who lived in great wealth in Europe. But in Brazil and along the South Atlantic seaboard of North America an enormously wealthy planter class, unlike the West Indians, remained in America after amassing their wealth.

In Europe, cities such as London and Liverpool in England, Glasgow in Scotland, and Nantes in France grew and became wealthy on the profits from the slave trade. Cities in the

Slaveholder negotiates for the sale of a slave on one of the Caribbean Islands. [Contemporary copper engraving by Charles Eisen. Bettmann Archive]

During 1693 and 1694 Captain Thomas Phillips carried slaves from Africa to Barbados on the Hannibal. *The financial backer of the voyage was the Royal African Company of London, which held an English crown monopoly on slavetrading. Phillips sailed to the west coast of Africa where he purchased the Africans who were sold into slavery by an African king. Then he set sail westward. In this passage from his journal he describes the deadly conditions of the voyage from the coast of West Africa across the Atlantic. Note the manner in which he equates the slaves only with money and the utterly detached fashion in which he describes their suffering and death. Such conditions were common on virtually all slavetrading ships. The loss of life of Africans so transported to America was staggeringly high.*

Having bought my complement of 700 slaves, 480 men and 220 women, and finish'd all my business at Whidaw [on the Gold Coast of Africa], I took my leave of the old king and his cappasheirs [attendants], and parted, with many affectionate expressions on both sides, being forced to promise him that I would return again the next year, with several things he desired me to bring from England. . . . I set sail the 27th of July in the morning, accompany'd with the *East-India Merchant*, who had bought 650 slaves, for the Island of St. Thomas . . . from which we took our departure on August 25th and set sail for Barbadoes.

We spent in our passage from St. Thomas to Barbadoes two months eleven days, from the 25th of August to the 4th of November following: in which time there happened such sickness and mortality among my poor men and Negroes. Of the first we buried 14, and of the last 320, which was a great detriment to our voyage, the Royal African Company losing ten pounds by every slave that died, and the owners of the ship ten pounds ten shillings, being the freight agreed on to be paid by the charter-party for every Negro delivered alive ashore to the African Company's agents at Barbadoes. . . . The loss in all amounted to near 6500 pounds sterling.

The distemper which my men as well as the blacks mostly died of was the white flux, which was so violent and inverterate that no medicine would in the least check it, so that when any of our men were seized with it, we esteemed him a dead man, as he generally proved. . . .

The Negroes are so incident to the small-pox that few ships that carry them escape without it, and sometimes it makes vast havock and destruction among them. But tho' we had 100 at a time sick of it, and that it went thro' the ship, yet we lost not above a dozen by it. All the assistance we gave the diseased was only as much water at they desir'd to drink, and some palm-oil to annoint their sores, and they would generally recover without any other helps but what kind nature gave them. . . .

But what the small pox spar'd, the flux swept off, to our great regret, after all our pains and care to give them their messes in due order and season, keeping their lodgings as clean and sweet as possible, and enduring so much misery and stench so long among a parcel of creatures nastier than swine, and after all our expectations to be defeated by their mortality. . . .

No gold-finders can endure so much noisome slavery as they do who carry Negroes; for those have some respite and satisfaction, but we endure twice the misery; and yet by their mortality our voyages are ruin'd, and we pine and fret ourselves to death, and take so much pains to so little purpose.

Thomas Phillips, "Journal," A Collection of Voyages and Travels, *Vol. VI, Edited by Awnsham and John Churchill (London, 1746) as quoted in Thomas Howard (Ed.),* Black Voyage: Eyewitness Accounts of the Atlantic Slave Trade *(Boston: Little, Brown and Company, 1971), pp. 85–87.*

British North American colonies profited from slavery sometimes by trading in slaves but more often from supplying other goods to the West Indian market. But it was not the New World planters and slave traders alone who were involved in the trade. Slavery touched most of the economy of the transatlantic world. All of the shippers who handled cotton, tobacco, and sugar depended on slavery, though they might have no direct contact with the institution.

There was a general triangle of trade that consisted of carrying goods to Africa to be exchanged for slaves, who were then taken to the West Indies, where they were traded for sugar and other tropical produce, which were then shipped to Europe. Not all ships necessarily covered all three legs of the triangle. Another major trade pattern existed between New England and the West Indies: New England fish or ship supplies were traded for sugar. But no matter what the exact configuration of this trade, slavery was the institution that lay at its heart.

THE LIFE OF A SLAVE The slave trade was extensive, inhumane, and quite profitable. Spanish, Portuguese, Dutch, French, and English traders participated in it. Several million (perhaps over nine million) black Africans were forcibly imported to the New World. During the first four centuries of settlement far more black slaves came involuntarily to shores of the New World than did free European settlers. The conditions of their passage across the Atlantic were wretched in every respect. Quarters were unspeakably cramped; food was bad; disease was rampant. Many Africans died on the crossing. Yet the trade persisted because of the demand for labor in America where it was cheaper to import new slaves than it was to rear slave children to adulthood. The mortality rate of slaves in the West Indies and elsewhere was very high. More and more new Africans had to be bought into slavery simply to keep a steady supply, as slaves already imported to or born in America died.

The life conditions of slaves differed from colony to colony. Black slaves living in Portuguese areas had the fewest legal protections. In the Spanish colonies the Church attempted to provide some small protection for black slaves but devoted much more effort toward protecting the native Americans. Slave codes were developed in the British and the French colonies during the seventeenth century. However, they provided only the most limited protection. Virtually all slaveowners feared a slave revolt and the legislation and other regulations were intended to prevent such an event. All slave laws looked out for the master rather than the slave. Slave masters were permitted to punish slaves by whipping and other exceedingly harsh corporal punishment. Furthermore, slaves were often forbidden any right to gather in large groups for fear that a revolt might be planned.

The daily life of most slaves during this period was one of very hard agricultural labor, relatively poor diet, and inadequate housing. Slave families could be separated by the owner or at the time of the death of the owner. The death rate among slaves was quite high. Their welfare and their lives were sacrificed to the ongoing expansion of the sugar, rice, and tobacco plantations that made their owners wealthy and that produced goods demanded by consumers in Europe.

The European settlers in the Americas and the slave traders also carried with them attitudes of prejudice against black Africans. Many Europeans thought Africans to be savage or less than civilized. Still others looked down upon them simply because they were slaves. These attitudes had been shared by both Christians and Muslims in the Mediterranean world where European slavery had for so long existed. Furthermore, many European languages and European cultures attached negative connotations to the idea and image of black. All of these factors formed the roots of racial prejudice that would plague all of these slave-based American colonies for the next two centuries.

The War of Jenkins' Ear

In the middle of the eighteenth century the West Indies had become a hotbed of trade rivalry: Spain attempted to tighten its monopoly and English smugglers, shippers, and pirates attempted to pierce it. Matters came to a climax in the late 1730s.

The Treaty of Utrecht (1713) included two special privileges for Great Britain in regard to the Spanish Empire. The British received a thirty-year *asiento*, or contract, to furnish slaves to the Spanish. Britain also gained the right to send one ship each year to the trading fair at Portobello, a major Caribbean seaport on the Panamanian coast. These two privileges allowed British traders and smugglers potential inroads into the Spanish market. Little but friction arose from these rights. The annual ship to Portobello was often supplied with additional goods during the night as it lay in port. Much to the chagrin of the British, the Spanish government took its own alleged trading monopoly seriously and maintained coastal patrols, which boarded and searched English vessels to look for contraband.

In 1731, during one such boarding operation, there was a fight, and an English captain named Robert Jenkins had his ear cut off by the Spaniards. Thereafter he carried about his severed ear preserved in a jar of brandy. This incident was of little importance until 1738, when Jenkins appeared before the British Parliament, reportedly brandishing his ear as an example of Spanish atrocities to British merchants in the West Indies. The British merchant and West Indies interests put great pressure on Parliament to do something about Spanish intervention in their trade. Robert Walpole attempted to reach a solution through negotiations. However, Parliament—and especially the members who believed that the war would drive Walpole from office—refused all accommodation. In late 1739 Great Britain went to war with Spain.

At the outbreak of hostilities, the French, under the administration of Cardinal Fleury, stood ready to profit from the British–Spanish conflict. They expected to see British trade harmed and eventually to receive Spanish commercial favors for aid. None of the major European powers except Britain had any standing grudge against France. The years of Fleury's cautious policy were about to pay off. Then, quite literally overnight, the situation on the Continent changed.

Mid-Century Wars

The War of the Austrian Succession (1740–1748)

In December 1740, after possessing the throne of Prussia for less than seven months, Frederick II ordered his troops to occupy the Austrian province of Silesia. The invasion shattered the provisions of the Pragmatic Sanction and upset the continental balance of power as established by the Treaty of Utrecht. The young king of Prussia had treated the House of Habsburg simply as another German state rather than as the leading state in the region. The province of Silesia itself rounded out Prussia's possessions, and Frederick was determined to keep his ill-gotten prize.

MARIA THERESA PRESERVES THE HABSBURG EMPIRE Maria Theresa was twenty-three years old and had succeeded to the Austrian crown only two months before Frederick's move. Her army was weak, her bureaucracy inefficient, and the loyalty of her subjects uncertain. She herself was inexperienced and was more usually guided by the values of piety than by hard-headed statecraft. Yet she succeeded in rallying to her side the Magyars of Hungary and the aristocratic leaders of her other domains. They were genuinely sympathetic to her plight and inspired by her courage. Maria Theresa's great achievement was not the reconquest of Silesia, which eluded her, but the preservation of the Habsburg Empire as a major political power.

The seizure of Silesia could have marked the opening of a general hunting season on Habsburg holdings and the beginning of revolts by Habsburg subjects. Instead it proved the occasion for new political allegiances. Maria Theresa achieved these new loyalties, especially between herself and the Magyars, not merely through heroism but more specifically by granting new privileges to the nobles of the various Habsburg realms. The empress recognized Hungary as the most important of her crowns and promised the Magyars considerable local autonomy. In this fashion she preserved the Habsburg state, but at considerable cost to the power of the central monarchy. Hungary would continue in the future to be, as it had been in the past, a particularly troublesome area in the Habsburg Empire. When the monarchy enjoyed periods of strength and security, guarantees made to Hungary were sometimes ignored. At times of weakness or when the Magyars could stir sufficient opposition, the monarchy made new promises or concessions.

FRANCE DRAWS GREAT BRITAIN INTO THE WAR The war over the Austrian succession and the British–Spanish commer-

Maria Theresa Agrees to Appoint Hungarian Councilors

Maintaining the loyalty of Hungary was always one of the chief difficulties of the Habsburg dynasty. Maria Theresa's coronation as monarch of Hungary occurred in 1741 shortly after Frederick the Great's invasion of Silesia; therefore, she especially needed Hungarian support. Toward the end of the ceremonies there occurred a famous scene in which the Hungarian nobles pledged their loyalty to the young queen as she stood before them holding her infant. However, Maria Theresa had paid a high price for this loyalty and the continuation of stable Habsburg rule. She had agreed to a series of laws that convinced the Hungarians that they would be secure under her rule and be able largely to direct their own affairs. These agreements were typical of the kind of bargaining in which Habsburg monarchs found themselves required to engage with their various realms.

Law XI of the agreement of 1741 included the following provisions.

On Hungarian affairs and business: that these are to be conducted through Hungarians.

1. Her Majesty has further graciously resolved that She will conduct, and have conducted, the affairs and business of the country, both inside and outside the country, through Hungarians.

2. Consequently, also in Her august Court, in matters dependent on the supreme power enjoyed by Her, She will, in accordance with Her august judgment and royal prerogative, make use of the assistance and counsel of Her loyal Hungarian Councilors.

. . . .

4. And She will deign to take men of Hungarian nationality into the Ministry of State itself.

5. And inside the Kingdom [of Hungary] She will in the future also duly conduct all administration and matters concerning the public affairs of the same Kingdom in the manner determined by the laws of the land, through the channel of the Vice-Regal Council. . . .

6. And in cases of future vacancies in the said Vice-Regal Council She will appoint suitable landed Hungarians from all parts of the Kingdom, men acquainted with the business and constitution of the Kingdom.

C. A. Macartney (Ed.), The Habsburg and Hohenzollern Dynasties in the Seventeenth and Eighteenth Centuries (New York: Walker and Company, 1970), pp. 135–136.

cial conflict could have remained separate disputes. They were neither logically nor necessarily politically related. What ultimately united them was the role of France. Cardinal Fleury understood that the long-range interests of France lay in the direction of commercial growth. However, just as British merchant interests had pushed Robert Walpole into war, a group of court aristocrats led by the count of Belle Isle compelled the elderly Fleury to abandon his planned naval attack on British trade and to support the Prussian aggression against Austria. This proved to be one of the most fateful decisions in French history.

Even though the Habsburgs had been the historic enemy of France, a war against Austria was not in the French interest in 1741. In the first place, aid to Prussia had the effect of con-

The Battle of Fontenoy was fought in 1745 during the War of Austrian Succession. The French under Marechal de Saxe defeated an English army that was defending the territory of Maria Theresa in the Austrian Netherlands. [Giraudon]

solidating a new and powerful state in Germany. That new power could, and indeed later did, endanger France. Second, the French move against Austria brought Great Britain into the continental war. The British, as usual, wanted to see the Low Countries remain in friendly hands. In the eighteenth century that policy required continued Habsburg control of the Austrian Netherlands. In 1744 the British–French conflict expanded beyond the Continent, as France decided to support Spain against Britain in the New World. As a result, French military and economic resources became badly divided. France could not bring sufficient strength to the colonial struggle. Having chosen to continue a struggle from the past with Austria, France lost the struggle for the future against Great Britain.

TREATY OF AIX-LA-CHAPELLE By 1748 the war had become a military stalemate for all concerned. Austria had not been able to

regain Silesia, but it had fended off further aggression from other German states. The French army, led by Marshal Maurice de Saxe (1696–1750), won a series of splendid victories over the British and the Austrians in the Netherlands during 1747 and 1748. Britain, for its part, had pursued a very successful colonial campaign. Its forces in America captured the fortress of Louisburg at the mouth of the Saint Lawrence River, and the British more than held their own on the Indian subcontinent. Warfare on French commerce had been highly effective. These victories overseas compensated for the poor showing on the Continent.

Consequently, the war was brought to a close by the Treaty of Aix-la-Chapelle (1748). In effect the treaty restored the conditions that had existed before the war, with the exception that Prussia retained Silesia. Spain renewed the *asiento* agreement with Great Britain. All observers believed that the treaty constituted a truce rather than a permanent peace.

The "Diplomatic Revolution" of 1756

Before the rivalries again erupted into war, a dramatic shift of alliances took place. In 1756 Prussia and Great Britain signed the Convention of Westminster. It was a defensive alliance aimed at preventing the entry of foreign troops into the Germanies. Frederick II feared invasions by both Russia and France. The convention meant that Great Britain, the ally of Austria since the wars of Louis XIV, had now joined forces with Austria's major eighteenth-century enemy.

Maria Theresa was despondent over this development. However, her foreign minister, Count Wenzel Anton Kaunitz (1711–1794), was delighted. This brilliant diplomat and servant of the Habsburg dynasty had long hoped for an alliance between Austria and France for the dismemberment of Prussia. The Convention of Westminster made this alliance, unthinkable a few years earlier, possible.

Count Kaunitz (1711–1794) was foreign minister of the Habsburg Monarchy. He negotiated the famous reversal of alliances (1756) by which France entered the Seven Years' War allied with Austria against Prussia and Britain. [Bildarchiv der Osterreichischen Nationalbibliothek, Vienna]

France was agreeable because Frederick had not consulted it before coming to his understanding with Britain. Consequently, later in 1756, France and Austria signed a defensive alliance. Kaunitz had succeeded in completely reversing the direction of French foreign policy from Richelieu through Fleury. France would now fight to restore Austrian supremacy in central Europe. But the French monarchy, though having changed its German ally, would remain diverted from its commercial interests on the high seas.

The Seven Years' War (1756–1763)

The Treaty of Aix-la-Chapelle had brought peace in Europe, but the conflict between France and Great Britain continued unofficially on the colonial front. There were continuous clashes between American and French settlers in the Ohio River valley and in upper New England. These were the prelude to what is known in American history as the French and Indian War. These colonial skirmishes would certainly have led in time to a broader conflict. However, once again the factor that opened a general European war that extended into a colonial theater was the action of the king of Prussia.

FREDERICK THE GREAT OPENS HOSTILITIES In August 1756 Frederick II invaded the kingdom of Saxony. He regarded this invasion as a continuation of the defensive strategy of which the Convention of Westminster had been a part. Frederick believed that there existed an international conspiracy on the part of Saxony, Austria, and France to undermine and destroy Prussian power. The attack on Saxony was in Frederick's mind a pre-emptive strike. The invasion itself created the very destructive alliance that Frederick feared. In the spring of 1757 France and Austria made a new alliance dedicated to the destruction of Prussia. They were eventually joined by Sweden, Russia, and the smaller German states.

Prussia was surrounded by enemies, and Frederick II confronted the gravest crisis of his career. It was after these struggles that he came to be called Frederick the Great. He won several initial battles, the most famous of which was Rossbach on November 5, 1757. Thereafter, however, the Prussians experienced a long

Frederick the Great Rallies His Officers for Battle

In December 1757 Frederick the Great of Prussia addressed his officers before the battle of Leuthen. Although he had recently won the battle of Rossbach, the monarch remained in a difficult position with his capital in the hands of enemy forces. In addressing his officers, he announces a daring attack and then appeals on the one hand to their patriotism and on the other hand to their fears of humiliation.

You are aware, gentlemen, that Prince Karl of Lorraine has succeeded in taking Schweidnitz, defeating the duke of Bevern and making himself master of Breslau, while I was engaged in checking the advance of the French and imperial forces. A part of Schleswig, my capital, and all the military stores it contained, are lost, and I should feel myself in dire straits indeed if it were not for my unbounded confidence in your courage, your constancy, and your love for the fatherland, which you have proved to me on so many occasions in the past.

. . . I should feel that I had accomplished nothing if Austria were left in possession of Schleswig. Let me tell you that I propose, in defiance of all the rule of the art of war, to attack the army of Prince Karl, three times as large as ours, wherever I find it. It is here no question of the numbers of the enemy nor of the importance of the positions they have occupied; all this I hope to overcome by the devotion of my troops and the careful carrying out of my plans. I must take this step or all will be lost; we must defeat the enemy, else we shall all lie buried under his batteries. So I believe—so I shall act.

Communicate my decision to all the officers of the army; prepare the common soldier for the exertions that are to come, and tell him that I feel justified in expecting unquestioning obedience from him. Remember that you are Prussians and you cannot show yourselves unworthy of that distinction.

. . . The regiment of cavalry that does not immediately on the receipt of orders throw itself upon the enemy I will have unmounted immediately after the battle and make it a garrison regiment. The battalion of infantry that even begins to hesitate, no matter what the danger may be, shall lose its flags and its swords and have the gold lace stripped from its uniforms.

And now, gentlemen, farewell; erelong we shall either have defeated the enemy or we shall see each other no more.

Quoted in James Harvey Robinson (Ed.), Readings in European History *(New York: Ginn & Company, 1906), 2: 323–324.*

series of defeats that might have destroyed the state.

Two factors in addition to Frederick's stubborn leadership saved Prussia. The first was major financial aid from Great Britain. The British contributed as much to the Prussian war effort as did the Prussian treasury itself. Second, in 1762 Empress Elizabeth of Russia died. Her successor was Tsar Peter III (he also died in the same year), whose admiration for Frederick knew almost no bounds. He immedi-

ately made peace with Prussia, thus relieving the country of one enemy and allowing it to hold its own against Austria and France. The treaty of Hubertusburg of 1763 closed the continental conflict with no significant changes in prewar borders. Silesia remained Prussia's province, and Prussia clearly stood in the ranks of the great powers.

WILLIAM PITT'S STRATEGY FOR WINNING NORTH AMERICA The sur-

William Pitt the Elder guided the armies and navies of Great Britain to a stunning victory in the Seven Years' War. [National Portrait Gallery, London]

vival of Prussia was less impressive to the rest of Europe than the victories of Great Britain over France in every theater of conflict. The architect of these victories was William Pitt the Elder (1708–1778). He came from a family that had made its fortune from commerce. His grandfather, "Diamond" Pitt, had laid the foundations of the family's wealth by commercial ventures in India. The grandson was no less dedicated to the growth of British trade and economic interests. Pitt was a person of colossal ego and administrative genius. From the time of the War of Jenkins' Ear he had criticized the government as being too timid in its colonial policy. He had been strongly critical of all continental involvement, including the Convention of Westminster.

During the 1750s he had gained the favor of the London merchant interest. Once war had begun again, these groups clamored for his appointment to the cabinet. In 1757 he was named the secretary of state in charge of the war. He soon drew into his own hands all the power he could grasp. A person of supreme confidence, he once told his friends, "I am sure that I can save the country, and that no one else can."

Once in office Pitt changed his attitude toward British involvement on the Continent. He came to regard the German conflict as a way to divert French resources and attention from the colonial struggle. He pumped huge financial subsidies to Frederick the Great and later boasted of having won America on the plains of Germany. North America was the center of Pitt's real concern. Put quite simply, he wanted all of North America east of the Mississippi for Great Britain, and that was exactly what he won. He turned more than forty thousand regular English and colonial troops against the French in Canada. Never had so many soldiers been devoted to a colonial field of warfare. He achieved unprecedented cooperation with the American colonies, whose leaders realized that they might finally defeat their French neighbors.

The French government was unwilling and unable to direct similar resources against the English in America. Their military administration was corrupt; the military and political command in Canada was divided; and the food supply to the French army failed. In September 1759, on the Plains of Abraham overlooking the valley of the Saint Lawrence River at Quebec City, the British army under General James Wolfe defeated the French under Lieutenant General Louis Joseph Montcalm. The French empire in Canada was coming to an end.

However, Pitt's colonial vision extended beyond the Saint Lawrence valley and the Great Lakes basin. The major islands of the French West Indies fell to the British fleets. Income from the sale of captured sugar helped finance the British war effort. British slave interests captured the bulk of the French slave trade. Between 1755 and 1760 the value of the French colonial trade fell by over 80 per cent. On the Indian subcontinent the British forces under the command of Robert Clive defeated the French in 1757 at the Battle of Plassey. This victory opened the way for the eventual

The British victory at the Battle of the Plains of Abraham at Quebec in 1759 meant the end of French rule in Canada. [Courtesy of the Trustees, National Maritime Museum, Greenwich, England]

conquest of Bengal and later of all India by the British East India Company. Never had Great Britain or any other European power experienced such a complete worldwide military victory.

THE TREATY OF PARIS OF 1763

The Treaty of Paris of 1763 reflected somewhat less of a victory than Britain had won on the battlefield. Pitt was no longer in office. George III (1760–1820) had succeeded to the British throne in 1760. He and Pitt had quarreled over policy, and the minister had departed. His replacement was the earl of Bute, a favorite of the new monarch. The new minister was responsible for the peace settlement. Britain received all of Canada, the Ohio River valley, and the eastern half of the Mississippi River valley. Britain partially surrendered the conquest in India by giving France footholds at Pondicherry and Chandernagore. The sugar islands of Guadeloupe and Martinique were restored to the French. Britain could have gained more territory only with further war involving more taxation, against which the country was already complaining.

The Seven Years' War had been a vast conflict. Tens of thousands of soldiers had been killed or wounded. Major battles had been fought around the globe. At great internal sacrifice Prussia had permanently wrested Silesia from Austria and had turned the Holy Roman Empire into an empty shell. Habsburg power now depended largely on the Hungarian domains. France, though still possessing sources of colonial income, was no longer a great colonial power. The Spanish Empire remained

CONFLICTS OF THE MID-EIGHTEENTH CENTURY	
1713	Treaty of Utrecht
1739	Outbreak of War of Jenkins' Ear between England and Spain
1740	War of the Austrian Succession commences
1748	Treaty of Aix-la-Chapelle
1756	Convention of Westminster between England and Prussia
1756	Seven Years' War opens
1757	Battle of Plassey
1759	British forces capture Quebec
1763	Treaty of Hubertusburg
1763	Treaty of Paris

Fort William in Calcutta was the base from which Clive was able to conquer Bengal.
[The British Library]

largely intact, but the British were still determined to penetrate its markets.

On the Indian subcontinent the British East India Company was in a position to continue to press against the decaying indigenous governments and to impose its own authority. The results of that situation would be felt until the middle of the twentieth century. In North America the British government faced the task of organizing its new territories. From this time until World War II, Great Britain assumed the status not simply of a European but also of a world power.

The quarter century of warfare also caused a long series of domestic crises among the European powers. The French defeat convinced many people in the nation of the necessity of political and administrative reform. The financial burdens of the wars had astounded all contemporaries. Every power had to begin to find ways to increase revenues to pay its war debt and to finance its preparation for the next combat. Nowhere did this search for revenue lead to more far-ranging consequences than in the British colonies in North America.

The American Revolution and Europe

The revolt of the British colonies in North America was an event in transatlantic and European history. It erupted from problems of revenue collection common to all the major powers after the Seven Years' War. The War of the American Revolution was a continuation of the conflict between France and Great Britain. The French support of the Americans deepened the existing financial and administrative difficulties of the monarchy.

Events in the British Colonies

The political ideals of the Americans had roots in the thought of John Locke and other English political theorists. The colonists raised questions of the most profound nature about monarchy, political authority, and constitutionalism. These questions had ramifications for all European states. Part of the difficulties from the British side arose because of the characteristic European political friction between the monarch and the aristocracy. Finally, many Europeans saw the Americans as inaugurating a new era in the history of European peoples and indeed of the world.

After the Treaty of Paris of 1763 the British government faced three imperial problems. The first was the sheer cost of empire, which the British felt they could no longer carry alone. The national debt had risen considerably, as had taxation. The American colonies had been the chief beneficiaries of the conflict. It made rational sense that they should henceforth bear part of the cost of their protection and administration. The second problem was the vast expanse of new territory in North America that the British had to organize. This included all the land from the mouth of the Saint Lawrence River to the Mississippi River with its French settlers and, more important, its Indian possessors.

As the British ministers pursued solutions to these difficulties, a third and more serious issue arose. The British colonists in North America resisted taxation and were suspicious of the imperial policies toward the western lands. Consequently the British had to search for new ways to exert their authority over the colonies. The Americans became increasingly resistant because their economy had outgrown the framework of mercantilism, because the removal of the French relieved them of dependence on the British army, and because they believed that their liberty was in danger.

STAMP ACT CRISIS The British drive for revenue commenced in 1764 with the passage of the Sugar Act under the ministry of George Grenville (1712–1770). The measure attempted to produce more revenue from imports into the colonies by the rigorous collection of what was actually a lower tax. Smugglers who violated the law were to be tried in admiralty courts without juries. The next year Parliament passed the Stamp Act, which put a tax on legal documents and certain other items such as newspapers. The British considered these taxes legal because they

had been passed by Parliament. The taxes seemed just because the money was to be spent in the colonies.

The Americans responded that they had the right to tax themselves and that they were not represented in Parliament. The colonists quite simply argued there should be no taxation without representation. Moreover, because the king had granted most of the colonial charters, the Americans claimed that their legal connection to Britain was through the monarch rather

MAP 17-2 NORTH AMERICA IN 1763 *In the year of the victory of France, the English colonies lay along the Atlantic seaboard. The difficulties of organizing authority over the previous French territory in Canada and west of the Appalachian mountains would contribute to the coming of the American Revolution.*

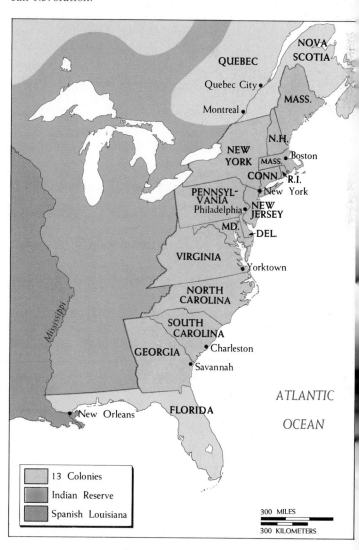

13 Colonies

Indian Reserve

Spanish Louisiana

300 MILES

300 KILOMETERS

than through the Parliament. The expenditure in the colonies of the revenue levied by Parliament did not reassure the colonists. They feared that if colonial government were financed from outside, they would lose control over their government.

In October 1765 the Stamp Act Congress met in America and drew up a protest to the crown. There was much disorder in the colonies, particularly in Massachusetts. The colonists agreed to refuse to import British goods. In 1766 Parliament repealed the Stamp Act, but through the Declaratory Act it said that Parliament had the power to legislate for the colonies.

The Stamp Act crisis set the pattern for the next ten years. Parliament, under the leadership of a royal minister, would approve a piece of revenue or administrative legislation. The Americans would then resist by reasoned argument, economic pressure, and violence. Then the British would repeal the legislation, and the process would begin again. Each time, tempers on both sides became more frayed and positions more irreconcilable.

TOWNSEND ACTS In 1767 Charles Townshend (1725–1767), as Chancellor of the Exchequer, led Parliament to pass a series of revenue acts relating to colonial imports. The colonists again resisted. The ministry sent over its own customs agents to administer the laws. To protect these new officers, the British sent troops to Boston in 1768. The obvious

This view of the "Boston Massacre" of March 5, 1770 by Paul Revere owes more to propaganda than fact. There was no order to fire and the innocent citizens portrayed here were really an angry, violent mob. [Library of Congress]

tensions resulted, and in March 1770 the Boston Massacre, in which British troops killed five citizens, took place. That same year Parliament repealed all of the Townshend duties except for the one on tea.

In May 1773 Parliament passed a new law relating to the sale of tea by the East India Company. The measure permitted the direct importation of tea into the American colonies. It actually lowered the price of tea while retaining the tax imposed without the colonists' consent. In some cities the colonists refused to permit the unloading of the tea; in Boston a shipload of tea was thrown into the harbor. The British ministry of Lord North (1732–1792) was determined to assert the authority of Parliament over the resistant colonies. During 1774 Parliament passed a series of laws known in American history as the Intolerable Acts. These measures closed the port of Boston, reorganized the government of Massachusetts, allowed troops to be quartered in private homes, and removed the trials of royal customs officials to England.

The same year Parliament approved the Quebec Act for the future administration of that province. It extended the boundaries of Quebec to include the Ohio River valley. The Americans regarded the Quebec Act as an attempt to prevent the extension of their mode of self-government westward beyond the Appalachian Mountains.

THE COMING OF THE REVOLUTION
During these years committees of correspondence composed of citizens critical of Britain had been established throughout the colonies. They made the various sections of the eastern seaboard aware of common problems and aided united action. In September 1774 these committees organized the gathering of the First Continental Congress in Philadelphia. This body hoped to persuade Parliament to restore self-government in the colonies and to abandon its attempt at direct supervision of colonial affairs. However, conciliation was not forthcoming. By April 1775 the battles of Lexington and Concord had been fought. In June the colonists suffered defeat at the Battle of Bunker Hill. Despite the defeat, the colonial assemblies soon began to meet under their own authority rather than under that of the king.

The Second Continental Congress gathered in May 1775. It still sought conciliation with Britain, but the pressure of events led that assembly to begin to conduct the government of the colonies. By August 1775 George III had declared the colonies in rebellion. During the winter Thomas Paine's pamphlet *Common Sense* galvanized public opinion in favor of separation from Great Britain. A colonial army and navy were organized. In April 1776 the Continental Congress opened American ports to the trade of all nations. And on July 4, 1776, the Continental Congress adopted the Declaration of Independence. Thereafter the War of the American Revolution continued until 1781, when the forces of George Washington defeated those of Lord Cornwallis at Yorktown.

However, early in 1778 the war had widened into a European conflict when Benjamin Franklin persuaded the French government to support the rebellion. In 1779 the Spanish also came to the aid of the colonies. The 1783 Treaty of Paris concluded the conflict, and the thirteen American colonies had established their independence.

This series of events is generally familiar to American readers. The relationship of the American Revolution to European affairs and the European roots of the American revolutionary ideals are less familiar.

NEW IDEOLOGY The political theory of the American Declaration of Independence derived from the writings of seventeenth-century English Whig theorists, such as John Locke, and eighteenth-century Scottish moral philosophers, such as Francis Hutcheson. Their political ideas had arisen in large measure out of the struggle of seventeenth-century English aristocrats and gentry against the absolutism of the Stuarts. The American colonists looked to the English Revolution of 1688 as having established many of their own fundamental political liberties as well as those of the English. The colonists claimed that through the measures imposed from 1763 to 1776, George III and the British Parliament had attacked those liberties; furthermore, it dissolved the bonds of moral and political allegiance that had formerly united the two peoples. Consequently, the colonists employed a theory that had developed to justify an aristocratic rebellion in order to support their own popular revolution.

Common Sense, *written by Tom Paine, was the most important political pamphlet published during 1776 when the American colonies were deciding to make a final break with Great Britain. [Left: Culver Pictures, Inc. Right: The Granger Collection]*

COMMON SENSE.

Of the Origin and Deſign of GOVERNMENT *in general, with conciſe Remarks on the* ENGLISH CONSTITUTION.

SOME writers have ſo confounded ſociety with government, as to leave little or no diſtinction between them; whereas, they are not only different, but have different origins. Society is produced by our wants, and government by our wickedneſs; the former promotes our happineſs *poſitively* by uniting our affections, the latter *negatively* by reſtraining our vices. The one encourages intercourſe, the other creates diſtinctions. The firſt is a patron, the laſt a puniſher.

Society in every ſtate is a bleſſing, but Government even in its beſt ſtate is but a neceſſary evil; in its worſt ſtate an intolerable one: for when we ſuffer, or are expoſed to the ſame miſeries *by a Government*, which we might expect in a country *without Government*, our calamity is heightened by

B   reflect-

These Whig political ideas were only a part of the English ideological heritage that affected the Americans. Throughout the eighteenth century they had become familiar with a series of British political writers called the *Commonwealthmen.* They held republican political ideas and had their intellectual roots in the most radical thought of the Puritan revolution. During the early eighteenth century these writers had relentlessly criticized the government patronage and parliamentary management of Robert Walpole and his successors. They argued that such government was corrupt and that it undermined liberty. They regarded much parliamentary taxation as simply a means of financing political corruption. They also attacked standing armies, which they considered instruments of tyranny.

In Great Britain this political tradition had only a marginal impact. The writers were largely ignored because most British subjects regarded themselves as the freest people in the world. However, over three thousand miles away in the colonies, these radical books and pamphlets were read widely and were often accepted at face value. The events in Great Britain following the accession of King George III made many colonists believe that the worst fears of the Commonwealth writers were coming true.

Events in Great Britain

George III (1760–1820) believed that his two immediate royal predecessors had been improperly bullied and controlled by their ministers. Royal power had in effect amounted to little more than the policies carried out by a

William Pitt the Elder Pleads the Cause
of the American Colonies

As Prime Minister, William Pitt had led Britain to its great victory and worldwide empire in the Seven Years' War. In January 1775 the elderly Pitt, addressing the House of Lords as Earl of Chatham, criticized the policies of George III, which had led to turmoil in Britain's relations with the American colonies. He specifically called for the repeal of the Intolerable Acts and for the removal of British troops from Boston. He compared the American resistance to taxation with the struggle of the Parliament against the Stuart monarchy a century earlier. In closing he contended that the policy of coercing the Americans would play into the hands of France and Spain. Pitt's appeals fell on deaf ears, and in April 1775 warfare broke out between the British Army and the colonists in Massachusetts.

If illegal violences have been, as it is said, committed in America [by the colonists resisting British policy], prepare the way, open the door of possibility, for acknowledgement and satisfaction: but proceed not to such coercion, such proscription; cease your indiscriminate inflictions; amerce not thirty thousand; oppress not three millions, for the fault of forty or fifty individuals. Such severity of injustice must for ever render incurable the wounds you have already given your colonies; you irritate them to unappeasable rancour. What though you march from town to town, and from province to province; though you should be able to enforce a temporary and local submission, which I only suppose, not admit—how shall you be able to secure the obedience of the country you leave behind you in your progress, to grasp the dominion of eighteen hundred miles of continent, populous in numbers, possessing valour, liberty, and resistance? . . . The spirit which now resists your taxation in America is the same which formerly opposed loans, benevolences, and ship-money in England: the same spirit which called England on its legs, and by the Bill of Rights vindicated the English constitution; the same spirit which established the great fundamental, essential maxim of your liberties, that no subject of England shall be taxed but by his own consent. . . . As an American, I would recognize to England her supreme right of regulating commerce and navigation: as an Englishman by birth and principle, I recognize to the Americans their supreme unalienable right in their property; a right which they are justified in the defence of to the last extremity. . . . I trust it is obvious to your Lordships, that all attempts to impose servitude upon such men, to establish despotism over such a mighty continental nation, must be vain, must be fatal. We shall be forced ultimately to retract; let us retract while we can, not when we must. . . . Avoid, then, this humiliating, disgraceful necessity. With a dignity becoming your exalted situation, make the first advances to concord, to peace and happiness: for that is your true dignity, to act with prudence and justice. . . . Every motive, therefore, of justice and of policy, of dignity and of prudence, urges you to ally the ferment in America—by a removal of your troops from Boston—by a repeal of your acts of parliament—and by demonstration of amicable dispositions towards your colonies. . . . Foreign war hanging over your heads by a slight and brittle thread: France and Spain watching your conduct, and waiting for the maturity of your errors;—with a vigilant eye to America, and the temper of your colonies, more than to their own concerns, be they what they may.

Correspondence of William Pitt, Earl of Chatham *(London:* 1840), *4: 380–384 as quoted in Elizabeth Kimball Kendall,* Source-book of English History for the Use of Schools and Readers *(New York: The Macmillan Company, 1900), pp. 350–353.*

few powerful Whig families. The new king intended to rule through Parliament, but he was determined to have ministers of his own choice. Moreover George III believed that Parliament should function under royal rather than aristocratic management. When William Pitt resigned after a disagreement with George over war policy, the king appointed the earl of Bute as his first minister. In doing so, he ignored the great Whig families that had run the country since 1715. The king sought the aid of politicians whom the Whigs hated. Moreover, he attempted to use the same kind of patronage techniques developed by Walpole to achieve royal control of the House of Commons.

Between 1761 and 1770 George tried one minister after another, but each in turn failed to gain sufficient support from the various factions in the House of Commons. Finally, in 1770 he turned to Lord North (1732–1792), who remained the king's first minister until 1782. The Whig families and other political spokesmen claimed that George III was at-

George III (1760–1820). Although he never sought to make himself a tyrant as his critics charged, George did try to reassert the political influence of the monarchy which had been eroded under the first two Hanoverian kings, George I and George II. [New York Public Library Picture Collection]

tempting to impose a tyranny. What they meant was that the king was attempting to curb the power of a particular group of the aristocracy. George III certainly was seeking to restore more royal influence to the government of Great Britain, but he was not attempting to make himself a tyrant.

THE CHALLENGE OF JOHN WILKES

Then, in 1763, began the affair of John Wilkes (1725–1797). This London political radical and member of Parliament published a newspaper called *The North Briton*. In issue Number 45 of this paper Wilkes strongly criticized Lord Bute's handling of the peace negotiations with France. Wilkes was arrested under the authority of a general warrant issued by the secretary of state. He pled the privileges of a member of Parliament and was released. The courts also later ruled that the vague kind of general warrant by which he had been arrested was illegal. However, the House of Commons ruled that issue Number 45 of *The North Briton* was a libel and expelled Wilkes from the Commons. He soon fled the country and was outlawed. Throughout these procedures there was very widespread support for Wilkes, and many demonstrations were held in his cause.

In 1768 Wilkes returned to England and again stood for election to Parliament. He won the election, but the House of Commons, under the influence of George III's friends, refused to seat him. He was elected three more times. After the fourth election the House of Commons simply ignored the election results and seated the government-supported candidate. As earlier in the decade, large popular demonstrations of shopkeepers, artisans, and small property owners supported Wilkes. He also received aid from some aristocratic politicians who wished to humiliate George III. Wilkes himself contended during all of his troubles that his cause was the cause of English liberty. "Wilkes and Liberty" became the slogan of all political radicals and many noble opponents of the monarch. Wilkes was finally seated in 1774, after having become the lord mayor of London.

The American colonists followed all of these developments of the 1760s very closely. The contemporary events in Britain confirmed their fears about a monarchical and parliamentary conspiracy against liberty. The king, as their Whig friends told them, was behaving

This satirical portrait of John Wilkes was made by William Hogarth. It suggests the unattractive personal character of Wilkes and also tends to question the sincerity of his calls for liberty. [Charles Farrell Collection]

like a tyrant. The Wilkes affair displayed the arbitrary power of the monarch, the corruption of the House of Commons, and the contempt of both for popular electors. That same monarch and Parliament were attempting to overturn the traditional relationship of Great Britain to its colonies by imposing parliamentary taxes. The same government had then landed troops in Boston, changed the government of Massachusetts, and undermined the traditional right of jury trial. All of these events fulfilled too exactly the portrait of political tyranny that had developed over the years in the minds of articulate colonists.

MOVEMENT FOR PARLIAMENTARY REFORM

The political influences between America and Britain operated both ways. The colonial demand for no taxation without representation and the criticism of the adequacy of the British system of representation struck at the core of the eighteenth-century British political structure. Colonial arguments could be adopted by British subjects at home who were no more directly represented in the House of Commons than were the Americans. The colonial questioning of the taxing authority of the House of Commons was related to the protest of John Wilkes. Both the Americans and Wilkes were challenging the power of the monarch and the authority of Parliament. Moreover, both the colonial leaders and Wilkes appealed over the head of legally constituted political authorities to popular opinion and popular demonstrations. Both were protesting the power of a largely self-selected aristocratic political body. The British ministry was fully aware of these broader political implications of the American troubles.

The American colonists also demonstrated to Europe how a politically restive people in the old regime could fight tyranny and protect political liberty. They established revolutionary but orderly political bodies that could function outside the existing political framework: the congress and the convention. These began with the Stamp Act Congress of 1765 and culminated in the Constitutional Convention of 1787. The legitimacy of those congresses and conventions lay not in existing law but in the alleged consent of the governed. This approach represented a new way to found a government.

Toward the end of the War of the American Revolution, calls for parliamentary reform were voiced in Britain itself. The method proposed for changing the system was the extralegal Association Movement.

THE YORKSHIRE ASSOCIATION MOVEMENT

By the close of the 1770s there was much resentment in Britain about the mismanagement of the war, the high taxes, and Lord North's ministry. In northern England in 1778 Christopher Wyvil (1740–1822), a landowner and retired clergyman, organized the Yorkshire Association Movement. Property owners or freeholders of Yorkshire met in a mass meeting to demand rather moderate changes in the corrupt system of parliamentary elections. They organized corresponding societies elsewhere. They intended that the association examine—and suggest reforms

Major Cartwright Calls for the Reform of Parliament

During the years of the American Revolution there were many demands in England itself for a major reform of Parliament. In this pamphlet of 1777 Major John Cartwright demanded that a much larger number of English citizens be allowed to vote for members of the House of Commons. He also heaped contempt on the opponents of reform.

Suffering as we do, from a deep parliamentary corruption, it is no time to tamper with silly correctives, and trifle away the life of public freedom: but we must go to the bottom of the stinking sore and cleanse it thoroughly: we must once more infuse into the constitution the vivifying spirit of liberty and expel the very last dregs of this poison. *Annual parliaments with an equal representation of the commons* are the only specifics in this case: and they would effect a radical cure. That a house of commons, formed as ours is, should maintain septennial elections, and laugh at every other idea is no wonder. The wonder is, that the British nation which, but the other day, was the greatest nation on earth, should be so easily laughed out of its liberties. . . .

Those who now claim the *exclusive* right of sending to parliament the 513 representatives for about six million souls (amongst whom are one million five hundred thousand males, *competent as electors*) consist of about two hundred and fourteen thousand persons; and 254 of these representatives are elected by 5,723. . . . Their pretended rights are many of them, derived from *royal favour*; some from antient usage and prescription; and some indeed from act of parliament; but neither the most authentic acts of royalty, nor precedent, nor prescription, nor even parliament can establish any flagrant injustice; much less can they strip one million two hundred and eighty six thousand of an inalienable right, to vest it in a number amounting to only one seventh of that multitude. . . .

John Cartwright, Legislative Rights of the Commonality Vindicated, *cited in S. Maccoby,* The English Radical Tradition, 1763–1914 *(London: Adam and Charles Black, 1966), pp. 32–33.*

for—the entire government. The Association Movement was thus a popular attempt to establish an extralegal institution to reform the government.

The movement collapsed during the early 1780s because its supporters, unlike Wilkes and the American rebels, were not willing to appeal for broad popular support. Nonetheless, the agitation of the Association Movement provided many people with experience in political protest. Several of its younger figures lived to raise the issue of parliamentary reform after 1815.

Parliament was not insensitive to the demands of the Association Movement. In April 1780 the Commons passed a resolution that called for lessening the power of the crown. In 1782 Parliament adopted a measure for "economical" reform, which abolished some patronage at the disposal of the monarch. However, these actions did not prevent George III from appointing a minister of his own choice. In 1783 shifts in Parliament obliged Lord North to form a ministry with Charles James Fox (1749–1806), a long-time critic of George III. The monarch was most unhappy with the arrangement.

In 1783 he approached William Pitt the Younger (1759–1806), son of the victorious war minister, to manage the House of Commons. During the election of 1784 Pitt received immense patronage support from the crown and constructed a House of Commons favorable to the king. Thereafter, Pitt sought to formulate trade policies that would give his ministry broad popularity. He attempted in 1785 one measure of modest parliamentary reform. When it failed, the young prime minister, who had been only twenty-four at the time of his appointment, abandoned the cause of reform.

By the mid-1780s George III had achieved a part of what he had sought beginning in 1761. He had reasserted the influence of the monarchy in political affairs. It proved a temporary victory because his own mental illness, which would finally require a regency, weakened the royal power. The cost of his years of dominance had been very high. On both sides of the Atlantic the issue of popular sovereignty had been raised and widely discussed. The American colonies had been lost. Economically this loss did not prove disastrous. British trade with America after independence actually increased.

However, the Americans—through the state constitutions, the Articles of Confederation, and the federal Constitution—had demonstrated to Europe the possibility of government without kings and without aristocracies. They had established the example of a nation in which written documents based on popular consent and popular sovereignty—rather than on divine law, natural law, tradition, or the will of kings—stood as the highest political

and legal authority. Writers throughout western Europe sensed that a new kind of political era was dawning. It was to be an age of constituent assemblies, constitutions, and declarations of rights.

EVENTS IN BRITAIN AND AMERICA RELATING TO THE AMERICAN REVOLUTION	
1760	George III ascends the English throne
1763	Treaty of Paris concludes the Seven Years' War
1763	John Wilkes publishes issue Number 45 of *The North Briton*
1764	Sugar Act
1765	Stamp Act
1766	Stamp Act repealed and Declaratory Act passed
1767	Townshend Acts
1768	Parliament refuses to seat John Wilkes after his election
1770	Lord North becomes George III's chief minister
1770	Boston Massacre
1773	Boston Tea Party
1774	Intolerable Acts
1774	First Continental Congress
1775	Second Continental Congress
1776	Declaration of Independence
1778	France enters the war on the side of America
1778	Yorkshire Association Movement founded
1781	British forces surrender at Yorktown
1783	Treaty of Paris concludes War of the American Revolution

---

Throughout the eighteenth century the great European powers fought in two major arenas— their overseas commercial empires and central Europe.

In the New World Britain, France, and Spain battled for commercial dominance. France and Britain also clashed over their spheres of influence in India. By the third quarter of the century Britain had succeeded in ousting France from most of its major holdings in North America and from all of its presence in India. Spain, though no longer a military power of the first order, had managed to maintain its vast colonial empire in Latin America and a large measure of trade monopoly.

On the continent France, Austria, and Prus-

sia collided over conflicting territorial and dynastic ambitions. Britain became involved as it sought to protect its continental interests and to use the continental wars to dominate in the colonial arena. By the third quarter of the century Prussia with British aid had emerged as a major continental power. Austria had lost considerable territory to Prussia. France had accumulated a vast debt.

The mid-century conflicts in turn led to major changes in all the European states. Each of the monarchies needed more money and attempted to govern themselves more efficiently. This problem led Britain to attempt to tax the North American colonies where soon a revolution arose resulting in the loss of those colonies. *Already deeply in debt, the French monarchy aided the Americans, fell into a deeper financial crisis, and soon sharply clashed with the nobility as royal ministers attempted to find new revenues. That clash eventually unleashed the French Revolution. Spain moved to administer its Latin American empire more efficiently with revolutionary discontent arising in the early nineteenth cen-* tury. *In preparation for future wars the rulers of Prussia, Austria, and Russia pursued a mode of activist government known as Enlightened Absolutism. This will be examined in the next chapter. In that regard the mid-eighteenth-century wars set in motion most of the major political developments of the next half century.*

Suggested Readings

B. BAILYN, *The Ideological Origins of the American Revolution* (1967). An important work illustrating the role of English radical thought in the perceptions of the American colonists.

B. BAILYN, *The Peopling of British North America: An Introduction* (1988). A study of the immigrants to the British colonies on the eve of the Revolution.

C. BECKER, *The Declaration of Independence: A Study in the History of Political Ideas* (1922). An examination of the political and imperial theory of the Declaration.

C. BONWICK, *English Radicals and the American Revolution* (1977). Explores the relationship between English radical politics and events in America.

J. BREWER, *Party Ideology and Popular Politics at the Accession of George III* (1976). An important series of essays on popular radicalism.

J. BREWER, *The Sinews of Power: War, Money, and the English State, 1688–1783* (1989). A study that emphasizes the financial power behind British military success.

J. BROOKE, *King George III* (1972). The best biography.

I. R. CHRISTIE, *Stress and Stability in Late Eighteenth-Century Britain: Reflections on the British Avoidance of Revolution* (1985). Thoughtful essays by one of the most important of eighteenth-century British historians.

D. B. DAVIS, *The Problem of Slavery in Western Culture* (1966). A brilliant and far-ranging discussion.

D. B. DAVIS, *The Problem of Slavery in the Age of Revolution, 1770–1823* (1975). A major work for both European and American history.

R. DAVIS, *The Rise of the Atlantic Economies* (1973). A major synthesis.

WALTER DORN, *Competition for Empire, 1740–1763* (1940). Still one of the best accounts of the mid-century struggle.

C. GIBSON, *The Aztecs Under Spanish Rule: A History of the Indians of the Valley of Mexico* (1964). An exceedingly interesting book.

C. GIBSON, *Spain in America* (1966). A splendidly clear and balanced discussion.

L. H. GIPSON, *The British Empire Before the American Revolution*, 13 vols. (1936–1967). A magisterial account of the mid-century wars from an imperial viewpoint.

L. HANKE, *Bartolomé de Las Casas: An Interpretation of His Life and Writings* (1951). A classic work.

F. KATZ, *The Ancient American Civilizations* (1972). An excellent introduction.

B. KEEN AND M. WASSERMAN, *A Short History of Latin America* (1984). A good survey with very helpful bibliographical guides.

P. LANGFORD, *A Polite and Commercial People: England 1717–1783* (1989). An excellent survey of mid-century Britain based on the most recent scholarship covering social history as well as politics, the overseas wars, and the American Revolution.

J. LOCKHARDT AND S. B. SCHWARTZ, *Early Latin America: A History of Colonial Spanish America and Brazil* (1983). The new standard work.

J. R. McNEIL, *Atlantic Empires of France and Spain: Louisbourg and Havana, 1700–1763* (1985). An examination of imperial policies in terms of two key overseas outposts.

R. MIDDLETON, *The Bells of Victory: The Pitt-Newcastle Ministry and the Conduct of the Seven Years' War, 1757–1762* (1985). A careful study of the intricacies of eighteenth-century cabinet government that questions the centrality of Pitt's role in the British victory.

S. W. MINTZ, *Sweetness and Power: The Place of Sugar in Modern History* (1985). Traces the role of sugar in the world economy and the manner in which sugar has had an impact on world culture.

R. PARES, *King George III and the Politicians* (1953). An important analysis of the constitutional and political structures.

J. H. PARRY, *Trade and Dominion: The European Overseas Empires in the Eighteenth Century* (1971). A comprehensive account with attention to the European impact on the rest of the world.

J. G. A. POCOCK, *The Machiavellian Moment: Florentine Political Thought and the Atlantic Republican Tradition* (1975). An exceedingly important book that traces the origins of Anglo-American radicalism to Renaissance Florence.

J. G. A. POCOCK, *Virtue, Commerce, and History:*

Essays on Political Thought and History, Chiefly in the Eighteenth Century (1985). Important articles.

C. D. RICE, *The Rise and Fall of Black Slavery* (1975). An excellent survey of the subject with careful attention to the numerous historiographical controversies.

G. RUDÉ, *Wilkes and Political Liberty* (1962). A close analysis of popular political behavior.

I. K. STEELE, *The English Atlantic, 1675–1740: An Exploration of Communication and Community* (1986). An exploration of culture and commerce in the trans-Atlantic world.

S. J. STEIN AND B. H. STEIN, *The Colonial Heritage of Latin America: Essays on Economic Dependence in Perspective* (1970). An important work emphasizing the long-range impact of the colonial economy.

R. L. STEIN, *The French Sugar Business in the Eighteenth Century* (1988). A study that covers all aspects of the French sugar trade.

G. WILLS, *Inventing America: Jefferson's Declaration of Independence* (1978). An important study that challenges much of the analysis in the Becker volume noted above.

G. S. WOOD, *The Creation of the American Republic, 1776–1787* (1969). A far-ranging work dealing with Anglo-American political thought.

ENLIGHTENMENT AND REVOLUTION

B etween approximately 1750 and 1850, certain extraordinary changes occurred in Western civilization. Although of immediate significance primarily for the nations of Europe and the Americas, these developments produced in the long run an immense impact throughout the world. No other civilizations eventually escaped the influence of the European intellectual ferment and political turmoil of these years. Most of the intellectual, political, economic, and social characteristics associated with the *modern* world came into being during this era. Europe became the great exporter of ideas and technologies that in time transformed one area after another of the human experience.

Intellectually, the ideals of reform and of challenge to traditional cultural authority captured the imagination of numerous writers. That movement, known as the *Enlightenment*, drew confidence from the scientific worldview that had emerged during the seventeenth century. Its exponents urged the application of the spirit of critical rationalism in one area of social and political life after another. They posed serious historical and moral questions to the Christian faith. They contended that laws of society and economics could be discovered and could then be used to improve the human condition. They embraced the idea of economic growth and development. They called for political reform and more efficient modes of government. They upheld the standard of rationality in order to cast doubt on traditional modes of thought and behavior that seemed to them less than rational. As a result of their labors, in Europe and ultimately throughout the world, the idea of change that has played so important a role in modern life came for the first time to have a generally positive value attached to it.

For many people, however, change seemed to come too rapidly and violently when revolution erupted n France in 1789. Commencing as an aristocratic revolt against the monarchy, the revolution rapidly spread to every corner of French political and social life. The rights of man and citizen displaced those of the monarchy, the aristocracy, and the Church. By 1792, the revolution had become a genuinely popular movement and had established a French republic whose armies challenged the other major European monarchies. The reign of terror that saw the execution of the French king unleashed domestic violence unlike anything witnessed in Europe since the age of the religious wars. By the end of the 1790s, to restore order, French political leaders turned themselves over to the leadership of Napoleon. Thereafter, for more than a decade, his armies uprooted institutions of the old regime across the continent. Only in 1815, after the battle of Waterloo, was the power of France and Napoleon finally contained.

The French Revolution in one way or another served as a model for virtually all later popular revolutions. It unleashed new forces and political creeds in one area of the world after another. The French Revolution, with its broad popular base, brought *the people* to the forefront of world political history. In the early revolutionary goals of establishing a legal framework of limited monarchical power, of securing citizen rights, and of making possible relatively free economic activity, the supporters of the revolution spawned the political creed of *liberalism.*

The wars of the French Revolution and of Napoleon, stretching from 1792 to 1815, awakened the political force of *nationalism,* which has proved to be the single most powerful ideology of the modern world. Loyalty to the nation defined in terms of a common language, history, and culture replaced loyalty to dynasties. As a political ideology, nationalism could be used both to liberate a people from the domination of another nation and to justify wars of aggression. Nationalism was put to both uses in Europe and throughout the rest of the world in the two centuries following the revolution in France. Nationalism became a kind of secular religion that aroused a degree of loyalty and personal self-sacrifice previously called forth only by the great religious traditions.

Finally, between 1750 and 1850, Europe became not only an exporter of reform and revolution but also of manufactured commodities. The technology and the society associated with industrialism took root throughout the western portion of the continent. Europeans achieved a productive capacity that, in cooperation with their naval power, permitted them to dominate the markets of the world. Thereafter, to be strong, independent, and modern seemed to mean to become industrialized and to imitate the manufacturing techniques of Europe and later of the United States.

But industrialism and its society fostered immense social problems, dislocations, and injustices. The major intellectual and political response was *socialism,* several varieties of which emerged from European social and economic turmoil of the 1830s and 1840s. History eventually proved the most important of these to be that espoused by Karl Marx, whose *Communist Manifesto* appeared in 1848.

Remarkable ironies are attached to the European achievements of the late eighteenth and the early nineteenth centuries. Enlightenment, revolution, and industrialism contributed to an awakening of European power that permitted the continent to dominate the world for a time at the end of the nineteenth century. Yet those same movements produced various intellectual critiques, political ideas, and economic skills that twentieth-century non-European peoples would turn against their temporary European masters. It is for that reason that the age of enlightenment and revolution in the West was of such significance not simply in Europe but in the history of the entire modern world.

*Jean Jacques Rousseau contributed to the political thought
of the Enlightenment. Many of his writings also challenged
the ideas of other Enlightenment writers. [Giraudon/Art Resource]*

18

THE AGE OF ENLIGHTENMENT: EIGHTEENTH-CENTURY THOUGHT

During the eighteenth century the conviction began to spread throughout the literate sectors of European society that change and reform were both possible and desirable. This attitude is now commonplace, but it came into its own only after 1700. It represents one of the primary intellectual inheritances from that age. The movement of people and ideas that fostered such thinking is called the Enlightenment.

Its leading voices combined confidence in the human mind inspired by the Scientific Revolution and faith in the power of rational criticism to challenge the intellectual authority of tradition and the Christian past. These writers stood convinced that human beings could comprehend the operation of physical nature and mold it to the ends of material and moral improvement. The rationality of the physical universe became a standard against which the customs and traditions of society could be measured and criticized. Such criticism penetrated every corner of contemporary society, politics, and religious opinion. As a result the spirit of innovation and improvement came to characterize modern Europe and Western society.

The writers associated with the Enlightenment explored virtually every aspect of contemporary social and economic life. They sought to encourage economic development and the spread of prosperity. They wrote in favor of legal reform and supported the then radical idea of religious toleration. They were highly critical of the militarism that characterized so much European life during the mid-century wars.

Some of their ideas had a direct impact on several rulers in central and eastern Europe. These rulers, whose policies became known by the term Enlightened Absolutism, sought to centralize their authority so as to reform their countries. They often attempted to restructure religious authority and to sponsor economic growth. Although they were often associated with the writers of the Enlightenment, many of their policies were in direct opposition to enlightened ideals. Nonetheless, both the Enlightenment writers and the monarchs were forces for the modernization of European life.

Formative Influences

The Newtonian worldview, the stability and prosperity of Great Britain after 1688, and the degradation that the wars of Louis XIV had brought to France were the chief factors that fostered the discussion of Enlightenment and reform throughout Europe.

Ideas of Newton and Locke

Isaac Newton (1642–1727) and John Locke (1632–1704) were the major intellectual forerunners of the Enlightenment. Newton's formulation of the laws of universal gravitation exemplified the powers of the human mind. His example and his writing encouraged Europeans to approach the study of nature directly and to avoid metaphysics and supernaturalism. Newton had formulated general laws but had always insisted on a foundation of specific empirical evidence for those laws. Empirical experience had provided a constant check on his rational speculation.

This emphasis on concrete experience became a keystone for Enlightenment thought. Moreover, Newton had discerned a pattern of rationality in natural physical phenomena. During the eighteenth century the ancient idea of following nature became transformed under the Newtonian influence into the idea of following reason. Because nature was rational, society should be organized in a rational manner.

As explained in Chapter 14, Newton's scientific achievement had inspired his countryman John Locke to seek a human psychology based on experience. In An Essay Concerning Human Understanding (1690), Locke argued that each human being enters the world as a tabula rasa, or blank page. His or her personality is consequently the product of the sensations that impinge from the external world throughout the course of life. The significant conclusion that followed from this psychology was that human nature is changeable and can be molded by modification of the surrounding physical and social environment. Locke's was a reformer's psychology. It suggested that improvement in the human situation was possible. Locke also, in effect, rejected the Christian view of humankind as creatures permanently flawed by sin. Human beings need not wait for the grace of God or other divine aid to better their lives. They could take charge of their own destiny.

The Example of British Toleration and Stability

Newton's physics and Locke's psychology provided the theoretical basis for reform. The domestic stability of Great Britain after the Revolution of 1688 furnished a living example of a society in which enlightened reforms functioned for the benefit of all concerned. England permitted religious toleration to all creeds except Unitarianism and Roman Catholicism, whose believers were not actually persecuted. Relative freedom of the press and free speech prevailed. The monarchy was limited in its authority, and political sovereignty resided in the Parliament. The courts protected citizens from arbitrary government action. The army was quite small. These liberal policies had produced not disorder and instability but economic prosperity and loyalty to the political system.

The continental view of England was somewhat idealized. Nevertheless, the country was sufficiently freer than any other nation to make the point that the reformers sought.

627

THE AGE OF
ENLIGHTENME.
EIGHTEENTH
CENTURY
THOUGHT

Science captured much of the imagination in the eighteenth century and inspired enlightenment writers. In this famous painting by Joseph Wright of Derby, eager observers surround an experiment with an air pump. [Tate Gallery, London]

Need for Reform in France

If the example of Great Britain suggested that change need not be disastrous to a nation and society, France exhibited many of the practices and customs of European politics and society that most demanded reform. Louis XIV had build his power on the bases of absolute monarchy, a large standing army, heavy taxation, and a religious unity requiring persecution. However, the enemies of France had defeated that nation in war. Its people were miserable, and celebrations had marked the death of the great king. His successors had been unable to reform the state. Critics of the monarchy were subject to arbitrary arrest. There was no freedom of worship. Political and religious censors interfered with the press and other literary productions. Offending authors could be imprisoned, although some achieved cooperative relations with the authorities. State regulations hampered economic growth. Many aristocrats regarded themselves as a military class and upheld militaristic values.

Yet throughout the French social structure there existed people who wanted to see changes brought about. These people read and supported the *philosophes* of their nation and of other countries. Consequently, France became the major center for the Enlightenment, for there, more than in any other state, the demand for reform daily confronted writers and political thinkers.

The *Philosophes*

The writers and critics who forged this new attitude favorable to change and who championed change and reform were the *philosophes.* They were not usually philosophers in a formal sense; rather, they were people who sought to apply the rules of reason and common sense to nearly all the major institutions and social practices of the day. The most famous of their number included Voltaire, Mon-

These philosophes *gathered at the salon of Madame Geoffrin in 1755. The Parisian salons presided over by fashionable, intelligent women were the places where the ideas of the Enlightenment were discussed and propagated. [Musée de Malmaison]*

tesquieu, Diderot, Rousseau, Hume, Gibbon, Smith, Bentham, Lessing, and Kant.

A few of these *philosophes* occupied professorships in universities. However, most were free agents who might be found in London coffeehouses, Edinburgh drinking spots, the salons of fashionable Parisian ladies, the country houses of reform-minded nobles, or the courts of the most powerful monarchs on the Continent. In eastern Europe persons of this outlook were often to be found in the royal bureaucracies. They were not an organized group; they disagreed on many issues. Their relationship with each other and with lesser figures of the same turn of mind has quite appropriately been compared with that of a family, in which despite quarrels and tensions a basic unity still remains.[1]

The chief unity of the *philosophes* lay in their desire to reform thought, society, and government for the sake of human liberty. As Peter Gay has suggested, this goal included "freedom from arbitrary power, freedom of speech, freedom of trade, freedom to realize one's talents, freedom of aesthetic response, freedom, in a word, of moral man to make his way in the world."[2] No other single set of ideas has done so much to shape the modern world. The literary vehicles through which the *philosophes* delivered their message included books, pamphlets, plays, novels, philosophical treatises, encyclopedias, newspapers, and magazines. During the Reformation and the religious wars writers had used the printed word to debate the proper mode of faith in God. The *philosophes* of the Enlightenment employed the printed word to proclaim a new faith in the capacity of humankind to improve itself without the aid of God.

Many of the *philosophes* were middle class in their social origins. The bulk of their readership was also drawn from the prosperous commercial and professional people of the eigh-

[1] *Peter Gay*, The Enlightenment: An Interpretation *(New York: Knopf, 1967), 1:4.*

[2] *Gay, 1:3.*

629

THE AGE OF
ENLIGHTENMEN
EIGHTEENTH
CENTURY
THOUGHT

Immanuel Kant Defines Enlightenment

*Immanuel Kant was one of the most important German philoso-
phers associated with the Enlightenment. His work is more fully
discussed in Chapter 20. The passage below is from one of his
more accessible articles written in 1784 for a broad audience. He
equates Enlightenment with the individual human being's daring
to use his or her reason. He indicates that this is difficult because
so many people have come by habit to depend upon the reasoning
of others to guide their lives. He discusses the courage required to
use reason and the freedom that is necessary for its use.*

Enlightenment is man's emergence from his self-imposed nonage. Nonage is the inability to use one's own understanding without another's guidance. This nonage is self-imposed if its causes lie not in lack of understanding but in indecision and lack of courage to use one's own mind without another's guidance. *Dare to know! (Sapere aude)* "Have the courage to use your own understanding," is therefore the motto of the enlightenment.

Laziness and cowardice are the reasons why such a large part of mankind gladly remain minors all their lives, long after nature has freed them from external guidance. They are the reasons why it is so easy for others to set themselves up as guardians. It is so comfortable to be a minor. If I have a book that thinks for men, a pastor who acts as my conscience, a physician who prescribes my diet, and so on—then I have no need to exert myself. I have no need to think, if only I can pay; others will take care of that disagreeable business for me. . . .

Thus it is very difficult for the individual to work himself out of the nonage which has become almost second nature to him. He has even grown to like it and is at first really incapable of using his own understanding, because he has never been permitted to try it. Dogmas and formulas, these mechanical tools designed for reasonable use—or rather abuse—of his natural gifts, are the fetters of an everlasting nonage. The man who casts them off would make an uncertain leap over the narrowest ditch, because he is not used to such movement. That is why there are only a few men who walk firmly, and who have emerged from nonage by cultivating their own minds.

It is more nearly possible, however, for the public to enlighten itself; indeed, if it is only given freedom, enlightenment is almost inevitable. There will always be a few independent thinkers, even among the self-appointed guardians of the multitude. Once such men have thrown off the yoke on nonage, they will spread about them the spirit of a reasonable appreciation of man's value and of his duty to think for himself. . . .

This enlightenment requires nothing but *freedom*—and the most innocent of all that may be called "freedom": freedom to make public use of one's reason in all matters.

From Kant, "What is Enlightenment?" Peter Gay, trans., in Introduction to Contemporary Civilization in the West, *2nd edition (New York: Columbia University Press, 1954), 2:1071–1072.*

teenth-century towns and cities. These people discussed the reformers' writings and ideas in local philosophical societies, Freemason lodges, and clubs. They had sufficient income and leisure time to buy and read the *philosophes'* works. Although the writers of the Enlightenment did not consciously champion the goals or causes of the middle class, they did provide an intellectual ferment and a major source of ideas that could be used to undermine existing social practices and political structures. They taught their contemporaries how to pose pointed, critical questions. Moreover, the *philosophes* generally supported the economic growth, the expansion of trade, and the improvement of transport which were transforming the society and the economy of the eighteenth century and enlarging the middle class.

The Enlightenment evolved over the course of the century and involved a number of writers living at different times in various countries. Its early exponents popularized the rationalism and scientific ideas of the seventeenth century (see Chapter 14). They worked to expose contemporary social and political abuses and argued that reform was necessary and possible. The advancement of their cause and ideas was anything but steady. They confronted the obstacles of vested interests, political oppression, and religious condemnation.

Yet by the mid-century they had brought enlightened ideas to the European public in a variety of formats. The *philosophes*' "family" had come into being. They corresponded with each other, wrote for each other as well as for the general public, and defended each other against the political and religious authorities.

By the second half of the century they were sufficiently safe to quarrel among themselves on occasion. They had stopped talking in generalities, and their major advocates were addressing themselves to specific abuses. Their books and articles had become more specialized and more practical. They had become more concerned with politics than with religion. Having convinced Europeans that change was a good idea, they began to suggest exactly what changes were most desirable. They had become honored figures.

Voltaire's Agenda of Intellectual Reform

One of the earliest and by far the most influential of the *philosophes* was François Marie Arouet, known to posterity as Voltaire (1694–1778). During the 1720s Voltaire had offended the French authorities by certain of his writings. He was arrested and put in prison for a brief time.

Later Voltaire went to England, where he visited in the best literary circles, observed the

Philosopher, dramatist, poet, historian, scientist— Voltaire (1694–1778) was the most famous and influential of the eighteenth-century philosophes. [Bulloz]

tolerant intellectual and religious climate, felt free in the atmosphere of moderate politics, and admired the science and the economic prosperity. In 1733 he published *Letters on the English*, which appeared in French the next year. The book praised the virtues of the English and indirectly criticized the abuses of French society. In 1738 he published *Elements of the Philosophy of Newton*, which popularized the thought of the great scientist. Both works were well received and gave Voltaire a reputation as an important writer.

Thereafter Voltaire lived part of the time in France and part near Geneva, just across the French border, where the royal authorities could not bother him. He wrote essays, history, plays, stories, and letters that made him the literary dictator of Europe. He brought the bitter venom of his satire and sarcasm against one evil after another in French and European life. His most famous satire is *Candide* (1759), in which he attacked war, religious persecution, and what he regarded as unwarranted optimism about the human condition.

Like most *philosophes*, Voltaire believed that improvement of human society was necessary and possible. But he was never certain that reform, if achieved, would be permanent. The optimism of the Enlightenment constituted a tempered hopefulness rather than a glib certainty. Pessimism provided an undercurrent to most of the works of the period.

The Encyclopedia

The mid-century witnessed the publication of one of the greatest monuments of the Enlightenment. Under the heroic leadership of Denis Diderot (1713–1784), and Jean le Rond d'Alembert (1717–1783), the first volume of the *Encyclopedia* appeared in 1751. The project reached

The title page of the first volume of the Encyclopedia *is shown here. The early volumes of the text received the approval of the royal censor, as noted on the last line, but when it became evident that the work challenged many widely held religious and political views, its opponents obtained withholding of approval for later volumes which were eventually published. [The Mansell Collection]*

completion in 1772, numbering seventeen volumes of text and eleven of plates (illustrations).

The *Encyclopedia* was the product of the collective effort of more than one hundred authors, and its editors had at one time or another solicited articles from all the major French *philosophes*. The project reached fruition only after numerous attempts to censor it and to halt its publication. The *Encyclopedia* set forth the most advanced critical ideas in religion, government, and philosophy. This criticism often had to be hidden in obscure articles or under the cover of irony. The articles represented a collective plea for freedom of expression. However, the large volumes also provided important information on manufacturing, canal building, ship construction, and improved agriculture.

Between fourteen and sixteen thousand copies of various editions of the *Encyclopedia* were sold before 1789. The project had been designed to secularize learning and to undermine the intellectual assumptions remaining from the Middle Ages and the Reformation. The articles on politics, ethics, and society ignored concerns about divine law and concentrated on humanity and its immediate well-being. The encyclopedists looked to antiquity rather than to the Christian centuries for their intellectual and ethical models. The future welfare of humankind lay not in pleasing God or following divine commandments but rather in harnessing the power and resources of the earth and in living at peace with one's fellow human beings. The good life lay here and now and was to be achieved through the application of reason to human relationships.

With the publication of the *Encyclopedia*, enlightened thought became more fully diffused over the Continent. Enlightened ideas penetrated German and Russian intellectual and political circles. The *philosophes* of the latter part of the century turned from championing the general cause of reform and discussed specific areas of practical application. Gotthold Lessing wrote plays to plead for religious toleration. Adam Smith attacked the mercantile system. Cesare Beccaria and Jeremy Bentham called for penal and legal reforms. By this time the concepts of reform and the rationalization of existing institutions had become deeply impressed on European thinking and society. The issue then became—and

631

THE AGE OF
ENLIGHTENMEN
EIGHTEENTH-
CENTURY
THOUGHT

would remain for over a century—how best to implement those reforms.

The Enlightenment and Religion

Throughout the century, in the eyes of the *philosophes* the chief enemy of the improvement of humankind and the enjoyment of happiness was the existence and influence of ecclesiastical institutions. The hatred of the *philosophes* for the Church and Christianity was summed up in Voltaire's cry of "Crush the Infamous Thing." Almost all varieties of Christianity, but especially Roman Catholicism, invited the criticism of the *philosophes*.

Intellectually the churches perpetuated a religious rather than a scientific view of humankind and physical nature. The clergy taught that human beings were basically depraved and that they required divine grace to become worthy creatures. The doctrine of original sin in either its Catholic or its Protestant formulation suggested that meaningful improvement in human nature on earth was impossible. Religious concerns turned human interest away from this world to the world to come. In the view of the *philosophes* the concept of predestination suggested that the condition of the human soul after death had little or no relationship to virtuous living during this life. Through disagreements over obscure doctrines the various churches favored the politics of intolerance and bigotry that in the past had caused human suffering, torture, and war.

To attack the Christian churches in this manner was to raise major questions about the life and the society of the old regime. Politically and socially the churches were deeply enmeshed in the power structure. They owned large amounts of land and collected tithes from peasants before any other taxes were collected. Most of the clergy were legally exempt from taxation and made only annual voluntary grants to the government. The upper clergy in most countries were relatives of aristocrats. Churchmen were actively involved in politics, serving in the British House of Lords and advising princes on the Continent. In Protestant countries the local clergyman of a particular parish was usually appointed by the local major landowner. Across the Continent membership in the predominant denomination of the kingdom gave certain subjects political advantages. Nonmembership often excluded other subjects from political participation.

Clergymen of all faiths preached the sinfulness of political disobedience, and they provided the intellectual justification for the social and political status quo. They were active where possible in exerting religious and literary censorship. The churches were thus privileged and powerful corporate bodies of the old regime. The *philosophes* chose to attack both their ideas and their power.

Deism

The *philosophes* believed that religion should be reasonable and should lead to moral behavior. The Newtonian worldview had convinced many writers that nature was rational. Therefore, the God who had created nature must also be rational, and the religion through which that God was worshiped should be rational. Moreover, Lockean psychology, which limited human knowledge to empirical experience, raised the question whether such a thing as divine revelation to humankind was, after all, possible. These considerations gave rise to a movement for enlightened religion known as *deism*.

The title of one of its earliest expositions, *Christianity Not Mysterious* (1696) by John Toland, indicates the general tenor of this religious outlook. Toland and later writers wished to consider religion a natural and rational, rather than a supernatural and mystical, phenomenon. In this respect the deists made a departure from the general piety of Newton and Locke, both of whom regarded themselves as distinctly Christian. Newton had believed that God might interfere with the natural order, whereas the deists regarded God as resembling a divine watchmaker who had set the mechanism of nature to work and had then departed from the scene.

There were two major points in the deists' creed. The first was a belief in the existence of God. They thought that this belief could be empirically deduced from the contemplation of nature. Joseph Addison's poem on the spacious firmament (1712) illustrates this idea:

> The spacious firmament on high,
> With all the blue ethereal sky,
> And spangled heav'n, a shining frame,

633

THE AGE (
ENLIGHTENM
EIGHTEENT
CENTURY
THOUGH

Voltaire Attacks Religious Fanaticism

The chief complaint of the philosophes *against Christianity was that it bred a fanaticism that led people to commit crimes in the name of religion. In this passage from his* Philosophical Dictionary *(1764) Voltaire directly reminded his readers of the intolerance of the Reformation era and indirectly referred to examples of contemporary religious excesses. He argued that the philosophical spirit can overcome fanaticism and foster toleration and more humane religious behavior. In a manner that shocked many of his contemporaries, he praised the virtues of Confucianism over those of Christianity.*

Fanaticism is to superstition what delirium is to fever and rage to anger. The man visited by ecstasies and visions, who takes dreams for realities and his fancies for prophecies, is an enthusiast; the man who supports his madness with murder is a fanatic. . . .

The most detestable example of fanaticism was that of the burghers of Paris who on St. Bartholomew's Night [1572] went about assassinating and butchering all their fellow citizens who did not go to mass, throwing them out of windows, cutting them in pieces.

Once fanaticism has corrupted a mind, the malady is almost incurable. . . .

The only remedy for this epidemic malady is the philosophical spirit which, spread gradually, at last tames men's habits and prevents the disease from starting; for once the disease has made any progress, one must flee and wait for the air to clear itself. Laws and religion are not strong enough against the spiritual pest; religion, far from being healthy food for infected brains, turns to poison in them. . . .

Even the law is impotent against these attacks of rage; it is like reading a court decree to a raving maniac. These fellows are certain that the holy spirit with which they are filled is above the law, that their enthusiasm is the only law they must obey.

What can we say to a man who tells you that he would rather obey God than men, and that therefore he is sure to go to heaven for butchering you?

Ordinarily fanatics are guided by rascals, who put the dagger into their hands; these latter resemble that Old Man of the Mountain who is supposed to have made imbeciles taste the joys of paradise and who promised them an eternity of the pleasures of which he had given them a foretaste, on condition that they assassinated all those he would name to them. There is only one religion in the world that has never been sullied by fanaticism, that of the Chinese men of letters. The schools of philosophy were not only free from this pest, they were its remedy; for the effect of philosophy is to make the soul tranquil, and fanaticism is incompatible with tranquility. If our holy religion has so often been corrupted by this infernal delirium, it is the madness of men which is at fault.

Voltaire, Philosophical Dictionary, *trans. by P. Gay (New York: Basic Books, 1962), pp. 267–269.*

Their great Original proclaim:
Th' unwearied Sun, from day to day,
Does his Creator's power display,
And publishes to every land
The work of an Almighty hand.

Because nature provided evidence of a rational God, that deity must also favor rational morality. Consequently, the second point in the deists' creed was a belief in life after death, when rewards and punishments would be meted out according to the virtue of the life a person led on this earth.

Deism was empirical, tolerant, reasonable, and capable of encouraging virtuous living. It was the major positive religious component of the Enlightenment. Voltaire declared:

> The great name of Deist, which is not sufficiently revered, is the only name one ought to take. The only gospel one ought to read is the great book of Nature, written by the hand of God and sealed with his seal. The only religion that ought to be professed is the religion of worshiping God and being a good man.[3]

If such a faith became widely accepted, the fanaticism and rivalry of the various Christian sects might be overcome. Religious conflict and persecutions encouraged by the fulsome zeal would end. There would also be little or no necessity for a priestly class to foment fanaticism, denominational hatred, and bigotry.

David Hume (1711–1776), the Scottish philosopher, argued against belief in miracles and, implicitly, against belief in Christianity itself. [National Galleries of Scotland]

Criticism of Religion

The *philosophes* did not rest with the formulation of a rational religious alternative to Christianity. They also attacked the churches and the clergy with great vehemence. Voltaire repeatedly questioned the truthfulness of priests and the morality of the Bible. In his *Philosophical Dictionary* (1764) he humorously pointed out inconsistencies in biblical narratives and immoral acts of the biblical heroes. The Scottish *philosophe* David Hume (1771–1776) published his *Inquiry into Human Nature* in 1748. In his chapter "Of Miracles" he argued that divine miracles, in which the churches put great store, were not grounded in rational belief or empirical evidence. For Hume, the greatest miracle was to believe in miracles. In *The Decline and Fall of the Roman Empire* (1776), Edward Gibbon (1737–1794), the English historian, examined the early history of Christianity and explained the rise of that faith in terms of natural causes rather than through the influence of miracles and piety.

A few *philosophes* went further. Baron d'Holbach (1723–1789) and Julien Offray de La Mettrie (1709–1751) embraced positions very near to atheism and materialism. Theirs was distinctly a minority position, however. Most of the *philosophes* sought not the abolition of

religion but its transformation into a humane force that would encourage virtuous living.

The *philosophes'* criticisms of Christianity also held negative implications for Judaism. The attack on biblical miracles and on the validity of biblical history undermined the authority of the Hebrew scriptures as well as the Christian. The satirical portrayals of personalities from the Bible were almost inevitably pointed at Jewish characters. In some cases Judaism came to appear as a much more primitive faith than Christianity. Consequently, the *philosophes'* harsh attitude toward traditional religion in general carried with it an implicit contempt for the Jewish as well as the Christian faith. In this manner the Enlightenment view of religion sometimes further undermined the position of Judaism and its adherents in the eyes of non-Jewish Europeans.

Toleration

A primary social condition for a virtuous life according to the *philosophes*, was the establishment of religious toleration. Again Voltaire took the lead in championing this cause. In 1762 the Roman Catholic political authorities in Toulouse ordered the execution of a Hugue-

---

[3] Quoted in J. H. Randall, The Making of the Modern Mind, rev. ed. (New York: Houghton Mifflin, 1940), p. 292.

not named Jean Calas. He stood accused of having murdered his son to prevent him from converting to Roman Catholicism. Calas had been viciously tortured and publicly strangled without ever having confessed his guilt. The confession would not have saved his life, but it would have given the Catholics good propaganda to use against Protestants.

Voltaire learned of the case only after Calas' death. He made the dead man's cause his own. In 1763 he published a *Treatise on Tolerance* and hounded the authorities for a new investigation. Finally, in 1765, the judicial decision against the unfortunate man was reversed. For Voltaire the case illustrated the fruits of religious fanaticism and the need for rational reform of judicial processes. Somewhat later in the century, the German playwright and critic Gotthold Lessing (1729–1781) wrote *Nathan the Wise* (1779) as a plea for toleration not only of different Christian sects but also of religious faiths other than Christianity.

635

THE AGE OF
ENLIGHTENMEN
EIGHTEENTH
CENTURY
THOUGHT

Beccaria Objects to Capital Punishment

In the eighteenth century the death penalty was commonly applied throughout Europe for small as well as great crimes. The young north Italian nobleman Cesare Beccaria thought the penalty was unproductive of law and order and was also unenlightened. On Crimes and Punishments *appeared when he was only twenty-six, and Voltaire, Bentham, and Catherine the Great professed to admire the work. His 1764 comments are a good example of the Enlightenment application of the criteria of reason and utility to social problems.*

Is the death penalty really *useful* and *necessary* for the security and good order of society? Are torture and torments *just*, and do they attain the *end* for which laws are instituted? What is the best way to prevent crimes? Are the same punishments equally effective for all times? What influence do they have on customary behavior? These problems deserve to be analyzed with that geometric precision which the mist of sophisms, seductive eloquence, and timorous doubt cannot withstand. . . . If, by defending the rights of man and of unconquerable truth, I should help to save from the spasm and agonies of death some wretched victim of tyranny or of no less fatal ignorance, the thanks and tears of one innocent mortal in his transports of joy would console me for the contempt of all mankind.

. . . .

If one were to cite against me the example of all the ages and of almost all the nations that have applied the death penalty to certain crimes, my reply would be that the example reduced itself to nothing in the face of truth, against which there is no prescription; that the history of men leaves us with the impression of a vast sea of errors; among which, at great intervals, some rare and hardly intelligible truths appear to float on the surface. Human sacrifices were once common to almost all nations, yet who will dare to defend them? That only a few societies, and for a short time only, have abstained from applying the death penalty, stands in my favor rather than against me, for that conforms with the usual lot of great truths, which are about as long-lasting as a lightning flash in comparison with the long dark night that envelops mankind. The happy time has not yet arrived in which truth shall be the portion of the greatest number, as error has heretofore been.

Cesare Beccaria, On Crimes and Punishments, *trans. by Henry M. Paolucci (Indianapolis: Bobbs-Merrill, 1963), pp. 10, 51.*

All of these calls for toleration stated, in effect, that life on earth and human relationships should not be subordinated to religion. Secular values and considerations were more important than religious ones.

The Enlightenment and Society

Although the *philosophes* wrote much on religion, humanity was the center of their interest. As one writer in the *Encyclopedia* observed, "Man is the unique point to which we

Jeremy Bentham applied the principle of "the greatest good for the greatest number" to his criticism of and attempts to reform English law. [National Portrait Gallery, London]

must refer everything, if we wish to interest and please amongst considerations the most arid and details the most dry."[4] The *philosophes* believed that the application of human reason to society would reveal laws in human relationships similar to those found in physical nature.

Although the term did not appear until later, the idea of social science originated with the Enlightenment. The purpose of discovering social laws was the removal of the inhumanity that existed through ignorance of them. These concerns became especially evident in the work of the *philosophes* on law and prison procedures.

Beccaria and Reform of Criminal Law

In 1764 Cesare Beccaria (1738–1794), an Italian *philosophe*, published *On Crimes and Punishments*, in which he applied critical analysis to the problem of making punishments both effective and just. He wanted the laws of monarchs and legislatures—that is, positive law—to conform with the rational laws of nature. He rigorously and eloquently attacked both torture and capital punishment. He thought that the criminal justice system should ensure speedy trial, sure punishment, and punishment intended to deter further crime. The purpose of laws was not to impose the will of God or some other ideal of perfection; its purpose was to secure the greatest good or happiness for the greatest number of human beings. This utilitarian philosophy based on happiness in this life permeated most of the Enlightenment writing on practical reforms.

Bentham and Utilitarianism

Although utilitarianism did not originate with him, it is particularly associated with the English legal reformer Jeremy Bentham (1748–1832). He sought to create codes of scientific law that were founded on the principle of utility, that is, the greatest happiness for the greatest number. In the *Fragment on Government* (1776) and *The Principles of Morals and Legislation* (1789), Bentham explained that the ap-

---

[4]*Quoted in F. L. Baumer,* Main Currents of Western Thought, *4th ed. (New Haven, Conn.: Yale University Press, 1978), p. 374.*

plication of the principle of utility would overcome the special interests of privileged groups who prevented rational government. Bentham regarded the existing legal and judicial systems as burdened by traditional practices that harmed the very people whom the law should

637

THE AGE C
ENLIGHTENME
EIGHTEENTH
CENTURY
THOUGHT

Jeremy Bentham Champions the Principle of Utility

Jeremy Bentham was a major philosopher of English legal reform. He believed that the legal system in particular and political thought in general could be based on the principle of utility that sought to achieve the greatest happiness for the greatest number. In this passage from An Introduction to the Principles of Morals and Legislation (1789) *he asserts that only the recognition of utility will allow a legislator to think clearly about human nature as it relates to the laws. He also suggests that the good of the community is the sum of the good of the individual members of the community. The tension between individual and community good proved an ongoing problem for utilitarian philosophy.*

Nature has placed mankind under the governance of two sovereign masters, *pain* and *pleasure*. It is for them alone to point out what we ought to do, as well as to determine what we shall do. On the one hand the standard of right and wrong, on the other the chain of causes and effects, are fastened to their throne. They govern us in all we do, in all we say, in all we think: every effort we can make to throw off our subjection will serve but to demonstrate and confirm it. In words a man may pretend to abjure their empire, but in reality he will remain subject to it all the while. The *principle of utility* recognizes this subjection and assumes it for the foundation of that system, the object of which is to read the fabric of felicity by the hands of reason and of law. Systems which attempt to question it deal in sounds instead of sense, in caprice instead of reason, in darkness instead of light.
. . . .
. . . By the principle of utility is meant that principle which approves or disapproves of every action whatsoever, according to the tendency which it appears to have to augment: or what is the same thing in other words, to promote or to oppose that happiness. I say of every action whatsoever; and therefore not only of every action of a private individual, but of every measure of government.

By utility is meant that property in any object, whereby it tends to produce benefit, advantage, pleasure, good, or happiness (all this in the present case comes to the same thing), or (what comes again to the same thing) to prevent the happening of mischief, pain, evil, or unhappiness to the party whose interest is considered: if that party be the community in general, then the happiness of the community; if a particular individual, then the happiness of that individual.

. . . The community is a fictitious *body*, composed of the individual persons who are considered as constituting as it were its *members*. The interest of the community then is—what? The sum of the interests of the several members who compose it.

It is in vain to talk of the interest of the community, without understanding what is the interest of the individual.

From An Introduction to the Principles of Morals and Legislation (1789) *as quoted in Edwin A. Burt (Ed.),* The English Philosophers from Bacon to Mill *(New York: The Modern Library, 1939), pp. 791–792.*

serve. The application of reason and utility would remove the legal clutter that prevented justice from being realized.

The Physiocrats and Economic Freedom

Another area of social relationships where the *philosophes* saw existing legislation and administration preventing the operation of natural social laws was the field of economic policy. They believed that mercantilist legislation and the labor regulations established by various governments and guilds actually hampered the expansion of trade, manufacture, and agriculture. In France these economic reformers were called the *physiocrats*. Their leading spokesmen were François Quesnay (1694–1774) and Pierre Dupont de Nemours (1739–1817).

They believed that the primary role of government was to protect property and to permit freedom in the use of property. They particularly felt that all economic production was dependent on sound agriculture. They favored the consolidation of small peasant holdings into larger, more efficient farms. Here as elsewhere there was a close relationship between the rationalism of the Enlightenment and the spirit of improvement at work in eighteenth-century European economic life.

Adam Smith and The Wealth of Nations

The most important Enlightenment exposition of economics was Adam Smith's (1723–1790) *Inquiry into the Nature and Causes of the Wealth of Nations* (1776). Smith, who was for a time a professor at Glasgow, urged that the mercantile system of England—including the navigation acts, the bounties, most tariffs, special trading monopolies, and the domestic regulation of labor and manufacture—be abolished. Smith believed that these modes of economic regulation by the state interfered with the natural system of economic liberty. They were intended to preserve the wealth of the nation, to capture wealth from other nations, and to assure a maximum amount of work for the laborers of the country.

However, Smith regarded such regulations as preventing the wealth and production of the country from expanding. He wanted to encour-

Adam Smith was one of the most important members of what may be called the Class of 1776—the astonishing outburst of British historical writing that centered on that year. In addition to Smith's Inquiry into the Nature and Causes of the Wealth of Nations, *Gibbon published the first volume of* The Decline and Fall, *Dr. Charles Burney (1726–1814) published the first volume of* A General History of Music *(completed in 1789), and Sir John Hawkins (1719–1789) managed to publish the entire five volumes of his* A General History of the Science and Practice of Music. *Moreover, in 1774, Thomas Warton (1728–1790) published the first volume of* The History of English Poetry *(third volume 1781; never completed), while in 1777 the Scottish historian William Robertson (1721–1793) published his* History of America. *[Culver Pictures]*

age economic growth and a consumer-oriented economy. The means to those ends was the unleashing of individuals to pursue their own selfish economic interest. The free pursuit of economic self-interest would ensure economic expansion as each person sought enrichment by meeting the demands of the marketplace. Consumers would find their wants met as manufacturers and merchants sought their business.

Smith's book challenged the concept of scarce goods and resources that lay behind mercantilism and the policies of the guilds.

Smith saw the realm of nature as a boundless expanse of water, air, soil, and minerals. The physical resources of the earth seemed to demand exploitation for the enrichment and comfort of humankind. In effect, Smith was saying that the nations and peoples of Europe need not be poor.

The idea of the infinite use of nature's goods for the material benefit of humankind—a concept that has dominated Western life until recent years—stemmed directly from the Enlightenment. When Smith wrote, the population of the world was smaller, its people were poorer, and the quantity of undeveloped resources per capita was much greater. For people of the eighteenth century it was in the uninhibited exploitation of natural resources that the true improvement of the human condition seemed to lie.

Smith is usually regarded as the founder of *laissez-faire* economic thought and policy, which has argued in favor of a very limited role for the government in economic life and regulation. However, *The Wealth of Nations* was a very complex book. Smith was no simple dogmatist. For example, he was not opposed to all government activity touching on the economy. The state should provide schools, armies, navies, and roads. It should also undertake certain commercial ventures, such as the opening of dangerous new trade routes that were economically desirable but too expensive or risky for private enterprise.

Smith's reasonable tone and recognition of the complexity of social and economic life displayed a very important point about the *philosophes*. Most of them were much less rigid and doctrinaire than any brief summary of their thought may tend to suggest. They recognized the passions of humanity as well as its reason. They adopted reason and nature as tools of criticism through which they might create a climate of opinion that would allow the fully developed human personality to flourish.

Political Thought of the *Philosophes*

Nowhere did the appreciation of the complexity of the problems of contemporary society become more evident than in the *philosophes'*

639

THE AGE O
ENLIGHTENME
EIGHTEENTH
CENTURY
THOUGHT

political thought. Nor did any other area of their reformist enterprise so clearly illustrate the tension and conflict within the "family" of the Enlightenment. Most *philosophes* were discontent with certain political features of their countries, but they were especially discontented in France. There the corruptness of the royal court, the blundering of the bureaucracy, the less than glorious mid-century wars, and the power of the Church compounded all problems. Consequently the most important political thought of the Enlightenment occurred in France. However, the French *philosophes* stood quite divided as to the proper solution. Their attitudes spanned the whole spectrum from aristocratic reform to democracy to absolute monarchy.

Montesquieu and The Spirit of the Laws

Charles Louis de Secondat, Baron de Montesquieu (1689–1755), was a lawyer, noble of the robe, and a member of a provincial parlement. He also belonged to the Bordeaux Academy of Science, before which he presented papers on scientific topics.

Although living comfortably within the bosom of French society, he saw the need for reform. In 1721 he published *The Persian Letters* to satirize contemporary institutions. The book consisted of letters purportedly written by two Persians visiting Europe. They explained to friends at home how European behavior contrasted with Persian life and customs. Behind the humor lay the cutting edge of criticism and an exposition of the cruelty and irrationality of much contemporary European life.

In his most enduring work, *The Spirit of the Laws* (1748), Montesquieu held up the example of the British constitution as the wisest model for regulating the power of government. With his interest in science, his hope for reform, and his admiration for Britain, he embodied all of the major elements of the Enlightenment mind.

Montesquieu's *The Spirit of the Laws* may well have been the single most influential book of the century. It is a work that exhibits the internal tensions of the Enlightenment. Montesquieu pursued an empirical method, taking illustrative examples from the political experience of both ancient and modern nations. From these he concluded that there could be no single set of political laws that applied to all peoples at all times and in all places. Rather, there existed a large number of political variables, and the good political life depended on the relationship of those variables. Whether a monarchy or a republic was the best form of government was a matter of the size of the political unit and its population, its social and religious customs, its economic structure, its traditions, and its climate. Only a careful examination and evaluation of these elements could reveal what mode of government would prove most beneficial to a particular people. A century later such speculations would have been classified as sociology.

So far as France was concerned, Montesquieu had some rather definite ideas. He believed in monarchical government, but with a monarchy whose power was tempered and limited by various sets of intermediary institutions. The latter included the aristocracy, the towns, and the other corporate bodies that enjoyed particular liberties that the monarch must respect. These corporate bodies might be said to represent various segments of the general population and thus of public opinion. In France he regarded the aristocratic courts, or *parlements*, as the major example of an intermediary association. Their role was to limit the power of the monarchy and thus to preserve the liberty of the subjects.

In championing these aristocratic bodies and the general role of the aristocracy, Montesquieu was a political conservative. However, he adopted that stance in the hope of achieving reform, for in his opinion it was the oppressive and inefficient absolutism of the monarchy that accounted for the degradation of French life.

One of Montesquieu's most influential ideas was that of division of power within any government. For his model of a government with authority wisely separated among different branches, he took contemporary Great Britain. There he believed he had found a system in which executive power resided in the king, legislative power in the Parliament, and judicial power in the courts. He thought any two branches could check and balance the power of the other. His perception of the eighteenth-century British constitution was incorrect because he failed to see how patronage and electoral corruption allowed a handful of powerful

Charles de Secondat, Baron de Montesquieu (1689–1744) was the author of The Spirit of the Laws, *possibly the most influential work of political thought of the eighteenth century. [Bulloz]*

aristocrats to dominate the government. Moreover, he was also unaware of the emerging cabinet system, which meant that the executive power was slowly becoming a creature of the Parliament.

Nevertheless, the analysis illustrated Montesquieu's strong sense of the need to limit the exercise of power through the constitutionalism and the formation of law by legislatures rather than by monarchs. In this manner, although Montesquieu set out to defend the political privileges of the French aristocracy, his ideas had a profound and still-lasting effect on the liberal democracies of the next two centuries.

Rousseau: A Radical Critique of Modern Society

Jean-Jacques Rousseau (1712–1778) held a view of the exercise and reform of political power quite different from Montesquieu's.

Rousseau was a strange, isolated genius who never felt particularly comfortable with the other *philosophes*. Yet perhaps more than any

641

THE AGE OF
ENLIGHTENMEN
EIGHTEENTH-
CENTURY
THOUGHT

Montesquieu Defends the Separation of Powers

The Spirit of the Laws (1748) was probably the most influential political work of the Enlightenment. In this passage Montesquieu explained how the division of powers within a government would make that government more moderate and would protect the liberty of its subjects. This idea was adopted by the writers of the United States Constitution when they devised the checks and balances of the three branches of government.

Democratic and aristocratic states are not in their own nature free. Political liberty is to be found only in moderate governments; and even in these it is not always found. It is there only when there is no abuse of power. But constant experience shows us that every man invested with power is apt to abuse it, and to carry his authority as far as it will go. . . .

To prevent this abuse, it is necessary from the very nature of things that power should be a check to power. . . .

In every government there are three sorts of power: the legislative; the executive in respect to things dependent on the law of nations; and the executive in regard to matters that depend on the civil law [the realm of the judiciary]. . . .

The political liberty of the subject is a tranquillity of mind arising from the opinion each person has of his safety. In order to have this liberty, it is requisite that government be so constituted as one man need not be afraid of another.

When the legislative and executive powers are united in the same person, or in the same body of magistrates, there can be no liberty; because apprehensions may arise, lest the same monarch or senate should enact tyrannical laws, to execute them in a tyrannical manner.

Again, there is no liberty, if the judiciary power be not separated from the legislative and executive. Were it joined with the legislative, the life and liberty of the subject would be exposed to arbitrary control; for the judge would be then the legislator. Were it joined to the executive power, the judge might behave with violence and oppression.

There would be an end to everything, were the same man or the same body, whether of the nobles or of the people, to exercise those three powers, that of enacting laws, that of executing the public resolutions, and of trying the causes of individuals.

Baron de Montesquieu, The Spirit of the Laws, trans. by Thomas Nugent (New York: Hafner Press, 1949), pp. 150–152.

other writer of the mid-eighteenth century he transcended the thought and values of his own time. Rousseau had a deep antipathy toward the world and the society in which he lived. It seemed impossible for human beings living according to contemporary commercial values to achieve moral, virtuous, or sincere lives. In 1750, in his *Discourse on the Moral Effects of the Arts and Sciences,* he contended that the process of civilization and enlightenment had corrupted human nature. Human beings in the state of nature had been more dignified. In

1755, in a *Discourse on the Origin of Inequality,* Rousseau blamed much of the evil in the world on maldistribution of property.

In both works Rousseau brilliantly and directly challenged the social fabric of the day. He drew into question the concepts of material and intellectual progress and the morality of a society in which commerce and industry were regarded as the most important of human activities. He felt that the real purpose of society was to nurture better people. In this respect Rousseau's vision of reform was much more

Jean-Jacques Rousseau's (1712–1778) writings raised some of the most profound social and ethical questions of the Enlightenment. [Metropolitan Museum of Art]

radical than that of other contemporary writers. The other *philosophes* believed that human life would be improved if people could enjoy more of the fruits of the earth or could produce more goods. Rousseau raised the more fundamental question of what the good life is. This question has haunted European social thought ever since the eighteenth century.

Rousseau carried these same concerns into his political thought. His most extensive discussion of politics appeared in *The Social Contract* (1762). Although the book attracted rather little immediate attention, by the end of the century it was widely read in France. *The Social Contract*, as compared to Montesquieu's *Spirit of the Laws*, is a very abstract book. It does not propose specific reforms but outlines the kind of political structure that

Rousseau Argues That Inequality Is Not Natural

Jean-Jacques Rousseau was one of the first writers to assert the social equality of human beings. He argued, as in this 1755 passage, that inequality had developed through the ages and was not "natural." He directly questioned the sanctity of property based on the assumed natural inequality of human beings.

I have endeavoured to trace the origin and progress of inequality, and the institution and abuse of political societies, as far as these are capable of being deduced from the nature of man merely by the light of reason, and independently of those sacred dogmas which give the sanction of divine right to sovereign authority. It follows from this survey that, as there is hardly any inequality in the state of nature, all the inequality which now prevails owes its strength and growth to the development of our faculties and the advance of the human mind, and becomes at last permanent and legitimate by the establishment of property and laws. Secondly, it follows that moral inequality, authorized by positive right alone, clashes with natural right, whenever it is not proportionate to physical inequality—a distinction which sufficiently determines what we think of that species of inequality which prevails in all civilized countries; since it is plainly contrary to the law of nature, however defined, that children should command old men, fools wise men, and that the privileged few should gorge themselves with superfluities while the starving multitude are in want of the bare necessities of life.

Jean-Jacques Rousseau, The Social Contract and Discourses, *trans. by G. D. H. Cole (London: J. M. Dent & Sons, 1950), pp. 271–272.*

Rousseau believed would overcome the evils of contemporary politics and society.

In the tradition of Thomas Hobbes and John Locke, most eighteenth-century political thinkers regarded human beings as individuals and society as a collection of such independent individuals pursuing personal, selfish goals. These writers wished to liberate these individuals from the undue bonds of government. Rousseau picked up the stick from the other end. His book opens with the declaration, "All men are born free, but everywhere they are in chains."[5] The rest of the volume constitutes a *defense* of the chains of a properly organized society over its members.

Rousseau suggested that society is more important than its individual members, because they are what they are only because of their relationship to the larger community. Independent human beings living alone can achieve very little. Through their relationship to the larger community, they become moral creatures capable of significant action. The question then becomes what kind of community allows people to behave morally. In his two previous discourses Rousseau had explained that contemporary European society was not such a community. It was merely an aggregate of competing individuals whose chief social goal was to preserve selfish independence in spite of all potential social bonds and obligations.

Rousseau sought to project the vision of a society in which each person could maintain personal freedom while behaving as a loyal member of the larger community. To that end Rousseau drew on the traditions of Plato and Calvin to define freedom as obedience to law. In his case the law to be obeyed was that created by the general will. This concept normally indicated the will of the majority of voting citizens who acted with adequate information and under the influence of virtuous customs and morals. Such democratic participation in decision making would bind the individual citizen to the community. Rousseau believed that the general will must always be right and that to obey the general will is to be free. This argument led him to the notorious conclusion that under certain circumstances some people must be forced to be free. Rousseau's politics thus constituted a justification for radical direct democracy and for collective action against individual citizens.

Rousseau had in effect launched an assault on the eighteenth-century cult of the individual and the fruits of selfishness. He stood at odds with the commercial spirit that was transforming the society in which he lived. Rousseau would have disapproved of the main thrust of Adam Smith's *Wealth of Nations*, which he may or may not have read, and would no doubt have preferred a study on the virtue of nations. Smith wanted people to be prosperous; Rousseau wanted them to be good even if being good meant that they might remain economically poor. He saw human beings not as independent individuals but as creatures enmeshed in neccessary social relationships. He believed that loyalty to the community should be encouraged. As one device to that end he suggested a civic religion based on the creed of deism. Such a shared tolerant religious faith would provide unity for the society.

643

THE AGE (
ENLIGHTENM
EIGHTEENT
CENTURY
THOUGH

MAJOR PUBLICATION DATES OF THE ENLIGHTENMENT

1687	Newton's *Principia Mathematica*
1690	Locke's *Essay Concerning Human Understanding*
1696	Toland's *Christianity Not Mysterious*
1721	Montesquieu's *Persian Letters*
1733	Voltaire's *Letters on the English*
1738	Voltaire's *Elements of the Philosophy of Newton*
1748	Montesquieu's *Spirit of the Laws*
1748	Hume's *Inquiry into Human Nature* with the chapter "Of Miracles"
1750	Rousseau's *Discourse on the Moral Effects of the Arts and Sciences*
1751	First volume of the *Encyclopedia* edited by Diderot
1755	Rousseau's *Discourse on the Origin of Inequality*
1762	Rousseau's *Social Contract*
1763	Voltaire's *Treatise on Toleration*
1764	Voltaire's *Philosophical Dictionary*
1764	Beccaria's *On Crimes and Punishments*
1776	Gibbon's *Decline and Fall of the Roman Empire*
1776	Bentham's *Fragment on Government*
1776	Smith's *Wealth of Nations*
1779	Lessing's *Nathan the Wise*

[5]*Jean-Jacques Rousseau, The Social Contract and Discourses, trans. by G. D. H. Cole (New York: Dutton, 1950), p. 3.*

Rousseau's chief intellectual inspiration arose from his study of Plato and the ancient Greek *polis*. Especially in Sparta he thought he had discovered human beings dwelling in a moral society inspired by a common purpose. He hoped that modern human beings might also create such a moral commonwealth in which virtuous living would become subordinate to commercial profit.

Rousseau's thought had only a marginal impact on his own time. The other *philosophes* questioned his critique of material improvement. Aristocrats and royal ministers could hardly be expected to welcome his proposal for radical democracy. Too many people were either making or hoping to make money to appreciate his criticism of commercial values. However, he proved to be a figure to whom later generations returned. Many leaders in the French Revolution were familiar with his writing. Thereafter, his ideas were important to most writers who felt called on to criticize the general tenor and direction of Western culture. Rousseau hated much about the emerging modern society in Europe, but he contributed much to modernity by exemplifying for later generations the critic who dared to call into question the very foundations of social thought and action.

Enlightened Absolutism

Most of the *philosophes* favored neither Montesquieu's reformed and revived aristocracy nor Rousseau's democracy as a solution to contemporary political problems. Like other thoughtful people of the day in other stations and occupations, they looked to the existing monarchies. The *philosophes* hoped in particular that the French monarchy might assert really effective power over the aristocracy and the Church to bring about significant reform. Voltaire was a very strong monarchist. He and others—such as Diderot, who visited Catherine II of Russia, and physiocrats, who were ministers to the French kings—did not wish to limit the power of monarchs. Rather, they sought to redirect that power toward the rationalization of economic and political structures and the liberation of intellectual life. Most *philosophes* were not opposed to power if they could find a way of using it for their own purposes.

During the last third of the century it seemed to some observers that several European rulers had actually embraced many of the reforms set forth by the *philosophes. Enlightened absolutism* is the term used to describe this phenomenon. The phrase indicates monarchical government dedicated to the rational strengthening of the central absolutist administration at the cost of other lesser centers of political power. The monarchs most closely associated with it are Frederick II of Prussia, Joseph II of Austria, and Catherine II of Russia. They often found that the political and social realities of their realms caused them to moderate the degree of both enlightenment and absolutism in their policies.

Frederick II corresponded with the *philosophes*, for a time provided Voltaire with a place at his court, and even wrote history and political tracts. Catherine II, who was a master at what would later be called public relations, consciously sought to create the image of being enlightened. She read the works of the *philosophes*, became a friend of Diderot and Voltaire, and made frequent references to their ideas, all in the hope that her nation might seem more modern and Western. Joseph II continued numerous initiatives begun by his mother, Maria Theresa. He imposed a series of religious, legal, and social reforms that contemporaries believed he had derived from suggestions of the *philosophes.*

Despite such appearances, the relationship between these rulers and the writers of the Enlightenment was rather more complicated. They did wish to see their subjects enjoy better health, somewhat more accessible education, the benefits of a more rational political administration, and economic prosperity. In many of these policies they were more advanced than the rulers of western Europe.

However, the humanitarian and liberating zeal of the Enlightenment directed only part of their policies. Frederick II, Joseph II, and Catherine II were also determined that their nations would play major diplomatic and military roles in Europe. In no small measure they sought the rational economic and social integration of their realms so they could achieve military strength. All of the states of Europe had emerged from the Seven Years' War understanding that they would require stronger armed forces in future conflicts and looking for new sources of taxation to finance their armies. The search for new revenues and further internal political support for their rule was an additional factor that led these central and eastern European monarchs to make "enlightened" reforms. Consequently, they and their advisers used rationality to pursue many goals admired by the *philosophes* but also to further what the *philosophes* considered irrational militarism.

Frederick the Great of Prussia

After the mid-century wars, during which Prussia had suffered badly and had almost been defeated, Frederick II (1740–1786) hoped to achieve recovery and consolidation. At grave military and financial cost he had succeeded in retaining Silesia, which he had seized from Austria in 1740. He worked to stimulate its potential as a manufacturing district. Like his Hohenzollern forebears he continued to import workers from outside Prussia. He directed new attention to Prussian agriculture. Under state supervision, swamps were drained, new crops introduced, and peasants encouraged and sometimes compelled to migrate. For the first time in Prussia, potatoes and turnips came into general production. Frederick also established a Land-Mortgage Credit Association to aid landowners in raising money for agricultural improvements.

Throughout this process, the impetus for development came from the state. The monarchy and its bureaucracy were the engine for change. Despite new policies and personal exhortations, the general populace of Prussia did not prosper under Frederick's reign. The burden of taxation still fell disproportionally on peasants and townspeople.

In less material ways Frederick pursued enlightened policies with somewhat more success. He continued the Hohenzollern policy of toleration. He allowed Catholics and Jews to settle in his predominantly Lutheran country, and he protected the Catholics living in Silesia. It should be noted, however, that despite this broad policy of freedom of religious observance, Frederick virtually always appointed Protestants to major positions in the government and army.

Frederick also ordered a new codification of Prussian law, which was completed after his death. The policy of toleration allowed foreign workers to contribute to the economic growth

Frederick the Great, here shown visiting a factory where women workers were employed, was concerned to see the Prussian economy grow and prosper. Such policies were associated with Enlightened absolutism throughout eastern Europe.

of the state. The new legal code was to rationalize the existing system, to make it more efficient, to eliminate regional peculiarities, and to eliminate excessive aristocratic influence. The enlightened monarchs were very concerned about legal reforms, primarily as a means of extending and strengthening royal power.

Frederick liked to describe himself as "the first servant of the State." That image represented an important change in the European conception of monarchy. The idea of an impersonal state was beginning to replace the concept of a personal monarchy. Kings might come and go, but the impersonal apparatus of government—the bureaucracy, the armies, the laws, the courts, and the citizens' loyalty arising from fear of state power and from appreciation of state services and protection—remained. The state as an entity separate from the personality of the ruler came into its own after the French Revolution, but it was born in the monarchies of the old regime.

Joseph II of Austria

No eighteenth-century ruler so embodied rational, impersonal force as the emperor Joseph

II of Austria. He was the son of Maria Theresa and co-ruler with her from 1765 to 1780. During the next ten years he ruled alone. He has been aptly described as "an imperial puritan and a good deal of a prig."[6] During much of his life he slept on straw and ate little but beef. He prided himself on a narrow, passionless rationality, which he sought to impose by his own will on the various Habsburg domains. Despite his eccentricities and the coldness of his personality, Joseph II genuinely and sincerely wished to improve the lot of his people. He was much less a political opportunist and cynic than either Frederick the Great of Prussia or Catherine the Great of Russia. The ultimate result of his well-intentioned efforts was a series of aristocratic and peasant rebellions extending from Hungary to the Austrian Netherlands.

CENTRALIZATION OF AUTHORITY As explained in Chapter 15, of all the rising states of the eighteenth century, Austria was the most diverse in its people and problems. Robert Palmer likened it to "a vast holding company."[7] The Habsburgs never succeeded in creating either a unified administrative structure or a strong aristocratic loyalty. The price of the preservation of the monarchy during the War of the Austrian Succession (1740–1748) had been guarantees of considerable aristocratic independence, especially in Hungary.

However, during and after the conflict Maria Theresa had taken major steps to strengthen the power of her crown in other of her realms. In Austria and Bohemia, through major administrative reorganization, she imposed a much more efficient system of tax collection that extracted funds even from the clergy and the nobles. She also established several central councils to deal with governmental problems. Her government became, in that regard, more bureaucratic than that of previous Habsburg rulers. She was particularly concerned about bringing all educational institutions into the service of the crown so that she could have a sufficiently large group of educated persons to serve as her officials; and she expanded primary education on the local level.

Maria Theresa was also quite concerned about the welfare of the peasants and serfs. The extension of the authority of the royal bureaucracy over that of the local nobilities was of some assistance to the peasants, as were the empress's decrees limiting the amount of labor, or *robot*, that could be demanded from the peasantry by the landowners. This concern was not particularly humanitarian; rather, it arose from her desire to assure a good military recruitment pool in the population. In all these policies and in her general desire to stimulate prosperity and military strength by royal initiative, Maria Theresa anticipated the policies of her son.

However, Joseph II was more determined, and his projected reforms were more wide-ranging than his mother's. He was aiming to extend the borders of his territories in the direction of Poland, Bavaria, and the Ottoman Empire. But his greatest ambition lay in changing the authority of the Habsburg emperor over his various realms. He sought to overcome the pluralism of the Habsburg holdings by increasing the power of the central monarchy in areas of political and social life where Maria Theresa had wisely chosen not to exert authority.

In particular, Joseph sought to lessen the very considerable autonomy enjoyed by Hungary. To that end, he refused to have himself crowned king of Hungary and even had the Crown of Saint Stephen sent to the Imperial Treasury in Vienna. By that means, he avoided having to guarantee existing or new Hungarian privileges at the time of his coronation. He reorganized local government in Hungary so as to increase the authority of his own officials. He also required the use of the German language in all governmental matters. Eventually, in 1790, Joseph had to rescind most of the imperial centralizing measures he had attempted to impose on Hungary as the Magyar nobility resisted one measure after another.

ECCLESIASTICAL POLICIES Another target of Joseph's assertion of royal absolutism was the Church. From the reign of Charles V in the sixteenth century to that of Maria Theresa, the Habsburgs had been the single most important dynastic champion of Roman Catholicism. Maria Theresa was quite devout, but she

[6] R. J. White, Europe in the Eighteenth Century (New York: St. Martin's, 1965), p. 214.

[7] Robert R. Palmer, The Age of Democratic Revolution (Princeton, N.J.: Princeton University Press, 1959), 1:103.

647

THE AGE O
ENLIGHTENME
EIGHTEENTH
CENTURY
THOUGHT

Maria Theresa and Joseph II of Austria Debate the Question of Toleration

In 1765 Joseph, the eldest son of the Empress Maria Theresa, had become co-regent with his mother. He began to believe that some measures of religious toleration should be introduced into the Habsburg realms. Maria Theresa, whose opinions on many political issues were quite advanced, adamantly refused to consider adopting a policy of toleration. This exchange of letters sets forth their sharply differing positions. The toleration of Protestants in dispute related only to Lutherans and Calvinists. Maria Theresa died in 1780; the next year Joseph issued an edict of toleration.

Joseph to Maria Theresa, July 20, 1777

. . . [I]t is only the word "toleration" which has caused the misunderstanding. You have taken it in quite a different meaning [from mine expressed in an earlier letter]. God preserve me from thinking it a matter of indifference whether the citizens turn Protestant or remain Catholic, still less, whether they cleave to, or at least observe, the cult which they have inherited from their fathers! I would give all I possess if all the Protestants of your states would go over to Catholicism.

The word "toleration," as I understand it, means only that I would employ any persons, without distinction of religion, in purely temporal matters, allow them to own property, practice trades, be citizens, if they were qualified and if this would be of advantage to the State and its industry. Those who, unfortunately, adhere to a false faith, are far further from being converted if they remain in their own country than if they migrate into another, in which they can hear and see the convincing truths of the Catholic faith. Similarly, the undisturbed practice of their religion makes them far better subjects and causes them to avoid irreligion, which is a far greater danger to our Catholics than if one lets them see others practice their religion unimpeded. . . .

Maria Theresa to Joseph, Late July, 1777

Without a dominant religion? Toleration, indifference are precisely the true means of undermining everything, taking away every foundation; we others will then be the greatest losers. . . . He is no friend of humanity, as the popular phrase is, who allows everyone his own thoughts. I am speaking only in the political sense, not as a Christian; nothing is so necessary and salutary as religion. Will you allow everyone to fashion his own religion as he pleases? No fixed cult, no subordination to the Church—what will then become of us? The result will not be quiet and contentment; its outcome will be the rule of the stronger and more unhappy times like those which we have already seen. A manifesto by you to this effect can produce the utmost distress and make you responsible for many thousands of souls. And what are my own sufferings, when I see you entangled in opinions so erroneous? What is at stake is not only the welfare of the State but your own salvation. . . . Turning your eyes and ears everywhere, mingling your spirit of contradiction with the simultaneous desire to create something, you are ruining yourself and dragging the Monarchy down with you into the abyss. . . . I only wish to live so long as I can hope to descend to my ancestors with the consolation that my son will be as great, as religious as his forebears, that he will return from his erroneous views, from those wicked books whose authors parade their cleverness at the expense of all that is most holy and most worthy of respect in the world, who want to introduce an imaginary freedom which can never exist and which degenerates into license and into complete revolution.

C. A. Macartney (Ed.), The Habsburg and Hohenzollern Dynasties in the Seventeenth and Eighteenth Centuries *(New York: Walker, 1970), pp. 151–153.*

had not allowed the Church to limit her authority. Although she had attempted to discourage certain of the more extreme modes of Roman Catholic popular religious piety, such as public flagellation, she stood adamantly opposed to toleration.

Joseph II was also a believing Catholic, but from the standpoint of both enlightenment and pragmatic politics, he favored a policy of toleration. In October 1781, Joseph issued a Toleration Patent (decree) that extended freedom of worship to Lutherans, Calvinists, and the Greek Orthodox. They were permitted to have their own places of worship, to sponsor schools, to enter skilled trades, and to hold academic appointments and positions in the public service. From 1781 through 1789 Joseph also issued a series of patents and other enactments that relieved the Jews in his realms of certain taxes and signs of personal degradation. He also extended to them the right of private worship. Although the Jews benefited from these actions, they still did not enjoy general legal rights equal to those of other Habsburg subjects.

Joseph also sought to bring the various institutions of the Roman Catholic church directly under the control of royal authority. He forbade direct communication between the bishops of his realms and the pope. He regarded orders of monks and nuns as generally unproductive. Consequently, he dissolved over six hundred monasteries and confiscated their lands, although he excepted certain orders that ran schools or hospitals. He dissolved the traditional Roman Catholic seminaries, which he believed taught priests too great a loyalty to the papacy and too little concern for duties to their future parishioners. Having dissolved the existing seminaries, he chose to sponsor eight general seminaries for the training of priests, with an emphasis on parish duties. He also issued decrees that areas needing more priests because of the number of people living there should be supplied with priests. He used funds from the confiscation of the monasteries to pay for these new parishes.

In effect, Joseph's policies made Roman Catholic priests the employees of the state and brought the influence of the Roman Catholic church as an independent institution in Habsburg lands to a close. Joseph was willing and even eager to have religious faith and practice flourish, but religious institutions and the people they employed had to stand subordinate to the authority of the government. In many respects the ecclesiastical policies of Joseph II, known as *Josephinism*, prefigured those of the French Revolution.

ECONOMIC AND AGRARIAN REFORM

Like Frederick of Prussia, Joseph sought to improve the economic life of his domains. He abolished many internal tariffs and encouraged road building and the improvement of river transport. He went on personal inspection tours of farms and manufacturing districts. Joseph also reconstructed the judicial system to make laws more uniform and rational and to lessen the influence of local landlords. National courts with power over the landlord courts were established. All of these improvements were expected to bring new unity to the state and more taxes into the coffers at Vienna.

In his policies toward serfdom and the land, Joseph II again pursued policies initiated by Maria Theresa to more far-reaching ends. Over the years of his reign Joseph II introduced a series of reforms that touched the very heart of the rural social structure. He did not seek to abolish the authority of landlords over their peasants, but he did seek to make that authority more moderate and subject to the oversight of royal officials. He abolished the legal status of serfdom defined in terms of servitude to another person. He gave peasants a much wider arena of personal freedom. They could marry without approval of the landlord, and they could also engage in skilled work or have their children trained in such skills without permission of the landlord.

The procedures of the manorial courts were reformed, and avenues of appeal to royal officials were opened. Joseph also encouraged landlords to change land leases so that it would be easier for peasants to inherit them or to transfer them to another peasant without bringing into doubt the landlord's title of ownership. In all of these actions Joseph believed that the lessening of traditional burdens would make the peasant tillers of the land more productive and industrious.

Near the end of his reign Joseph proposed a new and daring system of land taxation. He decreed in 1789 that all proprietors of the land were to be taxed regardless of social status. No longer were the peasants alone to bear the burden of taxation. He abolished *robot* (the services due a landlord from peasants) and commuted it into a monetary tax, only part of which would in the future go to the landlord while the remainder would revert to the state. The decree was made, but resistance from the nobles led to a delay in its implementation. Then, in 1790, Joseph died, and the decree never went into effect. However, it and others of his measures had stirred up turmoil throughout the Habsburg realms. Peasants revolted over disagreements about the interpretation of their newly granted rights. The nobles of the various realms protested the taxation scheme. The Hungarian Magyars resisted Joseph's centralization measures and compelled him to rescind them.

On Joseph's death, the crown went to his brother Leopold II (1790–1792). Although quite sympathetic to Joseph's goals, Leopold found himself compelled to repeal many of the most controversial decrees, such as that in regard to taxation. In other areas, Leopold thought his brother's policies simply wrong. For example, he returned much political and administrative power to local nobles because he thought it expedient for them to have a voice in government. Still, there was no wholesale repudiation of Joseph's policies, especially in regard to religion and such political centralization as Leopold thought possible to retain.

Joseph II had possessed a narrow vision attached to an unbending will. For all his intellectual brilliance and hard work, he had failed to understand that his policies enjoyed few supporters outside the royal bureaucracy. He had ruled without consulting any political constituency. The nobles, the Church, the towns with their chartered liberties, and the absence of a strong bureaucracy or army stood as barriers to the realization of his absolutism. His was a mind of classical rationalism in conflict with political and social realities of baroque complexity.

Catherine the Great of Russia

Joseph II never grasped the practical necessity of cultivating political support for his policies. Catherine II (1762–1796), who had been born a German princess but who became empress of Russia, understood only too well the fragility of the Romanov dynasty's base of power.

After the death of Peter the Great in 1725, the court nobles and the army repeatedly determined the Russian succession. As a result, the crown fell primarily into the hands of people with little talent. Peter's wife, Catherine I, ruled for two years (1725–1727) and was succeeded for three years by Peter's grandson Peter II. In 1730 the crown devolved on Ann, who was a niece of Peter the Great. During 1740 and 1741 a child named Ivan VI, who was less than a year old, was the nominal ruler. Finally, in 1741, Peter the Great's daughter Elizabeth came to the throne. She held the title of empress until 1762, but her reign was not notable for new political departures or sound administration. Her court was a shambles of political and romantic intrigue. Needless to say, much of the power possessed by the tsar at the opening of the century had vanished.

At her death in 1762 Elizabeth was succeeded by Peter III, one of her nephews. He was a weak ruler whom many contemporaries considered mad. He immediately exempted the nobles from compulsory military service and then made rapid peace with Frederick the Great, for whom he held unbounded admiration. That decision probably saved Prussia from military defeat. The one positive feature of this unbalanced creature's life was his marriage in 1745 to a young German princess born in Pomerania. This was the future Catherine the Great.

For almost twenty years she lived in misery and frequent danger at the court of Elizabeth. During that time she befriended important nobles and read widely in the books of the *philosophes*. She was a shrewd person whose experience in a court crawling with rumors, intrigue, and conspiracy had taught her how to survive. She had neither love nor loyalty for her demented husband. After a few months of rule Peter III was deposed and murdered with the approval, if not the aid, of Catherine. On his deposition she was immediately proclaimed empress.

Catherine's familiarity with the Enlightenment and the general culture of western Europe convinced her that Russia was very backward and that it must make major reforms if it was to remain a great power. She understood that any major reform must have a wide

649

THE AGE OF
ENLIGHTENMENT
EIGHTEENTH-
CENTURY
THOUGHT

sions in the law and government of Russia. There were over five hundred delegates drawn from all sectors of Russian life. Before the commission convened, Catherine issued a set of *Instructions*, partly written by herself. They contained numerous ideas drawn from the political writings of the *philosophes*. The commission considered the *Instructions* as well as other ideas and complaints raised by its members.

The revision of Russian law, however, did not occur for more than half a century. In 1768 Catherine dismissed the commission before several of its key committees had reported. Yet the meeting had not been useless, for a vast amount of information had been gathered about the conditions of local administration and economic life throughout the realm. The inconclusive debates and the absence of programs from the delegates themselves suggested that most Russians saw no alternative to an autocratic monarchy. For her part, it was clear that Catherine had no intention of departing from absolutism.

LIMITED ADMINISTRATIVE REFORM

Catherine proceeded to carry out limited reforms on her own authority. She gave strong support to the rights and local power of the nobility. In 1777 she reorganized local government to solve problems brought to light by the Legislative Commission. She put most local offices in the hands of nobles rather than creating a royal bureaucracy. In 1785 Catherine issued the Charter of the Nobility, which guaranteed many noble rights and privileges. In part the empress had no choice but to favor the nobles. They had the capacity to topple her from the throne. There were too few educated subjects in her realm to establish an independent bureaucracy, and the treasury could not afford an army strictly loyal to the crown. So Catherine wisely made a virtue of necessity. She strengthened the stability of her crown by making convenient friends with her nobles.

base of political and social support. Such was especially the case because she herself had assumed the throne through a palace coup. Consequently, in 1767, she summoned a Legislative Commission to advise her on revi-

ECONOMIC GROWTH

Part and parcel of Catherine's program was a continuation of the economic development begun under Peter the Great. She attempted to suppress internal bar-

This English cartoon illustrates the territorial ambitions of Catherine the Great in the eastern Mediterranean and Black Seas.

riers to trade. Exports of grain, flax, furs, and naval stores grew dramatically. She also favored the expansion of the small Russian middle class. Russian trade required such a vital urban class. And through all of these departures Catherine attempted to maintain ties of friendship and correspondence with the *philosophes*. She knew that if she treated them kindly, they would be sufficiently flattered and would give her a progressive reputation throughout Europe.

TERRITORIAL EXPANSION The limited administrative reforms and the policy of economic growth had a counterpart in the diplomatic sphere. The Russian drive for warm-water ports continued. This goal required warfare with the Turks. In 1769, as a result of a minor Russian incursion, the Ottoman Empire declared war on Russia. The Russians responded in a series of strikingly successful military moves.

During 1769 and 1770 the Russian fleet sailed all the way from the Baltic Sea into the eastern Mediterranean. The Russian army won several major victories that by 1771 gave Russia control of Ottoman provinces on the Danube River and the Crimean coast of the Black Sea. The conflict dragged on until 1774, when it was closed by the Treaty of Kuchuk-Kainardji. The treaty gave Russia a direct outlet on the Black Sea, free navigation rights in its waters, and free access through the Bosporus. Moreover, the province of the Crimea became an independent state, which Catherine painlessly annexed in 1783.

The Partition of Poland

These military successes obviously brought the empress much domestic political support. However, they made the other states of eastern Europe uneasy. These anxieties were overcome by an extraordinary division of Polish territory known as the First Partition of Poland.

The Russian victories along the Danube River were most unwelcome to Austria, which also harbored ambitions of territorial expansion in that direction. At the same time, the Ottoman Empire was pressing Prussia for aid against Russia. Frederick the Great made a proposal to Russia and Austria that would give each something it wanted, prevent conflict

among the powers, and save appearances. After long, complicated, secret negotiations the three powers agreed that Russia would abandon the conquered Danubian provinces. In compensation Russia received a large portion of Polish territory with almost two million inhabitants. As a reward for remaining neutral,

651

THE AGE OF
ENLIGHTENME[NT]
EIGHTEENTH-
CENTURY
THOUGHT

MAP 18-1 EXPANSION OF RUSSIA 1689–1796
The overriding territorial aim of Peter the Great in the first quarter and of Catherine the Great in the last half of the eighteenth century was the securing of northern and southern navigable-water outlets for the vast Russian Empire. Hence Peter's push to the Baltic Sea and Catherine's to the Black Sea. Catherine also managed to acquire large areas of Poland through the partitions of that country.

Prussia annexed most of the territory between East Prussia and Prussia proper. This land allowed Frederick to unite two previously separate sections of his realm. Finally, Austria took Galicia, with its important salt mines, and other Polish territory with over two and one-half million inhabitants.

In September 1772 the helpless Polish aristocracy, paying the price for the maintenance of their internal liberties, ratified this seizure of their territory. The Polish state had lost approximately one third of its territory. That loss was not necessarily fatal to the continued existence of Poland, and a considerable national political revival took place after the partition. Real attempts were made to adjust the Polish political structures to the realities of the time. These proved to be too little and too late. The political and military strength of Poland could not match that of its stronger, more ambitious neighbors.

There were two additional partitions of Poland by Russia and Prussia in 1793, and by all three powers in 1795. These partitions occurred in 1793 and 1795 and removed Poland from the map of Europe. Each time the great powers contended that they were saving themselves, and by implication the rest of Europe, from Polish anarchy. The fact of the matter was that the political weakness of Poland made the country and its resources a rich field for plunderous aggression. The last two partitions took place during the French Revolution. The three eastern European absolute monarchies objected to certain reforms undertaken by the Polish nobles for fear than even minor Polish reform might endanger the stability of their own societies.

MAP 18-2 PARTITIONS OF POLAND, 1772–1793–1795 *The callous eradication of Poland from the map displayed eighteenth-century power politics at its most extreme. Poland, without strong central governmental institutions, fell victim to those states in central and eastern Europe that had developed such institutions.*

The End of the Eighteenth Century in Central and Eastern Europe

During the last two decades of the eighteenth century, all three regimes based on enlightened absolutism became more conservative and politically repressive. In Prussia and Austria the innovations of the rulers stirred resistance among the nobility. In Russia fear of peasant unrest was the chief factor.

Frederick the Great lived much removed from his people during his old age. The aristocracy, looking out for its own self-interest, filled the major Prussian military and administrative posts. There also developed a strong reaction against Enlightenment thought among Prussian Lutheran writers.

Joseph II confronted growing frustration and political unrest over his plans for restructuring the society and administration of his realms. As a result, he made more and more use of censorship and the secret police. Throughout his realms the nobles called for an end to innovation.

653

THE AGE OF
ENLIGHTENMENT
EIGHTEENTH
CENTURY
THOUGHT

This French engraving is a satirical comment on the first partition of Poland (1772) by Russia, Austria, and Prussia. The distressed monarch attempting to retain his crown is Stanislaus of Poland. Catherine of Russia, Joseph of Austria, and Frederick of Prussia point out their respective shares of the loot.

Catherine the Great never fully recovered from the fears of social and political upheaval raised by Pugachev's rebellion (1771–1775). Once the French Revolution broke out in 1789, the Russian empress censored books based on Enlightenment thought and sent offensive authors into Siberian exile. By the close of the century fear of and hostility to change permeated the ruling classes throughout the region. Those attitudes had come into existence before 1789, but the events in France froze them for almost half a century. Paradoxically, nowhere did the humanity and liberalism of the Enlightenment encounter more difficulty than in those states that had been governed by "enlightened" rulers.

Although the enlightened absolute monarchs lacked the humanity of the *philosophes*, they had embraced the Enlightenment spirit of innovation. They wanted to change the political, social, and economic structures of their realms. From the close of the Seven Years' War (1763) until the opening of the French Revolution in 1789, the monarchies of both western and eastern Europe had been the major forces working for significant institutional change. In every case they had stirred up considerable aristocratic and some popular resistance and resentment. George III of Britain fought for years with Parliament and lost the colonies of North America in the process. Frederick II of Prussia carried out his program of reform only because he accepted new aristocratic influence over the bureaucracy and the army. Catherine II of Russia had to come to terms with her nobility. Joseph II left his domains in turmoil by imposing changes without consulting the nobility.

These monarchs pushed for innovations because of their desire for increased revenue. The same problem existed in France. There the royal drive for adequate fiscal resources also led to aristocratic rebellion. However, in France neither the monarchy nor the aristocracy could control the social and political forces unleashed by their quarrel.

The writers of the Enlightenment, known as philosophes, *charted a major new path of modern European and Western thought. Through their admiration for Newton they directly associated the cause of the new science with the cause of reformist thinking. In* one area of human activity after another they brought to the fore the criterion of reason. At the same time they believed that passions and feelings were essential parts of human nature. Throughout their writings they tended to champion reasonable moderation in social life. More than any other previous group of Western thinkers they strongly opposed the authority of the established churches and especially of Roman Catholicism. Most of them championed some form of religious toleration. They also sought to achieve a science of society so as to maximize human productivity and human happiness in a material sense. The great dissenter among them was Rousseau, who also wished to reform society but in the name of virtue rather than material happiness.

The political influence of these writers went in several divergent directions. The founding fathers of the American republic looked to them for political guidance as did moderate liberal reformers throughout Europe, especially within royal bureaucracies. The later revolutionaries in France would honor them. At the same time the autocratic rulers of eastern Europe consulted with the philosophes and believed their ideas might allow them to rule more efficiently. This diverse assortment of followers illustrates in itself the diverse character of the philosophes themselves. The diversity also suggests that their thought cannot be reduced to a single formula. Rather it should be seen as an outlook that championed change and reform within a world in which human beings and their welfare on earth stood at the center, instead of God or human welfare in the hereafter.

Suggested Readings

R. P. BARTLETT, Human Capital: The Settlement of Foreigners in Russia, 1762–1804 (1979). Examines Catherine's policy of attracting farmers and skilled workers to Russia.

D. BEALES, Joseph II: In the Shadow of Maria Theresa, 1741–1780 (1987). The best treatment in English of the early political life of Joseph II.

C. BECKER, The Heavenly City of the Eighteenth Century Philosophers (1932). An influential but very controversial discussion.

C. B. A. BEHRENS, Society, Government, and the Enlightenment: The Experiences of Eighteenth-Century France and Prussia (1985). A wide-ranging comparative study.

P. P. BERNARD, Joseph II (1968). A brief biography.

T. BESTERMANN, Voltaire (1969). A biography by the editor of Voltaire's letters.

D. D. BIEN, The Calas Affair: Persecution, Toleration, and Heresy in Eighteenth-Century Toulouse (1960). The standard treatment of the famous case.

E. CASSIRER, The Philosophy of the Enlightenment (1951). A brilliant but difficult work by one of the great philosophers of the twentieth century.

H. CHISICK, The Limits of Reform in the Enlightenment: Attitudes Toward the Education of the Lower Classes in Eighteenth-Century France (1981). An attempt to examine the impact of the Enlightenment on nonelite classes.

G. R. CRAGG, The Church and the Age of Reason (1961). A general survey of eighteenth-century religious life.

R. DARNTON, The Business of Enlightenment: A Publishing History of the Encyclopedia, 1775–1800 (1979). A wide-ranging examination of the printing and dispersion of the Encyclopedia.

R. DARNTON, The Literary Underground of the Old Regime (1982). Essays on the world of printers, publishers, and booksellers.

P. FUSSELL, The Rhetorical World of Augustan Humanism (1969). Examines writers during the Enlightenment.

J. GAGLIARDO, Enlightened Despotism (1967). A discussion of the subject in its European context.

P. GAY, The Enlightenment: An Interpretation, 2 vols. (1966, 1969). The most important and far-reaching treatment.

C. C. GILLISPIE, Science and Polity in France at the End of the Old Regime (1980). A major survey of the subject.

N. HAMPSON, A Cultural History of the Enlightenment (1969). A useful introduction.

M. C. JACOB, The Radical Enlightenment: Pantheists, Freemasons, and Republicans (1981). A treatment of frequently ignored figures in the age of the Enlightenment.

R. KREISER, Miracles, Convulsions, and Ecclesiastical Politics in Early Eighteenth-Century Paris (1978). An important study of the kind of religious life that the philosophes opposed.

C. A. MACARTNEY, The Habsburg Empire, 1790–1918 (1971). Provides useful coverage of major mid-eighteenth-century developments.

J. W. MCCLELLAN III, Science Reorganized: Scientific Societies in the Eighteenth Century (1985). An examination of the organization of science and its relationship to popular culture.

I. DE MADARIAGA, Russia in the Age of Catherine the Great (1981). The best discussion in English.

F. MANUEL, The Eighteenth Century Confronts the Gods (1959). A broad examination of the philosophes' treatment of Christian and pagan religion.

R. R. PALMER, Catholics and Unbelievers in Eigh-

655

THE AGE O
ENLIGHTENME
EIGHTEENTH
CENTURY
THOUGHT

teenth Century France (1939). A discussion of the opponents of the *philosophes*.

G. RITTER, *Frederick the Great* (trans. 1968). A useful biography.

R. O. ROCKWOOD (Ed.), *Carl Becker's Heavenly City Revisited* (1958). Important essays qualifying Becker's thesis.

R. B. SHER, *Church and University in the Scottish Enlightenment: The Moderate Literati of Edinburgh* (1985). A major study that examines the role of religious moderates in aiding the goals of the Enlightenment.

J. N. SHKLAR, *Men and Citizens, a Study of Rousseau's Social Theory* (1969). A thoughtful and provocative overview of Rousseau's political thought.

D. SPADAFORA, *The Idea of Progress in Eighteenth Century Britain* (1990). A recent major study that covers many aspects of the Enlightenment in Britain.

R. E. SULLIVAN, *John Toland and the Deist Controversy: A Study in Adaptation* (1982). An important and informative discussion.

A. M. WILSON, *Diderot* (1972). A splendid biography of the person behind the project for the *Encyclopedia* and other major Enlightenment publications.

On July 14, 1789, crowds in Paris stormed the Bastille which was a prison.
*Although only a few prisoners were in the building, the events symbolized
the entrance of the populace of Paris onto the revolutionary scene.*
[Giraudon/Art Resource]

19

THE FRENCH REVOLUTION

In the spring of 1789 the long-festering conflict between the French monarchy and the aristocracy erupted into a new political crisis. This dispute, unlike earlier ones, quickly outgrew the issues of its origins and produced the wider disruption of the French Revolution. The quarrel that began as a struggle between the most exclusive elements of the political nation soon involved all sectors of French society and eventually every major state in Europe.

Before the turmoil settled, small-town provincial lawyers and Parisian street orators exercised more influence over the fate of the

Continent than did aristocrats, royal ministers, or monarchs. Armies commanded by persons of low birth and filled by conscripted village youths emerged victorious over forces composed of professional soldiers and directed by officers of noble birth. The very existence of the Roman Catholic faith in France was challenged. Politically and socially neither France nor Europe would ever be quite the same after these events.

The Crisis of the French Monarchy

Although the French Revolution constituted one of the central turning points in modern European history, it originated from the basic tensions and problems that characterized practically all late-eighteenth-century states. From the Seven Years' War (1756–1763) onward, the French monarchy was unable to handle its finances on a sound basis. It emerged from the conflict both defeated and in debt. The French support of the American revolt against Great Britain further deepened the financial difficulties of the government. On the eve of the revolution the interest and payments on the royal debt amounted to just over one half of the entire budget. Given the economic vitality of the nation, this debt was neither overly large nor disproportionate to the debts of other European powers. The problem lay with the inability of the royal government to tap the wealth of the French nation through taxes to service and repay the debt. Paradoxically France was a rich nation with an impoverished government.

The debt was symptomatic of the failure of the eighteenth-century French monarchy to come to terms with the resurgent social and political power of the aristocracy. For twenty-five years after the Seven Years' War there was a standoff between them. The monarchy attempted to pursue a program somewhat resembling that associated with enlightened absolutism in eastern Europe. However, both Louis XV (1715–1774) and Louis XVI (1774–1792) lacked the character and the resolution for such a departure. The moral corruption of the former and the indecision of the latter meant that the monarchy could not rally the French public to its side.

The Monarchy Seeks New Taxes

In place of a consistent policy to deal with the growing debt, the monarchy gave way to hesitancy, retreat, and even duplicity. In 1763 the monarchy issued a new set of tax decrees that would have extended the collection of certain taxes that were supposed to have been discontinued at the close of the war. There were also new tax assessments. This search for revenue was not unlike the one that led the British government to attempt to tax the American colonies. Several of the provincial *parlements* and finally the Parlement of Paris—all controlled by nobles—declared the taxes illegal. During the ensuing dispute the aristocratic *parlements* set themselves up as the spokesmen of the nation and as the protectors of French liberty against the illegal assertion of monarchical power. This was one of the political functions of the nobility that Montesquieu had outlined in *The Spirit of the Laws* (1748).

In 1770 Louis XV appointed René Maupeou (1714–1792) as chancellor. The new minister was determined to break the *parlements* and impose a greater part of the tax burden on the nobility. He abolished the *parlements* and exiled their members to different parts of the country. He then commenced an ambitious program of reform and efficiency. What ultimately doomed Maupeou's policy was less the resistance of the nobility than the death of Louis XV in 1774. His successor, Louis XVI, in an attempt to regain what he conceived to be popular support, restored all the *parlements* and confirmed their old powers. This action, in conjunction with the later aid to the American colonies, locked the monarchy into a continuing financial bind. Thereafter, meaningful fiscal or political reform through existing institutions was probably doomed.

Louis XVI's first minister was the physiocrat Jacques Turgot (1727–1781), who attempted various economic reforms, including the removal of restrictions on the grain trade and the elimination of the guilds. He transformed the *corvée*, or road-working obligation of peasants, into money payments. Turgot also intended to restructure the taxation system in order to tap the wealth of the nobility. These and other ideas represented a program of bold new departures for the monarchy. They proved too bold for the tremulous young king, who dismissed Turgot in 1776.

By 1781 the debt, as a result of the aid to America, was larger and the sources of revenues were unchanged. However, the new director-general of finances, Jacques Necker (1732–1804), a Swiss banker, produced a public report that suggested that the situation was not so bad as had been feared. He argued that if the expenditures for the American war were removed, the budget was in surplus. However, Necker's report also revealed that a large portion of the royal expenditure went to pensions for aristocrats and other royal court favorites. This information aroused the anger of court aristocratic circles against the banker, who soon left office. His financial sleight of hand, nonetheless, made it more difficult for later government officials to claim a real need to raise new taxes.

The monarchy hobbled along until 1786. By this time Charles Alexandre de Calonne (1734–1802) was the minister of finance. He was probably the most able administrator to serve

Well-meaning but weak and vacillating, Louis XVI (1774–1792) stumbled from concession to concession until he finally lost all power to save his throne. [Giraudon]

Louis XVI. More carefully than previous ministers he charted the size of the debt and the deficit. He submitted a program for reform quite similar to that presented by Turgot a decade earlier. Calonne proposed to encourage internal trade; to lower some taxes, such as the *gabelle* on salt; and to transform peasants' services to money payments.

More important, Calonne urged the introduction of a new land tax that would require payments from all landowners regardless of their social status. If this tax could have been imposed, the monarchy would have been able to abandon other indirect taxes. The government would also rarely have had to seek approval for further new taxes from the aristocratically dominated *parlements*. Calonne also intended to establish new local assemblies to approve land taxes; in these assemblies the voting power would depend on the amount of land owned rather than on the social status of the owner. All these proposals would have undermined both the political and the social power of the French aristocracy.

The Aristocracy and the Clergy Resist Taxation

A new clash with the nobility was unavoidable, and the monarchy had very little room to maneuver. The creditors were at the door; the treasury was nearly empty. Consequently, in 1787 Calonne met with an Assembly of Notables drawn from the upper ranks of the aristocracy and the Church to seek support and approval for his plan. The assembly adamantly refused any such action; rather, it demanded that the aristocracy be allowed a greater share in the direct government of the kingdom. The notables called for the reappointment of Necker, who they believed had left the country in sound fiscal condition. Finally, they claimed that they had no right to consent to new taxes and that such a right was vested only in the medieval institution of the Estates General of France, which had not met since 1614. The notables believed that the calling of the Estates General, which had been traditionally organized to allow aristocratic and Church dominance, would produce a victory for the nobility over the monarchy.

Again Louis XVI backed off. He dismissed Calonne and replaced him with Étienne Charles Loménie de Brienne (1727–1794), who was archbishop of Toulouse and the chief opponent of Calonne at the Assembly of Notables. Once in office, Brienne found, to his astonishment, that the situation was as bad as his predecessor had asserted. Brienne himself now sought to impose the land tax. However, the Parlement of Paris took the new position that it lacked authority to authorize the tax and said that only the Estates General could do so. Shortly thereafter Brienne appealed to the Assembly of the Clergy to approve a large subsidy to allow funding of that part of the debt then coming due for payment. The clergy, like the Parlement dominated by aristocrats, not only refused the subsidy but also reduced their existing contribution, or *don gratuit*, to the government.

As these unfruitful negotiations were transpiring at the center of political life, local aristocratic *parlements* and estates in the provinces were making their own demands. They wanted a restoration of the privileges they had

This French cartoon of 1789 shows a peasant carrying a priest and a nobleman on his back. The peasantry could least afford to pay but was most heavily taxed, while the clergy and aristocracy were largely tax exempt. [Giraudon]

Le tems passé

enjoyed during the early seventeenth century before Richelieu and Louis XIV had crushed their independent power. Consequently, in July 1788 the king, through Brienne, agreed to convoke the Estates General the next year. Brienne resigned and was replaced by Necker. The institutions of the aristocracy—and to a lesser degree, of the church—had brought the French monarchy to its knees. In the country of its origin, royal absolutism had been defeated.

The Revolutions of 1789

The year 1789 proved to be one of the most remarkable in the history of both France and Europe. The French aristocracy had forced Louis XVI to call the Estates General into session. Yet, the aristocratic triumph proved to be quite brief. From the moment the monarch summoned the Estates General, the political situation in France drastically changed. Social and political forces that neither the nobles nor the king could control were immediately unleashed.

The Estates General Becomes the National Assembly

The first new difficulties arose from clashes among the groups represented in the Estates General. The body was composed of three divisions: the First Estate of the clergy, the Second Estate of the nobility, and the Third Estate, which represented everyone else in the kingdom. During the widespread public discussions preceding the meeting of the Estates General, it became clear that the Third Estate, which included all the professional, commercial, and middle-class groups of the country, would not permit the monarchy and the aristocracy to decide the future course of the nation.

Their spirit was best displayed in a pamphlet published during 1789 in which the Abbé Sieyès (1748–1836) declared, "What is the Third Estate? Everything. What has it been in the political order up to the present? Nothing. What does it ask? To become something."[1]

---

[1] *Quoted in Leo Gershoy*, The French Revolution and Napoleon *(New York: Appleton-Century-Crofts, 1964), p. 102.*

Abbé Sieyes Presents the Cause of the Third Estate

*Among the many pamphlets that appeared after the calling of the
Estates General, one of the most famous was* What Is the Third
Estate? *by Abbé Emmanuel Sieyes. In the pamphlet Sieyes distinguished the Third Estate by its contributions to the nation and by
its exclusion from political and social privilege. He argues that it
is not properly represented in the Estates General. Sieyes then
explains how the aristocracy actually controls the French government. Note how he presents an image of the Third Estate in direct
conflict with the aristocracy rather than with the monarchy. On
the basis of this pamphlet many later observers and historians
argued that the revolution was a conflict between the middle
class and the aristocracy. However, the social structure of France
and the interactions of those two groups was much more complicated than Sieyes suggests. Both groups were very discontent
with the state of the monarchical government.*

Who, then would dare to say that the third
estate has not within itself all that is necessary to constitute a complete nation? It
is the strong and robust man whose one
arm remains enchained. If the privileged
order were abolished, the nation would be
not something less but something more.
Thus, what is the third estate? Everything;
but an everything shackled and oppressed. . . .

The third estate must be understood to
mean the mass of the citizens belonging to
the common order. Legalized privilege in
any form deviates from the common order,
constitutes an exception to the common
law, and, consequently, does not appertain
to the third estate at all. We repeat, a common law and a common representation are
what constitute ONE nation. It is only too
true that one is NOTHING in France
when one has only the protection of the
common law; if one does not possess some
privilege, one must resign oneself to enduring contempt, injury, and vexations of
every sort. . . .

But here we have to consider the order of
the third estate less in its civil status than
in its relation with the constitution. Let us
examine its position in the Estates General.

Who have been its so-called representatives? The ennobled or those privileged for
a period of years. These false deputies have
not even been always freely elected by the
people. . . .

Add to this appalling truth that, in one
manner or another, all branches of the executive power also have fallen to the case
which furnishes the Church, the Robe, and
the Sword. A sort of spirit of brotherhood
causes the nobles to prefer themselves . . .
to the rest of the nation. Usurpation is
complete; in truth they reign.

. . . it is a great error to believe that
France is subject to a monarchical regime.

. . . it is the court, and not the monarch,
that has reigned. It is the court that makes
and unmakes, appoints and discharges
ministers, creates and dispenses positions,
etc. And what is the court if not the head
of this immense aristocracy which over-
runs all parts of France; which through its
members attains all and everywhere does
whatever is essential in all parts of the
commonwealth?

John Hall Stewart, A Documentary Survey of the French Revolution *(New York: The Macmillan Company,
1966), pp. 44–45.*

DEBATE OVER ORGANIZATION AND VOTING The split between the aristocracy and the Third Estate occurred before the Estates General gathered. Debate over the proper organization of the body drew the lines of basic disagreement. Members of the aristocracy demanded an equal number of representatives for each estate. In September 1788 the Parlement of Paris ruled that voting in the Estates General should be conducted by order rather than by head—that is, that each estate, or order, should have one vote, rather than that each member should have one vote. That procedure would ensure that the aristocratic First and Second Estates could always outvote the Third. Both moves on the part of the aristocracy unmasked its alleged concern for French liberty and exposed it as a group determined to maintain its privileges. Spokesmen for the Third Estate denounced the arrogant claims of the aristocracy.

The royal council eventually decided that the cause of the monarchy and fiscal reform would best be served by a strengthening of the Third Estate. In December 1788 the council announced that the Third Estate would elect twice as many representatives as either the nobles or the clergy. This so-called doubling of the Third Estate meant that it could easily dominate the Estates General if voting were allowed by head rather than by order. It was correctly assumed that some liberal nobles and clergy would support the Third Estate. The method of voting was settled by the king only after the Estates General had gathered at Versailles in May 1789.

THE *CAHIERS DE DOLÉANCES* When the representatives came to the royal palace, they brought with them *cahiers de doléances*, or lists of grievances, registered by the local electors, to be presented to the king. Large numbers of these have survived and provide considerable information about the state of the country on the eve of the revolution. These documents recorded criticisms of government waste, indirect taxes, church taxes and corruption, and the hunting rights of the aristocracy. They included calls for periodic meetings of the Estates General, more equitable taxes,

The Estates-General opened at Versailles in 1789 with much pomp and splendor. In this print, Louis XVI is on the throne. The First Estate, the clergy, is on the left; the Second Estate, the nobility, sits at the upper right; and the more numerous Third Estate, dressed in black suits and capes, sits at the lower right. [Culver Pictures]

more local control of administration, unified weights and measures, and a free press. The overwhelming demand of the *cahiers* was for equality of rights among the king's subjects.

These complaints and demands could not be discussed until the questions of organization and voting had been decided. From the beginning, the Third Estate, whose members consisted largely of local officials, professional men, and lawyers, refused to sit as a separate order as the king desired. For several weeks there was a standoff. Then on June 1 the Third Estate invited the clergy and the nobles to join them in organizing a new legislative body. A few members of the lower clergy did so. On June 17 that body declared itself the National Assembly.

THE TENNIS COURT OATH Three days later, finding themselves accidentally locked out of their usual meeting place, the National Assembly moved to a nearby tennis court. There its members took an oath to continue to sit until they had given France a constitution. This was the famous Tennis Court Oath. Louis XVI ordered the National Assembly to desist from their actions, but shortly afterward a majority of the clergy and a large group of nobles joined the assembly.

On June 27 the king capitulated and formally requested the First and Second Estates to meet with the National Assembly, where voting would occur by head rather than by order. Had nothing further occurred, the government of France would have been transformed. Government by privileged orders had come to an end. The National Assembly, which renamed itself the National Constituent Assembly, was composed of persons from all three orders, who possessed shared liberal goals for the administrative, constitutional, and economic reform of the country. The revolution in the governing of France had commenced.

The Oath of the Tennis Court, June 20, 1789 *was painted by Jacques Louis David* (1748–1825). *In the center foreground are members of different Estates joining hands in cooperation as equals. The presiding officer is Jean Sylvain Bailly, soon to become mayor of Paris.* [Art Resource]

The National Assembly Decrees Civic Equality in France

These famous decrees of August 4, 1789, *in effect created civic equality in France. The special privileges previously possessed or controlled by the nobility were removed.*

1. The National Assembly completely abolishes the feudal regime. It decrees that, among the rights and dues . . . all those originating in real or personal serfdom, personal servitude, and those which represent them, are abolished without indemnification; all others are declared redeemable, and that the price and mode of redemption shall be fixed by the National Assembly. . . .

2. The exclusive right to maintain pigeon-houses and dove-cotes is abolished. . . .

3. The exclusive right to hunt and to maintain unenclosed warrens is likewise abolished. . . .

4. All manorial courts are suppressed without indemnification.

5. Tithes of every description and the dues which have been substituted for them . . . are abolished, on condition, however, that some other method be devised to provide for the expenses of divine worship, the support of the officiating clergy, the relief of the poor, repairs and rebuilding of churches and parsonages, and for all establishments, seminaries, schools, academies, asylums, communities, and other institutions, for the maintenance of which they are actually devoted. . . .

. . . .

7. The sale of judicial and municipal offices shall be suppressed forthwith. . . .

8. Pecuniary privileges, personal or real, in the payment of taxes are abolished forever. . . .

. . . .

11. All citizens, without distinction of birth, are eligible to any office or dignity, whether ecclesiastical, civil or military. . . .

Frank Maloy Anderson (Ed. and Trans.), The Constitutions and Other Select Documents Illustrative of the History of France, 1789–1907, 2nd. ed., rev. and enlarged (Minneapolis: H. W. Wilson, 1908), pp. 11–13.

Fall of the Bastille

Two new forces soon intruded on the scene. The first was Louis XVI himself, who attempted to regain the initiative by mustering royal troops in the vicinity of Versailles and Paris. It appeared that he might be contemplating disruption of the National Constituent Assembly. Such was the advice of Queen Marie Antoinette, his brothers, and the most conservative nobles, with whom he had begun to consult. On July 11, without consultation with the assembly leaders, Louis abruptly dismissed his minister of finance Necker. These actions marked the beginning of a steady, but consistently poorly executed, royal attempt to undermine the assembly and halt the revolution. Most of the National Constituent Assem-

bly wished to create some form of constitutional monarchy, but from the start Louis' refusal to cooperate thwarted that effort. The king fatally decided to throw his lot in with the aristocracy against the nation.

The second new factor to impose itself on the events at Versailles was the populace of Paris. The mustering of royal troops created anxiety in the city, where throughout the winter and spring of 1789 there had been several bread riots. The Parisians who had elected their representatives to the Third Estate had continued to meet after the elections. By June they were organizing a citizen militia and collecting arms. They regarded the dismissal of Necker as the opening of a royal offensive against the National Constituent Assembly and the city.

On July 14 somewhat over eight hundred

people, most of whom were small shopkeepers, tradespeople, artisans, and wage earners, marched to the Bastille in search of weapons for the militia. This great fortress, with ten-foot-thick walls, had once held political prisoners. Through miscalculations and ineptitude on the part of the governor of the fortress, the troops in the Bastille fired into the crowd, killing ninety-eight people and wounding many others. Thereafter the crowd stormed the fortress and eventually gained entrance. They released the seven prisoners, none of whom was there for political reasons, and killed several troops and the governor. They found no weapons.

On July 15 the militia of Paris, by then called the National Guard, offered its command to Lafayette. The hero of the American Revolution gave the guard a new insignia in the design of the red and blue stripes of the city of Paris separated by the white stripe of the king. This emblem became the revolutionary cockade (badge) worn by the soldiers and eventually the flag of revolutionary France.

The attack on the Bastille marked the first of many crucial *journées*, or days when the populace of Paris would redirect the course of the revolution. The fall of the fortress signaled that the political future of the nation would not be decided solely by the National Constituent Assembly. As the news of the taking of the Bastille spread, similar disturbances took place in the provincial cities. A few days later Louis XVI again bowed to the force of events and personally visited Paris, where he wore the revolutionary cockade and recognized the organized electors as the legitimate government of the city. The king also recognized the National Guard. The citizens of Paris were, for the time being, satisfied.

The Great Fear and the Surrender of Feudal Privileges

Simultaneously with the popular urban disturbances, a movement known as the *Great Fear* swept across much of the French countryside. Rumors had spread that royal troops

This is an eye-witness drawing of the fall of the Bastille, July 14, 1789. The mob was supported by rebel troops and artillery. [Mary Evans Picture Library]

would be sent into the rural districts. The result was an intensification of the peasant disturbances that had begun during the spring. The Great Fear witnessed the burning of chateaux, the destruction of records and documents, and the refusal to pay feudal dues. The peasants were determined to take possession of food supplies and land that they considered rightfully theirs. They were reclaiming rights and property that they had lost through the aristocratic resurgence of the last quarter century, as well as venting their general anger against the injustices of rural life.

On the night of August 4, 1789, aristocrats in the National Constituent Assembly attempted to halt the spreading disorder in the countryside. By prearrangement a number of liberal nobles and churchmen rose in the assembly and renounced their feudal rights, dues, and tithes. In a scene of great emotion, hunting and fishing rights, judicial authority, and special exemptions were surrendered. In a sense these nobles gave up what they had already lost and what they could not have regained without civil war in the rural areas. Later they would also, in many cases, receive compensation for their losses. Nonetheless, after the night of August 4, all French citizens were subject to the same and equal laws. That dramatic session of the assembly paved the way for the legal and social reconstruction of the nation. Without those renunciations the constructive work of the National Constituent Assembly would have been much more difficult.

Both the attack on the Bastille and the Great Fear displayed varieties of the rural and urban riots that had characterized much of eighteenth-century political and social life. Louis XVI first thought that the turmoil over the Bastille was simply another bread riot. The popular disturbances also were only partly related to the events at Versailles. A deep economic downturn had struck France during 1787 and had continued into 1788. The harvests for both years had been poor, and food prices in 1789 stood higher than at any time since 1703. Wages had not kept up with the rise in prices. Throughout the winter of 1788–1789, an unusually cold one, many people suffered from hunger. Several cities had experienced wage and food riots. These economic difficulties helped the revolution reach such vast proportions.

The political, social, and economic grievances of numerous sections of the country became combined. The National Constituent Assembly could look to the popular forces as a source of strength against the king and the conservative aristocrats. When the various elements of the assembly later fell into quarrels among themselves, their factions succumbed to the temptation of appealing to the politically sophisticated and well-organized shopkeeping and artisan classes for support. When this turn of events came to pass, the popular classes could demand a price for their cooperation.

The Declaration of the Rights of Man and Citizen

In late August 1789 the National Constituent Assembly decided that before writing a new constitution, it should set forth a statement of broad political principles. On August 27 the assembly issued the Declaration of the Rights of Man and Citizen. This declaration drew together much of the political language of the Enlightenment and was also influenced by the Declaration of Rights adopted by Virginia in America in June 1776.

The French declaration proclaimed that all men were "born and remain free and equal in rights." The natural rights so proclaimed were "liberty, property, security, and resistance to oppression." Governments existed to protect those rights. All political sovereignty resided in the nation and its representatives. All citizens were to be equal before the law and were to be "equally admissible to all public dignities, offices, and employments, according to their capacity, and with no other distinction than that of their virtues and talents." There were to be due process of law and presumption of innocence until proof of guilt. Freedom of religion was affirmed. Taxation was to be apportioned equally according to capacity to pay. Property constituted "an inviolable and sacred right."[2]

Although these statements were rather abstract, almost all of them were directed against specific abuses of the old aristocratic and absolutist regime. If any two principles of the fu-

---

[2] Quoted in Georges Lefebvre, The Coming of the French Revolution, trans. by R. R. Palmer (Princeton, N.J.: Princeton University Press, 1967), pp. 221–223.

ture governed the declaration, they were civic equality and protection of property. The Declaration of the Rights of Man and Citizen has often been considered the death certificate of the old regime.

The Royal Family Forced to Return to Paris

Louis XVI stalled before ratifying both the declaration and the aristocratic renunciation of feudalism. The longer he hesitated, the larger existing suspicions grew that he might again try to resort to the use of troops. Moreover bread continued to be in short supply. On October 5 a large crowd of Parisian women marched to Versailles demanding more bread. They milled about the palace, and many stayed the night. Under this pressure the king agreed to sanction the decrees of the assembly. The next day he and his family appeared on a balcony before the crowd. The Parisians were deeply suspicious of the monarch and believed that he must be kept under the watchful eye of the people. Consequently they demanded that Louis and his family return to Paris.

The monarch had no real choice in the matter. On October 6, 1789, his carriage followed the crowd into the city, where he and his family settled in the palace of the Tuileries. The National Constituent Assembly also soon moved into Paris. Thereafter, both Paris and France remained relatively stable and peaceful until the summer of 1792.

The Reconstruction of France

Once established in Paris, the National Constituent Assembly set about reorganizing France. In government it pursued a policy of constitutional monarchy; in administration, rationalism; in economics, unregulated freedom; and in religion, anticlericalism. Throughout its proceedings the assembly was determined to protect property. It also sought to limit the impact on national life of the unpropertied elements of the nation and even of possessors of small amounts of property. Although championing civic equality before the law, the assembly spurned social equality and

The women of Paris marched to Versailles on October 5, 1789. The following day the royal family was forced to return to Paris with them. Henceforth, the French government would function under the constant threat of mob violence. [Mary Evans Picture Library]

extensive democracy. In all these areas the assembly charted a general course that, to a greater or lesser degree, nineteenth-century liberals across Europe would follow.

Political Reorganization

The Constitution of 1791, which was the product of the National Constituent Assembly's deliberations, established a constitutional monarchy. The major political authority of the nation would be a unicameral Legislative Assembly in which all laws would originate. The monarch was allowed a suspensive veto that could delay but not halt legislation. Powers of war and peace were vested in the assembly.

ACTIVE AND PASSIVE CITIZENS The constitution provided for an elaborate system of indirect elections intended to thwart direct popular pressure on the government. The citizens of France were divided into active and passive categories. Only active citizens—that is, men paying annual taxes equal to three days of local labor wages—could vote. They chose electors, who then in turn voted for the members of the legislature. At the levels of electors, or members, still further property qualifications were imposed. Only about fifty thousand citizens of a population of about twenty-five million could qualify as electors or members of the Legislative Assembly.

DEPARTMENTS REPLACE PROVINCES In reconstructing the local and judicial administration, the National Constituent Assembly applied the rational spirit of the Enlightenment. It abolished the ancient French provinces, such as Burgundy and Brittany, and established in their place eighty-three departments (départements) of generally equal size named after rivers, mountains, and other geographical features. The departments in turn were subdivided into districts, cantons, and communes. Most local elections were also indirect. The departmental reconstruction proved to be one of the most permanent achievements of the assembly. The departments exist to the present day.

All of the ancient judicial courts, including the seigneurial courts and the parlements, were also abolished. In their place were organized uniform courts with elected judges and prosecutors. Procedures were simplified, and

MAP 19-1 FRENCH PROVINCES AND THE REPUBLIC In 1789 the National Assembly redrew the map of France. The Ancient provinces (A) were replaced with a larger number of new, smaller departments (B). This redrawing of the map represented one of the efforts of the Assembly to achieve greater administrative rationality. The borders of the republic (C) changed as the French Army conquered new territory.

the most degrading punishments were removed from the books.

Economic Policy

In economic matters the National Constituent Assembly continued the policies formerly advocated by Louis XVI's reformist ministers. It suppressed the guilds and liberated the grain trade. The assembly established the metric system to provide the nation with uniform weights and measures.

WORKERS' ORGANIZATIONS FORBIDDEN These policies of economic freedom and uniformity disappointed both peasants and urban workers caught in the cycle of inflation. By decrees of 1789 the assembly placed the burden of proof on the peasants to rid themselves of the residual feudal dues for which compensation was to be paid. On June 14, 1791, the assembly crushed the attempts of urban workers to protect their wages by enacting the Chapelier Law, which forbade workers' associations. Peasants and workers were henceforth to be left to the freedom and mercy of the marketplace.

CONFISCATION OF CHURCH LANDS While these various reforms were being put into effect, the original financial crisis that had occasioned the calling of the Estates General persisted. The royal debt was not repudiated, because it was owed to the bankers, the merchants, and the commercial traders of the Third Estate. The National Constituent Assembly had suppressed many of the old, hated indirect taxes and had substituted new land taxes, but these proved insufficient. Moreover, there were not enough officials to collect them. The continuing financial problem led the assembly to take what may well have been, for the future of French life and society, its most decisive action. The assembly decided to finance the debt by confiscating and then sell-

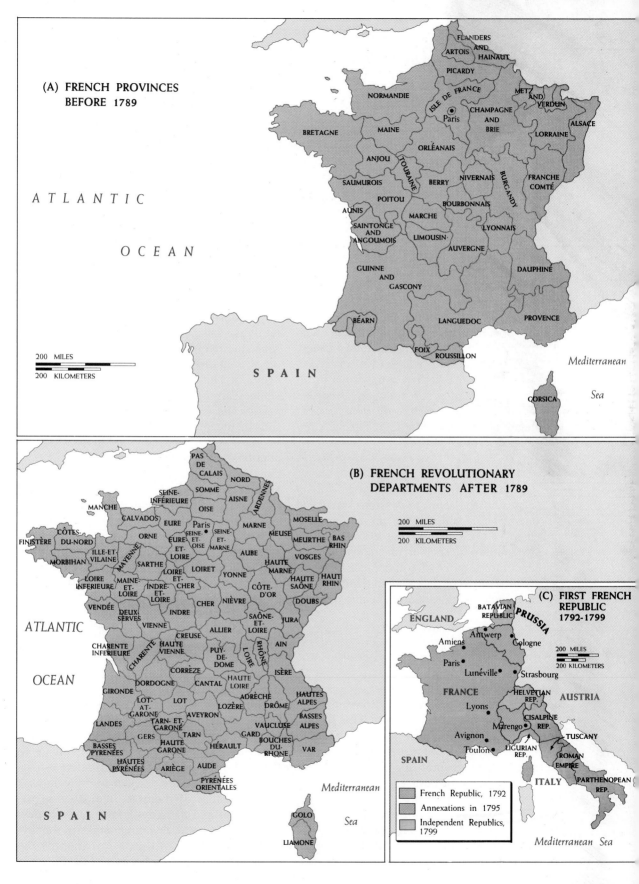

(A) FRENCH PROVINCES
BEFORE 1789

ATLANTIC

OCEAN

200 MILES
200 KILOMETERS

FLANDERS
AND
HAINAUT
ARTOIS
PICARDY
NORMANDIE
ISLE DE FRANCE
METZ AND VERDUN
Paris
CHAMPAGNE AND BRIE
ALSACE
BRETAGNE
MAINE
LORRAINE
ORLÉANAIS
ANJOU
TOURAINE
BERRY
NIVERNAIS
BURGANDY
FRANCHE COMTÉ
SAUMUROIS
POITOU
BOURBONNAIS
AUNIS
MARCHE
LYONNAIS
SAINTONGE AND ANGOUMOIS
LIMOUSIN
AUVERGNE
GUINNE AND GASCONY
DAUPHINÉ
BÉARN
LANGUEDOC
PROVENCE
FOIX
ROUSSILLON
Mediterranean Sea
CORSICA
SPAIN

(B) FRENCH REVOLUTIONARY
DEPARTMENTS AFTER 1789

200 MILES
200 KILOMETERS

ATLANTIC

OCEAN

SPAIN

PAS DE CALAIS
NORD
SEINE-INFÉRIEURE
SOMME
AISNE
ARDENNES
MANCHE
CALVADOS
OISE
MOSELLE
EURE
Paris
MARNE
MEUSE
MEURTHE
BAS RHIN
CÔTES-DU-NORD
FINISTÈRE
ORNE
SEINE-ET-OISE
SEINE-ET-MARNE
ILLE-ET-VILAINE
MAYENNE
SARTHE
EURE-ET-LOIRE
AUBE
HAUTE MARNE
VOSGES
HAUT RHIN
MORBIHAN
LOIRE-ET-CHER
LOIRET
YONNE
HAUTE SAÔNE
MAINE-ET-LOIRE
INDRE-ET-CHER
CÔTE-D'OR
DOUBS
LOIRE INFÉRIEURE
VENDÉE
DEUX-SERVES
VIENNE
INDRE
CHER
NIÈVRE
SAÔNE-ET-LOIRE
JURA
CHARENTE INFERIEURE
CHARENTE
CREUSE
HAUTE VIENNE
ALLIER
PUY-DE-DOME
LOIRE
RHÔNE
AIN
CORREZE
ISÈRE
DORDOGNE
CANTAL
HAUTE LOIRE
GIRONDE
LOT-ET-GARONE
LOT
AVEYRON
LOZÈRE
ADRÈCHE
DRÔME
HAUTES ALPES
LANDES
TARN-ET-GARONÉ
GERS
TARN
GARD
VAUCLUSE
BASSES ALPES
BASSES PYRÉNÉES
HAUTE GARONE
HÉRAULT
BOUCHES-DU-RHONE
VAR
HAUTES PYRÉNÉES
ARIÈGE
AUDE
PYRÉNÉES ORIENTALES
Mediterranean Sea
GOLO
LIAMONE

(C) FIRST FRENCH
REPUBLIC
1792-1799

200 MILES
200 KILOMETERS

ENGLAND
BATAVIAN REPUBLIC
PRUSSIA
Amiens
Antwerp
Cologne
Paris
Lunéville
Strasbourg
FRANCE
HELVETIAN REP.
AUSTRIA
Lyons
CISALPINE REP.
Avignon
Marengo
TUSCANY
Toulon
LIGURIAN REP.
ROMAN EMPIRE
ITALY
PARTHENOPEAN REP.
SPAIN
Mediterranean Sea

French Republic, 1792
Annexations in 1795
Independent Republics, 1799

669

The Revolutionary Government Forbids Worker Organizations

The Chapelier Law of June 14, 1791 was one of the most important pieces of revolutionary legislation. It abolished the kinds of labor organizations that had protected skilled workers under the old regime. The principles of this legislation prevented effective labor organization in France for well over half a century.

1. Since the abolition of all kinds of corporations of citizens of the same occupation and profession is one of the fundamental bases of the French Constitution, reestablishment thereof under any pretext or form whatsoever is forbidden.

2. Citizens of the same occupation or profession, entrepreneurs, those who maintain open shop, workers, and journeymen of any craft whatsoever may not, when they are together, name either president, secretaries, or trustees, keep accounts, pass decrees or resolutions, or draft regulations concerning their alleged common interests.

. . . .

4. If, contrary to the principles of liberty and the Constitution, some citizens associated in the same professions, arts, and crafts hold deliberations or make agreements among themselves tending to refuse by mutual consent or to grant only at a determined price the assistance of their industry or their labor, such deliberations and agreements, whether accompanied by oath or not, are declared unconstitutional, in contempt of liberty and the Declaration of the Rights of Man, and noneffective; administrative and municipal bodies shall be required so to declare them. . . .

. . . .

8. All assemblies composed of artisans, workers, journeymen, day laborers, or those incited by them against the free exercise of industry and labor appertaining to every kind of person and under all circumstances arranged by private contract, or against the action of police and the execution of judgments rendered in such connection, as well as against public bids and auctions of divers enterprises, shall be considered as seditious assemblies, and as such shall be dispersed by the depositories of the public force, upon legal requisitions made thereupon, and shall be punished according to all the rigor of the laws concerning authors, instigators, and leaders of the said assemblies, and all those who have committed assaults and acts of violence.

John Hall Stewart, A Documentary Survey of the French Revolution *(New York: The Macmillan Company, 1906), pp. 165–166.*

ing the land and property of the Roman Catholic church in France. The results were further inflation, religious schism, and civil war. In effect, the National Constituent Assembly had opened a new chapter in the relations of Church and state in Europe.

THE *ASSIGNATS* Having chosen to plunder the land of the Church, in December 1789 the assembly authorized the issuance of *assignats,* or government bonds. Their value was guaranteed by the revenue to be generated from the sale of Church property. Initially a limit was set on the quantity of *assignats* to be issued. However, the bonds proved so acceptable to the public that they began to circulate as currency. The assembly decided to issue an ever larger number of them to liquidate the national debt and to create a large body of new property owners with a direct stake in the revolution. However, within a few months the value of the *assignats* began to fall. Inflation

The assignats *were government bonds that were backed by confiscated church lands. They circulated as money. When the government printed too many of them, inflation resulted and their value fell. [Bettmann Archive]*

increased and put new stress on the lives of the urban poor.

The Civil Constitution of the Clergy

The confiscation of Church lands required an ecclesiastical reconstruction. In July 1790 the National Constituent Assembly issued the Civil Constitution of the Clergy, which transformed the Roman Catholic church in France into a branch of the secular state. This legislation reduced the number of bishoprics from 135 to 83 and brought the borders of the dioceses into conformity with those of the new departments. It also provided for the election of priests and bishops, who henceforth became salaried employees of the state. The assembly consulted neither the pope nor the French clergy about these broad changes. The king approved the measure only with the greatest reluctance.

The Civil Constitution of the Clergy was the major blunder of the National Constituent Assembly. The measure created immense opposition within the French church even from bishops who had long championed Gallican liberties over papal domination. In the face of this resistance the assembly unwisely ruled that all clergy must take an oath to support the Civil Constitution. Only seven bishops and about half the clergy did so. In reprisal the assembly designated the clergy who had not taken the oath as "refractory" and removed them from their clerical functions.

Further reaction was swift. Refractory priests attempted to celebrate Mass. In February 1791 the pope condemned not only the Civil Constitution of the Clergy but also the Declaration of the Rights of Man and Citizen. That condemnation marked the opening of a Roman Catholic offensive against liberalism and the revolution that continued throughout the nineteenth century. Within France itself the pope's action created a crisis of conscience and political loyalty for all sincere Catholics. Religious devotion and revolutionary loyalty became incompatible for many people. French citizens were divided between those who supported the constitutional priests and those who resorted to the refractory clergy. Louis XVI and his family favored the latter clergy.

Counterrevolutionary Activity

The revolution had other enemies besides the pope and the devout Catholics. As it became clear that the old political and social order was undergoing fundamental and probably permanent change, considerable numbers of aristocrats left France. Known as the *émigrés*, they settled in countries near the French border, where they sought to foment counterrevolution. Among the most important of their number was the king's younger brother, the count of Artois (1757–1836). In the summer of 1791 his agents and the queen persuaded Louis XVI to attempt to flee the country.

FLIGHT TO VARENNES On the night of June 20, 1791, Louis and his immediate family, disguised as servants, left Paris. They traveled as far as Varennes on their way to Metz. At Varennes the king was recognized, and his flight was halted. On June 24 a company of soldiers escorted the royal family back to Paris. The leaders of the National Constituent Assembly, determined to save the constitutional monarchy, announced that the king had been abducted from the capital. However, such a convenient public fiction could not cloak the reality that the chief counterrevolutionary in France now sat on the throne.

DECLARATION OF PILLNITZ Two months later, on August 27, 1791, under pressure from a group of *émigrés*, Emperor Leopold II of Austria, who was the brother of Marie Antoinette, and Frederick William II, the king of Prussia, issued the Declaration of Pillnitz. The two monarchs promised to intervene in France to protect the royal family and to preserve the monarchy *if* the other major European powers agreed. The latter provision rendered the statement meaningless because at the time Great Britain would not have given its consent. However, the declaration was not so read in France, where the revolutionaries saw the nation surrounded by aristocratic and monarchical foes.

The National Constituent Assembly drew to a close in September 1791. Its task of reconstructing the government and the administration of France had been completed. One of its last acts was the passage of a measure that forbade any of its own members to sit in the Legislative Assembly then being elected. The new body met on October 1 and had to confront the immense problems that had emerged during the earlier part of the year. Within the Legislative Assembly major political divisions also soon developed over the future course of the nation and the revolution.

A Second Revolution

By the autumn of 1791 the government of France had been transformed into a constitutional monarchy. Virtually all of the other administrative and religious structures of the nation had also been reformed. The situation both inside and outside France, however, remained quite unstable. Louis XVI had reluctantly accepted the constitution. French aristocrats resented their loss of position and plotted to overthrow the new order. In the

west of France, peasants resisted the revolutionary changes especially as they affected the Church. In Paris many groups of workers believed the revolution had not gone far enough. The same was true of radical members of the new Legislative Assembly. The major foreign powers saw the French revolution as dangerous to their own domestic political order. By the spring of 1792 all of these unstable elements had begun to overturn the first revolutionary settlement and led to a second series of revolutionary changes far more radical and extensive than the first.

End of the Monarchy

The issues of the Civil Constitution of the Clergy and the trustworthiness of Louis XVI undermined the unity of the revolution. Much factionalism displayed itself throughout the short life of the Legislative Assembly (1791–1792). Ever since the original gathering of the Estates General, deputies from the Third Estate had organized themselves into clubs composed of politically like-minded persons. The most famous and best organized of these were the Jacobins, whose name derived from the fact that Dominican friars were called *Jacobins*, and the group met in a Dominican monastery in Paris. The Jacobins had also established a network of local clubs throughout the provinces. They had constituted the most advanced political group in the National Constituent Assembly and had pressed for a republic rather than a constitutional monarchy. The events of the summer of 1791 led them to renew those demands.

In the Legislative Assembly a group of Jacobins known as the *Girondists* (because many of them came from the department of the Gironde) assumed leadership.[3] They were determined to oppose the forces of counterrevolution. They passed a measure ordering the *émigrés* to return or suffer loss of property and another requiring the refractory clergy to support the Civil Constitution or lose their state pensions. The king vetoed both acts.

Furthermore, on April 20, 1792, the Girondists led the Legislative Assembly to declare war on Austria, by this time governed by Fran-

---

[3] *The Girondists are also frequently called the* Brissotins *after Jacques-Pierre Brissot (1754–1793), who was their chief spokesman in early* 1792.

cis II (1768–1835) and allied to Prussia. The Girondists believed that the war would preserve the revolution from domestic enemies and bring the most advanced revolutionaries to power. Paradoxically Louis XVI and other monarchists also favored the war. They thought that the conflict would strengthen the executive power (i.e., the monarchy). The king also entertained the hope that French forces might be defeated and the old regime restored. Both sides were playing dangerously foolish politics.

The war radicalized the revolution and led to what is usually called the *second revolution,* which overthrew the constitutional monarchy and established a republic. Initially the war effort went quite poorly. Both the country and the revolution seemed in danger. In July 1792 the duke of Brunswick, commander of the Prussian forces, issued a manifesto promising the destruction of Paris if harm came to the French royal family. This statement stiffened support for the war and increased the already significant distrust of the king.

Late in July, under radical working-class pressure, the government of the city of Paris passed from the elected council to a committee, or commune, of representatives from the sections (municipal wards) of Paris. On August 10, 1792, a very large Parisian crowd invaded the Tuileries palace and forced Louis XVI and Marie Antoinette to take refuge in the Legislative Assembly itself. The crowd fought with the royal Swiss guards. When Louis was finally able to call off the troops, several hundred of them and a large number of Parisian citizens lay dead. The monarchy itself was also a casualty of that melee. Thereafter the royal family was imprisoned in comfortable quarters, but the king was allowed to perform none of his political functions.

The Convention and the Role of the Sans-culottes

Early in September the Parisian crowd again made its will felt. During the first week of the month, in what are known as the *September*

Marie Antoinette (1755–1793) was beautiful, elegant, and more intelligent than her husband, but her reputation for extravagance and her reactionary political intrigues (she favored war in 1792) were to help destroy the monarchy. [Art Resource]

Massacres, the Paris Commune summarily executed or murdered about twelve hundred people who were in the city jails. Many of these people were aristocrats or priests, but the majority were simply common criminals. The crowd had assumed that the prisoners were all counterrevolutionaries.

The Paris Commune then compelled the Legislative Assembly to call for the election by universal manhood suffrage of a new assembly to write a democratic constitution. That body, called the *Convention* after its American counterpart of 1787, met on September 21, 1792. The previous day the French army had halted the Prussian advance at the battle of Valmy in eastern France. The victory of democratic forces at home had been confirmed by victory on the battlefield. As its first act, the Convention declared France a republic, that is, a nation governed by an elected assembly without a king.

GOALS OF THE SANS-CULOTTES The second revolution had been the work of Jacobins more radical than the Girondists and of the people of Paris known as the *sans-culottes*. The name of the latter means "without breeches" and derived from the long trousers that, as working people, they wore instead of aristocratic knee breeches. The sans-culottes were shopkeepers, artisans, wage earners, and, in a few cases, factory workers. The persistent food shortages and the revolutionary inflation had made their generally difficult lives even more burdensome. The politics of the old regime had ignored them, and

A Pamphleteer Describes a Sans-culotte

This pamphlet is a 1793 description of a sans-culotte written either by one or by a sympathizer. It describes the sans-culotte as a hardworking, useful, patriotic citizen who bravely sacrifices himself to the war effort. It contrasts those virtues to the lazy and unproductive luxury of the noble and the personally self-interested plottings of the politician.

A sans-culotte you rogues? He is someone who always goes on foot, who has no millions as you would all like to have, no chateaux, no valets to serve him, and who lives simply with his wife and children, if he has any, on a fourth or fifth storey.

He is useful, because he knows how to work in the field, to forge iron, to use a saw, to use a file, to roof a house, to make shoes, and to shed his last drop of blood for the safety of the Republic.

And because he works, you are sure not to meet his person in the Café de Chartres, or in the gaming houses where others conspire and game; nor at the National theatre . . . nor in the literary clubs. . . .

In the evening he goes to his section, not powdered or perfumed, or smartly booted in the hope of catching the eye of the citizenesses in the galleries, but ready to support good proposals with all his might, and to crush those which come from the abominable faction of politicians.

Finally, a sans-culotte always has his sabre sharp, to cut off the ears of all enemies of the Revolution; sometimes he even goes out with his pike; but at the first sound of the drum he is ready to leave for the Vendée, for the army of the Alps or for the army of the North. . . .

"Reply to an Impertinent Question: What is a Sans-culotte?" April 1793. Reprinted in Walter Markov and Albert Soboul (Eds.), Die Sansculotten von Paris, and republished trans. by Clive Emsley in Merryn Williams (Ed.), Revolutions: 1775–1830 (Baltimore: Penguin Books, in association with the Open University, 1971), pp. 100–101.

the policies of the National Constituent Assembly had left them victims of unregulated economic liberty. However, the nation required their labor and their lives if the war was to succeed. From the summer of 1792 until the summer of 1794 their attitudes, desires, and ideals were the primary factors in the internal development of the revolution.

The sans-culottes generally knew what they wanted. The Parisian tradespeople and artisans sought immediate relief from food shortages and rising prices through the vehicle of price controls. They believed that all people had a right to subsistence and profoundly resented most forms of social inequality. This attitude led them to intense hostility toward the aristocracy and toward the original leaders of the revolution, who they believed simply wanted to take over the social privileges of the aristocracy. Their hatred of inequality did not go so far as to demand the abolition of property. Rather, they advocated a community of relatively small property owners.

In politics they were antimonarchical, strongly republican, and suspicious even of representative government. They believed that the people should make the decisions of government to as great an extent as possible. In Paris, where their influence was most important, the sans-culottes' political experience had been gained in meetings of the Paris sections. Those gatherings exemplified direct community democracy and were not unlike a New England town meeting. The economic hardship of their lives made them impatient to see their demands met.

THE POLICIES OF THE JACOBINS The goals of the sans-culottes were not wholly compatible with those of the Jacobins. The latter were republicans who sought representative government. Jacobin hatred of the aristocracy did not extend to a general suspicion of wealth. Basically, the Jacobins favored an unregulated economy. However, from the time of Louis XVI's flight to Varennes onward, the more extreme Jacobins began to cooperate with leaders of the Parisian sans-culottes and the Paris Commune for the overthrow of the monarchy. Once the Convention began its deliberations, these Jacobins, known as the *Mountain* because of their seats high in the assembly hall, worked with the sans-culottes

to carry the revolution forward and to win the war. This willingness to cooperate with the forces of the popular revolution separated the Mountain from the Girondists, who were also members of the Jacobin Club.

EXECUTION OF LOUIS XVI By the spring of 1793 several issues had brought the Mountain and its sans-culottes allies to domination of the Convention and the revolution. In December 1792 Louis XVI was put on trial as mere "Citizen Capet," the family name of extremely distant forebears of the royal family. The Girondists looked for some way to spare his life, but the Mountain defeated the effort. Louis was convicted, by a very narrow majority, of conspiring against the liberty of the people and the security of the state. He was condemned to death and was beheaded on January 21, 1793.

The next month the Convention declared war on Great Britain, Holland, and Spain. Soon thereafter the Prussians renewed their offensive and drove the French out of Belgium. To make matters worse, General Dumouriez, the Girondist victor of Valmy, deserted to the enemy. Finally, in March 1793 a royalist revolt led by aristocratic officers and priests erupted in the Vendée in western France and roused much popular support. Consequently the revolution found itself at war with most of Europe and much of the French nation. The Girondists had led the country into the war but had proved themselves incapable either of winning it or of suppressing the enemies of the revolution at home. The Mountain stood ready to take up the task. Every major European power was now hostile to the revolution.

Europe at War with the Revolution

Initially the attitude of the rest of Europe toward the revolutionary events in France had been ambivalent. Those people who favored political reform regarded the revolution as wisely and rationally reorganizing a corrupt and inefficient government. The major foreign governments thought that the revolution meant that France would cease to be an important factor in European affairs for several years.

Louis XVI was executed on January 21, 1793. [New York Public Library Picture Collection]

Edmund Burke Attacks the Revolution

In 1790, however, the Irish-born writer and British statesman Edmund Burke (1729–1799) argued a different position in *Reflections on the Revolution in France.* Burke regarded the reconstruction of French administration as the application of a blind rationalism that ignored the historical realities of political development and the complexities of social relations. He also forecast further turmoil as persons without political experience attempted to govern France. As the revolutionaries proceeded to attack the Church, the monarchy, and finally the rest of Europe, Burke's ideas came to have many admirers. His *Reflections* became the handbook of European conservatives for decades.

By the time of the commencement of the war with Austria in April 1792, the other European monarchies recognized the danger of both the ideas and the aggression of revolutionary France. The ideals of the Rights of Man and Citizen were highly exportable and applicable to the rest of Europe. One government after another turned to repressive domestic policies.

Suppression of Reform in Britain

In Great Britain William Pitt the Younger (1759–1806), the prime minister, who had unsuccessfully supported moderate reform of Parliament during the 1780s, turned against both reform and popular movements. The government suppressed the London Corresponding

Society, founded in 1792 as a working-class reform group. In Birmingham the government sponsored mob action to drive Joseph Priestley (1733–1804), a chemist and a radical political thinker, out of the country. In early 1793 Pitt secured parliamentary approval for acts suspending habeas corpus and making it possible to commit treason in writing. With less success Pitt attempted to curb freedom of the press. All political groups who dared to oppose the action of the government were in danger of becoming associated with revolutionary sedition.

The End of Enlightened Absolutism in Eastern Europe

In eastern Europe the revolution brought to a close the existence of enlightened absolutism. The aristocratic resistance to the reforms of

Burke Condemns the Work of the French National Assembly

Edmund Burke was undoubtedly the most important and articulate foreign critic of the French Revolution. He believed that governments could not be quickly created or organized, as seemed to have occurred in France. He was also deeply opposed to democracy, which he thought would lead to unwise, extreme actions on the part of government. Burke left a legacy of brilliantly argued conservative thought that remained a comfort to many followers and a serious challenge to liberals in nineteenth-century Europe. This passage is from his 1790 Reflections on the Revolution in France.

To make a government requires no great prudence. Settle the seat of power; teach obedience: and the work is done. To give Freedom is still more easy. It is not necessary to guide; it only requires to let go the rein. But to form a free government; that is, to temper together these opposite elements of liberty and restraint in one consistent work, requires much thought, deep reflection, a sagacious, powerful, and combining mind. This I do not find in those who take the lead in the National Assembly. Perhaps they are not so miserably deficient as they appear. I rather believe it. It would put them below the common level of human understanding. But when the leaders choose to make themselves bidders at an auction of popularity, their talents, in the construction of the state, will be of no service. They will become flatterers instead of legislators; the instruments, not the guides, of the people. If any of them should happen to propose a scheme of liberty, soberly limited, and defined with proper qualifications, he will be immediately outbid by his competitors, who will produce something more splendidly popular. Suspicions will be raised of his fidelity to his cause. Moderation will be stigmatized as the virtue of cowards; and compromise as the prudence of traitors; until, in hopes of preserving the credit which may enable him to temper, and moderate, on some occasions, the popular leader is obliged to become active in propagating doctrines, and establishing powers, that will afterwards defeat any sober purpose at which he ultimately might have aimed.

. . . The improvements of the National Assembly are superficial, their errors fundamental.

Edmund Burke, Reflections on the Revolution in France, *in* The Works of the Right Honourable Edmund Burke, *Vol. 2 (London: Henry G. Bohn, 1864), pp. 515–516.*

Mary Wollstonecraft Urges the Vindication of the Rights of Women

Edmund Burke's Reflections on the Revolution in France *provoked a very large number of replies. In 1790 Mary Wollstonecraft, an English writer, published a tract entitled* A Vindication of the Rights of Men. *Two years later she published her now more famous work* A Vindication of the Rights of Women (1972). *In that book she argued that existing social and educational arrangements, as well as the absence of political rights, treated women as if they were less than rational creatures and often prescribed for women less than rational roles in life. She argued that women must receive education and social roles like other rational beings and that the consequence would be beneficial to humanity.*

I wish to sum up what I have said in a few words, for I here threw down my gauntlet, and deny the existence of sexual virtues, not excepting modesty. For man and woman, truth, if I understand the meaning of the word, must be the same; yet the fanciful female character, so prettily drawn by poets and novelists, demanding the sacrifice of truth and sincerity, virtue becomes a relative idea, having no other foundation than utility, and of that utility men pretend arbitrarily to judge, shaping it to their own convenience.

Women, I allow, may have different duties to fulfil; but they are *human* duties, and the principles that should regulate the discharge of them, I sturdily maintain, must be the same.

To become respectable, the exercise of their understanding is necessary, there is no other foundation for independence of character; I mean explicitly to say that they must only bow to the authority of reason, instead of being the *modest* slaves of opinion.

In the superior ranks of life how seldom do we meet with a man of superior abilities, or even common acquirements? The reason appears to me clear, the state they are born in was an unnatural one. The human character has ever been formed by the employments the individual, or class, pursues; and if the faculties are not sharpened by necessity, they must remain obtuse. The argument may fairly be extended to women; for, seldom occupied by serious business, the pursuit of pleasure gives that insignificancy to their character which renders the society of the *great* so insipid. The same want of firmness, produced by a similar cause, forces them both to fly from themselves to noisy pleasures, and artificial passions, till vanity takes place of every social affection, and the characteristics of humanity can scarcely be discerned. Such are the blessings of civil governments, as they are at present organized, that wealth and female softness equally tend to debase mankind, and are produced by the same cause; but allowing women to be rational creatures, they should be incited to acquire virtues which they may call their own, for how can a rational being be ennobled by any thing that is not obtained by its *own* exertions?

Mary Wollstonecraft, A Vindication of the Rights of Women, *Carol H. Poston (Ed.) (New York: Norton, 1975),* pp. 45, 51–52.

Joseph II in the Habsburg lands led his brother, Leopold II, to come to terms with the landowners. Leopold's successor, Francis II (1792–1835), became a major leader of the counterrevolution. In Prussia Frederick William II (1786–1797), the nephew of Frederick the Great, looked to the leaders of the Lutheran church and the aristocracy to discourage any potential popular uprisings, such as those of the downtrodden Silesian weavers. In Russia Catherine the Great burned the works of her onetime friend Voltaire. She also exiled Alexander Radishchev (1749–1802) to Siberia for publishing his *Journey from Saint Petersburg to Moscow,* a work critical of Russian social conditions.

In 1793 and 1795 the eastern powers once again combined against Poland. In that unhappy land aristocratic reformers had finally achieved the abolition of the *liberum veto* and had organized a new constitutional monarchy in 1791. Russia and Prussia, which already had designs on Polish territory, saw or pretended to see a threat of revolution in the new Polish constitution. In 1793 they annexed large sections of the country; in 1795 Austria joined the two other powers in a final partition that removed Poland from the map of Europe until after World War I. The governments of eastern Europe had used the widely shared fear of further revolutionary disorder to justify old-fashioned eighteenth-century aggression.

War with Europe

In a paradoxical fashion the very success of the revolution in France brought to a rapid close reform movements in the rest of Europe. The French invasion of the Austrian Netherlands and the revolutionary reorganization of that territory roused the rest of Europe to the point of active hostility. In November 1792 the Convention declared that it would aid all peoples who wished to cast off the burdens of aristocratic and monarchical oppression. The Convention had also proclaimed the Scheldt River in the Netherlands open to the commerce of all nations and thus had broken a treaty that Great Britain had made with Austria and Holland. The British were on the point of declaring war on France over this issue when the Convention in February 1793 issued its own declaration of hostilities.

By April 1793, when the Mountain began to direct the French government, the nation stood at war with Austria, Prussia, Great Britain, Spain, Sardinia, and Holland. The governments of those nations were attempting to protect their social structures, political systems, and economic interests against the aggression of the revolution.

The Reign of Terror

The outbreak of war in the winter and spring of 1793 brought new, radical political actions within France. The government mobilized both itself and the nation for conflict. Throughout the nation there was the sense that a new kind of war had erupted. In this war the major issue was not protection of national borders as such but rather the defense of the bold new republican political and social order that had been established in France during the past four years. The French people understood that nothing less than the achievements of the revolution itself stood endangered. It was to protect those achievements that the government undertook extraordinary actions that touched almost every aspect of national life.

The Republic Defended

To mobilize for war, the revolutionary government organized a collective executive in the form of powerful committees. These in turn then sought to organize all French national life on a wartime footing. The result of this organization was the achievement of an immense military effort dedicated to both the protection and the advance of revolutionary ideals. This war effort also led to the suppression of much liberty within France itself and ultimately to a search for internal enemies of the revolution.

THE COMMITTEE OF PUBLIC SAFETY In April 1793 the Convention established a Committee of General Security and a Committee of Public Safety to perform the executive duties of the government. The latter committee became more important and eventually enjoyed almost dictatorial power. The most prominent leaders of the Committee of Public Safety were Jaques Danton (1759–1794), who had provided heroic leadership in September

The Committee of Public Safety met in 1793. The committee had twelve members, but it was said that they never all sat at the same table at the same time, since some were always stationed in the provinces. [Library of Congress]

1792; Maximilien Robespierre (1758–1794), who became for a time the single most powerful member of the committee; and Lazare Carnot (1753–1823), who was in charge of the military. All of these men and the other figures on the committee were strong republicans who had opposed the weak policies of the Girondists. They conceived of their task as saving the revolution from mortal enemies at home and abroad. They generally enjoyed a working political relationship with the sans-culottes of Paris, but this was an alliance of expediency on the part of the committee.

THE LEVÉE EN MASSE The major problem was to wage the war and to secure domestic support for the effort. In early June 1793 the Parisian sans-culottes invaded the Convention and successfully demanded the expulsion of the Girondist members. That action further radicalized the Convention and gave the Mountain complete control. On June 22 the Convention approved a fully democratic constitution but suspended its operation until the conclusion of the war emergency. On August 23 Carnot began a mobilization for victory by issuing a *levée en masse*, or general military requisition of the population, which conscripted males into the army and directed economic production for military purposes. On September 17 a ceiling on prices was established in accord with sans-culotte demands. During these same months the armies of the

revolution also successfully crushed many of the counterrevolutionary disturbances in the provinces.

Never before had Europe seen a nation organized in this way nor one defended by a citizen army. Other events within France astounded Europeans even more. The Reign of Terror had begun. Those months of quasi-judicial executions and murders stretching from the autumn of 1793 to the midsummer of 1794 are probably the most famous or infamous period of the revolution. They can be understood only in the context of the war on one hand and the revolutionary expectations of the Convention and the sans-culottes on the other.

The Republic of Virtue

The presence of armies closing in on the nation created a situation in which it was relatively easy to dispense with legal due process. However, the people who sat in the Convention and composed the Committee of Public Safety also believed that they had made a new departure in world history. They had established a republic in which civic virtue rather than aristocratic and monarchical corruption might flourish. The republic of virtue manifested itself in many ways: in the renaming of streets from the egalitarian vocabulary of the revolution; in republican dress copied from that of the sans-culottes or the Roman Republic; in the absence of powdered wigs; in the

PORTFOLIO IV
THE OLD REGIME
AND REVOLUTION

The social life of the eighteenth century was one of extremely marked social and economic contrasts among classes and among different regions of Europe. In Britain an energetic commercial society was emerging. France and the Low Countries also enjoyed considerable commercial life. However, the farther east one moved the more agriculture dominated and the greater the poverty of those who tilled the land. Transportation also was less well developed as one moved east.

Although many aristocrats worked very hard on their estates, they were frequently portrayed in settings of luxury and leisure. Aristocratic life came to be associated with decadence and unearned privilege. [Fête Champêtre by Antoine Watteau. National Gallery of Scotland, Edinburgh. Bridgeman Art Library/Art Resource]

Aristocracy

The aristocracy, though itself not always wealthy, enjoyed major social and political privileges. The wealthier aristocrats lived in great country houses and might also possess city townhouses. These various residences were often lavishly decorated to emphasize the wealth of their owners. Paintings of the aristocracy often pictured them on their large landed estates. Aristocratic women were usually portrayed in opulent surroundings. Aristocrats were associated with a carefree life that made them look socially irresponsible and possibly immoral.

The churches of the eighteenth century were also part of the world of social privilege. Bishops and other upper clergy often seemed to possess privilege and power without responsibility. Major cathedrals and abbeys were often decorated to emphasize the relationship of church officials to the life of the aristocracy and the government. By contrast, parish priests frequently lived in quiet poverty-stricken surroundings.

*Throughout the eighteenth century the Roman Catholic Church on the continent was closely associated with monarchs and aristocrats. Here Charles of Bourbon is depicted visiting Pope Benedict XIV. [*Charles of Bourbon Visiting Benedict XIV at the Quirinale *by Pannini. Capodimonte, Naples. Scala/Art Resource]*

Right *The life of ordinary people in the countryside was one of hardship and frequent poverty. This painting by Thomas Gainsborough illustrates an English country woman going to market. [Royal Holloway College, University of London, Egham Surrey. Bridgeman Art Library/Art Resource]*

Left *By the middle of the eighteenth century iron production was growing in Europe and especially in England. Throughout the countryside and also in cities blacksmiths ran large forges to produce metal products. [*The Iron Forge *by Joseph Wright of Derby. The Broadlands Collection. Bridgeman Art Library/Art Resource]*

Working People

This wealthy and politically privileged aristocratic and clerical world differed sharply from that of peasants, craftsmen, small tradesmen, physicians, and lawyers. Peasants across the continent lived in various kinds of dependence to landowners. Resentment over this situation led to numerous peasant rebellions during the century. The most violent of these occurred in Russia and the Habsburg lands. Urban craftsmen generally belonged to guilds which attempted to protect the economic value of their skills and to maintain their wages. The tradesmen and professional people generally prospered during the course of the eighteenth century. They also became socially more confident and expected greater political recognition by their respective governments.

The famous painting depicts the Oath of the Horatii brothers who according to legend represented Rome in combat with the Albans during the early years of the Republic. Their values of self-denial in the cause of patriotic virtue were seen as contrasting with the sometimes frivolous values and self-indulgence of the eighteenth-century aristocracy. [The Oath of the Horatii *by Jacques-Louis David. The Louvre, Paris. Giraudon/Art Resource]*

Contrasts in Values

The aristocratic world sharply contrasted with the lives of all these working and professional people. It also contrasted with the vision of ancient virtue, patriotism, and austerity that spread throughout the century. Writers associated with the Enlightenment often praised the values of ancient republican Rome. The widespread eighteenth-century fascination with

those ancient values served to emphasize the apparent decadence of aristocratic luxury and the refusal of aristocracies to bear a major portion of the tax burden. Such luxury seemed out of place to many people in a century that witnessed enormous suffering in naval and land warfare. Furthermore, the commercial and professional classes liked to contrast their virtues of industry and thrift with the luxury and irresponsibility of the aristocracy.

The French Revolution

The events of the French Revolution overthrew that aristocratic world. For almost ten years France was in a state of turmoil. The legislation of the early Revolution dismantled most of the privileges of the aristocracy, but virtually all other classes were also touched. The Civil Constitution of the Clergy (1790) transformed the relationship of Church and State. The Chapelier Law (1791) removed the protection of the guilds from French workers. The French monarchy fell and both the King and Queen were eventually executed. However, the Reign of Terror also found many of its victims in the peasants of the countryside who resisted changes in the Church. Finally, during the Reign of Terror many of the leaders of the Revolution itself were executed. The events of Thermidor (1794) brought the revolution to a close, and France sought stability under the Directory.

Left   *One of the most dramatic and memorable events of the French Revolution was the storming of the Bastille on* July 14, 1789. *The ancient prison actually held few prisoners, but its overthrow symbolized the collapse of the old order and marked the first major revolutionary activity by the people of Paris. [*Taking the Bastille. *Musee Carnavalet, Paris. Giraudon/Art Resource]*

Right   *On* August 10, 1792, *the Swiss Guards of Louis XVI fought with Parisians who attacked the Tuileries palace. Several hundred troops and citizens were killed, and Louis XVI and his family were forced to take refuge with the Legislative Assembly. After this event, the monarch exercised virtually no influence over events in France. [*Prise des Tuileries cour du Caroussel *by Jean Duplessi-Bertaux. Château de Versailles. Giraudon/Art Resource]*

It was not long until Napoleon came to power and led the citizen army created by the Revolution to victory after victory across Europe. The wars of the French Revolution and Napoleon disrupted Europe for almost a quarter-century. They also transformed the aristocratically led armies of the Old Regime into armies of citizens led by generals who more often than not were appointed for merit.

The Napoleonic Wars contributed to further social and political changes in Europe. Napoleon saw himself as a great modern legislator whose laws, though imposed by conquering armies, would liberate people from aristocratic bondage. Wherever his armies went, they changed laws and social customs. Furthermore, in efforts to rally support to oppose Napoleon, governments especially in the Germanies reformed themselves and in some cases abolished serfdom. Popular resistance to Napoleon in Spain and later in the Germanies served to foster nationalism. At the same time these wars saw enormous cruelty and suffering.

Above *This portrait records Napoleon in an heroic pose leading his troops across the Alps. Note that at the bottom of the picture on the stones are carved along with Napoleon's name those of Hannibal and Charlemagne who centuries earlier had led armies across the Alps to conquer Italy.* [Bonaparte Crossing the Alps on Horseback *by Jacques-Louis David. Chateau Malmaison. Giraudon/Art Resource*]

Below *In 1804 Napoleon in the presence of the Pope crowned himself emperor. The lavish ceremony illustrated how far the French government had moved away from the ideal of the revolution and toward a new form of monarchical domination.* [The Coronation of Napoleon *by Jacques-Louis David. The Louvre, Paris. Art Resource*]

Above   *The French invasion of Spain during the Napoleonic era led to especially brutal warfare. In this painting by Goya the French troops are shown executing citizens of Madrid in 1808. Such treatment served to ignite Spanish national resistance against French domination. [*The Third of May *by Goya. The Prado, Madrid. Scala/Art Resource]*

Below   *Theodore Gericault's painting of the* Raft of the Medusa *presented survivors of a ship wreck. The painting may also be seen as illustrating human beings caught in the great political and social forces of history upon which they ride as upon a turbulent ocean. Many romantic writers thought such to be the situation of human beings in the processes of history. [The Louvre, Paris. Giraudon/Art Resource]*

A New Era of Peace

The battle of Waterloo of 1815 brought to a close the Napoleonic Wars, and the Congress of Vienna reorganized the continent. Almost a half century of international peace followed. The politics of that era were often quite conservative. There was a nostalgia for a quiet rural order without the factories as in Great Britain and the urban expansion that was virtually everywhere. A widespread religious revival associated with romantic religion also occurred. Poets and painters associated with Romanticism often suggested that human beings were almost insignificant creatures struggling against the upheavals of the natural order. In that respect, they reflected the sentiment of many people who had lived from the Old Regime through the Revolution and Wars and who felt they had been fragile creatures on the waves of vast historical change.

Right After the quarter century of turmoil associated with the French Revolution and the Napoleonic Wars, many Europeans wanted to turn toward a more tranquil life. In this painting of pastoral calm the English painter John Constable illustrated the quiet of rural and village life that was also the scene of people working at productive labor. [Tate Gallery/Art Resource]

Left Many Romantic writers and artists were concerned about the relationship of human beings to nature. Quite often, as in this painting of the German artist Caspar David Friedrich, nature was portrayed as a vast force that overpowered and totally encompassed human life. [Kunsthistoriches Museum, Vienna. Saskia/Art Resource]

suppression of plays that were insufficiently republican; and in a general attack against crimes, such as prostitution, that were supposedly characteristic of aristocratic society.

DECHRISTIANIZATION The most dramatic departure of the republic of virtue, and one that illustrates the imposition of political values that would justify the Terror, was an attempt by the Convention to dechristianize France. In October 1793 the Convention proclaimed a new calendar dating from the first day of the French Republic. There were twelve months of thirty days with names associated with the seasons and climate. Every tenth day, rather than every seventh, was a holiday. Many of the most important events of the next few years became known as their dates on the revolutionary calendar.[4] In November 1793 the convention decreed the Cathedral of Notre Dame to be a Temple of Reason. The legislature then sent trusted members, known as *deputies on mission*, into the provinces to enforce dechristianization by closing churches, persecuting clergy and believers, and occasionally forcing priests to marry. Needless to say, this religious policy roused much opposition and deeply separated the French provinces from the revolutionary government in Paris.

ROBESPIERRE During the crucial months of late 1793 and early 1794 the person who emerged as the chief figure on the Committee of Public Safety was Robespierre. He was a complex person who has remained controversial to the present day. He was utterly selfless and from the earliest days of the revolution had favored a republic. The Jacobin Club provided his primary forum and base of power. A shrewd and sensitive politician, he had opposed the war in 1792 as a measure that might aid the monarchy. He largely depended on the support of the sans-culottes of Paris, but he continued to dress as he had before the revolution and opposed dechristianization as a political blunder. For him the republic of virtue meant wholehearted support of republican government and the renunciation of selfish

Maximilien Robespierre (1758–1794) emerged as the most powerful revolutionary figure in 1793–1794 and dominated the Committee of Public Safety. He considered the Terror essential for the success of the revolution. [Giraudon]

gains from political life. He once told the Convention,

> If the mainspring of popular government in peacetime is virtue, amid revolution it is at the same time virtue and terror: virtue, without which terror is fatal; terror, without which virtue is impotent. Terror is nothing but prompt, severe, inflexible justice; it is therefore an emanation of virtue.[5]

He and those who supported his policies were among the first apostles of secular ideologies who, in the name of humanity, would bring so much suffering to European polities of the left and the right in the next two centuries.

Progress of the Terror

The Reign of Terror manifested itself through a series of revolutionary tribunals established by the Convention during the summer of 1793. They were to try the enemies of the republic, but the definition of *enemy* remained uncertain and shifted as the months passed. The

---

[4] *From summer to spring the months on the revolutionary calendar were Messidor, Thermidor, Fructidor, Vendémiaire, Brumaire, Frimaire, Nivose, Pluviose, Ventose, Germinal, Floreal, and Prairial.*

---

[5] *Quoted in Richard T. Bienvenu,* The Ninth of Thermidor: The Fall of Robespierre *(New York: Oxford University Press, 1968), p. 38.*

On the way to her execution in 1793, Marie Antoin-
ette was sketched from life by David, as her tumbril
passed his window. [Giraudon]

enemies included those who might aid other European powers, those who endangered republican virtue, and finally good republicans who opposed the policies of the dominant faction of the government. In a very real sense the terror of the revolutionary tribunals systematized and channeled the popular resentment that had manifested itself in the September Massacres of 1792.

The first victims of the Terror were Marie Antoinette, other members of the royal family, and some aristocrats, who were executed in October 1793. They were followed by certain Girondist politicians who had been prominent in the Legislative Assembly.

By the early months of 1794 the Terror had moved to the provinces, where the deputies on mission presided over the summary execution of thousands of people who had allegedly supported internal opposition to the revolution. One of the most infamous incidents occurred in Nantes, where several hundred people were simply tied to rafts and drowned in the river. The victims of the Terror were now coming from every social class, including the sansculottes.

REVOLUTIONARIES TURN AGAINST THEMSELVES In Paris during the late winter Robespierre began to orchestrate the Terror against republican political figures of the left and right. On March 24 he secured the execution of certain extreme sans-culottes leaders known as the *enragés*. They had wanted further measures regulating prices, securing social equality, and pressing dechristianization. Robespierre then turned against more conservative republicans, including Danton. They were insufficiently militant on the war, had profited monetarily from the revolution, and had rejected any link between politics and moral virtue. Danton was executed during the first week in April. In this fashion Robespierre exterminated the leadership from both groups that might have threatened his position. Fi-

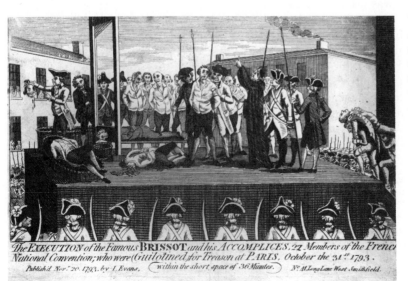

The EXECUTION of the Famous BRISSOT and his ACCOMPLICES, 27 Members of the French
National Convention; who were (Guillotined) for Treason at PARIS, October the 31st 1793.
Publish'd Nov.r 20. 1793. by J. Evans. (within the short space of 36 Minutes.) N.o 41 Long Lane West Smithfield.

The execution of the Girondists in October 1793 *left the Jacobins in full control of the revolution, and marked the victory of Paris over the provinces. [British Library]*

nally, on June 10, he secured passage of the Law of 22 Prairial, which permitted the revolutionary tribunal to convict suspects without hearing substantial evidence. The number of executions was growing steadily.

FALL OF ROBESPIERRE In May 1794, at the height of his power, Robespierre, considering the worship of Reason too abstract for most citizens, abolished it and established the Cult of the Supreme Being. This deistic cult was in line with Rousseau's idea of a civic religion that would induce morality among citizens. However, Robespierre did not long preside over his new religion.

On July 26 he made an ill-tempered speech in the Convention declaring that there existed among other leaders of the government a conspiracy against himself and the revolution. Such accusations against unnamed persons had usually preceded his earlier attacks. On July 27—the Ninth of Thermidor—by prearrangement, members of the Convention shouted him down when he rose to make another speech. That night Robespierre was arrested, and the next day he was executed. The revolutionary sans-culottes of Paris would not save him because he had deprived them of their chief leaders. The other Jacobins turned against him because after Danton's death they feared becoming the next victims. Robespierre had destroyed rivals for leadership without creating supporters for himself. In that regard, he was the selfless creator of his own destruction.

The fall of Robespierre might simply have been one more shift in the turbulent politics of the revolution. Those who brought about his demise were motivated by instincts of self-preservation rather than by major policy differences. They had generally supported the Terror and the executions. Yet within a short time the Reign of Terror, which ultimately claimed

The fall of Robespierre occurred literally overnight on July 26–27, 1794, when his enemies in the Convention had him and his supporters arrested and executed. In this print he lies on the table a prisoner, clutching a handkerchief to his wounded jaw, where he had been shot when he was arrested. A few hours later he was guillotined. The Terror died with him. [Library of Congress]

The Convention Establishes the Worship
of the Supreme Being

On May 7, 1794, the Convention passed one of the most extraordinary pieces of revolutionary legislation. It established the worship of the Supreme Being as a state cult. Although the law drew on the religious ideas of deism, the point of the legislation was to provide a religious basis for the new secular French state. The reader should pay particular attention to Article 7, which outlines the political and civic values that the Cult of the Supreme Being was supposed to nurture.

1. The French people recognize the existence of the Supreme Being and the immortality of the soul.

2. They recognize that the worship worthy of the Supreme Being is the observance of the duties of man.

3. They place in the forefront of such duties detestation of bad faith and tyranny, punishment of tyrants and traitors, succoring of unfortunates, respect of weak persons, defence of the oppressed, doing to others all the good that one can, and being just towards everyone.

4. Festivals shall be instituted to remind man of the concept of the Divinity and of the dignity of his being.

5. They shall take their names from the glorious events of our Revolution, or from the virtues most dear and most useful to man, or from the greatest benefits of nature.

. . . .

7. On the days of *décade* [the name given to a particular day in each month of the revolutionary calendar] it shall celebrate the following festivals:

To the Supreme Being and to nature; to the human race; to the French people; to the benefactors of humanity; to the martyrs of liberty; to liberty and equality; to the Republic; to the liberty of the world; to the love of the *Patrie* [Fatherland]; to the hatred of tyrants and traitors; to truth; to justice; to modesty; to glory and immortality; to friendship; to frugality; to courage; to good faith; to heroism; to disinterestedness; to stoicism; to love; to conjugal love; to paternal love; to maternal tenderness; to filial piety; to infancy; to youth; to manhood; to old age; to misfortune; to agriculture; to industry; to our forefathers; to posterity; to happiness.

John Hall Stewart, A Documentary Survey of the French Revolution *(New York: Macmillan*, 1951), pp. 526–527.

over twenty-five thousand victims, did come to a close. The largest number of executions had involved peasants and sans-culottes who had joined rebellions against the revolutionary government. By the late summer of 1794 those provincial uprisings had been crushed, and the war against foreign enemies was also going well. Those factors, combined with the feeling in Paris that the revolution had consumed enough of its own children, brought the Terror to an end.

The Thermidorian Reaction

The tempering of the revolution called the *Thermidorian Reaction* began in July 1794. It consisted of the destruction of the machinery of terror and the institution of a new constitutional regime. It was the result of a widespread feeling that the revolution had become too radical. In particular it displayed a weariness of

The Festival of the Supreme Being that took place in June 1794 inaugurated Robespierre's new civic religion. Its climax occurred when a statue of Atheism was burned and another statue of Wisdom rose from the ashes. [Giraudon]

the terror and a fear that the sans-culottes were exerting far too much political influence.

The End of the Terror

The influence of generally wealthy middle-class and professional people soon replaced that of the sans-culottes. Within days and weeks of Robespierre's execution the Convention allowed the Girondists who had been in prison or hiding to return to their seats. There was a general amnesty for political prisoners. The Convention restructured the Committee of Public Safety and gave it much less power. The Convention also repealed the notorious Law of 22 Prairial. Some, though by no means all, of the people responsible for the Terror were removed from public life. Leaders of the Paris Commune and certain deputies on mission were executed. The Paris Commune itself was outlawed. The Paris Jacobin Club was closed, and Jacobin clubs in the provinces were forbidden to correspond with each other.

The executions of former terrorists marked the beginning of "the white terror." Throughout the country people who had been involved in the Reign of Terror were attacked and often murdered. Jacobins were executed with little more due process than they had extended to their victims a few months earlier. The Convention itself approved some of these trials. In other cases gangs of youths who had aristocratic connections or who had avoided serving in the army roamed the streets beating known Jacobins. In Lyons, Toulon, and Marseilles these "bands of Jesus" dragged suspected terrorists from prisons and murdered them much as alleged royalists had been murdered during the September Massacres of 1792.

The republic of virtue gave way, if not to one of vice, at least to one of frivolous pleasures. The dress of the sans-culottes and the Roman Republic disappeared among the middle class and the aristocracy. New plays appeared in the theaters, and prostitutes again roamed the streets of Paris. Families of victims of the Reign of Terror gave parties in which they appeared with shaved necks like the victims of the guillotine and red ribbons tied about them. Although the Convention continued to favor the Cult of the Supreme Being, it allowed Catholic services to be held. Many refractory priests returned to the country. One of the unanticipated results of the Thermidorian Reaction was a genuine revival of Catholic worship.

Establishment of the Directory

The Thermidorian Reaction also involved still further political reconstruction. The fully democratic constitution of 1793, which had never gone into effect, was abandoned. The Convention issued in its place the Constitution of the Year III, which reflected the Thermidorian determination to reject both consti-

The closing of the Jacobin Club in November 1794 was a major event in the Thermidorean Reaction *that began with the fall of Robespierre. [The Granger Collection]*

tutional monarchy and democracy. The new document provided for a legislature of two houses. Members of the upper body, or Council of Elders, were to be men over forty years of age who were either husbands or widowers. The lower Council of Five Hundred was to consist of married or single men at least thirty years old. The executive body was to be a five-person Directory chosen by the Elders from a list submitted by the Council of Five Hundred. Property qualifications limited the franchise except for soldiers, who even without property were permitted to vote.

Thermidor became a term associated with political reaction. However, if the French Revolution had originated in political conflicts characteristic of the eighteenth century, it had by 1795 become something very different. A society and a political structure based on rank and birth had given way to one based on civic

equality and social status stemming from the ownership or nonownership of property. People who had never been allowed direct, formal access to political power had, to different degrees, been admitted to those activities. Their entrance had given rise to questions of property distribution and economic regulations that could not again be totally ignored. Representation had been established as a principle of practical politics. Henceforth the question before France and eventually before all of Europe would be which new groups would be admitted to representation. In the *levée en masse* the French had demonstrated to Europe the power of the secular ideal of nationhood.

All of these stunning changes in the political and social contours of Europe are not to be forgotten in a consideration of the post-Thermidorian course of the French Revolution. What triumphed in the Constitution of the

Year III was the revolution of the holders of property. For this reason the French Revolution has often been considered a victory of the bourgeoisie, or middle class. However, the property that won the day was not industrial wealth but the wealth stemming from commerce and the professions. Moreover the largest new propertied class to emerge from the revolutionary turmoil was the peasantry, who as a result of the destruction of aristocratic privileges, had achieved personal ownership of the land. Unlike peasants liberated from traditional landholding in other parts of Europe during the next century, French peasants had to pay no monetary compensation.

Removal of the Sans-culottes from Political Life

The most decisively reactionary element in the Thermidorian Reaction and the new constitution was the removal of the sans-culottes from political life. With the war effort succeeding, the Convention severed its ties with the sans-culottes. True to their belief in an unregulated economy, the Thermidorians repealed the ceiling on prices. As a result, the winter of 1794–1795 brought the worst food shortages of the period. There were numerous food riots, which the Convention put down with force to prove that the era of the sans-culottes *journées*

The French Convention Calls Up the Entire Nation

This proclamation of the levée en masse, *August 23, 1793, marked the first time in European history that all citizens of a nation were called to contribute to a war effort. The decree set the entire nation on a wartime footing under the centralized direction of the Committee of Public Safety.*

1. From this moment until that in which the enemy shall have been driven from the soil of the Republic, all Frenchmen are in permanent requisition for the service of the armies.

The young men shall go to battle; the married men shall forge arms and transport provisions; the women shall make tents and clothing and shall serve in the hospitals; the children shall turn old linen into lint; the aged shall betake themselves to the public places in order to arouse the courage of the warriors and preach the hatred of kings and the unity of the Republic.

2. The national buildings shall be converted into barracks, the public places into workshops for arms, the soil of the cellars shall be washed in order to extract therefrom the saltpetre.

3. The arms of the regulation calibre shall be reserved exclusively for those who shall march against the enemy; the service of the interior shall be performed with hunting pieces and side arms.

4. The saddle horses are put in requisition to complete the cavalry corps; the draught-horses, other than those employed in agriculture, shall convey the artillery and the provisions.

5. The Committee of Public Safety is charged to take all the necessary measures to set up without delay an extraordinary manufacture of arms of every sort which corresponds with the ardor and energy of the French people. . . .

. . . .

8. The levy shall be general. . . .

Frank Maloy Anderson (Ed. and Trans.), The Constitutions and Other Select Documents Illustrative of the History of France, 1789–1907, *2nd ed., rev. and enlarged (Minneapolis: H. W. Wilson, 1908), pp. 184–185.*

had come to a close. Royalist agents, who aimed to restore the monarchy, tried to take advantage of their discontent. On October 5, 1795—13 Vendémiaire—the sections of Paris led by the royalists rose up against the Convention. The government turned the artillery against the royalist rebels. A general named Napoleon Bonaparte (1769–1821) commanded the cannon, and with a "whiff of grapeshot" he dispersed the crowd.

By the Treaty of Basel in March 1795, the Convention concluded peace with Prussia and Spain. However, the legislators feared a resurgence of both radical democrats and royalists in the upcoming elections for the Council of Five Hundred. Consequently the Convention ruled that at least two thirds of the new legislature must have been members of the older body. The Thermidorians did not even trust the property owners as voters.

The next year the newly established Directory again faced social unrest. In Paris Gracchus Babeuf (1760–1797) led the Conspiracy of Equals. He and his followers called for more

The Society of Equals Calls for Social Revolution

Gracchus Babeuf led a small group of Parisians known as the Society of Equals. It was not an especially important political organization, but it combined many of the standard political doctrines of the revolution with a demand for further social revolution. These demands seemed very dangerous to the propertied classes who supported the Directory. In 1796 the Babeuvists combined these demands with a rejection of the Constitution of 1795 which had established the Directory and attempted a small uprising that was quickly crushed. Their doctrines outlined in this document of May 1796 look forward to the socialist ideas of the nineteenth century.

1. Nature has bestowed upon each and every individual an equal right to the enjoyment of property.

2. The purpose of society is to defend such equality, often assailed by the strong and the wicked in the state of nature, and to augment the general welfare through the cooperation of all.

3. Nature has imposed upon each and every individual the obligation to work; anyone who evades his share of labor is a criminal.

4. Both work and benefits must be common to all.

5. There is oppression when one person is exhausted by labor and is destitute of everything, while another lives in luxury without doing any work at all.

6. Anyone who appropriates exclusively to himself the products of the earth or of manufacture is a criminal.

7. In a real society there ought to be neither rich nor poor.

8. The rich who are not willing to renounce their surplus in favor of the poor are enemies of the people.

9. No one, by accumulating to himself all power, may deprive another of the instruction necessary for his welfare. Education ought to be common to all.

10. The aim of the French Revolution is to destroy inequality and to re-establish the general welfare.

11. The Revolution is not complete, because the rich monopolize all the property and govern exclusively, while the poor toil like slaves, languish in misery, and count for nothing in the state.

John Hall Stewart, A Documentary Survey of the French Revolution *(New York: The Macmillan Company, 1966), pp. 656–657.*

THE FRENCH REVOLUTION

1789

May 5	The Estates General opens at Versailles
June 17	The Third Estate declares itself the National Assembly
June 20	The National Assembly takes the Tennis Court Oath
July 14	Fall of the Bastille in the city of Paris
Late July	The Great Fear spreads in the countryside
August 4	The nobles surrender their feudal rights in a meeting of the National Constituent Assembly
August 27	Declaration of the Rights of Man and Citizen
October 5–6	Parisian women march to Versailles and force Louis XVI and his family to return to Paris

1790

July 12	Civil Constitution of the Clergy adopted
July 14	A new constitution is accepted by the king

1791

June 20–24	Louis XVI and his family attempt to flee France and are stopped at Varennes
August 27	The Declaration of Pillnitz
October 1	The Legislative Assembly meets

1792

April 20	France declares war on Austria
August 10	The Tuileries palace is stormed, and Louis XVI takes refuge with the Legislative Assembly
September 2–7	The September Massacres
September 20	France wins the battle of Valmy
September 21	The Convention meets, and the monarchy is abolished

1793

January 21	Louis XVI is executed
February 1	France declares war on Great Britain
March	Counterrevolution breaks out in the Vendée
April	The Committee of Public Safety is formed
June 22	The Constitution of 1793 is adopted but not put into operation
July	Robespierre enters the Committee of Public Safety
August 23	*Levée en masse* proclaimed
September 17	Maximum prices set on food and other commodities
October 16	Queen Marie Antoinette is executed
November 10	The Cult of Reason is proclaimed; the revolutionary calendar beginning on September 22, 1792, is adopted

1794

March 24	Execution of the Hébertist leaders of the *sans-culottes*
April 6	Execution of Danton
May 7	Cult of the Supreme Being proclaimed
June 8	Robespierre leads the celebration of the Festival of the Supreme Being
June 10	The Law of 22 Prairial is adopted
July 27	The Ninth of Thermidor and the fall of Robespierre
July 28	Robespierre is executed

1795

August 22	The Constitution of the Year III is adopted, establishing the Directory

radical democracy and for more equality of property. Babeuf was arrested, tried, and executed. This quite minor plot became famous many decades later when European socialists attempted to find their historical roots in the French Revolution.

The suppression of the sans-culottes, the narrow franchise of the constitution, the rule of the two thirds, and the Catholic royalist revival presented the Directory with problems that it never succeeded in overcoming. It lacked any broad base of meaningful political support. It particularly required active loyalty because France remained at war with Austria and Great Britain. Consequently, the Directory came to depend on the power of the army rather than on constitutional processes for governing the country. All of the soldiers could vote. Moreover, within the army, created and sustained by the revolution, stood officers who were eager for power and ambitious for political conquest. The results of the instability of the Directory and the growing role of the army held profound consequences not only for France but for the entire Western world.

The French Revolution is the central political event of modern European history. It unleashed political and social forces that determined the next two centuries of change in Europe and in much of the rest of the world as well. The revolution commenced with a clash between the monarchy and the nobility. However, once the Estates General gathered, the political discontent could not be contained within the traditional boundaries of eighteenth-century political life. The Third Estate in all of its vast diversity demanded a voice and real influence. Initially that meant the entrance upon the scene of middle-class members of the Estates General but quite soon the people of Paris and the peasants of the countryside made their demands known. Thereafter, the years of the revolution saw the general force of popular nationalism exerted on French political life and the political destiny of Europe.

The revolutionary legislation and the popular uprisings in Paris, across the countryside, and in other cities transformed the social as well as the political life of the nation. Nobles surrendered traditional social privileges. The Church saw its property confiscated and its general functioning brought under state control. For a time there was an attempt to dechristianize the nation. Vast amounts of landed property changed hands, and France became a nation of peasant landowners. Urban workers lost much of the protection they had enjoyed under the guilds and became much more subject to the forces of the marketplace.

Enormous violence accompanied many of the revolutionary changes. The reign of terror took the lives of thousands. France also found itself at war with virtually all of the rest of Europe. Resentment and fear brought the terror to an end as a desire for new stability came to the fore. That desire along with a determination to achieve victory against the foreign enemies of the revolution and to carry the revolution abroad would in turn work to the advantage of the army. Eventually Napoleon Bonaparte would claim leadership in the name of stability and national glory.

Suggested Readings

K. M. BAKER AND C. LUCAS (eds.), *The French Revolution and the Creation of Modern Political Culture*, 3 vols. (1987). A splendid collection of important original articles on all aspects of politics during the revolution.

R. COBB, *The Police and the People: French Popular Protest, 1789–1820* (1970). An interesting and imaginative treatment of the question of social control during the revolution.

R. COBB, *The People's Armies* (1987). The best treatment in English of the revolutionary army.

A. COBBAN, *Aspects of the French Revolution* (1970). Essays on numerous subjects.

W. DOYLE, *Origins of the French Revolution* (1980). An outstanding summary of historiographical interpretations.

J. EGRET, *The French Pre-Revolution, 1787–88* (1978). A useful survey of the coming crisis for the monarchy.

K. EPSTEIN, *The Genesis of German Conservatism* (1966). A major study of antiliberal forces in Germany before and during the revolution.

A. FORREST, *The French Revolution and the Poor* (1981). A study that expands consideration of the revolution beyond the standard social boundaries.

M. FREEMAN, *Edmund Burke and the Critique of Political Radicalism* (1980). A study of Burke's thought in the general context of modern political theory.

F. FURET, *Interpreting the French Revolution* (1981). A collection of controversial revisionist essays that cast doubt on the role of class conflict in the revolution.

J. GODECHOT, *The Taking of the Bastille, July 14, 1789* (1970). The best modern discussion of the subject and one that places the fall of the Bastille in the context of crowd behavior in the eighteenth century.

J. Godechot, *The Counter-Revolution: Doctrine and Action, 1789–1803* (1971). An examination of opposition to the revolution.

A. Goodwin, *The Friends of Liberty: The English Democratic Movement in the Age of the French Revolution* (1979). A major new work that explores the impact of the French Revolution on English radicalism.

L. Hunt, *Politics, Culture, and Class in the French Revolution* (1986). A series of essays that focus on the modes of expression of the revolutionary values and political ideals.

D. Johnson (Ed.), *French Society and the Revolution* (1976). A useful collection of important essays on the social history of the revolution.

E. Kennedy, *A Cultural History of the French Revolution* (1989). An important examination of the role of the arts, schools, clubs, and intellectual institutions.

M. Kennedy, *The Jacobin Clubs in the French Revolution: The First Years* (1982). A careful scrutiny of the organizations chiefly responsible for the radicalizing of the revolution.

M. Kennedy, *The Jacobin Clubs in the French Revolution: The Middle Years* (1988). A continuation of the previously listed study.

G. Lefebvre, *The French Revolution*, 2 vols. (1962–1964). A major study by one of the most important modern writers on the subject.

G. Lewis and C. Lucas (eds.), *Beyond the Terror: Essays in French Regional and Social History, 1794–1815* (1983). An important collection of essays on French developments after the Terror.

M. Lyons, *France Under the Directory* (1975). A brief survey of the post-Thermidorian governmental experiment.

M. Ozouf, *Festivals and the French Revolution* (1988). A pioneering study of the role of the public festivals in the revolution.

R. R. Palmer, *The Age of Democratic Revolution: A Political History of Europe and America, 1760–1800*, 2 vols. (1941). A clear narrative and analysis of the policies and problems of the committee.

R. R. Palmer, *Twelve Who Ruled: The Committee of Public Safety During the Terror* (1959, 1964). An impressive survey of the political turmoil in the transatlantic world.

S. Schama, *Patriots and Liberators: Revolution in the Netherlands, 1780–1813* (1977). One of the best and most thorough studies of the revolutionary era outside France.

A. Soboul, *The Parisian Sans-Culottes and the French Revolution, 1793–94* (1964). The best work on the subject.

A. Soboul, *The French Revolution* (trans., 1975). An important work by a Marxist scholar.

B. S. Stone, *The Parlement of Paris, 1774–1789* (1981). An examination of a key aristocratic institution responsible for precipitating the revolutionary crisis.

B. S. Stone, *The French Parlements and the Crisis of the Old Regime* (1988). A study that considers the role of the aristocratic courts in bringing on the collapse of monarchical government.

D. G. Sutherland, *France, 1789–1815: Revolution and Counterrevolution* (1986). A major synthesis based on recent scholarship in social history.

T. Tackett, *Religion, Revolution, and Regional Culture in Eighteenth-Century France: The Ecclesiastical Oath of 1791.* (1986). The most important study of this topic.

J. M. Thompson, *Robespierre*, 2 vols. (1935). The best biography.

C. Tilly, *The Vendée* (1964). A significant sociological investigation.

M. Walzer (ed.), *Regicide and Revolution: Speeches at the Trial of Louis XVI* (1974). An important and exceedingly interesting collection of documents with a useful introduction.

Napoleon in his study. This portrait was painted by Jacques-Louis David (1748–1825) in 1812 at the height of Napoleon's power, when he was about to invade Russia. [National Gallery of Art, Samuel H. Kress Collection]

20

THE AGE OF
NAPOLEON AND
THE TRIUMPH
OF ROMANTICISM

By the late 1790s there existed a general wish for stability in France especially among property owners who now included the peasants. The government of the Directory did not seem capable of providing a long-term stable government. The one force that did seem able to take charge of the nation as a symbol of both order and popular national will was the army. The most politically astute of the army generals was Napoleon Bonaparte. He had been a radical during the early revolution, a victorious general in Italy, and a supporter of the at-

tempt to bring revolutionary disturbances to an end after Thermidor. Furthermore, as a general, he was a leader in the French army, the institution seen most clearly to embody the popular values of the nation and the revolution.

Once in power Napoleon consolidated many of the revolutionary achievements. He also repudiated much of the revolution by establishing an empire. Thereafter, his ambitions led him to draw France into wars of conquest and liberation throughout the continent. For over a decade Europe experienced warfare with brief periods of armed truce. In leading the French armies across the continent Napoleon spread many of the ideas and institutions of the revolution and overturned much of the old political and social order. He also provoked popular nationalism in opposition to his conquest. This new force and the great diplomatic alliances eventually defeated him.

Throughout these Napoleonic years new ideas and sensibilities grew throughout Europe. These are known by the term Romanticism. Many of the ideas had originated in the eighteenth century, but the turmoil of the French Revolution and the Napoleonic Wars allowed them to flourish. The events and values of the revolution spurred the imagination of poets, painters, and philosophers. Some romantic ideas, such as romantic nationalism, supported the revolution; others, such as the emphasis on the value of history and religion, opposed the values of the revolution.

The Rise of Napoleon Bonaparte

The chief danger to the Directory came from the royalists, who hoped to restore the Bourbon monarchy by legal means. Many of the émigrés had drifted back into France. Their plans for a restoration drew support from devout Catholics and from those citizens whom the excesses of the revolution had disgusted. Monarchy seemed to hold the promise of stability. The spring elections of 1797 turned out most of the incumbents and replaced them with a majority of constitutional monarchists and their sympathizers.

To prevent an end to the republic and a peaceful restoration of monarchy, the anti-monarchist Directory staged a coup d'état on 18 Fructidor (September 4, 1797). They put their own supporters into the legislative seats won by their opponents. They then imposed censorship and exiled some of their enemies. Napoleon Bonaparte, the general in charge of the Italian campaign, had made these political actions possible. At the request of the Directors, he had sent one of his subordinates to Paris to guarantee the success of the coup. In 1797, as in 1795, the army and Bonaparte had saved the day for the government installed in the wake of the Thermidorian Reaction.

Napoleon Bonaparte was born in 1769 to a poor family of lesser nobles at Ajaccio, Corsica. Because France had annexed Corsica in the previous year, he went to French schools, pursued a military career, and in 1785 obtained a commission as a French artillery officer. He strongly favored the revolution and was a fiery Jacobin. In 1793 he played a leading role in recovering the port of Toulon from the British. In reward for his service the government appointed him a brigadier general. His radical associations threatened his career during the Thermidorian Reaction, but his defense of the new regime on 13 Vendémiaire restored him to favor and won him another promotion and a command in Italy.

Early Military Victories

By 1795 French arms and diplomacy had shattered the enemy coalition, but France's annexation of Belgium guaranteed continued fighting with Britain and Austria. The attack on Italy was aimed at depriving Austria of the provinces of Lombardy and Venetia. In a series of lightning victories Bonaparte crushed the Austrian and Sardinian armies. On his own initiative, and in many ways contrary to the wishes of the government in Paris, he concluded the Treaty of Campo Formio in October 1797. The treaty took Austria out of the war and crowned Napoleon's campaign and independent policy with success. Before long all of Italy and Switzerland had fallen under French domination.

In November 1797 the triumphant Bonaparte returned to Paris to be hailed as a hero and to confront France's only remaining enemy, Britain. He judged it impossible to cross the channel and invade England at that time. Instead, he chose to capture Egypt from

695

THE AGE O
NAPOLEON
AND THE
TRIUMPH O
ROMANTICIS

the Ottoman Empire. By this strategy he hoped to drive the British fleet from the Mediterranean, cut off British communications with India, damage British trade, and threaten the British Empire.

The invasion of Egypt was a failure. Admiral Horatio Nelson (1758–1805) destroyed the French fleet at Abukir on August 1, 1798. The French army could then neither accomplish anything of importance in the Near East nor get home. To make matters worse, the situation in Europe was deteriorating. The French invasion of Egypt had alarmed Russia, which had its own ambitions in the Near East. The Russians, the Austrians, and the Ottomans soon joined Britain to form the Second Coalition. In 1799 the Russian and Austrian armies defeated the French in Italy and Switzerland and threatened to invade France.

The Constitution of the Year VIII

Economic troubles and the dangerous international situation eroded the already fragile support of the Directory. One of the Directors, the Abbé Sieyès, proposed a new constitution. The author of the pamphlet *What Is the Third Estate?* (1789) wanted to establish a vigorous executive body independent of the whims of electoral politics, a government based on the principle of "confidence from below, power from above." The change would require another *coup d'état* with military support. News of France's diplomatic misfortunes had reached Napoleon in Egypt. Without orders and leaving his doomed army behind, he returned to France in October 1799. He received much popular acclaim, although some people thought that he deserved a court-martial for desertion. He soon joined Sieyès. On 19 Brumaire (November 10, 1799) his troops drove out the legislators and permitted the success of the *coup*.

Sieyès appears to have thought Napoleon could be used and then dismissed, but if so, he badly misjudged his man. The proposed constitution divided executive authority among three consuls. Bonaparte quickly pushed it aside, as he did Sieyès, and in December 1799 he issued the Constitution of the Year VIII. Behind a screen of universal manhood suffrage that suggested democratic principles, a complicated system of checks and balances that appealed to republican theory, and a Council of

Admiral Viscount Horatio Nelson (1758–1805) was the greatest naval commander of his age. Between 1798 and his death at the battle of Trafalgar in 1805, he won a series of brilliant victories that gave Britain mastery of the seas. [National Portrait Gallery, London]

State that evoked memories of Louis XIV, the constitution in fact established the rule of one man—the First Consul, Bonaparte. To find a reasonably close historical analogy, one must go back to Caesar and Augustus and the earlier Greek tyrants. The career of Bonaparte, however, pointed forward to the dictators of the twentieth century. He was the first modern political figure to use the rhetoric of revolution and nationalism, to back it with military force, and to combine those elements into a mighty weapon of imperial expansion in the service of his own power and ambition.

The Consulate in France (1799–1804)

The establishment of the Consulate, in effect, closed the revolution in France. The leading elements of the Third Estate—that is, officials, landowners, doctors, lawyers, and financiers—

had achieved most of their goals by 1799. They had abolished hereditary privilege, and the careers thus opened to talent allowed them to achieve the wealth and status they sought. The peasants were also satisfied. They had acquired the land they had always wanted and had destroyed oppressive feudal privileges as well. The newly established dominant classes were profoundly conservative. They had little or no desire to share their recently won privileges with the lower social orders. Bonaparte seemed just the person to give them security. When he submitted his constitution to the voters in a plebiscite, they approved it by 3,011,077 votes to 1,567.

Suppressing Foreign Enemies and Domestic Opposition

Bonaparte quickly justified the public's confidence by setting about achieving peace with France's enemies. Russia had already quarreled with its allies and left the Second Coalition. A campaign in Italy brought another victory over Austria at Marengo in 1800. The Treaty of Lunéville early in 1801 took Austria out of the war and confirmed the earlier settlement of Campo Formio. Britain was now alone and, in 1802, concluded the Treaty of Amiens, which brought peace to Europe.

Bonaparte was equally effective in restoring peace and order at home. He employed generosity, flattery, and bribery to win over some of his enemies. He issued a general amnesty and employed in his own service persons from all political factions. He required only that they be loyal to him. Some of the highest offices were occupied by persons who had been extreme radicals during the Reign of Terror, others by persons who had fled the Terror and favored constitutional monarchy, and still others by former high officials of the old regime.

On the other hand, Bonaparte was ruthless and efficient in suppressing opposition. He established a highly centralized administration in which all departments were managed by prefects directly responsible to the central government in Paris. He employed secret police. He stamped out once and for all the royalist rebellion in the west and made the rule of Paris effective in Brittany and the Vendée for the first time in many years.

Nor was Napoleon above using or even inventing opportunities to destroy his enemies. When a plot on his life surfaced in 1804, he used the event as an excuse to attack the Jacobins, even though the bombing was the work of the royalists. In 1804 his forces invaded the sovereignty of Baden to seize the Bourbon duke of Enghien. The duke was accused of participation in a royalist plot and put to death, even though Bonaparte knew him to be innocent. The action was a flagrant violation of international law and of due process. Charles Maurice de Talleyrand-Périgord (1754–1838), Bonaparte's foreign minister, later termed the act "worse than a crime—a blunder," because it helped to provoke foreign opposition. On the other hand, it was popular with the former Jacobins, for it seemed to preclude the possibility of a Bourbon restoration. The person who killed a Bourbon was hardly likely to restore the royal family. The execution seems to have put an end to royalist plots.

Prince Charles Maurice de Talleyrand was one of the most talented and adaptable diplomats of the age. Born into the highest French aristocracy, he had been a bishop before the Revolution. Later he became foreign minister, first for the Directory, then for Napoleon, and finally for Louis XVIII, whom he represented in 1814–1815 at the Congress of Vienna. [New York Public Library]

Concordat with the Roman Catholic Church

A major obstacle to internal peace was the steady hostility of French Catholics. Refractory clergy continued to advocate counterrevolution. The religious revival that dated from the Thermidorian Reaction increased discontent with the secular state created by the revolution. Bonaparte regarded religion as a political matter. He approved its role in preserving an orderly society but was suspicious of any such power independent of the state.

In 1801 Napoleon concluded a concordat with Pope Pius VII, to the shock and dismay of his anticlerical supporters. The settlement gave Napoleon what he most wanted. Both the refractory clergy and those who had accepted the revolution were forced to resign. Their replacements received their spiritual investiture from the pope, but the state named the bishops and paid their salaries and the salary of one

697

THE AGE OF
NAPOLEON
AND THE
TRIUMPH OF
ROMANTICISM

Napoleon Makes Peace with the Papacy

In 1801 Napoleon concluded a concordat with Pope Pius VII. This document was the cornerstone of Napoleonic religious policy. The concordat, which as announced on April 8, 1802, allowed the Roman Catholic Church to function freely in France only within the limits of Church support for the government as indicated in the oath included in Article 6.

The Government of the French Republic recognizes that the Roman, catholic and apostolic religion is the religion of the great majority of French citizens.

His Holiness likewise recognizes that this same religion has derived and in this moment again expects the greatest benefit and grandeur from the establishment of the catholic worship in France and from the personal profession of it which the consuls of the Republic make.

In consequence, after this mutual recognition, as well for the benefit of religion as for the maintenance of internal tranquility, they have agreed as follows:

1. The catholic, apostolic and Roman religion shall be freely exercised in France: its worship shall be public, and in conformity with the police regulations which the government shall deem necessary for the public tranquility.

. . . .

4. The First Consul of the Republic shall make appointments, within the three months which shall follow the publication of the bull of His Holiness, to the archbishoprics and bishoprics of the new circumscription. His Holiness shall confer the canonical institution, following the forms established in relation to France before the change of government.

. . . .

6. Before entering upon their functions, the bishops shall take directly, at the hands of the First Consul, the oath of fidelity which was in use before the change of government, expressed in the following terms:

"I swear and promise to God, upon the holy scriptures, to remain in obedience and fidelity to the government established by the constitution of the French Republic. I also promise not to have any intercourse, nor to assist by any counsel, nor to support any league, either within or without, which is inimical to the public tranquility; and if, within my diocese or elsewhere, I learn that anything to the prejudice of the state is being contrived, I will make it known to the government."

F. M. Anderson, The Constitution and Other Select Documents Illustrative of the History of France 1789–1907, *2nd ed. (Minneapolis: H. W. Wilson, 1908), pp. 296–297.*

priest in each parish. In return, the Church gave up its claims on its confiscated property.

The concordat declared that "Catholicism is the religion of the great majority of French citizens." This was merely a statement of fact and fell far short of what the pope had wanted: religious dominance for the Roman Catholic church. The clergy had to swear an oath of loyalty to the state. The Organic Articles of 1802, which were actually distinct from the concordat, established the supremacy of State over Church. Similar laws were applied to the Protestant and Jewish religious communities as well, reducing still further the privileged position of the Catholic church.

The Napoleonic Code

Peace and efficient administration brought prosperity and security to the French and gratitude and popularity to Bonaparte. In 1802 a plebiscite appointed him consul for life, and he soon produced still another new constitution, which granted him what amounted to full power. The years of the Consulate were employed in reforming and establishing the basic laws and institutions of France. The settlement imposed by Napoleon was an ambiguous combination of liberal principles derived from the Enlightenment and the early years of the revolution and conservative principles and practices going back to the old regime or adapted to the conservative spirit that had triumphed at Thermidor.

All privileges based on birth were abolished and equality before the law was established. All authority except that of the national state and all legal distinctions based on class or locality disappeared. Purchased offices were replaced by salaried officials chosen for merit. These changes represented the application of rationality and the achievement of goals sought by the people who had made the revolution. Most of these were embodied in the general codification of laws carried out under Bonaparte's direction. This was especially true of the Civil Code of 1804, usually called the Napoleonic Code. However, these laws stopped far short of the full equality advocated by liberal rationalists. Fathers were granted extensive control over their children and men over their wives. Labor unions were still forbidden, and the rights of workers were inferior to those of their employers.

In the political arena and in administration

Napoleonic institutions ran contrary to the tendencies of the revolution. They aimed at a kind of enlightened absolutism that was similar to but more effective than what had existed in the old regime. Representative government, local autonomy, and personal freedom were rejected in favor of the centralization of all power and the subordination of personal rights and political freedom to the needs of the state as interpreted by the First Consul. All of this was acceptable to the dominant bourgeoisie and the peasantry. They accepted censorship, the arbitrary and sometimes brutal suppression of dissent, and even the restoration of a new quasi nobility in the Legion of Honor as long as order, prosperity, and security of property were preserved.

Establishing a Dynasty

In 1804 Bonaparte seized on the bomb attack on his life to make himself emperor. He argued that the establishment of a dynasty would make the new regime secure and make further attempts on his life useless. Another new constitution was promulgated in which Napoleon Bonaparte was called Emperor of the French, instead of First Consul of the Republic. This constitution was also overwhelmingly ratified in a plebiscite.

To conclude the drama, Napoleon invited the pope to Notre Dame to take part in the coronation. But at the last minute the pope agreed that Napoleon should place the crown on the emperor's own head. The emperor had no intention of allowing anyone to think that his power and authority depended on the approval of the Church. Henceforth, he was called Napoleon I. This act was the natural goal of his career. His aims had always been profoundly selfish: power and glory for himself and his family. Had Napoleon wished it, Europe might well have had peace; but his ambition would not permit it.

Napoleon's Empire
(1804–1814)

In the decade between his coronation as emperor and his final defeat at Waterloo (1815), Napoleon conquered most of Europe in a series of military campaigns that astonished the world. France's victories changed the map of

The coronation of Napoleon, December 2, 1804 was painted by David. Having first crowned himself, the emperor is shown about to place the crown on the head of Josephine. Napoleon instructed David to paint Pope Pius VII with his hand raised in blessing. [Giraudon]

Europe. The wars put an end to the old regime and its feudal trappings in western Europe and forced the eastern European states to reorganize themselves to resist Napoleon's armies.

Everywhere Napoleon's advance unleashed the powerful force of nationalism. His weapon was the militarily mobilized French nation, one of the achievements of the revolution. Napoleon could put as many as 700,000 men under arms at one time, risk as many as 100,000 troops in a single battle, endure heavy losses, and come back to fight again. He could conscript citizen soldiers in unprecedented numbers, thanks to their loyalty to the nation and to their remarkable leader. No single enemy could match such resources. Even coalitions were unsuccessful until Napoleon at last overreached himself and made mistakes that led to his own defeat.

Conquering an Empire

The Peace of Amiens (1802) between France and Great Britain was doomed to be merely a truce. Napoleon's unlimited ambitions shattered any hope that it might last. He sent an army to restore the rebellious island of Haiti to French rule. This move aroused British fears that he was planning the renewal of a French empire in America, because Spain had restored Louisiana to France in 1800. More serious were his interventions in the Dutch Republic, Italy, and Switzerland and his role in the reorganization of Germany. The Treaty of Campo Formio had required a redistribution of territories along the Rhine River, and the petty princes of the region engaged in a shameful scramble to enlarge their holdings. Among the results were the reduction of Austrian influence in Germany and the emergence of a smaller number of larger German states in the west, all dependent on Napoleon.

BRITISH NAVAL SUPREMACY The British found all of these developments alarming enough to justify an ultimatum. When Napoleon ignored it, Britain declared war in May 1803. William Pitt the Younger returned to of-

William Pitt, the Younger (1759–1806), as prime minister, opposed any policy that recognized French domination of Europe. [New York Public Library Picture Collection]

fice as prime minister in 1804 and began to construct the Third Coalition. By August 1805 he had persuaded Russia and Austria to move once more against French aggression. A great naval victory soon raised the fortunes of the allies. On October 21, 1805, the British admiral Horatio, Lord Nelson destroyed the combined French and Spanish fleets at the Battle of Trafalgar just off the Spanish coast. Nelson died in the battle, but the British lost no ships. The victory of Trafalgar put an end to all French hope of an invasion of Britain and guaranteed British control of the sea for the rest of the war.

NAPOLEONIC VICTORIES IN CENTRAL EUROPE On land the story was very different. Even before Trafalgar Napoleon had marched to the Danube River to attack his continental enemies. In mid-October he forced a large Austrian army to surrender at Ulm and soon occupied Vienna. On December 2, 1805, in perhaps his greatest victory, Napoleon defeated the combined Austrian and Russian forces at Austerlitz. The Treaty of Pressburg, which followed, won major concessions from

Napoleon commands the field of Austerlitz. Austerlitz is considered Napoleon's most brilliant victory: 73,000 French crushed an Austro-Russian army of 86,000 under the command of the Tsar and the Emperor of Austria. [Library of Congress]

Austria. The Austrians withdrew from Italy and left Napoleon in control of everything north of Rome. He was recognized as king of Italy.

Extensive changes also came about in Ger-many. In July 1806 Napoleon organized the Confederation of the Rhine, which included most of the western German princes. The withdrawal of these princes from the Holy Roman Empire led Francis II of Austria to dis-

Napoleon Advises His Brother to Rule Constitutionally

As Napoleon conquered Europe, he set his relatives on the throne in various of the conquered kingdoms and then imposed written constitutions. In this letter of November 1807 Napoleon sent his brother Jerome a constitution for the Kingdom of Westphalia in Germany. The letter provides a good description of the manner in which Napoleon spread the political ideas and institutions of the French Revolution across Europe. However, Napoleon ignored the possibility of nationalistic resentment that French conquest aroused even when that conquest brought more liberal political institutions. Such nationalism would be one of the causes of his downfall.

I enclose the constitution for your Kingdom. You must faithfully observe it. I am concerned for the happiness of your subjects, not only as it affects your reputation, and my own, but also for its influence on the whole European situation.

Don't listen to those who say that your subjects are so accustomed to slavery that they will feel no gratitude for the benefits you give them. There is more intelligence in the Kingdom of Westphalia than they would have you believe; and your throne will never be firmly established except upon the trust and affection of the common people. What German opinion impatiently demands is that men of no rank, but of marked ability, shall have an equal claim upon your favour and your employment, and that every trace of serfdom, or of a feudal hierarchy between the sovereign and the lowest class of his subjects shall be done away with. The benefits of the Code Napoleon, public trial, and the introduction of juries, will be the leading features of your Government. And to tell you the truth, I count more upon their effects, for the extension and consolidation of your rule, than upon the most resounding victories. I want your subjects to enjoy a degree of liberty, equality, and prosperity hitherto unknown to the German people. . . . Such a method of government will be a stronger barrier between you and Prussia than the Elbe, the fortresses, and the protection of France. What people will want to return under the arbitrary Prussian rule, once it has tasted the benefits of a wise and liberal administration? In Germany, as in France, Italy, and Spain, people long for equality and liberalism. I have been managing the affairs of Europe long enough now to know that the burden of the privileged classes was resented everywhere. Rule constitutionally. Even if reason, and the enlightenment of the age, were not sufficient cause, it would be good policy for one in your position; and you will find that the backing of public opinion gives you a great natural advantage over the absolute kings who are your neighbors.

J. M. Thompson (Ed.), Napoleon's Letters *(London: Dent, 1954), pp. 190–191 as quoted in Maurice Hutt (Ed.),* Napoleon *(Englewood Cliffs, NJ: Prentice-Hall, Inc., 1972), p. 34.*

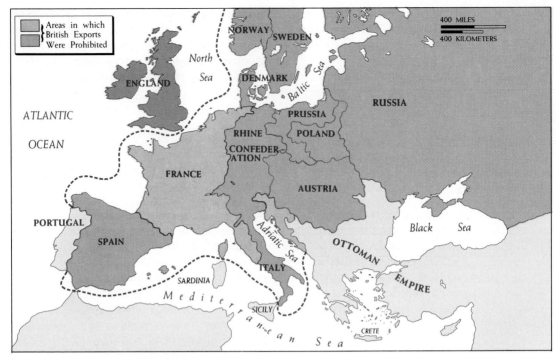

MAP 20-1 THE CONTINENTAL SYSTEM, 1806–1810 *Napoleon hoped to cut off all British trade with the European continent and thereby drive the British from the war.*

solve that ancient political body and henceforth to call himself only emperor of Austria.

Prussia, which had carefully remained neutral up to this point, was now provoked into war against France. The famous Prussian army was quickly crushed at the battles of Jena and Auerstädt on October 14, 1806. Two weeks later Napoleon was in Berlin. There, on No-

vember 21, he issued the Berlin Decrees forbidding his allies to import British goods. On June 13, 1807, Napoleon defeated the Russians at Friedland and was able to occupy Königsberg, the capital of East Prussia. The French emperor was master of all Germany.

TREATY OF TILSIT Unable to fight another battle and unwilling to retreat into Russia, Tsar Alexander I (1801–1825) was ready to make peace. He and Napoleon met on a raft in the middle of the Niemen River while the two armies and the nervous king of Prussia watched from the bank. On July 7, 1807, they signed the Treaty of Tilsit, which confirmed France's gains. Moreover, the Prussian state was reduced to half its size and was saved from extinction only by the support of Alexander. Prussia openly and Russia secretly became allies of Napoleon in his war against Britain.

Napoleon organized conquered Europe much like the domain of a great Corsican family. The great French Empire was ruled directly by the head of the clan, Napoleon. On its borders lay a number of satellite states carved out as the portions of the several family members.

NAPOLEON AND THE CONTINENTAL SYSTEM

1806 (Nov. 21)—Napoleon establishes the Continental System prohibiting all trade with England.

1807 (July 7)— The peace conference at Tilsit results in Russia joining the Continental System and becoming an ally of Napoleon.

1809 and 1810— Napoleon at the peak of his power.

1810 (Dec. 31)—Russia withdraws from the Continental System and resumes relations with Britain. Napoleon plans to crush Russia militarily.

1812 (June–December)—Napoleon invades Russia. The Russians adopt a scorched-earth policy and burn Moscow. The thwarted Napoleon deserts his dwindling army and rushes back to Paris.

Napoleon met Tsar Alexander I (1801–1825) at Tilsit in 1807. [New York Public Library]

His stepson ruled Italy for him, and three of his brothers and his brother-in-law were made kings of other conquered states. Napoleon denied a kingdom to his brother Lucien, of whose wife he disapproved. The French emperor expected his relatives to take orders without question. When they failed to do so, he rebuked and even punished them. This establishment of the Napoleonic family as the collective sovereign of Europe was offensive to the growing national feeling in many states and helped to create nationalism in others. The rule of puppet kings was unpopular and provoked political opposition that needed only encouragement and assistance to flare up into serious resistance.

The Continental System

After the Treaty of Tilsit such assistance could come only from Britain, and Napoleon knew that he must defeat the British before he could feel safe. Unable to compete with the British navy, he continued the economic warfare begun by the Berlin Decree. His plan was to cut off all British trade with the European continent. In this manner he hoped to cripple the commercial and financial power on which Britain depended. He wanted to cause domestic unrest and revolution, and thus to drive the British from the war. The Milan Decree of 1807 attempted to stop neutral nations from trading with Britain. For a time it appeared that this Continental System, as it was called, might work. British exports dropped, and riots broke out in England. But in the end the system failed and may even have contributed significantly to Napoleon's defeat.

The British economy survived because of its access to the growing markets of North and South America and of the eastern Mediterranean, all assured by the British control of the seas. At the same time, the Continental System did great harm to the European economies. The system was meant not only to hurt Britain but also to help France economically. Napoleon resisted advice to turn his empire into a free-trade area. Such a policy would have been both popular and helpful. Instead, his tariff policies favored France, increased the resentment of foreign merchants, and made them less willing to enforce the system and more ready to engage in smuggling. It was in part to prevent smuggling that Napoleon invaded Spain in 1808. The resulting peninsular campaign in Spain and Portugal helped to bring on his ruin.

European Response to the Empire

Napoleon's conquests stimulated the two most powerful political forces in nineteenth-century Europe: liberalism and nationalism. The export of his version of the French Revolution directly and indirectly spread the ideas and values of the Enlightenment and the principles of 1789. Wherever Napoleon ruled, the Napoleonic Code was imposed and class distinction was abolished. Feudal dues disappeared and the peasants were freed from serfdom and manorial dues. In the towns, the guilds and the local oligarchies that had been dominant for centuries were dissolved or deprived of their power. New freedom thus came to serfs, artisans, workers, and entrepreneurs outside the privileged circles. The established churches were deprived of their traditional independence and were made subordinate to the state. Church monopoly of religion was replaced by general toleration.

These reforms were not undone by the fall of Napoleon. Along with the demand for representative, constitutional government, they

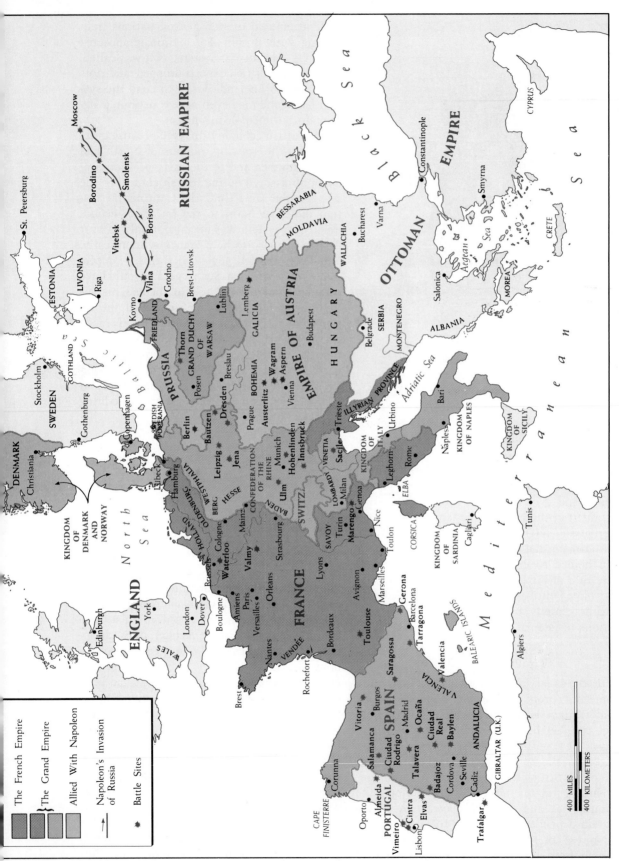

MAP 20-2 NAPOLEONIC EUROPE IN LATE 1812 By mid-1812 the areas shown in brown were incorporated into France, and most of the rest of Europe was directly controlled by or allied with Napoleon. But Russia had

Legend

- The French Empire
- The Grand Empire
- Allied With Napoleon
- Napoleon's Invasion of Russia
- Battle Sites

RUSSIAN EMPIRE

OTTOMAN EMPIRE

EMPIRE OF AUSTRIA

PRUSSIA

FRANCE

SPAIN

PORTUGAL

ENGLAND

DENMARK

SWEDEN

Black Sea

Baltic Sea

North Sea

Mediterranean Sea

Adriatic Sea

Aegean Sea

GRAND DUCHY OF WARSAW

CONFEDERATION OF THE RHINE

KINGDOM OF ITALY

KINGDOM OF NAPLES

KINGDOM OF SICILY

KINGDOM OF SARDINIA

KINGDOM OF DENMARK AND NORWAY

HUNGARY

BOHEMIA

GALICIA

ILLYRIAN PROVINCE

SWITZ.

HOLLAND

WESTPHALIA

HESSE

BERG

BADEN

OLDENBURG

SWEDISH POMERANIA

LIVONIA

ESTONIA

GOTHLAND

MOLDAVIA

BESSARABIA

WALLACHIA

SERBIA

MONTENEGRO

ALBANIA

MOREA

CRETE

CYPRUS

CORSICA

ELBA

BALEARIC ISLANDS

GIBRALTAR (U.K.)

VENETIA

LOMBARDY

SAVOY

VENDÉE

ANDALUCIA

VALENCIA

WALES

CAPE FINISTERRE

Moscow

Borodino

Smolensk

Vitebsk

Borisov

Vilna

Grodno

Brest-Litovsk

St. Petersburg

Riga

Stockholm

Gothenburg

Copenhagen

Christiania

Kovno

Friedland

Thorn

Posen

Lublin

Lemberg

Breslau

Dresden

Bautzen

Berlin

Hamburg

Lübeck

Prague

Vienna

Wagram

Aspern

Austerlitz

Budapest

Belgrade

Bucharest

Varna

Constantinople

Smyrna

Salonica

Leipzig

Jena

Munich

Hohenlinden

Innsbruck

Trieste

Urbino

Bari

Naples

Rome

Leghorn

Genoa

Milan

Turin

Marengo

Nice

Ulm

Mainz

Cologne

Strasbourg

Valmy

Waterloo

Brussels

Amiens

Paris

Versailles

Orleans

Lyons

Avignon

Marseilles

Toulon

Toulouse

Bordeaux

Rochefort

Nantes

Brest

London

Dover

York

Edinburgh

Gerona

Barcelona

Tarragona

Valencia

Saragossa

Vitoria

Burgos

Salamanca

Ciudad Rodrigo

Madrid

Ocaña

Ciudad Real

Talavera

Badajoz

Baylen

Cordova

Seville

Cadiz

Almeida

Elvas

Oporto

Vimeiro

Cintra

Lisbon

Corunna

Trafalgar

Cagliari

Tunis

Algiers

400 MILES

400 KILOMETERS

remained the basis of later liberal reforms. However, at the same time it became increasingly clear that Napoleon's policies were intended first and foremost for his own glory and that of France. The Continental System demonstrated that France, rather than Europe generally, was to be enriched by Napoleon's rule. Consequently, before long the conquered states and peoples became restive.

German Nationalism and Prussian Reform

The German response to Napoleon's success was particularly interesting and important. There had never been a unified German state. The great German writers of the Enlightenment, such as Immanuel Kant, Friedrich von Schiller, and Gotthold Lessing, were neither political nor nationalistic.

At the beginning of the nineteenth century the Romantic movement had begun to take hold. One of its basic features in Germany was the emergence of nationalism. This movement went through two distinct stages. Initially, nationalistic writers emphasized the unique and admirable qualities of German culture, which, they argued, arose from the peculiar history of the German people. Such cultural nationalism prevailed until Napoleon's humiliation of Prussia at Jena in 1806.

At that point many German intellectuals began to urge resistance to Napoleon on the basis of German nationalism. The French conquest endangered the independence and achievements of the German people. Many nationalists were also critical of the German princes, who ruled selfishly and inefficiently and who seemed ever ready to lick the boots of Napoleon. No less important in forging a German national sentiment was the example of France, which had attained greatness by enlisting the active support of the entire people in the patriotic cause. Henceforth many Germans sought to solve their internal political problems by establishing a unified German state, reformed to harness the energies of the entire people.

After Tilsit only Prussia could arouse such patriotic feelings. Elsewhere German rulers were either under Napoleon's thumb or actively collaborating with him. Defeated, humiliated, and shrunk in size, Prussia continued to resist, however feebly. To Prussia fled German nationalists from other states, calling for reforms and unification that were, in fact, feared and hated by Frederick William III and the *Junker* nobility. Reforms came about in spite of such opposition because the defeat at Jena had made clear the necessity of new departures for the Prussian state.

The Prussian administrative and social reforms were the work of Baron von Stein (1757–1831) and Count von Hardenberg (1750–1822). Neither of these reformers intended to reduce the autocratic power of the Prussian monarch or to put an end to the dominance of the *Junkers*, who formed the bulwark of the state and of the army officer corps. Rather, they aimed at fighting the revolution and French power with their own version of the French weapons. As Hardenberg declared:

> Our objective, our guiding principle, must be a revolution in the better sense, a revolution leading directly to the great goal, the elevation of humanity through the wisdom of those in authority. . . . Democratic rules of conduct in a monarchical administration, such is the formula . . . which will conform most comfortably with the spirit of the age.[1]

Although the reforms came from the top, they brought important changes in Prussian society.

Stein's reforms put an end to the existing system of Prussian landownership. The *Junker* monopoly of landholding was broken. Serfdom was generally abolished. However, the power of the *Junkers* did not permit the total end of the system, as in the western principalities of Germany. Peasants remaining on the land were forced to continue manorial labor, although they were free to leave the land if they chose. They could obtain the ownership of the land they worked only at the price of forfeiting a third of it to the lord. The result was that *Junker* holdings grew larger. Some peasants went to the cities to find work; others became agricultural laborers; and some did actually become small freeholding farmers. Serfdom had come to an end, but new social problems had been created as a landless labor force was enlarged by the population explosion.

Military reforms sought to increase the supply of soldiers and to improve their quality. Jena had shown that an army of free patriots commanded by officers chosen on merit rather

705

THE AGE O
NAPOLEON
AND THE
TRIUMPH O
ROMANTICIS

---

[1] *Quoted in Geoffrey Brunn,* Europe and the French Imperium *(New York: Harper & Row, 1938), p. 174.*

than by birth could defeat an army of serfs and mercenaries commanded by incompetent nobles. To remedy the situation, the Prussian reformers abolished inhumane punishments, sought to inspire patriotic feelings in the soldiers, opened the officer corps to commoners, gave promotions on the basis of merit, and organized war colleges that developed new theories of strategy and tactics.

These reforms soon put Prussia in a condition to regain its former power. However, because Napoleon had put a strict limit on the size of the Prussian army, universal conscription could not be introduced until 1813. Before that date the Prussians got around the limit of 42,000 men in arms by training one group each year, putting them into the reserves, and then training a new group the same size. In this manner Prussia could boast an army of 270,000 by 1814.

The Wars of Liberation

SPAIN In Spain more than elsewhere in Europe national resistance to France had deep social roots. Spain had achieved political unity as early as the sixteenth century. The Spanish peasants were devoted to the ruling dynasty and especially to the Roman Catholic church. France and Spain had been allies since 1796. In 1807, however, a French army came into the Iberian Peninsula to force Portugal to abandon

Arthur Wellesley, the duke of Wellington, first led troops against Napoleon in Spain and later defeated him at the battle of Waterloo, June 18, 1815. Unlike his great naval contemporary, Nelson, he lived to become an elder statesman of Britain. The portrait is by the celebrated Spanish painter Francisco Goya (1746–1828). [The Granger Collection]

Goya was horrified by the atrocities perpetrated by both sides during the guerrilla warfare that followed Napoleon's occupation of Spain. He entitled this drawing of the fighting "They are like wild beasts." [The Metropolitan Museum of Art, Rogers Fund, 1922]

its traditional alliance with Britain. The army stayed in Spain to protect lines of supply and communication. When a revolt broke out in Madrid in 1808, Napoleon used it as a pretext to depose the Spanish Bourbon dynasty and to place his brother Joseph on the Spanish throne. Attacks on the privileges of the Church increased public outrage. Many members of the upper classes were prepared to collaborate with Napoleon, but the peasants, urged on by the lower clergy and the monks, rose in a general rebellion.

Napoleon faced a new kind of warfare. Guerilla bands cut lines of communication, killed stragglers, destroyed isolated units, and then disappeared into the mountains. The British landed an army under Sir Arthur Wellesley (1769–1852), later the duke of Wellington, to support the Spanish insurgents. Thus began the long peninsular campaign that would drain French strength from elsewhere in Europe and play a critical role in Napoleon's eventual defeat.

AUSTRIA The French troubles in Spain encouraged the Austrians to renew the war in 1809. Since their defeat at Austerlitz they had sought a war of revenge. The Austrians counted on Napoleon's distraction in Spain, French war weariness, and aid from other German princes. However, Napoleon was fully in command in France; and the German princes did not move. The French army marched swiftly into Austria and won the battle of Wagram. The resulting Peace of Schönbrunn deprived Austria of much territory and three and a half million subjects.

Another spoil of victory was the Austrian Archduchess Marie Louise, daughter of the emperor. Napoleon's wife, Josephine de Beauharnais, was forty-six and had borne him no children. His dynastic ambitions, as well as the desire for a marriage matching his new position as master of Europe, led him to divorce his wife and to marry the eighteen-year-old Austrian princess. Napoleon had also considered the sister of Tsar Alexander but had received a polite rebuff.

The Invasion of Russia

The failure of Napoleon's marriage negotiations with Russia emphasized the shakiness of the Franco-Russian alliance concluded at Til-

sit. The alliance was unpopular with Russian nobles because of the liberal politics of France and because of the prohibition of the Continental System on timber sales to Britain. Only French aid in gaining Constantinople could justify the alliance in their eyes, but Napoleon gave them no help against the Ottoman Empire. The organization of the Grand Duchy of Warsaw as a Napoleonic satellite on the Russian doorstep and its enlargement in 1809 after the battle of Wagram angered Alexander I. Napoleon's annexation of Holland in violation of the Treaty of Tilsit, his recognition of the French Marshal Bernadotte as King Charles XIV of Sweden, and his marriage to an Austrian princess further disturbed the tsar. At the end of 1810 Russia withdrew from the Continental System and began to prepare for war.

Napoleon was determined to put an end to the Russian military threat. He amassed an army of over 600,000 men, including a core of Frenchmen and over 400,000 other soldiers drawn from the rest of his empire. He intended the usual short campaign crowned by a decisive battle, but the Russians disappointed him by retreating before his advance. His vast superiority in numbers—the Russians had only about 160,000 troops—made it foolish for them to risk a battle. Instead they followed a "scorched-earth" policy, destroying all food and supplies as they retreated. The so-called Grand Army of Napoleon could not live off the country, and the expanse of Russia made supply lines too long to maintain. Terrible rains, fierce heat, shortages of food and water, and the courage of the Russian rear guard eroded the morale of Napoleon's army. Napoleon's advisers urged him to abandon the venture, but he feared that an unsuccessful campaign would undermine his position in the empire and in France. He pinned his faith on the Russians' unwillingness to abandon Moscow without a fight.

In September 1812 Russian public opinion forced the army to give Napoleon the battle he wanted in spite of the canny Russian General Kutuzov's wish to avoid the fight and to let the Russian winter defeat the invader. At Borodino, not far west of Moscow, the bloodiest battle of the Napoleonic era cost the French 30,000 casualties and the Russians almost twice as many. Yet the Russian army was not destroyed. Napoleon won nothing substantial, and the battle was regarded as a defeat for him.

707

THE AGE OF
NAPOLEON
AND THE
TRIUMPH OF
ROMANTICISM

Fires, set by the Russians, soon engulfed Moscow and left Napoleon far from home with a badly diminished army lacking adequate supplies as winter came to a vast and unfriendly country. Napoleon, after capturing the burned city, addressed several peace offers to Alexander, but the tsar ignored them. By October what was left of the Grand Army was forced to retreat. By December Napoleon realized that the Russian fiasco would encourage plots against him at home. He returned to Paris, leaving the remnants of his army to struggle westward. Perhaps only as many as 100,000 lived to tell the tale of their terrible ordeal.

European Coalition

Even as the news of the disaster reached the west, the total defeat of Napoleon was far from certain. He was able to put down his opponents in Paris and to raise another army of 350,000 men. Neither the Prussians nor the Austrians were eager to risk another bout with Napoleon, and even the Russians hesitated. The Austrian foreign minister, Prince Klemens von Metternich (1773–1859), would have been glad to make a negotiated peace that would leave Napoleon on the throne of a shrunken and chastened France rather than see Europe dominated by Russia. Napoleon might have won a reasonable settlement by negotiation had he been willing to make concessions that would have split his jealous opponents. However, he would not consider that solution. As he explained to Metternich,

Your sovereigns born on the throne can let themselves be beaten twenty times and re-

The French entered Moscow on September 14, 1812. Despite his expectations, Napoleon found that the fall of their capital did not force the Russians to sue for peace. Within a month, the onset of winter had forced the French to retreat. [Art Resource]

The leading statesmen of the Congress of Vienna are here portrayed in a single group. Metternich, in white breeches, is standing on the left. Lord Castlereagh is sitting in the center with his legs crossed. Talleyrand is seated on the right with his arm on the table. [Royal Library, Windsor Castle. By gracious permission of HM the Queen]

turn to their capitals. I cannot do this because I am an upstart soldier. My domination will not survive the day when I cease to be strong, and therefore feared.[2]

In 1813 patriotic pressure and national ambition brought together the last and most powerful coalition against Napoleon. The Russians drove westward and were joined by Prussia and then Austria. All were assisted by vast amounts of British money. From the west Wellington marched his peninsular army into France. Napoleon's new army was inexperienced and poorly equipped. His generals had lost confidence and were tired. The emperor himself was worn out and sick. Still he was able to wage a skillful campaign in central Europe and to defeat the allies at Dresden. In October, however, he met the combined armies of

the enemy at Leipzig in what the Germans called the Battle of the Nations and was decisively defeated. At the end of March 1814 the allied army marched into Paris. A few days later Napoleon abdicated and went into exile on the island of Elba off the coast of northern Italy.

The Congress of Vienna and the European Settlement

Fear of Napoleon and hostility to his ambitions had held the victorious coalition together. As soon as he was removed, the allies began to pursue their own separate ambitions. The key person in achieving eventual agreement among the allies was Robert Stewart, Viscount Castlereagh (1769–1822), the British foreign secretary. Even before the victorious

[2] *Quoted in Felix Markham,* Napoleon and the Awakening of Europe *(New York: Macmillan, 1965), pp. 115–116.*

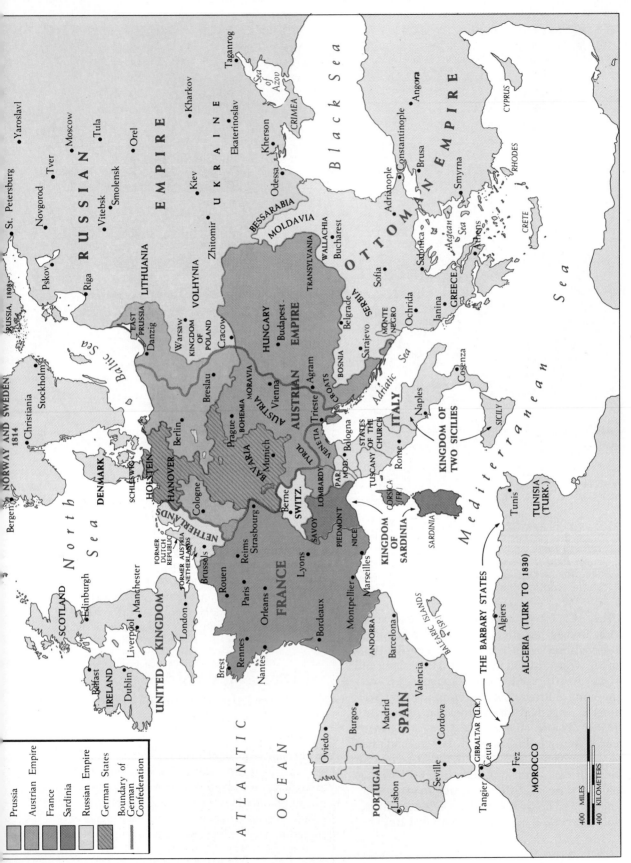

MAP 20-3 EUROPE, AFTER THE CONGRESS OF VIENNA 1815 *The Congress of Vienna achieved the post-Napoleonic territorial adjustments shown on the map. The most notable arrangements dealt with areas along*

armies had entered Paris, he brought about the signing of the Treaty of Chaumont on March 9, 1814. It provided for the restoration of the Bourbon dynasty to the French throne and the contraction of France to its frontiers of 1792. Even more important was the agreement by Britain, Austria, Russia, and Prussia to form a Quadruple Alliance for twenty years to guarantee the peace terms and to act together to preserve whatever settlement they later agreed on. Remaining problems—and they were many—and final details were left for a conference to be held at Vienna.

Territorial Adjustments

The Congress of Vienna assembled in September 1814 but did not conclude its work until November 1815. Although a glittering array of heads of state attended the gathering, the four great powers conducted the important work of the conference. The only full session of the congress met to ratify the arrangements made by the big four. The easiest problem facing the great powers was France. All the victors agreed that no single state should be allowed to dominate Europe, and all were determined to see that France should be prevented from doing so again. The restoration of the French Bourbon monarchy, which was again popular, and a nonvindictive boundary settlement kept France calm and satisfied.

In addition the powers constructed a series of states to serve as barriers to any new French expansion. They established the kingdom of the Netherlands, including Belgium, in the north and added Genoa to Piedmont in the south. Prussia, whose power was increased by accessions in eastern Europe, was given important new territories in the west along the Rhine River to deter French aggression in that area. Austria was given full control of northern Italy to prevent a repetition of Napoleon's conquests there. As for the rest of Germany, most of Napoleon's arrangements were left untouched. The venerable Holy Roman Empire, which had been dissolved in 1806, was not revived. In all these areas the congress established the rule of legitimate monarchs and rejected any hint of the republican and democratic politics that had flowed from the French Revolution.

On these matters agreement was not difficult, but the settlement of eastern Europe sharply divided the victors. Alexander I of Russia wanted all Poland under his rule. Prussia was willing if it received all of Saxony. But Austria was unwilling to surrender its share of Poland or to see the growth of Prussian power and the penetration of Russia deeper into central Europe. The Polish-Saxon question brought the congress to a standstill and almost brought on a new war among the victors. But defeated France provided a way out. The wily Talleyrand, now representing France at Vienna, suggested that the weight of France added to that of Britain and Austria might bring Alexander to his senses. When news of a secret treaty among the three leaked out, the tsar agreed to become ruler of a smaller Poland, and Frederick William III of Prussia agreed to accept only part of Saxony. Thereafter, France was included as a fifth great power in all deliberations.

MAP 20-4 THE GERMAN STATUS AFTER 1815 *As noted, German states were also reorganized.*

Prussian States

German States

Boundary of the German Confederation, 1815

Napoleon Announces His Return from Exile

After his abdication in 1814 Napoleon went into exile on Elba, an island off the coast of Italy. The great powers believed he had been defeated and these nations had already begun to negotiate the peace settlement in Vienna. Then Napoleon returned to France from Elba and called his troops once more to arms. In a stirring public letter he asked his soldiers once more to accept his leadership and to cast out the restored Bourbon monarchy imposed on France by the other great powers. The army of France responded but only to meet defeat four months later on June 18 at Waterloo. Napoleon's letter was dated March 1, 1815. Note in particular the emphasis he places on the symbols of the Bourbon monarchy and the symbols of the revolutionary army.

Soldiers! In exile I heard your voice. Now I have landed [in France]. . . .

Your general, made king by the voice of the people and raised to the throne upon your shields, has returned: come and join him. Renounce the [Bourbon] colors which the nation has proscribed and which for twenty-five years have served to rally the enemies of France. Unfurl instead the tricolor which you carried in the day of our greatness! . . . Take up once more the eagles which you carried at Ulm, at Austerlitz, at Jena, Eylau, Friedland, Moscow. . . .

We must forget that we were the master of the continent; but we must not let anyone meddle in our affairs. . . . Your rank, fortune, and glory, and those of your children, have no greater enemy than these [Bourbon] princes whom foreigners have imposed upon us. . . .

Soldiers, rally round the standard of your leader; his interests, his honor, his glory are the same, the very same, as your own. Victory will advance at the double. The eagle, bearing the national colors [of blue, white, red] will fly from steeple to steeple, right to the towers of Notre Dame [in Paris]. And then you will be able to show your scars with honor, then once again you will be able to boast of what you have done. You will be the liberators of your country . . . and in your old age . . . you will be able to say with pride, . . . "I cleansed Paris of the stain with which treason and the presence of the enemy there had sullied her."

Quoted from Napoleon, Correspondence, M. Hutt, trans., in Maurice Hutt, Napoleon (Englewood Cliffs, NJ: Prentice-Hall, Inc., 1972), p. 66.

The Hundred Days and the Quadruple Alliance

Unity among the victors was further restored by Napoleon's return from Elba on March 1, 1815. The French army was still loyal to the former emperor, and many of the French thought that their fortunes might be safer under his rule than under that of the restored Bourbons. The coalition seemed to be dissolving in Vienna. Napoleon seized the opportunity, escaped to France, and was soon restored to power. He promised a liberal constitution and a peaceful foreign policy. The allies were not convinced. They declared Napoleon an outlaw (a new device under international law) and sent their armies to crush him. Wellington, with the crucial help of the Prussians under Field Marshal von Blücher, defeated Napoleon at Waterloo in Belgium on June 18, 1815. Napoleon again abdicated and was sent into exile on Saint Helena, a tiny Atlantic island off the coast of Africa, where he died in 1821.

The Hundred Days, as the period of Napoleon's return is called, frightened the great powers and made the peace settlement harsher for France. In addition to some minor territorial adjustments, the victors imposed a war indemnity and an army of occupation on France. Alexander proposed a Holy Alliance, whereby the monarchs promised to act in accordance with Christian principles. Austria and Prussia signed; but Castlereagh thought it absurd, and England abstained. The tsar, who was then embracing mysticism, believed his proposal a valuable tool for international relations. The Holy Alliance soon became a symbol of extreme political reaction. The Quadruple Alliance between England, Austria, Prussia, and Russia was renewed on November 20, 1815.

The chief aims of the Congress of Vienna were to prevent a recurrence of the Napoleonic nightmare and to arrange an acceptable settlement for Europe that might produce lasting peace. It was remarkably successful in achieving these goals. France accepted the new situation without undue resentment. The victorious powers settled difficult problems in a reasonable way. They established a legalistic balance of power and methods for adjusting to change.

The work of the congress has been criticized for failing to recognize and provide for the great forces that would stir the nineteenth century—nationalism and democracy. But such criticism is inappropriate. The settlement, like all such agreements, was aimed at solving past ills, and in that it succeeded. If the powers failed to anticipate future problems or to yield to forces of which they disapproved, they were more than human to have done so. Perhaps it was unusual enough to produce a settlement that remained essentially intact for almost half a century and that allowed Europe to suffer no general war for a hundred years.

The Romantic Movement

The years of the French Revolution and the conquests of Napoleon saw the emergence of a new and very important intellectual movement throughout Europe. Romanticism in its various manifestations was a reaction against much of the thought of the Enlightenment. Romantic writers opposed what they consid-

NAPOLEONIC EUROPE

1797	Napoleon concludes the Treaty of Campo Formio
1798	Nelson defeats the French navy in the harbor of Abukir
1799	Consulate established in France
1801	Concordat between France and the papacy
1802	Treaty of Amiens
1803	War renewed between France and Britain
1804	Execution of Duke of Enghien
1804	Napoleonic Civil Code issued
1804	Napoleon crowned as emperor
1805	Nelson defeats French fleet at Trafalgar (October 21)
1805	Austerlitz (December 2)
1806	Jena
1806	Continental System established by Berlin Decrees
1807	Friedland
1807	Treaty of Tilsit
1808	Beginning of Spanish resistance to Napoleonic domination
1809	Wagram
1809	Napoleon marries Archduchess Marie Louise of Austria
1812	Invasion of Russia and French defeat at Borodino
1813	Leipzig (Battle of the Nations)
1814	Treaty of Chaumont (March) establishes Quadruple Alliance
1814	Congress of Vienna convenes (September)
1815	Napoleon returns from Elba (March 1)
1815	Waterloo (June 18)
1815	Holy Alliance formed at Congress of Vienna (September 26)
1815	Quadruple Alliance renewed at Congress of Vienna (November 20)
1821	Napoleon dies on Saint Helena

ered the excessive scientific narrowness of the eighteenth-century *philosophes*. The latter stood accused of subjecting everything to geometrical and mathematical models and thereby demeaning feelings and imagination. Romantic thinkers refused to conceive of human nature as primarily rational. They wanted to interpret both physical nature and human society in organic rather than in mechanical terms and categories. The Enlightenment *philosophes* had often criticized religion and faith; the Romantics in contrast saw religion as basic to human nature and faith as a means to knowledge.

Some historians, most notably Arthur O. Lovejoy, have warned against speaking of a single European-wide Romantic movement. They have pointed out that a variety of such movements—occurring almost simultaneously in Germany, England, and France—arose independently and had their own particular courses of development. Such considerations have not, however, prevented the designation of a specific historical period, dated roughly from 1780 to 1830, as the Age of Romanticism or of the Romantic movement.

Despite national differences, a shared reaction to the Enlightenment marked all of these writers and artists. They generally saw the imagination or some such intuitive intellectual faculty supplementing the reason as a means of perceiving and understanding the world. Many of these writers urged a revival of Christianity such as had permeated Europe during the Middle Ages. And unlike the *philosophes*, the Romantics liked the art, the literature, and the architecture of medieval times. They were also deeply interested in folklore, folk songs, and fairy tales. The Romantics were fascinated by dreams, hallucinations, sleepwalking, and other phenomena that suggested the existence of a world beyond that of empirical observation, sensory data, and discursive reasoning.

Romantic Questioning of the Supremacy of Reason

Several historical streams fed the Romantic movement. These included the individualism of the Renaissance and the Reformation, the pietism of the seventeenth century, and the eighteenth-century English Methodist movement. The latter influence encouraged a heartfelt, practical religion in place of dogmatism, rationalism, and deism. The sentimental novels of the eighteenth century, such as Samuel Richardson's *Clarissa*, also paved the way for thinkers who would emphasize feeling and emotion. The so-called *Sturm und Drang* ("storm and stress") period of German literature and German idealist philosophy were important to the Romantics. However, two writers who were also closely related to the Enlightenment provided the immediate intellectual foundations for Romanticism. They

were Jean-Jacques Rousseau and Immanuel Kant, both of whom raised questions about the sufficiency of the rationalism so dear to the *philosophes.*

Rousseau and Education

It has already been pointed out in Chapter 18 that Jean-Jacques Rousseau, though sharing in the reformist spirit of the Enlightenment, opposed many of its other facets. What Romantic writers especially drew from Rousseau was his conviction that society had corrupted human nature. In the two *Discourses* and others of his works, Rousseau had portrayed humankind as created happy and innocent by nature and originally living in a state of equilibrium, able to do what it desired and desiring only what it was able to do. For humankind to become happy again, it must remain true to its natural being, while still attempting to realize the new moral possibilities of life in society. In the *Social Contract* (1762) Rousseau had provided his prescription for the reorganization of political life that would achieve that goal.

Rousseau set forth his view on the individual's development toward the good and happy life in a novel entitled *Émile* (1762). Initially this treatise on education was far more influential than the *Social Contract*. In *Émile* Rousseau stressed the difference between children and adults. He distinguished the stages of human maturation and urged that in rearing children, one must give them maximum individual freedom. Each child should be allowed to grow freely, like a plant, and to learn by trial and error what reality is and how best to deal with it. The parent or teacher would help most by providing the basic necessities of life and warding off what was manifestly harmful. Otherwise the adult should stay completely out of the way, like a gardener who waters and weeds a garden but otherwise lets nature take its course.

This was a revolutionary concept of education in an age accustomed to narrow, bookish, and highly regimented vocational education and learning. Rousseau thought that the child's sentiments as well as its reason should be permitted to flourish. To Romantic writers this concept of human development vindicated the rights of nature over those of artificial society. They thought that such a form of education would eventually lead to a natural

715

THE AGE OF
NAPOLEON
AND THE
TRIUMPH OF
ROMANTICIS[M]

Immanuel Kant (1724–1804) was an eighteenth-century philosopher. Romantic writers saw his philosophy as a decisive refutation of the narrow rationality of the Enlightenment. [Bettmann Archive]

society. In its fully developed form, this view of life led the Romantics to place a high value on the uniqueness of each individual person and to explore in great detail the experiences of childhood. Like Rousseau the Romantics saw humankind, nature, and society as organically related to each other.

Kant and Reason

Immanuel Kant (1724–1804) wrote the two greatest philosophical works of the late eighteenth century: *The Critique of Pure Reason* (1781) and *The Critique of Practical Reason* (1788). He sought to accept the rationalism of the Enlightenment and still to preserve a belief in human freedom, immortality, and the existence of God. Against Locke and other philosophers who saw knowledge rooted in sensory experience alone, Kant argued for the subjective character of human knowledge. For Kant the human mind did not simply reflect the world around it like a passive mirror; rather, it actively imposed on the world of sensory experience "forms of sensibility" and "categories of understanding." These categories were generated by the mind itself. In other words, the human mind perceives the world as it does because of its own internal mental categories. What this meant was that human perceptions were as much the product of the mind's own activity as of sensory experience.

Kant found the sphere of reality that was accessible to pure reason to be quite limited.

However, he believed that beyond the phenomenal world of sensory experience, over which "pure reason" was master, there existed what he called the "noumenal" world. This world was a sphere of moral and aesthetic reality known by "practical reason" and conscience. Kant thought that all human beings possessed an innate sense of moral duty or an awareness of what he called a *categorical imperative*. This term referred to an inner command to act in every situation as one would have all other people always act in the same situation. Kant regarded the existence of this imperative of conscience as incontrovertible proof of humankind's natural freedom. On the basis of humankind's moral sense Kant went on to postulate the existence of God, eternal life, and future rewards and punishments. He believed that these transcendental truths could not be proved by discursive reasoning. Still, he was convinced that they were realities to which every reasonable person could attest.

To many Romantic writers Kantian philosophy was a decisive refutation of the narrow rationality of the Enlightenment. Whether they called it "practical reason," "fancy," "imagination," "intuition," or simply "feeling," the Romantics believed in the presence of a special power in the human mind that could penetrate beyond the limits of human understanding as set forth by Hobbes, Locke, and Hume. Most of them also believed that poets and artists generally possessed these powers in particular abundance. Other Romantic writers appealed to the limits of human reason in order to set forth new religious ideas or political thought that was often at odds with that of Enlightenment writers.

Romantic Literature

The term *romantic* appeared in English and French literature as early as the seventeenth century. Neoclassical writers then used the word to describe literature that they considered unreal, sentimental, or excessively fanciful. In the eighteenth century the English writer Thomas Warton associated *romantic* with medieval romances. In Germany, a major center of the Romantic literary movement, Johann Gottfried Herder used the terms *romantic* and *Gothic* interchangeably. In both England and Germany the term came to be applied to all literature that failed to observe classical forms and rules and that gave free play to the imagination.

As an alternative to such dependence on the classical forms, August Wilhelm von Schlegel praised the "romantic" literature of Dante, Petrarch, Boccaccio, Shakespeare, the Arthurian legends, Cervantes, and Calderón. According to Schlegel, Romantic literature was to classical literature what the organic and living were to the merely mechanical. He set forth his views in *Lectures on Dramatic Art and Literature* (1809–1811).

The Romantic movement had peaked in Germany and England before it became a major force in France under the leadership of Madame de Staël (1766–1817) and Victor Hugo (1802–1885). So influential was the classical tradition in France that not until 1816 did a French writer openly declare himself a Romantic. That was Henri Beyle (1783–1842), who wrote under the pseudonym Stendhal. He praised Shakespeare and Lord Byron and criticized his own countryman, the seventeenth-century classical dramatist Racine.

The English Romantic Writers

The English Romantics believed that poetry was enhanced by freely following the creative impulses of the mind. In this belief they directly opposed Lockean psychology, which regarded the mind as a passive receptor and poetry as a mechanical exercise of "wit" following prescribed rules. For William Blake and Samuel Taylor Coleridge the artist's imagination was God at work in the mind. As Coleridge expressed his views, the imagination was "a repetition in the finite mind of the eternal act of creation in the infinite I AM." So conceived of, poetry could not be considered idle play. It was the highest of human acts, humankind's self-fulfillment in a transcendental world.

BLAKE   William Blake (1757–1827) considered the poet a seer and poetry translated vision. He thought it a great tragedy that so many people understood the world only rationally and could perceive no innocence or beauty in it. In the 1790s he experienced a period of deep personal depression, which seems to have been related to his own inability to perceive the world as he believed it to be. The better

one got to know the world, the more the life of the imagination and its spiritual values seemed to recede. Blake saw this problem as evidence of the materialism and injustice of English society. He was deeply impressed by the strong sense of contradiction between a true childlike vision of the world and conceptions of it based on actual experience.

COLERIDGE   Samuel Taylor Coleridge (1772–1834) was the master of Gothic poems of the supernatural. His three poems "Christabel," "The Ancient Mariner," and "Kubla Khan" are of this character. "The Ancient Mariner" relates the story of a sailor cursed for killing an albatross. The poem treats the subject as a crime against nature and God and raises the issues of guilt, punishment, and the redemptive possibilities of humility and penance. At the end of the poem the mariner discovers the unity and beauty of all things. Having repented, he is delivered from his awful curse, which has been symbolized by the dead albatross hung around his neck:

> O happy living things! no tongue
> Their beauty might declare:
> A spring of love gushed from my heart,
> And I blessed them unaware . . .
> The self-same moment I could pray;
> And from my neck so free
> The Albatross fell off, and sank
> Like lead into the sea.

Coleridge also made major contributions to Romantic literary criticism in his lectures on Shakespeare and in *Biographia Literaria* (1817), which presents his theories of poetry.

WORDSWORTH   William Wordsworth (1770–1850) was Coleridge's closest friend. Together they published *Lyrical Ballads* in 1798 as a manifesto of a new poetry that rejected the rules of eighteenth-century criticism. Among Wordsworth's most important later poems is his "Ode on Intimations of Immortality" (1803), written in part to console Coleridge, who was in the midst of a deep personal crisis. Its subject is the loss of poetic vision, something Wordsworth also keenly felt at this time in himself. Nature, which he had worshipped, no longer spoke freely to him, and he feared that it might never speak to him again:

> There was a time when meadow, grove, and
>   stream,

717

THE AGE O
NAPOLEON
AND THE
TRIUMPH O
ROMANTICIS

The Romantic Movement's glorification of the individual is captured in this drawing entitled Newton *by William Blake (1757–1827). It is not, of course, a portrait of Sir Isaac Newton. Instead, it portrays a God-like scientist solving the mysteries of the universe. [The Tate Gallery, London/Art Resource]*

The earth, and every common sight,
  To me did seem
  Appareled in celestial light,
The glory and the freshness of a dream.
It is not now as it hath been of yore—
  Turn whereso'er I may,
    By night or day,
The things which I have seen I now can
    see no more.

What he had lost was the vision that he believed that all human beings lose in the necessary process of maturation: their childlike vision and closeness to spiritual reality. For both Wordsworth and Coleridge childhood was the bright period of creative imagination. Wordsworth held a theory of the soul's preexistence

Samuel Taylor Coleridge (1772–1834) was a true Romantic. He saw his poetry as similar to the God-like act of creation. [National Portrait Gallery, London]

in a celestial state before its creation. The child, being closer in time to its eternal origin and undistracted by much worldly experience, recollects the supernatural world much more easily. Aging and urban living corrupt and deaden the imagination, making one's inner feelings and the beauty of nature less important. In his book-length poem *The Prelude* (1850), Wordsworth presented a long autobiographical account of the growth of the poet's mind.

LORD BYRON   A true rebel among the Romantic poets was Lord Byron (1788–1824). At home, even the other Romantic writers distrusted and generally disliked him. He had little sympathy for their views of the imagination. However, outside England Byron was regarded as the embodiment of the new person of the French Revolution. He rejected the old traditions (he was divorced and famous for his amours) and championed the cause of personal liberty. Byron was outrageously skeptical and mocking, even of his own beliefs. In *Childe Harold's Pilgrimage* (1812) he created the figure of a brooding, melancholy romantic hero. In *Don Juan* (1819) he wrote with ribald humor, acknowledged nature's cruelty as well as its beauty, and even expressed admiration for urban life.

Byron tended to be content with the world as he directly knew it. He found his own experience of nature and love—objectively described and reported without embellishment—sufficient for poetic inspiration. He had the rare ability to encompass in his work the whole of his age and to write on subjects that other Romantics considered unworthy of poetry.

The German Romantic Writers

Much Romantic poetry was also written on the Continent, but almost all major German Romantics wrote at least one novel. Romantic novels tended to be highly sentimental and often borrowed material from medieval romances. The characters of Romantic novels were treated as symbols of the larger truth of life. Purely realistic description was avoided. The first German Romantic novel was Ludwig Tieck's *William Lovell* (1793–1795). It contrasts the young Lovell, whose life is built on love and imagination, with those who live by cold reason alone and who thus become an easy prey to unbelief, misanthropy, and ego-

George Gordon, Lord Byron (1788–1824) was brooding, melancholy, aristocratic, dissolute. He lived the life of a true Romantic hero, dying in the struggle for Greek independence in 1824. [National Portrait Gallery, London]

ism. As the novel rambles to its conclusion, Lovell is ruined by a mixture of philosophy, materialism, and skepticism, which are administered to him by two women whom he naively loves.

SCHLEGEL   Friedrich Schlegel (1767–1845) wrote a very progressive early Romantic novel, *Lucinde* (1799), which attacked contemporary prejudices against women as capable of being little more than lovers and domestics. Schlegel's novel reveals the ability of the Romantics to become involved in the social issues of their day. He depicted Lucinde as the perfect friend and companion, as well as the unsurpassed lover, of the hero. Like other early Romantic novels the work shocked contemporary morals by frankly discussing sexual activity and by describing Lucinde as equal in all ways to the male hero.

GOETHE   Towering above all of these German writers stood the figure of Johann Wolfgang von Goethe (1749–1832). Perhaps the greatest German literary figure of modern times, Goethe defies any easy classification. Part of his literary production fits into the Romantic mold, and part of it was a condemnation of Romantic excesses. The book that made his early reputation was *The Sorrows of*

Johann Wolfgang von Goethe (1749–1832), the greatest German writer of modern times, is portrayed here in the garb of a pilgrim against a Romantic background of classical ruins in the fields outside Rome. [Ursula Edelmann]

Young Werther, published in 1774. This novel, like many of the eighteenth century, is composed of a series of letters. The hero falls in love with Lotte, another man's wife. The letters explore this relationship and display the kind of emotional sentimentalism that was characteristic of the age. Eventually Werther and Lotte part, but in his grief over his abandoned love Werther takes his own life. This novel became very popular throughout Europe. Virtually all later Romantic authors, and especially those in Germany, admired it because of its emphasis on feeling and on living outside the bounds of polite society.

Much of Goethe's early poetry was also erotic in nature. However, as he became older, Goethe became much more serious and self-consciously moral. He published numerous other works, including *Wilhelm Meister's Apprenticeship* and *Iphigenia at Tauris*, that explored the manner in which human beings come to live moral lives while still acknowledging the life of the senses.

Goethe's greatest masterpiece was *Faust*, a long dramatic work of poetry in two parts. Part I was published in 1808. It tells the story of Faust, who, weary of life, makes a pact with the Devil: he will exchange his soul for greater knowledge than other human beings. As the story progresses, Faust seduces a young woman named Gretchen. She dies but is received into heaven as the grief-stricken Faust realizes that he must continue to live.

In Part II, completed in the year of Goethe's death (1832), Faust is taken through a series of strange adventures involving witches and various mythological characters. This portion of the work has never been admired as much as Part I. However, at the conclusion, Faust dedicates his life, or what remains of it, to the improvement of humankind. In this dedication he feels that he has found a goal that will allow him to overcome the restless striving that first made him make the pact with the Devil. That new knowledge breaks the pact. Faust then dies and is received by angels.

In this great work Goethe obviously was criticizing much of his earlier thought and that of contemporary Romantic writers. He was also attempting to portray the deep spiritual problems that Europeans would encounter as the traditional moral and religious values of Christianity were abandoned. Yet Goethe himself could not reaffirm those values. In that respect both he and his characters symbolized the spiritual struggle of the nineteenth century.

Religion in the Romantic Period

During the Middle Ages the foundation of religion had been the Church. The Reformation leaders had appealed to the authority of the

Bible. Then, later Enlightenment writers had attempted to derive religion from the rational nature revealed by Newtonian physics. Romantic religious thinkers, on the other hand, appealed to the inner emotions of humankind for the foundation of religion. Their forerunners were the mystics of Western Christianity. One of the first great examples of a religion characterized by Romantic impulses—Methodism—arose in England.

Methodism

Methodism originated in the middle of the eighteenth century as a revolt against deism and rationalism in the Church of England. The Methodist revival formed an important part of the background of English Romanticism. The leader of the Methodist movement was John Wesley (1703–1791). His education and religious development had been carefully supervised by a remarkable mother, Susannah Wesley, who bore eighteen children in addition to John.

While at Oxford, Wesley organized a religious group known as the "Holy Club." He soon left England to give himself to missionary work in Georgia in America, where he arrived

John Wesley (1703–1791), the founder of Methodism is shown here preaching in London. Methodism emphasized the role of enthusiastic emotional experience as part of Christian conversion. [New York Public Library Picture Collection]

in 1735. While crossing the Atlantic, he had been deeply impressed by a group of German Moravians on the ship. These German pietists exhibited unshakable faith and confidence during a violent storm at sea while Wesley despaired of his life. Wesley concluded that they knew far better than he the meaning of justification by faith. When he returned to England in 1738 after an unhappy missionary career, Wesley began to worship with Moravians in London. There, in 1739, he underwent a conversion experience that he described in the words, "My heart felt strangely warmed." From that point on, he felt assured of his own salvation.

Wesley discovered that he could not preach his version of Christian conversion and practical piety in Anglican church pulpits. Therefore, late in 1739, he began to preach in the open fields near the cities and towns of western England. Literally thousands of humble people responded to his message of repentance and good works. Soon he and his brother Charles, who became famous for his hymns, began to organize Methodist societies. By the late eighteenth century the Methodists had become a separate church. They ordained their own clergy and sent missionaries to America, where the Methodists eventually achieved their greatest success and most widespread influence.

The essence of Methodist teaching lay in its stress on inward, heartfelt religion and the possibility of Christian perfection in this life. John Wesley described Christianity as "an inward principle . . . the image of God impressed on a created spirit, a fountain of peace and love springing up into everlasting life." True Christians were those who were "saved in this world from all sin, from all unrighteousness . . . and now in such a sense perfect as not to commit sin and . . . freed from evil thoughts and evil tempers."[3]

Many people, weary of the dry rationalism that derived from deism, found Wesley's ideal relevant to their own lives. The Methodist preachers emphasized the role of enthusiastic emotional experience as part of Christian conversion. After Wesley, religious revivals became highly emotional in style and content.

[3] Quoted in Albert C. Outler (Ed.), John Wesley: A Representative Collection of His Writings (New York: Oxford University Press, 1964), p. 220.

New Directions in Continental Religion

Similar religious developments based on feeling appeared on the Continent. After the Thermidorian Reaction, a strong Roman Catholic revival took place in France. Its followers were people who had disapproved of both the religious policy of the revolution and the anticlericalism of the Enlightenment. The most important book to express these sentiments was *The Genius of Christianity* (1802) by Vicomte François René de Chateaubriand (1768–1848). In this work, which became known as the "Bible of Romanticism," Chateaubriand argued that the essence of religion was "passion." The foundation of faith in the Church was the emotion that its teachings and sacra-

721

THE AGE O
NAPOLEON
AND THE
TRIUMPH O
ROMANTICIS

Chateaubriand Describes the Appeal of a Gothic Church

Throughout most of the eighteenth century, writers had harshly criticized virtually all aspects of the Middle Ages, which were then considered an unenlightened time. One of the key elements of Romanticism was a new appreciation of all things medieval. In this passage from The Genius of Christianity *Chateaubriand praised the beauty of the Middle Ages and the strong religious feelings produced by stepping into a Gothic church. The description exemplifies the typically Romantic emphasis on feelings as the chief foundation of religion.*

You could not enter a Gothic church without feeling a kind of awe and a vague sentiment of the Divinity. You were all at once carried back to those times when a fraternity of cenobites [a particular order of monks], after having meditated in the woods of their monasteries, met to prostrate themselves before the altar and to chant the praises of the Lord, amid the tranquility and the silence of the night. . . .

Everything in a Gothic church reminds you of the labyrinths of a wood; every thing excites a feeling of religious awe, of mystery, and of the Divinity.

The two lofty towers erected at the entrance of the edifice overtop the elms and yew trees of the church yard, and produce the most picturesque effect on the azure of heaven. Sometimes their twin heads are illumined by the first rays of dawn; at others they appear crowned with a capital of clouds or magnified in a foggy atmosphere. The birds themselves seem to make a mistake in regard to them, and to take them for the trees of the forests; they hover over their summits, and perch upon their pinnacles. But, lo! confused noises suddenly issue from the tops of these towers and scare away the affrighted birds. The Christian architect, not content with building forests, has been desirous to retain their murmurs; and, by means of the organ and of bells, he has attached to the Gothic temple the very winds and thunders that roar in the recesses of the woods. Past ages, conjured up by these religious sounds, raise their venerable voices from the bosom of the stones, and are heard in every corner of the vast cathedral. The sanctuary reechoes like the cavern of the ancient Sibyl; loud-tongued bells swing over your head, while the vaults of death under your feet are profoundly silent.

Vicomte François René de Chateaubriand, The Genius of Christianity, *trans. by C. I. White (Baltimore: J. Murphy, 1862), as quoted in Howard E. Hugo (Ed.),* The Romantic Reader *(New York: Viking, 1957), pp. 341–342.*

ments inspired in the heart of the Christian.

Against the Newtonian view of the world and of a rational God, the Romantics found God immanent in nature. No one stated the Romantic religious ideal more eloquently or with greater impact on the modern world than Friedrich Schleiermacher (1768–1834). In 1799 he published *Speeches on Religion to Its Cultured Despisers*. It was a response to Lutheran orthodoxy, on the one hand, and to Enlightenment rationalism, on the other. The advocates of both were the "cultured despisers" of real or heartfelt religion. According to Schleiermacher, religion was neither dogma nor a system of ethics. It was an intuition or feelings of absolute dependence on an infinite reality. Religious institutions, doctrines, and moral activity expressed that primal religious feeling only in a secondary or indirect way.

Although Schleiermacher considered Christianity the "religion of religions," he also believed that every world religion was unique in its expression of the primal intuition of the infinite in the finite. He thus turned against the universal natural religion of the Enlightenment, which he termed "a name applied to loose, unconnected impulses," and defended the meaningfulness of the numerous world re-

The philosopher J. G. Fichte (1762–1814), shown here in the uniform of a Berlin home guard. Fichte glorified the role of the great individual in history. [Bildarchiv Preussischer Kulturbesitz]

ligions. Every such religion was seen to be a unique version of the emotional experience of dependence on an infinite being. In so arguing, Schleiermacher interpreted the religions of the world in the same way that other Romantic writers interpreted the variety of unique peoples and cultures.

Romantic Views of Nationalism and History

One of the most distinctive features of Romanticism, especially in Germany, was its glorification of both the individual person and individual cultures. Behind these views lay the philosophy of German idealism, which understood the world as the creation of subjective egos. J. G. Fichte (1762–1814), an important

MAJOR PUBLICATION DATES IN THE ROMANTIC MOVEMENT

1762	Rousseau's *Émile*
1774	Goethe's *Sorrow of Young Werther*
1781	Kant's *Critique of Pure Reason* *
1788	Kant's *Critique of Practical Reason* *
1789	Blake's *Songs of Innocence*
1794	Blake's *Songs of Experience*
1798	Wordsworth and Coleridge's *Lyrical Ballads*
1799	F. Schlegel's *Lucinde*
1799	Schleiermacher's *Speeches on Religion to Its Cultured Despisers*
1802	Chateaubriand's *Genius of Christianity*
1806	Hegel's *Phenomenology of Mind*
1808	Goethe's *Faust*, Part I
1812	Byron's *Childe Harold's Pilgrimage*
1819	Byron's *Don Juan*

* Kant's books were not themselves part of the Romantic movement, but they were fundamental to later Romantic writers.

German philosopher and nationalist, identified the individual ego with the Absolute that underlies all existing things. According to him and other similar philosophers, the world is truly the creation of humankind. The world is as it is because especially strong persons conceive of it in a particular way and impose their wills on the world and other people. Napoleon served as the contemporary example of such a great person. This philosophy has ever since served to justify the glorification of great persons and their actions in overriding all opposition to their will and desires.

Herder and Culture

In addition to this philosophy the influence of new historical studies lay behind the German glorification of individual cultures. German Romantic writers went in search of their own past in reaction to the copying of French manners in eighteenth-century Germany, the im-

723

THE AGE O
NAPOLEON
AND THE
TRIUMPH O
ROMANTICIS

Fichte Calls for the Regeneration of Germany

Johann Gottlieb Fichte (1762–1814) began to deliver his famous Addresses to the German Nation *late in 1807 as a series of Sunday lectures in Berlin. Earlier that year Prussia had been crushed by Napoleon's armies. In this passage from his concluding lecture, presented in early 1808, Fichte challenged the younger generation of Germans to recognize the national duty that historical circumstances had placed on their shoulders. They might either accept their defeat and the consequent slavery or revive the German nation and receive the praise and gratitude of later generations. It is important to note that Fichte saw himself speaking to all Germans as citizens of a single cultural nation rather than as the subjects of various monarchs and princes.*

Review in your own minds the various conditions between which you now have to make a choice. If you continue in your dullness and helplessness, all the evils of serfdom are awaiting you; deprivations, humiliations, the scorn and arrogance of the conqueror; you will be driven and harried in every corner, because you are in the wrong and in the way everywhere; until, by the sacrifice of your nationality and your language, you have purchased for yourselves some subordinate and petty place, and until in this way you gradually die out as a people. If, on the other hand, you bestir yourselves and play the man, you will continue in a tolerable and honorable existence, and you will see growing up among and around you a generation that will be the promise for you and for the Germans of most illustrious renown. You will see in spirit the German name rising by means of this generation to be the most glorious among all peoples; you will see this nation the regenerator and recreator of the world.

It depends on you whether you want to be the end, and to be the last of a generation unworthy of respect and certain to be despised by posterity even beyond its due—a generation of whose history . . . your descendants will read the end with gladness, saying its fate was just; or whether you want to be the beginning and the point of development for a new age glorious beyond all your conceptions, and the generation from whom posterity will reckon the year of their salvation. Reflect that you are the last in whose power this great alteration lies.

Johann Gottlieb Fichte, Addresses to the German Nation, *George Armstrong Kelly (Ed.) (New York: Harper Torchbooks, 1968), pp. 215–216.*

pact of the French Revolution, and the imperialism of Napoleon. An early leader in this effort was Johann Gottfried Herder (1744–1803). Herder had early resented the French cultural preponderance in Germany. In 1778 he published an influential essay entitled "On the Knowing and Feelings of the Human Soul." In it he vigorously rejected the mechanical explanation of nature so popular with Enlightenment writers. He saw human beings and societies as developing organically, like plants, over time. Human beings were different at different times and places.

Herder revived German folk culture by urging the collection and preservation of distinctive German songs and sayings. His most important followers in this regard were the Grimm brothers, Jakob (1785–1863) and Wilhelm (1786–1859), famous for their collection of fairy tales. Believing that each language and culture was the unique expression of a people, Herder opposed both the concept and the use of a "common" language, such as French, and "universal" institutions, such as those imposed on Europe by Napoleon. These, he believed, were forms of tyranny over the individuality of a people. Herder's writings led to a broad revival of interest in history and philosophy. Although initially directed toward the identification of German origins, such work soon expanded to embrace other world cultures as well. Eventually the ability of the Romantic imagination to be at home in any age or culture spurred the study of non-Western religion, comparative literature, and philology.

This lithograph of G. W. F. Hegel shows him attired in the robes of a university professor. Hegel was the most important philosopher of history in the Romantic period. [Bildarchiv Preussischer Kulturbesitz]

725

THE AGE OF
NAPOLEON
AND THE
TRIUMPH OF
ROMANTICISM

Hegel Explains the Role of Great Men in History

Hegel believed that behind the development of human history from one period to the next lay the mind and purpose of what he termed the "World Spirit," a concept somewhat resembling the Christian God. Hegel thought particular heroes from the past (such as Caesar) and in the present (such as Napoleon) were the unconscious instruments of that Spirit. In this passage from his lectures on the philosophy of history Hegel explained how these heroes could change the course of history. All of these concepts are characteristic of the Romantic belief that human beings and human history are always intimately connected with larger, spiritual forces at work in the world.

Such are all great historical men—whose own particular aims involve those large issues which are the will of the World-Spirit. They may be called Heroes, inasmuch as they have derived their purposes and their vocation, not from the calm, regular course of things, sanctioned by the existing order, but from a concealed fount—one which has not attained to phenomenal, present existence—from that inner Spirit, still hidden beneath the surface, which, impinging on the outer world as on a shell, bursts it in pieces, because it is another kernel than that which belonged to the shell in question. They are men, therefore, who appear to draw the impulse of their life from themselves; and whose deeds have produced a condition of things and a complex of historical relations which appear to be only *their* interest, and *their* work.

Such individuals had no consciousness of the general Idea they were unfolding, while prosecuting those aims of theirs; on the contrary, they were practical, political men. But at the same time they were thinking men, who had an insight into the requirements of the time—*what was ripe for development*. This was the very Truth for their age, for their world; the species next in order, so to speak, and which was already formed in the womb of time. It was theirs to know this nascent principle; the necessary, directly sequent step in progress, which their world was to take; to make this their aim, and to expend their energy in promoting it. World-historical men—the Heroes of an epoch—must, therefore, be recognized as its clear-sighted ones; *their* deeds, *their* words are the best of that time.

G. W. F. Hegel, The Philosophy of History, *trans. by J. Sibree (New York: Dover, 1956), pp. 30–31.*

Hegel and History

Perhaps the most important person to write about history during the Romantic period was the German Georg Wilhelm Friedrich Hegel (1770–1831). He is one of the most difficult philosophers in the history of Western civilization, and he is also one of the most important.

Hegel believed that ideas develop in an evolutionary fashion that involves conflict. At any given time a predominant set of ideas, which

he termed the *thesis*, holds sway. They are challenged by other conflicting ideas, which he termed the *antithesis*. As these patterns of thought clash, there emerges a *synthesis*, which eventually becomes the new thesis. Then the process begins all over again. Periods of world history receive their character from the patterns of thought predominating during them.

A number of important philosophical conclusions followed from this analysis. One of the most significant was the belief that all periods of history have been of almost equal value because each was, by definition, necessary to the achievements of those that came later. Also all cultures are valuable because each contributes to the necessary clash of values and ideas that allows humankind to develop. Hegel discussed these concepts in *The Phenomenology of Mind* (1806), *Lectures on the Philosophy of History* (1822–1831), and numerous other works, many of which were published only after his death. During his lifetime his ideas became widely known through his university lectures at Berlin.

These various Romantic ideas made a major contribution to the emergence of nationalism, which proved to be one of the strongest motivating forces of the nineteenth and twentieth centuries. The writers of the Enlightenment had generally championed a cosmopolitan outlook on the world. But the emphasis of the Romantic thinkers was on the individuality and worth of each separate people and culture. The factors that helped to define a people or a nation were common language, common history, a homeland that possessed historical associations, and common customs. This cultural nationalism gradually became transformed into a political creed. It came to be widely believed that every people, ethnic group, or nation should constitute a separate political entity, and that only when it so existed could the nation be secure in its own character.

The example of France under the revolutionary government and then Napoleon had demonstrated the power of nationhood. Other peoples came to desire similar strength and confidence. Napoleon's toppling of ancient political structures, such as the Holy Roman Empire, demonstrated the need for new political organization in Europe. By 1815 these were the aspirations of only a few Europeans, but as time passed, such yearnings came to be shared by scores of peoples from Ireland to the Ukraine. The Congress of Vienna could ignore such feelings, but for the rest of the nineteenth century, statesmen had to confront the growing reality of their power.

Suggested Readings

M. H. ABRAMS, *The Mirror and the Lamp: Romantic Theory and the Critical Tradition* (1958). A standard text on Romantic literary theory that looks at English Romanticism in the context of German Romantic idealism.

M. H. ABRAMS, *Natural Supernaturalism: Tradition and Revolution in Romantic Literature* (1971). A brilliant survey of Romanticism across west European literature.

J. S. ALLEN, *Popular French Romanticism: Authors, Readers, and Books in the Nineteenth Century* (1981). Relates Romanticism to popular culture.

L. BERGERON, *France Under Napoleon* (1981). An in-depth examination of Napoleonic administration.

J. F. BERNARD, *Talleyrand: A Biography* (1973). A useful account.

H. BLOOM, *The Visionary Company*, rev. ed. (1971). A standard reading of the major English Romantic poetic texts.

E. CASSIRER, *Kant's Life and Thought* (1981). A brilliant work by one of the major philosophers of this century.

D. G. CHANDLER, *The Campaigns of Napoleon* (New York, 1966). A good military study.

D. G. CHARLTON, *New Images of the Natural in France* (1984). An examination of the changing attitude toward nature in France during the Romantic era.

K. CLARK, *The Romantic Rebellion* (1973). A useful discussion that combines both art and literature.

O. CONNELLY, *Napoleon's Satellite Kingdoms* (1965). The rule of Napoleon and his family in Europe.

A. D. CULLER, *The Victorian Mirror of History* (1985). Studies in the writing of the nineteenth century with emphasis on Romantic influences.

H. C. DEUTSCH, *The Genesis of Napoleon's Imperialism, 1801–1805* (1938). Basic for foreign policy.

J. ENGELL, *The Creative Imagination: Enlightenment to Romanticism* (1981). An important book on the role of the imagination in Romantic literary theory.

M. GLOVER, *The Peninsular War, 1807–1814: A Concise Military History* (1974). An interesting account of the military campaign that so drained Napoleon's resources in western Europe.

F. W. J. HEMMINGS, *Culture and Society in France: 1789–1848* (1987). Discusses French romantic literature, theater, and art.

H. HONOUR, *Romanticism* (1979). The best introduction to the subject in terms of the fine arts.

H. KISSINGER, *A World Restored: Metternich, Castlereagh and the Problems of Peace, 1812–1822*

727

THE AGE O
NAPOLEON
AND THE
TRIUMPH O
ROMANTICIS

(1957). A provocative study by an author who became an American Secretary of State.

S. KÖRNER, *Kant* (1955). A very clear introduction to a difficult thinker.

M. LeBRIS, *Romantics and Romanticism* (1981). A lavishly illustrated work that relates politics and Romantic art.

G. LEFEBVRE, *Napoleon*, 2 vols., trans. by H. Stockhold, (1969). The fullest and finest biography.

F. MARKHAM, *Napoleon and the Awakening of Europe* (1954). Emphasizes the growth of nationalism.

F. MARKHAM, *Napoleon* (1963). A good biography strong on military questions.

H. NICOLSON, *The Congress of Vienna* (1946). A good, readable account.

R. PLANT, *Hegel: An Introduction* (1983). Emphasis on his political thought.

Z. A. PELCZYNSKI, *The State and Civil Society: Studies in Hegel's Political Philosophy* (1984). An important series of essays.

R. PORTER AND M. TEICH, (Ed.), *Romanticism in National Context* (1988). Essays on the phenomenon of Romanticism in the major European nations.

S. PRAWER (Ed.), *The Romantic Period in Germany* (1970). Contributions covering all facets of the movement.

B. M. G. REARDON, *Religion in the Age of Romanticism: Studies in Early Nineteenth-Century Thought* (1985). The best recent introduction to this important subject.

S. B. SMITH, *Hegel's Critique of Liberalism: Rights in Context* (1989). An excellent introduction to Hegelian political thought.

J. L. TALMON, *Romanticism and Revolt: Europe, 1815–1848* (1967). An effort to sketch the Romantic movements and relate them to one another and to the larger political history of the period.

C. TAYLOR, *Hegel* (1975). The best one-volume introduction.

J. M. THOMPSON, *Napoleon Bonaparte: His Rise and Fall* (1952). A sound biography.

J. E. TOEWS, *Hegelianism: The Path Toward Dialectical Humanism, 1805–1841* (1980). A brilliant treatment of German philosophy after Hegel.

B. YACK, *The Longing for Total Revolution: Philosophic Sources of Social Discontent from Rousseau to Marx and Nietzsche* (1986). A major exploration of the political philosophy associated with Romanticism.

A. WALICKI, *Philosophy and Romantic Nationalism: The Case of Poland* (1982). Examines the manner in which philosophy influenced the character of Polish nationalism.

This contemporary print depicting the "Peterloo" Massacre of 1819 in Manchester,
England, was intended to evoke sympathy for political radicalism. Note that in
addition to being dedicated to Henry "Orator" Hunt, it is also dedicated to women
who supported political reform. A large number of women and children
had been present at the political rally the authorities turned into a massacre.
[The Mansell Collection.]

21

RESTORATION, REACTION, AND REFORM (1815–1832)

The defeat of Napoleon and the diplomatic settlement of the Congress of Vienna restored a conservative political and social order in Europe. The upholders of the settlement wanted to see little or no political or social change either in their own nations or in neighboring ones. The major pillars of conservatism *were legitimate monarchies, landed aristocracies, and established churches. The institutions themselves were ancient, but the self-conscious alliance of throne, land, and altar was new. Throughout the eighteenth century these groups had engaged in frequent conflict. Only the upheavals of the French Revolution*

729

and the Napoleonic era transformed them into natural, if sometimes, reluctant, allies.

These conservative forces retained their former arrogance but neither their former privileges nor their old confidence. They knew they could be toppled by the political groups that hated them. They understood that revolution in one country could spill over into another. The conservatives regarded themselves as surrounded by enemies and as standing permanently on the defensive against the forces of liberalism, nationalism, and popular sovereignty. These potential sources of unrest had to be confronted both at home and abroad.

The major critics of the conservative order were groups, usually known as liberals, *who wanted to achieve moderate political reform and establish freer economic markets. Another set of critics of the conservative order were* nationalists *who wished to see the map of Europe drawn according to the boundaries*

of nationalities or ethnic groups. These goals threatened the dominance of the aristocracies and the rule of monarchs who governed by virtue of dynastic inheritance rather than by virtue of nationality. Still another set of enemies were the nations of Latin America who wished to achieve independence of Europe as had the British colonies of North America and the French colony of Haiti.

For the first fifteen years after the Congress of Vienna the forces of conservatism were successful except for the failure of Spain to retain control of Latin America. Late in the 1820s, however, the conservative forces met stronger efforts at either reform or revolution. Thereafter, certain major liberal goals were achieved as a major revolution occurred in France in 1830 and a sweeping reform bill passed the British Parliament in 1832. During the same period, political and social change continued to be resisted in central and eastern Europe as well as in Russia.

Conservative Governments on the Domestic Scene

The course of nineteenth-century history is frequently associated with the emergence of the liberal, national state and industrial society. But the staying power of the restored conservative institutions, especially in Great Britain and eastern Europe, is an equally and perhaps even more striking feature of the century. Actually not until World War I did their power and pervasive influence come to an end.

The more theoretical political and religious ideas of the conservative classes were associated with Romantic thinkers, such as Burke and Hegel. Conservatives shared other, less formal attitudes forged by the revolutionary experience. The fate of Louis XVI convinced most monarchs that they could trust only aristocratic governments or governments of aristocrats in alliance with the very wealthiest middle-class and professional people. The European aristocracies believed that their property and influence would rarely be safe under any form of genuinely representative government. All conservatives spurned the idea of a written constitution unless they were permitted to promulgate the document themselves.

Even then, some could not be reconciled to the concept.

The churches were equally apprehensive of popular movements except their own revivals. The ecclesiastical leaders throughout the Continent regarded themselves as entrusted with the educational task of supporting the social and political status quo. They also feared and hated most of the ideas associated with the Enlightenment because those rational concepts and reformist writings enshrined the critical spirit and undermined revealed religion. Conservative Europeans came to regard as *liberal* any idea or institution that they opposed. However, as will be seen, that word actually had rather different meanings in different countries.

Alexander I and Russian Autocracy

The pursuit of Napoleon's army across Europe after the burning of Moscow created a new image of vast Russian power. The image remained until the Russian defeat in the Crimean War (1854–1856). In Vienna Tsar Alexander I had played a more important personal role than any other participating monarch.

Both in those negotiations and in his governance of Russia, Alexander was and has remained a puzzling figure. He was torn between an intellectual attraction to the doctrines of the Enlightenment and reform and a very pragmatic adherence to traditional autocracy.

EARLY INTEREST IN REFORM Alexander I came to the Russian throne in 1801 after the murder of his father, Tsar Paul. The son had condoned the palace revolution. Paul had been an unstable person who ruled in an arbitrary and unpredictable manner. Paul had attempted to reverse the policies of his mother, Catherine the Great, whom he loathed. He attacked the privileges of the nobility. The result was a *coup d' état* led by court nobles and the army.

Tsar Alexander I (1802–1825). A mild reformer when he succeeded to the throne, Alexander became increasingly reactionary after 1815. [Royal Library, Windsor Castle. By gracious permission of HM the Queen]

Alexander I intended to return to the policies of his grandmother and to consider at least the possibility of political and administrative change in Russia. He confirmed the privileges of the nobles and abolished the security police. He was well educated in the ideas of the Enlightenment. In 1801, he appointed a government reform committee composed of liberal friends. Little came from the reformist plans submitted by this group. By 1803 Alexander had declared that no group had a right to challenge the legality of the decrees of the tsar.

Once Alexander had led Russia into war against Napoleon, even the mild reformist tendencies began to wane. In 1807 the security police were, in effect, reestablished. Yet the military reverses of the campaign and his personal admiration of Napoleon's administrative genius convinced the tsar that a reconstruction of the Russian government was necessary.

In 1808 he turned to Michael Speransky (1772–1839) to guide his thinking on matters of administrative reform. This enlightened minister, who held a series of government appointments, drew up a plan for constitutional government that included an elected legislative body. He even dared talk about an eventual, gradual abolition of serfdom. The tsar could not support such bold departures. Speransky had to be satisfied with a restructuring of the ministries and the bureaucracy. In 1812 he introduced new, progressive taxes on landed income. Each of these policies alienated the nobility. In March 1812 Alexander, fearing the discontent among the nobles, dismissed his once-trusted minister. Again reform came to a close almost without having begun.

AUTOCRACY REASSERTED Thereafter, Alexander, though occasionally using liberal rhetoric, became an increasingly hardened conservative. For the renewed struggle against Napoleon, he needed the support of his nobility and the army. Also, during this post-Speransky period, he was deeply drawn to those mystical religious feelings that lay behind his project for forming the Holy Alliance in 1815. The tsar came to regard the Enlightenment, the French Revolution, and Napoleon as one vast attack on Christianity. His new chief adviser was Alexis Arakcheiev (1769–1834), a general and a political opponent of Speransky. This reactionary military figure became the most powerful person in the country except for

Alexander himself. Together they pursued a consistently conservative policy. By the early 1820s, the tsar, whose early years had seemed to hold out the promise of possible reform, had become a leading symbol of conservative reaction.

Liberalism and Nationalism Resisted in Austria and the Germanies

The early nineteenth-century statesman who more than any other epitomized conservatism was the Austrian Prince Metternich. This devoted servant of the Habsburg emperor had been, along with Castlereagh, the chief architect of the Vienna settlement. It was he who seemed to exercise chief control over the forces of the European reaction. The conservative foreign and domestic policy that he forged for Austria stemmed from the pragmatic needs of that peculiar state rather than from ideology.

DYNASTIC INTEGRITY IN AUSTRIA The Austrian government could make no serious compromises with the new political forces in Europe. To no other country were the programs of liberalism and nationalism potentially more dangerous. The Habsburg domains were peopled with Germans and Hungarians, as well as Poles and other nationalities or ethnic groups. Through puppet governments Austria also dominated the Italian peninsula.

Pursuit of dynastic integrity required Austrian domination of the newly formed German Confederation to prevent the formation of a German national state that might absorb the heart of the empire and exclude the other realms governed by the Habsburgs. So far as Metternich and other officials were concerned, the recognition of the political rights and aspirations of any of the various national groups would mean the probable dissolution of the empire. If Austria permitted representative government, Metternich feared that the national groups would fight their battles internally at the probable cost of Austrian international influence.

During the immediate postwar years Metternich's primary concern lay with Germany. The Congress of Vienna had created the German Confederation to replace the defunct

Holy Roman Empire. It consisted of thirty-nine states under Austrian leadership. Each state remained more or less autonomous, but Austria was determined to prevent any movement toward constitutionalism in as many of them as possible.

DEFEAT OF PRUSSIAN REFORM The majority victory for this holding policy came in Prussia. In 1815 Frederick William III (1797–1840), during the exhilaration after the War of Liberation, as Germans termed the last part of their conflict with Napoleon, had promised some mode of constitutional government. However, he immediately stalled on keeping his pledge. In 1817 he formally reneged and created a new Council of State, which did bring about more efficient administration but which was not a constitutional mode of government.

In 1819 the king moved further away from thoughts of reform. After a major disagreement over the organization of the army, his chief reform-minded ministers resigned. The monarch replaced them with hardened conservatives. On their advice in 1823 Frederick William III established eight provincial estates, or diets. They were dominated by the *Junkers* and exercised only an advisory function. The old alliance between the Prussian monarchy, the army, and the landholders stood reestablished. This conservative alliance opposed German nationalist aspirations that seemed to threaten the social and political order.

STUDENT NATIONALISM AND THE CARLSBAD DECREES Three south German states—Baden, Bavaria, and Württemberg—had received constitutions after 1815 as their monarchs attempted to secure wider political support. Each of these constitutions was a very limited document that refused to recognize popular sovereignty and that defined political rights as the gift of the monarch. But the nationalist and liberal aspirations raised by the collective national experience of defeating the French armies remained alive in the hearts and minds of many young Germans.

The most important of these groups was the university students. They had grown up during the days of the reforms of Stein and Hardenburg and the initial circulation of the writings of Fichte and other German nationalists. Many of them had fought Napoleon. When

Prince Clemens von Metternich (1773–1859) was the statesman who epitomized nineteenth-century conservatism. [Royal Library, Windsor Castle. By gracious permission of HM the Queen]

they went to the universities, they continued to dream their dream of a united Germany. They formed *Burschenschaften*, or student associations. Like student groups today, these clubs served numerous social functions—one of them was severing old provincial loyalties and replacing them with loyalty to the concept of a united German state.

In 1817 in Jena one such student club organized a large celebration of the fourth anniversary of the battle of Leipzig and of the tercentenary of Luther's Ninety-five Theses. There were bonfires, songs, and processions as more than five hundred people gathered for the festivities. The event made German rulers uneasy, for it was known that some republicans were involved with the student clubs. Two years later, in March 1819, a young man named Karl Sand, who was a *Burschenschaft* member, assassinated the conservative dramatist August von Kotzebue. Sand, who was tried, condemned, and publicly executed, became a martyr in the eyes of some nationalists. Although the assassin had acted alone, Metternich decided to use the incident to suppress the student clubs and other potential institutions of liberalism.

Metternich Criticizes the Political Activity of the Middle Class

In 1820 the emperor of Austria asked Prince Klemens von Metternich to compose a political "confession of faith" to be sent to Alexander I of Russia. In the course of that document Metternich described what he regarded as the political evil of middle-class liberals. He argued that liberals sought to undermine the natural loyalty of subjects to monarchs. This action stemmed from the intellectual pride or presumption of these liberals, who had adopted many of the ideas of the Enlightenment. Metternich also pointed to the role of a free press in causing political unrest. Metternich himself did much to foster extensive press censorship in eastern Europe.

The evil exists and it is enormous. We do not think we can better define it and its cause at all times and in all places than we have already done by the word "presumption," that inseparable companion of the half-educated, that spring of an unmeasured ambition, and yet easy to satisfy in times of trouble and confusion.

It is principally the middle classes of society which this moral gangrene has affected, and it is only among them that the heads of the party [working for liberal reform] are found. . . .

Europe thus presents itself to the impartial observer under an aspect at the same time deplorable and peculiar. We find everywhere the people praying for the maintenance of peace and tranquility, faithful to God and their Princes, remaining proof against the efforts and seductions of the factious who call themselves friends of the people and who wish to lead them to an agitation which the people themselves do not desire!

The Governments, having lost their balance, are frightened, intimidated, and thrown into confusion by the cries of the intermediary class of society, which placed between Kings and their subjects, breaks the sceptre of the monarch, and usurps the cry of the people. . . .

We see this intermediary class abandon itself with a blind fury and animosity which proves much more of its own fears than any confidence in the success of its enterprises, to all the means which seem proper to assuage its thirst for power, applying itself to the task of persuading Kings that their rights are confined to sitting upon a throne, while those of the people are to govern, and to attack all that centuries have bequeathed as holy and worthy of man's respect—denying, in fact, the value of the past, and declaring themselves the masters of the future. . . . It takes possession of the press, and employs it to promote impiety, disobedience to the laws of religion and the State, and goes so far as to preach murder as a duty for those who desire what is good. . . .

If the same elements of destruction which are now throwing society into convulsion have existed in all ages . . . yet ours, by the single fact of the liberty of the press, possesses more than any preceding age the means of contact, seduction, and attraction whereby to act on these different classes of men.

Prince Richard Metternich (Ed.), Memoirs of Prince Metternich, 1815–1829, *Vol. 5 (New York: Charles Scribner's, 1881), pp. 465–466, 468, 472–473.*

In July 1819 Metternich persuaded representatives of the major German states to issue the Carlsbad Decrees, which dissolved the *Burschenschaften*. The decrees also provided for university inspectors and press censors. The next year the German Confederation promulgated the Final Act, which limited the subjects that might be discussed in the constitutional chambers of Bavaria, Württemberg, and Baden. The measure also asserted the right of the monarchs to resist demands of constitutionalists. Thereafter, for many years the secret police of the various German states harassed potential dissidents. In the opinion of the princes these included almost anyone who sought even moderate social or political change.

Repression in Great Britain

The years 1819 and 1820 marked a high tide for conservative influence and repression in western as well as eastern Europe. After 1815 Great Britain experienced two years of poor harvests. There was also considerable industrial unemployment, to which discharged sailors and soldiers added their numbers.

LORD LIVERPOOL'S MINISTRY AND POPULAR UNREST The Tory ministry of Lord Liverpool (1770–1828) was unprepared to deal with these problems of postwar dislocation. Instead, it sought to protect the interests of the landed and other wealthy classes. In 1815 Parliament passed a Corn Law to maintain high prices for domestically produced grain through import duties on foreign grain. The next year Parliament abolished the income tax paid by the wealthy and replaced it with excise or sales taxes on consumer goods paid by both the wealthy and the poor. These laws represented a continuation of previous legislation through which the British ruling class had abandoned much of its traditional role of paternalistic protector of the poor.

In 1799 Parliament had passed the Combination Acts forbidding workers' organizations or unions. During the war, wage protection had been removed. The taxpaying classes grumbled about supporting the poor law that provided public relief for those destitute or without work; many people called for its abolition.

In light of these policies and the postwar economic downturn, it is hardly surprising that the lower social orders began to doubt the wisdom of their rulers and to call for a reform of the political system. Mass meetings calling for the reform of Parliament were held. Reform clubs were organized. Radical newspapers, such as William Cobbett's *Political Registrar*, demanded political change. In the hungry, restive agricultural and industrial workers the government could see only images of continental sans-culotte crowds ready to hang aristocrats from the nearest lamppost. Government ministers regarded radical leaders, such as Cobbett (1763–1835), Major John Cartwright (1740–1824), and Henry 'Orator' Hunt (1773–1835), as demagogues who were seducing the people away from allegiance to their natural leaders.

The answer of the government to the discontent was repression. In December 1816 a very

This caricature depicts George IV (1820–1830) as a self-indulgent voluptuary. Although a discerning patron of the arts, George was extremely unpopular both as Prince of Wales and as king. His extravagant, dissolute way of life cast the monarchy itself into disrepute. [The Mansell Collection]

unruly mass meeting took place at Spa Fields near London. This disturbance provided an excuse to pass the Coercion Act of March 1817. These measures temporarily suspended habeas corpus and extended existing laws against seditious gatherings.

"PETERLOO" AND THE SIX ACTS

This initial repression, accompanied by improved harvests, brought calm for a time to the political landscape. However, by 1819 the people were restive again. Throughout the industrial north a large number of well-organized mass meetings were held to demand the reform of Parliament. Major radical leaders gave speeches to thousands of people. The radical reform campaign culminated on August 16, 1819, with a meeting in Manchester at Saint Peter's Fields. Royal troops and the local militia were on hand to ensure order. Just as the speeches were about to begin, a local magistrate ordered the militia to move into the audience. The result was panic and death. At least eleven people in the crowd were killed; scores were injured. The event became known as the "Peterloo" Massacre through a contemptuous comparison with the victory at Waterloo.

Peterloo had been the act of the local Manchester officials. However, the Liverpool ministry felt that those officials must be supported. The Cabinet also decided to act once and for all to end these troubles. Most of the radical leaders were arrested and thus taken out of circulation. In December 1819, a few months after the German Carlsbad Decrees, Parliament passed a series of laws called the Six Acts. These (1) forbade large unauthorized, public meetings, (2) raised the fines for seditious libel, (3) speeded up the trials of political agitators, (4) increased newspaper taxes, (5) prohibited the training of armed groups, and (6) allowed local officials to search homes in certain disturbed counties. In effect, the Six Acts attempted to remove the instruments of agitation from the hands of radical leaders and to provide the authorities with new powers.

The Cato Street conspirators were arrested in 1820. This half-baked plot was used by the government as a pretext for further repression. [The Mansell Collection]

Two months after the passage of the Six Acts, the Cato Street Conspiracy was unearthed. Under the guidance of a possibly demented figure named Thistlewood, a group of extreme radicals had plotted to blow up the entire British Cabinet. The plot was foiled. The leaders were arrested and tried, and four of them were executed. The conspiracy had been little more than a half-baked plot, but it provided new support for repression by the government. More important, the conspiracy helped further to discredit the movement for parliamentary reform.

Bourbon Restoration in France

The abdication of Napoleon in 1814 opened the way for a restoration of Bourbon rule in the homeland of the great revolution. The new king was the former count of Provence and a brother of Louis XVI. The son of the executed monarch had died in prison. Royalists had regarded the dead boy as Louis XVII, and so his uncle became Louis XVIII (1814–1824). This fat, awkward man had become a political realist during his more than twenty years of exile. He understood that he could not govern if he attempted to turn back the clock. France had undergone too many irreversible changes. Consequently, Louis XVIII agreed to become a constitutional monarch, but under a constitution of his own making.

THE CHARTER The constitution of the French restoration was the Charter. It provided for a hereditary monarchy and a bicameral leg-

Unlike his more reactionary supporters, who were said to be "more royalist than the king," Louis XVIII (1814–1824) was a political realist and agreed to reign as a constitutional monarch. [Library of Congress]

islature. The monarch appointed the upper house; the lower house, the Chamber of Deputies, was elected according to a very narrow franchise that upheld a high property qualification. The Charter guaranteed most of the rights enumerated by the Declaration of the Rights of Man and Citizen. There was to be religious toleration, but Roman Catholicism was designated as the official religion of the nation. Most important for thousands of the French at various stations of life who had profited from the revolution, the Charter promised not to disturb the property changes brought about by the confiscation and sale of aristocratic and Church land. In this manner Louis XVIII attempted to reconcile to his restored regime those classes that had benefited from the revolution.

ULTRAROYALISM This moderate spirit did not penetrate deeply into the ranks of royalist supporters. Their families had suffered much at the hands of the revolution. They now demanded their revenge. The king's brother, the count of Artois (1757–1836), served as a rallying point for those people who were more royalist than the monarch. In the months after

Napoleon's final defeat at Waterloo, royalists in the south and west carried out a White Terror against former revolutionaries and supporters of the deposed emperor. The king could do little or nothing to halt this bloodbath of royalist revenge. Similar extreme royalist sentiment existed in the Chamber of Deputies. The ultraroyalist majority elected in 1816 proved so dangerously reactionary that the king soon dissolved the chamber. The majority returned by the second election were more moderate.

Under the ministry of the duke of Richelieu the country paid off the war indemnity to the allies, and the occupation troops withdrew in 1818. Yet royalist discontent remained. Louis XVIII attempted to pursue a policy of mild accommodation with liberals through his minister Decazes, who took office in 1818. But the king's younger brother, the count of Artois, pushed for reactionary departures.

This give and take might have continued for some time. However, in February 1820 the duke of Berri, son of Artois and heir to the throne after his father, was murdered by a lone assassin. The ultraroyalists persuaded Louis XVIII that the murder was the result of Decazes' cooperation with liberal politicians. The duke of Richelieu was recalled. The electoral laws were revised to give wealthy electors two votes. Press censorship was imposed. Persons suspected of dangerous political activity could be easily arrested. By 1821 the direction of secondary education in France had been put under the control of the Roman Catholic bishops.

All of these actions revealed the basic contradiction of the French restoration. There had been no intention of creating a genuinely parliamentary system. The king rather than the Chamber of Deputies chose the ministers. The government constantly tinkered with the electoral apparatus to disqualify opponents from voting. By the early 1820s the veneer of constitutionalism had worn away. Liberals were being driven out of legal political life and into near-illegal activity.

The Conservative International Order

At the Congress of Vienna, the major powers— Russia, Austria, Prussia, and Great Britain— had agreed to consult with each other from

THE PERIOD OF POLITICAL REACTION

1812	Alexander I of Russia dismisses Speransky
1814	Louis XVIII restored in France under the Charter
1815	Holy Alliance formed among Russia, Austria, and Prussia
1815	Quadruple Alliance renewed among Russia, Austria, Prussia, and Britain
1817	Wartburg Festival at Jena
1818	Congress of Aix-la-Chapelle
1819	(March 23) Assassination of Kotzebue
1819	(July) Carlsbad Decrees
1819	(August 16) Peterloo Massacre
1819	(December) Six Acts passed in Great Britain
1820	(January) Spanish revolution
1820	(February 13) Assassination of the Duke of Berri
1820	(October) Congress of Troppau
1821	(January) Congress of Laibach
1821	(February) Greek revolution
1822	Congress of Verona
1823	France intervenes to crush the Spanish revolution

time to time on matters affecting Europe as a whole. The vehicle for this consultation was a series of postwar congresses. Later, as differences arose among the powers, the consultations became more informal. This mode of working out issues of foreign policy was known as the *Concept of Europe.* It meant that no one nation could take a major action in international affairs without the assent of the others. The major goal of the Concert of Europe was to maintain the balance of power against new French aggression and against the military might of Russia. The Concert of Europe continued to function on large and small issues until the third quarter of the century.

The Congress System

The years that witnessed the domestic conservative consolidation of power also saw a generally successful functioning of the congress system. The first congress occurred in 1818 at Aix-la-Chapelle. As a result of this congress the four major powers removed their troops from France, which had paid its war reparations, and readmitted that nation to good standing among European nations. Despite unanimity on these decisions, problems did arise during the conference. Tsar Alexander I, displaying his full reactionary colors, suggested that the Quadruple Alliance agree to uphold the borders and the existing governments of all European countries. Castlereagh, representing Britain, flatly rejected the proposal. He contended that the Quadruple Alliance was intended only to prevent future French aggression. These disagreements appeared somewhat academic until a series of revolutions began in southern Europe in 1820.

The Spanish Revolution of 1820

The Spanish rebelled against Ferdinand VII (1814–1833). When placed on his throne at the time of Napoleon's downfall, this Bourbon monarch had promised to govern according to a written constitution. Once securely in power, Ferdinand simply ignored that pledge. He dissolved the parliament (the Cortes) and ruled alone. In 1820 a group of army officers about to be sent to suppress revolution in Spain's Latin American colonies rebelled. In March Ferdinand once again announced that

he would abide by the provisions of the constitution. For the time being, the revolution had succeeded.

Almost at the same time, in July 1820, the revolutionary spirit erupted in Naples, where the king of the Two Sicilies very quickly accepted a constitution. There were other, lesser revolts in Italy, but none of them succeeded.

These events frightened the ever-nervous Metternich. Italian disturbances were especially troubling to him. Austria hoped to dominate the peninsula to provide a buffer against the spread of revolution on its own southern flank. The other powers were divided on the best course of action. Britain opposed joint intervention in either Italy or Spain. Metternich turned to Prussia and Russia for support. The three eastern powers, along with unofficial delegations from Britain and France, met at the Congress of Troppau in late October 1820. The members of the Holy Alliance, led by Alexander of Russia, issued the Protocol of Troppau. This declaration asserted that stable governments might intervene to restore order in countries experiencing revolution. Yet even Russia hesitated to authorize Austrian intervention in Italian affairs. That decision was finally reached in January 1821 at the Congress of Laibach. Shortly thereafter Austrian troops marched into Naples and restored the king of the Two Sicilies to unconstitutional government.

The final postwar congress took place in October 1822 at Verona. Its primary purpose was to resolve the situation in Spain. Once again Britain balked at joint action. Shortly before the meeting Castlereagh had committed suicide. George Canning (1770–1827), the new foreign minister, was much less sympathetic to Metternich's goals. At Verona, Britain, in effect, withdrew from continental affairs. Austria, Prussia, and Russia agreed to support French intervention in Spain. In April 1823 the French army crossed the Pyrenees and within a few months suppressed the Spanish revolution. Liberals and revolutionaries were tortured, executed, and driven from the country. The intervention in Spain in 1823 was one of the most bloody examples of reactionary politics during the entire century.

There was a second diplomatic result of the Congress of Verona and the Spanish intervention. George Canning was much more interested in the fate of British commerce and trade than Castlereagh had been. Consequently, Canning sought to prevent the politics of European reaction from being extended to the Spanish colonies then revolting in Latin America (to be discussed later). He intended to use those South American revolutions as the occasion for British penetration of the old Spanish trading monopoly in that area. To that end the British foreign minister supported the American Monroe Doctrine in 1823, prohibiting further colonization and intervention by European powers in the Americas. Britain soon recognized the Spanish colonies as independent states. Through the rest of the century British commercial interests dominated Latin America. In this fashion Canning may be said

to have brought to a successful conclusion the War of Jenkins' Ear (1739).

The Greek Revolution of 1821

While the powers were plotting the new restorations in Italy and Spain, a third Mediterranean revolt had erupted in Greece. The Greek revolution became one of the most famous of the century because it attracted the support and participation of many illustrious literary figures. Liberals throughout Europe, who were seeing their own hopes crushed at home, imagined that the ancient Greek democracy was being reborn. Lord Byron went to fight and in

Greece Dying on the Ruins of Missolonghi, *by Eugene Delacroix (1799–1863), illustrates how small nationalities were sentimentalized by Romantic artists in Western Europe. Greece is personified as a beautiful, defenceless woman appealing for help against the triumphant Turk pictured in the background. The painting was inspired by the fall of the fortress of Missolonghi in southern Greece to the Turks. Lord Byron died of typhus during the siege. [Giraudon]*

1824 died in the cause of Greek liberty. Philhe-llenic societies were founded in nearly every major country.

The Greeks were rebelling against the Otto-man Empire. The weakness of that empire troubled Europe for the entire century and raised what was known as the *eastern question.* The residue of the problem remains alive today in the tensions between Greece and Tur-key and in the instability in the Middle East.

Most of the major powers were interested in what happened to the Ottoman holdings. Rus-sia and Austria coveted land in the Balkans. France and Britain were concerned with the empire's commerce and with control of key naval positions in the eastern Mediterranean. There was also the issue of protection of Chris-tian access to the shrines in the Holy Land.

These conflicting interests, as well as mu-tual distrust, prevented any direct intervention in Greek affairs for several years. In 1827 a joint British, French, and Russian fleet sup-ported the Greek revolt. The fleet was enforc-ing the Treaty of London of 1827, in which those powers demanded Turkish recognition of Greek independence. They had decided that their domestic security would not be endan-gered by an independent Greek State; and in fact their several foreign-policy concerns in the area would prosper from such a new nation. In 1828 Russia sent troops against the Ottoman holdings in what is today Romania. By the treaty of Adrianople of 1829, Russia gained ef-fective control of that territory. The treaty fur-ther stipulated that the Turks would allow Britain, France, and Russia to decide the future of Greece.

In 1830 Greece was declared an independent kingdom by a second Treaty of London. Two years later Otto I (1832–1862), the son of the king of Bavaria, was chosen as the first king of the new Greek royal dynasty. The Greek revolt was the only successful national revolution of the first quarter of the century. Elsewhere, the conservative powers had defeated the attempts at revolution.

The Wars of Independence in Latin America

The wars of the French Revolution, and more particularly those of Napoleon, sparked move-ments for independence from European domi-

Toussaint L'Ouverture (1743–1803) began the re-volt that led to Haitian independence in 1804. [Cul-ver Pictures]

nation throughout Latin America. In less than two decades, between 1804 and 1824, France was driven from Haiti, Portugal lost control of Brazil, and Spain lost control of all but Cuba and Puerto Rico. Three centuries of Iberian colonial government over the South American continent came to an end.

Haiti achieved independence in 1804 follow-ing a slave revolt that began in 1794, led by Toussaint L'Ouverture and Jean-Jacques Des-salines. Such a revolution, involving the popu-lar uprising of a repressed social group, was the great exception in the Latin American drive for liberty from European masters. Generally speaking, on the South American continent, the creole elite, composed of Spanish mer-chants, landowners, and professional persons born in America, led the movements against Spain and Portugal. Very few Indians, blacks, people of mixed race, or slaves became in-volved or benefited from the end of Iberian rule. Indeed, the example of the Haitian slave revolt haunted the creoles. They were determined that any drive for political independence from Spain and Portugal should not cause social disruption or the loss of their existing social and economic privileges.

CREOLE DISCONTENT There were several sources of creole discontent with Spanish colonial government. (The Brazilian situation will be discussed separately.) Some of the creole complaints against Spain resembled those of the American colonists against Great Britain. Latin American merchants wanted to trade more freely within the region and throughout the North American and European markets. They wanted commercial regulations that would benefit them rather than Spain. The late-eighteenth-century Bourbon imperial reforms, through liberating trade, had hurt Latin American exports. Creoles also feared that Spanish imperial regulations might attempt to make changes in landholding, access to army officer commissions, local government, and the treatment of slaves and Indians. The creoles deeply resented the favors granted to persons born in Spain and the clear discrimination against themselves in matters of appointments and patronage in the colonial government, Church, and army.

Creole leaders had read the Enlightenment *philosophes* and regarded their reforms as potentially beneficial to the region. They were also well aware of the events and the political philosophy of the American Revolution. But something more than reform programs and revolutionary example was required to transform creole discontent into revolt against the Spanish government. That transforming event occurred in Europe when Napoleon toppled the Portuguese monarchy in 1807 and the Spanish government in 1808 and placed his own brother on those thrones. The Portuguese royal family fled to Brazil and established its government there. But the Bourbon monarchy of Spain stood, for the time being, wholly vanquished. That situation created an imperial political vacuum throughout Spanish Latin America and provided both the opportunity and the necessity for action by creole leaders.

The creole elite feared that a liberal Napoleonic monarchy in Spain would attempt to impose reforms in Latin America that would harm their economic and social interests. They also feared that a Spanish monarchy controlled by France would attempt to drain the region of the wealth and resources needed for Napoleon's wars. To protect their interests and to seize the opportunity to take over direction of their own political destiny, between 1808 and 1810 various creole *juntas*, or political committees, claimed the right to govern different regions of Latin America. Many of them quite insincerely declared that they were ruling in the name of the deposed Spanish monarch Ferdinand VII.

After the establishment of these local juntas, the Spanish would not again directly govern the continent; after ten years of politically and economically exhausting warfare, they were required to make Latin American independence permanent.

REGIONAL LIBERATORS The vast size of Latin America, its geographical barriers, and its distinct regional differences meant that there would be several different paths to independence. The first region to assert itself was the Río de la Plata, or modern Argentina. In 1810, the junta in Buenos Aires not only thrust off Spanish authority but also sent forces against both Paraguay and Uruguay in the cause of liberation from Spain and control by their own region. The armies were defeated, but Spanish control was lost in the two areas. Paraguay asserted its own independence. Uruguay was eventually absorbed by Brazil.

The Buenos Aires government was not discouraged by these early defeats and remained determined to liberate Peru, the greatest stronghold of royalist power. By 1814, José de San Martín had become the leading general of the Río de la Plata forces. He organized a disciplined army and led his forces in a daring march over the Andes Mountains. By early 1817, he had occupied Santiago in Chile, where the Chilean independence leader Bernardo O'Higgins was established as supreme dictator. From Santiago, San Martín oversaw the construction and organization of a naval force that, in 1820, he used to carry his army by sea to an assault on Peru. The next year, San Martín drove royalist forces from the city of Lima and took for himself the title of Protector of Peru.

While the army of San Martín had been liberating the southern portion of the continent, Simón Bolívar had been pursuing a similar task in the north. Bolívar had been involved in the organization of a liberating junta in Caracas,

Simón Bolívar and José de San Martín were the liberators of South America during the Wars of Independence. They eventually clashed over the future of the continent with San Martín favoring monarchical government and Bolívar favoring republics. [Both: The Granger Collection]

Venezuela, in 1810. He was a firm advocate of both independence and republican modes of government. Between 1811 and 1814, civil war took place throughout Venezuela as both royalists, on the one hand, and slaves and *llaneros* (Venezuelan cowboys), on the other, challenged the authority of the republican government. Bolívar had to go into exile first in Colombia and then in Jamaica. In 1816, with help from Haiti, he launched a new invasion against Venezuela. He first captured Bogotá, capital of New Granada (including modern Colombia, Bolivia, and Ecuador), to secure a base for the attack of Venezuela. The tactic worked. By the summer of 1821, Bolívar's forces had captured Caracas, and he had been named president.

A year later, in July 1822, the armies of Bolívar and San Martín joined as they moved to liberate Quito. At a famous meeting of the two liberators in Guayaquil, a sharp disagreement occurred about the future political structure of Latin America. San Martín believed that monarchies were required; Bolívar maintained his republicanism. Not long after the meeting, San Martín quietly retired from public life and went into exile in Europe. Meanwhile Bolívar purposely allowed the political situation in Peru to fall into confusion, and in 1823 he sent in troops to establish his control. On December 9, 1824, at the battle of Ayacucho, the Spanish royalist forces suffered a major defeat at the hands of the liberating army. The battle marked the conclusion of the Spanish effort to retain their American empire.

The drive for independence in New Spain (present-day Mexico) illustrates better than that of any other region the socially conservative outcome of the Latin American colonial revolutions. As elsewhere, a local governing junta was organized. But before it had undertaken any significant measures, a creole priest, Miguel Hidalgo y Costilla, issued a call for rebellion to the Indians in this parish. They and other repressed groups of black and mestizo urban and rural workers responded. Father Hidalgo set forth a program of social change, including hints of changes in landholding. Soon he stood at the head of a rather unorganized group of eighty thousand followers who captured several major cities and then marched on Mexico City.

Hidalgo's forces and the royalist army that opposed them committed numerous atrocities. In July 1811 the revolutionary priest was cap-

ATLANTIC

OCEAN

Rio Grande

San Antonio

MEXICO 1821

Gulf of Mexico

Mexico City

Veracruz

CUBA

HAITI 1804

PUERTO RICO

BR. HONDURAS

Guatemala

Caribbean Sea

TRINIDAD

UNITED PROVINCES OF CENTRAL AMERICA 1823-1839

Panama

Caracas

BR. GUIANA
DUTCH GUIANA
FR. GUIANA

Bogotá

GRAN COLOMBIA 1819-1830

GALAPAGOS IS.

Quito

Amazon

PACIFIC

PERU 1821

Lima

INDEFINITE BOUNDARY

EMPIRE OF BRAZIL 1822

Bahia

OCEAN

BOLIVIA 1825

Sucre

PARAGUAY 1813

Asunción

Rio de Janeiro

CHILE 1817

Santiago

URUGUAY 1828

Buenos Aires

Montevideo

UNITED PROVINCES OF LA PLATA 1816

Father Miguel Hidalgo y Costilla (d. 1811) led an unsuccessful peasant revolt in 1810–1811 that marked the beginning of the struggle for Mexican independence. [Organization of American States]

tured and executed. Leadership then fell to José María Morelos y Pavón, a mestizo priest. Far more radical then Hidalgo, he called for an end to forced labor and substantial land reforms before his execution in 1815. These five years of popular uprising that ended with Morelos' death had resulted in thousands of other fatalities.

The popular uprising and demand for fundamental social reform united all conservative political groups in Mexico whether they were creole or Spanish. These groups were unwilling to undertake any kind of reform that might cause loss of their privileges. In 1820 they found their recently achieved security challenged from an unexpected source. As already explained, the revolution in Spain had forced Ferdinand VII to accept a liberal constitution.

MAP 21-1 LATIN AMERICA IN 1830. *By 1830 Latin America had been liberated from European government. This map illustrates the early borders of the states of the region with the dates of their independence.*

Conservative Mexicans feared that the new liberal monarchy would attempt to impose liberal reforms in Mexico. Therefore, for the most conservative of reasons, they rallied to a former royalist general, Agustín de Iturbide, who in 1821 declared Mexico independent of Spain. Shortly thereafter, Iturbide was declared emperor. His own regime did not last long, but an independent Mexico governed by persons determined to resist any significant social reform had been created.

BRAZILIAN INDEPENDENCE Brazilian independence, in contrast to that of Spanish Latin America, came relatively simply and peacefully. As already noted, the Portuguese royal family took refuge in Brazil in 1807. The prince regent João addressed many of the local complaints, equivalent to those of the Spanish creoles, by measures such as the expansion of trade. In 1815, he made Brazil a kingdom, which meant that it was no longer to be regarded merely as a colony of Portugal. Then, in 1820, a revolution occurred in Portugal, and its leaders demanded João's return to Lisbon. They also demanded the return of Brazil to colonial status. João left his son Dom Pedro as regent in Brazil and encouraged him to be sympathetic to the political aspirations of the Brazilians. In September 1822 Dom Pedro embraced the cause of Brazilian independence against the recolonializing efforts of Portugal. By the end of the year, he had become emperor of an independent Brazil, which maintained that form of government until 1889.

The era of the wars of independence left Latin America liberated from direct colonial control but economically exhausted. The new republics felt themselves to be very weak and vulnerable and looked to Britain for protection and for markets and capital investment.

The most disadvantaged citizens received only the most marginal improvements as a result of independence. Caste distinctions and most racial distinctions were removed from the law, but the societies themselves remained very conscious of class and racial divisions. The Indian populations were not incorporated into political life. Landowners replaced urban colonial officials as the major governing sections in the nations. Very considerable portions of the populations of each republic felt little or no loyalty to the new regimes, which more often than not functioned almost entirely in the interests of the creole elites that had brought them into being.

Liberalism in the Early Nineteenth Century

The nineteenth century is frequently considered the great age of *isms*. Throughout the Western world, secular ideologies began to take hold of the popular and learned imagination in opposition to the political and social status quo. These included liberalism, nationalism, socialism, republicanism, and communism. One noted historian has called all such words "trouble-breeding and usually thought-obscuring terms."[1] They are just that, if one uses them as an excuse to avoid thinking or if one fails to see the variety of opinions concealed beneath each word.

It was just such intellectual laziness that characterized European conservatives as they faced their political opposition after the Napoleonic wars. They tended to call "liberal" almost anything or anyone who drew into questions their own political, social, or religious values. Moreover, the word *liberal* for twentieth-century Americans carries with it meanings and connotations that have little or nothing to do with its significance to nineteenth-century Europeans. European conservatives of the last century saw liberals as more radical than they actually were; present-day Americans think of them as being more conservative than they were.

Political Liberalism

Liberals derived their political ideas from the writers of the Enlightenment, the example of English liberties, and the so-called principles of 1789 as embodied in the French Declaration of the Rights of Man and Citizen. Liberal political figures sought to establish a framework of legal equality, religious toleration, and freedom of the press. Their general goal was a political structure that would limit the arbitrary power of the government against the persons and property of individual citizens. They generally believed that the legitimacy of government emanated from the freely given consent of the governed. The popular basis of such government was to be expressed through elected, representative, or parliamentary bodies. Most important, free government required that state or crown ministers be responsible to the representatives rather than to the monarch.

These goals may seem very limited, and they were. However, such responsible government existed in none of the major European countries in 1815. Even in Great Britain the Cabinet ministers were at least as responsible to the monarch as the House of Commons. The kinds of people who espoused these changes in government tended to be those who were excluded from the existing political processes but whose wealth and education made them feel that such exclusion was unjustified. Liberals were often academics, members of the learned professions, and people involved in the rapidly expanding commercial and manufacturing segments of the economy. They believed in and were products of the career open to talent. The existing monarchical and aristocratic regimes often failed to recognize sufficiently their new status and to provide for their economic and professional interests.

Although the liberals wanted broader political participation, they were *not* advocates of democracy. Second only to their hostility to the privileged aristocracies was their general contempt for the lower, unpropertied classes. Liberals transformed the eighteenth-century concept of aristocratic liberty into a new concept of privilege based on wealth and property rather than on birth. As the French liberal theorist Benjamin Constant (1767–1830) wrote in 1814:

> *Those whom poverty keeps in eternal dependence are no more enlightened on public affairs than children, nor are they more interested than foreigners in national prosperity, of which they do not understand the basis and of which they enjoy the advantages only indirectly. Property alone, by giving sufficient leisure, renders a man capable of exercising his political rights.*[2]

By the middle of the century this widely shared attitude meant that throughout Europe liberals had separated themselves from both the rural and the urban working class.

---

[1] *Arthur O. Lovejoy,* The Great Chain of Being: A Study in the History of an Idea *(New York: Harper Torchbooks, 1936), p. 6.*

[2] *Quoted in Frederick B. Artz,* Reaction and Revolution, 1814–1832 *(New York: Harper, 1934), p. 94.*

Liberal Economic Goals

The economic goals of the liberals also furthered that important future split in European politics and society. Here the Enlightenment and the economic thought deriving from Adam Smith set the pattern. The manufacturers of Great Britain, the landed and manufacturing

Benjamin Constant Discusses the Character of Modern Liberty

In 1819 the French liberal theorist Benjamin Constant delivered lectures on the character of ancient and modern liberty. In the passage below, he emphasized the close relationship of modern liberty to freedom of action in economic activity and to general freedom in the private lives of human beings. He then tied that desire for a free private life to the need for representative government. Modern life did not leave people enough time to make the kind of political commitment that had been required by the ancient polis. *Consequently, modern citizens turned over much of their political concern and activity to representatives. In this discussion Constant clearly set forth the desire of nineteenth-century liberals to maximize private freedom of action and to minimize areas of life in which government might interfere.*

[Modern liberty] is, for each individual, the right not to be subjected to anything but the law, not to be arrested, or detained, or put to death, or mistreated in any manner, as a result of the arbitrary will of one or several individuals. It is each man's right to express his opinions, to choose and exercise his profession, to dispose of his property and even abuse it, to come and go without obtaining permission and without having to give an account of either his motives or his itinerary. It is the right to associate with other individuals, either to confer about mutual interests or profess the cult that he and his associates prefer or simply to fill his days and hours in the manner most conforming to his inclinations and fantasies. Finally, it is each man's right to exert influence on the administration of government, either through the election of some or all of its public functionaries, or through remonstrances, petitions, and demands which authorities are more or less obliged to take into account. . . .

Just as the liberty we now require is distinct from that of the ancients, so this new liberty itself requires an organization different from that suitable for ancient liberty. For the latter, the more time and energy a man consecrated to the exercise of his political rights, the more free he believed himself to be. Given the type of liberty to which we are now susceptible, the more the exercise of our political rights leaves us time for our private interests, the more precious we find liberty to be. From this . . . stems the necessity of the representative system. The representative system is nothing else than an organization through which a nation unloads on several individuals what it cannot and will not do for itself. Poor men handle their own affairs; rich men hire managers. This is the story of ancient and modern nations. The representative system is the power of attorney given to certain men by the mass of the people who want their interests defended but who nevertheless do not always have the time to defend these interests themselves.

Benjamin Constant, Ancient and Modern Liberty, *as translated and quoted in Stephen Holmes,* Benjamin Constant and the Making of Modern Liberalism *(New Haven, Conn.: Yale University Press, 1984), pp. 66, 74.*

The Paris tolls were abolished May 1, 1791. Most European countries had a system of internal tolls by which goods entering a city or region were taxed as if they were foreign imports. Nineteenth-century liberals considered these a barrier to trade and worked for their removal. [Mary Evans Picture Library]

middle class of France, and the commercial interests of Germany and Italy sought the removal of the economic restraints associated with mercantilism. They wanted to be able to manufacture and sell goods freely. To that end they favored the general removal of internal barriers to trade and of international tariffs. Economic liberals opposed the old paternalistic legislation that established wages and labor practices by government regulation or by guild privileges. Labor was simply one more commodity to be bought and sold freely.

Liberals sought an economic structure in which people were at liberty to use whatever talents and property they possessed to enrich themselves. By this means, the liberals contended, there would be more goods and more services for everyone at lower prices. Such a system of economic liberty was to provide the basis for material progress.

Because the social and political circumstances of various countries differed, the specific programs of their liberals also differed. Great Britain already possessed institutions, such as Parliament, that could be reformed to provide more nearly representative government. The monarchy was already limited, and most individual liberties had been secured. Links between land, commerce, and industry existed. French liberals possessed a code of modern law in the Napoleonic Code. They could appeal to the widely accepted "principles of 1789." As in England, representatives of the different economic interests had worked together. Their problem was to protect the civil liberties of law, to define the respective powers of the monarch and the elected representative body, and to expand the electorate moderately while avoiding democracy.

The situation in Germany was quite different and very complex. Distinct social divisions existed between the aristocratic landowning classes, which filled the bureaucracies and officer corps, and the small middle-class commercial and industrial interests. There was little or no precedent for the latter groups' participating in the government or the army. There was no strong tradition of civil or individual liberty. From the time of Martin Luther through Kant and Hegel, freedom in Germany had meant conformity to a higher moral law rather than participation in politics.

Consequently, the mainstream of German liberalism differed from its British and French counterparts. There was much greater opposition from both the monarchs and the aristocracies. German liberals had little direct access to political influence. Most of them favored a united Germany that was to be created through the instrument of either the Austrian or the Prussian monarchy. This policy meant that they tended to stress the power of the state and the monarchy rather more than did other liberals. Once unification had been achieved, a freer social and political order might be established. The great difficulty for German liberals was the refusal of the Austrian or the Prussian monarchy to cooperate. Thus, in Germany, liberals were generally frustrated and had to remain satisfied with the lowering of internal trade barriers.

Nationalism

Nationalism proved to be the single most powerful European political ideology of the nineteenth and early twentieth centuries. As a political outlook, it was based on the concept that a nation was and should be composed of people joined naturally together by the bonds of common language, customs, culture, and history. It was directly opposed to the idea that monarchies or dynasties provided the basis for political unity. Quite often drawing upon Romantic writers, nationalists saw qualities of nationality as organic and politically and culturally as natural as the laws and structures of physical nature. Some nationalists regarded nations as the creations of God that resembled the species of organic nature.

Behind the concept of nationalism usually, though not always, lay the idea of popular sovereignty since the qualities of a people rather than of rulers determined national characters.

The liberal idea of the career open to talent could be applied to suppressed national groups who were not permitted to realize their cultural or political potential. The efficient government and administration required by expanding commerce and industry would lead to the replacement of petty dynasties of the small German and Italian states with larger political units. Moreover, nationalistic groups in one country could gain the sympathy of liberals in other nations by espousing the cause of representative government and political liberty.

The idea of nationhood based on language and ethnic bonds was not necessarily or even logically linked to liberalism. There were conservative nationalists, and there were nationalists who wished their own particular national group to dominate smaller national or ethnic groups within a particular region. This was very much the case of the Hungarian Magyars who sought to gain political control over non-Magyar peoples living within the historical boundaries of Hungary.

Nonetheless, although liberalism and nationalism were not identical, they were often compatible. Indeed, during most of the first half of the nineteenth century nationalists espoused such liberal political goals. Such was certainly the case within Germany, Italy, and much of the Austrian Empire. In Italy many of them, such as Giuseppe Mazzini, wanted to establish a republic. In Germany liberals wanted some kind of representative institutions and greater economic integration through free markets. In Austria they pressed for liberal political institutions.

However, nationalists also often defined their own national group in opposition to other national groups whom they might regard as cultural inferiors or as historical enemies. This darker side of nationalism would emerge much more starkly in the second half of the nineteenth century. And it would poison much European political life during the first half of the twentieth century.

Movements for Liberal Reform and Revolution

During the first half of the decade of the 1820s the institutions of the restored conservative order had successfully resisted the forces of

Mazzini Defines Nationality

No political force in the nineteenth century was stronger than nationalism. It replaced dynastic political loyalty with loyalty based on ethnic considerations. In 1835 the Italian nationalist and patriot Giuseppe Mazzini explained his understanding of the concept. Note the manner in which he combined a generally democratic view of politics with a religious concept of the divine destiny of nations.

The essential characteristics of a nationality are common ideas, common principles and a common purpose. A nation is an association of those who are brought together by language, by given geographical conditions or by the role assigned them by history, who acknowledge the same principles and who march together to the conquest of a single definite goal under the rule of a uniform body of law.

The life of a nation consists in harmonious activity (that is, the employment of all individual abilities and energies comprised within the association) towards this single goal. . . .

But nationality means even more than this. Nationality also consists in the share of mankind's labors which God assigns to a people. This mission is the task which a people must perform to the end that the Divine Idea shall be realized in this world; it is the work which gives a people its rights as a member of Mankind; it is the baptismal rite which endows a people with its own character and its rank in the brotherhood of nations. . . .

Nationality depends for its very existence upon its sacredness within and beyond its borders.

If nationality is to be inviolable for all, friends and foes alike, it must be regarded inside a country as holy, like a religion, and outside a country as a grave mission. It is necessary too that the ideas arising within a country grow steadily, as part of the general law of Humanity which is the source of all nationality. It is necessary that these ideas be shown to other lands in their beauty and purity, free from any alien mixture, from any slavish fears, from any skeptical hesitancy, strong and active, embracing in their evolution every aspect and manifestation of the life of the nation. These ideas, a necessary component in the order of universal destiny, must retain their originality even as they enter harmoniously into mankind's general progress.

The people must be the basis of nationality; its logically derived and vigorously applied principles its means; the strength of all its strength; the improvement of the life of all and the happiness of the great possible number its results; and the accomplishment of the task assigned to it by God its goal. This is what we mean by nationality.

Herbert H. Rown (Ed.), From Absolutism to Revolution, 1648–1848, 2nd ed. (New York: The Macmillan Company; London: Collier-Macmillan Limited, 1969), pp. 277, 280.

liberalism. The exceptions were the Greek Revolution and the Latin American Wars of Independence. Both the latter movements lay at the outer edges of the European world, one in the eastern Mediterranean, the other across the Atlantic. Elsewhere in Europe the restored order held sway. However, beginning in the middle of the 1820s, the conservative governments of Russia, France, and Great Britain faced new stirrings of political discontent. In Russia, the result was suppression; in France, revolution; and in Britain, accommodation.

Russia: The Decembrist Revolt of 1825

During the mid-1820s Russia took the lead in suppressing both liberal and nationalistic tendencies within its domains. In the process of driving Napoleon's army across Europe and then of occupying defeated France, many officers in the Russian army were introduced to the ideas of the French Revolution and the Enlightenment. They realized how economically backward and politically stifled their own nation remained. The domestic repression in Russia hardened as Alexander I became more conservative.

UNREST IN THE ARMY Under these conditions groups within the army officer corps formed secret societies. One such reformist coterie was the Southern Society. Led by an officer named Pestel, these men sought a representative government and the abolition of serfdom. Pestel himself favored democracy and a moderately independent Poland. The Northern Society was a second, more moderate group. It favored constitutional monarchy and the abolition of serfdom but protection for the interests of the aristocracy. Both societies were very small; there was much friction between them. They agreed only that there must be a change in the government of Russia. Sometime during 1825 they seem to have decided to carry out a *coup d'état* in 1826.

DYNASTIC CRISIS Other events intervened. In late November 1825 Tsar Alexander I suddenly and unexpectedly died. His death created two crises. The first was a dynastic one. Alexander had no direct heir. His brother Constantine stood next in line to the throne. However, Constantine, who was then the commander of Russian forces in occupied Poland, had married a woman who was not of royal blood. He had thus excluded himself from the throne and was more than willing to renounce any claim. Through a series of secret instructions made public only after his death, Alexander had named his younger brother, Nicholas (1825–1855), as the new tsar.

Once Alexander was dead, the legality of these instructions became uncertain. Constantine acknowledged Nicholas as tsar, and Nicholas acknowledged Constantine. This family muddle continued for about three weeks, during which Russia actually had no ruler, to the astonishment of all Europe. Then, during the early days of December, the army command reported to Nicholas the existence of a conspiracy among certain officers. Able to wait no longer for the working out of legal niceties, Nicholas had himself declared tsar, much to the delight of the by-now-exasperated Constantine.

The second crisis now proceeded to unfold. There was a plot devised by a number of junior officers intent on rallying the troops under their command to the cause of reform. On December 26, 1825, the army was to take the oath of allegiance to Nicholas, who was less popular than Constantine and was regarded as more conservative. Nearly all of the regiments did so. But the Moscow regiment, whose chief

Tsar Nicholas I (1825–1855) resisted all attempts to reform Russia and offered the use of Russian troops to other rulers threatened by revolution. [Culver Pictures]

A Decembrist Writes of the Sources
of His Political Ideals

After the failure of the Decembrist uprising, Tsar Nicholas I personally presided over the Commission that investigated the revolt. Much of our later knowledge of the ideas of the leaders of the uprising comes from the testimony given to that Commission and other materials collected by it. The following passage is taken from a letter written by Petr Grigor'evich Kakhovskii dated February 24, 1826. Notice the manner in which he associates his political ideas with those of the French and American Revolutions.

One must seek the origin of the [Secret, in this case Northern] Society in the spirit of the time and in our state of mind. I know a few belonging to the Secret Society but am inclined to think the membership is not very large. However, among my many acquaintances who do not adhere to any secret societies, very few are opposed to my opinions. Frankly I can state that among thousands of young men there are hardly a hundred who do not passionately long for freedom. These youths, inflamed with a strong, pure passion for the welfare of their fatherland and for true enlightenment, are growing mature.

The peoples of the world have conceived a sacred truth—that they do not exist for governments, but that governments must be organized for them. This is the cause of struggle in all countries; people, after tasting the sweetness of enlightenment and freedom, strive toward them; and governments, entrenched behind millions of bayonets, attempt to repel these peoples back into the darkness of ignorance. But all these efforts will prove in vain; impression once received can never be erased. Liberty, that torch of intellect and warmth of life, has always and everywhere been the attribute of peoples emerged from primitive ignorance. We are unable to live like our ancestors, like barbarians or slaves. . . .

. . . .

Emperor Alexander [I] promised us much; it could be said that, like a giant, he stirred the minds of the people toward the sacred rights of humanity. Later he altered his principles and intentions. The people became frightened, but the seed had sprouted and the roots had grown deep. The latter half of the past century and the events of our own time are so full of various revolutions that we have no need to refer to more distant eras. We are witnesses to great events. The discovery of the New World, and the United States of America, by virtue of its form of government, have forced Europe into rivalry with her. The United States will shine as an example even to distant generations. The name of Washington, the friend and benefactor of the people, will be passed on from generation to generation; the memory of his devotion to the welfare of the fatherland will stir the hearts of citizens.

George Vernadsky (Ed.), A Source Book for Russian History from Early Times to 1917 *(New Haven: Yale University Press, 1972), 2:519.*

officers, surprisingly, were not secret society members, marched into the Senate Square in Saint Petersburg and refused to swear allegiance. Rather, they called for Constantine and a constitution. Attempts to settle the situation peacefully failed. Late in the afternoon Nicholas ordered the cavalry and the artillery to attack the insurgents. Over sixty people were killed. Early in 1826 Nicholas himself presided over the commission that investigated the Decembrist Revolt and the secret army societies. Five of the plotters were executed and over one hundred other officers were exiled to Siberia.

THE AUTOCRACY OF NICHOLAS I

Although the Decembrist Revolt completely failed, it was the first rebellion in modern Russian history whose instigators had had specific political goals. They wanted constitutional government and the abolition of serfdom. As the century passed, the Decembrists, in their political martyrdom, came to symbolize the yearnings of all Russian liberals, whose numbers were always quite small. The more immediate result of the revolt was the crushing of liberalism as even a moderate political influence in Russia. Nicholas I was determined that never again would his power come under question. He eventually epitomized the most extreme form of nineteenth-century autocracy.

Nicholas was neither an ignorant nor a bigoted reactionary. He was quite simply afraid of change. He knew that Russia required reforms

Uvarov Praises the Policy of Official Nationality

Uvarov was the Russian minister of education under Nicholas I. In that capacity he was largely responsible for the policy of Official Nationality and its program of orthodoxy, autocracy, and nationality. In 1843 he explained that this ideology was to prevent Russia from experiencing the political turmoil that had occurred in western Europe.

In the midst of rapid collapse in Europe of religious and civil institutions, at the time of a general spread of destructive ideas, at the sight of grievous phenomena surrounding us on all sides, it was necessary to establish our fatherland on firm foundations upon which is based the well-being, strength, and life of a people; it was necessary to find the principles which form the distinctive character of Russia, and which belong only to Russia; it was necessary to gather into one whole the sacred remnants of Russian nationality and to fasten to them the anchor of our salvation. Fortunately, Russia had retained a warm faith in the sacred principles without which she cannot prosper, gain in strength, live. Sincerely and deeply attached to the church of his fathers, the Russian has of old considered it the guarantee of social and family happiness. Without a love for the faith of its ancestors a people, as well as an individual must perish. A Russian devoted to his fatherland, will agree as little to the loss of a single dogma of our *Orthodoxy* as to the theft of a single pearl from the tsar's crown. *Autocracy* constitutes the main condition of the political existence of Russia. The Russian giant stands on it as on the cornerstone of his greatness. An innumerable majority of the subjects of *Your Majesty* feel this truth; they feel it in full measure although they are placed on different rungs of civil life and although they vary in education and in their relations to the government. The saving conviction that Russia lives and is protected by the spirit of a strong, humane, and enlightened autocracy must permeate popular education and must develop with it. Together with these two national principles there is a third, no less important, no less powerful: *nationality.*

Cited in Nicholas Riasanovsk, Nicholas I and Official Nationality in Russia, 1825–1855 *(Berkeley: University of California Press, 1959), pp. 74–75.*

for economic growth and social improvement. In 1842 he told his State Council, "There is no doubt that serfdom, in its present form, is a flagrant evil which everyone realizes, yet to attempt to remedy it now would be, of course, an evil more disastrous."[3] To remove serfdom would necessarily, in his view, have undermined the nobles' support of the tsar. Consequently Nicholas turned his back on this and practically all other reforms. Literary and political censorship and a widespread system of secret police flourished throughout his reign. There was little attempt to forge even an efficient and honest administration. The only significant reform of his rule was a codification of Russian law published in 1833.

OFFICIAL NATIONALITY In place of reform Nicholas and his closest advisers embraced a program called *Official Nationality*. Its slogan, published repeatedly in government documents, newspapers, journals, and schoolbooks, was "Orthodoxy, Autocracy, and Nationalism." The Russian Orthodox faith was to provide the basis for morality, education, and intellectual life. The Church, which since the days of Peter the Great had been an arm of the secular government, controlled the schools and universities. Young Russians were taught to accept their place in life and to spurn rising in the social structure.

The program of autocracy championed the unrestrained power of the tsar as the only authority that could hold the vast expanse of Russia and its peoples together in an orderly fashion. Political writers stressed that only under the autocracy of Peter the Great, Catherine the Great, and Alexander I had Russia prospered and exerted a major influence on world affairs.

Through the glorification of Russian nationality, the country was urged to see its religion, language, and customs as a source of perennial wisdom that separated the nation from the moral corruption and political turmoil of the West. The person who presided over the program of Official Nationality was Count S. S. Uvarov, minister of education from 1833 to 1849. The result of his efforts and those of the tsar was the profound alienation of serious Russian intellectual life from the tsarist government.

REPRESSION IN POLAND Nicholas I also manifested extreme conservatism in foreign affairs. After the Congress of Vienna, Poland had been given a constitutional government, but within the limits of the Russian domination that dated back to the eighteenth-century partitions of Poland. Grand Duke Constantine, the brother of Alexander I and Nicholas I, was in charge of the Polish government by authority delegated by the tsars. Although both tsars frequently infringed on the constitutional arrangement and quarreled with the Polish Diet, the constitution itself remained. Nevertheless Polish nationalists continued to agitate for change.

In late November 1830, after the news of the French and Belgian revolutions of that summer had penetrated Poland, a small military insurrection broke out in Warsaw. Disturbances soon spread throughout the rest of the country. On December 18 the Polish Diet declared the revolution to be a nationalist movement. In early January 1831 the Diet voted to depose Nicholas as ruler of Poland. The tsar reacted by sending troops into the country. After several months the revolt was thoroughly suppressed. In February 1832 Nicholas issued the Organic Statute, which declared Poland to be an integral part of the Russian empire. The statute guaranteed certain Polish liberties, but they were systematically ignored. The Polish uprising had confirmed all the tsar's worst fears. Henceforth Russia and Nicholas became the gendarme of Europe, ever ready to provide troops to suppress liberal and nationalist movements.

Revolution in France (1830)

The Polish revolt was the most distant of several disturbances that flowed from the overthrow of the Bourbon dynasty in France during July 1830. In 1824 Louis XVIII had died. He was succeeded by his brother, the count of Artois, who became Charles X (1824–1830). The new king, who had been the chief leader of the ultraroyalists at the time of the restoration, considered himself a monarch by divine right.

THE REACTIONARY POLICIES OF CHARLES X His first action was to have

---

[3] *Quoted in Michael T. Florinsky*, Russia: A History and an Interpretation *(New York: Macmillan, 1953), 2:755.*

Liberty Leading the People *by Eugene Delacroix is a very famous depiction of the Revolution of 1830. [Giraudon]*

the Chamber of Deputies in 1824 and 1825 provide for the indemnification of aristocrats who had lost their lands in the revolution. The existing land settlement was confirmed. However, by lowering the interest rates on government bonds, the Chamber created a fund from which the survivors of the *émigrés* who had forfeited land would be paid an annual sum of money. The middle-class bondholders, who lost income, naturally resented this measure. Another measure restored the rule of primogeniture, whereby only the eldest son of an aristocrat inherited the family domains. Charles X supported the Roman Catholic church by a law punishing sacrilege with sentences of imprisonment or death. Liberals disapproved of all of these measures.

The results of the elections of 1827 compelled Charles X to appease the liberals, who in conjunction with more moderate royalists could muster a majority in the Chamber of Deputies. He appointed a less conservative ministry. Laws directed against the press and those allowing the government to dominate education were eased. Yet the liberals, who wanted a genuinely constitutional regime, remained unsatisfied. In 1829 the king decided that his policy of accommodation had failed. He dismissed his ministers and in their place appointed an ultraroyalist ministry headed by the Prince de Polignac (1780–1847). The opposition was now forced to the desperate action of opening negotiations with the liberal Orléanist branch of the royal family.

THE JULY REVOLUTION In 1830 Charles X called for new elections, in which the liberals scored a stunning victory. He might have relented and tried to accommodate the new Chamber of Deputies. Instead, the king and his ministers decided to attempt a royalist seizure of power. In June and July 1830 Polignac had sent a naval expedition against Algeria. On July 9 reports of its victory reached

Paris. The foundation of a French empire in North Africa had been laid. On July 25, 1830, under the euphoria of this foreign diversion, Charles X issued the Four Ordinances, which amounted to a royal *coup d'état*. The ordinances (1) restricted freedom of the press, (2) dissolved the recently elected Chamber of Deputies, (3) restricted the franchise to the wealthiest people in the country, and (4) called for new elections under the new royalist franchise.

The Four Ordinances provoked swift and decisive popular political reactions. Liberal newspapers called on the nation to reject the monarch's actions. The laboring populace of Paris, burdened since 1827 by an economic downturn, took to the streets and erected barricades. The king called out troops, and over eighteen hundred people died during the ensuing battles in the city.

On August 2 Charles X abdicated and left France for exile in England. The liberals in the Chamber of Deputies named a new ministry composed of constitutional monarchists. They proclaimed Louis Philippe (1830–1848), the duke of Orléans, the new monarch. The July Days had brought to a final close the rule of the Bourbon dynasty in France.

In the Revolution of 1830 the liberals of the Chamber of Deputies had filled a power vacuum created by the popular Paris uprising and the failure of effective royal action. Had Charles X provided himself with sufficient troops in Paris, the outcome could have been quite different. Moreover, had the liberals, who favored constitutional monarchy, not acted quickly, the workers and shopkeepers of Paris might have formed a republic. By seizing the moment, the middle class, the bureaucrats, and the moderate aristocratic liberals overthrew the restoration monarchy and still avoided a republic. These liberals feared a new popular revolution such as had swept France in 1792 on the overthrow of the old monarchy. They had no desire for another sans-culotte republic. Consequently, a fundamental political and social tension marked the new monarchy. The hard-pressed laborers and the prosperous middle-class people whose temporary alliance had achieved the revolution realized that their basic goals had been quite different.

MONARCHY UNDER LOUIS PHILIPPE

Politically the July Monarchy, as it was called,

was more liberal than the restoration government. Louis Philippe was called the king of the French rather than king of France. The tricolor flag of the revolution replaced the white flag of the Bourbons. The new constitution was regarded as a right of the people rather than a concession of the monarch. Catholicism became the religion of the majority of the people rather than the official religion. Censorship was abolished. The franchise became somewhat wider but remained on the whole restricted. The king had to cooperate with the Chamber of Deputies; he could not dispense with laws on his own authority.

Socially, however, the Revolution of 1830 proved quite conservative. The hereditary peerage was abolished in 1831, but the everyday economic, political, and social influence of the landed oligarchy continued. Money was the path to power and influence in the government. There was much corruption.

Most important, the liberal monarchy displayed little or no sympathy for the lower and working classes. The Paris workers in 1830 had called for the protection of jobs, better wages, and the preservation of the traditional crafts rather than for the usual goals of political liberalism. The government of Louis Philippe ignored their demands and their plight. The laboring classes of Paris and the provincial cities seemed just one more possible source of disorder. In late 1831 troops suppressed a workers' revolt in the city of Lyons. In July 1832 an uprising occurred in Paris during the funeral of a popular Napoleonic general. Again the government called out troops and over eight hundred people were killed or wounded. In 1834 a very large strike of silkworkers in Lyons was crushed. Such discontent might be smothered for a time, but without attention to the social and economic conditions creating that tension, new turmoil would eventually erupt.

Belgium Becomes Independent (1830)

The July Days in Paris sent sparks to other political tinder on the Continent. The revolutionary fires first lighted in neighboring Belgium. The former Austrian Netherlands, Belgium, had in 1815 been merged with the kingdom of Holland. The upper classes of Belgium had never reconciled themselves to rule

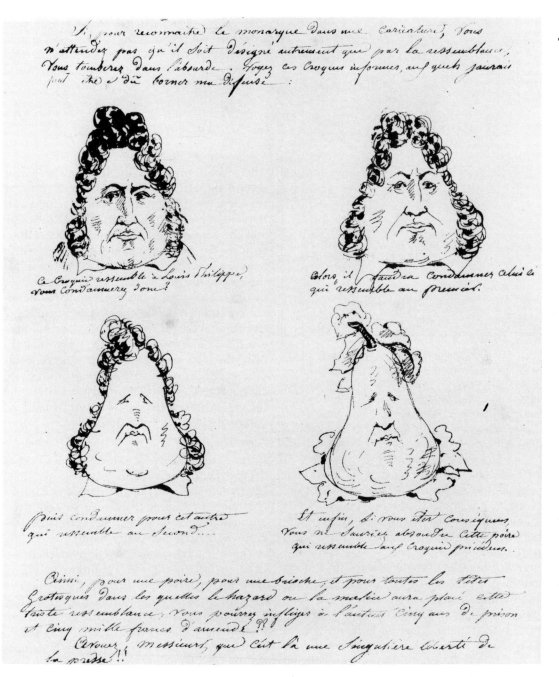

Despite laws forbidding disrespect to the government, political cartoonists had a field day with Louis Philippe. Here, the artist emphasizes the king's resemblance to a pear and in the process attacks restraints on freedom of the press. [Library of Congress]

by a country with a different language, religion, and economic life.

On August 25, 1830, disturbances broke out in Brussels following the performance of an opera that portrayed a rebellion of Naples against Spanish rule. To put an end to the riot-

ing, the municipal authorities and persons from the propertied classes formed a provisional national government. When compromise between the Belgians and the Dutch failed, William of Holland sent troops and ships against Belgium. By November 10, 1830,

MAP 21-2 CENTERS OF REVOLUTION, 1820–1830 *Conservative governments and cooperation among repressive great powers in post-Napoleonic Europe were challenged by uprisings and revolutions, beginning in 1820–1821 in Spain, Naples, and Greece and appearing in Russia, France, and Belgium later in the decade.*

the Dutch had been defeated. A national congress then wrote a liberal Belgian constitution, which was promulgated in 1831.

The major powers saw the revolution in Belgium as upsetting the boundaries established by the Congress of Vienna. Russia could not intervene because of the Polish revolt. Prussia and the other German states were suppressing small risings in their own domains. The Austrians were busy putting down disturbances in Italy. France under Louis Philippe favored an independent Belgium and hoped to dominate it. Britain felt that it could tolerate a liberal Belgium as long as it was free of foreign domination.

In December 1830 Lord Palmerston (1784–1865), the British foreign minister, gathered representatives of the powers in London. Through skillful negotiations he persuaded them to recognize Belgium as an independent and neutral state. In July 1831 Leopold of Saxe-Coburg (1831–1865) became king of the Belgians. By the Convention of 1839 the great powers guaranteed the neutrality of Belgium. For almost a century Belgian neutrality re-

mained one of the articles of faith in European international relations. In 1914 it was German violation of the neutrality convention that technically brought Great Britain into World War I.

The Great Reform Bill in Britain (1832)

The revolutionary year of 1830 saw in Great Britain the election of a House of Commons that debated the first major bill to reform Parliament. The death of George IV (1820–1830) and the accession of William IV (1830–1837) required the calling of an election. It was once believed that the July revolution in France had influenced the British elections in the summer of 1830. This theory has been shown to be incorrect through a close analysis of the time and character of the individual county and borough elections. The passage of the Great Reform Bill, which became law in 1832, was the result of a series of events very different from those that occurred on the Continent. In Britain the forces of conservatism and reform made accommodations with each other.

POLITICAL AND ECONOMIC REFORM Several factors made this situation possible. First, there was a larger commercial and industrial class in Britain than in other countries. No matter what group might control the government, British prosperity required attention to those economic interests. Second, there existed in Britain the long tradition of liberal Whig aristocrats, who regarded themselves as the protectors of constitutional liberty. They saw their role as that of making moderate political changes that would render revolutionary changes unnecessary. Their early sympathy for the French Revolution had lessened their influence. However, after 1815 they reentered the political arena and waited to be recalled to power. Finally, there also existed in British law, tradition, and public opinion a strong respect for civil liberties.

In 1820, the year after the passage of the notorious Six Acts, Lord Liverpool shrewdly moved to change his cabinet. The new members continued to favor generally conservative policies, but they also believed the government must accommodate itself to the changing social and economic life of the nation. They favored policies of greater economic freedom and repealed earlier Combination Acts that had prohibited labor organizations.

CATHOLIC EMANCIPATION ACT Economic considerations had generally led to these moderate reforms. English determination to maintain the union with Ireland brought about another key reform. England's relationship to Ireland was similar to that of Russia's to Poland or Austria's to its several national groups. In 1800, fearful that Irish nationalists might again rebel as they had in 1798 and perhaps turn Ireland into a base for a French invasion, William Pitt the Younger had

---

Thomas Babington Macaulay Defends the Great Reform Bill

Macaulay (1800–1859) was a member of the House of Commons that passed the Great Reform Bill in 1831, only to have it rejected by the House of Lords before another measure was successfully enacted in 1832. His speeches in support of the bill derived from his views on the need for Parliament to give balanced representation to major elements in the population. Specifically, he supported the Great Reform Bill because, without creating a democratic government, it allowed the middle class to obtain political influence. He saw the reform of Parliament as a way to prevent political revolution in England. His argument had wide appeal.

[The principle of the ministers] is plain, rational, and consistent. It is this,—to admit the middle class to a large and direct share in the Representation, without any violent shock to the institutions of our country. . . . I hold it to be clearly expedient, that in a country like this, the right of suffrage should depend on a pecuniary qualification. Every argument . . . which would induce me to oppose Universal Suffrage, induces me to support the measure which is now before us. I oppose Universal Suffrage, because I think that it would produce a destructive revolution. I support this measure, because I am sure that it is our best security against a revolution. . . . I . . . do entertain great apprehension for the fate of my country. I do in my conscience believe, that unless this measure, or some similar measure, be speedily adopted, great and terrible calamities will befall us. Entertaining this opinion, I think myself bound to state it, not as a threat, but as a reason. I support this measure as a means of Reform: But I support it still more as a measure of conservation. That we may exclude those whom it is necessary to exclude, we must admit those whom it may be safe to admit. . . . All history is full of revolutions, produced by causes similar to those which are now operating in England. A portion of the community which had been of no account, expands and becomes strong. It demands a place in the system, suited, not to its former weakness, but to its present power. If this is granted, all is well. If this is refused, then comes the struggle between the young energy of one class, and the ancient privileges of another. . . . Such . . . is the struggle which the middle classes in England are maintaining against an aristocracy of mere locality. . . .

Hansard's Parliamentary Debates, *3rd series, Vol. 2, pp. 1191–1197.*

Daniel O'Connell was the most dynamic and effective Irish nationalist leader in the first half of the nineteenth century. This portrait was made in 1834 when O'Connell was fifty-nine.

persuaded Parliament to pass the Act of Union between Ireland and England. Ireland now sent one hundred members to the House of Commons. However, only Protestant Irishmen could be elected to represent their overwhelmingly Roman Catholic nation.

During the 1820s, under the leadership of Daniel O'Connell (1775–1847), Irish nationalists organized the Catholic Association to agitate for Catholic emancipation. In 1828 O'Connell secured his own election to Parliament, where he could not legally take his seat. The British ministry of the duke of Wellington realized that henceforth an entirely Catholic delegation might be elected from Ireland. If they were not seated, civil war might erupt across the Irish Sea. Consequently, in 1829 Wellington and Robert Peel steered the Catholic Emancipation Act through Parliament. Roman Catholics would now become Members of Parliament. This measure, together with the repeal in 1828 of restrictions against Protestant nonconformists, meant that the Anglican monopoly on British political life was over.

Catholic emancipation was a liberal measure that was passed for the conservative purpose of preserving order in Ireland. It included a provision raising the franchise in Ireland so that only the wealthier Irish could vote. Nonetheless, this measure alienated many of Wellington's Anglican Tory supporters in the House of Commons. In the election of 1830 a large number of supporters of parliamentary reform were returned to Parliament. Even some Tories believed that parliamentary reform was necessary because they had concluded that Catholic emancipation could have been passed only by a corrupt House of Commons. The Wellington ministry soon fell. The Tories were badly divided. Consequently King William IV turned to The Whigs under the leadership of Earl Grey (1764–1845) to form a government.

LEGISLATING CHANGE The Whig ministry soon presented the House of Commons with a major reform bill that had two broad goals. The first was to abolish "rotten" boroughs, which had small numbers of voters, and to replace them with representatives for the previously unrepresented manufacturing districts and cities. Second, the number of voters in England and Wales was increased by about 50 per cent through a series of new franchises. In 1831 the House of Commons narrowly defeated the bill. Grey called for a new election,

EVENTS ASSOCIATED WITH LIBERAL REFORM AND REVOLUTION	
1824	Charles X becomes king of France
1825	Decembrist Revolt in Russia
1829	Catholic Emancipation Act in Great Britain
1830	(July 9) News of French victory in Algeria reaches Paris
1830	(July 25) Charles X issues the Four Ordinances
1830	(August 2) Charles X abdicates; Louis Philippe proclaimed king
1830	(August 25) Belgian revolution
1830	(November 29) Polish revolution
1832	Great Reform Bill passed in Great Britain

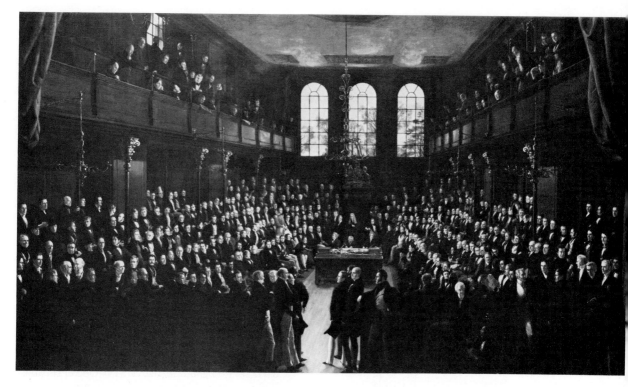

At the first meeting of the reformed House of Commons in 1833 most seats were still filled by the gentry and the wealthy. But the elimination of rotten boroughs and the election of members from the new urban centers began to transform the House of Commons into a representative national body. [National Portrait Gallery, London]

in which a majority in favor of the bill was returned. The House of Commons passed the reform bill, but the House of Lords rejected it. Mass meetings were held throughout the country. Riots broke out in several cities.

Finally, William IV agreed to create enough new peers to give a third reform bill a majority in the House of Lords. Under this pressure the House of Lords yielded, and in 1832 the measure became law.

The Great Reform Bill expanded the size of the English electorate, but it was not a democratic measure. The number of voters was increased by over 200,000 persons, or by almost 50 per cent. However, the basis of voting remained a property qualification. (Gender was also a qualification. No thought was given to enfranchising women.) Some working-class voters actually were disenfranchised because of the abolition of certain old franchise rights. New urban boroughs were created to allow the growing cities to have a voice in the House of Commons. Yet the passage of the reform act did not, as it was once thought, constitute the triumph of the middle-class interest in England. For every new urban electoral district, a new rural district was also drawn. It was expected that the aristocracy would dominate the rural elections.

The success of the reform bill was its reconciliation of previously unrepresented property owners and economic interests to the existing political institutions of the country. The act created a political situation in which further reforms of the Church, the municipal government, and commercial policy could be achieved in an orderly fashion. Revolution in Britain was unnecessary because the people who sought change had been admitted to the political forum that could legislate those changes. In this manner the historic institutions of Great Britain were maintained while the persons and groups who influenced them became more diverse.

The fifteen years between the conclusion of the Congress of Vienna and the Revolution of 1830 was a period of challenge to and defense of the post-Napoleonic settlement. The Congress system succeeded in holding back revolutionary and nationalistic disturbances throughout most of the continent. The exception occurred in Greece with its revolution in 1821. However, it was the exception. In Russia the Decembrist Revolt of 1825 failed almost before it had begun. The only truly successful revolutionary activity during these years occurred in Latin America, where the centuries-old colonial domination of Spain ended with the wars of independence.

Nonetheless, during the 1820s liberal political ideas and some liberal political figures began to make inroads into the otherwise conservative order. In 1830 revolution and reform again began to move across Europe. The French rejected the restored Bourbon monarchy and established a more liberal monarchy. Belgium also achieved independence with a liberal government. Perhaps most important, Great Britain moved slowly toward a more liberal position. During the 1820s Great Britain had become unenthusiastic about a political role that placed it in opposition to all change. For its own commercial reasons it favored independence for Latin America. Popular pressures at home led the British aristocratic leadership to enact a moderate reform bill in 1832. Thereafter, it would be viewed as the leading liberal state in Europe and one that would support nationalistic causes.

While throughout Europe political change occurred quite slowly, major social and economic changes were transforming the continent and bringing new political ideas and forces to the fore.

Suggested Readings

D. BEALES, *From Castlereagh to Gladstone, 1815–1885* (1969). A survey to be read in conjunction with Briggs (below).

R. M. BERDAHL, *The Politics of the Prussian Nobility: The Development of a Conservative Ideology, 1770–1848* (1988). A major examination of German conservative outlooks.

G. DE BERTIER DE SAUVIGNY, *The Bourbon Restoration* (trans., 1966), and *Metternich and His Times* (1962). Sympathetic, but not uncritical, studies of the forces of political conservatism.

R. J. BEZUCHA, *The Lyon Uprising of 1834: Social and Political Conflict in the Early July Monarchy* (1974). An excellent discussion of the tensions in France after the Revolution of 1830.

A. BRIGGS, *The Making of Modern England* (1959). The best survey of English history during the first half of the nineteenth century.

M. BROCK, *The Great Reform Act* (1974). The standard work.

G. A. CRAIG, *The Politics of the Prussian Army, 1640–1945* (1955). A splendid study of the conservative political influence of the army on Prussian development.

D. DAKIN, *The Struggle for Greek Independence* (1973). An excellent explanation of the intricacies of the Greek independence question.

J. DROZ, *Europe Between Revolutions, 1815–1848* (1967). An examination of Europe as created by the Vienna settlement.

E. HALÉVY, *England in 1815* (1913). One of the most important and influential books written on nineteenth-century Britain.

E. J. HOBSBAWM, *The Age of Revolution, 1789–1848* (1962). A very comprehensive survey emphasizing the social ramifications of the liberal democratic and industrial revolutions.

S. HOLMES, *Benjamin Constant and the Making of Modern Liberalism* (1984). An outstanding study of a major liberal theorist.

A. JARDIN AND A. J. TUDESQ, *Restoration and Reaction, 1815–1848* (1984). Surveys this period in France.

W. B. KAUFMANN, *British Policy and the Independence of Latin America, 1802–1828* (1951). A standard discussion of an important relationship.

H. KOHN, *The Idea of Nationalism: A Study in Its Origin and Background* (1944). An examination of the roots of nationalism in Western culture.

W. B. LINCOLN, *Nicholas I: Emperor and Autocrat of All the Russians* (1978). A serious scholarly treatment.

J. LYNCH, *The Spanish American Revolutions, 1808–1826* (1973). An excellent one-volume treatment.

C. A. MACARTNEY, *The Habsburg Empire, 1790–1918* (1971). An outstanding survey.

J. MERRIMAN (Ed.), *1830 in France* (1976). A collection of important essays on the Revolution of 1830.

A. PALMER, *Alexander I: Tsar of War and Peace* (1974). An interesting biography that captures much of the rather mysterious personality of this ruler.

D. H. Pinkney, *The French Revolution of* 1830 (1972). The best account in English.

M. Raeff, *The Decembrist Movement* (1966). An examination of the unsuccessful uprising, with documents.

N. V. Riasanovsky, *Nicholas I and Official Nationality in Russia,* 1825–1855 (1959). A lucid discussion of the conservative ideology that made Russia the major opponent of liberalism.

C. A. Ruud, *Fighting Words: Imperial Censorship and the Russian Press,* 1804–1906 (1982). Examines the government attempt to shape and control public opinion.

J. Sheehan, *German History,* 1770–1866 (1989). A very long work which is now the best available survey of the subject.

A. B. Ulam, *Russia's Failed Revolutionaries* (1981). Contains a useful discussion of the Decembrists as a background for other nineteenth-century Russian revolutionary activity.

P. S. Wandycz, *The Lands of Partitioned Poland,* 1795–1918 (1974). The best study of Poland during the nineteenth century.

Iron and coal transformed the European economy during the nineteenth century. They made possible iron bridges, locomotives, steam ships, as well as other heavy manufacturing equipment. [National Trust Photographic Library, photographed by Michael Holford]

22

ECONOMIC ADVANCE AND SOCIAL UNREST (1830–1850)

By 1830 Europe was headed toward an industrial society. Only Great Britain had already attained that status, but the pounding of new machinery and the grinding of railway engines soon began to echo across the entire continent. Further urbanization, the disintegration of traditional social bonds and work habits, and eventually class conflict accompanied the economic development. However, what characterized the second quarter of the century was not the triumph of industrialism but the final gasps of those economic groups who opposed it. Intellectually the period saw the formulation of the major creeds supporting and criticizing the new society.

These were years of uncertainty for almost everyone. Even the most confident entrepre-neurs knew that the trade cycle might bankrupt them in a matter of weeks. For the industrial workers and the artisans unemployment became a haunting and recurring problem. For the peasants the question was sufficiency of food. It was a period of self-conscious transition that culminated in 1848 with a continentwide outbreak of revolution. People knew that one mode of life was passing, but they were uncertain about what would replace it.

Toward an Industrial Society

During the first half of the nineteenth century industrial production of both manufacturing and consumer goods that had begun earlier in Great Britain spread across much of the European continent. In doing so, industrialism transformed virtually every aspect of social and economic life and soon contributed to new political unrest. This slow but steady conversion of the European economy to industrial manufacturing generally took place in cities. Consequently it brought about new migrations of people from the countryside to urban settings and caused a painful reorganization of the life of European workers. Many of those who possessed valuable pre-industrial skills saw those skills displaced by machines. Industrialism and the accompanying urban growth no less than the political revolutions that derived from the French Revolution overturned the social order of the Old Regime.

Britain's Industrial Leadership

The Industrial Revolution had begun in eighteenth-century Great Britain with the advances in textile production described in Chapter 16. Natural resources, adequate capital, native technological skills, a growing food supply, a social structure that allowed considerable mobility, and strong foreign and domestic demand for goods had given Britain an edge in achieving a vast new capacity for production in manufacturing. Its factories and recently invented machines allowed British producers to furnish customers with a greater number and higher quality products at lower prices than any competitors could. At the same time

the French Revolution and the wars of Napoleon had brought about the final collapse of the French Atlantic trade and had for two decades disrupted continental economic life.

The British advance especially in textiles was linked to a vast worldwide economic network. Much of the raw cotton that fed the new British textile mills came from the plantations of the southern United States. In that regard the British textile industry was dependent upon the labor of black American slaves even though Britain itself had since 1807 been attempting to end the worldwide slave trade. Then in turn the finished textiles were shipped all over the world along sea lanes protected by the British navy. The wealth that Britain acquired through textile production and its other industries of ironmaking, shipbuilding, china production, and the manufacture of other finished goods was invested all over the world but most particularly in the United States and Latin America. This enormous activity provided the economic foundation for British dominance of the world scene in the nineteenth century.

Despite the economic lag the continental nations were beginning to make material progress. By the 1830s, in Belgium, France, and Germany the number of steam engines in use was growing steadily. Exploitation of the coalfields of the Ruhr and the Saar basins had begun. Coke was replacing charcoal in iron and steel production.

Industrial areas were generally less concentrated than in Britain, and large manufacturing districts, such as the British Midlands, did not yet exist on the continent. There were major pockets of production in western Europe, such as the cities of Lyons, Rouen, Liège, and Lille, but most continental manufacturing still took place in the countryside. New machines were integrated into the existing domestic system. The extreme slowness of continental imitation of the British example meant that at mid-century, peasants and urban artisans remained more important politically than industrial factory workers.

Population and Migration

While the process of industrialization spread, the population of Europe continued to grow on the base of the eighteenth-century population explosion. The number of people in France rose from 32.5 million in 1831 to 35.8 million in 1851. The population of Germany rose from 26.5 million to 33.5 million during approximately the same period. That of Britain grew from 16.3 million to 20.8 million. More and more of the people of Europe lived in cities. By mid-century one half of the population of England and Wales had become town-dwellers; the proportion for France and Germany was about one quarter.

The sheer numbers of human beings put considerable pressure on the physical resources of the cities. Migration from the countryside meant that existing housing, water, sewers, food supplies, and lighting were completely inadequate. Slums with indescribable filth grew, and disease, especially cholera, ravaged the population. Crime increased and became a way of life for those who could make a living in no other manner. Human misery and degradation in numerous early nineteenth-century cities seemed to have no bounds.

The situation in the countryside was little or no better. During the first half of the century the productive use of the land still remained the overwhelming fact of life for the majority of Europeans. The enclosures of the late eighteenth century, the land redistribution of the French Revolution, and the emancipation of serfs in Prussia and later in Austria (1848) and Russia (1861) commercialized landholding. Liberal reformers had hoped that the legal revolution in ownership would transform peasants into progressive, industrious farmers. Most of them had instead become very conservative landholders who possessed too little soil to innovate or, in many cases, even to support themselves.

The specter of poor harvests still haunted

767

ECONOM
ADVANCE A
SOCIAL
UNREST
(1830–185

Starving Irish peasants begged for relief in 1847. The failure of the Irish potato crop in 1845–1847 led to the worst famine of nineteenth-century Europe. About 500,000 people starved and more than one million emigrated. [Mary Evans Picture Library]

Europe. The worst such experience of the century was the Irish famine of 1845–1847. Perhaps as many as half a million Irish peasants with no land or small plots simply starved when disease blighted the potato crop. Hundreds of thousands emigrated. By mid-century the revolution in landholding had led to greater agricultural production. It also resulted in a vast uprooting of people from the countryside into cities and from Europe into the rest of the world.

Railways

Industrial advance itself had also contributed to this migration. The decades of the 1830s and 1840s were the great age of railway building. The Stockton and Darlington Line opened in England in 1825. By 1830 another major line had been built between Manchester and Liverpool and had several hundred daily passengers. Belgium had undertaken railway construction by 1835. The first French line opened in 1832, but serious construction came only in the 1840s. Germany entered the railway age in 1835. At mid-century Britain had 9,797 kilometers of railway; France, 2,915; and Germany, 5,856.

The railroads, plus canals and improved regular roads, meant that people could leave the place of their birth more easily than ever before. The improvement in transportation also allowed cheaper and more rapid passage of raw materials and finished products.

Railways epitomized the character of the industrial economy during the second quarter

Stockport was an English industrial center shown here in about 1840. Note the railway viaduct running through the city. [Mary Evans Picture Library]

769

ECONOMIC
ADVANCE AN
SOCIAL
UNREST
(1830–1850

Sydney Smith Explores the Impact of the Railway

Sydney Smith was a witty British writer whose work appeared in numerous journals. In 1842 in a letter to the editor of The Morning Leader *he described the manner in which the rapidity of railway travel had changed contemporary life. He then complained in a satirical manner of the problem of early railway regulation. He criticized the lack of safety arising from the practice of locking all passengers in a railway car in order to ensure that all had paid. He then suggested that once a very important person has been injured the practice will change.*

Railway travelling is a delightful improvement of human life. Man is become a bird; he can fly longer and quicker than a solan-goose. The mamma rushes sixty miles in two hours to the aching finger of her conjugating and declining grammar-boy. The early Scotchman scratches himself in the morning mists of the north, and has his porridge in Piccadilly [in London] before the setting sun. . . . But, though charming and fascinating as all this is, we must not shut our eyes to the price we shall pay for it. There will be every three or four years some dreadful massacre—whole trains will be hurled down a precipice, and two hundred or three hundred persons will be killed on the spot. There will be every now and then a great combustion of human bodies, as there has been at Paris; then all the newspapers up in arms—a thousand regulations, forgotten as soon as the directors dare—loud screams of the velocity whistle—monopoly locks and bolts as before. [Locks permitting only one person to open the railway car.]

The locking plea of directors is philan-thropy; and I admit that to guard men from the commission of moral evil is as philanthropical as to prevent physical suffering. There is, I allow, a strong propensity in mankind to travel on railways without paying; and to lock mankind in till they have completed their share of the contract is benevolent, because it guards the species from degrading and immoral conduct; but to burn or crush a whole train, merely to prevent a few immoral insides from not paying, is, I hope, a little more than Ripon or Gladstone [two government cabinet ministers] will permit.

We have been, up to this point, very careless of our railway regulations. The first person of rank who is killed will put everything in order, and produce a code of the most careful rules. . . . From that moment the bad effects of the monopoly are destroyed; no more fatal deference to the directors; no despotic incarceration, no barbarous inattention to the anatomy and physiology of the human body; no commitment to locomotive prisons with warrant. . . .

Quoted in R. B. Morgan, Readings in English Social History from Contemporary Literature, *Vol. 5, 1688–1837 (Cambridge: Cambridge University Press, 1922), pp. 113–114.*

of the century. They represented investment in capital goods rather than in consumer goods. There was consequently somewhat of a shortage of consumer goods at cheap prices. This favoring of capital over consumer production was one reason that the working class often found itself able to purchase so little for its wages. The railways in and of themselves also brought about still more industrialization. Embodying the most dramatic application of the steam engine, they created a sharply increased demand for iron and steel and then for a more skilled labor force. The new iron and steel capacity soon permitted the construction

An 1837 *view of one of the first French railways, the line between Paris and the suburb of St. Germain. The line was built by Baron James de Rothschild, of the famous Jewish banking family. [Mary Evans Picture Library]*

of ironclad ships and iron rather than wooden machinery. These great capital industries led to the formation of vast industrial fortunes that would be invested in still newer enterprises. Industrialism had begun to grow on itself.

The Labor Force

The composition and experience of the early nineteenth-century labor force was quite varied. No single description could include all of the factory workers, urban artisans, domestic system craftsmen, household servants, countryside peddlers, farm workers, or railroad navvies. The work force was composed of some persons who were reasonably well off, enjoying steady employment and decent wages. It also numbered the "laboring poor," who held jobs but whose wages allowed them little more than subsistence. The condition of any particular working-class family depended on the skills of its members, the nature of the local labor market, and the trade cycle.

All of these working people faced possible unemployment, with little or no provision for their security. They confronted over the course of their lives the dissolution of many of the traditional social ties of custom and community. Most of the economic relationships in their lives became those of the marketplace or, as Thomas Carlyle said, of the "cash nexus."

Historians of the nineteenth century have traditionally emphasized the role and experience of industrial factory workers within the life of this immensely various European work force. In many respects this emphasis has been correct because factory labor and factory discipline did constitute the wave of the economic future. In the long run the industrial system affected almost every aspect of economic and social life.

However, during the first half of the century only the textile-manufacturing industry became thoroughly mechanized and moved into the factory setting. A vastly larger number of the nonrural, nonagricultural work force consisted of skilled urban artisans. They were attempting to maintain the value of their skills and control over their trades in the face of changing features of production.

Proletarianization of Factory Workers and Urban Artisans

During the century both artisans and factory workers underwent a process of *proletarianization*. This term is used to indicate the entry of workers into a wage economy and their gradual loss of significant ownership of the means of production, such as tools and equipment, and of control over the conduct of their own trades. The process occurred rapidly wherever the factory system arose. The factory owner provided the financial capital to construct the factory, to purchase the machinery, and to secure the raw materials. The factory workers contributed their labor for a wage.

Those factory workers also submitted to various kinds of factory discipline. This discipline meant that in large measure, work conditions became determined by the demands for smooth operation of the machines. Closing of factory gates to late workers, fines for such

lateness, dismissal for drunkenness, and public scolding of faulty laborers constituted attempts to create human discipline that would match the regularity of the cables, wheels, and pistons. The factory worker had no direct say in regard to the quality of the product or its price. For all the difficulties of factory conditions, however, the situation was often better than for the textile workers who resisted the factory mode of production. In particular English handloom weavers, who continued to work in their homes, experienced decades of declining trade and growing poverty in their unsuccessful competition with power looms.

Urban artisans in the nineteenth century experienced proletarianization more slowly than factory workers, and machinery had little to do with the process. The emergence of factories in and of itself did not harm urban artisans. Many even prospered from the development. For example, the construction and maintenance of the new machines generated major demand for metalworkers, who consequently prospered. The actual erection of fac-

771

ECONOMIC
ADVANCE AND
SOCIAL
UNREST
(1830–185

British metal workers toiled in the ship-building industry, c. 1840. Skilled laborers such as these often prospered with increasing industrialization. [National Trust Photographic Library, photographed by Michael Holford]

tories and the expansion of cities benefited all craftsmen in the building trades, such as carpenters, roofers, joiners, and masons. The lower prices for machine-made textiles aided artisans involved in the making of clothing, such as tailors and hatters, by reducing the costs of their raw materials. Where the urban artisans encountered difficulty and where they found their skills and livelihood threatened was in the organization of production.

In the eighteenth century a European town or city workplace had usually consisted of a few artisans laboring for a master. They labored first in the capacity of apprentices and then as journeymen, according to established guild regulations and practices. The master owned the workshop and the larger equipment, and the apprentices and journeymen owned their tools. The journeyman could well expect to become a master. This guild system had allowed very considerable worker control over labor recruitment and training, pace of production, quality of product, and price.

In the nineteenth century the situation of the urban artisan underwent very considerable change. It became increasingly difficult for artisans to continue to exercise corporate or guild direction and control over their trades. The legislation of the French Revolution had outlawed such organizations in France. Across Europe political and economic liberals disapproved of labor and guild organizations and attempted to make them illegal.

Other destructive forces were also at work. The masters often found themselves under increased competitive pressure from larger, more heavily capitalized establishments or from the possibility of the introduction of machine production into a previously craft-dominated industry. In many workshops masters began to follow a practice, known in France as *confection,* whereby goods such as shoes, clothing, and furniture were produced in standard sizes and styles rather than by special orders for individual customers.

The result of this practice was to increase the division of labor in the workshop. Each artisan produced a smaller part of the more-or-less uniform final product. Consequently, less skill was required of each artisan, and the particular skills possessed by a worker became less valuable. Masters also attempted to increase production and reduce their costs by lowering the wages paid for piecework. Those

attempts often led to work stoppages or strikes. Migrants from the countryside or small towns into the cities created, in some cases, a surplus of relatively unskilled workers. They were willing to work for lower wages or under less favorable and protected conditions than traditional artisans.

This dilution of skills and possible lower wages was caused not by machinery but by changes in the organization of artisan production. This situation made it much more difficult for urban journeymen ever to hope to become masters with their own workshops, in which they would be in charge. Increasingly these artisans became lifetime wage laborers whose skills were simply bought and sold in the marketplace.

Working-class Political Action: The Example of British Chartism

By the middle of the century, such artisans, proud of their skills and frustrated in their social expectations, became the most radical political element in the European working class. From at least the 1830s onward, these artisans took the lead in one country after another in attempting to formulate new ways of protecting their social and economic interests. Within the workplace they bargained and sometimes carried out strikes, as did the shoemakers of Marseilles in 1845. Other attempts to improve their situation included the formation of mutual aid societies; workers contributed in order to look after their needs in time of poor health or to ensure that they would have a proper funeral. Other artisans became involved in the various early socialist ideologies and the early trade-union movements. But repeatedly, artisans turned to collective action of a political nature. The most important of these in the first half of the century was British Chartism.

By the late 1830s the British working class had turned to direct political activity. They linked the solution of their economic plight to a program of political reform known as *Chartism.* In 1836 William Lovett (1800–1877) and other London radical artisans formed the London Working Men's Association. In 1838 the group issued the Charter, demanding six specific reforms. The Six Points of the Charter included universal manhood suffrage, annual election of the House of Commons, the secret ballot, equal electoral districts, abolition of

773

ECONOMI
ADVANCE A
SOCIAL
UNREST
(1830–185

This engraving depicts a Chartist procession in London. Chartism constituted the first large-scale working-class political movement. [The Mansell Collection]

property qualifications for Members of Parliament, and payment of members.

For over ten years the Chartists, who were never tightly organized, agitated for their reforms. On three occasions the Charter was presented to Parliament, which refused to pass it. Mass petitions were presented to the House of Commons with millions of signatures. Strikes were called. A Chartist newspaper called *The Northern Star* was published. Feargus O'Connor (1794–1855), the most important Chartist leader, made speeches up and down the island. Despite this vast activity Chartism as a national movement failed. Its ranks were split between those who favored violence and those who wanted to use peaceful tactics. However, locally the Chartists scored several successes and controlled the city councils in Leeds and Sheffield.

The economic foundation of Chartism had been the depression of the late 1830s and early 1840s. As prosperity returned, many working people abandoned the movement. Chartism came to a close in March 1848. A mass march on Parliament planned for that month fizzled. The reviving economy took care of the rest of the problem. Nevertheless, the Chartist movement constituted the first large-scale working-class political movement. It had specific goals

and largely working-class leadership. Eventually several of the Six Points were enacted into law. Continental working-class observers saw in Chartism the kind of mass movement that workers must eventually adopt if they were to improve their situation.

Family Structures and the Industrial Revolution

It is more difficult to write in generalities about the European family structure in the age of early industrialism than under the old regime. The reasons are that industrialism developed at very different rates across the continent and because the impact of industrialism cannot be separated from that of migration and urbanization. Furthermore, industrialism did not touch all families directly. In that regard, the structures and customs of many peasant families changed relatively little in the early and even in the later nineteenth century.

Yet the process of factory expansion, proletarianization, and the growth of commercial and service sectors related to industrialism did change the structures of much family life and the character of gender roles within families.

Much more is known about the relationships of the new industry to the family in Great Britain than elsewhere. It would seem that many of the British developments foreshadowed those in other countries as the factory system spread.

The Family in the Early Factory System

Contrary to the opinion once held, the adoption of new machinery and factory production did not destroy the working-class family. Before the late-eighteenth-century revolution in textile production in England, the individual family involved in textiles was the chief unit of production. The earliest textile inventions, such as the spinning jenny, did not change that

Concern about the plight of child labor in England only became acute in the 1830s when whole families ceased to work in the mills together, and children had to toil without their parents being present. [The Mansell Collection]

situation. The new machine was simply brought into the home to spin the thread. It was the mechanization of weaving that led to the major change. The father who became a machine weaver was employed in a factory. His work was thus separated from his home. However, the structure of early English factories allowed the father to preserve many of his traditional family roles as they had existed before the factory system.

In the domestic system of the family economy the father and mother had worked with their children in textile production as a family unit. They had trained and disciplined the children within the home setting. Their home life and their economic life were largely the same. In the early factories the father was permitted to employ his wife and children as his assistants. The tasks of education and discipline were not removed from the workplace nor from the institution of the family. Parental training and discipline were thus transferred from the home into the early factory. In some cases, in both Britain and France, whole families would move near a new factory so that the family as a unit could work there.

A major shift in this family and factory structure began in the mid-1820s in England and had been more or less completed by the mid-1830s. As spinning and weaving were put under one roof, the size of factories and of the machinery became larger. These newer machines required fewer skilled operators but many relatively unskilled attendants. The machine tending became the work of unmarried women and children. Factory owners found that they would accept lower wages and were less likely than adult men to attempt any form of worker or union organization.

However, factory wages for skilled adult males became sufficiently high to allow some fathers to remove their children from the factory and to send them to school. The children who were now working in the factories as assistants were often the children of the economically depressed handloom weavers. The wives of the skilled operatives also tended no longer to be working in the factories. Consequently, the original links of the family in the British textile factory that had existed for well over a quarter century largely disappeared.

CONCERN FOR CHILD LABOR It was at this point in the 1830s that much concern about the plight of child labor came to dominate workers' attention. They were concerned about the treatment of factory children because discipline was no longer being exercised by parents over their own children in the factories. The English Factory Act of 1833 was passed to protect children by limiting their workday to eight hours and requiring two hours of education paid for by the factory owner. The effect was to further divide work and home life. The workday for adult males remained twelve hours. Children often worked in relays of four or six hours. Consequently, the parental link was thoroughly broken. The education requirement began the process of removing nurturing and training from the home and family and setting them into a school, where a teacher rather than the parents was in charge of education.

After this act was passed, many of the working class demanded shorter workdays for adults. They desired to reunite, in some manner, the workday of adults with that of their children, or at least to allow adults to spend more hours with their children. In 1847 Parliament mandated a ten-hour day. By present standards this was very long. But at that time it allowed parents and children more hours together as a domestic unit since their relationship as a work or production unit had ceased wherever the factory system prevailed. By the middle of the 1840s, in the lives of industrial workers the role of men as breadwinners and men as fathers and husbands had become distinct in the British textile industry.

CHANGING ECONOMIC ROLE FOR THE FAMILY What occurred in Britain presents a general pattern for what would happen elsewhere with the spread of industrial capitalism and of public education. The European family was in the process of passing from the chief unit of both production and consumption to becoming the chief unit of consumption alone. This development did not mean the end of the family as an economic unit. However, parents and children now came to depend on sharing of wages often derived from several sources rather than on sharing of work in the home or in the factory.

Ultimately the wage economy meant that families were somewhat less closely bound together than in the past. Because wages could be sent over long distances to parents, children might now move farther away from home. Once they moved far away, the economic link was, in time, often broken. On the other hand, when a family settled in an industrial city, the wage economy might, in that or the next generation, actually discourage children from leaving home as early as they had in the past. Children could find wage employment in the same city and then live at home until they had accumulated enough savings to marry and begin their own household. That situation meant that children often remained with their parents to a later age than in the past.

Women in the Early Industrial Revolution

The industrial economy ultimately produced an immense impact on the home and the family life of women. First, it took virtually all productive work out of the home and put it elsewhere and allowed many families to live from the wages of the male spouse. That transformation prepared the way for a new concept of gender-determined roles in the home and in domestic life generally. Women came to be associated with domestic duties such as housekeeping, food preparation, child rearing and nurturing, and household management. The man came to be associated almost exclusively with breadwinning. Children were reared to match these expected gender patterns. Previously this domestic division of labor had prevailed among the relatively small middle class and gentry class. During the nineteenth century it came to characterize the working class as well.

Second, industrialization created for many young women new modes of employment that allowed them to earn enough money to marry or, if necessary, to support themselves independently. Third, industrialism, though fostering more employment for women, lowered the skills required of employed women.

Opportunities and Exploitation in Employment

Because the early Industrial Revolution had begun in textile production, women and their labor were deeply involved from the very start. While both spinning and weaving were still

775

ECONOMI
ADVANCE A
SOCIAL
UNREST
(1830–185

Women Industrial Workers Explain
Their Economic Situation

In 1832 there was much discussion in the British press about factory legislation. Most of that discussion was concerned with the employment of children, but the Examiner *newspaper made the suggestion that any factory laws should not only address the problem of child labor but also in time eliminate women from employment in factories. That article provoked the following remarkable letter to the editor, composed by or on behalf of women factory workers, which eloquently stated the very real necessity of such employment for women and the very unattractive alternatives.*

Sir,

Living as we do, in the densely populated manufacturing districts of Lancashire, and most of us belonging to that class of females who earn their bread either directly or indirectly by manufactories, we have looked with no little anxiety for your opinion on the Factory Bill. . . . You are for doing away with our services in manufactories altogether. So much the better, if you had pointed out any other more eligible and practical employment for the surplus female labour, that will want other channels for a subsistence. If our competition were withdrawn, and short hours substituted, we have no doubt but the effects would be as you have stated, "not to lower wages, as the male branch of the family would be enabled to earn as much as the whole had done," but for the thousands of females who are employed in manufactories, who have no legitimate claim on any male relative for employment or support, and who have, through a variety of circumstance, been early thrown on their own resources for a livelihood, what is to become of them?

In this neighbourhood, hand-loom has been almost totally superseded by power-loom weaving, and no inconsiderable number of females, who must depend on their own exertions, or their parishes for support, have been forced, of necessity into the manufactories, from their total inability to earn a livelihood at home.

It is a lamentable fact, that, in these parts of the country, there is scarcely any other mode of employment for female industry, if we except servitude and dress-making. Of the former of these, there is no chance of employment for one-twentieth of the candidates that would rush into the field, to say nothing of lowering the wages of our sisters of the same craft; and of the latter, galling as some of the hardships of manufactories are (of which the indelicacy of mixing with the men is not the least), yet there are few women who have been so employed, that would change conditions with the ill-used genteel little slaves, who have to lose sleep and health, in catering to the whims and frivolities of the butterflies of fashion.

We see no way of escape from starvation, but to accept the very tempting offers of the newspapers, held out as baits to us, fairly to ship ourselves off to Van Dieman's Land [Tasmania] on the very delicate errand of husband hunting, and having safely arrived at the "Land of Goshen," jump ashore, with a "Who wants me?" . . .

THE FEMALE OPERATIVES
OF TODMORDEN

The Examiner, *February 26, 1832, as quoted in Ivy Pinchbeck,* Women Workers and the Industrial Revolution, 1750–1850 *(New York: Augustus M. Kelley, 1969), pp. 199–200.*

777

ECONOMI
ADVANCE A
SOCIAL
UNREST
(1830–185

domestic industries, women usually worked in all stages of production. Hand spinning was virtually always a woman's task. When spinning was moved into factories and involved large machines, women tended to be displaced by men. The higher wages commanded by male cotton-factory workers allowed many women to stop work or to work only to supplement their husband's wages.

WOMEN IN FACTORIES With the next generation of machines in the 1820s, unmarried women rapidly became employed in the factories. However, in the factories their jobs tended to demand fewer skills than those they had previously exercised in the home production of textiles. They also required less skill than most work done by men. Tending a machine required less skill than actually spinning or weaving or acting as foreman. There was thus a certain paradox in the impact of the factory on women. Many new jobs were opened to women, but the level of skills was lowered.

Moreover, almost always, the women in the factories were young single women or widows. On marriage or perhaps the birth of the first child, they usually found that their husband earned enough money for them to leave the factory. Or they found themselves unwanted by the factory owners, who disliked employing married women because of the likelihood of pregnancy, the influence of their husbands, and the duties of child rearing.

WORK ON THE LAND AND IN THE HOME In Britain and elsewhere by mid-century, industrial factory work accounted for less than half of all employment for women. The largest group of employed women in France continued to work on the land. In England they were domestic servants. Domestic industries such as lacemaking, glove making, garment making, and other kinds of needlework employed a vast number of women. In almost all such cases their conditions of labor were harsh, whether they worked in their homes or in sweated workshops. Generally it cannot be overemphasized that all work by

Machinery in early textile mills was often tended by unmarried women or widows. There were many such jobs, but the women were paid less than men because it was unskilled labor. [Bettmann Archive]

women commanded low wages and involved low skills. They had virtually no effective modes of protecting themselves from exploitation. The charwoman, in that regard, was a common sight across the continent and symbolized the plight of working women.

Changing Expectations in Marriage

Movement to cities and entrance into the wage economy gave women wider opportunities for marriages. Cohabitation before marriage seems not to have been uncommon. Parents had less to do with arranging marriages than in the past. Marriage also now generally meant that a woman would leave the work force to live on her husband's earnings. If all went well, that arrangement might improve the woman's situation. However, if the husband became ill or died, or if the husband deserted his wife, she would find herself again required to enter the market for unskilled labor at a much advanced age.

Despite all of these changes, many of the traditional practices associated with the family economy survived into the industrial era. As a young woman came of age, both family needs and her desire to marry still directed what she would do with her life. The most likely early occupation for a young woman was domestic service. A girl born in the country normally migrated to a nearby town or city for such employment, often living initially with a relative. As in the past, she would attempt to earn enough in wages to give her a dowry, so that she might marry and establish her own household. If she became a factory worker, she would probably live in a supervised dormitory. Such dormitories were one of the ways that factory owners attracted young women into their employ by convincing parents that they would be safe.

The life of young women in the cities seems to have been more precarious than earlier. There seem to have been fewer family and community ties. There were also perhaps more available young men. These men, who worked for wages rather than in the older apprenticeship structures, were more mobile, so that relationships between men and women seem to have been more fleeting. In any case, illegitimate births increased. That is to say, fewer women who became pregnant before marriage found the father willing to marry them.

Marriage in the wage industrial economy was also different in certain respects from earlier marriages. Marriage still involved the starting of a separate household, but the structure of gender relationships within the household was different. Marriage was less an economic partnership. The husband's wages might well be able to support the entire family. The wage economy and the industrialization separating workplace and home made it very difficult for women to combine domestic duties with work. When married women worked, it was usually in the nonindustrial sector of the economy. More often than not, children were sent to work rather than the wife. This may provide one explanation for the increase of fertility within marriages, as children in the wage economy tended to be an economic asset. Married women worked outside the home only when family needs or illness or the death of a spouse really required them to do so. As Louise Tilly and Joan Scott wrote,

> Most women resolved the conflict between home and work by withdrawing from permanent employment, becoming temporary workers when their family need for their wages outweighed the advantages of their remaining at home and fulfilling economically important, but unpaid, domestic responsibilities.[1]

In the home, working-class women were by no means idle. Their domestic duties were an essential factor in the family wage economy. If work took place elsewhere, someone had to be directly in charge of maintaining the home front. Homemaking came to the fore when a life at home had to be organized that was separate from the place of work. Wives were primarily concerned with food and cooking, but they often also were in charge of the family's finances. The role of the mother expanded when the children still living at home became wage earners. She was now providing home support for her entire wage-earning family. She created the environment to which the family members returned after work. The longer period of home life of working children may also have increased and strengthened familial bonds of affection between those children and their hardworking, homebound mothers.

---

[1] Louise A. Tilly and Joan W. Scott, Women, Work, and Family (New York: Holt, Rinehart and Winston, 1978), p. 136.

Problems of Crime and Order

Throughout the nineteenth century the political and economic elite in Europe were profoundly concerned about social order. The revolutions of the late eighteenth and early nineteenth centuries made them fearful of future disorder and threats to life and property. The process of industrialization and urbanization also contributed to this problem of order. Thousands of Europeans migrated from the countryside to the towns and cities. There they often encountered poverty or unemployment and general social frustration and disap-

779

ECONOMIC
ADVANCE AND
SOCIAL
UNREST
(1830–185

A French Physician Describes a Working-class Slum in Lille

The work of medical doctors frequently carried them into working-class areas of industrial cities rarely visited by other members of the middle class. Louis Villermé was such a French physician. He wrote extensive descriptions of the slums and the general living conditions of industrial workers. The passage quoted below describes a particularly notorious section of Lille, a major cotton-manufacturing town in northern France.

The poorest live in the cellars and attics. These cellars . . . open onto the streets or courtyards, and one enters them by a stairway which is very often at once the door and the window. . . . Commonly the height of the ceiling is six or six and a half feet at the highest point, and they are only ten to fourteen or fifteen feet wide.

It is in these somber and sad dwellings that a large number of workers eat, sleep, and even work. The light of day comes an hour later for them than for others, and the night an hour earlier.

Their furnishings normally consist, along with the tools of their profession, of a sort of cupboard or a plank on which to deposit food, a stove . . . a few pots, a little table, two or three poor chairs, and a dirty pallet of which the only pieces are a straw mattress and scraps of a blanket. . . .

In their obscure cellars, in their rooms, which one would take for cellars, the air is never renewed, it is infected; the walls are plastered with garbage. . . . If a bed exists, it is a few dirty, greasy planks; it is damp and putrescent straw; it is a coarse cloth whose color and fabric are hidden by a layer of grime; it is a blanket that resembles a sieve. . . . The furniture is dislocated, worm-eaten, covered with filth. Utensils are thrown in disorder all over the dwelling. The windows, always closed, are covered by paper and glass, but so black, so smoke-encrusted, that the light is unable to penetrate . . . everywhere are piles of garbage, of ashes, of debris from vegetables picked up from the streets, of rotten straw; of animal nests of all sorts; thus, the air is unbreathable. One is exhausted, in these hovels, by a stale, nauseating, somewhat piquante odor, odor of filth, odor of garbage. . . .

And the poor themselves, what are they like in the middle of such a slum? Their clothing is in shreds, without substance, consumed, covered, no less than their hair, which knows no comb, with dust from the workshops. And their skin? . . . It is painted, it is hidden, if you wish, by indistinguishable deposits of diverse exudations.

Louis René Villermé, Tableau de l'état physique et moral des employés dans les manufactures de coton, de laine et de soie *(Paris, 1840), as quoted and trans. in William H. Sewell, Jr.,* Work and Revolution in France: The Language of Labor from the Old Regime to 1848 *(Cambridge: Cambridge University Press, 1980), p. 224.*

pointment. Cities became places associated with criminal activity and especially crimes against property, such as theft and arson. Throughout the first sixty years of the nineteenth century, there appears to have occurred a relatively slow but steady increase in crime, which then more or less plateaued.

Historians and social scientists are divided about the reasons for this rise in the crime rate. So little is known about crime in rural settings that comparisons are difficult. There are also many problems with crime statistics in the nineteenth century. No two nations kept them in the same manner. Different legal codes and systems of judicial administration were in effect in different areas of the continent, thus giving somewhat different legal definitions of criminal activity. The result has been confusion, very difficult research, and tentative conclusions.

New Police Forces

From the propertied elite classes there emerged, during the nineteenth century, two major views about containing crime and criminals. These were prison reform and better systems of police. The result of these efforts was the triumph in Europe of the concept of a policed society. This concept means the presence of a paid, professionally trained group of law-enforcement officers charged with keeping order, protecting property and lives, investigating crime, and apprehending offenders. These officers are distinct from the army and are charged specifically with domestic security. It is to them that the civilian population normally turns for law enforcement. One of the key features of the theory of a policed society is that crime may be prevented by the visible presence of law-enforcement officers. These police forces, at least in theory, did not perform a political role, though in many countries that distinction was often ignored.

Such professional police forces did not really exist until the early nineteenth century. They differed in the various countries in terms of both authority and organization, but their creation proved to be one of the main keys to the emergence of an orderly European society. Although police were viewed with a certain suspicion at various times, the remarkable fact is that by the end of the century most Europeans held friendly views toward police and regarded them as their protectors. Persons from the upper and middle classes felt their property to be more secure. Persons from the working class also frequently turned to the police to protect their lives and property and to aid them in other ways in emergencies. It is, of course, important to add that such was not the attitude toward political or secret police, who were hated and dreaded wherever governments created them.

THE FRENCH SYSTEM   In the late eighteenth century France was regarded as the best-policed state in Europe. Paris was regarded as the safest city on the Continent. Louis XIV had originally created the Paris police force. During the French Revolution the various revolutionary governments devised several different police organizations. There were important experiments that gave local municipalities responsibility for police enforcement. There was always fear that the police would be used by one political group against another. Under Napoleon the *police général* was a force used for political surveillance. There were further attempts to reorganize the police forces under the restored Bourbon government, but politics again came to the fore. From the revolution onward, the French governments depended on the *gendarmerie*, or military police, to patrol the provincial highways and, when necessary, to put down public disturbances.

In 1828 a new departure was taken. A new concept of policing was announced by the prefect of Paris:

> Safety by day and night, free traffic movement, clean streets, the supervision of and precaution against accidents, the maintenance of order in public places, the seeking out of offences and their perpetrators. . . . The municipal police is a parental police.[2]

The next year *sergents* in blue uniforms appeared on the streets of Paris. The uniform was important because it meant that the police officers could not disappear like a secret agent. They were very lightly armed to distinguish them from soldiers. There were never very many police in Paris or in other French cities during the nineteenth century. Paris had fewer than 500 at mid-century, and in the second

---

[2] Quoted in Clive Emsley, Policing and Its Context, 1750–1870 (London: Macmillan, 1983), p. 58.

781

ECONOMI
ADVANCE A
SOCIAL
UNREST
(1830–185

half of the century only about 4,000. In 1900 Marseilles had fewer than 300 police. The rapidly changing French governments tended to tolerate a rather confused and decentralized system of police. Those governments also continued to depend on the *gendarmerie* to put down major public and political disturbances.

THE PRUSSIAN SYSTEM The situation in Prussia was not unlike that in France. There was always a combination of small local police forces and troops to ensure order. The militarized character of Prussian society meant that many subjects lived in cities or towns where there were regularly stationed military garrisons. After the revolution of 1848, a new police force called the *Schutzmannschaft* was organized in Berlin. Originally a civilian force, it became over the years much more military in character. The police president of Berlin established a network of information with police presidents in other Prussian cities to increase criminal and political surveillance. Yet, at the same time, these Prussian police improved the delivery of municipal services and the general administration of their cities. This latter activity would appear to be one reason why many

people, especially those of the middle classes, accepted the political activity of the police as well.

THE BRITISH SYSTEM The most famous example of the creation of a domestic police force that came to command immense public confidence occurred in Great Britain. The British had always resisted the introduction of a professional police force. They feared that any such force would resemble the secret police of the major continental powers. However, in the early nineteenth century the British confronted two major problems. Local authorities using amateur constables and troops had not been able to maintain order. The Peterloo Massacre of 1819 had made that problem all too clear. Second, despite the fact that scores of capital offenses were on the law books, the threat of capital punishment was not deterring crimes against property. Gradually but dramatically, Britain lowered the number of capital offenses from more than two hundred in 1800 to eleven in 1841. After that date, only murder actually led to execution except during wartime. The reduction in penalties was tied to an effort to see that juries would actually convict

These men were London policemen in 1850. Professional police forces did not exist before the early nineteenth century. The London police force was created by Parliament in 1828. [The Mansell Collection]

and that criminals would actually be apprehended.

In 1828 Parliament passed the Metropolitan Police Act, creating a new police force for London. The minister who sponsored this legislation was Sir Robert Peel, after whom the members of the force came to be known as *bobbies.* By 1830 there were almost three thousand police serving in London. In 1839 Parliament extended permissive legislation to the countryside by permitting counties to organize police forces; in 1856 it mandated the establishment of those county forces. The English police during the nineteenth century tended to enjoy much popular support from all classes in the society. Members of the working class no less than members of the middle class turned to the police to ensure order and to apprehend persons who had disturbed their lives.

Prison Reform

The motives for establishing and reorganizing police forces were straightforward desires for order. Prison reform involved the impulse for both order and humanitarian improvement of the situation of prisoners. Before the nineteenth century European prisons tended to be local jails, quite large in the case of cities, or state prisons, such as the Bastille, or prison ships called *hulks.* Some nations sentenced prisoners to naval galleys, where, chained to their benches, they rowed until they died or were eventually released. Prisoners in prisons lived under the most wretched of conditions. Men and women were housed together. Children might be housed with adults. Persons guilty of minor offenses were left in the same room with persons guilty of the most serious offenses.

The late eighteenth century saw several developments that eventually fostered reform. The philosophy of the Enlightenment, as noted in Chapter 18, had raised questions about the treatment of criminals. Then, reformers such as John Howard in England made visits to prisons and widely publicized the terrible conditions. In 1813 Elizabeth Frey took up the cause of prison reform. In France Charles Lucas demanded change. All of these efforts made very slow progress. There was a host of local authorities to convince, and the building of new and better prisons was very expensive.

BRITISH REFORMS The British government had for sometime used the penalty of *transportation* for persons convicted of the most serious offenses. Beginning in the late eighteenth century these people were shipped to the colony of New South Wales in Australia. Transportation was regarded as an alternative to capital punishment. It was used by the British until the middle of the nineteenth century, when the colonies began to object. Thereafter, the British government established public works prisons in Britain to house long-term prisoners. The point of this mode of imprisonment was punishment and removing offenders from society. These had been the general purposes of imprisonment for decades in Europe.

However, in the 1840s both the French and the English undertook several bold efforts in prison reform. New prisons were designed according to what were regarded as scientific modes of understanding criminals and criminal reform. These prisons were intended to rehabilitate the criminal and to transform him or her during the period of incarceration. The original models for these prisons had been established in the United States. All of these experiments depended on various ways of separating prisoners from each other. One was known as the Auburn system after the Auburn Prison in New York State. According to it, prisoners were separated during the night but could associate in worktime during the day. The other was the Philadelphia system, in which prisoners were kept rigorously separated at all times.

Europeans used various versions of these systems. The keys to all of these systems were an individual cell for each prisoner and long periods of separation and silence between prisoners. The most famous example of this kind of prison in Europe was the Pentonville Prison near London. There, each prisoner was placed in a separate cell. The prisoners were never allowed to speak to each other while working or to see each other. They wore masks when in the prison yard, and in the chapel they had separate stalls. The point of the system was to turn the prisoner's mind in on itself to a mode of contemplation that would reform the criminal. As time passed, the system was allowed to become more relaxed because the intense isolation led to mental collapse.

Prisoners at the Brixton prison in Britain, around 1830, worked on the treadmill. It was advocated by social reformers as a way of improving discipline. [Library of Congress]

FRENCH PRISONS In France imprisonment became more repressive as the century passed. French prisons similar to Pentonville were constructed in the 1840s. One of the strongest advocates of the Philadelphia system in France was Alexis de Tocqueville, the author of *Democracy in America* (1833). Inspection of American prisons had been the occasion of his famous journey through the United States. The growing rigor of French prisons and the general treatment of crimes seems to have been closely related to fears of social and political disorder.

In 1851 the French government adopted transportation to the colonies at about the time the English gave up that system. In 1875 the French also adopted a firm general policy of isolation of prisoners in prison. This policy led to the construction of sixty prisons based on that principle by 1908. Prisoners were supposed to be trained in some kind of trade or skill while in prison so that they could re-emerge as reformed citizens. It was the vast increase in repeat offenses that led the French

government in 1885 to declare transportation the penalty for repeated offenses of serious crimes. The idea of this transportation to places, such as the infamous Devil's Island off the coast of South America, was literally to purge the nation of its worst criminals and to ensure that they would never return.

All of these attempts to create a police force and to reform prisons illustrate the new post–French Revolution concern about order and stability on the part of the European political and social elites. They also reflect attempts to impose some kind of new order on European social order. That order was put under immense pressures by a growing and migrating population, the emergence of industrial modes of production, urbanization, and political and economic discontent. New disturbances of a serious nature would occur, such as the revolutions of 1848 to be discussed later in this chapter. But on the whole, by the end of the century an orderly society had been established and the new police and prisons had no small role in that development.

Classical Economics

Economists whose thought largely derived from Adam Smith's *Wealth of Nations* (1776) dominated private and public discussions of industrial and commercial policy. Their ideas are generally associated with the phrase *laissez-faire*. Although they thought that the government should perform many important functions, the classical economists favored economic growth through competitive free enterprise. The economists conceived of society as consisting of atomistic individuals whose competitive efforts met the demands of the consumers in the marketplace. Most economic decisions should be made through the mechanism of the marketplace. They distrusted government action, believing it to be mischievous

Thomas Robert Malthus in his Essay on the Principle of Population *set forth a vision of human society drawn into misery by overpopulation. [Roger-Viollet]*

and corrupt. The government should maintain a sound currency, enforce contracts, protect property, impose low tariffs and taxes, and leave the remainder of economic life to private initiative. The economists naturally assumed that the state would maintain sufficient armed forces and naval power to protect the economic structure and the foreign trade of the nation. The emphasis on thrift, competition, and personal industriousness voiced by the political economists appealed to the middle classes.

Malthus on Population

The classical economists suggested complicated and very pessimistic ideas about the working class. Thomas Malthus (1766–1834) and David Ricardo (1772–1823), probably the most influential of all these writers, suggested, in effect, that the condition of the working class could not be improved. In 1798 Malthus published the first edition of his *Essay on the Principle of Population*. His ideas have haunted the world ever since. He contended that population must eventually outstrip the food supply. Although the human population grows geometrically, the food supply can expand only arithmetically. There was little hope of averting the disaster, in Malthus' opinion, except through late marriage, chastity, and contraception, the last of which he considered a vice. It took three quarters of a century for contraception to become a socially acceptable method of containing the population explosion.

Malthus contended that the immediate plight of the working class could only become worse. If wages were raised, the workers would simply produce more children, who would, in turn, consume both the extra wages and more food. Later in his life Malthus suggested, in a more optimistic vein, that if the working class could be persuaded to adopt a higher standard of living, their increased wages might be spent on consumer goods rather than on more children.

Ricardo on Wages

In the *Principles of Political Economy* (1817), David Ricardo transformed the concepts of Malthus into the Iron Law of Wages. If wages were raised, more children would be produced.

They, in turn, would enter the labor market, thus expanding the number of workers and lowering wages. As wages fell, working people would produce fewer children. Wages would then rise, and the process would start all over again. Consequently, in the long run, wages would always tend toward a minimum level. These arguments simply confirmed employers in their natural hesitancy to raise wages. These concepts also provided strong theoretical support for opposition to labor unions. The ideas of the economists were spread to the public during the 1830s through journals, newspapers, and even short stories, such as Harriet Martineau's series of *Illustrations of Political Economy.*

Government Policies Based on Classical Economics

The working class of France and Great Britain, needless to say, resented these attitudes, but the governments embraced them. Louis Philippe and his minister François Guizot told the French to go forth and enrich themselves. People who simply displayed sufficient energy need not be poor. A goodly number of the French middle class did just that. The July Monarchy saw the construction of major social overhead capital, such as roads, canals, and railways. Little was done about the poverty in the cities and the countryside.

In Germany the middle classes made less headway. However, the Prussian reformers after the Napoleonic wars had seen the desirability of abolishing internal tariffs that impeded economic growth. In 1834 all the major German states, with the exception of Austria, formed the *Zollverein,* or free trading union. Classical economics had somewhat less influence in Germany because of the tradition dating from enlightened absolutism of state direction of economic development. The German economist Friedrich List (1789–1846) argued for this approach to economic growth during the second quarter of the century.

Britain was the home of the major classical economists, and their policies were widely accepted. In 1834 the reformed House of Commons passed a new Poor Law. This measure established a Poor Law Commission, which set out to make poverty the most undesirable of all social situations. Government poor relief was to be disbursed only in workhouses. Life

785

ECONOMIC
ADVANCE AN
SOCIAL
UNREST
(1830–185

Harriet Martineau (1802–1876) was one of the most important popularizers of the ideas of the British classical economists. She illustrated their principles through moral tales. [The Granger Collection]

in the workhouse was consciously designed to be more unpleasant than life outside. Husbands and wives were separated; the food was bad; and the work assigned in the house was distasteful. The social stigma of the workhouse was even worse. The law and its administration presupposed that people would not work because they were lazy. The laboring class, not unjustly, regarded the workhouses as new "bastilles."

The second British monument to applied classical economics was the repeal of the Corn Laws in 1846. The Anti-Corn Law League, organized by manufacturers, had sought this goal for over six years. The league wanted the tariffs protecting the domestic price of grain to be abolished. That change would lead to lower food prices, which would then allow lower wages at no real cost to the workers. In turn, the prices on British manufactured goods could be lowered to allow a stronger competitive position in the world market.

The actual reason for Robert Peel's repeal of the Corn Laws in 1846 was the Irish famine. Peel had to open British ports to foreign grain to feed the starving Irish. He realized that the Corn Laws could not be reimposed. Peel accompanied the abolition measure with a program for government aid to modernize British agriculture and to make it more efficient. The repeal of the Corn Laws was the culmination of the lowering of British tariffs that had begun during the 1820s. The repeal marked the opening of an era of free trade that continued until late in the century.

Early Socialism

During the twentieth century the socialist movement, in the form of either communist or social democratic political parties, has constituted one of the major political forces in Europe. Less than 150 years ago the advocates of socialism lacked any meaningful political following. Their doctrines were blurred and often seemed silly to their contemporaries. The confusion in early socialist thought reflected its pioneering nature. The social and economic conditions being analyzed were new, and the exact problems to be solved still had to be defined.

The early socialists generally applauded the new productive capacity of industrialism. However, they denied that the free market could adequately produce and distribute goods in the fashion claimed by the classical economists. The socialists saw primarily mismanagement, low wages, maldistribution of goods, and suffering arising from the unregulated industrial system. Moreover, the socialists thought that human society should be organized as a community rather than merely as a conglomerate of atomistic, selfish individuals.

Utopian Socialism

Among the earliest people to define the social question were a group of writers called the *utopian socialists* by their later critics. They were considered utopian because their ideas were often visionary and because they frequently advocated the creation of ideal communities. They were called *socialists* because they questioned the structures and values of the existing capitalistic framework. In some cases they actually deserved neither description.

SAINT-SIMONIANISM   Count Claude Henri de Saint-Simon (1760–1825) was the earliest of the socialist pioneers. As a young liberal French aristocrat he had fought in the American Revolution. Later he welcomed the French Revolution, during which he made and

lost a fortune. By the time of Napoleon's ascendancy he had turned to a career of writing and social criticism.

Above all else Saint-Simon believed that modern society would require rational management. Private wealth, property, and enterprise should be subject to an administration other than that of its owners. His ideal government would have consisted of a large board of directors organizing and coordinating the activity of individuals and groups to achieve social harmony. In a sense he was the ideological father of technocracy. Not the redistribution of wealth but its management by experts would alleviate the poverty and social dislocation of the age.

When Saint-Simon died in 1825, he had persuaded only a handful of people that his ideas were correct. Interestingly enough, several of those disciples later became leaders in the French railway industry during the 1850s.

OWENISM   The major British contributor to the early socialist tradition was Robert Owen (1771–1858), a self-made cotton manufacturer. In his early twenties Owen became a partner in one of the largest cotton factories in Britain at New Lanark, Scotland. Owen was a firm believer in the environmentalist psychology of the Enlightenment. If human beings were placed in the correct surroundings, they and their character could be improved. Moreover Owen saw no incompatibility between creating a humane industrial environment and making a good profit.

At New Lanark he put his ideas into practice. Workers were provided with good quarters. Recreational possibilities abounded, and the children received an education. There were several churches, although Owen himself was a notorious freethinker on matters of religion and sex. In the factory itself various rewards were given for good work. His plant made a fine profit. Visitors flocked from all over Europe to see what Owen had accomplished through enlightened management.

In numerous articles and pamphlets, as well as in letters to influential people, Owen pleaded for a reorganization of industry based on his own successful model. He envisioned a series of communities shaped like parallelograms in which factory and farm workers might live together and produce their goods in cooperation. During the 1820s Owen sold his

Equitably → Fairly (not Evenly or Equally)

A dance recital by the students in the factory school in New Lanark. Robert Owen's industrial community there included free schooling for the children of his workers. [The Mansell Collection]

New Lanark factory and then went to the United States, where he established the community of New Harmony, Indiana. When quarrels among the members led to the community's failure, he refused to give up his reformist causes. He returned to Britain, where he became the moving force behind the organization of the Grand National Union. This was an attempt to draw all British trade unions into a single body. It collapsed with other labor organizations during the early 1830s.

Owen possessed an exaggerated sense of his own importance and was a difficult person. His version of socialism amounted to little more than old-fashioned paternalism transported to the industrial setting. However, he contributed to the socialist tradition a strong belief in the practicality of cooperative production and proof that industrial production and humane working conditions were compatible.

FOURIERISM Charles Fourier (1772–1837) was the French intellectual counterpart of Owen. He was a commercial salesman who never succeeded in attracting the same kind of public attention as Owen. He wrote his books and articles and waited at home each day at noon, hoping to meet a patron who would undertake his program. No one ever arrived to meet him. Fourier believed that the industrial order ignored the passionate side of human nature. Social discipline ignored all the pleasures that human beings naturally seek.

Fourier advocated the construction of communities, called *phalanxes,* in which liberated living would replace the boredom and dullness of industrial existence. Agrarian rather than industrial production would predominate in these communities. Sexual activity would be relatively free, and marriage was to be reserved only for later life. Fourier also urged that no person be required to perform the same kind of work for the entire day. People would be both happier and more productive if they moved from one task to another. Through his emphasis on the problem of boredom Fourier isolated one of the key difficulties of modern economic life.

Saint-Simon, Owen, and Fourier expected some existing government to carry out their ideas. They failed to confront the political difficulties of their envisioned social transformations. Other figures paid more attention to the politics of the situation. In 1839 Louis Blanc (1811–1882) published *The Organization of Labor.* Like other socialist writers this Frenchman demanded an end to competition, but he did not seek a wholly new society. He called for political reform that would give the vote to the working class. Once so empowered, workers could use the vote to turn the political processes to their own economic advantage. A state controlled by a working-class electorate would finance workshops to employ the poor. In time such workshops might replace private enterprise, and industry would be organized to ensure jobs. Blanc recognized the power of the state to improve life and the conditions of labor. The state itself could become the great employer of labor.

Anarchism

Other writers and activists of the 1840s, however, rejected both industry and the dominance of government. These were the anarchists. They are usually included in the socialist tradition although they do not exactly fit. Some favored programs of violence; others were peaceful. Auguste Blanqui (1805–1881) was a major spokesman for terror and was one of Europe's earliest professional revolutionaries. He spent most of his adult life in jail. Blanqui urged the development of a professional revolutionary vanguard to attack capitalist society. He sought the abolition of both capitalism and the state. His ideas for the new society were quite vague, but in his call for professional revolutionaries he foreshadowed Lenin.

Pierre Joseph Proudhon (1809–1865) represented the other strain of anarchism. In his most famous work, *What Is Property?* (1840), Proudhon attacked the banking system, which so rarely extended credit to small property owners or the poor. He wanted credit expanded to allow such people to engage in economic enterprise. Society should be organized on the basis of mutualism, which amounted to a system of small businesses. There would be peaceful cooperation and exchange of goods among these groups. With such a social system the state as it then existed would be unneces-

sary. His ideas later influenced the French labor movement, which generally avoided political activity.

These various strains of early socialist thought provided the background and the context for the emergence of Marxist socialism. But they did more than that. They influenced the ideas and activities of European socialists and trade unions well into the third quarter of the century. Too often the history of socialism is regarded as a linear development leading naturally or necessarily to the triumph of Marxism. Nothing could be further from the truth. Marxism did eventually triumph over much, though not all, of Europe, but only through competition with other socialist formulas. At mid-century the ideas of Karl Marx were simply one more contribution to a heady mixture of concepts and programs criticizing the emerging industrial capitalist society. Marxist ideology differed from its competitors in the brilliance of its author, its claim to rigorous scientific accuracy, and its message of the inevitable collapse of the capitalistic order.

Marxism

Karl Marx was born in 1818 in the Rhineland. His Jewish middle-class parents sent him to the University of Berlin, where he became deeply involved in Hegelian philosophy and radical politics. During 1842 and 1843 he edited the radical *Rhineland Gazette (Rheinische Zeitung).* Soon the German authorities drove him from his native land. He lived as an exile in Paris, then in Brussels, and finally, after 1849, in London.

PARTNERSHIP WITH ENGELS In 1844 Marx met Friedrich Engels (1820–1895), another young middle-class German, whose father owned a textile factory in Manchester, England. The next year Engels published *The Conditions of the Working Class in England,* which presented a devastating picture of industrial life. The two men became fast friends. Late in 1847 they were asked to write a pamphlet for a newly organized and ultimately short-lived secret Communist League. *The Communist Manifesto,* published in German, appeared early in 1848. Marx, Engels, and the league had adopted the name *communist* because the term was much more self-consciously radical than *socialist.* Commu-

789

ECONOMI◦
ADVANCE A
SOCIAL
UNREST
(1830–185◦

The socialist philosophy of Karl Marx eventually triumphed over most alternative versions of socialism in Europe—even though varying interpretations, criticisms, and revisions of his monumental work continue to today. [Bettmann Archive]

sis into a new intellectual synthesis. For Marx the conflict between dominant and lesser social groups generated conditions that led to the emergence of a new dominant social group. These new social relationships, in turn, generated new discontent, conflict, and development.

The French socialists provided Marx with a portrayal of the evils of capitalist society and had raised the issue of property redistribution. Both Hegel and Saint-Simon had led Marx to see society and economic conditions as developing through historical stages. The classical economists had produced the analytical tools for an empirical, scientific examination of industrial capitalist society. Marx later explained to a friend:

> *What I did that was new was to prove: (1) that the* existence of classes *is bound up with* particular historical phases in the development of production; *(2) that the class struggle necessarily leads to the* dictatorship of the proletariat; *(3) that this dictatorship itself only constitutes the transition to the* abolition of all classes and to a classless society.[3]

REVOLUTION THROUGH CLASS CONFLICT In *The Communist Manifesto* Marx and Engels contended that human history must be understood rationally and as a whole. It is the record of humankind's coming to grips with physical nature to produce the goods necessary for survival. That basic productive process determines the structures, values, and ideas of a society. Historically, the organization of the means of production has always involved conflict between the classes who owned and controlled the means of production and those classes who worked for them. That necessary conflict has provided the engine for historical development; it is not an accidental by-product of mismanagement or bad intentions. Consequently, piecemeal reforms cannot eliminate the social and economic evils that are inherent in the very structures of production. What is required is a radical social transformation. Such a revolution will occur as the inevitable outcome of the development of capitalism.

In Marx's and Engels' eyes, during the nineteenth century the class conflict that had char-

nism implied the outright abolition of private property rather than some less extensive rearrangement of society. The *Manifesto* itself was a work of less than fifty pages. It would become the most influential political document of modern European history, but that development lay in the future. At the time it was simply one more political tract. Moreover neither Marx nor his thought had any effect on the revolutionary events of 1848.

SOURCES OF MARX'S IDEAS The major ideas of the *Manifesto* and of Marx's later work, including *Capital* (Vol. I, 1867), were derived from German Hegelianism, French socialism, and British classical economics. Marx applied to social and economic development Hegel's concept that thought develops from the clash of thesis and antithe-

---

[3]*Albert Fried and Ronald Sanders (Eds.),* Socialist Thought: A Documentary History *(Garden City, N.Y.: Anchor Doubleday, 1964), p. 295.*

Karl Marx Analyzes the Character of Class Conflict

In a pamphlet of 1847 entitled The Poverty of Philosophy *Karl Marx very succinctly set forth the concept of class conflict leading to a total revolution. He argued that the concentration of capital among large bourgeois manufacturing concerns had generated the existence of a working class that had in turn come to have a collective sense of its own revolutionary goals. Thereafter, conflict with the bourgeoisie was an inevitable, necessary part of commercial, manufacturing society that he termed "civil society."*

Economic conditions first transformed the mass of the people of the country [England] into workers. The combination of capital has created for this mass a common situation, common interests. This mass is thus already a class as against capital, but not yet for itself. In the struggle . . . this mass becomes united, and constitutes itself as a class for itself. The interests it defends become class interests. But the struggle of class against class is a political struggle.

An oppressed class is the vital condition for every society founded on the antagonism of classes. The emancipation of the oppressed class thus implies necessarily the creation of a new society. For the oppressed class to be able to emancipate itself it is necessary that the productive powers already acquired and the existing social relations should no longer be capable of existing side by side. Of all the instruments of production, the greatest productive power is the revolutionary class itself. The organization of revolutionary elements as a class supposes the existence of all the productive forces which could be engendered in the bosom of the old society.

Does this mean that after the fall of the old society there will be a new class domination culminating in a new political power? No.

The condition for the emancipation of the working class is the abolition of every class, just as the condition for the liberation of the third estate, of the bourgeois order, was the abolition of all estates and all orders.

The working class, in the course of its development, will substitute for the old civil society an association which will exclude classes and their antagonism, and there will be no more political power properly so called, since political power is precisely the official expression of antagonism in civil society.

Meanwhile the antagonism between the proletariat and the bourgeoisie is a struggle of class against class, a struggle which carried to its highest expression is a total revolution. . . .

Robert Tucker (Ed.), The Marx-Engels Reader, *2nd ed. (New York: W. W. Norton & Company, 1978), pp. 218–219.*

acterized previous Western history had become simplified into a struggle between the bourgeoisie and the proletariat, or between the middle class and the workers. The character of capitalism ensured the sharpening of the struggle. Capitalist production and competition would steadily increase the size of the unpropertied proletariat. Large-scale mechanical production crushed both traditional and smaller industrial producers into the ranks of the proletariat. As the business structures grew larger and larger, smaller middle-class units would be squeezed out by the competitive pressures. Competition among the few remaining giant concerns would lead to more intense suffering on the part of the proletariat.

As the workers suffered increasingly from the competition among the ever-enlarging firms, they would eventually begin to foment revolution. Finally they would overthrow the few remaining owners of the means of production. For a time the workers would organize the means of production through a dictatorship of the proletariat. This would eventually give way to a propertyless and classless communist society.

This proletarian revolution was inevitable, according to Marx and Engels. The structure of capitalism required competition and consolidation of enterprise. Although the class conflict involved in the contemporary process resembled that of the past, it differed in one major respect. The struggle between the capitalistic bourgeoisie and the industrial proletariat would culminate in a wholly new society that would be free of class conflict. The victorious proletariat, by its very nature, could not be a new oppressor class: "The proletarian movement is the self-conscious, independent movement of the immense majority, in the interest of the immense majority."[4] The result of the proletarian victory would be "an association, in which the free development of each is the condition for the free development of all."[5] The victory of the proletariat over the bourgeoisie would represent the culmination of human history. For the first time in human history one group of people would not be oppressing another.

Marx's analysis was conditioned by his own economic environment. The 1840s had been a period of much unemployment and deprivation. However, capitalism did not collapse as he had predicted, nor did the middle class during the rest of the century become proletarianized. Rather, more and more people came to benefit from the industrial system. Nonetheless, within a generation Marxism had captured the imagination of many socialists and large segments of the working class. The doctrines were based on the empirical evidence of hard economic fact. This scientific aspect of Marxism helped the ideology as science became more influential during the second half of the century.

Marx had made the ultimate victory of socialism seem certain. His writings had also portrayed, for the first time, the actual magnitude of the revolutionary transformation. His works suggested that the path to socialism lay with revolution rather than with reform. The days of the utopians were over.

MAJOR WORKS OF ECONOMIC AND POLITICAL COMMENTARY	
1776	Adam Smith, *The Wealth of Nations*
1798	Thomas Malthus, *Essay on the Principle of Population*
1817	David Ricardo, *Principles of Political Economy*
1830s	Harriet Martineau, *Illustrations of Political Economy*
1839	Louis Blanc, *The Organization of Labor*
1844	Friedrich Engels, *The Condition of the Working Class in England*
1848	Karl Marx and Friedrich Engels, *The Communist Manifesto*

1848: Year of Revolutions

In 1848 a series of liberal and nationalistic revolutions spread across the Continent. No single factor caused this general revolutionary ground swell; rather, a number of similar conditions existed in several countries. Severe food shortages had prevailed since 1846. The harvests of grain and potatoes had been very poor. The famine in Ireland was simply the worst example of a more widespread situation. The commercial and industrial economy was also in a period of downturn. Unemployment was very widespread. All systems of poor relief were overburdened. These difficulties, added to the wretched living conditions in the cities, heightened the sense of frustration and discontent of the urban artisan and laboring classes.

However, the dynamic force for change in 1848 originated not with the working classes but with the political liberals, who were generally drawn from the middle classes. Throughout the Continent liberals were pushing for their program of more representative government, civil liberty, and unregulated economic

---

[4] *Robert C. Tucker (Ed.),* The Marx-Engels Reader *(New York: W. W. Norton, 1972), p. 353.*
[5] *Ibid.*

life. The repeal of the English Corn Laws and the example of peaceful agitation by the Anti-Corn Law League encouraged them. The liberals on the Continent wanted to pursue similar peaceful tactics. However, to put additional pressure on their governments, they began to appeal for the support of the urban working classes. The goals of the latter were improved working and economic conditions rather than a liberal framework of government. Moreover, the tactics of the working classes were frequently violent rather than peaceful. The temporary alliance of liberals and workers in several states overthrew or severely shook the old order; then the allies commenced to fight each other.

Finally, outside France nationalism was an important common factor in the uprisings. Germans, Hungarians, Italians, and smaller national groups in eastern Europe sought to create national states that would reorganize or replace existing political entities. The Austrian Empire, as usual, was the state most profoundly endangered by nationalism. The nationalists were also frequently liberal and sometimes benefited from lower- and working-class economic discontent in the major cities.

The immediate results of the 1848 revolutions were quite stunning. The French monarchy fell, and many of the others were badly shaken. Never in a single year had Europe known so many major uprisings. Yet the revolutions proved a false spring for progressive Europeans. Without exception they failed to establish genuinely liberal or national states. The conservative order proved stronger and more resilient than anyone had expected. Moreover, the liberal middle-class political malcontents in each country discovered that they could no longer push for political reform without at the same time raising the social question. The liberals refused to follow political revolution with social reform and thus isolated themselves from the working classes. Once separated from potential mass support, the liberal revolutions became an easy prey to the armies of the reactionary classes.

France: The Second Republic and Louis Napoleon

As twice before, the revolutionary tinder first blazed in Paris. The liberal political opponents of the corrupt regime of Louis Philippe and his minister Guizot had organized a series of political banquets. These occasions were used to criticize the government and to demand further middle-class admission to the political process. The poor harvests of 1846 and 1847 and the resulting high food prices and unemployment brought working-class support to the liberal campaign. On February 21, 1848, the government forbade further banquets. A very large one had been scheduled for the next day. On February 22 disgruntled Parisian workers paraded through the streets demanding reform and Guizot's ouster. The next morning the crowds grew, and by afternoon Guizot had resigned. The crowds had erected barricades, and numerous clashes had occurred between the citizenry and the municipal guard. On February 24, 1848, Louis Philippe abdicated and fled to England.

THE NATIONAL ASSEMBLY AND PARIS WORKERS The liberal opposition, led by the poet Alphonse de Lamartine (1790–1869), organized a provisional government. They intended to call an election for an assembly that would write a republican constitution. The various working-class groups in Paris had other ideas; they wanted a social as well as a political revolution. Led by Louis Blanc, they demanded representation in the Cabinet. Blanc and two other radical leaders were made ministers. Under their pressure the provisional government organized national workshops to provide work and relief for thousands of unemployed workers.

On Sunday, April 23, an election based on universal manhood suffrage chose the new National Assembly. The result was a legislature dominated by moderates and conservatives. In the French provinces there had been much resentment against the Paris radicals. The Church and the local notables still exercised considerable influence. Small landowning peasants feared possible confiscation of their holdings by Parisian socialists. The new conservative National Assembly had little sympathy for the very expensive national workshops, which they incorrectly perceived to be socialistic.

Throughout May government troops and the Parisian crowd of unemployed workers and artisans clashed. As a result, the assembly closed the workshops to new entrants and

This engraving gives a view from behind the barricade in Paris 1848. The street barricade was a hallmark of the revolutionary outbreaks that erupted across Europe in the 1830s and 1840s. Constructed of paving stones, carts, barrels, and whatever else was handy, these barricades across narrow, twisting streets could present formidable obstacles to troops. [Library of Congress]

planned the removal of many enrolled workers. By the latter part of June barricades again appeared in Paris. On June 24, under orders from the government, General Cavaignac, with troops drawn largely from the conservative countryside, moved to destroy the barricades and to quell potential disturbances. During the next two days over four hundred people were killed. Thereafter, troops hunted down another three thousand persons in street-to-street fighting. The drive for social revolution had come to an end.

EMERGENCE OF LOUIS NAPOLEON

The so-called June Days confirmed the political predominance of conservative property holders in French life. They wanted a republic, but a republic safe for small property. This search for social order received further confirmation late in 1848. The victor in the presidential election was Louis Napoleon Bonaparte (1808–1873), a nephew of the great emperor. For most of his life he had been an adventurer living outside France. Twice he had unsuccessfully attempted to lead a *coup* against the July Monarchy. The disorder of 1848 provided him a new opportunity to enter the French political scene. After the corruption of Louis Philippe and the turmoil of the early months of the Second Republic, the voters

Paris Workers Complain About the Actions of Their Government

In the late spring of 1848 the government of the recently formed French Republic abolished the national workshops that it had created a few weeks earlier to provide aid for the unemployed. The first selection below illustrates the anger caused by the abolition of the workshops and the sense of betrayal felt by the workers. The second document describes the experience of a cabinetmaker who had for a time enrolled in one of the workshops.

To the Finance Minister of the Republic

Are you really the man who was the first finance minister of the Republic, of the Republic won at the cost of blood thanks to the workers' courage, of this Republic whose first vow was to provide bread every day for all its children by proclaiming the universal right to work? Work, who will give it to us if not the state at a time when industry has everywhere closed its workshops, shops and factories? Yesterday martyrs for the Republic out on the barricades, today its defenders in the ranks of the national guard, the workers might consider it owed them something. . . .

Why do the national workshops so rouse your reprobation . . . ? You are not asking for their reform, but for their total abolition. But what is to be done with this mass of 110,000 workers who are waiting each day for their modest pay, for the means of existence for themselves and their families? Are they to be left a prey to the evil influences of hunger and of the excesses that follow in the wake of despair?

A Letter to a Newspaper Editor

I live in the fauborg [working class neighborhood]; by trade I am a cabinet-maker and I am enrolled in the national workshops, waiting for trade to pick up again.

I went into the workshops when I could no longer find bread elsewhere. Since then people have said we were given charity there. But when I went in I did not think that I was becoming a beggar. I believed that my brothers who were rich were giving me a little of what they had to spare simply because I was their brother.

I admit that I have not worked very hard in the national workshops, but then I have done what I could. I am too old now to change my trade easily—that is one explanation. But there is another: the fact is that, in the national workshops, there is absolutely nothing to do.

Roger Price (Ed. and Trans.), 1848 in France (Ithaca, N.Y.: Cornell University Press, 1975), pp. 103–104. Used by permission of the publisher.

turned to the name of Bonaparte as a source of stability and greatness.

The election of the "Little Napoleon" doomed the Second Republic. Louis Napoleon was dedicated to his own fame rather than to republican institutions. He was the first of the modern dictators who, by playing on unstable politics and social insecurity, greatly changed European life. He constantly quarreled with the National Assembly and claimed that he rather than they represented the will of the nation. In 1851 the assembly refused to amend the constitution to allow the president to succeed himself. Consequently, on December 2, 1851, the anniversary of the great Napoleon's victory at Austerlitz, Louis Napoleon seized personal power. Troops dispersed the assembly, and the president called for new elections. Over 200 people died resisting the *coup,* and over 26,000 persons were arrested throughout the country. Almost 10,000 persons who opposed the *coup* were transported to Algeria.

Yet, in the plebiscite of December 21, 1851, over 7.5 million voters supported the actions of Louis Napoleon and approved a new constitution that consolidated his power. Only about 600,000 citizens dared to vote against him. A year later, in December 1852, an Empire was proclaimed, and Louis Napoleon became Emperor Napoleon III. Again a plebiscite approved the action. For the second time in just over fifty years France had turned from republicanism to caesarism.

The Habsburg Empire: Nationalism Resisted

The events of February 1848 in Paris immediately reverberated throughout the Habsburg domains. The empire was susceptible to revolutionary challenge on every score. Its government rejected liberal institutions. Its geographical borders disregarded the principle of nationalism. Its society perpetuated serfdom. During the 1840s even Metternich had urged reform, but none was forthcoming. In 1848 the regime confronted major rebellions in Vienna, Prague, Hungary, and Italy. It was also intimately involved in the disturbances that broke out in Germany.

THE VIENNA UPRISING The Habsburg troubles began on March 3, 1848, when Louis Kossuth (1802–1894), a Magyar nationalist, attacked Austrian domination of Hungary. He called for the independence of Hungary and a responsible ministry under the crown of Habsburg. Ten days later, inspired by Kossuth's demands, students led a series of major disturbances in Vienna. The army failed to restore order. Metternich resigned and fled the country. The feeble-minded Emperor Ferdinand (1835–1848) promised a moderately liberal constitution. Unsatisfied, the radical students then formed democratic clubs to press the revolution further. On May 17 the emperor and the imperial court fled to Innsbruck. The government of Vienna at this point lay in the hands of a committee of over two hundred persons primarily concerned with alleviating the economic plight of Viennese workers.

What the Habsburg government most feared was not the urban rebellions but a potential uprising of the serfs. Already there had been

795

ECONOMIC
ADVANCE AN
SOCIAL
UNREST
(1830–185(

Louis Kossuth (1802–1894), Hungarian nationalist, led the revolution of 1848 in Budapest. [The Granger Collection]

isolated instances of serfs invading manor houses and burning records. Almost immediately after the Vienna uprising, the imperial government had emancipated the serfs in large areas of Austria. The Hungarian Diet also abolished serfdom in March 1848. These actions smothered the most serious potential threat to order in the empire. The emancipated serfs now had little reason to support the revolutionary movement in the cities.

THE MAGYAR REVOLT The Vienna revolt had further encouraged the Hungarians. The leaders of the Hungarian March revolution were primarily liberal Magyars supported by Magyar nobles who wanted their aristocratic liberties guaranteed against the central government in Vienna. The Hungarian Diet passed a series of March Laws that ensured equality of religion, jury trials, the election of a lower chamber, a relatively free press, and payment of taxes by the nobility. Emperor Ferdinand approved these measures because in the spring of 1848 he was in a position to do little else.

The Magyars also hoped to establish a separate Hungarian state within the Habsburg domains. They would retain considerable local autonomy while Ferdinand remained their emperor. As part of this scheme for a partially independent state, the Hungarians attempted to annex Transylvania, Croatia, and other territories on the eastern border of the Habsburg empire. That policy of annexation would bring Romanians, Croatians, and Serbs under Magyar government. These national groups re-

This caricature shows the flight of Metternich in March 1848. *Although he had advocated limited reform of the Austrian government during the 1840s, Metternich in the eyes of the people was the symbol of reaction. His fall evoked great popular rejoicing.* [Culver Pictures]

sisted the drive toward Magyarization. They believed that they had a better chance of maintaining their national or ethnic identity and self-interest under Habsburg control. Consequently, they turned against Hungary. In late March the Vienna government sent Baron Joseph Jellachich to aid the national groups who were rebelling against the rebellious Hungarians. By early September 1848 he was leading an invasion force against Hungary.

CZECH NATIONALISM In the middle of March 1848, with Vienna and Budapest in revolt, Czech nationalists had demanded that Bohemia and Moravia be permitted to constitute an autonomous Slavic state within the empire similar to that just constituted in Hungary. Conflict immediately developed, however, between the Czechs and the Germans living in these areas. The Czechs summoned a congress of the Slavs, which met in Prague during early June. On June 12, the day the congress closed, a radical insurrection broke out in the city. General Alfred von Windischgraetz, whose wife had been killed by a stray bullet, moved his troops to repress the uprising. The local middle class was happy to see the radicals suppressed, which they were by June 17. The Germans in the area approved the smothering of Czech nationalism. The policy of "divide and conquer" had succeeded.

REBELLION IN NORTHERN ITALY
While confronting the Hungarian and Czech bids for autonomy, the Habsburg government also faced war in northern Italy. A revolution against Habsburg domination began in Milan on March 18. Five days later the Austrian commander General Joseph Wenzel Radetzky retreated from the city. King Charles Albert of Piedmont (1831–1849), who wanted to expand the influence of his kingdom in the area, aided the rebels in Lombardy (the state of which Milan is the capital). The Austrian force fared badly until July, when Radetzky, reenforced by new troops, defeated Piedmont and suppressed

the revolution. For the time being, Austria had held its position in northern Italy.

Vienna and Hungary remained to be recaptured. In midsummer the emperor returned to the capital. A newly elected assembly was attempting to write a constitution. However, within the city the radicals continued to press for further concessions. The imperial government decided to reassert its control. When a new insurrection occurred in October, the imperial army bombarded Vienna and crushed the revolt. On December 2 Emperor Ferdinand, now clearly too feeble to govern, abdicated in favor of his young nephew Francis Joseph (1848–1916). Real power now lay with Prince Felix Schwarzenberg (1800–1852), who intended to use the army with full force.

On January 5, 1849, troops occupied Budapest. By March the triumphant Austrian forces had imposed military rule over Hungary, and the new emperor repudiated the recent constitution. The Magyar nobles attempted one last revolt. It was crushed in August by Austrian troops reenforced by 200,000 soldiers happily furnished by Tsar Nicholas I of Russia. The imperial Habsburg government had survived its gravest internal challenge because of the diversions among its enemies and its own willingness to use military force with a vengeance.

Italy: Republicanism Defeated

The brief Piedmont-Austrian war of 1848 marked only the first stage of the Italian revolution. Many Italians hoped that King Charles Albert of Piedmont would drive Austria from the peninsula and thus prepare the way for Italian unification. The defeat of Piedmont was a sharp disappointment. Liberal and nationalist hopes then shifted to the pope. Pius IX (1846–1878) had a liberal reputation. He had reformed the administration of the Papal States. Nationalists believed that some form of a united Italian state might emerge under the leadership of this pontiff.

In Rome, however, as in other cities, political radicalism was on the rise. On November 15, 1848, a democratic radical assassinated Count Pelligrino Rossi, the liberal minister of the Papal States. The next day popular demonstrations forced the pope to appoint a radical ministry. Shortly thereafter Pius IX fled to Naples for refuge. In February 1849 the radicals

proclaimed the Roman Republic. Republican nationalists from all over Italy, including Giuseppe Mazzini (1805–1872) and Giuseppe Garibaldi (1807–1882), two of the most prominent, flocked to Rome. They hoped to use the new republic as a base of operations to unite the rest of the peninsula under a republican government.

In March 1849 radicals in Piedmont forced Charles Albert to renew the patriotic war against Austria. The almost immediate defeat of Piedmont at the battle of Novara gave the king an opportunity to abdicate in favor of his son, Victor Emmanuel II (1849–1878). The defeat meant that the Roman Republic must defend itself alone. The troops that attacked Rome and restored the pope came from France. The French wanted to prevent the rise of a strong, unified state on their southern border. Moreover, protection of the pope was good domestic politics for the French Republic and its president, Louis Napoleon. In early June 1849 ten thousand French soldiers laid siege to the Eternal City. By the end of the month the Roman Republic had dissolved. Garibaldi attempted to lead an army north against Austria but was defeated. On July 3 Rome fell to the French forces, which continued to occupy it as protection for the pope until 1870.

Pius IX returned, having renounced his previous liberalism. He became one of the archconservatives of the next quarter century. Leadership toward Italian unification would have to come from another direction.

Germany: Liberalism Frustrated

The revolutionary contagion had also spread rapidly through numerous states of Germany. Württemberg, Saxony, Hanover, and Bavaria all experienced insurrections calling for liberal government and greater German unity. The major revolution, however, occurred in Prussia.

REVOLUTION IN PRUSSIA By March 15, 1848, large popular disturbances had erupted in Berlin. Frederick William IV (1840–1861), believing that the trouble stemmed from foreign conspirators, refused to turn his troops on the Berliners. He even announced certain limited reforms. Nevertheless, on March 18, several citizens were killed when troops cleared a square near the palace.

797

ECONOMIC
ADVANCE AND
SOCIAL
UNREST
(1830–1850)

The monarch was still hesitant to use his troops forcefully, and there was much confusion in the government. The king also called for a Prussian constituent assembly to write a constitution. The next day, as angry Berliners crowded around the palace, Frederick William IV appeared on the balcony to salute the corpses of his slain subjects. He made further concessions and implied that henceforth Prussia would aid the movement toward German unification. For all practical purposes the Prussian monarchy had capitulated.

Frederick William IV appointed a cabinet headed by David Hansemann (1790–1864), a widely respected moderate liberal. However, the Prussian constituent assembly proved to be radical and democratic. As time passed, the king and his conservative supporters decided that they would ignore the assembly. The lib-

eral ministry resigned and was replaced by a conservative one. In April 1849 the assembly was dissolved, and the monarch proclaimed his own constitution. One of its key elements was a system of three-class voting. All adult males were allowed to vote. However, they voted according to three classes arranged by ability to pay taxes. Thus the largest taxpayers, who constituted only about 5 per cent of the population, elected one third of the Prussian Parliament. This system prevailed in Prussia until 1918. In the finally revised Prussian constitution of 1850, the ministry was responsible to the king alone. Moreover, the Prussian army and officer corps swore loyalty directly to the monarch.

THE FRANKFURT PARLIAMENT While Prussia was moving from revolution to reac-

The Frankfurt Parliament met in a church in that city in September 1848. *Its deputies wanted to create a liberal, united Germany. However, as their debate dragged out, the forces of reaction regained strength and the parliament failed. [Bettmann Archive]*

799

ECONOMI(
ADVANCE A[
SOCIAL
UNREST
(1830–185(

The King of Prussia Declines the Crown Offered by the Frankfurt Parliament

In the spring of 1849 the Frankfurt Parliament completed the writing of a constitution for a united Germany that would exclude Austria. The Parliament offered the crown of a constitutional German monarchy to Frederick William IV of Prussia. He declined the offer. This letter of May 15, 1849 was addressed to the people of Prussia. In it the monarch explained his reasons and attacked the liberal political thought of the Parliament and the revolutionary events that had allowed it to be called in the first place.

Taking as a pretense the interests of Germany, the enemies of the fatherland have raised the standard of revolt, first in neighboring Saxony, then in several districts of south Germany. To my deep chagrin, even in parts of our own land some have permitted themselves to be seduced into following this standard and attempting, in open rebellion against the legal government, to overturn the order of things established by both divine and human sanction. In so serious and dangerous a crisis I am moved publicly to address a word to my people.

I was not able to return a favorable reply to the offer of a crown on the part of the German National Assembly [the Frankfurt Parliament], because the Assembly has not the right, without the consent of the German governments, to bestow the crown which they tendered me, and moreover, because they offered the crown upon condition that I would accept a constitution which could not be reconciled with the rights and safety of the German states.

I have exhausted every means to reach an understanding with the German National Assembly. . . . Now the Assembly has broken with Prussia. The majority of its members are no longer those men upon whom Germany looked with pride and confidence. The greater part of the deputies voluntarily left the Assembly when they saw that it was on the road to ruin, and yesterday I ordered all the Prussian deputies who had not already withdrawn to be recalled. The other governments [of the several German states] will do the same.

A party now dominates the Assembly which is in league with the terrorists. While they urge the unity of Germany as a pretense, they are really fighting the battle of godlessness, perjury, and robbery, and kindling a war against monarchy; but if monarchy were overthrown, it would carry with it the blessings of law, liberty, and property. . . .

James Harvey Robinson (Ed.), Readings in European History *(Boston: Ginn and Co., 1906), pp. 571–572.*

tion, other events were unfolding in Germany as a whole. On May 18, 1848, representatives from all the German states gathered in Saint Paul's Church in Frankfurt to revise the organization of the German Confederation. The Frankfurt Parliament intended to write a moderately liberal constitution for a united Germany. The liberal character of the Frankfurt Parliament alienated both German conserva-

tives and the German working class. The offense to the conservatives was simply the challenge to the existing political order. The Frankfurt Parliament lost the support of the industrial workers and artisans by refusing to restore the protection once afforded by the guilds. The liberals were too much attached to the concept of a free labor market to offer meaningful legislation to workers. This failure

The Revolutionary Crisis of 1848–1851

1848

February 22–24	Revolution in Paris forces the abdication of Louis Philippe
February 26	National workshops established in Paris
March 3	Kossuth attacks the Habsburg domination of Hungary
March 13	Revolution in Vienna
March 15	The Habsburg emperor accepts the Hungarian March Laws
	Revolution in Berlin
March 18	Frederick William IV of Prussia promises a constitution
	Revolution in Milan
March 19	Frederick William IV is forced to salute the corpses of slain revolutionaries in Berlin
March 22	Piedmont declares war on Austria
April 23	Election of the French National Assembly
May 15	Worker protests in Paris lead the National Assembly to close the national workshops
May 17	Habsburg Emperor Ferdinand flees from Vienna to Innsbruck
May 18	The Frankfurt Assembly gathers to prepare a German constitution
June 17	A Czech revolution in Prague is suppressed
June 23–26	A workers' insurrection in Paris is suppressed by the troops of the National Assembly
July 24	Austria defeats Piedmont
September 17	General Jellachich invades Hungary
October 31	Vienna falls to the bombardment of General Windischgraetz
November 15	Papal minister Rossi is assassinated in Rome
November 16	Revolution in Rome
November 25	Pope Pius IX flees Rome
December 2	Habsburg Emperor Ferdinand abdicates and Francis Joseph becomes emperor
December 10	Louis Napoleon is elected president of the Second French Republic

1849

January 5	General Windischgraetz occupies Budapest
February 2	The Roman Republic is proclaimed
March 12	War is resumed between Piedmont and Austria
March 23	Piedmont is defeated, and Charles Albert abdicates the crown of Piedmont in favor of Victor Emmanuel II
March 27	The Frankfurt Parliament completes a constitution for Germany
March 28	The Frankfurt Parliament elects Frederick William IV of Prussia to be emperor of Germany
April 21	Frederick William IV of Prussia rejects the crown offered by the Frankfurt Parliament
June 18	The remaining members of the Frankfurt Parliament are dispersed by troops
July 3	Collapse of the Roman Republic after invasion by French troops
August 9–13	The Hungarian forces are defeated by Austria aided by the troops of Russia

1850

November 29	The Punctation of Olmütz

1851

December 2	*Coup d'état* of Louis Napoleon

marked the beginning of a profound split between German liberals and the German working class. For the rest of the century German conservatives would be able to play on that division.

As if to demonstrate its disaffection from

workers, in September 1848 the Frankfurt Parliament called in troops of the German Confederation to suppress a radical insurrection in the city. The liberals in the parliament wanted nothing to do with workers who erected barricades and threatened the safety of property.

The Frankfurt Parliament floundered on the issue of unification as well as on the social question. Members differed over the inclusion of Austria in the projected united Germany. The large German *(grossdeutsch)* solution favored inclusion, whereas the small German *(kleindeutsch)* solution advocated exclusion. The latter formula prevailed because Austria rejected the whole notion of German unification. It raised too many other nationality problems within the Habsburg domains. Consequently, the Frankfurt Parliament looked to Prussian leadership.

On March 27, 1849, the parliament produced its constitution. Shortly thereafter its delegates offered the crown of a united Germany to Frederick William IV of Prussia. He rejected the offer, asserting that kings ruled by the grace of God rather than by the wisdom of man-made constitutions. On his refusal the Frankfurt Parliament began to dissolve. Not long afterward troops drove off the remaining members.

German liberals never fully recovered from this defeat. The Frankfurt Parliament had alienated the artisans and the working class without gaining any compensating support from the conservatives. The liberals had proved themselves to be awkward, hesitant, unrealistic, and ultimately dependent on the armies of the monarchies. They had failed to unite Germany or to confront effectively the realities of political power in the German states. What was achieved through the various revolutions was an extension of the franchise in some of the German states and the establishment of conservative constitutions. The gains were not negligible, but they were a far cry from the hopes of March 1848.

THE PUNCTATION OF OLMÜTZ The events of 1848 and 1849 had one important footnote for Frederick William IV. He gave much more thought to possible German unification under Prussia. In 1850 he attempted to create a German federation, which would have been a union of princes headed by the king of Prussia and excluding Austria. The Austrian Empire firmly rejected the proposal, which would have diminished Habsburg influence in Germany. In November 1850, in what is known as the Punctation of Olmütz, the Prussian monarch renounced his scheme at the demand of Austria. Prussian historians later called this event the Humiliation of Olmütz.

801

ECONOMIC
ADVANCE AND
SOCIAL
UNREST
(1830–1850

The first half of the nineteenth century had witnessed enormous, unprecedented social change in Europe. The foundations of the industrial economy were laid. Virtually no existing institution failed to be touched by that emerging economy. Railways crossed the continent. New consumer goods were available. Family patterns changed as did the social and economic expectations of women. The crowding of cities presented new social and political problems. Issues of social order came to the fore with the new concern about crime and the establishment of new police forces. An urban working class became one of the chief facts of both political and social life. The ebb and flow of the business cycle caused increased economic anxiety for workers and property owners alike.

While all of these fundamental social changes took place, Europe was also experiencing ongoing political strife. The turmoil of 1848 through 1850 brought to a close the era of liberal revolution that had begun in 1789. Liberals and nationalists had discovered that rational argument and small insurrections would not achieve their goals. The political initiative passed for a time to the conservative political groups. Nationalists henceforth were less romantic and more hardheaded. Railways, commerce, guns, soldiers, and devious diplomacy rather than language and cultural heritage became the weapons of national unification. The working class also adopted new tactics and organization. The era of the riot and urban insurrection was coming to a close. In the future, workers would turn to trade unions and political parties to achieve their political and social goals.

Perhaps most important after 1848 the European middle class ceased to be revolutionary. It became increasingly concerned about the protection of its property against radical political and social movements associated with socialism and increasingly as the century passed with Marxism. The middle class remained politically liberal only so long as liberalism seemed to promise economic stability and social security for its own style of life.

Suggested Readings

S. AVINERI, *The Social and Political Thought of Karl Marx* (1969). An advanced treatment.

I. BERLIN, *Karl Marx: His Life and Environment* (1948). An excellent introduction.

R. B. CARLISLE, *The Proffered Crown: Saint-Simonianism and the Doctrine of Hope* (1987). The best treatment of the broad social doctrines of Saint-Simonianism.

W. COLEMAN, *Death Is a Social Disease: Public Health and Political Economy in Early Industrial France* (1982). One of the first works in English to study this problem.

I. DEAK, *The Lawful Revolution: Louis Kossuth and the Hungarians, 1848–1849* (1979). The most significant study of the topic in English.

J. ELSTER, *An Introduction to Karl Marx* (1985). The best volume to provide a discussion of Marx's fundamental concepts.

T. HAMEROW, *Restoration, Revolution, and Reaction: Economics and Politics in Germany, 1815–1871* (1958). Traces the forces that worked toward the failure of revolution in Germany.

J. F. C. HARRISON, *Quest for the New Moral World: Robert Owen and the Owenites in Britain and America* (1969). Now the standard work.

R. HEILBRONER, *The Worldly Philosophers*, rev. ed. (1972). A useful, elementary introduction to nineteenth-century economic thought.

G. HIMMELFARB, *The Idea of Poverty: England in the Early Industrial Age* (1984). A major work covering the subject from the time of Adam Smith through 1850.

M. IGNATIEFF, *A Just Measure of Pain: The Penitentiary in the Industrial Revolution, 1750–1850* (1978). An important treatment of early English penal thought and practice.

K. KOLAKOWSKI, *Main Currents of Marxism: Its Rise, Growth, and Dissolution*, 3 vols. (1978). A very important and comprehensive survey.

D. LANDES, *The Unbound Prometheus: Technological Change and Industrial Development in Western Europe from 1750 to the Present* (1969). The best one-volume treatment of technological development in a broad social and economic context.

W. L. LANGER, *Political and Social Upheaval, 1832–1852* (1969). A remarkably thorough survey strong in both social and intellectual history as well as political narrative.

F. MANUEL, *The Prophets of Paris* (1962). A stimulating treatment of French utopian socialism and social reform.

T. W. MARGADANT, *French Peasants in Revolt: The Insurrection of 1851* (1979). A study of the rural resistance to Louis Napoleon.

J. M. MERRIMAN, *The Agony of the Republic: The Repression of the Left in Revolutionary France, 1848–1851* (1978). A major study of the manner in which the Second French Republic and popular support for it were suppressed.

J. M. MERRIMAN (Ed.), *Consciousness and Class Experience in Nineteenth-Century Europe* (1979). A collection of important revisionist essays in social and intellectual history covering topics across the Continent.

P. O'BRIEN, *The Promise of Punishment: Prisons in Nineteenth-Century France* (1982). An excellent treatment of the problems of life within the prison.

H. PERKIN, *The Origins of Modern English Society, 1780–1880* (1969). A provocative attempt to look at the society as a whole.

D. PHILIPS, *Crime and Authority in Victorian England: The Black Country 1835–1860* (1977). One of the few works to examine the problem in an industrial setting.

I. PINCHBECK, *Women Workers and the Industrial Revolution, 1750–1850* (1930, reprinted 1969). A pioneering study that remains of great value.

D. H. PINKNEY, *Decisive Years in France, 1840–47* (1986). A detailed and careful examination of the years leading up to the Revolution of 1848.

P. ROBERTSON, *An Experience of Women: Pattern and Change in Nineteenth-Century Europe* (1982). A useful survey.

W. H. SEWELL, JR., *Work and Revolution in France: The Language of Labor from the Old Regime to 1848* (1980). A very fine analysis of French artisans.

N. SMELZER, *Social Change in the Industrial Revolution: An Application of Theory to the British Cotton Industry* (1959). Important sections on the working-class family.

D. SORKIN, *The Transformation of German Jewry, 1780–1840* (1987). An examination of the decades of Jewish emancipation in Germany.

P. STEARNS, *Eighteen Forty-Eight: the Tide of Revolution in Europe* (1974). A good discussion of the social background.

G. D. SUSSMAN, *Selling Mother's Milk: The Wet-nursing Business in France, 1715–1914* (1982). An examination of an important subject in the history of the family and of women.

A. J. TAYLOR (Ed.), *The Standard of Living in Britain in the Industrial Revolution* (1975). A collection of major articles on the impact of industrialism.

D. THOMPSON, *The Chartists: Popular Politics in the Industrial Revolution* (1984). An important new study.

E. P. THOMPSON, *The Making of the English Working Class* (1964). An important, influential, and controversial work.

L. A. TILLY AND J. W. SCOTT, *Women, Work, and Family* (1978). A useful and sensitive survey.

A. S. WOHL, *Endangered Lives: Public Health in Victorian Britain* (1983). An important and wide-ranging examination of the health problems created by urbanization and industrialization.

C. WOODHAM-SMITH, *The Great Hunger: Ireland, 1845–1849* (1962). A moving account of one of the great social tragedies of the nineteenth century.

G. WRIGHT, *Between the Guillotine and Liberty: Two Centuries of the Crime Problem in France* (1983). A useful overview.

H. ZEHR, *Crime and the Development of Modern Society: Patterns of Criminality in Nineteenth-Century Germany and France* (1976). An examination of crimes against property in urban society.

803

ECONOMIC
ADVANCE AND
SOCIAL
UNREST
(1830–1850)

TOWARD THE MODERN WORLD

The century between approximately 1850 and 1945 may quite properly be regarded as the European era of world history. The nations of Europe achieved and exercised an unprecedented measure of political, economic, and military power across the globe. No less impressive than the vastness of this influence was its brevity. By 1945, much of Europe, from Britain to the Soviet Union, literally lay in ruins. Within a few years, the United States and the Soviet Union would emerge as superpowers with whom no European state could compete. Furthermore, nations throughout Asia, Africa, and Latin America that had once experienced direct or indirect European rule would thrust off their colonial status. Both the rise and the decline of European world dominance fostered violence, warfare, and human exploitation all over the globe.

The half century after 1850 witnessed political consolidation and economic expansion that paved the way for the momentary dominance of Europe. The skillful diplomats and armies of the conservative monarchies of Piedmont and Prussia united Italy and Germany by military force. As a major new political and economic power in central Europe, Germany loomed as a potential rival to Great Britain, France, and Russia. For a time, shrewd diplomacy and a series of complex alliances contained that rivalry. At the same time, while sorting out the new power relationships on the continent, the nations of Europe exported potential conflicts overseas. The result of this externalized rivalry was a period of imperialistic ventures. By the turn of the century these had resulted in the outright partition of Africa into areas directly governed by Europeans and in the penetration of China by European merchants, administrators, and missionaries.

What permitted this unprecedented situation to arise was the economic and technological base of late-nineteenth-century European civilization. Europeans possessed the productive capacity to dominate world markets. Their banks controlled or influenced vast amounts of capital throughout the world economy. Their engineers constructed and later often managed railways on all the continents. Their military technology, especially their navies, allowed Europeans to back up economic power with armed force.

Simultaneously with the expansion of industrial power new political ideologies came to the fore in Europe. Across the continent socialists challenged the ideology of liberalism and spawned internal disputes that have influenced European political life to the present day. Nationalism was the other dominant political ideology whose supporters challenged the legitimacy of any political arrangement that failed to recognize a politics based on ethnicity. Nowhere was nationalism a more troubling force than in the multinational Habsburg Empire.

In 1914 the more general situation of European dominance came to an abrupt end when war growing out of imperialistic and nationalistic rivalry erupted among the major states of Europe. That conflict may be regarded as the central event of the twentieth century. Its effects continue to influence the world today. The Austro-Hungarian monarchy collapsed. Germany became a republic. The revolutionary socialist government of the Bolsheviks replaced the imperial government of the Russian tsars.

Social turmoil and economic dislocation accompanied the political revolutions. The victorious nations of Britain, France, and Italy had been bled white of young men, and much of their wealth had been exhausted by wartime expenditures. The military and financial participation of the United States blocked the establishment of independent economic policy by the European powers. Ongoing nationalistic resentments fostered by the Paris Peace Settlement of 1919, in combination with the political and economic pressures of the 1920s and 1930s, created conditions from which arose the authoritarian movements of Italian Fascism and German Nazism. By 1939 the aggression of Germany and the hesitant response of the other major powers led again to the outbreak of war in Europe. From that conflict, Europe failed to reemerge as the dominant political or economic force in the world.

Two other developments also contributed to the end of the European era of world history. First, the principle of national self-determination applied to Europeans in the 1919 settlement was adopted by colonial peoples seeking to assert their own right to national independence. Second, the demand for self-determination soon became linked to criticism of the foreign capitalistic domination of colonial economic life. The latter development flowed directly from the spread of communist ideas throughout the colonial world after the Russian Revolution. In this respect, the ideologies of nationalism and revolutionary socialism developed by Europeans in the nineteenth century to solve certain problems in their own political and economic life were turned against them as peoples in Asia, Africa, and Latin America sought to solve their own political problems in the mid-twentieth century.

*William I of Prussia was declared Emperor of Germany in the
Hall of Mirrors at Versailles after the defeat of France in
the Franco-Prussian War. Bismarck stands in the white
uniform toward the right of the picture. [Photo Corstensen]*

23

THE AGE OF NATION-STATES

The revolutions of 1848 collapsed in defeat for both liberalism and nationalism. Throughout the early 1850s authoritarian regimes entrenched themselves across the Continent. Yet only a quarter century later many of the major goals of early-nineteenth-century liberals and nationalists stood accomplished. Italy and Germany were each at long last united under constitutional monarchies. The Habsburg emperor had accepted constitutional government; the Hungarian Magyars had attained recognition of their liberties. In Russia the serfs had been emancipated. France was again a republic. Liberalism and even democracy flourished in Great Britain.

Paradoxically most of these developments occurred under the direction and leadership of conservative leaders. Events within European international affairs compelled some of them to pursue new policies at home as well as abroad. They had to find novel methods of maintaining the loyalty of their subjects. In some cases conservative leaders preferred to carry out a popular policy on their own terms so that they, rather than the liberals, would receive credit. Finally, some political leaders moved as they did because they had no choice.

The Crimean War
(1854–1856)

As has so often been true in modern European history, the impetus for change originated in war. The Crimean War (1854–1856) was rooted in the long-standing rivalry between Russia and the Ottoman Empire. There were two disputes that led to the conflict. First, the Ottoman Empire had recently granted Catholic France rather than Orthodox Russia the oversight of the Christian shrines in the Holy Land. Second, Russia wanted to extend its control over the Ottoman provinces of Moldavia and Walachia (now in Romania). The tsar's duty to protect Orthodox Christians in the Ottoman Empire furnished the pretext for the Russian aggression. Russia occupied the two provinces in the summer of 1853. The Ottoman Empire declared war on Russia in the autumn of that year.

The other great powers soon became involved, and a war among major European states resulted. Both France and Great Britain opposed Russian expansion in the eastern Mediterranean, where they had extensive naval and commercial interests. Napoleon III also thought that an activist foreign policy would shore up domestic support for his regime. On March 28, 1854, France and Britain declared war on Russia. Much to the disappointment of Tsar Nicholas I, Austria and Prussia remained neutral. The Austrians had their own ambitions in the Balkans, and after the humiliation of Olmütz, Prussia followed Austrian leadership for some time.

The war was ineptly waged on both sides. The ill-equipped and poorly commanded armies became bogged down along the Crimean coast of the Black Sea. In September 1855, after a long siege, the Russian fortress of Sevastopol finally fell. In March 1856 a conference in Paris concluded the Treaty of Paris, which was highly unfavorable to Russia. It required Russia to surrender territory near the mouth of the Danube River, to recognize the neutrality of the Black Sea, and to renounce claims of protection over Christians in the Ottoman Empire. Even before the conference, Austria had forced Russia to withdraw from Moldavia and Walachia. The image of an invincible Russia that had prevailed across Europe since the close of the Napoleonic wars was totally shattered.

Also shattered was the Concert of Europe (see Chapter 21) as a means of dealing with international relations on the Continent. There was much less fear of revolution than in the early part of the century and consequently much less reverence for the Vienna settlement. As historian Gordon Craig commented, "After 1856 there were more powers willing to fight to overthrow the existing order than there were to take up arms to defend it."[1] Napoleon III had little respect for the Congress of Vienna and favored redrawing the map along lines of nationality. The Austrians hoped to compensate for the poor figure they had cut in remaining neutral during the conflict by asserting more influence within the German Confederation. Prussia became increasingly discontented with a role in Germany subordinate to Austria's. Russia, which had been among the chief defenders of the Vienna settlement, now sought to overcome the disgrace of the 1856 Treaty of Paris. The mediocre display of British military prowess led that nation to hesitate about future continental involvement.

Consequently, for about twenty-five years after the Crimean War, instability prevailed in European affairs, allowing a largely unchecked adventurism in foreign policy. Without the restraining influence of the Concert of Europe, each nation believed that only the limits of its military power and its diplomatic influence should act as constraints on its international ambitions. Moreover, foreign policy increasingly became an instrument of domestic policy. The two most significant achievements to result from this new international situation were the unifications of Italy and of Germany. Those events, in turn, generated further pressures on neighboring countries.

Italian Unification

Nationalists had long wanted the small, absolutist principalities of the Italian peninsula united into a single state. However, during the

---

[1] The New Cambridge Modern History (Cambridge: Cambridge University Press, 1967), 10:273.

The Crimean War (1854–1856) was the first major military conflict recorded by photography. The British photographer Roger Fenton, who accompanied the expeditionary force to the siege of Sevastopol, took these pictures of a cavalry camp (above) and of the supply depot at Balaklava (below).

first half of the century there had existed broad differences of opinion about the manner and goals of unification.

Romantic Republicans

One approach to the issue had been that of romantic republicans. After the Congress of Vienna numerous secret republican societies were founded, the most famous of which was the *Carbonari* ("charcoal burners"). They were singularly ineffective.

Following the failure of nationalist uprisings in 1831, the leadership of romantic republican nationalism passed to Giuseppe Mazzini (1805–1872). He became the most important nationalist leader in all Europe and brought to the cause of nationalism new emotional fervor. He once declared, "Nationality is the role assigned by God to a people in the work of humanity. It is its mission, its task on earth, to the end that God's thought may be realized in the world."[2] In 1831 he founded the Young Italy Society for the purposes of driving Austria from the peninsula and establishing an Italian republic.

During the 1830s and 1840s Mazzini and fellow republican Giuseppe Garibaldi (1807–1882) led insurrections. Both were deeply involved in the ill-fated Roman Republic of 1849. Throughout the next decade they continued to conduct what amounted to guerilla warfare. Because both men spent much time in exile, they became well known across the Continent and in the United States.

Republican nationalism frightened the more moderate Italians, who wanted to rid themselves of Austrian domination but not at the cost of establishing a republic. For a time these people had looked to the pope as a possible vehicle for unification. That solution became impossible after the experience of Pius IX with the Roman Republic in 1849. Consequently, at mid-century "Italy" remained a geographical expression rather than a political entity.

However, between 1852 and 1860 the area was transformed into a national state. The process was carried out not by romantic republican nationalists but by Count Camillo Cavour (1810–1861), the moderately liberal prime

Giuseppi Mazzini (1805–1872) was a fervent republican nationalist. He excited emotional support for Italian unity, but also frightened moderate Italians. [Ullstein Bilderdienst]

Cavour was the moderately liberal prime minister of the Kingdom of Piedmont. He was determined to make the idea of a united Italy respectable and acceptable to the rest of Europe. [Culver Pictures]

---

[2] *Quoted in William L. Langer,* Political and Social Upheaval, 1832–1852 *(New York: Harper Torchbooks, 1969), p. 115.*

minister of Piedmont. The method of unification was that of force of arms tied to secret diplomacy. The spirit of Machiavelli must have smiled over the enterprise.

Cavour's Policy

Piedmont (officially styled the Kingdom of Sardinia), in northwestern Italy, was the most independent state on the peninsula. The Congress of Vienna had restored the kingdom as a buffer between French and Austrian ambitions in the area. As we have seen, during 1848 and 1849 King Charles Albert of Piedmont, after having promulgated a conservative constitution, twice unsuccessfully fought Austria. Following the second defeat, he abdicated in favor of his son, Victor Emmanuel II. In 1852 the new monarch chose as his prime minister Count Camillo Cavour.

Cavour Explains Why Piedmont Should Enter the Crimean War

As prime minister of Piedmont, Cavour attempted to prove that the Italians were capable of progressive government. In 1855, addressing the Parliament of Piedmont, he urged entry into the Crimean War so that the other Europeans would consider Piedmont a military power. Earlier politics in Italy had been characterized by petty absolute princes and Romantic nationalist conspiracies, both of which Cavour scorned. He understood that in the nineteenth century a nation must possess good government, economic prosperity, and a strong army.

The experience of recent years and previous centuries has proved (at least in my opinion) how little Italy has benefited by conspiracies, revolutions and disorderly uprisings. Far from helping her, they have been a tremendous calamity for this beautiful part of Europe. And not only, gentlemen, because individual people so often suffered from them, not only because revolutions became the cause or pretext for repression, but above all because continual conspiracies, repeated revolutions and disorderly uprisings damaged the esteem and, up to a certain point, the sympathy that other European peoples cherished for Italy.

Now, gentlemen, I believe that the principal condition for the improvement of Italy's fate, the condition that stands out above all others, is to lift up her reputation once more, so to act that all the peoples of the world, those governing and those governed, may do justice to her qualities. And for this two things are necessary: first, to prove to Europe that Italy has sufficient civic sense to govern herself freely and according to law, and that she is in a condition to adopt the very best forms of government; second, to prove that her military valor is as great as that of her ancestors.

You have done Italy one service by your conduct over the last seven years. You have shown Europe in the most luminous way that Italians are capable of governing themselves with wisdom, prudence, and trustworthiness. But it still remains for you to do Italy an equal, if not a greater, service; it is our country's task to prove that Italy's sons can fight valiantly on battlefields where glory is to be won. And I am sure, gentlemen, that the laurels that our soldiers will win in Eastern Europe will help the future state of Italy more than all that has been done by those people who hoped to regenerate her by rhetorical speeches and writings.

Denis Mack Smith (Ed. and Trans.), The Making of Italy, 1796–1870 *(New York: Walker and Company, 1968), pp. 199–200.*

A cunning statesman, Cavour had begun political life as a strong conservative but had gradually moved toward a moderately liberal position. He had made a personal fortune by investing in railroads, reforming agricultural methods on his own estates, and editing a newspaper. He was deeply imbued with the ideas of the Enlightenment, classical economics, and utilitarianism. Cavour was a nationalist of a new breed who had no respect for Mazzini's ideals. A strong monarchist, Cavour rejected republicanism. It was economic and material progress rather than romantic ideals that required a large, unified state on the Italian peninsula.

Cavour believed that if Italians proved themselves to be efficient and economically progressive, the great powers might decide that Italy could govern itself. He joined the Piedmontese Cabinet in 1850 and became premier two years later. He worked for free trade, railway construction, credit expansion, and agricultural improvement. He felt that such material and economic bonds, rather than fuzzy Romantic yearnings, must unite the Italians. However, Cavour also recognized the need to capture the loyalties of the Italians who possessed other varieties of nationalistic feelings. To that end he fostered the Nationalist Society, which established chapters in other Italian states to press for unification under the leadership of Piedmont. Finally, the prime minister believed that Italy could be unified only with the aid of France. The recent accession of Napoleon III in France seemed to open the way for such aid at some time in the future.

FRENCH SYMPATHIES Cavour used the outbreak of the Crimean War to enter the larger European picture. In 1855 Piedmont joined the conflict on the side of France and Britain and sent ten thousand troops to the front. This small but significant participation in the war allowed Cavour to raise the Italian question at the Paris conference. He left Paris with no diplomatic reward, but he had impressed everyone with his intelligence and political capacity. Cavour also gained the sympathy of Napoleon III. During the rest of the decade Cavour achieved further international respectability for Piedmont by opposing various plots of Mazzini, who was still attempting to lead nationalist uprisings. By the close of the decade Cavour represented a moderate liberal alternative to both republicanism and reactionary absolutism in Italy.

The Piedmontese prime minister continued to bide his time. Then, in January 1858, an Italian named Orsini attempted to assassinate Napoleon III. The incident made the French emperor, who had once belonged to a nationalist group, newly aware of the Italian issue. He began to fancy himself as continuing his more famous uncle's liberation of the peninsula. He also saw Piedmont as a potential ally against Austria. In July 1858 Cavour and Napoleon III met at Plombières. Riding alone in a carriage, with the emperor at the reins, the two men plotted to provoke a war in Italy that would permit their two nations to intervene against Austria. A formal treaty in December 1858 confirmed the agreement. France was to receive Nice and Savoy for its aid.

WAR WITH AUSTRIA During the winter and spring of 1859 tension grew between Austria and Piedmont as the latter country mobilized its army. On April 22 Austria presented Piedmont with an ultimatum ordering a halt to mobilization. That demand provided sufficient grounds for Piedmont to claim that Austria was provoking a war. France intervened to aid its ally. On June 4 the Austrians were defeated at Magenta and on June 24 at Solferino. In the meantime revolutions had broken out in Tuscany, Modena, Parma, and Romagna.

With the Austrians in retreat and the new revolutionary states calling for union with Piedmont, Napoleon III feared too extensive a Piedmontese victory. On July 11 he independently concluded a peace with Austria at Villafranca. Piedmont received Lombardy, but Venetia remained under Austrian control. Cavour felt betrayed by France, but nonetheless the war had driven Austria from most of northern Italy. Later that summer, Parma, Modena, Tuscany, and Romagna voted to unify with Piedmont.

GARIBALDI'S CAMPAIGN At this point the forces of romantic republican nationalism entered the picture and compelled Cavour to pursue the complete unification of northern and southern Italy. In May 1860 Garibaldi landed in Sicily with more than a thousand troops, who had been outfitted in the north. He captured Palermo and prepared to attack the mainland. By September the city and kingdom

Garibaldi represented the popular forces of romantic Italian nationalism. The landing of his Redshirts on Sicily and their subsequent invasion of southern Italy in 1860 forced Cavour to unite the entire peninsula sooner than he had intended. [Culver Pictures]

of Naples, probably the most corrupt example of Italian absolutism, lay under Garibaldi's control. The popular leader had for over two decades hoped to form a republican Italy, but Cavour moved to forestall that possibility. He rushed Piedmontese troops south to confront Garibaldi. On the way they conquered the Papal States except for the area around Rome, which remained under the direct control of the pope and was protected by French troops. Garibaldi's nationalism won out over his republicanism, and he unhappily accepted the Piedmontese domination. In late 1860 the southern Italian states joined the northern union forged by Piedmont.

The New Italian State

In March 1861 Victor Emmanuel II was proclaimed king of Italy. Three months later

Cavour died. The new state more than ever needed his skills because Italy had, in effect, been more nearly conquered than united by Piedmont. The republicans resented the treatment of Garibaldi. The clericals resented the conquest of the Papal States. In the south armed resistance continued until 1866 against the intrusion of Piedmontese administration. The economies of the two areas were incompatible. The south was rural, poor, and backward. In the north industrialism was under way. The social structures reflected those differences, with landholding groups being dominant in the south and an urban working class emerging in the north.

The political framework of the united Italy did little to help overcome the problems. The constitution, which was that promulgated for Piedmont in 1848, provided for a rather conservative constitutional monarchy. The Senate was appointed, and the Chamber of Deputies was elected on a very narrow franchise. Ministers were responsible to the monarch. These arrangements did not foster a vigorous parliamentary life. The major problems of the nation were often simply avoided by the political leaders. In place of efficient, progressive government such as Cavour had brought to Piedmont, a system of *transformismo* developed. This process meant the transformation of political opponents into government supporters through bribery and favors or inclusion in cabinet coalitions. Italian politics became a byword for corruption.

There also remained territories that many Italians believed should be added to their nation. The most important of these were Venetia and Rome. The former was gained in 1866 as one result of the Austro-Prussian War. Rome and the papacy continued to be guarded by French troops, first sent there in 1849, until the Franco-Prussian War of 1870 forced the withdrawal of the garrison. The Italian state then annexed Rome and transferred the capital there from Florence. The papacy remained confined to the Vatican, and its relations with the Italian state remained hostile until the Lateran Accord of 1929.

By 1870 only the small territories of Trent and Trieste remained outside the state. In and of themselves these areas were not important, but they served to fuel the continued hostility of Italian patriots toward Austria. The desire to bring *Italia Irredenta* or "Unredeemed Italy"

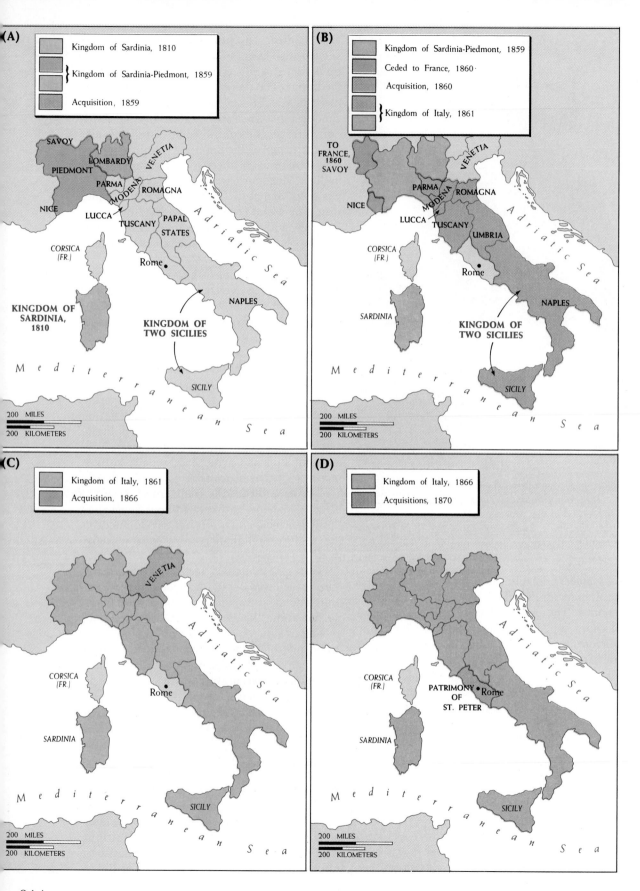

(A)

Kingdom of Sardinia, 1810

} Kingdom of Sardinia-Piedmont, 1859

Acquisition, 1859

SAVOY
PIEDMONT
LOMBARDY
VENETIA
PARMA
NICE
MODENA
ROMAGNA
LUCCA
TUSCANY
PAPAL STATES
CORSICA (FR.)
Rome
Adriatic Sea

KINGDOM OF SARDINIA, 1810

KINGDOM OF TWO SICILIES

NAPLES

SICILY

Mediterranean Sea

200 MILES
200 KILOMETERS

(B)

Kingdom of Sardinia-Piedmont, 1859

Ceded to France, 1860·

Acquisition, 1860

} Kingdom of Italy, 1861

TO FRANCE, 1860, SAVOY
VENETIA
NICE
PARMA
MODENA
ROMAGNA
LUCCA
TUSCANY
UMBRIA
CORSICA (FR.)
Rome
Adriatic Sea

KINGDOM OF TWO SICILIES

SARDINIA

NAPLES

SICILY

Mediterranean Sea

200 MILES
200 KILOMETERS

(C)

Kingdom of Italy, 1861

Acquisition, 1866

VENETIA
CORSICA (FR.)
Rome
Adriatic Sea

SARDINIA

SICILY

Mediterranean Sea

200 MILES
200 KILOMETERS

(D)

Kingdom of Italy, 1866

Acquisitions, 1870

CORSICA (FR.)
PATRIMONY OF ST. PETER
Rome
Adriatic Sea

SARDINIA

SICILY

Mediterranean Sea

200 MILES
200 KILOMETERS

814

MAP 23-1 THE UNIFICATION OF ITALY
Beginning with the association of Sardinia and Piedmont by the Congress of Vienna in 1800, unification was achieved through the expansion of Piedmont between 1859 and 1870. Both Cavour's statesmanship and the campaigns of ardent nationalists played large roles.

into the nation was one reason for the Italian support of the Allies against Austria and Germany in 1915.

German Unification

The construction of a united German nation was the single most important political development in Europe between 1848 and 1914. It transformed the balance of economic, military,

and international power. Moreover, the character of the united German state was largely determined by the method of its creation. Germany was united by the conservative army, monarchy, and prime minister of Prussia, among whose chief motives was the outflanking of Prussian liberals. The goal of a unified Germany, sought for two generations by German liberals, was actually achieved for the most illiberal of reasons.

During the 1850s German unification still seemed very far away. The major states continued to trade with each other through the *Zollverein* (tariff union), and railways linked the various economic regions. However, Frederick William IV of Prussia had given up his short-lived thoughts of unification under Prussian leadership. Austria continued to oppose any mode of closer union that might lessen its in-

MAP 23-2   THE UNIFICATION OF GERMANY   *Under Bismarck's leadership, and with the strong support of its royal house, Prussia used most of the available diplomatic and military means, on both the German and international stages, to force the unification of German states into a strong national entity.*

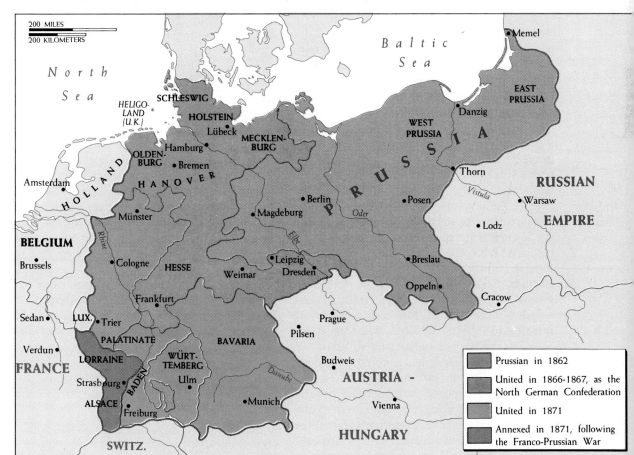

fluence. Liberal nationalists had not recovered from the humiliating experiences of 1848 and 1849. What modified this situation rather quickly was a series of domestic political changes and problems within Prussia.

In 1858 Frederick William IV was adjudged insane, and his brother William assumed the regency. William I (1861–1888), who became king in his own right in 1861, was less of an idealist than his brother and rather more of a Prussian patriot. In the usual tradition of the Hohenzollern dynasty, his first concern was for the strength of the Prussian army. In 1860 his war minister and chief of staff proposed to enlarge the army, to increase the number of officers, and to extend the period of conscription from two to three years. The Prussian Parliament, created by the Constitution of 1850, refused to approve the taxes necessary for the military expansion. The liberals, who dominated the body, did not wish to place so much additional power in the hands of the monarchy. A deadlock continued for two years between the monarch and the Parliament.

Bismarck

In September 1862 William I turned for help to the person who, more than any other single individual, shaped the next thirty years of European history: Otto von Bismarck (1815–1898). Bismarck came from *Junker* (noble landlord) stock. He attended the university, joined a *Burschenschaft*, and for a time displayed an interest in German unification. Then he retired to his father's estate. During the 1840s he was elected to the local provincial diet. At the time of the revolutions of 1848 his stand was so reactionary as to disturb even the king and the leading state ministers. Yet he had made his mark. From 1851 to 1859 Bismarck was the Prussian minister to the Frankfurt Diet of the German Confederation. Later he served as Prussian ambassador to Saint Petersburg. Just before William I called him to become prime minister of Prussia, Bismarck had been transferred to the post of ambassador to Paris.

Although Bismarck had entered public life as a reactionary, he had mellowed into a conservative. He opposed parliamentary government but not a constitutionalism that provided a strong monarch. His origins were those of a *Junker*, but he understood that Prussia—and later, Germany—must have a strong in-

Prince Otto von Bismarck (1815–1898). Through shrewd diplomacy and successful wars he made Germany a united nation. [German Information Center]

dustrial base. He was a fervent Prussian patriot. His years in Frankfurt arguing with his Austrian counterpart had only hardened that patriotism. In politics he was a pragmatist who put more trust in power and action than in ideas. As he declared in his first speech as prime minister, "Germany is not looking to Prussia's liberalism but to her power. . . . The great questions of the day will not be decided by speeches and majority decisions—that was the mistake of 1848–1849—but by iron and blood."[3] Yet this same minister, after having led Prussia into three wars, spent the next nineteen years seeking to ensure peace.

After being appointed prime minister in 1862, Bismarck immediately moved against the liberal Parliament. He contended that in the absence of new levies, the Prussian constitution permitted the government to carry out its functions on the basis of previously granted taxes. Therefore, taxes could be collected and spent despite the parliamentary refusal to vote them. The army and most of the bureaucracy supported this interpretation of the constitution. However, in 1863 new elections sustained the liberal majority in the Parliament.

---

[3] *Quoted in Otto Pflanze,* Bismarck and the Development of Germany: The Period of Unification: 1815–1871 *(Princeton, NJ: Princeton University Press, 1963), p. 177.*

Bismarck had to find some way to attract popular support away from the liberals and toward the monarchy and the army. To that end, Bismarck set about uniting Germany through the conservative institutions of Prussia. The tactic amounted to diverting public attention from domestic matters to foreign affairs.

THE DANISH WAR (1864)

Bismarck pursued a *kleindeutsch*, or small German, solution to the question of unification. Austria was to be ultimately excluded from German affairs when an opportunity presented itself. This maneuver required highly complex diplomacy. The Schleswig-Holstein problem provided the handle for Bismarck's policy. These two duchies had long been administered by Denmark without being incorporated into that kingdom. Their populations were a mixture of Germans and Danes. Holstein, where Germans predominated, belonged to the German Confederation. In 1863 the Danes moved to annex both duchies. The smaller states of the German Confederation proposed an all-German war to halt the annexation. Bismarck wanted Prussia to act alone or only in cooperation with Austria. Together the two large states defeated Denmark in a short war in 1864. They took over the joint administration of the two provinces in question.

The Danish defeat gave Bismarck new personal prestige. The joint holding of the duchies allowed him to prod Austria into war with Prussia. In August 1865 the two powers negotiated the Convention of Gastein, which put Austria in charge of Holstein and Prussia in charge of Schleswig. Bismarck then moved to mend other diplomatic fences. He had gained Russian sympathy by supporting the 1863 suppression of the Polish revolt. Conversations with Napoleon III achieved promises of neutrality in case of an Austro-Prussian conflict. In April 1866 Bismarck concluded a treaty with Italy that stated that Italy would annex Venetia in exchange for support of Prussia should war break out with Austria. Now the issue became the provocation of hostilities.

THE AUSTRO-PRUSSIAN WAR (1866)

There had been constant Austro-Prussian tension over the administration of Schleswig and Holstein. Bismarck ordered the Prussian forces to do whatever was necessary to be obnoxious to the Austrians. On June 1, 1866, Austria appealed to the German Confederation to intervene in the dispute. Bismarck claimed that the request violated the terms of the 1864 alliance and the Convention of Gastein. The Seven Weeks' War of the summer of 1866 led to the decisive defeat of Austria at Königgrätz. However, the Treaty of Prague, which ended the conflict on August 23, was quite lenient toward Austria. It lost no territory except Venetia, which was ceded to Napoleon III, who in turn ceded it to Italy. The exchange could not be direct because Austria had actually defeated Italy when the latter honored its commitment to Prussia. The Prussian defeat of Austria and the treaty permanently excluded the Habsburgs from German affairs. Prussia had become the only major power among the German states.

THE NORTH GERMAN CONFEDERATION

In 1867 the states of Hanover, Hesse, and Nassau, and the city of Frankfurt, which had supported Austria during the war, were incorporated into Prussia, and their ruling dynasties were deposed. Prussia and these newly incorporated territories, plus Schleswig and Holstein and the rest of the German states north of the Main River, constituted the North German Confederation. The constitution of this body provided for a federation under Prussian leadership. Each state retained its own local government, but the military forces were under federal control. The president of the federation was the king of Prussia, represented by his chancellor. There was a federal council, or *Bundesrat*, composed of nominated members. The lower house, or *Reichstag*, was chosen by universal manhood suffrage.

Bismarck had little fear of this broad franchise because he sensed that the peasants would tend to vote conservatively. Moreover, the *Reichstag* had little real power because the ministers were responsible only to the monarch. Even legislation did not originate in the *Reichstag*. The legislature did have the right to approve military budgets, but these were usually submitted to cover several years at a time. The constitution of the confederation, which after 1871 became the governing document of the German Empire, possessed some of the appearances but none of the substance of liberalism. Germany was in effect a military monarchy.

The spectacular success of Bismarck's policy

Bismarck Edits the Ems Dispatch

On July 13, 1870, William I of Prussia sent Bismarck a telegram reporting his meeting with Benedetti, the French ambassador, at Ems, a watering place in northwest Germany. The telegram also included a comment by the king's private secretary on later events of the day. Before releasing the dispatch to the press, Bismarck edited it so that the telegram appeared to report that the king of Prussia had treated the French ambassador in a brusque and insulting fashion. Bismarck thus hoped to goad France into a declaration of war. In the text of both telegrams "His Majesty" is William I, and "the Prince" is Charles Anthony, the father of Prince Leopold, the candidate for the Spanish throne. Throughout the negotiations Charles Anthony had spoken on behalf of his son.

The Original Message Sent by William I to Bismarck

"M. Benedetti intercepted me on the Promenade in order to demand of me most insistently that I should authorize him to telegraph immediately to Paris that I shall obligate myself for all future time never again to give my approval to the candidacy of the Hohenzollerns should it be renewed. I refused to agree to this, the last time somewhat severely, informing him that one dare not and cannot assume such obligations *à tout jamais* [forever]. Naturally, I informed him that I had received no news as yet, and since he had been informed earlier than I by way of Paris and Madrid, he could easily understand why my government was once again out of the matter."

Since then His Majesty has received a dispatch from the Prince. As His Majesty has informed Count Benedetti that he was expecting news from the Prince, His Majesty himself, in view of the above-mentioned demand and in consonance with the advice of Count Eulenburg and myself, decided not to receive the French envoy again but to inform him through an adjutant that His Majesty had now received from the Prince confirmation of the news which Benedetti had already received from Paris, and that he had nothing further to say to the Ambassador. His Majesty leaves it to the judgement of Your Excellency whether or not to communicate at once the new demand by Benedetti and its rejection to our ambassadors and to the press.

Bismarck's Edited Version Released to the Press

After the reports of the renunciation by the Hereditary Prince of Hohenzollern had been officially transmitted by the Royal Government of Spain to the Imperial Government of France, the French Ambassador presented to His Majesty the King at Ems the demand to authorize him to telegraph to Paris that His Majesty the King would obligate himself for all future time never again to give his approval to the candidacy of the Hohenzollerns should it be renewed.

His Majesty the King thereupon refused to receive the French envoy again and informed him through an adjutant that His Majesty had nothing further to say to the Ambassador.

Louis L. Snyder (Ed. and Trans.), Documents of German History (New Brunswick, NJ.: Rutgers University Press, 1958), pp. 215–216. Reprinted with permission of Rutgers University Press.

overwhelmed the liberal opposition in the Prussian Parliament. The liberals were split between those who prized liberalism and those who supported unification. In the end nationalism proved more attractive than liberalism. In 1866 the Prussian Parliament passed an indemnity measure that retroactively approved the earlier military budget. Bismarck had crushed the Prussian liberals by making the monarchy and the army the most popular institutions in the country. The drive toward unification had achieved Bismarck's domestic political goal.

The Franco-Prussian War and the German Empire (1870–1871)

Bismarck now awaited an opportunity to complete unification by bringing the states of southern Germany into the confederation. Events in Spain provided the excuse. In 1868 a revolution led by conservatives deposed the corrupt Bourbon queen of Spain. In searching for a new monarch, the Spaniards chose Prince Leopold of Hohenzollern-Sigmaringen, a cousin of William I of Prussia. On June 19, 1870, Leopold accepted the Spanish crown with Prussian blessings. Bismarck knew that France would react strongly against the idea of a second bordering state ruled by a Hohenzollern.

On July 2 the Spanish publicized Leopold's acceptance, and the French reacted as expected. France sent Count Vincent Benedetti (1817–1900) to consult with William I, who was vacationing at Bad Ems. They discussed the matter at several meetings. On July 12 Leopold's father renounced his son's candidacy for the Spanish throne, fearing that the issue would cause war between Prussia and France. William I seems to have been relieved that conflict had been avoided and that he had not been required to order Leopold to renounce his claim to the Spanish title.

There the matter might have rested had it not been for the impetuosity of the French and the guile of Bismarck. On July 13 the French government instructed Benedetti to ask William I for assurances that he would tolerate no future Spanish candidacy for Leopold. The king refused but said that he might take the question under further consideration. Later

that day he sent Bismarck, who was in Berlin, a telegram reporting the substance of the meeting. The chancellor, who desperately wanted a war with France to complete unification, had been disappointed by the peaceful resolution of the Spanish candidacy question. The telegram provided a new opportunity. Bismarck released an edited version of the dispatch. The revised Ems telegram made it appear that William I had insulted the French ambassador. The idea was to goad France into a declaration of war.

The French government of Napoleon III quickly fell for Bismarck's bait, and on July 19 the French declared war. The French emperor had been almost as eager for war as Bismarck

GERMAN AND ITALIAN UNIFICATION

1854	Crimean War opens
1855	Cavour leads Piedmont into the war on the side of France and England
1856	Treaty of Paris concludes the Crimean War
1858	(January 14) Attempt to assassinate Napoleon III
1858	(July 20) Secret conference between Napoleon III and Cavour at Plombières
1859	War of Piedmont and France against Austria
1860	Garibaldi lands his forces in Sicily and invades southern Italy
1861	(March 17) Proclamation of the Kingdom of Italy
1861	(June 6) Death of Cavour
1862	Bismarck becomes prime minister of Prussia
1864	Danish-Prussian War
1865	Convention of Gastein
1866	Austro-Prussian War
1866	Venetia ceded to Italy
1867	North German Confederation formed
1870	(June 19–July 12) Crisis over Hohenzollern candidacy for the Spanish throne
1870	(July 13) Bismarck publishes the Ems dispatch
1870	(July 19) France declares war on Prussia
1870	(September 1) France defeated at Sedan and Napoleon III captured
1870	(September 4) French Republic proclaimed
1870	(October 2) Italian state annexes Rome
1871	(January 18) Proclamation of the German Empire at Versailles
1871	(March 18–May 28) Paris Commune
1871	(May 1) Treaty of Frankfurt between France and Prussia

because he believed that victory over the North German Confederation would give his regime a new and stronger popular base of support. Once the conflict erupted, the south German states honored treaties signed with Prussia in 1866; they eagerly joined the northern cause against France, whose defeat was not long in coming. On September 1, at the Battle of Sedan, the Germans not only beat the French army but also captured the French emperor. By late September Paris stood besieged; it finally capitulated on January 28, 1871.

Ten days earlier, in the Hall of Mirrors at the Palace of Versailles, the German Empire had been declared. During the war the states of South Germany had joined the North German Confederation, and their princes had requested William I to accept the imperial title. The princes of the southern states retained their positions as heads of their respective states within the new federation. From the peace settlement with France, Germany received the additional territory of Alsace and part of Lorraine.

Both the fact and the manner of German unification produced long-range effects in Europe. A powerful new state had been created in north central Europe. It was rich in natural resources and talented citizens. Militarily and

The proclamation of the German Empire in the Hall of Mirrors at Versailles, January 18, 1871. *Kaiser Wilhelm I is standing at the top of the steps under the flags. Bismarck is in the center in a white uniform. [Bismarck Museum, Hamburg. Foto Carstensen]*

economically the German Empire would be stronger than Prussia had been alone. The unification of Germany was also a blow to European liberalism because the new state was a conservative creation. Conservative politics was now backed not by a weak Austria or an economically retrograde Russia but by the strongest state on the Continent.

The two nations most immediately affected by German and also Italian unification were France and Austria. The emergence of the two new unified states revealed the weakness of both France and the Habsburg Empire. Change had to come in each: France returned to republican government, and the Habsburgs organized a dual monarchy.

France: From Liberal Empire to the Third Republic

The reign of Emperor Napoleon III (1851–1870) is traditionally divided into the years of the authoritarian empire and those of the liberal empire. The point of division is 1860. Initially, after the *coup* in December 1851, Napoleon III had kept a close rein on the legislature, had strictly controlled the press, and had made life difficult for political dissidents. His support came from property owners, the French Catholic Church, and businessmen. They approved the security he brought to property, his protection of the pope, and his aid to commerce and railroad construction. The French victory in the Crimean War had further confirmed the emperor's popularity.

From the late 1850s onward, Napoleon III began to modify his policy. In 1860 he concluded a free trade treaty with Britain and permitted the legislature to discuss matters of state more freely. By the late 1860s he had relaxed the press laws and had permitted labor unions. In 1870 he allowed the leaders of the moderates in the legislature to form a ministry. That same year Napoleon III agreed to a liberal constitution that made the ministers responsible to the legislature.

All of these liberal moves were closely related to problems in foreign policy. He had lost control of the diplomacy of Italian unification. Between 1861 and 1867 he had supported a military expedition against Mexico led by

Archduke Maximilian of Austria. The venture ended in defeat and the execution of the archduke. In 1866 Napoleon III and France rather sat on the sidelines while Bismarck and Prussia reorganized German affairs. The liberal concessions on domestic matters were attempts to compensate for an increasingly unsuccessful foreign policy. The war of 1870 against Germany was simply Napoleon III's last and most disastrous attempt to shore up French foreign policy and to secure domestic popularity.

Whether Napoleon III would have succeeded in sustaining liberal government or his own position became a moot point. The Second Empire, but not the war, came to an inglorious end with the Battle of Sedan in September 1870. The emperor was captured, imprisoned, and then allowed to go to England, where he

From September 1870 to January 1871, Paris was besieged by the Germans and cut off from the rest of France. This photo shows the escape from the city of Leon Gambetta (1838–1882), the Minister of War in the Government of National Defense. Gambetta left Paris to organize French resistance to the Germans. [Bildarchiv Preussischer Kulturbesitz]

died in 1873. Shortly after news of the Sedan disaster reached Paris, a republic was proclaimed and a Government of National Defense was established. Paris itself was soon under Prussian siege. During the siege of Paris, the French government was transferred to Bordeaux. Paris finally surrendered in January 1871, but the rest of France had been ready to sue for peace long before the capital surrendered.

The Paris Commune

The division between the provinces and Paris became even more decided after the fighting stopped. Monarchists dominated the new National Assembly elected in February. For the time being, executive power was turned over to Adolphe Thiers (1797–1877), who had been active in French politics since 1830. He negotiated a settlement with Prussia (the Treaty of Frankfurt) whereby France was charged with a large indemnity, remained occupied by Prussian troops until the indemnity had been paid,

and surrendered territories in Alsace and Lorraine.

The city of Paris, which had suffered much during the siege, resented what it regarded as a betrayal by the monarchist National Assembly sitting at Versailles. Thiers, familiar with a half-century of Parisian political turmoil, ordered the disarmament of the Paris National Guard on March 17. The attempt on the next day to seize the guard's cannon was bungled. Paris then regarded the National Assembly as its new enemy.

The Parisians elected a new municipal government, called the *Paris Commune.* It was formally proclaimed on March 28, 1871. Its goal was to administer the city separately from the rest of the country. Political radicals and socialists of all stripes participated in the Paris Commune at one time or another. The National Assembly moved rapidly against the commune. By early April, Paris was again a besieged city, but this time it stood surrounded by a French army. On May 8 the Army bombarded Paris. On May 21, the day on which the

Mass graves were dug for the thousands of Parisians killed or executed during the fighting that marked the suppression of the Paris Commune in 1871. [Snark International]

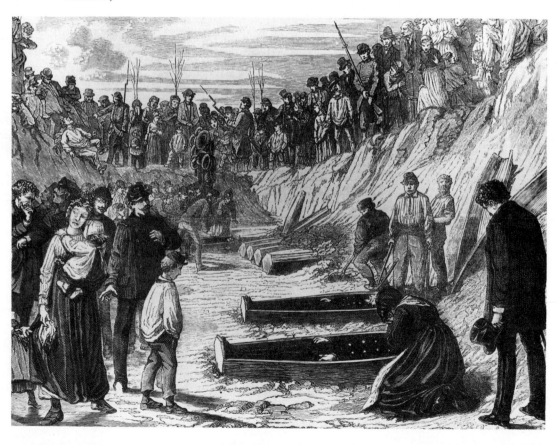

The Paris Commune Is Proclaimed

In September 1870 the French Republic was proclaimed, and shortly thereafter a National Assembly was elected. The city of Paris, which had held out against Prussia longer than any other part of France, was hostile to the National Assembly. On March 18, 1871, a revolt against the assembly occurred in Paris. The National Guard of Paris sought to organize the city as a separate part of France. Below is an excerpt of the proclamation of March 28 of the separation of Paris into an autonomous commune. The rebellious Parisians wanted all of France to be organized into a federation of politically autonomous communes. This communal concept was directly opposed to that of the large national state. Two months after this proclamation the troops of the assembly crushed the commune.

By its revolution of the 18th March, and the spontaneous and courageous efforts of the National Guard, Paris has regained its autonomy. . . . On the eve of the sanguinary and disastrous defeat suffered by France as the punishment it has to undergo for the seventy years of the Empire, and the monarchical, clerical, parliamentary, legal and conciliatory reaction, our country again rises, revives, begins a new life, and retakes the tradition of the Communes of old and of the French Revolution. This tradition, which gave victory to France, and earned the respect and sympathy of past generations, will bring independence, wealth, peaceful glory and brotherly love among nations in the future.

Never was there so solemn an hour. The Revolution which our fathers commenced and we are finishing . . . is going on without bloodshed, by the might of the popular will. . . . To secure the triumph of the Communal idea . . . it is necessary to determine its general principles, and to draw up . . . the programme to be realized. . . .

The Commune is the foundation of all political states, exactly as the family is the embryo of human society. It must have autonomy; that is to say, self-administration and self-government, agreeing with its particular genius, traditions, and wants; preserving, in its political, moral, national, and special groups its entire liberty, its own character, and its complete sovereignty, like a citizen of a free town.

To secure the greatest economic development, the national and territorial independence, and security, association is indispensable; that is to say, a federation of all communes, constituting a united nation.

The autonomy of the Commune guarantees liberty to its citizens; and the federation of all the communes increases, by the reciprocity, power, wealth, markets, and resources of each member, the profit of all. It was the Communal idea . . . which triumphed on the 18th of March, 1871. It implies, as a political form, the Republic, which is alone compatible with liberty and popular sovereignty.

G. A. Kertesz (Ed.), Documents in the Political History of the European Continent, 1815–1939 (Oxford: Clarendon Press, 1968), pp. 312–313.

formal treaty with Prussia was signed, the National Assembly forces broke through the city's defenses. During the next seven days the troops restored order to Paris and in the process killed about twenty thousand inhabitants.

The communards claimed their own victims as well.

The short-lived Paris Commune very quickly became a legend throughout France and Europe. Marxists regarded it as a genuine proletarian government which the troops of the French bourgeoisie had suppressed. This interpretation is largely mistaken. The commune, though of shifting composition, was dominated by petty bourgeois members. The socialism that was a part of the commune had its roots in Blanqui and Proudhon's anarchism rather than in Marx's concept of class conflict. The goal of the commune was not a worker's republic but a nation composed of relatively independent, radically democratic enclaves. The suppression of the commune consequently represented not only the protection of property but also the triumph of the centralized nation-state over an alternative mode of political organization. Just as the armies of Piedmont and Prussia had united the small states of Italy and Germany, the army of the French National Assembly destroyed the particularistic political tendencies of Paris and, by implication, those of any other French community.

The Third Republic

The National Assembly put down the commune directly, but it backed into a republican form of government indirectly and much against its will. The monarchists, who constituted its majority, were divided in loyalty between the House of Bourbon and the House of Orléans. They could have surmounted this problem because the Bourbon claimant had no children. He could have become king on the condition that the Orléanist heir would follow him to the throne. However, the Bourbon count of Chambord refused to become king if the nation retained the revolutionary tricolor flag. Even the conservative monarchists would not return to the white flag of the Bourbons, which symbolized extreme political reaction.

While the monarchists quarreled over the proper heir, and the heir over the proper flag, time passed and events marched on. By September 1873 the indemnity had been paid and the Prussian occupation troops had withdrawn. Thiers was ousted from office because he had displayed clear republican sentiments. The monarchists wanted a person more sympathetic with their goals to be executive. They elected as president Marshal MacMahon (1808–1893), who was conservative and who was expected to prepare for an eventual monarchist restoration. In 1875 the National As-

sembly, still monarchist in sentiment but unable to find a candidate for the throne, decided to regularize the political system. It adopted a law that provided for a Chamber of Deputies elected by universal manhood suffrage, a Senate chosen indirectly, and a president elected by the two legislative houses. This relatively simple republican system had resulted from the bickering and frustration of the monarchists.

MacMahon remained as president. He would have liked to transform that office into a much stronger position. After numerous quarrels with the Chamber of Deputies, he resigned in 1879. His departure meant that people dedicated to a republic generally controlled the national government. But France remained an uncertain and unconfident republic.

A considerable body of public opinion within the army, the Church, and the wealthy families still favored government by a single strong figure. During the late 1880s they looked to General Georges Boulanger (1837–1891) as such a leader. In 1886 and 1887 he had been a popular minister of war who initiated a number of military reforms. When a financial scandal touched several major political figures, Boulanger became all the more appealing for his honesty and integrity. He was elected to the Chamber of Deputies from numerous districts, though afterward he sat only for one. In 1889 there was much talk and expectation of his carrying out a *coup d' état*. Nothing came of these speculations. The good general had talked with too many different political groups to be trusted by any. He also lacked real drive and political ambition. In the end he left France for life with his Belgian mistress and in 1891 committed suicide on her grave in Brussels.

The political structure of the Third Republic proved much stronger than many citizens suspected at the time. It was able to survive a series of major scandals. In the late 1880s the son-in-law of the president was discovered to be selling positions in the Legion of Honor. Early in the next decade a number of ministers and deputies were implicated in the Panama affair. Ferdinand de Lesseps, who had constructed the Suez Canal, organized a company to build a canal in Panama. Various people in authority in France accepted bribes for their public support of the venture. These two *causes célèbres* made the republic look rather sleazy in the eyes of its conservative enemies. But the institutions of the republic allowed new ministers to replace those whose corruption was exposed.

The Dreyfus Affair

The greatest trauma of the republic occurred over the Dreyfus affair. On December 22, 1894, a French military court found Captain Alfred Dreyfus (1859–1935) guilty of passing secret information to the German army. The evidence supporting his guilt was at best flimsy and was later revealed to have been forged. Someone in the officer corps had been passing documents to the Germans, and it suited the army investigators to accuse Dreyfus, who was Jewish. However, after Dreyfus had been sent to Devil's Island, secrets continued to flow to the German army. In 1896 a new head of French counterintelligence reexamined the Dreyfus file and found evidence of forgery. A different officer was implicated, but a military court quickly acquitted him of all charges. The officer who had discovered the forgeries was transferred to a distant post.

By then the matter had become one of widespread and sometimes near-hysterical public debate. The army, the French Catholic church, political conservatives, and vehemently anti-Semitic newspapers repeatedly contended that Dreyfus was guilty. Such anti-Dreyfus opinion was quite powerful at the beginning of the affair. In 1898, however, the novelist Émile Zola published a newspaper article entitled *"J' accuse"* ("I Accuse") in which he contended that the army had consciously denied due process to Dreyfus and had plotted to suppress evidence and to forge other evidence. Zola was convicted of libel and received a one-year prison sentence, which he avoided only by leaving France for exile in England.

Zola was only one of numerous liberals, radicals, and socialists who had begun to demand a new trial for Dreyfus. Although these forces of the political left had come to Dreyfus' support rather slowly, they soon realized that his cause could aid their own public image. They portrayed the conservative institutions of the nation as having denied Dreyfus the rights belonging to any citizen of the republic. They also claimed, and quite properly so, that Dreyfus had been singled out so that the guilty persons, who were still in the army, could be pro-

The most serious political crisis of the Third Republic surrounded the trials of Captain Alfred Dreyfus, here shown standing on the right at his military trial. [Bettmann Archive]

tected. In August 1898 further evidence of forged material came to light. The officer responsible for those forgeries committed suicide in jail. A new military trial took place, but Dreyfus was again found guilty by officers who refused to admit the original mistake. The president of France immediately pardoned the captain, and eventually, in 1906, a civilian court set aside the results of both previous military trials.

The Dreyfus case divided France as no issue had done since the Paris Commune. By its conclusion the conservative political forces of the nation stood on the defensive. They had for a number of years allowed themselves to persecute an innocent person and to manufacture false evidence against him to protect themselves from disclosure. They had also embraced a strongly anti-Semitic posture. On the political left, radicals, republicans, and socialists developed an informal alliance that outlived the fight over the Dreyfus case itself. These groups realized that republican institutions must be preserved in a conscious fashion if the political left were to achieve any of its goals.

Outside political circles, ever larger numbers of French citizens understood that their rights and liberties were safer under a republic than under some alternative mode of conservative government. The divisions, suspicions, and hopes growing out of the Dreyfus affair would continue to mark and divide the Third French Republic until its defeat by Germany in 1940.

The Habsburg Empire

After 1848 the Habsburg Empire remained a problem both to itself and to the rest of Europe. An ungenerous critic remarked that the empire was supported by a standing army of soldiers, a kneeling army of priests, and a crawling army of informers. In the age of national states, liberal institutions, and industrialism, the Habsburg domains remained primarily dynastic, absolutist, and agrarian. The response to the revolts at the end of the 1840s had been the reassertion of absolutism. Francis Joseph, who became emperor in 1848 and ruled until 1916, was honest, hardworking, and unimaginative. He reacted to events but rarely commanded them.

During the 1850s his ministers attempted to impose a centralized administration on the empire. The system amounted to a military and bureaucratic government dominated by German-speaking Austrians. The Vienna government abolished all internal tariffs in the empire. It divided Hungary, which had been so revolutionary in 1848, into military districts. The Roman Catholic church received control of education. Although these actions stirred much domestic resentment and opposition, this system of neoabsolutism actually floundered because of a series of major setbacks in Habsburg foreign policy.

Austrian refusal to support Russia during the Crimean War meant that the new tsar would not in the future help to preserve Habsburg rule in Hungary as Nicholas I had done in 1849. An important external support of Habsburg power for the past half-century thus disappeared. The Austrian defeat in 1859 at the hands of France and Piedmont and the subsequent loss of territory in Italy confirmed the necessity for new structures of domestic government. For seven years the emperor, the civil servants, the aristocrats, and the politicians attempted to construct a viable system of government.

Formation of the Dual Monarchy

In 1860 Francis Joseph issued the October Diploma, which created a federation among the states and provinces of the empire. There were to be local diets dominated by the landed classes and a single imperial parliament. The Magyar nobility of Hungary rejected the plan.

Consequently, in 1861 the emperor promulgated the February Patent. Technically it interpreted the Diploma, but in point of fact it constituted an entirely different form of government. It established a bicameral imperial parliament, or *Reichsrat*, with an appointed upper chamber and an indirectly elected lower chamber. Again the Magyars refused to cooperate in a system designed to permit German-speaking Austrian domination of the empire. The Hungarians sent no delegates to the legislature. Nevertheless, for six years, the February Patent governed the empire, and it prevailed in Austria proper until World War I. There was no ministerial responsibility to the *Reichsrat*. Few genuine guarantees existed for civil liberties. Armies could be levied and taxes raised without parliamentary consent. When the *Reichsrat* was not in session, the emperor could simply promulgate laws on his own authority.

Meanwhile, negotiations continued between the emperor and the Magyars. These produced no concrete result until the defeat of Austria by Prussia in the summer of 1866 and the consequent exclusion of Austria from German affairs. The military disaster compelled Francis Joseph to come to terms with the Magyars. The subsequent *Ausgleich*, or Compromise, of 1867 transformed the Habsburg Empire into a dual monarchy.

Francis Joseph was separately crowned king of Hungary in Budapest. Except for the com-

The coronation of Francis Joseph as King of Hungary in 1867 is depicted in this painting. The so-called Ausgleich, or Compromise, of 1867 transformed the Habsburg Empire into a dual monarchy in which Austria and Hungary became almost separate states except for defense and foreign affairs. [Bildarchiv der Osterreichischen Nationalbibliothek, Vienna]

The Austrian Prime Minister Explains the Dual Monarchy

The multinational character of the Austrian Empire had long been a source of internal weakness and political discontent. After the defeat of Austria by Prussia in 1886, the Austrian government attempted to regain the loyalty of the Hungarians by making Hungary a separate kingdom within a dual monarchy known thereafter as Austria-Hungary.

The dangers which Austria has to face are of a twofold nature. The first is presented by the tendency of her liberal-minded German population to gravitate toward that larger portion of the German-speaking people . . . the second is the diversity of language and race in the empire. Of Austria's large Slav population, the Poles have a natural craving for independence after having enjoyed and heroically fought for it for centuries; while the other nationalities are likely at a moment of dangerous crisis to develop pro-Russian tendencies.

Now my object is to carry out a bloodless revolution—to show the various elements of this great empire that it is to the benefit of each of them to act in harmony with its neighbor. . . . But to this I have made one exception. Hungary is an ancient monarchy, more ancient as such than Austria proper. . . . I have endeavoured to give Hungary not a new position

with regard to the Austrian empire, but to secure her in the one which she has occupied. The Emperor of Austria is King of Hungary; my idea was that he should revive in his person the Constitution of which he and his ancestors have been the heads. The leading principles of my plan are . . . the resuscitation of an old monarchy and an old Constitution; not the separation of one part of the empire from the other, but the drawing together of the two component parts by the recognition of their joint positions, the maintenance of their mutual obligations, their community in questions affecting the entire empire, and their proportional pecuniary responsibility for the liabilities of the whole State. It is no plan of separation that I have carried out: on the contrary, it is one of close union, not by the creation of a new power, but by the recognition of an old one. . . .

Memories of Friedrich Ferdinand Count von Beust, Vol. I, ed. by Baron Henry de Worms (London: Remington, 1887), pp. xx–xxvi.

mon monarch, Austria and Hungary became almost wholly separate states. They shared ministers of foreign affairs, defense, and finance, but the other ministers were different for each state. There were also separate parliaments. Each year sixty parliamentary delegates from each state were to meet to discuss matters of mutual interest. Every ten years Austria and Hungary were to renegotiate their trade relationship. By this cumbersome machinery, unique in all European history, the Hungarian Magyars were reconciled to Habsburg rule.

They had achieved the free hand they had long wanted in local Hungarian matters.

Unrest of Nationalities

The Compromise of 1867 had introduced two very different principles of political legitimacy into the two sections of the Habsburg Empire. In Hungary the principle of political loyalty was based on nationality because Hungary had been recognized as a distinct part of the monarchy on the basis of nationalism. In effect,

Hungary had been recognized as a distinct Magyar nation under the Habsburg emperor. Throughout the rest of the domains the principle of legitimacy was dynastic loyalty to the emperor. Many of the other nationalities wished to test the basis of that loyalty or to strike out on their own independent paths or to unite with fellow nationals who lived across the borders of the empire.

Many of those other national groups—including the Czechs, the Ruthenians, the Romanians, and the Serbo-Croations—opposed the Compromise of 1867 that in effect had permitted the German-speaking Austrians and the Hungarian Magyars to dominate all other nationalities within the empire. The most vocal critics were the Czechs of Bohemia. They favored a policy of trialism or triple monarchy. In 1871 Francis Joseph was willing to accept this concept. However, the Hungarian Magyars vetoed the proposal for fear that they might have to make similar concessions to their own subject nationalities. Furthermore, the Germans in the empire who lived near the Czechs opposed the idea for fear they would have the Czech language imposed on them and their children.

For over twenty years an extension of generous Austrian patronage and admission to the Austrian bureaucracy conciliated the Czechs. However, by the 1890s Czech nationalism again became more strident. In 1897, through a series of ordinances, Francis Joseph gave the Czechs and the Germans equality of language in various localities. Thereafter, the Germans in the Austrian *Reichsrat* set out on a course of parliamentary disruption to oppose these measures. The Czechs replied in kind. By the turn of the century this obstructionist activity, which included the playing of musical instruments in the parliament chamber, had paralyzed parliamentary life. The emperor ruled by imperial decree with the support of the bureaucracy. In 1907 universal manhood suffrage was introduced in Austria, but it did not change the situation in the *Reichsrat*. In effect, by 1914 constitutionalism was a dead letter in Austria. It flourished in Hungary, but only because the Magyars relentlessly exercised political supremacy over all other competing national groups.

The unrest of the various nationalities within the Habsburg empire not only caused internal political difficulties, but also constituted one of the major sources of political instability for all of central and eastern Europe. Virtually all the nationality problems entailed a foreign policy as well as a domestic political dimension. Both the Serbo-Croations and the Poles believed they deserved a wholly independent state in union with their fellow nationals who lived outside the borders of the empire. Other national groups, such as Ukranians, Romanians, and Bosnians, saw themselves as potentially linked to Russia, to Romania, to Serbia, or to a larger yet-to-be established Slavic state. Many of these nationalities looked to Russia to protect their interests or to exert some kind of protective influence on the government in Vienna. Out of these tensions emerged much of the turmoil that would spark the First World War.

The dominant German population of Austria proper generally saw itself as loyal to the emperor. However, a significant segment of the Austrian German population was strongly nationalistic and yearned to be part of the united German state being established by Bismarck. These nationalistic Germans in the Austrian empire often hated the other smaller non-German national groups. Among these nationalistic German groups anti-Semitism often flourished. Such attitudes would influence the youth and young adulthood of Adolph Hitler.

Finally, these nationality problems in one way or another touched all three of the great central and eastern European empires—the German, the Russian, and the Austrian. All

---

MAJOR DATES IN LATE NINETEENTH-CENTURY HABSBURG EMPIRE

1848	Francis Joseph becomes emperor
1860	October Diploma
1861	February Patent
1866	Defeat by Prussia
1867	Compromise between emperor and Hungary establishing the Dual Monarchy
1897	Ordinances giving equality of language between Germans and Czechs in the Empire
1907	Universal manhood suffrage introduced

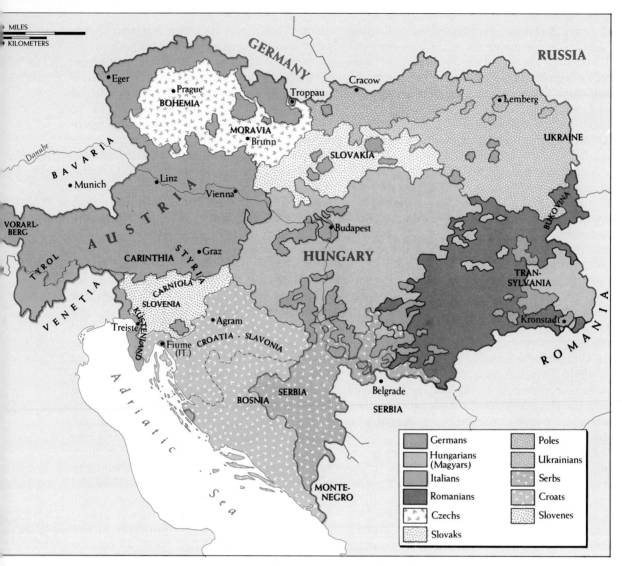

MAP 23-3   NATIONALITIES WITHIN THE HABSBURG EMPIRE   *The patchwork appearance reflects the unusual problem of the numerous ethnic groups that the Habsburgs could not, of course, meld into a modern national state. Only the Magyars were recognized in 1867, leaving nationalist Czechs, Slovaks, and the others chronically dissatisfied.*

had Poles within their borders. Each shared at least two other major national groups. Each nationality regarded its own aspirations and discontents as more important than the larger good or even survival of the empires that they inhabited. The stirrings of nationalism affected the fate of all three empires from the 1860s through the outbreak of World War I. The government of each of those empires would be overturned during the war, and the Austrian empire would disappear from the map. Those same unresolved problems of central and eastern European nationalism would then lead directly to World War II. For the next

century of European and even world history the significance of this nationalist unrest within the late-nineteenth-century Austrian empire and its neighbors can hardly be overestimated.

Russia: Emancipation and Revolutionary Stirrings

The last half of the nineteenth century witnessed remarkable changes in Russia. The long-standing problem of serfdom was finally addressed, and the government undertook other major administrative reforms. During the same period, however, radical revolutionary groups began to organize. These groups attempted to draw the peasants into revolutionary activity and assassinated major government officials including the tsar. The response was a new era of repression following the years of reform.

Reforms of Alexander II

The defeat in the Crimean War and the humiliation of the Treaty of Paris compelled the Russian government to reconsider its domestic situation. Nicholas I had died in 1855 during the conflict. Because of extensive travel in Russia and an early introduction to government procedures, Nicholas' son Alexander II (1855–1881) was quite familiar with the chief difficulties facing the nation. The debacle of the war had created a situation in which reform was both necessary and possible. Alexander II took advantage of this turn of events to institute the most extensive restructuring of Russian society and administration since Peter the Great. Like Peter, Alexander imposed his reforms from the top.

ABOLITION OF SERFDOM In every area of economic and public life a profound cultural gap existed between Russia and the rest of Europe. Nowhere was this fact more true than in the matter of serfdom. Everywhere else on the Continent it had been abandoned. In Russia the institution had changed very little since the eighteenth century. Landowners had a very free hand with their serfs, and the serfs had little recourse against the lords. In March 1856, at the conclusion of the Crimean War, Alexander II announced his intention to abolish serfdom. He had decided that only abolition of the institution would permit Russia to organize its human and natural resources so as to maintain its status as a great power.

Serfdom had become economically inefficient. The threat of large or small revolts of serfs was always present; the serfs recruited into the army had performed poorly in the Crimean conflict. The moral opinion of the day had come increasingly to condemn serfdom. Only Russia, Brazil, and certain portions of the United States among the Western nations still retained such forms of involuntary servitude.

For over five years government commissions wrestled over the way to implement the tsar's desire. Finally, in February 1861, against much opposition from the nobility and the landlords, Alexander II promulgated the long statute ending serfdom in Russia.

The technicalities of the emancipation statute meant that freedom was often more theoretical than practical. The procedures were so complicated and the results so limited that many serfs believed that real emancipation was still to come. Serfs immediately received the personal rights to marry without their landlord's permission as well as to purchase and sell property freely, to engage in court actions, and to pursue trades. What they did not receive immediately was free title to their land. They were required to pay the landlords for frequently insufficient allotments of land over a period of forty-nine years. They were also charged interest during this period. The serfs made the payments to the government, which had already reimbursed the landlords for their losses. The serfs did not receive title to the land until the debt was paid.

Life in Russian villages during the 1870s was very difficult. Serfdom had ended but peasants still had to pay off debts for the land received and the standard of living, as seen in these mud streets, was low. [The Granger Collection]

The redemption payments led to almost unending difficulty. Poor harvests caused the debts to fall into arrears, and the situation was not remedied until 1906. With widespread revolutionary unrest following the Japanese defeat of Russia in 1905, the government grudgingly completed the process of emancipation by canceling the remaining debts.

REFORM OF LOCAL GOVERNMENT AND JUDICIAL SYSTEM The abolition of serfdom required the reorganization of local government and the judicial system. The authority of village communes replaced that of the landlord over the peasant. The village elders settled family quarrels, imposed fines, issued internal passports, and collected taxes. In many cases also, the emancipated serfs owned land communally rather than individually. The nobility were permitted a larger role in local administration through a system of provincial and county *zemstvos*, or councils, organized in 1864. These councils were to oversee local matters such as bridge and road repair, education, and agricultural improvement. However, because the councils received inadequate funds, local government never became vigorous.

The flagrant inequities and abuses of the preemancipation judicial system could not continue. In 1864 Alexander II promulgated a new statute on the judiciary. For the first time principles of western European legal systems were introduced into Russia. These included equality before the law, impartial hearings, uniform procedures, judicial independence, and trial by jury. The new system was far from perfect. The judges were not genuinely independent, and the tsar could increase as well as reduce sentences. For certain offenses, such as those involving the press, jury trials were not held. Nonetheless, the system was an improvement both in its efficiency and in its relative lack of the old corruption.

MILITARY REFORM Reforms were also instituted in the army. Russia possessed the largest military establishment on the Continent, but it had floundered badly in the Crimean War. The usual period of recruitment was twenty-five years. Villages had to provide quotas of serfs. Often the recruiters had come to the villages and simply seized serfs from their families. Once in the army, the recruits

rarely saw their homes again. Life in the army was exceedingly harsh, even by the usually brutal standards of most mid-century armies. In the 1860s the army lowered the period of recruitment to fifteen years and slightly relaxed disciplinary procedures. In 1874 the enlistment period was lowered to six years of active duty, followed by nine years in the reserves. All males were subject to military service after the age of twenty.

REPRESSION IN POLAND Alexander's reformist departures became more measured shortly after the Polish Rebellion of 1863. As in 1830, Polish nationalists attempted to overthrow Russian dominance. Once again the Russian army suppressed the rebellion. Alexander II then moved to "russify" Poland. In 1864 he emancipated the Polish serfs as a move against the politically restive Polish nobility. Russian law, language, and administration were imposed on all areas of Polish life. Henceforth, until the close of World War I, Poland was treated merely as one other Russian province.

As revealed by the Polish suppression, Alexander II was a reformer only within the limits of his own autocracy. His changes in Russian life failed to create new loyalty or gratitude among his subjects. The serfs felt that their emancipation had been inadequate. The nobles and the wealthier educated segments of Russian society resented the tsar's persistent refusal to allow them a meaningful role in government and policymaking. Consequently, although Alexander II became known as the Tsar Liberator, he was never a popular ruler. He could be very indecisive and was rarely open to new ideas. These characteristics became more pronounced after 1866, when an attempt was made on his life. Thereafter, Russia increasingly became a police state. This new repression fueled the activity of radical groups within Russia. Their actions, in turn, made the autocracy more reactionary.

Revolutionaries

The tsarist regime had long had its critics. One of the most prominent was Alexander Herzen (1812–1870), who lived in exile. From London he published a newspaper called *The Bell* in which he set forth reformist positions. The initial reforms of Alexander II had raised great hopes among Russian students and intellectuals, but they soon became discontented with the limited character of the restructuring. Drawing on the ideas of Herzen and other radicals, these students formed a revolutionary movement known as *Populism*. They sought a social revolution based on the communal life of the Russian peasants. The chief radical society was called *Land and Freedom*.

In the early 1870s hundreds of young Russians, including both men and women, took their revolutionary message into the countryside. They intended to live with the peasants, to gain their trust, and to teach them about the peasant role in the coming revolution. The bewildered and distrustful peasants turned most of the youths over to the police. In the winter of 1877–1878 almost two hundred students were tried. Most were acquitted or given very light sentences, because they had been held for months in preventive detention and because the court believed that a display of mercy might lessen public sympathy for the young revolutionaries. The court even suggested that the tsar might wish to pardon those students given heavier sentences. The tsar refused and let it become known that he favored heavy penalties for all persons involved in revolutionary activity.

Thereafter the revolutionaries decided that the tsarist regime must be attacked directly. They adopted a policy of terrorism. In January 1878 Vera Zasulich attempted to assassinate

the military governor of Saint Petersburg. At her trial the jury acquitted her because the governor she had shot had a special reputation for brutality. Some people at the time also believed that Zasulich had a personal rather than a political grievance against her victim. Nonetheless, the verdict further encouraged the terrorists.

In 1879 Land and Freedom split into two groups. One held to the idea of educating the peasants, and it soon dissolved. The other, known as *People's Will*, was dedicated to the overthrow of the autocracy. Its members decided to assassinate the tsar himself. Several assassination attempts failed, but on March 1, 1881, a bomb hurled by a member of People's

The assassination of Tsar Alexander II (1855–1881) on March 1, 1881 is shown here. Two bombs were thrown. The first wounded several Imperial guards. The Tsar stopped his carriage to see to the wounded. The assassins then threw another bomb which killed Alexander. [Bildarchiv Preussischer Kulturbesitz]

The People's Will Issues a Revolutionary Manifesto

In the late 1870s a more extreme revolutionary movement appeared in Russia calling itself The People's Will. It called for the overthrow of the tsarist government and the election of an Organizing Assembly to form a government based on popular representation. It directly embraced terrorism as a path toward its goal of the Russian people governing themselves. Eventually members of this group assassinated Alexander II in 1881.

Although we are ready to submit wholly to the popular will, we regard it as none the less our duty, as a party, to appear before the people with our program. . . . It is as follows:

1. Perpetual popular representation, . . . having full power to act in all national questions.

2. General local self-government, secured by the election of all officers, and the economic independence of the people.

3. The self-controlled village commune as the economic and administrative unit.

4. Ownership of the land by the people.

5. A system of measures having for their object the turning over to the laborers of all mining works and factories.

6. Complete freedom of conscience, speech, association, public meeting, and electioneering activity.

7. The substitution of a territorial militia for the army.

. . . .

In view of the stated aim of the party its operations may be classified as follows:

1. *Propaganda and agitation.* Our propaganda has for its object the popularization, in all social classes, of the idea of a political and popular revolution as a means of social reform, as well as popularization of the party's own program. Its essential features are criticism of the existing order of things, and a statement and explanation of revolutionary methods. The aim of agitation should be to incite the people to protest as generally as possible against the present state of affairs, to demand such reforms as are in harmony with the party's purposes, and, especially, to demand the summoning of an Organizing Assembly. . . .

2. *Destructive and terroristic activity.* Terroristic activity consists in the destruction of the most harmful persons in the Government, the protection of the party from spies, and the punishment of official lawlessness and violence in all the more prominent and important cases in which such lawlessness and violence are manifested. The aim of such activity is to break down the prestige of Governmental power, to furnish continuous proof of the possibility of carrying on a contest with the Government, to raise in that way the revolutionary spirit of the people and inspire belief in the practicability of revolution, and, finally, to form a body suited and accustomed to warfare.

Quoted in George Kennan, Siberia and the Exile System *(New York: The Century Co., 1891), 2:495–499.*

Will killed Tsar Alexander II. Four men and two women were sentenced to death for the deed. All of them had been willing to die for their cause. The emergence of such dedicated revolutionary opposition constituted as much a part of the reign of Alexander II as did his reforms. The limited character of those reforms convinced many people from various walks of life that the autocracy could never truly redirect Russian society.

The reign of Alexander III (1881–1894) further underscored that pessimistic conviction.

He possessed all the autocratic and repressive characteristics of his grandfather Nicholas I and none of the better qualities of his father. Some slight attention was directed toward the improvement of life in the Russian factories, but primarily Alexander III sought to roll back the reforms of the third quarter of the century. He favored centralized bureaucracy over the new limited modes of self-government. He strengthened the secret police and increased press censorship. In effect, he confirmed all the evils that the revolutionaries saw inherent in autocratic government. His son, Nicholas II, who became tsar in 1894, would discover that autocracy could not survive the pressures of the twentieth century.

Great Britain: Toward Democracy

While the continental nations became unified and struggled toward internal political restructuring, Great Britain continued to symbolize the confident liberal state. Britain was not without its difficulties and domestic conflicts, but it seemed able to deal with these through existing political institutions. The general prosperity of the third quarter of the century took the edge off the social hostility of the 1840s. A large body of shared ideas emphasizing competition and individualism was accepted by the members of all classes. Even the leaders of trade unions during these years asked for little more than to receive a portion of the fruits of prosperity and to prove their own social respectability. Parliament itself continued to provide an institution that permitted the absorption of new groups and interests into the existing political processes. In short, the British did not have to create new liberal institutions and then learn how to live within them.

Lord Palmerston (1855–1865)

The major political figure of mid-century was Henry John Temple, Lord Palmerston (1784–1865). He became prime minister early in 1855 as the nation became weary of blunders in the conduct of the Crimean War. Except for a seventeen-month interlude in 1858 and 1859, he governed until late 1865. Palmerston was a liberal Whig whose chief interest was foreign policy. He generally championed free trade and the right of European nationalities to determine their own political destinies. His bombastic patriotism made him very popular with voters; he rarely hesitated to parade British naval power before the world.

Yet Palmerston was a person of the past. He had little sympathy with those political and working-class figures who wanted to extend the franchise beyond the limits of the Great Reform Act of 1832. By the time of his death Palmerston had become the chief obstacle to further political and social reform.

The Second Reform Act (1867)

By the early 1860s it had become clear to most observers that in one way or another the franchise would again have to be expanded. The prosperity and the social respectability of the working class convinced many politicians that the workers truly deserved the vote. Organizations such as the Reform League, led by John Bright (1811–1889), were agitating for parliamentary action. In 1866 Lord John Russell's Liberal ministry introduced a reform bill that was defeated by a coalition of traditional Conservatives and antidemocratic liberals. Russell resigned, and the Tory Lord Derby replaced him. What then occurred surprised everyone.

The Conservative ministry, led in the House of Commons by Benjamin Disraeli (1804–1881), introduced its own reform bill in 1867. As the debate proceeded, Disraeli accepted one amendment after another and expanded the electorate well beyond the limits earlier proposed by the Liberals. When the final measure was passed, the number of voters had been increased from approximately 1,430,000 to 2,470,000. Britain had taken a major step toward democracy. Large numbers of male working-class voters had been admitted to the electorate.

Disraeli hoped that by sponsoring the measure, the Conservatives would receive the gratitude of the new voters. Because reform was bound to come, it was best for the Conservatives to enjoy the credit. Disraeli thought that eventually significant portions of the working class would support Conservative candidates who proved themselves responsive to social issues. He also thought that the growing suburban middle class would become more conservative. In the long run, his intuition proved correct, for in the past century the Conservative Party has dominated British politics.

The immediate election of 1868, however, dashed Disraeli's hopes. William Gladstone (1809–1898) became the new prime minister. Gladstone had begun political life in 1833 as a strong Tory, but over the next thirty-five years he moved steadily toward liberalism. He had supported Robert Peel, free trade, repeal of the Corn Laws, and efficient administration. As chancellor of the exchequer during the 1850s and early 1860s he had lowered taxes and government expenditures. He had also championed Italian nationalism. For many years he continued to oppose a new reform bill. Yet by the early 1860s he had also modified his position on that issue. In 1866 he had been Russell's spokesman in the House of Commons for the unsuccessful liberal reform bill.

Gladstone's Great Ministry (1868–1874)

Gladstone's ministry of 1868–1874 witnessed the culmination of classical British liberalism. Those institutions that still remained the preserve of the aristocracy and the Anglican church were opened to people from other classes and religious denominations. By an Order in Council of 1870, competitive examinations replaced patronage as a means of entering the civil service. In 1871 the purchase of officers' commissions in the army was abolished. The same year saw the removal of Anglican religious requirements for the faculties of Oxford and Cambridge universities. The Ballot Act of 1872 introduced voting by secret ballot.

The most momentous measure of Gladstone's first ministry was the Education Act of 1870. For the first time in British history, the government assumed the responsibility for establishing and running elementary schools. Previously British education had been a task relegated to the religious denominations, which received small amounts of state support for the purpose.

All of these reforms were typically liberal. They sought to remove long-standing abuses without destroying existing institutions and to permit all able citizens to compete on the grounds of ability and merit. They attempted

to avoid the potential danger to a democratic state of an illiterate citizenry. These reforms also constituted a mode of state building because they created new bonds of loyalty to the nation by abolishing many sources of present and future discontent.

Disraeli in Office (1874–1880)

The liberal policy of creating popular support for the nation through the extension of political liberty and the reform of abuses had its conservative counterpart in concern about social reform. Disraeli succeeded Gladstone as prime minister in 1874, when the election produced sharp divisions among Liberal Party voters over matters of liquor regulation, religion, and education.

The two men had stood on different sides of most issues for over a quarter century. Whereas Gladstone looked to individualism, free trade, and competition to solve social problems, Disraeli believed that the ruling classes of the country must confront those matters through paternalistic legislation. Disraeli believed in state action to protect weak groups of citizens. In his view such paternalistic legislation would alleviate class antagonism.

Disraeli personally talked a better line than he produced. He had very few specific programs or ideas. The significant social legislation of his ministry stemmed primarily from the efforts of his Home Secretary, Richard Cross. The Public Health Act of 1875 consolidated previous sanitary legislation and reaffirmed the duty of the state to interfere with private property on matters of health and physical well-being. Through the Artisans Dwelling Act of 1875, the government became actively involved in providing housing for the working class. The same year, in an important symbolic gesture, the Conservative majority in Parliament passed a law that gave new protection to British trade unions and allowed them to raise picket lines. The Gladstone ministry, although recognizing the legality of unions, had refused such extensive protection.

The Irish Question

In 1880 a second Gladstone ministry took office as an agricultural depression and unpopu-

A House of Commons debate: Gladstone, standing on the right, is attacking Disraeli, who is sitting with legs crossed and arms folded. [Mary Evans Picture Library]

lar foreign policy undermined Disraeli's popularity. In 1884, with Conservative cooperation, a third reform act was passed, extending the vote to most male farm workers. However, the major issue of the decade was Ireland. From the late 1860s onward Irish nationalists had sought to achieve home rule for Ireland, by which they meant more Irish control of local government.

During his first ministry Gladstone had addressed the Irish question through two major pieces of legislation. In 1869 he carried a measure to disestablish the Church of Ireland, which was the Irish branch of the Anglican church. Henceforth, Irish Roman Catholics would not pay taxes to support the hated Protestant church, to which only a small fraction of the population belonged. Second, in 1870 the Liberal ministry sponsored a land act that provided compensation to evicted Irish tenants and loans for tenants who wished to purchase their land.

Throughout the 1870s the Irish question continued to fester. Land remained the center of the agitation. Today the matter of Irish economic development seems more complicated and who owned the land seems less important than the methods of management and cultivation. Nevertheless, the organization of the Irish Land League in the late 1870s brought a period of intense agitation and intimidation against the landlords, who were often English. The leader of the Irish movement for a just land settlement and for home rule was Charles Stewart Parnell (1846–1891). In 1881 the second Gladstone ministry passed another Irish land act, which provided further guarantees of tenant rights. This measure only partly satisfied Irish opinion because it was accompanied by a Coercion Act intended to restore law and order to Ireland.

By 1885 Parnell had organized eighty-five Irish members of the House of Commons into a tightly disciplined party that often voted as a bloc. They pursued disruptive tactics to gain attention for the cause of home rule. They bar-

William Gladstone Pleads for Irish Home Rule

Since 1800 Ireland had been governed as part of Great Britain, sending representatives to the British Parliament in Westminster. Throughout the century there had been tension and violent conflict between the Irish and their English governors. Agitation for Home Rule whereby the Irish would directly control many of their own affairs reached a peak in the 1880s. In 1886 William Gladstone introduced a Home Rule Bill into Parliament. The evening when Parliament voted on the measure Gladstone made a long speech, part of which is quoted here, asking Parliament to reject the traditions of the past and to grant Ireland this measure of independence. That night the Home Rule Bill of 1886 went down to defeat, but the problem remained to vex British politics from that time to the present.

What is the case of Ireland at this moment? . . . Can anything stop a nation's demand, except its being proved to be immoderate and unsafe? But here are multitudes, and, I believe, millions upon millions, out-of-doors, who feel this demand to be neither immoderate nor unsafe. In our opinion, there is but one question before us about this demand. It is as to the time and circumstance of granting it. There is no question in our minds that it will be granted. . . .

. . . .

Ireland stands at your bar expectant, hopeful, almost suppliant. Her words are the words of truth and soberness. She asks a blessed oblivion of the past, and in that oblivion our interest is deeper than even hers. My right honourable Friend the Member [of Parliament] for East Edinburgh asks us tonight to abide by the traditions of which we are the heirs. What traditions? By the Irish traditions? Go into the length and breadth of the world, ransack the literature of all countries, find, if you can, a single voice, a single book, find, I would almost say, as much as a single newspaper article, unless the product of the [present] day, in which the conduct of England towards Ireland is anywhere treated except with profound and bitter condemnation. Are these the traditions by which we are exhorted to stand? No; they are a sad exception to the glory of our country. They are a broad and black blot upon the pages of its history; and what we want to do is to stand by the traditions of which we are the heirs in all matters except our relations with Ireland, and to make our relations with Ireland to conform to the other traditions of our country. So we treat our traditions—so we hail the demand of Ireland for what I call a blessed oblivion of the past. She also asks a boon [a favor] for the future; and that boon for the future, unless we are much mistaken, will be a boon to us in respect of honour, no less than a boon to her in respect of happiness, prosperity, and peace. Such . . . is her prayer. Think, I beseech you, think well, think wisely, think, not for the moment, but for the years that are to come, before you reject this Bill.

Quoted in Hans Kohn (Ed.), The Modern World: 1848 to the Present, *2nd ed. (New York: The Macmillan Company; London: Collier-Macmillan Limited, 1968), pp. 116, 118.*

gained with the two English political parties. In the election of 1885 the Irish Party emerged with the balance of power between the English Liberals and Conservatives. The Irish could decide which party would take office. In December 1885 Gladstone announced support of

Charles Stewart Parnell (1846–1891) led the fight for Irish home rule, until his political career ended in scandal when his affair with a married woman became public knowledge. [Library of Congress]

the House of Lords Act of 1911, which curbed the power of that body, the bill had to pass the Commons three times over a Lord's veto to become law. The third passage occurred in the summer of 1914, and the implementation of the home rule provisions of the bill was suspended for the duration of World War I.

The Irish question affected British politics in a manner not unlike that of the Austrian nationalities problem. Normal British domestic issues could not be adequately addressed because of the political divisions created by Ireland. The split of the Liberal Party proved especially harmful to the cause of further social and political reform. The people who could agree on matters of reform could not agree on Ireland, and the latter problem seemed more

home rule for Ireland. Parnell gave his votes to the formation of a Liberal ministry. However, the issue split the Liberal Party. In 1886 a group of Liberals known as the Liberal Unionists joined with the Conservatives to defeat Gladstone's Home Rule Bill. Gladstone called for a new election, in which Liberals were defeated. They remained a permanently divided party.

The new Conservative ministry of Lord Salisbury (1830–1903) attempted to reconcile the Irish to English government through public works and administrative reform. The policy, which was tied to further coercion, had only marginal success. In 1892 Gladstone returned to power. A second Home Rule Bill passed the House of Commons but was defeated in the House of Lords. There the Irish question stood until after the turn of the century. The Conservatives sponsored a land act in 1903 that carried out the final transfer of land to tenant ownership. Ireland became a country of small farms. In 1912 a Liberal ministry passed the third Home Rule Bill. Under the provisions of

MAJOR DATES IN LATE-NINETEENTH-CENTURY BRITAIN	
1855–1865	Palmerston dominates British politics
1867	Second Reform Act
1868	Gladstone becomes prime minister
1869	Disestablishment of Church of Ireland
1870	Education Act and First Irish Land Act
1871	Purchase of army officers' commissions abolished
1871	Religious tests abolished at Oxford and Cambridge
1872	Ballot Act
1874	Disraeli becomes prime minister
1875	Public Health Act and Artisan Dwelling Act
1880	Beginning of Gladstone's Second Ministry
1881	Second Irish Land Act and Irish Coercion Act
1884	Third Reform Act
1885	Gladstone announces support of Irish Home Rule
1886	Home Rule Bill defeated and Lord Salisbury becomes the Conservative prime minister
1892	Gladstone begins his third ministry and Second Irish Home Rule Bill defeated
1903	Third Irish Land Act
1912	Third Irish Home Rule Bill passed
1914	Provisions of Irish Home Rule Bill suspended because of the outbreak of World War I

important. As the two traditional parties failed to deal with the social questions, by the turn of the century a newly organized Labour Party began to fill the vacuum.

Between 1850 and 1875 the major contours of the political systems that would dominate Europe until World War I had been drawn. Those systems and political arrangements solved, so far as such matters can be solved, many of the political questions and problems that had troubled the Europeans during the first half of the nineteenth century. The concept of the nation-state had on the whole triumphed. Support for governments no longer stemmed from loyalty to dynasties but from various degrees of citizen participation. Moreover, the unity of nations was no longer based on dynastic links but on ethnic, cultural, linguistic, and historical bonds. The parliamentary governments of western Europe and the autocracies of eastern Europe were quite different, but both political systems had been compelled to recognize the force of nationalism and the larger role of citizens in political affairs. Only Russia failed to make such concessions, but the emancipation of serfs had constituted a concession to a mode of popular opinion.

The major sources of future discontent would arise from the demands of labor to enter the political processes and the still unsatisfied aspirations of subject nationalities. Those two areas of unrest would trouble Europe for the next forty years and would eventually undermine the political structures created during the third quarter of the nineteenth century.

Suggested Readings

M. BENTLEY, *Politics Without Democracy, 1815–1914* (1984). A well-informed survey of British development.

R. BLAKE, *Disraeli* (1967). The best biography.

J. BLUM, *Lord and Peasant in Russia from the Ninth to the Nineteenth Century* (1961). A clear discussion of emancipation in the later chapters.

W. L. BURN, *The Age of Equipoise* (1964). A thoughtful and convincing discussion of Victorian social stability.

G. CHAPMAN, *The Dreyfus Affair: A Reassessment* (1955). A detached treatment of a subject that still provokes strong feelings.

G. CRAIG, *Germany, 1866–1945* (1978). An excellent survey.

S. EDWARDS, *The Paris Commune of 1871* (1971). A useful examination of a complex subject.

S. ELWITT, *The Making of the Third Republic: Class and Politics in France, 1868–1884* (1975). An excellent introduction.

S. ELWITT, *The Third Republic Defended: Bourgeois Reform in France, 1880–1914* (1986). A study that continues the survey of the previously listed volume.

E. HOBSBAWM, *The Age of Empire, 1875–1914* (1987). A stimulating survey that covers cultural as well as political developments.

I. V. HULL, *The Entourage of Kaiser Wilhelm II, 1888–1918* (1982). An important discussion of the scandals of the German court.

R. A. KANN, *The Multinational Empire*, 2 vols. (1950). The basic treatment of the nationality problem of Austria-Hungary.

G. KITSON KLARK, *The Making of Victorian England* (1962). The best introduction.

R. R. LOCKE, *French Legitimists and the Politics of Moral Order in the Early Third Republic* (1974). An excellent study of the social and intellectual roots of monarchist support.

A. J. MAY, *The Habsburg Monarchy, 1867–1914* (1951). Narrates in considerable detail and with much sympathy the fate of the dual monarchy.

N. M. NAIMARK, *Terrorists and Social Democrats: The Russian Revolutionary Movement Under Alexander III* (1983). Based on the most recent research.

C. C. O'BRIEN, *Parnell and His Party* (1957). An excellent treatment of the Irish question.

J. P. PARRY, *Democracy and Religion: Gladstone and the Liberal Party, 1867–1876* (1987). An important study of the role of religious denominations in the British Liberal Party.

O. PFLANZE, *Bismarck and the Development of Germany* (1963). Carries the story through the achievement of unification.

A. PLESSIS, *The Rise and Fall of the Second Empire, 1852–1871* (1985). A useful survey of France under Napoleon III.

R. SHANNON, *Gladstone: 1809–1865* (1982). Best coverage of his early career.

D. M. SMITH, *The Making of Italy, 1796–1870* (1968). A narrative that incorporates the major documents.

D. M. Smith, *Cavour* (1984). An excellent biography.

A. J. P. Taylor, *The Habsburg Monarchy, 1809–1918* (1941). An opinionated but highly readable work.

J. M. Thomson, *Louis Napoleon and the Second Empire* (1954). A straightforward account.

R. Tombs, *The War Against Paris, 1871* (1981). Examines the role of the army in suppressing the Commune.

A. B. Ulam, *Russia's Failed Revolutionaries* (1981). A study of revolutionary societies and activities prior to the Revolution of 1917.

F. Venturi, *The Roots of Revolution* (trans., 1960). A major treatment of late-nineteenth-century revolutionary movement.

H. S. Watson, *The Russian Empire, 1801–1917* (1967). A far-ranging narrative.

H. U. Wehler, *The German Empire, 1871–1918* (1985). An important, controversial work.

J. Wertheimer, *Unwelcome Strangers: East European Jews in Imperial Germany* (1987). Examines the difficult position of Jews in Wilhelminian German.

R. Williams, *The World of Napoleon III*, rev. ed. (1965). Examines the cultural setting.

C. B. Woodham-Smith, *The Reason Why* (1953). A lively account of the Crimean War and the charge of the Light Brigade.

T. Zeldin, *France: 1848–1945*, 2 vols. (1973, 1977). Emphasizes the social developments.

R. E. Zelnick, *Labor and Society in Tsarist Russia: The Factory Workers of St. Petersburg, 1855–1870* (1971). An important volume that considers the early stages of the Russian industrial labor force in the era of serf emancipation.

A British suffragette stands on a London street selling newspapers for the cause of votes for women. As indicated by the poster, some women believed opposition to their cause justified violent action. [The Bettmann Archive]

24

THE BUILDING OF EUROPEAN SUPREMACY: SOCIETY AND POLITICS TO WORLD WAR I

Between 1860 and 1914 the extensive spread of industrialism created an unparalleled productive capacity in Europe. The age of the automobile, the airplane, the bicycle, the refrigerated ship, the telephone, the radio, the typewriter, and the electric light bulb dawned. The world's economies, based on the gold standard, became increasingly interdependent. European goods flowed into markets all over the globe. In turn, foreign products, raw materials, and foodstuffs were imported.

During this half-century European political, economic, and social life assumed many of the features characteristic of our world today. Nation-states with large electorates, political parties, centralized bureaucracies, and universal military service emerged. Business adopted large-scale corporate structures, and the labor force organized itself into trade unions. Large numbers of white-collar workers appeared. Urban life came to predominate throughout western Europe. Socialism became a major ingredient in the political life of all nations. The foundations of the welfare state and of vast military establishments were laid. Taxation increased accordingly.

Europe had also quietly become dependent on the resources and markets of the rest of the world. Changes in the weather conditions in Kansas, Argentina, or New Zealand might now affect the European economy. However, before World War I the dependence was concealed by Europe's industrial, military, and financial supremacy. At the time people rather assumed that such supremacy was a natural situation, but the twentieth century would reveal it to have been quite temporary.

Population Trends and Migration

There seem to have been more Europeans proportionally about 1900 than ever before or since. Europe then contained just under one quarter of the estimated world population. Demographic expansion continued through the second half of the century. The number of Europeans rose from approximately 266 million in 1850 to 401 million in 1900 and 447 million in 1910. However, the rate of European growth began to slow, whereas the population expansion elsewhere did not recede. Depending on the country in Europe, the birth rate either fell or remained stationary. The death rate did likewise. In the long run that ratio meant a more slowly growing population. This situation also meant that the grave demographic differential between the developed and the undeveloped world—which is so much a part of the present food and resource crisis—had been established.

Europe's peoples were on the move in the last half of the century as never before. Legal movement and migration became easier as the role of the landlords lessened. Railways, steamships, and better roads allowed greater physical mobility. The development of the European economy and the economies of North America, Latin America, and Australia meant better wages and cheap land, which enticed people to move.

Europeans migrated away from their continent in record numbers. Between 1846 and 1932 over fifty million Europeans left their homelands. The major areas to benefit from this movement were the United States, Canada, Australia, South Africa, Brazil, and Argentina. At mid-century most of the emigrants were from Great Britain (and especially Ireland), Germany, and Scandinavia. After 1885 the migration drew its numbers from southern and eastern Europe. This exodus helped to relieve the social and population pressures on the Continent. The outward movement of peoples in conjunction with Europe's economic and technological superiority contributed heavily to the Europeanization of the world. Not since the sixteenth century had European civilization produced such an impact on other cultures.

The Second Industrial Revolution

As historian David Landes suggested, "The period from 1850 to 1873 was the continental industry's coming-of-age."[1] The gap that had existed for half a century between British

---

[1] David S. Landes, The Unbound Prometheus: Technological Change and Industrial Development in Western Europe from 1750 to the Present (Cambridge: Cambridge University Press, 1969), p. 193.

845

THE BUIL
OF EURO
SUPREMA
SOCIETY
POLITICS
WORLD W

European immigrants are shown on their way to the United States, 1906. Between 1846 and 1932, over 50 million Europeans immigrated to the United States, Canada, South America, Australia, and South Africa. [Library of Congress]

and continental economic development was closed. The basic heavy industries of Belgium, France, and Germany underwent major expansion. In particular, the expansion of German industry was stunning. Coal mining, iron and steel production, and the chemical industry made rapid progress. German steel production surpassed that of Britain in 1893 and had almost doubled the British effort by the outbreak of World War I. This emergence of an industrial Germany was the major fact of European economic and political life at the turn of the century.

The Second Industrial Revolution witnessed a shift in the European economic balance of power. In almost all areas of the new industrial expansion, Great Britain, which had pioneered the first Industrial Revolution, fell behind the continent and especially Germany. This situation greatly affected the international political rivalry of the two powers.

New Industries

Initially the economic expansion of the third quarter of the century involved the spread of industries similar to those pioneered earlier in Great Britain. In particular the expansion of railway systems on the Continent spurred economic growth. Thereafter, however, wholly new industries emerged. It is this latter development that is usually termed the Second Industrial Revolution. The first industrial revolution was associated with textiles, steam, and iron; by contrast, the second was associated with steel, chemicals, electricity, and oil.

In the 1850s Henry Bessemer (1830–1898), an English engineer, discovered a new process, named after him, for manufacturing steel cheaply in large quantities. In 1860 Great Britain, Belgium, France, and Germany had produced 125,000 tons of steel. By 1913 the figure had risen to 32,020,000 tons.

The chemical industry also came of age during this period. The Solway process of alkali production replaced the older Leblanc process. The new process allowed more chemical by-products to be recovered. More sulfuric acid could be produced and so could more laundry soap. New dyestuffs and plastics were also developed. In this growth of the chemical industry, for the first time formal scientific re-

This is the Krupp armaments works at Essen, Germany. In the late nineteenth century, Krupp was one of the largest industrial firms in Europe, employing some 30,000 workers. In the Second Industrial Revolution Germany, not Britain, led the way. [Culver Pictures]

search aided industrial development. As in so many other fields of the Second Industrial Revolution, Germany led the way in fostering scientific research and education.

New Sources of Energy

The most significant change for industry and eventually for everyday life involved the application of electrical energy to production. Electricity was the most versatile and transportable source of power ever discovered. It could be used to run either large or small machines and to make factory construction more efficient. Electricity was a mode of energy that could be taken to the machinery. The first major public power plant was constructed in Great Britain in 1881. Soon electric poles, lines, and generating stations dotted the European landscape. Electric lights were beginning to be used in homes. Streetcar and subway systems were electrified.

The turn of the century also saw the emergence of the first large European demand for petroleum. The internal combustion engine was invented in 1886. When the German engineer Gottlieb Daimler (1834–1900) put it on four wheels and obtained a French patent in 1887, the automobile was born. France initially took the lead in auto manufacture, but for many years the car remained a novelty item that only the wealthy could afford. It was the

American Henry Ford (1863–1947) who later made the automobile accessible to large numbers of people.

The automobile and the new industrial and chemical uses for oil greatly expanded the demand for petroleum. Before the 1890s petroleum had been used primarily for lighting; soon it became the basis for transportation and much of the new chemical industry. Europe, then as now, was almost wholly dependent on imported oil. The major supplying companies were Standard Oil of the United States, British Shell Oil, and Royal Dutch.

Economic Difficulties

Despite the vast expansion of new industries the second half of the century was not a period of uninterrupted or smooth economic growth. The years from 1850 to 1873 saw a general boom in both industry and agriculture. The last quarter of the century witnessed economic advance but of a much slower nature. Bad weather and foreign competition put grave pressures on European agriculture. From the consumers' standpoint these developments meant lower food prices. Nevertheless, the difficulties in the agricultural sector put a drag on the economy. Many of the emigrants who left Europe during these years came from the coun-

tryside or from those parts of Europe where industrialization was least advanced.

During 1873 a number of major banks failed, and the rate of capital investment slowed. During the next two decades stagnation, which many contemporaries regarded as a depression, occurred in several industries. Prices and profits fell. Wages also became lower, but the simultaneous fall in prices meant that real wages generally held firm, and in some countries even improved. There were pockets of unemployment (a word that was coined during this period) and frequent occurrences of strikes and other labor unrest. The economic difficulties fed the growth of trade unions and socialist political parties. However, despite the stagnation, the general standard of living in the industrialized nations improved over the course of the half-century. Yet many workers still lived and labored in abysmal conditions.

Consumerism

What brought the economy out of stagnation was a new expansion of consumer demand by the end of the century. The new industries of the late century were largely directed toward consumer goods. The lower food prices eventually allowed all classes to spend a marginally larger amount of their income on those con-

847

THE BUILDI
OF EUROPE
SUPREMAC
SOCIETY AN
POLITICS T
WORLD WA

The invention of electricity revolutionized European life, not least in public transport. Before the 1890s, streetcars in European cities were pulled by horses, which severely limited their size and speed. The electric trolley was bigger, faster, cleaner, and cheaper. This photograph was taken in Berlin in 1901 when electric streetcars were rapidly replacing horsedrawn buses. [Ullstein Bilderdienst]

sumer goods. Urbanization naturally created a larger market. People living in cities simply saw more things they wanted to buy than they would have seen in the countryside. Retailing techniques changed. Department stores, retail chains, new packaging techniques, mail-order catalogs, and advertising were developed. Marketing itself was creating new demand. The foundations of a consumer economy were being laid. Furthermore, the overseas imperialism of this period also opened new markets for European consumer goods.

The Middle Classes in Ascendancy

The sixty years before World War I were definitively the age of the middle classes. The Great Exhibition of 1851 held in the Crystal Palace in London had displayed the products and the new material life they had forged. Thereafter, the middle classes became the arbiter of much consumer taste and the defender of the status quo. After the revolutions of 1848 the middle classes ceased to be a revolutionary group. Most of their political goals had been attained, even if imperfectly. Once the question of social equality had been raised, large and small property owners across the continent moved to protect what they possessed.

Social Distinctions within the Middle Classes

The middle classes, which had never been perfectly homogeneous, now became even more diverse. Their most prosperous members were the owners and managers of great businesses and banks. They lived in a splendor that rivaled and sometimes excelled that of the aristocracy. Some, such as W. H. Smith, the owner of railway newsstands in England, were made members of the House of Lords. The Krupp family of Germany were pillars of the state and received visits from the German emperor and his court.

Only a few hundred families acquired such wealth. Beneath them were the comfortable small entrepreneurs and professional people, whose incomes permitted private homes, large quantities of furniture, pianos, pictures, books, journals, education for their children, and vacations. There were also the shopkeepers, the schoolteachers, the librarians, and others who had either a bit of property or a skill derived from education that provided respectable, nonmanual employment.

Finally, there was a wholly new element, namely the white-collar workers. These included secretaries, retail clerks, and lower-level bureaucrats in business and government. The white-collar labor force was often working class in its origins and might even belong to unions, but its aspirations for lifestyle were middle class. This lower-middle-class or petty-bourgeois element in society consciously sought to set itself off from the lifestyle of the working class. People from the lower middle class actively pursued educational opportunities and chances for even the slightest career advancement for themselves and their children. They also tended to spend a considerable portion of their disposable income on consumer goods, such as stylish clothing and furniture, that were distinctively middle class in appearance.

Middle-Class Social Anxieties

Significant tensions began to exist among the various strata of middle-class society during

849

THE BUILDIN
OF EUROPEA
SUPREMACY
SOCIETY AN
POLITICS T(
WORLD WA

Paris Department Stores Expand Their Business

The department store in Europe and the United States became a major institution of retailing in the last half of the nineteenth century. It was one of the reasons for the expansion in late-century consumer demand. This description, written by the Frenchman E. Levasseur in 1907, follows the growth of such stores in Paris and explains why they exerted such considerable economic power. The reader will notice how many of their techniques of retailing are still used today.

It was in the reign of Louis-Philippe [1830–1848] that department stores for fashion goods and dresses . . . began to be distinguished. The type was already one of the notable developments of the Second Empire; it became one of the most important ones of the Third Republic. These stores have increased in number and several of them have become extremely large. Combining in their different departments all articles of clothing, toilet articles, furniture and many other ranges of goods, it is their special object so to combine all commodities as to attract and satisfy customers who will find conveniently together an assortment of a mass of articles corresponding to all their various needs. They attract customers by permanent display, by free entry into the shops, by periodic exhibitions, by special sales, by fixed prices, and by their ability to deliver the goods purchased to customers' homes, in Paris and to the provinces. Turning themselves into direct intermediaries between the producer and the consumer, even producing sometimes some of their articles in their own workshops, buying at lowest prices because of their large orders and because they are in a position to profit from bargains, working with large sums, and selling to most of their customers for cash only, they can transmit these benefits in lowered selling prices. They can even decide to sell at a loss, as an advertisement or to get rid of out-of-date fashions. . . .

The success of these department stores is only possible thanks to the volume of their business, and this volume needs considerable capital and a very large turnover. Now capital, having become abundant, is freely combined nowadays in large enterprises. . . . [T]he large urban agglomerations, the ease with which goods can be transported by the railways, the diffusion of some comforts to strata below the middle classes, have all favoured these developments. . . .

According to the tax records of 1891, these stores in Paris, numbering 12, employed 1,708 persons and rated their site values at 2,159,000 francs; the largest had then 542 employees. These same stores had, in 1901, 9,784 employees; one of them over 2,000 and another over 1,600; their site value was doubled.

Sidney Pollard and Colin Holmes, Documents of European Economic History, *Vol. 3 (London: Edward Arnold, 1972), pp. 95–96.*

the latter part of the century. The small businessmen and shopkeepers, whose numbers rose steadily until shortly after 1900, often resented the power of the great capitalists. The little people of the middle class feared being edged out of the marketplace by large companies, with whom they could not hope to compete. The shopkeeping class always had to work very hard simply to maintain their lifestyle and were often dependent on banks for commercial credit. Department stores and mail-order catalogs endangered their livelihood.

There is also good reason to believe that the learned professions were becoming overcrowded. To be a professional person no longer ensured a sound income. The new white-collar work force had just attained respectability and a non-working-class status. They profoundly feared slipping back to their social origins.

Jewish Emancipation

One of the most important social changes to occur throughout Europe during the nineteenth century was the emancipation of European Jews from the narrow life of the ghetto into a world of equal or nearly equal citizen-

Throughout the first three-quarters of the nineteenth century European Jews received a general extension of civil rights. This Jewish family in England is pictured celebrating the feast of Passover. [The Granger Collection]

ship and social status. This transformation represented one of the major social impacts of political liberalism on European life. The slow and never fully completed process of Jewish emancipation began in the late eighteenth century and continued throughout the nineteenth. It moved at very different paces in different countries.

Differing Degrees of Citizenship

In 1782 Joseph II, the Habsburg emperor, issued a decree that placed the Jews of his empire under more or less the same laws as Christians. In France the National Assembly recognized Jews as French citizens in 1789. During the turmoil of the Napoleonic wars, Jewish communities in Italy and Germany were allowed to mix on a generally equal footing with the Christian population. These various steps toward political emancipation were always somewhat uncertain and were frequently limited or partially repealed with changes in rulers or governments. Certain freedoms granted were often later partially withdrawn. Even in countries that had advanced some political rights, Jews could not own land and could be subject to special discriminatory taxes. Nonetheless, during the first half of the century European Jews in western Europe and to a much lesser extent in central and eastern Europe began to acquire significant rights of equal or more nearly equal citizenship.

In Russia, by contrast, the traditional modes of prejudice and discrimination continued unabated until World War I. There the government undermined Jewish community life, limited publication of Jewish books, restricted areas where Jews might live, required internal passports from Jews, banned Jews from many forms of state service, and excluded Jews from many institutions of higher education. The police and others were allowed to conduct pogroms or organized riots against Jewish neighborhoods and villages. Jews were treated as aliens under Russian rule.

Broadened Opportunities

During the first half of the century various limitations remained on Jewish emancipation, especially in eastern Europe. However, after the revolutions of 1848 there occurred a general improvement in the situation of European Jews that lasted for several decades. Throughout Germany, Italy, the Low Countries, and Scandinavia Jews were allowed full rights of citizenship during these years. After 1858 Jews in Great Britain could sit in Parliament. In Austria-Hungary full legal rights were extended to Jews in 1867. Indeed, from approximately 1850 to 1880 there was relatively little organized or overt prejudice toward Jews. They entered the professions and other occupations once closed to them. They participated fully in the literary and cultural life of their nations. They were active in the arts and music. They became leaders in science and education. Jews intermarried freely with non-Jews as legal secular prohibitions against such marriages were repealed during the last quarter of the century.

Outside of Russia Jewish political figures entered cabinets and served in the highest offices of the state. Politically they tended to be aligned with liberal parties because these were the groups that had championed equal rights. Later in the century, especially in eastern Europe, many Jews became associated with the socialist parties.

The former prejudice that was associated with religious attitudes toward Jews seemed for a time to have dissipated. Although it still appeared on the local level in Russia and other parts of eastern Europe. From these regions hundreds of thousands of European Jews immigrated to the United States. Almost anywhere in Europe Jews might encounter prejudice on a personal level. But in western Europe, including England, France, Italy, and Germany as well as the Low Countries, the Jewish populations seem to have felt themselves relatively secure from the dangers of legalized persecution and discrimination that had haunted so much of the Jewish past.

That situation began to change during the last two decades of the nineteenth century. During the economic stagnation of the 1870s anti-Semitic sentiments were voiced when the problems were blamed on Jewish bankers and financial interests. In the 1880s organized anti-Semitism erupted in Germany as it did in France at the time of the Dreyfus Affair. As will be seen in the next chapter, those developments gave rise to the birth of Zionism. However, it was initially a minority movement within the Jewish community. Most Jewish leaders believed the attacks on Jewish life con-

stituted merely temporary recurrences of older modes of prejudice; they felt that their communities would remain safe under the legal protections that had been extended over the course of the century. That analysis would be proved disastrously wrong during the second quarter of the twentieth century.

851

THE BUILD
OF EUROPF
SUPREMAC
SOCIETY A
POLITICS
WORLD W

Late-Nineteenth-Century Urban Life

Europe became more urbanized than ever in the last half of the nineteenth century as migration continued toward the cities. In France the percentage of the urban population within the whole population rose between 1850 and 1911 from approximately 25 per cent to 44 per cent, and in Germany the shift was from 30 per cent to 60 per cent. In other countries of western Europe by 1900, similar proportions of national populations lived in urban areas.

The rural migrants to the cities were largely uprooted from traditional social ties. They often confronted poor housing, social anonymity, and potential unemployment because they rarely possessed skills that would make them easily employable. People from different ethnic backgrounds had difficulties in mixing socially. The competition for too few jobs generated new varieties of urban political and social discontent, such as were experienced by the thousands of Russian Jews who migrated to western Europe. Much of the political anti-Semitism of the latter part of the century had its social roots in these problems of urban migration.

GROWTH OF MAJOR EUROPEAN CITIES
(FIGURES IN THOUSANDS)

	1850	1880	1910
Berlin	419	1,122	2,071
Birmingham	233	437	840
Frankfurt	65	137	415
London	2,685	4,470	7,256
Madrid	281	398	600
Paris	1,053	2,269	2,888
Vienna	444	1,104	2,031

The Redesign of Cities

The inward urban migration placed new social and economic demands on already strained city resources and gradually produced significant transformations in the patterns of urban living. The central portions of many major European cities were redesigned during the second half of the century. Previously the central areas of cities had been places where large numbers of people from all social classes both lived and worked. From the middle of the century onward, these areas became transformed into districts where relatively few people resided and where businesses, government offices, large retail stores, and theaters were located. Commerce, trade, government, and leisure activities now dominated central cities.

DEVELOPMENT OF SUBURBS The commercial development of the central portion of cities, the clearing of slums, and the building of railways into cities displaced large numbers of people who had previously lived in city centers. These developments also raised the price of centrally located urban land and of the rents charged on buildings located in the center of cities. Consequently, both the middle classes and the working class began to seek housing elsewhere. The middle classes looked for neighborhoods removed from urban congestion. The working class was in search of affordable housing. Thus in virtually all countries, suburbs arose outside the urban center proper, to house the families whose breadwinner worked in the central city or in factories located within the city limits.

The expansion of railways with cheap workday fares and the introduction of mechanical and later electric tramways allowed tens of thousands of workers from all classes to move daily between the city and the outlying suburbs. For hundreds of thousands of Europeans, home and work became physically separated as never before.

THE NEW PARIS This remarkable social change and the values it reflected became embodied in the new designs of many European cities. The most famous and extensive transformation of a major city occurred in Paris. Like so many other European cities, Paris had expanded from the Middle Ages onward with little or no design or planning. Great public buildings and squalid hovels stood near each other. The Seine River was little more than an open sewer. The streets were narrow, crooked, and crowded. It was impossible to cross easily from one part of Paris to another either on foot or by carriage. In 1850 a fully correct map of the city did not even exist. Of more concern to the government of Napoleon III, those streets had for sixty years provided the battleground for urban insurrections that had, on numerous occasions, most recently in 1848, toppled French governments.

Napoleon III personally determined that Paris must be redesigned to be beautiful and to reflect the achievements of his regime and of modern technology. The person whom he put in charge of the rebuilding program was Georges Haussmann. As prefect of the Seine from 1853 to 1870, Haussmann oversaw a vast urban reconstruction program. Whole districts were destroyed to open the way for the broad boulevards and streets that became the hallmark of modern Paris. Much, though by no means all, of the purpose of this street planning was political. The wide vistas were not only beautiful but also allowed for the quick deployment of troops to put down riots. The eradication of the many small streets and alleys removed areas where barricades could be and had been erected.

The project was also political in another sense. In addition to the new boulevards, there were also constructed or completed parks, such as the Bois de Boulogne, and major public buildings, such as the Paris Opera. These projects, along with the demolition and street building, created a vast number of public jobs for thousands of people. Many other laborers found employment in the private construction that paralleled the public action.

The Franco-Prussian War ended the Second Empire, and the Paris Commune brought destruction to parts of the city. Further rebuilding and redesign took place under the Third Republic. There was much private construction of department stores, office complexes, and largely middle-class apartment buildings. By the late 1870s mechanical trams were operating in Paris. After long debate a subway system (the "Métro") was begun in 1895, long after that of London (1863). New railway stations were also erected near the close of the century. This transport linked the refurbished central city to the suburbs.

In 1889 the Eiffel Tower was built, originally as a temporary structure for the international trade exposition of that year. Not all the new structures of Paris bespoke the impact of middle-class commerce and the reign of iron and steel. Between 1873 and 1914 the French Roman Catholic church oversaw the construction of the Basilica of the Sacred Heart high atop Montmartre as an act of national penance for the sins that had led to French defeat in the Franco-Prussian War. Those two landmarks—the Eiffel Tower and the Basilica of the Sacred Heart—visibly symbolized the social and political divisions between liberals and conservatives in the Third Republic.

Urban Sanitation

The efforts of governments and of the increasingly conservative middle classes to maintain public order after 1848 led to a growing concern with the problems of public health and housing for the poor. There arose a widespread feeling that only when the health and housing of the working class were improved would the middle class' health also be secure and the political order stable.

IMPACT OF CHOLERA These concerns first manifested themselves as a result of the great cholera epidemics of the 1830s and 1840s. During this period thousands of Europeans, especially those in cities, had died from this disease of Asian origin, previously unknown in Europe. Unlike many other common deadly diseases of the day that touched only the poor, cholera struck persons from all classes and thus generated much middle-class demand for a solution. Before the development of the bacterial theory of disease (which was achieved only late in the century) physicians and sanitary reformers believed that cholera and other diseases were spread through infection from miasmas in the air. The miasmas, the presence of which was noted by their foul odors, were believed to arise from filth. The way to get rid of the dangerous, foul-smelling air was to clean up the cities.

During the 1840s numerous medical doctors and some government officials had begun to publicize the dangers posed by the unsanitary conditions associated with overcrowding in cities and with businesses such as basement slaughterhouses. In 1840 Louis René Villermé

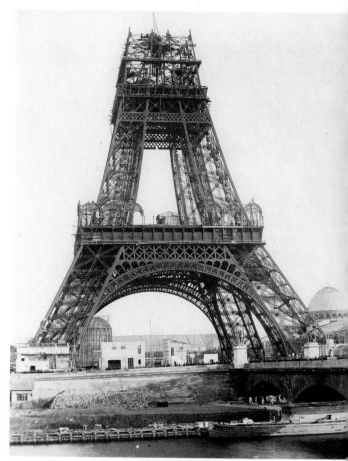

The Eiffel Tower, here photographed during its construction, became one of the symbols of the newly redesigned city of Paris. Its steel structure was also regarded as a symbol of industrial strength. [Roger-Viollet]

published his *Tableau de l'état physique et moral des ouvriers (Catalog of the Physical and Moral State of Workers)*. In 1842 Edwin Chadwick's *Report on the Sanitary Condition of the Labouring Population* shocked the English public. In Germany, Rudolf Virchow published similar findings. These and various other private and public commission reports closely linked the issues of wretched living conditions and public health. They also demonstrated that these dangers were removable and that the threat to health was preventable through sanitary reform. These reports have become some of the most important sources of information about working-class living conditions in the middle of the nineteenth century.

NEW WATER AND SEWER SYSTEMS The proposed solution to the health hazard was cleanliness, to be achieved through new

Sewers were built in the Albert Embankment along the Thames in London. New water and sewer systems did much to lower the mortality rate in nineteenth-century cities. [Mary Evans Picture Library]

water and sewer systems. The construction of these facilities proceeded very slowly. They were usually first begun in capital cities and then much later in provincial cities. Some major urban areas did not have good water systems until after the turn of the century. Nonetheless, the building of these systems constituted one of the major health and engineering achievements of the second half of the nineteenth century. The sewer system of Paris became one of the most famous parts of Haussmann's rebuilding program. In London the construction of the Albert Embankment along the Thames involved not only large sewers discharging into the river but gas mains and water pipes as well; it was all encased in thick walls of granite and concrete, the latter being one of the new building materials of the day.

Major Dates Relating to Sanitation Reform

1830s and 1840s	Cholera epidemics
1840	Villermé's *Catalog of the Physical and Moral State of Workers*
1842	Chadwick's *Report on the Sanitary Condition of the Labouring Population*
1848	British Public Health Act
1851	French Melun Act

Wherever these sanitary reforms were undertaken, considerable decreases in the mortality rate resulted.

EXPANDED GOVERNMENT INVOLVEMENT IN PUBLIC HEALTH This concern with public health led to a considerable expansion of governmental power on various levels. In Britain the Public Health Act of 1848, in France the Melun Act of 1851, and various laws in the still-disunited German states, as well as later legislation, introduced new restraints on private life and enterprise. This legislation allowed medical officers and building inspectors to enter homes and other structures in the name of public health. Private property could be condemned for posing health hazards. Private land could be excavated for the construction of the sewers and water mains required to protect the public. New building regulations put restraints on the activities of private contractors.

When the bacterial theory of disease had become fully accepted at the close of the century, the necessity of cleanliness assumed an ever greater role in public life. The discoveries of Louis Pasteur in France, Robert Koch in Germany, and Joseph Lister in Britain paved the way for the slow acceptance of the use of antiseptics in the practice of medicine and in public health policy. Thereafter, throughout Europe, issues related to the maintenance of public health and the physical well-being of national populations repeatedly opened the way for new modes of government intervention in the lives of citizens. The social roles of medical and scientific experts and governmental bureaucracies were expanded to vast new dimensions.

Housing Reform

The information about working-class living conditions brought to light by the sanitary reformers also led to heated debates over the housing problem. The wretched dwellings of the poor were themselves a cause of poor sanitation and thus became one of the newly perceived health hazards. Furthermore, middle-class reformers and bureaucrats found themselves shocked by the domestic arrangements of the poor, whose large families might live in a single room lacking all forms of personal privacy. A single toilet facility might be furnished for a whole block of tenements. After the revolutions of 1848, the overcrowding in housing and the social discontent that it generated also appeared as a political danger that demanded remedy.

HOUSING AND CHARACTER Middle-class reformers thus turned to housing reform as a solution to the medical, moral, and political dangers posed by slums. They praised the home, as it was understood by the middle class, as a remedy for these dangers. Proper, decent housing would foster a good home life, which would in turn lead to a healthy, moral, and politically stable population. As A. V. Huber, one of the early German housing reformers, declared,

> Certainly it would not be too much to say that the home is the communal embodiment of family life. Thus the purity of the dwelling is almost as important for the family as is the cleanliness of the body for the individual. Good or bad housing is a question of life and death if ever there was one.[2]

Later advocates of housing reform, such as Jules Simon in France, saw good housing as leading to good family life and then to strong national patriotism on the part of the well-housed family. It was widely believed that if the poor and the working class could enjoy adequate, respectable, cheap housing, much social and political discontent would be overcome. It was also believed that the personal saving and investment required for owning a home would lead the working class to adopt the thrifty habits of the middle classes.

PRIVATE EFFORTS The first attacks on the housing problem came from private philanthropy. Companies that operated on a very low margin of profit or that loaned money for housing construction at low interest rates encouraged the building of housing for the poor. Some major industrial companies undertook similar housing programs. They tended to favor the construction of small individual houses or cottages that would ensure for the working class the kind of detached dwellings associated with the middle classes. Model

This photo shows working-class housing in the slums of Glasgow around 1870. Nineteenth-century Glasgow was the booming industrial center of Scotland, but slums such as this, filthy, vermin-infested, disease-ridden, had not changed for centuries. [Library of Congress]

housing projects and industrial communities were constructed by industrial firms, such as the German Krupp armament concern, in all the major European nations. All of them were seeking to ensure a contented, healthy, and stable work force. These early private efforts to address the housing problem reflected the usual liberal tendency to favor private rather than governmental enterprise.

GOVERNMENT ACTION By the mid-1880s, as a result of record-breaking migration

---

[2] Quoted in Nicholas Bullock and James Read, The Movement for Housing Reform in Germany and France, 1840–1914 (Cambridge: Cambridge University Press, 1985), p. 42.

into the cities of Europe, the housing issue had come to the fore as a political question. Some form of governmental action seemed inescapable. The actual policies differed markedly in each country, but all were quite hesitant. In England the first steps toward public housing came in the form of an act of 1885 that lowered interest rates for the construction of cheap housing. A few years later, local town councils, especially that of London, began to construct public housing. In Germany action came somewhat later in the century, primarily through the initiative of local municipalities. In 1894 France passed legislation making credit available on an easier basis for the housing of the poor, and the terms of this legislation were somewhat expanded after the turn of the century.

No government had undertaken really large-scale housing experiments before World War I. Most legislation, though not all, was permissive in nature and facilitated the construction of cheap housing by the private sector.

By 1914 the housing problem stood fully recognized if not adequately addressed. What had been recognized was the necessity for planning and action. The middle-class housing reformers had, moreover, defined the terms of the debate and of future planning. The values and the character of the middle-class family house and home had become the ideal. The goal of housing reform across western Europe came to be that of a dwelling that would allow the working class to enjoy a family life more or less along the lines of the middle classes. It could be in the form of a detached house or some kind of affordable city apartment with several rooms, a private entrance, and separate toilet facilities.

Varieties of Late-Nineteenth-Century Women's Experience

The complexities of general European society reflected themselves in the variety of social experiences encountered by women. The lives of women in the various social ranks partook of the general lifestyle of those particular classes. Yet, within each of those social ranks, the experience of women was distinct from that of men. Women remained, generally speaking, in positions of economic dependence and legal inferiority, whatever their social class.

The pattern of gender-defined social roles had begun to develop in the early nineteenth century in the industrialized sections of western Europe. During the later part of the century it spread wherever industrialism and urbanization came to dominate, and especially wherever middle-class values predominated. Men worked as the chief family wage earner. Young women in the working class and the lower middle class still spent part of their youth working to support themselves and to accumulate enough money to marry. After these women married, they tended to work at home. Such was the expected social pattern for late-nineteenth-century women. The problem arose as the lives of many women did not or could not conform to this pattern. There was little or no provision for women who did not marry or who had to support themselves independently; they became very much the victims of the general social expectations of the lives of women.

New Employment Patterns for Women

During the decades of the Second Industrial Revolution, two major developments affected the economic lives of women. The first was an explosion in the variety of available jobs. The second was a significant withdrawal of married women from the work force. These two seemingly contradictory situations require some explanation.

AVAILABILITY OF NEW JOBS The expansion of governmental bureaucracies, the emergence of corporations and other large-scale businesses, the new and growing demand for schoolteachers resulting from compulsory education laws, and the vast expansion of retail stores opened many new employment opportunities for women. Technological inventions and innovations such as the typewriter and eventually the telephone exchange fostered female employment. Women by the thousands became secretaries and clerks for governments and for private businesses. Still more thousands became shop assistants.

Although these new jobs did mean new and often somewhat better employment opportunities for women, they still required relatively low levels of skill and involved minimal training. These jobs were occupied primarily by unmarried women or widows. Schoolteaching also became rapidly identified as a female occupation, but women very rarely entered the university world or the learned professions. They were even more rarely to be found in major positions of private or public management. Furthermore, employers continued to pay women low wages because they assumed, quite often knowing better, that a woman did not need to support herself independently but could expect additional financial support from her father or from her husband. Consequently, a woman who did need to support herself independently was almost always unable to find a job paying an adequate income—or a position that paid as well as one held by a man who was supporting himself independently.

WITHDRAWAL FROM THE LABOR FORCE Most of the women in this new service work force were young and unmarried. At the time of marriage, or certainly after the birth of her first child, a woman normally withdrew from the labor force. She either did not work or she worked at some occupation that could be pursued in the home. Such withdrawal was not new by the latter part of the century, but the extent of it was much more significant. The kinds of industrial occupations that women had filled in the middle of the nineteenth century, especially textile and garment making, were shrinking. There were consequently fewer opportunities for employment in those industries for either married or unmarried women. Employers in offices and retail stores seem to have preferred young, unmarried women whose family responsibilities would not interfere with their work. The shrinkage in the number of children being born also meant that fewer married women were needed to look after other women's children.

The real wages paid to male workers increased during this period, so that there was a somewhat reduced need for the supplementary wages of their wives. Also, men tended to live longer as a result of improving health conditions, and their wives had to enter the work force less frequently in emergencies. The smaller size of families also lowered the need

857

THE BUILD
OF EUROP
SUPREMAC
SOCIETY A
POLITICS
WORLD W

The invention of the telephone opened new employment for women such as these working in the London Central Telephone exchange. [Mary Evans Picture Library]

for supplementary wages. Working children stayed longer at home and continued to contribute to the family's wage pool.

Finally, the cultural dominance of the middle class, with its generally idle wives, established a pattern of social expectations: the more prosperous a working-class family became, the less involved in employment its women were supposed to be. Indeed, the less income-producing work a wife did, the more prosperous and stable the family was considered.

Yet behind these generalities stands a vast variety of different social and economic experiences encountered by women. As might be expected, the chief determinant of those individual experiences was social class.

Working-Class Women

Although the textile industry and garment making were much less dominant than earlier in the century, they continued to employ large numbers of women. The situation of women in the German clothing-making trades illustrates the kind of vulnerable economic situation that they could encounter as a result of their limited skills and the organization of the trade. The system of manufacturing mass-made clothes of uniform sizes in Germany was quite complex. It was designed to require minimal capital investment on the part of the manufacturers and to protect them from significant risk. A major manufacturer would arrange for the production of clothing through a putting-out system. He would purchase the material and then put it out for tailoring. The clothing was produced not in a factory but usually in numerous, independently owned, small sweatshops or by workers in their homes.

In Berlin in 1896 there were over eighty thousand garment workers, mostly women, who were so employed. When business was good and the demand strong, there was much employment for these women. But as the seasons shifted or business became poor, these workers became unemployed as less and less work was put out for production. In effect, the workers who actually sewed the clothing carried much of the risk of the enterprise. Some women did work in factories, but they, too, were subject to loss of work. Furthermore, women in the clothing trade were nearly always in positions less skilled than those of the male tailors or the male middlemen who owned the workshops.

In a very real sense the expectation of separate social and economic spheres for men and women and the definition of women's chief work as pertaining to the home contributed mightily to the exploitation of women workers outside the home. Because their wages were regarded merely as supplementing their husbands', they became particularly vulnerable to economic exploitation. The entire German putting-out system for clothing production and similar systems of clothing production elsewhere depended on this situation. What was regarded as an adequate wage for a woman was always seen in terms of a wage supplementary to the husband's. Consequently, women were nearly always treated as casual workers everywhere in Europe.

Prostitution

A major but little recognized social fact of most nineteenth-century cities was the presence of a very considerable surplus of women workers whose social situation did not conform to those normal expectations of working only to supplement a father's or a husband's wages. There were almost always many more women seeking employment than there were jobs. The economic vulnerability of women and the consequent poverty encountered by many of them were among the chief causes of prostitution. In any major late-nineteenth-century European city, there were thousands of prostitutes.

The presence of prostitution was, of course, not new. It had always been one way for very poor women to find some income. But in the late nineteenth century it seems to have been quite closely related to the difficulty encountered by very poor women who were attempting to make their way in an overcrowded female labor force. On the continent, prostitution was generally legalized and was subject to governmental and municipal regulations. Those regulations were, it should be noted, passed and enforced by male legislatures and councils and were enforced by male police and physicians. In Great Britain, prostitution received only minimal regulation.

POVERTY AND PROSTITUTION Numerous myths and much misunderstanding have surrounded the subject of prostitution. The most recent studies of the subject in England emphasize that most prostitutes were active on the streets for a very few years, generally from their late teens to about age twenty-five. They tended to be very poor women who had recently migrated from nearby rural areas. Others were born in the towns where they became prostitutes. Certain cities, such as towns with large army garrisons or naval ports or cities with large transient populations, such as London, fostered the presence of considerable numbers of prostitutes. There seem to have been many fewer prostitutes in manufacturing towns, where there were more opportunities for steady employment and where community life was more stable.

Women who became prostitutes tended to have minimal skills and education and to have come from families of unskilled workers. Many had been servants. They also tended to be from broken homes or to be orphaned. Contrary to many sensational late-century newspaper accounts, there seem to have been very few child prostitutes. Furthermore, rarely were these women seduced into their occupations by middle-class employers or middle-class clients. The customers of poor working-class prostitutes seem to have been primarily working-class men. Women remained prostitutes for relatively few years. Thereafter, they seem to have moved back into the regular work force or to have married.

GOVERNMENT REGULATION Poverty was not the only problem confronting English prostitutes. Venereal disease was another. Special institutions known as *lock hospitals* received women suffering from these diseases. It was nearly always assumed that a woman suffering from a venereal disease was a prostitute, and that she should be isolated from other patients. Because many people regarded venereal disease as the wages of vice, these hospitals were badly underfinanced. Within the hospitals women were submitted to rigorous moral and religious instruction. In contrast, men who suffered from venereal disease were not subjected to medical isolation or moral instruction.

Between 1864 and 1886 English prostitutes became subject to the Contagious Diseases Acts, which provided for the medical examina-

tion of prostitutes in certain naval and military cities. Any woman whom the police identified as or suspected of being a prostitute could be required to undergo immediate internal medical examination for venereal disease. Those found to have the disease could be confined to a lock hospital for a number of months. These measures, in effect, enacted the double standard of sexual morality into law. No action of any kind was taken against the male customers of these women.

By 1869 opposition to the Acts had arisen from a number of quarters. The most important of these opposition organizations was the Ladies' National Association for the Repeal of the Contagious Diseases Acts. This was a distinctly middle-class organization led by Josephine Butler. It achieved the suspension of the Acts in 1883 and their repeal in 1886. The advocates of repeal based their arguments on English liberty and on public repugnance at women being dragged from the streets on vague charges and then being forced to submit to physical examination.

Further, middle-class women were angered that the laws in no manner affected or penalized men. They also believed that the causes of prostitution lay primarily in the work conditions and the poverty imposed on so many working-class women. They saw poor women being made victims of the same kind of discrimination that prevented middle-class women from entering the universities and professions. Middle-class women were attempting to prove that they were just as human and rational as men and thus properly subject to equal treatment. The Contagious Diseases Acts were designed to prove that women were otherwise and to treat them as less than human and less than rational creatures. The laws literally took women's bodies from their own control and put them under the control of male customers, medical men, and the police.

The movement to repeal the Contagious Diseases Acts provided the first experience of many British middle-class women in the political arena. It also provided an example of one of the rare instances of active cooperation between women of markedly different social classes. Other results of the movement were purity crusades and calls for chastity to end the social evil of prostitution and venereal disease, and thus to make such repressive legislation unnecessary.

859

THE BUILDI
OF EUROPE
SUPREMAC
SOCIETY AN
POLITICS T
WORLD WA

Women of the Middle Class

A vast social gap lay between the experience of poor working-class women—whose economic situation led them into prostitution or into the sweated textile trades—and that of their middle-class counterparts. As their fathers' and husbands' incomes permitted, middle-class women participated in the vast expansion of consumerism and domestic comfort that marked the end of the nineteenth century and the early twentieth century. Their homes were filled with manufactured items, including clothing, china, furniture, carpets, drapery, wallpaper, and prints. They enjoyed all the improvements of sanitation and electricity. They could command the services of numerous domestic servants. They moved into the fashionable new houses being constructed in the rapidly expanding suburbs.

THE CULT OF DOMESTICITY For the middle classes the gender distinction between work and family had become complete and it constituted the model for all other social groups. Middle-class women, if at all possible, did not work. More than any other group of women, they became limited to the roles of wife and mother. That situation allowed them to enjoy much domestic luxury and comfort. But it also no less markedly circumscribed what they might do with their lives, their talents, their ambitions, and their intelligence. Middle-class women became, in large measure, the product of a particular understanding of social life. The home and its occupants were to have lives very different from the life of business and the marketplace. The home was not only to be distinct from the world of work and business, but it was also to be a private refuge from that life. This view was set forth in scores of women's journals across Europe.

As studies of the lives of middle-class women in northern France have suggested, this image of the middle-class home and of the role of women in the home is quite different from the one that had existed earlier in the nineteenth century. During the first half of the century the spouse of a middle-class husband might very well contribute directly to the business, handling accounts or correspondence. These women also frequently had little to do with rearing their children, leaving that task first to nurses and later to governesses. This situation was very different later in the century. The reasons for the change are not certain, but it would appear that men began to insist on doing business with other men. Magazines and books directed toward women began to praise motherhood, domesticity, religion, and charity as the proper work of women.

The cover of this French fashion magazine from March 1910 conveys an idealized portrait of middle-class femininity—modest, serene, elegant. Such a woman was expected to have no other role in life than that of dutiful daughter, wife, and mother. [Art Resource]

For these middle-class French women, as well as for middle-class women elsewhere, the home came to be praised as the center of virtue, of children, and of the proper life for women. Marriages were usually arranged for some kind of family economic benefit. Romantic marriage was presented as a danger to social stability. Most middle-class women in northern France married by the age of twenty-one. Children were expected to follow very soon

861

THE BUILD
OF EUROPE
SUPREMAC
SOCIETY AI
POLITICS 1
WORLD W

The Virtues of a French Middle-class Lady Praised

One of the chief social roles assigned to middle-class French women was that of charitable activity. This obituary of Mme. Émile Delesalle from a Roman Catholic church paper of the late nineteenth century describes the work of this woman among the poor. It is a very revealing document because it clearly shows the class divisions that existed in the giving of charity. It also is a document that instructed its women readers through the kind of virtues praised. Note the emphasis on home life, spirituality, and instruction of children in charitable acts.

The poor were the object of her affectionate interest, especially the shameful poor, the fallen people. She sought them out and helped them with perfect discretion which doubled the value of her benevolent interest. To those whom she could approach without fear of bruising their dignity, she brought, along with alms to assure their existence, consolation of the most serious sort—she raised their courage and their hopes. To others, each Sunday, she opened all the doors of her home, above all when her children were still young. In making them distribute these alms with her, she hoped to initiate them early into practices of charity.

In the last years of her life the St. Gabriel Orphanage gained her interest. Not only did she accomplish a great deal with her generosity, but she also took on the task of maintaining the clothes of her dear orphans in good order and in good repair. When she appeared in the courtyard of the establishment at recreation time, all her protégés surrounded her and lavished her with manifestations of their profound respect and affectionate gratitude.

Smith, Bonnie G., Ladies of the Leisure Class: The Bourgeois of Northern France in the Nineteenth Century. Copyright (c) 1981 by Princeton University Press, pp. 147–148.

after marriage. Quite often a child was born within the first year, and the rearing and nurturing of that child and of later children was the chief task in life for the woman. Such a woman would have had no experience of or training for any role other than that of a dutiful daughter, wife, and mother.

Within the home a middle-class woman performed major roles. She was largely in charge of the household. She oversaw virtually all domestic management and child care. She was in a very real sense in charge of the home as a major unit of consumption. It was for this reason that so much advertising was directed toward women. But all of this domestic activity occurred within the limits of the approved middle-class lifestyle that set relatively strict limits on a woman's initiative. She and her conspicuous idleness served to symbolize first her father's and then her husband's worldly success.

RELIGIOUS AND CHARITABLE ACTIVITIES

This cult of domesticity in France and elsewhere assigned to women very firm religious duties. The Roman Catholic church strongly supported these domestic and religious roles for French women. Frequent attendance at mass and religious instruction of their children were part of this role. Women were charged with observing meatless Fridays and with participating in religious observances. Prayer was a major part of their lives and daily rituals. Those portions of the Christian religion that stressed meekness and passivity became a major part of the mind set of these middle-class French women. In other countries as well, religion and religious activities became part of the expected work of women. For this reason women were regarded by political liberals as especially susceptible to the influence of priests. This close association between religion and a strict domestic life for women was one of the reasons for later tension between feminism and religious authorities.

Another important role for these middle-class women was the administration of charity. Women were judged especially prepared to carry out charitable roles because of their supposed innate spirituality and their capacity to instill domestic and personal discipline. Middle-class women were often in charge of clubs for poor youth, societies to protect poor young women, schools for infants, and societies for visiting the poor. Women were supposed to be particularly interested in the problems of poor women, their families, and their children. Quite often charity from middle-class women required the poor recipient to indicate in some manner the possession of a good character. By the end of the century middle-class women who were attempting to expand their spheres of activity became social workers either for the Church, for private charities, or for the government. It was a vocation that was a natural extension of the roles socially assigned to them.

SEXUALITY AND FAMILY SIZE The world of the middle-class wife and her family is now understood to have been much more complicated than was once thought. Not all such women or their families conformed to the stereotypes. First, recent studies have suggested that the middle classes of the nineteenth century enjoyed sexual relations within marriage far more fully than was once thought. Diaries, letters, and even early medical and sociological sex surveys indicate that sexual enjoyment rather than sexual repression was fundamental to middle-class marriages. Much of the inhibition about sexuality stemmed from the actual dangers of childbirth rather than from any dislike or disapproval of sexuality.

Second, one of the major changes in this regard during the second half of the century was the acceptance of small family size among the middle classes. The fertility rate in France dropped throughout the nineteenth century. It began to fall in England steadily from the 1870s onward. Middle-class married couples seem to have begun to make conscious decisions to limit the size of their families. During the last decades of the century, various new contraceptive devices became available and were used by middle-class families. One of the chief reasons for this change was the apparently conscious decision made by couples to maintain a relatively high level of material consumption by rearing fewer children. Children had become much more expensive to rear, and at the same time, more material comforts had become available. The presence of fewer children in the middle-class household probably meant that more attention was focused on the child and that mothers and their children became emotionally closer.

The Rise of Feminism

As can be seen from the previous discussion, liberal society and its values neither automatically nor inevitably improved the lot of women. Divorce was difficult everywhere. Most property laws until well into the second half of the century favored husbands or gave them virtually complete control over their wives' property. In France, for example, the major political legislation of the revolution and the Napoleonic Code excluded women from voting and made them subject to their husbands. There was a general apprehension among male political liberals that granting the vote to women would benefit political conservatives because it was widely assumed that women were unduly controlled by Roman Catholic priests. There was a similar apprehension about the alleged influence of the Anglican clergy over women in England. Consequently, anticlerical liberals had difficulty working with feminists.

Those few women who pioneered female entry into the professions, activity on government commissions and school boards, or dispersal of birth control information faced grave social obstacles, personal humiliation, and often outright bigotry. These women and their male supporters were challenging that clear separation of life into male and female spheres that had emerged in middle-class European social life during the nineteenth century. Women themselves were often hesitant to support feminist causes because they had been so thoroughly acculturated into the recently stereo-typed roles. Many women as well as men saw a real conflict between family responsibilities and feminism.

OBSTACLES TO ACHIEVING EQUAL-ITY

But there was another important reason for the frequent absence of support for feminist causes by women. Issues of gender constituted only one of several priorities in the minds and social concerns of women. Some women were very sensitive to their class and economic interests. Others subordinated feminist issues to national unity and nationalistic patriotism. Still others would not support particular feminist organizations because of differences over tactics. The various social and tactical differences among women led quite often to sharp divisions within the feminists' own ranks. Except in England, it was often difficult for working-class and middle-class women to cooperate. Roman Catholic feminists were uncomfortable with radical secularist feminists. There were other disagreements about which goals for improvement in women's legal and social conditions were most important.

Liberal society and law had set up many obstacles to women's developing their lives fully. The necessity of working within the political structures of liberal states raised many of the issues that divided women. However, the intellectual and political tools for feminists' social and political criticisms were also present in the ideology of liberal society. The rationalism and the penchant for self-criticism that have characterized modern Western society manifested themselves in the movement to emancipate women. As early as 1792 in Britain, Mary Wollstonecraft (1759–1797), in *The Vindication of the Rights of Woman* (see document in Chapter 19), had applied the revolutionary doctrines of the rights of man to the predicament of the members of her own sex. John Stuart Mill (1806–1873), in conjunction with his wife Harriet Taylor, had applied the logic of liberal freedom to the position of women in *The Subjection of Women* (1869). The arguments for utility and efficiency so dear to middle-class liberals could be used to expose the human and social waste implicit in the inferior role assigned to women.

Furthermore, the socialist criticism of capitalist society often, though by no means always, included a harsh indictment of the social and economic position to which women had been relegated. The earliest statements of feminism arose from critics of the existing order and were often associated with people who had unorthodox opinions about sexuality, family life, and property. This fact hardened resistance to the feminist message. This seems to have been especially true on the Continent. European feminists were never able to stir up massive public support or demonstrations as they were in Great Britain and the United States.

Much of the discussion of the social position of women remained merely theory and talk. Some women did gain meaningful employment in the professions, but their numbers were quite small. Women did not rise rapidly through the work force. However, to some extent, theory was transformed into practice, or at least into protest, as far as political life was concerned. The political tactics used by men to expand the electoral franchise and to influence the governing process earlier in the century were used later by women to pursue the same goal. The claims to political participation set forth by the respectable, prosperous, and educated working class applied equally well to respectable, prosperous, and educated women. Nonetheless, virtually everywhere, the feminist cause was badly divided.

BRITISH FEMINIST MOVEMENT

The most advanced women's movement in Europe was in Great Britain. There Millicent Fawcett (1847–1929) led the moderate National Union of Women's Suffrage Societies. Her view was that Parliament would grant women the vote only when convinced that women would be respectable and responsible in their political activity. In 1908 this organization could rally almost half a million women in London. Fawcett was the wife of a former liberal party Cabinet minister and economist. Her tactics were those of English liberals.

Emmeline Pankhurst (1858–1928) led a different and much more radical branch of British feminists. Pankhurst's husband, who had died near the close of the century, had been active in labor and Irish nationalist politics. Irish nationalists had developed numerous disruptive political tactics. Early labor politicians had also sometimes had confrontations with police over the right to hold meetings. In 1903 Pankhurst and her daughters, Christabel and Sylvia,

863

THE BUILDIN
OF EUROPEA
SUPREMACY
SOCIETY AN
POLITICS T
WORLD WA

Henry Asquith imprisoned many of the women and force-fed those who went on hunger strikes in jail. The government refused to extend the franchise. Only in 1918 did some British women receive the vote as a result of their contribution to the war effort.

FEMINISM ON THE CONTINENT How advanced the British women's movement was can be seen by the contrast in France and Germany. In France, Hubertine Auclert (1848–1914) had begun campaigning for the vote in the 1880s. She stood virtually alone. During the 1890s several women's organizations emerged. In 1901 the National Council of French Women (CNFF) was organized among upper-middle-class women, but it did not support the idea of the vote for women for several years. French Roman Catholic feminists such as Marie Mauguet (1844–1928) supported the franchise also. But almost all French feminists rejected any form of violence. They also were never able to organize mass rallies. The leaders of French feminism believed that the vote could be achieved through careful legalism. In 1919 the French Chamber of Deputies passed a bill granting the vote to women, but in 1922 the French Senate defeated the bill. It was not until after World War II that French women received the right to vote.

In Germany the situation of feminist awareness and action was even more underdeveloped. German law actually forbade German women from political activity. Because no group in the German Empire enjoyed extensive political rights, women were not certain that they would benefit from demanding them. Any such demand would be regarded as subversive not only of the political state but also of the society.

In 1894 the Union of German Women's Organizations (BDFK) was founded. By 1902 it was supporting a call for the right to vote. But it was largely concerned with improvement of women's social conditions, access to education, and other protections. The group also worked to see that women might be admitted to political or civic activity on the municipal level. This work usually included education,

founded the Women's Social and Political Union. For several years they and their followers, known derisively as *suffragettes*, lobbied publicly and privately for the extension of the vote to women. By 1910, having failed to move the government, they turned to the violent tactics of arson, window breaking, and sabotage of postal boxes. They marched en masse on Parliament. The Liberal government of

---

MAJOR DATES IN LATE-NINETEENTH-CENTURY
AND EARLY-TWENTIETH-CENTURY
WOMEN'S HISTORY

1864	Passage of Contagious Diseases Acts in Britain
1869	John Stuart Mill's *The Subjection of Women*
1886	Repeal of Contagious Diseases Acts in Britain
1894	Union of German Women's Organizations founded
1901	National Council of French Women founded
1903	British Women's Social and Political Union founded
1907	Norway permits women to vote on national issues
1910	British Suffragettes adopt radical tactics
1918	Vote extended to some British women
1918	Weimar constitution allows German women to vote
1922	French Senate defeats bill extending vote to women
1928	Britain extends vote to women on same basis as men

865

THE BUILDIN
OF EUROPEA
SUPREMACY
SOCIETY AN
POLITICS TO
WORLD WAI

An English Feminist Defends the Cause of the Female Franchise

Frances Power Cobbe wrote widely on numerous religious and social issues of the second half of the century. She had been a feminist since early adulthood. In this letter to an English women's feminist magazine in 1884, she explained why women should seek the vote. More important, she attempted to refute the argument that possession of the franchise would in some manner make women less womanly.

If I may presume to offer an old woman's counsel to the younger workers in our cause, it would be that they should adopt the point of view—that it is before all things our *duty* to obtain the franchise. If we undertake the work in this spirit, and with the object of using the power it confers, whenever we gain it, for the promotion of justice and mercy and the kingdom of God upon earth, we shall carry on all our agitation in a corresponding manner, firmly and bravely, and also calmly and with generous good temper. And when our opponents come to understand that this is the motive underlying our efforts, they, on their part, will cease to feel bitterly and scornfully toward us, even when they think we are altogether mistaken. . . .

The idea that the possession of political rights will destroy "womanliness," absurd as it may seem to us, is very deeply rooted in the minds of men; and when they oppose our demands, it is only just to give them credit for doing so on grounds which we should recognize as valid, *if their premises were true.* It is not so much that our opponents (at least the better part of them) despise women, as that they really prize what women now are in the home and in society so highly that they cannot bear to risk losing it by any serious change in their condition. These fears are futile and faithless, but there is nothing in them to affront us. To remove them, we must not use violent words, for every such violent word confirms their fears; but, on the contrary, show the world that while the revolutions wrought by men have been full of bitterness and rancor and stormy passions, if not of bloodshed, we women will at least strive to accomplish our great emancipation calmly and by persuasion and reason.

Letter to the Woman's Tribune, May 1, 1884, *quoted in Frances Power Cobbe,* Life of Frances Power Cobbe by Herself *(Boston: Houghton, Mifflin, 1894).*

child welfare, charity, and public health. The German Social Democratic Party supported women's suffrage, but this position made the demand all the more suspect in the eyes of the German authorities and especially in the view of German Roman Catholics. Women received the vote in Germany only in 1918, when the constitution of the Weimar Republic was promulgated after German defeat in war and revolution at home.

Throughout Europe in the years before World War I, the demands for women's rights were raised widely and vocally. But the extent of their success and their tactics tended in very large measure to reflect the political and class structures of the individual nations. Before World War I, only in Norway (1907) could women vote on national issues.

Labor, Socialism, and Politics to World War I

The late-century industrial expansion wrought further changes in the life of the labor force. In all industrializing continental countries the numbers of the urban proletariat rose. Proportionally there were many fewer artisans and highly skilled workers. For the first time factory wage-earners came to predominate. The increasingly mechanized factories often required less highly technical skills from their operatives. There also occurred considerable growth in the very unskilled work associated with shipping, transportation, and building. Work assumed a more impersonal character. Factories were located in cities, and almost all links between factory or day-labor employment and home life dissolved. Large corporate enterprise meant less personal contact between employers and their workers.

Workers still had to look to themselves for the improvement of their situation. However, after 1848 European workers ceased taking to the streets to voice their grievances in the form of riots. They also stopped trying to revive the paternal guilds and similar institutions of the past. After mid-century the labor force accepted the fact of modern industrial production and its general downgrading of skills and attempted to receive more benefits from that system. Workers turned to new institutions and ideologies. Chief among these were trade unions, democratic political parties, and socialism.

Trade Unionism

Trade unionism came of age as legal protections were extended to unions throughout the second half of the century. Unions became fully legal in Great Britain in 1871 and were allowed to picket in 1875. In France Napoleon III had first used troops against strikes, but as his political power waned, he allowed weak labor associations in 1868. The Third French Republic fully legalized unions in 1884. After 1890 they could function in Germany with little disturbance. Initially most trade unions entered the political process in a rather marginal fashion. As long as the representatives of the traditional governing classes looked after labor interests, members of the working class rarely sought office themselves.

The mid-century organizational efforts of the unions were directed toward skilled workers. The goal was the immediate improvement of wages and working conditions. By the close of the century, industrial unions for unskilled workers were being organized. They were very large and included thousands of workers. They confronted extensive opposition from employers, and long strikes were frequently required to bring about employer acceptance. In the pre-war decade there were an exceedingly large number of strikes throughout Europe as the unions attempted to raise wages to keep up with inflation. However, despite the advances of unions and the growth of their memberships (in 1910 to approximately 3 million in Britain, 2 million in Germany, and 977,000 in France) they never included a majority of the industrial labor force. What the unions did represent was a new collective fashion in which workers could associate to confront economic difficulties and to attain better security.

Democracy and Political Parties

The democratic franchise provided workers with direct political influence, which meant that they could no longer be ignored. With the exception of Russia all the major European states adopted broad-based, if not perfectly democratic, electoral systems. Great Britain passed its second voting-reform act in 1867 and its third in 1884. Bismarck brought universal manhood suffrage to the German Empire in 1871. The French Chamber of Deputies was democratically elected. Universal manhood suffrage was adopted in Switzerland in 1879, in Spain in 1890, in Belgium in 1893, in the Netherlands in 1896, and in Norway in 1898. Italy finally fell into line in 1912.

Democracy brought new modes of popular pressure to bear on all governments. It meant that discontented groups could now voice their grievances and advocate their programs within the institutions of government rather than from the outside.

The advent of democracy witnessed the formation for the first time in Europe of organized mass political parties, which had existed throughout the nineteenth century in the United States. In the liberal European states with narrow electoral bases, most voters had been people of property who knew what they had at stake in politics. Organization had been minimal. The new expansion of the electorate brought into the political processes many people whose level of political consciousness, awareness, and interest was quite low. This electorate had to be organized and taught the nature of power and influence in the liberal democratic state.

The organized political party—with its workers, newspapers, offices, social life, and discipline—was the vehicle that mobilized the new voters. The largest single group in these mass electorates was the working class. The democratization of politics presented the socialists with opportunities and required the traditional ruling classes to vie with the socialists for the support of the new voters.

Marx and the First International

Karl Marx himself made considerable accommodation to the new practical realities that developed during the third quarter of the century. He did not abandon the revolutionary doctrines of *The Communist Manifesto*, and in *Capital* (Vol. 1, 1867) he continued to predict the disintegration of capitalism. His private thoughts, as revealed in his letters, also remained quite revolutionary, but his practical, public political activity reflected a somewhat different approach.

In 1864 a group of British and French trade unionists founded the International Working Men's Association. Known as the First International, it encompassed in its membership a vast array of radical political types, including socialists, anarchists, and Polish nationalists. The First International allowed Marx, who was by then quite active in the London radical community, to write its inaugural address. In it he urged radical social change and the economic emancipation of the working class. But he also supported and approved efforts by workers and trade unions to reform the conditions of labor within the existing political and economic processes. He urged revolution but tempered the means. Privately he often criticized such reformist activity, but those writings were not made public until near the end of the century, and after his death.

During the late 1860s the First International gathered statistics, kept labor groups informed of mutual problems, provided a forum for the debate of socialist doctrine, and extravagantly proclaimed its own size and influence. From these debates and activities Marxism emerged as the single most important strand of socialism. In 1872 Marx and his supporters drove the anarchists out of the First International. Marx

was determined to preserve the role of the state against the anarchist attack on authority and large political organizations. Through the meetings and discussions of the First International, German socialists became deeply impressed by Marx's thought. Because, as will be seen, the German socialists became the most important socialist party in Europe, they became the chief channel for the preservation and development of Marxist thought.

The First International proved to be a very fragile structure. The events surrounding the Paris Commune presented the final blow to its existence. Few socialists and only one real Marxist were involved in the commune. However, Marx, in a major pamphlet, glorified the commune as a genuine proletarian uprising. British trade unionists, who in 1871 were finally receiving new legal protection, wanted no connection with the crimes of the Parisians. The French authorities used the uprising to suppress socialist activity. Throughout Europe the events in Paris cast a pall over socialism. The First International held its last European congress in 1873. Its offices were then transferred to the United States, where it was dissolved in 1876. Thereafter, the fate of socialism and the labor movement depended largely on the economic and political conditions of the individual European countries.

Great Britain: Fabianism and Early Welfare Programs

Neither Marxism nor any other form of socialism made significant progress in Great Britain, the most advanced industrial society of the day. There trade unions grew steadily and the members normally supported Liberal Party candidates. The "new unionism" of the late 1880s and the 1890s organized the dock workers, the gas workers, and similar unskilled groups. Employer resistance to unions heightened class antagonism. In 1892 Keir Hardie became the first independent working man to be elected to Parliament. The next year the small, socialist Independent Labour Party was founded, but it remained ineffective.

Until 1901 general political activity on the part of labor remained quite limited. The Taff Vale decision in that year by the House of Lords, however, removed the legal protection previously accorded union funds. The Trades Union Congress responded by launching the

867

THE BUILDIN
OF EUROPEA
SUPREMACY
SOCIETY AN
POLITICS T
WORLD WA

Labour Party. In the election of 1906 the fledgling party sent twenty-nine members to Parliament. Their goals as trade unionists did not yet encompass socialism. Along with this new political departure, the British labor movement became more militant. There were scores of strikes before the war, as workers fought for wages to meet the rising cost of living. The government took a larger role than ever before in mediating these strikes, which in 1911 and 1912 involved the railways, the docks, and the mines.

British socialism itself remained primarily the preserve of intellectuals. H. M. Hyndman (1842–1921), a wealthy graduate of Eton, and William Morris (1834–1896), the poet and designer, read Marx's works avidly. However, their Social Democratic Federation, founded in 1881, never had more than a few members.

The socialists who exerted the most influ-

Beatrice and Sidney Webb, in a photograph from the late 1920s. These most influential British Fabian socialists wrote many books on governmental and economic matters, served on special parliamentary commissions, and agitated for the enactment of socialist policies. [Radio Times Hulton Picture Library]

ence were the Fabian Society, founded in 1884. The society took its name from Q. Fabius Maximus, the Roman general whose tactics against Hannibal involved avoiding direct conflict that might lead to defeat. Through its name the society intended to indicate a gradual approach to major social reform. Its leading members were Sidney (1859–1947) and Beatrice (1858–1943) Webb, H. G. Wells (1866–1946), Graham Wallas (1858–1932), and George Bernard Shaw (1856–1950). Many of the Fabians were civil servants who believed that the problems of industry, the expansion of ownership, and the state direction of production could be achieved gradually, peacefully, and democratically. They sought to educate the country about the rational wisdom of socialism. They were particularly interested in modes of collective ownership on the municipal level, the so-called gas-and-water socialism.

The British government and the major political parties responded slowly to these various pressures. In 1903 Joseph Chamberlain launched his unsuccessful tariff-reform campaign to match foreign tariffs and to finance social reform through higher import duties. The campaign badly split the Conservative Party. After 1906 the Liberal Party, led by Sir Henry Campbell-Bannerman (1836–1908) and after 1908 by Herbert Asquith (1852–1928), pursued a two-pronged policy. Fearful of losing seats in Parliament to the new Labour Party, they restored the former protection of the unions. Then, after 1909, with Chancellor of the Exchequer David Lloyd George (1863–1945) as the guiding light, the Liberal ministry undertook a broad program of social legislation. This included the establishment of labor exchanges; the regulation of the sweated labor trades, such as tailoring and lacemaking; and the National Insurance Act of 1911, which provided unemployment benefits and health care.

The financing of these programs brought the House of Commons into conflict with the Conservative-dominated House of Lords. The result was the Parliament Act of 1911, which allowed the Commons to override the legislative veto of the upper chamber. The new taxes and social programs meant that in Britain, the home of nineteenth-century liberalism, the state was taking on an expanded role in the life of its citizens. The early welfare legislation was only marginally satisfactory to labor, many of whose members still thought they could gain more from the direct action of strikes.

France: "Opportunism" Rejected

French socialism gradually revived after the suppression of the Paris Commune. The institutions of the Third Republic provided a framework for legal activity. The major problem for French socialists was their own internal division rather than government opposition. There were no fewer than five separate parties, plus other independent socialists. They managed to elect approximately forty members to the Chamber of Deputies by the early 1890s. Despite the lack of a common policy, the socialist presence aided the passage of measures to relieve workers from carrying identity cards and to provide for factory safety inspection, health care, and limited working hours. In 1910 the republic inaugurated a scheme for voluntary pensions. However, the most important developments of French labor and socialism were not legislative.

At the turn of the century the two major factions of French socialism were led by Jean Jaurès (1859–1914) and Jules Guesde (1845–1922). Jaurès believed that socialists should cooperate with radical middle-class ministries to ensure the enactment of needed social legislation. Guesde opposed this policy, arguing that socialists could not, with integrity, support a bourgeois cabinet that they were theoretically dedicated to overthrow. The quarrel came to a head as a by-product of the Dreyfus affair. In 1899, as a means of uniting all supporters of Dreyfus, Prime Minister René Waldeck-Rousseau (1846–1904) appointed the socialist Allexander Millerand to the Cabinet.

By 1904 the issue of "opportunism," as such Cabinet participation by socialists was termed, came to be debated at the Amsterdam Congress of the Second International. This organization had been founded in 1889 in a new effort to unify the various national socialist parties and trade unions. The Amsterdam Congress condemned "opportunism" in France and ordered the French socialists to form a single party. Jaurès, believing socialist unity the most important issue in France, accepted the decision. French socialists began to work together, and by 1914 the recently united Socialist Party was the second largest group in the Chamber

Jean Jaurès was one of the great French socialist orators. In this contemporary drawing he is addressing a meeting being disrupted by the police. [Roger-Viollet]

of Deputies. Socialist Party members would not again serve in a French Cabinet until the Popular Front Government of 1936.

The French labor movement, with deep roots in the doctrines of anarchism, was uninterested in both politics and socialism. French workers tended to vote socialist, but the unions avoided active political participation. The Confédération Générale du Travail was founded in 1895 and regarded itself as a rival to the socialist parties. Its leaders sought to improve the workers' conditions through direct action. They embraced the doctrines of syndicalism, which were most persuasively expounded by Georges Sorel (1847–1922) in *Reflections on Violence* (1908). This book enshrined the idea of the general strike as a means of generating worker unity and power. The strike tactic was quite different from the socialist idea of aiding the situation of labor through the action of the state. Strike action on the part of unions flourished between 1905 and 1914, and the Radical ministry on more than one occasion used troops against the strikers.

Consequently, in France the forces of labor were suppressed by the liberal state, and the Socialist Party was locked into a doctrine of nonparticipation in the Cabinet, which effectively undermined its potential political influence.

Germany: Social Democrats and Revisionism

The judgment rendered by the Second International against French socialist participation in bourgeois ministries reflected a policy of permanent hostility to nonsocialist governments previously adopted by the German Social Democratic Party, or SPD. The organizational success of this party, more than any other single factor, kept Marxist socialism alive into the latter part of the century.

The party was founded in 1875. Its origins lay in the labor agitation of Ferdinand Lasalle (1825–1864), who wanted worker participation in German politics. His followers were joined by Wilhelm Liebknecht (1826–1900) and August Bebel (1840–1913), who were Marxists. Consequently, the party was divided from its founding between those who wanted reformist political activity and those who advocated revolution.

BISMARCK'S REPRESSION OF THE SPD The forging experience of the SPD was twelve years of persecution by Bismarck. The so-called Iron Chancellor believed that socialism would undermine German politics and society. Shortly after its founding, he moved against the young SPD. In 1878 there was an attempt to assassinate William I. Although the socialists were not involved, Bismarck used the opportunity to steer a number of antisocialist laws through the Reichstag. The measures suppressed the organization, meet-

ings, newspapers, and other public activities of the SPD. To remain a socialist meant to remove oneself from the mainstream of respectable German life and possibly to lose one's job. The antisocialist legislation proved politically counterproductive. From the early 1880s onward, the SPD steadily polled more and more votes in elections to the Reichstag.

As simple repression failed to separate German workers from socialist loyalties, Bismarck undertook a program of social welfare legislation. In 1883 the German Empire adopted a health insurance measure. The next year saw the enactment of accident insurance legislation. Finally, in 1889, Bismarck sponsored a plan for old age and disability pensions. These programs, to which both workers and employers contributed, represented a paternalistic, conservative alternative to socialism. The state itself would organize a system of social security that did not require any change in the system of property holding or politics. Germany became the first major industrial nation to enjoy this kind of welfare program.

THE ERFURT PROGRAM After forcing Bismarck's resignation, Emperor William II (1888–1918) allowed the antisocialist legislation to expire in hopes of thus building new support for the monarchy among the working class. Even under the repressive laws, members of the SPD could sit in the Reichstag. Now, however, the question became what attitude the recently legalized party should assume toward the German Empire.

The answer came in the Erfurt Program of 1891, formulated under the political guidance of Bebel and the ideological tutelage of Karl Kautsky (1854–1938). In good Marxist fashion the program declared the imminent doom of capitalism and the necessity of socialist ownership of the means of production. However, these goals were to be achieved by legal political participation rather than by revolutionary activity. Because by its very nature capitalism must fall, the immediate task of socialists was to work for the improvement of workers' lives rather than for the revolution, which was inevitable. In theory the SPD was vehemently hostile to the German Empire, but in practice the party functioned within its institutions. The SPD members of the Reichstag maintained clear consciences by refusing to enter the Cabinet (to which they were not invited anyway) and by refraining for many years from voting for the military budget.

THE DEBATE OVER REVISIONISM

The situation of the SPD, however, generated the most important internal socialist challenge to the orthodox Marxist analysis of capitalism and the socialist revolution. Eduard Bernstein (1850–1932) was the author of this socialist heresy. He had spent over a decade of his life in Great Britain and was quite familiar with the Fabians. Bernstein questioned whether Marx and his later orthodox followers, such as Kautsky, had been correct in their pessimistic appraisal of capitalism and the necessity of revolution. In *Evolutionary Socialism* (1899) Bernstein pointed to the rising standard of living in Europe. Ownership of capitalist industry was becoming more widespread through stockholding. The middle class was not falling into the ranks of the proletariat and was not identifying its problems with those of the workers. The inner contradictions of capitalism as expounded by Marx had simply not developed. Moreover, the opening of the franchise to the working class meant that revolutionary change might be achieved through parliamentary methods. What was required to realize a humane socialist society was not revolution but more democracy and social reform.

Bernstein's doctrines, known as *revisionism*, were widely debated among German socialists and were finally condemned as theory. His critics argued that evolution toward social democracy might be possible in liberal, parliamentary Britain, but not in authoritarian, militaristic Germany, with its basically powerless Reichstag. The critics were probably correct about the German political scene. Nonetheless, while still calling for revolution, the SPD pursued a course of action similar to that advocated by Bernstein. Its trade union members, prospering within the German economy, did not want revolution. Its grass-roots members wanted to consider themselves patriotic Germans as well as good socialists. Its leaders feared any actions that might renew the persecution that they had experienced under Bismarck.

Consequently, the party worked at elections, membership expansion, and short-term political and social reform. It prospered and became one of the most important institutions of imperial Germany. Even some middle-class Germans voted for it as a means of opposing the illiberal institutions of the empire. And in August 1914, after long debate among themselves, the SPD members of the Reichstag abandoned their former stance and unanimously voted for the war credits that would finance World War I.

Russia: Industrial Development and the Birth of Bolshevism

During the last decade of the nineteenth century Russia entered the industrial age and confronted many of the problems that the more advanced nations of the Continent had experienced fifty or seventy-five years earlier. Unlike

Eduard Bernstein was a major theorist within the German SPD. His volume Evolutionary Socialism *(1899) set forth the ideas associated with revisionism which were later rejected by the party. [Roger-Viollet]*

871

THE BUILDIN
OF EUROPEA
SUPREMACY
SOCIETY AN
POLITICS TO
WORLD WA

Eduard Bernstein Criticizes Orthodox Marxism

Eduard Bernstein was responsible for the emergence of "Revisionism" within the German Social Democratic Party. He was a dedicated socialist who believed that the Communist Manifesto *(1848) had not predicted the actual future of the European working classes. He believed that there would be no sudden collapse or catastrophe in the capitalist system and that socialists should change their tactics to work to achieve political rights and pursue reform instead of revolution.*

I set myself against the notion that we have to expect shortly a collapse of the bourgeois economy, and that social democracy should be induced by the prospect of such an imminent, great, social catastrophe to adapt its tactics to that assumption. . . .

The adherents of this theory of a catastrophe, base it especially on the conclusion of the *Communist Manifesto*. This is a mistake in every respect. . . .

Social conditions have not developed to such an acute opposition of things and classes as is depicted in the *Manifesto*. . . . The number of members of the possessing classes is to-day not smaller but larger. The enormous increase of social wealth is not accompanied by a decreasing number of large capitalists but by an increasing number of capitalists of all degrees. . . .

. . . .

In all advanced countries we see the privileges of the capitalist bourgeoisie yielding step by step to democratic organizations. . . . Factory legislation, the democratizing of local government, and the

extension of its area of work, the freeing of trade unions and system of co-operative trading from legal restrictions, the consideration of standard conditions of labour in the work undertaken by public authorities—all these characterize this phase of the evolution.

. . . .

The conquest of political power by the working classes, the expropriation of capitalists, are not ends in themselves but only means for the accomplishment of certain aims and endeavours. As such they are demands in the program of social democracy. . . . Nothing can be said beforehand as to the circumstances of their accomplishment; we can only fight for their realization. But the conquest of political power necessitates the possession of political *rights;* and the most important problem of tactics which German social democracy has at the present time to solve, appears to me to be to devise the best ways for the extension of the political and economic rights of the German working classes.

Eduard Bernstein, Evolutionary Socialism: A Criticism and Affirmation 1899 *(New York: Schocken Books, 1961), pp. xxiv–xxvi, xxix–xxx.*

those other countries, Russia had to deal with major political discontent and economic development simultaneously. Russian socialism reflected that peculiar situation.

WITTE'S PROGRAM FOR INDUSTRIAL GROWTH

The emancipation of the serfs in 1861 had brought little agricultural progress. The peasants remained burdened with redemp-

tion payments, local taxes, excessive national taxes, and falling grain prices. There were few attempts to educate the peasantry in the more advanced techniques of farming. Most of the land held by free peasants was owned communally through the *mir,* or village. This system of ownership was extremely inefficient and employed strip farming and the farming of small plots. Between 1860 and 1914 the popu-

PORTFOLIO V
WORKPLACES
IN THE NINETEENTH
CENTURY

During the course of the nineteenth century the workplaces of Europe became more varied than during any previous period of its history. This situation was the result of industrialization, the growth of cities, and the emergence of new services. At the same time many traditional areas of work, such as agriculture, continued; but even here changes in mechanization brought about major transformations.

*Iron and steel were used for all manner of construction and transportation needs during the nineteenth century. This painting from the 1840s portrays the Börsig ironworks in Berlin. [*Werk Börsig an der Chausseestrasse, 1847 *by Carl Eduard Biermann. Berlin Museum]*

Factories

In the late eighteenth century British workers began to move into factories. These factories were initially located in the countryside, but the steam engine soon allowed them to be moved into cities. A similar social and economic phenomenon occurred across the continent as industrialism slowly but steadily spread. Many of the early factories were quite small, but by the close of the century enormous factories had been constructed for heavy industries. Lighter industries, such as food production, might still use relatively small factories.

All metal production was quite complicated and involved several stages. In this factory scene from France in the 1860s, zinc ore was washed and sorted before being taken to vast ovens where it was melted down. [Workshop with Mechanical Sieves at the Factory of La Vieille Montagne by Francois Bonhomme. Paris, Conservatoire National des Arts et Metiers, Musee National des Techniques]

The Countryside

Although the nineteenth century is often identified with industrial factories, the majority of work occurred outside the factory setting. Throughout the century millions of Europeans still resided in the countryside and labored on the land. Many peasants, especially in eastern and central Europe, worked very much as had their eighteenth-century forebears. Other work in the countryside included the breaking of stones for paths and roads. By the close of the century machinery had begun to be used in the fields.

Right   *Cities were dependent upon workers in the countryside for the urban food supply. Here two cattle drivers from the province of Alsace during the 1850s are portrayed. [The Cattle Tender by Gustave Brion. York City Art Gallery]*

Below   *In the countryside, gleaners picked up grain left by the working groups who had harvested the grain. This division of labor and use of otherwise wasted food was a custom widespread across the continent. This painting by Francois Millet portrays gleaners in a French field. [The Gleaners by Francois Millet. The Louvre, Paris. Scala/Art Resource]*

European farmers and peasants herded sheep throughout the nineteenth century as they had for centuries before. They were often grazed on relatively barren land. The sheep provided wool for clothing and food. [The Sheepfold—Morning in Autumn by James Thomas Linnell. Wolverhampton Art Gallery, Staffs/ Bridgeman Art Gallery]

Stonebreaking was one form of very heavy labor in the countryside. Large stones could be used in construction of walls, fireplaces, and chimneys. Smaller stones could be used as gravel on roadways. [The Stone Breakers by Gustave Courbet. The Staatliche Kunstsammlungen, Dresden. Bridgeman Art Library]

Workshops

During the first half of the century thousands of small workshops employed a few skilled artisans. These were the people who by the middle of the century had been steadily displaced by machinery. However, those small workplaces and other labor that occurred in the home, such as handloom weaving, were among the most important places of manufacture during the early part of the century. It should never be forgotten that from the beginning through the end of the century thousands of Europeans, often women, worked in sweated trades, especially clothing manufacture and food preparation. In addition, large numbers of women from all classes spent their days working in their homes.

Above   *Very small factories or workshops employed tens of thousand of Europeans many of whom were women. They often manufactured articles of clothing. This painting illustrates women who were employed in the making of costume jewelry in Paris toward the end of the century. [*An Atelier for the Cutting of False Diamonds at Pré-Saint-Gervais *by Jules Adler. Bayeux. Musée Baron Gerard]*

Right   *Doing laundry was the employment of large numbers of poor women and widows. The task included gathering the dirty clothes, washing them, and, as in this picture, ironing the finished laundry. [*Woman Ironing *by Francois Bonvin. Philadelphia Museum of Art, John G. Johnson Collection]*

Shops and Services

In small towns and large cities thousands of merchants kept shops. These were the chief outlets for many of the goods manufactured in the factories. Small shops and later the department stores employed large numbers of workers, many of whom were women. Furthermore, by the close of the century service industries, such as insurance and telephone companies, employed large groups of people. Here again women quickly dominated this workforce. Schoolteaching was another profession that employed large numbers of people as the various nations became determined to make their new voting populations literate.

Working-class children often found casual employment which might or might not lead to better jobs. This London bootblack of the latter part of the century would have worked in different areas of the city finding customers wherever he could, usually from members of the middle class. [The London Bootblack by Jules Bastien-Lepage. Paris, Musee des Arts Decoratifs]

Transport and the Building Trades

Throughout the century both the manufacture and operation of transport industries grew. The railways required the production of the locomotives and cars, the rails and ties, and the laying of the tracks. Great bridges had to be constructed. Later the steamships for both war and peaceful transport created the demand for thousands of jobs. The coming of the trolley car and later the automobile further transformed economic life and the workplace. Each of these developments required people who could operate the equipment and serve the travellers whether across town or around the world. The transport industry also employed larger numbers of workmen on the docks loading and unloading goods for the everexpanding world trade.

In every major city significant portions of the population were involved in the building trades. Virtually all European cities saw major construction projects. These included the building of new streets, sewers, river embankments, government buildings, opera houses, and tens of thousands of private homes and apartments. As those cities grew and became more complex, the number of shops serving their populations expanded.

In these same cities large groups of people had little or no work. These people might beg or live as scavengers. They might also find temporary employment as day laborers. Always desperately poor, their lives constituted a culture of what seemed to be a permanent underclass.

Above   *The expansion of cities and growth of suburbs required new transportation between the central and outer cities. This painting illustrates the steam tram in Milan. Such urban transport created new jobs during the century.* [The Steam Tram *by Giannino Grassi. Museum of Milan. Scala/Art Resource*]

Below   *As the labor force attempted to improve its economic and social position, strikes were not uncommon. They involved hardship for both workers and their families.* [Strike at Saint-Ouen *by Delance. Paris, Musée d'Orsay. Giraudon/Art Resource*]

Domestic and Government Service

Until late in the century the single largest group of employed persons were domestic servants. Here again women predominated. Virtually every middle-class home and many more humble households had a maid or a cook.

Finally, as the century passed more and more people began to work for the government itself. An expansion of social services increased the number of both government clerks and postal delivery men. There was also the growth of men employed in the armies and navies of the great powers.

Left *The postal service was one of the major sources of government employment. This postman was Van Gogh's friend. [Portrait of Joseph Roulin by Vincent Van Gogh. Museum of Fine Arts, Boston. Acc. #35.1982]*

Below *Among the late nineteenth-century European workforce there emerged for the first time a significant number of paid professional politicians. Their presence was the result of the emergence of liberal states with large parliaments and with other representative institutions, such as city councils. This painting portrays a group of French political leaders. [A la Direction de la Republique Francaise by Henri Gervex. Paris, Orsay. Giraudon/Art Resource]*

lation of European Russia rose from approximately 50 million to approximately 103 million people. Land hunger spread among the peasants. There was intense agrarian discontent. Peasants with too little land still had to work on larger noble estates or for more prosperous peasant farmers known as *kulaks*. Uprisings in the countryside were a frequent problem. The agricultural sector benefited little from the late-century industrialism.

Alexander III and, after him, Nicholas II were determined that Russia should become an industrial power. Only by this means could the country maintain its military position and its diplomatic role in Europe. The person who led Russia into the industrial age was Sergei Witte (1849–1915). After a career in railways and other private business, he was appointed finance minister in 1892. Witte epitomized the nineteenth-century modernizer who pursued a policy of planned economic development, protective tariffs, high taxes, the gold standard, and efficiency. He established a strong financial link with the French money market, which led to later diplomatic cooperation between Russia and France.

Witte favored heavy industries. Between 1890 and 1904 the Russian railway system grew from 30,596 kilometers to 59,616 kilometers. The 5,000-mile Trans-Siberian Railroad was almost completed. Coal output more than tripled during the same period. There was a vast increase in pig-iron production, from 928,000 tons in 1890 to 4,641,000 tons in 1913. During the same period steel production rose from 378,000 tons to 4,918,000 tons. Textile manufacturing continued to expand and still constituted the single largest industry. The factory system began to be used more extensively throughout the country.

Industrialism brought considerable social discontent to Russia, as it had elsewhere. Landowners felt that foreign capitalists were earning too much of the profit. The peasants saw their grain exports and tax payments finance development that did not measurably improve their lives. A small but significant

MAJOR DATES IN THE DEVELOPMENT OF SOCIALISM	
1864	International Working Men's Association (The First International) founded
1875	German Social Democratic Party founded
1876	First International dissolved
1878	German antisocialist laws passed
1884	British Fabian Society founded
1889	Second International founded
1891	German antisocialist laws permitted to expire
1891	German Social Democratic Party's Erfurt Program
1895	French Confédération Générale du Travail founded
1899	Eduard Bernstein's *Evolutionary Socialism*
1902	Formation of the British Labour Party
1902	Lenin's *What Is to Be Done?*
1903	Bolshevik–Menshevik split
1904	"Opportunism" debated at the Amsterdam Congress of the Second International

industrial proletariat arose. At the turn of the century there were approximately three million factory workers in Russia. Their working and living conditions were very bad by any standard. They enjoyed little state protection,

Count Sergei Witte (1849–1915) sought to modernize Russia with a program of industrial development, protective tariffs, high taxes, and an adherence to the gold standard. [The Granger Collection]

A Russian Social Investigator Describes the Condition of Children in the Moscow Tailoring Trade

E. A. Oliunina was a young Russian woman who had been active among union organizers during the Revolution of 1905. Later, as a student at the Higher Women's Courses in Moscow, a school for women's postsecondary education, she began to investigate and to write about garment workers who were children.

Children begin their apprenticeship between the ages of twelve and thirteen, although one can find some ten- and eleven-year-olds working in the shops. . . .

Apprenticeship is generally very hard on children. At the beginning, they suffer enormously, particularly from the physical strain of having to do work well beyond the capacity of their years. They have to live in an environment where the level of morality is very low. Scenes of drunkenness and debauchery induce the boys to smoke and drink at an early age.

For example, in one subcontracting shop that made men's clothes, a fourteen-year-old boy worked together with twelve adults. When I visited there at four o'clock one Tuesday afternoon, the workers were half-drunk. Some were lying under the benches, others in the hallway. The boy was as drunk as the rest of them and lay there with a daredevil look on his face, dressed only in a pair of longjohns and a dirty, tattered shirt. He had been taught to drink at the age of twelve and could now keep up with the adults.

"Blue Monday" is a custom in most subcontracting shops that manufacture men's clothes. The whole workshop gets drunk,

and work comes to a standstill. The apprentices do nothing but hang around. Many of the workers live in the workshop, so the boys are constantly exposed to all sorts of conversations and scenes. In one shop employing five workers and three boys, "Blue Monday" was a regular ritual. Even the owner himself is prone to alcoholic binges. In these kinds of situations, young girls are in danger of being abused by the owner or his sons. . . .

In Russia, there have been no measures taken to improve the working conditions of apprentices. As I have tried to show, the situation in workshops in no way provides apprentices with adequate training in their trade. The young workers are there only to be exploited. Merely limiting the number of apprentices would not better their position, nor would it eradicate the influx of cheap labor. An incomparably more effective solution would be to replace apprenticeship with a professional educational system and well-established safeguards for child workers. However, the only real solution to the exploitation of unpaid child labor is to introduce a minimum wage for minors.

Victoria E. Bonnell, The Russian Worker: Life and Labor Under the Tsarist Regime *(Berkeley: University of California Press, 1983), pp. 177, 180–181, 182–183.*

and trade unions were illegal. In 1897 Witte did enact a measure providing for an 11½-hour workday. But needless to say, discontent and strikes continued.

New political departures accompanied the economic development. In 1901 the Social

Revolutionary Party was founded. Its members and intellectual roots went back to the Populists of the 1870s. The party opposed industrialism and looked to the communal life of rural Russia as a model for the economic future. In 1903 the Constitutional Democratic Party, or

875

THE BUILDI
OF EUROPE
SUPREMAC
SOCIETY AN
POLITICS T
WORLD WA

In this photograph taken in 1895 Lenin sits at the table in the midst of a group of other young Russian radicals from St. Petersburg. [Bettmann Archive]

Cadets, was formed. They were liberal in outlook and were drawn from people who participated in the local councils called *zemstvos*. They wanted a parliamentary regime with responsible ministries, civil liberties, and economic progress. The Cadets hoped to model themselves on the liberal parties of western Europe.

LENIN'S EARLY THOUGHT AND CAREER

The situation for Russian socialists differed radically from that of socialists in other major European countries. Russia had no representative institutions and only a small working class. The compromises and accommodations that had been achieved elsewhere were meaningless in Russia, where socialism in both theory and practice had to be revolutionary. The Russian Social Democratic Party had been established in 1898, but the repressive policies of the tsarist regime meant that the party had to function in exile. The party was Marxist, and its members greatly admired the German Social Democratic Party.

The leading late-nineteenth-century Russian Marxist was Gregory Plekhanov (1857–1918), who wrote from his exile in Switzerland. At the turn of the century his chief disciple was Vladimir Illich Ulyanov (1870–1924), who later took the name of Lenin. The future leader of the Communist Revolution had been born in 1870 as the son of a high bureaucrat. His older brother, while a student in Saint Petersburg, had become involved in radical politics. He was arrested for participating in a plot against Alexander III and was executed in 1887. In 1893 Lenin moved to Saint Petersburg, where he studied to become a lawyer. Soon he, too, was drawn to the revolutionary groups among the factory workers. He was arrested in 1895 and exiled to Siberia. In 1900, after his release, Lenin left Russia for the West.

He spent most of the next seventeen years in Switzerland.

Once in Switzerland Lenin became deeply involved in the organizational and policy disputes of the exiled Russian Social Democrats. They all considered themselves Marxists, but they held differing positions on the proper nature of a Marxist revolution in primarily rural Russia and on the structure of their own party. Unlike the backward-looking Social Revolutionaries, the Social Democrats were modernizers who favored further industrial development. The majority believed that Russia must develop a large proletariat before the revolution could come. This same majority hoped to mold a mass political party like the German SPD.

Lenin dissented from both positions. In *What Is to Be Done?* (1902) he condemned any accommodations, such as those practiced by the German SPD. He also criticized a trade unionism that settled for short-term gains rather than true revolutionary change for the working class. Lenin further rejected the concept of a mass party composed of workers. Revolutionary consciousness would not arise spontaneously from the working class. It must be carried to them by "people who make revo-

Lenin Argues for the Necessity of a Secret and Elite Party of Professional Revolutionaries

Social democratic parties in western Europe had mass memberships and generally democratic structures of organization. In this passage from What Is to Be Done? *(1902), Lenin explained why the autocratic political conditions of Russia demanded a different kind of organization for the Russian Social Democratic Party. Lenin's ideas became the guiding principles of Bolshevik organization.*

I assert that it is far more difficult [for government police] to unearth a dozen wise men than a hundred fools. This position I will defend, no matter how much you instigate the masses against me for my "anti-democratic" views, etc. As I have stated repeatedly, by "wise men," in connection with organisation, I mean *professional revolutionaries*, irrespective of whether they have developed from among students or working men. I assert: (1) that no revolutionary movement can endure without a stable organisation of leaders maintaining continuity; (2) that the broader the popular mass drawn spontaneously into the struggle, which forms the basis of the movement and participates in it, the more urgent the need for such an organisation, and the more solid this organisation must be . . . ; (3) that such an organisation must consist chiefly of people professionally engaged in revolutionary activity; (4) that in an autocratic state [such as Russia], the more we *confine* the membership of such an organisation to people who are professionally engaged in revolutionary activity and who have been professionally trained in the art of combating the political police, the more difficult will it be to unearth the organisation; and (5) the *greater* will be the number of people from the working class and from other social classes who will be able to join the movement and perform active work in it. . . .

The only serious organisation principle for the active workers of our movement should be the strictest secrecy, the strictest selection of members, and the training of professional revolutionaries.

Albert Fried and Ronald Sanders (Eds.), Socialist Thought: A Documentary History *(Garden City, NY: Anchor Doubleday, 1964), pp. 460, 468.*

On "Bloody Sunday," January 22, 1905 troops of Tsar Nicholas II fired on a peaceful procession of workers who sought to present a petition at the Winter Palace in St. Petersburg. After this day there was little chance that the Russian working class could be reconciled with the existing government. [Soviet Life from Sovfoto]

lutionary activity their profession."[3] Only a small elite party would possess the proper dedication to revolution and would be able to resist penetration by police spies. The guiding principle of that party should be "the strictest secrecy, the strictest selection of members, and the training of professional revolutionaries."[4]

In 1903, at the London Congress of the Rus-

sian Social Democratic Party, Lenin forced a split in the party ranks. During much of the congress Lenin and his followers lost votes on various questions put before the body. But near the close Lenin's group mustered a very slim majority. Thereafter Lenin's faction assumed the name _Bolsheviks_, meaning "majority," and the other, more moderate, democratic revolutionary faction became known as the _Mensheviks_, or "minority." There was, of course, a considerable public relations advantage to the name _Bolshevik_. (In 1912 the Bolsheviks organized separately.)

In 1905 Lenin complemented his organiza-

[3] Quoted in Albert Fried and Ronald Sanders (Eds.), Socialist Thought: A Documentary History (Garden City, NY: Anchor Doubleday, 1964), p. 459.

[4] Fried and Sanders, p. 468.

tional theory with a program for revolution in Russia. *Two Tactics of Social Democracy in the Bourgeois-Democratic Revolution* urged that the socialist revolution unite the proletariat and the peasants. Lenin grasped better than any other revolutionary the profound discontent in the Russian countryside. He knew that an alliance of workers and peasants in rebellion probably could not be suppressed. Lenin's two principles of an elite party and a dual social revolution allowed the Bolsheviks, in late 1917, to capture leadership of the Russian Revolution and to transform the political face of the modern world.

THE REVOLUTION OF 1905 AND ITS AFTERMATH

The quarrels among the Russian socialists and Lenin's doctrines had no

Peter Stolypin (1862–1911), the last great statesman of Imperial Russia, sought to counter the rising tide of discontent with a program that combined repression of rebellion with land reform. [Ullstein Bilderdienst]

immediate influence on events in their country itself. Industrialization proceeded and continued to stir resentment in many sectors. In 1903 Nicholas II dismissed Witte, hoping to quell the criticism. The next year Russia went to war with Japan, partly in expectation that public opinion would rally to the tsar. However, the result was Russian defeat and political crisis. The Japanese captured Port Arthur early in 1905. A few days later, on January 22, a priest named Father Gapon led several hundred workers to present a petition to the tsar for the improvement of industrial life. As the petitioners approached the Winter Palace in Saint Petersburg, the tsar's troops opened fire. About one hundred people were shot down in cold blood, and many more were wounded. Never again after this event, known as Bloody Sunday, would the Russian people see the tsar as their protector and "little father."

During the next ten months revolutionary disturbances spread throughout Russia: sailors mutinied; peasant revolts erupted; and property was attacked. The uncle of Nicholas II was assassinated. Liberal Constitutional Democrat leaders from the *zemstvos* demanded political reform. Student strikes occurred in the universities. Social Revolutionaries and Social Democrats were active among urban working groups. In early October 1905 strikes broke out in Saint Petersburg, and for all practical purposes worker groups, called *soviets*, controlled the city. Nicholas II recalled Witte and issued the October Manifesto, which promised Russia constitutional government.

Early in 1906 Nicholas II announced the election of a representative body, the Duma, with two chambers. However, he reserved to himself ministerial appointments, financial policy, military matters, and foreign affairs. The April elections returned a very radical group of representatives. The tsar dismissed Witte and replaced him with P. A. Stolypin (1862–1911), who had little sympathy for parliamentary government. Within four months Stolypin persuaded Nicholas to dissolve the Duma. A second assembly was elected in February 1907. Again cooperation proved impossible, and dissolution of that Duma came in June of that year. The tsar then changed the franchise to ensure a conservative Duma. The third Duma, elected on the new basis in late 1907, proved sufficiently pliable for the tsar

879

THE BUILDI
OF EUROPE.
SUPREMAC
SOCIETY AN
POLITICS T
WORLD WA

Count Witte Warns Tsar Nicholas II

In 1905 revolutionary disturbances shook the tsarist government after the events of "Bloody Sunday." Count Sergei Witte had been Tsar Nicholas II's chief minister and had presided over much of the modernization effort undertaken in Russia. In light of the troubles spreading across the country, he warned his monarch of revolution if steps were not taken to halt the spread of discontent. He sent this memorandum to the tsar on October 9, 1905.

The basic watchword of the present-day movement of public opinion in Russia is freedom.

. . . .

We live in a time dominated wholly by extremist ideas. No one stops to consider whether a given idea is realizable. To impetuous minds everything seems attainable and realizable, simply and easily.

Such a mood among the public is the most dangerous sign of an imminent explosion. The ranks of those who fervently advocate the regeneration of all aspects of Russian life, but only through peaceful evolution, are growing thinner each day. Each day it is becoming more and more difficult for them to restrain the movement.

. . . .

The inconsistent and clumsy actions and the indiscriminate methods the administration resorted to in the past, and which continue to this day, have produced fatal results. The public is not only dissatisfied; it has nurtured a hatred for the government which grows from day to day. The government is not respected and not trusted. The most beneficial undertakings inspire protest. At the same time the public has come to feel confident of its impor-tance and its powers, of its ability to withdraw support from the government and complete to capitulate. The daily course of events confirms public opinion as to the impotence, ignorance, and bewilderment of the authorities.

. . . .

The government should give real rather than fictitious leadership to the country. . . .

Leadership demands above all else a clearly formulated goal, an ideological, high-principled goal accepted by everyone.

The public has set such a goal, a goal of great and completely invincible significance, for justice and truth are on its side. The government must therefore accept it. The watchword of freedom should become the watchword of all government activity. There is no other way to save the state.

The course of historical progress cannot be stemmed. The idea of civil freedom will triumph, if not by reform then by revolution. But in the latter case it will be regenerated from the ashes of an overthrown millennial past. A Russian rebellion, mindless and merciless, will sweep everything away, will crumble everything into dust.

Geroge Vernadsky (Ed.), A Source Book from Russian History from Early Times to 1917 *(New Haven: Yale University Press, 1972), 3:703–704.*

and his minister. Thus, within two years of the 1905 Revolution, Nicholas II had recaptured much of the ground he had conceded.

Stolypin set about repressing rebellion, re-moving some causes of the revolt, and rallying property owners behind the tsarist regime. Early in 1907 special field courts-martial tried rebellious peasants, and almost seven hundred

Rasputin attracted the attention and support of numerous members of the court of Tsar Nicholas II. Here he is photographed surrounded by admirers. [Mansell Collection]

executions resulted. Before turning to this repression, the minister had cancelled any redemptive payments that the peasants still owed to the government from the emancipation of the serfs in 1861. This step, undertaken in November 1906, was part of a more general policy to eradicate communal land ownership. The peasants were encouraged to assume individual proprietorship of their land holdings and to abandon the communal system associated with the *mirs*. Stolypin believed that farmers working for themselves would be more productive. Agriculture did improve through this policy and through instruction of the peasants in better farming methods. The very small peasant proprietors who sold their land increased the size of the industrial labor force.

Russian moderate liberals who sat in the Duma approved of the new land measures. They liked the idea of competition and individual property ownership. The Constitutional Democrats wanted a more genuinely parliamentary mode of government, but they compromised out of fear of new revolutionary disturbances. There still existed widespread hatred of Stolypin among the older conservative groups in the country. The industrial workers were antagonistic to the tsar. In 1911 Stolypin was shot by a Social Revolutionary, who may have been a police agent in the pay of conservatives. Nicholas II found no worthy successor. His government simply continued to muddle along.

At court the monk Grigory Efimovich Rasputin (1871?–1916) came into ascendancy because of his alleged power to heal the tsar's hemophilic son, the heir to the throne. The undue influence of this strange and uncouth man, the continued social discontent, and the conservative resistance to any further liberal reforms rendered the position and the policy of the tsar uncertain after 1911. Once again, as in 1904, he and his ministers thought that some bold move on the diplomatic front might bring the regime the broad popular support that it so desperately needed.

881

THE BUILDI
OF EUROPE,
SUPREMAC
SOCIETY AN
POLITICS T
WORLD WA

The years from 1860 through 1914 saw the emergence of two apparently contradictory developments in European social life. On the one hand the lifestyle of the urban middle classes came to dominate. The lifestyle associated with a relatively small family living in its own house or large apartment with servants and a wife who did not work became the goal toward which hundreds of thousands of people aspired. Those people from the lower middle class who attained it soon feared losing such a style of living. These groups benefited from the many comforts emerging from the Second Industrial Revolution.

At the same time the forces of socialism and labor unions assumed a new and major role in European political life. The spokesmen for these new forces demanded greater social justice and a more fair distribution of the vast quantities of consumer goods being produced in Europe. Some of these socialists sought in one way or another to work within existing political systems. However, others—most particularly those in Russia—advocated direct revolution. It was the very growth in wealth and the availability of new goods and services that made the demands of labor and socialists so much more strident. The injustice of the situation of the poor and the contrast between their lives and those of the middle class were literally more visible. In Russia the strains of the early stages of industrialization added to the demands for social concern. In the wake of Russian military defeat those demands created temporarily in 1905 a revolutionary situation.

But the working class was not alone in demanding change. Women, for the first time in European history, were making strong demands for entrance into the political system. They were beginning to enter the professions in small numbers and were taking a significant role in the service economy, such as the new telephone companies. Those changes, as much as the demands of socialists, would in time raise questions about the adequacy of the much admired late nineteenth-century middle-class lifestyle.

Suggested Readings

J. ALBISETTI, *Secondary School Reform in Imperial Germany* (1983). Examines the relationship between politics and education.

L. R. BERLANSTEIN, *The Working People of Paris, 1871–1914* (1985). Interesting and comprehensive.

D. BLACKBOURN AND G. ELEY, *The Peculiarities of German History: Bourgeois Society and Politics in Nineteenth-Century Germany* (1985). An important and probing study.

N. BULLOCK AND J. READ, *The Movement for Housing Reform in Germany and France, 1840–1914* (1985). An important and wide-ranging study of the housing problem.

C. M. CIPOLLA, *The Economic History of World Population* (1962). A basic introduction.

R. J. EVANS AND W. R. LEE, *The German Family: Essays on the Social History of the Family in Nineteenth- and Twentieth-Century Germany* (1981). Very useful.

W. H. FRASER, *The Coming of the Mass Market, 1850–1914* (1981). Exploration of the expansion of consumer society.

P. GAY, *The Dilemma of Democratic Socialism: Eduard Bernstein's Challenge to Marx* (1952). A clear presentation of the problems raised by Bernstein's revisionism.

P. GAY, *The Bourgeois Experience: Victoria to Freud*, Vol. 1, *Education of the Senses* (1984). Vol. 2, *The Tender Passion* (1986). A major study of middle-class sexuality.

M. GIBSON, *Prostitution and the State in Italy, 1860–1915* (1986). An examination of state regulation of prostitution.

D. F. GOOD, *The Economic Rise of the Hapsburg*

Empire, 1750–1914 (1985). The best available study.

J. HARSIN, *Policing Prostitution in Nineteenth-Century Paris* (1985). A major study of this very significant subject in French social history.

S. C. HAUSE, *Women's Suffrage and Social Politics in the French Third Republic* (1984). A wide-ranging examination of the question.

S. C. HAUSE, *Herbertine Auclert, The French Suffragette* (1987). An excellent biography.

S. H. F. HICKEY, *Workers in Imperial Germany: The Miners of the Ruhr* (1985). A broad study of German working-class culture.

P. HILDEN, *Working Women and Socialist Politics in France,* 1880–1914 (1986). A study that traces both cooperation and tension between socialism and feminism in the French working class.

E. J. HOBSBAWM, *The Age of Capital* (1975). Explores the consolidation of middle-class life after 1850.

L. HOLCOMBE, *Wives and Property: Reform of the Married Women's Property Law in Nineteenth-Century England* (1983). The standard work on the subject.

S. S. HOLTON, *Feminism and Democracy: Women's Suffrage and Reform Politics in Britain,* 1900–1918 (1986). An excellent treatment of the subject.

K. H. JARAUSCH, *Students, Society, and Politics in Imperial Germany: The Rise of Academic Illiberalism* (1982). The reaction of the academic community to the threat of socialism.

P. JOYCE, *Work, Society, and Politics: The Culture of the Factory in Later Victorian England* (1980). Explores what actually happened in factories.

S. KERN, *The Culture of Time and Space,* 1880–1918 (1983). A lively discussion of the impact of the new technology.

K. KOLAKOWSKI, *Main Currents of Marxism: Its Rise, Growth, and Dissolution,* 3 vols. (1978). The relevant sections on the last years of the nineteenth century and the early years of the twentieth are especially good.

D. LANDES, *The Unbound Prometheus: Technological Change and Industrial Development in Western Europe from 1750 to the Present* (1969). Includes excellent discussions of late-nineteenth-century development.

A. MACLAREN, *Sexuality and Social Order: The Debate over the Fertility of Women and Workers in France,* 1770–1920 (1983). Examines the debate over birth control in France.

A. H. MCBRIAR, *Fabian Socialism and English Politics,* 1884–1918 (1962). The standard discussion.

W. O. MCCAGG, JR., *A History of Habsburg Jews,* 1670–1918 (1989). An excellent examination of the political and economic life of the Jews under Habsburg rule.

G. L. MOSSE, *German Jews beyond Judaism* (1985). Sensitive essays exploring the relationship of Jews to German culture in the nineteenth and early twentieth centuries.

P. G. NORD, *Paris Shopkeepers and the Politics of Resentment* (1986). An examination of the political attitudes of Paris shopkeepers in the wake of the redesign of the city.

R. A. NYE, *Crime, Madness, and Politics in Modern France: The Medical Concept of National Decline* (1984). Relevant to issues of family and women.

D. OLSEN, *The City as a Work of Art: London, Paris, Vienna* (1986). A splendidly illustrated survey of nineteenth-century urban growth and design.

H. PELLING, *The Origins of the Labour Party,* 1880–1900 (1965). Examines the sources of the party in the activities of British socialists and trade unionists.

M. PERROT, *Workers on Strike: France,* 1871–1890 (1987). A major exploration of the social and cultural dimensions of strikes.

D. H. PINKNEY, *Napoleon III and the Rebuilding of Paris* (1958). A classic study.

H. ROGGER, *Russia in the Age of Modernization and Revolution,* 1881–1917 (1983). The best synthesis of the period.

H. ROGGER, *Jewish Policies and Right-Wing Politics in Imperial Russia* (1986). A very learned examination of Russian anti-Semitism.

M. L. ROZENBLIT, *The Jews of Vienna,* 1867–1914: *Assimilation and Identity* (1983). Covers the cultural, economic, and political life of Viennese Jews.

D. L. RUSSEL (Ed.), *The Family in Imperial Russia* (1978). A collection of essays on a little investigated subject.

C. E. SCHORSKE, *German Social Democracy,* 1905–1917 (1955). A brilliant study of the difficulties of the Social Democrats under the empire.

J. SCOTT, *The Glassworkers of Carmaux: French Craftsmen and Political Action in a Nineteenth-Century City* (1974). A classic analysis of the manner in which highly skilled craftsmen confronted and were eventually defeated by the mechanization of their industry.

A. L. SHAPIRO, *Housing the Poor of Paris,* 1850–1902 (1985). Examines what happened to working-class housing at the time of the remodeling of Paris.

B. G. SMITH, *Ladies of the Leisure Class: The Bourgeoises of Northern France in the Nineteenth Century* (1981). Emphasizes the importance of the reproductive role of women.

R. A. SOLOWAY, *Birth Control and the Population Question in England,* 1877–1930 (1982). An important book that should be read with MacLaren (listed above).

N. STONE, *Europe Transformed* (1984). A sweeping

survey that emphasizes the difficulties of late-nineteenth-century liberalism.

F. M. L. THOMPSON, *The Rise of Respectable Society: A Social History of Victorian Britain, 1830–1900* (1988). A major survey.

A. B. ULAM, *The Bolsheviks: The Intellectual and Political History of the Triumph of Communism in Russia* (1965). Early chapters discuss prewar developments and the formation of Lenin's doctrines.

J. R. WALKOWITZ, *Prostitution and Victorian Society: Women, Class, and the State* (1980). A work of great insight and sensitivity.

E. WEBER, *Peasants into Frenchmen: The Modernization of Rural France, 1870–1914* (1976). An important and fascinating work on the transformation of French peasants into self-conscious citizens of the nation state.

M. J. WIENER, *English Culture and the Decline of the Industrial Spirit, 1850–1980* (1981). The best study of the problem.

883

THE BUILDI
OF EUROPE
SUPREMAC
SOCIETY AN
POLITICS T
WORLD WA

In two works of seminal importance, The Origin of Species *(1859)* and The Descent of Man *(1871), Charles Darwin (1809–1882) enunciated the theory of evolution by natural selection and applied that theory to human beings. The result was a storm of controversy that affected not only biology, but also religion, philosophy, sociology, and even politics. [National Portrait Gallery, London]*

25

THE BIRTH OF
CONTEMPORARY
EUROPEAN THOUGHT

During the same period that the modern nation-state developed and the Second Industrial Revolution laid the foundations for the modern material lifestyle, the ideas and concepts that have marked European thought for much of the present century took shape. Like previous intellectual changes, these arose from earlier patterns of thought. The Enlightenment provided late-nineteenth-century Europeans with a heritage of rationalism, toleration, cosmopolitanism, and appreciation of science. Romanticism led them to value feelings, imagination, national identity, and the autonomy of the artistic experience.

By 1900 these strands of thought had become woven into a new fabric. Many of the traditional intellectual signposts were disappearing. The death of God had been proclaimed. Christianity had undergone the most severe attack in its history. The picture of the physical world that had dominated since Newton had undergone major modification. The work of Darwin and Freud had challenged the special place that Western thinkers had assigned to humankind. The value long ascribed to rationality was being questioned. The political and humanitarian ideals of liberalism and socialism gave way for a time to new, aggressive nationalism. At the turn of the century European intellectuals were more daring than ever before, but they were also probably less certain and less optimistic.

The New Reading Public

The social context of intellectual life changed in the last half of the nineteenth century. For the first time in Europe, a mass reading public came into existence. In 1850 approximately half the population of western Europe and a much higher proportion of Russians were illiterate. Even those people who might technically be capable of reading and writing did so very poorly.

Advances in Primary Education

The literacy of the continent improved steadily, as from the 1860s onward one government after another undertook state-financed education. Hungary provided elementary education in 1868; Britain, in 1870; Switzerland, in 1874; Italy, in 1877; and France, between 1878 and 1881. The already advanced education system of Prussia was extended in various ways throughout the German Empire after 1871. The attack on illiteracy proved most successful in Britain, France, Belgium, the Netherlands, Germany, and Scandinavia, where by 1900 approximately 85 per cent or more of the people could read. Italy, Spain, Russia, Austria-Hungary, and the Balkans lagged well behind, with illiteracy rates of between 30 and 60 per cent.

The new primary education in the basic skills of reading and writing and elementary arithmetic reflected and generated social change. Both liberals and conservatives regarded such minimal training as necessary for orderly political behavior on the part of the newly enfranchised voters. There was also hope that literacy might help the poor to help themselves and might create a better, more productive labor force. This side of the educational crusade embodied the rationalist faith that right knowledge would lead to right action.

However, literacy and its extension soon became forces in their own right. The school-teaching profession grew rapidly in numbers and prestige. Those people who learned to read the little they were taught could continue to read much more on their own. They soon discovered that the education that led to better jobs and political influence was still open only to those who could afford it. Having created systems of primary education, the major nations had to give further attention to secondary education by the time of World War I. In yet another generation the question would become one of democratic university instruction.

Reading Material for the Mass Audience

The expanding literate population created a vast market for new reading material. There was nothing less than an explosion of printed matter. Advances in printing and paper technology lowered production costs. The number of newspapers, books, and libraries grew rapidly. Cheap mass-circulation newspapers, such as *Le Petit Journal* of Paris and the *Daily Mail* and *Daily Express* of London, enjoyed their first heyday. Newspapers with very specialized political or religious viewpoints were also published. The number of monthly and quarterly journals for families, women, and free-thinking intellectuals increased. Probably more people with different kinds of ideas could get into print in the late nineteenth century than ever before in European history. And more people could read their ideas than ever before.

The quantity of readers and reading material did not ensure quality. The cheap newspapers prospered on stories of sensational crimes and political scandal and on pages of advertising.

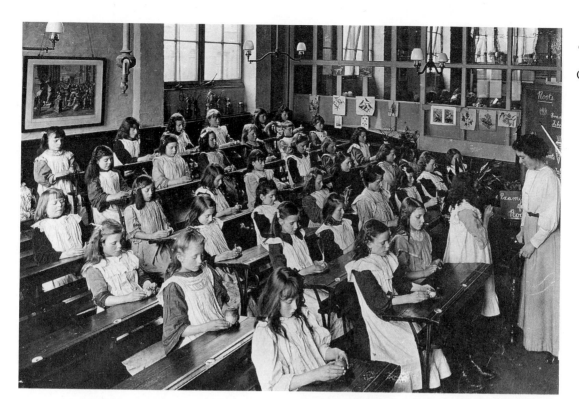

Wider public education spread across much of Europe during the second half of the nineteenth century. Here a class in an English School Board School is studying natural history. [Bettmann Archive/BBC Hulton]

Religious journals depended on denominational rivalry. A brisk market existed for pornography. There was much cutthroat journalism, as portrayed in George Gissing's (1857–1903) novel *New Grub Street* (1892). Newspapers became major factors in the emerging mass politics. The news could be managed, but in central Europe more often by the govern-

Travelers at an English railway station rush to buy newspapers in 1875. The late nineteenth century was the heyday of the cheap, mass-circulation newspaper. The enormous new reading public had an insatiable appetite for news. [New York Public Library Picture Collection]

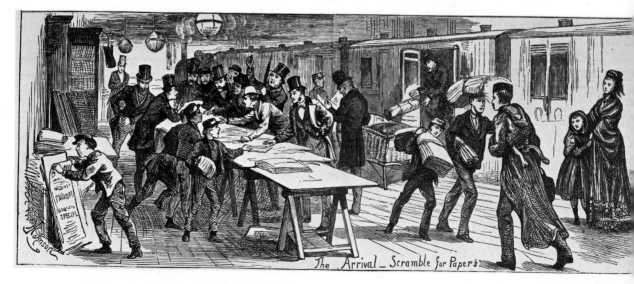

James Joyce transformed the modern novel and drew his readers into new modes of realism. [Culver Pictures, Inc.]

ment censor than by the publisher. Editorials appeared on the front page.

The mass audience and the new literary world created problems for the literary artist. Much of the contempt for democracy and for the "people" found in late-nineteenth-century literature arose in reaction to the recently established conditions for publication. The new sense of distance between the artist and the public was in part a result of the changed character of the literate public. As publishers sought to make profits, they often feared offending the sensibilities of their potential readership.

Some writers accepted this situation and happily wrote harmless verbiage that supported current moral and political opinion. Others, such as Matthew Arnold (1822–1888), worked to raise the level of popular taste. Still others, such as the French novelist Émile Zola

(1840–1902), deliberately offended the complaisant bourgeois values of their readers. These anxieties and tensions were closely related to some writers' criticism of democracy. Artists and their middle-class audience became the subjects of novels, such as James Joyce's (1882–1941) *Portrait of the Artist As a Young Man* (1914).

Because many of the new readers were only marginally literate and still quite ignorant on many scores, the books and journals catering to them seemed and often were thoroughly mediocre. Social and artistic critics were correct in pointing out this low level of public taste. Nevertheless, the new education, the new readers, and the hundreds of new books and journals permitted a monumental popularization of knowledge that has become a hallmark of the contemporary world. The new literacy was the intellectual equivalent of the railroad and the steamship. People could leave their original intellectual surroundings. Literacy is not an end in itself. It leads to other skills and the acquisition of other knowledge.

Science at Mid-Century

In about 1850 Voltaire would still have felt at home in a general discussion of scientific concepts. The basic Newtonian picture of physical nature that he had popularized still prevailed. Scientists continued to believe that nature operated as a vast machine according to mechanical principles.

During the first half of the century scientists had extended mechanistic explanation into several important areas. John Dalton (1766–1844) had formulated the modern theory of chemical composition. However, at mid-century and long thereafter atoms and molecules were thought to resemble billiard balls. During the 1840s several independent researchers had arrived at the concept of the conservation of energy, according to which energy is never lost in the universe but is simply transformed from one form to another. The principles of mechanism had been extended to geology through the work of Charles Lyell (1797–1875). His *Principles of Geology* (1830) postulated that various changes in geological formation were the result of the mechanistic operation of natural causes over great spans of time.

At mid-century the physical world was thus regarded as rational, mechanical, and dependable. Its laws could be ascertained objectively through experiment and observation. Scientific theory purportedly described physical nature as it really existed. Moreover, almost all scientists also believed, like Newton and the deists of the eighteenth century, that their knowledge of nature demonstrated the existence of a God or a Supreme Being.

uniformitarianism

Darwin's Theory of Natural Selection

In 1859 Charles Darwin (1809–1882) published *The Origin of Species*, which carried the mechanical interpretation of physical nature into the world of living things. The book proved to be one of the seminal works of Western thought and earned Darwin the honor of being regarded as the Newton of biology. Both Darwin and his book have been much misunderstood. He did not originate the concept of evolution, which had been discussed widely before he wrote. What he and Alfred Russel Wallace (1823–1913) did, working independently, was to formulate the principle of natural selection, which explained how species had changed or evolved over time. Earlier writers had believed that evolution might occur; Darwin and Wallace explained how it could occur.

Drawing on Malthus, the two scientists contended that more seeds and living organisms come into existence than can survive in their environment. Those organisms possessing some marginal advantage in the struggle for existence live long enough to propagate their kind. This principle of survival of the fittest Darwin called *natural selection*. The principle was naturalistic and mechanistic. Its operation required no guiding mind behind the development and change in organic nature. What neither Darwin nor anyone else in his day could explain was the origin of those chance variations that provided some living things with the marginal chance for survival. Only when the work on heredity of the Austrian monk Gregor Mendel (1822–1884) received public attention after 1900, several years following his death,

did the mystery of those variations begin to be unraveled.

Darwin's and Wallace's theory represented the triumph of naturalistic explanation, which removed the idea of purpose from organic nature. Eyes were not made for seeing according to the rational wisdom and purpose of God but had developed mechanistically over the course of time. In this manner the theory of evolution through natural selection not only contradicted the biblical narrative of the Creation but also undermined the deistic argument for the existence of God from the design of the universe. Moreover, Darwin's work undermined the whole concept of fixity in nature or the universe at large. The world was a realm of flux and change. The fact that physical and organic nature might be constantly changing allowed people in the late nineteenth century to believe that society, values, customs, and beliefs should also change.

In 1871 Darwin carried his work a step further. In *The Descent of Man* he applied the principle of evolution by natural selection to human beings. Darwin was hardly the first person to treat human beings as animals, but his arguments brought greater plausibility to that point of view. He contended that human-

Alfred Russel Wallace (1823–1913), here photographed in his later years, also came upon the principle of evolution by natural selection independently of Darwin. [The Granger Collection]

Darwin Defends a Mechanistic View of Nature

In the closing paragraphs of The Origin of Species (1859), *Charles Darwin contrasted the view of nature he championed with that of his opponents. He argued that interpreting the development of organic nature through mechanistic laws actually suggested a nobler concept of nature than interpreting its development in terms of some form of divine creation. Darwin, however, added the term* Creator *to these paragraphs in the second edition of the* Origin.

Authors of the highest eminence seem to be fully satisfied with the view that each species has been independently created. To my mind it accords better with what we know of the laws impressed on matter by the Creator, that the production and extinction of the past and present inhabitants of the world should have been due to secondary causes, like those determining the birth and death of the individual. When I view all beings not as special creations, but as the lineal descendants of some few beings which lived long before the first bed of the Cambrian [geological] system was deposited, they seem to me to become ennobled. . . .

It is interesting to contemplate a tangled bank, clothed with many plants of many kinds, with birds singing on the bushes, with various insects flitting about, and with worms crawling through the damp earth, and to reflect that these elaborately constructed forms, so different from each other, and dependent upon each other in so complex a manner, have all been produced by laws acting around us. These laws, taken in the largest sense, being Growth with Reproduction; Inheritance which is almost implied by reproduction; Variability from the indirect and direct action of the conditions of life, and from use and disuse: a Ratio of Increase so high as to lead to a Struggle for Life, and as a consequence to Natural Selection, entailing Divergence of Character and the Extinction of less-improved forms. Thus, from the war of nature, from famine and death, the most exalted object which we are capable of conceiving, namely the production of the higher animals, directly follows. There is grandeur in this view of life, with its several powers, having been originally breathed by the Creator into a few forms or into one; and that, whilst this planet has gone cycling on according to the fixed law of gravity, from so simple a beginning endless forms most beautiful and most wonderful have been, and are being evolved.

Charles Darwin, The Origin of Species and the Descent of Man *(New York: Modern Library, n.d.), pp. 373–374.*

kind's moral nature and religious sentiments, as well as its physical frame, had developed naturalistically in response largely to the requirements of survival. Neither the origin nor the character of humankind on earth, in Darwin's view, required the existence of a God for their explanation. Not since Copernicus had removed the earth from the center of the universe had the pride of Western human beings received so sharp a blow.

Darwin's theory of evolution by natural selection was very controversial from the moment of the publication of *The Origin of Species.* It encountered criticism from both the religious and the scientific communities. By the end of the century the concept of evolution was widely accepted by scientists, but not yet Darwin's mechanism of natural selection. The acceptance of the latter within the scientific community really dates from the 1920s and

1930s, when Darwin's theory became combined with the insights of modern genetics.

The Prestige of Science

Darwin's ideas remained highly controversial. They were widely debated in popular and scientific journals. He changed some of them in the course of his writings. However, at issue was not only the correctness of the theory and the place of humankind in nature but also the role of science and scientists in society. The prestige of Darwin's achievement, progress in medicine, and the links of science to the technology of the Second Industrial Revolution made the general European public aware of science as never before. The British Fabian Socialist Beatrice Webb recalled this situation from her youth:

> Who will deny that the men of science were the leading British intellectuals of that period; that it was they who stood out as men of genius with international reputations; that it was they who were the self-confident militants of the period; that it was they who were routing the theologians, confounding the mystics, imposing their theories on philosophers, their inventions on capitalists, and their discoveries on medical men; whilst they were at the same time snubbing the artists, ignoring the poets, and even casting doubts on the capacity of the politicians?[1]

Contemporaries spoke of a religion of science that would explain all without resort to supernaturalism. Popularizers, such as Thomas Henry Huxley (1825–1895) in Britain and Ernst Haeckel (1834–1919) in Germany, wrote and lectured widely on scientific topics. They argued that science held the answer to the major questions of life. They worked for government support of scientific research and for inclusion of science in the schools and universities.

COMTE AND POSITIVISM   Scientific knowledge and theories became models for thought in other fields even before the impact of Darwinian ideas. The French philosopher Auguste Comte (1798–1857), a late child of the Enlightenment and a one-time follower of Saint-Simon, developed a philosophy of

Auguste Comte (1798–1857), the founder of Positivism. Comte argued that all natural phenomena, including the workings of human society, could be explained by empirical scientific evidence— natural laws that human beings could describe and understand. [French Cultural Services, New York]

human intellectual development that culminated in science. In *The Positive Philosophy* (1830–1842), Comte argued that human thought had gone through three stages of development. In the theological stage, physical nature was explained in terms of the action of divinities or spirits. In the second or metaphysical stage, abstract principles became regarded as the operative agencies of nature. In the final or positive stage, explanations of nature became matters of exact description of phenomena, without recourse to an unobservable operative principle.

Physical science had, in Comte's view, entered the positive stage, and similar thinking should penetrate other areas of analysis. In particular Comte thought that positive laws of social behavior could be discovered in the same fashion as laws of physical nature. For this reason he is generally regarded as the father of sociology. Works like Comte's helped to convince learned Europeans that genuine knowledge in any area must resemble scientific knowledge. This belief had its roots in the Enlightenment and continues to permeate Western thought to the present day.

SCIENCE AND ETHICS   Theories of ethics were modeled on science during the last

---

[1] *Beatrice Webb, My Apprenticeship (London: Longmans, Green, 1926), pp. 130–131.*

half of the century. The concept of the struggle for survival was widely applied to human social relationships. The phrase "survival of the fittest" predated Darwin and reflected the competitive outlook of classical economics. Darwin's use of the phrase gave it the prestige associated with advanced science.

The most famous advocate of evolutionary ethics was Herbert Spencer (1820–1903), the British philosopher. Spencer, a strong individualist, believed that human society progressed through competition. If the weak received too much protection, the rest of humankind was the loser. In Spencer's work, struggle against one's fellow human beings became a kind of ethical imperative. The concept could be applied to justify the avoidance of aiding the poor and the working class or to justify the domina-

T. H. Huxley Criticizes Evolutionary Ethics

T. H. Huxley was a British scientist who had been among Darwin's strongest defenders. He was also one of the outspoken advocates of the advancement of science in the late nineteenth century. However, Huxley became a major critic of social Darwinism or evolutionary ethics that attempted to deduce human ethical behavior from the evolutionary processes of struggle in nature. Huxley drew a strong distinction between the cosmic process of evolution and the social process of ethical development. He argued that human ethical progress occurred through combating the cosmic process. These passages are taken from Evolution and Ethics *(1893).*

Men in society are undoubtedly subject to the cosmic process. As among other animals, multiplication goes on without cessation, and involves severe competition for the means of support. The struggle for existence tends to eliminate those less fitted to adapt themselves to the circumstances of their existence. The strongest, the most self-assertive, tend to tread down the weaker. But the influence of the cosmic process on the evolution of society is the greater the more rudimentary its civilization. Social progress means a checking of the cosmic process at every step and the substitution for it of another, which may be called the ethical process; the end of which is not the survival of those who may happen to be the fittest, in respect of the whole of the conditions which obtain, but of those who are ethically the best.

As I have already urged, the practice of that which is ethically best—what we call goodness or virtue—involves a course of conduct which, in all respects, is opposed to that which leads to success in the cosmic struggle for existence. In place of ruthless self-assertion it demands self-restraint; in place of thrusting aside, or treading down, all competitors, it requires that the individual shall not merely respect, but shall help his fellows; its influence is directed, not so much to the survival of the fittest, as to the fitting of as many as possible to survive. It repudiates the gladiatorial theory of existence.

It is from neglect of these plain considerations that the fanatical individualism of our time attempts to apply the analogy of cosmic nature to society. . . .

Let us understand, once for all, that the ethical progress of society depends, not on imitating the cosmic process, still less in running away from it, but in combating it.

T. H. Huxley, Evolution and Ethics *(London: Macmillan & Co., 1894) as quoted in Franklin L. Baumer,* Main Currents of Western Thought: Readings in Western European Intellectual History from the Middle Ages to the Present, *3rd ed., revised (New York: Alfred A. Knopf, 1970), pp. 561–562.*

tion of colonial peoples or to urge aggressively competitive relationships among nations. Evolutionary ethics and similar concepts, all of which are usually termed *social Darwinism*, often came very close to saying that might makes right.

Interestingly enough, one of the chief opponents of such thinking was Thomas Henry Huxley, the great defender of Darwin. In 1893 Huxley declared that the physical cosmic process of evolution was at odds with the process of human ethical development. The struggle in nature held no ethical implications except to demonstrate how human beings should not behave.

Scientists and their admirers enjoyed a supreme confidence during the last half of the century. They genuinely believed that they had, for all intents and purposes, discovered all that might be discovered. The issues for science in the future would be the extension of acknowledged principles and the refinement of measurement. However, the turn of the century held a much more brilliant future for science. That confident, self-satisfied world of late-nineteenth-century science and scientism vanished. A much more complicated picture of nature developed. Before examining those new departures, we must see how the cult of science affected religious thought and practice.

Christianity and the Church Under Siege

The nineteenth century was one of the most difficult periods in the history of the organized Christian churches. Many European intellectuals left the faith. The secular, liberal nation-states attacked the political and social influence of the Church. The expansion of population and the growth of cities challenged its organizational capacity to meet the modern age. Yet during all of this turmoil the Protestant and Catholic churches still made considerable headway at the popular level.

Intellectual Skepticism

The intellectual attack on Christianity arose on the grounds of its historical credibility, its scientific accuracy, and its pronounced morality. The *philosophes* of the Enlightenment had delighted in pointing out contradictions in the Bible. The historical scholarship of the nineteenth century brought new issues to the fore.

HISTORY In 1835 David Friederich Strauss (1808–1874) published a *Life of Jesus* in which he questioned whether the Bible provided any genuine historical evidence about Jesus. Strauss contended that the story of Jesus was a myth that had arisen from the particular social and intellectual conditions of first-century Palestine. Jesus' character and life represented the aspirations of the people of that time and place rather than events that had occurred. Other skeptical lives of Jesus were written and published elsewhere.

During the second half of the century scholars such as Julius Wellhausen (1844–1918) in Germany, Ernst Renan (1823–1892) in France, and William Robertson Smith (1847–1894) in Great Britain contended that the books of the Bible had been written and revised with the problems of Jewish society and politics in the minds of human authors. They were not inspired books but had, like the Homeric epics, been written by normal human beings in a primitive society. This questioning of the historical validity of the Bible caused more literate men and women to lose faith in Christianity than any other single cause.

SCIENCE The march of science also undermined Christianity. This blow was particularly cruel because many eighteenth-century writers had led Christians to believe that the scientific examination of nature provided a strong buttress for their faith. William Paley's (1743–1805) *Natural Theology* (1802) and books by numerous scientists had enshrined this belief. The geology of Charles Lyell (1797–1875) suggested that the earth was much older than the biblical records contended. By appealing to natural causes to explain floods, mountains, and valleys, Lyell removed the miraculous hand of God from the physical development of the earth. Darwin's theory cast doubt on the doctrine of the Creation. His ideas and those of other writers suggested that the moral nature of humankind could be explained without appeal to the role of God. Finally, anthropologists, psychologists, and sociologists suggested that religion itself and religious sentiments were just one more set of natural phenomena.

MORALITY Other intellectuals questioned the morality of Christianity. The old issue of immoral biblical stories was again raised. Much more important, the moral character of the Old Testament God came under fire. His cruelty and unpredictability did not fit well with the progressive, tolerant, rational values of liberals. They also wondered about the morality of the New Testament God, who would sacrifice for His own satisfaction the only perfect being ever to walk the earth. Many of the clergy began to ask themselves if they could honestly preach doctrines they felt to be immoral.

During the last quarter of the century this moral attack on Christianity came from another direction. Writers like Friedrich Nietzsche (1844–1900) in Germany portrayed Christianity as a religion of sheep that glorified weakness rather than the strength that life required. Christianity demanded a useless and debilitating sacrifice of the flesh and spirit rather than full-blooded heroic living and daring. Nietzsche once observed, "War and courage have accomplished more great things than love of neighbor."[2]

These widespread skeptical intellectual currents seem to have directly influenced only the upper levels of educated society. Yet they created a climate in which Christianity lost much of its intellectual respectability. Fewer educated people joined the clergy. More and more people found that they could lead their lives with little or no reference to Christianity. The secularism of everyday life proved as harmful to the faith as the direct attacks. This situation especially prevailed in the cities, which were growing faster than the capacity of the churches to meet the challenge. There was not even enough room in urban churches for the potential worshipers to sit. Whole generations of the urban poor grew up with little or no experience of the Church as an institution or of Christianity as a religious faith.

Conflict of Church and State

The secular state of the nineteenth century clashed with both the Protestant and the Roman Catholic churches. Liberals generally disliked the dogma and the political privileges of the established churches. National states were often suspicious of the supranational character of the Roman Catholic church. However, the primary area of conflict between the state and the churches was the expanding systems of education. The churches feared that future generations would emerge from the schools without the rudiments of religious teaching. The advocates of secular education feared the production of future generations more loyal to religion or the Church than to the nation. From 1870 through the turn of the century, the issue of religious education was heatedly debated in every major country.

GREAT BRITAIN In Great Britain the Education Act of 1870 provided for the construction of state-supported school-board schools, whereas earlier the government had given small grants to religious schools. The new schools were to be built in areas where the religious denominations failed to provide satisfactory education. There was rivalry not only between the Anglican church and the state but also between the Anglican church and the Nonconformist denominations, that is, those Christian denominations that were not part of the Church of England. There was intense local hostility among all these groups. The churches of all denominations had to oppose improvements in education because these increased the costs of their own schools. In the Education Act of 1902 the government decided to provide state support for both religious and nonreligious schools but imposed the same educational standards on each.

FRANCE The British conflict was relatively calm compared with that in France, where there existed a dual system of Catholic and public schools. Under the Falloux Law of 1850 the local priest provided religious education in the public schools. The very conservative French Catholic church and the Third French Republic were mutually hostile to each other. Between 1878 and 1886 the government passed a series of educational laws sponsored by Jules Ferry (1832–1893). The Ferry Laws replaced religious instruction in the public schools with civic training. Members of religious orders were no longer permitted to teach in the public schools, the number of which was to be expanded. After the Dreyfus affair the French Catholic church again paid a price for its reac-

[2] Walter Kaufmann (Ed. and trans.), The Portable Nietzsche (New York: Viking, 1967), p. 159.

tionary politics. The Radical government of Waldeck-Rousseau, drawn from pro-Dreyfus groups, suppressed the religious orders. In 1905 the Napoleonic Concordat was terminated, and Church and state were totally separated.

GERMANY AND THE KULTURKAMPF

The most extreme example of Church–state conflict occurred in Germany during the 1870s. At the time of unification the German Catholic hierarchy had wanted freedom for the churches guaranteed in the constitution. Bismarck left the matter to the discretion of each federal state, but he soon felt the activity of the Roman Catholic church and the Catholic Center Party to be a threat to the political unity of the new state. Through administrative orders in 1870 and 1871 Bismarck removed both Catholic and Protestant clergy from overseeing local education and set education under state direction. The secularization of education was merely the beginning of a concerted attack on the independence of the Catholic church in Germany.

The "May Laws" of 1873, which applied to Prussia and not the entire German Empire, required priests to be educated in German schools and universities and to pass state-administered examinations. The state could veto the appointments of priests. The disciplinary power of the pope and the Church over the clergy was abolished and transferred to the state. When the bishops and many of the clergy refused to obey these laws, Bismarck used the police against them. In 1876 he had either arrested or driven from Prussia all the Catholic bishops.

In the end, Bismarck's *Kulturkampf* ("cultural struggle") against the Catholic church failed. Not for the first time, Christian martyrs aided resistance to persecution. By the close of the decade the chancellor had abandoned his attack. He had gained state control of education and civil laws governing marriage only at the price of lingering Catholic resentment against the German state. The *Kulturkampf* was probably the greatest blunder of Bismarck's career.

Areas of Religious Revival

The successful German Catholic resistance to the intrusions of the secular state illustrates the continuing vitality of Christianity during

The conflict between Church and state disrupted German politics during the 1870s. In this contemporary cartoon Bismarck and Pope Pius IX are portrayed as playing chess, each having the goal of checkmating the other. [Archiv für Kunst und Geschichte, Berlin]

this period of intellectual and political hardship. In Great Britain both the Anglican church and the Nonconformist denominations experienced considerable growth in membership. Vast sums of money were raised for new churches and schools. In Ireland the 1870s saw a widespread Catholic devotional revival. Priests in France after the defeat by Prussia organized special pilgrimages to shrines by train for thousands of penitents who believed that France had been defeated because of their sins. The cult of the miracle of Lourdes originated during these years. There were efforts by churches of all denominations to give more attention to the urban poor.

In effect, the last half of the nineteenth century witnessed the final great effort to Christianize Europe. It was well organized, well led, and well financed. It failed not from want of effort but because the population had simply outstripped the resources of the churches. This persistent liveliness of the Church accounts in part for the intense hostility of its enemies.

The Roman Catholic Church and the Modern World

Perhaps the most striking feature of this religious revival amidst turmoil and persecution was the resilience of the papacy. The brief hope for a liberal pontificate from Pope Pius IX (1846–1878) vanished on the night in 1848 when he fled the turmoil in Rome. In the 1860s Pius IX, embittered by the mode of Italian unification, launched a counteroffensive against liberalism in thought and deed. In 1864 he issued the *Syllabus of Errors*, which condemned all the major tenets of political liberalism and modern thought. He set the Roman Catholic church squarely against the worlds of contemporary science, philosophy, and politics.

In 1869 the pope called into session the First Vatican Council. The next year, through the political manipulations of the pontiff and against much opposition from numerous members, the council promulgated the dogma of the infallibility of the pope when speaking officially on matters of faith and morals. No earlier pope had gone so far. The First Vatican Council came to a close in 1870, when Italian troops invaded Rome at the outbreak of the Franco-Prussian War.

Pius IX died in 1878 and was succeeded by Leo XIII (1878–1903). The new pope, who was sixty-eight years old at the time of his election, sought to make accommodation with the modern age and to address the great social ques-

tions. He looked to the philosophical tradition of Thomas Aquinas to reconcile the claims of faith and reason. His encyclicals of 1885 and 1890 permitted Catholics to participate in the politics of liberal states.

Leo XIII's most important pronouncement on public issues was the encyclical *Rerum Novarum* (1891). In that document Leo XIII defended private property, religious education, and religious control of the marriage laws; and he condemned socialism and Marxism. However, he also declared that employers should treat their employees justly, pay them proper wages, and permit them to organize labor unions. He supported laws and regulations to protect the conditions of labor. The pope urged that modern society be organized according to corporate groups, including people from various classes, who might cooperate according to Christian principles. The corporate society, derivative of medieval social organization, was to be an alternative to both socialism and competitive capitalism. On the basis of Leo XIII's pronouncements democratic Catholic parties and Catholic trade unions were founded throughout Europe.

Pope Leo XIII (1878–1903) led the Roman Catholic Church toward a recognition of the problems of industrial democracy. His encyclical Rerum Novarum (1891) *was the Church's major statement on social justice.* [Bildarchiv Preussischer Kulturbesitz]

Leo XIII Considers the Social Question in European Politics

In his 1891 encyclical Rerum Novarum, *Pope Leo XIII addressed the social question in European politics. It was the answer of the Catholic church to secular calls for social reforms. The pope denied the socialist claim that class conflict was the natural state of affairs. He urged employers to seek just and peaceful relations with workers.*

The great mistake that is made in the matter now under consideration is to possess oneself of the idea that class is naturally hostile to class; that rich and poor are intended by Nature to live at war with one another. So irrational and so false is this view that the exact contrary is the truth. . . . Each requires the other; capital cannot do without labour, nor labour without capital. Mutual agreement results in pleasantness and good order; perpetual conflict necessarily produces confusion and outrage. Now, in preventing such strife as this, and in making it impossible, the efficacy of Christianity is marvellous and manifold. . . . Religion teaches the labouring man and the workman to carry out honestly and well all equitable agreements freely made; never to injure capital, or to outrage the person of an employer; never to employ violence in representing his own cause, or to engage in riot or disorder; and to have nothing to do with men of evil principles, who work upon the people with artful promises and raise hopes which usually end in disaster and in repentance when too late. Religion teaches the rich man and the employer that their work people are not their slaves; that they must respect in every man his dignity as a man and as a Christian; that labour is nothing to be ashamed of, if we listen to right reason and to Christian philosophy, but is an honourable employment, enabling a man to sustain his life in an upright and creditable way; and that it is shameful and inhuman to treat men like chattels to make money by, or to look upon them merely as so much muscle or physical power. Thus, again, Religion teaches that, as among the workman's concerns are Religion herself and things spiritual and mental, the employer is bound to see that he has time for the duties of piety; that he be not exposed to corrupting influences and dangerous occasions; and that he be not led away to neglect his home and family or to squander his wages. Then, again, the employer must never tax his work people beyond their strength, nor employ them in work unsuited to their sex or age. His great and principal obligation is to give every one that which is just.

F. S. Nitti, Catholic Socialism, *trans. by Mary Mackintosh (London: S. Sonnenschein, 1895), p. 409.*

The emphasis of Pius X, who reigned from 1903 to 1914 and who has been proclaimed a saint, was intellectually reactionary. He hoped to restore traditional devotional life. Between 1903 and 1907 he condemned Catholic Modernism, a movement of modern biblical criticism within the Church, and in 1910 he required an anti-Modernist oath from all priests. By these actions Pius X set the Church squarely against the intellectual currents of the day, and the struggle between Catholicism and modern thought continued. Although Pius X did not strongly support the social policy of Leo XIII, the Catholic church continued to permit its members active participation in social and political movements.

Toward a Twentieth-Century Frame of Mind

World War I is often regarded as the point of departure into the contemporary world. Although this view is possibly true when applied to political and social developments, it is an incorrect assessment of intellectual history. The last quarter of the nineteenth century and the first decade of the twentieth century constituted the crucible of contemporary Western and European thought. During this period the kind of fundamental reassessment that Darwin's work had previously made necessary in biology and in understanding the place of human beings in nature became writ large in other areas of thinking. Philosophers, scientists, psychologists, and artists began to portray physical reality, human nature, and human society in ways quite different from those of the past. Their new concepts challenged the major presuppositions of mid-nineteenth-century science, rationalism, liberalism, and bourgeois morality.

Science: The Revolution in Physics

The modifications in the scientific world view originated within the scientific community itself. By the late 1870s considerable discontent existed over the excessive realism of mid-century science. It was thought that many scientists believed that their mechanistic models, solid atoms, and absolute time and space actually described the real universe.

In 1883 Ernst Mach (1838–1916) published *The Science of Mechanics*, in which he urged that the concepts of science be considered descriptive not of the physical world but of the sensations experienced by the scientific observer. Science could describe only the sensations, not the physical world that underlay the sensations. In line with Mach, the French scientist and mathematician Henri Poincaré (1854–1912) urged that the concepts and theories of scientists be regarded as hypothetical constructs of the human mind rather than as descriptions of the true state of nature. In 1911 Hans Vaihinger (1852–1933) suggested that the concepts of science be considered "as if" descriptions of the physical world. By World War I few scientists believed any longer that they could portray the "truth" about physical reality. Rather, they saw themselves as recording the observations of instruments and as setting forth useful hypothetical or symbolic models of nature.

X RAYS AND RADIATION New discoveries in the laboratory paralleled the philosophical challenge to nineteenth-century science. With those discoveries the comfortable world of supposedly "complete" nineteenth-century physics vanished forever. In December 1895 Wilhelm Roentgen (1845–1923) published a paper on his discovery of X rays, a form of energy that penetrated various opaque materials. The publication of his paper was followed within a matter of months by major steps in the exploration of radioactivity.

In 1896 Henri Becquerel (1852–1908), through a series of experiments following on Roentgen's work, found that uranium emitted a similar form of energy. The next year J. J. Thomson (1856–1940), working in the Cavendish Laboratory of Cambridge University, formulated the theory of the electron. The interior world of the atom had become a new area for human exploration. In 1902 Ernest Rutherford (1871–1937), who had been Thomson's assistant, explained the cause of radiation through the disintegration of the atoms of radioactive materials. Shortly thereafter he speculated on the immense store of energy present in the atom.

THEORIES OF QUANTUM ENERGY, RELATIVITY, AND UNCERTAINTY The discovery of radioactivity and discontent with the existing mechanical models led to revolutionary theories in physics. In 1900 Max Planck (1858–1947) pioneered the articulation of the quantum theory of energy, according to which energy is a series of discrete quantities or packets rather than a continuous stream. In 1905 Albert Einstein (1879–1955) published his first epoch-making papers on relativity. He contended that time and space exist not separately but rather as a combined continuum. Moreover, the measurement of space and time depend on the observer as well as on the entities being measured.

In 1927 Werner Heisenberg (1901–1976) set forth the uncertainty principle, according to which the behavior of subatomic particles is a matter of statistical probability rather than of exactly determinable cause and effect. So much that only fifty years earlier had seemed certain and unquestionable about the physical universe had now once again become problematical.

TWO CULTURES Nineteenth-century popularizers of science had urged its importance as a path to rational living and decision-making. By the early twentieth century the developments in the scientific world itself had dashed such optimistic hopes. The mathematical complexity of twentieth-century physics meant that despite valiant efforts science would rarely again be successfully popularized. However, at the same time, through applied technology and further research in physics and medicine, science affected daily living more than ever before in human history. Consequently, nonscientists in legal, business, and public life have been called on to make decisions involving technological matters that

The German physicist Albert Einstein's (1879–1955) theory of relativity, published in 1905, set the fundamental theory of physics in a new direction. [Brundy Library]

Marie (1869–1934) and Pierre Curie (1859–1906) were two of the most important figures in the advance of physics and chemistry. Marie was born in Poland but worked in France for most of her life. She is credited with the discovery of radium, for which she was awarded the Nobel Prize in Chemistry in 1911. [Ullstein Bilderdienst]

they rarely can or do understand in depth or detail.

By the middle of this century some writers—such as the English essayist, novelist, and physicist C. P. Snow (1905–1980)—spoke of the emergence of "two cultures," one of the scientists and one of literary persons. The problem was establishing ways in which they could communicate meaningfully with each other to address the major problems of human life.

Literature:
Realism and Naturalism

Between 1850 and 1914 the moral certainties of learned and middle-class Europeans underwent modifications no less radical than their concepts of the physical universe. The realist movement in literature portrayed the hypocrisy, the physical and psychic brutality, and the dullness that underlay bourgeois life and society. The realist and naturalist writers brought scientific objectivity and observation to their work. By using the mid-century cult of science so vital to the middle class, they confronted them with the harsh realities of life

Émile Zola (1840–1902) of France was the master of the realistic novel. [Bettmann Archive]

around them. Realism was a rejection of the Romantic idealization of nature, the poor, love, and polite society. Realist novelists portrayed the dark, degraded, and dirty side of life almost, so some people thought, for its own sake.

An earlier generation of writers, including Charles Dickens (1812–1870) and Honoré de Balzac (1799–1850), had portrayed the cruelty of industrial life and of a society based wholly on money. Other authors, such as George Eliot (born Mariann Evans) (1819–1880), had paid close attention to the details of the scenes and the characters portrayed. However, there had always been room in their works for play of the imagination, fancy, and artistry. They had felt a better moral world possible.

The major figures of late-century realism examined the dreary and unseemly side of life without being certain whether a better life was possible. In good Darwinian fashion they regarded and portrayed human beings as animals, subject to the passions, the materialistic determinism, and the pressures of the environment like any other animals. However, most of them also saw society itself as perpetuating evil.

FLAUBERT AND ZOLA Gustave Flaubert's (1821–1880) *Madame Bovary* (1856), with its story of colorless provincial life and a woman's hapless search for love inside and out of marriage, is often considered the first genuinely realistic novel. It portrayed life without heroism, purpose, or even simple civility.

The author who turned realism into a movement was Émile Zola (1840–1902). He found artistic inspiration in Claude Bernard's (1813–1878) *An Introduction to the Study of Experimental Medicine* (1865). Zola argued that he could write an experimental novel in which the characters and their actions would be observed and reported as the scientist might relate events within a laboratory experiment. He once declared, "I have simply done on living bodies the work of analysis which surgeons perform on corpses."[3] He believed that absolute physical and psychological determinism ruled human events in the same manner as

---

[3] *Quoted in George J. Becker,* Documents of Modern Literary Realism *(Princeton, NJ: Princeton University Press, 1963), p. 159.*

determinism prevailed in the physical world.

Between 1871 and 1893 Zola published twenty volumes of novels exploring subjects normally untouched by writers. In *L'Assommoir* (1877) he discussed the problem of alcoholism, and in *Nana* (1880) he followed the life of a prostitute. Others of his works considered the defeat of the French army and the social strife arising from attempts at labor organization. Zola refused to turn his pen or his readers' thoughts from the most ugly aspects of life. Nothing in his purview received the light of hope or the aura of romance. Although polite critics faulted his taste and middle-class moralists his subject matter, Zola enjoyed a wide following in France and elsewhere. As noted in Chapter 23, he took a leading role in the public defense of Captain Dreyfus.

IBSEN AND SHAW The Norwegian playwright Henrik Ibsen (1828–1906) carried realism into the dramatic presentation of domestic life. He sought to achieve new modes of social awareness and to strip away the illusory mask of middle-class morality. His most famous play is *A Doll's House* (1879). Its chief character, Nora, is the spouse of a narrow-minded middle-class husband who cannot tolerate any independence of character or thought on her part. When for the first time she fully confronts this situation, the play ends as she leaves him, slamming the door behind her. In *Ghosts* (1881) a respectable middle-class woman must deal with a son suffering from syphilis inherited from her husband. In *The Master Builder* (1892) an aging architect kills himself while trying to impress a young woman who perhaps loves him. Ibsen's works were extremely controversial. He had dared to strike at sentimentality in life, the female "angel of the house," and the cloak of respectability that hung so insecurely over the middle-class family.

One of Ibsen's greatest champions was the Irish writer George Bernard Shaw (1856–1950), who spent most of his life in England. During the late 1880s he had vigorously defended Ibsen's work. He went on to make his own realistic onslaught against Romanticism and false respectability. In *Mrs. Warren's Profession* (1893), a play long censored in England, he explored the matter of prostitution. In *Arms and the Man* (1894) and *Man and Superman* (1903)

he heaped scorn on the Romantic ideals of love and war, and in *Androcles and the Lion* (1913) he pilloried Christianity. Shaw added to the impact of his plays by writing long critical prefaces, in which he drove home the point of his social criticism.

TOLSTOY AND HARDY Realism struck the public ego in another fashion besides presenting unseemly social situations. The realists tended to see humankind as subject, and often helplessly so, to great physical or historical forces of determinism. Throughout *War and Peace* (1869) Leo Tolstoy (1828–1910) pictured his characters as being tossed on the seas of historical change. The characters of Thomas Hardy's (1840–1928) novels are repeatedly challenged by curious turns of fate. These writers felt that human beings in such settings could not control their lives and lacked the freedom to make conscious, meaningful moral

Henrik Ibsen's plays challenged middle-class values in one area of life after another. He particularly questioned the values surrounding marriage and the family. [Bildarchiv Preussischer Kulturbesitz]

choices. Their characters possess little or no nobility because the artists who created them had ceased to believe that human beings stood just a little lower than the angels or were creatures fully capable of rational behavior.

These realist writers and many others believed it the duty of the artist to portray reality and the commonplace. In dissecting what they considered the "real" world, they helped to change the moral perception of the good life. They refused to let existing public opinion dictate the subjects about which they wrote or the manner in which they treated them. By presenting their audiences with unmentionable subjects, they sought to remove the veneer of hypocrisy that had previously forbidden such discussion. They hoped to destroy social and moral illusions and to compel the public to confront reality. That change in itself seemed good. However, few of the realist writers who raised the problems had solutions. They often left their readers unable to sustain old values and uncertain about the sources of new ones.

Philosophy:
Revolt against Reason

Within philosophical circles the adequacy of rational thinking to address the human situation was being questioned.

FRIEDRICH NIETZSCHE No late-nineteenth-century writer better exemplified this new attitude than the German philosopher Friedrich Nietzsche (1844–1900), who had been educated as a classical philologist rather than as an academic philosopher. His books remained unpopular until late in his life, when his brilliance had deteriorated into an almost totally silent insanity. He was a person wholly at odds with the predominant values of the age. At one time or another he attacked Christianity, democracy, nationalism, rationality, science, and progress. He sought less to change values than to probe the very sources of values in the human mind and character. He wanted not only to tear away the masks of respectable life but also to explore the ways in which human beings made such masks.

His first important work was *The Birth of Tragedy* (1872), in which he urged that the nonrational aspects of human nature were as important and noble as the rational characteristics. Here and elsewhere he insisted on the positive function of instinct and ecstasy in human life. To limit human activity to strictly

Friedrich Nietzsche (1844–1900) was the most influential German philosopher of the late nineteenth century. His books challenged existing morality and values. He has exerted a vast influence on twentieth-century literature and philosophy. [New York Public Library Picture Collection]

rational behavior was to impoverish human life and experience. In this work Nietzsche regarded Socrates as one of the major contributors to Western decadence because of the Greek philosopher's appeal for rationality in human affairs. In Nietzsche's view the strength for the heroic life and the highest artistic achievement arose from sources beyond rationality.

In later works, such as the prose poem *Thus Spake Zarathustra* (1883), Nietzsche criticized democracy and Christianity. Both would lead only to the mediocrity of sheepish masses. He announced the death of God and proclaimed the coming of the Overman (*Übermensch*), who would embody heroism and greatness. This latter term was frequently interpreted as some mode of superman or super race, but such was not Nietzsche's intention. He was highly critical of contemporary racism and anti-Semitism. What he sought was a return to the heroism that he associated with Greek life in the Homeric age. He thought that the values of Christianity and of bourgeois morality prevented humankind from achieving life on a heroic level. Those moralities forbade too much of human nature from fulfilling and expressing itself.

Two of Nietzsche's most profound works are *Beyond Good and Evil* (1886) and *The Genealogy of Morals* (1887). Both are difficult books. Much of the former is written in brief, ambiguous aphorisms. Nietzsche sought to discover not what is good and what is evil but the social and psychological sources of the judgment of good and evil. He declared, "There are no moral phenomena at all, but only a moral interpretation of phenomena."[4] He dared to raise the question of whether morality itself was valuable: "We need a critique of moral values; the value of these values themselves must first be called in question."[5] In Nietzsche's view morality was a human convention that had no independent existence apart from humankind. For Nietzsche this discovery did not condemn morality but liberated human beings to create life-affirming instead of life-denying values. Christianity, utilitarianism, and middle-class respectability could, in good conscience, be abandoned. Human beings could, if they so willed, create a new moral order for themselves that would glorify pride, assertiveness, and strength rather than meekness, humility, and weakness.

What Nietzsche said about morality was indicative of what other philosophers were saying about similar subjects. There was a growing tendency to see all conceptual categories as useful creations rather than exact descriptions.

JAMES AND BERGSON The American philosopher William James (1842–1910) was one of the most influential figures to question the adequacy of nineteenth-century rationalism and science. He and his philosophy of pragmatism were very influential in Europe. James suggested that the truth of an idea or a description depended primarily on how well it worked. Knowledge was less an instrument for knowing than for acting.

The most important European philosopher to pursue such lines of thought was the Frenchman Henri Bergson (1859–1941). His most significant works were *Time and Free Will* (1889), *Creative Evolution* (1907), and *Two Sources of Morality and Religion* (1932). Bergson glorified instinct, will, and subjectivism. He regarded human beings as living in a world of becoming, where the only certain thing was their sense of themselves. The world was permeated with a great vital force in which all things participated to a greater or lesser degree. The evolutionary nature of the universe meant that both the knower and the object of knowledge were constantly changing. What Bergson did was to set down much of the thought of earlier mystics in the language of evolutionary science.

In their appeal to the feelings and the emotions and in their questioning of the adequacy of rationalism, these writers drew on the Romantic tradition. The kind of creative impulse that earlier Romantics had considered the gift of artists, these later writers saw as the burden of all human beings. The character of the human situation that these philosophers urged on their contemporaries was that of an ever-changing flux in which little or nothing but change itself was permanent. Human beings had to forge from their own inner will and determination the truth and values that were to exist in the world. These philosophies threw into doubt not only the rigid domestic and reli-

---

[4] *Walter Kaufman (Ed. and trans.), The Basic Writings of Nietzsche (New York: The Modern Library, 1968), p. 275.*
[5] *Kaufman, p. 456.*

gious morality of the nineteenth century but also the values of toleration, cosmopolitanism, and benevolence that had been championed during the Enlightenment.

The Birth of Psychoanalysis

A determination to probe beneath surface or public appearances united the major figures of late-nineteenth-century science, art, and philosophy. They sought to discern the various undercurrents, tensions, and complexities that lay beneath the smooth, calm surfaces of hard atoms, respectable families, rationality, and social relationships. Their theories and discoveries meant that articulate, educated Europe-

ans could never again view the surface of life with smugness or complacency or even much confidence. No single intellectual development more clearly and stunningly exemplified this trend than the emergence of psychoanalysis through the work of Sigmund Freud.

DEVELOPMENT OF FREUD'S EARLY THEORIES Freud was born in 1856 into an Austrian Jewish family that shortly thereafter settled in Vienna. He originally planned to become a lawyer but soon moved to the study of physiology and then to medicine. In 1886 he opened his medical practice in Vienna, where he continued to live until driven out by the Nazis in 1938, a year before his death. All of Freud's research and writing was done from the base of his medical practice. His earliest medical interests had been psychic disorders, to which he sought to apply the critical method of science. In late 1885 he had studied for a few months in Paris with Jean-Martin Charcot, who used hypnosis to treat cases of hysteria. In Vienna he collaborated with another physician, Josef Breuer (1842–1925), and in 1895 they published *Studies in Hysteria*.

In the mid-1890s Freud changed the technique of his investigations. He abandoned hypnosis and allowed his patients to talk freely and spontaneously about themselves. Repeatedly he found that they associated their particular neurotic symptoms with experiences related to earlier experiences, going back to childhood. He also noticed that sexual matters were significant in his patients' problems. For a time he thought that perhaps some sexual incident during childhood accounted for the illness of his patients.

However, by 1897 he had privately rejected this theory. In its place he formulated a theory of infantile sexuality, according to which sexual drives and energy exist in infants and do not simply emerge at puberty. In Freud's view human beings are creatures of sexuality from birth through adulthood. He thus questioned in the most radical manner the concept of childhood innocence. He also portrayed the little-discussed or little-acknowledged matter

Sigmund Freud (1856–1939) was photographed in his Vienna office in 1914. Freud revolutionized the concept of human nature in Western thought. After Freud it was no longer possible to see reason as the sole determinant of behavior. [Ullstein Bilderdienst]

Freud Explains an Obstacle to the Acceptance of Psychoanalysis

In addition to spawning numerous divergent views, the radical nature of Freud's theories caused them to be heard with misunderstanding, scorn, and opposition. In this 1915 passage, Freud was at pains to give a rational explanation for the nonrational popular reaction to his work. He contended that civilization had been built largely through channeling sexual energies into nonsexual activity. For him, psychoanalysis revealed this important role of the sexual impulses. By so revealing them, psychoanalysis tended to make people uncomfortable. Consequently, public opinion played down the discoveries of psychoanalysis by claiming it was either dangerous or immoral.

We believe that civilization has been built up, under the pressure of the struggle for existence, by sacrifices in gratification of the primitive impulses, and that it is to a great extent for ever being recreated, as each individual, successively joining the community, repeats the sacrifice of his instinctive pleasures for the common good. The sexual are among the most important of the instinctive forces thus utilized: they are in this way sublimated, that is to say, their energy is turned aside from its sexual goal and diverted towards other ends, no longer sexual and socially more valuable. But the structure thus built up is insecure, for the sexual impulses are with difficulty controlled; in each individual who takes up his part in the work of civilization there is a danger that a rebellion of the sexual impulses may occur, against this diversion of their energy. Society can conceive of no more powerful menace to its culture than would arise from the liberation of the sexual impulses and a return of them to their original goal. Therefore society dislikes this sensitive place in its development being touched upon; that the power of the sexual instinct should be recognized, and the significance of the individual's sexual life revealed, is very far from its interests; with a view to discipline it has rather taken the course of diverting attention away from this whole field. For this reason, the revelations of psychoanalysis are not tolerated by it, and it would greatly prefer to brand them as aesthetically offensive, morally reprehensible, or dangerous. . . . It is characteristic of human nature to be inclined to regard anything which is disagreeable as untrue, and then without much difficulty to find arguments against it.

Sigmund Freud, A General Introduction to Psychoanalysis, trans, by J. Riviere (Garden City, NY: Garden City Publishing Company, 1943), pp. 23–24.

of sex as one of the bases of mental order and disorder.

FREUD'S CONCERN WITH DREAMS
During the same decade Freud was also examining the psychic phenomena of dreams. Romantic writers had taken dreams very seriously, but most psychologists had not examined dreams scientifically. As a rational-ist Freud believed that there must exist a reasonable, scientific explanation for the irrational contents of dreams. That examination led him to a reconsideration of the general r ture of the human mind. He came to th clusion that when one dreamt; u wishes, desires, and drives that h cluded from everyday conscious life rience enjoyed relatively free play in ti

He argued, "The dream is the (disguised) fulfillment of a (suppressed, repressed) wish."[6] During the waking hours the mind repressed or censored those wishes, which were as important to one's psychological makeup as conscious thought. In fact, those unconscious drives and desires contributed to conscious behavior. Freud developed these concepts and related them to his idea of infantile sexuality in *The Interpretation of Dreams,* published in 1900. It was his most important book.

FREUD'S LATER THOUGHT In later books and essays Freud continued to urge the significance of the role played by the human unconscious. He portrayed a new internal organization of the mind. That inner realm was the arena for struggle and conflict among entities that he termed the *id,* the *ego,* and the *superego.* The id consisted of amoral, irrational, driving instincts for sexual gratification, aggression, and general physical and sensual pleasure. The superego constituted the external moral imperatives and expectations imposed on the personality by its society and culture. The ego stood as the mediator between the impulses of the id and the asceticism of the superego. The ego allowed the personality to cope with the inner and outer demands of its existence.

Consequently, everyday behavior displayed the activity of the personality as its inner drives were partially repressed through the ego's coping with the external moral expectations as interpreted by the superego. It has been a grave misreading of Freud to see him as urging humankind to thrust off all repression. He believed that excessive repression could lead to mental disorder but that a certain degree of repression of sexuality and aggression was necessary for civilized living and the survival of humankind.

Freud's work led to nothing less than a revolution in the understanding of human nature. As his views gained adherents just before and after World War I, new dimensions of human life became widely recognized. Human beings were seen as attaining rationality rather than merely exercising it. Civilization itself came to be regarded as a product of repressed or sublimated aggressions and sexual drive.

---

[6] *The Basic Writings of Sigmund Freud,* trans. by A. A. Brill (New York: The Modern Library, 1938), p. 235.

In Freud's appreciation of the role of instinct, will, dreams, and sexuality, his thought pertained to the Romantic tradition of the nineteenth century. However, Freud must stand as a son of the Enlightenment. Like the *philosophes* he was a realist who wanted human beings to live free of fear and illusions by rationally understanding themselves and their world. He saw the personalities of human beings as being determined by finite physical and mental forces in a finite world. He was hostile to religion and spoke of it as an illusion. Freud, like the writers of the eighteenth century, wished to see civilization and humane behavior prevail. However, more fully than those predecessors, he understood the immense sacrifice of instinctual drives required for civilized behavior. He understood how many previously unsuspected obstacles lay in the way of rationality. Freud believed that the sacrifice and struggle were worthwhile, but he was pessimistic about the future of civilization in the West.

DIVISIONS IN THE PSYCHOANALYTIC MOVEMENT Freud's work marked the beginning of the psychoanalytic movement. By 1910 he had gathered around him a small but highly able group of disciples. Several of his early followers soon moved toward theories of which the master disapproved. The most important of these dissenters was Carl Jung (1875–1961). He was a Swiss whom for many years Freud regarded as his most distinguished and promising student. Before World War I the two men had, however, come to a parting of the ways. Jung had begun to question the primacy of sexual drives in forming human personality and in contributing to mental disorder. He also put much less faith in the guiding light of reason.

Jung believed that the human subconscious contained inherited memories from previous generations of human beings. These collective memories, as well as the personal experience of an individual, constituted his or her soul. Jung regarded human beings in the twentieth century as alienated from these useful collective memories. One of his more famous books is entitled *Modern Man in Search of a Soul* (1933). Here and elsewhere Jung's thought tended toward mysticism and toward ascribing positive values to religion. Freud was highly critical of most of Jung's work. If Freud's thought derived primarily from the Enlightenment, Jung's was more dependent on Romanticism.

By the 1920s psychoanalysis had become even more fragmented as a movement. Nonetheless, in its several varieties, the movement touched not only psychology but also sociology, anthropology, religious studies, and literary theory. It has been one of the most important sets of ideas whereby intellectuals in the twentieth century have come to understand themselves and their civilization.

Retreat from Rationalism in Politics

Both nineteenth-century liberals and nineteenth-century socialists agreed that society and politics could be guided according to rational principles. Rational analysis could discern the problems of society and prepare solutions. They generally felt that once given the vote, individuals would behave in their rational political self-interest. Improvement of society and the human condition was possible through education. By the close of the century these views were under attack in both theory and practice. Political scientists and sociologists painted politics as frequently irrational. Racial theorists questioned whether rationality and education could affect human society at all.

WEBER During this period, however, one major social theorist stood profoundly impressed by the role of reason in human society. The German sociologist Max Weber (1864–1920) regarded the emergence of rationalism throughout society as the major development of human history. Such rationalization displayed itself in both the development of scientific knowledge and the rise of bureaucratic organization.

Weber saw bureaucratization as the most fundamental feature of modern social life. He used this view to oppose Marx's concept of the development of capitalism as the driving force in modern society. Bureaucratization involved the extreme division of labor as each individual began to fit himself or herself into a particular small role in much larger organizations. Furthermore, Weber believed that in modern society people derived their own self-images

Max Weber (1864–1920) considered bureaucratization as the most fundamental feature of modern social life. In contrast to Marx and Freud, Weber stressed the role of the individual and of rationality in human affairs. [German Information Center]

and sense of personal worth from their position in these organizations.

Weber also contended—again, in contrast to Marx—that noneconomic factors might account for major developments in human history. For example, in his most famous essay, *The Protestant Ethic and the Spirit of Capitalism* (1905), Weber traced much of the rational character of capitalist enterprise to the ascetic religious doctrines of Puritanism. The Puritans, in his opinion, had accumulated wealth and worked for worldly success less for its own sake than to furnish themselves the assurance that they stood among the elect of God.

THEORISTS OF COLLECTIVE BEHAVIOR In his emphasis on the individual and on the dominant role of rationality, Weber differed from many contemporary social scientists, such as Gustave LeBon, Émile Durkheim, and Georges Sorel in France; Vilfredo Pareto in Italy; and Graham Wallas in England. LeBon (1841–1931) was a psychologist who explored the activity of crowds and mobs. He believed that in crowd situations rational behavior was abandoned. Sorel (1847–1922) argued in *Reflections on Violence* (1908) that people did not pursue rationally perceived goals but were led to action by collectively shared ideals. Durkheim (1858–1917) and Wallas (1858–1932) became deeply interested in the necessity of shared values and activities in a society. These elements, rather than a logical analysis of the social situation, bound human beings together. Instinct, habit, and affections instead of reason directed human social behavior. Besides playing down the function of reason in society, all of these theorists emphasized the role of collective groups in politics rather than that of the individual formerly championed by liberals.

Racism

The same tendencies to question or even to deny the constructive activity of reason in human affairs and to sacrifice the individual to the group manifested themselves in theories of race. Racial thinking had long existed in Europe. Renaissance explorers had displayed considerable prejudice against nonwhite peoples. Since at least the eighteenth century, biologists and anthropologists had classified human beings according to the color of their skin, their language, and their stage of civilization.

Late-eighteenth-century linguistic scholars had observed similarities between many of the European languages and Sanskrit. They then postulated the existence of an ancient race called the *Aryans*, who had spoken the original language from which the rest derived. During the Romantic period writers had called the different cultures of Europe *races*.

The debates over slavery in the European colonies and the United States had given further opportunity for the development of racial theory. However, in the late nineteenth century the concept of race emerged as a single dominant explanation of the history and the character of large groups of people.

GOBINEAU Arthur de Gobineau (1816–1882), a reactionary French diplomat, enunciated the first important theory of race as the major determinant of human history. In his four-volume *Essay on the Inequality of the Human Races* (1853–1854), Gobineau portrayed the troubles of Western civilization as being the result of the long degeneration of the original white Aryan race. He claimed it had unwisely intermarried with the inferior yellow and black races, thus diluting the qualities of greatness and ability that originally existed in its blood. Gobineau was deeply pessimistic because he saw no way to reverse the degeneration that had taken place.

Gobineau's essay remained relatively obscure for many years. In the meantime a growing literature by anthropologists and explorers helped to spread racial thinking. In the wake of Darwin's theory, the concept of survival of the fittest was applied to races and nations. The recognition of the animal nature of humankind made the racial idea all the more persuasive.

CHAMBERLAIN At the close of the century Houston Stewart Chamberlain (1855–1927), an Englishman who settled in Germany, drew together these strands of racial thought into the two volumes of his *Foundations of the Nineteenth Century* (1899). He championed the concept of biological determinism through race, but he was somewhat more optimistic than Gobineau. Chamberlain believed that through genetics the human race could be improved and even that a superior race could be developed.

Chamberlain added another element. He

H. S. Chamberlain Exalts the Role of Race

Houston Stewart Chamberlain's Foundations of the Nineteenth Century (1899) *was one of the most influential works of the day to argue for the primary role of race in history. Chamberlain believed that most people in the world were racially mixed and that this mixture weakened those human characteristics most needed for physical and moral strength. However, as demonstrated in the passage below, he also believed that those persons who were assured of their racial purity could act with the most extreme self-confidence and arrogance. Chamberlain's views had a major influence on the Nazi Party in Germany and on others who wished to prove their alleged racial superiority for political purposes.*

Nothing is so convincing as the consciousness of the possession of Race. The man who belongs to a distinct, pure race, never loses the sense of it. The guardian angel of his lineage is ever at his side, supporting him where he loses his foothold, warning him like the Socratic Daemon where he is in danger of going astray, compelling obedience, and forcing him to undertakings which, deeming them impossible, he would never have dared to attempt. Weak and erring like all that is human, a man of this stamp recognises himself, as others recognise him, by the sureness of his character, and by the fact that his actions are marked by a certain simple and peculiar greatness, which finds its explanation in his distinctly typical and super-personal qualities. Race lifts a man above himself; it endows him with extraordinary—I might almost say supernatural—powers, so entirely does it distinguish him from the individual who springs from the chaotic jumble of peoples drawn from all parts of the world: and should this man of pure origin be perchance gifted above his fellows, then the fact of Race strengthens and elevates him on every hand, and he becomes a genius towering over the rest of mankind, not because he has been thrown upon the earth like a flaming meteor by a freak of nature, but because he soars heavenward like some strong and stately tree, nourished by thousands and thousands of roots—no solitary individual, but the living sum of untold souls striving for the same goal.

Houston Stewart Chamberlain, Foundations of the Nineteenth Century, *Vol. 1, trans. by John Lees (London: John Lane, 1912), p. 269.*

pointed to the Jews as the major enemy of European racial regeneration. Chamberlain's book and the lesser works on which it drew aided the spread of anti-Semitism in European political life. Also in Germany the writings of Paul de Lagarde and Julius Langbehn emphasized the supposed racial and cultural dangers posed by the Jews to traditional German national life.

LATE-CENTURY NATIONALISM Racial thinking was one part of a wider late-century movement toward more aggressive nationalism. Previously, nationalism had been a movement among European literary figures and liberals. The former had sought to develop what they regarded as the historically distinct qualities of particular national or ethnic literatures. The liberal nationalists had hoped to redraw the map of Europe to reflect ethnic boundaries. The drive for the unification of Italy and Germany had been major causes, as had been the liberation of Poland from foreign domination. The various national groups of the Habsburg Empire had also sought emancipation from Austrian domination.

From the 1870s onward, however, nationalism became a movement with mass support, well-financed organizations, and political parties. Nationalists tended to redefine nationality in terms of race and blood. The new nationalism opposed the internationalism of both liberalism and socialism. The ideal of nationality was used to overcome the pluralism of class, religion, and geography. The nation and its duties replaced religion in the lives of many secularized people. It sometimes became a secular religion in the hands of state schoolteachers, who were replacing the clergy as the instructors of youth. Nationalism of this aggressive racist variety would prove to be the most powerful ideology of the early twentieth century.

Anti-Semitism and the Birth of Zionism

Political and racial anti-Semitism, which have cast such dark shadows across the twentieth century, emerged in part from this atmosphere of racial thought and the retreat from rationality in politics. Religious anti-Semitism dated from at least the Middle Ages. Since the French Revolution, west European Jews had gradually gained entry into the civil life of Britain, France, and Germany. Popular anti-Semitism continued to exist as the Jewish community was identified with money and banking interests. During the last third of the century, as finance capitalism changed the economic structure of Europe, people pressured by the changes became hostile toward the Jewish community. This was especially true of the socially and economically insecure lower middle class.

ANTI-SEMITIC POLITICS In Vienna Mayor Karl Lueger (1844–1910) used such anti-Semitism as a major attraction to his successful Christian Socialist Party. In Germany the ultraconservative Lutheran chaplain Adolf Stoecker (1835–1909) revived anti-Semitism. The Dreyfus affair in France allowed a new flowering of hatred toward the Jews.

To this already ugly atmosphere, racial thought contributed the belief that no matter to what extent Jews assimilated themselves and their families into the culture of their country, their Jewishness—and thus their alleged danger to the society—would remain. The problem of race was not in the character but in the blood of the Jew. An important Jewish response to this new, rabid outbreak of anti-Semitism was the launching in 1896 of the Zionist movement to found a separate Jewish state. Its founder was the Austro-Hungarian Theodor Herzl (1860–1904).

HERZL'S RESPONSE Herzl was influenced by the conviction in 1894 of Captain Dreyfus in France and the election of Karl Lueger in 1895 as mayor of Vienna, as well as his personal experience of discrimination. He

Theodor Herzl (1860–1904), on a visit to Palestine in 1898. Herzl's vision of a Jewish state would eventually lead to the creation of Israel in 1948. [Bildarchiv Preussischer Kulturbesitz]

was convinced that liberal politics and the institutions of the liberal state could not protect the Jews in Europe or ensure that they would be treated justly. In 1896 Herzl published *The Jewish State,* in which he called for the organization of a separate state in which the Jews of

Herzl Calls for the Establishment of a Jewish State

In 1896 Theodor Herzl published his pamphlet entitled The Jewish State. *Herzl had lived in France during the turmoil and anti-Semitism associated with the Dreyfus Affair. He became convinced that only the establishment of a separate state for the Jewish people would bring a halt to the various outbreaks of anti-Semitism that characterized late-nineteenth-century European political and cultural life. Following the publication of this pamphlet, Herzl began to organize the Zionist movement among Jews in both eastern and western Europe.*

The idea which I develop in this pamphlet is an age-old one: the establishment of a Jewish State.

The world resounds with outcries against the Jews, and this is what awakens the dormant idea.

. . . .

I believe I understand anti-Semitism, a highly complex movement. I view it from the standpoint of a Jew, but without hatred or fear. I think I can discern in it the elements of vulgar sport, of common economic rivalry, of inherited prejudice, of religious intolerance—but also of a supposed need for self-defense. To my mind, the Jewish Question is neither a social nor a religious one, even though it may assume these and other guises. It is a national question, and to solve it we must first of all establish it as an international political problem which will have to be settled by the civilized nations of the world in council.

We are a people, *one* people.

Every where we have sincerely endeavored to merge with the national communities surrounding us and to preserve only the faith of our fathers. We are not permitted to do so. . . .

. . . .

And will some people say that the venture is hopeless, because even if we obtain the land and the sovereignty only the poor people will go along? They are the very ones we need first! Only desperate men make good conquerors.

Will anybody say, Oh yes, if it were possible it would have been done by now?

It was not possible before. It is possible now. As recently as a hundred, even fifty years ago it would have been a dream. Today it is all real. The rich, who have an epicurean acquaintance with all technical advance, know very well what can be done with money. And this is how it will be: Precisely the poor and plain people, who have no idea of the power that man already exercises over the forces of Nature, will have the greatest faith in the new message. For they have never lost their hope of the Promised Land.

. . . .

Now, all this may seem to be a long-drawn-out affair. Even in the most favorable circumstances it might be many years before the founding of the State is under way. In the meantime, Jews will be ridiculed, offended, abused, whipped, plundered, and slain in a thousand different localities. But no; just as soon as we begin to implement the plan, anti-Semitism will immediately grind to a halt everywhere. . . .

Theodor Herzl, The Jewish State *(New York: The Herzl Press, 1970), pp. 27, 33, 109 as quoted in William W. Hallo, David B. Ruderman, and Michael Stanislawski (Eds.),* Heritage: Civilization and the Jews Source Reader *(New York: Praeger, 1984), pp. 234–235.*

the world might be assured of those rights and liberties that they should be enjoying in the liberal states of Europe. Furthermore, Herzl followed the tactics of late-century mass democratic politics by particularly directing his appeal to the economically poor Jews who lived in the ghettos of eastern Europe and the slums of western Europe. The original call to Zionism thus combined a rejection of the anti-Semitism of Europe and a desire to establish some of the ideals of both liberalism and socialism in a state outside Europe.

By the opening of the twentieth century, European thought had achieved contours that seem familiar to us today. The study of science had led to virtually revolutionary changes in thinking about both biological and physical nature. Physicists had transformed the traditional views of matter and energy as they probed the mysteries of the atom. Through research in evolutionary biology human beings had come to be viewed as an essential part of the natural order and not as something distinct from it. In the minds of some writers science was expected to provide human beings with a basis for new ethical knowledge and moral values. Christianity had experienced the strongest challenge in modern times. In part this was a result of the strong new role for science but also because of other intellectual changes arising from the study of history and philosophy and the goals of the rulers of secular national states.

Simultaneous with this struggle between religion and science, there arose a tendency among certain major nonreligious thinkers and writers to question the primacy of reason. Nietzsche and Freud in their different ways questioned whether human beings were primarily creatures of reason. Weber and other social and political theorists doubted that politics could be entirely rational. All of these developments challenged the rational values associated with the Enlightenment. The racial theorists questioned whether mind and character were as important as alleged racial characteristics carried in the blood.

Racial thinking also allowed Europeans to believe that they were in some manner inherently superior to other peoples and cultures in the world. In both Europe and in the United States persons of color and other ethnic minority groups were regarded as inferior. Such racial thinking fostered racial anti-Semitism in Europe and racial discrimination against other ethnic minority groups. Similar racial attitudes also informed the minds of virtually all the colonial administrators of the European imperial powers.

Suggested Readings

J. L. ALTHOLZ, *The Churches in the Nineteenth Century* (1967). A useful overview.

R. ARON, *Main Currents in Sociological Thought*, 2 vols. (1965, 1967). An introduction to the founders of the science.

S. AVINERI, *The Making of Modern Zionism: The Intellectual Origins of the Jewish State* (1981). An excellent introduction to the development of Zionist thought.

S. BARROWS, *Distorting Mirrors: Visions of the Crowd in Late Nineteenth-Century France* (1981). An important and imaginative examination of crowd psychology as it related to social tension in France.

F. L. BAUMER, *Religion and the Rise of Scepticism* (1960). Traces the development of religious doubt from the seventeenth to the twentieth centuries.

F. L. BAUMER, *Modern European Thought: Continuity and Change in Ideas, 1600–1950* (1977). The best work on the subject for this period.

M. D. BIDDIS, *Father of Racist Ideology: The Social and Political Thought of Count Gobineau* (1970). Sets the subject in the more general context of nineteenth-century thought.

P. BOWLER, *The Eclipse of Darwinism: Anti-Darwinian Evolution Theories in the Decades Around 1900* (1983). A major study of the fate of Darwinian theory in the nineteenth-century scientific community.

P. BOWLER, *Evolution: The History of an Idea* (1989). An outstanding survey of the subject.

O. CHADWICK, *The Secularization of the European Mind in the Nineteenth Century* (1975). The best treatment available.

D. G. CHARLTON, *Positivist Thought in France During the Second Empire, 1852–1870* (1959), and *Secular Religions in France, 1815–1870* (1963). Two clear introductions to important subjects.

C. M. CIPOLLA, *Literacy and Development in the*

West (1969). Traces the explosion of literacy in the past two centuries.

A. DANTO, *Nietzsche as Philosopher* (1965). A very helpful and well-organized introduction.

P. GAY, *Freud: A Life for Our Time* (1988). The new standard biography.

C. C. GILLISPIE, *The Edge of Objectivity* (1960). One of the best one-volume treatments of modern scientific ideas.

H. S. HUGHES, *Consciousness and Society: The Reorientation of European Social Thought, 1890–1930* (1958). A wide-ranging discussion of the revolt against positivism.

C. JUNGNICKEL AND R. MCCORMMACH, *Intellectual Mastery of Nature: Theoretical Physics from Ohm to Einstein*, 2 vols. (1986). A demanding but powerful exploration of the creation of modern physics.

J. KATZ, *From Prejudice to Destruction: Anti-Semitism, 1700–1933* (1980). An excellent and far-reaching analysis.

J. T. KLOPPENBERG, *Uncertain Victory: Social Democracy and Progressivism in European and American Thought* (1986). An extremely important comparative study.

W. LACQUER, *A History of Zionism* (1989). The most extensive one-volume treatment.

B. LIGHTMAN, *The Origins of Agnosticism: Victorian Unbelief and the Limits of Knowledge* (1987). The best study of the subject.

T. A. KSELMAN, *Miracles and Prophesies in Nineteenth-Century France* (1983). A study of popular religion.

E. MAYR, *The Growth of Biological Thought: Diversity, Evolution, and Inheritance* (1982). A major survey by a scientist of note.

W. J. MCGRATH, *Freud's Discovery of Psychoanalysis: The Politics of Hysteria* (1986). A study of the relationship of Freud's cultural and political background to his scientific thought.

J. MCMANNERS, *Church and State in France, 1870–1914* (1972). The standard treatment.

J. T. MERZ, *A History of European Thought in the Nineteenth Century*, 4 vols. (1897–1914). Still a useful mine of information.

J. MOORE, *The Post-Darwinian Controversies: A Study of the Protestant Struggle to Come to Terms with Darwin in Great Britain and America, 1870–1900* (1979). A major examination of the impact of Darwinian thought on both science and religion.

J. MORRELL AND A. THACKRAY, *Gentlemen of Science: Early Years of the British Association for the Advancement of Science* (1981). An important study that examines the role of science in early and mid-nineteenth-century Britain.

G. L. MOSSE, *Toward the Final Solution: A History of European Racism* (1978). A sound introduction.

R. PASCAL, *From Naturalism to Expressionism: German Literature and Society, 1880–1918* (1973). A helpful survey.

H. W. PAUL, *From Knowledge to Power: The Rise of the Science Empire in France, 1860–1939* (1985). An extensive survey of both scientific thought and institutions in France.

L. POLIAKOV, *The Aryan Myth: A History of Racist and Nationalist Ideas in Europe* (1971). The best introduction to the problem.

P. G. J. PULZER, *The Rise of Political Anti-Semitism in Germany and Austria* (rev. 1989). A sound discussion of anti-Semitism in the world of central European politics.

C. E. SCHORSKE, *Fin de Siècle Vienna: Politics and Culture* (1980). Major essays on the explosively creative intellectual climate of Vienna.

J. SPERBER, *Popular Catholicism in Nineteenth-Century Germany* (1984). A significant new study.

F. STERN, *The Politics of Cultural Despair: A Study in the Rise of the German Ideology* (1965). An important examination of antimodern and anti-Semitic thought in imperial Germany.

F. M. TURNER, *The Greek Heritage in Victorian Britain* (1981). An examination of the role of Greek antiquity in Victorian thought.

A. VIDLER, *The Church in an Age of Revolution* (1961). A sound account of the problems of Church and state in the nineteenth century.

J. P. VON ARX. *Progress and Pessimism: Religion, Politics, and History in Late Nineteenth Century Britain* (1985). A major study that casts much new light on the nineteenth-century view of progress.

C. WELCH, *Protestant Thought in the Nineteenth Century*, 2 vols. (1972, 1985). The most extensive recent study.

British Prime Minister Lloyd George, French Premier Georges Clemenceau,
and American President Woodrow Wilson led the victorious Allies
at the Paris Peace Conference in 1919 which set the terms
of peace after World War I. [The Bettmann Archive]

26

IMPERIALISM, ALLIANCES, AND WAR

During the second half of the nineteenth century, and especially after 1870, European influence and control over the rest of the world grew to an unprecedented degree. North and South America, as well as Australia and New Zealand, became almost integral parts of the European world as the great streams of European immigrants populated them. Until the nineteenth century Asia (with the significant exception of India) and most of Africa had gone their own ways, having little contact with Europe. But the latter part of that century brought the partition of Africa among a number of European nations. Europe also established economic and political power from the eastern to the western borders of Asia. By the next century this growth of European dominance had brought every part of the globe into a single world economy. Events in any corner of the world were significant thousands of miles away.

These developments might have been expected to bring greater prosperity and good fortune. Instead, they helped to foster competition and hostility among the great powers of Europe and to bring on a terrible war that undermined Europe's strength and its influence in the world. The peace settlement, proclaimed as "a peace without victors," brought disillusionment among idealists in the West. It treated Germany with something like the harshness the Germans had in mind if they had been victorious. At the same time, the new system failed to provide realistic and effective safeguards against a return to power of a vengeful Germany. The withdrawal of the United States from world affairs into a disdainful isolation destroyed the basis for keeping the peace on which the hopes of Britain and France relied. The frenzy for imperial expansion that seized Europeans in the late nineteenth century had played an important part in destroying Europe's peace and prosperity and its dominant place in the world.

Expansion of European Power and the "New Imperialism"

The explosive developments in nineteenth-century science, technology, industry, agriculture, transportation, communication, and military weapons provided the chief sources of European power. They made it possible for a small number of Europeans (or Americans) to impose their will on other peoples many times their number by force or by the threat of force. Institutional as well as material advantages allowed Westerners to have their way. The growth of national states that commanded the loyalty, service, and resources of their inhabitants to a degree previously unknown was a Western phenomenon. It permitted the European nations to deploy their resources in the most effective way.

The Europeans also possessed another, less tangible weapon: a sense of superiority of their civilization and way of life. This gave them a confidence that often took the form of an unpleasant arrogance and that fostered the expansionist mood.

The expansion of European influence was not anything new. Spain, Portugal, France, and Britain had controlled territories overseas for centuries, but by the mid-nineteenth century only Great Britain retained extensive holdings. The first half of the century was generally a period of hostility to colonial expansion. Even the British had been sobered by their loss of the American colonies. The French acquired Algeria and part of Indochina. The British made some additional gains in territories adjacent to their holdings in Canada, India, Australia, and New Zealand. For the most part, however, the doctrine of free trade was dominant, and it opposed the idea of political interference in other lands.

Britain ruled the waves and had great commercial advantages as a result of being first in the Industrial Revolution. Therefore, the British were usually content to let commerce go forward without annexations. Yet they were quite prepared to interfere forcefully if some "backward" country placed barriers in the way of their trade. Still, at mid-century, in Britain as elsewhere, opinion stood predominantly against further political or military involvement overseas.

In the last third of the century, however, the European states swiftly spread their control over perhaps 10 million square miles and 150 million people—about a fifth of the world's land area and a tenth of its population. The movement has been called the *New Imperialism.*

Queen Victoria (1837–1901) works on state papers in 1893. Note the Indian attendant. The Queen was also Empress of India. India was by far the most important possession in the British Empire. [National Portrait Gallery, London]

The New Imperialism

Imperialism is a word that has come to be used so loosely as almost to be deprived of meaning. It may be useful to offer a definition that might be widely accepted: "the policy of extending a nation's authority by territorial acquisition or by the establishment of economic and political hegemony over other nations."[1] That definition seems to apply equally well to human actions as far back as ancient Egypt and Mesopotamia and to the performance of European nations in the late nineteenth century. But there were some new elements in the latter case. Previous imperialisms had taken the form either of seizing land and settling it with the conqueror's people or of establishing trading centers to exploit the resources of the dominated area. The New Imperialism did not completely abandon these devices, but it also introduced new ones.

The usual pattern of the New Imperialism was for the European nation to invest capital in the "backward" country, to build productive enterprises and improved means of trans-

portation, to employ great numbers of natives in the process. Thereby they transformed the entire economy and culture of the dominated area. To guarantee their investments, the European states would make favorable arrangements with the local government either by enriching the rulers or by threatening them.

If these arrangements proved inadequate, the dominant power established different degrees of political control. Sometimes this meant full annexation as a colony to protectorate status, whereby the local ruler was controlled by the dominant European state and maintained by its military power. In other instances, it meant "spheres of influence" status, whereby the European state received special commercial and legal privileges without direct political involvement. During this period European expansion went forward with great speed and participation in this expansion came to be regarded as necessary to retaining status as a great power.

Motives for the New Imperialism: The Economic Interpretation

There has been considerable debate about the motives for the New Imperialism, and after

---

[1] *American Heritage Dictionary of the English Language* (New York: Houghton Mifflin, 1969), p. 660.

more than a century there is still no agreement on this issue. The most widespread interpretation has been economic, most typically in the form given by the English radical economist J. A. Hobson and later adapted by Lenin. As Lenin put it, "Imperialism is the monopoly stage of capitalism,"[2] the last stage of a dying capitalist system. According to this interpretation, competition inevitably leads to the elimination of inefficient capitalists and, therefore, to monopoly. Powerful industrial and financial capitalists soon run out of profitable areas of investment in their own countries and persuade their governments to gain colonies in "backward" countries. Here they can find higher profits from their investments, new markets for their products, and safe sources of the needed raw materials.

The facts of the matter do not support this viewpoint. The European powers did export considerable amounts of capital in the form of investments abroad, but not in such a manner as to fit the model of Hobson and Lenin. Britain, for example, made heavier investments abroad before 1875 than during the next two decades. Only a very small percentage of British and European investments overseas, moreover, went to the new colonial areas. Most went into Europe itself or into older, well-established areas like the United States, Canada, Australia, and New Zealand. Even when investments were made in the new areas, they were not necessarily put into colonies held by the investing country.

The facts are equally discouraging for those who emphasize the need for markets and raw materials. Colonies were not usually important markets for the great imperial nations, and all were forced to rely on areas that they did not control as sources of vital raw materials. It is not even clear that control of the new colonies was particularly profitable. Britain, to be sure, benefited greatly from its rule of India. It is also true that some European businessmen and politicians hoped to find a cure for the great depression of 1873–1896 in colonial expansion.

Nevertheless, as one of the leading students of the subject has said, "No one can determine whether the accounts of empire ultimately closed with a favorable cash balance."[3] That is true of the European imperial nations collectively, but it is certain that for some of them, like Italy and Germany, empire was a losing proposition. Some individuals and companies, of course, were able to make great profits from particular colonial ventures, but such people were able to influence national policy only occasionally. Economic motives certainly played a part, but a full understanding of the New Imperialism requires a search for further motives as well.

Cultural, Religious, and Social Interpretations

Advocates of imperialism put forth various justifications. Some argued that it was the responsibility of the advanced European nations to bring the benefits of their higher culture and superior civilization to the people of "backward" lands. Few people were influenced by such arrogant arguments, though many shared the intellectual assumptions. Religious groups argued for the responsibility of Western nations to bring the benefits of Christianity to the heathen with more extensive efforts and aid from their governments. Some politicians and diplomats argued for imperialism as a tool of social policy. In Germany, for instance, some people suggested that imperial expansion might serve to deflect public interest away from domestic politics and social reform. Yet Germany acquired only a few colonies, and such considerations played little if any role.

In Britain such arguments were made, as was their opposite. The statesman Joseph Chamberlain argued for the empire as a source of profit and economic security that would finance a great program of domestic reform and welfare. To the extent that they had any influence, these arguments were not important as motives for imperialism because they were made well after the British had acquired most of their empire. Another common and apparently plausible justification was that colonies would provide a good place to settle surplus population. In fact, most European emigrants

---

[2]V. I. Lenin, Imperialism, the Highest Stage of Capitalism (New York: International Publishers, 1939), p. 88.

[3]D. K. Fieldhouse, The Colonial Empires (New York: Delacorte, 1966), p. 393.

Kipling Advises the Americans: The Responsibility for Empire

The White Man's Burden 1899

(The United States and the
Philippine Islands)

Take up the White Man's burden—
  Send forth the best ye breed—
Go bind your sons to exile
  To serve your captives' need;
To wait in heavy harness
  On fluttered folk and wild—
Your new-caught, sullen peoples,
  Half devil and half child.

Take up the White Man's burden—
  The savage wars of peace—
Fill full the mouth of Famine
  And bid the sickness cease;
And when your goal is nearest
  The end for others sought,
Watch Sloth and heathen Folly
  Bring all your hope to nought.

Take up the White Man's burden—
  An reap his old reward:
The blame of those ye better,
  The hate of those ye guard—
The cry of hosts ye humour
  (Ah, slowly!) toward the light:—
"Why brought ye us from bondage,
  "Our loved Egyptian night?"

Take up the White Man's burden—
  In patience to abide,
To veil the threat of terror
  And check the show of pride;
By open speech and simple,
  An hundred times made plain,
To seek another's profit,
  And work another's gain.

Take up the White Man's burden—
  No tawdry rule of kings,
But toil of serf and sweeper—
  The tale of common things.
The ports ye shall not enter,
  The roads ye shall not tread,
Go make them with your living,
  And mark them with your dead!

Take up the White Man's burden—
  Ye dare not stoop to less—
Nor call too loud on Freedom
  To cloak your weariness;
By all ye cry or whisper,
  By all ye leave or do,
The silent, sullen peoples
  Shall weigh your Gods and you.

Take up the White Man's burden—
  Have done with childish days—
The lightly proffered laurel,
  The easy, ungrudged praise.
Comes now, to search your manhood
  Through all the thankless years,
Cold-edged with dear-bought wisdom,
  The judgment of your peers!

"The White Man's Burden (1899)," from Rudyard Kipling's Verse: Definitive Edition (New York: Doubleday, 1940) pp. 321–323.

went to areas not controlled by their countries, chiefly to North and South America and Australia.

Strategic and Political Interpretations: The Scramble for Africa

Strategic and political considerations seem to have been more important in bringing on the New Imperialism. The scramble for Africa in the 1880s is one example.

GREAT BRITAIN Britain was the only great power with extensive overseas holdings on the eve of the scramble. The completion of the Suez Canal in 1869 made Egypt an area of vital interest to the British because it sat astride the shortest route to India. Under Disraeli, Britain purchased a major, but not a controlling, interest in the canal in 1875. When

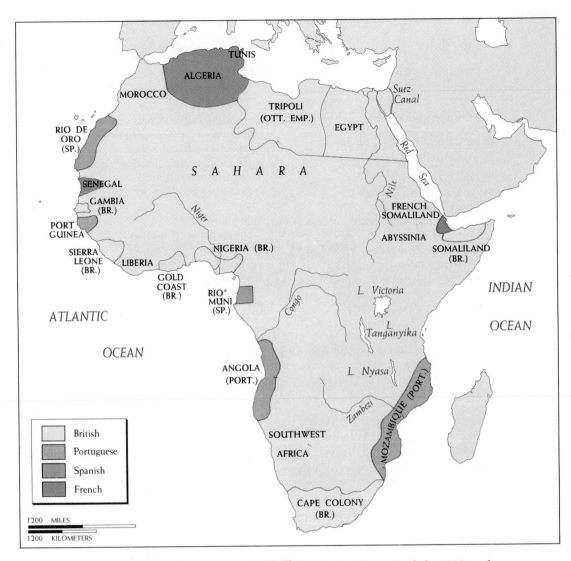

MAP 26-1 IMPERIAL EXPANSION IN AFRICA TO 1880 *Until the 1880s only a few European countries held colonies in Africa, mostly on its fringes.*

Egypt's stability was threatened by internal troubles in the 1880s, the British moved in and established a protectorate. Then, to protect Egypt, they advanced into the Sudan.

FRANCE AND SMALLER NATIONS
France became involved in Africa in 1830 by sending a naval expedition to Algeria to attack the pirates based there. Before long, French settlers arrived and established a colony. By 1882 France was in full control of Algeria. At about the same time, to prevent Tunisia from falling into Italy's hands, France took over that area of North Africa also.

Soon smaller states like Belgium, Portugal, Spain, and Italy were scrambling for African colonies. By the 1890s their intervention had compelled Britain to expand northward from the Cape of Good Hope into what is now Zimbabwe. Britain may have had significant strategic reasons for protecting the Suez and Cape routes to India, but France and the smaller European nations did not have such reasons. Their motives were political as well as economic, for they equated status as a great power (Britain stood as the chief model) with the possession of colonies. They therefore sought colonies as evidence of their own importance.

GERMANY Bismarck appears to have pursued an imperial policy, however brief, from coldly political motives. In 1884 and 1885 Ger-

Carl Peters Demands Colonies for Germany

Germany was a late arrival in the competition for colonies. The territories still available were neither profitable nor attractive for settlement by Europeans. Carl Peters (1856–1918) was one of the increasing number of Germans, who, nevertheless, were eager to acquire a colonial empire. He was the founder of German East Africa, now Tanzania. His arguments based on economic advantage and the prospects of German emigration proved to be absurd, but they provided a mask for less rational motives.

Manifesto of the Society for German Colonization April 1884

In the partition of the earth, as it has proceeded from the beginning of the fifteenth century up to our times, the German nation received nothing. All the remaining European culture-bearing peoples possess areas outside our continent where their languages and customs can take firm root and flourish. The moment that the German emigrant leaves the borders of the Reich behind him, he is a stranger sojourning on foreign soil. The German Reich, great in size and strength through its bloodily achieved unity, stands in the leading position among the continental European powers: her sons abroad must adapt themselves to nations which look upon us with either indifference or even hostility. For centuries the great stream of German emigration has been plunging down into foreign races where it is lost sight of. Germandom outside Europe has been undergoing a perpetual national decline.

This fact, so painful to national pride, also represents a great economic disadvantage for our *Volk*. Every year our Fatherland loses the capacity of approximately 200,000 Germans. The greatest amount of this capacity flows directly into the camp of our economic competitors and increases the strength of our rivals. Germany's imports of products from tropical zones originate in foreign settlements whereby many millions of German capital are lost every year to alien nations. German exports are dependent upon the discretion of foreign tariff policies. Our industry lacks an absolutely safe market for its goods because our *Volk* lacks colonies of its own.

The alleviation of this national grievance requires taking practical steps and strong action.

In recognition of this point of view, a society has been organized in Berlin with the goal of mobilizing itself for such steps and such action. The Society for German Colonization aims to undertake on its own, in a resolute and sweeping manner, carefully chosen colonization projects and thereby supplement the ranks of organizations with similar tendencies.

Its particular tasks will be:

1. to provide necessary sums of capital for colonization;
2. to seek out and lay claim to suitable districts for colonization;
3. to direct German emigrants to these regions.

Imbued as we are with the conviction that it is no longer permissible to hesitate in energetically mobilizing ourselves for this great national task, we venture to come before the German *Volk* with a plea for active support of the endeavors of our Society! The German nation has proven time and again its willingness to make sacrifices for general patriotic undertakings: may she also bring her full energies to play in the solution of this great historical task.

Every German whose heart beats for the greatness and the honor of our nation is entreated to come to the side of our Society. What is at stake is compensation for centuries of deprivation: to prove to the world that, along with the splendor of the Reich, the German *Volk* has inherited the old German national spirit of its forefathers!

Carl Peters, Die Grundung von Deutsch-Ostafrika [The Foundation of German East Africa], *Berlin*, 1906, *pp. 43–45. Trans. by Ralph A. Austen in* Modern Imperialism, *(Lexington, Mass.: D. C. Heath, 1969), pp. 62–63.*

This cartoon, "Cape to Cairo," by Lesley Sambourne appeared in Punch *in 1892. It shows Cecil Rhodes in British uniform astride the African continent. His dream of a railroad running through British colonies from South Africa to Egypt never came true. ["Cape to Cairo" by Sambourne. Publ. in* The Cartoon History of Britain *by Michael Wynn Jones. Photo by Elsa Peterson © 1990]*

many declared protectorates over Southwest Africa, Togoland, the Cameroons, and East Africa. None of these places was particularly valuable or of intrinsic strategic importance. Bismarck himself had no interest in overseas colonies and once compared them to fine furs worn by impoverished Polish nobles who had no shirts underneath. His concern lay in Germany's exposed position in Europe. On one occasion he said, "My map of Africa lies in Europe. Here is Russia, and there is France, and here in the middle are we. That is my map of Africa."[4] He acquired colonies chiefly to improve Germany's diplomatic position in Europe. He tried to turn France from hostility against Germany by diverting the French toward colonial interests. At the same time German colonies in Africa could be used as a subtle weapon with which to persuade the British to be reasonable.

The Irrational Element

Germany's annexations started a wild scramble by the other European powers to establish claims on what was left of Africa. By 1890 almost all of the continent was parceled out. Great powers and small expanded into areas neither profitable nor strategic for reasons less calculating and rational than Bismarck's. "Empire in the modern period," D. K. Fieldhouse observed, "was the product of European power: its reward was power or the sense of power."[5]

Such motives were not new. They had been well understood by the Athenian spokesman at Melos in 416 B.C., whose words were reported by Thucydides: "Of the gods we believe and of men we know clearly that by a necessity of their nature where they have the power they rule."[6]

In Asia the emergence of Japan as a great power in touch with the rest of the world frightened the other powers interested in China. The Russians were building a railroad across Siberia to Vladivostok and were afraid of any power that might threaten Manchuria. Together with France and Germany they applied diplomatic pressure that forced Japan out of the Liaotung Peninsula and its harbor, Port Arthur. All pressed feverishly for concessions in China. Fearing that China, its markets, and its investment opportunities would soon be closed to its citizens, the United States in 1899 proposed the "Open Door Policy." This policy opposed foreign annexations in China and allowed entrepreneurs of all nations to trade there on equal terms. The support of Britain helped win acceptance of the policy by all the powers except Russia.

[4] *Quoted by J. Remak in* The Origins of World War I, 1871–1914 *(New York: Holt, Rinehart & Winston, 1967), p. 5.*

[5] *Fieldhouse, p. 393.*

[6] *Thucydides,* The Peloponnesian War, *5.105.2.*

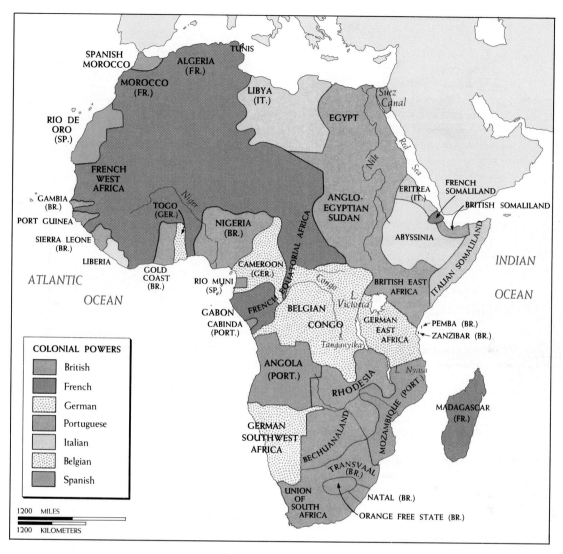

MAP 26-2 PARTITION OF AFRICA, 1880–1914 *Before 1880 European presence in Africa was largely the remains of early exploration by old imperialists and did not penetrate the heart of the continent. By 1914 the occupying powers included most large European states; only Liberia, and Abyssinia remained independent.*

The United States had only recently emerged as a force in international affairs. After freeing itself of British rule and consolidating its independence during the Napoleonic Wars, the Americans had busied themselves with westward expansion on the North American continent until the end of the nineteenth century. The Monroe Doctrine of 1823 had, in effect, made the entire Western Hemisphere an American protectorate. Cuba's attempt to gain independence from Spain was the spark for the new United States involvement in international affairs. Sympathy for the Cuban cause, American investments on the island, the de-

sire for Cuban sugar, and concern over the island's strategic importance in the Caribbean all helped win the Americans over to the idea of a war with Spain.

Victory in the Spanish-American War of 1898 brought the United States an informal protectorate over Cuba and the annexation of Puerto Rico and drove Spain completely out of the Western Hemisphere. The Americans also purchased the Philippine Islands and Guam, and Germany acquired the other Spanish islands in the Pacific. The Americans and the Germans also divided Samoa between them. What was left of the Pacific Islands was soon

In the Spanish-American War of 1898, Spain was driven from the western hemisphere and Cuba came under American influence. This picture shows the Tenth Cavalry Regiment, composed of black Americans, standing on San Juan Hill after the battle in July, 1898. [The Granger Collection]

taken by France and England. Hawaii had been under American influence for some time and had been asking for annexation, which was accomplished in 1898. This outburst of activity after the Spanish War made the United States an imperial and Pacific power.

Soon after the turn of the century most of the world had come under the control of the industrialized Western nations. The one remaining area of great vulnerability was the Ottoman Empire. However, its fate was closely tied up with European developments and must be treated in that context.

Emergence of the German Empire and the Alliance Systems (1873–1890)

Prussia's victories over Austria and France and its creation of a large, powerful German Empire in 1871 revolutionized European diplomacy. A vast new political unit had brought together the majority of the German people

MAP 26-3 ASIA 1880–1914 *As in Africa, the decades before World War I saw imperialism spread widely and rapidly in Asia. Two new powers, Japan and the United States joined British, French, and Dutch in extending control both to islands and to mainland and in exploiting an enfeebled China.*

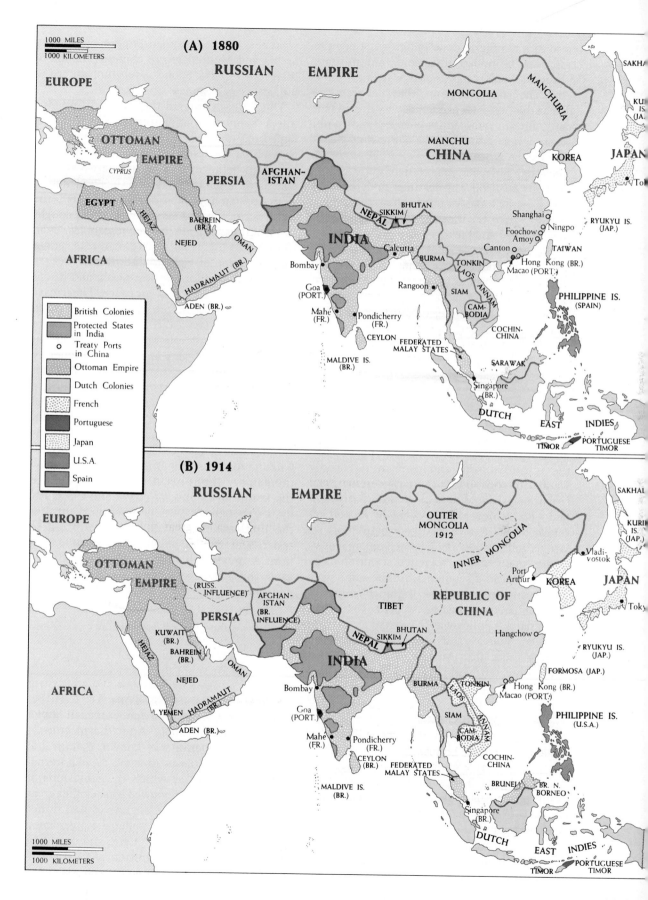

(A) 1880

1000 MILES
1000 KILOMETERS

EUROPE

RUSSIAN EMPIRE

MONGOLIA

MANCHURIA

SAKHA

KU
IS.
(JA.

OTTOMAN EMPIRE

CYPRUS

PERSIA

AFGHAN-ISTAN

MANCHU CHINA

KOREA

JAPAN

Tok

EGYPT

HEJAZ

BAHREIN (BR.)

NEJED

OMAN

NEPAL SIKKIM BHUTAN

Shanghai

Foochow Ningpo
Amoy

RYUKYU IS.
(JAP.)

AFRICA

HADRAMAUT (BR.)

ADEN (BR.)

INDIA

Calcutta

Bombay

Goa (PORT.)

Mahe (FR.)

Pondicherry (FR.)

CEYLON

MALDIVE IS. (BR.)

BURMA

Rangoon

SIAM

FEDERATED MALAY STATES

TONKIN
LAOS
ANNAM

CAM-BODIA

COCHIN-CHINA

SARAWAK

Singapore (BR.)

Canton

Macao (PORT.)

Hong Kong (BR.)

TAIWAN

PHILIPPINE IS. (SPAIN)

DUTCH EAST INDIES

TIMOR

PORTUGUESE TIMOR

Legend:

- British Colonies
- Protected States in India
- ○ Treaty Ports in China
- Ottoman Empire
- Dutch Colonies
- French
- Portuguese
- Japan
- U.S.A.
- Spain

(B) 1914

RUSSIAN EMPIRE

OUTER MONGOLIA 1912

INNER MONGOLIA

SAKHAL

KURI
IS.
(JAP.)

EUROPE

OTTOMAN EMPIRE

(RUSS. INFLUENCE)

PERSIA

AFGHAN-ISTAN (BR. INFLUENCE)

TIBET

REPUBLIC OF CHINA

Vladi-vostok

Port Arthur

KOREA

JAPAN

Toky

KUWAIT (BR.)

BAHREIN (BR.)

NEJED

OMAN

HEJAZ

NEPAL SIKKIM BHUTAN

Hangchow

RYUKYU IS. (JAP.)

AFRICA

YEMEN HADRAMAUT (BR.)

ADEN (BR.)

INDIA

Bombay

Goa (PORT.)

Mahe (FR.)

Pondicherry (FR.)

CEYLON (BR.)

MALDIVE IS. (BR.)

BURMA

SIAM

FEDERATED MALAY STATES

TONKIN
LAOS
ANNAM

CAM-BODIA

COCHIN-CHINA

Macao (PORT.)

Hong Kong (BR.)

FORMOSA (JAP.)

PHILIPPINE IS. (U.S.A.)

BRUNEI
BR. N. BORNEO

Singapore (BR.)

DUTCH EAST INDIES

TIMOR

PORTUGUESE TIMOR

1000 MILES
1000 KILOMETERS

925

to form a nation of great and growing population, wealth, industrial capacity, and military power. Its sudden appearance posed new problems. The balance of power that had been created at the Congress of Vienna was altered radically. Britain retained its position and so did Russia, even though it was somewhat weakened by the Crimean War.

Austria, however, had fallen quite a distance. Its position was destined to deteriorate further as the forces of nationalism threatened to disintegrate the Austro-Hungarian Empire. French power and prestige were badly damaged by the Franco-Prussian War and the German annexation of Alsace-Lorraine. The weakened French were afraid of their powerful new neighbor; at the same time they were resentful of the defeat, the loss of territory and population, and the loss of their traditional position of dominance in western Europe.

Bismarck's Leadership
(1873–1890)

Until 1890 Bismarck continued to guide German policy. He insisted after 1871 that Germany was a satisfied power and wanted no further territorial gains, and he meant it. He only wanted to consolidate the new international situation by avoiding a new war that might undo his achievement. Aware of French resentment, he tried to assuage it by friendly relations and by supporting French colonial aspirations in order to turn French attention away from European discontents. At the same time he prepared for the worst. If France could not be conciliated, it must be isolated. The kernel of Bismarck's policy was to prevent an alliance between France and any other European power—especially Austria or Russia—that would threaten Germany with a war on two fronts.

WAR IN THE BALKANS Bismarck's first move was to establish the Three Emperors' League in 1873. It brought together the three great conservative empires of Germany, Austria, and Russia. The league soon collapsed as a result of the Russo-Turkish War, which broke out in 1875 because of an uprising in the Ottoman Balkan provinces of Bosnia and Herzegovina. The tottering Ottoman Empire was held together chiefly by the competing aims of those powers who awaited its demise. The

weakness of the Ottoman Empire encouraged Serbia and Montenegro to come to the aid of their fellow Slavs. Soon the rebellion spread to Bulgaria.

Then Russia entered the fray and turned it into a major international crisis. The Russians hoped to pursue their traditional policy of expansion at Ottoman expense and especially hoped to achieve their most cherished goal: control of Constantinople and the Dardanelles. The Russian intervention also reflected the influence of the Pan-Slav movement. It sought to bring together all the Slavic peoples, even those under Austrian or Ottoman rule, under the protection of Holy Mother Russia.

The Ottoman Empire was weak, and before long it was forced to ask for peace. The Treaty of San Stefano of March 1878 was a Russian triumph. The Slavic states in the Balkans were freed of Ottoman rule, and Russia itself obtained territorial gains and a heavy monetary indemnity. But the Russian victory was not lasting. The other great powers were alarmed by the terms of the settlement. Austria feared that the great Slavic victory and the powerful increase in Russian influence in the Balkans would cause dangerous shock waves in its own Balkan provinces. The British were alarmed by the damage the Russian victory would do to the European balance of power and especially by the thought of possible Russian control of the Dardanelles. Disraeli was determined to resist, and British public opinion supported him. A music-hall song that became popular gave the language a new word for superpatriotism: jingoism.

> We don't want to fight,
> But by jingo if we do,
> We've got the men,
> We've got the ships,
> We've got the money too!

THE CONGRESS OF BERLIN Even before the Treaty of San Stefano, Disraeli sent a fleet to Constantinople. After the magnitude of Russia's appetite was known, Britain and Austria forced Russia to agree to an international conference at which the provisions of the treaty would be reviewed by the other great powers. The resulting Congress of Berlin met in June and July of 1878 under the presidency of Bismarck. The choice of site and presiding officer was a clear recognition of Germany's new importance and of its chancellor's claim that this policy called for no further territorial gains and aimed at preserving the peace.

Bismarck referred to himself as an "honest broker," and the title seems justified. He agreed to the congress simply because he wanted to avoid a war between Russia and Austria into which he feared Germany would be drawn with nothing to gain and much to lose. From the collapsing Ottoman Empire he wanted nothing. "The Eastern Question," he said, "is not worth the healthy bones of a single Pomeranian musketeer."[7]

The decisions of the congress were a blow to Russian ambitions. Bulgaria was reduced in size by two thirds and was deprived of access to the Aegean Sea. Austria-Hungary was given Bosnia and Herzegovina to "occupy and administer," although those provinces remained formally under Ottoman rule. Britain received Cyprus, and France gained permission to expand into Tunisia. These privileges were compensation for the gains that Russia was permitted to keep. Germany asked for nothing but got little credit from Russia for its restraint. The Russians believed that they had saved Prussia in 1807 from complete dismemberment by Napoleon and had expected a show of German gratitude. They were bitterly disappointed, and the Three Emperors' League was dead.

All of the Balkan states were also annoyed by the Berlin settlement. Romania wanted Bessarabia; Bulgaria wanted a return to the borders of the Treaty of San Stefano; and Greece wanted a part of the Ottoman spoils. The major trouble spot, however, was in the south Slavic states of Serbia and Montenegro. They deeply resented the Austrian occupation of Bosnia and Herzegovina, as did many of the natives of those provinces. The south Slavic question, no less than the estrangement between Russia and Germany, was a threat to the peace of Europe.

GERMAN ALLIANCES WITH RUSSIA AND AUSTRIA

For the moment Bismarck could ignore the Balkans, but he could not ignore the breach in his eastern alliance system. With Russia alienated, he turned to Austria and concluded a secret treaty in 1879. The resulting Dual Alliance provided that if either Germany or Austria were attacked by Russia

the ally would help the attacked party. If the signatory countries were attacked by someone else, each promised at least to maintain neutrality.

The treaty was for five years and was renewed regularly until 1918. As the central point in German policy, it was criticized at the time, and some have judged it mistaken in retrospect. It appeared to tie the German fortunes to those of the troubled Austro-Hungarian Empire and in that way to borrow trouble. At the same time, by isolating the Russians, it pushed them in the direction of seeking alliances in the West.

Bismarck was fully aware of these dangers but discounted them with good reason. At no time did he allow his Austrian alliance to drag Germany into Austria's Balkan quarrels. As he put it himself, in any alliance there is a horse and a rider, and in this one Bismarck meant Germany to be the rider. He made it clear to the Austrians that the alliance was purely defensive and that Germany would never be a party to an attack on Russia. "For us," he said, "Balkan questions can never be a motive for war."[8]

Bismarck believed that monarchical, reactionary Russia would not seek an alliance either with republican, revolutionary France or with increasingly democratic Britain. In fact, he expected the news of the Austro-German negotiations to frighten Russia into seeking closer relations with Germany, and he was right. Russian diplomats soon approached him, and by 1881 he had concluded a renewal of the Three Emperors' League on a firmer basis. The three powers promised to maintain friendly neutrality in case either of the others was attacked by a fourth power. Other clauses included the right of Austria to annex Bosnia-Herzegovina whenever it wished and close the Dardanelles to all nations in case of war.

The agreement allayed German fears of a Russian-French alliance and Russian fears of a combination of Austria and Britain against it, of Britain's fleet sailing into the Black Sea, and of a hostile combination of Germany and Austria. Most importantly, the agreement aimed at a resolution of the conflicts in the Balkans between Austria and Russia. Though it did not put an end to such conflicts, it was a significant step toward peace.

[7] Quoted by Hajo Holborn, A History of Modern Germany, 1840–1945 (New York: Knopf, 1969), p. 239.

[8] Quoted by J. Remak, p. 14.

THE TRIPLE ALLIANCE In 1882 Italy, ambitious for colonial expansion and annoyed by the French preemption of Tunisia, asked to join the Dual Alliance. The provisions of its entry were defensive and were directed against France. At this point Bismarck's policy was a complete success. He was allied with three of the great powers and friendly with the other, Great Britain, which held aloof from all alliances. France was isolated and no threat. Bismarck's diplomacy was a great achievement, but an even greater challenge was to maintain this complicated system of secret alliances in the face of the continuing rivalries among Germany's allies. In spite of another Balkan war that broke out in 1885 and that again estranged Austria and Russia, he succeeded.

Although the Three Emperors' League lapsed, the Triple Alliance (Germany, Austria, and Italy) was renewed for another five years. To restore German relations with Russia, he negotiated the Reinsurance Treaty of 1887, in which both powers promised to remain neutral

Bismarck and the young Kaiser William II meet in 1888. The two disagreed over many issues, and in 1890 *William dismissed the aged chancellor.* [German Information Center]

if either was attacked. All seemed smooth, but a change in the German monarchy soon overturned everything.

In 1888 William II (1888–1918) came to the German throne (reigned 1888–1918). He was twenty-nine years old, ambitious and impetuous. He was imperious by temperament and believed in monarchy by divine right. He had suffered an injury at birth that left him with a withered arm. He compensated for this disability by means of vigorous exercise, by a military bearing and outlook, and sometimes by an embarrassingly loud and bombastic rhetoric.

Like many Germans of his generation, William II was filled with a sense of Germany's destiny as the leading power of Europe. He wanted to achieve recognition at least of equality from Britain, the land of his mother and of his grandmother, Queen Victoria. To achieve a "place in the sun," he and his contemporaries wanted a navy and colonies like Britain's. These aims, of course, ran counter to Bismarck's limited continental policy. When William argued for a navy as a defense against a British landing in north Germany, Bismarck replied, "If the British should land on our soil, I should have them arrested." This was only one example of the great distance between the young emperor, or Kaiser, and his chancellor. In 1890 William used a disagreement over domestic policy to dismiss Bismarck.

As long as Bismarck held power, Germany was secure, and there was peace among the great European powers. Although he made mistakes and was not always successful, there was much to admire in his understanding and management of international relations in the hard world of reality. He had a clear and limited idea of his nation's goals. He resisted pressures for further expansion with few and insignificant exceptions. He understood and used the full range of diplomatic weapons: appeasement and deterrence, threats and promises, secrecy and openness. He understood the needs and hopes of other countries and, where possible, tried to help to accomplish them or used them to his own advantage. His system of alliances created a stalemate in the Balkans at the same time that it ensured German security.

During Bismarck's time Germany was a force for European peace and was increasingly understood to be so. This position would not, of course, have been possible without its great military power. But it also required the leadership of a statesman who was willing and able to exercise restraint and who could make a realistic estimate of what his country needed and what was possible.

Forging of the Triple Entente (1890–1907)

FRANCO-RUSSIAN ALLIANCE Almost immediately after Bismarck's retirement his system of alliances collapsed. His successor was General Leo von Caprivi (1831–1899), who had once asked, "What kind of jackass will dare to be Bismarck's successor?" Caprivi refused the Russian request to renew the Reinsurance Treaty, in part because he felt incompetent to continue Bismarck's complicated policy and in part because he wished to draw Germany closer to Britain. The results were unfortunate, as Britain remained aloof and Russia was alienated. Even Bismarck had assumed that ideological differences were too great to permit a Franco-Russian alliance. However, political isolation and the need for foreign capital unexpectedly drove the Russians toward France. The French, who were even more isolated, were glad to encourage their investors to pour capital into Russia if it would help produce an alliance and security against Germany. In 1894 the Franco-Russian alliance against Germany was signed.

BRITAIN AND GERMANY Britain now became the key to the international situation. Colonial rivalries pitted the British against the Russians in Central Asia and against the French in Africa. Traditionally Britain had also opposed Russian control of Constantinople and the Dardanelles and French control of the Low Countries. There was no reason to think that Britain would soon become friendly to its traditional rivals or abandon its accustomed friendliness toward the Germans.

Yet within a decade of William II's accession Germany had become the enemy in the minds of the British. Before the turn of the century popular British thrillers about imaginary wars portrayed the French as the invader; after the turn of the century the enemy was always German. This remarkable transformation has often been attributed to the economic rivalry of Germany and Britain, in which Germany made vast strides to challenge and even overtake British production in various materials and markets. There can be no doubt that Germany made such gains and that many Britons resented them. Yet the problem was not a serious cause of hostility and it waned as the first decade of the century wore on. The real problem lay in the foreign and naval policies of the German emperor and his ministers.

William II's attitude toward Britain was respectful and admiring, especially with regard to its colonial empire and its mighty fleet. At first, Germany tried to win the British over to the Triple Alliance, but when Britain clung to its policy of "splendid isolation," German policy took a different tack. The idea was to demonstrate Germany's worthiness as an ally by withdrawing support and even making trouble for Britain. This odd manner of gaining an ally reflected the Kaiser's confused feelings toward Britain, which consisted of dislike and jealousy mixed with admiration. These feelings reflected those of many Germans, especially in the intellectual community. Like William they were eager for Germany to pursue a "world policy" rather than Bismarck's limited one that confined German interests to Europe. They, too, saw England as the barrier to German ambitions. Their influence in the schools, the universities, and the press guaranteed popular approval of actions and statements hostile to Britain.

The Germans began to exert pressure against Britain in Africa by barring British attempts to build a railroad from Capetown to Cairo. They also openly sympathized with the Boers of South Africa in their resistance to British expansion. In 1896 William insulted the British by sending a congratulatory telegram to Paul Kruger (1825–1904), president of the Transvaal, for repulsing a British raid "without having to appeal to friendly powers for assistance."

In 1898 William's dream of a German navy began to achieve reality with the passage of a naval law providing for nineteen battleships. In 1900 a second law doubled that figure. The architect of the new navy was Admiral Alfred von Tirpitz (1849–1930), who openly proclaimed that Germany's naval policy was aimed at Britain. His "risk" theory argued that Germany could build a fleet strong enough, not to defeat the British, but to do sufficient damage to make the British navy inferior to that of other powers like France or the United

States. The theory was, in fact, absurd because as Germany's fleet became menacing, the British would certainly build ships to maintain their advantage, and British financial resources were greater than Germany's.

The naval policy, therefore, was doomed to failure. Over time its main achievements were to waste German resources and to begin a great naval race with Britain. It is not too much to say, moreover, that the threat posed by the German navy did more to antagonize British opinion than anything else. As the German navy grew and German policies seemed to become more threatening, the British were alarmed enough to abandon their traditional attitudes and policies.

At first, however, Britain was not unduly concerned. The British were embarrassed by the general hostility of world opinion during the Boer War (1899–1902), in which their great empire tried to crush a rebellion by South African farmers, and were suddenly alarmed that their isolation no longer seemed so splendid. The Germans had acted with restraint during the war. Between 1898 and 1901 Joseph Chamberlain, the colonial secretary, made several attempts to conclude an alliance with Germany. The Germans, confident that a British alliance with France or Russia was impossible, refused and expected the British to make greater concessions in the future.

THE ENTENTE CORDIALE The first breach in Britain's isolation came in 1902, when an alliance was concluded with Japan to relieve the pressure of defending British interests in the Far East against Russia. Next Britain abandoned its traditional antagonism toward France and in 1904 concluded a series of agreements with the French, collectively called the *Entente Cordiale*. It was not a formal treaty and had no military provisions, but it settled all outstanding colonial differences between the two nations. The Entente Cordiale was a long step toward aligning the British with Germany's great potential enemy.

Britain's new relationship with France was surprising, but in 1904 hardly anyone believed that the British whale and the Russian bear would ever come together. The Russo-Japanese war of 1904–1905 made such a development seem even less likely because Britain was allied with Russia's enemy. But Britain had behaved with restraint, and the Russians were chastened by their unexpected and humiliating defeat. The defeat also led to the Russian Revolution of 1905. Although the revolution was put down, it left Russia weak and reduced British apprehensions in that direction. At the same time the British were concerned that Russia might again drift into the German orbit.

THE FIRST MOROCCAN CRISIS At this point Germany decided to test the new understanding between Britain and France and to press for colonial gains. In March 1905 Emperor William II landed at Tangier, challenged the French protectorate there in a speech in favor of Moroccan independence, and by implication asserted Germany's right to participate in Morocco's destiny. Germany's chancellor, Prince Bernhard von Bülow (1849–1929), intended to show France how weak it was and how little it could expect from Britain. At the same time he hoped to gain significant colonial concessions.

The Germans might well have achieved their aims and driven a wedge between France and Britain, but they pushed too far and demanded an international conference to show their power more dramatically. The conference met in 1906 at Algeciras in Spain. Austria sided with its German ally, but Spain, Italy, and the United States voted with Britain and France. The Germans had overplayed their hand, receiving trivial concessions, and the French were confirmed in their position in Morocco. German bullying had, moreover, driven Britain and France closer together. In the face of the threat of a German attack on France, Sir Edward Grey, the British foreign secretary, without making a firm commitment, authorized conversations between the British and the French general staffs. Their agreements became morally binding as the years passed. By 1914 French and British military and naval plans were so mutually dependent that the two countries were effectively, if not formally, allies.

BRITISH AGREEMENT WITH RUSSIA Britain's fear of Germany's growing naval power, its concern over German ambitions in the Near East (as represented by the German-sponsored plan to build a railroad from Berlin to Baghdad), and its closer relations with France made it desirable for Britain to become more friendly with France's ally, Russia. With French support the British made overtures to the Russians and in 1907 concluded an agreement with them much like the Entente Cordiale with France. It settled Russo-British quarrels in Central Asia and opened the door for wider cooperation. The Triple Entente, an informal, but powerful association of Britain, France, and Russia, was now ranged against the Triple Alliance. Because Italy was unreliable, Germany and Austria-Hungary stood surrounded by two great land powers and Great Britain.

William II and his ministers had turned Bismarck's nightmare of the prospect of a two-front war with France and Russia into a reality. They had made it more horrible by adding Britain to the hostile coalition. The equilibrium that Bismarck had worked so hard to achieve was destroyed. Britain could no longer support Austria in restraining Russian ambitions in the Balkans. Germany, increasingly terrified by a sense of encirclement, was less willing to restrain the Austrians for fear of alienating them. In the Dual Alliance of Germany and Austria it had become less clear who was the horse and who was the rider.

Bismarck's alliance system had been intended to maintain peace, but the new one increased the risk of war and made the Balkans a likely spot for it to break out. Bismarck's diplomacy had left France isolated and impotent; the new arrangement found France associated with the two greatest superpowers in Europe apart from Germany. The Germans could rely only on Austria, and such was the condition of that troubled empire that it was less likely to provide aid than to need it.

World War I

The Road to War (1908–1914)

The situation in the Balkans in the first decade of this century was exceedingly complicated. The weak Ottoman Empire controlled the central strip running west from Constantinople to the Adriatic. North and south of it were the independent states of Romania, Serbia, and Greece, as well as Bulgaria, technically still part of the empire but legally autonomous and practically independent. The Austro-Hungar-

ian Empire included Croatia and Slovenia and since 1878 had "occupied and administered" Bosnia and Herzegovina.

With the exception of the Greeks and the Romanians, most of the inhabitants of the Balkans spoke variants of the same Slavic language and felt a cultural and historical kinship with one another. For centuries they had been ruled by Austrians, Hungarians, or Turks, and the growing nationalism that characterized late-nineteenth-century Europe made many of them eager for liberty. The more radical among them longed for a union of the south Slavic, or Yugoslav, peoples in a single nation. They looked to independent Serbia as the center of the new nation and hoped to detach all the Slavic provinces (especially Bosnia, which bordered on Serbia) from Austria. In this regard Serbia was to unite the Slavs at the expense of Austria, as Piedmont had united the Italians and Prussia the Germans.

In 1908 a group of modernizing reformers called the *Young Turks* brought about a revolution in the Ottoman Empire. Their actions threatened to revive the life of the empire and to interfere with the plans of the European jackals preparing to pounce on the Ottoman corpse. These events brought on the first of a series of Balkan crises that would eventually lead to war.

THE BOSNIAN CRISIS In 1908 the Austrian and Russian governments decided to act quickly before Turkey became strong enough to resist. They struck a bargain in which it was agreed that they would call an international conference where each of them would support the other's demands. Russia would agree to the Austrian annexation of Bosnia and Herzegovina, and Austria would support Russia's request to open the Dardanelles to Russian warships.

Austria, however, declared the annexation before any conference was called. The British, ever concerned about their own position in the Mediterranean, refused to agree to the Russian demand. The Russians, feeling betrayed by the British, were humiliated and furious. Their "little brothers," the Serbs, were frustrated and angered by the loss of Bosnia, which they had hoped one day to include in an independent south Slavic nation led by Serbia. The Russians were too weak to do anything but accept the new situation.

The Germans had not been warned in advance of Austria's plans and were unhappy because the action threatened their relations with Russia. But Germany felt so dependent of the Dual Alliance that it assured Austria of its support. Austria had been given a free hand, and to an extent German policy was being made in Vienna. It was a dangerous precedent. At the same time, the failure of Britain and France to support Russia strained the Triple Entente. This made it harder for them to oppose Russian interests again in the future if they were to retain Russian friendship.

THE SECOND MOROCCAN CRISIS

The second Moroccan crisis, in 1911, emphasized the French and British need for mutual support. When France sent in an army to put down a rebellion, Germany took the opportunity to "protect German interests" in Morocco as a means of extorting colonial concessions in the French Congo. To add force to their de-

This cartoon, "The Mailed Fist of the Kaiser Strikes Agadir," refers to the landing of the German gunboat Panther *at Agadir in Morocco in 1911. William II's purpose was to press the French to make colonial concessions to Germany in Africa and, perhaps, to break up the Entente between the French and the British. The result, instead, was the second Moroccan crisis, which drew the Entente closer together and helped bring on World War I.*

mands, the Germans sent the gunboat *Panther* to the port of Agadir, allegedly to protect German citizens there. Once again, as in 1905, the Germans went too far. The *Panther's* visit to Agadir provoked a strong reaction in Britain. For some time Anglo-German relations had been growing worse, chiefly because of the intensification of the naval race. In 1907 Germany had built its first new battleship of the dreadnought class, which Britain had developed in 1906. In 1908 Germany had passed still another naval law, which accelerated the schedule of production to challenge British naval supremacy.

These actions frightened and angered the British because of the clear threat to the security of the island kingdom and its empire. The German actions also forced Britain to increase taxes to pay for new armaments just when the Liberal government was launching its expensive program of social legislation. Negotiations failed to persuade William II and Tirpitz to slow down naval construction.

In this atmosphere the British heard of the *Panther's* arrival in Morocco. They wrongly believed that the Germans meant to turn Agadir into a naval base on the Atlantic. The crisis passed when France yielded some insignificant bits of the Congo and Germany withdrew from Morocco. The main result was to increase British fear and hostility and to draw the Britons closer to France. Specific military plans were formulated for a British expeditionary force to defend France in case of German attack, and the British and French navies agreed to cooperate. Without any formal treaty the German naval construction and the Agadir crisis had turned the Entente Cordiale into an alliance that could not have been more binding. If France were attacked by Germany, Britain must defend the French, for its own security was inextricably tied up with that of France.

WAR IN THE BALKANS

The second Moroccan crisis also provoked another crisis in the Balkans. Italy sought to gain colonies and to take its place among the great powers. It wanted Libya, which though worth little at the time was at least available. Italy feared that the recognition of the French protectorate in Morocco would encourage France to move into Libya. Consequently, in 1911, Italy attacked the Ottoman Empire to anticipate the French,

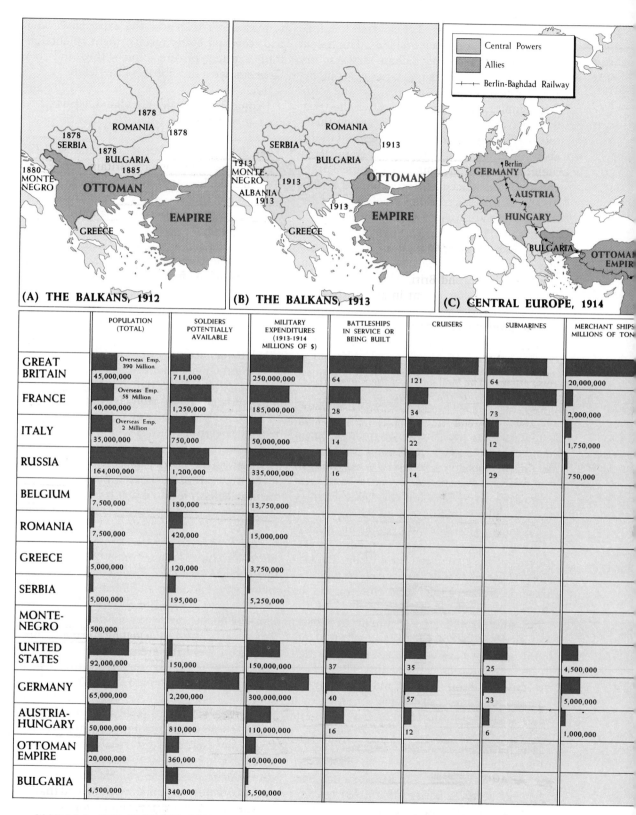

(A) THE BALKANS, 1912

(B) THE BALKANS, 1913

(C) CENTRAL EUROPE, 1914

Legend: Central Powers; Allies; Berlin-Baghdad Railway

	POPULATION (TOTAL)	SOLDIERS POTENTIALLY AVAILABLE	MILITARY EXPENDITURES (1913-1914 MILLIONS OF $)	BATTLESHIPS IN SERVICE OR BEING BUILT	CRUISERS	SUBMARINES	MERCHANT SHIPS MILLIONS OF TON
GREAT BRITAIN	45,000,000 (Overseas Emp. 390 Million)	711,000	250,000,000	64	121	64	20,000,000
FRANCE	40,000,000 (Overseas Emp. 58 Million)	1,250,000	185,000,000	28	34	73	2,000,000
ITALY	35,000,000 (Overseas Emp. 2 Million)	750,000	50,000,000	14	22	12	1,750,000
RUSSIA	164,000,000	1,200,000	335,000,000	16	14	29	750,000
BELGIUM	7,500,000	180,000	13,750,000				
ROMANIA	7,500,000	420,000	15,000,000				
GREECE	5,000,000	120,000	3,750,000				
SERBIA	5,000,000	195,000	5,250,000				
MONTENEGRO	500,000						
UNITED STATES	92,000,000	150,000	150,000,000	37	35	25	4,500,000
GERMANY	65,000,000	2,200,000	300,000,000	40	57	23	5,000,000
AUSTRIA-HUNGARY	50,000,000	810,000	110,000,000	16	12	6	1,000,000
OTTOMAN EMPIRE	20,000,000	360,000	40,000,000				
BULGARIA	4,500,000	340,000	5,500,000				

MAP 26-4   THE BALKANS, 1912–1913   *Two maps (A) and (B) show the Balkans before and after the two Balkan wars; note the Ottoman retreat. In panel C we see the geographical relationship of the Central Powers and their Bulgarian and Turkish allies. Tables give relative strength of World War I combatants.*

defeated the faltering Turks, and obtained Libya and the Dodecanese Islands. The Italian victory encouraged the Balkan states to try their luck. In 1912 Bulgaria, Greece, Montenegro, and Serbia joined an attack on the Ottoman Empire and won easily. After this First Balkan War, the victors fell out among themselves. The Serbs and the Bulgarians quarreled about the division of Macedonia, and in 1913 a Second Balkan War erupted. This time Turkey and Romania joined the other states against Bulgaria and stripped away much of what the Bulgarians had gained since 1878.

After the First Balkan War, the alarmed Austrians were determined to limit Serbian gains and especially to prevent the Serbs from gaining a port on the Adriatic. This policy meant keeping Serbia out of Albania, but the Russians backed the Serbs, and tensions mounted. An international conference sponsored by Britain in early 1913 resolved the matter in Austria's favor and called for an independent kingdom of Albania. But Austria felt humiliated by the public airing of Serbian demands. Then, for some time, the Serbs defied the powers and continued to occupy parts of Albania. Under Austrian pressure they withdrew, but in September 1913, after the Second Balkan War, the Serbs reoccupied sections of Albania. In mid-October Austria unilaterally issued an ultimatum to Serbia, and the latter country again withdrew its forces from Albania.

During this crisis many people in Austria had wanted an all-out attack on Serbia to remove its threat once and for all from the empire. Those demands had been resisted by Emperor Francis Joseph and the heir to the throne, Archduke Francis Ferdinand. At the same time Pan-Slavic sentiment in Russia pressed Tsar Nicholas II to take a firm stand, but Russia once again let Austria have its way in its confrontation with Serbia. Throughout the crisis Britain, France, and Germany restrained their respective allies, although each worried about seeming too reluctant to help its friends.

The lessons learned from this crisis of 1913 profoundly influenced behavior in the final crisis, the crisis of 1914. The Russians had once again, as in 1908, been embarrassed by their passivity; and their allies were more reluctant to restrain them again. The Austrians were embarrassed by what had resulted from accepting an international conference and were determined not to repeat the experience. They had seen that better results might be obtained from a threat of direct force; they and their German allies did not miss the lesson.

Sarajevo and the Outbreak of War (June–August 1914)

THE ASSASSINATION On June 28, 1914, a young Bosnian nationalist shot and killed the Austrian Archduke Francis Ferdinand, heir to the throne, and his wife as they drove in an open car through the Bosnian capital of Sarajevo. The assassin was a member of a conspiracy hatched by a political terrorist society called *Union or Death*, better known as the *Black Hand*. A major participant in the planning and preparation of the crime was the chief of intelligence of the Serbian army's general staff. Even though his role was not actually known at the time, it was generally believed that Serbian officials were involved. The glee of the Serbian press lent support to that belief.

The archduke was not a popular person in his own land, and his funeral evoked few signs of grief. He had been known to favor a form of federal government that would have given a higher status to the Slavs in the empire. This position alienated the conservatives and the Hungarians. It also alarmed radical Yugoslav nationalists, who feared that reform might end their dream of an independent south Slav state.

GERMANY AND AUSTRIA'S RESPONSE News of the assassination produced outrage and condemnation everywhere. To those Austrians who had long favored an attack on Serbia as a solution to the empire's Slavic problem, the opportunity seemed irresistible. But it was never easy for the Dual Monarchy to make a decision. Conrad von Hötzendorf, chief of the Austrian general staff, urged an attack as he had often done before. Count Stefan Tisza, speaking for Hungary, resisted. Leopold Berchtold, the Austro-Hungarian foreign minister, felt the need for strong action, but he knew that German support would be required in the likely event that Russia should decide to intervene to protect Serbia. He also knew that nothing could be done without Tisza's approval and that only German support could persuade the Hungarians to accept the policy of war. The question of peace or war, therefore, had to be answered in Berlin.

William II and Chancellor Theobald von Bethmann-Hollweg (1856–1921) readily promised German support for an attack on Serbia. It has often been said that they gave the Austrians a "blank check," but their message was firmer than that. They urged the Austrians to move swiftly while the other powers were still angry at Serbia. They also made the Austrians feel that a failure to act would be taken as evidence of Austria-Hungary's weakness and uselessness as an ally. Therefore, the Austrians never wavered in their determination to make war on Serbia. They hoped, with the protection of Germany, to fight a limited war that would not bring on a general European conflict, even though they were prepared to risk it. The Germans also knew that they risked a general war, but they hoped to "localize" the fight between Austria and Serbia.

Some scholars believe that Germany had long been plotting war, and some even think that a specific plan for war in 1914 was set in motion as early as 1912. However, the vast body of evidence on the crisis of 1914 gives little support to such notions. The German leaders plainly reacted to a crisis that they had not foreseen and just as plainly made decisions in response to events. The fundamental decision to support Austria made it very difficult if not impossible to avoid war. That decision was made by the emperor and chancellor without significant consultation with either their military or their diplomatic advisers.

William II appears to have reacted violently to the assassination. He was moved by his friendship for the archduke and by outrage at an attack on royalty. It is doubtful that a different provocation would have moved him so much. Bethmann-Hollweg was less emotional but under severe pressure. To resist the decision would have meant flatly to oppose the emperor. The chancellor, moreover, was suspected of being "soft" in the powerful military circles favored by his master. A conciliatory position would have been difficult.

Beyond these considerations, Bethmann-Hollweg, like many other Germans, viewed the future with apprehension. Russia was recovering its strength and would reach a military peak in 1917. The Triple Entente was growing more powerful, and Germany's only reliable ally was Austria. The chancellor recognized the danger of support for Austria, but he believed it to be even more dangerous to with-

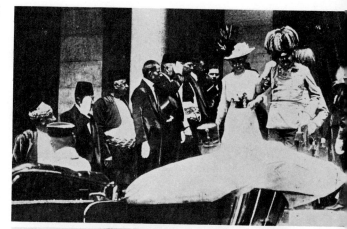

ABOVE: *The Austrian Archduke Franz Ferdinand and his wife visited Sarajevo on June 28, 1914. Later in the day the royal couple were assassinated by young revolutionaries trained and supplied in Serbia. The murders set off the crisis that led to World War I.* [Popperfoto, London]

BELOW: *Moments after the assassination the Austrian police captured one of the assassins in Sarajevo.* [Brown Brothers]

hold that support. If Austria did not crush Serbia, the empire would soon collapse before the onslaught of Slavic nationalism defended by Russia. If Germany did not defend its ally, the Austrians might look elsewhere for help. His policy was one of "calculated risk."

The calculations proved to be incorrect. Bethmann-Hollweg hoped that the Austrians would strike swiftly and present the powers with a *fait accompli* while the outrage of the assassination was still fresh. And he felt that German support would deter Russian involve-

The German Chancellor Theobald von Bethmann-Hollweg converses with Hakki Pascha, Ambassador from Turkey, in 1916. [Bildarchiv Preussischer Kulturbesitz]

ment. Failing that, he was prepared for a continental war that would bring rapid victory over France and allow a full-scale attack on the Russians, who were always slow to bring their strength into action. All of this policy depended on British neutrality; and the German chancellor convinced himself that the British could be persuaded to stand aloof.

However, the Austrians were slow to act. They did not even deliver their deliberately unacceptable ultimatum to Serbia until July 24, when the general hostility toward Serbia had begun to subside. Serbia further embarrassed the Austrians by returning so soft and conciliatory an answer that the mercurial German emperor thought it removed all reason for war. But the Austrians were determined not to turn back. On July 28 the Austrians declared war on Serbia, even though they could not put an army into the field until mid-August.

THE TRIPLE ENTENTE'S RESPONSE

The Russians, previously so often forced to back off, angrily responded to the Austrian demands on Serbia. The most conservative elements of the Russian government opposed war, fearing that it would bring on revolution as it had in 1905. But nationalists, Pan-Slavs, and most of the politically conscious classes in general demanded action. The government responded by ordering partial mobilization, against Austria only. This policy was militarily impossible, but its intention was the diplomatic one of putting pressure on Austria to hold back its attack on Serbia.

Mobilization of any kind, however, was a dangerous political weapon because it was generally understood to be equivalent to an act of war. It was especially alarming to General Helmuth von Moltke (1848–1916), head of the German general staff. The possibility that the Russians might start mobilization before the Germans could move would upset the delicate timing of Germany's only battle plan. The Schlieffen Plan, required an attack on France first, and would put Germany in great danger. From this point on, Moltke pressed for German mobilization and war. The pressure of military necessity mounted until it became irresistible.

The western European powers were not eager for war. France's president and prime minister were on their way back from a visit to Russia when the crisis flared up again on July 24. The Austrians had, in fact, timed their ultimatum precisely so that these two men would be at sea at the crucial moment. Had they been at their desks, they might have attempted to restrain the Russians. However, the French ambassador to Russia gave the Russians the same assurances that Germany had given its ally. The British worked hard to avoid trouble by traditional means: a conference of the powers. Austria, still smarting from its humiliation after the London Conference of 1913, would not hear of it. The Germans privately supported the Austrians but publicly took on a conciliatory tone in the hope of keeping the British neutral.

Soon, however, Bethmann-Hollweg came to realize what he should have known from the first: if Germany attacked France, Britain must fight. Until July 30 his public appeals to Austria for restraint were a sham. Thereafter, he sincerely tried to persuade the Austrians to negotiate and to avoid a general war, but it was too late. While Bethmann-Hollweg was urging restraint on the Austrians, General Moltke was pressing them to act. The Austrians wondered who was in charge in Berlin, but they could not turn back without losing their own self-respect and the respect of the Germans.

On July 30 Austria ordered mobilization against Russia. Bethmann-Hollweg resisted the enormous pressure to mobilize, not because he had any further hope of avoiding war but because he wanted Russia to mobilize against Germany first and appear to be the aggressor. Only in that way could he win the support of the German nation for war, especially the pacifistic Social Democrats. His luck was good for a change. The news of Russian general mobilization came only minutes before Germany would have mobilized in any case. The Schlieffen Plan went into effect. The Germans invaded Luxembourg on August 1 and Belgium on August 3. The latter invasion violated the treaty of 1839 in which the British had guaranteed Belgian neutrality. This factor undermined the considerable sentiment in Britain for neutrality and united the nation against Germany. Germany then invaded France, and on August 4 Britain declared war on Germany.

The Great War had begun. As Sir Edward Grey, the British foreign secretary, put it, the lights were going out all over Europe. They would come on again, but Europe would never be the same.

Strategies and Stalemate: 1914–1917

Throughout Europe jubilation greeted the outbreak of war. No general war had been fought since Napoleon, and the horrors of modern warfare were not yet understood. The dominant memory was of Bismarck's swift and decisive campaigns, in which costs and casualties were light and the rewards great. After the repeated crises of recent years and the fears and resentments they had created, war came as a release of tension. The popular press had increased public awareness of and interest in foreign affairs and had fanned the flames of patriotism. The prospect of war moved even a rational man of science like Sigmund Freud to say, "My whole libido goes out to Austria-Hungary."[9]

[9]Quoted in J. Remak, p. 134.

THE COMING OF WORLD WAR I

1871	The end of the Franco-Prussian War; creation of the German Empire; German annexation of Alsace-Lorraine
1873	The Three Emperors' League (Germany, Russia, and Austria-Hungary)
1875	The Russo-Turkish War
1878	The Congress of Berlin
1879	The Dual Alliance between Germany and Austria
1881	The Three Emperors' League is renewed
1882	Italy joins Germany and Austria in the Triple Alliance
1888	William II becomes the German emperor
1890	Bismarck is dismissed
1894	The Franco-Russian alliance
1898	Germany begins to build a battleship navy
1902	The British alliance with Japan
1904	The Entente Cordiale between Britain and France
1904–1905	The Russo-Japanese War
1905	The first Moroccan crisis
1907	The British agreement with Russia
1908–1909	The Bosnian crisis
1911	The second Moroccan crisis
1911	Italy attacks Turkey
1912–1913	The First and Second Balkan Wars
1914	Outbreak of World War I

Both sides expected to take the offensive, force a battle on favorable ground, and win a quick victory. The Triple Entente powers—or the Allies, as they came to be called—held superiority in numbers and financial resources as well as command of the sea. Germany and Austria, the Central Powers, had the advantages of internal lines of communication and of having launched their attack first.

After 1905 Germany's only war plan was the one developed by Count Alfred von Schlieffen (1833–1913), chief of the German general staff from 1891 to 1906. It aimed at going around the French defenses by sweeping through Belgium to the Channel, then wheeling to the south and east to envelop the French and to crush them against the German fortresses in Lorraine. The secret of success lay in making the right wing of the advancing German army immensely strong and deliberately weakening the left opposite the French frontier. The

The Kaiser's Comments on the Outbreak of the World War

On July 30, 1914, the German Foreign Office received the news that Russian mobilization had been started and would not be stopped. German strategy, based on the Schlieffen Plan, required an immediate mobilization and a swift attack on France before the weight of the Russian armies in the east could take full effect. The telegram from the German ambassador in Saint Petersburg, therefore, meant that war had come. The Kaiser, as usual, filled the margins of the document with his comments. On this occasion he concluded with a long note that reveals his own understanding of the situation.

If mobilization can no longer be retracted—WHICH IS NOT TRUE—why, then, did the Czar appeal for my mediation three days afterward without mention of the issuance of the mobilization order? That shows plainly that the mobilization appeared to him to have been precipitate, and that after he made this move *pro forma* in our direction for the sake of quieting his uneasy conscience, although he knew that it would no longer be of any use, as he did not feel himself to be strong enough to STOP the mobilization. Frivolity and weakness are to plunge the world into the most frightful war, which eventually aims at the destruction of Germany. For I have no doubt left about it: England, Russia and France have AGREED among themselves—after laying the foundation of the *casus foederis* for us through Austria—to take the Austro-Serbian conflict for an EXCUSE for waging a WAR OF EXTERMINATION against us. Hence Grey's [Sir Edward Grey, The British Foreign Secretary] cynical observation to Lichnowsky [The German Ambassador to Britain] "as long as the war is CONFINED to Russia and Austria, England would sit quiet, only when we and France MIXED INTO IT would he be compelled to make an active move against us ("); i.e., either we are shamefully to betray our allies, SACRIFICE them to Russia—thereby breaking up the Triple Alliance, or we are to be attacked in common by the Triple Entente for our FIDELITY TO OUR ALLIES and punished, whereby they will

weakness of the left was meant to draw the French into the wrong place while the war was decided on the German right. As one keen military analyst has explained,

> It would be like a revolving door—if a man pressed heavily on one side, the other side would spring round and strike him in the back. Here lay the real subtlety of the plan, not in the mere geographical detour.[10]

In the east the Germans planned to stand on the defensive against Russia until France had been crushed, a task they thought would take only six weeks.

The apparent risk, besides the violation of Belgian neutrality and the consequent alienation of Britain, lay in weakening the German defenses against a direct attack across the frontier. The strength of German fortresses and the superior firepower of German howitzers made that risk more apparent than real. The true danger was that the German striking force on the right through Belgium would not be powerful enough to make the swift progress vital to success. Schlieffen is said to have uttered the dying words, "It must come to a fight. Only make the right wing strong."

---

[10] *B. H. Liddell Hart, The Real War, 1914–1918 (Boston: Little, Brown, 1964; first published in 1930), p. 47.*

satisfy their jealousy by joining in totally RUINING us. That is the real naked situation *in nuce*, which, slowly and cleverly set going, certainly by Edward VII, has been carried on, and systematically built up by disowned conferences between England and Paris and Petersburg; finally brought to a conclusion by George V and set to work. And thereby the stupidity and ineptitude of our ally is turned into a snare for us. So the famous "CIRCUMSCRIPTION" of Germany has finally become a complete fact, despite every effort of our politicians and diplomats to prevent it. The net has been suddenly thrown over our head, and England sneeringly reaps the most brilliant success of her persistently prosecuted purely ANTI-GERMAN WORLD-POLICY, against which we have proved ourselves helpless, while she twists the noose of our political and economic destruction out of our fidelity to Austria, as we squirm ISOLATED in the net. A great achievement, which arouses the admiration even of him who is to be destroyed as its result! Edward VII is stronger after his death than am I who am still alive! And there have been people who believed that England could be won over or pacified, by this or that puny measure!!! Unremittingly, re-lentlessly she has pursued her object, with notes, holiday proposals, scares, Haldane, etc., until this point was reached. And we walked into the net and even went into the one-ship-program in construction with the ardent hope of thus pacifying England!!! All my warnings, all my pleas were voiced for nothing. Now comes England's so-called gratitude for it! From the dilemma raised by our fidelity to the venerable old Emperor of Austria we are brought into a situation which offers England the desired pretext for annihilating us under the hypocritical cloak of justice, namely, of helping France on account of the reputed "balance of power" in Europe, i.e., playing the card of all the European nations in England's favor against us! This whole business must now be ruthlessly uncovered and the mask of Christian peaceableness publicly and brusquely torn from its face in public, and the pharisaical hypocrisy exposed on the pillory!! And our consuls in Turkey and India, agents, etc., must fire the whole Mohammedan world to fierce rebellion against this hated, lying, conscienceless nation of shop-keepers; for if we are to be bled to death, England shall at least lose India.

Max Montgelas and Walther Schücking (Eds.), Outbreak of the World War: German Documents Collected by Karl Kautsky, *No. 401 (1924), pp. 348–350, trans. by Carnegie Endowment for International Peace. Reprinted by permission of Carnegie Endowment for International Peace.*

The execution of his plan, however, was left to Helmuth von Moltke, the nephew of Bismarck's most effective general. The younger Moltke (chief of staff 1906–1914) was a gloomy and nervous man who lacked the talent of his illustrious uncle and the theoretical daring of Schlieffen. He added divisions to the left wing and even weakened the Russian front for the same purpose. The consequence of this hesitant strategy was the failure of the Schlieffen Plan by a narrow margin.

THE WAR IN THE WEST The French had also put their faith in the offensive, but with less reason than the Germans. They badly un-derestimated the numbers and effectiveness of the German reserves and set too much store by the importance of the courage and spirit of their troops. These proved insufficient against modern weapons, especially the machine gun. The French offensive on Germany's western frontier failed totally. In a sense this defeat was better than a partial success because it released troops for use against the main German army. As a result the French and the British were able to stop the Germans at the Battle of the Marne in September 1914.

Thereafter, the nature of the war in the west changed completely and became one of position instead of movement. Both sides dug in

In 1914 few Europeans could imagine the carnage of modern war. These French cavalrymen with their brass breastplates, swords, and lances had no idea in August 1914 they were riding to a war of machine guns, poison gas, and trench warfare. [Bildarchiv Preussischer Kulturbesitz]

behind a wall of trenches protected by barbed wire that stretched from the North Sea to Switzerland. Strategically placed machine-gun nests made assaults difficult and dangerous. Both sides, nonetheless, attempted massive attacks prepared for by artillery barrages of unprecedented and horrible force and duration. Still the defense was always able to recover and to bring up reserves fast enough to prevent a breakthrough.

Sometimes assaults that cost hundreds of thousands of lives produced advances that could be measured only in hundreds of yards. The introduction of poison gas as a solution to the problem proved ineffective. In 1916 the British introduced the tank, which proved to

MAP 26-5 THE SCHLIEFFEN PLAN OF 1905 *Germany's grand strategy for quickly winning the war against France in 1914 is shown by the wheeling arrows on the map. The crushing blows at France were, in the original plan, to be followed by the release of troops for use against Russia on Germany's Eastern front. But the plan was not adequately implemented, and the war on the Western front became a long contest in place.*

Count Alfred von Schlieffen was chief of the German general staff from 1891 to 1906. He formulated the plan on which the Germans based their hopes for victory in 1914. [Archiv für Kunst und Geschichte, Berlin]

be the answer to the machine gun, but throughout the war defense was supreme. For three years after its establishment, the western front moved only a few miles in either direction.

THE WAR IN THE EAST In the east the war began auspiciously for the Allies. The Russians advanced into Austrian territory and inflicted heavy casualties, but Russian incompetence and German energy soon reversed the situation. A junior German officer, Erich Ludendorff (1865–1937), under the command of the elderly General Paul von Hindenburg (1847–1934), destroyed or captured an entire army at the Battle of Tannenberg and defeated the Russians at the Masurian Lakes. In 1915 the Central Powers pressed their advantage in the east and drove into the Baltic states and western Russia, inflicting over two million casualties in a single year. Russian confidence was badly shaken, but the Russian army stayed in the field.

As the battle lines hardened, both sides sought new allies. Turkey (because of its hostility to Russia) and Bulgaria (the enemy of Serbia) joined the Central Powers.

Italy seemed an especially valuable prize, and both sides bid for Italian support with promises of a division of the spoils of victory. Because what the Italians wanted most was held by Austria, the Allies were able to make the more attractive promises. In a secret treaty of 1915 the Allies agreed to deliver to Italy most of *Italia Irredenta* (i.e., the Trentino, the South Tyrol, Trieste, and some of the Dalma-

On the Western Front, the trenches were defended by barbed wire and machine guns, which gave the defense the advantage. The masks worn by the French soldiers in this picture were the response to the German attempt to break the deadlock by using poison gas. [Roger-Viollet]

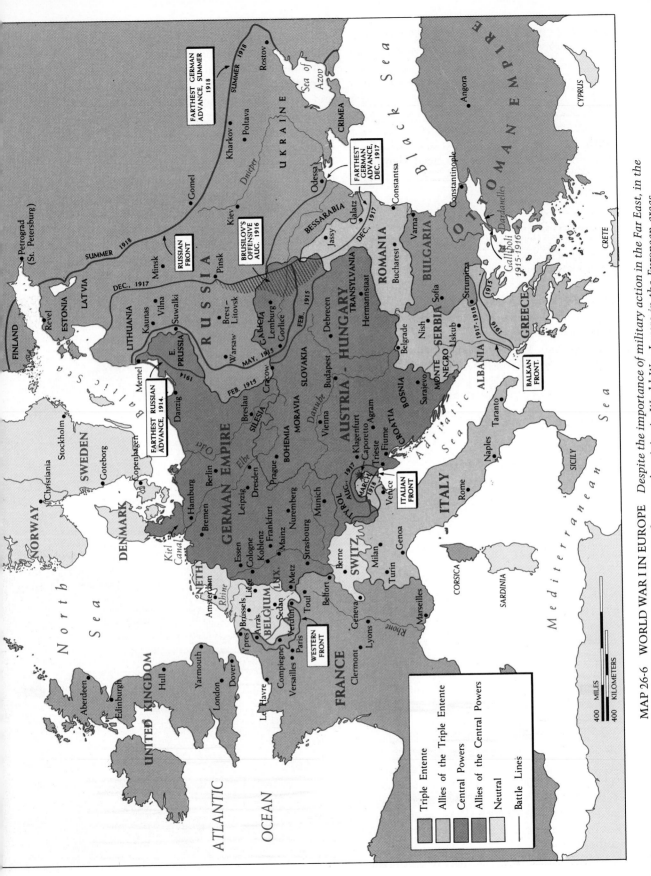

FARTHEST GERMAN ADVANCE, SUMMER 1918

SUMMER 1918

FARTHEST GERMAN ADVANCE, DEC. 1917

RUSSIAN FRONT

BRUSILOV'S OFFENSIVE AUG. 1916

DEC., 1917

FARTHEST RUSSIAN ADVANCE, 1914.

SUMMER 1918

FEB. 1915

MAY, 1915

FEB. 1915

1914

WESTERN FRONT

ITALIAN FRONT

BALKAN FRONT.

Place names and regions

- Petrograd (St. Petersburg)
- Rostov
- Sea of Azov
- Poltava
- Kharkov
- CRIMEA
- Revel
- ESTONIA
- FINLAND
- LATVIA
- Gomel
- UKRAINE
- Dnieper
- Kiev
- Pinsk
- RUSSIA
- Minsk
- Vilna
- Kaunas
- LITHUANIA
- Suwalki
- Brest-Litovsk
- BESSARABIA
- Jassy
- Galatz
- Odessa
- Constantsa
- Black Sea
- Angora
- CYPRUS
- OTTOMAN EMPIRE
- Constantinople
- Dardanelles
- Gallipoli 1915-1916
- CRETE
- Varna
- BULGARIA
- Sofia
- ROMANIA
- Bucharest
- TRANSYLVANIA
- Hermannstaat
- Debrecen
- Warsaw
- GALICIA
- Lemburg
- Gorlice
- Cracow
- SILESIA
- Breslau
- SLOVAKIA
- MORAVIA
- Budapest
- AUSTRIA-HUNGARY
- Vienna
- BOHEMIA
- Prague
- Memel
- Danzig
- E. PRUSSIA
- Oder
- Berlin
- Hamburg
- Bremen
- Leipzig
- Dresden
- Elbe
- GERMAN EMPIRE
- Essen
- Cologne
- Koblenz
- Frankfurt
- Mainz
- Nuremberg
- Munich
- Strasbourg
- Danube
- Klagenfurt
- TYROL
- AUG. 1917
- MARCH 1918
- Trieste
- Caporetto
- Fiume
- Agram
- CROATIA
- BOSNIA
- Sarajevo
- MONTE NEGRO
- SERBIA
- Belgrade
- Nish
- Uskub
- Strumitza
- ALBANIA 1917-1918
- 1915
- 1916
- GREECE
- Venice
- ITALY
- Rome
- Naples
- Taranto
- Genoa
- Turin
- Milan
- SWITZ.
- Berne
- Geneva
- Adriatic Sea
- CORSICA
- SARDINIA
- SICILY
- Mediterranean Sea
- Stockholm
- SWEDEN
- Goteborg
- Christiania
- NORWAY
- Copenhagen
- DENMARK
- Kiel Canal
- NETH.
- Amsterdam
- Rhine
- BELGIUM
- LUX.
- Brussels
- Liege
- Metz
- Sedan
- Ypres
- Arras
- Compiegne
- Paris
- Versailles
- Toul
- Verdun
- Belfort
- FRANCE
- Clermont
- Lyons
- Rhone
- Marseilles
- Baltic Sea
- North Sea
- UNITED KINGDOM
- Aberdeen
- Edinburgh
- Hull
- Yarmouth
- London
- Dover
- Le Havre
- ATLANTIC OCEAN

Legend

- Triple Entente
- Allies of the Triple Entente
- Central Powers
- Allies of the Central Powers
- Neutral
- Battle Lines

MILES 400
KILOMETERS 400

MAP 26-6 WORLD WAR I IN EUROPE   *Despite the importance of military action in the Far East, in the [...] and [...] the main theaters of activity in World War I were in the European areas.*

MAP 26-7 THE WESTERN FRONT 1914–1918
This map shows the crucial Western Front in detail.

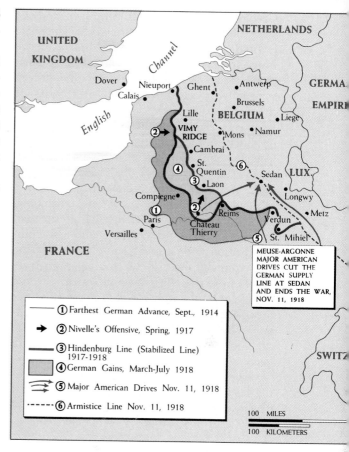

UNITED KINGDOM
NETHERLANDS
GERMA.
EMPIR
Channel
English
Dover
Nieuport
Ghent
Antwerp
Calais
Brussels
Liege
Lille
BELGIUM
Namur
VIMY RIDGE
Mons
②
Cambrai
St. Quentin
④
⑥
Sedan
LUX.
③
Laon
Longwy
Compiegne
①
②
Metz
Paris
Reims
Chateau Thierry
Verdun
Versailles
⑤
St. Mihiel
FRANCE
SWITZ

MEUSE-ARGONNE MAJOR AMERICAN DRIVES CUT THE GERMAN SUPPLY LINE AT SEDAN AND ENDS THE WAR, NOV. 11, 1918

① Farthest German Advance, Sept., 1914
② Nivelle's Offensive, Spring, 1917
③ Hindenburg Line (Stabilized Line) 1917-1918
④ German Gains, March-July 1918
⑤ Major American Drives Nov. 11, 1918
⑥ Armistice Line Nov. 11, 1918

100 MILES
100 KILOMETERS

tian Islands) after victory. By the spring of 1915 Italy was engaging Austrian armies. The Italian campaign drained the strength of the Central Powers to a degree. However, the alliance with Italy generally proved a disappointment to the Allies and never produced significant results. Romania joined the Allies in 1916 but was quickly defeated and driven from the war.

In the Far East, Japan honored its alliance with Britain and entered the war. The Japanese quickly overran the German colonies in China and the Pacific and used the opportunity to improve their own position against China.

Both sides also tried the tactic of subversion by appealing to nationalistic sentiment in areas held by the enemy. The Germans supported nationalist movements among the Irish, the Flemings in Belgium, and the Poles and the Ukrainians under Russian rule. They even tried to persuade the Turks to lead a Muslim uprising against the British and the French in North Africa.

The Allies also used the device of subversion, with greater success. They sponsored movements of national autonomy for the

A British tank is shown in action on the Western Front in 1917. The tank was impervious to machine gun fire. Had tanks been used in great numbers before 1918, they could have broken the stalemate in the West. [National Archives]

943

Czechs, the Slovaks, the south Slavs, and the Poles that were under Austrian rule. They also favored a movement of Arab independence from Turkey. Guided by Colonel T. E. Lawrence (1888–1935), this last scheme proved especially successful in the later years of the war.

In 1915 the Allies undertook to break the deadlock in the fighting by going around it. The idea came chiefly from Winston Churchill (1874–1965), First Lord of the British Admiralty. He proposed an attack on the Dardanelles and the swift capture of Constantinople. This policy would knock Turkey from the war, bring help to the Balkan front, and ease communication with Russia. The plan was daring but promising and, in its original form, presented little risk. British naval superiority and the element of surprise would allow the forcing of the straits and the capture of Constantinople by purely naval action. Even if the scheme failed, the fleet could escape with little loss.

Success depended on timing, speed, and daring leadership, but all of these were lacking. The execution of the attack was inept and overly cautious. Troops were landed, and as resistance continued, the Allied commitment increased. Before the campaign was abandoned, the Allies lost almost 150,000 men and diverted three times that number from more useful occupation.

RETURN TO THE WEST Both sides turned back to the west in 1916. General Erich von Falkenhayn (1861–1922), who had succeeded Moltke in September 1914, sought success by an attack on the French stronghold of Verdun. His plan was not to take the fortress or to break through the line but to inflict enormously heavy casualties on the French, who must defend it against superior firepower coming from several directions. He, too, underestimated the superiority of the defense. The French were able to hold Verdun with comparatively few men and to inflict almost as many casualties as they suffered. The commander of Verdun, Henri Pétain (1856–1951), became a national hero, and "They shall not pass" became a slogan of national defiance.

The Allies tried to end the impasse by launching a major offensive along the River Somme in July. Aided by a Russian attack in the east that drew off some German strength

Delegates to the peace conference of 1919 in Paris included: Standing in foreground is Prince Feisal (3rd son of King Hussein), Lawrence (of Arabia) (middle row second from right). Second from left is Brig. Gen. Nuri Pasha Said (Baghdad). [Bettmann Archive]

and by an enormous artillery barrage, they hoped at last to break through. Once again, the superiority of the defense was demonstrated. Enormous casualties on both sides brought no result. On all fronts the losses were great and the results meager. The war on land dragged on with no end in sight.

THE WAR AT SEA As the war continued, control of the sea became more important. The British ignored the distinction between war supplies (which were contraband according to international law) and food or other peaceful cargo (which was not subject to seizure). They imposed a strict blockade meant to starve out the enemy, regardless of international law. The Germans responded with submarine warfare meant to destroy British shipping and to starve the British. They declared the waters around the British Isles a war zone, where even neutral ships would not be safe. Both policies were unwelcome to neutrals, and especially to the United States, which conducted extensive trade in the Atlantic. Yet the sinking of neutral ships by German submarines was both more dramatic and more offensive.

In 1915 the British liner *Lusitania* was torpedoed by a German submarine. Among the 1,200 drowned were 118 Americans. President Woodrow Wilson (1856–1924) warned Germany that a repetition would not be accepted; the Germans desisted for the time being rather than further anger the United States. This development gave the Allies a considerable advantage. The German fleet that had cost so much money and had caused so much trouble played no significant part in the war. The only battle it fought was at Jutland in the spring of 1916. The battle resulted in a standoff and confirmed British domination of the surface of the sea.

AMERICA ENTERS THE WAR In December 1916 President Woodrow Wilson of the United States intervened in an attempt to bring about a negotiated peace. However, neither side was willing to renounce war aims that its opponent found unacceptable. The war seemed likely to continue until one or both sides reached exhaustion.

Two events early in 1917 changed the situation radically. On February 1 the Germans announced the resumption of unrestricted submarine warfare, which led the United States to

MAJOR CAMPAIGNS AND EVENTS OF WORLD WAR I

August 1914	Germans attack in West
August–September 1914	First Battle of the Marne
September 1914	Battles of Tannenberg and the Masurian Lakes
April 1915	British land at Gallipoli, start of Dardanelles Campaign
May 1915	Germans sink American ship Lusitania
February 1916	Germans attack Verdun
May–June 1916	Battle of Jutland
February 1917	Germans declare unrestricted submarine warfare
March 1917	Russian Revolution
April 1917	U.S. enters War
November 1917	Bolsheviks seize power
March 1918	Treaty of Brest-Litovsk
March 1918	German Offensive in the West
November 1918	Armistice

break off diplomatic relations. On April 6 the United States declared war on the Central Powers. One of the deterrents to an earlier American intervention had been the presence of autocratic tsarist Russia among the Allies. Wilson could conceive of the war only as an idealistic crusade "to make the world safe for democracy." That problem was resolved in March of 1917 by a revolution in Russia that overthrew the tsarist government.

The Russian Revolution

The March Revolution in Russia was neither planned nor led by any political faction. It was the result of the collapse of the monarchy's ability to govern. Although public opinion had strongly supported Russian entry into the war, the conflict put far too great demands on the resources of the country and the efficiency of the tsarist government.

Nicholas II was weak and incompetent and was suspected of being under the domination of his German wife and the insidious monk Rasputin, who was assassinated by a group of Russian noblemen in 1916. Military and domestic failures produced massive casualties, widespread hunger, strikes by workers, and disorganization in the army. The peasant dis-

The Outbreak of the Russian Revolution

The great Russian revolution of 1917 started with a series of ill-organized demonstrations in Petrograd early in the month of March. The nature of these actions and the incompetence of the government's response are described in the memoirs of Maurice Paléologue, the French ambassador.

Monday, March 12, 1917

At half-past eight this morning, just as I finished dressing, I heard a strange and prolonged din which seemed to come from the Alexander Bridge. I looked out: there was no one on the bridge, which usually presents such a busy scene. But, almost immediately, a disorderly mob carrying red flags appeared at the end which is on the right bank of the Neva, and a regiment came towards it from the opposite side. It looked as if there would be a violent collision, but on the contrary the two bodies coalesced. The army was fraternizing with revolt.

Shortly afterwards, someone came to tell me that the Volhynian regiment of the Guard had mutinied during the night, killed its officers and was parading the city, calling on the people to take part in the revolution and trying to win over the troops who still remain loyal.

At ten o'clock there was a sharp burst of firing and flames could be seen rising somewhere on the Liteïny Prospekt which is quite close to the embassy. Then silence.

Accompanied by my military attaché, Lieutenant-Colonel Lavergne, I went out to see what was happening. Frightened inhabitants were scattering through the streets. There was indescribable confusion at the corner of the Liteïny. Soldiers were helping civilians to erect a barricade. Flames mounted from the Law Courts. The gates of the arsenal burst open with a crash. Suddenly the crack of machine-gun fire split the air: it was the regulars who had just taken up position near the Nevsky Prospekt. The revolutionaries replied. I

content that had plagued the countryside before 1914 did not subside during the conflict. In 1916 the tsar adjourned the Duma Russian's parliament, and proceeded to rule alone. All political factions were in one way or another discontented.

The Provisional Government of the Mensheviks

In early March 1917 strikes and worker demonstrations erupted in Petrograd, as Saint Petersburg had been renamed. The ill-disciplined troops in the city refused to fire on the demonstrators. The tsar abdicated on March 15. The government of Russia fell into the hands of members of the reconvened Duma, who soon constructed a provisional government composed chiefly of Constitutional Democrats with Western sympathies.

At the same time the various socialists, including both Social Revolutionaries and Social Democrats of the Menshevik wing, began to organize the workers into soviets, councils of workers and soldiers. Initially they allowed the provisional government to function without actually supporting it. As relatively orthodox Marxists, the Mensheviks believed that a bourgeois stage of development must come to Russia before the revolution of the proletariat could be achieved. They were willing to work temporarily with the Constitutional Democrats (Cadets) in a liberal regime, but they became estranged as the Cadets failed to control the army or to purge "reactionaries" from the government.

had seen enough to have no doubt as to what was coming. Under a hail of bullets I returned to the embassy with Lavergne who had walked calmly and slowly to the hottest corner out of sheer bravado.

About half-past eleven I went to the Ministry for Foreign Affairs, picking up Buchanan [the British ambassador to Russia] on the way.

I told Pokrovski [the Russian foreign minister] everything I had just witnessed.

"So it's even more serious than I thought," he said.

But he preserved unruffled composure, flavoured with a touch of scepticism, when he told me of the steps on which the ministers had decided during the night:

"The sitting of the Duma has been prorogued to April and we have sent a telegram to the Emperor, begging him to return at once. With the exception of M. Protopopov [the Minister of the Interior, in charge of the police], my colleagues and I all thought that a dictatorship should be established without delay; it would be conferred upon some general whose prestige with the army is pretty high, General Russky for example."

I argued that, judging by what I saw this morning, the loyalty of the army was already too heavily shaken for our hopes of salvation to be based on the use of the "strong hand," and that the immediate appointment of a ministry inspiring confidence in the Duma seemed to me more essential than ever, as there is not a moment to lose. I reminded Pokrovski that in 1789, 1830, and 1848, three French dynasties were overthrown because they were too late in realizing the significance and strength of the movement against them. I added that in such a grave crisis the representative of allied France had a right to give the Imperial Government advice on a matter of internal politics.

Buchanan endorsed my opinion.

Pokrovski replied that he personally shared our views, but that the presence of Protopopov in the Council of Ministers paralyzed action of any kind.

I asked him:

"Is there no one who can open the Emperor's eyes to the real situation?"

He heaved a despairing sigh.

"The Emperor is blind!"

Deep grief was writ large on the face of the honest man and good citizen whose uprightness, patriotism and disinterestedness I can never sufficiently extol.

Maurice Paléologue, An Ambassador's Memoirs *(London: Doubleday & Company, Inc., Hutchinson Publishing Group Ltd., 1924), pp. 221–225. Reprinted by permission.*

In this climate the provisional government made the important decision to remain loyal to the existing Russian alliances and to continue the war against Germany. In this regard the provisional government was accepting the tsarist foreign policy and was associating itself with the source of much domestic suffering and discontent. The fate of the provisional government was sealed by the collapse of the new offensive in the summer of 1917. Disillusionment with the war, shortages of food and other necessities at home, and the growing demand by the peasants for land reform undermined the government. This occurred even after its leadership had been taken over by the moderate socialist Alexander Kerensky (1881–1970). Moreover, discipline in the army had badly disintegrated.

Lenin and the Bolsheviks

Ever since April the Bolshevik wing of the Social Democratic Party had been working against the provisional government. The Germans, in their most successful attempt at subversion, had rushed the brilliant Bolshevik leader V. I. Lenin in a sealed train from his exile in Switzerland across Germany to Petrograd. They hoped that he would cause trouble for the revolutionary government.

Lenin saw the opportunity to achieve the political alliance of workers and peasants that he had discussed theoretically before the war. In speech after speech he hammered away on the theme of peace, bread, and land. The Bolsheviks soon gained control of the soviets. They demanded that all political power go to the soviets. The failure of the summer offensive encouraged them to attempt a *coup*, but the effort was premature and a failure. Lenin fled to Finland, and his chief collaborator, Leon Trotsky (1877–1940), was imprisoned.

The failure of a right-wing counter *coup* gave the Bolsheviks another chance. Trotsky, released from prison, led the powerful Petrograd Soviet. Lenin returned in October, insisted to his doubting colleagues that the time was ripe to take power, and by the extraordinary force of his personality persuaded them to act. Trotsky organized the *coup* that took place on November 6 and that concluded with an armed assault on the provisional government. The Bolsheviks, almost as much to their own astonishment as to that of the rest of the world, had come to rule Russia.

The Communist Dictatorship

The victors moved to fulfill their promises and to assure their own security. The provisional government had decreed an election for late November to select a Constituent Assembly. The Social Revolutionaries won a large majority over the Bolsheviks. When the assembly gathered in January, it met for only a day before the Red Army, controlled by the Bolsheviks, dispersed it. All other political parties also ceased to function in any meaningful fashion. In November and January the Bolshevik government promulgated decrees that nationalized the land and turned it over to its peasant proprietors. Factory workers were put in charge of their plants. Banks were taken from their owners and seized for the state, and the debt of the tsarist government was repudiated. Property of the Church reverted to the state.

The Bolshevik government also took Russia out of the war, which they believed benefited only capitalism. They signed an armistice with Germany in December 1917. On March 3, 1918, they accepted the Treaty of Brest-Litovsk, by which Russia yielded Poland, the Baltic states, and the Ukraine. Some territory in the Transcaucasus region went to Turkey. In addition the Bolsheviks agreed to pay a heavy war indemnity.

These terms were a terribly high price to pay for peace, but Lenin had no choice. Russia was incapable of renewing the war effort, and the Bolsheviks needed time to impose their rule on a devastated and chaotic Russia. Moreover,

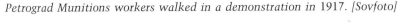

Petrograd Munitions workers walked in a demonstration in 1917. [Sovfoto]

Lenin Establishes His Dictatorship

After the Bolshevik coup in October, elections for the Constituent Assembly were held in November. The results gave a majority to the Social Revolutionary Party and embarrassed the Bolsheviks. Using his control of the Red Army, Lenin closed the Constituent Assembly in January 1918, after it had met for only one day, and established the rule of a revolutionary elite and his own dictatorship. Here is the crucial Bolshevik decree.

The Constituent Assembly, elected on the basis of lists drawn up prior to the October Revolution, was an expression of the old relation of political forces which existed when power was held by the compromisers and the Cadets. When the people at the time voted for the candidates for the Socialist-Revolutionary Party, they were not in a position to choose between the Right Socialist-Revolutionaries, the supporters of the bourgeoisie, and the Left Socialist-Revolutionaries, the supporters of Socialism. Thus the Constituent Assembly, which was to have been the crown of the bourgeois parliamentary republic, could not but become an obstacle in the path of the October Revolution and the Soviet power.

The October Revolution, by giving the power to the Soviets, and through the Soviets to the toiling and exploited classes, aroused the desperate resistance of the exploiters, and in the crushing of this resistance it fully revealed itself as the beginning of the socialist revolution . . . the majority in the Constituent Assembly which met on January 5 was secured by the party of the Right Socialist-Revolutionaries, the party of Kerensky, Avksentyev and Chernov. Naturally, this party refused to discuss the absolutely clear, precise, and unambiguous proposal of the supreme organ of Soviet power, the Central Executive Committee of the Soviets, to recognize the program of the Soviet power, to recognize the "Declaration of Rights of the Toiling and Exploited People," to recognize the October Revolution and the Soviet power. . . .

The Right Socialist-Revolutionary and Menshevik parties are in fact waging outside the walls of the Constituent Assembly a most desperate struggle against the Soviet power. . . .

Accordingly, the Central Executive Committee resolves: The Constituent Assembly is hereby dissolved.

Lenin believed that communist revolutions might soon sweep across other nations in Europe as a result of the war and the Russian example.

Until 1921 the New Bolshevik government confronted major domestic resistance. A civil war erupted between the "Red" Russians supporting the revolution and the "White" Russians, who opposed the Bolshevik triumph. In the summer of 1918 the tsar and his family were murdered. Loyal army officers continued to fight the revolution and eventually received aid from the Allied armies. However, under the leadership of Trotsky the Red Army eventually overcame the domestic opposition. By 1921 Lenin and his supporters were in firm control.

The End of World War I

The internal collapse of Russia and the later Treaty of Brest-Litovsk brought Germany to the peak of its success. The Germans con-

American troops move toward the trenches on the Western Front. The arrival of increasing numbers of fresh American troops in France in 1918 tipped the balance decisively in the Allies' favor. [National Archives]

trolled eastern Europe and its resources, especially food, and by 1918 they were free to concentrate their forces on the western front.

This turn of events would probably have been decisive had it not been balanced by American intervention. Still, American troops would not arrive in significant numbers for about a year, and both sides tried to win the war in 1917.

An Allied attempt to break through in the west failed disastrously, bringing heavy losses to the British and the French and causing a mutiny in the French army. The Austrians, supported by the Germans, defeated the Italians at Caporetto and threatened to overrun Italy, but they were checked with the aid of Allied troops. The deadlock continued, but time was running out for the Central Powers.

Germany's Last Offensive

In 1918 the Germans decided to gamble everything on one last offensive. (In this decision they were persuaded chiefly by Ludendorff, by then Quartermaster-General, second in command to Hindenburg, but the real leader of the army.) The German army pushed forward and even reached the Marne again but got no farther. They had no more reserves, and the entire

nation was exhausted. The Allies, on the other hand, were bolstered by the arrival of American troops in ever-increasing numbers. They were able to launch a counteroffensive that proved to be irresistible. As the Austrian fronts in the Balkans and Italy collapsed, the German high command knew that the end was imminent.

Ludendorff was determined that peace should be made before the German army could be thoroughly defeated in the field and that the responsibility should fall on civilians. For some time he had been the effective ruler of Germany under the aegis of the emperor. He now allowed a new government to be established on democratic principles and to seek peace immediately. The new government, under Prince Max of Baden, asked for peace on the basis of the Fourteen Points that President Wilson had declared as the American war aims. These were idealistic principles, including self-determination for nationalities, open diplomacy, freedom of the seas, disarmament, and establishment of a league of nations to keep the peace. Wilson insisted that he would deal only with a democratic German government because he wanted to be sure that he was dealing with the German people and not merely their rulers.

The disintegration of the German army forced William II to abdicate on November 9, 1918. The majority branch of the Social Democratic Party proclaimed a republic to prevent the establishment of a soviet government under the control of their radical, Leninist wing, which had earlier broken away as the Independent Socialist Party. Two days later this republican, socialist-led government signed the armistice that ended the war by accepting German defeat. At the time of the armistice the German people were, in general, unaware that their army had been defeated in the field and was crumbling. No foreign soldier stood on German soil. It appeared to many Germans that they could expect a negotiated and mild settlement. The real peace was quite different and embittered the German people. Many of them came to believe that Germany had not been defeated but had been tricked by the enemy and betrayed—even stabbed in the back—by republicans and socialists at home.

The victors rejoiced, but they also had much to mourn. The casualties on all sides came to about ten million dead and twice as many wounded. The economic and financial resources of the European states were badly strained. The victorious Allies, formerly creditors to the world, became debtors to the new American colossus, itself barely touched by the calamities of war.

The old international order, moreover, was dead. Russia was ruled by a Bolshevik dictatorship that preached world revolution and the overthrow of capitalism everywhere. Germany was in chaos. Austria-Hungary had disintegrated into a swarm of small national states competing for the remains of the ancient empire. These kinds of change stirred the colonial territories ruled by the European powers, and overseas empires would never again be as secure as they had seemed before the war. Europe was no longer the center of the world, free to interfere when it wished or to ignore the outer regions if it chose. Its easy confidence in material and moral progress was shattered by the brutal reality of four years of horrible war. The memory of that war lived on to shake the nerve of the victorious Western powers as they confronted the new conditions of the postwar world.

The representatives of the victorious states gathered at Versailles and other Parisian suburbs in the first half of 1919. Wilson speaking for the United States, David Lloyd George (1863–1945) for Britain, Georges Clemenceau (1841–1929) for France, and Vittorio Emanuele Orlando (1860–1952) for Italy made up the Big Four. Japan, now recognized for the first time as a great power, also had an important part in the discussions. The diplomats who met in Paris had a far more difficult task than the one facing those who had sat at Vienna a century earlier. Both groups attempted to restore order to the world after long and costly wars. However, at the earlier conference Metternich and his associates could confine their thoughts to Europe. France had acknowledged defeat and was willing to take part in and uphold the Vienna settlement. The diplomats at Vienna were not much affected by public opinion; and they could draw the new map of Europe along practical lines determined by the realities of power and softened by compromise.

Obstacles Faced by the Peacemakers

The negotiators at Paris in 1919 were not so fortunate. They represented constitutional, generally democratic governments, and public opinion had become a mighty force. Though there were secret sessions, the conference often worked in the full glare of publicity. Nationalism had become almost a secular religion, and Europe's many ethnic groups could not be relied on to remain quiet while they were distributed on the map at the whim of the great powers. World War I, moreover, had been transformed by propaganda and especially by the intervention of Woodrow Wilson into a moral crusade to achieve a peace that would be just as well as secure. The Fourteen Points set forth the right of nationalities to self-determination as an absolute value; but in fact there was no way to draw the map of Europe to match ethnic groups perfectly with their homelands. All these elements made compromise difficult.

Wilson's idealism, moreover, came into conflict with the more practical war aims of the victorious powers and with many of the secret

The Big Four at Versailles were Lloyd George of Britain, Orlando of Italy, Clemenceau of France, and Wilson of the United States. [National Archives]

treaties that had been made before and during the war. The British and French people had been told that Germany would be made to pay for the war. Russia had been promised control of Constantinople in return for recognition of the French claim to Alsace-Lorraine and British control of Egypt. Romania had been promised Transylvania at the expense of Hungary.

Some of the agreements contradicted others: Italy and Serbia had competing claims to the islands and shore of the Adriatic. During the war the British had encouraged Arab hopes of an independent Arab state carved out of the Ottoman Empire. But those plans conflicted with the Balfour Declaration (1917), in which the British seemed to accept Zionist ideology and to promise the Jews a national home in Palestine. Both of these plans stood in conflict with an Anglo-French agreement to divide the Near East between the two Western powers.

The continuing national goals of the victors presented further obstacles to an idealistic "peace without victors." France was keenly conscious of its numerical inferiority to Germany and of the low birth rate that would keep it inferior. So France was naturally eager to achieve a settlement that would permanently weaken Germany and preserve French superiority. Italy continued to seek the acquisition of *Italia Irredenta;* Britain continued to look to

its imperial interests; Japan pursued its own advantage in Asia. And the United States insisted on freedom of the seas, which favored American commerce, and on its right to maintain the Monroe Doctrine.

Finally, the peacemakers of 1919 faced a world still in turmoil. The greatest immediate threat appeared to be posed by the spread of Bolshevism. While Lenin and his colleagues were distracted by civil war, the Allies landed small armies at several places in Russia in the hope of overthrowing the Bolshevik regime. The revolution seemed likely to spread as communist governments were established in Bavaria and Hungary. Berlin also experienced a dangerous communist uprising led by the "Spartacus group." The Allies were sufficiently worried by these developments to allow and to support suppression of these communist movements by right-wing military forces. They even allowed an army of German volunteers to operate against the Bolsheviks in the Baltic states.

The fear of the spread of communism played a part in the thinking of the diplomats at Versailles, but it was far from dominant. The Germans kept playing on such fears as a way of getting better terms, but the Allies, and especially the French, would not hear of it. Fear of Germany remained the chief concern for

France. More traditional and more immediate interests governed the policies of the other Allies.

The Peace

The Paris settlement consisted of five separate treaties between the victors and the defeated powers. Formal sessions began on January 18, 1919, and the last treaty was signed on August 10, 1920. Wilson arrived in Europe to unprecedented acclaim. Liberals and idealists expected a new kind of international order achieved in a new and better way, but they were soon disillusioned. "Open covenants openly arrived at" soon gave way to closed sessions in which Wilson, Clemenceau, and Lloyd George made arrangements that seemed cynical to outsiders.

The notion of "a peace without victors" became a mockery when the Soviet Union (as Russia was now called) and Germany were excluded from the peace conference. The Germans were simply presented with a treaty and compelled to accept it in a manner that fully justified their complaint that the treaty had not been negotiated but dictated. The principle of national self-determination was violated many times, as was unavoidable. Still, the diplomats of the small nations were angered by their exclusion from decisions. The undeserved adulation accorded Wilson on his arrival gradually turned into equally undeserved scorn. He had not abandoned his ideals lightly but had merely given way to the irresistible force of reality.

THE LEAGUE OF NATIONS Wilson was able to make unpalatable concessions without abandoning his ideals because he put great faith in a new instrument for peace and justice, the League of Nations. Its covenant was an essential part of the peace treaty. The league was not intended as an international government but as a body of sovereign states who agreed to pursue some common practices and to consult in the common interest, especially when war threatened. In that case the members promised to submit the matter to arbitration or to an international court or to the League Council. Refusal to abide by this agreement would justify league intervention in the form of economic and even military sanctions. However, the league was unlikely to be effective because it had no armed forces at its disposal. Furthermore, any action required the unanimous consent of its council, consisting of Britain, France, Italy, the United States, and Japan, as well as four other states that had temporary seats. The Covenant of the League bound its members to "respect and preserve" the territorial integrity of all its members; this was generally seen as a device to ensure the security of the victorious powers. The exclusion from the League Assembly of Germany and the Soviet Union further undermined the league's claim to evenhandedness.

COLONIES Another provision of the covenant dealt with colonial areas. These were to be placed under the "tutelage" of one of the great powers under league supervision and encouraged to advance toward independence. Because there were no teeth in this provision, very little advance was made. Provisions for disarmament were doomed to be equally ineffective. Members of the league remained fully sovereign and continued to pursue their own national interests. Only Wilson seems to have put much faith in its future ability to produce peace and justice. This belief allowed him to approve territorial settlements that violated his own principles.

GERMANY In the west the main territorial issue was the fate of Germany. Although a united Germany was less than fifty years old, no one seems to have thought of undoing Bismarck's work and dividing it into its component parts. The French would have liked to detach the Rhineland and set it up as a separate buffer state, but Lloyd George and Wilson would not permit that. Still, they could not ignore France's need for protection against a resurgent Germany. France received Alsace-Lorraine and the right to work the coal mines of the Saar for fifteen years. Germany west of the Rhine and fifty kilometers east of it was to be a demilitarized zone; Allied troops on the west bank could stay there for fifteen years.

In addition to this physical barrier to a new German attack, the treaty provided that Britain and the United States would guarantee to aid France if it were attacked by Germany. Such an attack was made more unlikely by the permanent disarmament of Germany. Its army was limited to 100,000 men on long-term ser-

MAP 26-8 WORLD WAR I PEACE SETTLEMENT IN EUROPE AND THE MIDDLE EAST *The map of central and Eastern Europe, as well as that of the Middle East, underwent drastic revision after World War I. The enormous geographical losses suffered by Germany, Austria-Hungary, the Ottoman Empire, Bulgaria, and Russia were the other side of the coin represented by gains for France, Italy, Greece, and Romania and the appearance, or reappearance, of at least eight new independent states from Finland in the north to Yugoslavia in the south. The mandate system for former Ottoman territories outside Turkey proper laid foundations for several new, mostly Arab, states in the Middle East.*

vice; its fleet was all but eliminated; and it was forbidden to have war planes, submarines, tanks, heavy artillery, or poison gas. As long as these provisions were observed, France would be safe.

THE EAST The settlement in the east ratified the collapse of the great defeated empires that had ruled it for centuries. Germany's frontier was moved far to the west, excluding much of Silesia and most of Prussia. What was left of East Prussia was cut off from the rest of Germany by a corridor carved out to give the revived state of Poland access to the sea. The Austro-Hungarian Empire disappeared entirely, giving way to many smaller successor states. Most of its German-speaking people were gathered in the small Republic of Austria, cut off from the Germans of Bohemia and forbidden to unite themselves with Germany.

The Magyars occupied the much-reduced kingdom of Hungary. The Czechs of Bohemia and Moravia joined with the Slovaks and Ruthenians to the east to form Czechoslovakia, and this new state included several million unhappy Germans. The southern Slavs were united in the kingdom of Serbs, Croats, and Slovenes, or Yugoslavia. Italy gained the Trentino and Trieste. Romania was enlarged by receiving Transylvania from Hungary and Bessarabia from Russia. Bulgaria was diminished by the loss of territory to Greece and Yugoslavia. Russia lost vast territories in the west. Finland, Estonia, Latvia, and Lithuania became independent states, and a good part of Poland was carved out of formerly Russian soil.

The old Ottoman Empire disappeared. The new republic of Turkey was limited to little more than Constantinople and Asia Minor. The former Ottoman territories of Palestine and Iraq came under British control and Syria and Lebanon under French control as mandates of the League of Nations. Germany's former colonies in Africa were divided among Britain, France, and South Africa. The German Pacific possessions went to Australia, New Zealand, and Japan.

In theory the mandate system was meant to have the "advanced nations" govern the former colonies in the interests of the native peoples until they became ready to govern themselves. For this purpose they were divided into three categories, A, B, and C, in descending order of their readiness for independence.

In practice most mandated territories were treated as colonies by the powers under whose "tutelage" they came. Not even one Class A mandate had achieved full independence twenty years after the signing of the treaty. The legacy of colonialism was to remain a problem even after World War II.

REPARATIONS Perhaps the most debated part of the peace settlement dealt with reparations for the damage done by Germany during the war. Before the armistice the Germans promised to pay compensation "for all damages done to the civilian population of the Allies and their property." The Americans judged that the amount would be between $15 billion and $25 billion and that Germany would be able to pay that amount. However, France and Britain, worried about repaying their war debts to the United States, were eager to have Germany pay the full cost of the war, including pensions to survivors and dependents.

There was general agreement that Germany could not afford to pay such a sum, whatever it might be, and no sum was fixed at the conference. In the meantime Germany was to pay $5 billion annually until 1921. At that time a final figure would be set, which Germany would have to pay in thirty years. The French did not regret the outcome. Either Germany would pay and be bled into impotence, or Germany would refuse to pay and justify French intervention.

To justify these huge reparation payments, the Allies inserted the notorious Clause 231 into the treaty:

> The Allied and Associated Governments affirm, and Germany accepts, the responsibility of Germany and her allies for causing all the loss and damage to which the Allied and Associated Governments and their nationals have been subjected as a consequence of the war imposed upon them by aggression of Germany and her allies.

The Germans, of course, did not believe that they were solely responsible for the war and bitterly resented the charge. They had suffered the loss of vast territories containing millions of Germans and great quantities of badly needed natural resources. Yet they were presented with an astronomical and apparently unlimited reparations bill. To add insult to injury, they were required to admit to a war guilt that they did not feel.

Finally, to heap insult on insult, they were required to accept the entire treaty as it was written by the victors, without any opportunity for negotiation. Germany's Prime Minister Philipp Scheidmann (1865–1939) spoke of the treaty as the imprisonment of the German people and asked, "What hand would not wither that binds itself and us in these fetters?" But there was no choice. The Social Democrats and the Catholic Center Party formed a new government, and their representatives signed the treaty. These were the parties that formed the backbone of the Weimar government that ruled Germany until 1933. They never overcame the stigma of accepting the Treaty of Versailles.

Evaluation of the Peace

Few peace settlements have undergone more severe attacks than the one negotiated in Paris in 1919. It is natural that the defeated powers should object to it, but the peace soon came under bitter criticism in the victorious countries as well. Many of the French thought that it failed to provide adequate security for France, because it tied that security to promises of aid from the unreliable Anglo-Saxon countries. In England and the United States a wave of bitter criticism arose in liberal quarters because the treaty seemed to violate the idealistic and liberal aims that the Western leaders had professed.

It was not a peace without victors. It did not put an end to imperialism, but attempted to promote the national interests of the winning nations. It violated the principles of national self-determination by leaving significant pockets of minorities outside the borders of their national homelands.

THE ECONOMIC CONSEQUENCES OF THE PEACE The most influential critic was John Maynard Keynes (1883–1946), a brilliant British economist who took part in the peace conference. He resigned in disgust when he saw the direction it was taking and wrote a book called *The Economic Consequences of the Peace* (1920). It was a scathing attack, especially on reparations and the other economic aspects of the peace. It was also a skillful assault on the negotiators and particularly on Wilson, who was depicted as a fool and a hypocrite. Keynes argued that the Treaty of Versailles was both immoral and unworkable. He called it a Carthaginian peace, referring to the utter destruction of Carthage by Rome after the Third Punic War. He argued that such a

John Maynard Keynes served on the British delegation to the Paris peace conference of 1919. His denunciation of the Versailles Treaty helped undermine Western willingness to uphold its terms. [Bettmann/Hulton]

peace would bring economic ruin and war to Europe unless it were repudiated.

Keynes had a great effect on the British, who were already suspicious of France and glad of an excuse to withdraw from continental affairs. The decent and respectable position came to be one that aimed at revision of the treaty in favor of Germany. Even more important was the book's influence in the United States. It fed the traditional tendency toward isolationism and gave powerful weapons to Wilson's enemies. Wilson's own political mistakes helped prevent American ratification of the treaty. Consequently, America was out of the League of Nations and not bound to defend France. Britain, therefore, was also free from its obligation to France. France was left to protect itself without adequate means to do so for long.

Many of the attacks on the Treaty of Versailles are unjustified. It was not a Carthaginian peace. Germany was neither dismembered nor ruined. Reparations could be and were scaled down. Until the great world depression of the 1930s, the Germans recovered a high level of prosperity. Complaints against the peace should also be measured against the peace that the victorious Germans had imposed on Russia at Brest-Litovsk and the plans they had made for a European settlement in case of victory. Both were far more severe than anything enacted at Versailles. The attempt at achieving self-determination for nationalities was less than perfect, but it was the best solution Europe had ever accomplished in that direction.

DIVISIVE NEW BOUNDARIES AND TARIFF WALLS

The peace, nevertheless, was unsatisfactory in important ways. The elimination of the Austro-Hungarian Empire, however inevitable that might seem, created a number of serious problems. Economically it was disastrous, for it separated raw materials from manufacturing areas and producers from their markets by new boundaries and tariff walls. In hard times this separation created friction and hostility that aggravated other quarrels also created by the peace treaties. Po-

land contained unhappy German minorities, and Czechoslovakia was a collection of nationalities that did not find it easy to live together as a nation. Disputes over territories in eastern Europe promoted further tension.

The peace was inadequate on another level, as well. It rested on a victory that Germany did not admit. The Germans believed that they had been cheated rather than defeated. At the same time the high moral principles proclaimed by the Allies undercut the validity of the peace, for it plainly fell far short of those principles.

FAILURE TO ACCEPT REALITIES

Finally, the great weakness of the peace was its failure to accept reality. Germany and Russia must inevitably play an important part in European affairs, yet they were excluded from the settlement and from the League of Nations. Given the many discontented parties, the peace was not self-enforcing; yet no satisfactory machinery for enforcing it was established. The league was never a serious force for this purpose. It was left to France, with no guarantee of support from Britain and no hope of help from the United States, to defend the new arrangements. Finland, the Baltic states, Poland, Romania, Czechoslovakia, and Yugoslavia were created as a barrier to the expansion westward of Russian communism and as a threat in the rear to deter German revival. Most of these states, however, would have to rely on France in case of danger, and France was simply not strong enough for the task if Germany were to rearm.

The tragedy of the Treaty of Versailles was that it was neither conciliatory enough to remove the desire for change, even at the cost of war, nor harsh enough to make another war impossible. The only hope for a lasting peace required the enforcement of the disarmament of Germany while the more obnoxious clauses of the peace treaty were revised. Such a policy required continued attention to the problem, unity among the victors, and far-sighted leadership; but none of these was present in adequate supply during the next two decades.

The outburst of European imperialism in the last part of the nineteenth century brought the Western countries into contact with al- *most all the inhabited areas of the world. They intensified their activity in places where they had already been interested. The growth* of industry, increased ease of transportation and communication, and the growth of a world economic system all tended to bring previously remote and isolated places into the orbit of the West.

By the time of the outbreak of the war, European nations had divided all of Africa among themselves for exploitation in one way or another. The vast subcontinent of India had long been a British colony. The desirable parts of China were very much under European control for commercial purposes. Indo-China was under French rule and the islands of the Pacific had been divided up among the powers. Much of the Near East was under the nominal control of the Ottoman Empire, which was in its death throes and under European influence. The Monroe Doctrine made Latin America a protectorate of the United States. Japan, pushed out of its isolation, had itself become an imperial power at the expense of China and Korea.

But the world created by the New Imperialism did not last long. What began as yet another Balkan War involving the European powers became a general war that had a profound influence on much of the rest of the world. As the terrible war of 1914–1918 dragged on, the real motives that had driven the European powers to fight gave way to public affirmations of the principles of nationalism and self-determination. The peoples under colonial rule took the public statements—and sometimes promises made to them in private—seriously and sought to win their independence and nationhood.

For the most part, they were disappointed by the peace settlement. The establishment of the League of Nations and the system of mandates in place of the previous system of open colonial rule did not seem to change much. The British Empire grew even larger as it inherited vast territories from the defeated German and the defunct Ottoman Empire. The French retained and expanded their holdings in Africa, the Pacific, and the Near East. The Americans added to the islands they controlled in the Pacific. Japanese imperial ambitions were rewarded at the expense of China.

A glance at the new map of the world could give the impression that the old imperial nations, especially Britain and France, were more powerful than ever, but that impression would be superficial and misleading. The great Western European powers had paid an enormous price in lives, money, and will for their victory in the war. Colonial peoples pressed for the rights that were proclaimed as universal by the West but denied to their colonies; and some influential minorities in the countries that ruled them sympathized with colonial aspirations for independence. Tension between colonies and their ruling nations was a cause of serious instability in the world created by the Paris treaties of 1919.

Suggested Readings

L. ALBERTINI, *The Origins of the War of* 1914, 3 vols. (1952, 1957). Discursive but invaluable.

M. BALFOUR, *The Kaiser and His Times* (1972). A fine biography of William II.

V. R. BERGHAHN, *Germany and the Approach of War in 1914* (1973). A work similar in spirit to Fischer's [see below] but stressing the importance of Germany's naval program.

R. BOSWORTH, *Italy and the Approach of the First World War* (1983). A fine analysis of Italian policy.

L. L. FARRAR JR., *Arrogance and Anxiety: The Ambivalence of German Power 1848–1914.* (1981). A study of German politics and foreign policy.

S. B. FAY, *The Origins of the World War*, 2 vols. (1928). The best and most influential of the revisionist accounts.

M. FERRO, *The Great War, 1914–1918* (1973). A solid account of the course of World War I.

D. K. FIELDHOUSE, *The Colonial Experience: A Comparative Study from the Eighteenth Century* (1966). An excellent recent study.

F. FISCHER, *Germany's Aims in the First World War* (1967). An influential interpretation that stirred a great controversy in Germany and around the world by emphasizing Germany's role in bringing on the war.

F. FISCHER, *War of Illusions* (1975). A long and diffuse book that tries to connect German responsibility for the war with internal social, economic, and political developments.

I. GEISS, *July 1914* (1967). A valuable collection of documents by a student of Fritz Fischer's. The emphasis is on German documents and responsibility.

O. J. HALE, *The Great Illusion 1900–1914* (1971). A fine survey of the period, especially good on public opinion.

J. JOLL, *The Origins of the First World War* (1984). A brief but thoughtful analysis.

P. Kennedy, *The Rise of the Anglo-German Antagonism* 1860–1914 (1980). An unusual and thorough analysis of the political, economic, and cultural roots of important diplomatic developments.

J. M. Keynes, *The Economic Consequences of the Peace* (1920). The famous and influential attack on the Versailles Treaty.

V. G. Kiernan, *European Empires from Conquest to Collapse* 1815–1960 (1981). A study of the course of modern European imperialism.

L. Lafore, *The Long Fuse* (1965). A readable account of the origins of World War I that focuses on the problem of Austria-Hungary.

W. L. Langer, *The Diplomacy of Imperialism* (1935). A continuation of the previous study for the years 1890–1902.

W. L. Langer, *European Alliances and Alignments*, 2nd ed. (1966). A splendid diplomatic history of the years 1871–1890.

B. H. Liddell Hart, *The Real War* 1914–1918 (1964). A fine short account by an outstanding military historian.

D. C. B. Lieven, *Russia and the Origins of the First World War* (1983). A good account of the forces that shaped Russian policy.

E. Mantoux, *The Carthaginian Peace* (1952). A vigorous attack on Keynes' view [see Keynes, above].

W. J. Mommsen, *Theories of Imperialism* (1980). A study of the debate on the meaning of imperialism.

J. Steinberg, *Yesterday's Deterrent* (1965). An excellent study of Germany's naval policy and its consequences.

Z. Steiner, *Britain and the Origins of the First World War* (1977). A perceptive and informed account of the way British foreign policy was made in the years before the war.

A. J. P. Taylor, *The Struggle for Mastery in Europe*, 1848–1918 (1954). Clever but controversial.

L. C. F. Turner, *Origins of the First World War* (1970). Especially good on the significance of Russia and its military plans.

*There was much social and political disillusionment throughout Europe
during the 1920s. George Grosz in this painting satirized the various
conservative and rightwing groups in Weimar Germany including the army,
the courts, the newspapers, and the Nazi Party. [Bildarchiv Preussischer
Kulturbesitz]*

27

POLITICAL EXPERIMENTS OF THE 1920S

Pursuit of experimentation in politics and of normality in economic life marked the decade following the conclusion of the Paris settlement. In Great Britain the Labour Party came to power for the first time, and Ireland became an independent nation. Through war and revolution the Habsburg Empire became transformed into a series of successor states, only one of which became a successful democracy. Imperial Germany set out on the experiment of the Weimar Republic which encountered numerous determined violent opponents. In
Italy the political turmoil and social strains of the postwar era fostered the emergence of the authoritarian movement known as fascism. In the Soviet Union the Bolsheviks, having seized control of the government and winning the civil war, proceeded to reorganize every aspect of life in Russia.

Many of the political experiments failed, and the economic and social normality so many Europeans sought proved quite elusive. By the close of the decade the political path had been paved for the nightmares of brutally authoritarian governments and international aggression. Yet many of the people who had survived the Great War had hoped and worked for a better outcome. Authoritarianism and aggression were not the inescapable destiny of Europe. Their emergence was the result of failures in securing alternative modes of democratic political life and stable international relations.

Political and Economic Factors after the Paris Settlement

Political and economic life after 1919 was strikingly different than before the war. There were new governments in several nations. In all nations new political groups had become active. Many of them opposed certain aspects of the peace settlement; usually the objections were on nationalistic grounds. The peace treaties thus themselves became domestic political issues. The war and its financing radically changed European economic life. Across the continent governments became much more active in attempting to regulate their economies, a policy that had generally been rejected during the nineteenth century. Labor unions became much more active, and with the new democratic structures they were much more able to affect political life.

New Governments

In 1919 experimental political regimes studied the map of Europe. From Ireland to Russia new governments were seeking to gain the active support of their citizens and to solve the grievous economic problems caused by the war. In the Soviet Union the Bolsheviks regarded themselves as forging nothing less than a new kind of civilization. They gave little significant consideration to anything but an authoritarian rule.

The situation was different elsewhere on the Continent. Democratically elected parliamentary governments appeared where the autocratic, military empires of Germany and Austria-Hungary had previously held sway. Their goals were substantially more modest than those of the Bolsheviks. Yet to pursue parliamentary politics where it had never been meaningfully practiced proved no simple task. The Wilsonian vision of democratic, self-determined nations floundered on the harsh realities of economics, aggressive nationalism, and

revived political conservatism. Too often the will for democratic, parliamentary government, as well as experience in its exercise, was absent from the nations on which it had been bestowed. Moreover, in many of the new democracies important sectors of the citizenry believed that parliamentary politics was by its very nature corrupt or unequal to great nationalistic enterprise.

Demands for Revision of Versailles

Several other Europe-wide problems haunted the early interwar period and directly affected the decisions and actions of individual nations. The Paris settlement fostered both resentment and discontent in numerous countries. Germany had been humiliated. The arrangements for reparations led to seemingly endless haggling over payments. Various national groups in the successor states of eastern Europe felt that injustice had been done in their particular cases of self-determination. There were demands for further border adjustments.

On the other side the victorious powers, and especially France, often believed that the provisions of the treaty were being inadequately enforced. Consequently, throughout the 1920s, calls either to revise or to enforce the Paris treaties contributed to domestic political turmoil across the Continent. All too many political figures were willing to fish in these troubled international waters for a large catch of domestic votes.

Postwar Economic Problems

Simultaneous with the move toward political experiment and demands for revision of the recently established international order was a widespread desire to return to the economic prosperity of the prewar years. However, after 1918 it was impossible to restore what American President Warren Harding would shortly term "normalcy." During the conflict Europeans had turned against themselves and their civilization the vast physical power that they had created in the previous century.

More than 750,000 British soldiers had perished. The combat deaths for France and Germany were 1,385,000 and 1,808,000, respectively. Russia had lost no fewer than 1,700,000 troops. Scores of thousands more from other belligerent nations had also been killed. Still more millions had been wounded. These casualties meant not only the waste of human life and talent but also the loss of producers and consumers. There had also been widespread destruction of transport facilities, mines, and industry.

Another casualty of the conflict was the financial dominance and independence of Europe. At the opening of hostilities, Europe had been the financial and credit center of the world. At the close of the fighting, Europeans stood deeply in debt to each other and to the United States. The Bolsheviks had repudiated the debt of the tsarist government, much of which was owed to French creditors. Other nations could not pursue this revolutionary course. The Versailles settlement had imposed heavy financial obligations on Germany and its allies. The United States refused to ask reparations from Germany but firmly demanded repayment of war debts from its own allies.

On the one hand, the reparation and debt structure meant that no nation was fully in control of its own economic life. On the other hand, the absence of international economic cooperation meant that more than ever, individual nations felt compelled to pursue or to attempt to pursue selfish, nationalistic economic aims. It was perhaps the worst of all possible international economic worlds.

The market and trade conditions that had prevailed before 1914 had also changed radically. Russia, in large measure, withdrew from the European economic order. The political reconstruction of eastern and central Europe into the multitude of small successor states broke up the trade region formerly encompassed by Germany and Austria-Hungary.

One of the last British soldiers killed on the Western Front in November 1918. The millions killed or maimed in the war were one of the main causes for European weakness and instability in the 1920s and 1930s. [Library of Congress]

Most of those new states had weak economies hardly capable of competing in modern economic life. The new boundaries separated raw materials from the factories using them. Railway systems on which finished and unfinished products traveled might now lie under the control of two or more nations. Political and economic nationalism went together. New customs barriers were raised.

International trade also followed new patterns. The United States became less dependent on European production and assumed the status of a major competitor. During the war the belligerents had been forced to sell many of their holdings on other continents to finance the conflict. As a consequence, Europeans exercised less dominance over the world economy. Postwar economic growth within colonies or former colonies lowered the demand for European goods. The United States and Japan began to penetrate markets in Latin America and Asia that previously were dominated by European producers and traders.

New Roles for Government and Labor

The war effort in all countries occasioned new dimensions of state interference and direction in the economy. Large government bureaucracies had been organized to plan the course of production and the distribution of goods. Prices had been controlled, raw materials stockpiled, consumer goods rationed, and economic priorities set by government technocrats. The mechanism of the freely operating market so dear to nineteenth-century liberals had been rejected as a vehicle for economic decisionmaking. The economic planning skills learned during the war could be transferred to peacetime operations. Moreover, governments had learned about the immense productive and employment power of an economy placed under state control.

Labor had achieved new prominence within the wartime economic setting. The unions had actively supported the war effort of their nations. They had ensured labor peace for production. In turn, their members had received better wages, and their leaders had been admitted to high political councils. This wartime cooperation of unions and labor leaders with the various national governments destroyed the internationalism of the prewar labor move-

ment. However, it also meant that henceforth the demands of labor could not be ignored by governments. Although in peacetime wages might be lowered, they could very rarely be reduced to prewar levels. European workers intended to receive their just share of the fruits of their labor. Collective bargaining and union recognition brought on by the war also could not be abandoned. This improvement in both the status and the effective influence of labor was one of the most significant social and political changes to flow from World War I.

The social condition of the work force seemed to be improving while that of the middle class seemed to be stagnating or declining. Throughout the 1920s people from the various segments of the middle class remained very suspicious of the new role of labor and of socialist political parties. This suspicion and fear of potential loss of property on the part of the middle classes led them to seek to perpetuate the status quo and to fend off further social and economic advances of the working classes. In this regard, the European middle classes, once the vanguard of the liberal revolution, had become a thoroughly conservative political force.

The war and the peace settlement wrought one other major change that affected the course of political and economic life. The turn to liberal democracy resulted in the extension of the franchise to women and previously disenfranchised males. This meant that for the first time in European history the governments handling economic matters were responsible to mass electorates. Economics and politics had become more intimately connected than ever before. The economic and social anxieties of the electorate could and eventually did overcome its political scruples. Whereas previously economic discontent had been articulated through riots and later through unions, it could now be voiced through the ballot box.

Joyless Victors

France and Great Britain, with the aid of the United States, had won the war. France became the strongest military power on the Continent. Britain had escaped with almost no physical damage. Both nations, however, had lost vast numbers of young men in the conflict. Their economies were weak, and their overseas wealth and power stood much diminished. Compared with their contemporary events in Germany, Italy, and Russia, the interwar political development of the two major democracies seems rather tame. Neither experienced a revolution or a shift to authoritarian government. Yet this surface calm was largely illusory. Both were troubled democracies. To neither did victory in war bring the good life in peace.

France: The Search for Security

At the close of World War I, as after Waterloo, the revolution of 1848, and the defeat of 1871, the French voters elected a doggedly conservative Chamber of Deputies. The preponderance of military officers in blue uniforms among its members led to the nickname of the "Horizon Blue Chamber." The overwhelmingly conservative character of the chamber was registered in 1920 by its defeat of Georges Clemenceau's bid for the presidency. The crucial factor had been, of all things, the alleged leniency of the Paris treaties and the failure to establish a separate Rhineland state. The deputies wanted to achieve future security against Germany and Russian communism. They intended to make as few concessions to domestic social reform as possible. The 1920s were marked by fluctuations in ministries and a drift in domestic policy. The political turnstile remained ever active. Between the end of the war and January 1933, France was governed by no fewer than twenty-seven different cabinets.

NEW ALLIANCES During the first five years after the signing of the Treaty of Versailles, France accepted its role as the leading European power. The French plan was to enforce strictly the clauses of the treaty that were meant to keep Germany weak and, at the same time, to build a system of eastern alliances to replace the lost prewar alliance with Russia. In 1920 and 1921 three eastern states that had much to lose from revision of the treaty— Czechoslovakia, Romania, and Yugoslavia— formed the Little Entente. Before long France made military alliances with these states as well as with Poland. A dispute with Czechoslovakia over the control of Teschen prevented the Poles from joining the Little Entente, but the independent existence of Poland depended

on the maintenance of the Versailles settlement.

This new system of eastern alliances was the best France could do, but it was far weaker than the old Franco-Russian alliance. The new states combined were no match for the former power of imperial Russia, and they were neither united nor reliable. Poland and Romania were more concerned about Russia than about Germany, and the main target of the Little Entente was Hungary. If one of the eastern states were threatened by a resurgent Germany, there was considerable doubt that the others would be eager to come to its aid.

The formation of this new alliance system heightened the sense of danger and isolation felt by the two excluded powers, Germany and the Soviet Union. In 1922, while the European states were holding an economic conference at Genoa, the Russians and the Germans met at nearby Rapallo and signed a treaty of their own. It established diplomatic and economic relations that proved useful to both sides. Although the treaty contained no secret political or military clauses, such arrangements were suspected to exist. And it is now known that the Germans helped train the Russian army and gave their own army valuable experience in the use of tanks and planes in the Soviet Union. The news of Rapallo confirmed the French in their belief that Germany would not live up to the terms of the Versailles Treaty and helped move them to strong action.

QUEST FOR REPARATIONS In early 1923 the Allies, and France in particular, declared Germany to be in technical default of its reparations payments. Raymond Poincaré (1860–1934), France's powerfully nationalistic prime minister, took the opportunity to teach the Germans a lesson and force them to comply. On January 11, to ensure receipt of the hard-won reparations, the French government ordered its troops to occupy the Ruhr mining and manufacturing district. The response of the Weimar Republic was to order passive resistance. This policy amounted to calling a general strike in the largest industrial region of the nation. Confronted with this tactic, Poincaré sent French civilians to run the German mines and railroads. France got its way.

The Germans paid, but France also paid a great price for its victory. The English were alienated by the French heavy-handedness and

Raymond Poincaré (1860–1934). *As prime minister of France in the 1920s, Poincaré used force to compel Germany to pay reparations.* [Bildarchiv Preussischer Kulturbesitz]

took no part in the occupation. They became more suspicious of France and more sympathetic to Germany. The cost of the Ruhr occupation, moreover, vastly increased French as well as German inflation and damaged the French economy. As one scholar explained, the French "threatened to choke Germany to death; the Germans threatened to die. Neither side dared carry its threat to extremity."[1] From the French viewpoint, consequently, victory in the war and the achievement of considerable military power seemed to have brought the nation little of the prestige and effective influence it sought.

In 1924 the conservative ministry gave way to a coalition of leftist parties, the so-called *Cartel des Gauches,* led by Edouard Herriot (1872–1957). The chief policy changes of the new Cabinet were recognition of the Soviet Union and a more conciliatory policy toward Germany. Leadership on this score came from Aristide Briand (1862–1932), who was foreign minister for the remainder of the decade. He championed the League of Nations. He attempted to persuade his own nation that its

[1] A. J. P. Taylor, The Origins of the Second World War *(New York: Fawcett, 1961), p. 33.*

military power did not give it unlimited influence on the foreign affairs of Europe.

Under the leftist coalition a mild inflation also occurred. It had begun under the conservatives but picked up intensity in 1925. When the value of the franc fell sharply on the international money market in 1926, Poincaré returned to office as head of a national government composed of several parties. The value of the franc recovered somewhat, and inflation cooled. For the rest of the 1920s the conservatives remained in power. The country enjoyed a general prosperity that lasted until 1931, longer than in any other nation.

Great Britain: Economic Confusion

World War I profoundly changed British politics if not the political system. In 1918 Parliament expanded the electorate to include all men aged twenty-one and women aged thirty. (In 1928 the age for women voters was also lowered to twenty-one.) The prewar structure of parties and leadership also shifted. A coalition Cabinet composed of Liberal, Conservative, and Labour ministers had directed the war effort. The wartime ministerial participation of the Labour Party did much to dispel its radical image. For the Liberal Party, however, the conflict brought unexpected division.

Until 1916 Liberal Prime Minister Herbert Asquith had presided over the Cabinet. As disagreements over war management developed, he was ousted by fellow Liberal David Lloyd George. The party then became sharply split between followers of the two men. In 1918, against the wishes of both the Labour Party and the Asquith Liberals, Lloyd George decided to maintain the coalition through the tasks of the peace conference and the domestic reconstruction. The wartime coalition, now minus its Labour members, won a stunning victory at the polls. However, Lloyd George could thereafter remain prime minister only as long as his dominant Conservative partners wished to keep him.

During the 1918 election campaign there had been much talk about creating "a land fit for heroes to live in." It did not happen. Except for the three years immediately after the war, the British economy was depressed throughout the 1920s. Genuine postwar recovery simply

John Maynard Keynes Discusses the Future of Capitalism

Throughout the 1920s there arose much discussion about the future of capitalism. It had been repudiated in the Soviet Union. Across Europe the postwar capitalist economies were in difficulty. In 1924 the English economist John Maynard Keynes delivered a lecture at Oxford in which he attempted to clarify why people were having so much difficulty understanding the issues involved in the debate over capitalism. His own conclusion was that capitalism was a viable system if it were properly managed.

In Europe, or at least in some parts of Europe—but not, I think, in the United States of America—there is a latent reaction, somewhat widespread, against basing Society to the extent that we do upon fostering, encouraging, and protecting the money-motives of individuals. . . .

Confusion of thought and feeling leads to confusion of speech. Many people, who are really objecting to Capitalism as a way of life, argue as though they were objecting to it on the ground of its inefficiency in attaining its own objects. Contrariwise, devotees of Capitalism are often unduly conservative, and reject reforms in its technique, which might really strengthen and preserve it, for fear that they may prove to be first steps way from Capitalism itself. Nevertheless a time may be coming when we shall get clearer than at present as to when we are talking about Capitalism as an efficient or inefficient technique, and when we are talking about it as desirable or objectionable in itself. For my part, I think that Capitalism, wisely managed, can probably be made more efficient for attaining economic ends than any alternative system yet in sight, but that in itself it is in many ways extremely objectionable. Our problem is to work out a social organization which shall be as efficient as possible without offending our notions of a satisfactory way of life.

The next step forward must come, not from political agitation or premature experiments, but from thought. We need by an effort of the mind to elucidate our own feelings. At present our sympathy and our judgment are liable to be on different sides, which is a painful and paralyzing state of mind. . . . There is no party in the world at present which appears to me to be pursuing right aims by right methods. Material Poverty provides the incentive to change precisely in situations where there is very little margin of experiments. Material Prosperity removes the incentive just when it might be safe to take a chance. Europe lacks the means, America the will, to make a move. We need a new set of convictions which spring naturally from a candid examination of our own inner feelings in relation to the outside facts.

John Maynard Keynes, The End of Laissez-Faire *(London: Hogarth Press, 1916) as quoted in Hans Kohn, ed.,* The Modern World: 1848 to the Present, *2nd ed. (New York: The Macmillan Company; London: Collier-Macmillan Limited, 1968), pp. 243–244.*

did not get under way. Unemployment never dipped below 10 per cent and often hovered near 11 per cent. There were never fewer than a million workers unemployed. Government insurance programs to cover unemployed workers, widows, and orphans were expanded. There was no similar meaningful expansion in the number of jobs available. From 1922 onward, accepting the "dole" with little expectation of future employment became a wretched and degrading way of life for scores of thousands of poor British families.

THE FIRST LABOUR GOVERNMENT

In October 1922 the Conservatives dropped Lloyd George and replaced him with Bonar Law (1858–1923), one of their own. A Liberal would never again be prime minister. Stanley Baldwin (1867–1947) soon replaced Law, who fell victim to throat cancer. Baldwin decided to attempt to cure Britain's economic plight by abandoning free trade and imposing protective tariffs. The voters rejected the proposed policy in 1923. At the election the Conservative Party lost its majority in the House of Commons, but only votes from both Liberal and Labour party members could provide an alternative majority.

Labour had elected the second largest group of members to the Commons. Consequently, in December 1923, King George V (1910–1936) asked Ramsay MacDonald (1866–1937) to form the first Labour ministry in British history. The Liberal Party did not serve in the Cabinet but provided the necessary votes in the House of Commons to give the Labour ministry a working majority.

The Labour Party was socialistic in its platform, but not revolutionary. The party had expanded beyond its early trade-union base. MacDonald himself had opposed World War I and for a time had also broken with the party. His own version of socialism owed little, if anything, to Marx. His program consisted of plans for extensive social reform rather than for the nationalization or public seizure of industry. A sensitive politician, if not a great leader, MacDonald understood that the most important task facing the ministry was proving to the nation that the Labour Party was both respectable and responsible. His nine months in office achieved just that goal if little else of major importance. The establishment of Labour as a viable governing party signaled the permanent demise of the Liberal Party. It has continued to exist, but the bulk of its voters have drifted into either the Conservative or the Labour ranks.

THE GENERAL STRIKE OF 1926

The Labour government fell in the autumn of 1924 over charges of inadequate prosecution of a communist writer. Stanley Baldwin returned to office, where he remained until 1929. The problem of the stagnant economy remained uppermost in the public mind. Business and political leaders continued to believe that all would be well if they could restore the prewar conditions of trade. A major element in these conditions had been the gold standard as the basis for international trade. In 1925 the Conservative government returned to the gold standard, abandoned during the war, in hopes of re-creating the former monetary stability. However, the government set the conversion rate for the pound against other currencies too high and thus, in effect, raised the price of British goods to foreign customers.

In order to make their products competitive on the world market, British management attempted to lower prices by cutting wages. The coal industry was the sector most directly affected by the wage cuts. It was inefficient and poorly managed and had been in trouble ever since the end of the war.

Labor relations in the coal industry had been

Stanley Baldwin was the Conservative Party Prime Minister during the general strike of 1926. His solid, calm appearance suggested to many voters the qualities most needed in their government. [Bettmann Archive]

The British general strike of May 1926 produced much tension but little violence. Armored cars were used to protect food convoys in London and other big cities against attacks by strikers which never occurred. [Mary Evans Picture Library]

unruly for some time. In 1926, after cuts in wages and a breakdown in negotiations, the coal miners went out on strike. Soon thereafter, in May 1926, sympathetic workers in other industries engaged in a general strike lasting nine days. There was much tension but little violence. In the end the miners and the other unions capitulated. With such high levels of unemployment, organized labor was in a relatively weak position. After the general strike the Baldwin government attempted to reconcile labor primarily through an expansion of housing and reforms in the poor laws. Despite the economic difficulties of these years the actual standard of living of most British workers, including those receiving government insurance payments, actually improved somewhat.

EMPIRE World War I also modified Britain's imperial position. The aid given by the dominions, such as Canada and Australia, demonstrated a new independence on their part. Empire was a two-way proposition. The idea of self-determination as applied to Europe could not be prevented from filtering into imperial relationships. In India the Congress Party, led by Mohandas Gandhi (1869–1948), was beginning to attract widespread support. The British started to talk more about eventual self-government for the nation. Moreover, during the 1920s the Indian government achieved the right to impose tariffs for the protection of its own industry rather than for the advantage of British manufacturers. The British textile producers no longer had totally free access to the vast Indian market.

IRELAND A new chapter was written in the unhappy relations between Britain and Ireland during and after the war. In 1914 the Irish Home Rule Bill had passed Parliament, but its implementation was postponed for the duration of the conflict. As the war dragged on, Irish nationalists became determined to wait no longer. On Easter Monday, 1916, a national-

During the Easter Uprising in Dublin in 1916 several buildings were destroyed in the heart of the city. [Bettmann/Hulton]

ist uprising occurred in Dublin. It was the only rebellion of a national group to occur against any government engaged in the war. The British suppressed it in less than a week but then made a grave tactical blunder. They executed the Irish nationalist leaders who had been responsible for the uprising. Overnight those rebels became national martyrs. Leadership of the nationalist cause quickly shifted from the Irish Party in Parliament to the extremist Sinn Fein ("Ourselves Alone") movement.

In the election of 1918 the Sinn Fein Party won all but four of the Irish parliamentary seats outside Ulster. They refused to go to the Parliament at Westminster. Instead they constituted themselves into a Dail Eireann, or Irish Parliament. On January 21, 1919, they declared Irish independence. The military wing of Sinn Fein became the Irish Republican Army (IRA). The first president was Eamon De Valera (1882–1975), who had been born in the United States. Very quickly what amounted to a guerilla war broke out between the IRA and the British army supported by auxiliaries known as the Black and Tans. There was unu-

sually intense bitterness and hatred on both sides.

In late 1921 secret negotiations began between the two governments. In the treaty concluded in December 1921 the Irish Free State took its place beside the earlier dominions in the British Commonwealth: Canada, Australia, New Zealand, and South Africa. The six counties of Ulster, or Northern Ireland, were permitted to remain part of what was now called the United Kingdom of Great Britain and Northern Ireland, with provisions for home rule. No sooner had the treaty been signed than a new Irish civil war broke out between Irish moderates and diehards. The moderates supported the treaty; the diehards wanted the oath to the British monarch abolished and a totally independent republic established. The second civil war continued until 1923. De Valera, who supported the diehards, resigned the presidency and organized resistance to the treaty. In 1932 he was again elected president. The next year the Dail Eireann abolished the oath of allegiance to the monarch. During World War II the Irish Free State remained neutral. In 1949 it declared itself the wholly independent republic of Eire.

Trials of the New Democracies

Both France and Great Britain had prewar experience in liberal democratic government. Their primary challenges lay in responding to economic pressures and allowing new groups, such as the Labour Party, to share political power. In Germany, Poland, Austria, Czechoslovakia, and the other successor states, the challenge for the 1920s was to make new parliamentary governments function in a satisfactory and stable manner. Before the war both Germany and Austria-Hungary had possessed elected parliaments, but those bodies had not exercised genuine political power. The question after the war became whether those groups that had previously sat powerless in parliaments could assume both power and responsibility. Another question was how long conservative institutions, such as the armies and the conservative political groups, would tolerate or cooperate with the liberal experiments. At the same time all of these newly organized states confronted immense postwar economic difficulties.

Successor States in Eastern Europe

Only the barest outline can be given of the dreary political story of the successor states. It had been an article of faith among nineteenth-century liberals that only good could flow from the demise of Austria-Hungary. The new states in eastern Europe were to symbolize the principle of national self-determination and to provide a buffer against the westward spread of Bolshevism. However, they were in trouble from the beginning. They were poor and overwhelmingly rural nations in an industrialized world. Nationality problems continued to exist. The major social and political groups were generally unwilling to make compromises. With the exception of Czechoslovakia, all of these states succumbed to some form of authoritarian government.

HUNGARY In Hungary during 1919 the Bolsheviks had erected a socialist government led by Béla Kun (1885–1937). The Allies quickly authorized an invasion by Romanian troops to remove the communist danger. They then established Admiral Miklós Horthy (1858–1957) as regent, a position he held until 1944. During the 1920s the effective ruler of Hungary was Count Stephen Bethlen (1874–1947). He presided over a government that was parliamentary in form but aristocratic in character. In 1932 he was succeeded by General Julius Gömbös (1886–1936), who pursued policies of anti-Semitism and rigged elections. No matter how the popular vote turned out, the Gömbös party controlled the Parliament. There was also deep resentment in Hungary over the territory it had lost to other nations through the Paris settlement.

AUSTRIA The situation in Austria was little better. The new Austria consisted of a capital city surrounded by some other territory. A quarter of the eight million Austrians lived in Vienna. Viable economic life was almost impossible, and union with Germany was forbidden by the Paris settlement. Throughout the 1920s the leftist Social Democrats and the conservative Christian Socialists contended for power. Unwilling to use only normal political methods, both groups employed small armies to terrorize their opponents and to impress their followers.

In 1933 the Christian Socialist Engelbert Dollfuss (1892–1934) became chancellor. He tried to steer a course between the Austrian Social Democrats and the German Nazis, who had begun to penetrate Austria. In 1934 he outlawed all political parties except the Christian Socialists, the agrarians, and the paramilitary groups, which composed his own Fatherland Front. He used government troops against the Social Democrats. During an unsuccessful Nazi *coup* in 1934, Dollfuss was shot. His successor, Kurt von Schuschnigg (1897–1977) presided over Austria until Hitler annexed it in 1938.

SOUTHEASTERN EUROPE In southeastern Europe revision of the Versailles Treaty arrangements was somewhat less of an issue. Parliamentary government floundered nevertheless. In Yugoslavia (known as the kingdom of the Serbs, Croats, and Slovenes until 1929), the clash of nationalities eventually led to the imposition of royal dictatorship in 1929 under King Alexander I (1921–1934), himself a Serb. His dictatorship saw the outlawing of political parties and the jailing of popular politicians. Alexander I was assassinated in 1934, but the authoritarian government continued under the regency for his son.

Other royal dictatorships were imposed: in Romania by King Carol II (1930–1940) and in Bulgaria by King Boris III (1918–1943). They regarded their own illiberal regimes as countering even more extreme antiparliamentary movements and as quieting the discontent of the varied nationalities within their borders. In Greece the parliamentary monarchy floundered amidst military *coups* and calls for a re-

public. In 1936 General John Metaxas (1871–1941) instituted a dictatorship that for the time being ended parliamentary life in Greece.

POLAND   The nation whose postwar fortunes probably most disappointed liberal Europeans was Poland. For over a hundred years the country had been erased from the map. Restoration of an independent Poland had been one of Woodrow Wilson's Fourteen Points. When the country was finally reconstructed in 1919, nationalism proved an insufficient bond to overcome political disagreements stemming from class differences, diverse economic interests, and regionalism. The new Parliament was plagued with a vast number of small political parties. The constitution assigned too little power to the executive. In 1926 General Josef Pilsudski (1857–1935) carried out a military *coup*. He ruled personally until the close of the decade, when the government passed into the hands of a group of military leaders.

CZECHOSLOVAKIA   Only one central European successor state escaped the fate of self-imposed authoritarian government. Czechoslovakia possessed a strong industrial base, a substantial middle class, and a tradition of liberal values. During the war Czechs and Slovaks had cooperated to aid the Allies. They had learned to work together and to trust each other. After the war the new government had carried out agrarian reform and had broken up large estates in favor of small peasant holdings. In the person of Thomas Masaryk (1850–1937), the nation possessed a gifted leader of immense integrity and fairness. The country had a real chance of constructing a viable modern nation-state.

However, it was plagued with discontent among its smaller national groups, including the German population of the Sudetenland assigned to Czechoslovakia by the Paris settlement. The parliamentary regime might very well have been able to deal with this problem, but extreme German nationalists looked to Hitler for aid. For his part, the German dictator wished to expand into eastern Europe. In 1938, at Munich, the great powers divided liberal Czechoslovakia to appease the aggressive instincts of Hitler.

The fate of the successor states proved most disappointing to those who had hoped for political liberty to result from the dissolution of

Thomas Masaryk was the first president of the Czechoslovak Republic, which was the only successful democratic state in eastern Europe during the interwar period [UPI/Bettmann News Photos]

the Habsburg Empire and other border adjustments in eastern Europe. By the early 1930s, in most of those states, the authoritarianism of the Habsburgs had been replaced by that of other rulers. However, the most momentous democratic experiment between the wars was conducted in Germany. There, after a century of frustration and disappointment, a liberal state had been constructed. It was in Germany that parliamentary democracy and its future in Western civilization faced its major trial.

The Weimar Republic

The German Weimar Republic was born from the defeat of the imperial army, the revolution of 1918 against the Hohenzollerns, and the hopes of German Liberals and Social Democrats. Its name derived from the city in which its constitution was written and promulgated in August 1919. While the constitution was being debated, the republic, headed by the Social Democrats, accepted the humiliating terms of the Versailles Treaty. Although its officials had signed only under the threat of an Allied invasion, the republic was nevertheless permanently associated with the national disgrace and the economic burdens of the treaty.

Throughout the 1920s the government of the republic was required to fulfill the economic and military provisions imposed by the Paris settlement. It became all too easy for nationalists and military figures whose policies had brought on the tragedy and defeat of the war to blame the young republic and the socialists for the results of the conflict. In Germany, more than in other countries, the desire to revise the treaty was closely related to a desire to change the mode of domestic government.

CONSTITUTIONAL STRUCTURES The Weimar Constitution was a highly enlightened document. It guaranteed civil liberties and provided for direct election, by universal suffrage, of the Reichstag and the president. However, it also contained certain crucial structural flaws that allowed the eventual overthrow of its institutions. Within the Reichstag a complicated system of proportional representation was adopted. This system made it relatively easy for very small political parties to gain seats in the Reichstag. The result was shifting party combinations that led to considerable instabil-

ity. Ministers were technically responsible to the Reichstag, but the president appointed and removed the chancellor. Perhaps most importantly, Article 48 allowed the president, in times of emergency, to rule by decree. In this manner the constitution permitted the possibility of presidential dictatorship.

LACK OF BROAD POPULAR SUPPORT
Beyond the burden of the Versailles Treaty and these potential constitutional pitfalls, the Weimar Republic suffered from a lack of sympathy and a lack of loyalty on the part of many Germans. A social revolution had not accompanied the changes in political structure. Many important political figures actually favored a constitutional monarchy. The schoolteachers, civil servants, and judicial officials of the republic were generally the same people who had previously served the Kaiser and the empire. Before the war they had distrusted or even hated the Social Democratic Party, which figured so prominently in the establishment and the politics of the republic.

The officer corps was deeply suspicious of the government and profoundly resentful of the military provisions of the peace settlement. They and other nationalistic Germans perpetuated the myth that the German army had surrendered on foreign soil only because it had been stabbed in the back by civilians at home. In other words, large numbers of Germans in significant social and political positions wanted both to revise the peace treaty and to modify the system of government. The early years of the republic only solidified those sentiments.

A number of major and minor humiliations as well as considerable economic instability impinged on the new government. In March 1920 the right-wing Kapp *Putsch*, or armed insurrection, erupted in Berlin. Led by a conservative civil servant and supported by army officers, the attempted *coup* failed. But the collapse occurred only after government officials had fled the city and German workers had carried out a general strike. In the same month a series of strikes took place in the Ruhr mining district. The government sent in troops. Such extremism from both the left and the right would haunt the republic for all its days.

In May 1921 the Allies presented a reparations bill for 132 billion gold marks. The German republican government accepted this preposterous demand only after new Allied threats of occupation. Throughout the early 1920s there were numerous assassinations or attempted assassinations of important republican leaders. Violence was the hallmark of the first five years of the republic.

INVASION OF THE RUHR AND INFLATION

Inflation brought the major crisis of this period. The financing of the war and the continued postwar deficit spending generated an immense rise in prices. Consequently, the value of German currency fell. By early 1921 the German mark traded against the American dollar at a ratio of 64 to 1, compared with a ratio of 4.2 to 1 in 1914. The German financial community contended that the value of the currency could not be stabilized until the reparations issue had been solved. In the meantime the printing presses kept pouring forth paper

During the hyper-inflation that followed the French occupation of the Rhineland, Germans found it cheaper to burn money than to spend it on fuel. [Library of Congress]

money, which was used to redeem government bonds as they fell due.

The French invasion of the Ruhr in January 1923 and the German response of economic passive resistance produced cataclysmic inflation. The Weimar government paid subsidies to the Ruhr labor force, who had laid down their tools. Unemployment soon spread from the Ruhr to other parts of the country, creating a new drain on the treasury and also reducing tax revenues. The printing presses by this point had difficulty providing enough paper currency to keep up with the daily rise in prices. In November 1923 an American dollar was worth more than 800 million German marks. Money was literally not worth the paper it was printed on. Stores were unwilling to exchange goods for the worthless currency, and farmers withheld produce from the market.

The moral and social values of thrift and prudence were thoroughly undermined. The security of middle-class savings, pensions, and insurance policies was wiped out, as were investments in government bonds. Simultaneously, debts and mortgages could be paid off. Speculators in land, real estate, and industry made great fortunes. Union contracts generally allowed workers to keep up with rising prices. Inflation thus was not a disaster to everyone. However, to the middle class and the lower middle class the inflation was still one more traumatic experience coming hard on the heels of the military defeat and the peace treaty. Only when the social and economic upheaval of these months is grasped can the later German desire for order and security at almost any cost be comprehended.

HITLER'S EARLY CAREER

Late in 1923 Adolf Hitler (1889–1945) made his first major appearance on the German political scene. In 1889 he had been born the son of a minor Austrian customs official. By 1907 he had gone to Vienna, where his hopes of becoming an artist were soon dashed. He lived off money sent by his widowed mother and later off his Austrian orphan's allowance. He also painted postcards for further income and later found work as a day laborer. In Vienna he became acquainted with Mayor Karl Lueger's Christian Social Party, which prospered on an ideology of anti-Semitism and from the social anxieties of the lower middle class. Hitler's own relatively pre-

Lilo Linke Recalls the Mad Days of the German Inflation

In 1923 the presses that were printing paper currency in Germany could hardly keep up with the rising prices. This memoir recounts the difficulties of those days and the resentments that arose as money became worth less than the paper on which it was printed.

The whole population had suddenly turned into maniacs. Everyone was buying, selling, speculating, bargaining, and dollar, dollar, dollar was the magic word which dominated every conversation, every newspaper, every poster in Germany. Nobody understood what was happening. There seemed to be no sense, no rules in the mad game, but one had to take part in it if one did not want to be trampled underfoot at once. Only a few people were able to carry through to the end and gain by the inflation. The majority lost everything and broke down, impoverished and bewildered.

The middle class was hurt more than any other, the savings of a lifetime and their small fortunes melted into a few coppers. They had to sell their most precious belongings for ten milliard inflated marks to buy a bit of food or an absolutely necessary coat, and their pride and dignity were bleeding out of many wounds. Bitterness remained for ever in their hearts. Full of hatred, they accused the international financiers, the Jews and Socialists—their old enemies—of having exploited their distress. They never forgot and never forgave and were the first to lend a willing ear to Hitler's fervent preaching.

In the shop, notices announced that we should receive our salaries in weekly parts, after a while we queued up at the cashier's desk every evening, and before long we were paid twice daily and ran out during the lunch hour to buy a few things, because as soon as the new rate of exchange became known in the early afternoon our money had again lost half its value.

Lilo Linke, Restless Days *(New York: Knopf, 1935), pp. 131–132.*

carious situation and his own social observations taught him how desperately the lower middle class feared slipping into a working-class condition.

He also absorbed the rabid German nationalism and extreme anti-Semitism that flourished in Vienna. He came to hate Marxism, which he associated with Jews. During World War I Hitler fought in the German army and was wounded; he was promoted to the rank of corporal and awarded the Iron Cross for bravery. The war gave him his first sense of purpose.

This picture of Adolf Hitler was made in May 1927. At the time he was not yet a major political figure, and the Nazi movement was relatively small. [United Press International Photo]

Mein Kampf "Hitler

MAP 27-1 GERMANY'S WESTERN FRONTIER *The French-Belgian-German border area between the two world wars was sensitive. In spite of efforts to restrain tension in the twenty-year period, there were persistent difficulties related to the Ruhr, Rhineland, Saar, and Eupen-Malmedy regions that necessitated strong defenses.*

better known simply as the Nazis. The same year, the group began to parade under a red banner with a black swastika. It issued a platform, or program, of Twenty-five Points. Among other things these called for the repudiation of the Versailles Treaty, the unification of Austria and Germany, the exclusion of Jews from German citizenship, agrarian reform, the prohibition of land speculation, the confiscation of war profits, state administration of the giant cartels, and the replacement of department stores with small retail shops.

Originally the Nazis had called for a broad program of nationalization of industry in an attempt to compete directly with the Marxist political parties for the vote of the workers. As the tactic failed, the Nazis redefined the meaning of the word *socialist* in the party name so that it suggested a *nationalistic* outlook. In 1922 Hitler said:

> *Whoever is prepared to make the national cause his own to such an extent that he knows no higher ideal than the welfare of his nation; whoever has understood our great national anthem, Deutschland, Deutschland, über Alles ["Germany, Germany, over All"], to mean that nothing in the wide world surpasses in his eyes this Germany, people and land, land and people—that man is a Socialist.*[2]

This definition, of course, had nothing to do with traditional German socialism. The "socialism" that Hitler and the Nazis had in mind was not state ownership of the means of production but the subordination of all economic enterprise to the welfare of the nation. It often implied protection for very small economic enterprise. Increasingly over the years the Nazis discovered that their social appeal was to the lower middle class, which found itself squeezed between well-organized big business and socialist labor unions or political parties. The Nazis tailored their message to this very troubled economic group.

After the conflict Hitler settled in Munich. In the new surroundings he became associated with a small nationalistic, anti-Semitic political party that in 1920 adopted the name of National Socialist German Workers' Party,

---

[2] *Alan Bullock,* Hitler: A Study in Tyranny, *rev. ed. (New York: Harper & Row, 1962), p. 76.*

Hitler Denounces the Versailles Treaty

One of the chief complaints of the National Socialist movement was about the unfairness of the Versailles Treaty of 1919. Virtually all German public figures, including leaders of the Weimar Republic, hoped to see an eventual revision of that settlement. Hitler and his followers made denunciation of the treaty their single most uncompromising demand. In this speech of April 17, 1923, Hitler explained how the treaty had undermined the German nation.

With the armistice begins the humiliation of Germany. If the Republic on the day of its foundation had appealed to the country: "Germans, stand together! Up and resist the foe! The Fatherland, the Republic expects of you that you fight to your last breath," then millions who are now the enemies of the Republic would be fanatical Republicans. To-day they are the foes of the Republic not because it is a Republic but because this Republic was founded at the moment when Germany was humiliated, because it so discredited the new flag that men's eyes must turn regretfully towards the old flag.

It was no Treaty of Peace which was signed, but a betrayal of Peace.

The Treaty was signed which demanded from Germany that she should perform what was for ever impossible of performance. But that was not the worst; after all that was only a question of material values. This was not the end: Commissions of Control were formed! For the first time in the history of the modern world there were planted on a State agents of foreign Powers to act as Hangmen, and German soldiers were set to serve the foreigner. And if one of these Commissions was "insulted," a company of the German army had to defile before the French flag.

We no longer feel the humiliation of such an act; but the outside world says, "What a people of curs!"

So long as this Treaty stands there can be no resurrection of the German people: no social reform of any kind is possible! The Treaty was made in order to bring 20 million Germans to their deaths and to ruin the German nation. But those who made the Treaty cannot set it aside. At its foundation our Movement formulated three demands:

1. Setting aside of the Peace Treaty.
2. Unification of all Germans.
3. Land and soil to feed our nation.

Our Movement could formulate these demands, since it was not our Movement which caused the War, it has not made the Republic, it did not sign the Peace Treaty.

There is thus one thing which is the first task of this Movement: it desires to make the German once more National, that his Fatherland shall stand for him above everything else. It desires to teach our people to understand afresh the truth of the old saying: He who will not be a hammer must be an anvil. An anvil are we today, and that anvil will be beaten until out of the anvil we fashion once more a hammer, a German sword!

Norman H. Baynes (Ed.), The Speeches of Adolph Hitler, April 1922–1939 (Oxford: Oxford University Press, 1942).

Soon after the promulgation of the Twenty-five Points, the storm troopers or SA (*Sturmabteilung*), were organized under the leadership of Captain Ernst Roehm. It was a paramilitary organization that initially provided its members with food and uniforms and later in the decade with wages. In the mid-1920s the SA adopted its famous brown-shirted uniform.

Ernst Roehm Demands a Return to German Military Values

Ernst Roehm was the early Nazi leader who headed the SA (Sturmab-teilung, stormtroopers). He had fought in the First World War and saw himself primarily as a soldier. In this passage from his autobiography he emphasizes a soldier's understanding of German nationalism and the manner in which National Socialism may contribute to German renewal. Roehm himself became one of Hitler's victims in 1934 when he was executed along with other SA officers as Hitler consolidated his personal power.

I am a believer in plain talk and have not hid my heart like a skeleton in the closet.

I must write without fear, with defiance—just as it comes from my soul. . . .

Soldierly comradeship, cemented with blood, can perhaps temporarily relax, but it can never be torn out of the heart, it cannot be exterminated.

Still, all of Germany has not been awakened yet—despite National Socialism. My words shall be a trumpet call to those who are still asleep.

I am not appealing to the hustling and sneaky trader who has made accursed gold his God, but to the warrior who is struggling in the battle of life, who wants to win freedom and with it the kingdom of heaven.

I approve of whatever serves the purpose of German Freedom. I oppose whatever runs counter to it. Europe, aye, the whole world, may go down in flames—what concern is it of ours? Germany must live and be free.

One may call me a bigoted fool—I can't help that. I am opposed to sport in its present form and to its effects. Moreover, I consider it a definite national danger. We cannot rebuild the Fatherland with champions and artificially nurtured "big guns of sport." Only the most careful development which provides physical strength and capability, with spiritual elasticity and ethical backbone, can be of use to the Volk community. . . .

The Germans have forgotten how to hate.

Viral hate has been replaced by feminine lamentation. But he who is unable to hate cannot live either. Fanatical love and hate—their fires kindle flames of freedom.

Passionlessness, matter-of-factness, objectivity, are impersonality, are sophistry.

Only passion gives knowledge, creates wisdom.

"Peace and order" is the battle cry of people living on pensions. In the last analysis you cannot govern a state on the basis of the needs of pensioners. . . .

"Irresponsible dreamers" for years and years have called upon the people to rise up against enslavement and oppression. The "responsible politicians" of the new Germany in these same years have sold Germany lock, stock, and barrel. . . .

From time immemorial Germany was not suited to "diplomacy" and "politics." The sword has always determined the greatness of its history. . . .

Only the soldier could lead his people and Fatherland out of wretchedness and shame to freedom and honor.

Ernst Roehm, Die Geschichte eines Hochverraters *(Munich: Verlang Frz. Eher Nachf., 1928), pp. 365–367 (7th ed., 1934) as quoted in George L. Mosse,* Nazi Culture: Intellectual, Cultural, and Social Life in the Third Reich *(New York: Grosset & Dunlap, 1966), pp. 101–103.*

The storm troopers were the chief Nazi instrument for terror and intimidation before the party came into control of the government. They were a law unto themselves. The organization constituted a means of preserving military discipline and values outside the small army permitted by the Paris settlement. The existence of such a private party army was a sign of the potential for violence in the Weimar Republic. It also represented widespread contempt for the law and the institutions of the republic.

The social and economic turmoil following the French occupation of the Ruhr and the German inflation provided the fledgling party with an opportunity for direct action against the Weimar Republic; at that point it seemed incapable of providing military or economic security to the nation. By this time, because of his immense oratorical skills and organizational abilities, Hitler personally dominated the Nazi Party.

On November 9, 1923, Hitler and a band of followers, accompanied by General Ludendorff, attempted an unsuccessful *Putsch* at a beer hall in Munich. When the local authorities crushed the rising, sixteen Nazis were killed. Hitler and Ludendorff were arrested and tried for treason. The general was acquitted. Hitler employed the trial to make himself into a national figure. In his defense he condemned the republic, the Versailles Treaty, the Jews, and the weakened condition of his adopted country. He was convicted and sentenced to five years in prison. He actually spent only a few months in jail before being paroled. During this time he wrote *Mein Kampf* ("My Struggle"). Another result of the brief imprisonment was a decision on Hitler's part that in the future he and his party must seek to seize political power by legal methods.

THE STRESEMANN YEARS Elsewhere the officials of the republic were attempting to repair the damage from the inflation. Gustav Stresemann (1878–1929) was primarily responsible for the reconstruction of the republic and for its achievement of a sense of self-confidence. He served as chancellor only from August to November 1923, but he provided the nation with a new basis for stability. Stresemann abandoned the policy of passive resistance in the Ruhr. The country simply could

not afford it. Then, with the aid of banker Hjalmar Schacht, he introduced a new German currency. The rate of exchange was one trillion of the old German marks for one new *Rentenmark*.

Stresemann also moved against challenges from both the left and the right. He supported the crushing of both Hitler's abortive *Putsch* and smaller communist disturbances. In late November 1923 he resigned as chancellor and assumed the position of foreign minister, a post that he held until his death in 1929. In that office he exercised considerable influence over the affairs of the republic.

In 1924 the Weimar Republic and the Allies agreed to a new systematization of the reparation payments. The Dawes Plan, submitted by the American banker Charles Dawes, lowered the annual payments and allowed them to fluctuate according to the fortunes of the German economy. The French were to evacuate the Ruhr, and the last French troops left that region in 1925.

The same year Friedrich Ebert (1871–1925), the Social Democratic president of the republic, died. Field Marshal Paul von Hindenburg, a military hero and a conservative monarchist, was elected as his successor. He governed in strict accordance with the constitution, but his election suggested that a new conservative tenor had come to German politics. It looked as if conservative Germans had become reconciled to the republic. This conservatism was in line with the prosperity of the latter part of the decade. The new political and economic stability meant that foreign capital flowed into Germany, and employment, which had been poor throughout most of the postwar years, improved smartly. Giant industrial combines spread. The prosperity helped to establish broader acceptance and appreciation of the republic.

In foreign affairs Stresemann pursued a conciliatory course. He was committed to a policy of fulfilling the provisions of the Versailles Treaty, even as he attempted to revise it by diplomacy. He was willing to accept the settlement in the west but was a determined, if sometimes secret, revisionist in the east. He aimed to recover German territories lost to Poland and Czechoslovakia and possibly to unite with Austria, chiefly by diplomatic means. The first step, however, was to achieve

*The signing of the Locarno Agreements in October of 1925, which brought a new, if tempo-
rary, spirit of conciliation and hope to Europe. [United Press International Photo]*

respectability and economic recovery. That goal required a policy of accommodation and "Fulfillment," for the moment at least.

LOCARNO These developments gave rise to the Locarno Agreements of October 1925. The spirit of conciliation led politicians Austen Chamberlain for Britain and Aristide Briand for France to accept Stresemann's proposal for a fresh start. France and Germany both accepted the western frontier established at Versailles as legitimate. Britain and Italy agreed to intervene against the aggressor if either side violated the frontier or if Germany sent troops into the demilitarized Rhineland. Significantly, no such agreement was made about Germany's eastern frontier. However, the Germans made treaties of arbitration with Poland and Czechoslovakia, and France strengthened its ties with the Little Entente. France supported German membership in the League of Nations and agreed to withdraw its occupation troops from the Rhineland in 1930, five years earlier than specified at Versailles.

Germany was pleased to have achieved re-spectability and a guarantee against another Ruhr occupation, as well as the possibility of revision in the east. Britain was pleased to be allowed to play a more evenhanded role. Italy was glad to be recognized as a great power. The French were happy, too, because the Germans voluntarily accepted the permanence of their western frontier, which was also guaranteed by Britain and Italy, while France maintained its allies in the east. As A. J. P. Taylor put it, "Any French statesman of 1914 could have been bewildered with delight by such an achievement."[3]

The Locarno Agreements brought a new spirit of hope to Europe. Germany's entry into the League of Nations was greeted with enthusiasm. Chamberlain, Briand, and Stresemann jointly received the Nobel Peace Prize in 1926. The spirit of Locarno was carried even further when the leading European states, Japan, and the United States signed the Kellogg–Briand Pact in 1928, renouncing "war as an instrument of national policy."

[3] *Taylor, p. 58*

The joy and optimism were not justified. France had merely recognized its inability to coerce Germany without help. Britain had shown its unwillingness to uphold the settlement in the east. Austen Chamberlain declared that no British government ever would "risk the bones of a British grenadier" for the Polish corridor. Germany was by no means reconciled to the eastern settlement. It continued its clandestine military connections with the Soviet Union, which had begun with the Treaty of Rapallo, and planned to continue to press for revision of the Paris Settlement.

In both France and Germany, moreover, the conciliatory politicians represented only a part of the nation. In Germany, especially, most people continued to reject Versailles and regarded Locarno as only an extension of it. When the Dawes Plan ran out in 1929, it was replaced by the Young Plan. Named after the American businessman Owen D. Young, this plan lowered the reparation payments, put a term on how long they must be made, and removed Germany entirely from outside supervision and control. The intensity of the outcry in Germany against the continuation of any reparations showed how far the Germans were from accepting their situation.

In spite of these problems, major war was by no means inevitable. Europe, aided by American loans, was returning to prosperity. German leaders like Stresemann would certainly have continued to press for change, but there is little reason to think that they would have resorted to force, much less to a general war. Continued prosperity and diplomatic success might have won the loyalty of the German people for the Weimar Republic and moderate revisionism. But the Great Depression of the 1930s brought new forces to power.

The Fascist Experiment in Italy

While its wartime allies continued to pursue parliamentary politics and its former enemies set out on the troubled path of democracy, Italy moved toward a new form of authoritarian government. From the Italian Fascist movement of Benito Mussolini (1883–1945) was derived the general term of *fascist*, which has frequently been used to describe the vari-

ous right-wing dictatorships that arose between the wars.

The exact meaning of *fascism* as a political term remains much disputed among both historians and political scientists. However, a certain consensus does exist. The governments regarded as fascist were antidemocratic, anti-Marxist, antiparliamentary, and frequently anti-Semitic. They hoped to hold back the spread of Bolshevism, which seemed at the time a very real threat. They sought a world safe for the middle class, small businesses, owners of moderate amounts of property, and small farmers. The fascist regimes rejected the political inheritance of the French Revolution and of nineteenth-century liberalism.

Their adherents believed that normal parliamentary politics and parties sacrificed national honor and greatness to petty party disputes. They wanted to overcome the class conflict of Marxism and the party conflict of liberalism by consolidating the various groups and classes within the nation for great national purposes. As Mussolini declared in 1931, "The fascist conception of the state is all-embracing, and outside of the state no human or spiritual values can exist, let alone be desirable."[4] The fascist governments were usually single-party dictatorships characterized by terrorism and police surveillance. These dictatorships were rooted in the base of mass political parties.

The Rise of Mussolini

The Italian *Fasci di Combattimento* ("Band of Combat") was founded in 1919 in Milan. Its members came largely from Italian war veterans who felt that the sacrifices of the conflict had been in vain. They resented the failure of Italy to gain the city of Fiume, toward the northern end of the Adriatic Sea, at the Paris conference. They feared socialism and inflation.

Their leader, Benito Mussolini, had been born the son of a blacksmith. For a time he had been a schoolteacher, then a day laborer. He became active in Italian socialist politics and by 1912 had become editor of the socialist newspaper *Avanti*. In 1914 Mussolini broke with the socialists and supported Italian entry into the war on the side of the Allies. His inter-

---

[4]*Quoted in Denis Mack Smith,* Italy: A Modern History *(Ann Arbor: University of Michigan Press, 1959), p. 412.*

ventionist position lost him the editorship of *Avanti*. He then established his own paper, *Il Popolo d'Italia*. Later he served in the army and was wounded. In 1919, although of some prewar political stature, Mussolini was simply one of many Italian politicians. His *Fasci* organization was, for its part, simply one of numerous small political groups in a country characterized by such entities. As a politician Mussolini was an opportunist par excellence. He proved capable of changing his ideas and principles to suit every new occasion. Action for him was always more important than thought or rational justification. His one real rule was that of political survival.

POSTWAR ITALIAN POLITICAL TURMOIL Postwar Italian politics was a muddle. During the conflict the Italian Parliament had for all intents and purposes ceased to function. It had been quite willing to allow

Mussolini was a powerful public orator. His gestures, which often appear comic in hindsight, were part of a carefully cultivated public image designed to make him appear at all times a leader. [Culver Pictures]

ministers to rule by decree. However, the parliamentary system as it then existed had begun to prove quite unsatisfactory to large sectors of the citizenry. Many Italians besides those in Mussolini's band of followers felt that Italy had emerged from the war as less than a victorious nation, had not been treated as a great power at the peace conference, and had not received the territories it deserved.

The main spokesman for this discontent was the extreme nationalist poet and novelist Gabriele D'Annunzio (1863–1938). In 1919 he successfully led a force of patriotic Italians in an assault on Fiume. Troops of the Italian parliamentary government eventually drove him out. D'Annunzio had provided the example of the political use of a nongovernmental military force. The action of the government in removing him from Fiume gave the parliamentary ministry a somewhat-less-than-patriotic appearance.

Between 1919 and 1921 Italy also experienced considerable internal social turmoil. Numerous industrial strikes occurred, and workers occupied factories. Peasants seized uncultivated land from large estates. Parliamentary and constitutional government seemed incapable of dealing with this unrest. The Socialist Party had captured a plurality of seats in the Chamber of Deputies during the 1919 election. A new Catholic Popular Party had also done quite well. Both appealed to the working and agrarian classes. However, neither party would cooperate with the other, and parliamentary deadlock resulted. Under these conditions many Italians honestly and still others conveniently believed that there existed the danger of a communist revolution.

EARLY FASCIST ORGANIZATION Initially, Mussolini was uncertain of the direction of the political winds. He first supported the factory occupations and land seizures. However, never one to be concerned with consistency, he soon reversed himself. He had discovered that large numbers of both upper-class and middle-class Italians, who were pressured by inflation and who feared property loss, had no sympathy for the workers or the peasants. They wanted order rather than some vague social justice that might harm their own interests.

Consequently, Mussolini and his Fascists took direct action in the face of the govern-

Mussolini Heaps Contempt on Political Liberalism

The political tactics of the Italian Fascists wholly disregarded the liberal belief in the rule of law and the consent of the governed. In 1923 Mussolini explained why the Fascists so hated and repudiated these liberal principles. The reader should note his emphasis on the idea of the twentieth century as a new historical epoch requiring a new kind of politics and his undisguised praise of force in politics.

Liberalism is not the last word, nor does it represent the definitive formula on the subject of the art of government. . . . Liberalism is the product and the technique of the 19th century. . . . It does not follow that the Liberal scheme of government, good for the 19th century, for a century, that is, dominated by two such phenomena as the growth of capitalism and the strengthening of the sentiment of nationalism, should be adapted to the 20th century, which announces itself already with characteristics sufficiently different from those that marked the preceding century. . . .

I challenge Liberal gentlemen to tell if ever in history there has been a government that was based solely on popular consent and that renounced all use of force whatsoever. A government so constructed there has never been and never will be. Consent is an ever-changing thing like the shifting sand on the sea coast. It can never be permanent: It can never be complete. . . . If it be accepted as an axiom that any system of government whatever creates malcontents, how are you going to prevent this discontent from overflowing and constituting a menace to the stability of the State? You will prevent it by force. By the assembling of the greatest force possible. By the inexorable use of this force whenever it is necessary. Take away from any government whatsoever force—and by force is meant physical, armed force—and leave it only its immortal principles, and that government will be at the mercy of the first organized group that decides to overthrow it. Fascism now throws these lifeless theories out to rot. . . . The truth evident now to all who are not warped by [liberal] dogmatism is that men have tired of liberty. They have made an orgy of it. Liberty is today no longer the chaste and austere virgin for whom the generations of the first half of the last century fought and died. For the gallant, restless and bitter youth who face the dawn of a new history there are other words that exercise a far greater fascination, and those words are: order, hierarchy, discipline. . . .

Know then, once and for all, that Fascism knows no idols and worships no fetishes. It has already stepped over, and if it be necessary it will turn tranquilly and step again over, the more or less putrescent corpse of the Goddess of Liberty.

Benito Mussolini, "Force and Consent" (1923), as cited and trans. in Jonathan F. Scott and Alexander Baltzly, Readings in European History Since 1814 (New York: F. S. Crofts, 1931), pp. 680–682.

ment inaction. They formed local squads of terrorists who disrupted Socialist Party meetings, mugged Socialist leaders, and terrorized Socialist supporters. They attacked strikers and farm workers and protected strikebreakers. Conservative land and factory owners were grateful. The officers and institutions of the law simply ignored the crimes of the Fascist squads. By early 1922 the Fascists had turned their intimidation through arson, beatings, and murder against local officials in cities such as Ferrara, Ravenna, and Milan. They controlled the local government in many parts of northern Italy.

MARCH ON ROME In the election of 1921 Mussolini and thirty-four of his followers were sent to the Chamber of Deputies. Their importance grew as the local Fascists gained more direct power. The movement now had hundreds of thousands of supporters. In October 1922 the Fascists, dressed in their characteristic black shirts, began a march on Rome. King Victor Emmanuel III (1900–1946), because of both personal and political fear, refused to sign a decree that would have authorized the use of the army against the marchers. Probably no other single decision so ensured a Fascist seizure of power. The Cabinet resigned in protest. On October 29 the monarch telegraphed Mussolini in Milan and asked him to become prime minister. The next day Mussolini arrived in Rome by sleeping car and greeted his followers as head of the government when they entered the city.

Technically Mussolini had come into office by legal means. The monarch did possess the power to appoint the prime minister. However, Mussolini had no majority or even near majority in the Chamber of Deputies. Behind the legal facade of his assumption of power lay the months of terrorist disruption and intimidation and the threat of the Fascist march itself. The non-Fascist politicians, whose ineptitude had prepared the way for Mussolini, believed that his regime, like others of previous months, would be temporary. They failed to comprehend that he was not a traditional Italian politician.

The Fascists in Power

Mussolini had not really expected to be appointed prime minister. He moved cautiously to shore up his support and to consolidate his power. His success was the result of the impotence of his rivals, his own effective use of his office, his power over the masses, and his sheer ruthlessness. On November 23, 1922, the king and Parliament granted Mussolini dictatorial authority for one year to bring order to the lower levels of the government. Wherever possible Mussolini appointed Fascists to office.

REPRESSION OF OPPOSITION Late in 1924, under Mussolini's guidance, the Parliament changed the election law. Previously parties had been represented in the Chamber of

Deputies in proportion to the popular vote cast for them. According to the new election law, the party that gained the largest popular vote (within a minimum of at least 25 per cent) received two thirds of the seats in the chamber. Coalition government, with all its compromises and hesitant policies, would no longer be necessary. In the election of 1924 the Fascists won a great victory and complete control of the Chamber of Deputies. They used that majority to end legitimate parliamentary life. A series of laws passed in 1925 and 1926 permitted Mussolini, in effect, to rule by decree. In 1926 all other political parties were dissolved. By the close of that year Italy had been transformed into a single-party dictatorial state.

Their growing dominance over the government had not, however, diverted the Fascists from their course of violence and terror. They were put in charge of the police force, and the terrorist squads became institutionalized into government militia. In late 1924 their thugs murdered Giacomo Matteotti (1885–1924), a major non-Communist socialist leader. He had persistently criticized Mussolini and had exposed the criminality of the Fascist movement. In protest against the murder, a number of opposition deputies withdrew from the Chamber of Deputies. That tactic gave the prime minister an even freer hand. The deputies were refused readmission.

PARALLEL STRUCTURE OF PARTY AND GOVERNMENT The parallel organization of the party and the government sustained support for the regime. For every government institution there existed a corresponding party organization. In this manner the Fascist Party dominated the political structure at every level. When all other political parties were outlawed, the citizens had to look to the Fascists in their community for political favors. They also knew the high price of opposition. By the late 1920s the Grand Council of the party had become an organ of the state. It drew up and presented the list of persons who would stand for election to the Chamber of Deputies. Major policies to be approved by the chamber first passed the Grand Council. And Mussolini himself controlled the council.

The party used propaganda quite effectively. A cult of personality surrounded Mussolini. His skills in oratory and his general intelli-

The signing of the Lateran Accord occurred on February 11, 1929. Cardinal Gasparri, the Vatican's Secretary of State is seated at the center; Mussolini is sitting on his left. [Bildarchiv Preussischer Kulturbesitz]

gence allowed him to hold his own with both large crowds and the leaders of the more respectable portions of the community. The latter tolerated and often admired him in the belief that he had saved them from Bolshevism. The persons who did have the courage to oppose Mussolini were usually driven into exile, and some were murdered.

ACCORD WITH THE VATICAN The Italian dictator made one important domestic departure that brought him significant political dividends. Through the Lateran Accord of February 1929, the Roman Catholic church and the Italian state made peace with each other. Ever since the armies of Italian unification had seized papal lands in the 1860s, the Church had been hostile to the state. The popes had remained virtual prisoners in the Vatican after 1870. The agreement of 1929 recognized the pope as the temporal ruler of Vatican City. The Italian government agreed to pay an indemnity to the papacy for confiscated land. The state also recognized Catholicism as the religion of the nation, exempted Church property from taxes, and allowed Church law to govern the institution of marriage. The Lateran Accord brought further respectability to Mussolini's authoritarian regime.

The Beginning of the Soviet Experiment

The political right had no monopoly on authoritarianism between the wars. The consolidation of the Bolshevik Revolution in Russia established the most extensive and durable of all twentieth-century authoritarian governments. However, the dictatorship of the left and the right did differ from each other. Unlike the Italian Fascists or the German National Socialists, the Bolsheviks had seized power through revolution. For several years they confronted effective opposition, and their leaders long felt insecure about their hold on the country. The Communist Party was not a mass party nor a nationalistic one. Its early membership rarely exceeded 1 per cent of the Russian population.

The Bolsheviks confronted a much less industrialized economy than existed in Italy or Germany. They believed in and practiced the collectivization of economic life attacked by the right-wing dictatorships. The Marxist-Leninist ideology was far more all-encompassing than the nationalism of the Fascists and the racism of the Nazis. Communism was an exportable commodity. The Communists re-

The Third International Issues
Conditions of Membership

After the Russian Revolution, the Russian Communist Party organized the Third Communist International. Any communist party outside the Soviet Union was required to accept these Twenty-one Conditions, adopted in 1919, in order to join the International. In effect, this program demanded that all such parties adopt a distinctly revolutionary program. They also need to cease operating as legal parties within their various countries. By this means, the Soviet Union sought to achieve leadership of the socialist movement throughout Europe. The non-Russian socialist parties quickly split into social democratic parties that remained independent of Moscow and communist parties that adopted the policy imposed by the Russian Communist Party.

1. The daily propaganda and agitation must bear a truly communist character and correspond to the program and all the decisions of the Third International. All the organs of the press that are in the hands of the party must be edited by reliable communists who have proved their loyalty to the cause of the proletarian revolution. . . .

. . . .

3. The class struggle in almost all of the countries of Europe and America is entering the phase of civil war. Under such conditions the communists can have no confidence in bourgeois law. They must everywhere create a parallel illegal apparatus, which at the decisive moment could assist the party in performing its duty of revolution. . . .

4. The obligation to spread communist ideas includes the particular necessity of persistent, systematic propaganda in the army. . . .

5. It is necessary to carry on systematic and steady agitation in the rural districts. . . .

. . . .

7. The parties desiring to belong to the Communist International must recognize the necessity of a complete and absolute rupture with reformism . . . , and they must carry on propaganda in favor of this rupture among the broadest circles of the party membership. . . .

8. . . . . Every party desirous of belonging to the Third International must ruthlessly denounce the methods of "their own" imperialists in the colonies, supporting, not in words, but in deeds, every independence movement in the colonies. . . .

. . . .

14. Every party that desires to belong to the Communist International must give every possible support to the Soviet Republics in their struggle against all counterrevolutionary forces. . . .

. . . .

16. All decisions of the congresses of the Communist International . . . are binding on all parties affiliated to the Communist International. . . .

17. In connection with all this, all parties desiring to join the Communist International must change their names. Every party that wishes to join the Communist International must bear the name: *Communist party* of such-and-such country. This question as to name is not merely a formal one, but a political one of great importance. The Communist International has declared a decisive war against the entire bourgeois world and all the yellow social democratic parties. Every rank-and-file worker must clearly understand the difference between the communist parties and the old official "social democratic" or "socialist" parties which have betrayed the cause of the working class.

18. Members of the party who reject the conditions and thesis of the Communist International, on principle, must be expelled from the party.

International Communism in the Era of Lenin: A Documentary History, ed. by Helmut Gruber (Garden City, NY: Doubleday, 1972), pp. 241–246.

garded their government and their revolution not as local events in a national history but as epoch-making events in the history of the world and the development of humanity.

The Third International

The policies of the early Russian Communist Revolution directly and importantly affected the rise of the Fascists and the Nazis in western Europe. The success of the revolution in Russia had the paradoxical effect of dividing socialist parties and socialist movements in the rest of Europe. In 1919 the Soviet Communists founded the Third International of the European socialist movement. It became better known as the Comintern. A year after its inception the Comintern imposed its Twenty-one Conditions on any other socialist party that wished to become a member. The conditions included acknowledgment of leadership from Moscow, rejection of reformist or revisionist socialism, and repudiation of previous socialist leaders. The Comintern wished to make the Russian model of socialism, as developed by Lenin, the rule for all socialist parties outside the Soviet Union.

The decision whether to join or not to join the Comintern under these conditions split every major socialist party on the Continent. As a result, separate communist parties and social democratic parties emerged. The former modeled themselves after the Soviet party and pursued policies dictated by Moscow. The social democratic parties attempted to pursue both social reform and liberal parliamentary politics. Throughout the 1920s and early 1930s the communists and the social democrats tended to fight each other more intensely than they fought either capitalism or conservative political parties. This division of the European political left meant that right-wing political movements rarely had to confront a united opposition on the political left.

War Communism

Within the Soviet Union the Red Army under the organizational genius of Leon Trotsky (1879–1940) had suppressed internal and foreign military opposition to the new government. Within months of the revolution a new secret police, known as *Cheka*, appeared. Throughout the civil war Lenin had declared that the Bolshevik Party, as the vanguard of the revolution, was imposing the dictatorship

Lenin and Trotsky (saluting) in Red Square in Moscow in 1919, from a documentary film made by Herman Axelbank. Trotsky's organizational skill was largely responsible for the Red Army's victory in the Russian Civil War of 1918–1920. [United Press International Photo]

of the proletariat. Political and economic administration became highly centralized. All major decisions flowed from the top in a nondemocratic manner. Under the economic policy of "War Communism" the revolutionary government confiscated and then operated the banks, the transport facilities, and heavy industry. The state also forcibly requisitioned grain produced by the peasants and shipped it from the countryside to feed the army and the workers in the cities. The fact of the civil war permitted suppression of possible resistance to this economic policy.

"War Communism" aided the victory of the Red Army over its opponents. The revolution had survived and triumphed. However, the policy generated domestic opposition to the Bolsheviks, who in 1920 numbered only about 600,000 members. The alliance of workers and peasants forged by the slogan of "Peace, Bread, and Land" had begun to come apart at the seams. Many Russians were no longer willing to make the sacrifices demanded by the central party bureaucrats. In 1920 and 1921 major strikes occurred in numerous factories. Peasants were discontented and resisted the requisition of grain as they had since 1918. In March 1921 the Baltic fleet mutinied at Kronstadt.

Between 1918 and 1921 an estimated seven million Russians died from hunger or sickness. The famine was particularly severe during the winter of 1920–1921, when only massive relief from the United States prevented even more people from starving. Lenin's New Economic Policy, which sought to stimulate food production, was a reaction to these conditions. [Library of Congress]

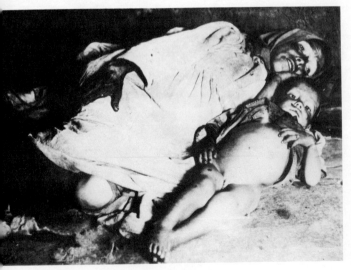

The Red Army crushed the rebellion with grave loss of life.

Each of these incidents suggested that the proletariat itself was opposing the dictatorship of the proletariat. Also, by late 1920 it had become clear that further revolution would not sweep across the rest of Europe. For the time being, the Soviet Union would constitute a vast island of revolutionary socialism in the larger sea of worldwide capitalism.

The New Economic Policy

Under these difficult conditions Lenin made a crucial strategic retreat. In March 1921, following the Kronstadt mutiny and in the face of peasant resistance to the requisition of grain that was needed to feed the urban population, he outlined the New Economic Policy, normally referred to as NEP. Apart from what he termed "the commanding heights" of banking, heavy industry, transportation, and international commerce, there was to be considerable private economic enterprise. In particular, peasants were to be permitted to farm for a profit. They would pay taxes like other citizens, but they could sell their surplus grain on the open market. The NEP was in line with Lenin's earlier conviction that the Russian peasantry held the key to the success of revolution in the nation.

After 1921 the countryside did become more stable, and a more secure food supply seemed assured for the cities. Similar free enterprise flourished within light industry and domestic retail trade. However, the implementation of NEP was not fully successful because the peasants found there were virtually no consumer goods to purchase with the money they received for their grain. Yet by 1927 industrial production had reached its 1913 level. The revolution seemed to have transformed Russia into a land of small, if frequently discontented, family farmers and owners of small, private shops and businesses.

Stalin Versus Trotsky

The New Economic Policy had caused sharp disputes within the Politburo, the highest governing committee of the Communist Party. The partial return to capitalism seemed to some members nothing less than a betrayal of sound Marxist principles. These frictions in-

Lenin and Stalin in the summer of 1922, after Stalin's appointment as General Secretary of the Communist Party. The following December Lenin suffered a paralytic stroke and was unable to check Stalin's increasing dominance of party affairs. Lenin died in January 1924.

creased as Lenin's firm hand disappeared. In 1922 he suffered a stroke that broke his health. He returned to work but never again dominated party affairs. In 1924 Lenin died.

As the power vacuum developed, an intense struggle for future leadership of the party began. Two factions emerged. One was led by Leon Trotsky; the other by Joseph Stalin (1879–1953), who had become general secretary of the party in 1922. Shortly before his death Lenin had criticized both men. He was especially harsh toward Stalin. However, the general secretary's base of power lay with the party membership and with the daily management of party affairs. Consequently, he was able to withstand the posthumous strictures of Lenin.

The issue between the two factions was power within the party, but the struggle was fought out over the question of Russia's path toward industrialization and the future of the communist revolutionary movement. Trotsky, speaking for what became known as the left wing, urged rapid industrialization financed through the expropriation of farm production. Agriculture should be collectivized, and the peasants should be made to pay for industrialization. Trotsky further argued that the revolution in Russia could succeed only if new revo-

lutions took place elsewhere in the world. Russia needed the skills and wealth of other nations to build its own economy. As Trotsky's influence within the party began to wane, he also demanded that party members be permitted to criticize the policies of the government and the party. However, Trotsky was very much a latecomer to the advocacy of open discussion. When in control of the Red Army, he had been known as an unflinching disciplinarian.

A right-wing faction opposed Trotsky. Its chief ideological voice was that of Nikolai Bukharin (1888–1938), the editor of *Pravda*, the official party paper. Stalin was the major political manipulator. In the mid-1920s in the face of uncertain economic recovery, this group pressed for the continuation of Lenin's NEP and a policy of relatively slow industrialization. At the time this position represented an economic policy based largely on decentralized economic planning. Stalin emerged as the victor in these intraparty rivalries.

Stalin had been born in 1879 into a very poor family. Unlike the other early Bolshevik leaders, he had not spent a long period of exile in western Europe. He was much less an intellectual and internationalist. He was also much more brutal. In his capacity as Commissar of

tion, Stalin gained power through his command of bureaucratic and administrative methods. He was neither a brilliant writer nor an effective public speaker. However, he mastered the crucial, if dull, details of party structure, including admission and promotion. That mastery meant that he could draw on the support of the lower levels of the party apparatus when he came into conflict with other leaders.

In the middle of the decade Stalin expediently supported Bukharin's position on economic development. In 1924 he also enunciated, in opposition to Trotsky, the doctrine of "socialism in one country." He urged that socialism could be achieved in Russia alone. Russian success did not depend on the fate of the revolution elsewhere. In this manner Stalin nationalized the previously international scope of the Marxist revolution. Stalin cunningly used the apparatus of the party and his control over the Central Committee of the Communist Party to edge out Trotsky and his supporters.

By 1927 Trotsky had been removed from all his offices, expelled from the party, and exiled to Siberia. In 1929 he was sent out of Russia and eventually took up residence in Mexico, where he was murdered in 1940, presumably by one of Stalin's agents. With the removal of Trotsky from all positions of influence, Stalin was firmly in control of the Soviet state. It remained to be seen where he would direct its course and what "socialism in one country" would mean in practice.

Nationalities, Stalin's handling of various recalcitrant national groups within Russia after the revolution had shocked even Lenin though not enough for the latter to dismiss him. As the Party General Secretary, a post disdained by party intellectuals as a mere clerical posi-

At the close of the 1920s it appeared that Europe had finally emerged from the difficulties of the World War I era. The initial resentments over the peace settlement seemed to have abated. The major powers were cooperating. Democracy was still functioning in Germany. The Labour Party was about to form its second ministry in Britain. France had settled into a less assertive international role. Mussolini's Fascism seemed to have little relevance to the rest of the Continent. The successor states had not fulfilled the democratic hopes of the Paris conference, but their troubles seemed their own. The Soviet Union, regarded in the West as harboring a communist menace, stood both isolated by the other powers and withdrawn into its own internal

development and power struggles.

The European economy seemed finally to be on an even keel. The frightening inflation was over, and unemployment had eased. American capital was flowing into the Continent. The reparation payments had been systematized by the Young Plan. Yet both this economic and this political stability proved illusory and temporary. What brought them to an end was the deepest economic depression in the modern history of the West. As the governments and electorates responded to the economic collapse, the search for liberty gave way in more than one instance to a search for security. The political experiments of the 1920s gave way to the political tragedies of the 1930s.

Suggested Readings

D. H. ALDCROFT, *From Versailles to Wall Street: The International Economy in the 1920s* (1976). A useful introduction.

I. BANAC, *The National Question in Yugoslavia: Origins, History, Politics* (1984). An outstanding treatment of the reorganization of east European political life.

R. BESSEL, *Political Violence and the Rise of Nazism: The Storm Troopers in Eastern Germany, 1925–1934* (1984). A study of the uses of violence by the Nazis.

K. D. BRACHER, *The German Dictatorship* (1970). A comprehensive treatment of both the origins and the functioning of the Nazi movement and government.

A. BULLOCK, *Hitler: A Study in Tyranny*, rev. ed. (1964). The best biography.

E. H. CARR, *A History of Soviet Russia*, 9 vols. (1950–19—). An extensive and important study.

S. F. COHEN, *Bukharin and the Bolshevik Revolution: A Political Biography, 1888–1938* (1973). An interesting examination of Stalin's chief opponent on the Communist right.

I. DEUTSCHER, *The Prophet Armed* (1954), *The Prophet Unarmed* (1959), and *The Prophet Outcast* (1963). A major biography of Trotsky.

E. EYCK, *A History of the Weimar Republic*, 2 vols. (trans. 1963). The story as narrated by a liberal.

L. FISCHER, *The Life of Lenin* (1964). A sound biography by an American journalist.

P. FUSSELL, *The Great War and Modern Memory* (1975). A brilliant account of the literature arising from World War I during the 1920s.

P. GAY, *Weimar Culture: The Outsider as Insider* (1968). A sensitive analysis of the intellectual life of Weimar.

H. J. GORDON, *Hitler and the Beer Hall Putsch* (1972). An excellent account of the event and the political situation in the early Weimar Republic.

N. GREENE, *From Versailles to Vichy: The Third Republic, 1919–1940* (1970). A useful introduction to a difficult subject.

H. GRUBER, *International Communism in the Era of Lenin: A Documentary History* (1967). An excellent collection of difficult-to-find documents.

P. KENEZ, *The Birth of the Propaganda State: Soviet Methods of Mass Mobilization, 1917–1929* (1985). An examination of the manner in which the Communist government inculcated popular support.

C. A. MACARTNEY AND A. W. PALMER, *Independent Eastern Europe: A History* (1962). A helpful one-volume survey.

C. S. MAIER, *Recasting Bourgeois Europe: Stabilization in France, Germany, and Italy in the Decade after World War I* (1975). An important interpretation written from a comparative standpoint.

A. MARWICK, *The Deluge: British Society and the First World War* (1965). Full of insights into both major and more subtle minor social changes.

E. NOLTE, *Three Faces of Fascism* (1963). An important, influential, and difficult work on France, Italy, and Germany.

R. PIPES, *The Formation of the Soviet Union*, 2nd ed. (1964). A study of internal policy with emphasis on Soviet minorities.

J. F. POLLARD, *The Vatican and Italian Fascism 1929–32: A Study in Conflict* (1985). Provides the background to the Lateran Pacts.

J. ROTHCHILD, *East Central Europe between the Two World Wars* (1974). A detailed and authoritative survey.

S. A. SCHUKER, *The End of French Predominance in Europe: The Financial Crisis of 1924 and the Adoption of the Dawes Plan* (1976). An excellent study of a very complicated issue.

H. SETON-WATSON, *Eastern Europe Between the Wars, 1918–1941* (1946). Somewhat dated but still a useful work.

D. P. SILVERMAN, *Reconstructing Europe after the Great War* (1982). Examines the difficulties confronted by the major powers.

D. M. SMITH, *Italy: A Modern History*, rev. ed. (1969). Very good chapters on the Fascists and Mussolini.

D. M. SMITH, *Italy and Its Monarchy* (1989). A major treatment of an important neglected subject.

R. J. SONTAG, *A Broken World, 1919–1939* (1971). An exceptionally thoughtful and well-organized survey.

M. STEINBERG, *Sabers and Brownshirts: The German Students' Path to National Socialism, 1918–1935* (1977). An interesting study of the recruitment of young Germans.

A. J. P. TAYLOR, *English History, 1914–1945* (1965). Lively and opinionated.

M. TRACTENBERG, *Reparations in World Politics: France and European Economic Diplomacy, 1916–1923* (1980). Points to the special role of reparations in French calculations.

R. TUCKER, *Stalin as Revolutionary, 1879–1929: A Study in History and Personality* (1973). A useful and readable account of Stalin's rise to power.

N. TUMARKIN, *Lenin Lives: The Lenin Cult in Soviet Russia* (1983). An interesting work on the uses of Lenin's reputation after his death.

T. WILSON, *The Downfall of the Liberal Party, 1914–1935* (1966). A close examination of the surprising demise of a political party in Britain.

E. WISKEMANN, *Fascism in Italy: Its Development and Influence* (1969). A comprehensive treatment.

R. WOHL, *The Generation of 1914* (1979). An important work that explores the effect of the war on political and social thought.

The dictatorships of Mussolini and Hitler achieved new modes of authoritarian government. [UPI/Bettman Newsphotos]

28

EUROPE AND THE GREAT DEPRESSION OF THE 1930S

In Europe, unlike in the United States, the 1920s had not been "roaring." Economically they had been a decade of much insecurity, of a search for elusive stability, of a short-lived upswing, and then of collapse in finance and production. The Great Depression that began in 1929 was the most severe downturn ever experienced by the capitalist economies. The unemployment, low production levels, financial instability, and contracted trade arrived and would not depart. Marxists thought that the final downfall of capitalism was at hand. Capitalist businessmen and political leaders despaired over the failure of the market mechanism to save them.

Voters looked for new ways out of the doldrums and politicians sought escapes from the pressures that the Depression had brought on them. One result of the fight for economic security was the establishment of the Nazi dictatorship in Germany. Another was the piecemeal construction of what has since become known as the mixed economy; that is, governments became directly involved in economic decisions. In both cases most of the political and economic guidelines of nineteenth-century liberalism were abandoned for good. Two other casualties of these years were decency and civility in political life.

Toward the Great Depression

Three factors combined to bring about the intense severity and the extended length of the Great Depression. There was a financial crisis that stemmed directly from the war and the peace settlement. To this was added a crisis in the production and distribution of goods in the world market. These two problems became intertwined in 1929, and as far as Europe was concerned, they reached the breaking point in 1931. Finally, both of these difficulties became worse than might have been necessary because of the absence of strong economic leadership and responsibility on the part of any major west European country or the United States. Without cooperation or leadership in the Atlantic economic community, the economic collapse in finance and production simply lingered and deepened.

The Financial Tailspin

Most European nations emerged from World War I with inflated currencies. Immediately after the armistice the unleashed demand for consumer and industrial goods continued to drive up prices. The price and wage increases generally subsided after 1921. Yet the problem of maintaining the value of their currencies still haunted political leaders—and even more after the German financial disaster of 1923. This frightening experience accounted in part for the refusal of most governments to run budget deficits when the Depression struck. They feared inflation as a political danger in the same manner that European governments since World War II have feared unemployment.

REPARATIONS AND WAR DEBTS The problems of reparation payments and international war-debt settlement further complicated the picture. France and the United States provided the stumbling blocks in these matters. France had paid reparations as a defeated nation after 1815 and 1871. As a victor it now intended to receive reparations and to finance its postwar recovery through them. The 1923 invasion of the Ruhr demonstrated French determination on this question.

The United States was no less determined to receive repayments of the wartime loans extended to its allies. There were also various debts that the European Allies owed to each other. It soon became apparent that German reparations were to provide the means of repaying the American and other Allied debts. Most of the money that the Allies collected from each other also went to the United States.

In 1922 Great Britain announced that it would collect payment on its own debts only to the extent that the United States required payments from Britain. However, the American government would not relent. The reparations and the war debts made normal business, capital investment, and international trade very difficult and expensive for the European nations. Various modes of government controls were exercised over credit, trade, and currency. Speculation in currency drew funds away from capital investment in productive enterprise. The monetary problems served to reinforce the general tendency toward high tariff policies. If a nation imported too many goods from abroad, it might have difficulty meeting those costs and the expenses of debt or reparation payments. The financial and money muddle thus discouraged trade and production and, in turn, harmed employment.

AMERICAN INVESTMENTS In 1924 the Dawes Plan brought more system to the administration and transfer of reparations. Those procedures, in turn, smoothed the debt repayments to the United States. Thereafter, large amounts of private American capital flowed into Europe and especially into Germany. Much of this money, which provided the basis for Europe's brief prosperity after 1925, was in the form of short-term loans.

In 1928 this lending began to contract as American money became diverted from European investments into the booming New York stock market. The crash of Wall Street in October 1929—the result of virtually unregulated financial speculation—saw the loss of large amounts of money. United States banks had made very large loans to customers who then invested the money in the stock market. When stock prices fell, the customers could not repay the banks. Consequently, within the United States there occurred a major contraction of all kinds of credit, and numerous banks failed. Thereafter, little American capital was available for investment in Europe. Furthermore, loans already made to Europeans were not re-

Crowds gathered on Wall Street in New York on October 29, 1929, the day the stock market crashed. The Depression in the United States meant that no American capital was available to loan to Europe. [Brown Brothers]

newed, as American banks used their available funds to cover domestic shortages.

THE END OF REPARATIONS

As the credit to Europe began to run out, a major financial crisis struck the continent. In May 1931 the Kreditanstalt, a major bank in Vienna, collapsed. It was a primary lending institution for much of central and eastern Europe. The German banking system came under severe pressure and was saved only through government guarantees. However, it became clear that under this crisis situation Germany would be unable to make its next reparation payment as stipulated in the 1929 Young Plan. As the German difficulties reached such large proportions, American President Herbert Hoover announced in June 1931 a one-year moratorium on all payments of international debts.

The Hoover moratorium was a prelude to the end of reparations. Hoover's action was a sharp blow to the French economy, for which

the flow of reparations had continued to be important. The French agreed to the moratorium most reluctantly but really had little alternative because the German economy was in a state of virtual collapse. The Lausanne Conference of the summer of 1932 in effect brought the era of reparations to a close. The next year the debts owed to the United States were settled either through small token pay-

MAJOR DATES OF THE ECONOMIC CRISIS	
1923	German inflation following French invasion of Ruhr
1924	Dawes Plan on reparations
1929	Young Plan on reparations
1929	Wall Street Crash
1931	(May) Collapse of Kreditanstalt in Vienna
1931	(June) Hoover announces moratorium on reparations
1932	Lausanne Conference ends reparations

ments or simply through default. Nevertheless the financial politics of the 1920s had done its damage.

Problems in Agricultural Commodities

In addition to the dramatic financial turmoil and collapse there was also a less dramatic, but equally fundamental, downturn in production and trade. The 1920s witnessed a contraction in the market demand for European goods relative to the continent's productive capacity.

Part of this problem originated within Europe and part outside. In both instances the difficulty arose from agriculture. Better methods of farming, improved strains of wheat, expanded tillage, and more extensive transport facilities all over the globe vastly increased the quantity of grain produced. World wheat prices fell to record lows. This development was, of course, initially good for consumers. However, it meant lower incomes for European farmers and especially for those of central and eastern Europe.

At the same time higher industrial wages

The League of Nations Reports the Collapse of European Agriculture

A crisis in agriculture was as much a cause of the Depression as was the turmoil in the financial community. The League of Nations reported in 1931 how, in part, the desperate situation in agriculture had developed.

It is the lowness of prices that constitutes the agricultural crisis. It is becoming difficult to sell products, and in many cases prices have reached a level at which they are scarcely, if at all, sufficient to cover the cost of production.

The reason for the crisis and for its continuance is to be found in the fact that agricultural prices are low in comparison with the expenditure which the farmer must meet. . . . Agricultural products cost a lot to produce and then fetch very little in the market. In spite of the great technical progress achieved, operating costs remain implacably higher than selling prices, farmers obtain no longer a fair return on their labour or on their capital. Frequently the returns of agricultural undertakings are not enough to cover the necessary outlay for the purchase of the material or products necessary for continued operation or for the payment of wages and taxes and so forth.

This disproportion between the income and expenditure of agricultural undertakings . . . appears to constitute the dominant and decisive element of the prevailing agricultural depression.

Until 1929, prices were low as compared with prices of industrial products, but were above pre-war prices. The predominating tendency to a fall which was observed was not altogether general nor was it abnormally rapid. The general character of the price movement completely changed in 1930. A fall, sometimes catastrophic, spread with extreme violence to almost all agricultural produce. It was so rapid that at the end of the year, whilst some products reached the pre-war level of prices, others fell as low as one-quarter or one-half below the 1913 level. . . . Farmers throughout the world have suffered from it.

League of Nations, Economic Committee, The Agricultural Crisis, *Vol. 1 (1931), pp. 7–8, reprinted in S. B. Clough, T. Moodie, and C. G. Moodie,* Economic History of Europe: The Twentieth Century *(New York: Harper & Row, 1968), pp. 216–217.*

raised the cost of the industrial goods used by the farmer or peasant. The farmers could not purchase those products. Moreover, farmers began to have difficulty paying off their mortgages and normal annual operation debts. They borrowed money to plant their fields, expecting to pay the debt when the crops were sold. The fall in commodity prices raised problems of repayment.

The difficulties of agricultural finance became especially pressing in eastern Europe. Immediately after the war numerous land-reform programs had been undertaken in this region. The democratic franchise in the successor states had opened the way for considerable redistribution of tillable soil. In Romania and Czechoslovakia large amounts of land changed hands. This occurred to a lesser extent in Hungary and Poland.

However, the new relatively small farmers proved to be inefficient and were unable to earn sufficient incomes. Protective tariffs often prevented the export of grain among European countries. The credit and cost squeeze on east European farmers and on their counterparts in Germany played a major role in their disillusionment with liberal politics. For example, in Germany farmers provided the Nazis with a major source of political support.

Outside Europe similar problems affected other producers of agricultural commodities. The prices that they received for their products plummeted. Government-held reserves accumulated to record levels. This glut of major world commodities involved the supplies of wheat, sugar, coffee, rubber, wool, and lard. The people who produced these goods in underdeveloped nations could no longer make enough money to buy finished goods from industrial Europe. As world credit collapsed, the economic position of these commodity producers became all the worse. Commodity production had simply outstripped world demand.

The result of the collapse in the agricultural sector of the world economy and the financial turmoil was stagnation and depression for European industry. Coal, iron, and textiles had depended largely on international markets. Unemployment spread from these industries to those producing finished consumer goods. The persistent unemployment of Great Britain and to a lesser extent of Germany during the 1920s had already meant "soft" domestic markets. The policies of reduced government

spending with which the governments confronted the Depression further weakened domestic demand. By the early 1930s the Great Depression was growing on itself.

Areas of Growth Within the Depressed Economies

Despite the Great Depression, some economic growth did take place between the wars. Depression did not mean economic regression. The economic growth was spotty, unsteady, and concentrated in special areas. Three of these industries deserve brief mention. They were radios, automobiles, and synthetic goods. The technological basis for each of them had been developed before World War I, but their major impact on the economy occurred afterward.

RADIO Radio and radio technology came of age in the 1920s and 1930s. The wartime requirements for communication had speeded up the development and the production of the wireless. In 1922 broadcasting facilities had been established in Britain. The nationalized British Broadcasting Corporation was organized in 1926. Other radio broadcasting facilities spread across the Continent during the same years. The radio was a consumer gadget of the first order. The expanding electrical systems made its use possible. The radio itself was sold and then required other businesses to supply service parts. The radio industry, in turn, expanded the scope and transformed the nature of advertising.

By the end of the 1920s millions of radios were in European homes. It was a product bought not by the wealthy, who had various other modes of leisure, but by the relatively poor and middle-class groups of the population. It was the first product of sophisticated electrical technology to capture the mass market. Radio—like its successor, television—transformed European life and tended to produce a more nearly uniform culture. Radio also helped to make the propaganda programs of the authoritarian states possible.

AUTOMOBILES Automobiles were a second interwar growth industry. Only during those years did the motor car become a product of widespread consumption. In France Louis Renault and André Citroën built cars that the

This is a Citroën automobile of the late 1920s with Michelin tires. In the interwar period, France had more private automobiles than any other country except the United States. [Bilderdienst Suddeutscher Verlag]

middle class wanted and could afford to buy. The automobile revolutionized European life rather less than it did American life. But the auto did bring new mobility and also possessed obvious military uses. Its production called forth new demand for steel, glass, rubber, petroleum, and highways. The automobile, like the radio, required a sales and service—as well as a production—industry.

SYNTHETICS During these years the production of synthetic goods began to assume major economic significance. Rayon, invented before World War I, led the way in this area. Its production and consumption for hose and underwear grew rapidly. The product itself was soon much improved through the acetate process. Rayon began to replace cotton as the cheap textile for everyday use. The production of this synthetic fabric proved especially attractive to governments, such as those of Germany and Italy, that sought economic self-sufficiency. The prospect of war in the late 1930s led various governments to encourage the chemical industries to search for other synthetic substances that might replace natu-

ral products if foreign sources for the latter were shut off.

Depression and Government Policy

It is important to remember these areas of industrial expansion between the wars. The Great Depression did not mean absolute economic decline. Nor did it mean that everyone was out of a job. The numbers of employed always well exceeded those without work. What the economic downturn did mean was the spread of actual or potential insecurity. People in nearly all walks of life feared that their own economic security and lifestyle might be the next to go. The Depression also brought on a frustration of social and economic expectations. People with jobs frequently improved their standard of living or received promotion much more slowly than they might have under sound economic conditions. Although they were employed, they seemed in their own eyes to be going nowhere. Their anxieties created a major source of social discontent.

Motor Cars Become More Popular in France

The Depression came to France later than to other countries. During the late 1920s and early 1930s the motor-car industry grew. More French citizens drove cars, and the manufacture of cars became more standardized. This passage from a report on the French economy describes this development and emphasizes the desire of French consumers to have real choices in regard to motor-car styles.

Nearly twelve times as many passenger cars are in use today in France as there were in 1913, the number of registered or tax-paying passenger cars having grown from 107,857 in that year to 1,279,142 at the end of 1932; since 1928, when the number was 757,668, the increase has been over half a million. . . .

In the French motor-car industry noteworthy progress has been made in standardization during the last seven years. The industry is one in which there was particular scope for the introduction of some form of standardization, for owing to the multiplicity of small manufacturers (50 or more of whom produced between them only about 10 per cent of the total output of the country, each seeking to strike a note of individuality), there was an inevitable tendency towards an unduly large variety of designs and dimensions, even of the most ordinary parts. A normalization bureau was set up in 1926 by the association of accessory and spare parts manufacturers, and by 1928 standards had been established for 29 parts, resulting in price reductions, in some cases, of 86 to 95 per cent. For instance, the number of different types of caps for radiators and petrol tanks has been reduced from 88 to five. . . .

Government departments and public utility concerns, such as the Ministry of War and the motor transport concession holders working in collaboration with the railways, are lending useful support to the normalization movement by inserting a clause in their specifications requiring suppliers of vehicles to employ only parts conforming to the accepted standards. . . .

The tendency towards standardization was further manifested about 1929, by a fairly general decision of leading French motor-car manufacturers, whereby each firm concentrated its energies on two or three types of cars, instead of trying to cater for the whole range of motor-car users, private and industrial; the Citroën and Peugeot firms, in particular, being prominent protagonists of the new policy. The individualistic French temperament, however, proved itself too strong for this policy to be followed for long; and at the motor shows of 1931–1933 a reversion to the former practice of putting on the markets as many different types of cars as each producer thought he had a chance of selling, was clearly apparent.

J. R. Cahill, Economic Conditions in France (London: 1934), pp. 253, 257–258, as cited in Sidney Pollard and Colin Holmes, Documents of European Economic History, Vol. 3 (London: Edward Arnold, 1973), pp. 587–588.

The governments of the late 1920s and the early 1930s were not particularly well fitted in either structure or ideology to confront these problems. The demand from the electorates was to do something. What the government did depended in large measure on the severity of the Depression in a particular country and the self-confidence of the nation's political system.

The Keynesian theory of governments'

spending the economy out of Depression was not yet available. John Maynard Keynes' *General Theory of Employment, Interest, and Money* was not published until 1936. The orthodox economic policy of the day called for cuts in government spending so as to prevent inflation. It was then expected that eventually the market mechanism would bring the economy back to prosperity. However, the length and severity of the Depression, plus the possibility of direct democratic political pressure, led governments across Europe to interfere with the economy as never before.

Government participation in economic life was not new. One need only recall the policies of mercantilism and the government encouragement of railway building. But from the early 1930s onward, government involvement increased rapidly. Private economic enterprise became subject to new trade, labor, and currency regulations. The political goals of the restoration of employment and the provision for defense established new state-related economic priorities. Generally speaking, as in the past, the extent of state intervention increased as one moved from west to east across the continent. These new economic policies, in most cases, also involved further political experimentation.

Confronting the Great Depression in the Democracies

The Great Depression brought to an end the business-as-usual attitude that had marked the political life of Great Britain and France during the late 1920s. In Britain the emergency led to

George Orwell Observes a Woman in the Slums

Although Great Britain was beginning to emerge from the Great Depression by the late 1930s, much poverty and human degradation remained. This scene, described in 1937 by the social critic and novelist George Orwell (1903–1950), captures a glimpse of the sadness and hopelessness that many British citizens experienced every day of their lives.

The train bore me away, through the monstrous scenery of slag-heaps, chimneys, piled scrap-iron, foul canals, paths of cindery mud crisscrossed by the prints of clogs. . . . As we moved slowly through the outskirts of the town we passed row after row of little grey slum houses running at right angles to the embankment. At the back of one of the houses a young woman was kneeling on the stones, poking a stick up the leaden waste-pipe which ran from the sink inside, and which I suppose was blocked. I had time to see everything about her—her sacking apron, her clumsy clogs, her arms reddened by the cold. . . . She had a round pale face, the usual exhausted face of the slum girl who is twenty-five and looks forty, thanks to miscarriages and drudgery; and it wore, for the second in which I saw it, the most desolate, hopeless expression I have ever seen. It struck me then that we are mistaken when we say that "It isn't the same for them as it would be for us," and that people bred in the slums can imagine nothing but the slums. For what I saw in her face was not the ignorant suffering of an animal. She knew well enough what was happening to her—understood as well as I did how dreadful a destiny it was to be kneeling there in the bitter cold, on the slimy stones of a slum backyard, poking a stick up a foul drain-pipe.

George Orwell, The Road to Wigan Pier *(New York: Berkley Medallion Books, 1967; originally printed in 1937), p. 29.*

a new coalition government and the abandonment of economic policies considered almost untouchable for a century. The economic stagnation in France proved to be the occasion for a bold political and economic program sponsored by the parties of the left. The relative success of the British venture gave the nation new confidence in the democratic processes; the new departures in France created social and political hostilities that undermined faith in republican institutions.

Great Britain:
The National Government

In 1929 a second minority Labour government, headed by Ramsay MacDonald, assumed office. As the number of British unemployed rose to more than 2.5 million workers in 1931, the ministry became divided over the remedy for the problem. MacDonald believed that the budget should be slashed, government salaries reduced, and the benefits to people on government unemployment insurance lowered. This was a bleak program for a Labour government. MacDonald's strong desire to make the Labour Party respectable led him away from more radical programs. Many of the Cabinet ministries rejected MacDonald's proposals. They would not consent to taking income away from the poor and the unemployed. The prime minister requested the resignations of his Cabinet and arranged for a meeting with King George V.

Everyone assumed that the entire Labour ministry was about to leave office. However, to the surprise of his party and the nation, MacDonald did not resign. At the urging of the king and probably of his own ambition, MacDonald formed a coalition ministry called the *National Government* composed of Labour, Conservative, and Liberal ministers. The bulk of the Labour Party believed that their leader had sold out. In the election of 1931 the National Government received a very comfortable majority. After the election, however, MacDonald, who remained prime minister until 1935, was little more than a tool of the Conservatives. They held a majority in their own right in the House of Commons, but the appearance of a coalition was useful for imposing unpleasant programs.

The National Government took three decisive steps to attack the Depression. To balance the budget, it raised taxes, cut insurance benefits to the unemployed and the elderly, and lowered government salaries. Its leaders argued that the fall in prices that had taken place meant that lowering those benefits and salaries did not appreciably cut real income. In September 1931 the National Government went off the gold standard. The value of the British pound on the international money market fell by about 30 per cent. Exports were somewhat stimulated by this move. In 1932 Parliament passed the Import Duties Bill, which placed a 10 per cent *ad valorem* tariff on all imports except those from the empire. In the context of previous British policy, all of these steps were nothing less than extraordinary. Gold and free trade, the hallmarks of almost a century of British commercial policy, stood abandoned.

The policies of the National Government produced significant results. Great Britain avoided the banking crisis that hit other countries. By 1934 industrial production had expanded somewhat beyond the level for 1929. Britain was the first nation to achieve restoration of that level of production. Of course, the mediocre British industrial performance of the 1920s made the British task easier. The government also encouraged lower interest rates. These, in turn, led to the largest private housing boom in British history. Industries related to housing and the furnishing of homes prospered.

Those people who were employed generally experienced an improvement in their standard of living. Nonetheless, the hard core of unemployment remained. In 1937 the number of jobless had fallen to just below 1.5 million. That same year, when George Orwell described the laboring districts of the nation in *The Road to Wigan Pier*, the poverty and the workless days of the people whom he met dominated his picture.

Britain had entered the Depression with a stagnant economy and left the era with a stagnant economy. Yet the political system itself was not fundamentally challenged. There were demonstrations of the unemployed, but social insurance, though hardly generous, did support them. To the employed citizens of the country the National Government seemed to pursue a policy that avoided the extreme wings of both the Labour and the Conservative parties. When MacDonald retired in 1935, Stanley Baldwin again took office. He was succeeded in 1937 by

The cabinet of the National Government that was formed in Britain in January 1931. Ramsay MacDonald is seated in the center with Stanley Baldwin on his right. Neville Chamberlain, who would become prime minister in 1937, is standing second from the right. [AP]

Neville Chamberlain (1869–1940). The new prime minister is today known for the disaster of the Munich agreement. When he took office, he was known as one of the more progressive thinkers on social issues in the Conservative Party.

Britain did see one movement that flirted with the extreme right-wing politics of the Continent. In 1932 Sir Oswald Mosley (1896–1980) founded the British Union of Fascists. He had held a minor position in the second Labour government and was disappointed in its feeble attack on unemployment. Mosley urged a program of direct action through a new corporate structure for the economy. His group wore black shirts and attempted to hold mass meetings. He gained only a few thousand adherents. Mosley's popularity reached its height in 1934. Thereafter his anti-Semitism began to alienate supporters, and by the close of the decade he had become little more than a political oddity.

France: The Popular Front

The timing of the Great Depression in France was the reverse of that in Britain. It came later and lasted much longer. Only in 1931 did the economic slide begin to affect the French economy. Even then unemployment did not become the major problem that it did elsewhere. Rarely were more than half a million workers without jobs. However, in one industry after another, wages were lowered. Tariffs were raised to protect French goods and especially French agriculture. Ever since that time French farmers have enjoyed unusual protection from the government. These measures helped to maintain the home market but did little to overcome industrial stagnation. Relations between labor and management were tense.

The first political fallout of the Depression was the election of another Radical coalition government in 1932. Fearful of contributing to inflation as it had after 1924, the Radical government pursued a generally deflationary policy. In the same year that the new ministry took office, reparation payments had stopped. As the economic crisis tightened, normal parliamentary and political life became difficult and confused.

RIGHT-WING VIOLENCE Outside the Chamber of Deputies politics assumed a very ugly face. The old divisions between left and right hardened. Various right-wing groups with authoritarian tendencies became active. These leagues included the *Action Française*, founded before World War I in the wake of the Dreyfus affair, and the *Croix de Feu* ("Cross of Fire"), composed of army veterans. The memberships of these and other similar groups numbered somewhat more than two million persons. Some members wanted a monarchy; others favored what would have amounted to military rule. They were hostile to the idea of parliamentary government, socialism, and communism. They wanted what they regarded as the greater good and glory of the nation to be set above the petty machinations of political parties. In this regard they resembled the Fascists and the Nazis.

The activities and propaganda of these leagues aided the dissolution of loyalty to republican government and injected bitterness and vindictiveness into French political life. They also created one moment of extraordinary havoc that produced important long-range political consequences.

The incident grew out of the Stavisky affair, the last of those curious *causes célèbres* that punctuated the political fortunes of the Third Republic. Serge Stavisky was a small-time gangster who appears to have had good connections within the government. In 1933 he became involved in a fraudulent bond scheme. When finally tracked down by the police, he committed suicide in January 1934. The official handling of the matter suggested a political cover-up. It was alleged that people in high places wished to halt the investigation. To the right wing in France the Stavisky incident symbolized all the seaminess, immorality, and corruption of republican politics.

On February 6, 1934, a very large demonstration of the right-wing leagues took place in Paris. The exact purpose and circumstances of the rally remain uncertain, but the crowd did attempt to march on the Chamber of Deputies. Violence erupted between right and left political groups and between them and the police. Fourteen demonstrators were killed; scores of others were injured. It was the largest disturbance in Paris since the Commune of 1871.

In the wake of the night of February 6, the Radical ministry of Edouard Daladier (1884–1970) resigned and was replaced by a national coalition government composed of all living former premiers. The Chamber of Deputies permitted the ministry to deal with economic matters by decree. However, the major result of the right-wing demonstrations was a political self-reassessment by the parties of the left. Radicals, Socialists, and Communists began to realize that a right-wing *coup* might be possible in France.

Right-wing crowds attempted to storm the French Parliament on February 6, 1934 in the wake of the Stavisky scandal. [Ullstein Bilderdienst]

EMERGENCE OF SOCIALIST–COMMUN-
IST COOPERATION Consequently, between 1934 and 1936, the French left began to
make peace within its own ranks. This was no
easy task. French Socialists, led by Léon Blum
(1872–1950), had been the major target of the
French Communists since the split over joining the Comintern in 1920. Only Stalin's fear
of Hitler as a danger to the Soviet Union made
this new cooperation possible. In spite of deep
suspicions on all sides, the Popular Front had
been established by Bastille Day in 1935. Its
purpose was to preserve the republic and to
press for social reform.

The election of 1936 gave the Popular Front
a majority in the Chamber of Deputies. The
Socialists were the largest single party for the
first time in French history. Consequently,
they organized the Cabinet as they had long
promised they would do when they constituted the majority party of a coalition. Léon
Blum assumed the premiership on June 5,
1936. From the early 1920s this Jewish intellectual and humanitarian had opposed the
communist version of socialism. Cast as the

successor to Jean Jaurès, who had been assassinated in 1914, Blum wanted socialism in the
context of democratic, parliamentary government. He hoped to bring France a program akin
to the New Deal that President Franklin Roosevelt had carried out in the United States.

BLUM'S GOVERNMENT During May
1936, before the Popular Front came to power,
strikes had begun to spread throughout French
industry. Immediately after assuming office on
June 6, the Blum government faced further
spontaneous work stoppages involving over
half a million workers who had occupied factories in sit-down strikes. These were the most
extensive labor disturbances in the history of
the Third Republic. They aroused new fears in
the conservative business community, which
had already been frightened by the election of
the Popular Front.

Blum acted swiftly to bring together representatives of labor and management. On June 8
he announced the conclusion of the Matignon
Accord, which reorganized labor–management
relations in France. Wages were immediately

*Leaders of the French Popular front display unity at a Bastille Day rally in Paris, July
14, 1935. Léon Blum of the Socialist Party is on the left with Mme. Blum; Maurice
Thorez (1900–1964), the Secretary of the French Communist Party, stands beside him
on the right. [Globe Photos]*

French Management and Labor Reach an Agreement

When the Popular Front government came to power in France in 1936, it immediately confronted widespread strikes. Premier Léon Blum called together the representatives of labor and management. The result of these negotiations was the Matignon Accord, which gave the unions more secure rights, raised wages, and brought the strikes to an end.

The delegates of the General Confederation of French Production (CGPF) and the General Confederation of Labour (CGT) have met under the chairmanship of the Premier (Léon Blum) and have concluded the following agreement, after arbitration by the Premier:

1. The employer delegation agrees to the immediate conclusion of collective agreements.

2. These agreements must include, in particular, articles 3. . . .

3. All citizens being required to abide by law, the employers recognize the freedom of opinion of workers and their right to freely join and belong to trade unions.

In their decisions on hiring, organization or assignment of work, disciplinary measures or dismissals, employers agree not to take into consideration the fact of membership or nonmembership in a union. . . .

The exercise of trade union rights must not give rise to acts contrary to law.

4. The wages actually paid to all workers as of 25 May 1936 will be raised, as of the resumption of work, by a decreasing percentage ranging from 15 per cent for the lowest rates down to 7 per cent for the highest rates. In no case must the total increase in any establishment exceed 12 per cent. . . .

The negotiations, which are to be launched at once, for the determination by collective agreement of minimum wages by regions and by occupations must take up, in particular, the necessary revision of abnormally low wages. . . .

. . . .

6. The employer delegation promises that there will be no sanctions for strike activities.

7. The CGT delegation will ask the workers on strike to return to work as soon as the managements of establishments have accepted this general agreement and as soon as negotiations for its application have begun between the managements and the personnel of the establishments.

V. R. Lorwin, The French Labour Movement (Cambridge: Harvard University Press, 1954), pp. 313–315.

raised from 7 to 15 per cent, depending on the job involved. Employers were required to recognize unions and to bargain collectively with them. Annual, paid two-week vacations for workers were adopted. The forty-hour week was established throughout French industry. Blum hoped to overcome labor hostility to French society, to establish a foundation for justice in labor–management relations, and to increase the domestic consumer demand of the nation.

Blum followed his labor policy with other bold departures. He raised the salaries of civil servants and instituted a program of public works. Government loans were extended to small industry. Spending on armaments was increased, and some armament industries were nationalized. To aid agriculture, he set up a National Wheat Board to manage the production and sale of grain. Initially he had promised to resist devaluation of the franc. However, by the autumn of 1936 international monetary pressure forced him to devalue. He did so again in the spring of 1937. The devaluations brought little aid to French exports because they came too late.

All of these moves enraged the conservative banking and business community. In March 1937 they brought sufficient influence to bear on the ministry to cause Blum to halt the program of reform. It was not taken up again. Blum's Popular Front colleagues considered the pause in reform an unnecessary compromise. In June 1937 Blum resigned. The Popular Front ministry itself held on until April 1938, when it was replaced by a Radical ministry under Daladier.

The Popular Front had brought much hope to labor and to socialists, but it did not lead France out of the Great Depression. Some of its programs actually harmed production. The business community, because of its apprehensions and hostility, became even less venturesome after the Popular Front reforms. Not until 1939 did French industrial production reach the level of 1929. In a sense the Popular Front had come too late to give either the economy or French political life new vitality. Internal divisions and conservative opposition meant that the Popular Front had enjoyed less than a free hand.

By the close of the 1930s citizens from all walks of life had begun to wonder if the republic was worth preserving. The left continued to remain divided. Business people found the republic inefficient and, in their opinion, too much subject to socialist pressures. The right wing hated the republic in principle. When the time came in 1940 to defend the republic, there were too many citizens who were less than sure that it was worth defending.

Germany: The Nazi Seizure of Power

The most remarkable political event caused by the uncertainty and turmoil of the Great Depression was the coming to power of the National Socialists (Nazis) in Germany. By the late 1920s the Nazis were a major political presence in the Weimar Republic, but not real contenders for political dominance. The financial crisis, economic stress, and social anxiety associated with the onset of the Depression rapidly changed the political landscape in Germany. All of the fragility of the Weimar constitution was exposed and the path opened for the most momentous and far-reaching event of the decade, the Nazi seizure of power.

Depression and Political Deadlock

The outflow of foreign, and especially American, capital from Germany beginning in 1928 undermined the economic prosperity of the Weimar Republic. The resulting economic crisis brought parliamentary government to an end. In 1928 a coalition of center parties and the Social Democrats governed. All went reasonably well until the Depression struck. Then the coalition partners differed sharply on economic policy. The Social Democrats wanted no reduction in social and unemployment insurance. The more conservative parties, remembering the inflation of 1923, insisted on a balanced budget. The coalition dissolved in March 1930.

To resolve the parliamentary deadlock in the Reichstag, President von Hindenburg appointed Heinrich Brüning (1885–1970) as chancellor. Lacking a majority in the Reichstag, the new chancellor governed through emergency presidential decrees as authorized

DEPRESSION YEARS IN GREAT BRITAIN AND FRANCE	
1929	Second Labour Government comes to power in Britain with Ramsay MacDonald as prime minister
1931	Formation of National Government in Britain
1931	British Government goes off the gold standard
1932	Oswald Mosely founds British Union of Fascists
1933–1934	Stavisky Affair in France
1934	(February 6) Right-wing riots in France
1935	Stanley Baldwin becomes British prime minister
1936	(June 5) Popular Front government in France under Blum
1936	(June 8) Matignon Labor Accord in France
1937	Neville Chamberlain becomes British prime minister
1938	Popular Front replaced by Radical Ministry in France

by Article 48 of the constitution. The party divisions in the Reichstag prevented the overriding of the decrees. In this manner the Weimar Republic was transformed into a presidential dictatorship.

German unemployment rose from 2,258,000

The Nazis Proclaim Their Assumption of Power in Cologne

The Nazi assumption of power occurred on the local scene as well as on the national level. In Cologne the Nazis had held only a few seats in the city council. However, in March 1933, the Nazis simply took over the institutions of municipal government and cast out of office Konrad Adenauer, the Catholic Center Party mayor, who would become the most important national leader in postwar Germany. The local Nazi leader Joseph Grohé in a speech to a large gathering in the city hall explained the significance of the changes. His condemnation of Marxists included both Communists and Social Democrats.

It is a great hour that we celebrate today. The proudest, most heroic, and most industrious people in the world were torn apart and plunged into a gruesome abyss by the revolt of November 1918. The most exemplary people on earth became a conglomeration of selfish interest groups and a chaotic tangle of class hatred and obscurantist caste prejudice. A people of power and outstanding honor became the plaything of other nations and a victim of international capitalistic exploiters.

. . . .

Now the day has dawned for the reestablishment of German existence in Cologne. What the history of our city has so far never been able to record (without doubt, the result of the oppression and endeavours of our enemies) has now become reality; the people of Cologne have overwhelmingly avowed their faith in German Volkdom and in the national unity of a great German Reich. (Loud shouts of "Bravo!") And this, German men and women, we owe to the German *Volksmann* Adolf Hitler, who, from nothing and as an unknown among the millions of our people, began the battle against degradation and stupidity and who, in the face of countless difficulties, awakened in the German people the national revolution which we have celebrated with unbounded jubilation in these last weeks and days.

. . . .

Everybody has to come to terms with the fact that this has been the last multiparty election [the election of March, 1933]. (Applause.) . . .

With the assumption of power, Adolf Hitler and his fellow warriors have once and for all overcome the system of coalitions and barter.

. . . .

But we want to make it absolutely clear that we are determined to eradicate ruthlessly all those who endanger the people, and that we shall not under any circumstances permit corruption and the propagation of any special interests that are inimical to the common welfare.

As a matter of principle, we deny Marxists the right to any activity within Germany.

From Peter Schmidt, Zwansig Jahre Soldat Adolf Hitlers, Zehn Jarhe Gauleiter: Ein Buch von Kampf and Treue Cologne: Verlag Westdeutscher Beobacter, 1941), pp. 198–204 as quoted in George L. Mosse, ed., Nazi Culture: Intellectual, Cultural and Social Life in the Third Reich (New York: Grosset & Dunlap, 1966), pp. 378–481.

in March 1930 to over 6,000,000 in March 1932. There had been persistent unemployment during the 1920s, but nothing of such magnitude or duration. The economic downturn and the parliamentary deadlock worked to the advantage of the more extreme political parties. In the election of 1928 the Nazis had won only 12 seats in the Reichstag, and the Communists had won 54 seats. Two years later, after the election of 1930, the Nazis held 107 seats and the Communists 77.

The power of the Nazis in the streets was also on the rise. The unemployment fed thousands of men into the storm troopers (SA), which had 100,000 members in 1930 and almost 1 million in 1933. The SA freely and viciously attacked Communists and Social Democrats. For the Nazis, politics meant the capture of power through the instruments of terror and intimidation as well as by legal elections. Anything resembling decency and civility in political life vanished. The Nazis held rallies that resembled secular religious revivals. They paraded through the streets and the countryside. They gained powerful supporters and sympathizers in the business, military, and newspaper communities. Some intellectu-

als were also sympathetic. The Nazis were able to transform this discipline and enthusiasm born of economic despair and nationalistic frustration into impressive electoral results.

Hitler Comes to Power

For two years Brüning continued to govern through the confidence of Hindenburg. The economy did not improve, and the political situation deteriorated. In 1932 the eighty-three-year-old president stood for reelection. Hitler ran against him and forced a runoff. In the first election the Nazi leader garnered 30.1 per cent of the vote, and he later gained 36.8 per cent in the second. Although Hindenburg was returned to office, the results of the poll convinced him that Brüning no longer commanded sufficient confidence from conservative German voters.

On May 30, 1932, he dismissed Brüning, and on the next day he appointed Franz von Papen (1878–1969) in his place. The new chancellor was one of a small group of extremely conservative advisers on whom the aged Hindenburg had become increasingly dependent. Others

S.S. troops were a familiar sight in German streets once the Nazis came to power. They were an essential part of the apparatus of authoritarian rule. [Bildarchiv Preussischer Kulturbesitz]

President von Hindenburg (1847–1934) appears with Chancellor Hitler in 1930 at the anniversary of the battle of Tannenberg. To Hitler's left are two prominent Nazis: Hermann Göring (1893–1946) and Ernst Roehm (1887–1934), the commander of the SA, who later was murdered by Hitler. [Library of Congress]

included the president's son and several military figures. With the continued paralysis in the Reichstag, their influence over the president virtually amounted to control of the government. Consequently, the crucial decisions of the next several months were made by only a handful of people.

Papen and the circle around the president wanted to find some way to draw the Nazis into cooperation with them without giving any effective power to Hitler. The government needed the mass popular support that only the Nazis seemed able to generate. The Hindenburg circle decided to convince Hitler that the Nazis could not come to power on their own. Papen removed the ban on Nazi meetings that Brüning had imposed. Furthermore, he called a Reichstag election for July 1932. The Nazis won 230 seats and polled 37.2 per cent of the vote. As the price for his entry into the Cabinet, Hitler demanded appointment as chancellor. Hindenburg refused. Another election was called in November, partly as a means of wearing down the Nazis' financial resources. It was successful in that regard. The number of Nazi seats fell to 196, and their percentage of the popular vote dipped to 33.1 per cent. The advisers around Hindenburg still refused to appoint Hitler to office.

In November 1932 Papen resigned, and Kurt von Schleicher (1882–1934) became chancellor in December. There now existed much fear of civil war between groups on the left and the right. Schleicher decided to attempt the construction of a broad-based coalition of conservative groups and trade unionists. The prospect of such a coalition, including groups from the political left, frightened the Hindenburg circle even more than the prospect of Hitler. They did not trust Schleicher's motives, which have never been very clear. Consequently, they persuaded Hindenburg to appoint Hitler as chancellor. To control him and to see that he did little mischief, Papen was named vice-chancellor, and other traditional conservatives were appointed to the Cabinet. On January 30, 1933, Adolph Hitler became the chancellor of Germany.

Hitler's Consolidation of Power

Hitler had come into office by legal means. All of the proper legal forms and procedures had been observed. This fact was very important, for it permitted the civil service, the courts, and the other agencies of the government to support him with good conscience. He had forged a rigidly disciplined party structure and had mastered the techniques of mass politics and propaganda. He understood how to touch

*The Reichstag fire in 1933 provided the occasion for Hitler to consolidate his power.
[Ullstein Bilderdienst]*

the raw social and political nerves of the electorate. His major support came from the lower middle class, the farmers, and the young. Each of these groups had especially suffered from the insecurity of the 1920s and the Depression of the early 1930s. Hitler promised them security against communists and socialists, effective government in place of the petty politics of the other parties, and an uncompromising nationalist vision of a strong, restored Germany.

Much credit was once given to German big business for the rise of Hitler. However, little evidence exists that business money financed the Nazis in a fashion that made any crucial difference to their success or failure. Hitler's supporters were frequently suspicious of business and giant capitalism. They wanted a simpler world and one in which small property would be safe from both socialism and large-scale capitalist consolidation. These people looked to Hitler and the Nazis rather than to the Social Democrats because the latter,

though concerned with social issues, never appeared sufficiently nationalistic. The Nazis won out over other conservative nationalistic parties because, unlike the latter, they did address themselves to the problem of lower-middle-class social insecurity.

Once in office Hitler moved with almost lightning speed to consolidate his control. This process had three facets: the capture of full legal authority, the crushing of alternative political groups, and the purging of rivals within the Nazi Party itself.

On February 27, 1933, a mentally ill Dutch Communist set fire to the Reichstag building in Berlin. The Nazis quickly turned the incident to their own advantage by claiming that the fire proved the existence of an immediate Communist threat against the government. To the public it seemed plausible that the Communists might attempt some action against the state now that the Nazis were in power. Under Article 48 Hitler made the Emergency Decree suspending civil liberties and proceeded to arrest Communists or alleged Communists. This decree was not revoked for as long as Hitler ruled Germany.

In early March another Reichstag election took place. The Nazis still received only 43.9 per cent of the vote. However, the arrest of the newly elected Communist deputies and the political fear aroused by the fire meant that Hitler could control the Reichstag. On March 23, 1933, the Reichstag passed an Enabling Act that permitted Hitler to rule by decree. Thereafter, there were no legal limits on his exercise of power. The Weimar Constitution was never formally repealed or amended. It had simply been supplanted by the February Emergency Decree and the March Enabling Act.

Perhaps better than anyone else Hitler understood that he and his party had not inevitably come to power. All of his potential opponents had stood divided between 1929 and 1933. He intended to prevent them from regrouping. In a series of complex moves Hitler outlawed or undermined various German institutions that might have served as rallying points for opposition. In early May 1933 the offices, banks, and newspapers of the free trade unions were seized, and their leaders were arrested. The Nazi Party itself, rather than any government agency, undertook this action. In late June and early July all of the other German political parties were outlawed. By July 14, 1933, the National Socialists were the only legal party in Germany. During the same months the Nazis had moved against the governments of the individual federal states in Germany. By the close of 1933 all major institutions of potential opposition had been eliminated.

The final element in Hitler's consolidation of power involved the Nazi Party itself. By late 1933 the SA, or storm troopers, consisted of approximately one million active members and a larger number of reserves. The commander of this party army was Ernst Roehm, a possible rival to Hitler himself. The German army officer corps, on whom Hitler depended to rebuild the national army, were jealous of the SA leadership. Consequently, to protect his own position and to shore up support with the regular army, on June 30, 1934, Hitler personally ordered the murder of key SA officers, including Roehm. Others killed between June 30 and July 2 included the former chancellor General Kurt von Schleicher and his wife. The exact number of victims purged is unknown, but it has been estimated to have exceeded one

At an anti-Jewish rally in Berlin, 1935, the banners read: "The Jews are our ruin." "The Jews are our disaster." [AP]

hundred persons. The German army, which was the only institution in the nation that might have prevented the murders, did nothing.

A month later, on August 2, 1934, President Hindenburg died. Thereafter the offices of chancellor and president were combined. Hitler was now the sole ruler of Germany and of the Nazi Party.

The Police State and Anti-Semitism

Terror and intimidation had been a major factor in the Nazi march to office. As Hitler consolidated his power, he oversaw the organization of a police state. The chief vehicle of police surveillance was the SS (Schutzstaffel), or security units, commanded by Heinrich

The Nazis Pass Their Racial Legislation

Anti-Semitism had been a fundamental tenet of the Nazi Party and became a major policy of the Nazi government. This comprehensive legislation of September 15, 1935, carried anti-Semitism into all areas of public life and into some of the most personal areas of private life as well. It was characteristically titled the Law for the Protection of German Blood and Honor. Hardly any aspect of Nazi thought and action was so shocking to the non-German world as was this policy toward the Jews.

Imbued with the knowledge that the purity of German blood is the necessary prerequisite for the existence of the German nation, and inspired by an inflexible will to maintain the existence of the German nation for all future times, the Reichstag has unanimously adopted the following law, which is now enacted:

Article I: (1) Any marriages between Jews and citizens of German or kindred blood are herewith forbidden. Marriages entered into despite this law are invalid, even if they are arranged abroad as a means of circumventing this law.

(2) Annulment proceedings for marriages may be initiated only by the Public Prosecutor.

Article II: Extramarital relations between Jews and citizens of German or kindred blood are herewith forbidden.

Article III: Jews are forbidden to employ as servants to their households female subjects of German or kindred blood who are under the age of forty-five years.

Article IV: (1) Jews are prohibited from displaying the Reich and national flag and from showing the national colors.

(2) However, they may display the Jewish colors. The exercise of this right is under state protection.

Article V: (1) Anyone who acts contrary to the prohibition noted in Article I renders himself liable to penal servitude.

(2) The man who acts contrary to the prohibition of Article II will be punished by sentence to either a jail or penitentiary.

(3) Anyone who acts contrary to the provisions of Articles III or IV will be punished with a jail sentence up to a year and with a fine, or with one of these penalties.

Article VI: The Reich Minister of Interior, in conjunction with the Deputy to the Führer and the Reich Minister of Justice, will issue the required legal and administrative decrees for the implementation and amplification of this law.

Article VII: This law shall go into effect on the day following its promulgation, with the exception of Article III, which shall go into effect on January 1, 1936.

Louis L. Snyder (ed. and trans.), Documents of German History (New Brunswick, N.J.: Rutgers University Press, 1958), pp. 427–428.

During the night of November 9, 1938 (Kristallnacht), all across Germany the windows of stores owned by Jews were smashed and synagogues burned. The Nazis then confiscated the insurance money and refused to allow the Jewish businesses to be compensated for their losses. [AP]

1013

EUROPE ANI
THE GREAT
DEPRESSION ɪ
THE 1930S

Himmler (1900–1945). This group had originated in the mid-1920s as a bodyguard for Hitler and had become a more elite paramilitary organization than the larger SA. In 1933 the SS was composed of approximately fifty-two thousand members. It was the instrument that carried out the blood purges of the party in 1934. By 1936 Himmler had become head of all police matters in Germany and stood second only to Hitler in power and influence.

The police character of the Nazi regime was all-pervasive, but the people who most consistently experienced the terror of the police state were the German Jews. Anti-Semitism had been a key plank of the Nazi program. It was anti-Semitism based on biological racial theories stemming from late-nineteenth-century thought rather than from religious discrimination. Before World War II the Nazi attack on the Jews went through three stages of increasing intensity. In 1933, shortly after assuming power, the Nazis excluded Jews from offices in the civil service. For a time they also attempted to enforce boycotts of Jewish shops and businesses. The boycotts won relatively little public support.

In 1935 a series of measures known as the *Nuremberg Laws* robbed German Jews of their citizenship. All persons with at least three Jewish grandparents were defined as Jews. The professions and the major occupations were closed to Jews. Marriage and sexual intercourse between Jews and non-Jews were prohibited. Legal exclusion and humiliation of the Jews became the order of the day.

The persecution of the Jews increased again in 1938. Business careers were forbidden. In November 1938, under orders from the Nazi Party, thousands of Jewish stores and synagogues were burned or otherwise destroyed. The Jewish community itself was required to pay for the damage because the government confiscated the insurance money. In all manner of other ways, large and petty, the German Jews were harassed. This persecution allowed the Nazis to inculcate the rest of the population with the concept of a master race of pure German "Aryans" and also to display their own contempt for civil liberties.

MAJOR DATES IN THE NAZI SEIZURE OF POWER

1928	National Socialists win 12 seats in the Reichstag
1930	National Socialists win 107 seats in the Reichstag
1930	Brüning appointed Chancellor
1932	(April 10) Hindenburg defeats Hitler for presidency
1932	(May 31) Von Papen replaces Brüning
1932	(July 31) National Socialists win 230 seats in the Reichstag
1932	(November 6) Indecisive Reichstag election
1932	(November 17) Von Papen resigns
1932	(December 2) Von Schleicher appointed Chancellor
1933	(January 28) Von Schleicher resigns
1933	(January 30) Hitler appointed chancellor
1933	(February 27) Reichstag Fire
1933	(March 5) National Socialists win 288 seats in the Reichstag
1933	(March 23) Enabling Act Passed
1933	(July 14) National Socialists declared the only legal party
1934	(June 30) Murder of major SA officers
1934	(August 2) Death of Von Hindenburg
1935	Passage of Nuremberg Laws
1938	(November 9) Night of attack on Jewish businesses and synagogues (Kristallnacht)

After the war broke out, Hitler decided in 1942 to destroy the Jews in Europe. Over six million Jews, mostly from east European nations, died as a result of that staggering decision, unprecedented in its scope and implementation.

Nazi Economic Policy

Besides consolidating power and persecuting allegedly inferior races, Hitler still had to confront the reality of the Great Depression. German unemployment had been a major factor in

May 1, 1938: *Hitler introduces the first* volkswagen *("people's car"). The volkswagens were supposed to provide cheap transportation for German workers. The coming of war, however, meant that few volkswagens were built. [Ullstein Bilderdienst]*

his rise to power. The Nazis attacked this problem and achieved a degree of success that astonished and frightened the rest of Europe. By 1936, while the rest of the European economy continued to stagnate, the specter of unemployment and other difficulties associated with the Great Depression for all intents and purposes no longer haunted Germany.

As far as the economic crisis was concerned, Hitler had become the most effective political leader in Europe. This fact was a most important element in accounting for the internal strength and support of his tyrannical regime. The Nazi success against the Great Depression provided the regime with considerable contemporary credibility. As might be expected, the cost in terms of liberty and human dignity had been very high.

Hitler reversed the deflationary policy of the cabinets that had preceded him. He instituted what amounted to a massive program of public works and spending. Many of these projects related directly or indirectly to rearmament. Canals were built, and land was reclaimed. Construction of a large system of highways with clear military uses was begun. Some unemployed workers were sent back to farms if they had originally come from there. Other laborers were frozen in their jobs and were not permitted to change employment.

In 1935 renunciation of the military provisions of the Versailles Treaty led to open rearmament and expansion of the army with little opposition, as will be explained in Chapter 29. These measures essentially restored full employment. In 1936, Hitler instructed Hermann Göring (1893–1946), who had headed the air force since 1933, to undertake a Four-Year Plan to prepare the army and the economy for war. The state determined that Germany must be economically self-sufficient. Armaments received top priority. This economic program satisfied both the yearning for social and economic security and the desire for national fulfillment.

Nazi economic policies maintained private property and private capitalism. However, all significant economic enterprise and decisions became subordinated to the goals of the state. Prices were controlled and investments restricted. Currency regulation interfered with trade. Production that related to the military buildup received top priority and even redirected some industries. For example, in the

Hermann Göring (1892–1946) talking with Dr. Josef Goebbels (1897–1945). Göring was Hitler's second in command, head of the air force, and director of Germany's plan for rearmament. Goebbels was the Nazi Minister of Propaganda, in control of the press, radio, and cinema. [Library of Congress]

late 1930s, the German chemical producers diverted a large proportion of their resources toward the manufacture of various synthetics.

With the crushing of the trade unions in 1933, strikes became illegal. There was no genuine collective bargaining. The government handled labor disputes through compulsory arbitration. Both workers and employers were required to participate in the Labor Front; this organization was intended to prove that class conflict had ended. It sponsored a "Strength Through Joy" program that provided vacations and other forms of recreation for the labor force.

However, behind the direction of both business and labor stood the Nazi terror and police. The Nazi economic experiment proved that with the sacrifice of all political and civil liberty, of a free trade-union movement, of private exercise of capital, and of consumer satis-

faction, full employment for the purposes of war and aggression could be achieved.

Women in Nazi Germany

Although Nazi spokesmen adopted modern technology, they also frequently rejected many of the chief features of modern social life. The Nazi outlook on the role of women exemplified this rejection of modern changes and the championing of traditional attitudes.

Hitler and other Nazis thought there were naturally separate social spheres for men and women. The former belonged in the world of action; the latter, in the home. The two spheres should not mix. Women who sought to liberate themselves and to adopt roles traditionally followed by men in public life were considered as symbols of a cultural decline. The respect that women should receive was to arise from their function as wives and mothers.

These attitudes stood in direct opposition to many of the social changes that the lives of German women, like women elsewhere in Europe, had undergone during the first three decades of the twentieth century. German women had become much more active and assertive. More German women worked in factories or were independently employed. Women had begun to enter the professions in Germany. Under the Weimar constitution they voted. Throughout the Weimar period there was also a lively discussion of issues surrounding women's emancipation. The Nazis saw many of these developments as signs of cultural weakness. They generally urged a much more traditional role for women in their new society.

IN THE HOME First and foremost Nazi writers portrayed the proper role of women as wives and mothers. This point of view allowed the Nazis to draw support from women of a generally conservative outlook and women who were following traditional roles as housewives. The Nazi attitudes allowed these women to believe they had made the proper choice about the direction of their lives. Men were also drawn to this view because during the years of high unemployment the attitude tended to discourage women from competing with men for employment. Such competition had commenced during World War I and was regarded by many Nazis as an indication of the social confusion that had followed upon the German defeat.

The Nazi discussion of the role of women was also deeply rooted in the racism of Nazi ideology. Nazi writers argued that the superiority of the pure German race depended upon the purity of the blood of each and every individual. It was the special task of German women in their role as mothers to preserve racial purity. Hitler particularly championed this view of women. They were to breed the strong sons and daughters for the German nation. Nazi journalists often compared the role of women in childbirth to that of men in battle. Each served the state in particular social and gender roles. In both cases, the good of the nation was regarded as superior to that of the individual.

Most Nazis who discussed the role of women relegated them to the home. They also generally attacked feminist outlooks. They wanted women to bear large numbers of children. They believed the declining German birth rate was the result of emancipated women who had spurned their natural and proper role as mothers. The Nazis established special medals for women who bore large families. They also sponsored schools that taught women how to care for and rear children.

For the Nazis women were also intended to be educators of the young. In that role they were the special protectors of German cultural values. Through cooking, dress, music, and stories mothers were to instill a love for the nation. As consumers for the home, women were to aid German-owned shops, to buy German-produced goods, and to avoid Jewish merchants.

IN THE WORKPLACE Nazi ideology held a place for employed women, but it was regarded as second to that of wives and mothers living in the home. The Nazis recognized that in the midst of the Depression many women would need to work, but the party urged that they pursue employment that was natural to their character as women. These tasks included agricultural work, teaching, nursing, social service, and domestic service. The Nazis seem to have achieved the political support of women because the roles they assigned to them were those in which most German women actually found themselves. Interestingly enough, despite some variation in the early and mid-1930s, the percentage of women employed in Germany was 37 per cent in 1928 and the same again in 1939. Thereafter, the war effort saw the need to recruit large numbers of women into the German workforce.

There were also a few Nazi feminists, who hoped that women could achieve new standing in the Nazi order. They appealed to ancient German history to prove that German men and women had once been equal. They also contended that only by allowing a broader role to women could Nazi society actually attain major achievements. They argued that if sons were not reared to respect deeply their mothers, then those mothers could not carry out their role as educators of children for the nation. It would appear that most of these Nazi feminists were professional women who hoped to support the party and to maintain their position in German society. They had only a minimal influence on the policies of the party and really none on the major leaders.

Italy: Fascist Economics

The Fascists had promised to bring order to the instability of Italian social and economic life. Discipline was a substitute for economic policy and creativity. During the 1920s Mussolini undertook programs of public works, such as draining the Pontine Marshes near Rome for settlement. The shipping industry was subsidized, and protective tariffs were introduced. Mussolini desperately sought to make Italy self-sufficient. He embarked on the "battle of wheat" to prevent foreign grain from appearing in products on Italian tables. There was an extraordinary expansion of wheat farming in Italy. However, these policies did not keep the Great Depression from affecting Italy. Production, exports, and wages fell. Even the increased wheat production backfired. So much poor marginal land that was expensive to cultivate came into production that the domestic price of wheat, and thus of much food, actually rose.

Syndicates

Both before and during the Depression the Fascists sought to steer an economic course between socialism and a liberal *laissez-faire* system. Their policy was known as *Corporatism*. It constituted a planned economy linked to the private ownership of capital and to government arbitration of labor disputes. Major industries were first organized into syndicates representing labor and management. The two groups negotiated labor settlements within this framework and submitted differences to compulsory government arbitration. The Fascists contended that class conflict would be avoided if both labor and management looked to the greater goal of productivity for the nation.

It is a matter of considerable dispute whether this arrangement favored workers or managers. What is certain is that from the mid-1920s Italian labor unions lost the right to strike and to pursue their own independent economic goals. In that respect management clearly profited.

Corporations

After 1930 these industrial syndicates were further organized into entities called *corporations.* These bodies included all industries relating to a major area of production, such as agriculture or metallurgy, from raw materials through finished product and distribution. A total of twenty-two such corporations was established to encompass the whole economy. In 1938 Mussolini abolished the Italian Chamber of Deputies and replaced it with a Chamber of Corporations.

This vast organizational framework did not increase production; instead, it led to excessive bureaucracy and corruption. The corporate state allowed the government to direct much of the nation's economic life without a formal change in ownership. Consumers and owners simply no longer could determine what was to be produced. The Fascist government gained further direct economic power through the Institute for Industrial Reconstruction, which extended loans to businesses in financial difficulty. The loans, in effect, established partial state ownership.

How corporatism might have affected the Italian economy in the long run cannot really be calculated. In 1935 Italy invaded Ethiopia. Economic life was put on a formal wartime footing. The League of Nations imposed eco-

nomic sanctions, urging member nations to refrain from purchasing Italian goods. The sanctions had little effect. Thereafter taxes rose. During 1935 the government imposed a forced loan on the citizenry by requiring property owners to purchase bonds. Wages continued to be depressed. As the international tensions increased during the late 1930s, the Italian state assumed more and more direction over the economy. The order of Fascism in Italy had not proved to be an order of prosperity. It had brought economic dislocation and a falling standard of living.

The Soviet Union: Central Economic Planning and Party Purges

While the capitalist economies of western Europe floundered in the doldrums of the Great Depression, the Soviet Union entered on a period of tremendous industrial advance. Like similar eras of past Russian economic progress, the direction and impetus came from the top. Stalin far exceeded his tsarist predecessors in the intensity of state coercion and terror he brought to the task. Russia achieved its stunning economic growth during the 1930s only at the cost of literally millions of human lives and the degradation of still other millions. Stalin's economic policy clearly proved that his earlier rivalry with Trotsky had been a matter of political power rather than one of substantial ideological difference.

The Decision for Rapid Industrialization

Through 1927 Lenin's New Economic Policy (NEP), as championed by Bukharin with Stalin's support, had charted the course of Soviet economic development. Private ownership and enterprise were permitted to flourish in the countryside as a means of ensuring an adequate food supply for the workers in the cities. Even though the industrial production level of 1913 had been achieved by 1927, there was little indication that future industrial growth would be substantial. During 1927 the Party Congress decided to move toward the goal of rapid industrialization. This policy, which be-

Stalin Praises the Results of the First Five-Year Plan

The first Five-Year Plan was carried out between 1928 and 1932. The goal was to transform Soviet industry and agriculture so that the nation could compete with the capitalist world. The plan involved immense disruption of Russian society, and most especially of agriculture, in the pursuit of industrialism. In this passage of 1933, Stalin explained what the purpose of the plan had been and boasted of its successes with only the barest indication of the resistance that the Communist Party had encountered in the countryside. These disturbances were so considerable that Stalin had had to pull back from the full implementation of the plan, but that fact was never openly admitted.

The fundamental task of the Five-Year Plan was to transfer our country, with its backward, and in part medieval, technique, to the lines of new, modern technique.

The fundamental task of the Five-Year Plan was to convert the U.S.S.R. from an agrarian and weak country, dependent upon the caprices of the capitalist countries, into an industrial and powerful country, fully self-reliant and independent of the caprices of world capitalism.

The fundamental task of the Five-Year Plan was, in converting the U.S.S.R. into an industrial country, fully to eliminate the capitalist elements, to widen the front of socialist forms of economy, and to create the economic base for the abolition of classes in the U.S.S.R., for the construction of socialist society.

The fundamental task of the Five-Year Plan was to create such an industry in our country as would be able to re-equip and reorganize, not only the whole of industry, but also transport and agriculture—on the basis of socialism.

The fundamental task of the Five-Year Plan was to transfer small and scattered agriculture to the lines of large-scale collective farming, so as to ensure the economic base for socialism in the rural districts and thus to eliminate the possibility of the restoration of capitalism in the U.S.S.R.

Finally, the task of the Five-Year Plan was to create in the country all the necessary technical and economic prerequisites for increasing to the utmost the defensive capacity of the country, to enable it to organize the determined resistance to any and every attempt at military intervention from outside, to any and every attempt at military attack from without.

. . . The object of the Five-Year Plan in the sphere of agriculture was to unite the scattered and small individual peasant farms, which lacked the opportunity of utilizing tractors and modern agricultural machinery, into large collective farms, equipped with all the modern implements of highly developed agriculture, and to cover unoccupied land with model state farms. . . .

The party has succeeded in routing the kulaks as a class, although they have not yet been dealt the final blow; the laboring peasants have been emancipated from kulak bondage and exploitation and a firm economic basis for the Soviet government, the basis of collective farming, has been established in the countryside.

The party has succeeded in converting the U.S.S.R. from a land of small peasant farming into a land where agriculture is run on the largest scale in the world.

Joseph Stalin, Selected Writings *(New York: International Publishers, 1942), pp. 242, 253–254.*

ginning in 1928 was carried out through a series of centrally constructed and directed Five-Year Plans, marked a sharp departure from NEP.

The scope of the industrial achievement of the Soviet Union between 1928 and World War II stands as one of the most striking accomplishments of the twentieth century. Russia made a more rapid advance toward economic growth than any other nation in the Western world during any similar period of time.

By even the conservative estimates of Western observers, Soviet industrial production rose approximately 400 per cent between 1928 and 1940. Emphasis was place on the production of iron, steel, coal, electrical power, tractors, combines, railway cars, and other heavy machinery. Few consumer goods were produced. The labor for this development was supplied internally, Capital was raised from the export of grain even at the cost of internal shortage. The technology was generally borrowed from already industrialized nations. All of these elements actually paralleled the manner in which the tsarist government had pursued industrialization in the late nineteenth century.

Unlike the tsarist drive toward an industrial economy, Stalin's organizational vehicle for industrialization was a series of Five-Year Plans first begun in 1928. The State Planning Commission, or Gosplan, oversaw the program. It set goals of production and organized the economy to meet them. The task of coordinating all facets of production was immensely difficult and complicated. Deliveries of materials from mines or factories had to be assured before the next unit could carry out its part of the plan. There was many a slip between the cup and the lip. The troubles in the countryside were harmful. A vast program of propaganda was undertaken to sell the Five-Year Plans to the Russian people and to elicit cooperation. However, the industrial labor force soon became subject to regimentation similar to that being imposed on the peasants.

By the close of the 1930s the accomplishment of the three Five-Year Plans was truly impressive and probably allowed the Soviet Union to survive the German invasion. Industries that had never existed in Russia now challenged and in some cases, such as tractor production, surpassed their counterparts in the rest of the world. Large, new industrial cities had been built and populated by hundreds of thousands of people.

The Collectivization of Agriculture

The decision to industrialize rapidly brought momentous consequence for Soviet agriculture. Under NEP a few farmers, the *kulaks*, had become quite prosperous. They probably numbered less than 5 per cent of the rural population. They and other farmers remained discontent with their situation because of the absence of consumer goods to purchase with the cash they received for their crops. They had frequently withheld grain from the market throughout the decade and did so again during 1928 and 1929. Food shortages occurred in the cities and provided a cause of potential unrest against the government.

During these troubled months Stalin came to a momentous decision. Agriculture must be collectivized to produce sufficient grain for food and export, to achieve control over the farm sector of the economy, and to free peasant labor for the factories in the expanding industrial sector. The implementation of this pro-

Russian collective farmers march in 1931. Stalin's forced collectivization of Russian agriculture gave the Soviet government control of the food supply, but it also led to the Soviet Union's chronic inability to produce enough grain to feed its citizens. [Wide World Photos]

gram of collectivization, which basically embraced Trotsky's earlier economic position, unleashed nothing less than a second Russian revolution. The costs and character of "Socialism in One Country" now became clear.

In 1929 Stalin ordered party agents into the countryside to confiscate any hoarded wheat. The *kulaks* bore the blame for the grain shortages. As part of the general plan to erase the private ownership of land and to collectivize farming, the government undertook a program to eliminate the *kulaks* as a class. However, the definition of a *kulak* soon embraced anyone who opposed Stalin's policy. In the countryside there was extensive resistance from peasants and farmers at all levels of wealth. The stubborn peasants were determined to keep their land. They wreaked their own vengeance on the policy of collectivization by slaughtering more than 100 million horses and cattle between 1929 and 1933. The situation in the countryside amounted to nothing less than open warfare. The peasant resistance caused Stalin to call a brief halt to the process in March 1930. He justified the slowdown on the grounds of "dizziness from success."

Soon thereafter the drive to collectivize the farms was renewed with vehemence, and the costs remained very high. As many as ten million peasants were killed, and millions of others were sent forcibly to collective farms or labor camps. Initially, because of the turmoil on the land, agricultural production fell. There was famine in 1932 and 1933. Milk and meat remained in short supply because of the livestock slaughter. Yet Stalin persevered. The uprooted peasants were moved to thousand-acre collective farms. The machinery for these units was provided by the state through machine-tractor stations. In this fashion the state retained control over major farm machines. That monopoly was a powerful weapon.

The upheaval of collectivization did change Russian farming in a very dramatic way. In 1928 approximately 98 per cent of Russian farmland consisted of small peasant holdings. Ten years later, despite all the opposition, over 90 per cent of the land had been collectivized; and the quantity of farm produce directly handled by the government had risen by 40 per cent. Those shifts in control meant that the government now had primary direction over the food supply. The farmers and peasants could no longer determine whether there would be stability or unrest in the cities. Stalin and the Communist Party had won the battle of the wheat fields, but they had not solved the problem of producing sufficient quantities of grain. That difficulty has continued to plague the Soviet Union to the present day.

Foreign Reactions and Repercussions

Many non-Russian contemporaries looked at the Soviet economic experiment quite uncritically. While the capitalist world lay in the throes of the Great Depression, the Soviet economy had grown at a pace never realized in the West. The American writer Lincoln Steffens reported after a trip to Russia, "I have seen the future and it works." Beatrice and Sidney Webb, the British Fabian Socialists, spoke of "a new civilization" in the Soviet Union. These and other similar writers ignored the shortages in consumer goods and the poor housing. More important, they seem to have had little idea of the social cost of the Soviet achievement. Millions of human beings had been killed and millions more uprooted. The total picture of suffering and human loss during those years will probably never be known; however, the deprivation and sacrifice of Soviet citizens far exceeded anything described by Marx and Engels in relation to nineteenth-century industrialization in western Europe.

The internal difficulties caused by collectivization and industrialization led Stalin to make an important shift in foreign policy. In 1934 he began to fear that the nation might be left isolated against future aggression by Nazi Germany. The Soviet Union was not yet strong enough to withstand such an attack. Consequently that year he ordered the Comintern to permit Communist parties in other countries to cooperate with non-Communist political parties against Nazism and Fascism. This marked a reversal of the Comintern policy established by Lenin as part of the Twenty-one Conditions in 1919. The new Stalinist policy originating from Moscow allowed the formation of the Popular Front Government in France. After more than a decade of vicious rivalry between Communists and Democratic Socialists, for a few years the two groups would attempt to cooperate against the common right-wing foe.

The Purges

Stalin's decisions to industrialize rapidly, to move against the peasants, and to reverse the Comintern policy did arouse internal political opposition. They were all departures from the policies of Lenin. In 1929 Stalin forced Bukharin, the fervent supporter of the NEP and his own former ally, off the Politburo. Little detailed information is known about further opposition, but it does seem to have existed among lower-level party followers of Bukharin and other previous opponents of rapid industrialization. Sometime in 1933 Stalin began to fear loss of control over the party apparatus and the emergence of possibly effective rivals. These fears were probably produced as much by his own paranoia as by real plots. Nevertheless they resulted in the Great Purges, one of the most mysterious and horrendous political events of this century. The purges were not understood at the time and have not been fully comprehended either inside or outside the Soviet Union to the present day.

On December 1, 1934, Sergei Kirov (1888–1934), the popular party chief of Leningrad (formerly Saint Petersburg and Petrograd) and a member of the Politburo, was assassinated. In the wake of the shooting thousands of people were arrested, and still larger numbers were expelled from the party and sent to labor camps. At the time it was believed that Kirov had been murdered by opponents of the regime. Direct or indirect complicity in the crime became the normal accusation against the persons whom Stalin attacked. It now seems almost certain that Stalin himself authorized Kirov's assassination in fear of eventual rivalry with the Leningrad leader.

The purges after Kirov's death were just the beginning of a larger process. Between 1936 and 1938 a series of spectacular show trials were held in Moscow. Previous high Soviet leaders, including former members of the Politburo, publicly confessed all manner of political crimes. They were convicted and executed. It is still not certain why they made their palpably false confessions. Still other leaders and lower-level party members were tried in private and shot. Thousands of people received no trial at all. The purges touched persons in all areas of party life. There was apparently little rhyme or reason to why some were executed, others sent to labor camps, and still others left unmolested.

After the civilian party members had been purged, the prosecutors turned against the army. Important officers, including heroes of the civil war, were sent to their deaths. Within the party itself hundreds of thousands of members were expelled, and applicants for membership were removed from the rolls. The exact numbers of executions, imprisonments, and expulsions are unknown but certainly ran into the millions.

The trials and purges astonished Western observers. Nothing quite like this phenomenon had been seen before. Political murders and executions were not new, but the absurd confessions were novel. The scale of the political turmoil was also unprecedented. The Russians themselves did not believe or comprehend what was occurring. There existed no national emergency or crisis. There were only accusations of sympathy for Trotsky or of complicity in Kirov's murder or of other nameless crimes.

If a rational explanation is to be sought, it probably must be found in Stalin's concern over his own power. In effect, the purges created a new party structure absolutely loyal to him. The "old Bolsheviks" of the October Revolution were among his earliest targets. They and others active in the first years of the revolution knew how far Stalin had moved from Lenin's policies. New, younger members ap-

MAJOR DATES IN SOVIET HISTORY DURING
THE FIVE-YEAR PLANS AND PURGES

1928	Decision to undertake the first Five-Year Plan
1929	Beginning of collectivization of agriculture
1929	Expulsion of Bukharin from Politburo serves to affirm Stalin's central position
1930	Call of Stalin for moderation in his policy of agricultural collectivization because of "dizziness from success"
1934	Assassination of Kirov
1936	Major purge trials

peared to replace all of the party members executed or expelled. The newcomers had little knowledge of old Russia or of the ideals of the original Bolsheviks. They had not been loyal to Lenin, to Trotsky, or to any Soviet leader except Stalin himself.

By the middle of the 1930s dictators of the right and the left had established themselves across much of Europe. Political tyranny was hardly new to Europe, but several factors combined to give these rules unique characteristics. They drew their immediate support from well-organized political parties. Except for the Bolsheviks, these were mass parties. The roots of support for the dictators lay in nationalism, the social and economic frustration of the Great Depression, and political ideologies that promised to transform the social and political order. As long as the new rulers seemed successful, they were not lacking in support. They had in the eyes of many citizens brought an end to the pettiness of everyday politics.

After coming to power, these dictators possessed a practical monopoly over mass communications. Through armies, police forces, and party discipline, they also held a monop-oly on terror and coercive power. They could propagandize large populations and compel large groups of people to obey them and their followers. Finally, as a result of the Second Industrial Revolution, they commanded a vast amount of technology and a capacity for immense destruction. Earlier rulers in Europe may have shared the ruthless ambitions of Hitler, Mussolini, and Stalin, but they had not found at their disposal the ready implements of physical force to impose their wills.

Mass political support, monopoly of police and military power, and technological capacity meant that the dictators of the 1930s held more extensive sway over their nations than any other group of rulers who had ever governed on the continent. Soon the issue would become whether they would be able to maintain peace among themselves and with their democratic neighbors.

Suggested Readings

W. S. ALLEN, *The Nazi Seizure of Power: The Experience of a Single German Town, 1930–1935* (1965). A classic treatment of Nazism in a microcosmic setting.

K. E. BAILES, *Technology and Society Under Lenin and Stalin: Origins of the Soviet Technical Intelligentsia, 1917–1941* (1978). An important study of the people who actually put the programs of modernization into place.

N. BRANSON AND M. HEINEMANN, *Britain in the Nineteen Thirties* (1971). Primarily considers the social and economic problems of the day.

T. CHILDERS, *The Nazi Voter: The Social Foundations of Fascism in Germany, 1919–1933* (1983). An attempt to examine who in the German voting population voted for the Nazis.

J. COLTON, *Léon Blum: Humanist in Politics* (1966). One of the best biographies of any twentieth-century political figure.

R. CONQUEST, *The Great Terror: Stalin's Purges of the Thirties* (1968). The best treatment of the subject to this date.

R. CONQUEST, *The Harvest of Sorrow: Soviet Collectivization and the Terror-Famine* (1986). A study of the manner in which Stalin used starvation against his own subjects.

G. CRAIG, *Germany, 1866–1945* (1978). An important survey.

I. DEUTSCHER, *Stalin: A Political Biography*, 2nd ed. (1967). The best biography in English.

M. DOBB, *Soviet Economic Development Since 1917*, 6th ed. (1966). A basic introduction.

R. F. HAMILTON, *Who Voted for Hitler?* (1982). An examination of voting patterns.

E. C. HELMREICH, *The German Churches Under Hitler: Background, Struggle, and Epilogue* (1979). A useful study.

J. JACKSON, *The Politics of Depression in France, 1932–1936* (1985). A detailed examination of the political struggles prior to the Popular Front.

J. JACKSON, *The Popular Front in France: Defending Democracy, 1934–1938* (1988). The best recent treatment.

H. JAMES, *The German Slump: Politics and Economics, 1914–1936* (1986). A rather difficult but quite informative examination of the German experience of the Great Depression.

C. KINDLEBERGER, *The World in Depression, 1929–1939* (1973). An account by a leading economist whose analysis is comprehensible to the layperson.

C. KINDLEBERGER, *A Financial History of Western Europe* (1984). A major study.

D. LANDES, *The Unbound Prometheus: Technological Change and Industrial Development in West-*

ern Europe from 1750 to the Present (1969). Includes an excellent analysis of both the Great Depression and the few areas of economic growth.

E. MENDELSOHN, The Jews of East Central Europe Between the World Wars (1983). The best survey of the subject.

D. J. K. PEUKERT, Inside Nazi Germany: Conformity, Opposition, and Racism in Everyday Life (1987). An excellent discussion of life under Nazi rule.

L. J. RUPP, Mobilizing Women for War: German and American Propaganda, 1939–1945 (1978). Although concentrating on a later period, it includes an excellent discussion of general Nazi attitudes toward women.

D. SCHOENBAUM, Hitler's Social Revolution: Class and Status in Nazi Germany (1966). A fascinating analysis of Hitler's appeal to various social classes.

D. M. SMITH, Mussolini's Roman Empire (1976). A general description of the Fascist regime in Italy.

W. D. SMITH, The Ideological Origins of Nazi Imperialism (1986). A study that links Nazi expansionist thought to earlier German foreign policy.

A. SOLZHENITSYN, The Gulag Archipelago, 3 vols. (1974–1979). A major examination of the labor camps under Stalin by one of the most important of contemporary writers.

J. STEPHENSON, The Nazi Organization of Women (1981). Examines the attitude and policies of the Nazis toward women.

H. A. TURNER, JR., German Big Business and the Rise of Hitler (1985). An important major study of the subject.

Reference should also be made to the works cited in Chapter 27.

GLOBAL CONFLICT, COLD WAR, AND NEW DIRECTIONS

The people of Europe and the United States regarded the great conflict of 1914–1918 as a world war, but by far the largest part of the fighting and suffering was confined to the European continent. The second great political and military upheaval of the twentieth century, the war of 1939–1945, was truly global in scope and even more devastating than the first. Heavy fighting took place in Africa and Asia as well as in Europe. The people of every inhabited continent were involved. Battle casualties were many, and the assault on civilians was unprecedented. Massive aerial bombardment of cities began with the German attack on Britain in 1940 and concluded with the use of the new and terrifying atomic weapons against Japan in 1945. The cost of World War II in life and property was even greater than that of World War I.

After World War II the hopes of many for peace and stability rested with a new international organization, the United Nations. Unlike the League of Nations, which the United States had never joined, the new organization included all the victorious powers and came to include almost all the nations of the world. Its success, however, required the cooperation of the great powers. It was just such cooperation that proved elusive as the Second World War drew to an end.

The coalition of the victors had always been a tenuous one because of the differences between the political and economic system of the Western nations and those of the Soviet Union and because of the mutual suspicion between them. The Western powers' insistence on free, democratic elections in the lib-erated states of eastern Europe was incompatible with the Soviet Union's desire to establish secure control over the areas on its western border. Disputes over Poland, the Balkan states, and Germany led to a division of Germany and of all Europe into east and west. Thus began a period of competition and sometimes open hostility called the *Cold War.* The division hardened with the formation of the North Atlantic Treaty Organization (NATO) in 1949 and the Warsaw Pact in 1955. From that time through the mid-1980s the former allies faced each other across what Winston Churchill called an "Iron Curtain" with ever-increasing collections of deadly weapons and with continuing tension, occasionally relaxed by hopes for cooperation.

The Cold War quickly spread to Asia, where the Communist Party under Mao Tse-tung gained control of China and allied itself with the Soviet Union. They supported the Communist regime in North Korea against South Korea, which was in turn supported by the United States and its allies. Later, the same alignment appeared in Vietnam, but by the 1960s a split between the Chinese and the Russians became apparent and international relations became even more complex. During the 1970s the sharp exchanges of the Cold War gave way to a period of hesitant cooperation under the American policy known as *detente.* Negotiation replaced confrontation between the United States and the Soviet Union.

Throughout the postwar era the influence of the United States touched Europe as never before. The NATO alliance, trade relations, and an enormous annual wave of tourists brought Americans into a series of close relationships with Europeans. At the same time, the nations of western Europe began to forge new economic links among themselves through the establishment of the European Economic Community founded in 1957. By the opening of the 1990s the members of the Community looked forward to unprecedented economic cooperation and unhindered movement of peoples and goods across their borders.

From the late 1940s through the mid-1980s the Soviet bloc including the Soviet Union and its eastern European neighbors had lived under authoritarian political systems dominated by Communist parties. Their economies were centrally controlled. In 1956 in Poland and Hungary and in 1968 in Czechoslovakia, the Soviet Union had demonstrated either politically or militarily its determination to dominate and control those nations. That situation underwent marked change first in Poland with the activities of the Solidarity trade union. Then in 1985 Mikhail Gorbachev began to lead the Soviet Union into new directions of economic and political liberalization. The year 1989 saw popular uprisings throughout eastern Europe against the political domination of the Communist Party and the Soviet Union. The full impact of these changes has yet to be realized. Nonetheless, it seems clear that the era of the Cold War has ended and a new political geography is emerging on the European continent.

*Winston Churchill, Prime Minister of Great Britain, walks through
the rubblestrewn streets of London after the city had experienced a
night of German bombing. [UPI/Bettmann Newsphotos]*

29

WORLD WAR II

The more idealistic survivors of the First World War, especially in the United States and Great Britain, thought of it as "the war to end all wars" and a war "to make the world safe for democracy." Only in those ways could they justify the horrible slaughter, expense, and upheaval of that terrible conflict. How appalled they would have been had they known that only twenty years after the peace treaties a second great war would break out that would be more terribly global than the first. In this war the democracies would be fighting for their lives against militaristic, nationalistic, authoritarian, and totalitarian states in Europe and in Asia and they would be allied with the communist Soviet Union in the struggle. The defeat of the militarists and dictators would not bring the peace they longed for, but a Cold War. In this Cold War the European states would become powers of the second class, subordinate to the two new great powers, partially or fully non-European: the Soviet Union and the United States.

1028

GLOBAL
CONFLICT,
OLD WAR,
AND NEW
DIRECTIONS

Again the Road to War
(1933–1939)

World War I and the Versailles Treaty themselves had only a marginal relationship to the world depression of the 1930s. But in Germany, where the reparations settlement had contributed to the vast inflation of 1923, economic and social discontent focused on the Versailles settlement as the cause of all ills. Throughout the late 1920s Adolf Hitler and the Nazi Party had never ceased denouncing Versailles as the source of all Germany's trouble. The economic woes of the early 1930s seemed to bear them out. Nationalism and attention to the social question, along with party discipline, had been the sources of Nazi success. They continued to influence Hitler's foreign policy after he became chancellor in early 1933. Moreover, the Nazi destruction of the Weimar Constitution and of political opposition meant that to an extraordinary degree German foreign policy lay in Hitler's own hands. Consequently, it is important to know what his goals were and what plans he had for achieving them.

Hitler's Goals

For almost twenty years after the outbreak of World War II there was general agreement that the war was the outcome of Hitler's expansionist ambitions. Those ambitions might have been unlimited, and they certainly included vast conquests in eastern Europe and dominance of the European continent. A more recent view is that Hitler was not very much different from any other German statesman: he wanted only a revision of Germany's eastern boundaries, elimination of the restrictions of the Versailles Treaty, "and then to make Germany the greatest power in Europe by her natural weight."[1] The same view asserts that Hitler did not have a consistent plan in foreign policy but was an opportunist. He went the way that events and opportunity took him, emphasizing his own statement: "I go the way that Providence dictates with the assurance of a sleepwalker."[2]

[1] A. J. P. Taylor, The Origins of the Second World War (New York: Atheneum, 1968), p. 70.

[2] Quoted by Alan Bullock in "Hitler and the Origins of the Second World War," in E. M. Robertson (Ed.), The Origins of the Second World War (London: Macmillan, 1971), p. 192.

The truth appears to be a combination of these apparently contradictory views. From the first expression of his goals in a book written in jail, Mein Kampf, to his last days in the bunker where he died, Hitler's racial theories and goals held the central place in his thought. He meant to go far beyond Germany's 1914 boundaries, which were the limit of the vision of his predecessors. He meant to bring the entire German people (Volk), understood as a racial group, together into a single nation.

The new Germany would include all the Germanic parts of the old Habsburg Empire, including Austria. This virile and growing nation would need more space to live (Lebensraum), which would be taken from the Slavs, a lesser race, fit only for servitude. The new Germany would be purified by the removal of the Jews, another inferior race in Nazi theory. The plan always required the conquest of Poland and the Ukraine as the primary areas for the settlement of Germans and for the provision of badly needed food. Neither Mein Kampf nor later statements of policy were blueprints for action. Hitler was a brilliant improviser who sought after and made good use of opportunities as they arose. But he never lost sight of his goal, which would almost certainly require a major war.

GERMANY DISARMS When Hitler came to power, Germany was far too weak to permit the direct approach. The first problem was to shake off the fetters of Versailles and to make Germany a formidable military power. In October of 1933 Germany withdrew from an international disarmament conference and also from the League of Nations. Hitler argued that because the other powers had not disarmed as they had promised, it was wrong to keep Germany helpless. These acts alarmed the French but were merely symbolic. In January of 1934 Germany made a nonaggression pact with Poland that was of greater concern, for it put into question France's chief means of containing the Germans. At last, in March 1935, Hitler formally renounced the disarmament provisions of the Versailles Treaty with the formation of a German air force, and soon he reinstated conscription, which aimed at an army of half a million men.

THE LEAGUE OF NATIONS FAILS His path was made easier by growing evidence that the League of Nations was ineffective as a de-

Hitler Describes His Goals in Foreign Policy

From his early career, Hitler had certain long-term general views and goals. They were set forth in his Mein Kampf, *which appeared in 1925, and included consolidation of the German* Volk *(People), provision of more land for the Germans, and contempt for such "races" as Slavs and Jews. Here are some of Hitler's views on land.*

The National Socialist movement must strive to eliminate the disproportion between our population and our area—viewing this latter as a source of food as well as a basis for power politics—between our historical past and the hopelessness of our present impotence. . . .

The demand for restoration of the frontiers of 1914 is a political absurdity of such proportions and consequences as to make it seem a crime. Quite aside from the fact that the Reich's frontiers in 1914 were anything but logical. For in reality they were neither complete in the sense of embracing the people of German nationality, nor sensible with regard to geomilitary expediency. . . .

As opposed to this, we National Socialists must hold unflinchingly to our aim in foreign policy, namely, to secure for the German people the land and soil to which they are entitled on this earth. . . .

. . . The soil on which some day German generations of peasants can beget powerful sons will sanction the invest-ment of the sons of today, and will some day acquit the responsible statesmen of blood-guilt and sacrifice of the people, even if they are persecuted by their contemporaries. . . .

Much as all of us today recognize the necessity of a reckoning with France, it would remain ineffectual in the long run if it represented the whole of our aim in foreign policy. It can and will achieve meaning only if it offers the rear cover for an enlargement of our people's living space in Europe. . . .

If we speak of soil in Europe today, we can primarily have in mind only *Russia* and her vassal border states. . . .

. . . See to it that the strength of our nation is founded, not on colonies, but on the soil of our European homeland. Never regard the Reich as secure unless for centuries to come it can give every scion of our people his own parcel of soil. Never forget that the most sacred right on this earth is a man's right to have earth to till with his own hands, and the most sacred sacrifice the blood that a man sheds for this earth.

Adolf Hitler, Mein Kampf, *trans. by Ralph Manheim (Boston: Houghton, Mifflin, 1943), pp. 646, 649, 652, 653, 656.*

vice for keeping the peace and that collective security was a myth. In September 1931 Japan occupied Manchuria, provoking an appeal to the League of Nations by China. The league responded by sending out a commission under the Earl of Lytton. The Lytton Report condemned the Japanese for resorting to force, but the powers were unwilling to impose sanctions. Japan withdrew from the league and kept control of Manchuria.

When Hitler announced his decision to rearm Germany, the league formally condemned that action, but it took no steps to prevent Germany's rearming. The response of France and Britain was hostile, but they felt unable to object because they had not carried out their own promises to disarm. Instead, they met with Mussolini in June 1935 to form the so-called Stresa Front, making an agreement to use force to maintain the status quo in Europe. But Britain, desperate to maintain superiority at sea, even contrary to the Stresa

1030

GLOBAL
CONFLICT,
COLD WAR,
AND NEW
DIRECTIONS

accords and at the expense of French security needs, soon made a separate naval agreement with Hitler. This pact allowed him to rebuild the German fleet to 35 per cent of the British navy. Italy's expansionist ambitions in Africa soon brought it into conflict with the Western powers. Hitler had taken a major step toward his goal without provoking serious opposition.

Italy Attacks Ethiopia

The Italian attack on Ethiopia made the impotence of the League of Nations and the timidity of the Allies even clearer. Using a border incident as an excuse, Mussolini attacked Ethiopia in October 1935. His purpose was to avenge a humiliating defeat that the Italians had suffered in 1896, to begin the restoration of

Emperor Haile Selassie of Ethiopia (1892–1975) appealed in Geneva to the League of Nations in June 1936 for help against the Italian invasion of his country. The League condemned Italian aggression but took no practical steps to counter it. [Bilderdienst Suddeutscher Verlag]

Roman imperial glory, and, perhaps, to turn the thoughts of Italians away from the corruption of the Fascist regime and their economic misery.

France and Britain were eager to appease Mussolini in order to offset the growing power of Germany. They were prepared to allow him the substance of conquest if he would only maintain Ethiopia's formal independence. But for Mussolini the form was more important than the substance. His attack outraged opinion in the West, and the French and British governments were forced at least to appear to resist.

The League of Nations condemned Italian aggression and, for the first time, voted economic sanctions. It imposed an arms embargo that limited loans and credits to and imports from Italy. But Britain and France were afraid of alienating Mussolini, so they refused to place an embargo on oil, the one economic sanction that could have prevented Italian victory. Even more important, the British fleet did not prevent the movement of Italian troops and munitions through the Suez Canal. The results of this wavering policy were disastrous. The League of Nations and collective security were totally discredited, and Mussolini was alienated as well. He now turned to Germany, and by November 1, 1936, he could speak publicly of a Rome–Berlin "Axis."

Remilitarization of the Rhineland

No less important a result of the Ethiopian affair was its effect on Hitler's evaluation of the strength and determination of the western powers. On March 7, 1936, he took his greatest risk yet, sending a small armed force into the demilitarized Rhineland. This was a breach not only of the Versailles Treaty but of the Locarno Agreements of 1925 as well—agreements that Germany had made voluntarily. It also removed one of the most important elements of French security. France and Britain had every right to resist; and the French especially had a claim to retain the only element of security left after the failure of the Allies to guarantee its defense. Yet neither did anything but make a feeble protest with the League of Nations. British opinion would not permit any support for France. The French themselves were paralyzed by internal division and by mil-

General Francisco Franco led the uprising against the duly elected government of Spain in 1936, producing a bloody civil war. Here he marches through the city of Burgos, in northern Spain. [Mary Evans Picture Library]

itary ideas that concentrated on defense and feared taking the offensive. Both countries were further weakened by a growing pacifism.

In retrospect it appears that the Allies lost a great opportunity to stop Hitler before he became a serious menace. The failure of his gamble, taken against the advice of his generals, might have led to his overthrow; at the least it would have made German expansion to the east dangerous if not impossible. Nor is there much reason to doubt that the French army could easily have routed the tiny German force in the Rhineland. As the German General Alfred Jodl said some years later, "The French covering army would have blown us to bits."[3]

A Germany that was rapidly rearming and had a defensible western frontier presented a completely new problem to the western powers. Their response was the policy of "appeasement." It was based on the assumption that Germany had real grievances and that Hitler's goals were limited and ultimately acceptable. They believed that the correct policy was to bring about revision by negotiation and con-

cession before a crisis could arise and lead to war.

Behind this approach was the general horror at the thought of another war. Memories of the losses in the last war were still fresh, and the advent of aerial bombardment made the thought of a new war terrifying. A firmer policy, moreover, would have required rapid rearmament. British leaders especially were reluctant to pursue this path because of the expense and because of the widespread belief that the arms race had been a major cause of the last war. As Germany armed, the French huddled behind their newly constructed defensive wall, the Maginot Line, and the British hoped things would go well.

The Spanish Civil War

The new European alignment that found the Western democracies on one side and the fascist states on the other was made clearer by the Spanish Civil War, which broke out in July 1936. In 1931 the Spaniards had driven out their king and established a democratic republic. The new government followed a program of moderate reform that antagonized landowners, the Catholic church, nationalists, and con-

---

[3] *Quoted by W. L. Shirer in* The Collapse of the Third Republic *(New York: Simon & Schuster, 1969), p. 281.*

1032

GLOBAL
CONFLICT,
COLD WAR,
AND NEW
DIRECTIONS

servatives without satisfying the demands of peasants, workers, Catalan separatists, or radicals. Elections in February 1936 brought to power a Spanish Popular Front government ranging from republicans of the left to communists and anarchists. The defeated groups, especially the Falangists, the Spanish version of fascists, would not accept defeat at the polls. In July, General Francisco Franco (1892–1975) led an army from Spanish Morocco in rebellion against the republic.

Thus began a civil war that lasted almost three years, cost hundreds of thousands of lives, and provided a training ground for World

MAP 29-1   THE SPANISH CIVIL WAR, 1936–1939   *The shaded area on the map shows the large portion of Spain quickly overrun by Franco's insurgent armies during the first year of the war. In the following two years, progress came more slowly for the fascists as the war became a kind of international rehearsal for the coming World War II. Madrid's fall to Franco in the spring of 1939 had been preceded by that of Barcelona a few weeks earlier.*

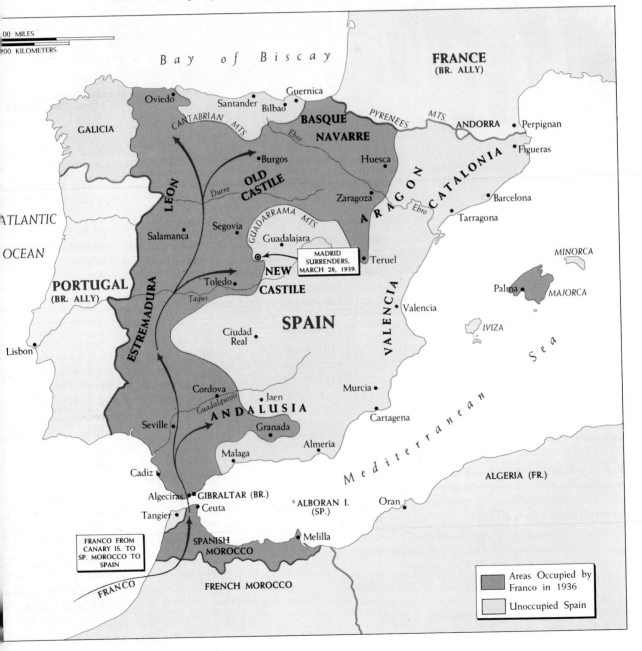

War II. Germany and Italy aided Franco with troops, airplanes, and supplies. The Soviet Union sent airplanes, equipment, and advisers to the republicans. Liberals and leftists from Europe and America volunteered to fight in the republican ranks against fascism.

The civil war, fought on blatantly ideological lines, had a profound effect on world politics. It brought Germany and Italy closer together, leading to the Rome–Berlin Axis Pact. The Axis powers were joined in the same year by Japan in the Anti-Comintern Pact, ostensibly against communism but really a new and powerful diplomatic alliance. Western Europe, especially France, had a great interest in preventing Spain from falling into the hands of a fascist regime closely allied with Germany and Italy. However, the appeasement mentality reigned. Although international law permitted the sale of weapons and munitions to the legitimate republican government, France and Britain forbade the export of war materials to either side, and the United States passed new neutrality legislation to the same end. When the city of Barcelona fell to Franco early in 1939, the fascists had won effective control of Spain.

Austria and Czechoslovakia

Hitler made good use of his new friendship with Mussolini. He had always planned to make his native Austria a part of the new Germany. In 1934 the Nazi Party in Austria assassinated the prime minister and tried to seize power. Mussolini had not yet allied with Hitler and was suspicious of German intentions. He moved an army to the Brenner Pass in the Alps between Austria and Italy, preventing German intervention and causing the *coup* to fail.

In 1938 the new diplomatic situation encouraged Hitler to try again. He seems to have hoped to achieve his goal by propaganda, bullying, and threats, but the Austrian Premier Kurt Schuschnigg refused to collapse. The premier announced a plebiscite for March 13, in which the Austrian people could decide the question of union with Germany for themselves. Hitler dared not let the plebiscite take place and sent his army into Austria on March 12. To his great relief Mussolini made no objection and Hitler could march into Vienna to the cheers of his Austrian sympathizers. This peaceful

outcome was fortunate for the Germans. Their army was far from ready for combat, and a high percentage of German tanks and trucks broke down along the roads of Austria.

The *Anschluss,* or union of Germany and Austria, was another clear violation of Versailles. Because the treaty was now a dead letter, the latest violation produced no reaction from the West. It had great strategic significance, however, especially for the position of Czechoslovakia, one of the bulwarks of French security. The union with Austria left the Czechs surrounded by Germany on three sides.

The very existence of Czechoslovakia was an affront to Hitler. It was democratic and pro-Western; it had been created as a check on Germany and was allied both to France and to the Soviet Union. It also contained about 3.5 million Germans who lived in the Sudetenland near the German border. These Germans had been the dominant class in the old Austro-Hungarian Empire and resented their new minority position. Supported by Hitler and led by Konrad Henlein, the chief Nazi in Czechoslovakia, they made ever-increasing demands for privileges and autonomy within the Czech state. The Czechs made many concessions, but Hitler did not want to improve the lot of the Sudeten Germans. He wanted to destroy Czechoslovakia. He told Henlein, "We must always demand so much that we can never be satisfied."[4]

As pressure mounted, the Czechs grew nervous. In May 1938 they received false rumors of an imminent attack by Germany and mobilized their army. The French, British, and Russians all issued warnings that they would support the Czechs. Hitler, who had not planned an attack at that time, was forced to make a public denial of any designs on Czechoslovakia. The public humiliation infuriated him, and from that moment he planned a military attack on the Czechs. The affair stiffened Czech resistance, but it appears to have frightened the French and British. The French, as had become their custom, deferred to British leadership. The British prime minister was Neville Chamberlain, a man thoroughly committed to the policy of appeasement. He was determined not to allow Britain to come close to war again. He put pressure on the Czechs to

---

[4] *Quoted by Alan Bullock in* Hitler, A Study in Tyranny *(New York: Harper & Row, 1962), p. 443.*

1034

GLOBAL
CONFLICT,
COLD WAR,
AND NEW
DIRECTIONS

make further concessions to Germany, but no concession was enough.

On September 12, 1938, Hitler made a provocative speech at the Nuremberg Nazi Party rally. His assertions led to rioting in the Sudetenland and the declaration of martial law by the Czech government. German intervention seemed imminent. Chamberlain, aged sixty-nine, had never flown before, but between September 15 and September 29 he made three flights to Germany in an attempt to appease Hitler at Czech expense and thus to avoid war. At Hitler's mountain retreat, Berchtesgaden, on September 15 Chamberlain accepted the separation of the Sudetenland from Czechoslovakia. And he and the French premier, Daladier, forced the Czechs to agree by threatening to desert them if they did not. A week later Chamberlain flew yet again to Germany only to find that Hitler had raised his demands: he wanted cession of the Sudetenland in three days and immediate occupation by the German army.

Munich

Chamberlain returned to England thinking that he had failed, and France and Britain prepared for war. Almost at the last moment Mus-solini proposed a conference of Germany, Italy, France, and Britain. It met on September 29 at Munich. Hitler received almost everything he had demanded. The Sudetenland, the key to Czech security, became part of Germany, thus depriving the Czechs of any chance of self-defense. In return the powers agreed to spare the rest of Czechoslovakia. Hitler promised, "I have no more territorial demands to make in Europe." Chamberlain returned to England with the Munich agreement and told a cheering crowd that he had brought "peace with honour. I believe it is peace for our time."

Even in the short run the appeasement of Hitler at Munich was a failure. Soon Poland and Hungary tore bits of territory from Czechoslovakia, and the Slovaks demanded autonomy. Finally, on March 15, 1939, Hitler broke his promise and occupied Prague, putting an end to Czechoslovakia and to illusions that his only goal was to restore Germans to the Reich. Defenders of the appeasers have argued that their policy was justified because it bought valuable time in which the West could prepare for war. But that argument was not made by the appeasers themselves, who thought that they were achieving peace, nor does the evidence appear to support it.

On September 29–30, 1938, Hitler met with the leaders of Britain and France at Munich, to decide the fate of Czechoslovakia. The western leaders abandoned the small democratic nation in a vain attempt to appease Hitler and avoid war. Hitler sits in the center of the picture. To his right is British Prime Minister Neville Chamberlain. [Ullstein Bilderdienst]

If the French and the British had been willing to attack Germany from the west while the Czechs fought in their own defense, there is reason to think that their efforts might have been successful. High officers in the German army were opposed to Hitler's risky policies and might have overthrown him. Even failing such developments, a war begun in October 1938 would have forced Hitler to fight without the friendly neutrality and material assistance of the Soviet Union—and without the resources of eastern Europe that became available to him as a result of appeasement. If, moreover, the West ever had a chance of alliance with the Soviet Union against Hitler, the exclusion of the Russians from Munich and the appeasement policy helped destroy it. Munich remains an example of short-sighted

policy that helped bring on a war in disadvantageous circumstances because of the very fear of war and the failure to prepare for it.

Hitler's occupation of Prague discredited appeasement in the eyes of the British people. In the summer of 1939 a Gallup Poll showed that three quarters of the British public believed it worth a war to stop Hitler. Though Chamberlain himself had not lost all faith in his policy, he felt the need to respond to public opinion, and he responded to excess.

It was apparent that Poland was the next target of German expansion. In the spring of 1939 the Germans put pressure on Poland to restore the formerly German city of Danzig and to allow a railroad and a highway through the Polish Corridor to connect East Prussia with the rest of Germany. When the Poles would

MAP 29-2 PARTITIONS OF CZECHOSLOVAKIA AND POLAND, 1938–1939 *The immediate backround of World War II is found in the complex international drama unfolding on Germany's eastern frontier in 1938 and 1939. Germany's expansion inevitably meant the victimization of Austria, Czechoslovakia, and Poland. With the failure of the Western powers' appeasement policy and the signing of a German-Soviet pact, the stage for the war was set.*

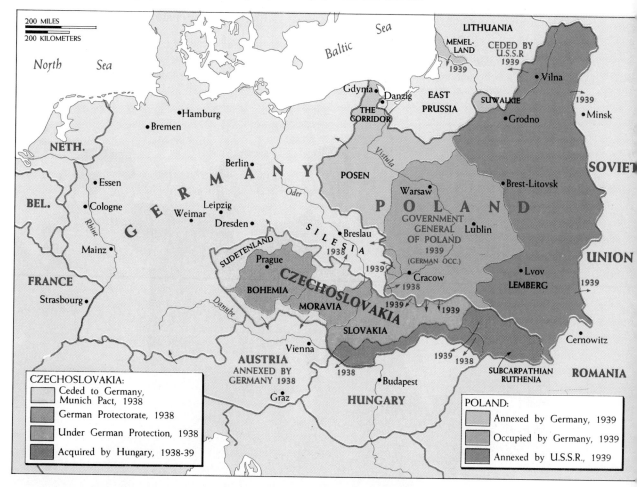

1036

GLOBAL
CONFLICT,
COLD WAR,
AND NEW
DIRECTIONS

not yield, the usual propaganda campaign began, and the pressure mounted. On March 31 Chamberlain announced a Franco-British guarantee of Polish independence. Hitler appears to have expected to fight a war with Poland but not with the western allies, for he did not take their guarantee seriously. He had come to hold their leaders in contempt. He knew that both countries were unprepared for war and that large segments of their populations were opposed to fighting a war to save Poland.

Belief in the Polish guarantee was further undermined by the inability of France and Britain to get effective help to the Poles. An attack on Germany's western front was out of the question for the French, still dominated by the defensive mentality of the Maginot Line. The only way to defend Poland was to bring Russia into the alliance against Hitler, but a Russian alliance posed many problems. Each side was profoundly suspicious of the other. The French and the British were hostile to Russia's communist ideology; and since Stalin's purge of the officer corps of the Red Army, they stood unconvinced of the military value of an alliance with Russia. Besides, the Russians could not help Poland without the right of transit through Romania and the right of entry into Poland. Both nations, suspicious of Russian intentions, and with good reason, refused to grant these rights. As a result Western negotiations with Russia moved forward slowly and cautiously.

The Nazi–Soviet Pact

The Russians had at least equally good reason to hesitate. They resented being left out of the Munich agreement. They were annoyed by the low priority that the West seemed to give to negotiations with Russia compared with the urgency with which they dealt with Hitler. They feared, quite rightly, that the western powers meant them to bear the burden of the war against Germany. As a result they opened negotiations with Hitler, and on August 23, 1939, the world was shocked to learn of a Nazi–Soviet nonaggression pact.

Its secret provisions, which were easily

The Nazi-Soviet Pact of August, 1939, which shocked the world, sealed the fate of Poland and made the imminent outbreak of World War II inevitable. This photo shows Soviet foreign minister Molotov (1890–1986) signing the treaty, while Nazi foreign minister von Ribbentrop (1893–1946) and Stalin (1879–1953) look on. [Library of Congress]

guessed and soon carried out, divided Poland between the two powers and allowed Russia to take over the Baltic states and to take Bessarabia from Romania. The most bitter ideological enemies had become allies. Communist parties in the West changed their line overnight from the ardent advocacy of resistance to Hitler to a policy of peace and quiet. Ideology gave way to political and military reality. The West offered the Russians danger without much prospect of gain. Hitler offered Stalin gain without immediate danger. There could be little doubt about the decision.

The Nazi–Soviet Pact sealed the fate of Poland, and the Franco-British commitment guaranteed a general war. On September 1, 1939, the Germans invaded Poland. Two days later Britain and France declared war on Germany. World War II had begun.

World War II (1939–1945)

World War II has a better claim to its name than its predecessor, for it was truly global. Fighting took place in Europe and Asia, the Atlantic and the Pacific oceans, the Northern and Southern Hemispheres. The demand for the fullest exploitation of material and human resources for increased production, the use of blockades, and the intensive bombing of civilian targets made the war of 1939 even more "total"—that is, comprehensive and intense—than that of 1914.

The German Conquest of Europe

The German attack on Poland produced swift success. The new style of "lightning warfare," or *Blitzkrieg*, employed fast-moving, massed armored columns supported by air power. The Poles were inferior in tanks and planes, and their defense soon collapsed. The speed of the German victory astonished everyone, not least the Russians, who hastened to collect their share of the booty before Hitler could deprive them of it.

On September 17 Russia invaded Poland from the east, dividing the country with the Germans. They then forced the encircled Baltic countries to sign treaties with them. By

THE COMING OF WORLD WAR II	
1919	(June) The Versailles Treaty
1923	(January) France occupies the Ruhr
1925	(October) The Locarno Agreements
1931	(Spring) Onset of the Great Depression in Europe
1933	(January) Hitler comes to power
	(October) Germany withdraws from the League of Nations
1935	(March) Hitler renounces disarmament, starts an air force, and begins conscription
	(October) Mussolini attacks Ethiopia
1936	(March) Germany reoccupies and remilitarizes the Rhineland
	(July) Outbreak of the Spanish Civil War
	(October) Formation of the Rome–Berlin Axis
1938	(March) *Anschluss* with Austria
	(September) The Munich Conference and partition of Czechoslovakia
1939	(March) Hitler occupies Prague; France and Great Britain guarantee Polish independence
	(August) The Nazi–Soviet pact
	(September 1) Germany invades Poland
	(September 3) Britain and France declare war on Germany

1940 Estonia, Latvia, and Lithuania were absorbed as constituent republics into the USSR (Union of Soviet Socialist Republics, or the Soviet Union). In November 1940 the Russians invaded Finland, but the Finns put up a surprisingly effective resistance. Although they were finally worn down and compelled to yield territory and bases to Russia, they retained their independence. Russian difficulties in Finland may well have encouraged Hitler to invade the Soviet Union in June 1941, just twenty-two months after the 1939 treaty.

Through the fall of 1939 and the winter of 1939–1940, the western front was quiet. The French remained quiet behind the Maginot Line while Hitler and Stalin swallowed Poland and the Baltic states. Britain hastily rearmed and reorganized the traditional naval blockade. Cynics in the West called it the phony war, or "*Sitzkrieg*," but Hitler shattered the stillness in the spring of 1940. In April, without warning and with swift success, the Germans invaded Denmark and Norway. Hitler's northern

1038

GLOBAL
CONFLICT,
COLD WAR,
AND NEW
DIRECTIONS

Churchill Breathes Defiance After Dunkirk

By the end of May 1940 the German army had driven to the Channel coast, eager to capture and destroy the British forces in France. Extraordinary efforts by the soldiers and by individual Englishmen who came with small boats of their own to help with the evacuation allowed most of the British army to get home by the fourth of June to fight another day. The miraculous escape did not conceal the terrible blow that had struck the nations allied against Hitler. In this dark hour, when defeat and invasion threatened, Prime Minister Winston S. Churchill roused his people to defiance and resistance.

Our thankfulness at the escape of our Army and so many men, whose loved ones have passed through an agonizing week, must not blind us to the fact that what has happened in France and Belgium is a colossal military disaster. The French Army has been weakened, the Belgian Army has been lost, a large part of those fortified lines upon which so much faith had been reposed is gone, many valuable mining districts and factories have passed into the enemy's possession, the whole of the Channel ports are in his hands, with all the tragic consequences that follow from that, and we must expect another blow to be struck almost immediately at us or at France. We are told that Herr Hitler has a plan for invading the British Isles. This has often been thought of before. When Napoleon lay at Boulogne for a year with his flat-bottomed boats and his Grand Army, he was told by someone, 'There are bitter weeds in England.' There are certainly a great many more of them since the British Expeditionary Force returned.

Turning once again, and this time more generally, to the question of invasion, I would observe that there has never been a period in all these long centuries of which we boast when an absolute guarantee against invasion, still less against serious raids, could have been given to our people. In the days of Napoleon the same wind which would have carried his transports across the Channel might have driven away the blockading fleet. There was al-

front was secure, and he now had both air and naval bases closer to Britain. A month later a combined land and air attack struck Belgium, the Netherlands, and Luxembourg. German airpower and armored divisions were irresistible. The Dutch surrendered in a few days; the Belgians, though aided by the French and the British, surrendered less than two weeks later.

The British and French armies in Belgium were forced to flee to the English Channel to seek escape from the beaches of Dunkirk. By the heroic effort of hundreds of Britons manning small boats, over 200,000 British and 100,000 French soldiers were saved. However, casualties were high and much valuable equipment was abandoned.

The Maginot Line ran from Switzerland to the Belgian frontier. Until 1936 the French had expected the Belgians to continue the fortifications along their German border. After Hitler remilitarized the Rhineland without opposition, the Belgians lost faith in their French alliance and returned to neutrality, leaving the Maginot Line exposed on the left flank. Hitler's swift advance through Belgium therefore circumvented France's main line of defense.

The French army, poorly and hesitantly led by superannuated generals who lacked a proper understanding of the use of tanks and planes, quickly collapsed. Mussolini, eager to claim the spoils of victory when it was clearly safe to do so, sent an army across the French border on June 10. Less than a week later the new French government, under the ancient hero of Verdun, Henri Philippe Pétain, asked for an armistice. In two months Hitler had accomplished what

ways the chance, and it is that chance which has excited and befooled the imaginations of many Continental tyrants. Many are the tales that are told. We are assured that novel methods will be adopted, and when we see the originality of malice, the ingenuity of aggression, which our enemy displays, we may certainly prepare ourselves for every kind of novel stratagem and every kind of brutal and treacherous manoeuvre. I think that no idea is so outlandish that it should not be considered and viewed with a searching, but at the same time, I hope, with a steady eye. We must never forget the solid assurances of sea-power and those which belong to air-power if it can be locally exercised.

I have, myself, full confidence that if all do their duty, if nothing is neglected, and if the best arrangements are made, as they are being made, we shall prove ourselves once again able to defend our island home, to ride out the storm of war, and to outlive the menace of tyranny, if necessary for years, if necessary alone. At any rate, that is what we are going to try to do. That is the resolve of His Majesty's Government— every man of them. That is the will of Parliament and the nation. The British Empire and the French Republic, linked together in their cause and in their need, will defend to the death their native soil, aiding each other like good comrades to the utmost of their strength. Even though large tracts of Europe and many old and famous States have fallen or may fall into the grip of the Gestapo and all the odious apparatus of Nazi rule, we shall not flag or fail. We shall go on to the end, we shall fight in France, we shall fight on the seas and oceans, we shall fight with growing confidence and growing strength in the air, we shall defend our island, whatever the cost may be, we shall fight on the beaches, we shall fight on the landing grounds, we shall fight in the fields and in the streets, we shall fight in the hills; we shall never surrender, and even if, which I do not for a moment believe, this island or a large part of it were subjugated and starving, then our Empire beyond the seas, armed and guarded by the British Fleet, would carry on the struggle, until, in God's good time, the new world, with all its power and might, steps forth to the rescue and the liberation of the old.

Charles Eade, comp., The War Speeches of Winston Churchill, *vol. 1 Boston, Little, Brown & Co., 1953, pp. 193–195.*

Germany had failed to achieve in four years of bitter fighting in the previous war.

The terms of the armistice, signed June 22, 1940, allowed the Germans to occupy more than half of France, including the Atlantic and English Channel coasts. In order to prevent many of the French from fleeing to North Africa to continue the fight, and even more to prevent the French from turning their fleet over to Britain, Hitler left southern France unoccupied. Pétain set up a dictatorial regime at the resort city of Vichy and followed a policy of collaboration with the Germans in order to preserve as much autonomy as possible. Most of the French were too stunned to resist. Many thought that Hitler's victory was certain and saw no alternative to collaboration.

A few French, most notably General Charles de Gaulle (1890–1969), fled to Britain. There they organized the French National Committee of Liberation, or "Free French." The Vichy government controlled most of French North Africa and the navy, but the Free French began operating in central Africa. From London they beamed messages of hope and defiance to their compatriots in France. As the passage of time dispelled expectations of a quick German victory, a French underground movement arose that organized many forms of resistance.

The Battle of Britain

The fall of France left Britain isolated, and Hitler expected the British to come to terms. He was prepared to allow Britain to retain its empire in return for a free hand for Germany on

1040

GLOBAL
CONFLICT,
COLD WAR,
AND NEW
DIRECTIONS

German troops stage a victory parade past the Arc de Triomphe in Paris in June, 1940. [Ullstein Bilderdienst]

the Continent. The British had never been willing to accept such an arrangement and had fought the long and difficult war against Napoleon to prevent the domination of the Continent by a single power. If there was any chance that the British would consider such terms, that chance disappeared when Winston Churchill (1874–1965) replaced Chamberlain as prime minister in May of 1940.

Churchill had been an early and forceful critic of Hitler, the Nazis, and the policy of appeasement. He was a descendant and biographer of the duke of Marlborough (1650–1722), who had fought to prevent the domination of Europe by Louis XIV in the seventeeth century. Churchill's sense of history, his feeling for British greatness, and his hatred of tyranny and love of freedom made him reject any thought of compromise. His skill as a speaker and a writer allowed him to infuse the British people with his own courage and determination and to undertake what seemed almost a hopeless fight. Hitler and his allies, including

the Soviet Union, controlled all of Europe. Japan was having its way in Asia. The United States was neutral, dominated by isolationist sentiment, and determined to avoid involvement outside the Western Hemisphere.

One of Churchill's greatest achievements was establishing a close relationship with the American President Franklin D. Roosevelt. Roosevelt found ways to help the British in spite of strong political opposition. In 1940 and 1941, before the United States was at war, America sent military supplies, traded badly needed warships for leases on British naval bases, and even convoyed ships across the Atlantic to help the British survive.

As weeks passed and Britain remained defiant, Hitler was forced to contemplate an invasion, and that required control of the air. The first strikes by the German air force *(Luftwaffe)*, directed against the airfields and fighter planes in southeastern England, began in August 1940. There is reason to think that if these attacks had continued, Germany might soon have gained control of the air and, with it, the chance of a successful invasion.

In early September, however, seeking revenge for some British bombing raids on German cities, the *Luftwaffe* made London its major target. For two months London was bombed every night. Much of the city was destroyed and about fifteen thousand people were killed. But the theories of victory through air power alone proved vain. Casualties were many times fewer than expected and morale was not shattered. In fact, the bombings brought the British people together and made them more resolute. At the same time the Royal Air Force (RAF) inflicted heavy losses on the *Luftwaffe*. Aided by the newly developed radar and an excellent system of communications, the Spitfire and Hurricane fighter planes destroyed more than twice as many enemy planes as were lost by the RAF. Hitler had lost the Battle of Britain in the air and was forced to abandon his plans for invasion.

The German Attack on Russia

From the first, the defeat of Russia and the conquest of the Ukraine to provide *Lebensraum* ("living room") for the German people had been a major goal for Hitler. Even before the assault on Britain he had informed his staff of his intention to attack Russia as soon as conditions were favorable. In December of 1940, even while the bombing of England continued, he ordered his generals to prepare for an invasion of Russia by May 15, 1941. He appears to have thought that a *Blitzkrieg* victory in the east would destroy all hope and bring the British to their senses.

Operation Barbarossa, the code name for the invasion of Russia, was aimed at knocking Russia out of the war before winter could set in. Success depended in part on an early start, but here Hitler's Italian alliance proved costly. Mussolini was jealous of Hitler's success and annoyed by the treatment he had received from the German dictator. He was unable to make progress against the French army even while Hitler was crushing the part of it that was on his own frontier. Mussolini was not allowed any gain at the expense of France or even of French Africa. Instead he launched an attack against the British in Egypt and drove them back some sixty miles. Encouraged by this success, he invaded Greece from his base

Londoners returning home after a raid. Despite many casualties and wide-spread devastation, the German bombing of London did not break British morale or prevent the city from functioning. [UPI/ Bettmann Newsphotos]

in Albania (which he had seized in 1939). His purpose was revealed by his remark to his son-in-law, Count Ciano: "Hitler always faces me with a *fait accompli*. This time I am going to pay him back in his own coin. He will find out in the newspapers that I have occupied Greece."[5]

However, in North Africa the British counterattacked and drove the Italians back into Libya. The Greeks themselves pushed into Albania. In March 1941 the British sent help to the Greeks, and Hitler was forced to divert his

[5] *Quoted by Gordon Wright,* The Ordeal of Total War, *1939–1945 (New York: Harper & Row, 1968), pp. 35–36.*

With Göring on the podium, Hitler announces the invasion of Russia to the Reichstag on June 22, 1941. "The world," he said, "will hold its breath." [Reuters/Bettmann Newsphotos]

German tanks roll across the plains of the Ukraine in June, 1941. Despite many signs that war was imminent, the German invasion took the Soviets by surprise. German armies were able to penetrate to the edge of Moscow before stiffening Russian resistance—and the onset of winter—halted them. [Library of Congress]

attention to the Balkans and to Africa. General Erwin Rommel (1891–1944), later to earn the title "The Desert Fox," went to Africa and soon got the British out of Libya and back into Egypt. In the Balkans the German army swiftly occupied Yugoslavia and crushed Greek resistance. However, the price was a delay of six weeks. The diversion caused by Mussolini's vanity proved to be costly the following winter in the Russian campaign.

Operation Barbarossa was launched against Russia on June 22, 1941, and it came very close to success. In spite of their deep suspicion of Germany (and the excuse later offered by apologists for the Soviet Union that the Nazi–Soviet Pact was meant to give Russia time to prepare), the Russians were taken quite by surprise. Stalin appears to have panicked. He had not fortified his frontier, nor had he issued orders for his troops to withdraw when attacked. In the first two days some two thousand planes were destroyed on the ground. By November Hitler had gone further into Russia than Napoleon: the German army stood at the gates of Leningrad, on the outskirts of Moscow, and on the Don River. Of the 4.5 million troops with which the Russians had begun the fighting, they had lost 2.5 million; of their 15,000 tanks only 700 were left. Moscow was in panic, and a German victory seemed imminent.

Yet the Germans could not deliver the final blow. In August there was a delay in their advance to decide on a course of action. One plan was to drive directly for Moscow and take it before winter. There is some reason to think that such a plan might have worked and brought victory. Unlike the situation in Napoleon's time, Moscow was the hub of the Russian system of transportation. Hitler, however, imposed his own view on his generals and diverted a significant part of his forces to the south. By the time he was ready to return to the offensive near Moscow, it was too late. Winter struck the German army, which was neither dressed nor equipped to face it.

Given precious time, Stalin was able to restore order and to build defenses for the city. Even more important, there was time for troops to come from Siberia, where they had been placed to check a possible Japanese attack. In November and December the Russians were able to counterattack. The *Blitzkrieg* had turned into a war of attrition, and the Germans began to have visions of Napoleon's retreat.

Hitler's Plans for Europe

Hitler often spoke of the "new order" that he meant to impose after he had established his Third Reich throughout Europe. The first two German empires *(Reich)* were those of Charlemagne in the ninth century and William II in the nineteenth. Hitler predicted that his own would last for a thousand years. If his organization of Germany before the war is a proper index, he had no single plan of government but relied frequently on intuition and pragmatism. His organization of conquered Europe had the same characteristics of spontaneity and patchwork. Some conquered territory was annexed to Germany; some was administered directly by German officials; some lands were nominally autonomous but were ruled by puppet governments.

The demands and distractions of war and the fact that Hitler's defeat prevented him from fully carrying out his plans make it hard to be sure what his intentions were. But the measures he took before his death provide indications. They give evidence of a regime probably unmatched in history for carefully planned terror and inhumanity. His plan of giving *Lebensraum* to the Germans was to be accomplished at the expense of people he deemed inferior. Hitler established colonies of Germans in parts of Poland, driving the local people from their land and employing them as cheap labor. He had similar plans on an even higher scale for Russia. The Russians would be driven eastward to central Asia and Siberia; they would be kept in check by frontier colonies of German war veterans. The more desirable lands of European Russia would be settled by Germans.

Hitler's long-range plans included Germanization as well as colonization. In lands inhabited by people racially akin to the Germans, like the Scandinavian countries, the Netherlands, and Switzerland, the natives would be absorbed into the German nation. Such peoples would be reeducated and purged of dissenting elements, but there would be little or no colonization. He even had plans, only slightly realized, of adopting selected people from the lesser races into the master race. One of these plans involved bringing half a million Ukrainian girls into Germany as servants and finding German husbands for them; about fifteen thousand actually did reach Germany.

In the economic sphere Hitler regarded the conquered lands merely as a source of plunder. From eastern Europe he removed everything useful, including entire industries. In Russia and Poland the Germans simply confiscated the land. In the west the conquered countries were forced to support the occupying army at a rate several times the real cost. The Germans used the profits to buy up everything useful and desirable, stripping the conquered peoples of most necessities. The Nazis were frank about their policies. One of Hitler's high officials said, "Whether nations live in prosperity or starve to death interests me only insofar as we need them as slaves for our culture."[6]

---

[6] *Quoted by Gordon Wright,* The Ordeal of Total War, *1939–1945 (New York: Harper & Row, 1968), p. 117.*

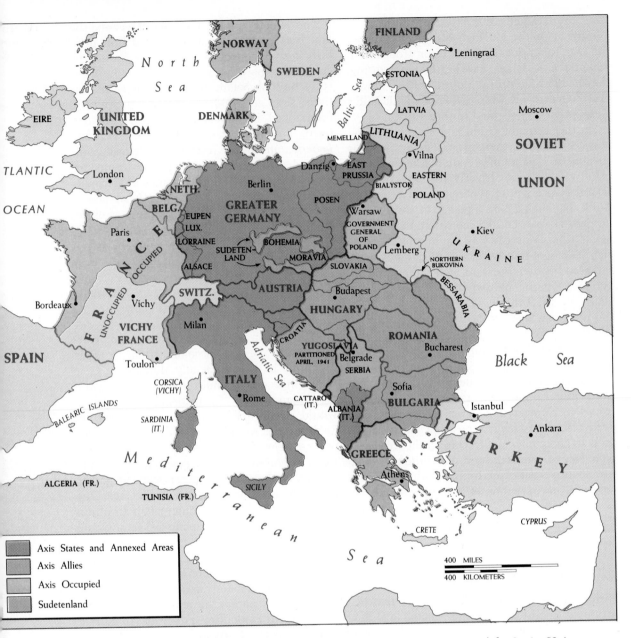

MAP 29-3   AXIS EUROPE, 1941   *On the eve of the German invasion of the Soviet Union the Germany-Italy Axis bestrode most of Western Europe by annexation, occupation, or alliance—from Norway and Finland in the north to Greece in the south and from Poland to France. Britain, the Soviets, a number of insurgent groups, and, finally, America had before them the long struggle of conquering this Axis "fortress Europe."*

Racism and the Holocaust

The most horrible aspect of the Nazi rule in Europe arose not from military or economic necessity but from the inhumanity and brutality inherent in Hitler's racial doctrines. He considered the Slavs *Untermenschen*, subhuman creatures like beasts who need not be thought of or treated as people. In parts of Po-land the upper and professional classes were entirely removed—either jailed, deported, or killed. Schools and churches were closed; marriage was controlled by the Nazis to keep down the Polish birth rate; and harsh living conditions were imposed.

In Russia things were even worse. Hitler spoke of his Russian campaign as a war of extermination. Heinrich Himmler, head of Hit-

A Jewish couple in Berlin in October 1941 wear yellow stars of David marked Jude (Jew). The wearing of the stars was required of all German Jews by a law passed the previous month. The final step in the Nazi's anti-Jewish campaign, the deportation of Jews to death camps in Eastern Europe, began in early 1942. [Wide World Photos]

These are the dead at the Nordhausen concentration camp, which was liberated by the American army in April 1945. The Nazis set up their first concentration camps in Germany 1933 to hold opponents of their regime. After the conquest of Poland, new camps were established there as part of the "final solution," the extermination of the Jews. About six million Jews were murdered in these camps. Even in those camps not dedicated to extermination, in which political prisoners and "undesirables," such as gypsies, homosexuals, and Jehovah's Witnesses, were held, conditions were brutal in the extreme, and tens of thousands died. The crimes of the Nazi regime have no precedent in human history. [National Archives]

1046

GLOBAL
CONFLICT,
COLD WAR,
AND NEW
DIRECTIONS

Mass Extermination at Belzec

Hitler's calculated plan to wipe out Europe's Jews, along with millions of other people he considered undesirable for racial and other reasons, was not widely known during the war. Care was taken to keep the mass murders secret. Even when news of them leaked out many were reluctant to believe what they heard, and participants in the crimes were naturally not eager to talk about them. Kurt Gerstein, a colonel in the SS, was part of the apparatus of extermination. However, unlike most people involved and at great risk to himself, he tried to tell the world what was taking place. The following is an account of what he saw at the death camp at Belzec in 1942.

A train arrived from Lemberg [Lvov]. There were forty-five cars containing 6,700 people, 1,450 of whom were already dead. Through the gratings on the windows, children could be seen peering out, terribly pale and frightened, their eyes filled with mortal dread . . . The train entered the station, and two hundred Ukrainians wrenched open the doors and drove the people out of the carriages with their leather whips. Instructions came through a large loudspeaker telling them to remove all their clothing, artificial limbs, glasses, etc. They were to hand over all objects of value at the counter . . . Shoes were to be carefully tied together, for otherwise no one would ever again have been able to find shoes belonging to each other in a pile that was a good eighty feet high. Then the women and girls were sent to the barber who, with two or three strokes of his scissors, cut off all their hair and dropped it into potato sacks. "That's for some special purpose or other on U-Boats, for packing or something like that," I was told by an SS-Unterscharfuhrer . . .

Then the column moved off. Headed by an extremely pretty young girl, they walked along the avenue, all naked, men, women, and children, with artificial limbs removed. I myself was stationed up on the ramp between the [gas] chambers with Captain Wirth.

Mothers with babies at their breasts came up, hesitated, and entered the chambers of death. At the corner stood a burly SS man with a priest-like voice. "Nothing at all is going to happen to you!" he told the poor wretches. "All you have to do

ler's elite SS guard, planned the elimination of thirty million Slavs to make room for the Germans; he formed extermination squads for the purpose. The number of Russian prisoners of war and deported civilian workers who died under Nazi rule may have reached six million.

Hitler had special plans for the Jews. He meant to make all Europe *Judenrein* ("free of Jews"). For a time he thought of sending them to the island of Madagascar. Later he arrived at the "final solution of the Jewish problem": extermination. The Nazis built extermination camps in Germany and Poland and used the latest technology to achieve the most efficient means of killing millions of men, women, and children for no other reason than their birth into the designated group. Before the war was over, perhaps six million Jews had died in what has come to be called the *Holocaust*. Only about a million remained alive, those mostly in pitiable condition.

World War II was unmatched in modern times in cruelty. When Stalin's armies conquered Poland and entered Germany, they raped, pillaged, and deported millions to the East. The British and American bombing of Germany killed thousands of civilians, and the dropping of atomic bombs on Japan inflicted terrible harm on civilian populations. The bombings, however, were thought of as acts of

when you get into the chambers is to breathe in deeply. That stretches the lungs. Inhaling is necessary to prevent disease and epidemics." When asked what would be done with them, he replied: "Well, of course, the men will have to work building houses and roads, but the women won't need to work. They can do housework or help in the kitchen, but only if they want to." For some of these poor creatures, this was a small ray of hope that was enough to make them walk the few steps to the chambers without resistance. Most of them knew what was going on. The smell told them what their fate was to be. They went up the small flight of steps and saw everything. Mothers with their babies clasped to their breasts, small children, adults, men, women, all naked; they hesitated, but they entered the chambers of death, thrust forward by the others behind them or by the leather whips of the SS [Storm Troopers]. Most went in without a word . . . Many were saying prayers. I prayed with them. I pressed myself into a corner and cried aloud to my God and theirs. How gladly I should have gone into the chambers with them; how gladly I should have died with them. Then they would have found an SS officer in uniform in their gas chambers; they would have believed it was an accident and the story would have been buried and forgotten. But

I could not do that yet. First, I had to make known what I had seen here. The chambers were filling up. Fill them up well— that was Captain Wirth's order. The people were treading on each other's feet. There were 700–800 of them in an area of 270 square feet, in 1,590 cubic feet of space. The SS crushed them together as tightly as they possibly could. The doors closed. Meanwhile, the rest waited out in the open, all naked. "It's done exactly the same way in winter," I was told. "But they may catch their death!" I said. "That's what they're here for," an SS man said . . . The Diesel exhaust gases were intended to kill those unfortunates. But the engine was not working . . . The people in the gas chambers waited, in vain. I heard them weeping, sobbing . . . After 2 hours and 49 minutes, measured by my stop watch, the Diesel started. Up to that moment, men and women had been shut up alive in those four chambers, four times 750 people in four times 1,590 cubic feet of space. Another twenty-five minutes dragged by. Many of those inside were already dead. They could be seen through the small window when the electric light went on for a moment and lit up the inside of the chamber. After twenty-eight minutes, few were left alive. At the end of thirty-two minutes, all were dead.

From Saul Friedlaender, Pius XII and the Third Reich: A Documentation (New York: Alfred A. Knopf, 1966, pp. 126–128).

war that would help defeat the enemy. Stalin's atrocities were not widely known in the West at the time or even today.

The victorious Western Allies, therefore, were shocked by what they saw when they came on the Nazi extermination camps and their pitiful survivors. Little wonder that they were convinced that the effort of resistance to the Nazis and all the pain it had cost were well worth it.

Japan and America's Entry into the War

The sympathies of the American government were very much on the British side. In fact, the various forms of assistance that Roosevelt gave Britain would have justified a German declaration of war. Hitler, however, held back. It is not clear that the United States government would have overcome isolationist sentiment and entered the war in the Atlantic if war had not been thrust on America in the Pacific.

Since the Japanese conquest of Manchuria in 1931, American policy toward Japan had been suspicious and unfriendly. The outbreak of the war in Europe emboldened the Japanese to move forward more quickly in their drive to dominate Asia. They allied themselves with Germany and Italy, made a treaty of neutrality with the Soviet Union, and penetrated into

The successful Japanese attack on the American base at Pearl Harbor in Hawaii on December 7, 1941, together with simultaneous attacks on other Pacific bases, brought the United States into war against the Axis powers. This picture shows the effects of the Japanese bombing upon the battleships Arizona, Tennessee, *and* West Virginia. *[Official United States Navy Photograph]*

Indochina at the expense of defeated France. At the same time they continued their war in China and made plans to gain control of Malaya and the East Indies at the expense of beleaguered Britain and the conquered Netherlands. The only barrier to Japanese expansion was the United States.

The Americans had temporized, unwilling to cut off vital supplies of oil and other materials for fear of provoking a Japanese attack on Southeast Asia and Indonesia. The Japanese seizure of Indochina in July 1941 changed that policy, which had already begun to stiffen. The United States froze Japanese assets and cut off oil supplies; the British and Dutch did the same. Japanese plans for expansion could not continue without the conquest of the Indonesian oil fields and Malayan rubber and tin.

In October a war faction led by General Hideki Tojo (1885–1948) took power in Japan and decided to risk a war rather than yield. On Sunday morning, December 7, 1941, even while Japanese representatives were discussing a settlement in Washington, Japan launched an air attack on Pearl Harbor, Hawaii, the chief American naval base in the Pacific. The technique was similar to the one Japan had used against the Russian fleet at Port Arthur in 1904, and it caught the Americans equally by surprise. A large part of the American fleet and many airplanes were destroyed; the American capacity to wage war in the Pacific was destroyed for the time being. The next day the United States and Britain declared war on Japan. Three days later Germany and Italy declared war on the United States.

The Tide Turns

The potential power of the United States was enormous, but right after Pearl Harbor, America was ill prepared for war. Though conscription had been introduced in 1940, the army was tiny, inexperienced, and ill supplied. American industry was not ready for war. The Japanese swiftly captured Guam, Wake Island, and the Philippine Islands. At the same time they attacked Hong Kong, Malaya, Burma, and Indonesia. By the spring of 1942 they controlled these places and the Southwest Pacific as far as New Guinea. They were poised for an attack on Australia, and it seemed that nothing could stop them.

In the same year the Germans advanced deeper into Russia and almost reached the Caspian Sea in their drive for Russia's oil fields. In Africa, too, Axis fortunes were high. Rommel drove the British back into Egypt toward the Suez Canal and finally was stopped at El Alamein, only seventy miles from Alexandria. Relations between the democracies and their Soviet ally were still far from close. German submarine warfare was threatening British supplies. The Allies were being thrown back on every front and the future looked bleak.

The first good news for the Allied cause in the Pacific came in the spring of 1942. A naval battle in the Coral Sea sent many Japanese ships to the bottom and gave security to Australia. A month later the United States defeated the Japanese in a fierce air and naval battle off Midway Island; thus they blunted the chance of another assault on Hawaii and did enough damage to halt the Japanese advance. Soon American Marines landed on Guadalcanal in the Solomon Islands and began in a small way to reverse the momentum of the war. The war in the Pacific was far from over, but Japan was checked sufficiently to allow the Allies to concentrate their efforts first in Europe.

The nations opposed to the Axis powers numbered more than twenty and were located all over the world. But the main combatants were Great Britain, the Soviet Union, and the United States. The two Western democracies cooperated in everything to an unprecedented degree, but suspicion between them and their Soviet ally continued. The Russians accepted all the aid they could get. Nevertheless, they did not trust their allies, complained of inadequate help, and demanded that the democracies open a "second front" on the mainland of Europe.

In 1942 American preparation and production were inadequate for an invasion of Europe. Control of the Atlantic by German submarines was such as to prevent safe crossing by the required number of troops. Not until 1944 were conditions right for the invasion, but in the meantime other developments forecast the doom of the Axis.

ALLIED LANDINGS IN AFRICA, SICILY, AND ITALY In November 1942 an Allied force landed in French North Africa. Even before that landing, the British Field Marshal Bernard Montgomery (1887–1976), after stopping Rommel at El Alamein, had begun a drive to the west. Furthermore, the American General Dwight D. Eisenhower (1890–1969) had pushed eastward through Morocco and Algeria. The two armies caught the German army between them in Tunisia and crushed it. The Suez Canal and the Mediterranean were now under Allied control, and southern Europe was exposed.

In July and August 1943 the Allies took Sicily. Mussolini was driven from power. The new government tried to make peace but the Germans moved into Italy. The Allies landed in Italy, and Marshal Pietro Badoglio (1871–1956), the leader of the new Italian government, went over to their side, declaring war on Germany. Churchill had spoken of Italy as the "soft underbelly" of the Axis, but German resistance was tough and determined. Still the need to defend Italy put a strain on the Germans' energy and resources and left them vulnerable on other fronts.

BATTLE OF STALINGRAD The Russian campaign became especially demanding. In the summer of 1942 the Germans resumed the offensive on all fronts but were unable to get very far except in the south. Their goal was the oil fields near the Caspian Sea. They got as far as Stalingrad on the Volga, a key point for the protection of the flank of the German army in the south. Hitler was determined to take the city and Stalin to hold it. The Battle of Stalingrad raged for months with unexampled ferocity. The Russians lost more men than the Americans lost in combat during the entire

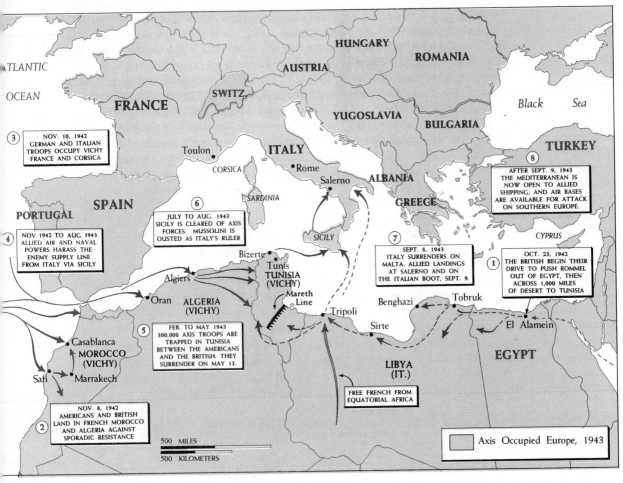

MAP 29-4 NORTH AFRICAN CAMPAIGNS, 1942–1945 *Control of North Africa was important to the Allies in order to have access to Europe from the south. The map diagrams this theater of the war from Morocco to Egypt and the Suez Canal.*

Map labels:

③ NOV. 10, 1942 GERMAN AND ITALIAN TROOPS OCCUPY VICHY FRANCE AND CORSICA

④ NOV. 1942 TO AUG. 1943 ALLIED AIR AND NAVAL POWERS HARASS THE ENEMY SUPPLY LINE FROM ITALY VIA SICILY

⑥ JULY TO AUG. 1943 SICILY IS CLEARED OF AXIS FORCES. MUSSOLINI IS OUSTED AS ITALY'S RULER

⑧ AFTER SEPT. 9, 1943 THE MEDITERRANEAN IS NOW OPEN TO ALLIED SHIPPING, AND AIR BASES ARE AVAILABLE FOR ATTACK ON SOUTHERN EUROPE.

⑦ SEPT. 8, 1943 ITALY SURRENDERS ON MALTA. ALLIED LANDINGS AT SALERNO AND ON THE ITALIAN BOOT, SEPT. 9.

① OCT. 23, 1942 THE BRITISH BEGIN THEIR DRIVE TO PUSH ROMMEL OUT OF EGYPT, THEN ACROSS 1,000 MILES OF DESERT TO TUNISIA

⑤ FEB. TO MAY 1943 300,000 AXIS TROOPS ARE TRAPPED IN TUNISIA BETWEEN THE AMERICANS AND THE BRITISH. THEY SURRENDER ON MAY 13.

② NOV. 8, 1942 AMERICANS AND BRITISH LAND IN FRENCH MOROCCO AND ALGERIA AGAINST SPORADIC RESISTANCE

FREE FRENCH FROM EQUATORIAL AFRICA

500 MILES
500 KILOMETERS

Axis Occupied Europe, 1943

war, but their heroic defense prevailed. Because Hitler again overruled his generals and would not allow a retreat, an entire German army was lost.

Stalingrad marked the turning point of the Russian campaign. Thereafter, the Americans provided material help. Even more important, increased production from their own industry, which had been moved to or built up in the safety of the central and eastern regions of the U.S.S.R., allowed the Russians to gain and keep the offensive. As the German military and material resources dwindled, the Russians advanced westward inexorably.

The German defeat at Stalingrad, February 1943, marked the turning point of the Russian campaign. Thereafter, the Russians advanced inexorably westward. [Sovfoto]

STRATEGIC BOMBING In 1943 the Allies began to gain ground in production and logistics as well. The industrial might of the United States began to come into full force, and at the same time new technology and tactics made great strides in eliminating the submarine menace.

In the same year the American and British air forces began a series of massive bombardments of Germany by night and day. The Americans were more committed to the theory of the "precision bombing" of military and industrial targets vital to the enemy war effort, so they flew the day missions. The British regarded precision bombing as impossible and therefore useless. They preferred indiscriminate "area bombing" aimed at destroying the morale of the German people; this kind of mission could be done at night. It does not appear that either kind of bombing had much effect on the war until 1944. Then the Americans introduced long-range fighters that could protect the bombers and allow accurate missions by day.

By 1945 the Allies had cleared the skies of German planes and could bomb at will. Concentrated attacks on industrial targets, especially communications centers and oil refineries, did very real damage and helped to shorten the war. Terror bombing continued, too, but seems not to have had any useful result. The bombardment of Dresden in February 1945 was especially savage and destructive. It was much debated within the British government and has raised moral questions since. The aerial war over Germany took a heavy toll of the German air force and diverted vital resources away from other military purposes.

The Defeat of Nazi Germany

On June 6, 1944 ("D-Day"), American, British, and Canadian troops landed in force on the coast of Normandy. The "second front" was

American troops land in Normandy on D-Day, June 6, 1944. [UPI Bettmann Newsphotos]

MAP 29-5 DEFEAT OF THE AXIS IN EUROPE, 1942–1945 *Here we see some major steps in the progress toward allied victory against Axis Europe. From the south through Italy, the west through France, and the*

The Axis
Allied with the Axis
Occupied by the Axis

1 AXIS TROOPS OCCUPY VICHY FRANCE, NOV. 10 and 11, 1942

3 ALLIES INVADE SICILY & ITALY, JULY–SEPT. 1943

4 ITALIAN SURRENDER SEPT. 8, 1943

5 NORMANDY INVASION JUNE 5, 1944

6 RUSSIAN FRONT JUNE 23, 1944

7 ALLIES LAND IN PROVENCE AUG. 15, 1944

8 BATTLE OF THE BULGE DEC. 1944

9 RHINE CROSSING, 9 MARCH 7, 1945

10 GERMAN SURRENDER IN REIMS, MAY 7, 1945 AND BERLIN MAY 8, 1945

FARTHEST AXIS ADVANCE, NOV. 1942

FARTHEST AXIS ADVANCE, DEC., 1941

AXIS TROOPS EVACUATED, 2 MAY, 1943

300 MILES
300 KILOMETERS

opened. General Dwight D. Eisenhower, the commander of the Allied armies, faced a difficult problem. The European coast was heavily fortified. Amphibious assaults, moreover, are especially vulnerable to changes of wind and weather. Success depended on meticulous planning, advance preparation by heavy bombing, and successful feints to mask the point of attack. The German defense was strong, but the Allies were able to establish a beachhead and then to break out of it. In mid-August the Allies landed in southern France to put more pressure on the enemy. By the beginning of September, France had been liberated.

THE BATTLE OF THE BULGE All went smoothly until December, when the Germans launched a counterattack on the Belgian front through the Forest of Ardennes. Because the Germans were able to push forward into the Allied line, this was called the Battle of the Bulge. It brought heavy losses and considerable alarm to the Allies. That effort, however, was the last gasp for the Germans. The Allies recovered the momentum and pushed eastward. They crossed the Rhine in March of 1945, and German resistance crumbled. This time there could be no doubt that the Germans had lost the war on the battlefield.

THE CAPTURE OF BERLIN In the east the Russians swept forward no less swiftly. By March 1945 they were within reach of Berlin. Because the Allies insisted on unconditional surrender, the Germans fought on until May. Hitler and his intimates committed suicide in an underground hideaway in Berlin on May 1, 1945. The Russians occupied Berlin by agreement with their Western allies. The Third Reich had lasted a dozen years instead of the millennium predicted by Hitler.

Fall of the Japanese Empire

The war in Europe ended on May 8, 1945, and by then victory over Japan was in sight. The original Japanese attack on the United States had been a calculated risk against the odds. The longer the war lasted, the greater was the advantage to the American superiority in industrial production and human resources.

AMERICANS RECAPTURE THE PACIFIC ISLANDS Beginning in 1943 the American forces, still relatively small in number, began a campaign of "island hopping." They did not try to recapture every Pacific island held by the Japanese but selected major bases and places strategically located along the enemy supply line. Starting from the Solomons, they moved northeast toward the Japanese homeland. By June of 1944 they had reached the Mariana Islands, which they could use as bases for bombing the Japanese in the Philippines, in China, and in Japan itself.

In October of the same year the Americans recaptured most of the Philippines and drove the Japanese fleet back into its home waters. In 1945 Iwo Jima and Okinawa fell, in spite of a determined Japanese resistance that included "kamikaze" attacks, or suicide missions in which specially trained pilots deliberately flew their explosive-filled planes into American warships. From these new bases, closer to Japan, the American bombers launched a terrible wave of bombings that destroyed Japanese industry and disabled the Japanese navy. But still the Japanese government, dominated by a military clique, refused to surrender.

Confronted with Japan's determination, the Americans made plans for a frontal assault on the Japanese homeland. They calculated it might cost a million American casualties and even greater losses for the Japanese. At this point science and technology presented the Americans with another choice.

THE ATOMIC BOMB Since early in the war a secret program had been in progress. Its staff, made up in significant part of exiles from Hitler's Europe, was working to use atomic energy for military purposes. On August 6, 1945, an American plane dropped an atomic bomb on the city of Hiroshima. The city was destroyed, and more than 70,000 of its 200,000 residents were killed. Two days later the Soviet Union declared war on Japan and invaded Manchuria. The next day a second atomic bomb fell, this time on Nagasaki. Even then the Japanese did not yield. The Japanese Cabinet was prepared to resist further, to face an invasion rather than give up.

The unprecedented intervention of Emperor Hirohito finally convinced the government to surrender on August 14. Even then they made the condition that Japan could keep its emperor. Although the Allies had continued to insist on unconditional surrender, President

1054

GLOBAL
CONFLICT,
COLD WAR,
AND NEW
DIRECTIONS

Hiroshima was destroyed by the explosion of an atomic bomb on August 6, 1945. Stubborn Japanese resistance ended with surrender only after another atomic bomb was dropped on Nagasaki. [The Granger Collection]

MAJOR CAMPAIGNS AND EVENTS OF WORLD WAR II

September 1939	Germany and Soviet Union invade Poland
November 1939	Soviet Union invades Finland
April 1940	Germany invades Denmark and Norway
May 1940	Germany invades Belgium, Netherlands, Luxembourg, and France
June 1940	Fall of France
August 1940	Battle of Britain begins
June 1941	Germany invades Soviet Union
July 1941	Japan takes Indo-China
December 1941	Japan attacks Pearl Harbor, U.S. enters war against Axis Powers
June 1942	Battle of Midway
November 1942	Battle of Stalingrad begins
November 1942	Allies land in North Africa
February–August 1943	Allies take Sicily, land in Italy
June 1944	Allies land in Normandy
May 1945	Germany surrenders
August 1945	Atomic bombs dropped on Hiroshima and Nagasaki
September 1945	Japan surrenders

Harry S. Truman (1884–1972), who had come to office on April 12, 1945, on the death of Franklin D. Roosevelt, accepted the condition. Peace was formally signed aboard the U.S.S. *Missouri* in Tokyo Bay on September 2, 1945.

Revulsion and horror at the only use of atomic bombs as well as hindsight arising from the Cold War have surrounded with debate the decision to use the bomb against Japanese cities. Some have suggested that the bombings were unnecessary to win the war and that their main purpose was to frighten the Russians into a more cooperative attitude after the war. Others have emphasized the bureaucratic, almost automatic nature of the decision, once it had been decided to develop the bomb. To the decisionmakers and their contemporaries, however, matters were simpler. The bomb was a way to end the war swiftly without the need of invasion or an extended period of bombardment, and it would save American lives. The decision to use it was conscious, not automatic, and required no ulterior motive.

The Cost of War

World War II was the most terrible war in history. Military deaths are estimated at some fif-

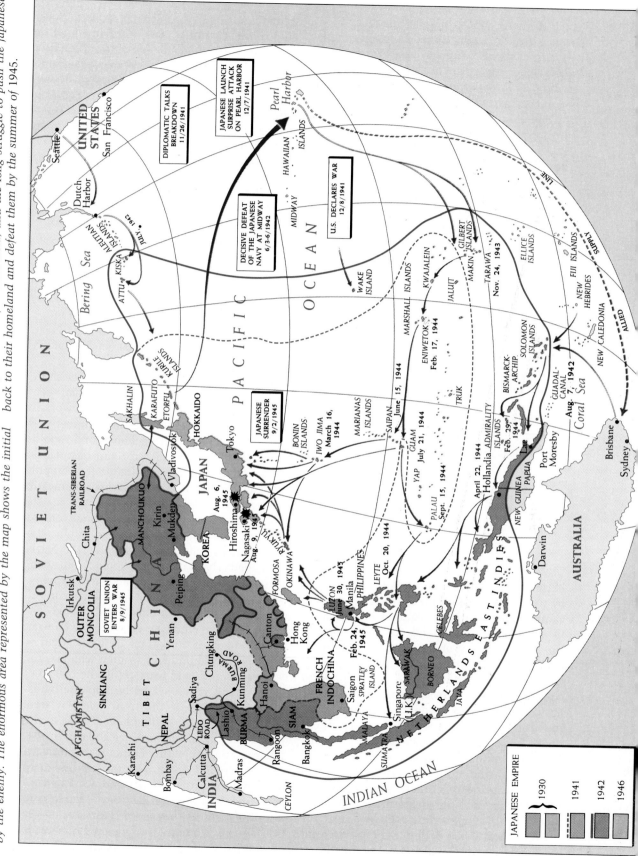

...areas that had been quickly taken earlier as huge sections of eastern Asia, and the long struggle to push the Japanese by the enemy. The enormous area represented by the map shows the initial back to their homeland and defeat them by the summer of 1945.

1055

1056

GLOBAL
CONFLICT,
COLD WAR,
AND NEW
DIRECTIONS

teen million, and at least as many civilians were killed. If deaths linked indirectly to the war, from disease, hunger, and other causes, are included, the figure of victims might reach as high as forty million. Most of Europe and significant parts of Asia were devastated. Yet the end of so terrible a war brought little opportunity for relaxation. The dawn of the Atomic Age and the dramatic end it brought to the war made people conscious that another major war might bring an end to humanity. Everything depended on the conclusion of a stable peace, but even as the fighting came to an end, conflicts among the victors made the prospects of a lasting peace doubtful.

The Domestic Fronts

World War II represented an effort of total war on the part of all the belligerents. Never before in European or world history had so many men and women and so many resources been devoted to military effort. One result was the carnage that occurred on the battlefields and at sea. Another was an unprecedented organization of civilians on the various home fronts. Each domestic effort and experience was different, but in every case almost no one escaped the impact of the conflict. Everywhere there were shortages, propaganda campaigns, and new political developments.

Germany:
From Apparent Victory
to Defeat

Hitler had expected to defeat all his enemies by a series of rapid strokes, *blitzkrieg*. Such campaigns would have required little change in Germany's society and economy. During the first two years of the war, in fact, Hitler demanded few important sacrifices from the German people. Spending on domestic projects continued, and food was plentiful; the economy as a whole was not on a full wartime footing. The failure of the Soviet Union to accept quick defeat and the resistance the Germans encountered there changed everything. Food could no longer be imported from the east in needed quantities, Germany had to mobilize for total war, and the government demanded major sacrifices from the people.

A great expansion of the army and of military production began in 1942. As Minister for

Armaments and Munitions, Albert Speer guided the economy, and Germany met its military needs instead of making consumer goods. The government sought the cooperation of major German business enterprises to aid the growth of wartime production. Between 1942 and late 1944 the output of military products tripled; as the war went on, more men were drawn away from industry into the army, and this hurt even the production of military goods.

As the manufacture of armaments replaced the production of consumer goods, the German people experienced a serious shortage of everyday products. Prices and wages were controlled, but the standard of living of German workers fell. Burdensome food rationing began in April, 1942, and shortages were severe until the Nazi government provided more food by seizing it from the occupied regions of Europe. To preserve their own home front, the Nazis passed on the suffering to their defeated neighbors.

By 1943 there were also serious labor shortages. The Nazis required young German teenagers and retired workers to undertake work in the factories, and increasing numbers of women joined them. To achieve total mobilization, the Germans closed retail businesses, raised the age of women eligible for compulsory service, shifted non-German domestic workers to wartime industry, moved artists and entertainers into military service, closed theaters, and reduced such basic public services as mail and railways. Finally, the Nazis compelled thousands of people from conquered lands to do forced labor in Germany.

Hitler assigned women a special place in the war effort. The celebration of motherhood continued, with an emphasis on women who were the mothers of important military figures. Films portrayed ordinary women who became especially brave and patriotic in the course of the war and remained faithful to their husbands who were at the front. Women were thereby shown as mothers and wives who would send their sons and husbands off to war. The government pictured other wartime activities of women as the natural fulfillment of their maternal roles. As air raid wardens they protected their families; as factory workers in munitions plants they aided their sons on the front lines. Women working on farms were providing for their soldier-sons and husbands;

as housewives they were helping to win the war by conserving food and managing their households in a frugal manner. Finally, by their faithful chastity German women were protecting racial purity. They were not to marry or to engage in sexual relations with men who were not Germans. In these ways German women were supposed to demonstrate the kind of service and courage required of women by the war.

The war years also saw an intensification of political propaganda on the domestic front beyond what occurred in other countries. Hitler and other Germans genuinely believed that weak domestic support had led to Germany's defeat in World War I; they were determined that this situation would not happen again. Nazi propaganda blamed the outbreak of the war on the British and its prolongation on the policy of Germany's opponents. It also stressed the might of Germany and the inferiority of its foes.

Propaganda Minister Josef Goebbels used both radio and films to boost the Nazi cause. Movies of the collapse of Poland, Belgium, Holland, and France were shown in Germany to demonstrate German military might. Throughout the conquered territories the

Nazis used the same mass media to frighten inhabitants about the possible consequences of an Allied victory. Later in the war the ministry broadcast exaggerated claims of Nazi victories. As the German armies were checked on the battlefield, especially in Russia, propaganda became a substitute for victory. To stiffen German resolve the propaganda aimed to frighten the German population itself about the consequences of defeat.

After May 1943, when the Allies began their major bombing offensive over Germany, the German people had much to fear. One German city after another endured heavy bombing, fires, and destruction. Although the bombing took a fearful toll of the German air force, the *Luftwaffe,* it was ineffective in undermining German morale. It may even have confirmed the general fear of defeat at the hands of such savage opponents and increased German resistance.

World War II brought increased power to the Nazi Party in Germany. Every area of the economy and society came under the direct influence or control of the party. The Nazis were determined that they, rather than the traditionally honored German officer corps, would profit from the new authority flowing to the

The allied campaign of aerial bombardment did terrible damage to German cities. Here a wounded man makes his way through the ruined streets of Hamburg in 1945. [Ullstein Bilderdienst]

1058

GLOBAL
CONFLICT,
COLD WAR,
AND NEW
DIRECTIONS

central government as a result of the war effort. Throughout the war years there was virtually no serious opposition to Hitler or his ministers. In 1944 a small group of army officers made an attempt to assassinate Hitler; the effort failed, and there were few indications of significant popular support for this act.

The war brought great changes to Germany, but what transformed the country was the experience of defeat accompanied by vast physical destruction, invasion, and occupation. Hitler and the Nazis had brought the nation to such a complete and disastrous defeat that only a new kind of state with new political structures could emerge.

France: Defeat, Collaboration, and Resistance

After its swift defeat in 1940 France was divided into an occupied zone and an ostensibly free region with its capital at Vichy and under a government led by the aged hero of World War I, Henri Pétain. In fact, the Vichy government cooperated closely with the Germans for a variety of reasons.

Some of the collaborators believed that the Germans were sure to win the war and wanted to be on the victorious side. A few sympathized with the ideas and plans of the Nazis. Many conservatives regarded the French defeat as a judgment on what they saw as the corrupt, secularized, liberal ways of the Third Republic. Most of the French were not active collaborators but were helpless and demoralized by defeat and the evidence of German power.

Many conservatives and extreme rightists saw the Vichy government as a device for reshaping the French national character and for halting the decadence they associated with political and religious liberalism. The Roman Catholic clergy, who had lost power and influence under the Third Republic, gained status under Vichy. The Church supported Pétain; and his government restored religious instruction in the state schools and increased financial support for Catholic schools. Vichy adopted the Church's views of the importance of family and spiritual values. The government passed a law forbidding divorce during the first three years of marriage and made subsequent divorce difficult; tangible rewards were offered to encourage large families.

The Vichy regime encouraged an intense, chauvinistic nationalism. It encouraged the longstanding prejudice against foreigners working in France and also encouraged resentment even against French men and women who were not regarded as genuinely and thoroughly French. The chief victims were French Jews. Anti-Semitism was not new in France, as the Dreyfus affair had demonstrated. Even before Germany undertook Hitler's "final solution" in 1942, the French had begun to remove Jews from positions of influence in government, education, and publishing. In 1941 the Germans began to intern Jews living in occupied France; soon they carried out assassinations and imposed large fines collectively on the Jews of the occupied zone. In the spring of 1942 they began to deport Jews, ultimately over 60,000 in number, to the extermination camps of eastern Europe. The Vichy government had no part in these decisions, but it made no protest, and its own anti-Semitic policies made the whole process easier to carry out.

A few Frenchmen had fled to join Charles de Gaulle's Free French forces soon after the defeat of 1940. Serious internal resistance to the German occupiers and to the Vichy government, however, began to develop only late in 1942. The Germans attempted to force young people in occupied France to work in German factories; some of them fled into Vichy, France and joined the Resistance, but the number of all the resisters was small. Many were deterred by fear of harsh punishment by the Germans. Some disliked the violence inevitably connected with resistance to a powerful tyrant nation. So long as it appeared that the Germans would win the war, moreover, resistance seemed imprudent and futile. For these reasons the organized resistance never attracted vast numbers of followers; well under 5 per cent of the adult French population appear to have been involved.

By early 1944 the tide of battle had shifted. It seemed only a matter of time before the Allies won, and it was clear that the Vichy government would not survive; only then did an active resistance assert itself. General de Gaulle spoke confidently for Free France from his base in London and urged the French people to resist their conquerors and their lackeys in the Vichy government. Within France resistance groups joined forces to plan for a better day. From Algiers on August 9, 1944, the Commit-

This classic photo shows the liberation of Paris by Americans, 1944. Free French Fighters joined by gendarmes lead group of Nazi prisoners jeered at by populace. [Bettmann Archive]

tee of National Liberation declared the authority of Vichy illegitimate. Soon French soldiers joined in the liberation of Paris and established a government for Free France. On October 21, 1945 France voted to end the Third Republic and adopted a new constitution as the basis of the Fourth Republic. The French people had experienced defeat, disgrace, deprivation, and suffering in the war. Hostility and bitter quarrels over who had done what during the occupation and the Vichy period divided them for decades.

Great Britain: Organization for Victory

On May 22, 1940 the British Parliament enacted a law giving the government emergency powers. Together with others already in effect, this measure allowed the government to institute compulsory military service, food rationing, and various controls over the economy.

To deal with the crisis facing them, the British political parties joined in a national government under Winston Churchill. Churchill and the British war cabinet moved as quickly as possible to mobilize the nation. Perhaps the most pressing immediate need was the production of airplanes to fight the Germans in the battle of Britain. This effort was led by Lord Beaverbrook, one of Britain's most important newspaper publishers. The demand for more planes and other armaments inspired a massive campaign to reclaim scrap metal. Wrought-iron fences, kitchen pots and pans, and every conceivable kind of scrap metal were collected for the war effort. This was only one successful example of the many ways the civilian population was enthusiastically engaged in the struggle.

By the end of 1941 British production had already surpassed Germany's. To meet the heavy demands on the labor force, factory hours were extended and women were brought into the work force in great numbers. Unemployment disappeared, and the working classes had more money to spend than they had enjoyed for many years. To avoid inflation caused

1060

GLOBAL
CONFLICT,
COLD WAR,
AND NEW
DIRECTIONS

by increased demand for an inadequate supply of consumer goods, savings were encouraged and taxes were raised to absorb the excess purchasing power.

The British people had reason to fear a German invasion of their islands. They had seen German forces overwhelm one nation after another on the Continent. In the dark days after the evacuation of the British army at Dunkirk in 1940, many believed that invasion and defeat were imminent. The British took the threat so seriously as to devise plans to confuse a German invading army: street and road signs were changed and road maps destroyed. The government interned Germans living in England, many of them refugees from the Nazis, who were considered security risks. Only the Royal Air Force (RAF) stood between the British and invasion.

The RAF barely managed to outlast the Luftwaffe, in large part because of the German decision to shift its attacks from air bases to London and other British cities. The "blitz" of the winter and spring of 1940–1941 was the most immediate and dramatic experience of the war to the British people themselves. The German air raids killed many people and destroyed the homes of many others. Once the bombing began many families removed their children to the countryside. Ironically, the rescue effort improved the standard of living of many of the children, for they received meals and medication subsidized by the government. Gas masks were issued to thousands of city-dwellers, who were frequently compelled to take shelter from the bombs in the London subways.

After the spring of 1941 Hitler needed most of his air force for use on the Russian front, but the bombing of Britain continued, killing more than thirty thousand people. Terrible as it was, this toll was much smaller than the number of Germans killed by Allied bombing later in the war. In England, as in Germany, however, the bombing did not break the people's spirit but seems to have made them more determined.

During the worst months of the "blitz" the remarkable speeches of Winston Churchill cheered and encouraged the British people. He united them with a sense of common suffering and of a common purpose. They were called upon to make many sacrifices: transportation facilities were strained simply from carrying enough coal for domestic heating and for running factories. Food and clothing for civilians was in short supply, and the government adopted strict rationing to achieve a fair distribution. Every scrap of land was farmed, increasing the productive portion by almost four million acres. Gasoline was in short supply, so private vehicles gave way to public transportation almost entirely.

The British established their own propaganda machine to influence the continent. The British Broadcasting Company (BBC) sent programs to every country in Europe in the local language to encourage resistance against the Nazis. At home the government used the radio to unify the nation. Soldiers at the front heard the same programs as their families at home. The most famous program, second only to Churchill's speeches, was *It's That Man Again*, a humorous broadcast filled with imaginary figures that the entire nation came to treasure.

For the broad mass of the population, strangely enough, the standard of living improved over the course of the war. The general health of the nation also improved for reasons that are still not clear. These improvements should not be exaggerated, but they did occur, and many connected them with the active involvement of the government in the economy and the lives of the citizens. This wartime experience may have contributed to the Labour party's victory in 1945; many feared that a return to Conservative Party rule would bring a return to the economic problems and unemployment of the 1930s.

The Soviet Union: "The Great Patriotic War"

The war against Germany came as a great surprise to Stalin and the Soviet Union. The German attack violated the 1939 pact with Hitler and put the government of the Soviet Union on the defensive both militarily and politically. It showed the failure of Stalin's foreign policy and the ineptness of his preparation for war. He claimed that the pact had given the nation an extra year and a half to prepare for war, but this was clearly a lame and implausible excuse in light of the ease of Germany's early victories. Within days a large part of the western Soviet Union was occupied by German troops. The Communist government feared that Soviet citizens who had been conquered by the Germans, many of them not ethnic Russians, might welcome the conquerors as liberators; these Soviet citizens had been oppressed by the Russians and had lived under harsh conditions.

No nation suffered greater loss of life or more extensive physical destruction during World War II than the Soviet Union. Perhaps as many as 16 million people were killed, and vast numbers of Soviet troops were taken prisoner. Hundreds of cities and towns, and well over half of the industrial and transportation facilities of the country were devastated. From 1942 on the Germans sent thousands of Soviet prisoners to work in factories in Germany as forced labor. The Germans also confiscated grain supplies and drew mineral resources and oil from the Soviet Union to serve their own war effort.

Stalin conducted the war as virtual chief of the armed forces, and the State Committee for Defense provided strong central coordination. In the decade before the war Stalin had already made the Soviet Union a highly centralized nation; he had attempted to manage the entire economy centrally by means of the Five-Year Plans, the collectivization of agriculture, and the purges. The country was thus on what amounted to a wartime footing long before the conflict erupted. When the war began millions of citizens entered the army, but the army itself did not grow in influence at the expense of the state and the Communist Party, that is, of Stalin. He was suspicious of the generals even though he had presumably eliminated officers of doubtful loyalty in the purges of the late 1930s. As the war continued, however, the army gained some degree of independence, and after a while the generals were no longer subservient to party commissars. The army in that way gained some freedom of action. However, it was still sharply limited by suspicions, by the power of Stalin, and by the nature of Soviet government and society.

Soviet propaganda differed in many ways from that of other nations. Because the Soviet government distrusted the loyalty of its citizens, it confiscated many radios to prevent the people from listening to German propaganda. In large cities the government erected large loudspeakers to broadcast to the people in place of radios. The Soviets, moreover, turned away from traditional Marxist propaganda that

stressed class conflict, in favor of unifying propaganda that emphasized Russian patriotism. The conflict was called "The Great Patriotic War." As in other countries, writers and playwrights contributed to the effort to sustain public support for the war. Sometimes they drew on communist themes, but they also portrayed the common Soviet citizen as contributing to a great patriotic struggle.

As the war dragged on, Russian patriotism rather than communist ideology became the main theme. Great Russian novels of the past were republished; more than half a million copies of Tolstoy's *War and Peace* were pub-

During the terrible German siege of Leningrad that lasted for two and a half years, starvation and disease reduced the population from 4 to 2.5 million. Civilian morale, however, did not collapse. Here a group of girls are on their way to work on rebuilding the city. [SOVFOTO]

lished during the siege of Leningrad. Other authors wrote straightforward propaganda fostering hatred of the Germans. Serge Eisenstein, the great filmmaker, produced a vast epic entitled *Ivan the Terrible*, which glorified one of the most brutal tsars of the Russian past. Musicians, such as Dimitri Shostakovich, produced scores that sought to contribute to the struggle and evoke heroic emotions. The most important of these was Shostakovich's *Seventh Symphony*, also known as the *Leningrad Symphony*.

The pressure of war led Stalin to make peace with the Russian Orthodox Church. He pursued friendly relations with Church leaders and allowed them to enter the premises of the Kremlin. Stalin hoped that this new policy would give him more support at home and permit the Soviet Union to be viewed more favorably in other areas of Europe where the Orthodox church predominated, especially in the Balkans.

Within occupied portions of the western Soviet Union an active resistance movement arose against the Germans. The swiftness of the German invasion had left thousands of Soviet troops stranded. Many were shipped to Germany as prisoners of war, but others escaped and carried on irregular resistance warfare behind the enemy lines. Stalin supported partisan forces in lands held by the enemy for two reasons: he wanted to cause as much difficulty as possible for the Germans; also the Soviet-sponsored resistance served to remind the peasants in the conquered regions that the Soviet government, with its policies of collectivization, had not disappeared. Stalin feared that the peasants' hatred of the Communist government might lead them to collaborate with the invaders. When the Soviet army moved westward toward the end of the war it incorporated the partisans into the regular army.

As the Soviet armies reclaimed the occupied areas and then moved across eastern and central Europe, the Soviet Union established itself as a world power second only to the United States. Stalin had entered the war a reluctant belligerent, but he emerged a major victor. In that respect, the war and the extraordinary patriotic effort and sacrifice it generated consolidated the power of Stalin and the party more effectively than the political and social policies of the previous decade.

Preparations for Peace

The split between the Soviet Union and its wartime allies should cause no surprise. As the self-proclaimed center of world communism, the Soviet Union was openly dedicated to the overthrow of the capitalist nations. However, this message was muted when the occasion demanded. On the other side, the western allies were no less open about their hostility to communism and its chief purveyor, the Soviet Union. Though they had been friendly to the early stages of the Russian Revolution, they had sent troops in hopes of overthrowing the Bolshevik regime. The United States did not grant formal recognition to the Union of Soviet Socialist Republics until 1933. The Western powers' exclusion of the Soviets from the Munich conference and Stalin's pact with Hitler did nothing to improve relations.

Cooperation against a common enemy and strenuous propaganda efforts in the West helped improve Western feeling toward the Soviet ally. Still, Stalin remained suspicious and critical of the Western war effort, and Churchill never ceased planning to contain the Soviet advance into Europe. For some time Roosevelt seems to have been hopeful that the Allies could continue to work together after the war, but even he was losing faith as the war and his life drew to a close. Differences in historical development and ideology, as well as traditional conflicts over political power and influence, soon dashed hopes of a mutually satisfactory peace settlement and continued cooperation to uphold it.

The Atlantic Charter

In August 1941, even before the Americans were at war, Roosevelt and Churchill had met on a ship off Newfoundland and agreed to the Atlantic Charter. This broad set of principles in the spirit of Wilson's Fourteen Points provided a theoretical basis for the peace they sought. When Russia and the United States joined Britain in the war, the three powers entered a purely military alliance in January 1942, leaving all political questions aside. The first political conference was the meeting of foreign ministers in Moscow in October 1943. The ministers reaffirmed earlier agreements to fight on until the enemy surrendered without condition and to continue cooperating after the war in a united-nations organization.

Tehran: Agreement on a Second Front

The first meeting of the three leaders of state took place at Tehran, the capital of Iran, in 1943. Western promises to open a second front in France the next summer (1944) and Stalin's agreement to join in the war against Japan when Germany was defeated created an atmosphere of goodwill in which to discuss a postwar settlement. Stalin wanted to retain what he had gained in his pact with Hitler and to dismember Germany. Roosevelt and Churchill were conciliatory, but they made no firm commitments.

The most important decision was the one that chose Europe's west coast as the point of attack instead of southern Europe, by the way of the Mediterranean. That meant, in retrospect, that Soviet forces would occupy eastern Europe and control its destiny. At Tehran in 1943 the Western allies did not foresee this clearly, for the Russians were still fighting deep within their own frontiers, and military considerations were paramount everywhere.

CHURCHILL AND STALIN By 1944, the situation was different. In August, Soviet armies were in sight of Warsaw, which had risen in expectation of liberation. But the Russians halted, allowing the Polish rebels to be annihilated while they turned south into the Balkans. They gained control of Romania and Hungary, advances of which centuries of expansionist tsars had only dreamed. Alarmed by these developments, Churchill went to Moscow and met with Stalin in October. They agreed to share power in the Balkans on the basis of Soviet predominance in Romania and Bulgaria, Western predominance in Greece, and equality of influence in Yugoslavia and Hungary. These agreements were not enforceable without American approval and the Americans were known to be hostile to such un-Wilsonian devices as "spheres of influence."

GERMANY Agreement on European questions was more difficult. The three powers easily agreed on Germany—its disarmament and denazification and its division into four zones of occupation by France and the Big Three (the

U.S.S.R., Britain, and the United States). Churchill, however, began to balk at Stalin's plan to dismember Germany. He objected to Stalin's demand for reparations in the amount of $20 billion as well as forced labor from all the zones, with Russia to get half of everything. These matters were left undecided to fester and to cause dissension in the future.

EASTERN EUROPE The settlement of eastern Europe was no less a problem. Everyone agreed that the Soviet Union deserved neighboring governments that were friendly, but the West insisted that they also be independent, autonomous, and democratic. The Western leaders, and especially Churchill, were not eager to see eastern Europe fall under Russian domination. They were also, especially Roosevelt, truly committed to democracy and self-determination.

However, Stalin knew that independent, freely elected governments in Poland and Romania would not be safely friendly to Russia. He had already established a subservient government in Poland at Lublin in competition with the Polish government-in-exile in London. Under pressure from the Western leaders, however, he agreed to reorganize the government and to include some Poles friendly to the West. He also signed a Declaration on Liberated Europe promising self-determination and free democratic elections. Stalin may have been eager to avoid conflict before the war with Germany was over. He never was free of the fear that the Allies might still make an arrangement with Germany and betray him. And he probably thought it worth endorsing some meaningless principles as the price of continued harmony. In any case, he wasted little time in violating these agreements.

Yalta

The next meeting of the Big Three was at Yalta in the Crimea in February 1945. The western armies had not yet crossed the Rhine, and the Soviet army was within a hundred miles of Berlin. The war with Japan continued, and no atomic explosion had yet taken place. Roosevelt, faced with an invasion of Japan and prospective heavy losses, was eager to bring the Russians into the Pacific war as soon as possible. As a true Wilsonian he also suspected Churchill's determination to maintain the

MAP 29-7 YALTA TO THE SURRENDER *"The Big Three", Roosevelt, Churchill, Stalin, met at Yalta in the Crimea in February of 1945. At the meeting concessions were made to Stalin concerning the settlement of Eastern Europe, as Roosevelt was eager to bring the Russians into the Pacific war as soon as possible. This map shows the positions held at the time of the surrender.*

Map labels: North Sea; SWEDEN; DENMARK; LATVIA; LITHUANIA; Memel; Baltic Sea; NETH.; BELG.; LUX.; FRANCE; Metz; Strasbourg; Nice; Milan; ITALY; Bologna; Florence; SWITZ.; Brenner Pass; Flensburg; Lübeck; Wismar; Hamburg; Bremen; Cologne; Remagen; Frankfurt; Mannheim; Nurnburg; Munich; Kassel; Magdeburg; Berlin; Torgau; Leipzig; Chemnitz; Karlsbad; Prague; Pilsen; Brunn; CZECHOSLOVAKIA; GERMANY; Danzig; Breslau; POLAND; AUSTRIA; Linz; Vienna; Graz; Budapest; HUNGARY; Trieste; YUGOSLAVIA; Rhine; Elbe; Danube; BRITAIN; CANADA; U.S.

MUCH OF YUGOSLAVIA WAS HELD BY TITO'S COMMUNIST PARTISANS

Legend:
- Conquered by the Russians to the Time of Surrender.
- German-Held Areas at the Time of Surrender, May 7–9, 1945.
- ---- Battleline at the Time of the Yalta Conference, Feb. 1945.

MILES / KILOMETERS

British Empire and Britain's colonial advantages. The Americans thought that Churchill's plan to set up British spheres of influence in Europe would encourage the Russians to do the same and lead to friction and war. To encourage Russian participation in the war against Japan, Roosevelt and Churchill made extensive concessions to Russia in Sakhalin and the Kurile Islands, in Korea, and in Manchuria.

Again in the tradition of Wilson, Roosevelt laid great stress on a united-nations organization: "Through the United Nations, he hoped to achieve a self-enforcing peace settlement that would not require American troops, as well as an open world without spheres of influence in which American enterprise could work freely."[7] Soviet agreement on these points seemed well worth concessions elsewhere.

Potsdam

The Big Three met for the last time in the Berlin suburb of Potsdam in July 1945. Much had changed since the last conference. Germany was defeated, and news of the successful experimental explosion of an atomic weapon reached the American president during the meetings. The cast of characters was also different: President Truman replaced the deceased Roosevelt, and Clement Attlee (1883–1967), leader of the Labour Party that had defeated Churchill's Conservatives in a general election, replaced Churchill as Britain's spokesman during the conference. Previous agreements were reaffirmed, but progress on undecided questions was slow.

Russia's western frontier was moved far into what had been Poland and included part of German East Prussia. In compensation Poland was allowed "temporary administration" over the rest of East Prussia and Germany east of the Oder–Neisse river line, a condition that

[7] *Robert O. Paxton,* Europe in the Twentieth Century *(New York: Harcourt Brace Jovanovich, 1975), p. 487.*

NEGOTIATIONS AMONG THE ALLIES

August 1941	Churchill and Roosevelt meet off Newfoundland to sign Atlantic Charter
October 1943	American, British, and Soviet Foreign Ministers meet in Moscow
November 1943	Churchill, Roosevelt, and Stalin meet at Tehran
October 1944	Churchill meets with Stalin in Moscow
February 1945	Churchill, Roosevelt, and Stalin meet at Yalta
July 1945	Attlee, Stalin, and Truman meet at Potsdam

This photograph shows the "Big Three" at Potsdam. By the summer of 1945, only Stalin remained among the leaders of the major allies. Roosevelt and Churchill had been replaced by Harry Truman and Clement Attlee. [UPI/Bettmann Newsphotos]

became permanent. In effect, Poland was moved about a hundred miles west, at the expense of Germany, to accommodate the Soviet Union. The Allies agreed that Germany would be divided into occupation zones until the final peace treaty was signed. As no such treaty has ever been made, Germany remains divided to this day. Recent developments in eastern Europe, however, make it likely that Germany will soon be reunited.

A Council of Foreign Ministers was established to draft peace treaties for Germany's allies. Growing disagreements made the job difficult, and it was not until February 1947 that Italy, Romania, Hungary, Bulgaria, and Finland signed treaties. The Russians were dissatisfied with the treaty that the United States made with Japan in 1951 and signed their own agreements with the Japanese in 1956. These disagreements were foreshadowed at Potsdam.

The second great war of the twentieth century (1939–1945) grew out of the unsatisfactory resolution of the first. In retrospect, the two wars appear to some people to be one continuous conflict, a kind of twentieth-century "Thirty Years' War," with the two main periods of fighting separated by an uneasy truce. To others that point of view seems to oversimplify and distort the situation by implying that the second war was the inevitable result of the first and its inadequate peace treaties. The latter opinion seems more sound, for, whatever the flaws of the treaties of Paris, the

world suffered an even more terrible war than the first because of failures of judgment and will on the part of the victorious democratic powers.

The United States, which had become the wealthiest and potentially the strongest nation in the world, disarmed almost entirely and withdrew into a short-sighted and foolish isolation. Therefore, it could play no important part in restraining the angry and ambitious dictators who would bring on the war. Britain and France refused to face the reality of the threat posed by the Axis powers until

1066

GLOBAL
CONFLICT,
COLD WAR,
AND NEW
DIRECTIONS

the most deadly war in history was required to put it down. If the victorious democracies had remained strong, responsible, and realistic, they could easily have remedied whatever injustices or mistakes arose from the treaties without any danger to the peace.

The second war itself was so plainly a world war that little need be said to indicate its global character. There is good reason to think that if the Japanese occupation of Manchuria in 1931 was not technically a part of that war, it was a significant precursor. Morever, there was Italy's attack on the African nation of Ethiopia in 1935; the Italian, German, and Soviet interventions in the Spanish Civil War (1936–1939); and Japan's attack on China in 1937. These acts revealed that aggressive forces were on the march around the globe and that the defenders of the world order lacked the will to stop them. The formation of the Axis between Germany, Italy, and Japan guaranteed that when the war came it would be fought around the world.

There was fighting and suffering in Asia, Africa, the islands of the Pacific, and Europe; and men and women from all the inhabited continents took part in it. The use of atomic weapons brought the frightful struggle to a close. Still, what are called conventional weapons did almost all the damage; their level of destructiveness threatened the survival of civilization, even without the use of atomic or nuclear devices.

This war ended not with unsatisfactory peace treaties but with no treaty at all in the European area where the war had begun. The world quickly split into two unfriendly camps: the western led by the United States, and the eastern led by the Soviet Union. This division, among other things, hastened the liberation of former colonial territories. The bargaining power of the new nations that emerged from them was temporarily increased as the two rival great powers tried to gain their friendship or allegiance. It has become customary to refer to these nations as "the Third World," with the Soviet Union and the United States and their respective allies being the first two. The passage of time has shown that the differences between these newer nations are so great as to make the name not very helpful.

The surprising treatment received by the defeated powers of the second war was also largely the result of the emergence of the Cold War. Instead of their being held back, democratic governments were installed in them. They were taken into the Western alliance and assisted in their economic recovery to the point where Japan and West Germany are among the richest nations in the world and Italy is more prosperous than it has ever been.

By the last decade of the twentieth century Japan had become one of the greatest industrial, commercial, and financial powers in the world and a major investor in the American economy. The rapid growth of the Japanese economy and its effective competition against American producers had produced concern among its major competitors in the United States and western Europe and considerable sentiment in favor of protective tariffs to fight off the competition.

Germany, divided between East and West by the war, never ceased to hope for eventual unification. The startling events of 1989 that saw the Soviet Union ease its hold over Eastern Europe produced a situation in which the unification of Germany took place. That event again poses the question of how a unified Germany can fit into Europe, a question at the root of the two great wars of the twentieth century.

Suggested Readings

A. ADAMTHWAITE, France and the Coming of the Second World War, 1936–1939 (1977). A careful account making good use of the newly opened French archives.

J. ADLER, The Jews of Paris and the Final Solution: Communal Response and Internal Conflicts, 1940–1944 (1987). Written by a former member of the French resistance.

E. R. BECK, Under the Bombs: The German Home Front, 1942–1945 (1986). An interesting examination of a generally unstudied subject.

A. BULLOCK, Hitler: A Study in Tyranny, rev. ed. (1964). A brilliant biography.

W. S. CHURCHILL, The Second World War, 6 vols. (1948–1954). The memoirs of the great British leader.

H. FEIS, From Trust to Terror: The Onset of the Cold War, 1945–1950 (1970). The best general account.

H. W. GATZKE, Stresemann and the Rearmament of Germany (1954). An important monograph.

M. GILBERT, The Holocaust: A History of the Jews of

Europe during the Second World War (1985). The best and most comprehensive treatment.

M. GILBERT AND R. GOTT, *The Appeasers*, rev. ed. (1963). A revealing study of British policy in the 1930s.

M. HARRISON, *Soviet Planning in Peace and War, 1938–1945* (1985). An examination of the Soviet wartime economy.

B. H. Liddell Hart, *History of the Second World War*, 2 vols. (1971). A good military history.

K. HILDEBRAND, *The Foreign Policy of the Third Reich* (1970).

M. KNOX, *Mussolini Unleashed* (1982). An outstanding study of Fascist Italy's policy and strategy in World War II.

G. KOLKO, *The Politics of War* (1968). An interesting example of the new revisionist school that finds the causes of the Cold War in economic considerations and emphasizes American responsibility.

W. L. LANGER AND S. E. GLEASON, *The Challenge of Isolation* (1952). American foreign policy in the 1930s.

S. MARKS, *The Illusion of Peace* (1976). A good discussion of European international relations in the 1920s and early 1930s.

V. MASTNY, *Russia's Road to the Cold War* (1979). Written by an expert on the Soviet Union and eastern Europe.

W. MURRAY, *The Change in the European Balance of Power 1938–1939* (1984). A brilliant study of the relationship between strategy, foreign policy, economics, and domestic politics in the years before the war.

N. RICH, *Hitler's War Aims*, 2 vols. (1973–1974).

M. SHERWIN, *A World Destroyed: The Atomic Bomb and the Grand Alliance* (1975). An analysis of the role of the atomic bomb in the years surrounding the end of World War II.

R. J. SONTAG, *A Broken World 1919–1939* (1971). An excellent survey.

A. J. P. TAYLOR, *The Origins of the Second World War* (1966). A lively, controversial, even perverse study.

H. THOMAS, *The Spanish Civil War*, 3rd ed. (1986). The best account in English.

C. THORNE, *The Approach of War 1938–1939* (1967). A careful analysis of diplomacy.

G. WRIGHT, *The Ordeal of Total War 1939–1945* (1968). An excellent survey.

The erection of the Berlin wall in August, 1961, separating East and West Berlin came to symbolize the tensions of the Cold War Era. Here the wall is being repaired in 1963. [UPI/Bettmann Newsphotos]

30

THE ERA OF
THE COLD WAR
AND SUPERPOWER CONFRONTATION

From approximately 1848 to 1948 the nation-state characterized European political life and rivalry. Generally these countries sought to expand their political influence and economic power at each other's expense. During the same century Europe's economic and technological supremacy allowed certain of its states to rule or administer vast areas of the globe

1070

GLOBAL
CONFLICT,
COLD WAR,
AND NEW
DIRECTIONS

inhabited by non-European peoples. Although those nation-states continued to exist, the economic and political collapse occasioned by World War II caused them to experience over four decades of political subordination to the United States and the Soviet Union.

Since 1945 the rivalry between the United States and the Soviet Union, the two superpowers with nuclear arsenals, was the most fundamental political fact of life for Europe and the rest of the world. Europe stood at the center of the ongoing confrontation known as the Cold War between the two superpowers. For over two decades the rivalry of the Cold War threatened the peace of Europe and disrupted the peace of other parts of the world. During the past two decades the United States and the Soviet Union have tended to work out their differences through negotiations.

The new role of the United States in Europe and indeed throughout the world represented a major shift in American policy. Having learned the dangers of retreat from the world scene after 1919, the United States following World War II actively assumed a position of military, political, and economic leadership. It moved to oppose what it regarded as the expansion of Soviet power and communist influence across the globe. This policy of active leadership led to the introduction of the Marshall Plan, the formation of NATO, the intervention in Korea, and the decision to intervene in Vietnam. Superpower tensions also manifested themselves in the Middle East.

The Onset of the Cold War

Tensions had arisen between the United States and the Soviet Union in the closing months of the Second World War. Some scholars attribute the hardening of the atmosphere to the advent of Harry Truman in place of the more sympathetic Franklin Roosevelt and to the American possession of an effective atomic bomb. The fact is that Truman was trying to carry Roosevelt's policies forward, and there is evidence that Roosevelt himself had become distressed by Soviet actions in eastern Europe. Nor did Truman use the successful test of the atomic bomb to try to keep Russia out of the Pacific. On the contrary, he worked hard to ensure Russian intervention against Japan. In part, the new coldness among the Allies arose from the mutual feeling that each had violated previous agreements. The Russians were plainly asserting permanent control of Poland and Romania under puppet communist governments. The United States, on the other hand, was taking a harder line on the extent of German reparations to the Soviet Union.

The Lines Drawn

In retrospect, however, it appears unlikely that friendlier styles on either side could have avoided a split that rested on basic differences of ideology and interest. The Soviet Union's attempt to extend its control westward into central Europe and the Balkans and southward into the Middle East was a continuation of the policy of tsarist Russia. It had been Britain's traditional role to try to restrain Russian expansion into these areas. Therefore it was not surprising that the United States should inherit that task as Britain's power waned.

The Americans made no attempt to roll back Soviet power where it existed. And at the time American military forces were the greatest in their history, American industrial power was unmatched in the world, and atomic weapons were an American monopoly. In less than a year from the war's end, American forces in Europe were reduced from 3.5 million to half a million. The speed of the withdrawal was the result of pressure to "get the boys home" but was fully in accord with American plans and peacetime goals.

These goals were the traditional ones of support for self-determination, autonomy, and democracy in the political area, free trade, freedom of the seas, no barriers to investment, and the Open Door in the economic sphere. These goals agreed with American principles, and they served American interests well. As the strongest, richest nation in the world, the one with the greatest industrial plant and the strongest currency, the United States would benefit handsomely if such an international order were established.

THE IRON CURTAIN American hostility to colonial empires created tension with

MAP 30-1 TERRITORIAL CHANGES AFTER
WORLD WAR II *The map pictures the shifts in
territory following the defeat of the Axis. No treaty
of peace has formally ended the war with Germany.*

——— Post World War II
Boundaries

▨ Territorial Changes
Resulting From
World War II

Berlin and Vienna were
Under 4-Power Control

The Saar and the Free
Territory of Triest
were Under Special Control

The Saar was returned
to Germany in 1957

400 MILES
400 KILOMETERS

France and Britain, but these were minor. The
main conflict came with the Soviet Union.
From the Soviet perspective the extension of
its frontiers and the domination of formerly
independent states in eastern Europe were necessary for the security of the U.S.S.R. They
were seen as a proper compensation for the
fearful losses that the Russians had suffered in
the war. American resistance to the new state
of things could be seen as a threat to the Soviets' security and legitimate aims. American
objections over Poland and other states could
be seen as attempts to undermine regimes
friendly to Russia and to encircle the Soviet
Union with hostile neighbors. Such behavior
might be seen to justify Russian attempts to
overthrow regimes friendly to the United
States in western Europe and elsewhere.

The growth in France and Italy of large Communist parties plainly taking orders from Moscow led the Americans to believe that Stalin
was engaged in a great worldwide plot to destroy capitalism and democracy by subversion.
In the absence of reliable evidence about Stalin's intentions, certainty is not possible, but
most people in the West thought the suspicions plausible. Rivalry between the Soviet
Union and the United States dominated international relations for the next three decades. In
the flawed world of reality it is hard to see how
things could have been otherwise. The important question was whether the conflict would
take a diplomatic or a military form.

Evidence of the new mood of hostility
among the former allies was not long in coming. In February 1946 both Stalin and his foreign minister, Vyacheslav Molotov, gave public speeches in which they spoke of the
western democracies as enemies. A month
later Churchill gave a speech in Fulton, Missouri, in which he viewed Russian actions in
eastern Europe with alarm. He spoke of an *Iron
Curtain* that had descended on Europe, dividing a free and democratic West from an East
under totalitarian rule. He warned against
communist subversion and urged Western
unity and strength as a response to the new
menace. In this atmosphere difficulties grew.

1072

GLOBAL
CONFLICT,
COLD WAR,
AND NEW
DIRECTIONS

Churchill Invents the Iron Curtain; Cold War Declared

In 1946 Winston Churchill chose an American audience (at Westminster College in Fulton, Missouri) for the speech that contributed iron curtain *to the language. More important, it defined the existence of what came to be known as the* Cold War *between the communist and the democratic camps.*

A shadow has fallen upon the scenes so lately lighted by the Allied victory. Nobody knows what Soviet Russia and its Communist international organization intends to do in the immediate future, or what are the limits, if any, to their expansive and proselytizing tendencies. . . .

From Stettin in the Baltic to Trieste in the Adriatic, an iron curtain has descended across the Continent. Behind that line lie all the capitals of the ancient states of central and eastern Europe. Warsaw, Berlin, Prague, Vienna, Budapest, Belgrade, Bucharest and Sofia; all these famous cities and the populations around them lie in the Soviet sphere and all are subject in one form or another, not only to Soviet influence but to a very high and increasing measure of control from Moscow. Athens alone, with its immortal glories, is free to decide its future at an election under British, American, and French observation. The Russian-dominated Polish government has been encouraged to make enormous and wrongful inroads upon Germany, and mass expulsions of millions of Germans on a scale grievous and undreamed of are now taking place. The Communist parties, which were very small in all these eastern states of Europe, have been raised to preeminence and power far beyond their numbers and are seeking everywhere to obtain totalitarian control. Police governments are prevailing in nearly every case, and so far except in Czechoslovakia, there is no true democracy. . . .

. . . I do not believe that Soviet Russia desires war. What they desire is the fruits of war and the indefinite expansion of their power and doctrines. . . .

. . . If the western democracies stand together in strict adherence to the principles of the United Nations Charter, their influence for furthering these principles will be immense and no one is likely to molest them. If, however, they become divided or falter in their duty, and if these all-important years are allowed to slip away, then indeed catastrophe may overwhelm us all.

"Winston Churchill's Speech at Fulton," in Vital Speeches of the Day, Vol. 12 (New York: City News Publishing), March 15, 1946, pp. 331–332.

Early Frustrations of the United Nations

The formation of the United Nations had been one of Roosevelt's major goals toward the end of the war. He hoped that the United Nations could represent a postwar organization that would permit international military intervention against aggression as well as be a site for postwar negotiation and consultation. The U.S. commitment to such an international organization indicated that it would accept the responsibilities of a world power and not retreat from that responsibility as it had after World War I. The new organization would be located in the United States.

The United States had taken the leading role in devising the organization of the United Nations; it was formally founded in February 1945. It was organized with a large General

1073

THE ERA
THE COL
WAR AN
SUPERPOW
CONFRONTA

Assembly in which all member nations sat and a smaller Security Council that included the five major allied powers (Great Britain, France, China, the Soviet Union, and the United States) as permanent members and other nations who sat as temporary members. Within the Security Council, which rapidly became the center of U.N. authority, each of the permanent members had the right to veto any measure that was presented.

By the late 1940s hopes that the United Nations would resolve the world's major conflicts had been disappointed. Like the League of Nations, it was (and is) dependent on voluntary contributions of money and troops. The U.N. Charter, moreover, forbids interference in the internal affairs of nations, and many of the problems of the late 1940s were internal in nature. Finally, during the late 1940s and throughout the 1950s the Soviet Union repeatedly used its veto in the Security Council and thus frustrated the capacity of the United Nations to resolve existing problems.

The attempt to deal with the problem of atomic energy was an early victim of the Cold War and the difficulties encountered in the United Nations. The Americans put forward a plan to place the manufacture and control of atomic weapons under international control. The Russians balked at the proposed requirements of on-site inspection and for limits on the veto power in the United Nations. The plan fell through. The United States continued to develop its own atomic weapons in secrecy, and the Russians did the same. By 1949, with the help of information obtained by Soviet spies in Britain and the United States, the Soviet Union exploded its own atomic bomb, and

The first meeting of the United Nations took place in San Francisco in April, 1945. Initial hopes that the U.N. would be able to resolve international conflicts soon foundered on the realities of great power conflict in the post-war world. [AP/Wide World Photos]

1074

GLOBAL
CONFLICT,
COLD WAR,
AND NEW
DIRECTIONS

the race for nuclear weapons was on. The presence of such weapons in the arsenal of the two superpowers has been one of the major concerns of all arms negotiations since that time.

Containment

Western resistance to what the West increasingly perceived as Soviet intransigence and communist plans for subversion and expansion took clearer form in 1947. Since 1944 civil war had been raging in Greece between the royalist government restored by Britain and insurgents supported by the communist countries, chiefly Yugoslavia. In 1947 Britain informed the United States that it was financially no longer able to support the Greeks. On March 12 President Truman asked Congress for legislation to support Greece and also Turkey, which was under Soviet pressure to yield

The Truman Doctrine

In 1947 the British informed the United States that they could no longer support the Greeks in their fight against a Communist insurrection supported from the outside. On March 12 of that year, President Truman asked Congress for legislation in support of both Greece and Turkey, which was also in danger. The spirit behind that request, which became known as the Truman Doctrine, *appears in the following selections from Truman's speech to the Congress.*

One of the primary objectives of the foreign policy of the United States is the creation of conditions in which we and other nations will be able to work out a way of life free from coercion. This was a fundamental issue in the war with Germany and Japan. Our victory was won over countries which sought to impose their will, and their way of life, upon other nations.

To insure the peaceful development of nations, free from coercion, the United States has taken a leading part in establishing the United Nations. The United Nations is designed to make possible lasting freedom and independence for all its members. We shall not realize our objectives, however, unless we are willing to help free peoples to maintain their free institutions and their national integrity against aggressive movements that seek to impose upon them totalitarian regimes. . . .

At the present moment in world history nearly every nation must choose between alternative ways of life. The choice is too often not a free one.

One way of life is based upon the will of the majority, and is distinguished by free institutions, representative government, free elections, guaranties of individual liberty, freedom of speech and religion, and freedom from political oppression.

The second way of life is based upon the will of a minority forcibly imposed upon the majority. It relies upon terror and oppression, a controlled press and radio, fixed elections, and the suppression of personal freedoms.

I believe that it must be the policy of the United States to support free peoples who are resisting attempted subjugation by armed minorities or by outside pressures.

I believe that we must assist free peoples to work out their own destinies in their own way.

I believe that our help should be primarily through economic and financial aid, which is essential to economic stability and orderly political processes.

Senate Committee on Foreign Relations, A Decade of American Foreign Policy: Basic Documents 1941–1949 *(1950), pp. 1235–1237.*

control of the Dardanelles. Congress voted funds to aid Greece and Turkey, but the Truman Doctrine, as enunciated in a speech of March 12, had a broader significance. The president advocated a policy of supporting "free people who are resisting attempted subjugation by armed minorities or by outside pressures," by implication anywhere in the world.

THE MARSHALL PLAN

American aid to Greece and Turkey took the form of military equipment and advisers, but the threat in western Europe was the growth of Communist parties fed by postwar poverty and hunger. To deal with this menace, the Americans devised the European Recovery Program, named the Marshall Plan after George C. Marshall, the secretary of state who introduced it. This was a plan for broad economic aid to European states on condition only that they work together for their mutual benefit. The invitation included the Soviet Union and its satellites. Finland and Czechoslovakia were willing to participate, and Poland and Hungary showed interest. The Soviets, fearing that American economic aid would attract many satellites out of their orbits, forbade them to take part.

The Marshall Plan was a great success in restoring prosperity to western Europe and in setting the stage for Europe's unprecedented postwar economic growth. It also led to the waning of communist strength in the West and to the establishment of solid democratic regimes.

REVIVAL OF THE COMINTERN

From the Western viewpoint this policy of "containment" was a new and successful response to the Soviet and communist challenge. To Stalin it may have seemed a renewal of the old Western attempt to isolate and encircle the U.S.S.R. His answer was to put an end to all multi-party governments behind the Iron Curtain and to replace them with thoroughly communist regimes completely under his control. He also called a meeting of all Communist parties around the world at Warsaw in the autumn of 1947. There they organized the Communist Information Bureau (Cominform), a revival of the old Comintern, dedicated to spreading revolutionary communism throughout the world. The era of the popular front was officially over. Communist leaders in the West who favored friendship, collaboration, and reform were re-

placed by hard-liners who attempted to sabotage the new structures.

In February 1948 a more dramatic and brutal display of Stalin's new policy took place in Prague. The Communists expelled the democratic members of what had been a coalition government and murdered Jan Masaryk, the foreign minister and son of the founder of Czechoslovakia, Thomas Masaryk. President Eduard Beneš (1884–1948) was also forced to resign, and Czechoslovakia was brought fully under Soviet rule.

These Soviet actions, especially those in Czechoslovakia, increased American determination to go ahead with its own arrangements in Germany. The wartime Allies had never agreed on the details of a German settlement and kept putting off decisions. At first they all agreed on the dismemberment of Germany but not on the form it should take. By the time of Yalta, Churchill had come to fear Russian control of eastern and central Europe and began to oppose dismemberment.

There were differences in economic policy, too. The Russians proceeded swiftly to dismantle German industry in the eastern zone, but the Americans acted differently. They concluded that such a policy would require the United States to support Germany for the foreseeable future. It would also cause political chaos and open the way for communism. They preferred, therefore, to try to make Germany self-sufficient, and this meant restoring rather than destroying its industrial capacity. To the Soviets the restoration of a powerful industrial Germany, even in the western zones only, was frightening and unacceptable. The same difference of approach hampered agreement on reparations. The Soviets claimed the right to the industrial equipment in all the zones, and the Americans resisted their demands.

BERLIN BLOCKADE

Disagreement over Germany produced the most heated of postwar debates. When the Western powers agreed to go forward with a separate constitution for the western sectors of Germany in February 1948, the Soviets walked out of the joint Allied Control Commission. In the summer of that year the Western powers issued a new currency in their zone. Berlin, though well within the Soviet zone, was governed by all four powers. The Soviets feared the new currency that was circulating in Berlin at better rates than their

1075

THE ERA O
THE COLI
WAR AND
SUPERPOW
CONFRONTAT

This photo shows the American airlift in action during the Berlin blockade. Every day for almost a year a stream of planes supplied the city until Stalin lifted the blockade in May, 1949. [Bildarchiv Preussischer Kulturbesitz]

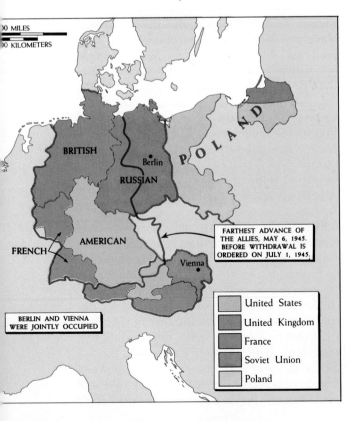

FARTHEST ADVANCE OF THE ALLIES, MAY 6, 1945. BEFORE WITHDRAWAL IS ORDERED ON JULY 1, 1945.

BERLIN AND VIENNA WERE JOINTLY OCCUPIED

United States
United Kingdom
France
Soviet Union
Poland

own. They chose to seal the city off by closing all railroads and highways to West Germany. Their purpose was to drive the Western powers out of Berlin. The Western allies responded to the Berlin Blockade with an airlift of supplies to the city that lasted almost a year. In May 1949 the Russians were forced to back down and to open access to Berlin.

However, the incident was decisive. It greatly increased tensions and suspicions between the opponents, and it hastened the separation of Germany into two states. West Germany formally became the German Federated Republic in September 1949, and the eastern region became the German Democratic Republic a month later. Ironically Germany had been dismembered in a way no one had planned or expected.

NATO and the Warsaw Pact

Meanwhile the nations of western Europe had been coming closer together. The Marshall Plan encouraged international cooperation. Consequently, in March 1948 Belgium, the Netherlands, Luxembourg, France, and Britain signed the Treaty of Brussels, providing for cooperation in economic and military matters. In April 1949 these nations joined with Italy, Denmark, Norway, Portugal, and Iceland to sign a treaty with Canada and the United States that formed the North Atlantic Treaty Organization (NATO). NATO committed its members to mutual assistance in case any of them was attacked. For the first time in history the United States was committed to defend allies outside the Western Hemisphere. The NATO treaty formed the West into a bloc. A few years later West Germany, Greece, and Turkey joined the alliance.

Soviet relations with the states of eastern Europe were governed by a series of bilateral treaties providing for close ties and mutual assistance in case of attack. In 1949 the Coun-

MAP 30-2 OCCUPIED GERMANY AND AUSTRIA *At the war's end, defeated Germany, including Austria, was occupied by the victorious Allies in the several zones shown here. Austria, by prompt agreement, was reerected into an independent, neutral state, no longer occupied. The German zones hardened into an "East" Germany (the former Soviet zone) and a "West" Germany (the former British, French, and American zones). Berlin, within the Soviet zone, was similarly divided.*

MAP 30-3 MAJOR EUROPEAN ALLIANCE SYSTEMS *The North Atlantic Treaty Organization, which includes both Canada and the United States, stretches as far east as Turkey. By contrast, the Warsaw Pact nations were contiguous communist states of eastern Europe, with the Soviet Union, of course, as the dominant member.*

cil of Mutual Assistance (COMECON) was formed to integrate the economies of these states. Unlike the NATO states, the Eastern alliance system was under direct Soviet domination through local Communist parties controlled from Moscow and overawed by the presence of the Red Army. The Warsaw Pact of May 1955, which included Albania, Bulgaria, Czechoslovakia, East Germany, Hungary, Poland, Romania, and the Soviet Union, merely gave formal recognition to a system that already existed. Europe was divided into two unfriendly blocs. The Cold War had taken firm shape in Europe.

The Korean Conflict

While early stages of the Cold War took place in Europe, the United States found itself confronting armed aggression in Asia. As part of a U.N. police action, it intervened militarily in Korea according to the same principles of foreign policy that were informing its actions in Europe.

1078

GLOBAL
ONFLICT,
OLD WAR,
ND NEW
RECTIONS

Between 1910 and 1945, Japan, as an Asian colonial power in its own right, occupied and exploited Korea. By the close of World War II the Japanese had been driven out of the Korean

MAP 30-4 KOREA, 1950–1953 *The North Korean invasion of South Korea in 1950 and the bitter three-year war to repulse the invasion and stabilize a firm boundary near the thirty-eighth parallel are outlined here. The war was a dramatic application of the American policy of "containment" of communism.*

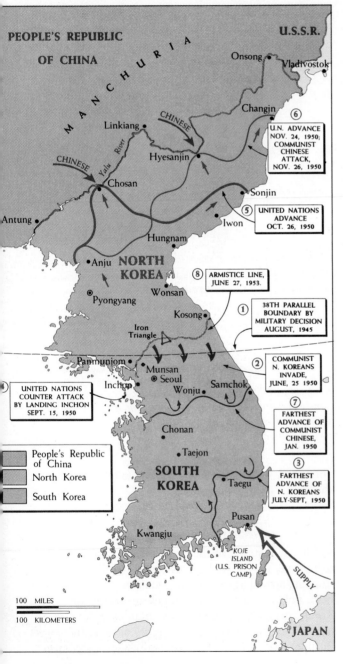

PEOPLE'S REPUBLIC OF CHINA

MANCHURIA

U.S.S.R.

Onsong
Vladivostok

Changjin ⑥

⑥ U.N. ADVANCE NOV. 24, 1950; COMMUNIST CHINESE ATTACK, NOV. 26, 1950

Linkiang
CHINESE
Hyesanjin
CHINESE
Chosan
Antung
Sonjin

⑤ UNITED NATIONS ADVANCE OCT. 26, 1950

Iwon
Hungnam

Anju NORTH KOREA
Pyongyang
Wonsan

⑧ ARMISTICE LINE, JUNE 27, 1953.

Kosong ①

① 38TH PARALLEL BOUNDARY BY MILITARY DECISION AUGUST, 1945

Iron Triangle
Panmunjom
Munsan
Inchon Seoul
Wonju Samchok

② COMMUNIST N. KOREANS INVADE, JUNE, 25 1950

⑦

⑦ FARTHEST ADVANCE OF COMMUNIST CHINESE, JAN. 1950

④ UNITED NATIONS COUNTER ATTACK BY LANDING INCHON SEPT. 15, 1950

Chonan

Taejon

People's Republic of China
North Korea
South Korea

SOUTH KOREA
Taegu

③ FARTHEST ADVANCE OF N. KOREANS JULY-SEPT, 1950

Pusan
Kwangju

KOJE ISLAND (U.S. PRISON CAMP)

SUPPLY

100 MILES
100 KILOMETERS

JAPAN

peninsula. At home, under the direction of the United States, the Japanese nation was politically reconstructed into a democracy. Maintenance of a democratic Japan was to be a cornerstone of postwar United States policy.

The Japanese empire still had to be dealt with. Consequently, the United States and the Soviet Union presided over the division of Korea into two parts with the thirty-eighth parallel as the line of separation. It was anticipated that the country would eventually be reunited. However, by 1948 two separate states had been organized: the Democratic People's Republic of Korea under Kim Il Sung in the north and the Republic of Korea under Syngman Rhee in the south. The former was supported by the Soviet Union and the latter by the United States.

Numerous border clashes occurred between the two states. In late June 1950 forces from North Korea invaded across the thirty-eighth parallel. The United States intervened and was soon supported by a mandate of the United Nations. Great Britain, Turkey, and Australia sent token forces. The troops were commanded by General Douglas MacArthur (1880–1964). The Korean police action was technically a United Nations venture to halt aggression. (It had been made possible by a boycott by the Soviet ambassador to the United Nations at the time of the key vote.) From the standpoint of the United States the point of the Korean conflict was to contain the spread and to halt the aggression of communism. The United States policymakers tended to conceive of the communist world as a single unit directed from Moscow. The movement of forces into South Korea was, in their view, simply another example of communist pressure against a noncommunist state similar to that previously confronted in Europe.

General MacArthur's forces had initially repelled the North Koreans. He then pushed them almost to Manchuria. Late in 1950, however, the Chinese, responding to the pressure against their border, sent troops to support North Korea. The American forces had to retreat. The United States policymakers believed that the Chinese, who since 1949 had been under the Communist government of Mao Tse-tung (1893–1976), were simply the puppets of Moscow. For over two years the war bogged down. Eventually a border near the thirty-eighth parallel was restored. The war lasted until June 16, 1953, when an armistice was signed.

In Korea limited military action had halted and contained the military advance of a communist nation. The lessons of the Cold War learned in Europe appeared to have been successfully applied to Asia. The American government was confirmed in its faith in a policy of containment.

The onset of the Cold War in Europe and the hardening of the rivalry between the United States and the Soviet Union provided a major backdrop for the domestic political development of both nations.

The American Domestic Scene since World War II

Three major themes have characterized the postwar American experience. These have been opposition to any further spread of communism, expansion of civil rights to blacks and other minorities at home, and determination to achieve ongoing economic growth. Virtually all of the major postwar political debates and social divisions arose from one or more of these issues.

The Truman and Eisenhower Administrations

As explained in the previous section, the foreign policy of President Harry Truman was directed against communist expansion in Europe through the enunciation of the Truman Doctrine and the implementation of the Marshall Plan. He also led the United States to support the United Nations intervention against aggression in Korea. Domestically the Truman administration, under the term *Fair Deal*, pursued what may be regarded as a continuation of the *New Deal* policies of Franklin Roosevelt; these expanded the role of the federal government in the economy.

However, those efforts became frustrated as fear of a domestic communist menace swept

MAJOR DATES OF EARLY COLD WAR CONFRONTATION	
1945	Yalta Conference
1945	Founding of the United Nations
1946	Churchill's Iron Curtain speech
1947	(March) Truman Doctrine regarding Greece and Turkey
1947	(June) Announcement of Marshall Plan
1948	Communist takeover in Czechoslovakia
1948	Communist takeover in Hungary
1948–1949	Berlin Blockade
1949	NATO founded
1949	East and West Germany emerge as separate states
1950–1953	Korean Conflict
1955	Warsaw Pact founded

President Dwight Eisenhower of the United States and Premier Nikita Khrushchev of the Soviet Union were the two dominant world leaders during the late 1950s. [U.S. Navy Photo from the Eisenhower Library]

1080

GLOBAL
CONFLICT,
COLD WAR,
AND NEW
DIRECTIONS

much of the country in the early 1950s. Senator Joseph McCarthy of Wisconsin led the campaign against a perceived communist danger said to exist within the ranks of American citizens and within agencies of the government. The patriotism and loyalty of scores of prominent Americans came under public scrutiny and question. That development, frustration with the war in Korea, and perhaps the natural weariness of the electorate after twenty years of Democratic Party government led to the election of war hero Dwight Eisenhower in 1952.

In retrospect the Eisenhower years have come to seem a period of calm after the war years of the 1940s and before the turmoil of the 1960s. Eisenhower, personally popular, brought the Korean War to a conclusion. The country was generally prosperous. Homebuilding increased dramatically, and the vast interstate highway system was initiated. He was by design a less activist president than either Roosevelt or Truman.

Beneath the apparent quiet of the Eisenhower years there stirred several forces that would lead to the disruptions of the 1960s. For example, during the Eisenhower administration major foreign policy commitments were made throughout the world to oppose the advance of communism. It was the honoring of those commitments that led to the American involvement in Vietnam. Indeed that involvement began under Eisenhower.

Another key event in the Eisenhower years was the Cuban Revolution. The establishment of a Communist government in Cuba so near to the shores of the United States became a major factor in both domestic politics and foreign policy.

The Cuban Revolution

Cuba had remained a colony of Spain until the Spanish-American War of 1898. Thereafter, it achieved independence within a sphere of U.S. influence, which took the form of economic domination and occasional military intervention. The fluctuating governments of the island had been both ineffective and corrupt. During the 1950s, Fulgencio Batista (1901–1973), a dictator supported by the U.S. government, ruled Cuba.

Over the decades, there had been much political unrest in Cuba. During the 1940s, vari-

Fidel Castro's successful achievement of power in Cuba brought the tensions of the Cold War very near to the shores of the United States. [Elliot Erwitt © Magnum Photos, Inc.]

ous university student groups led antigovernment agitation. Among the students thus politicized in those years was Fidel Castro Ruz (b. 1926), the son of a wealthy landowner. On July 26, 1953, he and others unsuccessfully attacked a government army barracks. The revolutionary movement that he came to lead in exile took its name from that date: the Twenty-sixth of July Movement. In 1956, Castro and a handful of followers set sail on a yacht from Mexico and landed in Cuba. They took refuge in the Sierra Maestra mountains, from which they organized guerilla attacks on Batista's government and supporters. By late 1958, Castro's forces were in a position to topple Batista, who fled Cuba on New Year's Day in 1959. By the middle of the month, Castro had arrived in Havana as the revolutionary victor.

Castro undertook the most extensive political, economic, and social reconstruction seen in recent Latin American history. He rejected parliamentary democracy and chose to govern

Cuba in an authoritarian manner. For approximately the first decade of the revolution, he ruled in a very personal manner; by the early 1970s, though Castro continued to dominate, executive power was vested in a council. The revolutionary government carried out major land redistribution. In some cases, groups of relatively small landowners were established. On other parts of the island, large state farms became the model.

In foreign affairs, the Cuban Revolution was characterized by a sharp break with the United States and a close relationship with the Soviet Union. Very shortly after achieving power, Castro aligned himself with the Cuban Communist Party and thereafter with the Soviet bloc. The United States, under both Republican and Democratic administrations, pursued a policy of hostility toward Castro and toward the presence of a communist state less than a

108

The Era
the Co
War an
Superpov
Confront

Castro Asserts the Necessary Marxist Character of Revolution

In a speech delivered at the University of Havana in 1967 Fidel Castro discussed the relationship of Cuban revolutionaries to the wider Marxist ideology. His fervent Marxism and the use of Cuba as a base for exporting Marxist revolution into other parts of Latin America made Castro one of the major concerns of the United States foreign policy from the late 1950s onward.

Anyone can give himself the name of "eagle" without having a single feather on his back. In the same way, there are people who call themselves communists without having a communist hair on their heads. The international communist movement, to our way of thinking, is not a church. It is not a religious sect or a Masonic lodge that obliges us to hallow any weakness, any deviation; that obliges us to follow a policy of a mutual admiration with all kinds of reformists and pseudo-revolutionaries.

Our stand regarding communist parties will be based on strictly revolutionary principles. The parties that have a line without hesitations and capitulationism, the parties that in our opinion have a consistent revolutionary line, will receive our support in all circumstances; but the parties that entrench themselves behind the name of communists or Marxists and believe themselves to have a monopoly on revolutionary sentiment—what they really monopolize is reformism—will not be treated by us as revolutionary par-

ties. . . . For every true revolutionary, who bears within him the revolutionary spirit, revolutionary vocation, will always come to Marxism! It is impossible for a man, traveling the road of revolution, not to arrive at Marxism! And every revolutionary on the continent who is deserving of the name will arrive at the Marxist conception of society! What is important are the revolutionaries, those who are capable of making revolution and developing themselves in revolutionary theory.

Many times practice comes first and then theory. Our people too, are an example of that. Many, the immense majority of those who today proudly call themselves Marxist-Leninists, arrived at Marxism-Leninism by way of the revolutionary struggle. To exclude, to deny, to reject a priori all those who from the beginning did not call themselves communists is an act of dogmatism and unqualified sectarianism. Whoever denies that it is the road of revolution which leads the people to Marxism is no Marxist, although he may call himself a communist.

Martin Kenner and James Petras, Fidel Castro Speaks *(New York: Grove Press, 1969), p. 131.*

1082

GLOBAL
CONFLICT,
COLD WAR,
AND NEW
DIRECTIONS

hundred miles from the Florida mainland. In 1961, the United States and Cuban exiles launched the unsuccessful Bay of Pigs invasion. The close Cuban relationship to the Soviet Union prepared the ground for the missile crisis of 1962, which will be discussed later in this chapter. Thereafter followed about a decade of cool relations without overt acts of hostility. During the late 1970s and the 1980s, a dialogue of sorts was undertaken between Cuba and the United States, but formal diplomatic relations have not resumed. An atmosphere of mutual distrust continues.

Perhaps more important, ever since 1959, Cuba has served as a center for the export of communist revolution throughout Latin America, and—in the case of the sending of Cuban troops to Angola in the late 1970s—in Africa as well. A key policy of the U.S. government, pursued with differing intensities and strategies under different administrations, has been to prevent the establishment of a second Communist-dominated state in Latin America. That goal has led to direct and indirect intervention in other revolutionary situations and to support for authoritarian governments in Latin America dedicated to resistance to Marxist revolution.

Civil Rights

In 1954 the United States Supreme Court in the decision of *Brown v. Board of Education of Topeka* declared segregation of the black and white races unconstitutional and ordered the desegregation of schools. For the next ten years the struggle over school integration and civil rights for black Americans in general stirred the nation. Various southern states attempted to resist school desegregation. In 1957 Eisenhower sent troops into Little Rock, Arkansas to integrate the schools, but resistance continued to appear in various forms in other southern states.

While the battle raged over the schools, an awakened civil rights movement among American blacks began to protest segregation in other areas of national life. In 1955 Rev. Martin Luther King, Jr. organized a boycott against segregated buses in Montgomery, Alabama. The Montgomery bus boycott marked the beginning of the use of civil disobedience to fight racial discrimination in the United States. Drawing upon the ideas of the American Henry David Thoreau and the experience of Gandhi in India, the leaders of the civil rights movement went to jail rather than obey laws they believed to be unjust. The civil rights struggle continued well into the 1960s. One of its most dramatic moments was the march in 1963 on Washington by tens of thousands of supporters of civil rights legislation.

The greatest achievements of the movement were the passage of the Civil Rights Act of 1964, which desegregated public accommodations, and the Voting Rights Act of 1965, which cleared the way for large numbers of blacks to vote. The results of that legislation as well as ongoing protests in areas of housing and job discrimination brought black Americans nearer to the mainstream of American life than ever before.

However, much yet remained to be done. In 1967 major race riots occurred in several American cities with significant loss of life. Those riots followed by the assassination of Martin Luther King, Jr. in 1968 greatly weakened the civil rights movement. Despite new

Rev. Martin Luther King stood as the foremost civil rights leader in the United States. His tactic of nonviolent resistance mobilized thousands of black Americans to demand an end to segregation. [Library of Congress]

1083

THE ERA (
THE COLI
WAR ANI
SUPERPOW
CONFRONTA

The United States Supreme Court Declares Segregation Unconstitutional

In 1954, the United States Supreme Court in Brown v. the School Board of Topeka reversed the decisions of Plessy v. Ferguson of 1896. The Court declared that separate facilities were inherently unequal. This decision was one of the major sparks to the Civil Rights Movement of the 1950s and 1960s.

In approaching this problem, we cannot turn the clock back to 1868 when the [Fourteenth] Amendment was adopted, or even to 1896 when *Plessy v. Ferguson* was written. We must consider public education in the light of its full development and its present place in American life throughout the Nation. Only in this way can it be determined if segregation in public schools deprives these plaintiffs of the equal protection of the laws.

Today, education is perhaps the most important function of state and local governments. Compulsory school attendance laws and the great expenditures for education both demonstrate our recognition of the importance of education to our democratic society. It is required in the performance of our most basic public responsibilities, even service in the armed forces. It is the very foundation of good citizenship. Today it is a principal instrument in awak-

ening the child to cultural values, in preparing him for later professional training, and in helping him to adjust normally to his environment. In these days, it is doubtful that any child may reasonably be expected to succeed in life if he is denied the opportunity of an education. Such an opportunity where the state has undertaken to provide it, is a right which must be made available to all on equal terms.

We come to the question presented: Does segregation of children in public schools solely on the basis of race, even though the physical facilities and other "tangible" factors may be equal, deprive the children of the minority group of equal educational opportunities? We believe that it does. . . .

We conclude that in the field of public education the doctrine of "separate but equal" has no place. Separate educational facilities are inherently unequal.

Brown v. Board of Education of Topeka, 1954, *as quoted in Henry Steel Commager,* Documents of American History, *8th ed. (New York: Appleton-Century-Crofts, 1968), 2: 607–608.*

efforts to fight discrimination, a major national leader of the civil rights movement was missing. Not until the late 1980s did a new leader emerge in the person of the Rev. Jesse Jackson, who actively contested the Democratic Party nomination for the presidency.

New Social Programs

The advance of the civil rights movement in the late 1950s and early 1960s represented the cutting edge of a new advance of political liberalism. In 1960 John F. Kennedy narrowly won the presidential election. He saw himself as

attempting to set the country moving again after the years of Eisenhower calm and defined his goals as seeking to move toward a *New Frontier.* For example, he set the goal of the United States putting a man on the moon. He also attempted unsuccessfully to expand medical care under the social security program. In terms of the civil rights movement he basically reacted rather than led.

However, the reaction to Kennedy's assassination in 1963 provided the occasion for his successor Lyndon Johnson to press for activist legislation. In order to fulfill Kennedy's programs and to launch those of his own, Johnson

1084

GLOBAL
CONFLICT,
COLD WAR,
AND NEW
DIRECTIONS

pushed through Congress the Civil Rights Act of 1964 and the tax cut of that year. Johnson then set forth a bold domestic program known as the War on Poverty that established major federal programs to create jobs and to provide job training. Furthermore, new entitlements were added to the social security program, including Medicare. Johnson's drive for what he termed the *Great Society* may be seen as the close of the era of major federal government initiatives that had commenced under Franklin Roosevelt. The liberal impulse remained alive in American politics, but by the late sixties it can now be seen that the electorate had commenced a move toward a much more conservative stance.

The Vietnam War and Domestic Turmoil

Johnson's activist domestic vision was very quickly wrecked on the rock of the U.S. involvement in Vietnam, which will be considered more fully later in this chapter. By 1965 Johnson had made the decision to send tens of thousands of Americans to Vietnam. This policy led to the longest of American wars. At home the Vietnam involvement resulted in vast public protests over the war and more particularly over the draft. The overwhelming majority of young American men who were drafted went into the armed forces. However, very significant numbers resisted the draft. Large-scale protests involving civil disobedience, often patterned after those of the civil rights movements, erupted on college and university campuses. In some cases units of the national guard were sent to restore calm. In the case of Kent State University in Ohio in 1970 protesters were killed. The Vietnam War divided the nation as had no conflict since the Civil War.

The national unrest led Lyndon Johnson to decide against seeking reelection in 1968. Richard Nixon led the Republicans to victory. His election may be seen as marking the beginning of an era of American politics dominated by conservative policies, though some might say the nomination of Senator Barry Goldwater by the Republicans in 1964 marked that beginning. Nixon pressed his campaign on a platform of law and order. He also stressed his experience in foreign policy. In that regard, perhaps the most important act of Nixon's administration was his reestablishment of relations with the People's Republic of China after a quarter century of no diplomatic relations between the two nations. Initially, his

The clash between protesting students and the Ohio National Guard at Kent State University was the most violent moment in the protests against the United States involvement in Vietnam. [Kent State University News Service]

policies toward Vietnam were no more successful than those of Johnson. Half of the war casualties occurred under his administration. Nonetheless, he concluded the war in 1972. That same year Nixon was reelected. Very soon thereafter the Watergate Scandal began to unfold.

The Watergate Scandal

On the surface the Watergate scandal involved a burglary of the Democratic Party National headquarters at the Watergate Hotel by White House operatives. The deeper issues related to questions of the extent of presidential authority and the right of the government to intrude into the personal lives of citizens. In 1973 Congress established a committee to investigate the scandal. Testimony before that committee revealed that President Nixon had recorded large numbers of conversations in the White House. The special prosecutor, who had been appointed to investigate the charges, finally gained access to the tapes in the summer of 1974 through a decision of the Supreme Court. In the meantime, the Judiciary Committee of the House of Representatives voted three articles of impeachment against Nixon. Shortly thereafter certain of the newly released tapes revealed that Nixon had ordered federal agencies to try to cover up the participation of the White House in the burglary. After this revelation, Nixon became the only president in American history to resign the presidency.

The Watergate Scandal further shook public confidence in the government. It had also proved a remarkable distraction from the major problems facing the country. One of the chief of these was inflation, which had resulted from fighting the war in Vietnam while pursuing the expansion of federal domestic expenditures under Johnson. The subsequent administrations of Gerald Ford (1974–1977) and Jimmy Carter (1977–1981) battled the inflation and high interest rates without any significant success. Furthermore, the Carter administration became bogged down in the Iran hostage crisis of 1980 when more than forty American Embassy personnel were held hostage in Iran for over a year.

The Reagan Presidency

In 1980, Ronald Reagan (b. 1911) was elected president by a large majority. He was reelected four years later. Reagan was the first ideological conservative to be elected in the postwar era. His goals were relatively straightforward. In foreign policy, he took a tough line toward the Soviet Union and vastly increased defense spending. For all eight years of his administration, he also sought to contain the Sandinistas in Nicaragua. At the same time, he had concluded a major missile reduction treaty with the Soviet Union by the end of his second term.

In domestic policy, Reagan sought to reduce the role of the federal government in American life. The chief vehicle to this end was a major tax cut and reform of the taxation system. The consequence of the defense spending and the tax policy was the accumulation of the largest fiscal deficit in American history. However, in the process the inflation came under control and the economy experienced its longest peacetime expansion in American history.

The straightforward conservatism of the Reagan administration proved offensive to numerous groups of Americans who had traditionally supported a liberal political and social

1085

THE ERA
THE COL
WAR AN
SUPERPOW
CONFRONTA

MAJOR DATES IN U.S. HISTORY SINCE 1945	
1945–1953	Truman presidency
1953–1961	Eisenhower presidency
1953	*Brown v. Board of Education of Topeka*
1955	Montgomery Bus Boycott
1958	Cuban Revolution
1961–1963	Kennedy presidency
1961	Unsuccessful Bay of Pigs Invasion
1963	Kennedy assassination
1963–1969	Johnson presidency
1964	Civil Rights Act
1968	Martin Luther King assassination
1969	First U.S. landing on the moon
1969–1974	Nixon presidency
1970	Shootings of students at Kent State
1970	Nixon reestablishes relations with China
1972–1974	Watergate Scandal
1974	Nixon resignation
1974–1977	Ford presidency
1977–1981	Carter presidency
1979–1981	Iran Hostage crises
1981–1989	Reagan presidency
1990	Mobilization in the Persian Gulf

1086

GLOBAL
CONFLICT,
COLD WAR,
AND NEW
DIRECTIONS

This 1988 meeting of President Ronald Reagan, Vice-President Bush, and President Gorbachev symbolized the new co-operative relationship that has begun to develop between the United States and the Soviet Union. [Photo: Jean Louis Atlan/Sygma]

agenda. It was regarded as being hostile to blacks and to the expansion of rights for women. A number of scandals took place that involved directly or indirectly some high administration officials. The most important of these scandals surrounded the sale of military arms to Iran in exchange for the release of American hostages being held in Lebanon. Despite all of these difficulties during his second term, Reagan left office as probably the most popular and successful of the post-World War II American presidents.

In 1988 Vice President George Bush was elected to succeed Reagan. He was immediately confronted by the major changes that Gorbachev was carrying out in the Soviet Union and the extraordinary transformations that occurred in Eastern Europe, discussed in the next chapter. Bush worked to keep the NATO alliance in an ongoing close relationship to the United States at a time when observers had begun to question its utility. In 1989 he sent troops into Panama to oust the Panamanian dictator, Manuel Noriega. In the summer of 1990 in response to the invasion of

Kuwait by Iraq, discussed later in this chapter, he commenced the largest mobilization of American troops since the Vietnam War. In this latter instance he worked closely with the United Nations to forge a collective response to the Iraqi aggression.

All of these domestic developments provided the backdrop for the American rivalry with the Soviet Union. General opposition to the expansion of communist governments first unfolded itself in Europe but then manifested itself in American opposition to the spread of communism in Asia and Latin America.

The Soviet Union during the Cold War

During the 1930s and 1940s Stalin had placed his mark and control on virtually every aspect of Soviet politics, life, and culture. With his death in 1953 the Soviet system had to deal with his legacy. For a time there was a moderate relaxation of control under Nikita Khrushchev. Then from the mid-sixties through the mid-eighties a fully authoritarian political structure dominated the Soviet Union.

The Last Years of Stalin

Many Russians had hoped that the end of World War II would signal a lessening of Stalinism. No other nation had suffered greater losses or more deprivation than the Soviet Union. Its people anticipated some immediate reward for their sacrifice and heroism. They desired a reduction in the scope of the police state and a redirection of the economy away from heavy industry to consumer products. They were disappointed. Stalin did little or nothing to modify the character of the regime he had created. The police remained ever-present. The cult of personality expanded, and

the central bureaucracy continued to grow. Heavy industry was still favored over production for consumers. Agriculture continued to be troubled. Stalin's personal authority over the party and the nation remained unchallenged.

In foreign policy, Stalin moved to solidify Soviet control over eastern Europe for the purposes of both communist expansion and Soviet national security. He attempted to impose the Soviet model on those nations. The Cold War stance of the United States simply served to confirm Stalin in his ways.

By late 1952 and early 1953 it appeared that Stalin might be ready to unloose a new series of purges. In January 1953 a group of Jewish physicians was arrested and charged with plotting the deaths of important leaders. Charges of extensive conspiracy appeared in the press. All of these developments were similar to the

1087

THE ERA
THE COL
WAR AN
SUPERPOW
CONFRONTA

By the late 1930s the cult of Stalin was an ever-present fact of Soviet life. Even at beach resorts his picture was always near. In this 1950 photograph swimmers in the Black Sea carry large pictures of him on small rafts. Note the warships in the background. [Sovfoto]

1088

GLOBAL
CONFLICT,
COLD WAR,
AND NEW
DIRECTIONS

events that had preceded the purges of the 1930s. Then, quite suddenly, in the midst of this new furor, on March 6, 1953, Stalin died.

For a time no single leader replaced Stalin. Rather the Presidium (the renamed Politburo) pursued a policy of collective leadership. Gradually, however, power and influence began to devolve on Nikita Khrushchev (1894–1971), who in 1953 had been named party secretary. Three years later Khrushchev himself became premier. His rise constituted the end of collective leadership, but at no time did he enjoy the extraordinary powers of Stalin.

The Rise and Fall of Khrushchev

The Khrushchev era, which lasted until the autumn of 1964, witnessed a marked retreat from Stalinism, though not from extreme authoritarianism. Indeed, the political repression of Stalin had been so extensive that there was considerable room for relaxation of surveil-

lance within the limits of tyranny. Politically the demise of Stalinism meant shifts in leadership and party structure by means other than purges.

In 1956, at the Twentieth Congress of the Communist Party, Khrushchev made a secret speech (later published outside the Soviet Union) in which he denounced Stalin and his crimes against socialist justice during the purges of the 1930s. The speech caused shock and consternation in party circles and opened the way for limited, but genuine, internal criticism of the Soviet government. Gradually the strongest supporters of Stalinist policies were removed from the Presidium. By 1958 all of Stalin's former supporters were gone, but none had been executed.

INTELLECTUAL LIFE Under Khrushchev, intellectuals were somewhat more free to express their opinions. This so-called thaw in the cultural life of the country was closely related to the premier's interest in the opinions of experts on problems of industry and agriculture. He often went outside the usual bureaucratic channels in search of information and new ideas. Novels such as Aleksandr Solzhenitsyn's (b. 1918) *One Day in the Life of Ivan Denisovich* (1963) could be published. However, Boris Pasternak (1890–1960), the author of *Dr. Zhivago*, was not permitted to accept the Nobel prize for literature in 1958. The intellectual liberalization of Soviet life during this period should not be overestimated. It looked favorable only in comparison with what had preceded it and continued to seem so because of the decline of such freedom of expression after Khrushchev's fall.

ECONOMIC EXPERIMENTS The economic policy also somewhat departed from the strict Stalinist mode. By 1953 the economy had recovered from the strains and destruction of the war, but consumer goods and housing still remained in very short supply. The problem of an adequate food supply also continued. Malenkov had favored improvements in meeting the demand for consumer goods; Khru-

In 1957 the Soviet Union launched its first satellite, Sputnik, into space. The achievement shocked American public opinion and eventually led to the American commitment to land on the moon. [Sovfoto]

1089

THE ERA (
THE COLI
WAR AND
SUPERPOWI
CONFRONTAT

Khrushchev Denounces the Crimes of Stalin: The Secret Speech

In 1956 Khrushchev denounced Stalin in a secret speech to the Party Congress. The New York Times *published a text of that speech smuggled from Russia.*

Stalin acted not through persuasion, explanation, and patient cooperation with people, but by imposing his concepts and demanding absolute submission to his opinion. Whoever opposed this concept or tried to prove his viewpoint and the correctness of his position was doomed to removal from the leading collective [group] and to subsequent moral and physical annihilation. . . .

Stalin originated the concept of "enemy of the people." This term automatically rendered it unnecessary that the ideological errors of a man or men engaged in a controversy be proved; this term made possible the usage of the most cruel repression violating all norms of revolutionary legality, against anyone who in any way disagreed with Stalin, against those who were only suspected of hostile intent, against those who had bad reputations.

This concept "enemy of the people" actually eliminated the possibility of any kind of ideological fight or the making of one's views known on this or that issue, even those of a practical character. In the main, and in actuality, the only proof of guilt used, against all norms of current legal science, was the "confession" of the accused himself; and, as a subsequent probing proved, "confessions" were acquired through physical pressures against the accused. . . .

Lenin used severe methods only in the most necessary cases, when the exploiting classes were still in existence and were vigorously opposing the revolution, when the struggle for survival was decidedly assuming the sharpest forms, even including civil war.

Stalin, on the other hand, used extreme methods and mass repressions at a time when the revolution was already victorious, when the Soviet State was strengthened, when the exploiting classes were already liquidated and Socialist relations were rooted solidly in all phases of national economy, when our party was politically consolidated and had strengthened itself both numerically and ideologically. It is clear that here Stalin showed in a whole series of cases his intolerance, his brutality and his abuse of power. Instead of proving his political correctness and mobilizing the masses, he often chose the path of repression and physical annihilation, not only against actual enemies, but also against individuals who had not committed any crimes against the party and the Soviet Government. . . .

The New York Times, June 5, 1956, pp. 13–16.

shchev also favored such a departure. Khrushchev also moved in a moderate fashion to decentralize economic planning and execution. During the late 1950s he often boasted that Soviet production of consumer goods would overtake that of the West. Steel, oil, and electric-power production continued to grow, but the consumer sector improved only marginally.

However, the ever-growing defense budget and the space program that successfully launched the first human-engineered satellite of the earth, *Sputnik*, in 1957 made major demands on the nation's productive resources. Economically Khrushchev was attempting to move the country in too many directions at once.

Khrushchev strongly redirected Stalin's agri-

1090

GLOBAL
CONFLICT,
COLD WAR,
AND NEW
DIRECTIONS

cultural policy. He recognized that in spite of the collectivation of the 1930s the Soviet Union had not produced an agricultural system capable of feeding its own people. Administratively Khrushchev removed many of the most restrictive regulations on private cultivation. The machine tractor stations were abandoned. Existing collective farms were further amalgamated. The government undertook an extensive "virgin lands" program to extend wheat cultivation by hundreds of thousands of acres. This policy initially increased grain production to new records. However, in a very few years the new lands became subject to erosion. The farming techniques applied had been inappropriate for the soil. The agricultural problem has simply continued to grow. Currently the Soviet Union imports vast quantities of grain from the United States and other countries. United States grain imports have constituted a major facet of the policy of detente.

FOREIGN POLICY Adventuresomeness also characterized Khrushchev's foreign policy. In 1956 the Soviet Union adopted the phrase "peaceful coexistence" in regard to its relationship with the United States. The policy implied no less competition with the capitalist world but suggested that war might not be the best way to pursue communist expansion. The previous year Khrushchev had participated in the Geneva summit meeting alongside Bulganin. Thereafter followed visits around the world, culminating with one to the United States in 1959.

By the early 1960s it had become clear that Khrushchev had made few inroads on Western policy. He was under increasing domestic pressure and also pressure from the Chinese. The militancy of the denunciation of the U-2 flight, the aborting of the Paris summit meeting, the Berlin Wall, and the Cuban Missile Crisis were all responses to those pressures. The last of these adventures brought a clear Soviet retreat.

By 1964 numerous high Russian leaders and many people lower in the party had concluded that Khrushchev had tried to do too much too soon and had done it too poorly. On October 16, 1964, after defeat in the Central Committee of the Communist Party, Khrushchev resigned. He was replaced by Alexei Kosygin (1904–1980) as premier and Leonid Brezhnev (1906–1982) as party secretary. The latter eventually emerged as the dominant figure. In 1977 the constitution of the Soviet Union was

changed to combine the offices of president and party secretary. Brezhnev became president, and thus head of the state as well as of the party. He held more personal power than any Soviet leader since Stalin.

The Brezhnev Era

Domestically the Soviet government became markedly more repressive after 1964. All intellectuals enjoyed less and less freedom and little direct access to the government leadership. In 1974 the government expelled novelist Aleksandr Solzhenitsyn. Furthermore, Jewish citizens of the Soviet Union became subject to harassment. Major bureaucratic obstacles were placed in the way of the emigration of Soviet Jews to Israel. These policies suggested a return to the limitations of the Stalinist period.

DISSIDENTS The internal repression gave rise to a dissident movement. Certain Soviet citizens dared to criticize the regime in public and to carry out small demonstrations against the government. They accused the Soviet government of violating the human rights provision of the 1975 Helsinki Accords. The dissidents included a number of prominent citizens, such as the Nobel Prize physicist Andrei Sakharov. The response of the Soviet government was further repression.

In foreign policy the Brezhnev years witnessed attempts to reach accommodation with the United States. Simultaneously they continued to press for expanded Soviet influence and further attempts to maintain Soviet leadership of the communist movement. During the Vietnam war the Soviet Union pursued a policy of restrained support for North Vietnam. Under President Richard Nixon, the United States pursued a policy of detente based on arms limitation and trade agreements. Nonetheless, Soviet spending on defense, and particularly on naval expansion, continued to grow and harmed the consumer sectors of the Soviet economy.

INVASION OF AFGHANISTAN More important in leading to a new cooling of relations between the superpowers was the Soviet invasion of Afghanistan in December 1979. A Soviet presence had already existed in that country. But for reasons that still remain unclear the Soviet government felt that it was required to send in troops to ensure its influ-

Anti-Soviet freedom fighters in Afghanistan were active during the 1980s. From 1979 to 1988 the Soviet army was bogged down there in a bloody and expensive guerrilla war in an effort to prop up a puppet communist regime. [Raymond Deparon/Sygma]

1091

THE ERA
THE COL
WAR AN
SUPERPOW
CONFRONTA

ence in central Asia. The invasion brought a grain embargo on the part of the United States and a U.S. boycott of the 1980 Moscow Olympic games. It also dashed U.S. Senate ratification of the arms limitation treaty signed by President Carter and President Brezhnev in 1979. The commitment of forces in Afghanistan also proved to be a domestically unpopular move within the Soviet Union.

By the time of Brezhnev's death in 1982 the entire Soviet system appeared to both internal and external observers as extremely rigidified and less than capable of meeting the needs of its people or pursuing a successful foreign policy. This situation provided the background for the remarkable changes that would be undertaken a few years later by Mikhail S. Gorbachev (to be discussed in the next chapter).

Europe and the Soviet–American Rivalry

The first round of Cold War confrontation had culminated in the formation of NATO (1949) and the intervention of the United States and

United Nations forces in Korea (1950). The death of Stalin in 1953 and the armistice concluded in Korea later the same year produced hope that international tensions might lessen. In early 1955 Austria agreed to become a neutral state and Soviet occupation forces left.

Later that year the leaders of France, Great Britain, the Soviet Union, and the United

MAJOR DATES IN SOVIET HISTORY 1945–1985

1953	Death of Stalin
1956	Concept of peaceful coexistence announced
1958–1964	Khrushchev Era
1956	Khrushchev denounces Stalin
1956	Uprising in Hungary
1957	*Sputnik* launched
1959	Khrushchev visit to the United States
1960	Khrushchev aborts Geneva Summit
1961	Soviet Union erects Berlin Wall
1964	Khrushchev falls from power
1964–1982	Brezhnev era
1974	Solzhenitsyn expelled
1979	Afghanistan invaded

1092

GLOBAL
CONFLICT,
OLD WAR,
ND NEW
IRECTIONS

States held a summit conference at Geneva. Nuclear weapons and the future of divided Germany were the chief items on the agenda. Although there was much public display of friendliness among the participants, there were few substantial agreements on major problems. Nonetheless, the fact that world leaders were discussing problems and issues produced the so-called spirit of Geneva. This atmosphere proved to be short-lived, and the rivalry of power and polemics soon resumed.

The Crises of 1956

The year 1956 was one of considerable significance for both the Cold War and the recognition of the realities of European power in the postwar era. Great Britain and France intervened ineffectively in the Middle East. The Soviet Union confronted major political crises in Poland and Hungary. In the latter case the Soviets used troops to crush a popular revolt against Communist Party domination.

SUEZ In July President Gamal Abdel Nasser (1918–1970) of Egypt nationalized the Suez Canal. Great Britain and France feared that this action would close the canal to their sup-

plies of oil in the Persian Gulf. In October 1956 war broke out between Egypt and the eight-year-old state of Israel (for a discussion of the formation of Israel, see the section later in this chapter titled "The Arab–Israeli Conflict"). The British and the French seized the opportunity of this conflict to intervene. Publicly they spoke of acting to separate the combatants, but their real motive was to recapture the canal. The Anglo-French military operation was a fiasco of the first order that resulted in a humiliating diplomatic defeat. The United States refused to support the Anglo-French action. The Soviet Union protested in the most severe terms. The Anglo-French forces had to be withdrawn, and control of the canal remained with Egypt.

The Suez intervention proved that without the support of the United States the nations of western Europe could no longer undertake meaningful military operations. They could no longer impose their will on the rest of the world. At the same time it appeared that the United States and the Soviet Union had acted to restrain their allies from undertaking actions that might result in a wider conflict. The fact that neither of the superpowers wanted war put limitations on the actions of both Egypt and the Anglo-French forces.

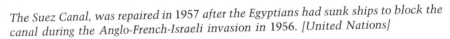

The Suez Canal, was repaired in 1957 after the Egyptians had sunk ships to block the canal during the Anglo-French-Israeli invasion in 1956. [United Nations]

In Budapest in October 1956, street battles raged for several days until Soviet tanks finally put down the Hungarian revolt. [Raymond Darolle/Sygma]

POLAND The autumn of 1956 also saw important developments in eastern Europe. These demonstrated in a similar fashion the limitations on independent action among the Soviet bloc nations. When the prime minister of Poland died, the Polish Communist Party leaders refused to choose as his successor the person selected by Moscow. Considerable tension developed. The Soviet leaders even visited Warsaw to make their opinions known. In the end, Wladyslaw Gomulka (1905–1982) emerged as the new Communist leader of Poland. He was the choice of the Poles. He also proved acceptable to the Soviets because he promised continued economic and military cooperation and most particularly continued Polish membership in the Warsaw Pact. Within those limits he moved to halt the collectivation of Polish agriculture and to improve the relationship between the Commu-

nist government and the Polish Roman Catholic Church.

UPRISING IN HUNGARY Hungary provided the second trouble spot for the Soviet Union. In late October, as the Polish problem was approaching a solution, demonstrations of sympathy for the Polish people occurred in Budapest. The Communist government moved to stop the demonstrations, and street fighting erupted. A new ministry headed by former premier Imre Nagy (1896–1958) was installed by the Hungarian Communist Party.

Nagy was a Communist who sought a more independent position for Hungary. He went much further in his demands than had Gomulka in Poland, and Nagy made direct appeals for political support from non-Communist groups in Hungary. Nagy called for the removal of Soviet troops and the ultimate neu-

1094

GLOBAL
CONFLICT,
COLD WAR,
AND NEW
DIRECTIONS

tralization of Hungary. He even went so far as to call for Hungarian withdrawal from the Warsaw Pact. These demands were wholly unacceptable to the Soviet Union. In early November Soviet troops invaded the country; deposed Nagy, who was later executed; and imposed Janos Kadar (b. 1912) as premier.

The Suez intervention had provided an international diversion that helped to permit free action with the Soviet Union. The Polish and Hungarian disturbances had several results. They demonstrated the limitations of independence within the Soviet bloc, but they did not bring an end to independent action. They also demonstrated that the example of Austrian neutrality would not be imitated elsewhere in eastern Europe. Finally, the failure of the United States to take any action in the Hungarian uprising demonstrated the hollowness of American political rhetoric about liberating the captive nations of eastern Europe.

Collapse of the Paris Summit Conference

The events of 1956 brought to a close the era of fully autonomous action by the European nation-states. In very different ways and to differing degrees the two superpowers had demonstrated the new political realities. After 1956 the Soviet Union began to talk about "peaceful coexistence" with the United States. In 1958 negotiations began between the two countries for limitations on the testing of nuclear weapons. However, that same year the Soviet Union announced that the status of West Berlin must be changed and the Allied occupation forces must be withdrawn. The demand was refused. In 1959 tensions relaxed sufficiently for several Western leaders to visit Moscow and for Soviet Premier Nikita Khrushchev to tour the United States. A summit meeting was scheduled for May 1960, and American President Dwight D. Eisenhower (1890–1969) was to go to Moscow.

The Paris Summit Conference of 1960 proved anything but a repetition of the friendly days of 1955. Just before the gathering, the Soviet Union shot down an American U-2 aircraft that was flying reconnaissance over Soviet territory. Khrushchev demanded an apology from President Eisenhower for this air surveillance. Eisenhower accepted full responsibility for the policy but refused to issue any apology. Khrushchev then refused to take part in the summit conference, just as the participants arrived in the French capital. The conference was thus aborted, and Eisenhower's proposed trip to the Soviet Union never took place.

The Soviet actions to destroy the possibility of the summit conference on the eve of its opening were not simply the result of the American spy flights. The Soviets had long been aware of the American flights but chose to protest at this time for two reasons. Khrushchev had hoped that the leaders of Britain, France, and the United States would be sufficiently divided over the future of Germany so that a united Allied front would be impossible. The divisions did not come about as he had hoped. Consequently, the conference would have been of little use to him.

Second, by 1960 the communist world itself had become split between the Soviets and the Chinese. The latter were portraying the Russians as lacking sufficient revolutionary zeal. Khrushchev's action was, in part, a response to those charges and proof of the hard-line attitude of the Soviet Union toward the capitalist world.

Kennedy: The Berlin Wall and the Cuban Missile Crisis

The abortive Paris conference opened the most difficult period of the Cold War. In 1961 the new U.S. president, John F. Kennedy (1917–1963), and Premier Khrushchev met in Vienna. The conference was inconclusive, but the American president left wondering if the two nations could avoid war. Throughout 1961 thousands of refugees from East Germany were crossing the border into West Berlin. This outflow was a political embarrassment to East Germany and a detriment to its economic life.

In August 1961 the East Germans erected a concrete wall along the border between East and West Berlin. Henceforth it was possible to cross only at designated checkpoints and with proper papers. The United States protested and sent Vice President Lyndon Johnson (1908–1973) to Berlin to reassure its citizens, but the Berlin Wall remained until 1989. The refugee stream was halted, and the United States'

President Kennedy and Nikita Khruschev met in Vienna in 1961. The discussions were very difficult, and both leaders left the talks with much distrust of each other. [Cornell Capa/Magnum Photos]

commitment to West Germany was brought into doubt.

A year later the most dangerous days of the Cold War occurred during the Cuban missile crisis. The Soviet Union attempted to place missiles in Cuba, which was a nation friendly to Soviet aims lying less than a hundred miles from the United States. The United States blockaded Cuba, halted the shipment of new missiles, and demanded the removal of existing installations. After a very tense week, with numerous threats and messages between Moscow and Washington, the crisis ended and the Soviets backed down.

The Cuban missile crisis was the last major Cold War confrontation that would have involved Europe directly because of the possibility of the launching of missiles over Europe or from European bases. Thereafter, the American–Soviet rivalry shifted to the war in Vietnam and the Arab–Israeli conflict in the Near East. A "hotline" communications system was installed between Moscow and Washington for more rapid and direct exchange of diplomatic messages in times of crisis.

President Kennedy Defines the Cold War Arena

This passage is from President John F. Kennedy's speech at the time of the Berlin Wall crisis of 1961. He called for a democratic challenge to communism throughout the world. The commitment to Southeast Asia would later lead to the major war in Vietnam.

The immediate threat to free men is in West Berlin. But that isolated outpost is not an isolated problem. The threat is worldwide. Our effort must be equally wide and strong, and not be obsessed by any single manufactured crisis. We face a challenge in Berlin, but there is also a challenge in Southeast Asia, where the borders are less guarded, the enemy harder to find, and the dangers of communism less apparent to those who have so little. We face a challenge in our own hemisphere, and indeed wherever else the freedom of human beings is at stake.

Public Papers of the Presidents of the United States, John F. Kennedy, January 20 to December 31, 1961, *ed. by Wayne C. Gover (Washington: U.S. Government Printing Office, 1962), p. 533.*

Detente and After

In 1963 the two powers concluded a Nuclear Test Ban Treaty. This agreement marked the beginning of a lessening in the tensions between the United States and the Soviet Union.

The German problem somewhat subsided in the late 1960s as West Germany, under Premier Willy Brandt (b. 1913), moved to improve its relations with the Soviet Union and eastern Europe. In 1968 the Soviet Union invaded Czechoslovakia to prevent its emergence into further independence. Although deplored by the United States, this action led to no renewal of tensions. During the presidency of Richard Nixon (1969–1974), the United States embarked on a policy of detente or reduction of tension with the Soviet Union. This policy involved trade agreements and mutual reduction of strategic armaments.

In 1975 President Gerald Ford attended a conference in Helsinki, Finland, that in effect recognized the Soviet sphere of influence in eastern Europe. The Helsinki Accords also committed its signatory powers, including the Soviet Union, to recognize and protect the human rights of their citizens.

The foreign policy of President Jimmy Carter (b. 1924) placed much stress on the observance of these human rights clauses. However, the Soviet invasion of Afghanistan in 1979, though not directly affecting Europe, hardened relations between Washington and Moscow. The United States refused to participate in the 1980 Olympic Games held in Moscow and

Soviet tanks entered Prague, in August, 1968. Unlike the Hungarians in 1956, the Czechs did not resist the Soviets. The invasion demonstrated that the nations of eastern Europe would be compelled to remain politically and economically tied to the Soviet Union. [Ullstein Bilderdienst]

placed an embargo on American grain being shipped to the Soviet Union. Furthermore, in 1979 President Carter signed a second Strategic Arms Limitation Treaty with the Soviet Union. The U.S. Senate refused to ratify it.

The administration of President Ronald Reagan adopted a much firmer policy and rhetoric toward the Soviet Union, although the United States relaxed the trade embargo and placed less emphasis on human rights. Initially, the Reagan administration sharply slowed arms limitation negotiations and successfully deployed a major new missile system in Europe. The United States also launched a new arms proposal, known as the Strategic Arms Defense Initiative, involving a system of highly developed technology designed to provide defense in outer space against nuclear attack (hence the name Star Wars given it by the press.) The proposal was very controversial, but it played a major role in recent arms negotiations between the United States and the Soviet Union.

President Reagan and Mikhail S. Gorbachev (b. 1931) held a friendly summit meeting in 1985, the first East-West Summit in six years. Other meetings followed. Arms negotiations continued with very hard bargaining on both sides until, in December 1987, the United States and the Soviet Union signed a major treaty in regard to nuclear missiles. The two powers have agreed to dismantle over two thousand medium and shorter-range missiles. The treaty also provides for mutual inspection. This action represents the most significant agreement since World War II between the two superpowers. In 1990 the two nations concluded an agreement limiting chemical weapons.

European Retreat from Empire

At the onset of World War II many of the nations of Europe were still imperial powers. Great Britain, France, the Netherlands, Belgium, Italy, and Portugal governed millions of non-European peoples. One of the most striking and significant postwar developments has been the decolonization of these imperial holdings and the consequent emergence of the so-called Third World political bloc.

The Effects of World War II

1097

THE ERA OF
THE COLD
WAR AND
SUPERPOWER
CONFRONTATION

The Effects of World War II

The decolonization that has occurred since 1945 has been a direct result of both the war itself and the rise of indigenous nationalist movements within the European colonial world. World War II drew the military forces of the colonial powers back to Europe. The Japanese conquests of Asia helped to turn out the European powers from that area. After the military and political dislocations of the war came the postwar economic collapse, which meant that the colonial powers could no longer afford to maintain their positions abroad.

The war aims of the Allies undermined colonialism. It was difficult to fight against tyranny in Europe while maintaining colonial dominance abroad. Moreover, the postwar policy of the United States generally opposed the continuation of European empires. Within the colonies there had also arisen nationalist movements of varying strength. These were often led by gifted persons who had been educated in Europe. The values and the political ideologies that they had learned in Europe itself helped them to present effective critiques of the colonial situation. Such leadership, as well as the frequently blatant injustice imposed on colonial peoples, paved the way for effective nationalist movements.

Major Areas of Colonial Withdrawal

There was a wide variety in decolonization. Some cases were relatively systematic; in others the European powers simply beat a hasty retreat. In 1947 Britain left India. The result of internal disputes, including religious differences, was the creation of two states, India and Pakistan. In 1948 Burma and Sri Lanka (formerly Ceylon) became independent. During the 1950s the British attempted to prepare colonies for self-government. Ghana (formerly the Gold Coast) and Nigeria—which became self-governing in 1957 and 1960, respectively—were the major examples of planned decolonization. In other areas, such as Malta and Cyprus, the British withdrawal occurred under the pressure of militant nationalist movements.

The smaller colonial powers had much less choice. The Dutch were forced from Indonesia

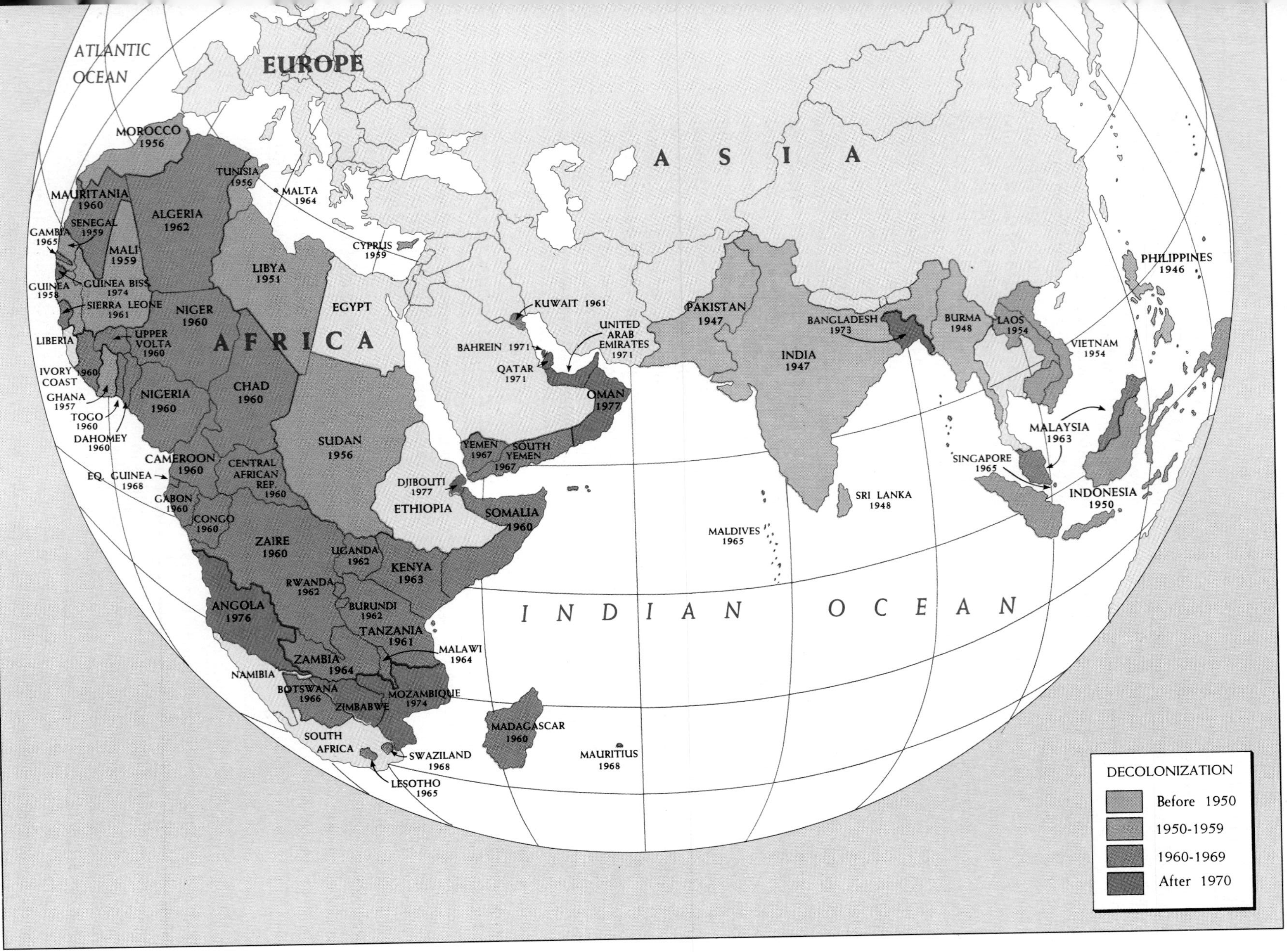

MAP 30-5 DECOLONIZATION SINCE WORLD WAR II *The extent of the rapid retreat from imperial-ism on the part of the Western powers after World War II is graphically shown on this outline map covering*

DECOLONIZATION

- Before 1950
- 1950-1959
- 1960-1969
- After 1970

EUROPE

ASIA

AFRICA

ATLANTIC OCEAN

INDIAN OCEAN

PHILIPPINES 1946
VIETNAM 1954
MALAYSIA 1963
SINGAPORE 1965
INDONESIA 1950
LAOS 1954
BURMA 1948
BANGLADESH 1973
INDIA 1947
PAKISTAN 1947
SRI LANKA 1948
MALDIVES 1965
KUWAIT 1961
UNITED ARAB EMIRATES 1971
BAHREIN 1971
QATAR 1971
OMAN 1977
SOUTH YEMEN 1967
YEMEN 1967
SOMALIA 1960
DJIBOUTI 1977
ETHIOPIA
MAURITIUS 1968
MADAGASCAR 1960
CYPRUS 1959
EGYPT
SUDAN 1956
MALAWI 1964
KENYA 1963
UGANDA 1962
BURUNDI 1962
TANZANIA 1961
RWANDA 1962
ZAMBIA 1964
MOZAMBIQUE 1974
ZIMBABWE 1966
SWAZILAND 1968
LESOTHO 1965
SOUTH AFRICA
BOTSWANA 1966
NAMIBIA
ANGOLA 1976
ZAIRE 1960
CONGO 1960
GABON 1960
CENTRAL AFRICAN REP. 1960
CAMEROON 1960
EQ. GUINEA 1968
MALTA 1964
LIBYA 1951
CHAD 1960
TUNISIA 1956
MOROCCO 1956
ALGERIA 1962
NIGER 1960
NIGERIA 1960
UPPER VOLTA 1960
MAURITANIA 1960
SENEGAL 1959
MALI 1959
GUINEA BISS 1974
GUINEA 1958
SIERRA LEONE 1961
GAMBIA 1965
LIBERIA
IVORY COAST 1960
GHANA 1957
TOGO 1960
DAHOMEY 1960

1098

in 1950. In 1960 the Belgian Congo, now Zaire, became independent in the midst of great turmoil. For a considerable time, as will be seen, France attempted to maintain its position in Southeast Asia but met defeat in 1954. It was similarly driven from North Africa. President Charles de Gaulle carried out a policy of referendums on independence within the remaining French colonial possessions. By the late 1960s only Portugal remained a traditional colonial power. In 1975 it finally abandoned its African colony of Angola.

France, the United States, and Vietnam

As far as the general history of the West is concerned, the decolonization policies of France produced the major postwar upheavals. French decolonization became an integral part of the Cold War and led directly to the involvement of the United States in the Southeast Asian country of Vietnam. The problem of decolonization helped to transfer the Cold War rivalry that had developed in Europe to other continents. Nowhere did those rivalries become more intense than in Asia. Moreover, there was a close relationship between events in Asia and in Europe.

Resistance to French Colonial Rule

During the years of the Korean conflict another war was being fought in Asia between France and the Viet Minh nationalist movement in Indochina. France, in its push for empire, had occupied this territory (which contained Laos, Cambodia, and Vietnam) between 1857 and 1883. France had administered the area and had invested heavily in it, but the economy of Indochina remained overwhelmingly agrarian. During World War I tens of thousands of Indochinese troops supported France. The French also educated many people from the colony. However, neither the aid during the war nor the achievement of Western education allowed the Vietnamese to escape discrimination from their French colonial rulers.

HO CHI MINH'S LEADERSHIP By 1930 a movement against French colonial rule had been organized by Ho Chi Minh (1892–

1969) into the Indochinese Communist Party. Ho had traveled throughout the world and had held jobs in several places in Europe before World War I. He and other Indochinese had lobbied at the Versailles Conference in 1919 to have the principle of self-determination applied to their country. In 1920 he was part of the wing of the French Socialist Party that formed the French Communist Party. In 1923 he was sent to Moscow. By 1925 he had formed the Vietnam Revolutionary Youth. After organizing the Indochinese Communist Party, he traveled in Asia and spent considerable time in the Soviet Union. Throughout the 1930s, however, the French succeeded in suppressing most activities by the Communist Party in their colony.

World War II provided new opportunities for Ho Chi Minh and other nationalists. When Japan invaded, it found the pro-Vichy French colonial administration ready to collaborate. Consequently, action against the Japanese thereafter meshed quite neatly with action against the French. It was during these wartime circumstances that Ho Chi Minh established his position as a major nationalist leader. He was a communist to be sure, but he was first and foremost a nationalist. Most important, he had achieved his position in Vietnam during the war independent of the support of the Chinese Communist movement.

In September 1945 Ho Chi Minh declared the independence of Vietnam under the Viet

Ho Chi Minh (1892–1969), center, and advisors meet during the war against the French in 1954. [Black Star]

1099

THE ERA C
THE COLI
WAR AND
SUPERPOW
CONFRONTAT

1100

GLOBAL
CONFLICT,
COLD WAR,
AND NEW
DIRECTIONS

Minh. There was considerable internal Vietnamese resistance to this claim of political control. The opposition arose from religious groups and non-Communist nationalists. After the war the French immediately took advantage of these divisions to establish a government favorable to their own interests. The United States, in line with its wartime anticolonialist position, urged the French to make some kind of accommodation with Ho Chi Minh.

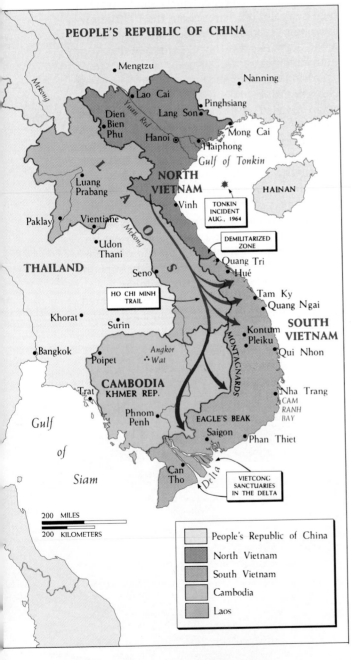

MAP 30-6 VIETNAM AND ITS NEIGHBORS
The Southeast Asia scene of the long and complex struggle centered in Vietnam is shown by the map.

In 1946, France and the Viet Minh reached an armistice. It proved to be quite temporary, and in 1947 full-fledged war broke out. The next year the French established a friendly Vietnamese government under Bao Dai. It was to be independent within a loose union with France. This arrangement would have meant very limited independence and was clearly unacceptable to both the Viet Minh and most other nationalists.

Until 1949 the United States had displayed only the most minimal concern about the Indochina War. However, the defeat of Chiang Kai-shek (1887–1975) and the establishment of the Communist People's Republic of China in 1949 changed that situation dramatically. This turn of events led the United States to regard the French colonial war against Ho Chi Minh as an integral part of the Cold War conflict. The French government, hoping for United States support, worked to maintain that point of view. Early in 1950 the United States recognized the Bao Dai government. At approximately the same time the Soviet Union and the People's Republic of China recognized the government of Ho Chi Minh. Indochina was thus transformed from a colonial battleground into an area of Cold War confrontation.

FRENCH DEFEAT AT DIEN BIEN PHU
In May 1950 the United States announced that it would supply financial aid to the French war effort. Between that time and 1954 more than $4 billion flowed from the United States to France. However, the war itself deteriorated for the French. In the spring of 1954 their army was overrun by the Viet Minh forces at the battle of Dien Bien Phu. Psychologically and militarily the French could not muster new energy for the war. Pierre Mendès-France (1907–1982) was elected premier in Paris on the promise of concluding the conflict. At this point the United States government was badly divided, but it decided against military intervention.

The Geneva Settlement and Its Aftermath

During the late spring and the early summer of 1954 a conference was held at Geneva to settle the Indochina conflict. All in all it proved a most unsatisfactory gathering. To one degree or another, all of the major powers were involved in the proceedings, but they did not sign the agreements. Technically the agreements existed between the armed forces of France and those of the Viet Minh. The precedents for such arrangements were the surrender of the German army in 1945 and the Korean Armistice of 1953.

NORTH AND SOUTH VIETNAM The Geneva conference provided for the division of Vietnam at the seventeenth parallel. This was to be a temporary border. By 1956, elections were to be held to reunify the country. North of the parallel, centered on the city of Hanoi, the Viet Minh were in charge; below it, the French were in charge, and Saigon was the major city. The prospect of elections meant that theoretically both groups could function politically in the territory of the other. In effect, the conference attempted to transform a military conflict into a political one.

The United States was less than happy about the results of the Geneva discussions. Its first major response came in September 1954, with the formation of the Southeast Asia Treaty Organization (SEATO). It was a collective security agreement that in some respects paralleled the European NATO alliance. However, it did not involve the integration of forces achieved in NATO, nor did it include all the major states of the region. Its membership consisted of the United States, Great Britain, France, Australia, New Zealand, Thailand, Pakistan, and the Philippines.

By 1955 American policymakers had begun to think about the Indochina region, and more especially Vietnam, largely in terms of the Korean example. The United States government assumed that the government being established in North Vietnam was, like the government of North Korea, basically a Communist puppet state. The same year French troops began to withdraw from the south. As they left, the various Vietnamese political groups began to fight for power.

THE UNITED STATES AND THE DIEM GOVERNMENT Into the turmoil of the military vacuum stepped the United States with military and economic aid. Among the Vietnamese politicians, it chose to support Ngo Dinh Diem. He was a strong non-Communist nationalist who had not collaborated with the French. The Americans hoped that he would become a leader around whom a non-Communist Vietnamese nationalist movement might rally. However, because the United States had publicly been deeply committed to the French, any government it supported would be, and was, viewed with suspicion by Vietnamese nationalists. In October 1955 Diem established a Republic of Vietnam in the territory for which the Geneva conference had made France responsible. By 1956 the United States was training troops and government officials, paying salaries, and providing military equipment.

In the meantime Diem announced that he and his newly established government were not bound by the Geneva agreements and that elections would not be held in 1956. The American government, which had not signed the Geneva documents, supported his position. Diem undertook an anti-Communist campaign, attacking many citizens who had earlier resisted the French. This was the beginning of a program of political repression that characterized his regime and those that followed.

There was a long series of ordinances that gave the government extraordinary power over its citizens. Diem alienated the peasants by restoring rents to landlords and generally strengthening large landowners. He abolished elected village councils and replaced them with his own officials, who had often come from the north. In fact, Diem's major base of political support lay with the more than one million Vietnamese who had migrated to the south after 1954.

By 1960 Diem's policy had created considerable internal resistance in South Vietnam. In that year the National Liberation Front was founded, with the goals of overthrowing Diem, unifying the country, reforming the economy, and ousting the Americans. It was anticolonial, nationalist, and Communist. Its military arm was called the Viet Cong. Sometime in the very late 1950s the government of North Vietnam began to aid the insurgent forces of the south. The Viet Cong and their supporters carried out a program of widespread terrorism and political disruption. They imposed an informal government through much of the countryside. Many peasants voluntarily supported them;

1101

THE ERA C
THE COLL
WAR AND
SUPERPOW
CONFRONTAT

others supported them from fear of reprisals.

In addition to the Communist opposition, Diem confronted mounting criticism from non-Communist citizens. The Buddhists agitated against the Roman Catholic president. The army was less than satisfied with him. Diem's response to all of these pressures was further repression and dependence on an ever smaller group of advisers.

The U.S. Involvement

The Eisenhower and early Kennedy administrations in the United States continued to support Diem while demanding reforms. The American military presence grew from somewhat more than six hundred persons in early 1961 to over sixteen thousand troops in late 1963. The political situation in Vietnam became increasingly unstable. On November 1, 1963, Diem was overthrown and murdered in an army *coup*. The United States was deeply involved in this plot. Its officials hoped that if the Diem regime were eliminated, the path would be opened for the establishment of a new government in South Vietnam capable of generating popular support. Thereafter, the political goal of the United States was to find a leader who could fill this need. It finally settled on Nguyen Van Thieu, who governed South Vietnam from 1966 to 1975.

President Kennedy was assassinated on November 22, 1963. His successor, Lyndon Johnson, continued and vastly expanded the commitment to South Vietnam. In August 1964, after an attack on an American ship in the Gulf of Tonkin, the first bombing of North Vietnam was authorized. In February 1965 major bombing attacks began that continued, with only brief pauses, until the early weeks of 1973. The land war grew in extent, with over 500,000 Americans stationed in South Vietnam.

United States marines patrol in Vietnam, May 1968. At the war's peak, more than 500,000 American troops were stationed in South Vietnam. For a decade, this effort seriously weakened the U.S. commitment to Western Europe. [Griffiths/Magnum]

In 1969 President Richard Nixon commenced a policy of gradual withdrawal of troops. The program was called *Vietnamization*. From the spring of 1968 onward, long-drawn-out peace negotiations were conducted in Paris. In January 1973 a cease-fire was finally arranged. The troops of the United States were pulled back, and prisoners of war held in North Vietnam were returned. Thereafter, violations of the cease-fire occurred on both sides. In early 1975 an evacuation of South Vietnamese troops from the northern part of their country turned into a complete rout as they were attacked by the troops of North Vietnam. On April 30, 1975, the city of Saigon fell to the troops of the Viet Cong and North Vietnam. The Second Indochina War had come to an end.

The Second Indochina War was, in effect, a continuation of the first war, which the French had lost. The United States saw the conflict as part of the Cold War and as a repetition of Korea. Aggression from the north had to be halted. There was also hope that the military power of the United States might buy time so that a strong nationalist, non-Communist regime could be established in South Vietnam.

The war grew out of a power vacuum left by decolonization. It produced a major impact on all the Western world. For a decade after the Cuban missile crisis the attention of the United States was largely diverted from Europe. American prestige suffered, and the American commitment to western Europe came into question. Moreover the American policy in Southeast Asia made many Europeans wonder about the basic wisdom of the American government. Many young Europeans—and not a few Americans—born after World War II came to regard the United States not as a protector of liberty but as an ambitious, aggressive, and cruel power trying to keep colonialism alive after the end of the colonial era.

The Arab–Israeli Conflict

A final area of East–West confrontation during the decades following World War II has been the Arab–Israeli conflict. Like Southeast Asia,

MAJOR DATES IN VIETNAM WAR	
1945	Ho Chi Minh proclaims Vietnam independence from French rule
1947–1954	War between France and Vietnamese
1950	U.S. financial aid to French
1954	French defeat at Dien Bien Phu
1954	Geneva Conference on Southeast Asia
1954	Southeast Asia Treaty Organization founded
1955	Diem establishes Republic of Vietnam in the south
1960	Foundation of National Liberation Front to overthrow the Diem government
1961	Six hundred American troops and advisers in Vietnam
1963	Diem overthrown and assassinated
1964	Bay of Tonkin Resolution
1965	Major U.S. troop commitment
1969	Nixon announces policy of Vietnamization
1973	Cease-fire announced
1975	Saigon falls to North Vietnamese troops

Palestine prior to World War II was governed by a European power, in this case Great Britain. The events in this area represent in one respect another example of the turmoil that has resulted from the retreat of a colonial power. Furthermore, this dispute has directly involved Europe because many of the citizens of Israel are immigrants from Europe and because Europe, like the United States, is highly dependent on oil from Arab countries.

British Balfour Declaration

The modern state of Israel was the achievement of the world Zionist movement founded in 1897 by Theodore Herzl and later led by Chaim Weizmann. The British Balfour Declaration of 1917 had favored the establishment of a national home for the Jewish people in Palestine. Between the wars thousands of Jews, mainly from Europe, immigrated into the area, which was then governed by Great Britain under a mandate of the League of Nations. During the interwar period the Yishuv or Jewish community in Palestine developed its own political parties, press, labor unions, and educational system. There were numerous conflicts with the Arabs already living in Pales-

1104

GLOBAL
CONFLICT,
COLD WAR,
AND NEW
DIRECTIONS

tine, for they considered the Jewish settlers intruders. The British rather unsuccessfully attempted to mediate those clashes.

This situation might have prevailed longer in Palestine except for the outbreak of World War II and the attempt by Hitler to exterminate the Jewish population of Europe. The Nazi persecution united Jews throughout the world behind the Zionist ideal of a Jewish state in Palestine. At the same time the knowledge of Nazi atrocities mobilized the conscience of the United States and other Western powers. It seemed morally right that something be done for Jewish refugees from Nazi concentration camps.

In 1947 the British turned over to the United Nations the whole problem of the relationship of Arabs and Jews in Palestine. That same year the United Nations passed a resolution calling for a division of the territory into a Jewish state and an Arab state. The Arabs in Palestine and the surrounding area resisted the United Nations resolution. Not unnaturally, they resented the influx of new settlers. Large numbers of Palestinian Arabs were displaced and themselves became refugees.

The Birth of the State of Israel

In May 1948 the Yishuv declared the independence of a new Jewish state called Israel. The United States, through President Truman, almost immediately recognized the new nation, whose first prime minister was David Ben-Gurion (1886–1973). During 1948 and 1949 Israel fought its war of independence against the Arabs. In that war Israel expanded its borders beyond the limits originally set forth by the United Nations. By 1949 Israel had, through force of arms, secured its existence and peace. However, it had not secured diplomatic recognition by its Arab neighbors— Egypt, Jordan, Syria, and Saudi Arabia, to name those closest. The peace amounted to little more than an armed truce.

Then in 1952 a group of Egyptian army officers seized power in Egypt. Their leader was Gamal Abdel Nasser. He established himself as a dictator and, more important, as a spokesman for militant Arab nationalism. His policy was marked by a clear hatred of all the old imperial powers. In 1956 Nasser nationalized the Suez Canal. That same year, as noted previously, Great Britain and France responded to Nasser's action by attacking the canal. Israel joined with France and Britain. This alliance helped Israel fend off certain Arab guerilla attacks but associated Israel with the former

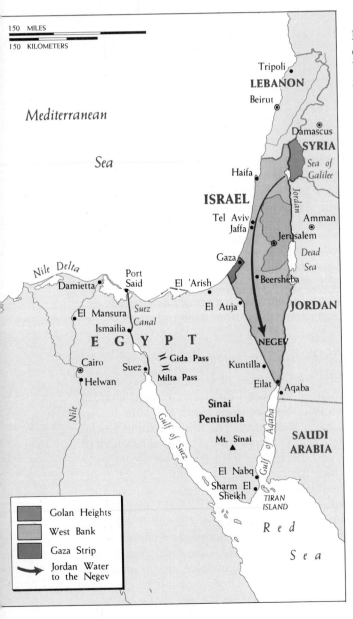

MAP 30-7 ISRAEL AND ITS NEIGHBORS *The map shows the geography of the difficult problem of Israel and its surrounding Arab neighbors. Syria, Jordan, and Egypt are the states with lands now occupied by Israel. The future of those lands and of earlier Palestinian refugees makes up the major set of problems still unresolved in the area.*

imperial powers. After 1956 a United Nations peacekeeping force separated the armies of Israel and Egypt. The bases of the U.N. force were located in Egypt. Still there was no official Arab recognition of the existence of Israel.

The 1967 Six Days' War

An uneasy peace continued until 1967. Meanwhile, the Soviet Union increased its influence in Egypt and the United States increased its influence in Israel. Both great powers supplied weapons to their friends in the area. In 1967 President Nasser made the calculation, which proved to be quite wrong, that the Arab nations could defeat Israel, which by then was nearly two decades old. He began to mass troops in the Sinai Peninsula, and he attempted to close the Gulf of Aqaba to Israeli shipping. He also demanded the withdrawal of the U.N. peacekeeping force. Diplomatic activity failed to stem the crisis and the Arab attempt to isolate Israel.

On June 5, 1967, the armed forces of Israel, under the direction of Defense Minister Moshe Dayan (1915–1981), attacked Egyptian airfields rather than endure additional provocation by Egypt. Almost immediately Syria and Jordan entered the war on the side of Egypt. Yet, by June 11, the Six Days' War was over, and Israel had won a stunning victory. The military forces of Egypt lay in shambles. Moreover, Israel had occupied the entire Egyptian Sinai Peninsula, as well as the West Bank region along the Jordan River that had previously been part of the state of Jordan. This victory marked the height of Israeli power and prestige.

Egyptian Policy under Anwar el-Sadat

In 1970 President Nasser died. He was succeeded by Anwar el-Sadat (1918–1981). Sadat had first to shore up his support at home. The existing tensions between Israel and the defeated Egypt, of course, continued, and the Soviet Union still poured weapons into Egypt. However, Sadat deeply distrusted the Russians and in 1972 ordered them to leave the country.

Sadat and his advisers also felt that only another war with Israel could return to Egypt the lands lost in 1967. In October 1973, on the Jewish holy day of Yom Kippur, the military forces of Egypt and Syria launched an attack across the Suez Canal into Israeli-held terri-

1105

THE ERA C
THE COLE
WAR AND
SUPERPOW
CONFRONTAT

Israeli troops occupy the Golan Heights in Syria during the Six Days' War of 1967. Israel annexed the Golan in 1981. [Black Star]

1106

GLOBAL
CONFLICT,
COLD WAR,
AND NEW
DIRECTIONS

tory. The invasion came as a complete surprise to the Israelis. Initially the Egyptian forces made considerable headway. Then the Israeli army thrust back the invasion. In November 1973 a truce was signed between the forces in the Sinai. Although Israel had been successful in repelling the Egyptians, the cost in troops and prestige was very high.

The Yom Kippur War added a major new element to the Middle East problem. In the fall of 1973, when the war broke out, the major Arab oil-producing states shut off the flow of oil to the United States and Europe. This dramatic move was an attempt to force the Western powers to use their influence to moderate the policy of Israel. The threat of the loss of oil was particularly frightening to Europeans, who possess almost no major sources of oil, on which their industry depends.

In November 1977, President Sadat of Egypt, in a dramatic personal gesture, flew to Israel. He addressed the Israeli Parliament and held discussions with Prime Minister Menachem Begin (b. 1913), although the two states were still technically at war. In effect, for the first time the head of a major Arab state recognized the existence of Israel. Previously all contacts had taken place through either the United Nations or other third parties.

The Camp David Accords and the PLO

The Sadat initiative, roundly condemned in many Arab quarters, resulted in direct conversations. The most important occurred at Camp David in the United States with President Carter as moderator. The Camp David Accords of September 1978 have provided one framework through which negotiations on Middle East questions have taken place. Since 1978 numerous meetings have occurred between Egyptian and Israeli officials.

Until 1986 no other Arab states joined these talks. The major stumbling block to future agreements has been the Palestine refugee problem. The Palestine Liberation Organization (PLO) remains the major spokesman for the refugees. The PLO continues to demand a separate Palestinian state. The government of Israel has steadily refused to recognize the PLO. Israel also believes that virtually any independent Palestinian state would be a threat to its own independence and ultimate survival.

In early 1981 Prime Minister Begin's coalition was reelected, but in October of that year President Sadat was assassinated by Muslim extremists. The death of the Egyptian president cast doubt on the long-range stability of

President Sadat of Egypt, President Carter, and Prime Minister Begin of Israel announced the historic Camp David Accords in 1978. [UPI]

1107

THE ERA (
THE COL
WAR AND
SUPERPOW
CONFRONTA

Beginning in the late 1980s Palestinian youth on the West Bank began active resistance to Israeli occupation. [Reuters/Bettmann Newsphotos]

the Camp David process. Further strains appeared in late December 1981, when the Israeli Parliament suddenly annexed the Golan Heights while the attention of most of the Western world was on the crisis in Poland.

Lebanon and the Intifada

In 1982 Israeli troops invaded Lebanon in an effort to destroy PLO bases and to disperse the PLO leadership. They were largely successful in that effort. However, at the same time the fragile Lebanese state, long racked by civil war, virtually collapsed. For a few months in 1983 the United States stationed marines in Lebanon. After a terrorist bombing killed more than three hundred troops, the marines were withdrawn. In 1985 Israeli troops withdrew. Syrian troops remain and battle with the various Lebanese factions and their armies. Vari-

MAJOR DATES IN ARAB-ISRAELI CONFLICT

1917	Balfour Declaration
1947	British turn Palestine problem over to the U.N.
1948	State of Israel proclaimed
1952	Nasser comes to power in Egypt
1956	Nasser nationalizes Suez Canal
1967	Six Days' War
1970	Anwar el-Sadat succeeds Nasser
1973	Yom Kippur War
1973	Arab Oil Boycott
1978	Camp David Accords
1981	Assassination of Sadat
1982	Israel invades Lebanon
1983	U.S. troops stationed temporarily in Lebanon
1985	Israel withdraws from Lebanon
1987	Arab uprisings on the West Bank commence
1990	Iraq invades Kuwait

1108

GLOBAL
CONFLICT,
OLD WAR,
AND NEW
DIRECTIONS

ous radical Arab factions have held British, French, and American citizens as hostages in order to attempt to put pressure on their governments. At present and into the foreseeable future, Lebanon remains a center of crisis and a base from which political terrorists may operate against all sides.

In 1983 Prime Minister Begin of Israel, who was in ill health, resigned. He was succeeded by a series of coalition governments. The most important recent developments in the region are the Arab uprisings against Israeli rule that commenced in 1987 on the West Bank (known as the Intifada). This area was conquered in the 1967 war but it has neither been annexed to Israel nor made independent. Since 1987 political and social unrest on the West Bank has led to the increasing use of Israeli troops to put down local revolts. This situation has created much division of opinion within Israel as well as much controversy within the world community over the actions being taken there.

The Persian Gulf Crisis

In August, 1990 a new crisis erupted in the Middle East with major consequences for Israel, the United States, and Europe. Iraq, under the leadership of Saddam Hussein, invaded the oil-rich principality of Kuwait on the Persian Gulf. Hussein invaded Kuwait to capture its oil-producing wealth and certain strategic islands that control Iraq's access to the Persian Gulf. Iraq possesses the largest army in the region and a vast supply of chemical weapons. Hussein has used such weapons against groups in his own nation. Iraq fought a long, brutal war with Iran during the 1980s from which it emerged as the victor. Iraq borders Saudi Arabia, another major oil producer which like Kuwait supplies much of the oil to the United States, Europe, and Japan. Its forces are also in

striking distance of other small emirates surrounding the Persian Gulf which are suppliers of oil to the industrialized world. Over the years Iraq has made numerous threats against Israel, which it could attack by crossing Jordan.

The response to the invasion was swift. The United States, working through the United Nations and with its NATO allies, imposed a naval blockade against Iraq in order to force Iraq to withdraw from Kuwait. The Soviet Union supported the United Nations actions. President Bush, in cooperation with Arab nations and several European nations, undertook a major military commitment to protect Saudi Arabia from invasion. The American mobilization to meet that commitment required the largest military buildup since the Vietnam War. Tens of thousands of American troops were immediately transported to the Gulf as were troops and equipment from other Western nations. In the meantime, Iraq held several thousand foreigners virtual hostages, threatening to place them where they would be killed or injured if any attack took place.

As this chapter is written, the Persian Gulf crisis remained unresolved. It could result in a major war. Whatever its eventual outcome, the crisis has transformed diplomatic and economic relations in the Middle East. For the time being, a major conflict among Arab nations has displaced the conflict between the Arabs and Israel though the outbreak of hostilities might involve Israel. The United States has clearly asserted a longterm involvement of military forces in Saudi Arabia. For the first time Arab nations have actually sought the presence of foreign military forces to protect them from another Arab nation. Once again as in the 1970s the United States and Europe have discovered their dependence upon Arabian oil sources. The military response to the Iraqi invasion has demonstrated the determination of both the United States and Europe to prevent those oil producing areas from falling into hostile hands.

The quarter century following the conclusion of World War II saw Europe decline in its relative political power on the world scene. The United States and the Soviet Union emerged as the two great superpowers pos- *sessed of economic and military strength. They confronted each other across the globe at one crisis point after another. In Europe the point of confrontation was often the divided city of Berlin. The United States voiced con-*

cern about eastern Europe but was never willing to exert significant influence in that region.

But there were other pressure points throughout the world. In Asia the United States twice intervened. First, it led the United Nations police action in Korea. Second, it became involved in the long war over the political future of Vietnam. The Cuban Revolution and the subsequent establishment of a Communist government provided another point of tension which in 1962 provoked the most dangerous crisis of the postwar era. In the Middle East both the Soviet Union and the United States confronted each other as they became involved in the Arab–Israeli conflict.

Following almost two decades of tension and crises the United States and the Soviet Union entered upon two decades marked by negotiation and climaxed by a significant arms reduction treaty. At some point in the mid-1980s it is generally agreed that the Cold War came to an end with the exact character of the new era not quite clear. During these same decades of superpower conflict the nations of Europe began to move in directions of unprecedented cooperation and prosperity.

1109

THE ERA C
THE COLI
WAR ANI
SUPERPOW
CONFRONTA

Suggested Readings

C. D. BLACK AND G. DUFFY (Eds.), *International Arms Control Issues and Agreements* (1985). Useful essays.

E. BOTTOME, *The Balance of Terror: Nuclear Weapons and the Illusion of Security, 1945–1985* (1986). A pessimistic evaluation.

L. T. CALDWELL AND W. DIEBOLD, JR., *Soviet American Relations in the 1980s: Superpower Politics and East-West Trade* (1980). An attempt to delineate the major problems in Soviet–American relations during the present decade.

R. V. DANIELS, *Year of the Heroic Guerilla: World Revolution and Counterrevolution in 1968* (1989). A worldwide examination of the events of that year.

A. W. DEPORTE, *Europe Between the Superpowers: The Enduring Balance* (1979). A very important study.

R. EMERSON, *From Empire to Nation: The Rise to Self-assertion of Asian and African Peoples* (1960). An important discussion of the origins of decolonization.

B. B. FALL, *The Two Vietnams: A Political and Military Analysis*, rev. ed. (1967). A discussion by a journalist who spent many years on the scene.

H. FEIS, *From Trust to Terror: The Onset of the Cold War, 1945–1950* (1970). The best general account.

D. J. GARROW, *Bearing the Cross: Martin Luther King, Jr. and the Southern Christian Leadership Conference 1955–1968* (1986). The best work on the subject.

D. HOLLOWAY, *The Soviet Union and the Arms Race* (1985). Excellent treatment of internal Soviet decision making.

D. KERNS, *Lyndon Johnson and the American Dream* (1976). A useful biography.

G. KOLKO, *The Politics of War* (1968). An interesting example of the revisionist school that finds the causes of the Cold War in economic considerations and emphasizes American responsibility.

S. I. KUTLER, *The Wars of Watergate: The Last Crisis of Richard Nixon* (1980). The first major treatment by a professional historian.

L. MARTIN (Ed.), *Strategic Thought in the Nuclear Age* (1979). A collection of useful essays on an issue that lies at the core of the American relationship to western Europe.

C. MURRAY, *Losing Ground: American Social Policy 1950–1980* (1983). A pessimistic assessment.

D. W. REINHARD, *The Republican Right since 1945* (1983). A useful overview.

Z. SCHIFF AND E. YA'ARI, *Intifada: The Palestinian Uprising—Israel's Third Front* (1990). An analysis of recent developments.

A. M. SCHLESINGER, JR., *A Thousand Days: John F. Kennedy in the White House* (1965). A biography by an adviser and major historian.

J. STEELE, *Soviet Power: The Kremlin's Foreign Policy—Brezhnev to Andropov* (1983). A broad survey.

A. ULAM, *Expansion and Coexistence: The History of Soviet Foreign Policy, 1917–1967* (1968). A major treatment.

The opening of the Berlin Wall in November, 1989, more than any other single event symbolized the collapse of the Communist governments in Eastern Europe. [Patrick Piel/Gamma-Liaison]

31

TOWARD A NEW EUROPE

Within a decade of the end of World War II all of the nations of western Europe realized that they could no longer exert independent *military or political power on the world scene, as it was dominated by the superpowers. They turned instead to the pursuit of na-*

1112

GLOBAL
CONFLICT,
COLD WAR,
AND NEW
DIRECTIONS

tional policies of social security for their people and economic prosperity. Their leaders believed this goal would prevent a new turn toward authoritarian government. Those west European nations also moved toward unprecedented economic cooperation in the form of the European Economic Community. The population of western Europe experienced unprecedented improvements in their standard of living.

In contrast, the nations of eastern Europe in the Soviet bloc experienced over forty years of very tight control from the Soviet Union. They also endured economic hardship. Over the course of the period the contrast between the living standards of eastern and western Europe became more and more pronounced. The Soviet bloc nations were governed by Communist parties that generally adopted the policies dictated by Moscow. The Soviet military suppression of the Hungarian Revolution of 1956 and the Czech experiment of 1968 indicated that Moscow would allow little or no freedom and independence for these nations.

However, commencing with events in Poland in 1980 followed by the reforms that *Mikhail Gorbachev has undertaken in the Soviet Union since 1985, the political face of eastern Europe has begun to change. The Revolutions of 1989 overturned Communist governments throughout the region and opened the way for the reunification of Germany. The entire structure of postwar Europe became transformed in a matter of months.*

Beyond prosperity and politics, however, new social attitudes and social developments have arisen in Europe. These have included a new role for women, an expanded university population accompanied by student activism, criticism of the influence of the United States, and a new concern for the environment. The existentialist movement challenged the concept of the rationality of human life and the possibility of religious faith. But no less important has been the ongoing role of the Christian heritage in Europe during the postwar years. These social and intellectual changes have provided the background for the political development of Europe during the second half of the century. Indeed, they have supplied many of the building blocks of a new European order.

New Patterns in the Work and Expectations of Women

The decades since World War II have witnessed notable changes in the work patterns and the social expectations of women. In all social ranks women have begun to assert larger economic and wider political roles. Women have entered the learned professions and have achieved more major managerial roles than ever before in European history.

More Married Women in Work Force

One of the patterns that was firmly established at the turn of the century has reversed itself. The number of married women in the work force has sharply risen. Both middle-class and working-class married women have sought to find jobs outside the home. The largest sector of employment became positions in service industries. The postwar population growth increased the demand for such services as were associated with the rearing of children. The larger number of children, in turn, spurred the growth of consumer industries that employed women.

Because there had been relatively few women born in the 1930s, there were, in turn, relatively few young single women to be employed in the years just after the war. Married women entered the job market to replace them. Some factories changed the nature of the hours and their workshifts in order to accommodate the needs of the married women in their employment. It was also easier for married women to enter the work force because improvements in health care and in consumer conveniences meant that child rearing demanded somewhat less time than in the past.

In the twentieth century, children were no longer expected to make substantial contributions to family income. They spent large amounts of their time in compulsory schools. If the family needed further income to supplement that of the father, the mother would now enter the work force. There is also considerable evidence to suggest that married women began to work in order to escape the boredom

In Europe, as in the United States, women have achieved new roles. Geraldine Bridgewater was the first woman to hold a seat on the London Stock Exchange. [Gamma-Liaison]

of housework and to find company among other female workers.

New Work Patterns

The work pattern of a European woman's life displayed much more continuity than it had in the nineteenth century. After schooling, the young single woman went to work. But she also continued to work after marriage. She might have withdrawn from the work force during her children's earliest years, and then returned to it when her children began to go to school. A number of factors created this new pattern, but one of the most important is the much longer life span of women.

At the time when women died relatively young, child rearing necessarily filled a large proportion of their short lives. The extension of the life span has meant that child rearing fills a much smaller proportion of women's lives. Consequently, women throughout the Western world have come to have new concerns about how they will spend those years when they are not involved in rearing children.

Many women have begun to choose to limit sharply the number of children they bear or to forego childbearing and child rearing altogether. Marriage remains a standard expectation of both men and women. However, the new kinds of careers open to women and the possibility of greater consumption on the part of childless married couples have led to a decline in the birth rate in some countries and to a sharp stabilization in others.

These changing patterns have spurred sharp social debates in Europe, as in the United States. Feminist groups in Europe have emphasized the need to assert the rights of women as equal citizens.

The liberalization of divorce laws has been one of the chief results of these demands. In turn, however, there has arisen much criticism of the new social expectations of women. The Roman Catholic church has often taken the lead in this matter. Generally speaking, the European women's movement is less well organized and has been somewhat less successful than its counterpart in the United States.

Transformations in Knowledge and Culture

Throughout the twentieth century the realms of knowledge and culture have rapidly transformed themselves. Institutions of higher education have rapidly expanded their numbers and the kinds of persons enrolled so as to make

1113

1114

GLOBAL
CONFLICT,
COLD WAR,
AND NEW
DIRECTIONS

knowledge available to more persons than ever before. At the same time intellectual movements, such as existentialism, have challenged many of the traditional intellectual attitudes of Europeans. Concerns about the environment have also brought new issues to the fore. Throughout this ferment the various spokespersons for the Christian faith have attempted to make their religious message relevant to the rapidly changing culture of Europe.

Expansion of the University Population and Student Rebellion

The rapid changes in communication and the increases in the quantity of accessible information have been accompanied by a growing number of Europeans who have received some form of university education. At the turn of the century in every major European country, only a few thousand people were enrolled in the universities. By the 1980s that figure had risen to hundreds of thousands even though university education is still less common in Europe than in the United States. More people from different kinds of social and economic backgrounds are receiving higher education. Equally important, for the first time large numbers of women are receiving such training.

This expansion has been closely related to the intense self-criticism of Europeans. Millions of citizens have become equipped with those critical intellectual skills that in previous centuries were usually the possession of very small literate elites. Television has given such critical voices a wide audience.

The "student experience"—that is, leaving home and settling for several years in a community composed primarily of late adolescents—has come to be widely shared. Previously only a relatively few privileged persons had known this experience in Europe. Since World War II it has become one of the major features of European society.

The expansion in the number of students has also meant a general increase in the numbers of university teachers. As a result, there have been more scientists, historians, economists, literary critics, and other professional intellectuals during the last seventy-five years than in all previous human history. Moreover, not since the early years of the Reformation

have university intellectuals exerted such widespread influence. The major intellectual developments of the seventeenth, eighteenth, and nineteenth centuries took place primarily, though not entirely, outside the university. In the twentieth century the university has become the most likely home for the intellectual. And the symbol of success for a writer in almost any field has been the inclusion of his or her work in the university curriculum.

One of the most striking and unexpected results of this expansion in the numbers of university students and the larger numbers of university intellectuals was the student rebellion of the 1960s. This development is still not well understood. Student uprisings began in the early 1960s in the United States and assumed major proportions as opposition grew to the war in Vietnam. The student rebellion then spread into Europe and other parts of the world. It was almost always associated with a radical political critique of the United States, though in eastern Europe some resentment was directed toward the Soviet Union. There was a general attitude of antimilitarism. In addition to political concerns, students raised questions about the adequacy of middle-class values, traditional sexual mores, and traditional family life.

The year 1968 may be regarded as the high point in this student movement. That year, students in the United States participated in demonstrations against U.S. involvement in Vietnam. The same year students at the Sorbonne in Paris were the leading instigators of major unrest against the government of Charles de Gaulle. Students were also in the forefront of the liberal socialist experiment in Czechoslovakia during 1968. All of these protests failed to move their respective government policies. The U.S. remained in Vietnam for several more years. De Gaulle's government survived the challenge of May, 1968. The Soviets suppressed the Czech experiment.

By the early 1970s the major era of student rebellion seemed to have passed. Students remained active in European movements against nuclear weapons and particularly against the placement of American nuclear weapons in Germany and elsewhere in Europe. However, from the middle of the 1970s European students, though maintaining a generally radical political stance, pursued a much more traditional middle-class career pattern.

In May, 1968, student demonstrators and police clashed in Paris. [© Marc Riboud/Magnum Photos]

Environmentalism

The lack of consumer goods after the war created pressure for economic growth associated with postwar reconstruction throughout the 1950s and 1960s. It had left little room for public debate about preserving the environment or challenging the ethic of economic expansion and efficiency. During the 1970s concern arose across Europe over matters relating to the environment. By the 1980s environmental issues began to have real impact on the political scene. For the first time groups addressing issues of pollution gained very considerable public and political prominence. Among the most important of these was the Club of Rome founded in 1972 and the German Greens who formed a political party in 1979. The latter immediately began to contest elections.

Several developments lay behind this new awareness of the dangers to the environment. The Arab oil embargo of 1973–1974 pressed home to Europeans their dependence upon foreign natural resources and the limited character of all such natural resources. By the 1970s the economic expansion of the three decades

following the war had begun to damage the environment in ways that no one could deny. Fish were dying in the Thames River in England. Industrial pollution was destroying the rivers of Germany and France. Acid rain had begun to kill trees throughout Germany. Finally, throughout Europe all the movements opposed to nuclear weapons in general or to their placement in Europe in particular based at least part of their opposition on environmentalist concerns.

The origins of the German Green movement were the radical student groups of the late 1960s. There was a tendency of these groups to be anticapitalist because they saw German and other European businesses as responsible for much of the pollution. The Greens, as well as other European environmentalists, assumed a strong antinuclear position. Unlike the students of the 1960s the Greens avoided violence and mass demonstrations. Rather, they sought to enter the electoral process directly. They succeeded in electing a small number of representatives to the West German Parliament as well as to local offices.

The 1986 nuclear disaster at the Chernobyl

1116

GLOBAL
CONFLICT,
COLD WAR,
AND NEW
DIRECTIONS

nuclear reactor in the Soviet Union brought new support to environmental issues and raised questions that no European government could ignore. The Soviet government had to confront deaths and injuries at the site and has had to relocate tens of thousands of people. Clouds of radioactive fallout spread westward across Europe. Environmentalists had always contended that their issues of preserving and protecting the environment and the health of people endangered by environmental disaster rose above national concerns. The Chernobyl fire demonstrated this to be true.

Since 1986 virtually all European govern- ments have begun to respond to issues relating to the environment. Some observers believe the environment may become a major political issue across the Continent. In the wake of Chernobyl the governments of the Soviet Union and eastern Europe found they must address the question.

Throughout western Europe leaders in the various parliamentary systems have begun to realize that the environmental groups com- mand significant numbers of votes. The move- ment toward further western European inte- gration in 1992 has opened the way to greater cooperation on addressing environmental con-

World Leaders Point to the Problems of the Environment

In 1989 a summit conference of leaders of the major industrial- ized nations, including the United States, Japan, Canada, the United Kingdom, France, Germany, and Italy, gathered in Paris for their annual meeting. In the statement issued from the confer- ence they addressed themselves to the problem of preserving and cleaning up the environment.

There is growing awareness throughout the world of the necessity to preserve bet- ter the global ecological balance. This in- cludes serious threats to the atmosphere, which could lead to future climate changes. We note with great concern the growing pollution of air, lakes, rivers, oceans and seas; acid rain; dangerous sub- stances; and the rapid desertification and deforestation. . . .

Decisive action is urgently needed to understand and protect the Earth's ecologi- cal balance. We will work together to achieve the common goals of preserving a healthy and balanced global environment in order to meet shared economic and so- cial objectives. . . .

We urge all countries to give further impetus to scientific research on environ- mental issues, to develop necessary tech- nologies and to make clear evaluations of the economic costs and benefits. . . .

In this connection, we ask all countries to combine their efforts in order to im- prove observation and monitoring on a global scale. . . .

We believe that international coopera- tion also needs to be enhanced in the field of technology and technology transfer in order to reduce pollution. . . .

We believe that industry has a crucial role in preventing pollution at the source, in waste minimization, in energy conser- vation, and in the design and marketing of cost-effective clean technologies. The agri- cultural sector must also contribute to tackling problems such as water pollution, soil erosion and desertification. . . .

Environmental protection is integral to issues such as trade, development, energy, transport, agriculture and economic plan- ning. Therefore, environmental considera- tions must be taken into account in eco- nomic decision-making.

The New York Times, July 17, 1989, p. A7.

cerns on a transnational level. It seems certain that the large new businesses that will grow as the European Economic Community solidifies will do so in a regulatory climate in which care for the environment plays an important role.

Existentialism

The single intellectual movement that perhaps best characterized the predicament and mood of mid-twentieth-century European culture was existentialism. It was symptomatic that most of the philosophers associated with this movement disagree with each other on major issues. Like the modern Western mind in general, existentialism, which has been termed the philosophy of Europe in the twentieth century, has been badly divided. The movement represents in part a continuation of the revolt against reason that began in the nineteenth century.

ROOTS IN NIETZSCHE AND KIERKE-GAARD Friedrich Nietzsche, whose thought was considered in Chapter 25, was one of the

Jean-Paul Sartre (1905–1980) and Simone de Beauvoir (1908–1986), were two leading French intellectuals of the mid-century. His was a major voice of the existentialist movement, and she wrote extensively on the social position, experience, and psychology of women. [United Press International Photo]

major forerunners of existentialism. Another was the Danish writer Sören Kierkegaard (1813–1855), who wrote during the second quarter of the nineteenth century but received little attention until after World War I. He was a rebel against Hegelian philosophy and Christianity as he found them in Denmark. In works such as *Fear and Trembling* (1843), *Either/Or* (1843), and *Concluding Unscientific Postscript* (1846), he urged that the truth of Christianity could not be contained in creeds, doctrines, and church organizations. It could be grasped only in the living experience of those who faced extreme human situations.

Kierkegaard also criticized Hegelian philosophy and, by implication, all modes of academic rational philosophy. Its failure, he felt, was the attempt to contain all of life and human experience within abstract categories. Kierkegaard spurned this faith in the power of mere reason. "The conclusions of passion," he once declared, "are the only reliable ones."[1]

The intellectual and ethical crisis of World War I brought Kierkegaard's thought to the fore and also created new interest in Nietzsche's critique of reason. The human sacrifice and the destruction of property made many people doubt whether human beings were actually in control of their own destiny. The conflict stood as an affront to the concept of human improvement and the view of human beings as creatures of rationality. The war itself had been fought with the instruments developed through rational technology. The pride in rational human achievement that had characterized much nineteenth-century European civilization lay in ruins. The sunny faith in rational human development and advancement had not been able to withstand the extreme experiences of war.

QUESTIONING OF RATIONALISM Existential thought came to thrive in this climate and received further encouragement from the trauma of World War II. The major existential writers included the Germans Martin Heidegger (1889–1976) and Karl Jaspers (1883–1969) and the French Jean-Paul Sartre (1905–1980) and Albert Camus (1913–1960). Their books are often very difficult and in some cases sim-

---

[1] *Quoted in Walter Kaufman (Ed.),* Existentialism from Dostoevsky to Sartre *(Cleveland: The World Publishing Company, 1962), p. 18.*

1118

GLOBAL
CONFLICT,
COLD WAR,
AND NEW
DIRECTIONS

ply obscure. And the writers frequently disagreed with each other. Yet all of them in one way or another questioned the primacy of reason and scientific understanding as ways of coming to grips with the human situation. Heidegger went so far as to argue, "Thinking

Sartre Discusses the Character of His Existentialism

Jean-Paul Sartre, dramatist, novelist, and philosopher, was the most important French existentialist. In the first paragraph of this 1946 statement Sartre asserted that all human beings must experience a sense of anguish or the most extreme anxiety when undertaking a major commitment. That anguish arises because consciously or unconsciously they are deciding whether all human beings should make the same decision. In the second paragraph Sartre argued that the existence or nonexistence of God would make no difference in human affairs. What humankind must do is to discover the character of its own situation by itself.

The existentialist frankly states that man is in anguish. His meaning is as follows— When a man commits himself to anything, fully realizing that he is not only choosing what he will be, but is thereby at the same time a legislator deciding for the whole of mankind—in such a moment a man cannot escape from the sense of complete and profound responsibility. There are many, indeed, who show no such anxiety. But we affirm that they are merely disguising their anguish or are in flight from it. Certainly, many people think that in what they are doing they commit no one but themselves to anything: and if you ask them, "What would happen if everyone did so?" they shrug their shoulders and reply, "Everyone does not do so." But in truth, one ought always to ask oneself what would happen if everyone did as one is doing; nor can one escape from that disturbing thought except by a kind of self-deception. The man who lies in self-excuse, by saying "Everyone will not do it" must be ill at ease in his conscience, for the act of lying implies the universal value which it denies. By its very disguise his anguish reveals itself.

Existentialism is nothing else but an attempt to draw the full conclusions from a consistently atheistic position. Its intention is not in the least that of plunging men into despair. And if by despair one means—as the Christians do—any attitude of unbelief, the despair of the existentialist is something different. Existentialism is not atheist in the sense that it would exhaust itself in demonstration of the nonexistence of God. It declares, rather, that even if God existed that would make no difference from its point of view. Not that we believe God does exist, but we think that the real problem is not that of His existence; what man needs is to find himself again and to understand that nothing can save him from himself, not even a valid proof of the existence of God. In this sense existentialism is optimistic. It is a doctrine of action, and it is only by self-deception, by confusing their own despair with ours that Christians can describe us as without hope.

Jean-Paul Sartre, Existentialism and Humanism, *trans. by Philip Mairet (London: Methuen), in Walter Kaufman (Ed.),* Existentialism from Dostoevsky to Sartre *(New York: Meridian Books, 1956), pp. 292, 310–311.*

only begins at the point where we have come to know that Reason, glorified for centuries, is the most obstinate adversary of thinking."[2]

The tradition of the Enlightenment suggested that analysis or the separation of human experience into its component parts was the proper path to understanding. Existential writers rejected this approach. They argued that the human condition was greater than the sum of its parts and must be grasped as a whole.

The Romantic writers of the early nineteenth century had also questioned the primacy of reason, but they did so in a much less radical manner than the existentialists. The Romantics emphasized the imagination and intuition, but the existentialists tended to dwell primarily on the extremes of human experience. Death, dread, fear, and anxiety provided their themes. The titles of their works illustrate their sense of foreboding and alienation: *Being and Time* (1962) by Heidegger; *Nausea* (1938) and *Being and Nothingness* (1943) by Sartre; *The Plague* (1947) and *The Stranger* (1942) by Camus. The touchstone of philosophic truth became the experience of individual human beings under such extreme situations.

The existentialists saw human beings as compelled to formulate their own ethical values rather than being able to find ethical guidance from traditional religion, rational philosophy, intuition, or social customs. This opportunity and necessity to lay down values for oneself became the dreadful freedom of existentialist philosophy.

In large measure the existentialists were protesting against a world in which reason, technology, and the political policies of war and genocide had produced unreasonable results. Their thought reflected the uncertainty of social institutions and ethical values that existed during the era of the two world wars. However, since the 1950s their thought has become the subject of study in universities throughout the world. They will probably continue to be subjects of philosophy and literature classes, but it seems unlikely that they will again achieve their former popularity.

In most ways Christianity has continued to be hard-pressed during the twentieth century as it had been in the late nineteenth. Material prosperity and political ideologies have replaced religious faith as the dominant factors in many people's lives. However, despite their loss of much popular support and former legal privileges, the Christian churches still exercise considerable social and political influence. In Germany the churches were one of the few major institutions not wholly conquered by the Nazis. Lutheran clergymen, such as Martin Neimöller and Dietrich Bonhoeffer, were leaders of the opposition to Hitler. After the war, in Poland and elsewhere in eastern Europe, the Roman Catholic church actively opposed the influence of communism.

In western Europe religious affiliation provided much of the initial basis for the Christian Democratic parties. Across the continent the churches have raised critical questions about colonialism, nuclear weapons, human rights, and other moral issues. Consequently, in the most secular of all ages, the Church has affected numerous issues of state.

Neo-Orthodoxy

A theological revival took place during the first half of the century. Nineteenth-century theologians had frequently softened the concept of sin and had tended to portray human nature as not very far removed from the divine. The horror of World War I destroyed that optimistic faith. Many Europeans felt that evil had stalked the continent.

The most important Christian response to this experience was the theology of Karl Barth (1886–1968). In 1919 this Swiss pastor published *A Commentary on the Epistle to the Romans*, which reemphasized the transcendence of God and the dependence of humankind on the divine. Barth portrayed God as wholly other than, and different from, humankind. In a sense Barth was returning to the Reformation theology of Luther, but the work of Kierkegaard had profoundly influenced his reading of the reformer. Barth, like the Danish writer, regarded the lived experience of men and women as the best testimony to the truth of

---

[2]*Quoted in William Barrett,* Irrational Man *(Garden City, NY: Doubleday, 1962), p. 20.*

1120

GLOBAL
CONFLICT,
COLD WAR,
AND NEW
DIRECTIONS

Pope John Paul II Discusses
International Social Justice

Pope John Paul II issued his encyclical entitled "The Social Concerns of the Church" in 1988. In the passages below he attempted to set concerns for justice among developed and developing nations into the larger context of Christian moral theology. He pointed out how the international system of trade and finance works to the disadvantage of poorer nations. He also emphasized that even though Christians await the return of Jesus, they are not thus relieved of acting upon concerns of social justice here and now. This encyclical illustrates the general desire of this pope to address the needs of developing nations in Latin America, Africa, and Asia where the Roman Catholic church has enjoyed very considerable growth. The Pope also urged the more radical Roman Catholic writers in Latin America to look to more traditional Christian teachings for their basis of their social policy.

The Church's social doctrine is not a "third way" between liberal capitalism and Marxist collectivism, nor even a possible alternative to other solutions less radically opposed to one another: rather, it constitutes a category of its own. Nor is it an ideology, but rather the accurate formulation of the results of a careful reflection on the complex realities of human existence, in society and in the international order, in the light of faith and of the Church's tradition. Its main aim is to interpret these realities, determining their conformity with or divergence from the lines of the Gospel teaching on man and his vocation, a vocation which is at once earthly and transcendent; its aim is thus to guide Christian behavior. It therefore belongs to the field, not of ideology, but of theology and particularly moral theology.

The international trade system today frequently discriminates against the products of the young industries of the developing countries and discourages the producers of raw materials. There exists, too, a kind of international division of labor, whereby the low-cost products of certain countries which lack effective labor laws or which are too weak to apply them are sold in other parts of the world at considerable profit for the companies engaged in this form of production, which knows not frontiers. . . .

. . . [H]umanity today is in a new and more difficult phase of its genuine development. It needs a greater degree of international ordering, at the service of the societies, economies and cultures of the whole world.

It is desirable, for example, that nations of the same geographical area should establish forms of cooperation which will make them less dependent on more powerful producers; they should open their frontiers to the products of the area; they should examine how their products might complement one another; they should combine in order to set up those services which each one separately is incapable of providing; they should extend cooperation to the monetary and financial sector.

The Church well knows that no temporal achievement is to be identified with the Kingdom of God, but that all such achievements simply reflect and in a sense anticipate the glory of the Kingdom, the Kingdom which we await at the end of history, when the Lord will come again. But that expectation can never be an excuse for lack of concern for people in their concrete personal situations and in their social, national, and international life, since the former is conditioned by the latter, especially today.

The New York Times, February 20, 1988, p. 4.

his theology. Those extreme moments of life described by Kierkegaard provided the basis for a real knowledge of humankind's need for God.

This view totally challenged much nineteenth-century writing about human nature. Barth's theology, which became known as *neo-orthodoxy*, proved to be very influential throughout the West in the wake of new political disasters and human suffering.

Liberal Theology

Liberal theology, however, was not swept away by neo-orthodoxy. The German-Ameri-can Paul Tillich (1886–1965) was the most important liberal theologian. He looked to a theology of culture and tended to regard religion as a human rather than a divine phenomenon. Whereas Barth saw God as dwelling outside humankind, Tillich believed that evidence of the divine had to be sought from within human nature and human culture.

Other liberal theologians, such as Rudolf Bultmann (1884–1976), continued to work out the problems of naturalism and supernaturalism that had plagued earlier writers. Bultmann's major writing took place before World War II but was popularized thereafter in

Pope John XXIII (1958–1963) convened the Vatican Council in October 1962. The council, known as Vatican II, *effected the most extensive changes in the Catholic Church since the Council of Trent in the sixteenth century. [AP/World Wide Photos]*

1122

GLOBAL
CONFLICT,
COLD WAR,
AND NEW
DIRECTIONS

Anglican Bishop John Robinson's *Honest To God* (1963). Another liberal Christian writer from Britain, C. S. Lewis (1878–1963), attracted millions of readers during and after World War II. He was a layman and his books were often in the form of letters or short stories. His most famous work is *The Screwtape Letters* (1942).

Roman Catholic Reform

The most significant postwar religious departures occurred within the Roman Catholic church. Pope John XXIII (1958–1963) undertook the most extensive changes to occur in Catholicism for over a century—and some would say, since the Council of Trent in the sixteenth century. In 1959 Pope John summoned the twenty-first ecumenical council of

the Church to be called since the series started under the emperor Constantine in the fourth century. It was known as *Vatican II*. He died before it had completed its work; but his successor, Pope Paul VI, continued the council, which met between 1962 and 1965. Among the numerous changes in liturgy, the Mass became celebrated in the vernacular. Free relations were established with other Christian denominations. More power was shared with bishops. Pope Paul also appointed a number of cardinals from nations of the former colonial world.

However, after having taken these very liberal moves, the pope firmly upheld the celibacy of priests and maintained the Church's prohibition on contraception. The former position caused many men and women to leave the priesthood and religious orders. And many of the laity deeply resented the policy on family planning.

Paul VI died in 1978, as did John Paul I, his immediate successor, whose reign lasted only thirty-four days. The second new pope of 1978, who also took the name John Paul, was Karol Wojtyla of Poland, the former archbishop of Cracow. John Paul II was the youngest pope to be elected in over a century.

John Paul II, who survived an assassination attempt in 1981, has pursued a three-pronged policy. He has reasserted a traditional policy in regard to the priesthood and the nature of family life. He has stressed the authority of the papacy in doctrinal matters. He also has attempted to limit doctrinal and liturgical experiment on the part of those Catholics regarded as either exceedingly liberal or exceedingly conservative. Finally, he has encouraged the expansion of the Church in the non-Western world. In this last effort he has stressed the need for social justice while at the same time limiting the political activity of priests. All of these policies have provoked controversy within the Church and between the Church and the rest of the world. These policies have also commanded broad support in the Church, largely because of the attractive and charismatic personal qualities of John Paul II.

Pope John Paul II (elected 1978), the first non-Italian to be elected pope since 1522, has reasserted traditional Catholic practices and values while also emphasizing the Church's commitment to social justice. [Ullstein Bilderdienst]

Internal Political Developments in Western Europe

After the war, with the exceptions of Portugal and Spain, which remained dictatorships until the mid-1970s, the nations of western Europe pursued the path of liberal democracy. However, their leaders realized that the prewar democratic political structures alone had been insufficient to ensure peace, stability, material prosperity, and domestic liberty for their peoples. It had become clear that democracy required a social and economic base as well as a political structure. Economic prosperity and social security in the eyes of most Europeans became a duty of government as a way of staving off the kind of turmoil that had brought on tyranny and war. They also regarded such programs as a means of avoiding communism.

Except for the British Labour Party, the vehicles of the new postwar politics were not, as might have been expected, the democratic socialist parties. On the whole those parties did not prosper after the onset of the Cold War. They stood opposed by both Communists and groups more conservative than themselves. Rather, the new departures were led by various Christian Democratic parties, usually leading coalition governments.

These Christian Democratic political parties were a major new feature of postwar politics. They were largely Roman Catholic in leadership and membership. Catholic parties had previously existed in Europe. But from the late nineteenth century through the 1930s they had been very conservative and had tended to protect the social, political, and educational interests of the Church. They had traditionally opposed communism but had few positive programs of their own. The postwar Christian Democratic parties of Germany, France, and Italy were progressive. They accepted democracy and advocated social reform. They welcomed non-Catholics to membership. Democracy, social reform, economic growth, and anticommunism were their hallmarks.

The events of the war years in large measure determined the political leadership of the postwar decade. On the Continent those groups and parties that had been active in the resistance against Nazism and Fascism held an initial advantage. Until 1947 those groups frequently included the Communist Party. Thereafter Communists were quite systematically excluded from all western European governments. This policy was quite naturally favored and encouraged by the United States. The immediate domestic problems after the war included not only those created by the physical damage of the conflict but often those that had existed in 1939. The war in most cases had not solved those prewar difficulties, but it had often opened new opportunities or possibilities for solution.

Great Britain: Socialism Back to Free Markets

In July 1945, the British electorate overwhelmingly voted for a Labour Party government. For the first time, the Labour Party commanded in its own right a majority of the House of Commons. Clement Attlee (1883–1967) replaced Winston Churchill as prime minister.

ATTLEE'S LABOUR MINISTRY Attlee's ministry was socialist but clearly non-Marxist. It made a number of bold departures in both economic and social policy. The government assumed ownership of certain major industries, including the Bank of England, the airlines, public transport, coal, electricity, and steel. The ministry also undertook a major housing program. Probably its most popular accomplishment was the establishment of new programs of social welfare legislation. This involved further unemployment assistance, old-age pensions, school lunches, and, most important, free medical service to all citizens.

The forward domestic policy of the Labour government was matched by a policy of gradual retreat on the world scene. In 1947, the enunciation of the Truman Doctrine in regard to Greece and Turkey marked Britain's admission that it could not afford to oversee the security of those areas. In the same year, Britain recognized the independence of Pakistan and India. In the postwar era, Britain would be repeatedly confronted by nationalist movements within the empire and would gradually, and usually gracefully, retreat from those outposts.

1124

GLOBAL
CONFLICT,
COLD WAR,
AND NEW
DIRECTIONS

THE CONSERVATIVE PARTY IN THE
1950s In 1951, the Conservative Party
under Churchill returned to office, remaining
there until 1964. This was the longest period of
continuous government by any party in modern British history. Under Churchill and then
under his successors, Sir Anthony Eden in
1955–1957, Harold Macmillan in 1957–1963,
and Sir Alec Douglas Home in 1963–1964, the
Conservatives attempted to draw a picture of
major differences between themselves and the
Labour Party. In reality, the differences were of
degree rather than of kind. The Conservative
government did return the steel industry to
private ownership, but it did not return to an
economy based wholly on private enterprise.
The program of national welfare and health
services continued, and the Conservatives actually undertook a building program larger
than that of the Labour Party.

The problem of decline of power and prestige
continued. From the mid-fifties onward, one
part of the empire after another became independent. The Suez intervention of 1956
brought an end to independent British military
intervention. Increasingly, British policy was
made subservient to that of the United States.
However, the economy constituted the most
persistent difficulty. Through the fifties, the
slogan "Export or die" was heard. Exports did
grow rapidly, yet more slowly than imports.
Productivity remained discouragingly low.
British unions were old-fashioned and less for-
ward-looking than those on the Continent.
Management was quite timid. Perhaps most
important, there was a low rate of capital investment in both privately and nationally
owned industries.

In 1964 the Labour Party returned to office
under Harold Wilson. For the next fifteen years
the Labour Party and the Conservatives moved
in and out of power with neither giving a fundamental direction to national policy. Then in
1979 Margaret Thatcher led the Conservative
Party to a major electoral victory, the first of
three to be achieved under her guidance. She
was the first woman to be the British prime
minister and one of the most forceful personalities in modern British political history.

THATCHERISM Within the context of the
British Conservative Party, Thatcher stood
very far to the right. Her Cabinet pursued a
policy of very high interest rates, sharp tax
cuts, and somewhat reduced government
spending. Generally Thatcher also took a very
hard line with the trade unions. The results of
these policies, popularly known as Thatcherism, led to mixed results. Inflation came under
limited control while the rate of British unemployment in the early 1980s reached the levels
of the Great Depression years.

The positive policies pursued by the government involved various forms of privatization
and a strong faith in the free market. Policies
pointing in these new directions included the
sale of public housing units to their inhabitants, thus creating a new property-owning
group in the nation, and the sale of shares in
various previously government-owned companies to the general public. Furthermore, the
government, through loans and other devices,
has attempted to foster small business ventures and a general atmosphere of free enterprise. Great profits were made in real estate
development in London and some other cities
in the south of England.

*Prime Minister Margaret Thatcher is shown at the
annual conference of the British Conservative Party
in 1979. Thatcher has been the most right-wing
prime minister of post-war Britain. [Magnum]*

During the summer of 1984 race riots erupted again in London. [Gerard Rancnam/Sygma]

The Thatcher decade saw major new strains within British society. For example, in the summer of 1981 riots broke out in several of the major cities, including Liverpool and London. These disturbances erupted among the large number of jobless British youth and among the tens of thousands of nonwhite immigrants who had come to settle in Britain from the nation's former colonies. Some of the riots of 1981, and later ones, involved racial clashes; others involved both white and non-white youths jointly attacking the police, who had come to be viewed in some urban areas as symbols of political repression. During 1984 and 1985 the nation was divided over a major strike by the coal mine workers. Here the issue was the power of the central government over a recalcitrant labor union. The chief issue was the determination of the government to close inefficient mines. In the end the Thatcher government came to be viewed as the victor.

THE FALKLANDS WAR In the spring of 1982, after years of fruitless negotiations over the question of legal ownership, the government of Argentina ordered the invasion of the Falkland Islands (Malvinas). Located in the South Atlantic off the shore of South America, these islands had been governed by Great Britain for over a century and a half. The Argentines claimed that the dispute involved the recapture of territory held by a colonial power. The British contended that the Argentines had committed an act of international aggression, an opinion in which the government of the United States concurred. The invasion occurred on April 3. Shortly thereafter the British dispatched a very large fleet to the South Atlantic. During the following weeks the largest naval engagements since World War II took place between the British and Argentine navies. Both forces sustained major losses before the British emerged the victors.

Children in Belfast stone British armored cars. An entire generation of Northern Irish children has grown up in an atmosphere of continuous violence. [Sygma]

The election of 1983 held in the wake of the Falklands military success proved a great victory for Thatcher. Her party retained firm control of Parliament. She achieved a third victory in 1987. In both elections the Labour Party was badly divided between its moderate and extreme left wing. Furthermore, since 1980 the Social Democrats, composed of relatively conservative Labour Party members, and the Liberal Party have represented a third force in British politics draining votes away from Labour. Even so, by the end of the decade the Social Democrats had failed to make a significant impact on British electoral politics.

THE TROUBLES IN NORTHERN IRELAND Since the late 1960s through both Labour and Conservative governments, Britain has confronted major internal disturbances in Northern Ireland. By the treaty of 1921 the Ulster counties remained part of the United Kingdom while retaining a large measure of self-government. The Protestant majority used its power to discriminate systematically against the Roman Catholic minority in the province. In 1968 a Catholic civil rights movement was launched. Units of the Provisional Wing of the Irish Republican Army became active in seeking to unite Ulster with the Irish Republic. In turn, militant Protestant organizations became mobilized. The British government sent in units of the army to restore order. Soon the army units became the target of both groups of militant Irish. In 1972 the British suspended the Northern Irish Parliament and began to govern the province directly. Since that time, despite a series of attempts to achieve peace, Northern Ireland has remained a territory stricken with civil war and violence.

France: Search for Stability and Glory

France experienced the most troubled immediate postwar domestic political scene of any major west European nation. After the defeat of 1940 a little-known general named Charles de Gaulle (1890–1970) had organized a Free French government in London. In 1944 De

Gaulle presided over the provisional government in liberated France. He was an immensely proud, patriotic person who seemed to regard himself as personally embodying the spirit of France. In 1946 De Gaulle, who hated the machinations of political parties, suddenly resigned from the government, believing that the newly organized Fourth Republic, like the Third, gave far too little power to the executive. The Fourth French Republic thus lost the single strong leader it had possessed. After De Gaulle's departure the republic returned to the rapid turnover of ministries that had characterized the Third Republic during the 1920s and 1930s.

A major source of domestic discontent related to colonial problems in North Africa and Indochina. By 1954 the government of Premier Mendes-France had withdrawn from Indochina after a protracted war and later granted independence to Tunisia. Morocco was also soon moving toward independence. The seemingly intractable problem lay in Algeria, which was regarded not as a colony but as part of France. An anticolonial revolt in Algeria deeply divided France.

CHARLES DE GAULLE AND THE FIFTH REPUBLIC

In 1958 with France on the brink of civil war over Algeria a group of politicians in Paris turned to Charles de Gaulle, whom the army trusted would uphold their cause in Algeria. De Gaulle came to power and created the Fifth French Republic, in which the president possesses extraordinary power. Having secured his own authority, De Gaulle moved to attack the Algerian problem. In the face of major domestic opposition he made large concessions to the Algerian Liberal Movement, and by 1962 Algeria was independent.

Throughout the rest of the 1960s De Gaulle pursued a policy of making France the leading nation in a united Europe. He presented himself as a strong nationalist in part no doubt to heal the wounds remaining from the Algerian problem. He pursued systematically good relations with Germany but was never friendly with Great Britain. He deeply resented the influence of the United States in western Europe.

De Gaulle wanted Europe to become a third force in the world between the superpowers. For that reason he pushed for the development of a French nuclear capacity and refused to

President Charles de Gaulle (1890–1969) was the most important and successful French political leader since World War II. [Magnum]

become a party to the 1963 Nuclear Test Ban Treaty. He took French military forces out of NATO in 1967 and caused its headquarters to be moved from Paris to Brussels, but he did not take France out of the alliance itself. He was highly critical of the American involvement in Vietnam. That American adventure served to convince him even further that Europe under French leadership must prepare to fend for itself.

For ten years De Gaulle succeeded in leading France according to his own lights. Then in 1968 he confronted domestic unrest in France. The troubles began among student groups in Paris, and then they spread to other major sectors of French life. Hundreds of thousands of workers went on strike. Having assured himself of the support of the army, De Gaulle made a brief television speech to rally his followers. Soon they, too, came into the streets to demonstrate for De Gaulle and stability. The strikes ended. Police often moved against the student groups. The government itself quickly moved to improve the wages and benefits of workers. May 1968 had revealed the fragile strength of the Fifth Republic. It had also revealed that the economic progress of France since the war had created a large body of citizens with sufficient stake in the status quo to fear and prevent disruption.

1128

GLOBAL
CONFLICT,
COLD WAR,
AND NEW
DIRECTIONS

In 1969 President de Gaulle resigned after some relatively minor constitutional changes were rejected in a referendum. His immediate successors and supporters, Georges Pompidou (1911–1974) and Valery Giscard D'Estaing (b. 1926), set about improving the economic conditions that had fostered discontent among factory workers in 1968. They also continued to support a strong policy favoring European unity. In 1973, three years after De Gaulle's death in political retirement, France permitted Great Britain to join the Common Market, the west European organization for economic co-operation, discussed more fully later in the chapter. Throughout the rest of the decade the French government pursued a center-right course and emphasized technocratic solutions to French economic problems.

FRANÇOIS MITTERAND AND THE SOCIALISTS The presidential election of 1980 witnessed a sharp turnaround in French politics. François Mitterand (b. 1916), the Socialist Party candidate, decisively defeated Giscard d'Estaing. A few weeks later the Socialists also captured control of the French Parliament. Giscard d'Estaing had become personally unpopular and was regarded as increasingly aloof from the French people. But no less important was Mitterand's successful effort throughout the 1970s to build a united politi-

François Mitterand, a socialist, was elected president in 1980, ending twenty-two years of right-wing domination of French politics. However, the right recaptured control of parliament in 1986. [UPI/ Bettmann Newsphotos]

cal left in France, thus overcoming the traditional divisions within the French left.

The Mitterand government initially pursued a policy of active socialism in rhetoric and rather moderate policies in action. Government ownership of several large industries increased. There was an unsuccessful attempt to reform the educational system to the detriment of Roman Catholic influence. In the realm of foreign policy Mitterand pursued a strong anti-Soviet line and a moderately strong pro-American position. This stance differed from the traditional Gaullist position, which had put France on a course of independent mediation between the two superpowers. Mitterand, however, strongly supported the continuation of the independent French nuclear capability.

The French parliamentary elections of 1986 resulted in two new situations for the Fifth Republic. First, the election saw the emergence on the national scene of the National Front, an extreme right-wing group led by Jean-Marie LePen. This group seemed to appeal to certain working-class voters among whom there had arisen racial and ethnic tensions as a result of the immigration of workers from North Africa into the French labor market. Second, a coalition of traditional French conservative parties won control of the National Assembly. The French Constitution, which had been tailored by and for De Gaulle, had not envisioned a situation in which the presidency would be held by one party and the assembly controlled by another. Through an arrangement known popularly as cohabitation the two parties managed to handle matters of state.

However, in 1987 Mitterand was elected to a new term in office. Shortly thereafter the left-wing parties won a narrow majority in the National Assembly, and cohabitation came to an end. The main result of that election was an apparent determination of the majority of the French electorate to pursue a middle political course and to avoid the extremes of traditional ideology.

West Germany: Democracy and Prosperity

The Federal Republic of Germany was organized in 1949 from the three Western allied occupation sectors. Its amazing material prog-

PORTFOLIO VI
THE NEW EUROPE

Three forces have forged the emerging face of a New Europe. These are technology, the military and economic alliances of Western Europe, and the revolutions that have swept across Eastern Europe and the Soviet Union during the 1980s.

Technology

After World War II all the nations of Europe rebuilt themselves and became more modern and technologically oriented. Western Europe became much more prosperous, but the drive toward a more modern technology occurred everywhere. This movement manifested itself in terms of nuclear power, expanding steel mills, high speed trains, and new architecture. European medical technology continued to move forward, keeping pace with that of the United States. In Germany virtually new cities replaced those destroyed in the bombing. In the Soviet Union there was a major drive toward the exploration of outer space.

European technology and production has made rapid strides. In a Volkswagen factory automobiles are assembled by robots. [R. Bossu/SYGMA]

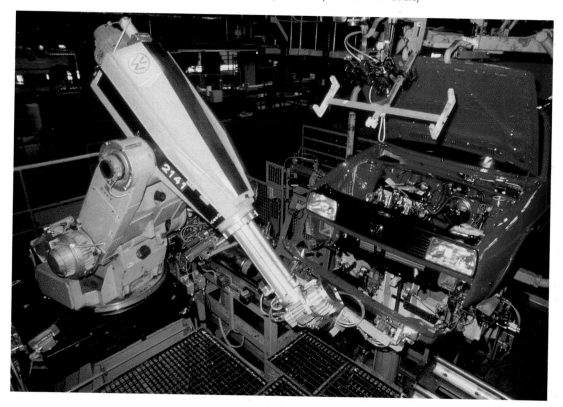

The Christian tradition has also frequently embraced modern architectural expression as in this church of Notre-Dame-due-Haut in Ronchamp, France, designed by Le Corbusier. [George Holton/Photo Researchers]

European architecture has attempted to break with the traditions of the past. Here in the Pompidou Center in Paris many of the stairways and other mechanical parts of the structure form an outer skeleton. [Steve Elmore]

Prosperity in Western Europe

Despite the general economic development that occurred throughout the continent, a much higher level of prosperity and far more consumer goods were present in Western Europe. The Marshall Plan sponsored by the United States had helped stimulate the rebuilding of Western Europe. In 1957 several of these nations had formed the European Economic Community which others joined over the next thirty years. The lowering of tariffs and other trade barriers and the achievement of unprecedented levels of economic cooperation led to very marked differences in the standards of living between Western Europe and Eastern Europe. In the latter centrally planned economies resulted in extreme shortages of consumer goods and food.

In 1985 the artist Christo carried out a massive, temporary work of art. He directed over three hundred workers in the wrapping of the Pont-Neuf in Paris with over four hundred thousand square feet of woven polyamide fabric which was held to the bridge by thousands of feet of rope and tons of iron weights in the river. The famous bridge remained so wrapped from 22 September through 7 October, 1985. [Project Director: Johannes Schaub. Copyright: C.V.J. Corp/Christo 1985. Photo: Wolfgang Volz.]

During the Cold War anti-United States billboards were to be found in Moscow.
This scene from 1968 illustrates Russian and Vietcong bullets wounding the arm
of an evil looking Uncle Sam. [Sovfoto]

NATO and
the Warsaw Pact

The economic differences were directly associated with the differing political systems. The democratic states of Western Europe were members of NATO while the one-party Communist states of Eastern Europe and the Soviet Union belonged to the Warsaw Pact.

Throughout Western Europe the NATO alliance, with its headquarters first in France and then in Belgium, provided a protective umbrella under which those nations prospered. The European Economic Community, with its headquarters in Brussels, and the European Parliament, situated in Strasbourg, provided the basis for a new economic integration. Both the presence of nuclear weapons within the alliance and the materialism associated with prosperity led many young people to criticize

and reject the newly emerging culture of the West. Many people feared the environmental consequences of economic growth.

Dissent was more difficult in Eastern Europe where Soviet troops crushed political and economic change in Hungary in 1956 and in Czechoslovakia in 1968. Indeed the Warsaw Pact functioned as much to police its own member nations as to halt potential military attacks. The Warsaw Pact served to maintain in power the various Communist Parties. These in turn led their nations to adopt centralized economic planning that resulted in a relatively low standard of living. Once it became clear in the late 1980s that the troops of the Warsaw Pact would no longer be used to support the local Communist Parties, bold experiments in both politics and economics took place.

Political Change in Eastern Europe and the Soviet Union

During the 1980s change occurred throughout Eastern Europe and the Soviet Union. The movement to challenge the dominance of the Soviet Union and of the various Communist Parties started in Poland with the activity of the Solidarity Trade Union. In 1985 Mikhail Gorbachev came to power in the Soviet Union and began a series of bold political and economic experiments to address the economic malaise of the nation.

The strikes and demonstrations of Solidarity in Poland during the early 1980s marked the first major challenge to Communist Party domination of Eastern Europe. [Georges Merillon/Gamma Liaison]

Through 1989 and into 1990 revolutionary stirrings spread across all of the Communist block nations. Thousands of people took to the streets to protest their Communist governments. In Poland and elsewhere noncommunist governments came to power. In Germany the Berlin Wall was breached. It soon became virtually certain that a reunified Germany would emerge. In Romania the dictator Nicholae Ceaucescu was overthrown and killed. Further change took place in the Soviet Union. Large popular demonstrations were held. Gorbachev led the Soviet Communist Party to renounce its monopoly on power. Ethnic unrest spread in both the Baltic and Islamic Republics.

The most emotionally symbolic moment in the Revolutions of 1989 occurred in November when the Berlin Wall was opened and crowds of Germans from both sides of the wall climbed over its top. [R. Bossu/SYGMA]

Far left *Lithuania has posed the gravest challenge to the territorial integrity of the post-World War II borders of the Soviet Union. [J. Langevin/SYGMA]*

Left *During the Revolutions of 1989 statues of Lenin and other Soviet heroes were removed from various cities in central Europe to indicate the determination to be independent of Soviet domination. [Patrick Forestier/SYGMA]*

The only truly violent revolution of 1989 occurred in Romania where troops were ordered to fire on demonstrators. Once that firing took place, there was a general resort to force. [P. Parrot/SYGMA]

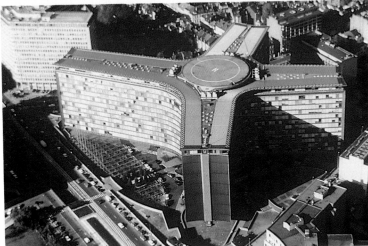

Below *Many Europeans whose nations are members of the European Economic Community now travel on a European Community passport rather than upon that of their own nations. This is another indication of the quickening pace of European unity and cooperation. [Courtesy European Communities]*

Top *The European Parliament meets in Strasbourg. In coming years it seems likely that major European political careers will be achieved in this forum as for the past century and a half they have been formed in the various national parliaments. [Courtesy European Communities]*

Bottom *This building houses the High Commission of the European Economic Community. The policies shaped in this structure have transformed the economic life of Western Europe. [Courtesy European Communities]*

An Uncertain Future

As the last decade of the century opened, a New Europe had clearly emerged. In the West there was remarkable economic prosperity and a movement toward still more extensive economic cooperation and even unity. In the East politics had taken a new, initially more democratic direction with the collapse of the postwar Communist regimes. The future of both NATO and the Warsaw Pact had become uncertain. The material prosperity of the West and its liberal political structures proved ultimately attractive to the peoples of Eastern Europe and the Soviet Union. The great challenges of the next decade will be the way the political and economic liberalization of Eastern Europe and the Soviet Union stabilizes itself and how Europeans address the issues arising from a reunified Germany.

ress arising from the ruins of the conflict became known as the economic miracle of postwar Europe. Between 1948 and 1964 West German industrial production grew by 600 per cent. Unemployment became almost unknown. All of this time the country remained the center of Cold War disputes and was occupied by thousands of foreign troops. In the midst of Cold War tensions the Germans prospered.

ECONOMIC MIRACLE The economic growth of the nation stemmed from a number of favorable factors. The Marshall Plan provided a strong impetus to recovery. The government of the republic throughout the 1950s and 1960s pursued a policy of giving private industry a relatively free hand while providing sufficient planning to avoid economic crisis. The goods produced by Germany proved attractive to the customers of other nations. *Volkswagen* became a household word throughout the world. Moreover, domestic demand was vigorous, and skilled labor and energetic management were available. Finally, Germany had very few foreign commitments or responsibilities. A relatively small portion of its national income had to be spent on defense. This situation aided capital formation.

In a very real sense postwar West Germany indulged in economic expansion rather than in politics or active international policy. Unlike the Weimar Constitution, the constitution of the Federal Republic did not permit the proliferation of splinter parties. Nor did the president possess extraordinary power. The Federal Republic returned to the arena of nations very slowly. In 1949 it participated in the Marshall Plan and two years later in the European Coal and Steel Community. In 1955 the nation joined NATO, and in 1957 it was one of the charter members of the European Economic Community. The Federal Republic has been perhaps the major champion of European cooperation.

CHRISTIAN DEMOCRATS Throughout this period political initiative lay with the Christian Democrats led by Konrad Adenauer (1876–1967). His domestic policies were relatively simple and consistent: West Germany must become genuinely democratic and economically stable and prosperous. His foreign policy was profoundly anti-Communist.

Under what was known as the Hallstein Doctrine, the Federal Republic refused to have diplomatic ties with any nation, except the Soviet Union, that extended diplomatic recognition to East Germany. Adenauer's position on East Germany contributed to the Cold War climate, and it may have led the United States to overestimate the threat of Communist aggression in Europe. The Hallstein Doctrine separated the Federal Republic from all the nations of eastern Europe.

Adenauer remained in office until 1963, when he retired at the age of eighty-seven. The Christian Democrats remained in power, led first by Ludwig Erhard (1897–1977) and later by Kurt Kiesinger (b. 1904). In 1966, however, they were compelled to form a coalition with the Social Democratic Party (SDP). After the war this party had revived but had been unable to capture a parliamentary majority. By the early 1960s the SDP had expanded its base beyond the working class and had become more a party of social and economic reform than a party of socialism. This shift reflected the growing prosperity of the German working class.

BRANDT AND OSTPOLITIK The major leader of the SDP in the 1960s was Willy Brandt (b. 1913), the mayor of West Berlin. In 1966 he became vice-chancellor in the coalition government. In 1969 Brandt and the SDP carried the election in their own right.

The most significant departure of the SDP occurred in the area of foreign policy. While continuing to urge further Western unity through the Common Market, Brandt moved carefully but swiftly to establish better relations with eastern Europe (a policy called *Ostpolitik*). In 1970 he met with the leadership of East Germany. Later that year he went to Moscow to sign a treaty of cooperation. By November 1970 Brandt had completed a reconciliation treaty with Poland that recognized the Oder–Neisse river line as the Polish western border. A treaty with Czechoslovakia soon followed. In 1973 both the Federal Republic of Germany and the German Democratic Republic were admitted to the United Nations. Brandt's moves were in part a subdevelopment of the policy of detente on the part of the United States and the Soviet Union. In 1974 Brandt resigned. He was succeeded by Helmut Schmidt (b. 1918) who continued a policy of

West German Premier Helmut Kohl seized the opportunity of the revolutions of 1989 in Eastern Europe to lead the movement toward German reunification. [Ullstein Bilderdienst]

nist leadership group was deposed in East Germany, he called for a new united Germany that would take the form of a confederation.

Events moved even more rapidly than Kohl or others anticipated. By early 1990 it had become clear that German reunification would indeed take place. Negotiations commenced to establish a common currency for the two Germanies. In February, 1990, the United States, the Soviet Union, Great Britain, and France announced their approval of a process of discussion of German unification that would take place in two stages. During the first, representatives of the two Germanies would undertake negotiations on matters relating to internal political arrangements. During the second, the four powers from World War II would enter the discussions to consider matters relating to external security and the relationship of the new united Germany to its European neighbors and European relations in general. Again events moved rapidly. On October 3, 1990 Germany became reunited, and it had been agreed by the other powers that it would continue its membership in NATO.

The newly united Germany will be a nation of approximately eighty million citizens, thus constituting the largest European nation west of the Soviet Union. Unification has already brought major changes to German domestic politics. Unification with West Germany has guaranteed that the East Germans will move into a democratic era. The Christian Democrats would seem to have emerged as the primary forgers of new German national unification. Yet they confront enormous political problems because of the virtual collapse of the economy in East Germany. The integration of that economy with the West Germany economy will involve numerous costs which may bring difficult political pressures to bear on the Christian Democrats.

The reunification of the two Germanies represents the most significant change among the European powers since 1945. In terms of these relations the predominant question will be the manner in which the ongoing German presence in NATO is accepted and addressed by future Soviet policy. The acceptance of this membership represented a major concession

conversations with the Communist bloc nations and Moscow. Schmidt also took a lead in asserting the necessity of close United States consultation with its west European allies on both economic and military matters.

KOHL'S MINISTRY In 1982 Helmut Kohl, a conservative Christian Democrat, became the West German chancellor. His first years in office were marked by a number of political and financial scandals. He also pursued a controversial policy of allowing Germany to begin to acknowledge more openly its Nazi epoch in an effort to bring about full reconciliation with Germany's allies. He visited World War I battlefields with President Mitterand of France. In 1985 he persuaded President Reagan to visit the German military cemetery at Bitburg among whose graves were those of SS officers. Kohl and his party also generally maintained the strength of the German economy.

GERMAN REUNIFICATION In 1989 Kohl immediately welcomed the revolutionary events in East Germany, which will be more fully discussed later in this chapter. Shortly after travel was restored between East and West Germany and the longtime Commu-

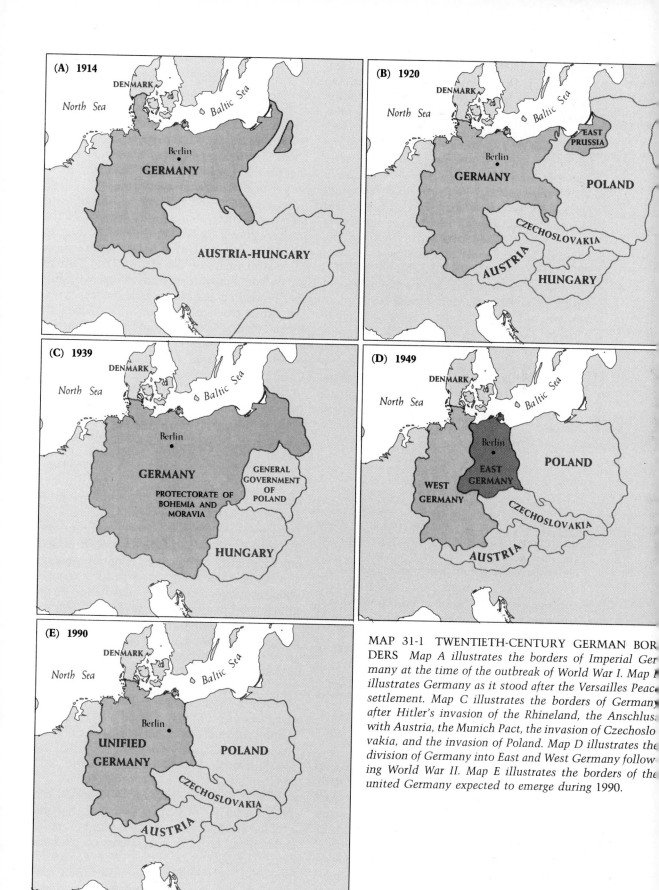

MAP 31-1 TWENTIETH-CENTURY GERMAN BOR-
DERS *Map A illustrates the borders of Imperial Germany at the time of the outbreak of World War I. Map B
illustrates Germany as it stood after the Versailles Peace
settlement. Map C illustrates the borders of Germany
after Hitler's invasion of the Rhineland, the Anschluss
with Austria, the Munich Pact, the invasion of Czechoslovakia, and the invasion of Poland. Map D illustrates the
division of Germany into East and West Germany following World War II. Map E illustrates the borders of the
united Germany expected to emerge during 1990.*

1132

GLOBAL
CONFLICT,
COLD WAR,
AND NEW
DIRECTIONS

on the part of the Soviet Union which had initially desired a neutral Germany. It remains to be seen how in the future the Soviet Union will regard that NATO membership. The presence of Germany in NATO is expected to preserve the Western orientation of Germany and to prevent Germany from becoming an overly powerful and aggressive state, as occurred in 1914 and 1939. Several of Germany's eastern neighbors, such as Poland, wished to preserve German association with NATO as a means of providing for their own security from both potential German expansion or renewed Soviet domination. NATO itself has been compelled to rethink its own goals and purposes in light of the collapse of the Communist government in eastern Europe and the marked changes in Soviet policy.

Whatever the short-range outcome of the debates over reunification, the presence of a unified German nation in the middle of Europe will become the most important political factor of the next decade and beyond in European history.

Toward Western European Unification

Since 1945, the nations of western Europe have taken unprecedented steps toward cooperation and potential unity. The moves toward unification have related primarily to economic integration. These actions arose from American encouragement in response to the Soviet domination of eastern Europe, and from a sense of lack of effective political power on the part of the states of western Europe. The process of economic integration has not been steady, nor is it near completion; but it has provided a major new factor in the domestic politics of the states involved.

Postwar Cooperation

The movement toward unity could have occurred in at least three ways: politically, militarily, or economically. The economic path was taken largely because the other paths were blocked. In 1949, ten European states organized the Council of Europe, which meets in Strasbourg, France. Its organization involved foreign ministers and a Consultative Assembly elected by the parliaments of the participants. The Council of Europe was and continues to be only an advisory body. Some persons hoped that the council might become a parliament of Europe. However, during the early 1950s none of the major states was willing to surrender any of its sovereignty to the newly organized body. The initial failure of the council to bring about significant political cooperation meant that for that time unity would not come about by political or parliamentary routes.

Between 1950 and 1954, there was some interest in a more thorough integration of the military forces of NATO. When the Korean War broke out, the United States began to urge the rearmament of Germany. The German forces would provide western Europe with further protection against possible Soviet aggression while the United States was involved in Korea. France continued to fear a German army. In 1951, the French government suggested the creation of a European Defense Community that would constitute a supranational military organization. It would require a permanent British commitment of forces to the Continent to help France, in effect, counter any future German threat. The proposal continued to be considered for some time, but in 1954 the French Parliament itself vetoed the program. In 1955, Germany was permitted to rearm and to enter NATO. Supranational military organization had not been achieved.

Rather than in politics or the military, the major moves toward European cooperation and potential unity came in the economic sphere. Unlike the other two possible paths of cooperation, economic activity involved little or no immediate loss of political sovereignty. Moreover, the material benefits of combined economic activity brought new popular support to all of the governments involved.

Many European leaders and civil servants believed that only through the abandonment of economic nationalism could the newly organized democratic states avoid the economic turmoil that had proved such fertile ground for dictatorship. Economic cooperation carried the possibility of greater efficiency, prosperity, and employment.

In 1950, Robert Schuman (1886–1963), the foreign minister of France, proposed that the coal and steel production of western Europe be undertaken on an integrated, cooperative basis. The next year, France, West Germany, Italy, and the "Benelux" countries (Belgium, the Netherlands, and Luxembourg) organized the European Coal and Steel Community. Its activity was limited to a single part of the economy, but that was a sector affecting almost all other industrial production. An agency called the *High Authority* administered the plan. The authority was genuinely supranational, and its members could not be removed during their appointed terms. The Coal and Steel Community prospered. By 1955, coal production had grown by 23 per cent. Iron and steel production was up by almost 150 per cent. The community both benefited from and contributed to the immense growth of material production in western Europe during this period. Its success reduced the suspicions of government and business groups about the concept of coordination and economic integration.

The European Economic Community

It took more than the prosperity of the European Coal and Steel Community to draw Euro-

---

The European Economic Community Is Established

The 1957 Treaty of Rome identified the major goals of the European Economic Community (Common Market) for the original six members.

Article 2: It shall be the aim of the Community, by establishing a Common Market and progressively approximating the economic policies of Member States, to promote throughout the Community a harmonious development of economic activities, a continuous and balanced expansion, an increased stability, an accelerated raising of the standard of living and closer relations between its Member States.

Article 3: For the purposes set out in the preceding Article, the activities of the Community shall include, under the conditions and with the timing provided for in this Treaty:

(a) the elimination, as between Member States, of customs duties and of quantitative restrictions in regard to the importation and exportation of goods, as well as of all other measures with equivalent effect;

(b) the establishment of a common customs tariff and a common commercial policy towards third countries;

(c) the abolition, as between Member States, of the obstacles to the free movement of persons, services and capital;

(d) the inauguration of a common agricultural policy;

(e) the inauguration of a common transport policy;

(f) the establishment of a system ensuring that competition shall not be distorted in the Common Market;

(g) the application of procedures which shall make it possible to co-ordinate the economic policies of Member States and to remedy disequilibria in their balances of payments;

(h) the approximation of their respective municipal law to the extent necessary for the functioning of the Common Market;

(i) the creation of a European Social Fund in order to improve the possibilities of employment for workers and to contribute to the raising of their standard of living;

(j) the establishment of a European Investment Bank intended to facilitate the economic expansion of the Community through the creation of new resources; and

(k) the association of overseas countries and territories with the Community with a view to increasing trade and to pursuing jointly their effort towards economic and social development.

Treaty Establishing the European Economic Community *(Brussels: Secretariat of the Interim Committee for the Common Market and Euratom, 1957), pp. 17–18.*

1134

GLOBAL
CONFLICT,
COLD WAR,
AND NEW
DIRECTIONS

pean leaders toward further unity. The unsuccessful Suez intervention and the resulting diplomatic isolation of France and Britain persuaded many Europeans that only through unified action could they exert any significant influence on the two superpowers or control their own destinies. Consequently, in 1957, through the Treaty of Rome, the six members of the Coal and Steel Community agreed to form a new organization: the European Economic Community. The *Common Market,* as the EEC soon came to be called, envisioned more than a free-trade union. Its members sought to achieve the eventual elimination of tariffs, a free flow of capital and labor, and similar wage and social benefits in all the participating countries. Its chief institutions were a Council of Foreign Ministers and a High Commission composed of technocrats. The former came to be the dominant body.

The Common Market achieved a stunning degree of success during its early years. By 1968, all tariffs among the six members had been abolished well ahead of the planned schedule. Trade and labor migration among the members grew steadily. Moreover, nonmember states began to copy the community and later to seek membership. In 1959, Britain, Denmark, Norway, Sweden, Switzerland, Austria, and Portugal formed the European Free Trade Area. However, by 1961 Great Britain had decided to seek Common Market membership. Twice, in 1963 and 1967, British membership was vetoed by President de Gaulle of France. The French president felt that Britain was too closely related to the United States and its policies to support the European Economic Community wholeheartedly.

Toward 1992

Despite the French actions, the Common Market survived and continued to prosper. In 1973, Great Britain, Ireland, and Denmark became members. Discussions continued on further steps toward integration including proposals for a common currency. However, during the late 1970s there seemed to be a loss of momentum. Norway and Sweden, with relatively strong economies, declined to join. Although in 1982 Spain, Portugal, and Greece applied for membership and were admitted, sharp disagreements and a sense of stagnation continued within the Community.

Then after almost a decade of disagreements and loss of direction, the leaders of the Community reached an extremely important decision early in 1988. They set upon the year 1992 as the goal for achieving a virtual free-trade zone throughout the Community. This momentous new step involves the elimination of remaining trade barriers and other restrictive trade policies. If carried to a successful conclusion, this new policy will establish all of western Europe as a zone for free trade not unlike that existing within the United States. This situation will create a vast new market immediately benefiting the large companies of western Europe and opening the possibility of the growth of new enterprises. These companies will be able to compete more easily with non-European rivals. In all likelihood there will be further cooperation in shipping, banking, and other major economic activity.

Politically, there are likely to be two immediate results. First, the new unity of the European Economic Community will change the nature of East–West relationships. Undoubtedly difficulties regarding the United States and the NATO alliance will arise as the Community develops more extensive trade relationships with the nations of eastern Europe and the Soviet Union. On the other side of the equation, those same trade relations may draw the eastern European nations away from the Soviet orbit. Virtually all of the new governments that emerged in eastern Europe after the revolutions of 1989 indicated a desire for closer economic relationships with the Community. Indeed, one of the reasons for the general discontent with the Communist Party-dominated regimes in eastern Europe was their failure to provide the kind of economic progress and prosperity that had developed in western Europe—and most particularly in the nations of the European Economic Community.

The second political implication of the new unity will be an increase in the importance of the European Community Parliament in Strasbourg. Ambitious European political figures will now have to decide whether to pursue their ambitions within their individual national parliaments or within the larger European parliament. Previously, the national political arenas were more important. That may no longer be the case after 1992.

It remains unclear how the emergence of a reunified Germany will affect the future of the

European Economic Community. The new German nation could simply become the strongest partner in the Community and lead the Community to expand its concerns further east. Another possibility would be for Germany to forge its own independent economic relationships that would eventually favor ties to eastern Europe over those to the Community. In both the late nineteenth and early twentieth centuries such links were very important for Germany. The tendency toward greater political cooperation and integration had developed during the middle of the 1980s. The political strength and ambitions of a united Germany could overcome and delay the process or even undermine it. As with so many questions in Europe at the present time, it is too early to know which direction will be pursued.

Communism and Western Europe

Throughout this century there existed in western Europe groups of intellectuals sympathetic to communism as well as organized Communist parties. The relationship of these groups to the western European political experience must be seen in a context that goes back to the Bolshevik victory itself. That event in 1918 cast all pre-World-War I European socialism into disarray. The western European socialist movement rapidly divided into independent democratic socialist parties and Soviet-dominated Communist parties that followed the directions of the Third International. Throughout the 1920s and 1930s those two groups generally fought against each other with only rare moments of cooperation, as during the French Popular Front in 1936. At the same time European left-wing intellectuals divided between those who supported socialism and those who supported communism. The results of those divisions and debates continued to influence western European political life through the 1980s.

The Intellectuals

During the 1930s, as liberal democracies floundered during the Great Depression and as right-wing regimes spread across the Continent, communism appeared to numerous peo-

ple at the time as a way to protect human values. Throughout Europe students in the universities were affiliated with the Communist Party. They and older intellectuals visited the Soviet Union and praised Stalin's achievements. Some of these writers did not know of Stalin's terror; others simply closed their eyes to it, somehow believing that human ends might come from inhumane methods; still others actually defended Stalinist terror. During the late 1920s and the 1930s communism became for some Europeans little less than a substitute religion. One group of former Communists, writing after World War II, described their attraction and later disillusionment with communism in a book entitled *The God That Failed* (1949).

Four events proved crucial to the disillusionment of the intellectuals. These were the great public purge trials of 1936 and later, the Spanish Civil War (1936–1939), the Nazi–Soviet Pact of 1939, and the Soviet invasion of Hungary in 1956. Arthur Koestler's novel *Darkness at Noon* (1940) recorded a former Communist's view of the purges. George Orwell, who had never been a Communist but who had

In his essays and novels, the most popular of which were Animal Farm *(1945) and* 1984 *(1949), George Orwell (1903–1950) attacked the totalitarian tendencies that threaten human values in the twentieth century. [Ullstein Bilderdienst]*

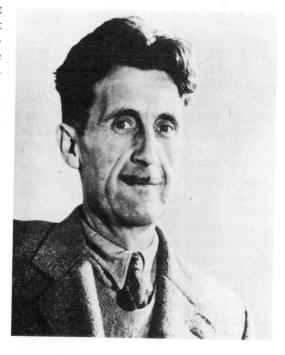

1136

GLOBAL
CONFLICT,
COLD WAR,
AND NEW
DIRECTIONS

sympathized, presented the disappointment with Stalin's policy in Spain in *Homage to Catalonia* (1938). The Nazi–Soviet Pact destroyed the image of Stalin as an opponent of fascism. Other intellectuals, such as the French philosopher Jean-Paul Sartre, long put faith in the Soviet Union, but the Hungarian Revolution cooled his ardor. The later invasion of Czechoslovakia simply confirmed a general disillusionment with Soviet policies on the part of even left-wing western European intellectuals.

Yet disillusionment with the Soviet Union or with Stalin did not in all cases mean disillusionment with Marxism or with radical socialist criticism of European society. Some writers and social critics looked to the establishment of alternative communist governments based

on non-Soviet models. During the decade after World War II, Yugoslavia provided the example of such a different path. Beginning in the late 1950s radical students and a few intellectuals looked for inspiration to the Chinese Revolution. Other groups hoped for the development of a European Marxist system. Among the more important contributors to this non-Soviet tradition was the Italian Communist Antonio Gramsci (1891–1937) and his work *Letters from Prison* (published posthumously in 1947). The thought of such non-Soviet communists became very important to Western European Communist parties, such as that of Italy, which hoped to gain office democratically.

Another mode of Marxist accommodation within mid-twentieth-century European thought was a redefinition of the basic message of Marx himself. During the 1930s a considerable body of previously unprinted essays by Marx was published. These books and articles are quite abstract and philosophical and were written by Marx before *The Communist Manifesto* of 1848. They make the "young Marx" appear to belong more nearly to the humanist than to the revolutionary tradition of European thought. Since World War II these works, including *Philosophic Manuscripts of 1844* and *German Ideology*, have been widely read. Today many people are more familiar with them than with the *Manifesto* or *Capital*. The writings of the young Marx allowed some people to consider themselves sympathetic to Marxism without also seeing themselves as revolutionaries or supporters of the Soviet Union.

The Rise and Fall of Euro-Communism

During the 1970s and early 1980s there appeared to be developing a new western European Marxist alternative known at the time as Euro-Communism. The term referred to an effort to accommodate western European Communist parties to the political realities of their positions in successfully functioning liberal democracies. The chief architect of this strategy was Enrico Berlinguer (1922–1984), the leader of the Italian Communist Party which was the largest and best organized in western Europe. The strategy was carried farther in Italy than in any other state.

MAJOR DATES IN WESTERN EUROPEAN DOMESTIC POLITICS

1945	Attlee leads Labour Party to victory in Britain
1946	De Gaulle resigns position in Fourth French Republic
1948–1949	Berlin blockade
1954	France retreats from Indochina
1955	West Germany joins NATO
1956	Suez Crisis
1957	European Economic Community (Common Market) founded
1958	De Gaulle returns to power, founding Fifth French Republic
1962	France recognizes Algerian independence
1967	French forces removed from NATO
1968	Student and factory worker unrest in Paris
1969	De Gaulle resigns French presidency
	Willie Brandt leads SDP to victory in West Germany
1970	West Germany recognizes Oder–Neisse line with Poland
1972	Northern Irish Parliament suspended
1979	Margaret Thatcher becomes British prime minister
1980	Mitterand leads Socialist victory in France
1982	Falklands War between Britain and Argentina
	Helmut Kohl becomes Christian Democratic Prime Minister of West Germany
1988	European Economic Community agrees to work toward free trade zone by 1992
1990	Reunification of Germany

During the mid-1970s the Italian Communist Party had begun to make inroads on national political life as a result of weariness with the corruption of the Christian Democratic Party that had governed since shortly after the end of World War II. The Communists had won a considerable number of municipal elections. During 1976 the Italian Communists won over 35 per cent of the popular vote for the Chamber of Deputies. However, they were refused admission to the Cabinet. In an effort to gain entry into the real arena of government, Berlinguer at that point set forth a policy that became known as the *Historic Compromise.*

Berlinguer's policy represented a major break not only with the previous stand of the Italian Communist Party but also with the Moscow-dominated Communist movement. By the "historic compromise" Berlinguer announced the willingness of the Italian Communist Party to enter a coalition government with the Christian Democrats and non-Communist parties. In other words, the Italian Communists in effect renounced revolution as the path to political power. They also agreed to participate in a government that they would not dominate or control. The Italian Communist Party also promised that as a partner in the coalition or as the governing party, should it be elected, it would govern constitutionally and would respect individuals' civil liberties. It also urged continued Italian participation in NATO and criticized the crackdown on the Solidarity Movement in Poland.

The "historic compromise" was never put to the test in Italy. There is little evidence that voters really believed the Communists would keep their word once in power. The Italian Communists reached their electoral peak in the early 1980s. Berlinguer died in 1984 and no strong successor emerged. The importance of Euro-Communism may have been overestimated at the time. Yet it marked still another development in the evolution of the communist movement in the West and in its attempts to separate itself from the Soviet model. The entire situation of the western European Communist parties became transformed during the second half of the 1980s: the electorates became more conservative and the Communist Party governments in eastern Europe collapsed and that of the Soviet Union underwent radical reform.

Brezhnev died in 1982. Both of his immediate successors, Yuri Andropov (1914–1984) and Constantine Chernenko (1911–1984), died after holding office for very short periods. In 1984 Mikhail S. Gorbachev came to power and soon emerged as the most significant political figure in the past half-century of European history. He immediately set about making the most remarkable changes that the Soviet Union has witnessed since the 1920s.

Economic Perestroika

The backdrop for these events has been the economic stagnation of the Soviet economy and the consequent disillusionment with the Soviet Communist Party. By the early 1980s the Soviet Union stood in a paradoxical situation. It was militarily stronger than it had ever been before. After the Soviet backdown during the Cuban Missile Crisis, the Soviet government embarked on a major military expansion that was both extensive and successful. However, virtually all of the nonmilitary side of the economy remained stagnant. The economic growth rate was declining. Worker absenteeism because of alcoholism was high. There was poor progress in all areas of technology except for defense. Shortages in all kinds of consumer goods were extensive.

Gorbachev believed that only drastic changes in the entire Soviet political and economic system could transform this situation. In attempting to carry out this radical transformation, Gorbachev has assumed a role in the tradition of those major figures in Russian and Soviet history who have attempted to impose major reforms from above. He and his supporters within the Communist Party and the Soviet government have challenged the traditional role of the bureaucracy in directing the economy and government policy. The term that has been applied to these economic changes, as well as to the major political changes, is *perestroika* or restructuring.

The target of this effort has been the various centralized economic ministries that were considerably reduced in size. A larger role has been allowed for private enterprise on the local level. By early 1990 in a clear abandonment of

1138

GLOBAL
CONFLICT,
OLD WAR,
AND NEW
DIRECTIONS

*Mikhail Gorbachev has led the Soviet Union in the boldest European political and
economic experience since the close of World War II. [Tass from Sovfoto]*

traditional Marxist ideology, Gorbachev had
begun to advocate private ownership of property. Within the Soviet context, Gorbachev's
approach has been genuinely radical. It has
challenged centralized planning and centralized Communist Party control. He and his
supporters have proved to be exceedingly critical of the corruption and inefficiencies in the
economy and the party bureaucracy. Yet by
1990 the Soviet economy had not significantly
improved.

By the opening of the 1990s, after more than
five years in power, Gorbachev had not been
able to effect most of his economic goals. Agricultural production had not increased and the
government formally announced major food
shortages. Virtually all other consumer goods
and housing remained in short supply. There
was extensive debate in the Soviet Union over
what economic course should be taken. Gorbachev and his chief advisors looked to a transformation of the existing centrally directed
Soviet economy into a more nearly free market
system. That outlook fostered much disagreement about the speed at which such a free

economy should be established. There were
fears of inflation and unemployment which
would put new political pressures on the government. In early 1990 Gorbachev announced
that a national referendum would be held on
the issues surrounding the move toward a free
market. What the nature or outcome of that
possible referendum would be cannot be predicted.

It is important to bear in mind that the very
serious economic difficulties of the Soviet
economy have had a very real impact on the
decisions that Gorbachev has made in regard
to both political restructuring and foreign policy. To some extent, he has pursued bold actions in those areas because of the absence of
progress in the economic realm.

Glasnost

Gorbachev has allowed, within the Soviet context, an extraordinarily broad public discussion and criticism of Soviet history and Soviet
Communist Party policy. This general development has been termed *glasnost* or openness.

Certain Communist figures from the 1920s, such as Burkharin, later purged by Stalin, have once again received official public recognition for their positive contributions to Soviet history. Within factories, workers have been able to criticize party officials and the economic plans set forth by the party and the government. Intellectuals have experienced extensive possibilities of free expression. Censorship has been relaxed. Many of the dissidents have been released from prison. In the summer of 1988 Gorbachev presided over a party congress that witnessed very full debates. Another manifestation of this more open atmosphere has taken the form of demands for great political autonomy on the part of certain national minorities.

Political Perestroika

Gorbachev has also fostered *perestroika* in the political arena. In 1988 a new constitution was adopted, permitting openly contested elections. The Supreme Soviet was elected in 1989 after actual political campaigning. Issues and personalities were discussed. One of the new members of the Supreme Soviet was the late Andrei Sakharov (1921–1989), the dissident physicist who was persecuted under Brezhnev. Once the Supreme Soviet met there was very lively debate. The latter body formally elected Gorbachev as president in 1989. However, in the future, as other provisions of the new constitution go into effect, the president of the Soviet Union will be elected by the Supreme Soviet. This will mean that Gorbachev, elected to that position in 1990, will then have a political power base beyond his position in the Communist Party and the Politburo.

In this respect, Gorbachev would appear to be moving toward establishing a new political structure. It would be characterized by a strong presidency in which his own authority and that of his government would be distinct from that of the Communist Party itself. It would seem that he believes or has been led by events to recognize a widespread discontent and lack of general popular support for the Party. Legal election by a broad electorate would give Gorbachev a new basis for power as well as enormous personal political authority.

The recent reforms in the Soviet Union have led to various popular demonstrations previously virtually unknown in Soviet life. This particular demonstration involved members of the Soviet scientific community. [Novosti from Sovfoto]

1140

GLOBAL
CONFLICT,
COLD WAR,
AND NEW
DIRECTIONS

It is, however, not entirely clear how free a hand Gorbachev may have as the political structures continue to evolve. Some political groups are much more conservative than he is. These include conservative Russian nationalist groups some of which resemble the right-

Andrei Sakharov Criticizes the Limits of Perestroika

Throughout the 1970s and early 1980s Andrei Sakharov was one of the foremost Soviet dissidents. A noted physicist, he was placed under arrest and exiled from Moscow. However, with the Gorbachev reforms he was allowed to enter Soviet political life. Before his death in 1989 he was an outspoken member of the Congress of People's Deputies which met in Moscow. At the close of the Congress he was permitted to deliver a speech criticizing the progress or lack thereof which he thought had occurred. He was not, however, permitted to deliver all of his remarks; these were later printed in the United States. He criticized the large powers that the Congress reserved for Gorbachev and urged the Congress to assert greater authority on its own. He also paid special attention to the possibility of ethnic strife in the Soviet Union.

We are in the throes of spreading economic catastrophe and a tragic worsening of interethnic relations; one aspect of the powerful and dangerous processes at work has been the general crisis of confidence in the nation's leadership. If we simply float with the current, hoping that things will gradually get better in the distant future, then the accumulating tensions could explore, with dire consequences to our society.

Comrade deputies, at this moment in history, an enormous responsibility has fallen to you. Political decisions are needed in order to strengthen the local Soviet organs and resolve our economic, social, ecological, and ethnic problems. If the Congress of People's Deputies cannot take power into its hands, then there is not the slightest hope that the soviets of Union Republics [the local governments of the separate Soviet Republics] regions, districts, and villages will do so. But without strong local soviets, it won't be possible to implement land reform or any agrarian policy other than nonsensical attempts to resuscitate uneconomic collective farms.

Without a strong Congress and strong and independent soviets, it won't be possible to overcome the dictates of the bureaucracy, to work out and implement new laws on commercial enterprises, to fight against ecological folly.

. . . .

We have inherited from Stalinism a constitutional structure that bears the stamp of imperial thinking and the imperial policy of "divide and rule." The smaller Union Republics and the autonomous national subdivisions, which are administratively subordinated to the Union Republics, are victims of this legacy. For decades they have been subjected to national oppression. Now these problems have come to the surface in dramatic fashion. But to an equal extent the more numerous ethnic groups have also suffered, and that includes the Russian people who have had to bear the main burden of imperial ambitions and the consequences of adventurism and dogmatism in foreign and domestic policy.

Andrei Sakharov, *"A Speech to the People's Congress,"* The New York Review of Books, August 17, 1989, *p. 25.*

wing parties of Western Europe during the 1930s with policies that include antisemitism. More traditional Soviet Communists either object to Gorbachev fundamentally or wish to move much more slowly. More radical groups include former dissidents who now sit in the Soviet Parliament. The late Andre Sakharov spoke for this group in his urging Gorbachev to move more rapidly. Among the radicals are Communists, such as Boris Yeltsin, who have argued for more radical change. Yeltsin, when a member of the central Politburo, openly opposed Gorbachev and was then removed from that body. In 1990, however, Yeltsin was elected president of the Russian Republic within the Soviet Union from which power base he may be expected to carry on his criticism of Gorbachev.

Finally, it is unclear whether the Soviet military command will continue to support Gorbachev. All of these groups, as well as still unanticipated events, will no doubt put increasing pressure on Gorbachev's personal political position and the stability of the Soviet government.

In pursuing this political reconstruction, Gorbachev made his most radical departure early in 1990. He proposed to the Central Committee of the Soviet Communist Party that it renounce its traditional monopoly on political power. In adopting this proposal after extensive and harsh debate, the Committee sharply departed from the Leninist position that the forging of a new Soviet society required a single elite party that constituted the vanguard of the revolution. The renunciation of a Communist monopoly of power represents a rejection of the entire seventy-year heritage of Soviet communist ideology. In setting out on this new direction, Gorbachev was following the example of the Communist parties of eastern Europe, which renounced their political monopolies after the revolutions of 1989.

Assuming this new policy is adopted by the general Soviet Communist Party Congress, henceforth the Soviet Union will function with a multi-party political system. The Soviet Communist Party would be only one of those parties. Opposition groups already exist. It is also possible that different wings of the Communist Party will split off and contest elections against each other.

Internal Soviet Ethnic Discontent

Numerous obstacles lie in the path of Gorbachev's domestic policies and perhaps even his continuation in power. The greatest internal challenge to Gorbachev's position and poli-

Ethnic unrest has been one of the major challenges confronting Gorbachev. In 1989 a number of civilians and soldiers were killed in the city of Tbilisi in Soviet Georgia. This photo records the funeral procession for the burial of the citizens killed in the clash. [Novosti from Sovfoto]

1142

GLOBAL
CONFLICT,
COLD WAR,
AND NEW
DIRECTIONS

Gorbachev Proposes the Soviet Communist Party Abandon Its Monopoly of Power

On February 5, 1990, President Mikhail Gorbachev delivered a major speech to the Central Committee of the Soviet Communist Party. He proposed that the Party abandon its position as the single legal party as provided in Article 6 of the Soviet Constitution. His proposal followed similar actions by several of the Communist Parties of eastern Europe. From the time of Lenin through Brezhnev the Soviet Communist Party portrayed itself as the sole vanguard of the revolution. Gorbachev argued that it should abandon that special role and compete for political power with other political parties that may organize within the Soviet Union. The policy outlined in this speech marked a dramatic turning point in Soviet Communist political thought.

The main thing that now worries Communists and all citizens of the country is the fate of perestroika, the fate of the country and the role of the Soviet Communist Party at the current, probably most crucial, stage of revolutionary transformation.

. . . .

[It is important to understand] . . . that the party will only be able to fulfill the mission of political vanguard if it drastically restructures itself, masters the art of political work in the present conditions and succeeds in cooperating with forces committed to perestroika.

The crux of the party's renewal is the need to get rid of everything that tied it to the authoritarian-bureaucratic system, a system that left its mark not only on methods of work and inter-relationships within the party, but also on ideology, ways of thinking and notions of socialism.

The [newly proposed] platform says: our ideal is a humane, democratic socialism, expressing the interests of the working class and all working people; and relying on the great legacy of Marx, Engels and Lenin, the Soviet Communist Party is creatively, developing socialist ideals to match present-day realities and with due account for the entire experience of the 20th century.

The platform states clearly what we should abandon. We should abandon the ideological dogmatism that became ingrained during past decades, outdated stereotypes in domestic policy and outmoded views on the world revolutionary process and world development as a whole.

We should abandon everything that led to the isolation of socialist countries from the mainstream of world civilization. We should abandon the understanding of progress as a permanent confrontation with a socially different world. . . .

The party's renewal presupposes a fundamental change in its relations with state and economic bodies and the abandonment of the practice of commanding them and substituting for their functions.

The party in a renewing of society can exist and play its role as vanguard only as a democratically recognized force. This means that its status should not be imposed through constitutional endorsement.

The Soviet Communist Party, it goes without saying, intends to struggle for the status of the ruling party. But it will do so strictly within the framework of the democratic process by giving up any legal and political advantages, offering its program and defending it in discussions, cooperating with other social and political forces, always working amidst the masses, living by their interests and their needs.

The New York Times, February 6, 1990, p. A16.

MAP 31-2 THE USSR *The USSR is divided into 15 republics. In recent years, these individual republics have been seeking various degrees of political and economic independence. These demands could cause political instability in the future.*

cies comes from nationalistic and ethnic discontent within the Soviet Union. The U.S.S.R. is, like the old Habsburg Empire, a multinational state. Many of the republics within the Soviet Union are composed of a single dominant ethnic group. These groups have resented being ruled by a Russian national state as much as by a Communist-dominated state. In various areas such as Soviet Georgia and Armenia there have been violent confrontations between nationalists and the government authorities with loss of lives.

THE BALTIC STATES The most direct actions have been taken within the three Baltic Republics of Estonia, Latvia, and Lithuania. They were independent republics until the eve of the Second World War. As part of secret arrangements involved in the Soviet–German Nonaggression Pact of 1939, they were turned over to the Soviet Union. That pact represented the only legal basis for Soviet control of the republics. During 1989 and 1990 the parliaments of those republics attempted in various ways to establish independence from the Soviet Union with Lithuania actually declaring independence. Other nationalist groups may attempt similar actions and thus challenge the very basis of the union of the Soviet Union.

1144

GLOBAL
CONFLICT,
OLD WAR,
AND NEW
DIRECTIONS

THE ISLAMIC REPUBLICS A second area of major ethnic unrest is to be found in the Soviet Islamic republics in central Asia. Major riots have occurred in Azerbaijan with considerable loss of life. They have also taken place in Tadzhikistan. These have usually involved clashes between Islamic populations and Christian minorities. Much of this upheaval represents in the Soviet Republics the outburst of the Islamic revival that has swept across so much of central Asia and North Africa.

Foreign Policy

In foreign policy Gorbachev has made a considerable effort to win over the public opinion of western Europe. The first major Soviet leader to have a rather clear understanding of the value of good public relations, he has traveled extensively in the West. He carried out negotiations with the Reagan administration, leading to the limitation on intermediate-range nuclear missiles. In 1988 the Soviet Union dramatically withdrew from its military engagement in Afghanistan. In 1989 Gorbachev personally visited China to restore normal diplomatic relations between the two great Communist powers that had quarreled for over a quarter century. In 1990 he accepted mutual troop reductions in Europe that would give the United States a numerical advantage.

The most dramatic of Gorbachev's foreign policy departures has been his attitude toward Soviet domination in eastern Europe. As the revolutions of 1989, which will be discussed in the next section, swept across eastern Europe, Gorbachev personally informed the relevant eastern European Communist leaders that he would not use Soviet troops to prevent those changes. In that manner he rejected the policy that had led to Soviet military intervention in Hungary in 1956 and in Czechoslovakia in 1968. Furthermore, Gorbachev indicated that he believed the nations of eastern Europe should work out their own destinies with only a minimum of direct Soviet influence.

In point of fact, this attitude coupled with those popular revolutions has led to the virtual collapse of the Warsaw Pact. Furthermore, Gorbachev contended that the Communist parties of eastern Europe must actively contest for power through open elections. This represented an abandonment of the monopoly on

political power in that region held by Soviet-dominated Communist parties achieved immediately after 1945. Finally, in 1990 the Soviet Union cooperated with efforts to reunify Germany and to resist Iraq's invasion of Kuwait.

Gorbachev's position remains a very difficult one. He has set out on a course of bold reform and reconstruction. The areas of ethnic discontent may lead to a series of civil wars between the republics and the central Soviet government. Gorbachev may also confront new and expanding opposition from Soviet Communist Party officials fearful of losing their influence or entrenched positions. The ongoing failure to produce an adequate food supply and more consumer goods may undermine his political support. Other groups may become fearful for Soviet security as they watch the retreat from power in eastern Europe and the reunification of Germany. As Soviet politics become more diverse and elections more fully contested, it is not certain whether ongoing order will prevail or whether the Soviet Union will enter a period of very real internal turmoil.

Transformations
in Eastern Europe

Immediately after World War II the Soviet Union attempted to construct people's democracies in eastern Europe. These governments were modeled in the Stalinist mold. They were one-party states in which the Communist Party directed the economy, education, and social life. By 1948 such states existed in Bulgaria, Romania, Hungary, Yugoslavia, Albania, Czechoslovakia, Poland, and East Germany. The establishment of these Soviet-dominated states was the most immediate cause of the Cold War between the United States and the Soviet Union. Yugoslavia, headed by Marshal Tito (1892–1980), pursued an independent course of action and was bitterly denounced by Stalin. Elsewhere, however, Soviet troops and Stalinist party leaders prevailed.

Soviet Domination
during the Cold War

The economies of those states were made to conform to the requirements of Soviet eco-

The Warsaw Pact Justifies the Invasion of Czechoslovakia

In 1968 the Soviet Union and its Warsaw Pact allies invaded Czechoslovakia to halt the political liberalization being carried out by that portion of the Czech Communist Party led by Alexander Dubcek. Their intention was to place other, less liberal Communists into power. The Dubcek government is here portrayed as in league with foreign powers and as an enemy to the interests of the Warsaw Pact nations. This invasion marked the occasion of the setting forth of the Brezhnev Doctrine claiming the right of these states to interfere in the internal affairs of their Communist neighbors.

Tass [the Soviet Government news agency] is authorized to state that [Communist] party and Government leaders of the Czechoslovak Socialist Republic have asked the Soviet Union and other allied states to render the fraternal Czechoslovak people urgent assistance, including assistance with armed forces. This request was brought about by the threat that has arisen to the socialist system existing in Czechoslovakia and to the statehood established by the Constitution—the threat emanating from the counterrevolutionary forces that have entered into a collusion with foreign forces hostile to socialism.

The events in Czechoslovakia and around her were repeatedly the subject of exchanges of views between leaders of fraternal socialist countries, including the leaders of Czechoslovakia. These countries are unanimous in that the support, consolidation and defense of the people's socialist gains is a common internationalist duty of all the socialist states. . . .

The Soviet Government and the Governments of the allied countries—the People's Republic of Bulgaria, the Hungarian People's Republic, the German Democratic Republic, the Polish People's Republic—proceeding from the principles of inseparable friendship and cooperation and in accordance with the existing contractual commitments, have decided to meet the above-mentioned request for rendering necessary help to the fraternal Czechoslovak people.

The decision is fully in accord with the right of states to individual and collective self-defense envisaged in treaties of alliance concluded between the fraternal socialist countries. This decision is also in line with vital interests of our countries in safeguarding European peace against forces of militarism, aggression and revenge, which have more than once plunged the peoples of Europe into wars.

Soviet armed units, together with armed units of the above-mentioned allied countries, entered the territory of Czechoslovakia on Aug. 21 [1968]. They will be immediately withdrawn from the Czechoslovak Socialist Republic as soon as the obtaining threat to the gains of socialism in Czechoslovakia, the threat to the security of the socialist countries, is eliminated and lawful authorities find that further presence of these armed units there is no longer necessary.

The actions which are being taken are not directed against any state and in no measure infringe state interests of anybody. They serve the purpose of peace and have been prompted by concern for its consolidation.

The New York Times, December 5, 1989, p. A15.

1146

GLOBAL
CONFLICT,
COLD WAR,
AND NEW
DIRECTIONS

nomic recovery and growth. The Soviet Union paid low prices for its imports from eastern Europe and demanded high prices for its exports. In this fashion and through outright reparations, it drained the resources of the region for its own uses. The Soviet Union prevented the eastern European nations from participating in the Marshal Plan and responded with its own Council for Economic Mutual Assistance in 1949. In 1955 it organized the Warsaw Pact to confront NATO.

The events in Poland and Hungary of 1956 demonstrated the refusal of the Soviet Union to tolerate significant independence in its eastern European neighbors. In 1968, during what became known as the Prague Spring, the government of Czechoslovakia under Alexander Dubcek (b. 1921) pursued a liberal Communist political experiment. Dubcek was permitting in Czechoslovakia the very kind of intellectual freedom and discussion that was simultaneously being suppressed within Russia itself. In the summer of 1968 the Soviet government sent troops into Czechoslovakia and installed Communist leaders more to its own liking.

At the time of the invasion, Soviet Party Chairman Brezhnev, in what came to be termed the "Brezhnev Doctrine," declared the right of the Soviet Union to interfere in the domestic politics of other Communist countries. No further direct intervention occurred after 1968. However, during the 1970s considerable economic subsidies flowed from the Soviet Union to the eastern European nations. Those nations were also highly dependent on the Soviet Union for raw materials and markets.

The Soviet domination of eastern Europe had historical as well as ideological roots. Twice during the twentieth century and under Napoleon during the previous century the lands of the Soviet Union had been invaded by western European powers across the plains of northern Europe. Soviet losses during World War II had been extraordinary. The block of eastern European satellites stood as a buffer against such future invasions.

Within the Soviet bloc there had arisen some independence in regard to economic policy. However, until the middle of the 1980s virtually all observers had thought these nations would continue with their one-party governments, with their aspirations for self-determination smothered, and with the most limited possibilities for independent political action. It was assumed that the situation of forty years would continue.

Communism and Solidarity in Poland

After 1956, the Polish Communist Party, led by Wladyslaw Gomulka (b. 1905), made peace

Lech Walesa (b. 1944) addresses the members of the Solidarity Committee in Gdansk in August 1980. At Soviet urging, Solidarity was suppressed after the Polish military took power in December 1981. Walesa was not imprisoned, but his activities were closely monitored. [Jean Gaumy/Magnum Photos]

with the Roman Catholic church, halted land collectivization, established trade with the West, and participated in cultural exchange programs with noncommunist nations. However, Poland experienced chronic economic mismanagement and persistent shortages in food and consumer goods. In 1970, food shortages led to a series of strikes, the most famous of which occurred in the shipyards of Gdansk. In December 1970, the Polish authorities broke the strike at the cost of a number of workers' lives. These events led to the departure of Gomulka. His successor was Edward Gierek (b. 1913).

In the decade after 1970, the Polish economy made very little progress. Food and other consumer goods remained in very short supply. In early July 1980, the Polish government raised meat prices. The result was hundreds of protest strikes across the country. On August 14, workers occupied the Lenin shipyard at Gdansk. The strike soon spread to other shipyards, transport facilities, and factories connected with the shipbuilding industry. The most important leader to emerge from among the strikers was Lech Walesa (b. 1944). He and the other strike leaders refused to negotiate with the government through any of the traditionally government-controlled unions. The Gdansk strike ended on August 31 with the workers having been promised the right to organize an independent union. The union was called Solidarity. The agreement with the government guaranteed the right of access to television and the press on the part of the union and the Polish Roman Catholic church.

Less than a week later, on September 6, Edward Gierek was dismissed as the head of the Polish Communist Party. He was replaced by Stanislaw Kania. Later in September, the Polish courts recognized Solidarity as an independent union, and the state-controlled radio for the first time in thirty years broadcast a Roman Catholic mass.

During the summer of 1981 no less remarkable events occurred within the governance of the Polish Communist Party. For the first time in any European communist state, secret elections for the congress of the party were permitted with real choices among the candidates. Poland remained a nation governed by a single party, but for the time being, real debate was permitted within the party congress.

The extraordinary Polish experiment came

This picture records the first freely printed edition of the Solidarity newspaper, which appeared in May, 1989. The person holding it is Tadeusz Mazowiecki, who became the first non-communist premier of Poland, in August, 1989. [Reuters/Bettmann Newsphotos]

to a rapid close in late 1981. General Wajciech Jaruzelski (b. 1923) became head of the party, and the army moved into the center of Polish events. In December 1981, martial law was declared in Poland. The government moved against Solidarity and arrested a number of its leaders. The Polish military leaders succeeded in repressing the Poles. However, they were not successful in addressing the major economic problems of the country.

By the late 1980s events in Poland took another turn. The government had modified martial law, though Jaruzelski remained in control. However, the economic situation continued to deteriorate. During 1987 the government released the last of the Solidarity prisoners through a sweeping amnesty. In 1988

1148

GLOBAL
CONFLICT,
COLD WAR,
AND NEW
DIRECTIONS

strikes again occurred, and as a result of consultations between the government and Solidarity, the union was legalized. Lech Walesa again came into the public spotlight as a kind of mediator between the government and the more independent elements of the trade union movement he had founded. On this occasion the Communist government was no longer able to control the situation.

Jaruzelski began to undertake a number of political reforms with the tacit consent of the Soviet Union. Martial law was repelled. The Communist government promised free elections in a more powerful parliament. In 1989 the Communists lost overwhelmingly to Solidarity candidates. Later in the year Jaruzelski was unable to find any Communist who could form a government that would receive the support of a majority in the parliament. Late that summer he turned to Solidarity to form a government and negotiated directly with Lech Walesa as to who would become the next prime minister.

On August 24, 1989, Tadeusz Mazowiecki (b. 1927) of Solidarity became the first non-

Communist prime minister of Poland since 1945. The appointment was made with the express approval of Gorbachev. Quite significantly the Communists continued to hold the ministries that direct the armed forces and the police. Furthermore, some observers believed the Communists had permitted Solidarity to come to power because it would not be able to solve the grave economic problems facing the country and would thus lose credibility. Whatever the motives of the Polish Communists and the Soviet Union, in the middle of 1989 Poland embarked on a new political road that had immediate implications for all of eastern Europe.

1989: Year of Revolutions in Eastern Europe

The establishment of a Solidarity government in Poland had been the result of almost a decade of struggle. Within a few months of that event relatively peaceful uprisings toppled the Communist Party governments elsewhere in eastern Europe. In each case at some point in the rush of events the ruling Communist Party renounced its monopoly of power in a fashion that foreshadowed the similar renunciation that occurred in the Soviet Union in 1990. These events rapidly transformed the entire political face of the continent and ushered in what appears to be a new era of European history and of East–West relations.

None of these revolutions could have taken place without the refusal of the Soviet Union to intervene militarily as it had done in 1956 and 1968. As events unfolded, it became clear that Gorbachev would not come to the aid of the old-line Communist governments and party leaderships in eastern Europe. Furthermore, in October 1989, Gorbachev formally renounced the Brezhnev Doctrine that had asserted the Soviet right to interfere in the internal affairs of its Communist neighbors. For the first time since the end of World War II, the people of eastern Europe knew they could work out their own political destinies without the almost certain military intervention of the Soviet Union. Once that situation was recognized, thousands of ordinary citizens took to the streets to denounce the local Communist Party rule and to assert their desire for democracy and a society free of Communist Party domination.

MAJOR DATES IN RECENT EASTERN EUROPEAN HISTORY

1968	Invasion of Czechoslovakia
1980	Solidarity founded in Poland
1981	Martial Law proclaimed in Poland
1982	Brezhnev dies and is succeeded by Andropov in the Soviet Union
1983	Pope John Paul II visits Poland Martial Law suspended in Poland Lech Walesa awarded Nobel Peace Prize
1984	Andropov dies and is succeeded by Chernenko in the Soviet Union
1985	Chernenko dies and Gorbachev comes to power in the Soviet Union
1986	Chernobyl nuclear disaster
1988	Full debates at Soviet Communist Party Congress Soviet withdrawal from Afghanistan
1989	Supreme Soviet elected after actual political campaigning Revolutions throughout Eastern Europe
1990	Gorbachev calls for the end of Communist monopoly on political power in the Soviet Union Reunification of Germany Lithuania declares independence

MAP 31-3 THE REAL NATIONS IN THE CENTER OF EUROPE *The rapid changes in Eastern Europe during the close of the 1980s has again brought to the fore various longstanding ethnic tensions in the region. This map illustrates the chief ethnic borders in the area and indicates where there are major ethnic enclaves within areas generally dominated by a single ethnic group. [Adapted from* The New York Times. *Copyright © 1990 by the New York Times Company, Reprinted by permission]*

It is important to note that the generally peaceful character of these revolutions (Romania being the exception) was not inevitable. It would appear to be in part the result of the very different kind of situation that occurred in the People's Republic of China in the late

1150

GLOBAL
CONFLICT,
OLD WAR,
AND NEW
DIRECTIONS

spring of 1989. During May of that year thousands of students and other Chinese citizens had gathered in Tiananmen Square in Beijing to demand economic and political reform. These round-the-clock demonstrations continued for weeks and were widely covered by television and newspapers. However, during the second week in June the Chinese Communist government turned army troops against the demonstrators. Although an official death toll is not known, certainly at least several hundred people were killed. The event shocked world opinion. As political demonstrations took place later in the year in eastern Europe, many government and military officials were determined not to repeat such a massacre in their own capitals even though some leaders contemplated such an alternative.

HUNGARY   Of the eastern European nations, Hungary had for some time demonstrated the most economic independence of the Soviet Union. The Hungarian government had emphasized the production of food and consumer goods. It had also allowed the presence of a small stock exchange. During the early months of 1989, as events unfolded in Poland, the Hungarian Communist government began to take other independent actions. In January its parliament passed legislation to permit independent political parties. Soon thereafter the government opened the Hungarian border with Austria and permitted free travel between the two nations. One immediate result was the movement of thousands of East Germans into Austria through Hungary. From Austria they proceeded into West Germany. This situation marked the first breach in the Iron Curtain.

Not long thereafter various political changes occurred in Hungary. In May Premier Janos Kadar, who had been installed after the Soviet intervention in 1956, was voted from office by the Parliament. Hungarians demonstrated their determination to indicate the reality of this change when thousands of people gave an honored burial to the body of Hungarian Premier Imre Nagy, who had been executed in 1956. The Hungarian Communist Party changed its name to the Socialist Party and permitted the emergence of other opposition political parties. In October Hungary proclaimed itself to be an independent republic. The Hungarian government promised free

elections. By 1990, a coalition of democratic parties controlled by the parliament governed the country.

EAST GERMANY   No part of Europe had so come to symbolize the tensions of the Cold War as the divided Germanies. The Berlin Wall had been erected in 1961 to halt the outflow of East Germans to the West. In the autumn of 1989 as thousands of East Germans moved into West Germany through Hungary and then Austria, popular demonstrations erupted in numerous German cities. The most important demonstrations occurred in Leipzig. The streets filled with people demanding democracy and an end to Communist Party rule.

In addition to the pressure of the popular demonstrations, the leaders of the East German Communist Party were told by Gorbachev that the Soviet Union would no longer support them. With a swiftness that could not have been expected, the Communist leaders of the East German government, including Premier Erich Honecker (b. 1912), resigned, making way for a younger generation of the Communist Party. The new leaders, who remained in office for only a matter of weeks, promised political and economic reform. They convinced few East Germans and the emigration to the West continued. In November, 1989, in one of the most emotional moments in European history since 1945 the government of East Germany ordered the opening of the Berlin Wall. That week tens of thousands of East Berliners crossed into West Berlin. Shortly thereafter free travel commenced between East and West Germany.

Further political transformation occurred in East Germany. For all intents and purposes the Communist-dominated party became thoroughly discredited. Enormous corruption among party officials became exposed. The East German Communist Party changed its name and claimed that henceforth it would be a social democratic party. Free elections in 1990 brought into parliament a conservative majority that sought rapid unification with West Germany.

The revolution in East Germany, more than those elsewhere in Europe, had broad ramifications on international relations. Within days of the events the issue of the reunification of the Germanies, discussed earlier in this chapter, was raised. Helmut Kohl, the prime minister of West Germany, set forth a tentative plan for reunification. Late in 1989 the ministers of the European Economic Community indicated an acceptance in principle of a future unification of Germany. By February 1990, some form of reunification had become a foregone conclusion and had been accepted by the United States, the Soviet Union, Great Britain, and France. But the decision lay only formally with those powers.

In the closing months of 1989 and the opening weeks of 1990 it had become very clear that the citizens of the two Germanies were determined to reunify. With the collapse of Communist Party government in East Germany, there was no longer a viable distinction between the two Germanies; they had remained divided largely on the excuse that their two governments were wholly incompatible. With the Communists in confusion, the forces of national self-determination came to the fore.

BULGARIA Todor Zhivkov had governed Bulgaria since 1954. The nation had been under strict Communist Party authority throughout the postwar period.

Throughout the 1980s the Bulgarian government had undertaken various measures that were hostile and repressive to ethnic Turks living in the country. For example, at one point all Turks were required to take Bulgarian names. During the spring of 1989 the Bulgarian government had undertaken a massive removal of ethnic Turks from Bulgaria into Turkey. Over three hundred thousand Turks were so removed. This process caused very considerable social and economic turmoil in Bulgaria. Zhivkov was the chief architect of these policies. Many of the cabinet leaders opposed them.

The chief of these opponents was Petar Mladenov, the foreign minister. During the summer of 1989 he was in contact with the government of the Soviet Union to gain support for a major political change in Bulgaria. On November 9, the same day as the decision to open the Berlin Wall, Mladenov gained sufficient support on the Bulgarian Politburo to remove Zhivkov. He began immediately to make moves in Bulgaria that resembled those of *glasnost* and *perestroika* in the Soviet Union. There would appear to be the likelihood of a more open Communist Party, and a multi-party system. Considerable political unrest has continued.

CZECHOSLOVAKIA The hard-line wing of the Czechoslovak Communist Party had been restored to power by the Soviet invasion of 1968. This wing of the party removed the Communist leaders of the 1968 "Prague Spring" from public life and retained virtually unquestioned authority for twenty years. Any opponents might find themselves imprisoned for their activities.

In November 1989, under popular pressures from street demonstrations and a well-organized political opposition, the Czechoslovakian Communist Party began a retreat from office. The patterns were similar to those occurring elsewhere. The old leadership resigned, and younger Communists replaced them. The changes they offered were inadequate.

The new popular Czech leader who led the forces against the party was Vaclav Havel (b. 1936), a playwright of international standing who had been frequently imprisoned by the

Vaclav Havel, an internationally recognized playwright, was elected the first non-communist president of Czechoslovakia after the collapse of Communist Party power. [Polak/Gamma-Liaison]

1152

GLOBAL
CONFLICT,
OLD WAR,
AND NEW
DIRECTIONS

government. He represented a group that called itself Civic Forum. They negotiated a series of changes with the government. These included an end to the political dominance of the Communist Party (which had been a part of the constitution), inclusion of non-Commu-nists in the government, elimination of tradi-tional Marxist education, the removal of travel restrictions, and relaxation of censorship. They succeeded in forcing the resignation of the Czech president and in guaranteeing a free election for his successor.

The Soviet Union and Warsaw Pact Reassess the 1968 Invasion of Czechoslovakia

In December 1989, the Soviet Union and the Warsaw Pact issued statements in which they condemned the 1968 invasion of Czechoslovakia. These statements represented a rejection of the Brezhnev Doctrine, according to which the Soviet Union and its Warsaw Pact Allies claimed the right to intervene in the affairs of their Communist neighbors. These statements should be com-pared with the justification of the invasion that appears on p. 1145.

Soviet Statement

The Czechoslovak society is at the state of a critical reassessment of the experience of its political and economic development.

This is a natural process. Many coun-tries undergo it in one way or another.

Regrettably, the need for constant so-cialist self-renewal and realistic appraisal of the events has not always been taken for granted, particularly in situations when such events intertwined in a contradictory way and required bold answers to the chal-lenges of times.

In 1968, the Soviet leadership of that time supported the stand of one side in an internal dispute in Czechoslovakia regard-ing objective pressing tasks.

The justification for such an unbal-anced, inadequate approach, an interfer-ence in the affairs of a friendly country, was then seen in an acute East-West con-frontation.

We share the view of the Presidium of the Central Committee of the Communist Party of Czechoslovakia and the Czecho-slovak Government that the bringing of armies of five socialist countries into Czechoslovak territory in 1968 was un-founded, and that the decision, in the light of all the presently known facts, was erro-neous.

Warsaw Pact Statement

Leaders of Bulgaria, Hungary, the German Democratic Republic, Poland, and the So-viet Union, who gathered for a meeting in Moscow on December 4 [1989], stated that the bringing of troops of their countries into Czechoslovakia in 1968 was an inter-ference in internal affairs of sovereign Czechoslovakia and should be condemned.

Disrupting the process of democratic renewal in Czechoslovakia, those illegal actions had long-term negative conse-quences.

History showed how important it is, even in the most complex international situation, to use political means for the solution of any problems, strictly to ob-serve the principles of sovereignty, inde-pendence and noninterference in internal affairs in relations among states, which is in keeping with the provisions of the War-saw Treaty.

The New York Times, December 5, 1989, p. A15.

Furthermore, early in December the tottering Communist government admitted that the invasion of 1968 was a mistake. The Soviet Union and Warsaw Pact did likewise. Shortly thereafter, Gustav Husak, who had been installed as the president of Czechoslovakia after the invasion, resigned. On December 28, 1989, Alexander Dubcek returned to public office as chairman of the Parliament. The next day Havel was elected president of the nation.

ROMANIA The most violent upheaval of 1989 occurred in Romania, where President Nicholae Ceausescu (1918–1989) had governed without opposition for almost a quarter century. He had been at odds with the Soviet government for some time. In the face of the reforms carried out by Gorbachev, the Romanian ruler had maintained an ongoing Stalinist regime. Romania was a one-party state with total centralized economic planning. Ceausescu was supported by an army and a smaller security force loyal to himself. He had also placed his closest relatives into major political positions where they personally profited through corrupt practices.

On December 15 troubles erupted in the city of Timisoara in western Romania. The security forces sought to arrest a clergyman who had attempted to protect the rights of ethnic Hungarians within Romania's borders. Over the next two days the Romanian security forces opened fire on demonstrators in Timisoara. There were very heavy casualties that ran into at least the hundreds and quite possibly higher. A few days later demonstrators in Bucharest publicly shouted against Ceausescu at a major rally. On December 22 the city of Bucharest was in full revolt. Major conflict involving many casualties broke out between the army, which supported the revolution, and the security forces loyal to Ceausescu. The revolutionaries gained control of the television station and broadcast the events of the spreading revolution. Ceausescu attempted to flee the country. He was captured. He was secretly tried along with his wife and was executed by firing squad on December 25. With his death the shooting between the army and security forces came to an end.

The provisional government in Bucharest announced that the first free elections since the end of World War II would take place in the spring of 1990. During the early months of the

Romanian youths climbed atop a truck in Bucharest to cheer the newly formed government in December, 1989. [© Leonard Freed/Magnum Photos]

year numerous demonstrations occurred both in favor and in opposition to the new government. Political turmoil seems likely to continue.

1989 *in Perspective*

The events of 1989 may be compared with those of 1848 in that revolutionary events in one nation quickly spread to others. In both cases nationalism provided a strong motive for action. Furthermore, in both 1848 and 1989 popular revolutionary forces cast from power political regimes that were perceived as corrupt and as upholders of an illiberal order. In

1154

GLOBAL
CONFLICT,
COLD WAR,
AND NEW
DIRECTIONS

both cases new popular political forces were unleashed that challenged the previous political stability.

Shortly after the outbreak of the revolutions of 1848, the powers of reaction crushed the revolts. It would appear that the revolutions of 1989 will have longer lasting results. The Soviet Union has refused to intervene in eastern Europe. Yet at the time of this writing it is not yet clear exactly what kind of governments will replace the Communist-dominated ones. Nor do we know how new political systems involving more than one political party will establish themselves. It is also uncertain what a change in the leadership of the Soviet Union would mean for the new emerging governments of eastern Europe.

There is still another link between 1848 and 1989. The revolutions of 1989 may also have brought to a close the era in the history of European socialism that commenced with the publication of Marx and Engels' *Communist Manifesto* in 1848. As traced in earlier chapters, Marxism dominated the debates over European socialism prior to World War I. The Bolshevik victory in the Russian Revolution and the foreign policy of Lenin and Stalin further supported the spread of Marxist versions of socialism in Europe and elsewhere. The European governments and economies fostered by the results of the Russian Revolution lie in a state of collapse across the Continent. It is an open question whether socialism itself now stands permanently on the defensive, but it does seem certain that the socialism that flowed from the thought of Marx through Lenin and Stalin stands generally discredited in Europe. A new era has opened requiring socialists to come to grips with the benefits of markets, economic decentralization, welfare systems, and political democracy.

The revolutions of 1989 have exerted profound effects on issues relating to European foreign policy. The Warsaw Pact can hardly be said to exist any longer. Most of the revolutionary governments have demanded the removal of Soviet troops from their borders. The demise of the Warsaw Pact has raised new concerns about the role of NATO. It was previously justified largely, though never entirely, by the danger of a Soviet ground attack upon western Europe. It will be more difficult to hold the alliance in place as that threat is diminished. The reunification of Germany also places new pressures on NATO as the debate occurs over German membership. France, Great Britain, Italy, as well as Poland and other eastern European nations, are just beginning to think through the implications of German reunification.

MAJOR EVENTS OF REVOLUTIONS OF 1989

January 11	Independent parties permitted in Hungary
April 5	Solidarity legalized in Poland and free elections accepted by government
May 2	Hungary dismantles barriers along its borders
May 8	Jonas Kadar removed from office in Hungary
May 17	Polish government recognizes Roman Catholic church
June 4	Solidarity victory in Polish parliamentary elections
July 25	Solidarity asked to join coalition government
August 19	Solidarity premier appointed in Poland
October 18	Erich Honeker removed from office in East Germany
October 23	Hungary proclaims itself a republic
October 25	Gorbachev renounces Brezhnev Doctrine
November 9	Berlin Wall opened Zhivkov removed as leader in Bulgaria
November 17	Large antigovernment demonstration in Czechoslovakia crushed by police
November 19	Czech opposition groups organize into Civic Forum and demand resignation of Communist leaders responsible for 1968 invasion
November 24	Czech Communist leadership resigns
December 1	New Czech Communist leaders denounce 1968 invasion. Soviet Union and Warsaw Pact express regret over 1968 invasion.
December 3	Czech government announces ministry with non-Communist members
December 16–17	Massacre of civilians in Timisoara, Romania
December 22	Ceausescu government overthrown in Romania with many casualties
December 25	Announcement of Ceausescu's execution
December 28	Alexander Dubcek elected as chairman of Czech Parliament
December 29	Vaclav Havel elected president of Czechoslovakia

Furthermore, there will be much debate over how the economies of eastern Europe are integrated into the economies of the European Economic Community. In that regard, it seems virtually certain that the new economic policies in the Soviet Union, combined with the need for new economic initiatives and investment in eastern Europe, have brought to a close the era of centrally directed Communist economies. Free markets will certainly play a far more important role in eastern Europe and the Soviet Union. Indeed, it seems clear that the prosperity generated by the economies of western Europe as contrasted with the shortages in goods and services in eastern Europe provided a major source of popular discontent with the Communist Party regimes.

It would, however, be a mistake to explain the collapse of the Communist governments of eastern Europe only in terms of economic stagnation and consumer dissatisfaction. For over forty years the citizens of all of those nations had lived without the possibility of exercising the broad array of civil liberties known throughout western Europe and the United States. Lacking a free press, the right to free speech, and the possibility of free open assembly, they had dwelled under the shadow of police surveillance and arbitrary arrest. Communist Party governments had jailed writers who voiced opposition and party officials who had advocated reform. The Communist Party governments had also repressed the Roman Catholic church and imposed martial law. The citizens of those countries could not travel freely. Workers could not organize independent trade unions.

When the people of eastern Europe took to the streets in the summer and autumn of 1989 and when Romanian students fell before the bullets of government troops, they carried banners and shouted slogans demanding democracy, fundamental political liberties, and human rights. They manifested in this generation the desire for constitutionalism and recognition of human dignity that have been major traditions of the Western political heritage, however troubled their realization may have been over the centuries.

Toward a New Europe and the Twenty-first Century

This edition of The Western Heritage *concludes in the wake of the most extraordinary events to take place in Europe since the end of World War II. The pace of historical change does not time itself to match publication deadlines. Further rapidly developing changes in Europe and the Persian Gulf may render parts of this chapter dated even as they are printed.*

The transformations in European life are indeed rapid and stunning, but they are still manifestations of peoples changing and reshaping their destinies in the context of Western civilization. The concern for constitutional government has again come to the fore. Throughout eastern Europe the Church has been a major player in revolutionary change. The Western penchant for critical self-examination manifested itself first secretly in the intellectual circles of eastern Europe and then publicly in the political debates following the revolutions of 1989. The desire of eastern Europeans for the prosperity made possible by technology and the influence of rapid technological communication on Soviet citizenry and politics have been key to recent events.

As Europeans move toward the next century, they are in the process of establishing a new kind of European society. In this regard, the most remarkable change during the second half of the twentieth century has been the apparent general demise of militant nationalism as a major political force in Europe. Twice in the first half of the century nationalism contributed to the outbreak of worldwide conflict. At the moment there seems little prospect for such a new turn of events.

In western Europe the emergence of the European Economic Community is the major manifestation of transnational cooperation. German reunification stands as the major challenge to the continuation of European political life based on international cooperation rather than upon nationalistic rivalry. There are, however, numerous indications that German leaders see themselves as leaders of a new Europe based on such cooperation. The

1156

GLOBAL
CONFLICT,
OLD WAR,
AND NEW
DIRECTIONS

example of Italy, which embraced aggressive nationalism earlier in the century only to reject it for the past half-century, suggests that such cooperative policies can be successfully pursued.

In eastern Europe the long years of Soviet domination tended to suppress nationalism. It is possible with the potential loosening of Soviet domination that new nationalistic forces and ethnic strife will emerge in that area. It is too early to predict. However, the desire for consumer goods and economic prosperity throughout eastern Europe which will require international cooperation, may serve to smother potential forces of nationalism and ethnic conflict. In eastern Europe as well as in western Europe it seems possible that the benefits flowing from extensive economic interdependency and the necessity of addressing major international environmental problems may overcome latent nationalistic tendencies.

During the second half of this century Europeans have become much less culturally isolated within their individual nations and within their continent. Touring and foreign vacations were once the preserve of the wealthy, but now they have become a major part of middle-class European culture. Such travel, as well as economic cooperation, has no doubt itself helped to overcome nationalistic outlooks. This marked lessening of nationalistic impulses will mean that the next century of European history will be very different from the last two centuries.

Europe has also become a much more consumer-oriented society. From the years immediately after the war when there were shortages of almost all goods, western Europe has moved toward the creation of a genuine consumer society. Electric household appliances, once rare, have become commonplace. More people than ever before drive automobiles. This world of consumption has become increasingly internationalized as Japanese electronic devices are sold across the continent and as American fast food chains, such as McDonald's, have appeared in virtually all major west European cities.

The prosperity that has spread throughout the recent decades and the accompanying changes in economic structure have lessened the class strife that marked domestic European politics from the French Revolution

through the opening of World War II. Many serious social problems continue to confront Europeans. Unemployment and the social strains of economic dislocation have not disappeared. Homeless people walk the streets of Europe as they do in the United States. There is much social tension surrounding the presence of workers from Turkey and North Africa in western Europe. The political turmoil that might occur should there be another major worldwide economic downturn cannot be really predicted. However, the kind of class conflict that marked European history for so many decades has clearly lessened.

Indeed, the expansion of technology itself may come to be seen as a more important force determining the historical events of this century than was class struggle. For some observers technology may appear to be an enemy and a threat to the environment. Yet science has touched in a positive manner the lives of more people than might have been imagined even fifty years ago. And it will be from scientific understanding that the problems of the environment and resource shortages will be resolved.

Rationalism in the processes of everyday life has never been more present, even though many intellectuals have praised the irrational. The use of reason still promises the best hope to humankind. Since World War II the problems of constitutional order and human rights have continued to be major concerns of political life and discussion. This process continues in a remarkably lively manner as west Europeans move toward unity and as eastern Europe and the Soviet Union experiment with perestroika.

These persistent features of European life have not ensured that its civilization, as well as the results flowing from it, will be morally good. Rather they have meant that Western civilization has possessed in itself the possibility of correcting and redirecting itself and of raising questions about what are the good life and the good society. The possibility of asking those questions is necessary before the desired improvement and reform can be attained. Perhaps the chief carriers of Western culture today are those who within its midst most criticize it and demand that it justify itself.

Suggested Readings

G. AMBROSIUS AND W. H. HUBBARD, *A Social and Economic History of Twentieth-Century Europe* (1989). The best one-volume treatment of the subject.

T. G. ASH, *The Magic Lantern: The Revolution of 89 Witnessed in Warsaw, Budapest, Berlin and Prague* (1990). Essays by a longtime observer of central Europe.

T. G. ASH, *The Uses of Adversity* (1989). Important essays on central European culture and politics prior to the events of 1989.

S. BEER, *Modern British Politics: Parties and Pressure Groups in the Collectivist Age* (1982). An excellent overview of the situation that brought Margaret Thatcher to power.

E. BRAMWELL, *Ecology in the 20th Century: A History* (1989). Traces the environmental movement to its late nineteenth-century origins.

W. M. BRINTON AND A. RINZLER, *Without Force or Lies: Voices from the Revolutions of Central Europe, 1989–90* (1990). Selections of major spokesmen for political change and reform.

R. CROSSMAN (Ed.), *The God That Failed* (1949). Essays by former communist intellectuals.

K. DAWISHA, *Eastern Europe, Gorbachev and Reform: The Great Challenge* (1988). A probing analysis of the potential impact of reform in the Soviet Union on eastern Europe.

P. DESAI, *Perestroika in Perspective: The Design and Dilemmas of Soviet Reform* (1989). A thoughtful essay on Gorbachev's reforms.

J. EISEN, *The Glasnost Reader* (1990). An anthology of selections relating to political change in the Soviet Union.

J. R. FEARS, *France in the Giscard Presidency* (1981). A survey.

M. FRANKLIN, *The Decline of Class Voting in Britain* (1986). The argument is stated in the title.

M. I. GOLDMAN, *Gorbachev's Challenge: Economic Reform in the Age of High Technology* (1988). Emphasizes the economic goals of Gorbachev's program.

W. F. HANRIEDER, *Germany, America, and Europe: Forty Years of German Foreign Policy* (1989). A major survey.

H. S. HUGHES, *Sophisticated Rebels: The Political Culture of European Dissent, 1968–1987* (1988). A series of thoughtful essays on recent cultural critics.

W. G. HYLAND, *The Cold War Is Over* (1990). Discussion of the end of Cold War tensions from the point of view of the United States.

W. LAQUER, *Soviet Realities: Culture and Politics from Stalin to Gorbachev* (1990). Essays on developments in Soviet intellectual life.

M. JAY, *The Dialectical Imagination* (1973). An important work on the development of Marxist thought among German intellectuals.

P. JENKINS, *Mrs. Thatcher's Revolution: The Ending of the Socialist Era* (1988). The best work on the subject.

W. W. KULSKI, *De Gaulle and the World: The Foreign Policy of the Fifth French Republic* (1968). A straightforward treatment of De Gaulle's drive toward French and European autonomy.

J. LAPALOMBARA, *Democracy Italian Style* (1987). The best book on the subject.

R. F. LESLIE, *The History of Poland since 1863* (1981). An excellent collection of essays that provides the background for the current turbulent decade.

Z. A. MEDVEDEV, *Gorbachev* (1986). The best available biography.

R. MEDVEDEV AND C. CHIESA, *Time of Change: An Insider's View of Russia's Transformation* (1989). An effort to explain recent changes through analysis of Soviet society and political structures.

G. MONTEFIORE, *Philosophy in France Today* (1983). A good introduction to one of the major centers of contemporary thought.

L. P. MORRIS, *Eastern Europe since 1945* (1984). Concentrates on the political and economic organization of the Soviet-dominated states.

B. NAHAYLO AND V. SWOBODA, *Soviet Disunion: A History of the Nationalities Problem in the USSR* (1990). A discussion of one of the major areas of challenge to Gorbachev.

M. POSTER, *Existential Marxism in Postwar France* (1975). An excellent and clear work.

G. ROSS, *Workers and Communists in France: From Popular Front to Eurocommunism* (1982). A useful survey.

J. ROTHCHILD, *Return to Diversity: A Political History of East Central Europe since World War II* (1989). A clear, well-organized introduction.

J. RUSCOE, *The Italian Communist Party, 1976–1981: On the Threshold of Government* (1982). Examines the party at the height of its influence.

H. SIMONIAN, *The Privileged Partnership: Franco-German Relations in the European Community (1969–1984)* (1985). An important examination of the dominant role of France and Germany in the European Economic Community.

C. TUGENHAT, *Making Sense of Europe* (1986). An evaluation of the Common Market by one of its commissioners.

H. A. TURNER, *The Two Germanies since 1945* (1987). The best brief introduction.

INDEX

885-1026

-1026